| | | NATIONAL INCOME AND PRODUCT ACCOUNTS | 1968 | 1969 | 1970 | 1971 | 1972 | 1973 | 1974 | 1975 | 1976 | 1977 |
|---|---|---|---|---|---|---|---|---|---|---|---|---|
| | | **EXPENDITURES APPROACH** | | | | | | | | | | |
| the sum of | 1 | Personal consumption expenditures | 558.0 | 605.2 | 648.5 | 701.9 | 770.6 | 852.4 | 933.4 | 1,034.4 | 1,151.9 | 1,278.6 |
| | 2 | Gross private domestic investment | 141.2 | 156.4 | 152.4 | 178.2 | 207.6 | 244.5 | 249.4 | 230.2 | 292.0 | 361.3 |
| | 3 | Government purchases | 209.4 | 221.5 | 233.8 | 246.5 | 263.5 | 281.7 | 317.9 | 357.7 | 383.0 | 414.1 |
| | 4 | Exports | 47.9 | 51.9 | 59.7 | 63.0 | 70.8 | 95.3 | 126.7 | 138.7 | 149.5 | 159.4 |
| less | 5 | Imports | 46.6 | 50.5 | 55.8 | 62.3 | 74.2 | 91.2 | 127.5 | 122.7 | 151.1 | 182.4 |
| equals | 6 | Gross domestic product | 910.0 | 984.6 | 1,038.5 | 1,127.1 | 1,238.3 | 1,382.7 | 1,500.0 | 1,638.3 | 1,825.3 | 2,030.9 |
| | | **INCOMES APPROACH** | | | | | | | | | | |
| the sum of | 7 | Compensation of employees | 524.3 | 577.6 | 617.2 | 658.9 | 725.1 | 811.2 | 890.2 | 949.1 | 1,059.3 | 1,180.5 |
| | 8 | Proprietors' income | 74.3 | 77.4 | 78.4 | 84.8 | 95.9 | 113.5 | 113.1 | 119.5 | 132.2 | 145.7 |
| | 9 | Rental income of persons | 20.9 | 21.2 | 21.4 | 22.4 | 23.4 | 24.3 | 24.3 | 23.7 | 22.3 | 20.7 |
| | 10 | Corporate profits | 98.8 | 95.4 | 83.6 | 98.0 | 112.1 | 125.5 | 115.8 | 134.8 | 163.3 | 192.4 |
| | 11 | Net interest | 27.1 | 32.7 | 39.1 | 43.9 | 47.9 | 55.2 | 70.8 | 81.6 | 85.5 | 101.1 |
| | 12 | Adjustments | 77.8 | 85.4 | 91.2 | 100.1 | 106.8 | 117.7 | 127.9 | 137.2 | 149.2 | 158.5 |
| equals | 13 | National income | 823.2 | 889.7 | 930.9 | 1,008.1 | 1,111.2 | 1,247.4 | 1,342.1 | 1,445.9 | 1,611.8 | 1,798.9 |
| plus | 14 | Indirect taxes minus subsidies | −7.7 | −9.1 | −5.5 | −3.6 | −8.0 | −16.6 | −20.1 | −8.3 | −8.6 | −18.3 |
| | 15 | Consumption of fixed capital | 88.4 | 97.9 | 106.7 | 115.0 | 126.5 | 139.3 | 162.5 | 187.7 | 205.2 | 230.0 |
| | 16 | Net factor incomes from rest of world | 6.1 | 6.1 | 6.4 | 7.6 | 8.6 | 12.6 | 15.5 | 13.0 | 16.9 | 20.3 |
| equals | 17 | Gross domestic product | 910.0 | 984.6 | 1,038.5 | 1,127.1 | 1,238.3 | 1,382.7 | 1,500.0 | 1,638.3 | 1,825.3 | 2,030.9 |
| | 18 | Real GDP (billions of 2000 dollars) | 3,652.7 | 3,765.4 | 3,771.9 | 3,898.6 | 4,105.0 | 4,341.5 | 4,319.5 | 4,311.2 | 4,540.9 | 4,750.5 |
| | 19 | Real GDP growth (percent per year) | 4.8 | 3.1 | 0.2 | 3.4 | 5.3 | 5.8 | −0.5 | −0.2 | 5.3 | 4.6 |
| | | **OTHER DATA** | | | | | | | | | | |
| | 20 | Population (millions) | 200.7 | 202.7 | 205.1 | 207.7 | 209.9 | 211.9 | 213.9 | 216.0 | 218.0 | 220.2 |
| | 21 | Labor force (millions) | 78.7 | 80.7 | 82.8 | 84.4 | 87.0 | 89.4 | 92.0 | 93.8 | 96.2 | 99.0 |
| | 22 | Employment (millions) | 75.9 | 77.9 | 78.7 | 79.4 | 82.1 | 85.1 | 86.8 | 85.8 | 88.8 | 92.0 |
| | 23 | Unemployment (millions) | 2.8 | 2.8 | 4.1 | 5.0 | 4.9 | 4.4 | 5.2 | 7.9 | 7.4 | 7.0 |
| | 24 | Labor force participation rate (percent) | 59.6 | 60.1 | 60.4 | 60.2 | 60.4 | 60.8 | 61.3 | 61.2 | 61.6 | 62.2 |
| | 25 | Unemployment rate (percent of labor force) | 3.6 | 3.5 | 4.9 | 5.9 | 5.6 | 4.9 | 5.6 | 8.5 | 7.7 | 7.0 |
| | 26 | Real GDP per person (2000 dollars per year) | 18,199 | 18,578 | 18,395 | 18,774 | 19,557 | 20,488 | 20,199 | 19,962 | 20,826 | 21,570.0 |
| | 27 | Growth rate of real GDP per person (percent per year) | 3.8 | 2.1 | −1.0 | 2.1 | 4.2 | 4.8 | −1.4 | −1.2 | 4.3 | 3.6 |
| | 28 | Quantity of money (M2, billions of dollars) | 566.8 | 587.9 | 626.4 | 710.1 | 802.1 | 855.3 | 901.9 | 1,016.0 | 1,151.7 | 1,269.9 |
| | 29 | GDP deflator (2000 = 100) | 24.9 | 26.1 | 27.5 | 28.9 | 30.2 | 31.8 | 34.7 | 38.0 | 40.2 | 42.8 |
| | 30 | GDP deflator inflation rate (percent per year) | 4.2 | 4.9 | 5.3 | 5.3 | 4.4 | 5.7 | 8.6 | 9.3 | 6.0 | 6.5 |
| | 31 | Consumer price index (1982–1984 = 100) | 34.8 | 36.7 | 38.8 | 40.5 | 41.8 | 44.4 | 49.3 | 53.8 | 56.9 | 60.6 |
| | 32 | CPI inflation rate (percent per year) | 4.2 | 5.5 | 5.7 | 4.4 | 3.2 | 6.2 | 11.0 | 9.1 | 5.8 | 6.5 |
| | 33 | Current account balance (billions of dollars) | 0.6 | 0.4 | 2.3 | −1.4 | −5.8 | 7.1 | 2.0 | 18.1 | 4.3 | −14.3 |

# MACROECONOMICS
seventh edition

# PARKIN

To change the way students see the world—that has been my aim throughout the seven editions of this book.

The cover depicts a landscape viewed through a geometric icon.

The landscape is the economic world. And the icon represents the clarity that economic science brings to our view and understanding of the economic world.

When we view the landscape without the economic lens, we see questions but not answers. The lens provides answers by enabling us to focus on the unseen forces that shape our world. It is a tool that enables us to see the invisible.

This book equips students with the economic lens, shows them how to use it, and enables them to gain their own informed and structured view of the economic world.

# Great news!
## MyEconLab can help you improve your grades!

With your purchase of a new copy of this textbook, you received a Student Access Kit for **MyEconLab** for Parkin, Seventh Edition. Your Student Access Kit looks like this:

## DON'T THROW IT AWAY!

What is **MyEconLab** and how will it help you? **MyEconLab** is an online learning environment for Economics. *Online Practice Tests* measure your progress and generate a personalized *Study Plan* to show you where to focus your study. *Exercises* and turorials give you ample opportunity to practice and improve. An advanced *graphing tool* helps you understand how the concepts, numbers, and graphs are connected. Each exercise links to the appropriate page in your eText, which includes animated graphs and an interactive glossary.

In addition **MyEconLab** includes valuable features that further your understanding of how economics impacts your life. **MyEconLab** also provides resources for extra help when you need it.

- *Economics in the News*—news links updated daily during the school year
- *Online Office Hours*—extra help from the author via email
- *eThemes of the Times*—articles from the *New York Times* accompanied by critical-thinking questions
- *Research Navigator*—a one-stop resource for college research assignments
- *Tutor Center*—phone, fax, and email access to live tutors, five days per week

If you did not purchase a new textbook or cannot locate the Student Access Kit and would like to access the resources in **MyEconLab** for Parkin, Seventh Edition, you may purchase a subscription online with a major credit card at www.myeconlab.com/parkin.

## To activate your prepaid subscription:

1. Locate the **MyEconLab** Student Access Kit that came bundled with your textbook.
2. Ask your instructor for your **MyEconLab** course ID.*
3. Go to www.myeconlab.com/parkin. Follow the instructions on the screen and use the access code in your **MyEconLab** Student Access Kit to register as a new user.

\* If your instructor does not provide you with a Course ID, you can still access some of the online resources listed above. Go to www.myeconlab.com/parkin to register.

# MACROECONOMICS
## seventh edition

# Michael Parkin
*University of Western Ontario*

Boston  San Francisco  New York
London  Toronto  Sydney  Tokyo  Singapore  Madrid
Mexico City  Munich  Paris  Cape Town  Hong Kong  Montreal

| | |
|---|---|
| *Editor-in-Chief* | Denise Clinton |
| *Acquisitions Editor* | Adrienne D'Ambrosio |
| *Senior Project Manager* | Mary Clare McEwing |
| *Digital Assets Manager* | Jason Miranda |
| *Senior Administrative Assistant* | Dottie Dennis |
| *Managing Editor* | James Rigney |
| *Senior Production Supervisor* | Nancy Fenton |
| *Senior Design Supervisor* | Gina Hagen Kolenda |
| *Technical Illustrator* | Richard Parkin |
| *Electronic Production Manager* | Scott Silva |
| *Executive Media Producer* | Michelle Neil |
| *Senior Media Producer* | Melissa Honig |
| *Copyeditor and Proofreader* | Kathy Smith |
| *Indexer* | Alexandra Nickerson |
| *Senior Manufacturing Buyer* | Hugh Crawford |
| *Media Buyer* | Ginny Michaud |
| *Executive Marketing Manager* | Stephen Frail |
| *Copywriter/Marketing Specialist* | Christine Lyons |

ISBN: 0-321-22658-5

Library of Congress Cataloging-in-Publication Data

Parkin, Michael, 1939–
    Macroeconomics/Michael Parkin. — 7th ed.
       p. cm.
    Includes index.
    ISBN 0-321-22658-5 (alk. paper)
    1. Macroeconomics.    I. Title.
    HB172.5.P36    2005
    339—dc22           2003067211
                           CIP

Copyright © 2005 by Pearson Education, Inc. publishing as Addison-Wesley.

All rights reserved. No part of this publication may be reproduced, stored in a retrieval system, or transmitted, in any form or by any means, electronic, mechanical, photocopying, recording, or otherwise, without the prior written permission of the publisher.

Printed in the United States of America.

1 2 3 4 5 6 7 8 10 –RNT–0807060504

Text and photo credits appear on page xxix, which constitutes a continuation of the copyright page.

to Robin

# ABOUT MICHAEL PARKIN

**Michael Parkin** received his training as an economist at the Universities of Leicester and Essex in England. Currently in the Department of Economics at the University of Western Ontario, Canada, Professor Parkin has held faculty appointments at Brown University, the University of Manchester, the University of Essex, and Bond University. He is a past president of the Canadian Economics Association and has served on the editorial boards of the *American Economic Review* and the *Journal of Monetary Economics* and as managing editor of the *Canadian Journal of Economics*. Professor Parkin's research on macroeconomics, monetary economics, and international economics has resulted in over 160 publications in journals and edited volumes, including the *American Economic Review,* the *Journal of Political Economy,* the *Review of Economic Studies,* the *Journal of Monetary Economics,* and the *Journal of Money, Credit and Banking*. He became most visible to the public with his work on inflation that discredited the use of wage and price controls. Michael Parkin also spearheaded the movement toward European monetary union. Professor Parkin is an experienced and dedicated teacher of introductory economics.

# PREFACE

This book presents economics as a serious, lively, and evolving science. Its goal is to open students' eyes to the "economic way of thinking" and to help them gain insights into how the economy works and how it might be made to work better.

I provide a thorough and complete coverage of the subject, using a straightforward, precise, and clear writing style.

Because I am conscious that many students find economics hard, I place the student at center stage and write for the student. I use language that doesn't intimidate and that allows the student to concentrate on the substance.

I open each chapter with a clear statement of learning objectives, a real-world student-friendly vignette to grab attention, and a brief preview. I illustrate principles with examples that are selected to hold the student's interest and to make the subject lively. And I put principles to work by using them to illuminate current real-world problems and issues.

I explain modern topics, such as dynamic comparative advantage, game theory, the principal-agent problem and the modern theory of the firm, public choice theory, information and uncertainty, rational expectations, new growth theory, and real business cycle theory, using the familiar core ideas and tools.

Today's course springs from today's issues—the information revolution and the new economy, the economic shockwaves after 9/11, corporate scandals, and the expansion of global trade and investment. But the principles that we use to understand these issues remain the core principles of our science.

Governments and international agencies place continued emphasis on long-term fundamentals as they seek to promote economic growth. This book reflects this emphasis.

To help promote a rich, active learning experience, I have developed a comprehensive online learning environment featuring a dynamic e-book, interactive tutorials and quizzes, daily news updates, and more.

## The Seventh Edition Revision

*MACROECONOMICS*, SEVENTH EDITION, RETAINS ALL OF the improvements achieved in its predecessor with its thorough and detailed presentation of modern economics, emphasis on real-world examples and critical thinking skills, diagrams renowned for pedagogy and precision, and path-breaking technology.

New to this edition are

- A refocused introductory chapter
- Revised and updated macroeconomics content
- **MyEconLab**

### Refocused Introductory Chapter

Chapter 1 has been refocused to place greater emphasis on the role of incentives in influencing people's choices and on the central question: Can choices made in the pursuit of self-interest also serve the social interest? This central question of economics is introduced through ten pressing issues in today's world that are explored further at various later points in the text.

### Revised and Updated Macroeconomics Content

In addition to thorough and extensive updating, including the major revision of the National Income and Product Accounts of December 2003, the macroeconomics chapters feature the following seven major revisions:

1. **A First Look at Macroeconomics** (Chapter 4): This new chapter overviews the macroeconomic landscape and previews the issues; it shows why economic growth matters by contrasting the magnitudes of the Lucas wedge and the Okun gap.

2. **Aggregate Supply and Aggregate Demand** (Chapter 7): This chapter includes a new section that defines and explains the Keynesian, classical, and monetarist schools of macroeconomic thought.

3. **The Economy at Full Employment: The Classical Model** (Chapter 8): This chapter combines two chapters of the sixth edition in a streamlined coverage of the labor market and capital market and the determination of potential GDP and its allocation between consumption and saving.

4. **Money** (Chapters 10 and 11): These chapters have been reorganized to place all the institutional material on money, banks, and the Fed in the first chapter and the monetary transmission mechanism in the second chapter.

5. **Money and Inflation** (Chapters 10, 11, and 12): These chapters, along with the growth chapter, are placed before the chapters on the business cycle and stabilization policy and lay the foundation for a deeper look at the sources of macroeconomic fluctuations. (Alternative routes through the material are possible because of the self-contained nature of the chapters.)

6. **Fiscal Policy** (Chapter 15): This chapter is heavily revised in two ways. First, it no longer relies on the Keynesian model to study stabilization policy. (For those wishing to use the Keynesian approach, Chapter 29, Expenditure Multipliers: The Keynesian Model, has a new appendix that covers the fiscal policy multipliers.) Second, the chapter includes an expanded coverage of supply-side effects of tax wedges on potential GDP and economic growth and a new section on generational accounting, fiscal imbalance, and the burden of the budget deficit on future generations.

7. **Monetary Policy** (Chapter 16): Another major reworking, this chapter covers the instruments, goals, and intermediate targets of monetary policy and provides an in-depth exploration of alternative rules for avoiding inflation and achieving sustainable long-term growth.

## MyEconLab

**MyEconLab** is a turnkey, online solution for your economics course. Featuring a new and powerful graphing tool and question bank, students are able to self-test and generate a study plan, and instructors are able to assign homework and capture grades. With a tight, everything-in-one-place organization around the new testing tool, questions include true-false, multiple-choice, fill-ins, numerical, and complete-the-graph. Because questions are generated algorithmically, there are about 40,000 questions per chapter!

Previous users of *Economics In Action* will find **MyEconLab** an exciting and powerful resource. Practice tests for each section of the textbook enable students to test their ability and identify the areas in which they need further work. Based on a student's performance on a practice test, a personalized study plan shows where further study is needed. Once students have received their study plan, additional practice exercises, keyed to the textbook, provide extensive practice and link directly to the eText, with animated graphs and other resources.

Users of **MyEconLab** will revel in the powerful graphing tool integrated into both the practice tests and practice exercises. This tool enables students to manipulate graphs and see how the concepts, numbers, and graphs are connected. Questions that use the graphing tool (like all other questions) can be submitted and graded online.

For review and self-assessment, **MyEconLab** provides tutorials launched directly from the practice exercises. Using the tutorial instruction, students can see a demonstration of step-by-step solutions to practice problems, or they can participate in guided tutorials that promote self-discovery.

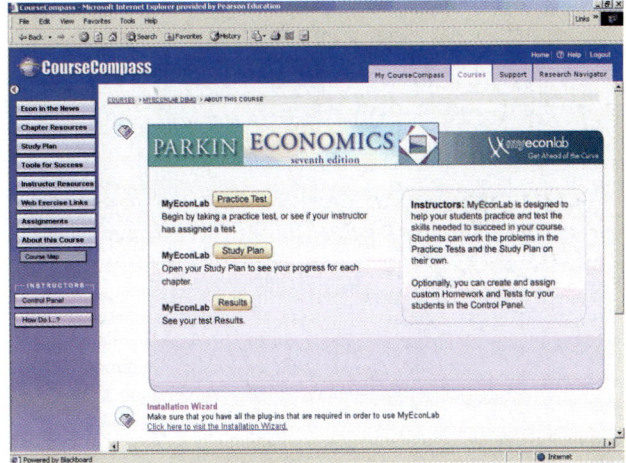

## Features to Enhance Teaching and Learning

HERE I DESCRIBE THE CHAPTER FEATURES THAT ARE designed to enhance the learning process. Each chapter contains the following learning aids.

### Chapter Opener

Each chapter opens with a one-page student-friendly, attention-grabbing vignette. The vignette raises questions that both motivate the student and focus the chapter. I carry this story into the main body of the chapter and relate it to the chapter-ending *Reading Between the Lines* feature for a cohesive learning experience.

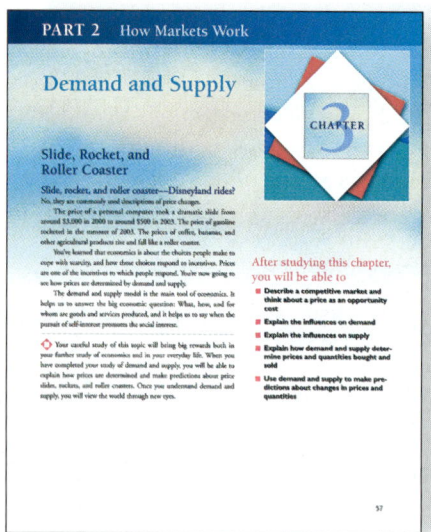

### Chapter Objectives

A list of learning objectives enables students to see exactly where the chapter is going and to set their goals before they begin the chapter. I link these goals directly to the chapter's major headings.

### In-Text Review Quizzes

A review quiz at the end of most major sections enables students to determine whether a topic needs further study before moving on.

### Key Terms

Highlighted terms within the text simplify the student's task of learning the vocabulary of economics. Each highlighted term appears in an end-of-chapter list with page numbers, in an end-of-book glossary with page numbers, boldfaced in the index, in the Web glossary, and in the Web Flash Cards.

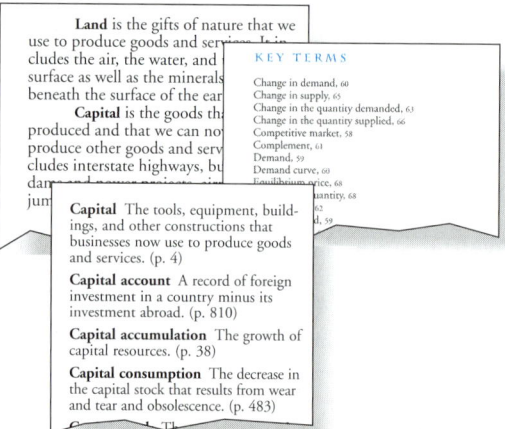

### Diagrams That Show the Action

Through seven editions, this book has set new standards of clarity in its diagrams. My goal has always been to show "where the economic action is." The diagrams in this book continue to generate an enormously positive response, which confirms my view that graphical analysis is the most powerful tool available for teaching and learning economics. But many students find graphs hard to work with. For this reason, I have developed the entire art program with the study and review needs of the student in mind.

The diagrams feature

- Original curves consistently shown in blue
- Shifted curves, equilibrium points, and other important features highlighted in red
- Color-blended arrows to suggest movement
- Graphs paired with data tables
- Diagrams labeled with boxed notes
- Extended captions that make each diagram and its caption a self-contained object for study and review.

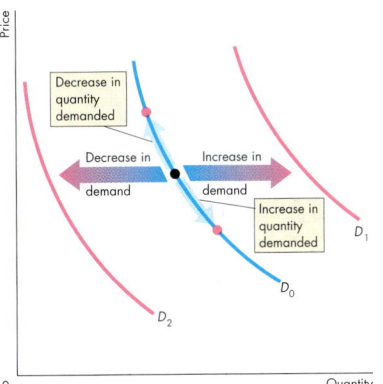

## Reading Between the Lines

In *Reading Between the Lines*, which appears at the end of each chapter, I show the student how to apply the tools they have just learned by analyzing an article from a newspaper or news Web site. The seventh edition features 17 new articles and 1 classic from the previous edition. I have chosen each article so that it sheds additional light on the questions first raised in the Chapter Opener.

Special "You're the Voter" sections in selected chapters invite students to analyze typical campaign topics and to probe their own stances on key public policy issues. Critical Thinking questions about the article appear with the end-of-chapter questions and problems.

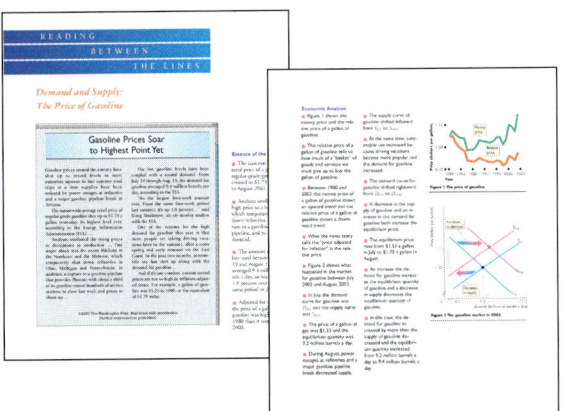

## End-of-Chapter Study Material

Each chapter closes with a concise summary organized by major topics, lists of key terms (all with page references), problems, critical thinking questions, and Web Exercises.

The end-of-chapter problems are organized in pairs. The solution to the odd-numbered problem in each pair may be found at **MyEconLab**; the parallel even-numbered problem is left for students to solve on their own. This arrangement offers help to students and flexibility to instructors who want to assign problems for credit.

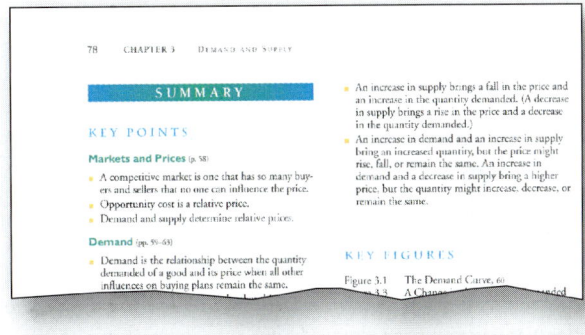

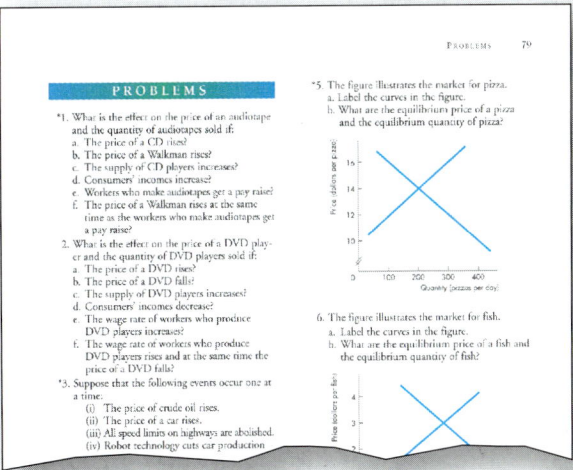

# For the Instructor

THIS BOOK ENABLES YOU TO ACHIEVE THREE OBJECTIVES in your principles course:

- Focus on the economic way of thinking
- Explain the issues and problems of our time
- Choose your own course structure

## Focus on the Economic Way of Thinking

You know how hard it is to encourage a student to think like an economist. But that is your goal. Consistent with this goal, the text focuses on and repeatedly uses the central ideas: choice; tradeoff; opportunity cost; the margin; incentives; the gains from voluntary exchange; the forces of demand, supply, and equilibrium; the pursuit of economic rent; the tension between self-interest and the social interest; and the scope and limitations of government actions.

## Explain the Issues and Problems of Our Time

Students must *use* the central ideas and tools if they are to begin to *understand* them. There is no better way to motivate students than by using the tools of economics to explain the issues that confront today's world. Issues such as globalization and the emergence of China as a major economic force; the new economy with new near-monopolies such as eBay and the widening income gap between rich and poor; the post-9/11 economy and the reallocation of resources toward counterterrorism and the defense that it entails; corporate scandals and the principal-agent problems and incentives faced by corporate managers; HIV/AIDS and the enormous cost of drugs for treating it; the disappearing tropical rainforests and the challenge that this problem of the commons creates; the challenge of managing the world's water resources; the persistent unemployment during the nation's jobless recovery of 2002 and 2003; the looming debt that arises from our newly emerged federal budget deficit and the even greater fiscal problems that arise from the Social Security obligations to an aging population; our vast and rising international deficit; and the tumbling value of the dollar on the foreign exchange market.

## Choose Your Own Course Structure

You want to teach your own course. I have organized this book to enable you to do so. I demonstrate the book's flexibility in the flexibility chart and alternative sequences table that appear on pp. xxvi–xxviii. You can use this book to teach a traditional course that blends theory and policy or a current policy issues course. Your micro course can emphasize theory or policy. You can structure your macro course to emphasize long-term growth and supply-side fundamentals. Or you can follow a traditional macro sequence and emphasize short-term fluctuations. The choices are yours.

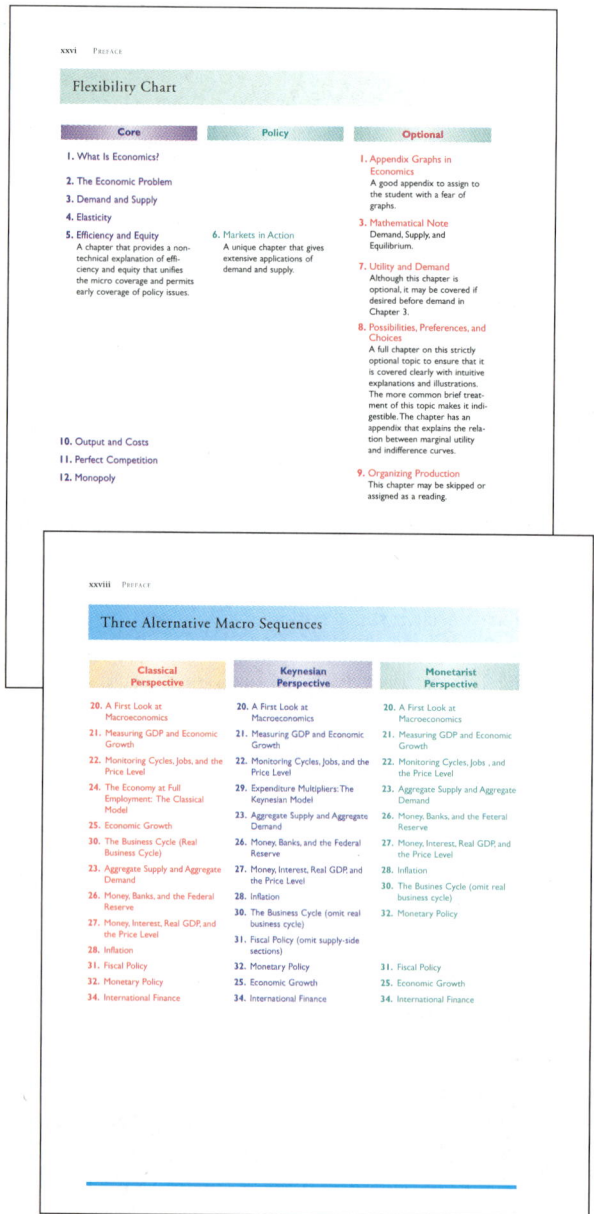

## Instructor's Manual

The Instructor's Manual (which I wrote with James Morley of Washington University, St. Louis) integrates the teaching and learning package and serves as a guide to all the supplements. Each chapter contains a chapter outline, what's new in the seventh edition, teaching suggestions, a look at where we have been and where we are going, a list of available overhead transparencies, a description of the electronic supplements, additional discussion questions, answers to the Review Quizzes, solutions to end-of-chapter problems, additional problems, and solutions to the additional problems. The chapter outline and teaching suggestions sections are keyed to the PowerPoint lecture notes.

**New Lecture Notes** This edition of the Instructor's Manual offers two new exciting features. Extensive lecture notes that incorporate alternative teaching examples—"Points of Interest"—enable a new user of Parkin to walk into a classroom well armed with engaging stories and explanations and a seasoned user to access a whole new set of fresh examples.

**New Worksheets** Another new and innovative feature is a set of Worksheets prepared by Patricia Kuzyk of Washington State University. These Worksheets ask students to contemplate real-world problems that illustrate economic principles. Examples include showing the effect of the catastrophic events of 9/11 using a marginal cost/marginal benefit diagram, and calculating the effects of funding Social Security for the huge number of baby-boomer retirees. Instructors can assign these as in-class group projects or as homework. There is a Worksheet for every chapter of the book.

## Three Test Banks

Three separate Test Banks with nearly 6,500 questions provide multiple-choice, true-false, numerical, fill-in-the-blank, short-answer, and essay questions. Mark Rush of the University of Florida reviewed and edited all existing questions to ensure their clarity and consistency with the seventh edition and incorporated over 1,000 new questions written by Constantin Ogloblin of Georgia Southern University and William Mosher of Clark University. These Test Banks are available in hard copy and electronically on an Instructor's CD-ROM and in the instructor's resources section of **MyEconLab**.

**New Problems** This edition features the addition of problems to the testing mix. Written by Constantin Ogloblin, these problems follow the style and format of the end-of-chapter text problems and provide the instructor with a whole new set of testing opportunities and/or homework assignments for every chapter.

**New Part Tests** These end-of-part tests contain questions that cover all the chapters in the part and feature integrative questions that span more than one chapter.

## PowerPoint Resources

Robin Bade and I have developed a full-color Microsoft PowerPoint Lecture Presentation for each chapter that includes all the figures from the text, animated graphs, and speaking notes. The slide outlines are based on the chapter outlines in the Instructor's Manual, and the speaking notes are based on the Instructor's Manual teaching suggestions. The presentations can be used electronically in the classroom or can be printed to create hard-copy transparency masters. This item is available for Macintosh and Windows.

## Overhead Transparencies

Full-color overhead transparencies of enlarged and simplified key figures from the text will improve the clarity of your lectures. They are available to qualified adopters of the text (contact your Addison-Wesley sales representative).

## Instructor's CD-ROM with Computerized Test Banks

This CD-ROM contains Computerized Test Bank files, Test Bank and Instructor's Manual files in Microsoft Word, and PowerPoint files. All three test banks are available in Test Generator Software (TestGen with QuizMaster). Fully networkable, it is available for Windows and Macintosh. TestGen's new graphical interface enables instructors to view, edit, and add questions; transfer questions to tests; and print different forms of tests. Tests can be formatted with varying fonts and styles, margins, and headers and footers, as in any word-processing document. Search and sort features let the instructor quickly locate questions and arrange them in a preferred order. QuizMaster, working with your school's computer network, automatically grades the exams, stores the results on disk, and allows the instructor to view or print a variety of reports.

## MyEconLab

The Web site that accompanies *Economics*, seventh edition breaks new ground by providing a structured environment in which students can practice what they learn and test their understanding and then pursue a study plan that is generated from their performance on practice tests. **MyEconLab** provides rich content resources keyed to the eText as well as flexible tools that enable instructors to easily and effectively customize online course materials to suit their needs.

Instructors can create and assign tests, quizzes, or graded homework assignments that incorporate graphing questions. **MyEconLab** saves instructors time by automatically grading all questions and tracking results in an online grade book. The complete Parkin Test Bank is also preloaded into **MyEconLab**, giving instructors ample material from which they can create assignments.

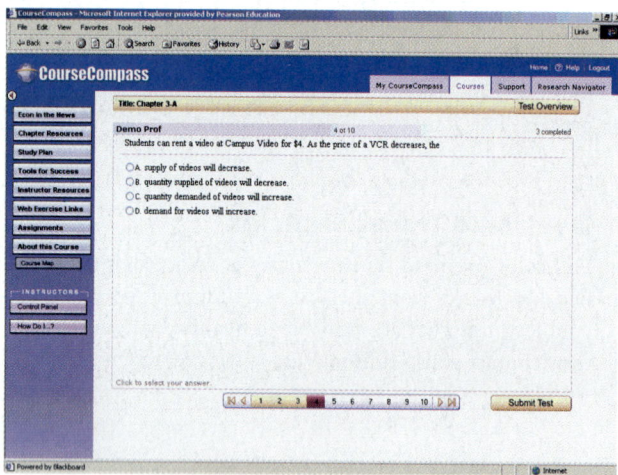

Once registered for **MyEconLab**, instructors have access to downloadable supplements such as Instructor's Manuals, PowerPoint lecture notes, and Test Banks. Instructors also have access to a "Consult the Author" feature that allows them to ask questions of and make suggestions to the author via e-mail and receive a response within 24 hours.

For more information about **MyEconLab**, or to request an Instructor Access Code, visit

http://www.myeconlab.com.

## For the Student

TWO OUTSTANDING SUPPORT TOOLS ARE AVAILABLE for the student:

- Study Guide
- **MyEconLab**

### Study Guide

The Seventh Edition Study Guide by Mark Rush of the University of Florida is carefully coordinated with the text, MyEconLab, and the Test Banks. Each chapter of the Study Guide contains

- Key concepts
- Helpful hints
- True/false/uncertain questions that ask students to explain their answers
- Multiple-choice questions
- Short-answer questions
- Common questions or misconceptions that the student explains as if he or she were the teacher

Each part allows students to test their cumulative understanding with sample midterm tests.

### MyEconLab

Packaged with every new book, **MyEconLab** puts students in control of their own learning through a suite of study and practice tools tied to the online, interactive version of the textbook and other media tools. At the core of **MyEconLab** are the following features:

- Practice tests
- Personalized study plan
- Additional practice exercises
- Tutorial instruction
- Powerful graphing tool

**Practice Tests** Practice tests for each section of the textbook enable students to test their understanding and identify the areas in which they need to do further work. Instructors can customize the practice tests or leave students to use the supplied pre-built tests.

**Personalized Study Plan** Based on a student's performance on a practice test, a personal study plan is generated that shows where further study is needed. This study plan consists of a series of additional practice exercises.

**Additional Practice Exercises** Generated by the student's own performance on a practice test, additional practice exercises keyed to the textbook provide extensive practice and link students to the eText with animated graphs and to other tutorial instruction resources.

**Tutorial Instruction** Launched from the additional practice exercises, tutorial instruction is provided in the form of solutions to problems, step-by-step explanations, and other media-based explanations.

**Powerful Graphing Tool** A powerful graphing tool integrated into the practice tests and additional practice exercises let students manipulate graphs so that they get a better feel for how the concepts, numbers, and graphs are connected. Questions that use the graphing tool (like all the other questions) can be submitted and graded.

**Additional MyEconLab tools**
1. eText (the entire textbook in electronic format)
2. eStudy guide (the entire Study Guide in electronic format and printable)
3. Animated figures (all the textbook figures in step-by-step animations with audio explanations of the action)
4. Electronic tutorials
5. Glossary—key terms from the textbook
6. Glossary Flashcards
7. Office Hours
8. Daily *Economics in the News* updates and archives
9. Links to the most useful economic data and information sources on the Internet
10. eThemes of the Times—archived articles from the *New York Times*, correlated to each textbook chapter and paired with critical thinking questions
11. Research Navigator—extensive help on the research process and four exclusive databases of credible and reliable source material including the *New York Times, The Financial Times*, and peer-reviewed journals.
12. Econ Tutor Center—Staffed by qualified, experienced college economics instructors, the Econ Tutor Center is open five days a week, seven hours a day. Tutors can be reached by phone, fax, e-mail or White Board technology. The Econ Tutor Center hours are designed to meet your students' study schedules, with evening hours Sunday through Thursday. Students receive one-on-one tutoring on examples, related exercises, and problems.

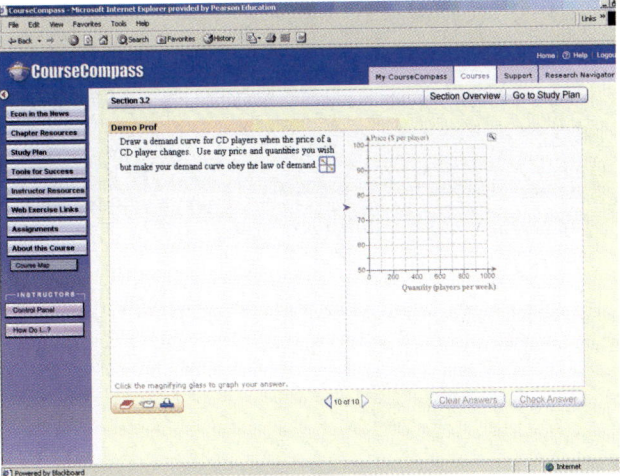

## Special Editions

THREE SPECIAL EDITIONS OF THE SEVENTH EDITION text are available:

- Economist.com Edition
- The Wall Street Journal Edition
- Financial Times Edition

### Economist.com Edition

The premier online source of economic news analysis, Economist.com provides your students with insight and opinion on current economic events. Through an agreement between Addison-Wesley and *The Economist*, your students can receive a low-cost subscription to this premium Web site for 12 weeks, including the complete text of the current issue of *The Economist* and access to *The Economist*'s searchable archives. Other features include Web-only weekly articles, news feeds with current world and business news, and stock market and currency data. Professors who adopt this special edition will receive a complimentary one-year subscription to Economist.com.

### The Wall Street Journal Edition

Addison-Wesley is also pleased to provide your students with access to *The Wall Street Journal*, the most respected and trusted daily source for information on business and economics. For a small additional charge, Addison-Wesley offers your students a subscription to *The Wall Street Journal* and WSJ.com. Ten-week and 15-week subscriptions are available. Adopting professors will receive a complimentary one-year subscription to *The Wall Street Journal* as well as access to WSJ.com.

### Financial Times Edition

Featuring international news and analysis from FT journalists in more than 50 countries, the *Financial Times* will provide your students with insights and perspectives on economic developments around the world. The *Financial Times Edition* provides your students with a 15-week subscription to one of the world's leading business publications. Adopting professors will receive a complimentary one-year subscription to the *Financial Times* as well as access to FT.com.

## Acknowledgments

I THANK MY CURRENT AND FORMER COLLEAGUES and friends at the University of Western Ontario who have taught me so much. They are Jim Davies, Jeremy Greenwood, Ig Horstmann, Peter Howitt, Greg Huffman, David Laidler, Phil Reny, Chris Robinson, John Whalley, and Ron Wonnacott. I also thank Doug McTaggart and Christopher Findlay, co-authors of the Australian edition, and Melanie Powell and Kent Matthews, co-authors of the European edition. Suggestions arising from their adaptations of earlier editions have been helpful to me in preparing this edition.

I thank the several thousand students whom I have been privileged to teach. The instant response that comes from the look of puzzlement or enlightenment has taught me how to teach economics.

It is a special joy to thank the many outstanding editors, media specialists, and others at Addison-Wesley who contributed to the concerted publishing effort that brought this edition to completion. Denise Clinton, Editor-in-Chief for Economics and Finance, was a constant source of inspiration and encouragement and provided overall direction to the project. Adrienne D'Ambrosio, Acquisitions Editor for Economics and my sponsoring editor, played a major role in shaping this revision and the many outstanding supplements that accompany it. Adrienne brings intelligence and insight to her work and has quickly become a pre-eminent economics editor. Mary Clare McEwing, Senior Project Manager, brought her huge experience and dedicated professionalism to the development effort and once again outperformed her own outstanding record of finding the very best reviewers. Dottie Dennis, Senior Administrative Assistant, worked tirelessly to bring reviews in on time and consolidate and summarize them. Michelle Neil, Executive Media Producer, ably helped by Melissa Honig, Senior Media Producer, developed the new version of **MyEconLab** and ensured that all the legacy of media assets from the sixth edition Web site, including the diagnostic quizzes and *Economics in Action*, translated smoothly and correctly into our powerful new learning and teaching environment. Jason Miranda, Digital Assets Manager, working with an outstanding team of authors, managed the creation of a large and complex supplements package. Stephen Frail, Executive Marketing Manager, provided inspired marketing strategy and direction. His brochures and his intimate involvement at all stages of the development of this edition had a significant impact on its shape. Christine Lyons provided copy that sparkled and that captured the essence and spirit of the book and package. Regina Hagen Kolenda, Senior Designer, designed the cover, text, and package and yet again surpassed the challenge of ensuring that we meet the highest design standards. Managing Editor James Rigney, Electronic Production Manager Scott Silva and his team, and especially Nancy Fenton, Senior Production Supervisor, worked miracles on a tight production schedule and coped calmly with late-changing content. Hugh Crawford, Senior Manufacturing Buyer, and Ginny Michaud, Media Buyer, ensured the highest standards of print and CD production. Kathy Smith copyedited and proofread the text manuscript and Sheryl Nelson the Instructor's Manual. I thank all of these wonderful people. It has been inspiring to work with them and to share in creating what I believe is a truly outstanding educational tool.

I thank our talented seventh edition supplements authors—Michael Stroup, Stephen F. Austin State University; James Morley, Washington University, St. Louis; Constantin Ogloblin, Georgia Southern University; William Mosher, Clark University; and Patricia Kuzyk, Washington State University. I especially thank Mark Rush, who yet again played a crucial role in creating another edition of this text and package. Mark has been a constant source of good advice and good humor. I thank the many exceptional reviewers who have shared their insights through the various editions of this book. Their contribution has been invaluable. I particularly thank John Graham, Mark Thoma, David Wharton, Steven Peterson, Francis Mummery, and Patricia Kuzyk for their extraordinarily careful accuracy reviews.

I thank the people who work directly with me. Jeannie Gillmore provided outstanding research assistance on many topics, including the *Reading Between the Lines* news articles. Richard Parkin created the electronic art files and offered many ideas that improved the figures in this book. And Laurel Davies managed an ever-growing and ever more complex **MyEconLab** database.

As with the previous editions, this one owes an enormous debt to Robin Bade. I dedicate this book to her and again thank her for her work. I could not have written this book without the unselfish help she has given me. My thanks to her are unbounded.

Classroom experience will test the value of this book. I would appreciate hearing from instructors and students about how I can continue to improve it in future editions.

*Michael Parkin*
London, Ontario, Canada
michael.parkin@uwo.ca

## Reviewers

Eric Abrams, Hawaii Pacific University
Christopher Adams, University of Vermont
Tajudeen Adenekan, Bronx Community College
Syed Ahmed, Cameron University
Frank Albritton, Seminole Community College
Milton Alderfer, Miami-Dade Community College
William Aldridge, Shelton State Community College
Donald L. Alexander, Western Michigan University
Terence Alexander, Iowa State University
Stuart Allen, University of North Carolina, Greensboro
Sam Allgood, University of Nebraska, Lincoln
Neil Alper, Northeastern University
Alan Anderson, Fordham University
Lisa R. Anderson, College of William and Mary
Jeff Ankrom, Wittenberg University
Fatma Antar, Manchester Community Technical College
Kofi Apraku, University of North Carolina, Asheville
Moshen Bahmani-Oskooee, University of Wisconsin, Milwaukee
Donald Balch, University of South Carolina
Mehmet Balcilar, Wayne State University
Paul Ballantyne, University of Colorado
Sue Bartlett, University of South Florida
Jose Juan Bautista, Xavier University of Louisiana
Valerie R. Bencivenga, University of Texas, Austin
Ben Bernanke, Princeton University
Margot Biery, Tarrant County Community College South
John Bittorowitz, Ball State University
David Black, University of Toledo
S. Brock Blomberg, Wellesley College
William T. Bogart, Case Western Reserve University
Giacomo Bonanno, University of California, Davis
Sunne Brandmeyer, University of South Florida
Audie Brewton, Northeastern Illinois University
Baird Brock, Central Missouri State University
Byron Brown, Michigan State University
Jeffrey Buser, Columbus State Community College
Alison Butler, Florida International University
Tania Carbiener, Southern Methodist University
Kevin Carey, American University
Kathleen A. Carroll, University of Maryland, Baltimore County
Michael Carter, University of Massachusetts, Lowell
Edward Castronova, California State University, Fullerton

Subir Chakrabarti, Indiana University-Purdue University
Joni Charles, Southwest Texas State University
Adhip Chaudhuri, Georgetown University
Gopal Chengalath, Texas Tech University
Daniel Christiansen, Albion College
John J. Clark, Community College of Allegheny County, Allegheny Campus
Meredith Clement, Dartmouth College
Michael B. Cohn, U. S. Merchant Marine Academy
Robert Collinge, University of Texas, San Antonio
Carol Condon, Kean University
Doug Conway, Mesa Community College
Larry Cook, University of Toledo
Bobby Corcoran, Middle Tennessee State University
Kevin Cotter, Wayne State University
James Peery Cover, University of Alabama, Tuscaloosa
Erik Craft, University of Richmond
Eleanor D. Craig, University of Delaware
Jim Craven, Clark College
Elizabeth Crowell, University of Michigan, Dearborn
Stephen Cullenberg, University of California, Riverside
David Culp, Slippery Rock University
Norman V. Cure, Macomb Community College
Dan Dabney, University of Texas, Austin
Andrew Dane, Angelo State University
Joseph Daniels, Marquette University
Gregory DeFreitas, Hofstra University
David Denslow, University of Florida
Mark Dickie, University of Georgia
James Dietz, California State University, Fullerton
Carol Dole, State University of West Georgia
Ronald Dorf, Inver Hills Community College
John Dorsey, University of Maryland, College Park
Eric Drabkin, Hawaii Pacific University
Amrik Singh Dua, Mt. San Antonio College
Thomas Duchesneau, University of Maine, Orono
Lucia Dunn, Ohio State University
Donald Dutkowsky, Syracuse University
John Edgren, Eastern Michigan University
David J. Eger, Alpena Community College
Harry Ellis, Jr., University of North Texas
Ibrahim Elsaify, State University of New York, Albany
Kenneth G. Elzinga, University of Virginia
Antonina Espiritu, Hawaii Pacific University
Gwen Eudey, University of Pennsylvania

M. Fazeli, Hofstra University
Philip Fincher, Louisiana Tech University
F. Firoozi, University of Texas, San Antonio
Nancy Folbre, University of Massachusetts at Amherst
Kenneth Fong, Temasek Polytechnic (Singapore)
Steven Francis, Holy Cross College
David Franck, University of North Carolina, Charlotte
Roger Frantz, San Diego State University
Mark Frascatore, Clarkson University
Alwyn Fraser, Atlantic Union College
Richard Fristensky, Bentley College
James Gale, Michigan Technological University
Susan Gale, New York University
Roy Gardner, Indiana University
Eugene Gentzel, Pensacola Junior College
Scott Gilbert, Southern Illinois University at Carbondale
Andrew Gill, California State University, Fullerton
Robert Giller, Virginia Polytechnic Institute and State University
Robert Gillette, University of Kentucky
James N. Giordano, Villanova University
Maria Giuili, Diablo College
Susan Glanz, St. John's University
Robert Gordon, San Diego State University
Richard Gosselin, Houston Community College
John Graham, Rutgers University
John Griffen, Worcester Polytechnic Institute
Wayne Grove, Syracuse University
Robert Guell, Indiana State University
Jamie Haag, University of Oregon
Gail Heyne Hafer, Lindenwood University
Rik W. Hafer, Southern Illinois University, Edwardsville
Daniel Hagen, Western Washington University
David R. Hakes, University of Northern Iowa
Craig Hakkio, Federal Reserve Bank, Kansas City
Ann Hansen, Westminster College
Seid Hassan, Murray State University
Jonathan Haughton, Northeastern University
Randall Haydon, Wichita State University
Denise Hazlett, Whitman College
Julia Heath, University of Memphis
Jac Heckelman, Wake Forest University
Jolien A. Helsel, Kent State University
James Henderson, Baylor University
Jill Boylston Herndon, University of Florida
Gus Herring, Brookhaven College
John Herrmann, Rutgers University

John M. Hill, Delgado Community College
Jonathan Hill, Florida International University
Lewis Hill, Texas Tech University
Steve Hoagland, University of Akron
Tom Hoerger, Vanderbilt University
Calvin Hoerneman, Delta College
George Hoffer, Virginia Commonwealth University
Dennis L. Hoffman, Arizona State University
Paul Hohenberg, Rensselaer Polytechnic Institute
Jim H. Holcomb, University of Texas, El Paso
Harry Holzer, Michigan State University
Linda Hooks, Washington and Lee University
Jim Horner, Cameron University
Djehane Hosni, University of Central Florida
Harold Hotelling, Jr., Lawrence Technical University
Calvin Hoy, County College of Morris
Julie Hunsaker, Wayne State University
Beth Ingram, University of Iowa
Jayvanth Ishwaran, Stephen F. Austin State University
Michael Jacobs, Lehman College
S. Hussain Ali Jafri, Tarleton State University
Dennis Jansen, Texas A&M University
Frederick Jungman, Northwestern Oklahoma State University
Paul Junk, University of Minnesota, Duluth
Leo Kahane, California State University, Hayward
Veronica Kalich, Baldwin-Wallace College
John Kane, State University of New York, Oswego
Eungmin Kang, St. Cloud State University
Arthur Kartman, San Diego State University
Gurmit Kaur, Universiti Teknologi (Malaysia)
Louise Keely, University of Wisconsin at Madison
Manfred W. Keil, Claremont McKenna College
Elizabeth Sawyer Kelly, University of Wisconsin at Madison
Rose Kilburn, Modesto Junior College
Robert Kirk, Indiana University—Purdue University, Indianapolis
Norman Kleinberg, City University of New York, Baruch College
Robert Kleinhenz, California State University, Fullerton
John Krantz, University of Utah
Joseph Kreitzer, University of St. Thomas
Patricia Kuzyk, Washington State University
David Lages, Southwest Missouri State University
W. J. Lane, University of New Orleans
Leonard Lardaro, University of Rhode Island
Kathryn Larson, Elon College
Luther D. Lawson, University of North Carolina, Wilmington
Elroy M. Leach, Chicago State University

Jim Lee, Fort Hays State University
Sang Lee, Southeastern Louisiana University
Robert Lemke, Florida International University
Mary Lesser, Iona College
Jay Levin, Wayne State University
Arik Levinson, University of Wisconsin, Madison
Tony Lima, California State University, Hayward
William Lord, University of Maryland, Baltimore County
Nancy Lutz, Virginia Polytechnic Institute and State University
Murugappa Madhavan, San Diego State University
K. T. Magnusson, Salt Lake Community College
Mark Maier, Glendale Community College
Beth Maloan, University of Tennessee, Martin
Jean Mangan, California State University, Sacramento
Michael Marlow, California Polytechnic State University
Akbar Marvasti, University of Houston
Wolfgang Mayer, University of Cincinnati
John McArthur, Wofford College
Amy McCormick, College of William and Mary
Russel McCullough, Iowa State University
Gerald McDougall, Wichita State University
Stephen McGary, Ricks College
Richard D. McGrath, College of William and Mary
Richard McIntyre, University of Rhode Island
John McLeod, Georgia Institute of Technology
Mark McLeod, Virginia Tech
B. Starr McMullen, Oregon State University
Mary Ruth McRae, Appalachian State University
Kimberly Merritt, Cameron University
Charles Meyer, Iowa State University
Peter Mieszkowski, Rice University
John Mijares, University of North Carolina, Asheville
Richard A. Miller, Wesleyan University
Judith W. Mills, Southern Connecticut State University
Glen Mitchell, Nassau Community College
Jeannette C. Mitchell, Rochester Institute of Technology
Khan Mohabbat, Northern Illinois University
Bagher Modjtahedi, University of California, Davis
W. Douglas Morgan, University of California, Santa Barbara
William Morgan, University of Wyoming
James Morley, Washington University in St. Louis
William Mosher, Clark University
Joanne Moss, San Francisco State University
Nivedita Mukherji, Oakland University
Francis Mummery, Fullerton College
Edward Murphy, Southwest Texas State University

Kevin J. Murphy, Oakland University
Kathryn Nantz, Fairfield University
William S. Neilson, Texas A&M University
Bart C. Nemmers, University of Nebraska, Lincoln
Melinda Nish, Salt Lake Community College
Anthony O'Brien, Lehigh University
Constantin Ogloblin, Georgia Southern University
Mary Olson, Washington University
Terry Olson, Truman State University
James B. O'Neill, University of Delaware
Farley Ordovensky, University of the Pacific
Z. Edward O'Relley, North Dakota State University
Donald Oswald, California State University, Bakersfield
Jan Palmer, Ohio University
Michael Palumbo, University of Houston
Chris Papageorgiou, Louisiana State University
G. Hossein Parandvash, Western Oregon State College
Randall Parker, East Carolina University
Robert Parks, Washington University
David Pate, St. John Fisher College
Donald Pearson, Eastern Michigan University
Steven Peterson, University of Idaho
Mary Anne Pettit, Southern Illinois University, Edwardsville
Kathy Phares, University of Missouri, St. Louis
William A. Phillips, University of Southern Maine
Dennis Placone, Clemson University
Charles Plot, California Institute of Technology, Pasadena
Mannie Poen, Houston Community College
Kathleen Possai, Wayne State University
Ulrika Praski-Stahlgren, University College in Gavle-Sandviken, Sweden
Edward Price, Oklahoma State University
Rula Qalyoubi, Colorado State University
K. A. Quartey, Talladega College
Herman Quirmbach, Iowa State University
Jeffrey R. Racine, University of South Florida
Peter Rangazas, Indiana University-Purdue University, Indianapolis
Vaman Rao, Western Illinois University
Laura Razzolini, University of Mississippi
Rob Rebelein, University of Cincinnati
J. David Reed, Bowling Green State University
Robert H. Renshaw, Northern Illinois University
Javier Reyes, University of Arkansas
Rupert Rhodd, Florida Atlantic University
W. Gregory Rhodus, Bentley College

Jennifer Rice, Indiana University, Bloomington
John Robertson, Paducah Community College
Malcolm Robinson, University of North Carolina, Greensboro
Richard Roehl, University of Michigan, Dearborn
Carol Rogers, Georgetown University
William Rogers, University of Northern Colorado
Thomas Romans, State University of New York, Buffalo
David R. Ross, Bryn Mawr College
Thomas Ross, St. Louis University
Robert J. Rossana, Wayne State University
Jeffrey Rous, University of North Texas
Rochelle Ruffer, Youngstown State University
Mark Rush, University of Florida
Allen R. Sanderson, University of Chicago
Gary Santoni, Ball State University
John Saussy, Harrisburg Area Community College
Don Schlagenhauf, Florida State University
David Schlow, Pennsylvania State University
Paul Schmitt, St. Clair County Community College
Jeremy Schwartz, Broward Community College
Martin Sefton, Indianapolis University
Esther-Mirjam Sent, University of Notre Dame
Rod Shadbegian, University of Massachusetts, Dartmouth
Gerald Shilling, Eastfield College
Dorothy R. Siden, Salem State College
Mark Siegler, California State University at Sacramento
Scott Simkins, North Carolina Agricultural and Technical State University
Chuck Skoro, Boise State University
Phil Smith, DeKalb College
William Doyle Smith, University of Texas, El Paso
Sarah Stafford, College of William and Mary
Frank Steindl, Oklahoma State University
Jeffrey Stewart, New York University
Allan Stone, Southwest Missouri State University
Courtenay Stone, Ball State University
Paul Storer, Western Washington University
Mark Strazicich, Ohio State University, Newark
Michael Stroup, Stephen F. Austin State University
Robert Stuart, Rutgers University
Della Lee Sue, Marist College
Abdulhamid Sukar, Cameron University
Terry Sutton, Southeast Missouri State University
Gilbert Suzawa, University of Rhode Island
David Swaine, Andrews University
Jason Taylor, University of Virginia

Mark Thoma, University of Oregon
Janet Thomas, Bentley College
Kiril Tochkov, SUNY at Binghamton
Kay Unger, University of Montana
Anthony Uremovic, Joliet Junior College
David Vaughn, City University, Washington
Don Waldman, Colgate University
Francis Wambalaba, Portland State University
Rob Wassmer, Wayne State University
Paul A. Weinstein, University of Maryland, College Park
Lee Weissert, St. Vincent College
Robert Whaples, Wake Forest University
David Wharton, Washington College
Mark Wheeler, Western Michigan University
Charles H. Whiteman, University of Iowa
Sandra Williamson, University of Pittsburgh
Brenda Wilson, Brookhaven Community College
Larry Wimmer, Brigham Young University
Mark Witte, Northwestern University
Willard E. Witte, Indiana University
Mark Wohar, University of Nebraska, Omaha
Laura Wolff, Southern Illinois University, Edwardsville
Cheonsik Woo, Clemson University
Douglas Wooley, Radford University
Arthur G. Woolf, University of Vermont
Ann Al Yasiri, University of Wisconsin, Platteville
John T. Young, Riverside Community College
Michael Youngblood, Rock Valley College
Peter Zaleski, Villanova University
Jason Zimmerman, South Dakota State University
David Zucker, Martha Stewart Living Omnimedia

**Supplements Authors**

James Cobbe, Florida State University
Carol Dole, State University of West Georgia
John Graham, Rutgers University
Jill Herndon, University of Florida
Sang Lee, Southeastern Louisiana University
Patricia Kuzyk, Washington State University
James Morley, Washington University, St. Louis
William Mosher, Clark University
Constantin Ogloblin, Georgia Southern University
Edward Price, Oklahoma State University
Mark Rush, University of Florida
Della Lee Sue, Marist College
Michael Stroup, Stephen F. Austin State University

# Flexibility Chart

## Core

1. What Is Economics?

2. The Economic Problem

3. Demand and Supply

4. Elasticity

5. Efficiency and Equity
   A chapter that provides a nontechnical explanation of efficiency and equity that unifies the micro coverage and permits early coverage of policy issues.

10. Output and Costs

11. Perfect Competition

12. Monopoly

## Policy

6. Markets in Action
   A unique chapter that gives extensive applications of demand and supply.

## Optional

1. Appendix Graphs in Economics
   A good appendix to assign to the student with a fear of graphs.

3. Mathematical Note
   Demand, Supply, and Equilibrium.

7. Utility and Demand
   Although this chapter is optional, it may be covered if desired before demand in Chapter 3.

8. Possibilities, Preferences, and Choices
   A full chapter on this strictly optional topic to ensure that it is covered clearly with intuitive explanations and illustrations. The more common brief treatment of this topic makes it indigestible. The chapter has an appendix that explains the relation between marginal utility and indifference curves.

9. Organizing Production
   This chapter may be skipped or assigned as a reading.

| Core | Policy | Optional |
|---|---|---|
| **13.** Monopolistic Competition and Oligopoly | **14.** Regulation and Antitrust Law  Introduces the public-choice theory of government, sets the scene for the following policy chapters, and explains the positive theory of regulation and antitrust law. | |
| | **15.** Externalities | |
| | **16.** Public Goods and Common Resources | |
| **17.** Demand and Supply in Factor Markets | **18.** Economic Inequality | **19.** Uncertainty and Information |
| **20.** A First Look at Macroeconomics | | |
| **21.** Measuring GDP and Economic Growth | | |
| **22.** Monitoring Cycles, Jobs, and the Price Level | | |
| **23.** Aggregate Supply and Aggregate Demand  This chapter may be delayed and studied after Chapter 25. | | **24.** The Economy at Full Employment: The Classical Model |
| **25.** Economic Growth  The chapter may be delayed and studied at any desired point. | | |
| **26.** Money, Banks, and the Federal Reserve | | |
| **27.** Money, Interest, Real GDP, and the Price Level | | |
| **28.** Inflation | | **29.** Expenditure Multipliers: The Keynsian Model  This chapter may be brought forward and studied at any point after Chapter 21. |
| | **31.** Fiscal Policy | **30.** The Business Cycle |
| | **32.** Monetary Policy | **33.** Trading with the World |
| | | **34.** International Finance |

# Three Alternative Macro Sequences

## Classical Perspective

20. A First Look at Macroeconomics
21. Measuring GDP and Economic Growth
22. Monitoring Cycles, Jobs, and the Price Level
24. The Economy at Full Employment: The Classical Model
25. Economic Growth
30. The Business Cycle (Real Business Cycle)
23. Aggregate Supply and Aggregate Demand
26. Money, Banks, and the Federal Reserve
27. Money, Interest, Real GDP, and the Price Level
28. Inflation
31. Fiscal Policy
32. Monetary Policy
34. International Finance

## Keynesian Perspective

20. A First Look at Macroeconomics
21. Measuring GDP and Economic Growth
22. Monitoring Cycles, Jobs, and the Price Level
29. Expenditure Multipliers: The Keynesian Model
23. Aggregate Supply and Aggregate Demand
26. Money, Banks, and the Federal Reserve
27. Money, Interest, Real GDP, and the Price Level
28. Inflation
30. The Business Cycle (omit real business cycle)
31. Fiscal Policy (omit supply-side sections)
32. Monetary Policy
25. Economic Growth
34. International Finance

## Monetarist Perspective

20. A First Look at Macroeconomics
21. Measuring GDP and Economic Growth
22. Monitoring Cycles, Jobs, and the Price Level
23. Aggregate Supply and Aggregate Demand
26. Money, Banks, and the Feteral Reserve
27. Money, Interest, Real GDP, and the Price Level
28. Inflation
30. The Busines Cycle (omit real business cycle)
32. Monetary Policy
31. Fiscal Policy
25. Economic Growth
34. International Finance

# CREDITS

Part 1: Adam Smith (p. 52), Corbis-Bettmann. Pin factory (p. 53), Culver Pictures. Silicon wafer (p. 53), Bruce Ando/Tony Stone Images.

Part 2: Alfred Marshall (p. 146), Stock Montage. Railroad bridge (p. 147), National Archives. Airport (p. 147), PhotoDisc, Inc.

Part 3: John Maynard Keynes (p. 174), Stock Montage. Worker destroying spinning jenny in England (p. 175), Corbis/Bettmann. AT&T Networking Center (p. 175), Hank Morgan.

Part 4: Joseph Schumpeter (p. 228), Corbis-Bettmann. McCormick's first reaping machine, ca. 1834 (p. 229), North Wind Picture Archives. Fiber optics (p. 229), PhotoDisc, Inc. Paul Romer (p. 230), Christopher Irion.

Part 5: Milton Friedman (p. 300), Marshall Henrichs/Addison-Wesley. German housewife burning Reichmarks in 1923 (p. 301), UPI/Corbis-Bettmann. Brazilians stocking up on food before price increase (p. 301), © Carlos Humberto TDC/Contact Press Images.

Part 6: Irving Fisher (p. 410), Yale University Archives, Manuscripts and Archives, Yale Library. Depositors outside door of closed bank (p. 411), Corbis-Bettmann. Boarded-up shop (p. 411), ©Susan van Etten. Peter N. Ireland (p. 412), L. Pellegrini.

Part 7: David Ricardo (p. 458), Corbis-Bettmann. Clipper ship (p. 459), North Wind Picture Archives. Container ship (p. 459), © M. Timothy O'Keefe/ Weststock.

# BRIEF CONTENTS

### PART 1  Introduction
Chapter 1  What Is Economics?
Chapter 2  The Economic Problem

### PART 2  How Markets Work
Chapter 3  Demand and Supply

### PART 3  Macroeconomic Overview
Chapter 4  A First Look at Macroeconomics
Chapter 5  Measuring GDP and Economic Growth
Chapter 6  Monitoring Cycles, Jobs, and the Price Level
Chapter 7  Aggregate Supply and Aggregate Demand

### PART 4  Aggregate Supply and Economic Growth
Chapter 8  The Economy at Full Employment: The Classical Model
Chapter 9  Economic Growth

### PART 5  Aggregate Demand, Money, and Inflation
Chapter 10  Money, Banks, and the Federal Reserve
Chapter 11  Money, Interest, Real GDP, and the Price Level
Chapter 12  Inflation

### PART 6  Economic Fluctuations and Stabilization Policy
Chapter 13  Expenditure Multipliers: The Keynesian Model
Chapter 14  The Business Cycle
Chapter 15  Fiscal Policy
Chapter 16  Monetary Policy

### PART 7  The Global Economy
Chapter 17  Trading with the World
Chapter 18  International Finance

# CONTENTS

## Part 1  Introduction  1

### Chapter 1  What Is Economics?  1

#### Understanding Our Changing World  1

#### Definition of Economics  2
- Microeconomics  2
- Macroeconomics  2

#### Two Big Microeconomic Questions  3
- What, How, and For Whom?  3
- When Is the Pursuit of Self-Interest in the Social Interest?  5

#### The Economic Way of Thinking  9
- Choices and Tradeoffs  9
- What, How, and For Whom Tradeoffs  9
- Choices Bring Change  10
- Opportunity Cost  10
- Choosing at the Margin  11
- Responding to Incentives  11
- Human Nature, Incentives, and Institutions  11

#### Economics: A Social Science  12
- Observation and Measurement  12
- Model Building  12
- Testing Models  12
- Obstacles and Pitfalls in Economics  13
- Agreement and Disagreement  14

*Summary (Key Points, Key Figures and Tables, and Key Terms), Problems, Critical Thinking, and Web Exercises appear at the end of each chapter.*

### Chapter 1  Appendix  17

#### Graphs in Economics  17

#### Graphing Data  17
- Time-Series Graphs  18
- Cross-Section Graphs  18
- Scatter Diagrams  19

#### Graphs Used in Economic Models  20
- Variables That Move in the Same Direction  20
- Variables That Move in Opposite Directions  21
- Variables That Have a Maximum or a Minimum  22
- Variables That Are Unrelated  23

#### The Slope of a Relationship  24
- The Slope of a Straight Line  24
- The Slope of a Curved Line  25

#### Graphing Relationships Among More Than Two Variables  26

xxxi

## Chapter 2     The Economic Problem   31

### Good, Better, Best!   31

### Production Possibilities and Opportunity Cost   32
Production Possibilities Frontier   32
Production Efficiency   33
Tradeoff Along the *PPF*   33
Opportunity Cost   33

### Using Resources Efficiently   35
The *PPF* and Marginal Cost   35
Preferences and Marginal Benefit   36
Efficient Use of Resources   37

### Economic Growth   38
The Cost of Economic Growth   38
Economic Growth in the United States and Hong Kong   39

### Gains from Trade   40
Comparative Advantage   40
Achieving the Gains from Trade   41
Absolute Advantage   43
Dynamic Comparative Advantage   43

### Economic Coordination   44
Firms   44
Markets   44
Circular Flows Through Markets   44
Coordinating Decisions   45

### READING BETWEEN THE LINES
### POLICY WATCH
The Cost and Benefit of Airport Security   46

### PART 1 Wrap-Up
**Understanding the Scope of Economics**   51
Probing the Ideas: The Sources of Economic Wealth   52
Talking with Lawrence H. Summers   54

## Part 2     How Markets Work   57

## Chapter 3     Demand and Supply   57

### Slide, Rocket, and Roller Coaster   57

### Markets and Prices   58

### Demand   59
The Law of Demand   59
Demand Curve and Demand Schedule   59
A Change in Demand   60
A Change in the Quantity Demanded Versus a Change in Demand   62

### Supply   64
The Law of Supply   64
Supply Curve and Supply Schedule   64
A Change in Supply   65
A Change in the Quantity Supplied Versus a Change in Supply   66

### Market Equilibrium   68
Price as a Regulator   68
Price Adjustments   69

### Predicting Changes in Price and Quantity   70
A Change in Demand   70
A Change in Supply   71
A Change in Both Demand and Supply   72

### READING BETWEEN THE LINES
Demand and Supply: The Price of Gasoline   74

**MATHEMATICAL NOTE**
Demand, Supply, and Equilibrium   76

### PART 2 Wrap-Up
**Understanding How Markets Work**   81
Probing the Ideas: Discovering the Laws of Demand and Supply   82
Talking with Charles Plott   84

## Part 3  Macroeconomic Overview  87

### Chapter 4  A First Look at Macroeconomics  87

**What Will Your World Be Like?**  87

**Origins and Issues of Macroeconomics**  88
  Short-Term Versus Long-Term Goals  88
  The Road Ahead  88

**Economic Growth and Fluctuations**  89
  Economic Growth in the United States  89
  Economic Growth Around the World  91
  The Lucas Wedge and the Okun Gap  93
  Benefits and Costs of Economic Growth  94
  Jobs and Unemployment  94
  Jobs  94
  Unemployment  94
  Unemployment in the United States  95
  Unemployment Around the World  96
  Why Unemployment Is a Problem  96

**Inflation**  97
  Inflation in the United States  97
  Inflation Around the World  98
  Is Inflation a Problem?  98

**Surpluses and Deficits**  99
  Government Budget Surplus and Deficit  99
  International Deficit  99
  Do Deficits Matter?  100

**Macroeconomic Policy Challenges and Tools**  101

**Policy Challenges and Tools**  101

**READING BETWEEN THE LINES**
  The 2003 Expansion  102

### Chapter 5  Measuring GDP and Economic Growth  107

**An Economic Barometer**  107

**Gross Domestic Product**  108
  GDP Defined  108
  GDP and the Circular Flow of Expenditure and Income  109
  Financial Flows  110
  How Investment Is Financed  110
  Gross and Net Domestic Product  111

**Measuring U.S. GDP**  113
  The Expenditure Approach  113
  The Income Approach  113

**Real GDP and the Price Level**  115
  Calculating Real GDP  115
  Calculating the Price Level  116
  Deflating the GDP Balloon  117

**Measuring Economic Growth**  118
  Economic Welfare Comparisons  118
  International Comparisons  120
  Business Cycle Forecasts  121

**READING BETWEEN THE LINES**
  Real GDP in the 2003 Expansion  122

## Chapter 6  Monitoring Cycles, Jobs, and the Price Level  127

### Vital Signs  127

#### The Business Cycle  128
- Business Cycle Dates  128
- The 2001 Recession  129

#### Jobs and Wages  130
- Population Survey  130
- Three Labor Market Indicators  130
- Aggregate Hours  132
- Real Wage Rate  133

#### Unemployment and Full Employment  135
- The Anatomy of Unemployment  135
- Types of Unemployment  137
- Full Employment  137
- Real GDP and Unemployment Over the Cycle  139

#### The Consumer Price Index  140
- Reading the CPI Numbers  140
- Constructing the CPI  140
- Measuring Inflation  142
- The Biased CPI  143
- The Magnitude of the Bias  143
- Some Consequences of the Bias  143

#### READING BETWEEN THE LINES
The Jobless Recovery of 2002–2003  144

## Chapter 7  Aggregate Supply and Aggregate Demand  149

### Production and Prices  149

#### Aggregate Supply  150
- Aggregate Supply Fundamentals  150
- Long-Run Aggregate Supply  150
- Short-Run Aggregate Supply  151
- Movements Along the *LAS* and *SAS* Curves  152
- Changes in Aggregate Supply  153

#### Aggregate Demand  155
- The Aggregate Demand Curve  155
- Changes in Aggregate Demand  156

#### Macroeconomic Equilibrium  158
- Short-Run Macroeconomic Equilibrium  158
- Long-Run Macroeconomic Equilibrium  159
- Economic Growth and Inflation  160
- The Business Cycle  160
- Fluctuations in Aggregate Demand  162
- Fluctuations in Aggregate Supply  163

#### U.S. Economic Growth, Inflation, and Cycles  164
- Economic Growth  164
- Inflation  165
- Business Cycles  165
- The Evolving Economy: 1963–2003  165

#### Macroeconomic Schools of Thought  166
- The Keynesian View  166
- The Classical View  166
- The Monetarist View  167
- The Way Ahead  167

#### READING BETWEEN THE LINES
Aggregate Supply and Aggregate Demand in Action  168

### PART 3 Wrap-Up
**Understanding the Themes of Macroeconomics  173**
- Probing the Ideas: Macroeconomic Revolutions  174
- Talking with Robert Barro  176

## Part 4  Aggregate Supply and Economic Growth  179

**Chapter 8**  **The Economy at Full Employment: The Classical Model**  179

### Our Economy's Compass  179

### The Classical Model: A Preview  180

### Real GDP and Employment  180
Production Possibilities  180
The Production Function  181

### The Labor Market and Potential GDP  182
The Demand for Labor  182
The Supply of Labor  184
Labor Market Equilibrium and Potential GDP  185

### Unemployment at Full Employment  187
Job Search  187
Job Rationing  188
Job Rationing and Unemployment  189

### Investment, Saving, and the Interest Rate  190
Investment Decisions  190
Investment Demand  191
Saving Decisions  192
Saving Supply  193
Equilibrium in the Capital Market  193

### The Dynamic Classical Model  195
Changes in Productivity  195
An Increase in Population  196
An Increase in Labor Productivity  197
Population and Productivity in the United States  199

### READING BETWEEN THE LINES
Productivity Growth in 2003  200

**Chapter 9**  **Economic Growth**  205

### Transforming People's Lives  205

### Long-Term Growth Trends  206
Growth in the U.S. Economy  206
Real GDP Growth in the World Economy  207

### The Causes of Economic Growth: A First Look  209
Preconditions for Economic Growth  209
Saving and Investment in New Capital  209
Investment in Human Capital  210
Discovery of New Technologies  210

### Growth Accounting  211
Labor Productivity  211
The Productivity Curve  211
Accounting for the Productivity Growth Slowdown and Speedup  213
Technological Change During the Productivity Growth Slowdown  214
Achieving Faster Growth  214

### Growth Theories  215
Classical Growth Theory  215
Neoclassical Growth Theory  217
New Growth Theory  219
Sorting Out the Theories  221

### READING BETWEEN THE LINES
### POLICY WATCH
Economic Growth in Asia  222

### PART 4 Wrap-Up
**Understanding Aggregate Supply and Economic Growth  227**
Probing the Ideas: Incentives to Innovate  228
Talking with Paul Romer  230

## Part 5  Aggregate Demand, Money, and Inflation  233

### Chapter 10  Money, Banks, and the Federal Reserve  233

**Money Makes the World Go Around  233**

**What Is Money?**  234
- Medium of Exchange  234
- Unit of Account  234
- Store of Value  235
- Money in the United States Today  235

**Depository Institutions**  237
- Commercial Banks  237
- Thrift Institutions  238
- Money Market Mutual Funds  238
- The Economic Functions of Depository Institutions  238
- Financial Regulation, Deregulation, and Innovation  239
- Deregulation in the 1980s and 1990s  240
- Financial Innovation  240
- Deregulation, Innovation, and Money  241

**How Banks Create Money**  242
- Reserves: Actual and Required  242
- Creating Deposits by Making Loans  242
- The Federal Reserve System  244
- The Fed's Goals and Targets  244
- The Structure of the Fed  244
- The Fed's Power Center  244
- The Fed's Policy Tools  245
- The Fed's Balance Sheet  246

**Controlling the Quantity of Money**  247
- How Required Reserve Ratios Work  247
- How the Discount Rate Works  247
- How an Open Market Operation Works  247
- The Monetary Base, the Quantity of Money, and the Money Multiplier  249
- The Size of the Money Multiplier  250

**READING BETWEEN THE LINES**
Electronic Money  252

### Chapter 11  Money, Interest, Real GDP, and the Price Level  257

**Ripple Effects of Money  257**

**The Demand for Money**  258
- The Influences on Money Holding  258
- The Demand for Money Curve  259
- Shifts in the Demand for Money Curve  259
- The Demand for Money in the United States  260

**Interest Rate Determination**  261
- Money Market Equilibrium  261
- Changing the Interest Rate  262

**Short-Run Effects of Money on Real GDP and the Price Level**  263
- Ripple Effects of Interest Rate  263
- The Fed Tightens to Avoid Inflation  264
- The Fed Eases to Avoid Recession  265

**Long-Run Effects of Money on Real GDP and the Price Level**  266
- An Increase in the Quantity of Money at Full Employment  266
- The Quantity Theory of Money  267
- The Quantity Theory and the *AS-AD* Model  268
- Historical Evidence on the Quantity Theory of Money  269
- International Evidence on the Quantity Theory of Money  269
- Correlation, Causation, and Other Influences  269

**READING BETWEEN THE LINES**
The Quantity Theory of Money in Argentina  272

## Chapter 12  Inflation  277

### From Rome to Rio de Janeiro  277

### Inflation and the Price Level  278

### Demand-Pull Inflation  279
- Initial Effect of an Increase in Aggregate Demand  279
- Money Wage Rate Response  279
- A Demand-Pull Inflation Process  280

### Cost-Push Inflation  281
- Initial Effect of a Decrease in Aggregate Supply  281
- Aggregate Demand Response  282
- A Cost-Push Inflation Process  282

### Effects of Inflation  284
- Unanticipated Inflation in the Labor Market  284
- Unanticipated Inflation in the Market for Financial Capital  284
- Forecasting Inflation  285
- Anticipated Inflation  285
- Unanticipated Inflation  286
- The Costs of Anticipated Inflation  286

### Inflation and Unemployment: The Phillips Curve  288
- The Short-Run Phillips Curve  288
- The Long-Run Phillips Curve  290
- Changes in the Natural Rate of Unemployment  290
- The U.S. Phillips Curve  291

### Interest Rates and Inflation  292
- How Interest Rates Are Determined  293
- Why Expected Inflation Influences the Nominal Interest Rate  293

#### READING BETWEEN THE LINES
The U.S. Phillips Curve: 2000–2003  294

### PART 5 Wrap-Up
**Understanding Aggregate Demand, Money, and Inflation  299**
- Probing the Ideas: Understanding Inflation  300
- Talking with Michael Woodford  302

## Part 6  Economic Fluctuations and Stabilization Policy  305

## Chapter 13  Expenditure Multipliers: The Keynesian Model  305

### Economic Amplifier or Shock Absorber?  305

### Fixed Prices and Expenditure Plans  306
- Expenditure Plans  306
- Consumption Function and Saving Function  306
- Marginal Propensities to Consume and Save  308
- Slopes and Marginal Propensities  309
- Other Influences on Consumption Expenditure and Saving  309
- The U.S. Consumption Function  310
- Consumption as a Function of Real GDP  311
- Import Function  311

### Real GDP with a Fixed Price Level  312
- Aggregate Planned Expenditure and Real GDP  313
- Actual Expenditure, Planned Expenditure, and Real GDP  313
- Equilibrium Expenditure  314
- Convergence to Equilibrium  315

### The Multiplier  316
- The Basic Idea of the Multiplier  316
- The Multiplier Effect  316
- Why Is the Multiplier Greater than 1?  317
- The Size of the Multiplier  317
- The Multiplier and the Marginal Propensities to Consume and Save  318
- Imports and Income Taxes  318
- Business Cycle Turning Points  319

### The Multiplier and the Price Level  321
- Aggregate Expenditure and Aggregate Demand  321
- Aggregate Expenditure and the Price Level  321
- Equilibrium Real GDP and the Price Level  323

#### READING BETWEEN THE LINES
Inventories in Expansion  326

#### MATHEMATICAL NOTE
The Algebra of the Keynesian Model  328

## Chapter 14 The Business Cycle 335

**Must What Goes Up Always Come Down? 335**

Cycle Patterns, Impulses, and Mechanisms 336
- Business Cycle Patterns 336
- Cycle Impulses and Mechanisms 336
- The Central Role of Investment and Capital 337
- The *AS-AD* Model 338

Aggregate Demand Theories of the Business Cycle 338
- Keynesian Theory 338
- Monetarist Theory 340
- Rational Expectations Theories 342
- *AS-AD* General Theory 344

Real Business Cycle Theory 345
- The RBC Impulse 345
- The RBC Mechanism 346
- Criticisms of Real Business Cycle Theory 348
- Defense of Real Business Cycle Theory 348

Expansion and Recession During the 1990s and 2000s 349
- The U.S. Expansion of the 1990s 349
- The U.S. Recession of 2001 350

The Great Depression 352
- Why the Great Depression Happened 353
- Can It Happen Again? 354

**READING BETWEEN THE LINES**
Explaining the 2002–2003 Expansion 356

## Chapter 15 Fiscal Policy 361

**Balancing Acts on Capitol Hill 361**

The Federal Budget 362
- The Institutions and Laws 362
- Highlights of the 2004 Budget 363
- The Budget in Historical Perspective 364
- The U.S. Government Budget in Global Perspective 367
- State and Local Budgets 367

The Supply Side: Employment and Potential GDP 368
- Full Employment and Potential GDP 368
- The Effects of the Income Tax 368
- Taxes on Expenditure and the Tax Wedge 369
- Some Real World Tax Wedges 369
- Does the Tax Wedge Matter? 369
- Tax Revenues and the Laffer Curve 370
- The Supply-Side Debate 370

The Supply Side: Investment, Saving, and Economic Growth 371
- The Sources of Investment Finance 371
- Taxes and the Incentive to Save 372
- Government Saving 373

Generational Effects of Fiscal Policy 374
- Generational Accounting and Present Value 374
- The Social Security Time Bomb 375
- Generational Imbalance 375
- International Debt 376

Stabilizing the Business Cycle 377
- The Government Purchases Multiplier 377
- The Tax Multiplier 377
- The Balanced Budget Multiplier 377
- Discretionary Fiscal Stabilization 377
- Limitations of Discretionary Fiscal Policy 379
- Automatic Stabilizers 379

**READING BETWEEN THE LINES**
**POLICY WATCH**
Fiscal Policy Today 382

### Chapter 16   Monetary Policy   387

**What Can Monetary Policy Do?   387**

Instruments, Goals, Targets, and the Fed's
Performance   388
    Price Level Stability   388
    Sustainable Real GDP Growth   389
    The Fed's Performance: 1973–2003   389

Achieving Price Level Stability   392
    Fixed-Rule Policies   392
    Feedback-Rule Policies   392
    Discretionary Policies   392
    A Monetarist Fixed Rule with Aggregate Demand
        Shocks   392
    A Keynesian Feedback Rule with Aggregate Demand
        Shocks   393
    Policy Lags and the Forecast Horizon   394
    Stabilizing Aggregate Supply Shocks   395
    Monetarist Fixed Rule with a Productivity Shock   395
    Feedback Rules with Productivity Shock   396
    Monetarist Fixed Rule with a Cost-Push Inflation
        Shock   397
    Feedback Rules with Cost-Push Inflation Shock   397

Policy Credibility   399
    A Surprise Inflation Reduction   399
    A Credible Announced Inflation Reduction   400
    Inflation Reduction in Practice   400

New Monetarist and New Keynesian Feedback
Rules   401
    The McCallum Rule   401
    The Taylor Rule   402
    Differences Between the Rules   403
    Choosing Between the Rules   403

**READING BETWEEN THE LINES**
**POLICY WATCH**
Monetary Policy Today   404

### Part 6   Wrap-Up
**Understanding Economic Fluctuations and
Stabilization Policy   409**
    Probing the Ideas: Business Cycles   410
    Talking with Peter Ireland   412

### Part 7   The Global Economy

### Chapter 17   Trading with the World   415

**Silk Routes and Sucking Sounds   415**

Patterns and Trends in International Trade   416
    Trade in Goods   416
    Trade in Services   416
    Geographical Patterns of International Trade   416
    Trends in the Volume of Trade   416
    Net Exports and International Borrowing   416

The Gains from International Trade   417
    Opportunity Cost in Farmland   417
    Opportunity Cost in Mobilia   418
    Comparative Advantage   418
    The Gains from Trade: Cheaper to Buy Than to
        Produce   418
    The Terms of Trade   418
    Balanced Trade   419
    Changes in Production and Consumption   419
    Calculating the Gains from Trade   421
    Gains for All   421
    Gains from Trade in Reality   421

International Trade Restrictions   423

The History of Tariffs   423
    How Tariffs Work   424
    Nontariff Barriers   426
    How Quotas and VERs Work   426
    The Case Against Protection   427
    The National Security Argument   427
    The Infant-Industry Argument   427
    The Dumping Argument   427
    Saves Jobs   428
    Allows Us to Compete with Cheap Foreign Labor   428
    Brings Diversity and Stability   429
    Penalizes Lax Environmental Standards   429
    Protects National Culture   429
    Prevents Rich Countries from Exploiting Developing
        Countries   430

Why Is International Trade Restricted?   430
    Tariff Revenue   430
    Rent Seeking   430
    Compensating Losers   431

**READING BETWEEN THE LINES**
**POLICY WATCH**
The Gains from Globalization   432

## Chapter 18 International Finance 437

### ¥€$! 437

### Financing International Trade 438
Balance of Payments Accounts  438
Borrowers and Lenders, Debtors and Creditors  440
Current Account Balance  441
Net Exports  441
The Three Sector Balances  442
Is U.S. Borrowing for Consumption or Investment?  442

### The Exchange Rate 443
Demand in the Foreign Exchange Market  444
The Law of Demand for Foreign Exchange  444
Changes in the Demand for Dollars  444
Supply in the Foreign Exchange Market  446
The Law of Supply of Foreign Exchange  446
Changes in the Supply of Dollars  447
Market Equilibrium  448
Changes in the Exchange Rate  448
Exchange Rate Expectations  449
The Fed in the Foreign Exchange Market  450

### READING BETWEEN THE LINES
The Sinking Dollar  452

### PART 7 Wrap-Up
**Understanding the Global Economy 457**
Probing the Ideas: Gains from International Trade  458
Talking with Jagdish Bhagwati  460

Glossary **G-1**

Index **I-1**

# PART 1  Introduction

# What Is Economics?

CHAPTER 1

## Understanding Our Changing World

**You are studying economics at a time of enormous** change and uncertainty. Much of the change is for the better. The information age of laptop computers with wireless connection to the Internet, MP3 music, DVD movies, cell phones, Palm Pilots, and a host of other gadgets and toys have transformed the way we work and play.

But some change is for the worse. After the hype of the new millennium and as 2001 began, the U.S. and global economies slipped into recession. Businesses fired hundreds of thousands of workers and cut production. Then, on September 11, 2001, terrorist attacks generated shockwaves that cut business and vacation travel and shrank our airlines and at the same time expanded our security and defense industries.

◆ The information age, recession, and the effects of terrorism are just some of the forces that are changing today's world. Your course in economics will help you to understand how these powerful forces shape our world. This chapter takes the first step. It describes the questions that economists try to answer, the way they think about those questions, and the methods they use in the search for answers. Economics makes extensive use of graphs, and an appendix provides a guide to these graphical methods.

### After studying this chapter, you will be able to

- **Define economics and distinguish between microeconomics and macroeconomics**
- **Explain the big questions of economics**
- **Explain the key ideas that define the economic way of thinking**
- **Explain how economists go about their work as social scientists**

## Definition of Economics

ALL ECONOMIC QUESTIONS ARISE BECAUSE WE want more than we can get. We want a peaceful and secure world. We want clean air, lakes, and rivers. We want long and healthy lives. We want good schools, colleges, and universities. We want spacious and comfortable homes. We want an enormous range of sports and recreational gear from running shoes to jet skis. We want the time to enjoy sports, games, novels, movies, music, travel, and hanging out with our friends.

What each one of us can get is limited by time, by the incomes we earn, and by the prices we must pay. Everyone ends up with some unsatisfied wants. What as a society we can get is limited by our productive resources. These resources include the gifts of nature, human labor and ingenuity, and tools and equipment that we have produced.

Our inability to satisfy all our wants is called *scarcity*. The poor and the rich alike face scarcity. A child wants a $1.00 can of soda and two 50¢ packs of gum but has only $1.00 in his pocket. He faces scarcity. A millionaire wants to spend the weekend playing golf *and* spend the same weekend at the office attending a business strategy meeting. She faces scarcity. A society wants to provide improved health care, install a computer in every classroom, explore space, clean polluted lakes and rivers, and so on. Society faces scarcity. Even parrots face scarcity!

Faced with scarcity, we must *choose* among the available alternatives. The child must *choose* the soda *or* the gum. The millionaire must *choose* the golf game *or* the meeting. As a society, we must *choose* among health care, national defense, and the environment.

The choices that we make depend on the incentives that we face. An **incentive** is a reward that encourages or a penalty that discourages an action. If the price of soda falls, the child has an *incentive* to choose more soda. If a profit of $10 million is at stake, the millionaire has an incentive to skip the golf game. As computer prices tumble, school boards have an *incentive* to connect more classrooms to the Internet.

**Economics** is the social science that studies the *choices* that individuals, businesses, governments, and entire societies make as they cope with *scarcity* and the *incentives* that influence and reconcile those choices. The subject divides into two main parts

- Microeconomics
- Macroeconomics

### Microeconomics

**Microeconomics** is the study of the choices that individuals and businesses make, the way these choices interact in markets, and the influence of governments. Some examples of microeconomic issues are: Why are people buying more SUVs and fewer minivans? How would a tax on e-commerce affect Amazon.com?

### Macroeconomics

**Macroeconomics** is the study of the performance of the national economy and the global economy. Some examples of macroeconomic issues are: Why did production and jobs shrink in 2001? Why has Japan's economy stagnated? Can the Federal Reserve bring prosperity by cutting interest rates?

> **REVIEW QUIZ**
>
> 1. List some examples of scarcity in the United States today.
> 2. Use the headlines in today's news to provide some examples of scarcity around the world.
> 3. Use today's news to illustrate the distinction between microeconomics and macroeconomics.

Not only do I want a cracker—we all want a cracker!

© The New Yorker Collection 1985
Frank Modell from cartoonbank.com. All Rights Reserved.

# Two Big Economic Questions

TWO BIG QUESTIONS SUMMARIZE THE SCOPE OF economics:

- How do choices end up determining *what*, *how*, and *for whom* goods and services get produced?
- When do choices made in the pursuit of *self-interest* also promote the *social interest*?

## What, How, and For Whom?

**Goods and services** are the objects that people value and produce to satisfy human wants. Goods are physical objects such as golf balls. Services are tasks performed for people such as haircuts. By far the largest part of what the United States produces today is services such as retail and wholesale trade, health care, and education. Goods are a small part of total production.

**What?** What we produce changes over time. Sixty years ago, almost 25 percent of Americans worked on farms. That number has shrunk to less than 3 percent today. Over the same period, the number of people who produce goods—in mining, construction, and manufacturing—has shrunk from 30 percent to 20 percent. The decrease in farming and manufacturing is reflected in an increase in services. Sixty years ago, 45 percent of the population produced services. Today, almost 80 percent of working Americans have service jobs. Figure 1.1 shows these trends.

What determines the quantities of corn, DVDs, and haircuts and all the other millions of items that we produce?

**How?** Goods and services are produced by using productive resources that economists call **factors of production**. Factors of production are grouped into four categories:

- Land
- Labor
- Capital
- Entrepreneurship

**Land** The "gifts of nature" that we use to produce goods and services are called **land**. In economics, land is what in everyday language we call *natural resources*.

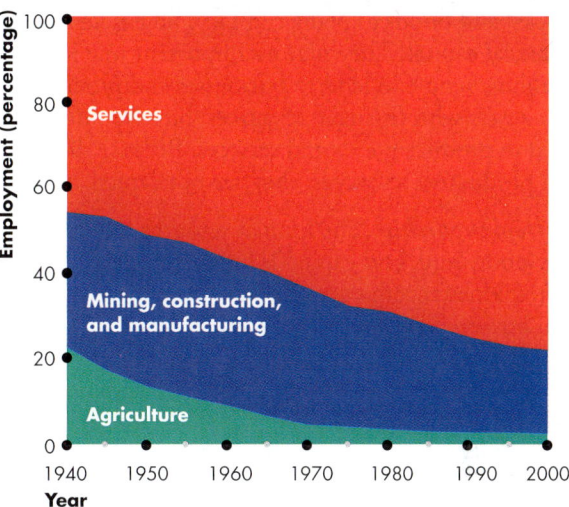

**FIGURE 1.1** Trends in What We Produce

Services have expanded and agriculture, mining, construction, and manufacturing have shrunk.

*Source:* U.S. Census Bureau, *Statistical Abstract of the United States.*

It includes land in the everyday sense together with metal ores, oil, gas and coal, water, and air.

Our land surface and water resources are renewable and some of our mineral resources can be recycled. But the resources that we use to create energy are nonrenewable—they can be used only once.

**Labor** The work time and work effort that people devote to producing goods and services is called **labor**. Labor includes the physical and the mental efforts of all the people who work on farms and construction sites and in factories, shops, and offices.

The *quality* of labor depends on **human capital**, which is the knowledge and skill that people obtain from education, on-the-job training, and work experience. You are building your own human capital right now as you work on your economics course, and your human capital will continue to grow as you become better at your job.

Human capital expands over time. Today, more than 80 percent of the population of the United States has completed high school and 25 percent have a college or university degree. Figure 1.2 shows a measure of the growth of human capital in the United States over the past century.

***Capital*** The tools, instruments, machines, buildings, and other constructions that businesses now use to produce goods and services are called **capital**.

In everyday language, we talk about money, stocks, and bonds as being capital. These items are financial capital. They play an important role in enabling people to lend to businesses and provide businesses with financial resources, but they are not used to produce goods and services. Because they are not productive resources, they are not capital.

***Entrepreneurship*** The human resource that organizes labor, land, and capital is called **entrepreneurship**. Entrepreneurs come up with new ideas about what and how to produce, make business decisions, and bear the risks that arise from these decisions.

How do the quantities of factors of production that get used to produce the many different goods and services get determined?

**For Whom?** Who gets the goods and services that are produced depends on the incomes that people earn. A large income enables a person to buy large quantities of goods and services. A small income leaves a person with few options and small quantities of goods and services.

People earn their incomes by selling the services of the factors of production they own:

- Land earns **rent**.
- Labor earns **wages**.
- Capital earns **interest**.
- Entrepreneurship earns **profit**.

Which factor of production earns most income? The answer is labor. Wages and fringe benefits are around 70 percent of total income. Land, capital, and entrepreneurship share the rest. These percentages have been remarkably constant over time.

Knowing how income is shared among the factors of production doesn't tell us how it is shared among individuals. You know of lots of people who earn very large incomes. Ray Romano gets $50 million for starring in the TV program "Everybody Loves Raymond." And Bill Gates has piled up more than $30 billion from the operations of Microsoft.

You know of even more people who earn very small incomes. Servers at McDonald's average around $6.35 an hour; checkout clerks, gas station attendants, and textile and leather workers all earn less than $10 an hour.

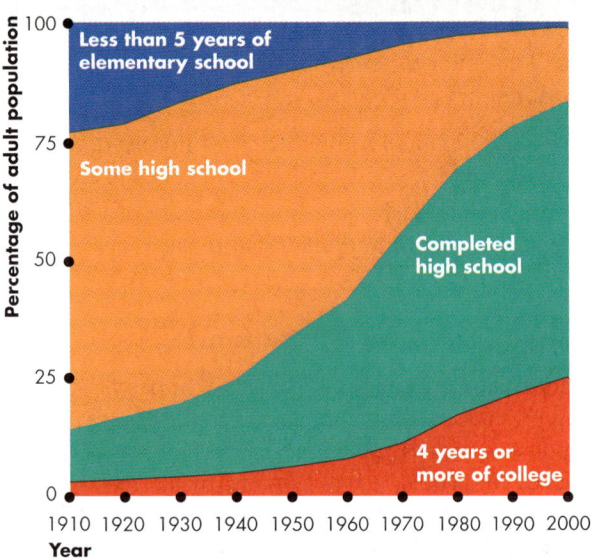

**FIGURE 1.2  A Measure of Human Capital**

Today, 25 percent of the population has 4 years or more of college, up from 3 percent in 1910. A further 58 percent have completed high school, up from 11 percent in 1910.

*Source:* U.S. Census Bureau, *Statistical Abstract of the United States.*

You probably know about other persistent differences in incomes. Men, on the average, earn more than women; whites more than minorities; college graduates more than high-school graduates.

We can get a good sense of who consumes the goods and services produced by looking at the percentages of total income earned by different groups of people. The 20 percent of people with the lowest incomes earn 4 percent of total income, while the richest 20 percent earn 49 percent of total income. So on the average, people in the top 20 percent earn more than 12 times the incomes of those in the bottom 20 percent.

Why is the distribution of income so unequal? Why do women and minorities earn less than white males?

Economics provides some answers to these questions about what, how, and for whom goods and services get produced.

The second big question of economics that we'll now examine is a harder question both to appreciate and to answer.

### When Is the Pursuit of Self-Interest in the Social Interest?

Every day, you and 292 million other Americans, along with 6.1 billion people in the rest of the world, make economic choices that result in "What," "How," and "For Whom" goods and services get produced.

Are the goods and services produced, and the quantities in which they are produced, the right ones? Do the factors of production employed get used in the best possible way? And do the goods and services that we produce go to the people who benefit most from them?

You know that your own choices are the best ones for you—or at least you think they're the best at the time that you make them. You use your time and other resources in the way that makes most sense to you. But you don't think much about how your choices affect other people. You order a home delivery pizza because you're hungry and want to eat. You don't order it thinking that the delivery person or the cook needs an income. You make choices that are in your **self-interest**—choices that you think are best for you.

When you act on your economic decisions, you come into contact with thousands of other people who produce and deliver the goods and services that you decide to buy or who buy the things that you sell. These people have made their own decisions—what to produce and how to produce it, who to hire or whom to work for, and so on. Like you, everyone else makes choices that they think are best for them. When the pizza delivery person shows up at your home, he's not doing you a favor. He's earning his income and hoping for a nice tip.

Could it be possible that when each one of us makes choices that are in our own best interest, it turns out that these choices are also the best for society as a whole? Choices that are the best for society as a whole are said to be in the **social interest**.

Economists have been trying to find the answer to this question since 1776, the year of American independence and the year in which Adam Smith's monumental book, *The Nature and the Causes of the Wealth of Nations*, was published. The question is a hard one to answer, but a lot of progress has been made. Much of the rest of this book helps you to learn what we know about this question and its answer. To help you start thinking about the question, we're going to illustrate it with ten topics that generate heated discussion in today's world. You're already at least a little bit familiar with each one of them. They are

- Privatization
- Globalization
- The new economy
- The post 9/11 economy
- Corporate scandals
- HIV/AIDS
- Disappearing tropical rainforests
- Water shortages
- Unemployment
- Deficits and debts

**Privatization** November 9, 1989 is a date that will long be recalled in the world's economic history books. On that day the Berlin Wall tumbled and with its destruction, two Germanys embarked on a path toward unity.

West Germany was a nation designed on the model of the United States and Western Europe. In these nations, people own property and operate businesses. Privately owned businesses produce goods and services and trade them freely with their customers in shops and markets. All this economic activity is conducted by people who pursue their own self-interest.

East Germany was a nation designed on the model of the Soviet Union—a communist state. In such a state, people are not free to operate businesses and trade freely with each other. The government owns the factories, shops, and offices, and it decides what to produce, how to produce it, and for whom to produce. Economic life is managed in detail by a government central economic planning agency, and each individual follows instructions. The entire economy is operated like one giant firm.

The Soviet Union collapsed soon after the fall of the Berlin Wall and splintered into a number of independent states, each of which embarked on a process of privatization. China, another communist state, began to encourage private enterprise and move away from sole reliance on public ownership and central economic planning during the 1980s.

Today, only Cuba, North Korea, and Vietnam remain communist states.

Do publicly owned businesses coordinated by the central planning system of communism serve the social interest better than private businesses that trade freely in markets like they do in the United States? Or is it possible that our economic system serves the social interest more effectively?

**Globalization** Whenever world leaders hold summit meetings, anti-globalization protests accompany them. Globalization—the expansion of international trade and investment—has been going on for centuries, but during the 1990s, advances in microchip, satellite, and fiber-optic technologies brought a dramatic fall in the cost of communication and accelerated the process. A phone call or even a video-conference with people who live 10,000 miles apart has become an everyday and easily affordable event. Every day, 20,000 people travel by air between the United States and East Asia, and close to that number travel between the United States and Europe.

The result of this explosion of communication is a globalization of production decisions. When Nike decides to increase the production of sports shoes, people who live in China, Indonesia, or Malaysia get more work. As more and more people use credit cards, people in Barbados get hired to key in the data from sales slips. When Sony wants to create a new game for PlayStation 2, or when Steven Spielberg wants a movie animation sequence, programmers in India or New Zealand write the code. And when China Airlines wants some new airplanes, it is most likely that Americans who work for Boeing will build them.

As part of the process of globalization, the United States produce more services and fewer manufactured goods. And China and the small economies in East Asia produce an expanding volume of manufactures.

The economies of Asia are also growing more rapidly than are those of the United States and Europe. China is already the world's second largest economy in terms of production and, on current trends, by 2013 it will be the world's largest economy. This rapid economic expansion in Asia will bring further changes to the global economy as the wealthier Chinese and other Asians begin to travel and buy more of the goods and services that the United States and other parts of the world produce. Globalization will proceed at an accelerated pace.

But globalization is leaving some behind. The nations of Africa and parts of South America are not sharing in the prosperity that globalization is bringing to other parts of the world.

Is globalization a good thing? Whom does it benefit? Globalization is pretty clearly in the interest of the owners of multinational firms that profit by producing in low-cost regions and selling in high-price regions. But is globalization in your interest and the interest of the young worker in Malaysia who sews your new running shoes? Is it in the social interest?

**The New Economy** The 1980s and 1990s were years of extraordinary economic change that have been called the *Information Revolution*. Economic revolutions don't happen very often. The previous one, the *Industrial Revolution*, occurred between 1760 and 1830 and saw the transformation from rural farm life to urban industrial life for most people. The revolution before that, the *Agrarian Revolution*, occurred around 12,000 years ago and saw the transformation from a life of hunting and gathering to a life of settled farming.

Placing the events of the last twenty years of the twentieth century on the status of those two previous revolutions might be a stretch. But the changes that occurred during those years were incredible. And they were based on one major technology: the microprocessor or computer chip. Moore's law predicted that the number of transistors that could be placed on one integrated chip would double every 18 months. This prediction turned out to be remarkably accurate. In 1980, a PC chip had 60,000 transistors. By 2000, chips with more than 40 million transistors were in machines like the one that sits on your lap.

The spinoffs from faster and cheaper computing were widespread. Telecommunications became much faster and cheaper, music and movie recording became more realistic and cheaper, millions of routine tasks that previously required human decision and action were automated. You encounter these automated tasks everyday when you check out at the supermarket, call directory assistance, or call a government department or large business.

All the new products and processes and the low-cost computing power that made them possible were produced by people who made choices in the pursuit of self-interest. They did not result from any grand design or government economic plan.

When Gordon Moore set up Intel and started making chips, no one had told him to do so, and he wasn't thinking how much easier it would be for you to turn in your essay on time if you had a faster PC. When Bill Gates quit Harvard to set up Microsoft, he wasn't trying to create the best operating system and improve people's computing experience. Moore and Gates and thousands of other entrepreneurs were in hot pursuit of the big payoffs that many of them achieved. Yet their actions did make everyone else better off. They did advance the social interest.

But could more have been done? Were resources used in the best possible way during the information revolution? Did Intel make the best possible chips and sell them in the right quantities for the right prices? Or was the quality of the chips too low and the price too high? And what about Microsoft? Did Bill Gates have to be paid $30 billion to produce the successive generations of Windows and Word? Were these programs developed in the social interest?

**The Economic Response to 9/11** The awful events of September 11, 2001 created economic shockwaves that will last for some years and changed "What," "How," and "For Whom."

The biggest changes in production occurred in travel, accommodation, and security. Much business travel was replaced by teleconferencing. Much vacation travel left the air and went onto the highway. Foreign trips were cut back. Airlines lost business and cut back on their own orders for new airplanes. Banks that had lent money to airlines wrote off millions of dollars in losses.

But sales of SUVs and RVs increased. And airports, although operating at lower capacity, beefed up their security services. Tens of thousands of new security agents were hired and state-of-the-art scanners were installed.

Thousands of people made choices in pursuit of their self-interest that lead to these changes in production. But were these changes also in the social interest?

**Corporate Scandals** In 2000, the names Enron and WorldCom meant corporate integrity and spectacular success. But today, they are tainted with scandal.

Founded in 1985, Enron expanded to become America's seventh largest business by 2001. But its expansion was built on an elaborate web of lies, deceit, and fraud. In October 2001, after revelations by one of its former executives, Enron's directors acknowledged that by inflating reported income and hiding debts, they had made the firm appear to be worth considerably more than it actually was. One Enron executive, Michael Kopper, pleaded guilty to charges of money laundering and wire fraud and helped federal investigators uncover the fraud that made millions of dollars for the firm's executives and wiped out its stockholders' wealth.

Scott Sullivan, a highly respected financial officer, joined WorldCom in 1992 and helped turn it into one of the world's telecommunications giants. In his last year with the company, Sullivan's salary was $700,000 and his bonus (in stock options) $10 million. But just ten years after joining the company, Sullivan was fired and arrested for allegedly falsifying the company's accounts, inflating its book profits by almost $4 billion, and inflating his own bonus in the process. Shortly after these events, WorldCom filed for bankruptcy protection in the largest bankruptcy filing in U.S. history, laid off 17,000 workers, and wiped out its stockholders' wealth.

These cases illustrate the fact that sometimes, in the pursuit of self-interest, people break the law. Such behavior is not in the social interest. Indeed, the law was established precisely to limit such behavior.

But some corporate behavior is legal yet regarded by some as inappropriate. For example, many people think that top executive salaries are out of control. In some cases, executives who have received huge incomes have brought ruin to the companies that they manage.

The people who hired the executives acted in their own self-interest and appointed the best people they could find. The executives acted in their own self-interest. But what became of the self-interest of the stockholders and the customers of these firms. Didn't they suffer? Aren't these glaring examples of conflict between self-interest and the social interest?

**HIV/AIDS** The World Health Organization and United Nations estimate that 42 million people were suffering from HIV/AIDS in 2002. During that year, 3 million died from the disease and there were 5 million new cases. Most of the HIV/AIDS cases—30 million of them in 2002—were in Africa, where incomes average around $7 a day. The most effective treatment for this disease is an antiretroviral drug made by the large multinational drug companies. The cost of this treatment is around $2,700 a year—more than $7 a day. For sales to poor countries, the cost has been lowered to around $1,200 a year—$3.30 a day.

Developing new drugs is a high-cost and high-risk activity. And if the activity were not in the self-interest of the drug companies, they would stop the effort. But once developed, the cost of producing a drug is just a few cents a dose. Would it be in the social interest for drugs to be made available at the low cost of producing them?

**Disappearing Tropical Rainforests** Tropical rainforests in South America, Africa, and Asia support the lives of 30 million species of plants, animals, and insects—approaching 50 percent of all species on the planet. These rainforests provides us with the ingredients for many goods including soaps, mouthwashes, shampoos, food preservatives, rubber, nuts, and fruits.

The Amazon rainforest alone converts about 1 trillion pounds of carbon dioxide into oxygen each year.

Yet tropical rainforests cover less than two percent of the Earth's surface and are heading for extinction. Logging, cattle ranching, mining, oil extraction, hydroelectric dams, and subsistence farming are destroying the equivalent to two football fields every second or an area larger than New York City every day. At the current rate of destruction, almost all the tropical rainforest ecosystems will be gone by 2030.

Each one of us makes economic choices that are in our self-interest to consume products, some of which are destroying this natural resource. Are our choices damaging the social interest? And if they are, what can be done to change the incentives we face and change our behavior?

**Water Shortages** The world is awash with water—it is our most abundant resource. But 97 percent of it is seawater. Another 2 percent is frozen in glaciers and ice. The 1 percent of the earth's water that is available for human consumption would be sufficient if only it were in the right places. Finland, Canada, and a few other places have more water than they can use, but Australia, Africa, and California (and many other places) could use much more water than they can get.

Some people pay less for water than others. California farmers, for example, pay less than California households. Some of the highest prices for water are faced by people in the poorest countries who must either buy from a water dealer's truck or carry water in buckets over many miles.

In the United Kingdom, water is provided by private water companies. In the United States, public enterprises deliver the water.

In India and Bangladesh, plenty of rain falls, but it falls during a short wet season and the rest of the year is dry. Dams could help, but not enough have been built in those countries.

Are the nation's and the world's water resources being managed properly? Are the decisions that we each make in our self-interest to use, conserve, and transport water also in the social interest?

**Unemployment** During the 1930s, in a period called the *Great Depression*, more than 20 percent of the labor force was unemployed. Even today, more than 40 percent of the African American teenage labor force is unemployed. Why can't everyone who wants a job find one? If economic choices arise from scarcity, how can resources be left unused?

People get jobs because other people think they can earn a profit by hiring them. And people accept jobs when they think the pay and other conditions are good enough. So the number of people with jobs is determined by the self-interest of employers and workers. But is the number of jobs also in the social interest?

**Deficits and Debts** Every single day since September 30, 2002, the U.S. government has run a budget deficit of $1.65 billion, which means that the government's debt has increased each day by that amount. On August 13, 2003, the day these words were written, your personal share of the outstanding government debt was $23,138.

Also, during 2003, Americans bought goods and services from the rest of the world in excess of what foreigners bought from America to the tune of $500 billion. To pay for these goods and services, we borrowed from the rest of the world.

These enormous deficits and the debts they create cannot persist indefinitely, and the debt will somehow have to be repaid. And they will most likely be repaid by you, not by your parents.

Are the choices that we vote for and make through our federal government and the choices we make when we buy from and sell to the rest of the world in the social interest?

We've just looked at ten topics that illustrate the big question: Do choices made in the pursuit of self-interest also serve the social interest?

You'll discover, as you work through this book, that much of what we do in the pursuit of our self-interest does indeed further the social interest. But there are areas in which the social interest and self-interest come into conflict. You'll discover the principles that help economists to figure out when the social interest is being served, when it is not, and what might be done when it is not.

### REVIEW QUIZ

1. Describe the broad facts about "What," "How," and "For Whom" goods and services get produced.
2. Use headlines from the recent news to illustrate the potential for conflict between self-interest and the social interest.

# The Economic Way of Thinking

THE DEFINITION OF ECONOMICS AND THE questions that you've just reviewed tell you about the *scope of economics*. But they don't tell you how economists *think* about these questions and go about seeking answers to them.

You're now going to begin to see how economists approach economic questions. First, in this section, we'll look at the ideas that define the *economic way of thinking*. This way of thinking needs practice, but it is powerful and as you become more familiar with it, you'll begin to see the world around you with a new and sharp focus.

## Choices and Tradeoffs

Because we face scarcity, we must make choices. And when we make a choice, we select from the available alternatives. For example, you can spend the weekend studying for your next economics test and having fun with your friends, but you can't do both of these activities at the same time. You must choose how much time to devote to each. Whatever choice you make, you could have chosen something else instead.

You can think about your choice as a tradeoff. A **tradeoff** is an exchange—giving up one thing to get something else. When you choose how to spend your weekend, you face a tradeoff between studying and hanging out with your friends.

**Guns Versus Butter** The classic tradeoff is between guns and butter. "Guns" and "butter" stand for any pair of goods. They might actually be guns and butter. Or they might be broader categories such as national defense and food. Or they might be any pair of specific goods or services such as cola and bottled water, baseball bats and tennis rackets, colleges and hospitals, realtor services and career counseling.

Regardless of the specific objects that guns and butter represent, the guns-versus-butter tradeoff captures a hard fact of life: If we want more of one thing, we must trade something else in exchange for it.

The idea of a tradeoff is central to the whole of economics. We'll look at some examples, beginning with the big questions: What, How, and For Whom? We can view each of these questions about the goods and services that get produced in terms of tradeoffs.

## What, How, and For Whom Tradeoffs

The questions what, how, and for whom goods and services are produced all involve tradeoffs that are similar to that between guns and butter.

**"What" Tradeoffs** What goods and services get produced depends on choices made by each one of us, by our government, and by the businesses that produce the things we buy.

Each of these choices involves a tradeoff. Each one of us faces a tradeoff when we choose how to spend our income. You go to the movies this week, but you forgo a few cups of coffee to buy the ticket. You trade off coffee for a movie.

The federal government faces a tradeoff when it chooses how to spend our tax dollars. Congress votes for more national defense but cuts back on educational programs—Congress trades off education for national defense.

Businesses face a tradeoff when they decide what to produce. Nike hires Tiger Woods and allocates resources to designing and marketing a new golf ball but cuts back on its development of a new running shoe. Nike trades off running shoes for golf balls.

**"How" Tradeoffs** How goods and services get produced depends on choices made by the businesses that produce the things we buy. These choices involve a tradeoff. For example, Krispy Kreme opens a new doughnut store with an automated production line and closes an older store with a traditional kitchen. Krispy Kreme trades off labor for capital.

**"For Whom" Tradeoffs** For whom goods and services are produced depends on the distribution of buying power. Buying power can be redistributed—transferred from one person to another—in three ways: by voluntary payments, by theft, or through taxes and benefits organized by government. Redistribution brings tradeoffs.

Each of us faces a "for whom" tradeoff when we choose how much to contribute to the United Nations' famine relief fund. You donate $50 and cut your spending. You trade off your own spending for a small increase in economic equality.

We make choices that influence redistribution by theft when we vote to make theft illegal and devote resources to law enforcement. We trade off goods and services for an increase in the security of our property.

We also vote for taxes and social programs that redistribute buying power from the rich to the poor. Government redistribution confronts society with what has been called the **big tradeoff**—the tradeoff between equality and efficiency. Taxing the rich and making transfers to the poor bring greater economic equality. But taxing productive activities such as running a business, working hard, and saving and investing in capital discourages these activities. So taxing productive activities means producing less. A more equal distribution means there is less to share.

You can think of the big tradeoff as being the problem of how to share a pie that everyone contributes to baking. If each person receives a share of the pie that reflects the size of her or his effort, everyone will work hard and the pie will be as large as possible. But if the pie is shared equally, regardless of contribution, some talented bakers will slacken off and the pie will shrink. The big tradeoff is one between the size of the pie and how equally it is shared. We trade off some production for increased equality.

### Choices Bring Change

What, how, and for whom goods and services are produced changes over time. And choices bring change. The quantity and range of goods and services available today in the United States is much greater than that in Africa. And the economic condition of the United States today is much better than it was a generation ago. But the quality of economic life (and its rate of improvement) doesn't depend purely on nature and on luck. It depends on many of the choices made by each one of us, by governments, and by businesses. And these choices involve tradeoffs.

One choice is that of how much of our income to consume and how much to save. Our saving can be channeled through the financial system to finance businesses and to pay for new capital that increases production. The more we save and invest, the more goods and services we'll be able to produce in the future. When you decide to save an extra $1,000 and forgo a vacation, you trade off the vacation for a higher future income. If everyone saves an extra $1,000 and businesses invest in more equipment that increases production, the average consumption per person rises. As a society, we trade off current consumption for economic growth and higher future consumption.

A second choice is how much effort to devote to education and training. By becoming better educated and more highly skilled, we become more productive and are able to produce more goods and services. When you decide to remain in school for another two years to complete a professional degree and forgo a huge chunk of leisure time, you trade off leisure today for a higher future income. If everyone becomes better educated, production increases and income per person rises. As a society, we trade off current consumption and leisure time for economic growth and higher future consumption.

A third choice, usually made by businesses, is how much effort to devote to research and the development of new products and production methods. Ford Motor Company can hire engineers to do research on a new robotic assembly line or to operate the existing plant and produce cars. More research brings greater productivity in the future but means smaller current production—a tradeoff of current production for greater future production.

Seeing choices as tradeoffs emphasizes the idea that to get something, we must give up something. What we give up is the cost of what we get. Economists call this cost the opportunity cost.

### Opportunity Cost

The highest-valued alternative that we give up to get something is the **opportunity cost** of the activity chosen. "There's no such thing as a free lunch" is not just a clever throwaway line. It expresses the central idea of economics: that every choice involves a cost.

You can quit school, or you can remain in school. If you quit school and take a job at McDonald's, you earn enough to buy some CDs, go to the movies, and spend lots of free time with your friends. If you remain in school, you can't afford these things. You will be able to buy these things when you graduate, and that is one of the payoffs from being in school. But for now, when you've bought your books, you have nothing left for CDs and movies. And doing assignments leaves no time for hanging around with your friends. The opportunity cost of being in school is the highest-valued alternative that you would have done if you had quit school.

All the "what," "how," and "for whom" tradeoffs that we've just considered involve opportunity cost. The opportunity cost of some guns is the butter forgone; the opportunity cost of a movie ticket is the number of cups of coffee forgone.

And the choices that bring change also involve opportunity cost. The opportunity cost of more goods and services in the future is less consumption today.

## Choosing at the Margin

You can allocate the next hour between studying and e-mailing your friends. But the choice is not all or nothing. You must decide how many minutes to allocate to each activity. To make this decision, you compare the benefit of a little bit more study time with its cost—you make your choice at the **margin.**

The benefit that arises from an increase in an activity is called **marginal benefit.** For example, suppose that you're spending four nights a week studying and your grade point average is 3.0. You decide that you want a higher grade and decide to study an extra night each week. Your grade now rises to 3.5. The marginal benefit from studying for one additional night a week is the 0.5 increase in your grade. It is *not* the 3.5 grade. The reason is that you already have the benefit from studying for four nights a week, so we don't count this benefit as resulting from the decision you are now making.

The cost of an increase in an activity is called **marginal cost.** For you, the marginal cost of increasing your study time by one night a week is the cost of the additional night not spent with your friends (if that is your best alternative use of the time). It does not include the cost of the four nights you are already studying.

To make your decision, you compare the marginal benefit from an extra night of study with its marginal cost. If the marginal benefit exceeds the marginal cost, you study the extra night. If the marginal cost exceeds the marginal benefit, you do not study the extra night.

By evaluating marginal benefits and marginal costs and choosing only those actions that bring greater benefit than cost, we use our scarce resources in the way that makes us as well off as possible.

## Responding to Incentives

Our choices respond to incentives. A change in marginal cost or a change in marginal benefit changes the incentives that we face and leads us to change our choice.

For example, suppose your economics instructor gives you a problem set and tells you that all the problems will be on the next test. The marginal benefit from working these problems is large, so you diligently work them all. In contrast, if your math instructor gives you a problem set and tells you that none of the problems will be on the next test, the marginal benefit from working these problems is lower, so you skip most of them.

The central idea of economics is that we can predict how choices will change by looking at changes in incentives. More of an activity is undertaken when its marginal cost falls or marginal benefit rises; less of an activity is undertaken when its marginal cost rises or marginal benefit falls.

Incentives are also the key to reconciling self-interest and the social interest. When our choices are *not* in the social interest, it is because we face the wrong incentives. One of the central challenges for economists is to figure out the incentive systems that result in self-interested choices leading to the social interest.

## Human Nature, Incentives, and Institutions

Economists take human nature as given and view people as acting in their self-interest. All people—consumers, producers, politicians, and public servants—pursue their self-interest.

Self-interested actions are not necessarily *selfish* actions. You might decide to use your resources in ways that bring pleasure to others as well as to yourself. But a self-interested act gets the most value for *you* based on *your* view about value.

If human nature is given and if people act in their self-interest, how can we take care of the social interest? Economists answer this question by emphasizing the crucial role that institutions play in influencing the incentives that people face as they pursue their self-interest.

Private property protected by a system of laws and markets that enable voluntary exchange are the fundamental institutions. You will learn as you progress with your study of economics that where these institutions exist, self-interest can indeed promote the social interest.

### REVIEW QUIZ

1 Provide three everyday examples of a tradeoff and describe the opportunity cost involved in each.
2 Provide three everyday examples to illustrate what we mean by choosing at the margin.
3 How do economists predict changes in choices?
4 What do economists say about the role of institutions in promoting the social interest?

## Economics: A Social Science

Economics is a social science (along with political science, psychology, and sociology). Economists try to discover how the economic world works, and in pursuit of this goal (like all scientists), they distinguish between two types of statements:

- What *is*
- What *ought to be*

Statements about what *is* are called *positive* statements and they might be right or wrong. We can test a positive statement by checking it against the facts. When a chemist does an experiment in her laboratory, she is attempting to check a positive statement against the facts.

Statements about what *ought to be* are called *normative* statements. These statements depend on values and cannot be tested. When Congress debates a motion, it is ultimately trying to decide what ought to be. It is making a normative statement.

To see the distinction between positive and normative statements, consider the controversy over global warming. Some scientists believe that centuries of the burning of coal and oil are increasing the carbon dioxide content of the earth's atmosphere and leading to higher temperatures that eventually will have devastating consequences for life on this planet. "Our planet is warming because of an increased carbon dioxide buildup in the atmosphere" is a positive statement. It can (in principle and with sufficient data) be tested. "We ought to cut back on our use of carbon-based fuels such as coal and oil" is a normative statement. You can agree with or disagree with this statement, but you can't test it. It is based on values. Health-care reform provides an economic example of the distinction. "Universal health care will cut the amount of work time lost to illness" is a positive statement. "Every American should have equal access to health care" is a normative statement.

The task of economic science is to discover positive statements that are consistent with what we observe and that help us to understand the economic world. This task can be broken into three steps:

- Observation and measurement
- Model building
- Testing models

### Observation and Measurement

Economists observe and measure data on such things as the quantities of natural and human resources, wages and work hours, the prices and quantities of the different goods and services produced, taxes and government spending, and the quantities of goods and services bought from and sold to other countries.

### Model Building

The second step toward understanding how the economic world works is to build a model. An **economic model** is a description of some aspect of the economic world that includes only those features of the world that are needed for the purpose at hand. A model is simpler than the reality it describes. What a model includes and what it leaves out result from assumptions about what is essential and what are inessential details.

You can see how ignoring details is useful—even essential—to our understanding by thinking about a model that you see every day: the TV weather map. The weather map is a model that helps to predict the temperature, wind speed and direction, and precipitation over a future period. The weather map shows lines called isobars—lines of equal barometric pressure. It doesn't show the interstate highways. The reason is that our theory of the weather tells us that the pattern of air pressure, not the location of the highways, determines the weather.

An economic model is similar to a weather map. For example, an economic model of a cell phone network might tell us the effects of the development of a new low-cost technology on the number of cell phone subscribers and the volume of cell phone use. But the model would ignore such details as the colors of the covers on people's cell phones and the tunes they use for ring tones.

### Testing Models

The third step is testing the model. A model's predictions might correspond to the facts or be in conflict with them. By comparing the model's predictions with the facts, we can test a model and develop an economic theory. An **economic theory** is a generalization that summarizes what we think we understand about the economic choices that people make and the performance of industries and entire economies. It is a bridge between an economic model and the real economy.

The process of building and testing models creates theories. For example, meteorologists have a theory that if the isobars form a particular pattern at a particular time of the year (a model), then it will snow (reality). They have developed this theory by repeated observation and by carefully recording the weather that follows specific pressure patterns.

Economics is a young science. It was born in 1776 with the publication of Adam Smith's *Wealth of Nations* (see p. 52). Over the years since then, economists have discovered many useful theories. But in many areas, economists are still looking for answers. The gradual accumulation of economic knowledge gives most economists some faith that their methods will, eventually, provide usable answers to the big economic questions.

But progress in economics comes slowly. Let's look at some of the obstacles to progress in economics.

## Obstacles and Pitfalls in Economics

We cannot easily do economic experiments. And most economic behavior has many simultaneous causes. For these two reasons, it is difficult in economics to unscramble cause and effect.

**Unscrambling Cause and Effect** By changing one factor at a time and holding all the other relevant factors constant, we isolate the factor of interest and are able to investigate its effects in the clearest possible way. This logical device, which all scientists use to identify cause and effect, is called *ceteris paribus*. **Ceteris paribus** is a Latin term that means "other things being equal" or "if all other relevant things remain the same." Ensuring that other things are equal is crucial in many activities, and all successful attempts to make scientific progress use this device.

Economic models (like the models in all other sciences) enable the influence of one factor at a time to be isolated in the imaginary world of the model. When we use a model, we are able to imagine what would happen if only one factor changed. But *ceteris paribus* can be a problem in economics when we try to test a model.

Laboratory scientists, such as chemists and physicists, perform experiments by actually holding all the relevant factors constant except for the one under investigation. In non-experimental sciences such as economics (and astronomy), we usually observe the outcomes of the simultaneous operation of many factors. Consequently, it is hard to sort out the effects of each individual factor and to compare them with what a model predicts. To cope with this problem, economists take three complementary approaches.

First, they look for pairs of events in which other things were equal (or similar). An example might be to study the effects of unemployment insurance on the unemployment rate by comparing the United States with Canada on the presumption that the people in the two economies are sufficiently similar. Second, economists use statistical tools—called econometrics. Third, when economists can, they perform experiments. This relatively new approach puts real subjects (usually students) in a decision-making situation and varies their incentives in some way to discover how they respond to a change in one factor at a time.

Economists try to avoid fallacies—errors of reasoning that lead to a wrong conclusion. But two fallacies are common, and you need to be on your guard to avoid them. They are the

- Fallacy of composition
- *Post hoc* fallacy

**Fallacy of Composition** The fallacy of composition is the (false) statement that what is true of the parts is true of the whole or that what is true of the whole is true of the parts. There are many everyday examples of this fallacy. Standing at a ball game to get a better view works for one person but not for all—what is true for a part of a crowd is not true for the whole crowd.

The fallacy of composition arises in many economic situations that stem from the fact that the parts interact with each other to produce an outcome for the whole that might differ from the intent of the parts.

For example, a firm fires some workers to cut costs and improve its profits. If all firms take similar actions, income falls and so does spending. The firm sells less, and its profits don't improve.

Or suppose that a firm thinks it can gain market share by cutting its price and mounting a large advertising campaign. Again, if the one firm takes these actions they work. But if all the firms in an industry take the same actions, they all end up with the same market share as before and lower profits.

**Post Hoc Fallacy** Another Latin phrase—*post hoc, ergo propter hoc*—means "after this, therefore because of this." The *post hoc* fallacy is the error of reasoning that a first event *causes* a second event because the first occurred before the second. Suppose you are a visitor from a far-off world. You observe lots of people shopping in early December, and then you see them opening gifts and partying in the holiday season. "Does the shopping cause the holiday season?," you wonder. After a deeper study, you discover that the holiday season causes the shopping. A later event causes an earlier event.

Unraveling cause and effect is difficult in economics. And just looking at the timing of events often doesn't help. For example, the stock market booms, and some months later the economy expands—jobs and incomes grow. Did the stock market boom cause the economy to expand? Possibly, but perhaps businesses started to plan the expansion of production because a new technology that lowered costs had become available. As knowledge of the plans spread, the stock market reacted to *anticipate* the economic expansion. To disentangle cause and effect, economists use economic models and data and, to the extent that they can, perform experiments.

Economics is a challenging science. Does the difficulty of getting answers in economics mean that anything goes and that economists disagree on most questions? Perhaps you've heard the joke "If you laid all the economists in the world end to end, they still wouldn't reach agreement." Surprisingly, perhaps, the joke does not describe reality.

### Agreement and Disagreement

Economists agree on a remarkably wide range of questions. And often the agreed-upon view of economists disagrees with the popular and sometimes politically correct view. When Federal Reserve Chairman Alan Greenspan testifies before the Senate Banking Committee, his words are rarely controversial among economists, even when they generate endless debate in the media and Congress.

Here are 12 propositions with which at least 7 out of every 10 economists broadly agree:

- Tariffs and import restrictions make most people worse off.
- A large budget deficit has an adverse effect on the economy.
- A minimum wage increases unemployment among young workers and low-skilled workers.
- Cash payments to welfare recipients make them better off than do transfers-in-kind of equal cash value.
- A tax cut can help to lower unemployment when the unemployment rate is high.
- The distribution of income in the United States should be more equal.
- Inflation is primarily caused by a rapid rate of money creation.
- The government should restructure welfare along the lines of a "negative income tax."
- Rent ceilings cut the availability of housing.
- Pollution taxes are more effective than pollution limits.
- The redistribution of income is a legitimate role for the U.S. government.
- The federal budget should be balanced on the average over the business cycle but not every year.

Which of these propositions are positive and which are normative? Notice that economists are willing to offer their opinions on normative issues as well as their professional views on positive questions. Be on the lookout for normative propositions dressed up as positive propositions.

### REVIEW QUIZ

1. What is the distinction between a positive statement and a normative statement? Provide an example (different from those in the chapter) of each type of statement.
2. What is a model? Can you think of a model that you might use (probably without thinking of it as a model) in your everyday life?
3. What is a theory? Why is the statement "It might work in theory, but it doesn't work in practice" a silly statement?
4. What is the *ceteris paribus* assumption and how is it used?
5. Try to think of some everyday examples of the fallacy of composition and the *post hoc* fallacy.

# SUMMARY

## KEY POINTS

### Definition of Economics (p. 2)

- All economic questions arise from scarcity—from the fact that wants exceed the resources available to satisfy them.
- Economics is the social science that studies the choices that people make as they cope with scarcity.
- The subject divides into microeconomics and macroeconomics.

### Two Big Economic Questions (pp. 3–8)

- Two big questions summarize the scope of economics:
  1. How do choices end up determining *what*, *how*, and *for whom* goods and services get produced?
  2. When do choices made in the pursuit of *self-interest* also promote the *social interest*?

### The Economic Way of Thinking (pp. 9–11)

- Every choice is a tradeoff—exchanging more of something for less of something else.
- The classic guns-versus-butter tradeoff represents all tradeoffs.
- All economic questions involve tradeoffs.
- The big social tradeoff is that between equality and efficiency.
- A macroeconomic tradeoff is the short-run tradeoff between output and inflation.
- The highest-valued alternative forgone is the opportunity cost of what is chosen.
- Choices are made at the margin and respond to incentives.

### Economics: A Social Science (pp. 12–14)

- Economists distinguish between positive statements—what is—and normative statements—what ought to be.
- To explain the economic world, economists develop theories by building and testing economic models.
- Economists use the *ceteris paribus* assumption to try to disentangle cause and effect and are careful to avoid the fallacy of composition and the *post hoc* fallacy.
- Economists agree on a wide range of questions about how the economy works.

## KEY TERMS

Big tradeoff, 10
Capital, 4
*Ceteris paribus*, 13
Economic model, 12
Economics, 2
Economic theory, 12
Entrepreneurship, 4
Factors of production, 3
Goods and services, 3
Human capital, 3
Incentive, 2
Interest, 4
Labor, 3
Land, 3
Macroeconomics, 2
Margin, 11
Marginal benefit, 11
Marginal cost, 11
Microeconomics, 2
Opportunity cost, 10
Profit, 4
Rent, 4
Scarcity, 2
Self-interest, 5
Social interest, 5
Tradeoff, 9
Wages, 4

## PROBLEMS

*1. Your friends go the movies one evening and you decide to stay home and do your economics assignment and practice test. You get 80 percent on your next economics exam compared with the 70 percent that you normally score. What is the opportunity cost of your extra points?

2. You go to the movies one evening instead of doing your economics assignment and practice test. You get 50 percent on your next economics exam compared with the 70 percent that you normally score. What is the opportunity cost of going to the movies?

*3. You plan to go to school this summer. If you do, you won't be able to take your usual job that pays $6,000 for the summer, and you won't be able to live at home for free. The cost of tuition is $2,000 and textbooks is $200, and living expenses are $1,400. What is the opportunity cost of going to summer school?

4. You plan to go skiing next weekend. If you do, you'll have to miss doing your usual weekend job that pays $100. You won't be able study for 8 hours and you won't be able to use your pre-paid college meal plan. The cost of your travel and accommodations will be $350, the cost of renting skis is $60, and your food will cost $40. What is the opportunity cost of the weekend ski trip?

*5. The local mall has free parking, but the mall is always very busy, and it usually takes 30 minutes to find a parking space. Today when you found a vacant spot, Harry also wanted it. Is parking really free at this mall? If not, what did it cost you to park today? When you parked your car today, did you impose any costs on Harry? Explain your answers.

6. The university has built a new movie house. Admission for students is free and there are always plenty of empty seats. But when the movie house screened *Lord of the Rings*, the lines were long. So the movie house decided to charge $4 per student. Cadbury Schweppes offered students a free soft drink. Compare the student's opportunity cost of seeing the movie *Lord of the Rings* with that of any other movie screened this year. Which is less costly and by how much?

\* Solutions to odd-numbered problems are available on **MyEconLab**.

## CRITICAL THINKING

1. Use the two big questions of economics and the economic way of thinking to organize a short essay about the economic life of a homeless man. Does he face scarcity? Does he make choices? Can you interpret his choices as being in his own best interest? Can either his own choices or the choices of others make him better off? If so, how?

## WEB EXERCISES

**Use the links on MyEconLab to work the following exercises.**

1. Visit *CNNfn*.
   a. What is the top economic news story today?
   b. With which of the big questions does it deal? (It must deal with at least one of them and might deal with more than one.)
   c. What tradeoffs does the news item discuss?
   d. Write a brief summary of the news item in a few bulleted points using as much as possible of the economic vocabulary that you have learned in this chapter and that is in the key terms list on p. 15.
2. Visit *Resources For Economists on the Internet*. This site is a good place from which to search for economic information on the Internet.
   a. Scroll down the page and click on General Interest.
   b. Visit the "general interest" sites and become familiar with the types of information they contain.
3. Visit the Bureau of Labor Statistics.
   a. What is the number of people employed (nonfarm employment) in your area?
   b. Has employment increased or decreased?
   c. What is income per person (per capita income) in your area?

# APPENDIX

## Graphs in Economics

### After studying this appendix, you will be able to

- Make and interpret a time-series graph, a cross-section graph, and a scatter diagram
- Distinguish between linear and nonlinear relationships and between relationships that have a maximum and a minimum
- Define and calculate the slope of a line
- Graph relationships among more than two variables

## Graphing Data

A GRAPH REPRESENTS A QUANTITY AS A DISTANCE ON a line. Figure A1.1 shows two examples. Here, a distance on the horizontal line represents temperature, measured in degrees Fahrenheit. A movement from left to right shows an increase in temperature. The point marked 0 represents zero degrees Fahrenheit. To the right of 0, the temperature is positive. To the left of 0 (as indicated by the minus sign), the temperature is negative. A distance on the vertical line represents altitude or height, measured in thousands of feet above sea level. The point marked 0 represents sea level. Points above 0 represent feet above sea level. Points below 0 (indicated by a minus sign) represent feet below sea level.

By setting two scales perpendicular to each other, as in Fig. A1.1, we can visualize the relationship between two variables. The scale lines are called *axes*. The vertical line is the *y*-axis, and the horizontal line is the *x*-axis. Each axis has a zero point, which is shared by the two axes. This zero point, common to both axes, is called the *origin*.

To show something in a two-variable graph, we need two pieces of information: the value of the *x* variable and the value of the *y* variable. For example, off the coast of Alaska on a winter's day, the temperature is 32 degrees—the value of *x*. A fishing boat is located at 0 feet above sea level—the value of *y*. These two bits of information appear as point *A* in Fig. A1.1. A climber at the top of Mount McKinley on a cold day is 20,320

**FIGURE A1.1  Making a Graph**

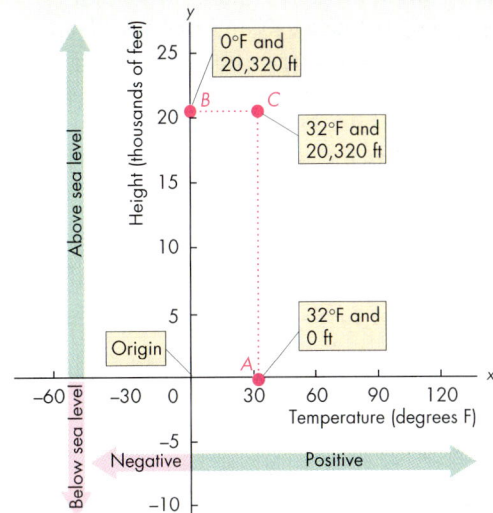

Graphs have axes that measure quantities as distances. Here, the horizontal axis (*x*-axis) measures temperature, and the vertical axis (*y*-axis) measures height. Point *A* represents a fishing boat at sea level (0 on the *y*-axis) on a day when the temperature is 32°F. Point *B* represents a climber at the top of Mt. McKinley 20,320 feet above sea level at a temperature of 0°F. Point *C* represents a climber at the top of Mt. McKinley, 20,320 feet above sea level at a temperature of 32°F.

feet above sea level in a zero-degree gale. These two pieces of information appear as point *B*. The position of the climber on a warmer day might be at the point marked *C*. This point represents the peak of Mt. McKinley at a temperature of 32 degrees.

We can draw two lines, called *coordinates*, from point *C*. One, called the *y*-coordinate, runs from *C* to the horizontal axis. Its length is the same as the value marked off on the *y*-axis. The other, called the *x*-coordinate, runs from *C* to the vertical axis. Its length is the same as the value marked off on the *x*-axis. We describe a point in a graph by the values of its *x*-coordinate and its *y*-coordinate.

Graphs like that in Fig. A1.1 can show any type of quantitative data on two variables. Economists use three types of graphs based on the principles in Fig. A1.1 to reveal and describe the relationships among variables. They are

- Time-series graphs
- Cross-section graphs
- Scatter diagrams

17

## Time-Series Graphs

A **time-series graph** measures time (for example, months or years) on the *x*-axis and the variable or variables in which we are interested on the *y*-axis. Figure A1.2 is an example of a time-series graph. It provides some information about the price of coffee.

In Fig. A1.2, we measure time in years running from 1970 to 2000. We measure the price of coffee (the variable that we are interested in) on the *y*-axis.

The point of a time-series graph is to enable us to visualize how a variable has changed over time and how its value in one period relates to its value in another period.

A time-series graph conveys an enormous amount of information quickly and easily, as this example illustrates. It shows:

- The *level* of the price of coffee—when it is *high* and *low*. When the line is a long way from the *x*-axis, the price is high, as it was, for example, in 1977. When the line is close to the *x*-axis, the price is low, as it was, for example, in 1992.
- How the price *changes*—whether it *rises* or *falls*. When the line slopes upward, as in 1976, the price is rising. When the line slopes downward, as in 1978, the price is falling.
- The *speed* with which the price changes—whether it rises or falls *quickly* or *slowly*. If the line is very steep, then the price rises or falls quickly. If the line is not steep, the price rises or falls slowly. For example, the price rose quickly between 1975 and 1977 and slowly between 1983 and 1984. The price fell quickly between 1977 and 1978 and slowly between 1988 and 1992.

A time-series graph also reveals whether there is a trend. A **trend** is a general tendency for a variable to move in one direction. A trend might be upward or downward. In Fig. A1.2, you can see that the price of coffee had a general tendency to fall from the mid-1970s to the early 1990s. That is, although the price rose and fell, the general tendency was for it to fall—the price had a downward trend.

A time-series graph also helps us to detect fluctuations in a variable around its trend. You can see some peaks and troughs in the price of coffee in Fig. A1.2.

Finally, a time-series graph also lets us compare the variable in different periods quickly. Figure A1.2 shows that the 1980s were different from the 1970s.

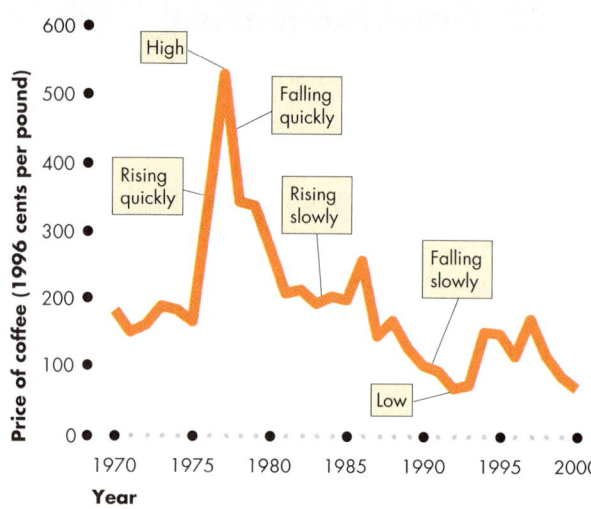

**FIGURE A1.2  A Time-Series Graph**

A time-series graph plots the level of a variable on the *y*-axis against time (day, week, month, or year) on the *x*-axis. This graph shows the price of coffee (in 1996 cents per pound) each year from 1970 to 2000. It shows us when the price of coffee was *high* and when it was *low*, when the price *increased* and when it *decreased*, and when it changed *quickly* and when it changed *slowly*.

The price of coffee fluctuated more violently in the 1970s than it did in the 1980s.

You can see that a time-series graph conveys a wealth of information. And it does so in much less space than we have used to describe only some of its features. But you do have to "read" the graph to obtain all this information.

## Cross-Section Graphs

A **cross-section graph** shows the values of an economic variable for different groups in a population at a point in time. Figure A1.3, called a *bar chart*, is an example of a cross-section graph.

The bar chart in Fig. A1.3 shows the population across the 10 largest metropolitan areas in the United States in 2000. The length of each bar indicates the population size. This figure enables you to compare the population in these 10 metropolitan areas. And you can do so much more quickly and clearly than by looking at a list of numbers.

APPENDIX: GRAPHS IN ECONOMICS    19

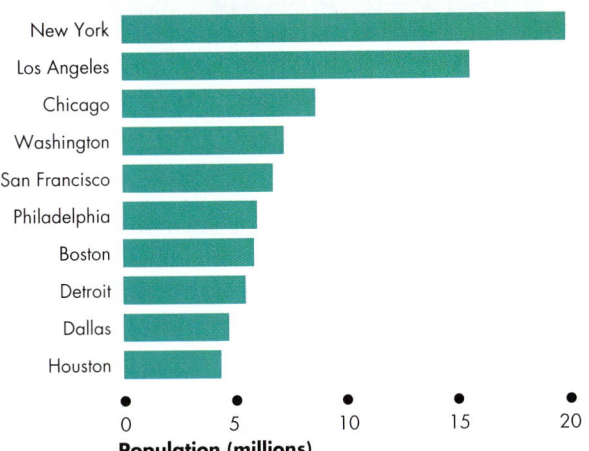

**FIGURE A1.3    A Cross-Section Graph**

A cross-section graph shows the level of a variable across the members of a population. This bar chart shows the population in each of the 10 largest metropolitan areas in the United States in 1999.

## Scatter Diagrams

A **scatter diagram** plots the value of one variable against the value of another variable. Such a graph reveals whether a relationship exists between two variables and describes their relationship. Figure A1.4(a) shows the relationship between expenditure and income. Each point shows expenditure per person and income per person in a given year from 1990 to 2000. The points are "scattered" within the graph. The point labeled A tells us that in 1996, income per person was $20,613 and expenditure per person was $18,888. The dots in this graph form a pattern, which reveals that as income increases, expenditure increases.

Figure A1.4(b) shows the relationship between the number of international phone calls and the price of a call. This graph shows that as the price per minute falls, the number of calls increases.

Figure A1.4(c) shows a scatter diagram of inflation and unemployment in the United States. Here, the dots show no clear relationship between these two variables. The dots in this graph reveal that there is no simple relationship between these variables.

**FIGURE A1.4    Scatter Diagrams**

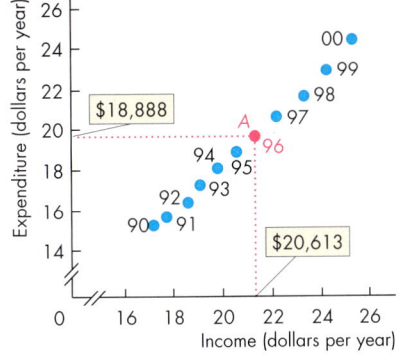

(a) Expenditure and income

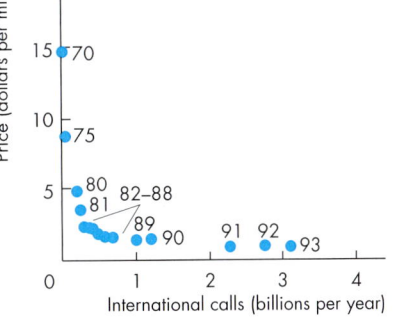

(b) International phone calls and prices

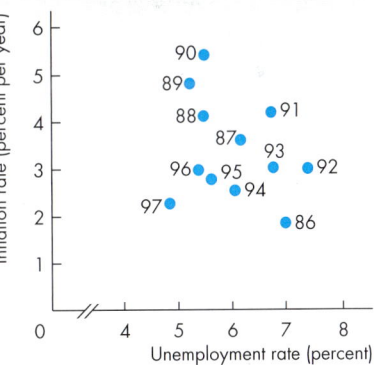

(c) Unemployment and inflation

A scatter diagram reveals the relationship between two variables. Part (a) shows the relationship between expenditure and income. Each point shows the values of the two variables in a specific year. For example, point A shows that in 1996, average income was $20,613 and average expenditure was $18,888. The pattern formed by the points shows that as income increases, expenditure increases.

Part (b) shows the relationship between the price of an international phone call and the number of calls made. This graph shows that as the price of a phone call falls, the number of calls made increases. Part (c) shows a scatter diagram of the inflation rate and unemployment rate in the United States. This graph shows that inflation and unemployment are not closely related.

**Breaks in the Axes** Two of the graphs you've just looked at, Fig. A1.4(a) and Fig. A1.4(c), have breaks in their axes, as shown by the small gaps. The breaks indicate that there are jumps from the origin, 0, to the first values recorded.

In Fig. A1.4(a), the breaks are used because the lowest value of expenditure exceeds $14,000 and the lowest value of income exceeds $16,000. With no breaks in the axes of this graph, there would be a lot of empty space, all the points would be crowded into the top right corner, and we would not be able to see whether a relationship exists between these two variables. By breaking the axes, we are able to bring the relationship into view.

Putting a break in the axes is like using a zoom lens to bring the relationship into the center of the graph and magnify it so the relationship fills the graph.

**Misleading Graphs** Breaks can be used to highlight a relationship. But they can also be used to mislead—to make a graph that lies. The most common way of making a graph lie is to use axis breaks and to either stretch or compress a scale. For example, suppose that in Fig. A1.4(a), the $y$-axis that measures expenditure ran from zero to $45,000 while the $x$-axis was the same as the one shown. The graph would now create the impression that despite a huge increase in income, expenditure had barely changed.

To avoid being misled, it is a good idea to get into the habit of always looking closely at the values and the labels on the axes of a graph before you start to interpret it.

**Correlation and Causation** A scatter diagram that shows a clear relationship between two variables, such as Fig. A1.4(a) or Fig. A1.4(b), tells us that the two variables have a high correlation. When a high correlation is present, we can predict the value of one variable from the value of the other variable. But correlation does not imply causation.

Sometimes a high correlation is a coincidence, but sometimes it does arise from a causal relationship. It is likely, for example, that rising income causes rising expenditure (Fig. A1.4a) and that the falling price of a phone call causes more calls to be made (Fig. A1.4b).

You've now seen how we can use graphs in economics to show economic data and to reveal relationships between variables. Next, we'll learn how economists use graphs to construct and display economic models.

# Graphs Used in Economic Models

THE GRAPHS USED IN ECONOMICS ARE NOT ALWAYS designed to show real-world data. Often they are used to show general relationships among the variables in an economic model.

An *economic model* is a stripped down, simplified description of an economy or of a component of an economy such as a business or a household. It consists of statements about economic behavior that can be expressed as equations or as curves in a graph. Economists use models to explore the effects of different policies or other influences on the economy in ways that are similar to the use of model airplanes in wind tunnels and models of the climate.

You will encounter many different kinds of graphs in economic models, but there are some repeating patterns. Once you've learned to recognize these patterns, you will instantly understand the meaning of a graph. Here, we'll look at the different types of curves that are used in economic models, and we'll see some everyday examples of each type of curve. The patterns to look for in graphs are the four cases in which

- Variables move in the same direction.
- Variables move in opposite directions.
- Variables have a maximum or a minimum.
- Variables are unrelated.

Let's look at these four cases.

## Variables That Move in the Same Direction

Figure A1.5 shows graphs of the relationships between two variables that move up and down together. A relationship between two variables that move in the same direction is called a **positive relationship** or a **direct relationship**. A line that slopes upward shows such a relationship.

Figure A1.5 shows three types of relationships, one that has a straight line and two that have curved lines. But all the lines in these three graphs are called curves. Any line on a graph—no matter whether it is straight or curved—is called a *curve*.

A relationship shown by a straight line is called a **linear relationship**. Figure A1.5(a) shows a linear

## FIGURE A1.5  Positive (Direct) Relationships

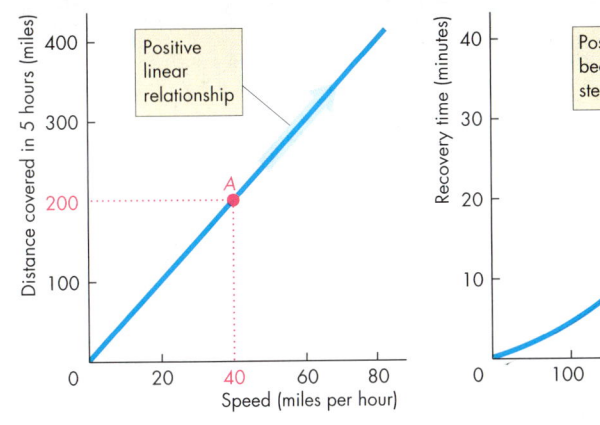
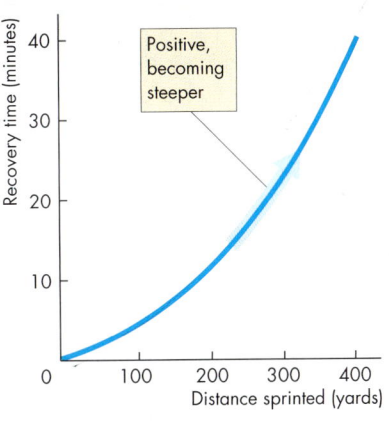
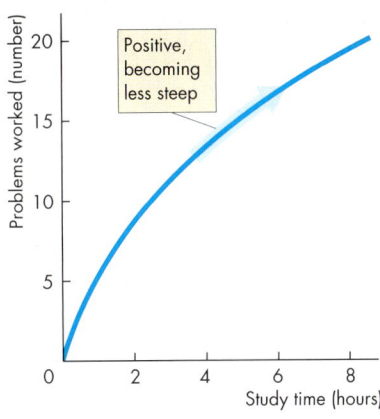

**(a) Positive linear relationship**  **(b) Positive, becoming steeper**  **(c) Positive, becoming less steep**

Each part of this figure shows a positive (direct) relationship between two variables. That is, as the value of the variable measured on the *x*-axis increases, so does the value of the variable measured on the *y*-axis. Part (a) shows a linear relationship—as the two variables increase together, we move along a straight line. Part (b) shows a positive relationship such that as the two variables increase together, we move along a curve that becomes steeper. Part (c) shows a positive relationship such that as the two variables increase together, we move along a curve that becomes flatter.

---

relationship between the number of miles traveled in 5 hours and speed. For example, point *A* shows that we will travel 200 miles in 5 hours if our speed is 40 miles an hour. If we double our speed to 80 miles an hour, we will travel 400 miles in 5 hours.

Figure A1.5(b) shows the relationship between distance sprinted and recovery time (the time it takes the heart rate to return to its normal resting rate). This relationship is an upward-sloping one that starts out quite flat but then becomes steeper as we move along the curve away from the origin. The reason this curve slopes upward and becomes steeper is because the additional recovery time needed from sprinting an additional 100 yards increases. It takes less than 5 minutes to recover from the first 100 yards but more than 10 minutes to recover from the third 100 yards.

Figure A1.5(c) shows the relationship between the number of problems worked by a student and the amount of study time. This relationship is an upward-sloping one that starts out quite steep and becomes flatter as we move away from the origin. Study time becomes less productive as you increase the hours worked and become more tired.

## Variables That Move in Opposite Directions

Figure A1.6 shows relationships between things that move in opposite directions. A relationship between variables that move in opposite directions is called a **negative relationship** or an **inverse relationship**.

Figure A1.6(a) shows the relationship between the number of hours available for playing squash and the number of hours for playing tennis when the total is 5 hours. One extra hour spent playing tennis means one hour less playing squash and vice versa. This relationship is negative and linear.

Figure A1.6(b) shows the relationship between the cost per mile traveled and the length of a journey. The longer the journey, the lower is the cost per mile. But as the journey length increases, the cost per mile decreases, and the fall in the cost is smaller, the longer the journey. This feature of the relationship is shown by the fact that the curve slopes downward, starting out steep at a short journey length and then becoming flatter as the journey length increases. This relationship arises because some of the costs are fixed, such as auto insurance, and the fixed costs are spread over a longer journey.

## FIGURE A1.6  Negative (Inverse) Relationships

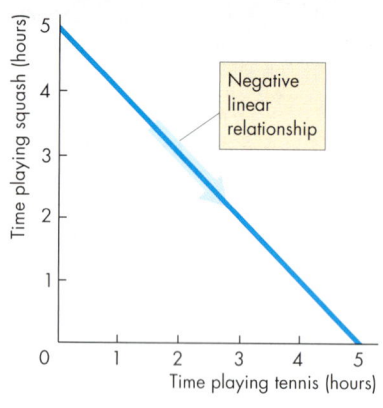
(a) Negative linear relationship

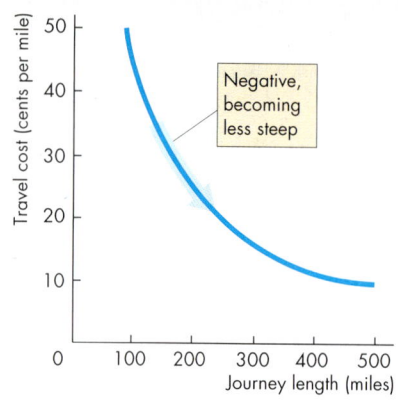
(b) Negative, becoming less steep

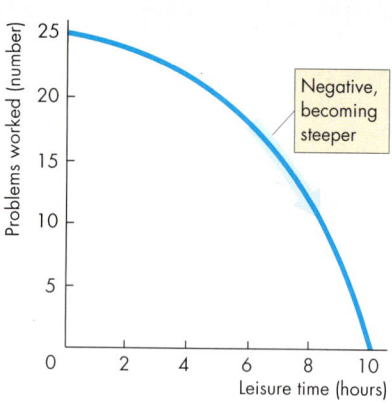
(c) Negative, becoming steeper

Each part of this figure shows a negative (inverse) relationship between two variables. That is, as the value of the variable measured on the x-axis increases, the value of the variable measured on the y-axis decreases. Part (a) shows a linear relationship. The total time spent playing tennis and squash is 5 hours. As the time spent playing tennis increases, the time spent playing squash decreases, and we move along a straight line. Part (b) shows a negative relationship such that as the journey length increases, the travel cost decreases as we move along a curve that becomes less steep. Part (c) shows a negative relationship such that as leisure time increases, the number of problems worked decreases as we move along a curve that becomes steeper.

Figure A1.6(c) shows the relationship between the amount of leisure time and the number of problems worked by a student. Increasing leisure time produces an increasingly large reduction in the number of problems worked. This relationship is a negative one that starts out with a gentle slope at a small number of leisure hours and becomes steeper as the number of leisure hours increases. This relationship is a different view of the idea shown in Fig. A1.5(c).

## Variables That Have a Maximum or a Minimum

Many relationships in economic models have a maximum or a minimum. For example, firms try to make the maximum possible profit and to produce at the lowest possible cost. Figure A1.7 shows relationships that have a maximum or a minimum.

Figure A1.7(a) shows the relationship between rainfall and wheat yield. When there is no rainfall, wheat will not grow, so the yield is zero. As the rainfall increases up to 10 days a month, the wheat yield increases. With 10 rainy days each month, the wheat yield reaches its maximum at 40 bushels an acre (point A). Rain in excess of 10 days a month starts to lower the yield of wheat. If every day is rainy, the wheat suffers from a lack of sunshine and the yield decreases to zero. This relationship is one that starts out sloping upward, reaches a maximum, and then slopes downward.

Figure A1.7(b) shows the reverse case—a relationship that begins sloping downward, falls to a minimum, and then slopes upward. Most economic costs are like this relationship. An example is the relationship between the cost per mile and speed for a car trip. At low speeds, the car is creeping in a traffic snarl-up. The number of miles per gallon is low, so the cost per mile is high. At high speeds, the car is traveling faster than its efficient speed, using a large quantity of gasoline, and again the number of miles per gallon is low and the cost per mile is high. At a speed of 55 miles an hour, the cost per mile is at its minimum (point B). This relationship is one that starts out sloping downward, reaches a minimum, and then slopes upward.

APPENDIX: GRAPHS IN ECONOMICS    23

## FIGURE A1.7    Maximum and Minimum Points

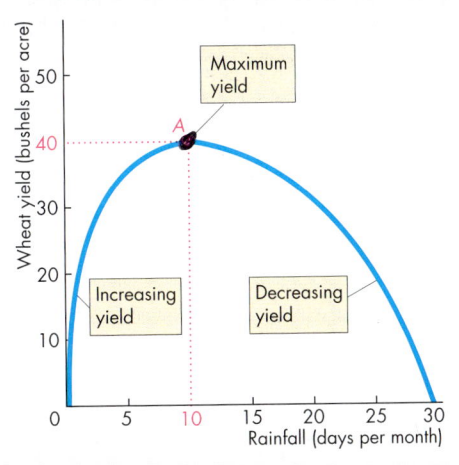

(a) Relationship with a maximum

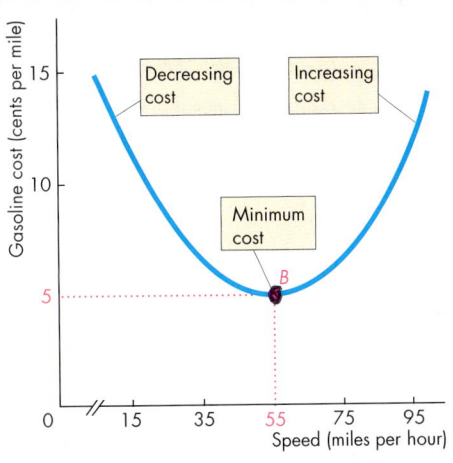

(b) Relationship with a minimum

Part (a) shows a relationship that has a maximum point, A. The curve slopes upward as it rises to its maximum point, is flat at its maximum, and then slopes downward.

Part (b) shows a relationship with a minimum point, B. The curve slopes downward as it falls to its minimum, is flat at its minimum, and then slopes upward.

## Variables That Are Unrelated

There are many situations in which no matter what happens to the value of one variable, the other variable remains constant. Sometimes we want to show the independence between two variables in a graph, and Fig. A1.8 shows two ways of achieving this.

In describing the graphs in Fig. A1.5 through A1.7, we have talked about curves that slope upward or slope downward, and curves that become less steep or steeper. Let's spend a little time discussing exactly what we mean by slope and how we measure the slope of a curve.

## FIGURE A1.8    Variables That Are Unrelated

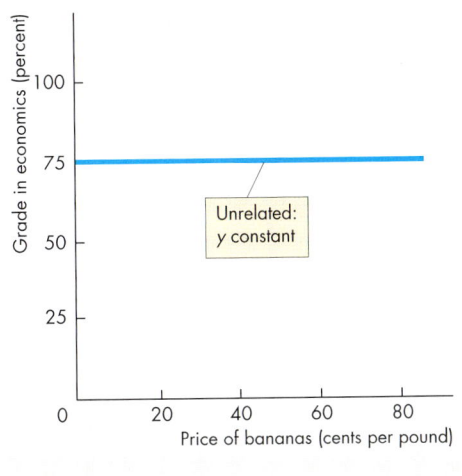

(a) Unrelated: y constant

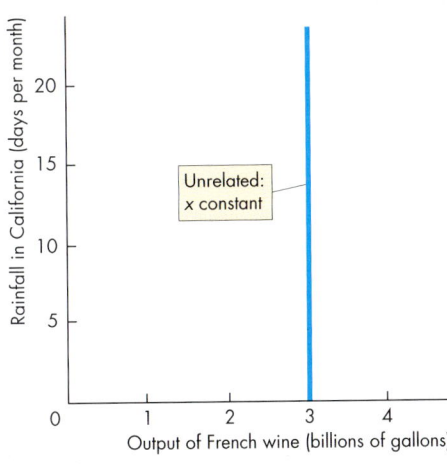

(b) Unrelated: x constant

This figure shows how we can graph two variables that are unrelated. In part (a), a student's grade in economics is plotted at 75 percent on the y-axis regardless of the price of bananas on the x-axis. The curve is horizontal.

In part (b), the output of the vineyards of France on the x-axis does not vary with the rainfall in California on the y-axis. The curve is vertical.

## The Slope of a Relationship

WE CAN MEASURE THE INFLUENCE OF ONE variable on another by the slope of the relationship. The **slope** of a relationship is the change in the value of the variable measured on the *y*-axis divided by the change in the value of the variable measured on the *x*-axis. We use the Greek letter $\Delta$ (*delta*) to represent "change in." Thus $\Delta y$ means the change in the value of the variable measured on the *y*-axis, and $\Delta x$ means the change in the value of the variable measured on the *x*-axis. Therefore the slope of the relationship is

$$\Delta y / \Delta x$$

If a large change in the variable measured on the *y*-axis ($\Delta y$) is associated with a small change in the variable measured on the *x*-axis ($\Delta x$), the slope is large and the curve is steep. If a small change in the variable measured on the *y*-axis ($\Delta y$) is associated with a large change in the variable measured on the *x*-axis ($\Delta x$), the slope is small and the curve is flat.

We can make the idea of slope clearer by doing some calculations.

### The Slope of a Straight Line

The slope of a straight line is the same regardless of where on the line you calculate it. The slope of a straight line is constant. Let's calculate the slopes of the lines in Fig. A1.9. In part (a), when *x* increases from 2 to 6, *y* increases from 3 to 6. The change in

**FIGURE A1.9**  The Slope of a Straight Line

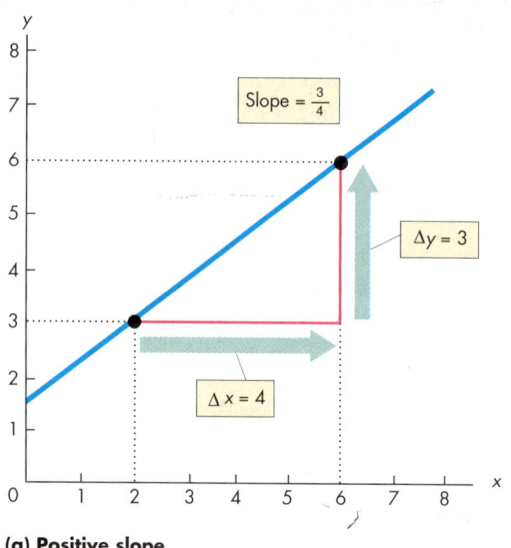

**(a) Positive slope**

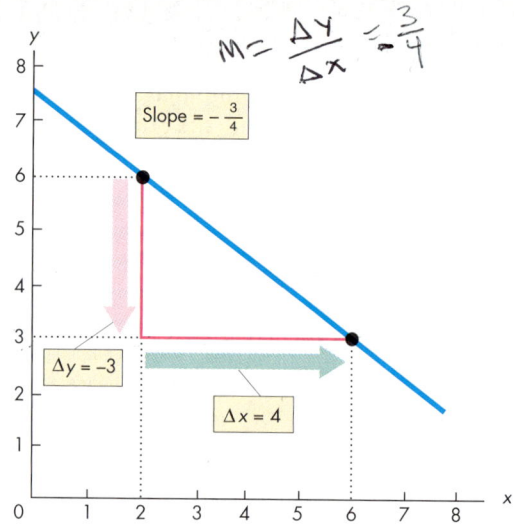

**(b) Negative slope**

To calculate the slope of a straight line, we divide the change in the value of the variable measured on the *y*-axis ($\Delta y$) by the change in the value of the variable measured on the *x*-axis ($\Delta x$), as we move along the curve. Part (a) shows the calculation of a positive slope. When *x* increases from 2 to 6, $\Delta x$ equals 4. That change in *x* brings about an increase in *y*

from 3 to 6, so $\Delta y$ equals 3. The slope ($\Delta y/\Delta x$) equals ¾. Part (b) shows the calculation of a negative slope. When *x* increases from 2 to 6, $\Delta x$ equals 4. That increase in *x* brings about a decrease in *y* from 6 to 3, so $\Delta y$ equals $-3$. The slope ($\Delta y/\Delta x$) equals $-¾$.

$x$ is +4—that is, $\Delta x$ is 4. The change in $y$ is +3—that is, $\Delta y$ is 3. The slope of that line is

$$\frac{\Delta y}{\Delta x} = \frac{3}{4}.$$

In part (b), when $x$ increases from 2 to 6, $y$ decreases from 6 to 3. The change in $y$ is *minus* 3—that is, $\Delta y$ is –3. The change in $x$ is *plus* 4—that is, $\Delta x$ is 4. The slope of the curve is

$$\frac{\Delta y}{\Delta x} = \frac{-3}{4}.$$

Notice that the two slopes have the same magnitude (¾) but the slope of the line in part (a) is positive (+3/+4 = ¾), while that in part (b) is negative (−3/+4 = −¾). The slope of a positive relationship is positive; the slope of a negative relationship is negative.

## The Slope of a Curved Line

The slope of a curved line is trickier. The slope of a curved line is not constant. Its slope depends on where on the line we calculate it. There are two ways to calculate the slope of a curved line: You can calculate the slope at a point, or you can calculate the slope across an arc of the curve. Let's look at the two alternatives.

**Slope at a Point** To calculate the slope at a point on a curve, you need to construct a straight line that has the same slope as the curve at the point in question. Figure A1.10 shows how this is done. Suppose you want to calculate the slope of the curve at point $A$. Place a ruler on the graph so that it touches point $A$ and no other point on the curve, then draw a straight line along the edge of the ruler. The straight red line is this line, and it is the tangent to the curve at point $A$. If the ruler touches the curve only at point $A$, then the slope of the curve at point $A$ must be the same as the slope of the edge of the ruler. If the curve and the ruler do not have the same slope, the line along the edge of the ruler will cut the curve instead of just touching it.

Now that you have found a straight line with the same slope as the curve at point $A$, you can calculate the slope of the curve at point $A$ by calculating the slope of the straight line. Along the straight line, as $x$

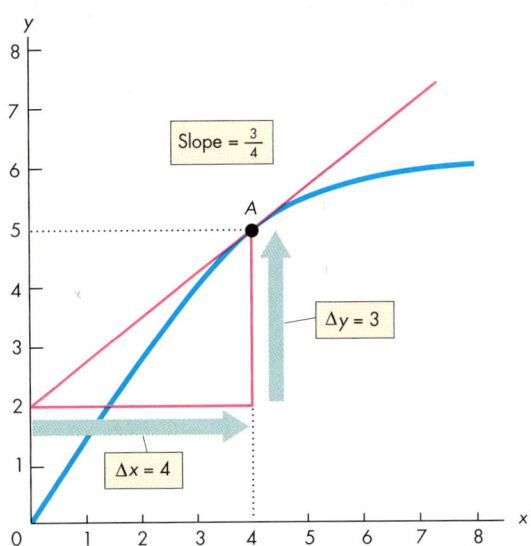

**FIGURE A1.10** Slope at a Point

To calculate the slope of the curve at point A, draw the red line that just touches the curve at A—the tangent. The slope of this straight line is calculated by dividing the change in y by the change in x along the line. When x increases from 0 to 4, $\Delta x$ equals 4. That change in x is associated with an increase in y from 2 to 5, so $\Delta y$ equals 3. The slope of the red line is ¾. So the slope of the curve at point A is ¾.

increases from 0 to 4 ($\Delta x = 4$) $y$ increases from 2 to 5 ($\Delta y = 3$). Therefore the slope of the line is

$$\frac{\Delta y}{\Delta x} = \frac{3}{4}.$$

Thus the slope of the curve at point $A$ is ¾.

**Slope Across an Arc** An arc of a curve is a piece of a curve. In Fig. A1.11, you are looking at the same curve as in Fig. A1.10. But instead of calculating the slope at point $A$, we are going to calculate the slope across the arc from $B$ to $C$. You can see that the slope at $B$ is greater than at $C$. When we calculate the slope across an arc, we are calculating the average slope between two points. As we move along the arc from $B$ to $C$, $x$ increases from 3 to 5 and $y$ increases from 4 to 5.5. The change in $x$ is 2 ($\Delta x = 2$), and the change

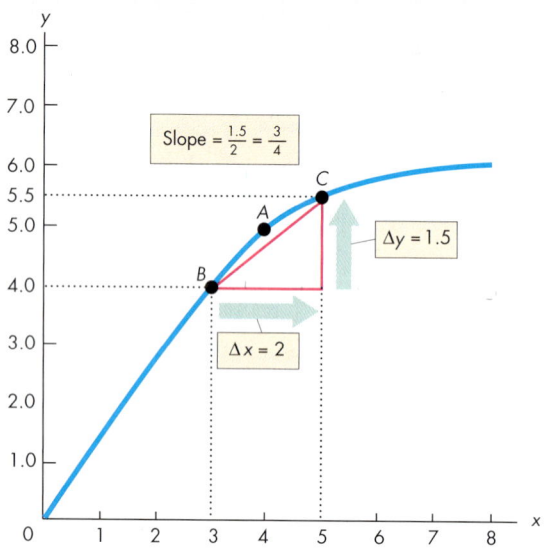

**FIGURE A1.11** Slope Across an Arc

To calculate the average slope of the curve along the arc BC, draw a straight line from B to C. The slope of the line BC is calculated by dividing the change in y by the change in x. In moving from B to C, Δx equals 2 and Δy equals 1.5. The slope of the line BC is 1.5 divided by 2, or ¾. So the slope of the curve across the arc BC is ¾.

in $y$ is 1.5 ($\Delta y = 1.5$). Therefore the slope of the line is

$$\frac{\Delta y}{\Delta x} = \frac{1.5}{2} = \frac{3}{4}.$$

Thus the slope of the curve across the arc $BC$ is ¾.

This calculation gives us the slope of the curve between points $B$ and $C$. The actual slope calculated is the slope of the straight line from $B$ to $C$. This slope approximates the average slope of the curve along the arc $BC$. In this particular example, the slope across the arc $BC$ is identical to the slope of the curve at point $A$. But the calculation of the slope of a curve does not always work out so neatly. You might have some fun constructing some more examples and some counterexamples.

You now know how to make and interpret a graph. But so far, we've limited our attention to graphs of two variables. We're now going to learn how to graph more than two variables.

# Graphing Relationships Among More Than Two Variables

WE HAVE SEEN THAT WE CAN GRAPH THE relationship between two variables as a point formed by the $x$- and $y$-coordinates in a two-dimensional graph. You may be thinking that although a two-dimensional graph is informative, most of the things in which you are likely to be interested involve relationships among many variables, not just two. For example, the amount of ice cream consumed depends on the price of ice cream and the temperature. If ice cream is expensive and the temperature is low, people eat much less ice cream than when ice cream is inexpensive and the temperature is high. For any given price of ice cream, the quantity consumed varies with the temperature; and for any given temperature, the quantity of ice cream consumed varies with its price.

Figure A1.12 shows a relationship among three variables. The table shows the number of gallons of ice cream consumed each day at various temperatures and ice cream prices. How can we graph these numbers?

To graph a relationship that involves more than two variables, we use the *ceteris paribus* assumption.

**Ceteris Paribus** We noted in the chapter (see p. 13) that every laboratory experiment is an attempt to create *ceteris paribus* and isolate the relationship of interest. We use the same method to make a graph when more than two variables are involved.

Figure A1.12(a) shows an example. There, you can see what happens to the quantity of ice cream consumed when the price of ice cream varies when the temperature is held constant. The line labeled 70°F shows the relationship between ice cream consumption and the price of ice cream if the temperature remains at 70°F. The numbers used to plot that line are those in the third column of the table in Fig. A1.12. For example, if the temperature is 70°F, 10 gallons are consumed when the price is 60¢ a scoop, and 18 gallons are consumed when the price is 30¢ a scoop. The curve labeled 90°F shows consumption as the price varies if the temperature remains at 90°F.

We can also show the relationship between ice cream consumption and temperature when the price of ice cream remains constant, as shown in

# FIGURE A1.12  Graphing a Relationship Among Three Variables

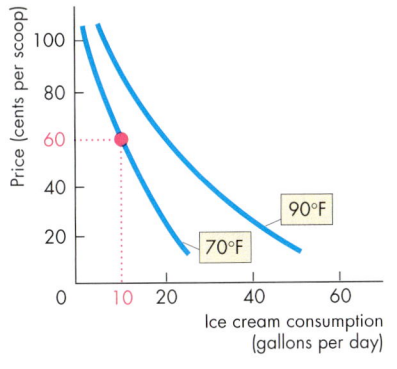
(a) Price and consumption at a given temperature

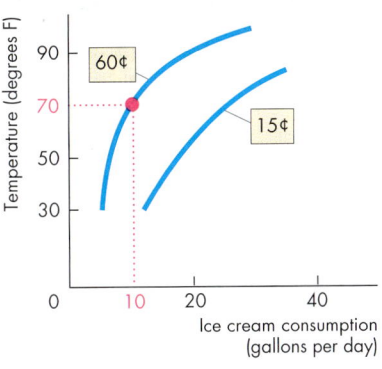
(b) Temperature and consumption at a given price

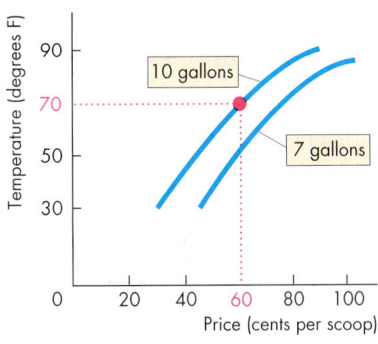
(c) Temperature and price at a given consumption

| Price (cents per scoop) | Ice cream consumption (gallons per day) | | | |
|---|---|---|---|---|
| | 30°F | 50°F | 70°F | 90°F |
| 15 | 12 | 18 | 25 | 50 |
| 30 | 10 | 12 | 18 | 37 |
| 45 | 7 | 10 | 13 | 27 |
| 60 | 5 | 7 | 10 | 20 |
| 75 | 3 | 5 | 7 | 14 |
| 90 | 2 | 3 | 5 | 10 |
| 105 | 1 | 2 | 3 | 6 |

The quantity of ice cream consumed depends on its price and the temperature. The table gives some hypothetical numbers that tell us how many gallons of ice cream are consumed each day at different prices and different temperatures. For example, if the price is 60¢ a scoop and the temperature is 70°F, 10 gallons of ice cream are consumed. This set of values is highlighted in the table and each part of the figure.

To graph a relationship among three variables, the value of one variable is held constant. Part (a) shows the relationship between price and consumption when temperature is held constant. One curve holds temperature at 90°F and the other at 70°F. Part (b) shows the relationship between temperature and consumption when price is held constant. One curve holds the price at 60¢ a scoop and the other at 15¢ a scoop. Part (c) shows the relationship between temperature and price when consumption is held constant. One curve holds consumption at 10 gallons and the other at 7 gallons.

Fig. A1.12(b). The curve labeled 60¢ shows how the consumption of ice cream varies with the temperature when ice cream costs 60¢ a scoop, and a second curve shows the relationship when ice cream costs 15¢ a scoop. For example, at 60¢ a scoop, 10 gallons are consumed when the temperature is 70°F and 20 gallons when the temperature is 90°F.

Figure A1.12(c) shows the combinations of temperature and price that result in a constant consumption of ice cream. One curve shows the combination that results in 10 gallons a day being consumed, and the other shows the combination that results in 7 gallons a day being consumed. A high price and a high temperature lead to the same consumption as a lower price and a lower temperature. For example, 10 gallons of ice cream are consumed at 70°F and 60¢ a scoop, at 90°F and 90¢ a scoop, and at 50°F and 45¢ a scoop.

◆ With what you have learned about graphs, you can move forward with your study of economics. There are no graphs in this book that are more complicated than those that have been explained in this appendix.

# SUMMARY

## KEY POINTS

### Graphing Data (pp. 17–20)

- A time-series graph shows the trend and fluctuations in a variable over time.
- A cross-section graph shows how variables change across the members of a population.
- A scatter diagram shows the relationship between two variables. It shows whether two variables are positively related, negatively related, or unrelated.

### Graphs Used in Economic Models (pp. 20–23)

- Graphs are used to show relationships among variables in economic models.
- Relationships can be positive (an upward-sloping curve), negative (a downward-sloping curve), positive and then negative (have a maximum point), negative and then positive (have a minimum point), or unrelated (a horizontal or vertical curve).

### The Slope of a Relationship (pp. 24–26)

- The slope of a relationship is calculated as the change in the value of the variable measured on the $y$-axis divided by the change in the value of the variable measured on the $x$-axis—that is, $\Delta y/\Delta x$.
- A straight line has a constant slope.
- A curved line has a varying slope. To calculate the slope of a curved line, we calculate the slope at a point or across an arc.

### Graphing Relationships Among More Than Two Variables (pp. 26–27)

- To graph a relationship among more than two variables, we hold constant the values of all the variables except two.
- We then plot the value of one of the variables against the value of another.

## KEY FIGURES

Figure A1.1 Making a Graph, 17
Figure A1.5 Positive (Direct) Relationships, 21
Figure A1.6 Negative (Inverse) Relationships, 22
Figure A1.7 Maximum and Minimum Points, 23
Figure A1.9 The Slope of a Straight Line, 24
Figure A1.10 Slope at a Point, 25
Figure A1.11 Slope Across an Arc, 26

## KEY TERMS

Cross-section graph, 18
Direct relationship, 20
Inverse relationship, 21
Linear relationship, 20
Negative relationship, 21
Positive relationship, 20
Scatter diagram, 19
Slope, 24
Time-series graph, 18
Trend, 18

# REVIEW QUIZ

1. What are the three types of graphs used to show economic data?
2. Give an example of a time-series graph.
3. List three things that a time-series graph shows quickly and easily.
4. Give three examples, different from those in the chapter, of scatter diagrams that show a positive relationship, a negative relationship, and no relationship.
5. Draw some graphs to show the relationships between two variables
   a. That move in the same direction.
   b. That move in opposite directions.
   c. That have a maximum.
   d. That have a minimum.
6. Which of the relationships in question 5 is a positive relationship and which a negative relationship?
7. What are the two ways of calculating the slope of a curved line?
8. How do we graph a relationship among more than two variables?

# PROBLEMS

The spreadsheet provides data on the U.S. economy: Column A is the year, column B is the inflation rate, column C is the interest rate, column D is the growth rate, and column E is the unemployment rate. Use this spreadsheet to answer problems 1, 2, 3, and 4.

|    | A    | B   | C   | D    | E   |
|----|------|-----|-----|------|-----|
| 1  | 1991 | 4.2 | 5.7 | −0.5 | 6.7 |
| 2  | 1992 | 3.0 | 3.6 | 3.0  | 7.4 |
| 3  | 1993 | 3.0 | 3.1 | 2.7  | 6.8 |
| 4  | 1994 | 2.6 | 4.6 | 4.0  | 6.1 |
| 5  | 1995 | 2.8 | 5.8 | 2.7  | 5.6 |
| 6  | 1996 | 3.0 | 5.3 | 3.6  | 5.4 |
| 7  | 1997 | 2.3 | 5.5 | 4.4  | 4.9 |
| 8  | 1998 | 1.6 | 5.4 | 4.3  | 4.5 |
| 9  | 1999 | 2.2 | 5.2 | 4.1  | 4.2 |
| 10 | 2000 | 3.4 | 6.2 | 4.1  | 4.0 |
| 11 | 2001 | 2.8 | 3.6 | 1.1  | 4.8 |

*1. a. Draw a time-series graph of the inflation rate.
   b. In which year(s) (i) was inflation highest, (ii) was inflation lowest, (iii) did it increase, (iv) did it decrease, (v) did it increase most, and (vi) did it decrease most?
   c. What was the main trend in inflation?

2. a. Draw a time-series graph of the interest rate.
   b. In which year(s) was the interest rate highest, (ii) was the interest rate lowest, (iii) did it increase, (iv) did it decrease, (v) did it increase most, and (vi) did it decrease most.
   c. What was the main trend in the interest rate?

*3. Draw a scatter diagram to show the relationship between the inflation rate and the interest rate. Describe the relationship.

4. Draw a scatter diagram to show the relationship between the growth rate and the unemployment rate. Describe the relationship.

*5. Draw a graph to show the relationship between the two variables $x$ and $y$:

| $x$ | 0 | 1 | 2 | 3 | 4  | 5  | 6  | 7  | 8  |
|-----|---|---|---|---|----|----|----|----|----|
| $y$ | 0 | 1 | 4 | 9 | 16 | 25 | 36 | 49 | 64 |

   a. Is the relationship positive or negative?
   b. Does the slope of the relationship increase or decrease as the value of $x$ increases?
   c. Think of some economic relationships that might be similar to this one.

6. Draw a graph that shows the relationship between the two variables $x$ and $y$:

| $x$ | 0  | 1  | 2  | 3  | 4 | 5 |
|-----|----|----|----|----|---|---|
| $y$ | 25 | 24 | 22 | 16 | 8 | 0 |

   a. Is the relationship positive or negative?
   b. Does the slope of the relationship increase or decrease as the value of $x$ increases?
   c. Think of some economic relationships that might be similar to this one.

*7. In problem 5, calculate the slope of the relationship between $x$ and $y$ when $x$ equals 4.

8. In problem 6, calculate the slope of the relationship between $x$ and $y$ when $x$ equals 3.

*9. In problem 5, calculate the slope of the relationship across the arc when $x$ increases from 3 to 4.

10. In problem 6, calculate the slope of the relationship across the arc when $x$ increases from 4 to 5.

*11. Calculate the slope of the relationship shown at point A in the following figure.

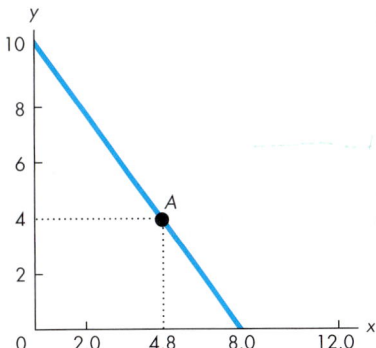

12. Calculate the slope of the relationship shown at point A in the following figure.

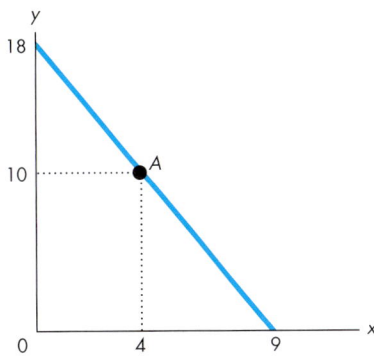

* Solutions to odd-numbered problems are available on **MyEconLab**.

*13. Use the following figure to calculate the slope of the relationship:

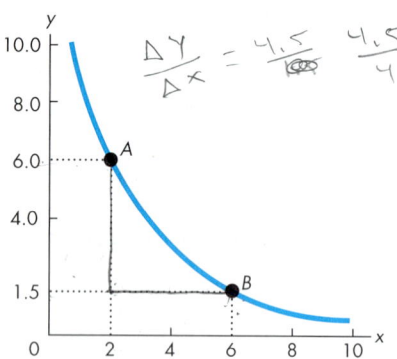

a. At points A and B.
b. Across the arc AB.

14. Use the following figure to calculate the slope of the relationship:

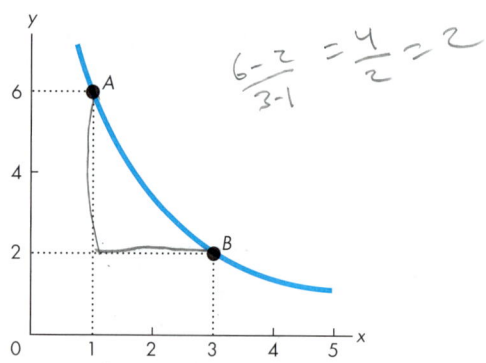

a. At points A and B.
b. Across the arc AB.

*15. The table gives the price of a balloon ride, the temperature, and the number of rides a day.

| Price (dollars per ride) | Balloon rides (number per day) | | |
|---|---|---|---|
| | 50°F | 70°F | 90°F |
| 5.00 | 32 | 40 | 50 |
| 10.00 | 27 | 32 | 40 |
| 15.00 | 18 | 27 | 32 |
| 20.00 | 10 | 18 | 27 |

Draw graphs to show the relationship between
a. The price and the number of rides, holding the temperature constant.
b. The number of rides and temperature, holding the price constant.
c. The temperature and price, holding the number of rides constant.

16. The table gives the price of an umbrella, the amount of rainfall, and the number of umbrellas purchased.

| Price (dollars per umbrella) | Umbrellas (number per day) | | |
|---|---|---|---|
| | 0 | 1 | 2 |
| | (inches of rainfall) | | |
| 10 | 7 | 8 | 12 |
| 20 | 4 | 7 | 8 |
| 30 | 2 | 4 | 7 |
| 40 | 1 | 2 | 4 |

Draw graphs to show the relationship between
a. The price and the number of umbrellas purchased, holding the amount of rainfall constant.
b. The number of umbrellas purchased and the amount of rainfall, holding the price constant.
c. The amount of rainfall and the price, holding the number of umbrellas purchased constant.

# WEB EXERCISES

**Use the links on MyEconLab to work the following exercises.**

1. Find Consumer Price Index (CPI) for the latest 12 months. Make a graph of the CPI. During the most recent month, was the CPI rising or falling? Was the rate of rise or fall increasing or decreasing?
2. Find the unemployment rate for the latest 12 months. Graph the unemployment rate. During the most recent month, was it rising or falling? Was the rate of rise or fall increasing or decreasing?
3. Use the data that you obtained in exercises 1 and 2. Make a graph to show whether the CPI and the unemployment rate are related to each other.
4. Use the data that you obtained in exercises 1 and 2. Calculate the percentage change in the CPI each month. Make a graph to show whether the percentage change in the CPI and the unemployment rate are related to each other.

# The Economic Problem

**CHAPTER 2**

## Good, Better, Best!

**We live in a style that surprises our grandparents** and would have astonished our great-grandparents. MP3s, video games, cell phones, gene splicing, and personal computers, which didn't exist even 25 years ago, have transformed our daily lives. For most of us, life is good and getting better. But we still make choices and face costs.

Perhaps the biggest change in the choices we're making and the costs we're facing arise from the climate of insecurity that prevails in today's world. We'll look at one of these choices in *Reading Between the Lines* at the end of this chapter.

When we make our choices, we pursue our self-interest. Do our choices also serve the social interest? And what do we mean by the social interest?

We see an incredible amount of specialization and trade in the world. Each one of us specializes in a particular job—as a lawyer, a journalist, a home maker. Why? How do we benefit from specialization and trade?

Over many centuries, social institutions have evolved that we take for granted. They include firms, markets, and a political and legal system that protects private property. Why have these institutions evolved?

◆ These are the questions that we study in this chapter. We begin with the core economic problem—scarcity and choice—and the concept of the production possibilities frontier. We then learn about the central idea of economics: that the pursuit of the social interest means using resources efficiently. We also discover how we can expand production by accumulating capital, expanding our knowledge, and specializing and trading with each other. What you will learn in this chapter is the foundation on which all economics is built.

### After studying this chapter, you will be able to

- **Define the production possibilities frontier and calculate opportunity cost**
- **Distinguish between production possibilities and preferences and describe an efficient allocation of resources**
- **Explain how current production choices expand future production possibilities**
- **Explain how specialization and trade expand our production possibilities**
- **Explain why property rights and markets have evolved**

31

# Production Possibilities and Opportunity Cost

EVERY WORKING DAY, IN MINES, FACTORIES, shops, and offices and on farms and construction sites across the United States, 138 million people produce a vast variety of goods and services valued at $50 billion. But the quantities of goods and services that we can produce are limited by both our available resources and by technology. And if we want to increase our production of one good, we must decrease our production of something else—we face tradeoffs. You are going to learn about the production possibilities frontier, which describes the limit to what we can produce and provides a neat way of thinking about and illustrating the idea of a tradeoff.

The **production possibilities frontier** (*PPF*) is the boundary between those combinations of goods and services that can be produced and those that cannot. To illustrate the *PPF*, we focus on two goods at a time and hold the quantities produced of all the other goods and services constant. That is, we look at a *model* economy in which everything remains the same (*ceteris paribus*) except for the production of the two goods we are considering.

Let's look at the production possibilities frontier for CDs and pizza, which stand for *any* pair of goods or services.

## Production Possibilities Frontier

The *production possibilities frontier* for CDs and pizza shows the limits to the production of these two goods, given the total resources available to produce them. Figure 2.1 shows this production possibilities frontier. The table lists some combinations of the quantities of pizzas and CDs that can be produced in a month given the resources available. The figure graphs these combinations. The *x*-axis shows the quantity of pizzas produced, and the *y*-axis shows the quantity of CDs produced.

The *PPF* illustrates *scarcity* because we cannot attain the points outside the frontier. They are points that describe wants that can't be satisfied. We can produce at all the points *inside* the *PPF* and *on* the *PPF*. They are attainable points. Suppose that in a typical month, we produce 4 million pizzas and 5 million CDs. Figure 2.1 shows this combination as point *E* and as possibility *E* in the table. The figure

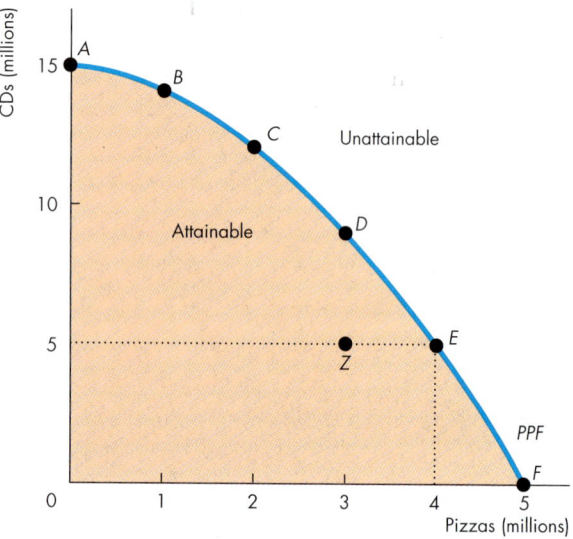

**FIGURE 2.1** Production Possibilities Frontier

| Possibility | Pizzas (millions) | | CDs (millions) |
|---|---|---|---|
| A | 0 | and | 15 |
| B | 1 | and | 14 |
| C | 2 | and | 12 |
| D | 3 | and | 9 |
| E | 4 | and | 5 |
| F | 5 | and | 0 |

The table lists six points on the production possibilities frontier for CDs and pizza. Row *A* tells us that if we produce no pizza, the maximum quantity of CDs we can produce is 15 million. Points *A*, *B*, *C*, *D*, *E*, and *F* in the figure represent the rows of the table. The line passing through these points is the production possibilities frontier (*PPF*).

The *PPF* separates the attainable from the unattainable. Production is possible at any point *inside* the orange area or *on* the frontier. Points outside the frontier are unattainable. Points inside the frontier such as point *Z* are inefficient because resources are wasted or misallocated. At such points, it is possible to use the available resources to produce more of either or both goods.

also shows other production possibilities. For example, we might stop producing pizza and move all the people who produce it into producing CDs. Point A in the figure and possibility A in the table show this case. The quantity of CDs produced increases to 15 million, and pizza production dries up. Alternatively, we might close the CD factories and switch all the resources into producing pizza. In this situation, we produce 5 million pizzas. Point F in the figure and possibility F in the table show this case.

## Production Efficiency

We achieve **production efficiency** if we cannot produce more of one good without producing less of some other good. When production is efficient, we are at a point *on* the *PPF*. If we are at a point *inside* the *PPF*, such as point Z, production is *inefficient* because we have some *unused* resources or we have some *misallocated* resources or both.

Resources are unused when they are idle but could be working. For example, we might leave some of the factories idle or some workers unemployed.

Resources are *misallocated* when they are assigned to tasks for which they are not the best match. For example, we might assign skilled pizza makers to work in a CD factory and skilled CD makers to work in a pizza shop. We could get more pizza *and* more CDs from these same workers if we reassigned them to the tasks that more closely match their skills.

If we produce at a point inside the *PPF* such as Z, we can use our resources more efficiently to produce more pizzas, more CDs, or more of *both* pizzas and CDs. But if we produce at a point *on* the *PPF*, we are using our resources efficiently and we can produce more of one good only if we produce less of the other. That is, along the *PPF*, we face a *tradeoff*.

## Tradeoff Along the *PPF*

Every choice *along* the *PPF* involves a *tradeoff*—we must give up something to get something else. On the *PPF* in Fig. 2.1, we must give up some CDs to get more pizza or give up some pizza to get more CDs.

Tradeoffs arise in every imaginable real-world situation, and you reviewed several of them in Chapter 1. At any given point in time, we have a fixed amount of labor, land, capital, and entrepreneurship. By using our available technologies, we can employ these resources to produce goods and services. But we are limited in what we can produce. This limit defines a boundary between what we can attain and what we cannot attain. This boundary is the real-world's production possibilities frontier, and it defines the tradeoffs that we must make. On our real-world *PPF*, we can produce more of any one good or service only if we produce less of some other goods or services.

When doctors say that we must spend more on AIDS and cancer research, they are suggesting a tradeoff: more medical research for less of some other things. When the President says that he wants to spend more on education and health care, he is suggesting a tradeoff: more education and health care for less national defense or less private spending (because of higher taxes). When an environmental group argues for less logging, it is suggesting a tradeoff: greater conservation of endangered wildlife for less paper. When your parents say that you should study more, they are suggesting a tradeoff: more study time for less leisure or sleep.

All tradeoffs involve a cost—an opportunity cost.

## Opportunity Cost

The *opportunity cost* of an action is the highest-valued alternative forgone. The *PPF* helps us to make the concept of opportunity cost precise and enables us to calculate it. Along the *PPF*, there are only two goods, so there is only one alternative forgone: some quantity of the other good. Given our current resources and technology, we can produce more pizzas only if we produce fewer CDs. The opportunity cost of producing an additional pizza is the number of CDs we *must* forgo. Similarly, the opportunity cost of producing an additional CD is the quantity of pizzas we *must* forgo.

For example, at point C in Fig. 2.1, we produce fewer pizzas and more CDs than at point D. If we choose point D over point C, the additional 1 million pizzas *cost* 3 million CDs. One pizza costs 3 CDs.

We can also work out the opportunity cost of choosing point C over point D in Fig. 2.1. If we move from point D to point C, the quantity of CDs produced increases by 3 million and the quantity of pizzas produced decreases by 1 million. So if we choose point C over point D, the additional 3 million CDs *cost* 1 million pizzas. One CD costs 1/3 of a pizza.

**Opportunity Cost Is a Ratio**  Opportunity cost is a ratio. It is the decrease in the quantity produced of one good divided by the increase in the quantity produced of another good as we move along the production possibilities frontier.

Because opportunity cost is a ratio, the opportunity cost of producing an additional CD is equal to the *inverse* of the opportunity cost of producing an additional pizza. Check this proposition by returning to the calculations we've just worked through. When we move along the *PPF* from *C* to *D*, the opportunity cost of a pizza is 3 CDs. The inverse of 3 is 1/3, so if we decrease the production of pizza and increase the production of CDs by moving from *D* to *C*, the opportunity cost of a CD must be 1/3 of a pizza. You can check that this number is correct. If we move from *D* to *C*, we produce 3 million more CDs and 1 million fewer pizzas. Because 3 million CDs cost 1 million pizzas, the opportunity cost of 1 CD is 1/3 of a pizza.

**Increasing Opportunity Cost** The opportunity cost of a pizza increases as the quantity of pizzas produced increases. Also, the opportunity cost of a CD increases as the quantity of CDs produced increases. This phenomenon of increasing opportunity cost is reflected in the shape of the *PPF*—it is bowed outward.

When a large quantity of CDs and a small quantity of pizzas are produced—between points *A* and *B* in Fig. 2.1—the frontier has a gentle slope. A given increase in the quantity of pizzas *costs* a small decrease in the quantity of CDs, so the opportunity cost of a pizza is a small quantity of CDs.

When a large quantity of pizzas and a small quantity of CDs are produced—between points *E* and *F* in Fig. 2.1—the frontier is steep. A given increase in the quantity of pizzas *costs* a large decrease in the quantity of CDs, so the opportunity cost of a pizza is a large quantity of CDs.

The *PPF* is bowed outward because resources are not all equally productive in all activities. People with several years of experience working for Sony are good at producing CDs but not very good at making pizzas. So if we move some of these people from Sony to Domino's, we get a small increase in the quantity of pizzas but a large decrease in the quantity of CDs.

Similarly, people who have spent years working at Domino's are good at producing pizzas, but they have no idea how to produce CDs. So if we move some of these people from Domino's to Sony, we get a small increase in the quantity of CDs but a large decrease in the quantity of pizzas. The more of either good we try to produce, the less productive are the additional resources we use to produce that good and the larger is the opportunity cost of a unit of that good.

**Increasing Opportunity Costs Are Everywhere**
Just about every activity that you can think of is one with an increasing opportunity cost. We allocate the most skillful farmers and the most fertile land to the production of food. And we allocate the best doctors and the least fertile land to the production of health-care services. If we shift fertile land and tractors away from farming to hospitals and ambulances and ask farmers to become hospital porters, the production of food drops drastically and the increase in the production of health-care services is small. The opportunity cost of a unit of health-care services rises. Similarly, if we shift our resources away from health care toward farming, we must use more doctors and nurses as farmers and more hospitals as hydroponic tomato factories. The decrease in the production of health-care services is large, but the increase in food production is small. The opportunity cost of a unit of food rises.

This example is extreme and unlikely, but these same considerations apply to any pair of goods that you can imagine.

> **REVIEW QUIZ**
>
> 1. How does the production possibilities frontier illustrate scarcity?
> 2. How does the production possibilities frontier illustrate production efficiency?
> 3. How does the production possibilities frontier show that every choice involves a tradeoff?
> 4. How does the production possibilities frontier illustrate opportunity cost?
> 5. Why is opportunity cost a ratio?
> 6. Why does the *PPF* for most goods bow outward so that opportunity cost increases as the quantity produced of a good increases?

We've seen that what we can produce is limited by the production possibilities frontier. We've also seen that production on the *PPF* is efficient. But we can produce many different quantities on the *PPF*. How do we choose among them? How do we know which point on the *PPF* is the best one?

# Using Resources Efficiently

YOU'VE SEEN THAT POINTS INSIDE THE *PPF* waste resources or leave them unused and are inefficient. You've also seen that points *on* the *PPF* are efficient—we can't produce more of one good unless we forgo some units of another good. But there are many such points on the *PPF*. Each point on the *PPF* achieves production efficiency. What quantities of CDs and pizzas best serve the social interest?

This question is an example of real-world questions of enormous consequence such as: How much should we spend on treating AIDS and how much on cancer research? Should we expand education and health-care programs or cut taxes? Should we spend more on the preservation of rainforests and the conservation of endangered wildlife?

To answer these questions, we must find a way of measuring and comparing costs and benefits.

## The *PPF* and Marginal Cost

The limits to production, which are summarized by the *PPF*, determine the marginal cost of each good or service. **Marginal cost** is the opportunity cost of producing *one more unit*. We can calculate marginal cost in a way that is similar to the way we calculate opportunity cost. *Marginal cost* is the opportunity cost of *one* additional pizza—the quantity of CDs that *must* be given up to get one more pizza—as we move along the *PPF*.

Figure 2.2 illustrates the marginal cost of pizza. If pizza production increases from zero to 1 million—a move from *A* to *B*—the quantity of CDs decreases from 15 million to 14 million. So the opportunity cost of a pizza is 1 CD.

If pizza production increases from 1 million to 2 million—a move from *B* to *C*—the quantity of CDs decreases by 2 million. So the opportunity cost of a pizza is 2 CDs.

You can repeat this calculation for an increase in pizza production from 2 million to 3 million, from 3 million to 4 million, and finally from 4 million to 5 million. Figure 2.2 shows the opportunity costs as a series of steps. Each additional pizza costs more CDs than the preceding pizza.

We've just calculated the opportunity cost of a pizza and generated the steps in Fig. 2.2(a). The opportunity cost of a pizza is also the *marginal cost* of producing a pizza. In Fig. 2.2(b), the line labeled *MC* shows the marginal cost.

**FIGURE 2.2** The *PPF* and Marginal Cost

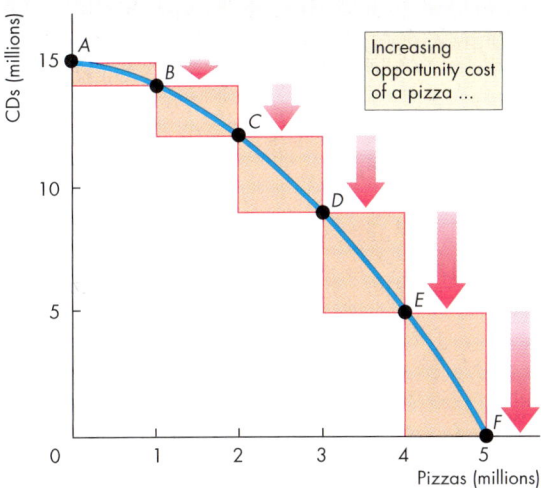

(a) *PPF* and opportunity cost

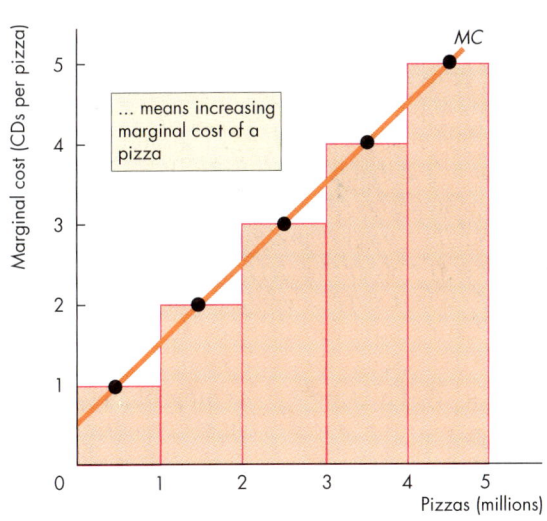

(b) Marginal cost

Opportunity cost is measured along the *PPF* in part (a). If the production of pizzas increases from zero to 1 million, the opportunity cost of a pizza is 1 CD. If the production of pizza increases from 1 million to 2 million, the opportunity cost of a pizza is 2 CDs. The opportunity cost of a pizza increases as the production of pizza increases. Part (b) shows the marginal cost of a pizza as the *MC* curve.

## Preferences and Marginal Benefit

Look around your classroom and notice the wide variety of shirts, caps, pants, and shoes that you and your fellow students are wearing today. Why is there such a huge variety? Why don't you all wear the same styles and colors? The answer lies in what economists call preferences. **Preferences** are a description of a person's likes and dislikes.

You've seen that we have a concrete way of describing the limits to production: the *PPF*. We need a similarly concrete way of describing preferences. To describe preferences, economists use the concept of marginal benefit. The **marginal benefit** of a good or service is the benefit received from consuming one more unit of it.

We measure the marginal benefit of a good or service by the most that people are *willing to pay* for an additional unit of it. The idea is that you are not willing to pay more for a good than it is worth to you. But you are willing to pay an amount up to what it is worth. So the willingness to pay for something measures its marginal benefit.

Economists use the marginal benefit curve to illustrate preferences. The **marginal benefit curve** shows the relationship between the marginal benefit of a good and the quantity of that good consumed. It is a general principle that the more we have of any good or service, the smaller is its marginal benefit and the less we are willing to pay for an additional unit of it. This tendency is so widespread and strong that we call it a principle—the *principle of decreasing marginal benefit*.

The basic reason why marginal benefit of a good or service decreases as we consume more of it is that we like variety. The more we consume of any one good or service, the more we can see other things that we would like better.

Think about your willingness to pay for pizza (or any other item). If pizza is hard to come by and you can buy only a few slices a year, you might be willing to pay a high price to get an additional slice. But if pizza is all you've eaten for the past few days, you are willing to pay almost nothing for another slice.

In everyday life, we think of what we pay for goods and services as the money that we give up—dollars. But you've learned to think about cost as other goods or services forgone, not a dollar cost. You can think about willingness to pay in the same terms. The price you are willing to pay for something is the quantity of other goods and services that you are willing to forgo. Let's continue with the example of CDs and pizzas and illustrate preferences this way.

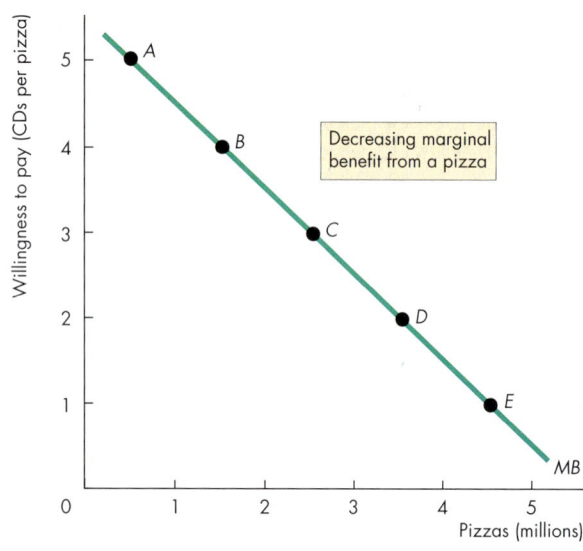

**FIGURE 2.3** Preferences and the Marginal Benefit Curve

| Possibility | Pizzas (millions) | Willingness to pay (CDs per pizza) |
|---|---|---|
| A | 0.5 | 5 |
| B | 1.5 | 4 |
| C | 2.5 | 3 |
| D | 3.5 | 2 |
| E | 4.5 | 1 |

The smaller the quantity of pizzas produced, the more CDs people are willing to give up for an additional pizza. If pizza production is 0.5 million, people are willing to pay 5 CDs per pizza. But if pizza production is 4.5 milllion, people are willing to pay only 1 CD per pizza. Willingness to pay measures marginal benefit. And decreasing marginal benefit is a universal feature of people's preferences.

Figure 2.3 illustrates preferences as the willingness to pay for pizza in terms of CDs. In row *A*, pizza production is 0.5 million, and at that quantity, people are willing to pay 5 CDs per pizza. As the quantity of pizza produced increases, the amount that people are willing to pay for it falls. When pizza production is 4.5 million, people are willing to pay only 1 CD per pizza.

Let's now use the concepts of marginal cost and marginal benefit to describe the efficient quantity of pizzas to produce.

## Efficient Use of Resources

When we cannot produce more of any one good without giving up some other good, we have achieved *production efficiency*, and we're producing at a point on the *PPF*. When we cannot produce more of any good without giving up some other good that we *value more highly*, we have achieved **allocative efficiency** and we are producing at the point on the *PPF* that we prefer above all other points.

Suppose in Fig. 2.4, we produce 1.5 million pizzas. The marginal cost of a pizza is 2 CDs and the marginal benefit from a pizza is 4 CDs. Because someone values an additional pizza more highly than it costs to produce, we can get more value from our resources by moving some of them out of producing CDs and into producing pizzas.

Now suppose we produce 3.5 million pizzas. The marginal cost of a pizza is now 4 CDs, but the marginal benefit from a pizza is only 2 CDs. Because the additional pizza costs more to produce than anyone thinks it is worth, we can get more value from our resources by moving some of them away from producing pizzas and into producing CDs.

But suppose we produce 2.5 million pizzas. Marginal cost and marginal benefit are now equal at 3 CDs. This allocation of resources between pizzas and CDs is efficient. If more pizzas are produced, the forgone CDs are worth more than the additional pizzas. If fewer pizzas are produced, the forgone pizzas are worth more than the additional CDs.

### REVIEW QUIZ

1. What is marginal cost? How is it measured?
2. What is marginal benefit? How is it measured?
3. How does the marginal benefit from a good change as the quantity produced of that good increases?
4. What is production efficiency and how does it relate to the production possibilities frontier?
5. What conditions must be satisfied if resources are used efficiently?

You now understand the limits to production and the conditions under which resources are used efficiently. Your next task is to study the expansion of production possibilities.

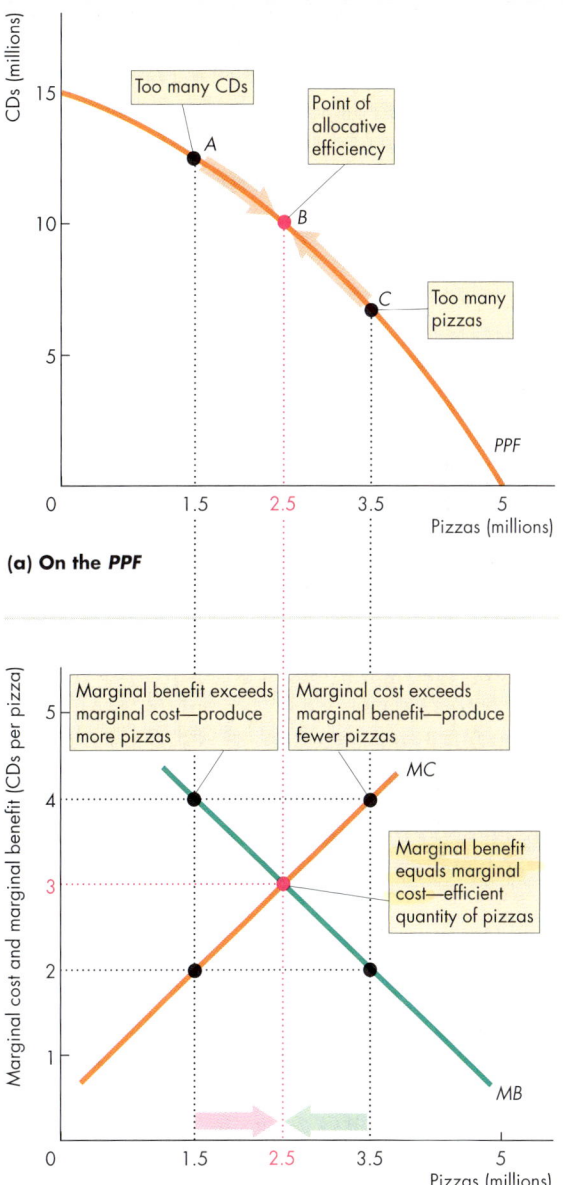

**FIGURE 2.4  Efficient Use of Resources**

(a) On the *PPF*

(b) Marginal benefit equals marginal cost

The greater the quantity of pizzas produced, the smaller is the marginal benefit (*MB*) from pizza—the fewer CDs people are willing to give up to get an additional pizza. But the greater the quantity of pizzas produced, the greater is the marginal cost (*MC*) of pizza—the more CDs people must give up to get an additional pizza. When marginal benefit equals marginal cost, resources are being used efficiently.

# Economic Growth

**D**URING THE PAST 30 YEARS, PRODUCTION PER person in the United States has doubled. Such an expansion of production is called **economic growth**. Economic growth increases our *standard of living*, but it doesn't overcome scarcity and avoid opportunity cost. To make our economy grow, we face a tradeoff—the faster we make production grow, the greater is the opportunity cost of economic growth.

## The Cost of Economic Growth

Two key factors influence economic growth: technological change and capital accumulation. **Technological change** is the development of new goods and of better ways of producing goods and services. **Capital accumulation** is the growth of capital resources, which includes *human capital*.

As a consequence of technological change and capital accumulation, we have an enormous quantity of cars that enable us to produce more transportation than was available when we had only horses and carriages; we have satellites that make global communications possible on a scale that is much larger than that produced by the earlier cable technology. But new technologies and new capital have an opportunity cost. To use resources in research and development and to produce new capital, we must decrease our production of consumption goods and services. Let's look at this opportunity cost.

Instead of studying the *PPF* of pizzas and CDs, we'll hold the quantity of CDs produced constant and examine the *PPF* for pizzas and pizza ovens. Figure 2.5 shows this *PPF* as the blue curve *ABC*. If we devote no resources to producing pizza ovens, we produce at point *A*. If we produce 3 million pizzas, we can produce 6 pizza ovens at point *B*. If we produce no pizza, we can produce 10 ovens at point *C*.

The amount by which our production possibilities expand depends on the resources we devote to technological change and capital accumulation. If we devote no resources to this activity (point *A*), our *PPF* remains at *ABC*—the blue curve in Fig. 2.5. If we cut the current production of pizza and produce 6 ovens (point *B*), then in the future, we'll have more capital and our *PPF* will rotate outward to the position shown by the red curve. The fewer resources we devote to producing pizza and the

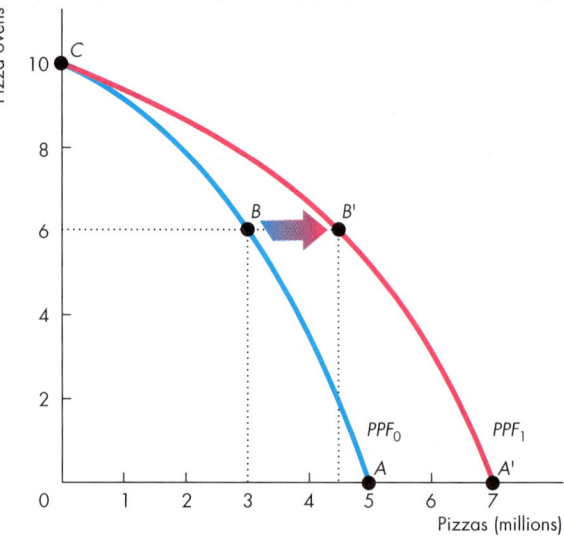

**FIGURE 2.5  Economic Growth**

$PPF_0$ shows the limits to the production of pizza and pizza ovens, with the production of all other goods and services remaining the same. If we devote no resources to producing pizza ovens and produce 5 million pizzas, we remain at point *A*. But if we decrease pizza production to 3 million and produce 6 ovens, at point *B*, our production possibilities expand. After one period, the *PPF* rotates outward to $PPF_1$ and we can produce at point *B'*, a point outside the original *PPF*. We can rotate the *PPF* outward, but we cannot avoid opportunity cost. The opportunity cost of producing more pizzas in the future is fewer pizzas today.

more resources we devote to producing ovens, the greater is the expansion of our production possibilities.

Economic growth is not free. To make it happen, we devote resources to producing new ovens and less to producing pizza. In Fig. 2.5, we move from *A* to *B*. There is no free lunch. The opportunity cost of more pizzas in the future is fewer pizzas today. Also, economic growth is no magic formula for abolishing scarcity. On the new production possibilities frontier, we continue to face a tradeoff and opportunity cost.

The ideas about economic growth that we have explored in the setting of the pizza industry also apply to nations. Let's look at two examples.

## Economic Growth in the United States and Hong Kong

If as a nation we devote all our resources to producing consumption goods and none to research and capital accumulation, our production possibilities in the future will be the same as they are today. To expand our production possibilities in the future, we must devote fewer resources to producing consumption goods and some resources to accumulating capital and developing technologies so that we can produce more consumption goods in the future. The decrease in today's consumption is the opportunity cost of an increase in future consumption.

The experiences of the United States and Hong Kong make a striking example of the effects of our choices on the rate of economic growth. In 1963, the production possibilities per person in the United States were more than four times those in Hong Kong (see Fig. 2.6). The United States devoted one fifth of its resources to accumulating capital and the other four fifths to consumption. In 1963, the United States was at point $A$ on its $PPF$. Hong Kong devoted one third of its resources to accumulating capital and two thirds to consumption. In 1963, Hong Kong was at point $A$ on its $PPF$.

Since 1963, both countries have experienced economic growth, but growth in Hong Kong has been more rapid than that in the United States. Because Hong Kong devoted a bigger fraction of its resources to accumulating capital, its production possibilities have expanded more quickly.

By 2003, the production possibilities per person in Hong Kong had reached 80 percent of those in the United States. If Hong Kong continues to devote more resources to accumulating capital than we do (at point $B$ on its 2003 $PPF$), it will continue to grow more rapidly than the United States. But if Hong Kong increases consumption and decreases capital accumulation (moving to point $D$ on its 2003 $PPF$), then its rate of economic growth will slow.

The United States is typical of the rich industrial countries, which include Western Europe and Japan. Hong Kong is typical of the fast-growing Asian economies, which include Taiwan, Thailand, South Korea, and China. Growth in these countries slowed during the Asia crisis of 1998 but quickly rebounded. Production possibilities expand in these countries by between 5 and almost 10 percent a year. If these high growth rates are maintained, these other Asian countries will eventually close the gap on the United States as Hong Kong has done.

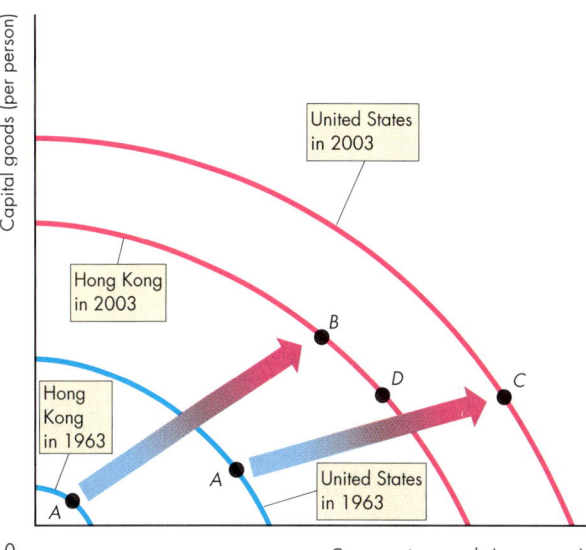

**FIGURE 2.6** Economic Growth in the United States and Hong Kong

In 1963, the production possibilities per person in the United States were much larger than those in Hong Kong. But Hong Kong devoted more of its resources to accumulating capital than did the United States, so its production possibilities frontier has shifted outward more quickly than has that of the United States. In 2003, Hong Kong's production possibilities per person were 80 percent of those in the United States.

### REVIEW QUIZ

1. What are the two key factors that generate economic growth?
2. How does economic growth influence the production possibilities frontier?
3. What is the opportunity cost of economic growth?
4. Why has Hong Kong experienced faster economic growth than the United States has?

Next, we're going to study another way in which we expand our production possibilities—the amazing fact that *both* buyers and sellers gain from specialization and trade.

# Gains from Trade

People can produce for themselves all the goods that they consume, or they can concentrate on producing one good (or perhaps a few goods) and then trade with others—exchange some of their own goods for those of others. Concentrating on the production of only one good or a few goods is called *specialization*. We are going to discover how people gain by specializing in the production of the good in which they have a *comparative advantage* and trading with each other.

## Comparative Advantage

A person has a **comparative advantage** in an activity if that person can perform the activity at a lower opportunity cost than anyone else. Differences in opportunity costs arise from differences in individual abilities and from differences in the characteristics of other resources.

No one excels at everything. One person is an outstanding pitcher but a poor catcher; another person is a brilliant lawyer but a poor teacher. In almost all human endeavors, what one person does easily, someone else finds difficult. The same applies to land and capital. One plot of land is fertile but has no mineral deposits; another plot of land has outstanding views but is infertile. One machine has great precision but is difficult to operate; another is fast but often breaks down.

Although no one excels at everything, some people excel and can outperform others in many activities. But such a person does not have a *comparative* advantage in each of those activities. For example, John Grisham is a better lawyer than most people. But he is an even better writer of fast-paced thrillers. So his *comparative* advantage is in writing.

Because people's abilities and the quality of their resources differ, they have different opportunity costs of producing various goods. Such differences give rise to comparative advantage. Let's explore the idea of comparative advantage by looking at two CD factories: one operated by Tom and the other operated by Nancy.

**Tom's Factory** To simplify the story quite a lot, suppose that CDs have just two components: a disc and a plastic case. Tom has two production lines: one for discs and one for cases. Figure 2.7 shows Tom's production possibilities frontier for discs and cases.

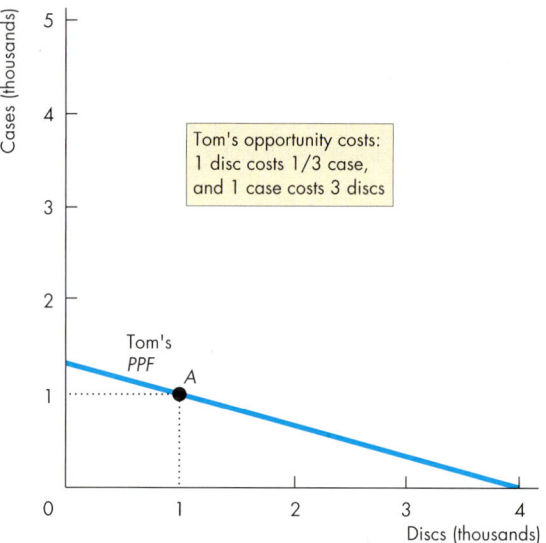

**FIGURE 2.7** Production Possibilities in Tom's Factory

Tom's opportunity costs: 1 disc costs 1/3 case, and 1 case costs 3 discs

Tom can produce discs and cases along the production possibilities frontier *PPF*. For Tom, the opportunity cost of 1 disc is ⅓ of a case and the opportunity cost of 1 case is 3 discs. If Tom produces at point *A*, he can produce 1,000 cases and 1,000 discs an hour.

It tells us that if Tom uses all his resources to make discs, he can produce 4,000 discs an hour. The *PPF* in Fig. 2.7 also tells us that if Tom uses all his resources to make cases, he can produce 1,333 cases an hour. But to produce cases, Tom must decrease his production of discs. For each case produced, he must decrease his production of discs by 3. So

Tom's opportunity cost of producing 1 case is 3 discs.

Similarly, if Tom wants to increase his production of discs, he must decrease his production of cases. And for each 1,000 discs produced, he must decrease his production of cases by 333. So

Tom's opportunity cost of producing 1 disc is 0.333 of a case.

Tom's *PPF* is linear because his workers have similar skills so if he reallocates them from one activity to another, he faces a constant opportunity cost.

**Nancy's Factory** The other factory, operated by Nancy, also produces cases and discs. But Nancy's factory has machines that are custom made for case production, so they are more suitable for producing cases than discs. Also, Nancy's work force is more skilled in making cases.

These differences between the two factories mean that Nancy's production possibilities frontier—shown along with Tom's *PPF* in Fig. 2.8—is different from Tom's. If Nancy uses all her resources to make discs, she can produce 1,333 an hour. If she uses all her resources to make cases, she can produce 4,000 an hour. To produce discs, Nancy must decrease her production of cases. For each 1,000 additional discs produced, she must decrease her production of cases by 3,000. So

Nancy's opportunity cost of producing 1 disc is 3 cases.

Similarly, if Nancy wants to increase her production of cases, she must decrease her production of discs. For each 1,000 additional cases produced, she must decrease her production of discs by 333. So

Nancy's opportunity cost of producing 1 case is 0.333 of a disc.

Suppose that Tom and Nancy produce both discs and cases and that each produces 1,000 discs and 1,000 cases—1,000 CDs—an hour. That is, each produces at point *A* on their production possibilities frontiers. Total production is 2,000 CDs an hour.

In which of the two goods does Nancy have a comparative advantage? Recall that comparative advantage is a situation in which one person's opportunity cost of producing a good is lower than another person's opportunity cost of producing that same good. Nancy has a comparative advantage in producing cases. Nancy's opportunity cost of producing a case is 0.333 of a disc, whereas Tom's is 3 discs.

You can see Nancy's comparative advantage by looking at the production possibilities frontiers for Nancy and Tom in Fig. 2.8. Nancy's production possibilities frontier is steeper than Tom's. To produce one more case, Nancy must give up fewer discs than Tom has to. Hence Nancy's opportunity cost of producing a case is less than Tom's. This means that Nancy has a comparative advantage in producing cases.

Tom's comparative advantage is in producing discs. His production possibilities frontier is less steep than Nancy's. This means that to produce one more

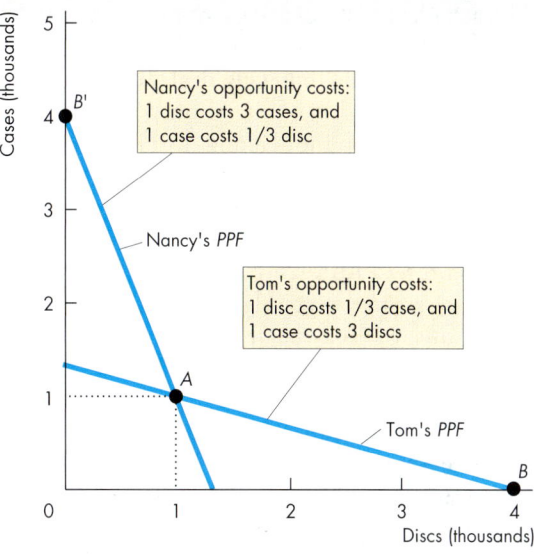

**FIGURE 2.8 Comparative Advantage**

Along Tom's *PPF*, the opportunity cost of 1 disc is ⅓ of a case and the opportunity cost of 1 case is 3 discs. Along Nancy's *PPF*, the opportunity cost of 1 disc is 3 cases. Like Tom, Nancy produces at point *A*, where she produces 1,000 cases and 1,000 discs an hour. Nancy's opportunity cost of cases is less than Tom's, so Nancy has a comparative advantage in cases. Tom's opportunity cost of discs is less than Nancy's, so Tom has a comparative advantage in discs.

disc, Tom must give up fewer cases than Nancy has to. Tom's opportunity cost of producing a disc is 0.333 of a case, which is less than Nancy's 3 cases per disc. So Tom has a comparative advantage in producing discs.

Because Nancy has a comparative advantage in producing cases and Tom has a comparative advantage in producing discs, they can both gain from specialization and trade with each other.

### Achieving the Gains from Trade

If Tom, who has a comparative advantage in producing discs, puts all his resources into that activity, he can produce 4,000 discs an hour—point *B* on his *PPF*. If Nancy, who has a comparative advantage in producing cases, puts all her resources into that activity, she can produce 4,000 cases an hour—point *B'* on her *PPF*. By specializing, Tom and Nancy together can produce 4,000 cases and 4,000 discs an hour, double the total production they can achieve without specialization.

By specialization and trade, Tom and Nancy can get *outside* their individual production possibilities frontiers. To achieve the gains from specialization, Tom and Nancy must trade with each other.

Figure 2.9 shows how Tom and Nancy gain from trade. They make the following deal: Tom agrees to increase his production of discs from 1,000 an hour to 4,000 an hour—a move along his *PPF* from point *A* to point *B* in Fig. 2.9(a). Nancy agrees to increase her production of cases from 1,000 an hour to 4,000 an hour—a move along her *PPF* from point *A* to point *B'* in Fig. 2.9(b).

They also agree to trade cases and discs at a "price" of one case for one disc. So Tom sells discs to Nancy for one case per disc, and Nancy sells cases to Tom for one disc per case.

With this deal in place, Tom and Nancy exchange along the red "Trade line." They exchange 2,000 cases and 2,000 discs, and each moves to point *C* (in both parts of the figure). At point *C*, each has 2,000 discs and 2,000 cases, or 2,000 CDs. So each now produces 2,000 CDs an hour—double the previous production rate. This increase in production of 2,000 CDs an hour is the gain from specialization and trade.

Both parties to the trade share the gains. Nancy, who can produce discs at an opportunity cost of 3 cases per disc, can buy discs from Tom at a cost of 1 case per disc. Tom, who can produce cases at an opportunity cost of 3 discs per case, can buy cases from Nancy at a cost of 1 disc per case.

For Nancy, the cost of a disc falls from 3 cases to 1 case. So she gets her discs more cheaply than she can produce them herself.

For Tom, the cost of a case falls from 3 discs to 1 disc. So he gets his cases more cheaply than he can produce them himself.

Because both Tom and Nancy obtain the items they buy from the other at a lower cost than that at which they can produce the items themselves, they both gain from specialization and trade.

The gains that we achieve from international trade are similar to those achieved by Tom and Nancy in this example. When Americans buy T-shirts from

## FIGURE 2.9  The Gains from Trade

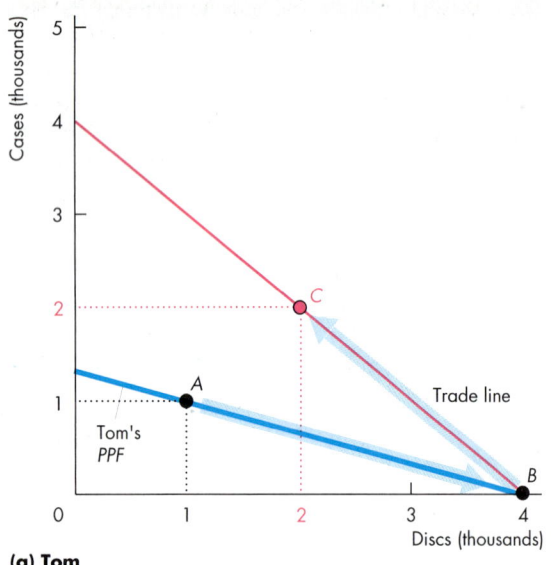

**(a) Tom**

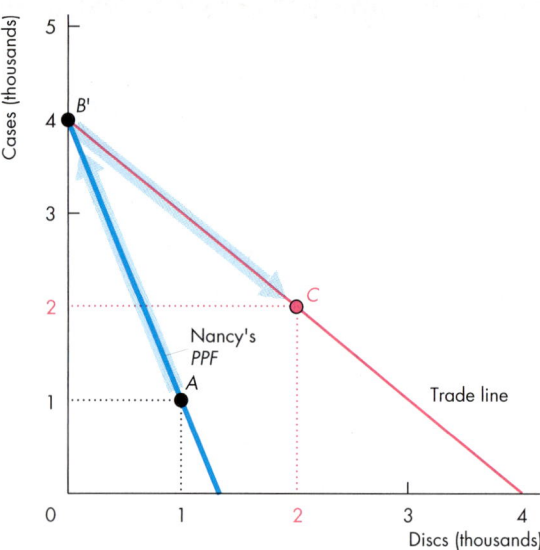

**(b) Nancy**

Tom and Nancy initially produce at point *A* on their respective *PPF*s. Tom has a comparative advantage in discs, and Nancy has a comparative advantage in cases. If Tom specializes in discs, he produces at point *B* on his *PPF*. If Nancy specializes in cases, she produces at point *B'* on her *PPF*. They exchange cases for discs along the red "Trade line." Nancy buys discs from Tom for less than her opportunity cost of producing them, and Tom buys cases from Nancy for less than his opportunity cost of producing them. Each goes to point *C*—a point outside his or her *PPF*—where each produces 2,000 CDs an hour. Tom and Nancy increase production with no change in resources.

China and when China buys Boeing 747 airplanes from the United States, both countries gain. We get our shirts at a lower cost than that at which we can produce them, and China gets its airplanes at a lower cost than that at which it can produce them.

Tom and Nancy are equally productive. Tom can produce the same quantities of discs as Nancy can produce cases. But this equal productivity is not the source of the gains from specialization and trade. The gains arise from comparative advantage and would be available even if one of the trading partners was much more productive than the other. To see that comparative advantage is the source of the gains, let's look at Tom and Nancy when Nancy is much more productive than Tom.

## Absolute Advantage

A person has an **absolute advantage** if that person can produce more goods with a given amount of resources than another person can. Absolute advantage arises from differences in productivity. A person who has a better technology, more capital, or is more skilled than another person has an absolute advantage. (Absolute advantage also applies to nations.)

The gains from trade arise from *comparative* advantage, so people can gain from trade in the presence of *absolute* advantage. To see how, suppose that Nancy invents and patents a new production process that makes her *four* times as productive as she was before in the production of both cases and discs. With her new technology, Nancy can produce 16,000 cases an hour (4 times the original 4,000) if she puts all her resources into making cases. Alternatively, she can produce 5,332 discs (4 times the original 1,333) if she puts all her resources into making discs. Nancy now has an absolute advantage.

But Nancy's *opportunity cost* of 1 disc is still 3 cases. And this opportunity cost is higher than Tom's. So Nancy can still get discs at a lower cost by exchanging cases for discs with Tom.

In this example, Nancy will no longer produce only cases. With no trade, she would produce 4,000 discs and 4,000 cases. With trade, she will increase her production of cases to 7,000 and decrease her production of discs to 3,000. Tom will produce 4,000 discs and no cases. Tom will provide Nancy with 2,000 discs in exchange for 2,000 cases. So Tom's CD production will increase from 1,000 to 2,000 as before. Nancy's CD production will increase from 4,000 to 5,000.

Both Tom and Nancy have gained 1,000 CDs by taking advantage of comparative advantage, the same gains as before.

The key point to recognize is that even though someone (or some nation) has an absolute advantage, this fact does not destroy comparative advantage.

## Dynamic Comparative Advantage

At any given point in time, the resources and technologies available determine the comparative advantages that individuals and nations have. But just by repeatedly producing a particular good or service, people become more productive in that activity, a phenomenon called **learning-by-doing**. Learning-by-doing is the basis of *dynamic* comparative advantage. **Dynamic comparative advantage** is a comparative advantage that a person (or country) possesses as a result of having specialized in a particular activity and, as a result of learning-by-doing, having become the producer with the lowest opportunity cost.

Hong Kong and Singapore are examples of countries that have pursued dynamic comparative advantage vigorously. They have developed industries in which initially they did not have a comparative advantage but, through learning-by-doing, became low opportunity cost producers in those industries. A specific example is the decision to develop a genetic engineering industry in Singapore. Singapore probably did not have a comparative advantage in genetic engineering initially. But it might develop one as its scientists and production workers become more skilled in this activity.

### REVIEW QUIZ

1. What gives a person a comparative advantage?
2. Is production still efficient when people specialize?
3. Why do people specialize and trade?
4. What are the gains from specialization and trade?
5. What is the source of the gains from trade?
6. Distinguish between comparative advantage and absolute advantage.
7. How does dynamic comparative advantage arise?

## Economic Coordination

PEOPLE GAIN BY SPECIALIZING IN THE PRODUCtion of those goods and services in which they have a comparative advantage and then trading with each other. Nancy and Tom, whose production of CDs we studied earlier in this chapter, can get together and make a deal that enables them to enjoy the gains from specialization and trade. But for billions of individuals to specialize and produce millions of different goods and services, their choices must somehow be coordinated.

Economic coordination does not require a central authority and a national economic plan. In fact, when such an arrangement was tried, as it was for 60 years in Russia, it was shown to be a failure.

Two complementary institutions have evolved to achieve economic coordination. They are:

- Firms
- Markets

### Firms

A **firm** is an economic unit that hires factors of production and organizes those factors to produce and sell goods and services. Examples of firms are your local gas station, Wal-Mart, and General Electric.

Firms coordinate a huge amount of economic activity. The CD maker TDK, for example, might buy the machines and labor services of Nancy and Tom and produce CDs *and* CD cases in a single firm.

But if a firm gets too big, it can't keep track of all the information that is needed to coordinate its activities. For this reason, firms themselves specialize and trade with each other. For example, Wal-Mart could produce all the things that it sells in its stores. And it could produce all the raw materials that are used to produce the things that it sells. But Sam Walton would not have become one of the wealthiest people in the world if he had followed that path. Instead, Wal-Mart buys from other firms that specialize in the production of a narrow range of items. And this trade takes place in markets.

### Markets

In ordinary speech, the word *market* means a place where people buy and sell goods such as fish, meat, fruits, and vegetables. In economics, a *market* has a more general meaning. A **market** is any arrangement that enables buyers and sellers to get information and to do business with each other. An example is the market in which oil is bought and sold—the world oil market. The world oil market is not a place. It is the network of oil producers, oil users, wholesalers, and brokers who buy and sell oil. In the world oil market, decision makers do not meet physically. They make deals throughout the world by telephone, fax, and direct computer link.

Markets have evolved because they facilitate trade. Without organized markets, we would miss out on a substantial part of the potential gains from trade. Enterprising individuals and firms, each pursuing their own self-interest, have profited from making markets—standing ready to buy or sell the items in which they specialize. But markets can work only when property rights exist.

### Property Rights
The social arrangements that govern the ownership, use, and disposal of resources, goods, and services are called **property rights**. *Real property* includes land and buildings—the things we call property in ordinary speech—and durable goods such as plant and equipment. *Financial property* includes stocks and bonds and money in the bank. *Intellectual property* is the intangible product of creative effort. This type of property includes books, music, computer programs, and inventions of all kinds and is protected by copyrights and patents.

Where property rights are enforced, people have the incentive to specialize and produce the goods in which each person has a comparative advantage. Where people can easily steal the production of others, then time, energy, and resources are devoted not to production but to protecting possessions. If we had not developed property rights, we would still be hunting and gathering like our Stone Age ancestors.

### Circular Flows Through Markets

Figure 2.10 shows the flows that result from the choices that households and firms make. Households specialize and choose the quantities of labor, land, capital, and entrepreneurship to sell or rent to firms. Firms choose the quantities of factors of production to hire. These (red) flows go through the *factor markets*. Households choose the quantities of goods and services to buy, and firms choose the quantities to produce. These (red) flows go through the *goods markets*. Households receive incomes and make expenditures on goods and services (the green flows).

How do markets coordinate all these decisions?

## FIGURE 2.10  Circular Flows in the Market Economy

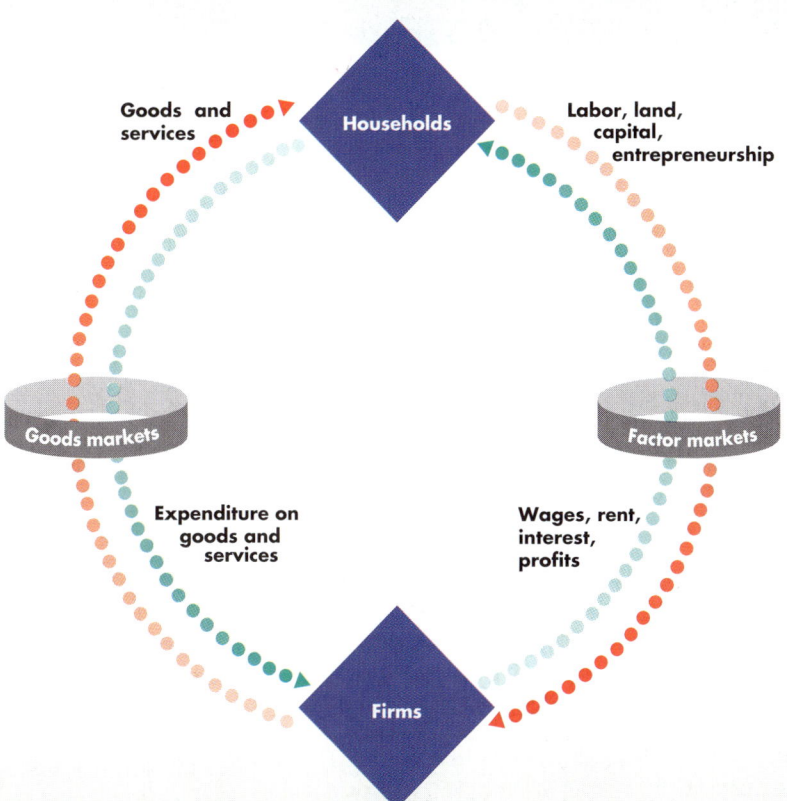

Households and firms make economic choices. Households choose the quantities of labor, land, capital, and entrepreneurship to sell or rent to firms in exchange for wages, rent, interest, and profit. Households also choose how to spend their incomes on the various types of goods and services available. Firms choose the quantities of factors of production to hire and the quantities of the various goods and services to produce.

Goods markets and factor markets coordinate these choices of households and firms. Factors of production and goods flow clockwise (red), and money payments flow counterclockwise (green).

### Coordinating Decisions

Markets coordinate individual decisions through price adjustments. To see how, think about your local market for hamburgers. Suppose that some people who want to buy hamburgers are not able to do so. To make the choices of buyers and sellers compatible, buyers must scale down their appetites or more hamburgers must be offered for sale (or both must happen). A rise in the price of hamburgers produces this outcome. A higher price encourages producers to offer more hamburgers for sale. It also encourages some people to change their lunch plans. Fewer people buy hamburgers, and more buy hot dogs. More hamburgers (and more hot dogs) are offered for sale.

Alternatively, suppose that more hamburgers are available than people want to buy. In this case, to make the choices of buyers and sellers compatible, more hamburgers must be bought or fewer hamburgers must be offered for sale (or both). A fall in the price of a hamburger achieves this outcome. A lower price encourages firms to produce a smaller quantity of hamburgers. It also encourages people to buy more hamburgers.

### REVIEW QUIZ

1 Why are social arrangements such as markets and property rights necessary?
2 What are the main functions of markets?

◆ You have now begun to see how economists approach economic questions. Scarcity, choice, and divergent opportunity costs explain why we specialize and trade and why property rights and markets have developed. You can see all around you the lessons you've learned in this chapter. *Reading Between the Lines* on pp. 46–47 gives an example. It explores the *PPF* for security services and other goods and services and the change in the efficient quantity of security services following the increase in terrorism in the United States.

# READING BETWEEN THE LINES

POLICY WATCH

## *The Cost and Benefit of Airport Security*

**LOS ANGELES TIMES, SEPTEMBER 2, 2003**

### LAX to Get U.S. Funds

The Department of Homeland Security will announce today that it is giving $256 million to the city's airport agency to help defray the cost of new baggage systems at Los Angeles and Ontario international airports. …

At LAX [Los Angeles international airport], the move is necessary to get the three-ton machines out of terminal lobbies, where they are contributing to long lines. It will also boost security, officials say, by allowing the city's airport agency to get rid of less efficient devices, such as those that look for trace amounts of explosives on luggage. …

The money will allow the city to rip out 1960s-era baggage conveyors at LAX and install more efficient computer-based systems. Officials need to replace about three miles of aging belts, making sure at the same time that about 150,000 bags make it onto the proper flights each day. LAX handles more luggage than any other U.S. airport.

The baggage systems that crisscross the lower levels of most of the airport's nine terminals run at only one speed and were not built to incorporate machines that inspect baggage for explosives…

The $1-million cost of each explosives-detection machine—about 60 at LAX and 10 at Ontario—is not included in the grant and will be paid by the federal government. The machines that are currently in airport lobbies will be shipped to other facilities. …

©2003 Los Angeles Times. Reprinted with permission.
Further reproduction prohibited.

### Essence of the Story

■ The Department of Homeland Security is providing $256 million toward the cost of new baggage systems at Los Angeles and Ontario international airports.

■ The airports will use the money to replace older-model baggage conveyors with new computer-based systems.

■ The current baggage conveyors are not designed to incorporate machines that inspect baggage for explosives.

■ Sixty explosives-detection machines will be installed at LAX and ten machines will be installed at Ontario, at a cost of $1 million each.

## Economic Analysis

- Figure 1 shows the *PPF* for security services and other goods and services.

- As we move from point *A* to point *B* we increase the production of security services and decrease the production of other goods and services.

- The news article tells us that an explosives-detection machine costs $1 million, but this is not its opportunity cost.

- The opportunity cost of an additional explosives-detection machine is the other goods and services that we must give up to produce it.

- Why are we producing more security machines?

- We have become more aware of the risk of terrorism attacks on air travel.

- Figure 2 shows that before September 11 the marginal benefit curve was $MB_0$, the marginal cost curve was *MC*, and the efficient quantity of security machines was 100.

- Following September 11, we are willing to pay more for each additional unit of security and the marginal benefit curve shifts rightward to $MB_1$.

- If we continue to produce 100 units of security services, the marginal benefit of security exceeds the marginal cost.

- Because someone values an additional unit of security services more highly than it costs to produce, resources are used more efficiently if the production of security services increases and the production of other goods and services decreases.

- If we produce 150 security services at the intersection of *MC* and $MB_1$ in Fig. 2, the allocation of resources between security services and other goods and services is efficient.

### You're The Voter

- Do you think increased security at airports should be paid for by the federal government or by air travelers?

- Would the same level of security be provided if travelers paid for it?

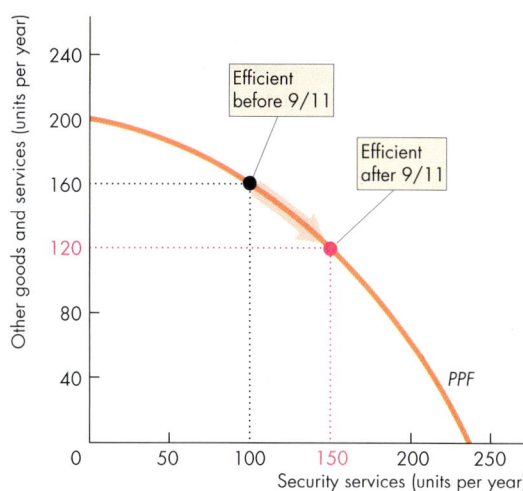

**Figure 1** The security *PPF*

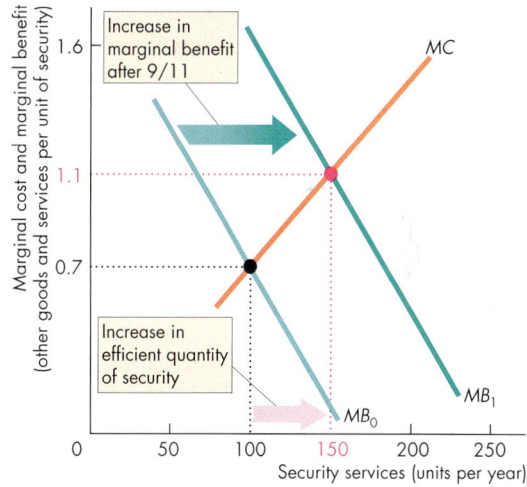

**Figure 2** Marginal benefit and marginal cost

# SUMMARY

## KEY POINTS

### Production Possibilities and Opportunity Cost (pp. 32–34)

- The production possibilities frontier, *PPF*, is the boundary between production levels that are attainable and those that are not attainable when all the available resources are used to their limit.
- Production efficiency occurs at points on the *PPF*.
- Along the *PPF*, the opportunity cost of producing more of one good is the amount of the other good that must be given up.
- The opportunity cost of all goods increases as the production of the good increases.

### Using Resources Efficiently (pp. 35–37)

- The marginal cost of a good is the opportunity cost of producing one more unit.
- The marginal benefit from a good is the maximum amount of another good that a person is willing to forgo to obtain more of the first good.
- The marginal benefit of a good decreases as the amount of the good available increases.
- Resources are used efficiently when the marginal cost of each good is equal to its marginal benefit.

### Economic Growth (pp. 38–39)

- Economic growth, which is the expansion of production possibilities, results from capital accumulation and technological change.
- The opportunity cost of economic growth is forgone current consumption.

### Gains from Trade (pp. 40–43)

- A person has a comparative advantage in producing a good if that person can produce the good at a lower opportunity cost than everyone else.
- People gain by specializing in the activity in which they have a comparative advantage and trading with others.
- Dynamic comparative advantage arises from learning-by-doing.

### Economic Coordination (pp. 44–45)

- Firms coordinate a large amount of economic activity, but there is a limit to the efficient size of a firm.
- Markets coordinate the economic choices of people and firms.
- Markets can work efficiently only when property rights exist.

## KEY FIGURES

Figure 2.1   Production Possibilities Frontier, 32
Figure 2.4   Efficient Use of Resources, 37
Figure 2.9   The Gains from Trade, 42
Figure 2.10  Circular Flows in the Market Economy, 45

## KEY TERMS

Absolute advantage, 43
Allocative efficiency, 37
Capital accumulation, 38
Comparative advantage, 40
Dynamic comparative advantage, 43
Economic growth, 38
Firm, 44
Learning-by-doing, 43
Marginal benefit, 36
Marginal benefit curve, 36
Marginal cost, 35
Market, 44
Preferences, 36
Production efficiency, 33
Production possibilities frontier, 32
Property rights, 44
Technological change, 38

# PROBLEMS

*1. Use the figure to calculate Wendell's opportunity cost of one hour of tennis when he increases the time he plays tennis from
a. 4 to 6 hours a week.
b. 6 to 8 hours a week.

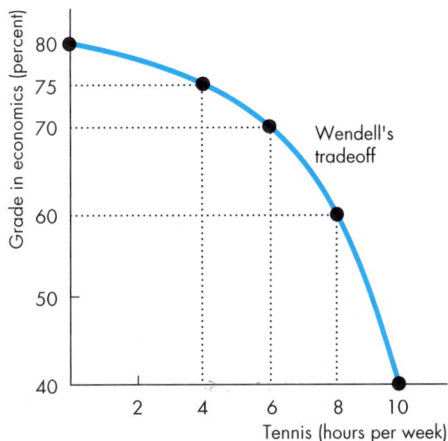

2. Use the figure to calculate Tina's opportunity cost of a day of skiing when she increases her time spent skiing from
a. 2 to 4 days a month.
b. 4 to 6 days a month.

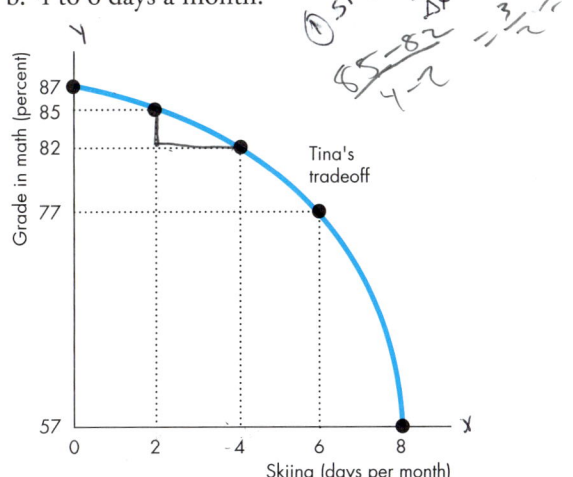

*3. In problem 1, describe the relationship between the time Wendell spends playing tennis and the opportunity cost of an hour of tennis.

4. In problem 2, describe the relationship between the time Tina spends skiing and the opportunity cost of a day of skiing.

*Solutions to odd-numbered problems are available on **MyEconLab**.

*5. Wendell, in problem 1, has the following marginal benefit curve:

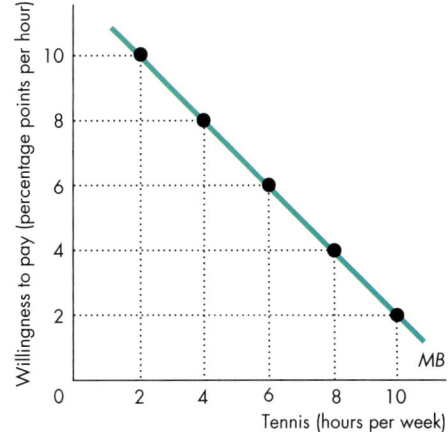

a. If Wendell is efficient, what is his grade?
b. Why would Wendell be worse off getting a higher grade?

6. Tina, in problem 2, has the following marginal benefit curve:

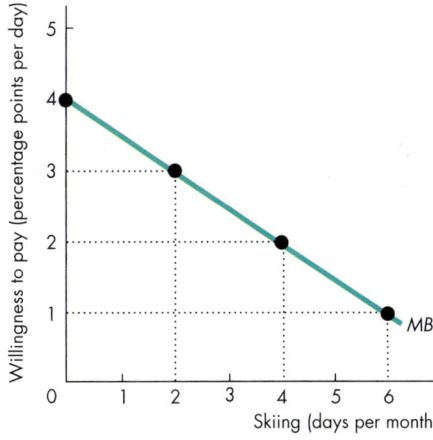

a. If Tina is efficient, how much does she ski?
b. Why would Tina be worse off spending more days a month skiing?

*7. Sunland's production possibilities are

| Food (pounds per month) | | Sunscreen (gallons per month) |
|---|---|---|
| 300 | and | 0 |
| 200 | and | 50 |
| 100 | and | 100 |
| 0 | and | 150 |

a. Draw a graph of Sunland's production possibilities frontier.

b. What are Sunland's opportunity costs of producing food and sunscreen at each output?

8. Jane's Island's production possibilities are

| Corn (pounds per month) | | Cloth (yards per month) |
|---|---|---|
| 6 | and | 0 |
| 4 | and | 2 |
| 2 | and | 4 |
| 0 | and | 6 |

   a. Draw a graph of the *PPF* on Jane's Island.
   b. What are Jane's opportunity costs of producing corn and cloth at each output in the table?

*9. In problem 7, to get a gallon of sunscreen the people of Sunland are willing to give up 5 pounds of food if they have 25 gallons of sunscreen, 2 pounds of food if they have 75 gallons of sunscreen, and 1 pound of food if they have 125 gallons of sunscreen.
   a. Draw a graph of Sunland's marginal benefit from sunscreen.
   b. What is the efficient quantity of sunscreen?

10. In problem 8, to get a yard of cloth Jane is willing to give up 1.5 pounds of corn if she has 2 yards of cloth; 1.0 pound of corn if she has 4 yards of cloth; and 0.5 pound of corn if she has 6 yards of cloth.
    a. Draw a graph of Jane's marginal benefit from cloth.
    b. What is Jane's efficient quantity of cloth?

*11. Busyland's production possibilities are

| Food (pounds per month) | | Sunscreen (gallons per month) |
|---|---|---|
| 150 | and | 0 |
| 100 | and | 100 |
| 50 | and | 200 |
| 0 | and | 300 |

Calculate Busyland's opportunity costs of food and sunscreen at each output in the table.

12. Joe's Island's production possibilities are

| Corn (pounds per month) | | Cloth (yards per month) |
|---|---|---|
| 12 | and | 0 |
| 8 | and | 1 |
| 4 | and | 2 |
| 0 | and | 3 |

What are Joe's opportunity costs of producing corn and cloth at each output in the table?

*13. In problems 7 and 11, Sunland and Busyland each produce and consume 100 pounds of food and 100 gallons of sunscreen per month, and they do not trade. Now the countries begin to trade with each other.
   a. What good does Sunland sell to Busyland and what good does it buy from Busyland?
   b. If Sunland and Busyland divide the total output of food and sunscreen equally, what are the gains from trade?

14. In problems 8 and 12, Jane's Island and Joe's Island each produce and consume 4 pounds of corn and 2 yards of cloth and they do not trade. Now the islands begin to trade.
   a. What good does Jane sell to Joe and what good does Jane buy from Joe?
   b. If Jane and Joe divide the total output of corn and cloth equally, what are the gains from trade?

## CRITICAL THINKING

1. After you have studied *Reading Between the Lines* on pp. 46–47, answer the following questions:
   a. Who bears the cost of improved baggage security systems at the two California airports?
   b. Who benefits from improved baggage security systems at the two airports?
   c. Why did the efficient quantity of security services increase after 9/11?
   d. If a new technology was invented that could deliver security services at half the current opportunity cost, how would the *PPF* change in Fig. 1 and how would the *MC* and *MB* curves and efficient quantity of security services change in Fig. 2?

## WEB EXERCISES

**Use the links on MyEconLab to work the following exercise.**

1. Use the link on the Parkin Web site and obtain data on the tuition and other costs of enrolling in the MBA program at a school that interests you.
   a. Draw a *PPF* that shows the tradeoff that you would face if you decided to enroll in the MBA program.
   b. Do you think the marginal benefit of an MBA exceeds the marginal cost?

# UNDERSTANDING THE SCOPE OF ECONOMICS

**PART 1**

## *Your Economic Revolution*

You are making progress in your study of economics. You've already encountered the big questions and big ideas of economics. And you've learned about the key insight of Adam Smith, the founder of economics: specialization and exchange create economic wealth.

You are studying economics at a time that future historians will call the *Information Revolution*. We reserve the word 'Revolution' for big events that influence all future generations.

During the *Agricultural Revolution*, which occurred 10,000 years ago, people learned to domesticate animals and plant crops. They stopped roaming in search of food and settled in villages and eventually towns and cities, where they developed markets in which to exchange their products.

During the *Industrial Revolution*, which began 240 years ago, people used science to create new technologies. This revolution brought extraordinary wealth for some but created conditions in which others were left behind. It brought social and political tensions that we still face today.

During today's *Information Revolution*, people who embraced the new technologies prospered on an unimagined scale. But the incomes and living standards of the less educated are falling behind, and social and political tensions are increasing. Today's revolution has a global dimension. Some of the winners live in previously poor countries in Asia, and some of the losers live here in the United States.

So you are studying economics at an interesting time. Whatever *your* motivation is for studying economics, *my* objective is to help you do well in your course, to enjoy it, and to develop a deeper understanding of the economic world around you.

There are three reasons why I hope that we both succeed: First, a decent understanding of economics will help you to become a full participant in the Information Revolution. Second, an understanding of economics will help you play a more effective role as a citizen and voter and enable you to add your voice to those who are looking for solutions to our social and political problems. Third, you will enjoy the sheer fun of *understanding* the forces at play and how they are shaping our world.

If you are finding economics interesting, think seriously about majoring in the subject. A degree in economics gives the best training available in problem solving, offers lots of opportunities to develop conceptual skills, and opens doors to a wide range of graduate courses, including the MBA, and to a wide range of jobs. You can read more about the benefits of an economics degree in Robert Whaples's essay in your *Study Guide*.

Economics was born during the Industrial Revolution. We'll look at its birth and meet its founder, Adam Smith. Then we'll talk about the progress that economists have made and some of the outstanding policy problems of today with one of today's most distinguished economists, Lawrence H. Summers, President of Harvard University.

# PROBING THE IDEAS

## The Sources of Economic Wealth

*"It is not from the benevolence of the butcher, the brewer, or the baker that we expect our dinner, but from their regard to their own interest."*

ADAM SMITH
*The Wealth of Nations*

### THE FATHER OF ECONOMICS

**Adam Smith** *was a giant of a scholar who contributed to ethics and jurisprudence as well as economics. Born in 1723 in Kirkcaldy, a small fishing town near Edinburgh, Scotland, Smith was the only child of the town's customs officer (who died before Adam was born).*

*His first academic appointment, at age 28, was as Professor of Logic at the University of Glasgow. He subsequently became tutor to a wealthy Scottish duke, whom he accompanied on a two-year grand European tour, following which he received a pension of £300 a year—ten times the average income at that time.*

*With the financial security of his pension, Smith devoted ten years to writing* An Inquiry into the Nature and Causes of **The Wealth of Nations**, *which was published in 1776. Many people had written on economic issues before Adam Smith, but he made economics a science. Smith's account was so broad and authoritative that no subsequent writer on economics could advance ideas without tracing their connections to those of Adam Smith.*

### THE ISSUES

Why are some nations wealthy while others are poor? This question lies at the heart of economics. And it leads directly to a second question: What can poor nations do to become wealthy?

**Adam Smith**, who is regarded by many scholars as the founder of economics, attempted to answer these questions in his book *The Wealth of Nations*, published in 1776. Smith was pondering these questions at the height of the Industrial Revolution. During these years, new technologies were invented and applied to the manufacture of cotton and wool cloth, iron, transportation, and agriculture.

Smith wanted to understand the sources of economic wealth, and he brought his acute powers of observation and abstraction to bear on the question. His answer:
- The division of labor
- Free markets

The division of labor—breaking tasks down into simple tasks and becoming skilled in those tasks—is the source of "the greatest improvement in the productive powers of labor," said Smith. The division of labor became even more productive when it was applied to creating new technologies. Scientists and engineers, trained in extremely narrow fields, became specialists at inventing. Their powerful skills accelerated the advance of technology, so by the 1820s, machines could make consumer goods faster and more accurately than any craftsman could. And by the 1850s, machines could make other machines that labor alone could never have made.

But, said Smith, the fruits of the division of labor are limited by the extent of the market. To make the market as large as possible, there must be no impediments to free trade both within a country and among countries. Smith argued that when each person makes the best possible economic choice, that choice leads as if by "an invisible hand" to the best outcome for society as a whole. The butcher, the brewer, and the baker each pursue their own interests but, in doing so, also serve the interests of everyone else.

## THEN

Adam Smith speculated that one person, working hard, using the hand tools available in the 1770s, might possibly make 20 pins a day. Yet, he observed, by using those same hand tools but breaking the process into a number of individually small operations in which people specialize —by the *division of labor*—ten people could make a staggering 48,000 pins a day. One draws out the wire, another straightens it, a third cuts it, a fourth points it, a fifth grinds it. Three specialists make the head, and a fourth attaches it. Finally, the pin is polished and packaged. But a large market is needed to support the division of labor: One factory employing ten workers would need to sell more than 15 million pins a year to stay in business.

## NOW

If Adam Smith were here today, the computer chip would fascinate him. He would see it as an extraordinary example of the productivity of the division of labor and of the use of machines to make machines that make other machines. From a design of a chip's intricate circuits, cameras transfer an image to glass plates that work like stencils. Workers prepare silicon wafers on which the circuits are printed. Some slice the wafers, others polish them, others bake them, and yet others coat them with a light-sensitive chemical. Machines transfer a copy of the circuit onto the wafer. Chemicals then etch the design onto the wafer. Further processes deposit atom-sized transistors and aluminum connectors. Finally, a laser separates the hundreds of chips on the wafer. Every stage in the process of creating a computer chip uses other computer chips. And like the pin of the 1770s, the computer chip of today benefits from a large market—a global market—to buy chips in the huge quantities in which they are produced efficiently.

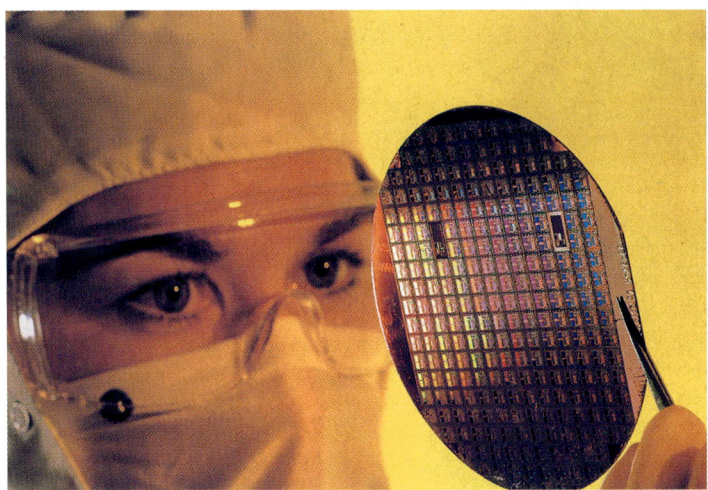

*Many economists have worked on the big themes that Adam Smith began. One of these is Lawrence H. Summers, President of Harvard University and a distinguished economist.*

# TALKING WITH

**Lawrence H. Summers**

***Lawrence H. Summers*** *is President of Harvard University. Born in 1954 in New Haven, Connecticut, into a family of distinguished economists, he was an undergraduate at the Massachusetts Institute of Technology and a graduate student at Harvard University. While still in his 20s, he became one of the youngest tenured economics professors at Harvard University. In Washington, he has held a succession of public service jobs at the World Bank and in the U.S. government, culminating in 1999 with his appointment as Secretary of the Treasury—the chief financial officer of the United States and the president's highest-ranking adviser.*

*Dr. Summers's research has covered an enormous range of macroeconomic and public policy issues that include capital taxation, unemployment, global financial crises, the transition to a market economy in Eastern Europe, and the problem of speeding progress in the developing countries.*

*Michael Parkin talked with Lawrence Summers about his career and the progress that economists have made since the pioneering days of Adam Smith.*

*How does Adam Smith's assessment of the nature and causes of the wealth of nations" look today in light of the lessons that economists have learned over the past two centuries?*

Adam Smith is looking very good today. I think one of the most important insights of the social sciences of the last several centuries is Smith's idea that good things can come from the invisible hand—from decentralization rather than from central planning and direction. But Smith is also prescient in recognizing the various qualifications to the argument for the invisible hand, whether involving fairness, externalities, or monopoly.

*What do we know today that Adam Smith didn't know?*

We know today much more than Smith did about economic fluctuations and about the role of money—about what we today call macroeconomics. We know more today about economic situations that involve bargaining, whether between two individuals or between small numbers of firms in an industry, or between a buyer and a seller. We know much more today about markets without perfect information. I know how good my used car is when I sell it—you don't when you buy it. I know whether I'm sick when I buy medical insurance, but you the insurance company have to try to figure it out. The role of information in markets, which turns out to be quite profound, is something we understand much better today. And we also understand much better today the role of politics and governments in shaping the economy, which is far larger than it was in Smith's day.

*Coincidentally, a few days before we're holding this conversation, a new nation was born—East Timor. What advice can economists offer a new and extremely poor nation as it takes its first steps?*

Much of economic success involves strong rights to property. Has anyone ever washed a rented car or taken as good care of their hotel room as their home? When people own their farmlands, they're much more likely to farm them sustainably. When businesses own their machinery, they're much more likely to take care of it. When individuals own what they produce, they're much more likely to work hard.

Strong property rights and the framework of laws that support them are profoundly important to the market-based exchanges that are essential to economic success. So also is stable money that can be a basis for exchange. So also is an educated and capable population. But if there is a single lesson that is important for a starting economy, it is that strong property rights can motivate individuals.

*One lesson that we've learned from your work at the World Bank is that the return to educating girls in developing countries is very high. What did you discover in that work?*

Primary education, and especially for girls, may be the highest return investment available in the developing world. Those who read produce more and therefore earn more. Girls who are educated grow up to be better mothers who have smaller, happier, healthier families. Women who are educated are empowered with greater career options. They are less likely to fall into prostitution, and that reduces the spread of AIDS. Women who are educated are much more likely to take care of the environment. So it is in many respects that primary education, and especially that of girls, generates very large returns.

*Are there any other activities that yield comparable returns for developing countries?*

Maybe some investments in health care that generate very large returns—it's a difficult evaluation to make. The really crucial lesson is that a country's most precious assets are its people, and investments in people are likely to be the most important investments of all.

*Some of your earliest research was on taxing the income from capital. Why isn't the income from capital just like the income from labor?*

Think about it this way: two individuals both earn a hundred dollars. One spends it all this year; the other saves half of it and earns 10 percent interest next year. Who should pay more total taxes? Plausibly, for fairness, both should pay the same tax. A tax on income will lead to the same taxes in the first year for the two individuals; and higher taxes in the second year for the individual who saved.

In effect, taxes on capital income are taxes on future consumption, and it is far from clear why a society should want to tax future consumption more highly than present consumption.

On the other hand, very large fortunes often show up as capital income, and so designing a workable and fair tax system that doesn't tax investment income is something that is very difficult to do.

> *"The really crucial lesson is that a country's most precious assets are its people, and investments in people are likely to be the most important investments of all."*

*Would you say that we have not yet managed to figure this one out?*

We'll all be working on finding the best tax systems for a long time to come. And it may mean that the income tax is, as Churchill said of democracy, terrible but the best alternative.

*The United States has a large and persistent current account deficit, a low personal saving rate, and a projected deficit in the Social Security and Medicare trust funds. Are you concerned about these problems?*

Herb Stein, who was a leading American policy economist, once said that the unsustainable cannot be sustained and must surely end!

This is a concern, given that U.S. national debt to foreigners is rising faster than U.S. income. And it's a concern in terms of the financing of Social Security and Medicare as our population ages. In a way, the solution to both these problems is more American saving, because that will put us in a stronger position as our population ages, and will allow us to have investment in the United States without incurring debts to foreigners.

Probably the most potent way of increasing a country's national savings is to improve the position of its budget. Whether to increase taxes or cut expenditures is a judgment for the congress to debate. My guess is that some combination would be appropriate. There are aspects of expenditures that are going to be hard to control. On the other hand, there are other aspects in terms of transfer payments and terms of various subsidies where economies probably are possible. And one virtue of a strong fiscal position is that it reduces interest expense down the road.

*Did you always want to be an economist? How did you choose economics?*

I thought I would be a mathematician or a physicist, but found myself very interested in questions of public policy. I was very involved in debate when I was in college. So I found myself wanting very much to combine an interest in public policy issues with an analytical approach, and economics gave me a way to do that. I also found that I had some aptitude, relative to my aptitude for pure mathematics or physics, so I gravitated to economics.

*What led a brilliant academic economist to Washington? What did you want to achieve?*

I hoped to put to use some of what I had learned in my studies in a direct way and to enhance my understanding of the way actual economies work by seeing how the policy process operated. I had a great time in Washington and feel that my economics training made a huge difference in everything I did. Whether it was thinking about how to respond to the Mexican and Asian financial crises or working on financial deregulation. Whether it was choosing optimal investments for the Customs Department in protecting our borders or designing tax incentives to promote saving. Whether it was supporting the protection of the Social Security trust fund or thinking about enforcement policies against corporate tax shelters. Principles of economics—in terms of maximizing benefits relative to costs, in terms of always thinking of the margin, in terms of always recognizing the opportunity cost of choices taken, in terms of always needing to see things add up—was quite valuable.

*And what insights does economics bring to the task of running a major university?*

I came to Harvard because I thought after my time in government the two most important resources that were going to shape the economies of the future were leaders and new ideas, and those are the two things that a university produces.

Successful leadership in a university is all about what economists think about all the time—incentives—whether it's for professors to do a good job teaching, attracting the best scholars in a particular area, or motivating concern and research about the most important problems.

Leadership and management for the university are very much about economics because they're very much about incentives. Some of them are pecuniary and involve money, but other incentives come from people's feelings of being appreciated; they come from the teams in which people have an opportunity to work; they come from the way in which the university is organized. If working at the treasury was heavily about applied macroeconomics, leadership in the university is heavily about applied microeconomics.

*What is your advice to a student who is just setting out to become an economist? What other subjects work well with economics?*

The best advice to students is, don't be a commodity that's available in a perfectly competitive market. Stand out by developing your own distinctive expertise in something you care deeply about. It matters much less what it is and much more that it be yours and it not be a hundred other people's.

I think there is enormous potential in almost every area of economics, but I think that the people who will contribute the most to economics over the next quarter century will be those who have some keen understanding of the context in which economics is playing out—the international context, the technological context, and the political context. So my hope would be that those interested in economics would understand that economics is very different from physics in that it is tracking a changing reality and that in order to do the best economics in a given period, you have to be able to track that changing reality, and that means understanding international, technological, and political contexts.

# PART 2   How Markets Work

# Demand and Supply

CHAPTER 3

## Slide, Rocket, and Roller Coaster

Slide, rocket, and roller coaster—Disneyland rides? No, they are commonly used descriptions of price changes.

The price of a personal computer took a dramatic slide from around $3,000 in 2000 to around $500 in 2003. The price of gasoline rocketed in the summer of 2003. The prices of coffee, bananas, and other agricultural products rise and fall like a roller coaster.

You've learned that economics is about the choices people make to cope with scarcity, and how those choices respond to incentives. Prices are one of the incentives to which people respond. You're now going to see how prices are determined by demand and supply.

The demand and supply model is the main tool of economics. It helps us to answer the big economic question: What, how, and for whom are goods and services produced. It also helps us to say when the pursuit of self-interest promotes the social interest.

◆ Your careful study of this topic will bring big rewards both in your further study of economics and in your everyday life. When you have completed your study of demand and supply, you will be able to explain how prices are determined and make predictions about price slides, rockets, and roller coasters. Once you understand demand and supply, you will view the world through new eyes.

### After studying this chapter, you will be able to

- Describe a competitive market and think about a price as an opportunity cost
- Explain the influences on demand
- Explain the influences on supply
- Explain how demand and supply determine prices and quantities bought and sold
- Use demand and supply to make predictions about changes in prices and quantities

57

## Markets and Prices

When you need a new pair of running shoes, want a bagel and a latte, plan to upgrade your stereo system, or need to fly home for Thanksgiving, you must find a place where people sell those items or offer those services. The place in which you find them is a *market*. You learned in Chapter 2 (p. 44) that a market is any arrangement that enables buyers and sellers to get information and to do business with each other.

A market has two sides: buyers and sellers. There are markets for *goods* such as apples and hiking boots, for *services* such as haircuts and tennis lessons, for *resources* such as computer programmers and earthmovers, and for other manufactured *inputs* such as memory chips and auto parts. There are also markets for money such as Japanese yen and for financial securities such as Yahoo! stock. Only our imagination limits what can be traded in markets.

Some markets are physical places where buyers and sellers meet and where an auctioneer or a broker helps to determine the prices. Examples of this type of market are the New York Stock Exchange and the wholesale fish, meat, and produce markets.

Some markets are groups of people spread around the world who never meet and know little about each other but are connected through the Internet or by telephone and fax. Examples are the e-commerce markets and currency markets.

But most markets are unorganized collections of buyers and sellers. You do most of your trading in this type of market. An example is the market for basketball shoes. The buyers in this $3 billion-a-year market are the 45 million Americans who play basketball (or who want to make a fashion statement). The sellers are the tens of thousands of retail sports equipment and footwear stores. Each buyer can visit several different stores, and each seller knows that the buyer has a choice of stores.

Markets vary in the intensity of competition that buyers and sellers face. In this chapter, we're going to study a **competitive market**—a market that has many buyers and many sellers, so no single buyer or seller can influence the price.

Producers offer items for sale only if the price is high enough to cover their opportunity cost. And consumers respond to changing opportunity cost by seeking cheaper alternatives to expensive items.

We are going to study the way people respond to *prices* and the forces that determine prices. But to pursue these tasks, we need to understand the relationship between a price and an opportunity cost.

In everyday life, the *price* of an object is the number of dollars that must be given up in exchange for it. Economists refer to this price as the **money price**.

The *opportunity cost* of an action is the highest-valued alternative forgone. If, when you buy a coffee, the highest-valued thing you forgo is some gum, then the opportunity cost of the coffee is the *quantity* of gum forgone. We can calculate the quantity of gum forgone from the money prices of coffee and gum.

If the money price of coffee is $1 a cup and the money price of gum is 50¢ a pack, then the opportunity cost of one cup of coffee is two packs of gum. To calculate this opportunity cost, we divide the price of a cup of coffee by the price of a pack of gum and find the *ratio* of one price to the other. The ratio of one price to another is called a **relative price**, and a *relative price is an opportunity cost.*

We can express the relative price of coffee in terms of gum or any other good. The normal way of expressing a relative price is in terms of a "basket" of all goods and services. To calculate this relative price, we divide the money price of a good by the money price of a "basket" of all goods (called a *price index*). The resulting relative price tells us the opportunity cost of the good in terms of how much of the "basket" we must give up to buy it.

The theory of demand and supply that we are about to study determines *relative prices,* and the word "price" means *relative* price. When we predict that a price will fall, we do not mean that its *money* price will fall—although it might. We mean that its *relative* price will fall. That is, its price will fall *relative* to the average price of other goods and services.

> ### REVIEW QUIZ
> 1. What is the distinction between a money price and a relative price?
> 2. Explain why a relative price is an opportunity cost.
> 3. Can you think of an example of a good whose money price and relative price have risen?
> 4. Can you think of an example of a good whose money price and relative price have fallen?

Let's begin our study of demand and supply, starting with demand.

# Demand

IF YOU DEMAND SOMETHING, THEN YOU

1. Want it,
2. Can afford it, and
3. Plan to buy it.

*Wants* are the unlimited desires or wishes that people have for goods and services. How many times have you thought that you would like something "if only you could afford it" or "if it weren't so expensive"? Scarcity guarantees that many—perhaps most—of our wants will never be satisfied. Demand reflects a decision about which wants to satisfy.

The **quantity demanded** of a good or service is the amount that consumers plan to buy during a given time period at a particular price. The quantity demanded is not necessarily the same as the quantity actually bought. Sometimes the quantity demanded exceeds the amount of goods available, so the quantity bought is less than the quantity demanded.

The quantity demanded is measured as an amount per unit of time. For example, suppose that you buy one cup of coffee a day. The quantity of coffee that you demand can be expressed as 1 cup per day, 7 cups per week, or 365 cups per year.

Many factors influence buying plans and one of them is price. We look first at the relationship between the quantity demanded of a good and its price. To study this relationship, we keep all other influences on buying plans the same and we ask: How, other things remaining the same, does the quantity demanded of a good change as its price changes?

The law of demand provides the answer.

## The Law of Demand

The **law of demand** states

> Other things remaining the same, the higher the price of a good, the smaller is the quantity demanded; and the lower the price of a good, the greater is the quantity demanded.

Why does a higher price reduce the quantity demanded? For two reasons:

- Substitution effect
- Income effect

**Substitution Effect** When the price of a good rises, other things remaining the same, its *relative* price—its opportunity cost—rises. Although each good is unique, it has *substitutes*—other goods that can be used in its place. As the opportunity cost of a good rises, people buy less of that good and more of its substitutes.

**Income Effect** When a price rises and all other influences on buying plans remain unchanged, the price rises *relative* to people's incomes. So faced with a higher price and an unchanged income, people cannot afford to buy all the things they previously bought. They must decrease the quantities demanded of at least some goods and services, and normally, the good whose price has increased will be one of the goods that people buy less of.

To see the substitution effect and the income effect at work, think about the effects of a change in the price of a recordable compact disc—a CD-R. Several different goods are substitutes for a CD-R. For example, an audiotape and prerecorded CD provide services similar to those of a CD-R.

Suppose that a CD-R initially sells for $3 and then its price falls to $1.50. People now substitute CD-Rs for audiotapes and prerecorded CDs—the substitution effect. And with a budget that now has some slack from the lower price of a CD-R, people buy more CD-Rs—the income effect. The quantity of CD-Rs demanded increases for these two reasons.

Now suppose that a CD-R initially sells for $3 each and then the price doubles to $6. People now substitute prerecorded CDs and audiotapes for CD-Rs—the substitution effect. And faced with a tighter budget, people buy fewer CD-Rs—the income effect. The quantity of CD-Rs demanded decreases for these two reasons.

## Demand Curve and Demand Schedule

You are now about to study one of the two most used curves in economics: the demand curve. And you are going to encounter one of the most critical distinctions: the distinction between *demand* and *quantity demanded*.

The term **demand** refers to the entire relationship between the price of the good and the quantity demanded of the good. Demand is illustrated by the demand curve and the demand schedule. The term *quantity demanded* refers to a point on a demand curve—the quantity demanded at a particular price.

Figure 3.1 shows the demand curve for CD-Rs. A **demand curve** shows the relationship between the quantity demanded of a good and its price when all other influences on consumers' planned purchases remain the same.

The table in Fig. 3.1 is the demand schedule for CD-Rs. A *demand schedule* lists the quantities demanded at each price when all the other influences on consumers' planned purchases remain the same. For example, if the price of a CD-R is 50¢, the quantity demanded is 9 million a week. If the price is $2.50, the quantity demanded is 2 million a week. The other rows of the table show the quantities demanded at prices of $1.00, $1.50, and $2.00.

We graph the demand schedule as a demand curve with the quantity demanded of CD-Rs on the *x*-axis and the price of a CD-R on the *y*-axis. The points on the demand curve labeled *A* through *E* correspond to the rows of the demand schedule. For example, point *A* on the graph shows a quantity demanded of 9 million CD-Rs a week at a price of 50¢ a disc.

**Willingness and Ability to Pay** Another way of looking at the demand curve is as a **willingness-and-ability-to-pay curve**. And the willingness and ability to pay is a measure of *marginal benefit*.

If a small quantity is available, the highest price that someone is willing and able to pay for one more unit is high. But as the quantity available increases, the marginal benefit of each additional unit falls and the highest price that someone is willing and able to pay also falls along the demand curve.

In Fig. 3.1, if only 2 million CD-Rs are available each week, the highest price that someone is willing to pay for the 2 millionth CD-R is $2.50. But if 9 million CD-Rs are available each week, someone is willing to pay 50¢ for the last CD-R bought.

## A Change in Demand

When any factor that influences buying plans other than the price of the good changes, there is a **change in demand**. Figure 3.2 illustrates an increase in demand. When demand increases, the demand curve shifts rightward and the quantity demanded is greater at each and every price. For example, at a price of $2.50, on the original (blue) demand curve, the quantity demanded is 2 million discs a week. On the new (red) demand curve, the quantity demanded is 6 million discs a week. Look closely at the numbers in the table in Fig. 3.2 and check that the quantity demanded is greater at each price.

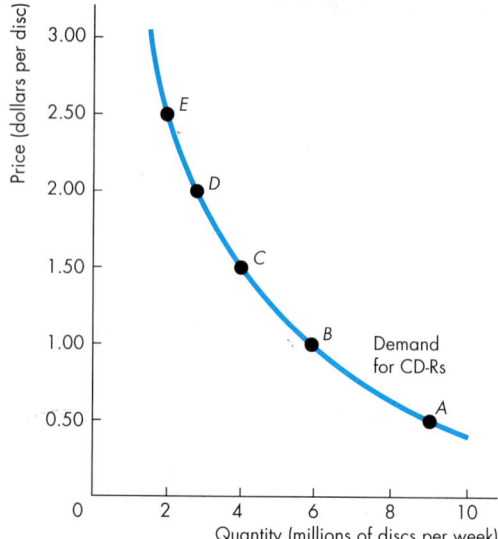

FIGURE 3.1    The Demand Curve

|   | Price (dollars per disc) | Quantity demanded (millions of discs per week) |
|---|---|---|
| A | 0.50 | 9 |
| B | 1.00 | 6 |
| C | 1.50 | 4 |
| D | 2.00 | 3 |
| E | 2.50 | 2 |

The table shows a demand schedule for CD-Rs. At a price of 50¢ a disc, 9 million a week are demanded; at a price of $1.50 a disc, 4 million a week are demanded. The demand curve shows the relationship between quantity demanded and price, everything else remaining the same. The demand curve slopes downward: As price decreases, the quantity demanded increases.

The demand curve can be read in two ways. For a given price, the demand curve tells us the quantity that people plan to buy. For example, at a price of $1.50 a disc, the quantity demanded is 4 million discs a week. For a given quantity, the demand curve tells us the maximum price that consumers are willing and able to pay for the last disc available. For example, the maximum price that consumers will pay for the 6 millionth disc is $1.00.

Six main factors bring changes in demand. They are changes in

1. The prices of related goods
2. Expected future prices
3. Income
4. Expected future income
5. Population
6. Preferences

**1. Prices of Related Goods** The quantity of CD-Rs that consumers plan to buy depends in part on the prices of substitutes for CD-Rs. A **substitute** is a good that can be used in place of another good. For example, a bus ride is a substitute for a train ride; a hamburger is a substitute for a hot dog; and a prerecorded CD is a substitute for a CD-R. If the price of a substitute for a CD-R rises, people buy less of the substitute and more CD-Rs. For example, if the price of a prerecorded CD rises, people buy fewer CDs and more CD-Rs. The demand for CD-Rs increases.

The quantity of CD-Rs that people plan to buy also depends on the prices of complements with CD-Rs. A **complement** is a good that is used in conjunction with another good. Hamburgers and fries are complements. So are spaghetti and meat sauce, and so are CD-Rs and CD-R burners. If the price of a CD burner falls, people buy more CD burners *and more* CD-Rs. A fall in the price of a CD burner increases the demand for CD-Rs in Fig. 3.2.

**2. Expected Future Prices** If the price of a good is expected to rise in the future and if the good can be stored, the opportunity cost of obtaining the good for future use is lower today than it will be when the price has increased. So people retime their purchases—they substitute over time. They buy more of the good now before its price is expected to rise (and less after), so the current demand for the good increases.

For example, suppose that Florida is hit by a frost that damages the season's orange crop. You expect the price of orange juice to rise in the future. So you fill your freezer with enough frozen juice to get you through the next six months. Your current demand for frozen orange juice has increased, and your future demand has decreased.

Similarly, if the price of a good is expected to fall in the future, the opportunity cost of buying the good today is high relative to what it is expected to be in the future. So again, people retime their purchases. They buy less of the good now before its price

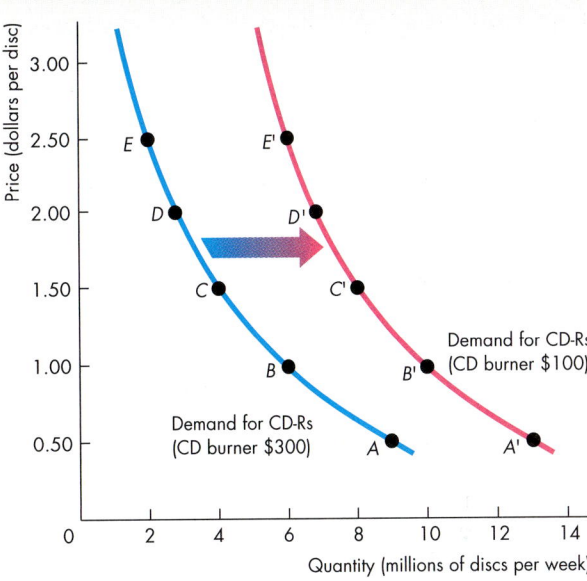

**FIGURE 3.2   An Increase in Demand**

| Original demand schedule CD burner $300 | | | New demand schedule CD burner $100 | | |
|---|---|---|---|---|---|
| | Price (dollars per disc) | Quantity (millions of discs per week) | | Price (dollars per disc) | Quantity (millions of discs per week) |
| A | 0.50 | 9 | A' | 0.50 | 13 |
| B | 1.00 | 6 | B' | 1.00 | 10 |
| C | 1.50 | 4 | C' | 1.50 | 8 |
| D | 2.00 | 3 | D' | 2.00 | 7 |
| E | 2.50 | 2 | E' | 2.50 | 6 |

A change in any influence on buyers' plans other than the price of the good itself results in a new demand schedule and a shift of the demand curve. A change in the price of a CD burner changes the demand for CD-Rs. At a price of $1.50 a disc, 4 million discs a week are demanded when a CD burner costs $300 (row C of the table) and 8 million CD-Rs a week are demanded when a CD burner costs $100. A *fall* in the price of a CD burner *increases* the demand for CD-Rs. The demand curve shifts *rightward*, as shown by the shift arrow and the resulting red curve.

falls, so the demand for the good decreases today and increases in the future.

Computer prices are constantly falling, and this fact poses a dilemma. Will you buy a new computer now, in time for the start of the school year, or will you wait until the price has fallen some more? Because people expect computer prices to keep falling, the current demand for computers is less (the future demand is greater) than it otherwise would be.

**3. Income** Consumers' income influences demand. When income increases, consumers buy more of most goods, and when income decreases, consumers buy less of most goods. Although an increase in income leads to an increase in the demand for *most* goods, it does not lead to an increase in the demand for *all* goods. A **normal good** is one for which demand increases as income increases. An **inferior good** is one for which demand decreases as income increases. Long-distance transportation has examples of both normal goods and inferior goods. As incomes increase, the demand for air travel (a normal good) increases and the demand for long-distance bus trips (an inferior good) decreases.

**4. Expected future income** When expected future income increases, demand might increase. For example, a sales person gets the news that she will receive a big bonus at the end of the year, so she decides to buy a new car right now.

**5. Population** Demand also depends on the size and the age structure of the population. The larger the population, the greater is the demand for all goods and services; the smaller the population, the smaller is the demand for all goods and services.

For example, the demand for parking spaces or movies or CD-Rs or just about anything that you can imagine is much greater in New York City (population 7.5 million) than it is in Boise, Idaho (population 150,000).

Also, the larger the proportion of the population in a given age group, the greater is the demand for the goods and services used by that age group.

For example, between 1988 and 1998, the number of Americans aged 20 to 24 years decreased by 2 million. As a result, the demand for college places decreased during those years. During those same years, the number of Americans aged 85 years and over increased by more than 1 million. As a result, the demand for nursing home services increased.

**TABLE 3.1  The Demand for CD-Rs**

**The Law of Demand**

*The quantity of CD-Rs demanded*

| Decreases if: | Increases if: |
|---|---|
| ■ The price of a CD-R rises | ■ The price of a CD-R falls |

**Changes in Demand**

*The demand for CD-Rs*

| Decreases if: | Increases if: |
|---|---|
| ■ The price of a substitute falls | ■ The price of a substitute rises |
| ■ The price of a complement rises | ■ The price of a complement falls |
| ■ The price of a CD-R is expected to fall in the future | ■ The price of a CD-R is expected to rise in the future |
| ■ Income falls* | ■ Income rises* |
| ■ Expected future income falls | ■ Expected future income rises |
| ■ The population decreases | ■ The population increases |

*A CD-R is a normal good.

**6. Preferences** Demand depends on preferences. *Preferences* are an individual's attitudes toward goods and services. For example, a rock music fanatic has a much greater preference for CD-Rs than does a tone-deaf technophobic. As a consequence, even if they have the same incomes, their demands for CD-Rs will be very different.

Table 3.1 summarizes the influences on demand and the direction of those influences.

## A Change in the Quantity Demanded Versus a Change in Demand

Changes in the factors that influence buyers' plans cause either a change in the quantity demanded or a change in demand. Equivalently, they cause either a movement along the demand curve or a shift of the demand curve. The distinction between a change in the quantity demanded and a change in demand is the same as that between a movement along the demand curve and a shift of the demand curve.

A point on the demand curve shows the quantity demanded at a given price. So a movement along the demand curve shows a **change in the quantity demanded**. The entire demand curve shows demand. So a shift of the demand curve shows a *change in demand*. Figure 3.3 illustrates and summarizes these distinctions.

**Movement Along the Demand Curve** If the price of a good changes but everything else remains the same, there is a movement along the demand curve. Because the demand curve slopes downward, a fall in the price of a good increases the quantity demanded of it and a rise in the price of the good decreases the quantity demanded of it—the law of demand.

In Fig. 3.3, if the price of a good falls when everything else remains the same, the quantity demanded of that good increases and there is a movement down the demand curve $D_0$. If the price rises when everything else remains the same, the quantity demanded of that good decreases and there is a movement up the demand curve $D_0$.

**A Shift of the Demand Curve** If the price of a good remains constant but some other influence on buyers' plans changes, there is a change in demand for that good. We illustrate a change in demand as a shift of the demand curve. For example, if the price of a CD burner falls, consumers buy more CD-Rs regardless of the price of a CD-R. That is what a rightward shift of the demand curve shows—more CD-Rs are bought at each and every price.

In Fig. 3.3, when any influence on buyers' planned purchases changes, other than the price of the good, there is a *change in demand* and the demand curve shifts. Demand *increases* and the demand curve *shifts rightward* (to the red demand curve $D_1$) if the price of a substitute rises, the price of a complement falls, the expected future price of the good rises, income increases (for a normal good), expected future income increases, or the population increases. Demand *decreases* and the demand curve *shifts leftward* (to the red demand curve $D_2$) if the price of a substitute falls, the price of a complement rises, the expected future price of the good falls, income decreases (for a normal good), expected future income decreases, or the population decreases. (For an inferior good, the effects of changes in income are in the direction opposite to those described above.)

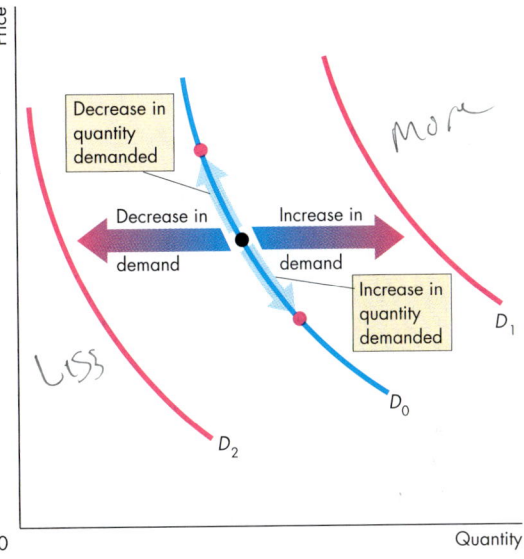

**FIGURE 3.3  A Change in the Quantity Demanded Versus a Change in Demand**

When the price of the good changes, there is a movement along the demand curve and *a change in the quantity demanded*, shown by the blue arrows on demand curve $D_0$. When any other influence on buyers' plans changes, there is a shift of the demand curve and a *change in demand*. An increase in demand shifts the demand curve rightward (from $D_0$ to $D_1$). A decrease in demand shifts the demand curve leftward (from $D_0$ to $D_2$).

### REVIEW QUIZ

1. Define the quantity demanded of a good or service.
2. What is the law of demand and how do we illustrate it?
3. If a fixed amount of a good is available, what does the demand curve tell us about the price that consumers are willing to pay for that fixed quantity?
4. List all the influences on buying plans that change demand, and for each influence say whether it increases or decreases demand.
5. What happens to the quantity of Palm Pilots demanded and the demand for Palm Pilots if the price of a Palm Pilot falls and all other influences on buying plans remain the same?

## Supply

IF A FIRM SUPPLIES A GOOD OR SERVICE, THE FIRM

1. Has the resources and technology to produce it,
2. Can profit from producing it, and
3. Plans to produce it and sell it.

A supply is more than just having the *resources* and the *technology* to produce something. *Resources and technology* are the constraints that limit what is possible.

Many useful things can be produced, but they are not produced unless it is profitable to do so. Supply reflects a decision about which technologically feasible items to produce.

The **quantity supplied** of a good or service is the amount that producers plan to sell during a given time period at a particular price. The quantity supplied is not necessarily the same amount as the quantity actually sold. Sometimes the quantity supplied is greater than the quantity demanded, so the quantity bought is less than the quantity supplied.

Like the quantity demanded, the quantity supplied is measured as an amount per unit of time. For example, suppose that GM produces 1,000 cars a day. The quantity of cars supplied by GM can be expressed as 1,000 a day, 7,000 a week, or 365,000 a year. Without the time dimension, we cannot tell whether a particular number is large or small.

Many factors influence selling plans and again, one of them is price. We look first at the relationship between the quantity supplied of a good and its price. And again, as we did when we studied demand, to isolate this relationship, we keep all other influences on selling plans the same and we ask: How, other things remaining the same, does the quantity supplied of a good change as its price changes?

The law of supply provides the answer.

### The Law of Supply

The **law of supply** states:

Other things remaining the same, the higher the price of a good, the greater is the quantity supplied; and the lower the price of a good, the smaller is the quantity supplied.

Why does a higher price increase the quantity supplied? It is because *marginal cost increases*. As the quantity produced of any good increases, the marginal cost of producing the good increases. (You can refresh your memory of increasing marginal cost in Chapter 2, p. 35.)

It is never worth producing a good if the price received for it does not at least cover the marginal cost of producing it. So when the price of a good rises, other things remaining the same, producers are willing to incur a higher marginal cost and increase production. The higher price brings forth an increase in the quantity supplied.

Let's now illustrate the law of supply with a supply curve and a supply schedule.

### Supply Curve and Supply Schedule

You are now going to study the second of the two most used curves in economics: the supply curve. And you're going to learn about the critical distinction between *supply* and *quantity supplied*.

The term **supply** refers to the entire relationship between the quantity supplied and the price of a good. Supply is illustrated by the supply curve and the supply schedule. The term *quantity supplied* refers to a point on a supply curve—the quantity supplied at a particular price.

Figure 3.4 shows the supply curve of CD-Rs. A **supply curve** shows the relationship between the quantity supplied of a good and its price when all other influences on producers' planned sales remain the same. The supply curve is a graph of a supply schedule.

The table in Fig. 3.4 sets out the supply schedule for CD-Rs. A *supply schedule* lists the quantities supplied at each price when all the other influences on producers' planned sales remain the same. For example, if the price of a CD-R is 50¢, the quantity supplied is zero—in row *A* of the table. If the price of a CD-R is $1.00, the quantity supplied is 3 million CD-Rs a week—in row *B*. The other rows of the table show the quantities supplied at prices of $1.50, $2.00, and $2.50.

To make a supply curve, we graph the quantity supplied on the *x*-axis and the price on the *y*-axis, just as in the case of the demand curve. The points on the supply curve labeled *A* through *E* correspond to the rows of the supply schedule. For example, point *A* on the graph shows a quantity supplied of zero at a price of 50¢ a CD-R.

## FIGURE 3.4  The Supply Curve

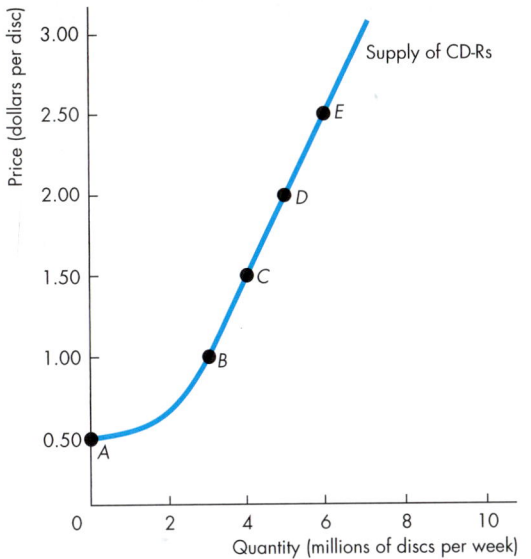

| | Price<br>(dollars per disc) | Quantity supplied<br>(millions of discs per week) |
|---|---|---|
| A | 0.50 | 0 |
| B | 1.00 | 3 |
| C | 1.50 | 4 |
| D | 2.00 | 5 |
| E | 2.50 | 6 |

The table shows the supply schedule of CD-Rs. For example, at a price of $1.00, 3 million discs a week are supplied; at a price of $2.50, 6 million discs a week are supplied. The supply curve shows the relationship between the quantity supplied and price, everything else remaining the same. The supply curve usually slopes upward: As the price of a good increases, so does the quantity supplied.

A supply curve can be read in two ways. For a given price, it tells us the quantity that producers plan to sell at that price. And for a given quantity, it tells us the minimum price that producers are willing to accept for that quantity.

**Minimum Supply Price**  Just as the demand curve has two interpretations, so too does the supply curve. The demand curve can be interpreted as a willingness-and-ability-to-pay curve. The supply curve can be interpreted as a **minimum-supply-price curve**. It tells us the lowest price at which someone is willing to sell another unit.

If a small quantity is produced, the lowest price at which someone is willing to sell one more unit is low. But if a large quantity is produced, the lowest price at which someone is willing to sell one more unit is high.

In Fig. 3.4, if 6 million CD-Rs a week are produced, the lowest price that a producer is willing to accept for the 6 millionth disc is $2.50. But if only 4 million CD-Rs are produced each week, the lowest price that a producer is willing to accept for the 4 millionth disc is $1.50.

## A Change in Supply

When any factor that influences selling plans other than the price of the good changes, there is a **change in supply**.

Five main factors bring changes in supply. They are changes in

1. The prices of resources used to produce the good
2. The prices of related goods produced
3. Expected future prices
4. The number of suppliers
5. Technology

**1. Prices of Productive Resources**  The prices of productive resources influence supply. The easiest way to see this influence is to think about the supply curve as a minimum-supply-price curve. If the price of a productive resource rises, the lowest price a producer is willing to accept rises, so supply decreases. For example, during 2001, the price of jet fuel increased and the supply of air transportation decreased. Similarly, a rise in the minimum wage decreases the supply of hamburgers. If the wages of disc producers rise, the supply of CD-Rs decreases.

**2. Prices of Related Goods Produced**  The prices of related goods and services that firms produce influence supply. For example, if the price of a prerecorded CD rises, the supply of CD-Rs decreases. CD-Rs and prerecorded CDs are *substitutes in production*—goods that can be produced by using the same resources. If the price of beef rises, the supply of cowhide increases. Beef and cowhide are *complements in production*— goods that must be produced together.

**3. Expected Future Prices** If the price of a good is expected to rise, the return from selling the good in the future is higher than it is today. So supply decreases today and increases in the future.

**4. The Number of Suppliers** The larger the number of firms that produce a good, the greater is the supply of the good. And as firms enter an industry, the supply in that industry increases. As firms leave an industry, the supply in that industry decreases.

**5. Technology** The term "technology" is used broadly to mean the way that factors of production are used to produce a good. Technology changes both positively and negatively. A positive technology change occurs when a new method is discovered that lowers the cost of producing a good. An example is new methods used in the factories that make CDs. A negative technology change occurs when an event such as extreme weather or natural disaster increases the cost of producing a good. A positive technology change increases supply, and a negative technology change decreases supply.

Figure 3.5 illustrates an increase in supply. When supply increases, the supply curve shifts rightward and the quantity supplied is larger at each and every price. For example, at a price of $1.00, on the original (blue) supply curve, the quantity supplied is 3 million discs a week. On the new (red) supply curve, the quantity supplied is 6 million discs a week. Look closely at the numbers in the table in Fig. 3.5 and check that the quantity supplied is larger at each price.

Table 3.2 summarizes the influences on supply and the directions of those influences.

## A Change in the Quantity Supplied Versus a Change in Supply

Changes in the factors that influence producers' planned sales cause either a change in the quantity supplied or a change in supply. Equivalently, they cause either a movement along the supply curve or a shift of the supply curve.

A point on the supply curve shows the quantity supplied at a given price. A movement along the supply curve shows a **change in the quantity supplied**. The entire supply curve shows supply. A shift of the supply curve shows a *change in supply*.

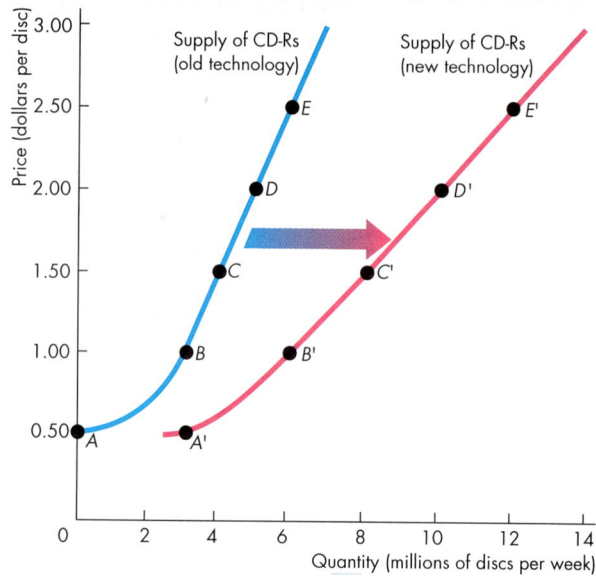

**FIGURE 3.5    An Increase in Supply**

| | Original supply schedule<br>Old technology | | | New supply schedule<br>New technology | |
|---|---|---|---|---|---|
| | Price<br>(dollars per disc) | Quantity<br>(millions of discs per week) | | Price<br>(dollars per disc) | Quantity<br>(millions of discs per week) |
| A | 0.50 | 0 | A' | 0.50 | 3 |
| B | 1.00 | 3 | B' | 1.00 | 6 |
| C | 1.50 | 4 | C' | 1.50 | 8 |
| D | 2.00 | 5 | D' | 2.00 | 10 |
| E | 2.50 | 6 | E' | 2.50 | 12 |

A change in any influence on sellers' plans other than the price of the good itself results in a new supply schedule and a shift of the supply curve. For example, if Imation Enterprises invents a new, cost-saving technology for producing CD-Rs, the supply of CD-Rs changes. At a price of $1.50 a disc, 4 million discs a week are supplied when producers use the old technology (row C of the table) and 8 million CD-Rs a week are supplied when producers use the new technology. An advance in technology *increases* the supply of CD-Rs. The supply curve shifts *rightward*, as shown by the shift arrow and the resulting red curve.

Figure 3.6 illustrates and summarizes these distinctions. If the price of a good falls and everything else remains the same, the quantity supplied of that good decreases and there is a movement down the supply curve $S_0$. If the price of a good rises and everything else remains the same, the quantity supplied increases and there is a movement up the supply curve $S_0$. When any other influence on selling plans changes, the supply curve shifts and there is a *change in supply*. If the supply curve is $S_0$ and if production costs fall, supply increases and the supply curve shifts to the red supply curve $S_1$. If production costs rise, supply decreases and the supply curve shifts to the red supply curve $S_2$.

### TABLE 3.2  The Supply of CD-Rs

#### The Law of Supply

The quantity of CD-Rs supplied

| Decreases if: | Increases if: |
|---|---|
| ■ The price of a CD-R falls | ■ The price of a CD-R rises |

#### Changes in Supply

The supply of CD-Rs

| Decreases if: | Increases if: |
|---|---|
| ■ The price of a resource used to produce CD-Rs rises | ■ The price of a resource used to produce CD-Rs falls |
| ■ The price of a substitute in production rises | ■ The price of a substitute in production falls |
| ■ The price of a complement in production falls | ■ The price of a complement in production rises |
| ■ The price of a CD-R is expected to rise in the future | ■ The price of a CD-R is expected to fall in the future |
| ■ The number of CD-R producers decreases | ■ The number of CD-R producers increases |
| ■ A less efficient technology for producing CD-Rs is used | ■ A more efficient technology for producing CD-Rs is used |

**FIGURE 3.6   A Change in the Quantity Supplied Versus a Change in Supply**

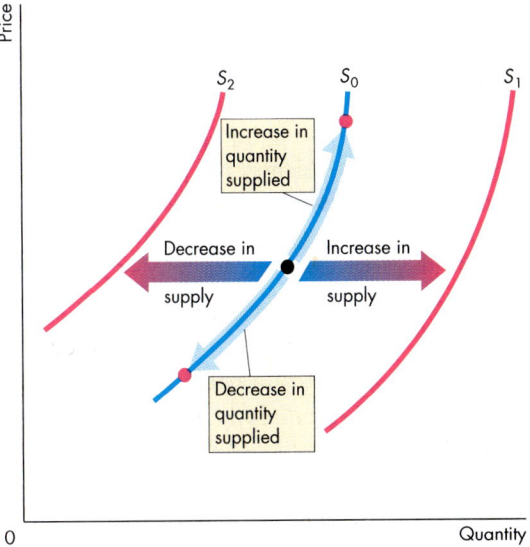

When the price of the good changes, there is a movement along the supply curve and *a change in the quantity supplied*, shown by the blue arrows on supply curve $S_0$. When any other influence on selling plans changes, there is a shift of the supply curve and a *change in supply*. An increase in supply shifts the supply curve rightward (from $S_0$ to $S_1$), and a decrease in supply shifts the supply curve leftward (from $S_0$ to $S_2$).

### REVIEW QUIZ

1. Define the quantity supplied of a good or service.
2. What is the law of supply and how do we illustrate it?
3. What does the supply curve tell us about the price at which firms will supply a given quantity of a good?
4. List all the influences on selling plans, and for each influence say whether it changes supply.
5. What happens to the quantity of Palm Pilots supplied and the supply of Palm Pilots if the price of a Palm Pilot falls?

Your next task is to use what you've learned about demand and supply and understand how prices and quantities are determined.

## Market Equilibrium

WE HAVE SEEN THAT WHEN THE PRICE OF A GOOD rises, the quantity demanded *decreases* and the quantity supplied *increases*. We are now going to see how prices coordinate the plans of buyers and sellers and achieve an equilibrium.

An *equilibrium* is a situation in which opposing forces balance each other. Equilibrium in a market occurs when the price balances the plans of buyers and sellers. The **equilibrium price** is the price at which the quantity demanded equals the quantity supplied. The **equilibrium quantity** is the quantity bought and sold at the equilibrium price. A market moves toward its equilibrium because

- Price regulates buying and selling plans.
- Price adjusts when plans don't match.

### Price as a Regulator

The price of a good regulates the quantities demanded and supplied. If the price is too high, the quantity supplied exceeds the quantity demanded. If the price is too low, the quantity demanded exceeds the quantity supplied. There is one price at which the quantity demanded equals the quantity supplied. Let's work out what that price is.

Figure 3.7 shows the market for CD-Rs. The table shows the demand schedule (from Fig. 3.1) and the supply schedule (from Fig. 3.4). If the price of a disc is 50¢, the quantity demanded is 9 million discs a week, but no discs are supplied. There is a shortage of 9 million discs a week. This shortage is shown in the final column of the table. At a price of $1.00 a disc, there is still a shortage, but only of 3 million discs a week. If the price of a disc is $2.50, the quantity supplied is 6 million discs a week, but the quantity demanded is only 2 million. There is a surplus of 4 million discs a week. The one price at which there is neither a shortage nor a surplus is $1.50 a disc. At that price, the quantity demanded is equal to the quantity supplied: 4 million discs a week. The equilibrium price is $1.50 a disc, and the equilibrium quantity is 4 million discs a week.

Figure 3.7 shows that the demand curve and the supply curve intersect at the equilibrium price of $1.50 a disc. At each price *above* $1.50 a disc, there is a surplus of discs. For example, at $2.00 a disc, the surplus

**FIGURE 3.7  Equilibrium**

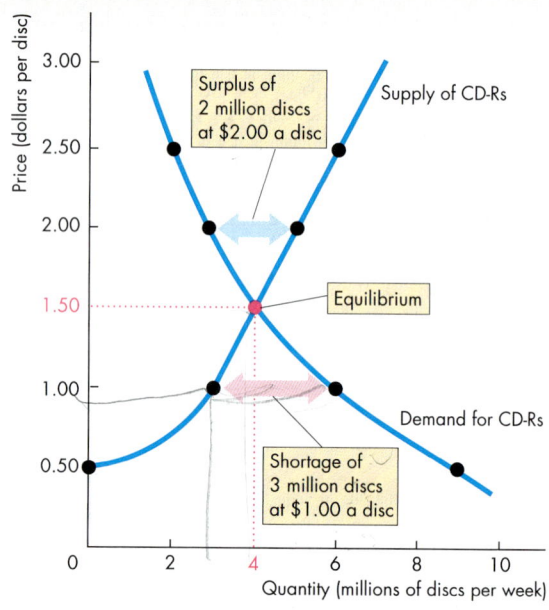

| Price (dollars per disc) | Quantity demanded | Quantity supplied | Shortage (–) or surplus (+) |
|---|---|---|---|
| | (millions of discs per week) | | |
| 0.50 | 9 | 0 | –9 |
| 1.00 | 6 | 3 | –3 |
| 1.50 | 4 | 4 | 0 |
| 2.00 | 3 | 5 | +2 |
| 2.50 | 2 | 6 | +4 |

The table lists the quantities demanded and quantities supplied as well as the shortage or surplus of discs at each price. If the price is $1.00 a disc, 6 million discs a week are demanded and 3 million are supplied. There is a shortage of 3 million discs a week, and the price rises.

If the price is $2.00 a disc, 3 million discs a week are demanded and 5 million are supplied. There is a surplus of 2 million discs a week, and the price falls.

If the price is $1.50 a disc, 4 million discs a week are demanded and 4 million are supplied. There is neither a shortage nor a surplus. Neither buyers nor sellers have any incentive to change the price. The price at which the quantity demanded equals the quantity supplied is the equilibrium price.

is 2 million discs a week, as shown by the blue arrow. At each price *below* $1.50 a disc, there is a shortage of discs. For example, at $1.00 a disc, the shortage is 3 million discs a week, as shown by the red arrow.

## Price Adjustments

You've seen that if the price is below equilibrium, there is a shortage and that if the price is above equilibrium, there is a surplus. But can we count on the price to change and eliminate a shortage or surplus? We can, because such price changes are beneficial to both buyers and sellers. Let's see why the price changes when there is a shortage or a surplus.

**A Shortage Forces the Price Up**  Suppose the price of a CD-R is $1. Consumers plan to buy 6 million discs a week, and producers plan to sell 3 million discs a week. Consumers can't force producers to sell more than they plan, so the quantity that is actually offered for sale is 3 million discs a week. In this situation, powerful forces operate to increase the price and move it toward the equilibrium price. Some producers, noticing lines of unsatisfied consumers, raise the price. Some producers increase their output. As producers push the price up, the price rises toward its equilibrium. The rising price reduces the shortage because it decreases the quantity demanded and increases the quantity supplied. When the price has increased to the point at which there is no longer a shortage, the forces moving the price stop operating and the price comes to rest at its equilibrium.

**A Surplus Forces the Price Down**  Suppose the price of a CD-R is $2. Producers plan to sell 5 million discs a week, and consumers plan to buy 3 million discs a week. Producers cannot force consumers to buy more than they plan, so the quantity that is actually bought is 3 million discs a week. In this situation, powerful forces operate to lower the price and move it toward the equilibrium price. Some producers, unable to sell the quantities of CD-Rs they planned to sell, cut their prices. In addition, some producers scale back production. As producers cut the price, the price falls toward its equilibrium. The falling price decreases the surplus because it increases the quantity demanded and decreases the quantity supplied. When the price has fallen to the point at which there is no longer a surplus, the forces moving the price stop operating and the price comes to rest at its equilibrium.

### The Best Deal Available for Buyers and Sellers

When the price is below equilibrium, it is forced up toward the equilibrium. Why don't buyers resist the increase and refuse to buy at the higher price? Because they value the good more highly than the current price and they cannot satisfy all their demands at the current price. In some markets—for example, the auction markets that operate on eBay—the buyers might even be the ones who force the price up by offering to pay higher prices.

When the price is above equilibrium, it is bid down toward the equilibrium. Why don't sellers resist this decrease and refuse to sell at the lower price? Because their minimum supply price is below the current price and they cannot sell all they would like to at the current price. Normally, it is the sellers who force the price down by offering lower prices to gain market share from their competitors.

At the price at which the quantity demanded and the quantity supplied are equal, neither buyers nor sellers can do business at a better price. Buyers pay the highest price they are willing to pay for the last unit bought, and sellers receive the lowest price at which they are willing to supply the last unit sold.

When people freely make offers to buy and sell and when demanders try to buy at the lowest possible price and suppliers try to sell at the highest possible price, the price at which trade takes place is the equilibrium price—the price at which the quantity demanded equals the quantity supplied. The price coordinates the plans of buyers and sellers, and no one has an incentive to change it.

### REVIEW QUIZ

1. What is the equilibrium price of a good or service?
2. Over what range of prices does a shortage arise?
3. Over what range of prices does a surplus arise?
4. What happens to the price when there is a shortage?
5. What happens to the price when there is a surplus?
6. Why is the price at which the quantity demanded equals the quantity supplied the equilibrium price?
7. Why is the equilibrium price the best deal available for both buyers and sellers?

# Predicting Changes in Price and Quantity

THE DEMAND AND SUPPLY THEORY THAT WE HAVE just studied provides us with a powerful way of analyzing influences on prices and the quantities bought and sold. According to the theory, a change in price stems from a change in demand, a change in supply, or a change in both demand and supply. Let's look first at the effects of a change in demand.

## A Change in Demand

What happens to the price and quantity of CD-Rs if the demand for CD-Rs increases? We can answer this question with a specific example. Between 1998 and 2001, the price of a CD burner fell from $300 to $100. Because the CD burner and CD-R discs are complements, the demand for discs increased, as is shown in the table in Fig. 3.8. The original demand schedule and the new one are set out in the first three columns of the table. The table also shows the supply schedule for CD-Rs.

When demand increases, there is a shortage at the original equilibrium price of $1.50 a disc. To eliminate the shortage, the price must rise. The price that makes the quantity demanded and quantity supplied equal again is $2.50 a disc. At this price, 6 million discs are bought and sold each week. When demand increases, both the price and the quantity increase.

Figure 3.8 shows these changes. The figure shows the original demand for and supply of CD-Rs. The original equilibrium price is $1.50 a CD-R, and the quantity is 4 million CD-Rs a week. When demand increases, the demand curve shifts rightward. The equilibrium price rises to $2.50 a CD-R, and the quantity supplied increases to 6 million CD-Rs a week, as highlighted in the figure. There is an *increase in the quantity supplied* but *no change in supply*—a movement along, but no shift of, the supply curve.

We can reverse this change in demand. Start at a price of $2.50 a disc with 6 million CD-Rs a week being bought and sold, and then work out what happens if demand decreases to its original level. Such a decrease in demand might arise from a fall in the price of an MP3 player (a substitute for CD-R technology). The decrease in demand shifts the demand curve leftward. The equilibrium price falls to $1.50 a disc, and the equilibrium quantity decreases to 4 million discs a week.

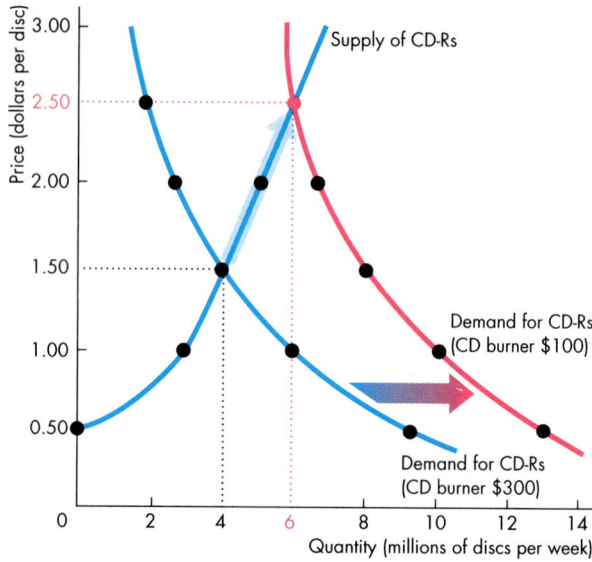

FIGURE 3.8 The Effects of a Change in Demand

| Price (dollars per disc) | Quantity demanded (millions of discs per week) | | Quantity supplied (millions of discs per week) |
|---|---|---|---|
| | CD burner $300 | CD burner $100 | |
| 0.50 | 9 | 13 | 0 |
| 1.00 | 6 | 10 | 3 |
| 1.50 | 4 | 8 | 4 |
| 2.00 | 3 | 7 | 5 |
| 2.50 | 2 | 6 | 6 |

With the price of a CD burner at $300, the demand for CD-Rs is the blue demand curve. The equilibrium price is $1.50 a disc, and the equilibrium quantity is 4 million discs a week. When the price of a CD burner falls from $300 to $100, the demand for CD-Rs increases and the demand curve shifts rightward to become the red curve.

At $1.50 a disc, there is now a shortage of 4 million discs a week. The price of a disc rises to a new equilibrium of $2.50. As the price rises to $2.50, the quantity supplied increases—shown by the blue arrow on the supply curve—to the new equilibrium quantity of 6 million discs a week. Following an increase in demand, the quantity supplied increases but supply does not change—the supply curve does not shift.

We can now make our first two predictions:

1. When demand increases, both the price and the quantity increase.
2. When demand decreases, both the price and the quantity decrease.

## A Change in Supply

When Imation and other producers introduce new cost-saving technologies in their CD-R production plants, the supply of CD-Rs increases. The new supply schedule (the same one that was shown in Fig. 3.5) is presented in the table in Fig. 3.9. What are the new equilibrium price and quantity? The answer is highlighted in the table: The price falls to $1.00 a disc, and the quantity increases to 6 million a week. You can see why by looking at the quantities demanded and supplied at the old price of $1.50 a disc. The quantity supplied at that price is 8 million discs a week, and there is a surplus of discs. The price falls. Only when the price is $1.00 a disc does the quantity supplied equal the quantity demanded.

Figure 3.9 illustrates the effect of an increase in supply. It shows the demand curve for CD-Rs and the original and new supply curves. The initial equilibrium price is $1.50 a disc, and the quantity is 4 million discs a week. When the supply increases, the supply curve shifts rightward. The equilibrium price falls to $1.00 a disc, and the quantity demanded increases to 6 million discs a week, highlighted in the figure. There is an *increase in the quantity demanded* but *no change in demand*—a movement along, but no shift of, the demand curve.

We can reverse this change in supply. If we start out at a price of $1.00 a disc with 6 million discs a week being bought and sold, we can work out what happens if supply decreases to its original level. Such a decrease in supply might arise from an increase in the cost of labor or raw materials. The decrease in supply shifts the supply curve leftward. The equilibrium price rises to $1.50 a disc, and the equilibrium quantity decreases to 4 million discs a week.

We can now make two more predictions:

1. When supply increases, the quantity increases and the price falls.
2. When supply decreases, the quantity decreases and the price rises.

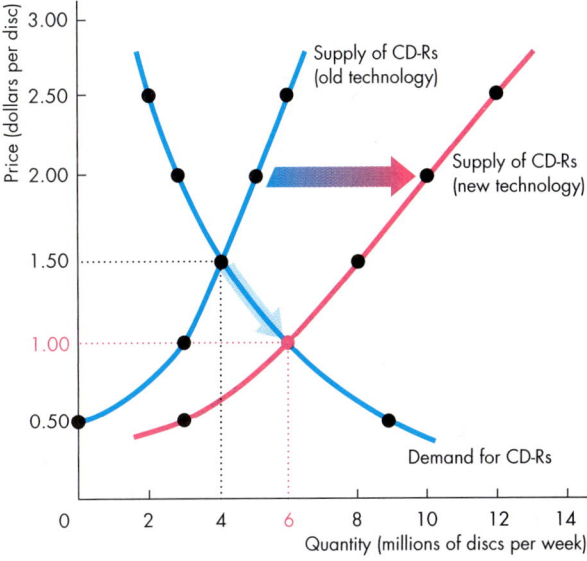

**FIGURE 3.9** The Effects of a Change in Supply

| Price (dollars per disc) | Quantity demanded (millions of discs per week) | Quantity supplied (millions of discs per week) | |
|---|---|---|---|
| | | Old technology | New technology |
| 0.50 | 9 | 0 | 3 |
| 1.00 | 6 | 3 | 6 |
| 1.50 | 4 | 4 | 8 |
| 2.00 | 3 | 5 | 10 |
| 2.50 | 2 | 6 | 12 |

With the old technology, the supply of CD-Rs is shown by the blue supply curve. The equilibrium price is $1.50 a disc, and the equilibrium quantity is 4 million discs a week. When the new technology is adopted, the supply of CD-Rs increases and the supply curve shifts rightward to become the red curve.

At $1.50 a disc, there is now a surplus of 4 million discs a week. The price of a CD-R falls to a new equilibrium of $1.00 a disc. As the price falls to $1.00, the quantity demanded increases—shown by the blue arrow on the demand curve—to the new equilibrium quantity of 6 million discs a week. Following an increase in supply, the quantity demanded increases but demand does not change—the demand curve does not shift.

## A Change in Both Demand and Supply

You can now predict the effects of a change in either demand or supply on the price and the quantity. But what happens if *both* demand and supply change together? To answer this question, we look first at the case in which demand and supply move in the same direction—either both increase or both decrease. Then we look at the case in which they move in opposite directions—demand decreases and supply increases or demand increases and supply decreases.

**Demand and Supply Change in the Same Direction** We've seen that an increase in the demand for CD-Rs raises its price and increases the quantity bought and sold. And we've seen that an increase in the supply of CD-Rs lowers its price and increases the quantity bought and sold. Let's now examine what happens when both of these changes occur together.

The table in Fig. 3.10 brings together the numbers that describe the original quantities demanded and supplied and the new quantities demanded and supplied after the fall in the price of the CD burner and the improved CD-R production technology. These same numbers are illustrated in the graph. The original (blue) demand and supply curves intersect at a price of $1.50 a disc and a quantity of 4 million discs a week. The new (red) supply and demand curves also intersect at a price of $1.50 a disc but at a quantity of 8 million discs a week.

An increase in either demand or supply increases the quantity. So when both demand and supply increase, so does the equilibrium quantity.

An increase in demand raises the price, and an increase in supply lowers the price, so we can't say whether the price will rise or fall when demand and supply increase together. In this example, the price does not change. But notice that if demand increases by slightly more than the amount shown in the figure, the equilibrium price will rise. And if supply increases by slightly more than the amount shown in the figure, the equilibrium price will fall.

We can now make two more predictions:

1. When *both* demand and supply increase, the quantity increases and the price might increase, decrease, or remain the same.
2. When *both* demand and supply decrease, the quantity decreases and the price might increase, decrease, or remain the same.

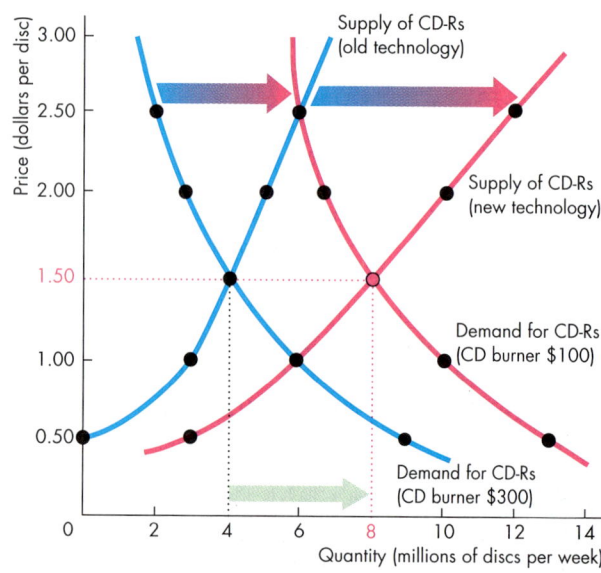

**FIGURE 3.10** The Effects of an Increase in Both Demand and Supply

|  | Original quantities (millions of discs per week) | | New quantities (millions of discs per week) | |
|---|---|---|---|---|
| Price (dollars per disc) | Quantity demanded CD burner $300 | Quantity supplied old technology | Quantity demanded CD burner $100 | Quantity supplied new technology |
| 0.50 | 9 | 0 | 13 | 3 |
| 1.00 | 6 | 3 | 10 | 6 |
| 1.50 | 4 | 4 | 8 | 8 |
| 2.00 | 3 | 5 | 7 | 10 |
| 2.50 | 2 | 6 | 6 | 12 |

When a CD burner costs $300 and firms use the old technology to produce discs, the price of a disc is $1.50 and the quantity is 4 million discs a week. A fall in the price of the CD burner increases the demand for CD-Rs, and improved technology increases the supply of CD-Rs. The new supply curve intersects the new demand curve at $1.50 a disc, the same price as before, but the equilibrium quantity increases to 8 million discs a week. These increases in demand and supply increase the quantity but leave the price unchanged.

**Demand and Supply Change in Opposite Directions** Let's now see what happens when demand and supply change together in *opposite* directions. A new production technology increases the supply of CD-Rs as before. But now the price of an MP3 download rises. An MP3 download is a *complement* of a CD-R. With more costly MP3 downloads, some people switch from buying CD-Rs to buying prerecorded CDs. The demand for CD-Rs decreases.

The table in Fig. 3.11 describes the original and new demand and supply schedules and the original (blue) and new (red) demand and supply curves. The original equilibrium price is $2.50 a disc, and the quantity is 6 million discs a week. The new supply and demand curves intersect at a price of $1.00 a disc and at the original quantity of 6 million discs a week.

A decrease in demand or an increase in supply lowers the price. So when a decrease in demand and an increase in supply occur together, the price falls.

A decrease in demand decreases the quantity, and an increase in supply increases the quantity, so we can't say for sure which way the quantity will change when demand decreases and supply increases at the same time. In this example, the quantity doesn't change. But notice that if demand had decreased by slightly more than is shown in the figure, the quantity would have decreased. And if supply had increased by slightly more than is shown in the figure, the quantity would have increased. So

1. When demand decreases and supply increases, the price falls and the quantity might increase, decrease, or remain the same.
2. When demand increases and supply decreases, the price rises and the quantity might increase, decrease, or remain the same.

### REVIEW QUIZ

1 What is the effect on the price of a CD-R and the quantity of CD-Rs if (a) the price of a PC falls or (b) the price of an MP3 download rises or (c) more firms produce CD-Rs or (d) CD-R producers' wages rise or (e) any two of these events occur together? (Draw the diagrams!)

◆ To complete your study of demand and supply, take a look at *Reading Between the Lines* on pp. 74–75, which looks at the rocketing price of gasoline in the summer of 2003.

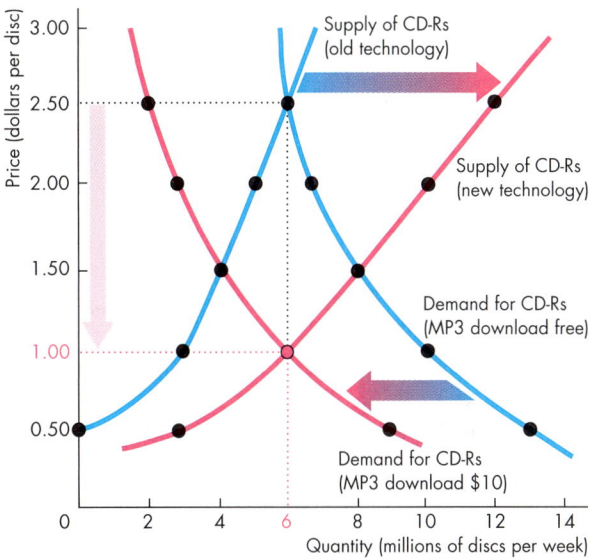

**FIGURE 3.11** The Effects of a Decrease in Demand and an Increase in Supply

|  | Original quantities (millions of CD-Rs per week) | | New quantities (millions of CD-Rs per week) | |
| --- | --- | --- | --- | --- |
| Price (dollars per disc) | Quantity demanded MP3 download free | Quantity supplied old technology | Quantity demanded MP3 download $10 | Quantity supplied new technology |
| 0.50 | 13 | 0 | 9 | 3 |
| 1.00 | 10 | 3 | 6 | 6 |
| 1.50 | 8 | 4 | 4 | 8 |
| 2.00 | 7 | 5 | 3 | 10 |
| 2.50 | 6 | 6 | 2 | 12 |

When MP3 downloads are free and firms use the old technology to produce discs, the price of a CD-R is $2.50 and the quantity is 6 million discs a week. A rise in the price of an MP3 download decreases the demand for CD-Rs, and improved technology increases the supply of CD-Rs. The new equilibrium price is $1.00 a disc, a lower price, but in this case the quantity remains constant at 6 million discs a week. This decrease in demand and increase in supply lower the price but leave the quantity unchanged.

# READING BETWEEN THE LINES

## Demand and Supply: The Price of Gasoline

**THE WASHINGTON POST, AUGUST 26, 2003**

### Gasoline Prices Soar to Highest Point Yet

Gasoline prices around the country have shot up to record levels as more motorists squeeze in late summer road trips at a time supplies have been reduced by power outages at refineries and a major gasoline pipeline break in Arizona.

The nationwide average retail price of regular-grade gasoline shot up to $1.75 a gallon yesterday, its highest level ever, according to the Energy Information Administration (EIA). ...

Analysts attributed the rising prices to disruptions in production ... One major shock was the recent blackout in the Northeast and the Midwest, which temporarily shut down refineries in Ohio, Michigan and Pennsylvania. In addition, a rupture in a gasoline pipeline that provides Phoenix with about a third of its gasoline caused hundreds of service stations to close last week and prices to shoot up. ...

The low gasoline levels have been coupled with a record demand. From July 19 through Aug. 15, the demand for gasoline averaged 9.4 million barrels per day, according to the EIA.

"It's the largest four-week amount ever. From the same four-week period last summer, it's up 1.8 percent..." said Doug MacIntyre, an oil market analyst with the EIA.

One of the reasons for the high demand for gasoline this year is that more people are taking driving vacations later in the summer, after a rainy spring and early summer on the East Coast. In the past two months, automobile use has shot up along with the demand for gasoline ...

And if it's any comfort, current record prices are not so high in inflation-adjusted terms. For example, a gallon of gasoline was $1.25 in 1980, or the equivalent of $2.79 today.

©2003 The Washington Post. Reprinted with permission. Further reproduction prohibited.

### Essence of the Story

■ The national average retail price of a gallon of regular-grade gasoline increased to $1.75 a gallon in August 2003.

■ Analysts attribute the high price to a blackout, which temporarily shut down refineries, a rupture in a gasoline pipeline, and to record demand.

■ The amount of gasoline used between July 19 and August 15 2003 averaged 9.4 million barrels a day, an increase of 1.8 percent over the same period in 2002.

■ Adjusted for inflation, the price of a gallon of gasoline was higher in 1980 than it was in 2003.

## Economic Analysis

- Figure 1 shows the money price and the relative price of a gallon of gasoline.

- The relative price of a gallon of gasoline tells us how much of a "basket" of goods and services we must give up to buy the gallon of gasoline.

- Between 1980 and 2003, the money price of a gallon of gasoline shows an upward trend and the relative price of a gallon of gasoline shows a downward trend.

- What the news story calls the "price adjusted for inflation" is the relative price.

- Figure 2 shows what happened in the market for gasoline between July 2003 and August 2003.

- In July, the demand curve for gasoline was $D_{JUL}$ and the supply curve was $S_{JUL}$.

- The price of a gallon of gas was $1.53 and the equilibrium quantity was 9.2 million barrels a day.

- During August, power outages at refineries and a major gasoline pipeline break decreased supply.

- The supply curve of gasoline shifted leftward from $S_{JUL}$ to $S_{AUG}$.

- At the same time, automobile use increased because driving vacations became more popular and the demand for gasoline increased.

- The demand curve for gasoline shifted rightward from $D_{JUL}$ to $D_{AUG}$.

- A decrease in the supply of gasoline and an increase in the demand for gasoline both increase the equilibrium price.

- The equilibrium price rose from $1.53 a gallon in July to $1.75 a gallon in August.

- An increase in the demand for gasoline increases the equilibrium quantity of gasoline and a decrease in supply decreases the equilibrium quantity of gasoline.

- In this case, the demand for gasoline increased by more than the supply of gasoline decreased and the equilibrium quantity increased from 9.2 million barrels a day to 9.4 million barrels a day.

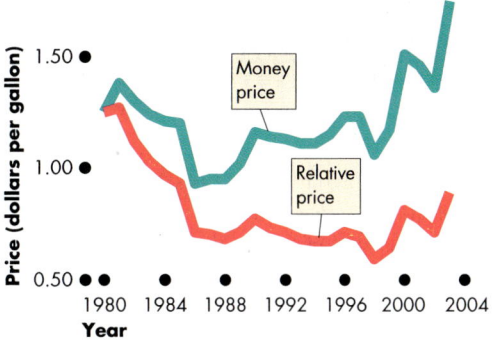

**Figure 1** The price of gasoline

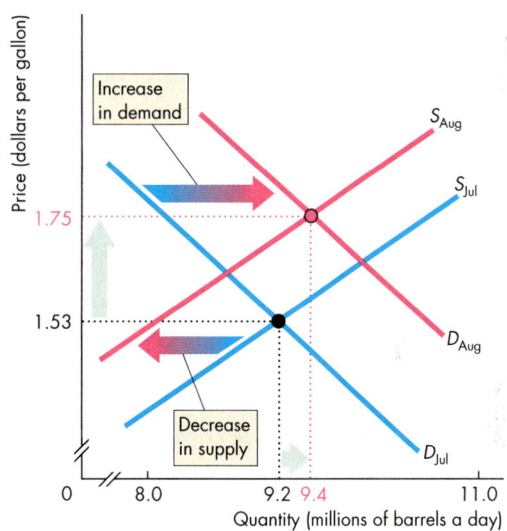

**Figure 2** The gasoline market in 2003

## Mathematical Note
### Demand, Supply, and Equilibrium

#### Demand Curve

The law of demand says that as the price of a good or service falls, the quantity demanded of that good or service increases. We illustrate the law of demand by setting out a demand schedule, drawing a graph of the demand curve, or writing down an equation. When the demand curve is a straight line, the following linear equation describes it:

$$P = a - bQ_D,$$

where $P$ is the price and $Q_D$ is the quantity demanded. The $a$ and $b$ are positive constants.

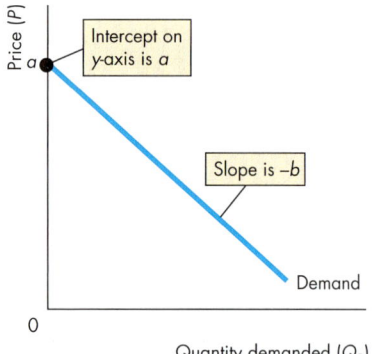

The demand equation tells us three things:

1. The price at which no one is willing to buy the good ($Q_D$ is zero). That is, if the price is $a$, then the quantity demanded is zero. You can see the price $a$ on the graph. It is the price at which the demand curve hits the $y$-axis—what we call the demand curve's "intercept on the $y$-axis."

2. As the price falls, the quantity demanded increases. If $Q_D$ is a positive number, then the price $P$ must be less than $a$. And as $Q_D$ gets larger, the price $P$ becomes smaller. That is, as the quantity increases, the maximum price that buyers are willing to pay for the good falls.

3. The constant $b$ tells us how fast the maximum price that someone is willing to pay for the good falls as the quantity increases. That is, the constant $b$ tells us about the steepness of the demand curve. The equation tells us that the slope of the demand curve is $-b$.

#### Supply Curve

The law of supply says that as the price of a good or service rises, the quantity supplied of that good or service increases. We illustrate the law of supply by setting out a supply schedule, drawing a graph of the supply curve, or writing down an equation. When the supply curve is a straight line, the following linear equation describes it:

$$P = c + dQ_S,$$

where $P$ is the price and $Q_S$ is the quantity supplied. The $c$ and $d$ are positive constants.

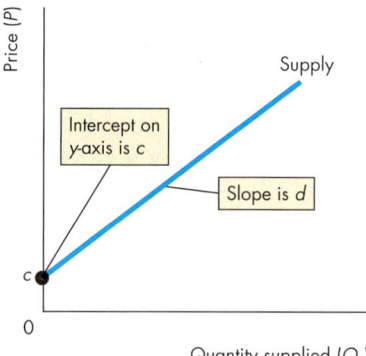

The supply equation tells us three things:

1. The price at which sellers are not willing to supply the good ($Q_S$ is zero). That is, if the price is $c$, then no one is willing to sell the good. You can see the price $c$ on the graph. It is the price at which the supply curve hits the $y$-axis—what we call the supply curve's "intercept on the $y$-axis."

2. As the price rises, the quantity supplied increases. If $Q_S$ is a positive number, then the price $P$ must be greater than $c$. And as $Q_S$ increases, the price $P$ get larger. That is, as the quantity increases, the minimum price that sellers are willing to accept rises.

3. The constant $d$ tells us how fast the minimum price at which someone is willing to sell the good rises as the quantity increases. That is, the constant $d$ tells us about the steepness of the supply curve. The equation tells us that the slope of the supply curve is $d$.

## Market Equilibrium

Demand and supply determine market equilibrium. The figure shows the equilibrium price ($P^*$) and equilibrium quantity ($Q^*$) at the intersection of the demand curve and the supply curve.

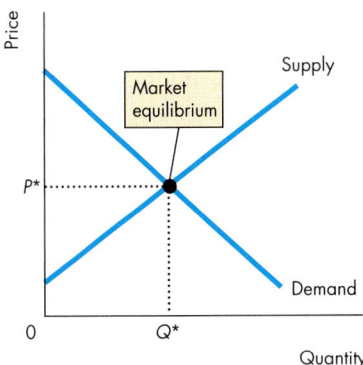

We can use the equations to find the equilibrium price and equilibrium quantity. The price of a good adjusts until the quantity demanded equals the quantity supplied. That is,

$$Q_D = Q_S.$$

So at the equilibrium price ($P^*$) and equilibrium quantity ($Q^*$),

$$Q_D = Q_S = Q^*.$$

To find the equilibrium price and equilibrium quantity, substitute $Q^*$ for $Q_D$ in the demand equation and $Q^*$ for $Q_S$ in the supply equation. Then the price is the equilibrium price ($P^*$), which gives

$$P^* = a - bQ^*$$
$$P^* = c + dQ^*.$$

Notice that

$$a - bQ^* = c + dQ^*.$$

Now solve for $Q^*$:

$$a - c = bQ^* + dQ^*$$
$$a - c = (b + d)Q^*$$
$$Q^* = \frac{a - c}{b + d}.$$

To find the equilibrium price, ($P^*$), substitute for $Q^*$ in either the demand equation or the supply equation.

Using the demand equation, we have

$$P^* = a - b\left(\frac{a - c}{b + d}\right)$$
$$P^* = \frac{a(b + d) - b(a - c)}{b + d}$$
$$P^* = \frac{ad + bc}{b + d}.$$

Alternatively, using the supply equation, we have

$$P^* = c + d\left(\frac{a - c}{b + d}\right)$$
$$P^* = \frac{c(b + d) + d(a - c)}{b + d}$$
$$P^* = \frac{ad + bc}{b + d}.$$

## An Example

The demand for ice-cream cones is

$$P = 800 - 2Q_D.$$

The supply of ice-cream cones is

$$P = 200 + 1Q_S.$$

The price of a cone is expressed in cents, and the quantities are expressed in cones per day.

To find the equilibrium price ($P^*$) and equilibrium quantity ($Q^*$), substitute $Q^*$ for $Q_D$ and $Q_S$ and $P^*$ for $P$. That is,

$$P^* = 800 - 2Q^*$$
$$P^* = 200 + 1Q^*.$$

Now solve for $Q^*$:

$$800 - 2Q^* = 200 + 1Q^*$$
$$600 = 3Q^*$$
$$Q^* = 200.$$

And

$$P^* = 800 - 2(200)$$
$$= 400.$$

The equilibrium price is $4 a cone, and the equilibrium quantity is 200 cones per day.

# SUMMARY

## KEY POINTS

### Markets and Prices (p. 58)

- A competitive market is one that has so many buyers and sellers that no one can influence the price.
- Opportunity cost is a relative price.
- Demand and supply determine relative prices.

### Demand (pp. 59–63)

- Demand is the relationship between the quantity demanded of a good and its price when all other influences on buying plans remain the same.
- The higher the price of a good, other things remaining the same, the smaller is the quantity demanded—the law of demand.
- Demand depends on the prices of substitutes and complements, expected future prices, income, expected future income, population, and preferences.

### Supply (pp. 64–67)

- Supply is the relationship between the quantity supplied of a good and its price when all other influences on selling plans remain the same.
- The higher the price of a good, other things remaining the same, the greater is the quantity supplied—the law of supply.
- Supply depends on the prices of resources used to produce a good, the prices of related goods produced, expected future prices, the number of suppliers, and technology.

### Market Equilibrium (pp. 68–69)

- At the equilibrium price, the quantity demanded equals the quantity supplied.
- At prices above equilibrium, there is a surplus and the price falls.
- At prices below equilibrium, there is a shortage and the price rises.

### Predicting Changes in Price and Quantity (pp. 70–73)

- An increase in demand brings a rise in the price and an increase in the quantity supplied. (A decrease in demand brings a fall in the price and a decrease in the quantity supplied.)
- An increase in supply brings a fall in the price and an increase in the quantity demanded. (A decrease in supply brings a rise in the price and a decrease in the quantity demanded.)
- An increase in demand and an increase in supply bring an increased quantity, but the price might rise, fall, or remain the same. An increase in demand and a decrease in supply bring a higher price, but the quantity might increase, decrease, or remain the same.

## KEY FIGURES

Figure 3.1    The Demand Curve, 60
Figure 3.3    A Change in the Quantity Demanded Versus a Change in Demand, 63
Figure 3.4    The Supply Curve, 65
Figure 3.6    A Change in the Quantity Supplied Versus a Change in Supply, 67
Figure 3.7    Equilibrium, 68
Figure 3.8    The Effects of a Change in Demand, 70
Figure 3.9    The Effects of a Change in Supply, 71

## KEY TERMS

Change in demand, 60
Change in supply, 65
Change in the quantity demanded, 63
Change in the quantity supplied, 66
Competitive market, 58
Complement, 61
Demand, 59
Demand curve, 60
Equilibrium price, 68
Equilibrium quantity, 68
Inferior good, 62
Law of demand, 59
Law of supply, 64
Money price, 58
Normal good, 62
Quantity demanded, 59
Quantity supplied, 64
Relative price, 58
Substitute, 61
Supply, 64
Supply curve, 64

# PROBLEMS

*1. What is the effect on the price of an audiotape and the quantity of audiotapes sold if
   a. The price of a CD rises?
   b. The price of a Walkman rises?
   c. The supply of CD players increases?
   d. Consumers' incomes increase?
   e. Workers who make audiotapes get a pay raise?
   f. The price of a Walkman rises at the same time as the workers who make audiotapes get a pay raise?

2. What is the effect on the price of a DVD player and the quantity of DVD players sold if
   a. The price of a DVD rises?
   b. The price of a DVD falls?
   c. The supply of DVD players increases?
   d. Consumers' incomes decrease?
   e. The wage rate of workers who produce DVD players increases?
   f. The wage rate of workers who produce DVD players rises and at the same time the price of a DVD falls?

*3. Suppose that the following events occur one at a time
   (i) The price of crude oil rises.
   (ii) The price of a car rises.
   (iii) All speed limits on highways are abolished.
   (iv) Robot technology cuts car production costs.

   Which of these events will increase or decrease (state which)
   a. The demand for gasoline?
   b. The supply of gasoline?
   c. The quantity of gasoline demanded?
   d. The quantity of gasoline supplied?

4. Suppose that the following events occur one at a time
   (i) The price of airfares halve.
   (ii) The price of beef falls.
   (iii) A cheap new strong cloth, a close substitute for leather, is invented.
   (iv) A new high-speed technology for cutting leather is invented.

   Which of these events will increase or decrease (state which)
   a. The demand for leather bags?
   b. The supply of leather bags?
   c. The quantity of leather bags demanded?
   d. The quantity of leather bags supplied?

*5. The figure illustrates the market for pizza.
   a. Label the curves in the figure.
   b. What are the equilibrium price of a pizza and the equilibrium quantity of pizza?

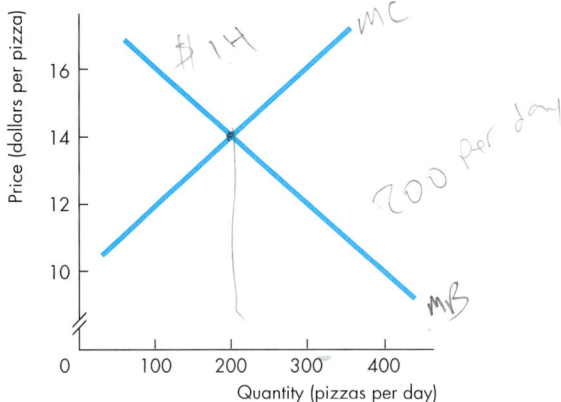

6. The figure illustrates the market for fish.
   a. Label the curves in the figure.
   b. What are the equilibrium price of a fish and the equilibrium quantity of fish?

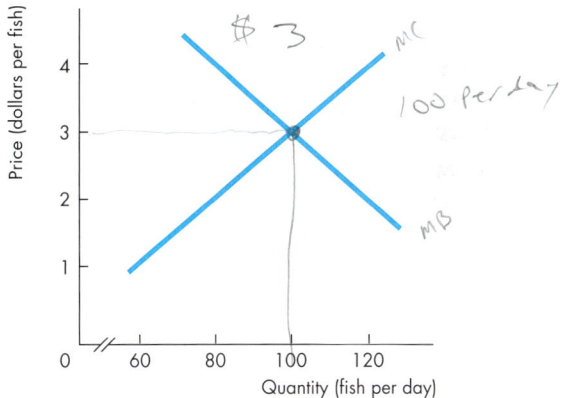

*7. The demand and supply schedules for gum are

| Price (cents per pack) | Quantity demanded | Quantity supplied |
|---|---|---|
| | (millions of packs a week) | |
| 20 | 180 | 60 |
| 30 | 160 | 80 |
| 40 | 140 | 100 |
| 50 | 120 | 120 |
| 60 | 100 | 140 |
| 70 | 80 | 160 |
| 80 | 60 | 180 |

   a. Draw a graph of the gum market and mark in the equilibrium price and quantity.

* Solutions to odd-numbered problems are available on MyEconLab.

b. Suppose that gum is 70 cents a pack. Describe the situation in the gum market and explain how the price of gum adjusts.

8. The demand and supply schedules for potato chips are

| Price (cents per bag) | Quantity demanded (millions of bags per week) | Quantity supplied (millions of bags per week) |
|---|---|---|
| 50 | 160 | 130 |
| 60 | 150 | 140 |
| 70 | 140 | 150 |
| 80 | 130 | 160 |
| 90 | 120 | 170 |
| 100 | 110 | 180 |

a. Draw a graph of the potato chip market and mark in the equilibrium price and quantity.
b. Suppose that chips are 60 cents a bag. Describe the situation in the market for chips and explain how the price adjusts.

*9. In problem 7, suppose that a fire destroys some gum-producing factories and the supply of gum decreases by 40 million packs a week.
  a. Has there been a shift of or a movement along the supply curve of gum?
  b. Has there been a shift of or a movement along the demand curve for gum?
  c. What are the new equilibrium price and equilibrium quantity of gum?

10. In problem 8, suppose a new dip comes onto the market, which is very popular and the demand for potato chips increases by 30 million bags per week.
  a. Has there been a shift of or a movement along the supply curve of potato chips?
  b. Has there been a shift of or a movement along the demand curve for potato chips?
  c. What are the new equilibrium price and equilibrium quantity of potato chips?

*11. In problem 9, suppose an increase in the teenage population increases the demand for gum by 40 million packs per week at the same time as the fire occurs. What are the new equilibrium price and quantity of gum?

12. In problem 10, suppose that a virus destroys several potato farms with the result that the supply of potato chips decreases by 40 million bags a week at the same time as the dip comes onto the market. What are the new equilibrium price and quantity of potato chips?

## CRITICAL THINKING

1. After you have studied *Reading Between the Lines* on pp. 74–75, answer the following questions:
   a. What happened to the relative price of gasoline between 1980 and 2003? In which year was the relative price the highest and in which was it the lowest?
   b. Why did the supply of gasoline decrease in August 2003?
   c. Why did the demand for gasoline increase in August 2003?
   d. Why did the equilibrium quantity of gasoline increase in August 2003?

## WEB EXERCISES

**Use the links on MyEconLab to work the following exercises.**

1. Obtain data on the prices and quantities of wheat.
   a. Make a figure similar to Fig. 3.7 on p. 68 to illustrate the market for wheat in 2001 and 2002.
   b. Show the changes in demand and supply and the changes in the quantity demanded and the quantity supplied that are consistent with the price and quantity data.

2. Obtain data on the price of oil.
   a. Describe how the price of oil has changed over the past five years.
   b. Draw a demand-supply graph to explain what happens to the price when there is an increase or a decrease in supply and no change in demand.
   c. What do you predict would happen to the price of oil if a new drilling technology permitted deeper ocean sources to be used?
   d. What do you predict would happen to the price of oil if a clean and safe nuclear technology were developed?
   e. What do you predict would happen to the price of oil if automobiles were powered by batteries instead of by internal combustion engines?

# UNDERSTANDING HOW MARKETS WORK

PART 2

## The Amazing Market

The four chapters that you've just studied explain how markets work. The market is an amazing instrument. It enables people who have never met and who know nothing about each other to interact and do business. It also enables us to allocate our scarce resources to the uses that we value most highly. Markets can be very simple or highly organized.

A simple market is one that the American historian Daniel J. Boorstin describes in The Discoverers (p. 161). In the late fourteenth century,

> The Muslim caravans that went southward from Morocco across the Atlas Mountains arrived after twenty days at the shores of the Senegal River. There the Moroccan traders laid out separate piles of salt, of beads from Ceutan coral, and cheap manufactured goods. Then they retreated out of sight. The local tribesmen, who lived in the strip mines where they dug their gold, came to the shore and put a heap of gold beside each pile of Moroccan goods. Then they, in turn, went out of view, leaving the Moroccan traders either to take the gold offered for a particular pile or to reduce the pile of their merchandise to suit the offered price in gold. Once again the Moroccan traders withdrew, and the process went on. By this system of commercial etiquette, the Moroccans collected their gold.

An organized market is the New York Stock Exchange, which trades many millions of stocks each day. Another is an auction at which the U.S. government sells rights to broadcasters and cellular telephone companies for the use of the airwaves.

All of these markets determine the prices at which exchanges take place and enable both buyers and sellers to benefit.

Everything and anything that can be exchanged is traded in markets. There are markets for goods and services; for resources such as labor, capital, and raw materials; for dollars, pounds, and yen; for goods to be delivered now and for goods to be delivered in the future. Only the imagination places limits on what can be traded in markets.

You began your study of markets in Chapter 3 by learning about the laws of demand and supply. There, you discovered the forces that make prices adjust to coordinate buying plans and selling plans. In Chapter 4, you learned how to calculate and use the concept of elasticity to predict the responsiveness of prices and quantities to changes in supply and demand. In Chapter 5, you studied efficiency and discovered the conditions under which a competitive market sends resources to uses in which they are valued most highly. And finally, in Chapter 6, you studied markets in action. There, you learned how markets cope with change and discovered how they operate when governments intervene to fix prices, impose taxes or quotas, or make some goods illegal.

The laws of demand and supply that you've learned and used in these four chapters were discovered during the nineteenth century by some remarkable economists. We conclude our study of demand and supply and markets by looking at the lives and times of some of these economists and by talking to one of today's most influential economists who studies markets using experimental methods.

# PROBING THE IDEAS

## Discovering the Laws of Demand and Supply

*"The forces to be dealt with are . . . so numerous, that it is best to take a few at a time. . . . Thus we begin by isolating the primary relations of supply, demand, and price"*

ALFRED
MARSHALL
*The Principles of Economics*

### THE ECONOMIST

**Alfred Marshall** *(1842–1924) grew up in an England that was being transformed by the railroad and by the expansion of manufacturing. Mary Paley was one of Marshall's students at Cambridge, and when Alfred and Mary married, in 1877, celibacy rules barred Alfred from continuing to teach at Cambridge. By 1884, with more liberal rules, the Marshalls returned to Cambridge, where Alfred became Professor of Political Economy.*

*Many others had a hand in refining the theory of demand and supply, but the first thorough and complete statement of the theory as we know it today was set out by Alfred Marshall, with the acknowledged help of Mary Paley Marshall. Published in 1890, this monumental treatise,* The Principles of Economics, *became the textbook on economics on both sides of the Atlantic for almost half a century. Marshall was an outstanding mathematician, but he kept mathematics and even diagrams in the background. His supply and demand diagram appears only in a footnote.*

### THE ISSUES

The laws of demand and supply that you studied in Chapter 3 were discovered during the 1830s by Antoine-Augustin Cournot (1801–1877), a professor of mathematics at the University of Lyon, France. Although Cournot was the first to use demand and supply, it was the development and expansion of the railroads during the 1850s that gave the newly emerging theory its first practical applications. Railroads then were at the cutting edge of technology just as airlines are today. And as in the airline industry today, competition among the railroads was fierce.

Dionysius Lardner (1793–1859), an Irish professor of philosophy at the University of London, used demand and supply to show railroad companies how they could increase their profits by cutting rates on long-distance business on which competition was fiercest and by raising rates on short-haul business on which they had less to fear from other transportation suppliers. Today, economists use the principles that Lardner worked out during the 1850s to calculate the freight rates and passenger fares that will give airlines the largest possible profit. And the rates calculated have a lot in common with the railroad rates of the nineteenth century. On local routes on which there is little competition, fares per mile are highest, and on long-distance routes on which the airlines compete fiercely, fares per mile are lowest.

Known satirically among scientists of the day as "Dionysius Diddler," Lardner worked on an amazing range of problems from astronomy to railway engineering to economics. A colorful character, he would have been a regular guest of David Letterman if late-night talk shows had been around in the 1850s. Lardner visited the École des Ponts et Chaussées (School of Bridges and Roads) in

Paris and must have learned a great deal from Jules Dupuit.

In France, Jules Dupuit (1804–1866), a French engineer/ economist, used demand to calculate the benefits from building a bridge and, once the bridge was built, for calculating the toll to charge for its use. His work was the forerunner of what is today called *cost-benefit analysis*. Working with the principles invented by Dupuit, economists today calculate the costs and benefits of highways and airports, dams, and power stations.

## THEN

Dupuit used the law of demand to determine whether a bridge or canal would be valued enough by its users to justify the cost of building it. Lardner first worked out the relationship between the cost of production and supply and used demand and supply theory to explain the costs, prices, and profits of railroad operations. He also used the theory to discover ways of increasing revenue by raising rates on short-haul business and lowering them on long-distance freight.

## NOW

Today, using the same principles that Dupuit devised, economists calculate whether the benefits of expanding airports and air-traffic control facilities are sufficient to cover their costs. Airline companies use the principles developed by Lardner to set their prices and to decide when to offer "seat sales." Like the railroads before them, the airlines charge a high price per mile on short flights, for which they face little competition, and a low price per mile on long flights, for which competition is fierce.

*Markets do an amazing job. And the laws of demand and supply help us to understand how markets work. But in some situations, a market must be designed and institutions must be created to enable the market to operate. In recent years, economists have begun to use experiments to design and create markets. And one of the chief architects of experimental methods in economics is Charles Plott, whom you can meet on the following pages.*

# TALKING WITH

***Charles R. Plott***, Edward S. Harkness Professor of Economics and Political Science at the California Institute of Technology, is a leading pioneer in the use of laboratory experimental methods in economics.

Born in 1938 in Frederick, Oklahoma, he was an undergraduate at Oklahoma State University and a graduate student at the University of Virginia.

Professor Plott's research has led to some of the most fundamental discoveries in economics and political science. He has studied such practical problems as those of allocating landing rights at airports, allocating resources on the International Space Station, operating markets for emissions permits, designing mechanisms for pricing the use of natural gas pipelines, electric power, and the right to use railroad tracks, and the design and implementation of auction markets for the frequency spectrum used by your cell phone.

Professor Plott has recently designed experimental tools that enable people from around the world to participate in a single experimental market.

Michael Parkin talked with Charles Plott about his career and the progress that economists have made in understanding behavior in markets by using experimental methods.

**Charles R. Plott**

*What sparked your interest in economics and led to your decision to become an economist?*

The beauty of economics as a coherent and immediately relevant science attracted me. Economics has an amazing capacity to summarize staggeringly complex phenomena by the application of only a handful of principles. Furthermore, it works. Economic principles lead to an understanding of the complex world around us better than any other branch of science or philosophy.

*The accuracy of the demand and supply model is an amazing fact of life. Why it works remains a mystery.*

*How does the demand and supply model of Alfred Marshall stand up today in the light of the progress that economists have made?*

The accuracy of the demand and supply model is an amazing fact of life. Why it works remains a mystery. We continue in our attempts to improve the principle, or replace it with a different set of principles but so far that has not happened. Through the application of experimental methods we can now understand features of its operation and how its operation can be influenced by institutions. But, Marshall's basic principle still remains as the best understanding of how markets work.

*What can we learn about how competitive markets work in classroom experiments?*

Learning economics through experiments is really the same as using experiments to learn about any other science. Experiments are used because naturally occurring phenomena, as they are found in nature, are too complex to understand. When left on her own, Nature does not create circumstances that allow us to clearly view the principles at work.

Science is also about communication and the building of knowledge. All science is about creating simple situations that can serve as the lens through which one person can experience for himself or herself what other persons report to have experienced.

In classroom experiments the students see for themselves the operations of the principles of economics reported in the book. For example, price determination when there are a few people on each side of a market is accurately described by the mathematical structure of the competitive model as found in the book. However, just because the principles are reported authoritatively in the book does not mean that the student should simply accept them. The principles are not sermons to be memorized, they are tools to be used, once they are understood. True understanding only follows evidence on how they work. The experiments demonstrate and clarify the principles that are in operation.

*Can we learn even more by doing Web-based experiments? What in particular are the gains from running global experiments like those that you've designed?*
The major advantages of web based experiments are size and complexity. Economies are large and interdependent. The creation of economies that are at once sufficiently simple to understand but also reflect the interdependence that is the substance of some central economic theories requires a large number of people. The web allows the creation of such economies. In addition, the web demonstrates that culture, location, personality, ethnic background, etc. have little to do with the basic principles of economics. This profound generality of the principles of economics is hard for people to accept and the web experiments allow them to see the evidence for themselves.

*What do the experiments that you and others have conducted tell us about the harmony or conflict between self-interested choices and the social interest?*
Adam Smith says it remarkably well. He tells us that social interest is served by self-interest but he leaves out a step that we know is needed. The relationship between self-interest and social interest depends on the social institutions. For example, the lack of appropriate property rights can transform a well functioning and wealth creating system into a commons dilemma. Failure to protect property can result in poverty because the self-interest of those who would steal is focused on wealth destroying activities as opposed to wealth creating activities. We seem to have little control over human nature but we do have control over the institutional environment within which humans interact. Economics tells us to look to the structure of that institutional environment if we are concerned about social issues. Experimental evidence supports that emphasis.

*Some people are skeptical about experiments.*
In all branches of science there are people who are skeptical of experimental methods. For the most part they are people who either do not understand the indirect and round about ways of science or are impatient. We have all heard comments to the effect that "It is great in the lab but has nothing to do with the real world." Such comments are heard in all sciences, not only in economics, and they seem directed as criticisms of basic science in general and not simply the use of experiments in that process.

Science is indirect and experiments are part of that process. Experiments are simple situations that inform us about principles. The principles inform us about theory. The resulting theory helps us understand phenomena that are vastly more complex than can be observed in experiments. The many successes of experiments in economics demonstrate the value of the methodology.

*What are some of the easily disposed of criticisms?*
Most criticisms are not of experiments or experimental methods in general. They are criticisms of particular experiments conducted. The criticisms suggest that the experiment did not answer a question that the critic wanted answered. For example, critics can be heard declaring that experimental economics is "irrelevant" because the subjects were students, were

not businessmen, did not have sufficient incentives, were not representative, etc. etc. In markets critics might say that there were too many subjects, or too few subjects or incorrect relative size of subjects or that the markets should have been organized differently, etc. etc. It is important to recognize that these are not criticisms of the use of experiments. They are actually a call for additional experiments of the sort that would address the issue posed by the critic. Of course, the particular questions about the effect of variables related to subject selection have been addressed experimentally many times and for the most part they are variables that have no effect at all on how the theories perform. Similarly, many different variations of markets and market organization have also been studied.

Basically, such criticisms are only complaints that the experimenter did not do the research that the critic would like done. Such critics want someone to do their research for them.

From time to time we notice that critics simply do not know what has been learned from experiments, or more importantly, they do not know how experiments are conducted. They imagine what experimentalists do and then direct their criticisms to what they have imagined. Of course, in those cases, their idea of what experimental economists do is nowhere near what is actually done.

### Are there any compelling criticisms of the experimental approach? How do you respond to them?

There are many important questions that cannot be answered by the use of experimental methods. That is the case in economics as it is the case in any other science. If one wants to know specific facts about the U.S. economy or any other economy then one must study the economy as it is found in nature. It is silly to think about creating the whole economy in a laboratory for replication and study. How does one respond when someone poses a question that experiments cannot answer? Just simply say that they are correct and add examples to the list.

Experimentation is a method that is sometimes useful and sometimes not. The fact that experiments cannot answer all questions does not mean that there are no questions at all that experiments can answer.

One can just as easily turn the discussion around by posing questions that can only be answered by application of experimental methods. Almost all subtle issues of theory fall in the latter class.

### Have experiments helped economists to design better auction markets or better allocations of resources? How do we know that we've achieved a better outcome?

Your question is about the jump from basic science to applications. It is like the jump from physics to engineering. There have been many successful applications for business and government.

When a process is designed and tested in the lab we know something about the principles at work. We know something about the reliability of those principles and we have measurements that inform us about how well the process is working. When one then moves from the laboratory and implements a design in nature, the controls and measuring devices of the laboratory are not available. Consequently, one never knows for sure that the process is working according to theory. However, we do know that the problem that the design was intended to fix no longer appears so in that sense we know that the design is working—for some reason or another. Of course, we do not really know that it is working for the right reasons—the right reasons being the theory that led to the design in the first place.

### What is your advice to a student who is just setting out to become an economist? Is economics a good subject in which to major?

Economics is a good background for all of the social sciences, business, management and law. It is also very useful in engineering. It is a central body of science with broad principles that have applications throughout most other fields. So, regardless of what the student plans as a profession, economics is a good place to start. Those who want to become professional economists should understand that it is a technical subject as is any other science or engineering.

### What other subjects work well with economics?

I think that both mathematics and statistics are important if one is going into the scientific end of economics.

# PART 3    Macroeconomic Overview

# A First Look at Macroeconomics

CHAPTER 4

## What Will Your World Be Like?

**During the past 100 years, the quantity of goods** and services produced in the nation's farms, factories, shops, and offices has expanded more than twentyfold. As a result, we have a much higher standard of living than our grandparents had. Will production always expand?

For most of us, a high standard of living means finding a good job. What kind of job will you find when you graduate? Will you have lots of choices, or will you face a labor market with a high unemployment rate in which jobs are hard to find?

A high standard of living means being able to afford to buy life's necessities and have some fun. If prices rise too quickly, some people get left behind and must cut back on what they buy. What will the dollar buy next year; in 10 years when you are paying off your student loan; and in 50 years when you are spending your life's savings in retirement?

Almost every year for the past 30 years, the U.S. government has spent more than it has raised in taxes. And most years, we have imported more goods and services from the rest of the world than we have exported to it. We have large and persistent government and international deficits. How will these deficits affect your future?

To keep production expanding and prevent an economic slowdown, the federal government and the Federal Reserve Board—the nation's financial managers—take policy actions. How do their actions influence production, jobs, prices, and the ability of Americans to compete in the global marketplace?

◆ These are the questions of macroeconomics that you are about to study. The macroeconomic events through which we are living today are tumultuous and exciting. With what you learn in these chapters, you will be able to understand these events, the policy challenges they bring, and the political debate they stir. You will be able to prepare yourself better for your world—the economic world that you enter when you graduate and in which you will earn your living.

### After studying this chapter, you will be able to

■ Describe the origins of macroeconomics and the problems it deals with

■ Describe the long-term trends and short-term fluctuations in economic growth, unemployment, inflation, and government and international deficits

■ Explain why economic growth, unemployment, inflation, and deficits matter

■ Identify the macroeconomic policy challenges and describe the tools available for meeting them

## Origins and Issues of Macroeconomics

ECONOMISTS BEGAN TO STUDY ECONOMIC growth, inflation, and international payments as long ago as the 1750s, and this work was the origin of macroeconomics. But modern macroeconomics did not emerge until the **Great Depression**, a decade (1929–1939) of high unemployment and stagnant production throughout the world economy. In the Depression's worst year, 1933, the production of U.S. farms, factories, shops, and offices was only 70 percent of its 1929 level and 25 percent of the labor force was unemployed. These were years of human misery on a scale that is hard to imagine today. They were also years of extreme pessimism about the ability of the market economy to work properly. Many people believed that private ownership, free markets, and democratic political institutions could not survive.

The science of economics had no solutions to the Great Depression. The major alternative system of central planning and socialism seemed increasingly attractive to many people. It was in this climate of economic depression and political and intellectual turmoil that modern macroeconomics emerged with the publication in 1936 of John Maynard Keynes' *The General Theory of Employment, Interest, and Money*.

### Short-Term Versus Long-Term Goals

Keynes' theory was that depression and high unemployment result from insufficient private spending and that to cure these problems, the government must increase its spending. Keynes focused primarily on the *short term*. He wanted to cure an immediate problem almost regardless of the *long-term* consequences of the cure. "In the long run," said Keynes, "we're all dead."

But Keynes believed that after his cure for depression had restored the economy to a normal condition, the long-term problems of inflation and slow economic growth would return. And he suspected that his cure for depression, increased government spending, might trigger inflation and might lower the long-term growth rate of production. With a lower long-term growth rate, the economy would create fewer jobs. If this outcome did occur, a policy aimed at lowering unemployment in the short run might end up increasing it in the long run.

By the late 1960s and through the 1970s, Keynes' predictions became a reality. Inflation increased, economic growth slowed, and in some countries unemployment became persistently high. The causes of these developments are complex. But they point to an inescapable conclusion: The long-term problems of inflation, slow growth, and persistent unemployment and the short-term problems of depression and economic fluctuations intertwine and are most usefully studied together. So although macroeconomics was reborn during the Great Depression, it has now returned to its older tradition. Today, macroeconomics is a subject that studies long-term economic growth and inflation as well as short-term business fluctuations and unemployment.

### The Road Ahead

There is no unique way to study macroeconomics. Because its rebirth was a product of depression, the common practice for many years was to pay most attention to short-term output fluctuations and unemployment but never to completely lose sight of the long-term issues. When a rapid inflation emerged during the 1970s, this topic returned to prominence. During the 1980s, when long-term growth slowed in the United States and other rich industrial countries but exploded in East Asia, economists redirected their energy toward economic growth. During the 1990s, as information technologies further shrank the globe, the international dimension of macroeconomics became more prominent. The result of these developments is that modern macroeconomics is a broad subject that studies all the issues we've just identified: long-term economic growth, unemployment, and inflation. It also studies two new problems: government budget deficit and U.S. international deficit.

Over the past 40 years, economists have developed a clearer understanding of the forces that determine macroeconomic performance and have devised policies that they hope will improve this performance. Your main goal is to become familiar with the theories of macroeconomics and the policies that they make possible. To set you on your path toward this goal, we're going to take a first look at economic growth, unemployment, inflation, and surpluses and deficits and learn why these macroeconomic phenomena merit our attention.

# Economic Growth and Fluctuations

YOUR PARENTS ARE RICHER THAN YOUR GRANDparents were when they were young. But are you going to be richer than your parents are? And are your children going to be richer than you? The answers depend on the rate of economic growth.

**Economic growth** is the expansion of the economy's production possibilities. It can be pictured as an outward shift of the production possibilities frontier (PPF).

We measure economic growth by the increase in real gross domestic product. **Real gross domestic product** (also called **real GDP**) is the value of the total production of all the nation's farms, factories, shops, and offices measured in the prices of a single year. Real GDP in the United States is currently measured in the prices of 2000 (called 2000 dollars). We use the dollar prices of a single year to eliminate the influence of *inflation*—the increase in the average level of prices—and determine how much production has grown from one year to another.

Real GDP is not a perfect measure of total production because it does not include everything that is produced. It excludes the things we produce for ourselves at home (preparing meals, doing laundry, house painting, gardening, and so on). It also excludes production that people hide to avoid taxes or because the activity is illegal—the underground economy. But despite its shortcomings, real GDP is the best measure of total production available. Let's see what it tells us about economic growth.

## Economic Growth in the United States

Figure 4.1 shows real GDP in the United States since 1962 and highlights two features of economic growth:

- The growth of potential GDP
- Fluctuations of real GDP around potential GDP

**The Growth of Potential GDP** When all the economy's labor, capital, land, and entrepreneurial ability are fully employed, the value of production is called **potential GDP**. Real GDP fluctuates around potential GDP and the rate of long-term economic growth is measured by the growth rate of potential GDP. It is shown by the steepness of the potential GDP line (the black line) in Fig. 4.1.

During the 1960s, real GDP grew at an unusually rapid rate. But the growth rate of output per person slowed during the 1970s, a phenomenon called the **productivity growth slowdown**. Real GDP began to grow more rapidly during the late 1980s and through the 1990s. But the high growth rate of the 1960s did not return.

Why did the productivity growth slowdown occur? The answer to this question is controversial. One possible cause is a sharp rise in the relative price of energy. We explore the causes of the productivity growth slowdown in Chapter 9. Whatever its cause, a productivity growth slowdown means that we all have smaller incomes today than we would have had if the economy had continued to grow at its rate of the 1960s.

Let's now look at GDP fluctuations.

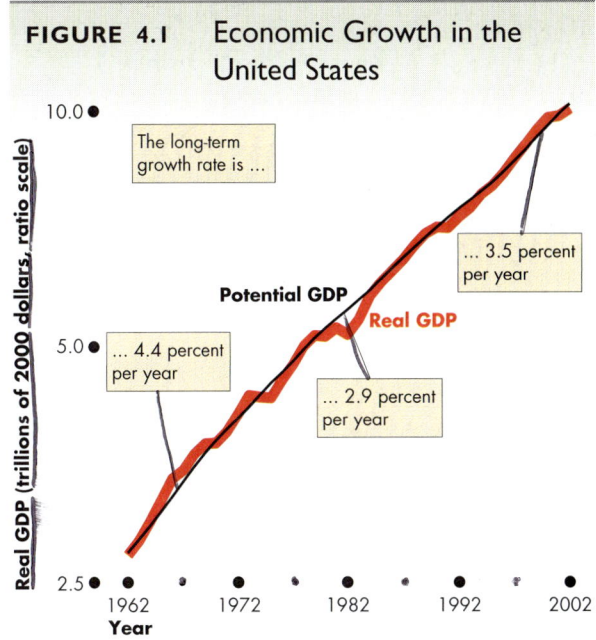

**FIGURE 4.1  Economic Growth in the United States**

The long-term economic growth rate, measured by the growth of potential GDP, was 4.4 percent a year during the 1960s. Growth slowed to 2.9 percent during the 1970s. Growth speeded up again during the 1980s and 1990s but did not return to its 1960s rate. Real GDP fluctuates around potential GDP.

*Source:* U.S. Department of Commerce, *National Income and Product Accounts of the United States.*

## Fluctuations of Real GDP Around Potential GDP

Real GDP fluctuates around potential GDP in a business cycle. A **business cycle** is the periodic but irregular up-and-down movement in production. It is measured by fluctuations in real GDP around potential GDP. When real GDP is less than potential GDP, some resources are underused. For example, some labor is unemployed and capital is underutilized. When real GDP is greater than potential GDP, resources are being overused. Many people work longer hours than they are willing to put up with in the long run, capital is worked so intensively that it is not maintained in prime working order, delivery times lengthen, bottlenecks occur, and backorders increase.

Business cycles are not regular, predictable, or repeating cycles like the phases of the moon. Their timing changes unpredictably, but they do have some things in common. Every business cycle has two phases:

1. A recession
2. An expansion

and two turning points:

1. A peak
2. A trough

Figure 4.2 shows these features of the most recent business cycle in the United States. A common definition of **recession** is a period during which real GDP decreases—its growth rate is negative—for at least two successive quarters. The most recent recession, which is highlighted in the figure, began in the first quarter of 2001 and ended in the third quarter of 2001. This recession lasted for three quarters. An **expansion** is a period during which real GDP increases. The most recent expansion began in the fourth quarter of 2001. The earlier expansion that began in the second quarter of 1991 was the longest expansion on record.

When an expansion ends and a recession begins, the turning point is called a *peak*. The most recent peak occurred in the fourth quarter of 2000. When a recession ends and a recovery begins, the turning point is called a *trough*. The most recent trough occurred in the fourth quarter of 2001.

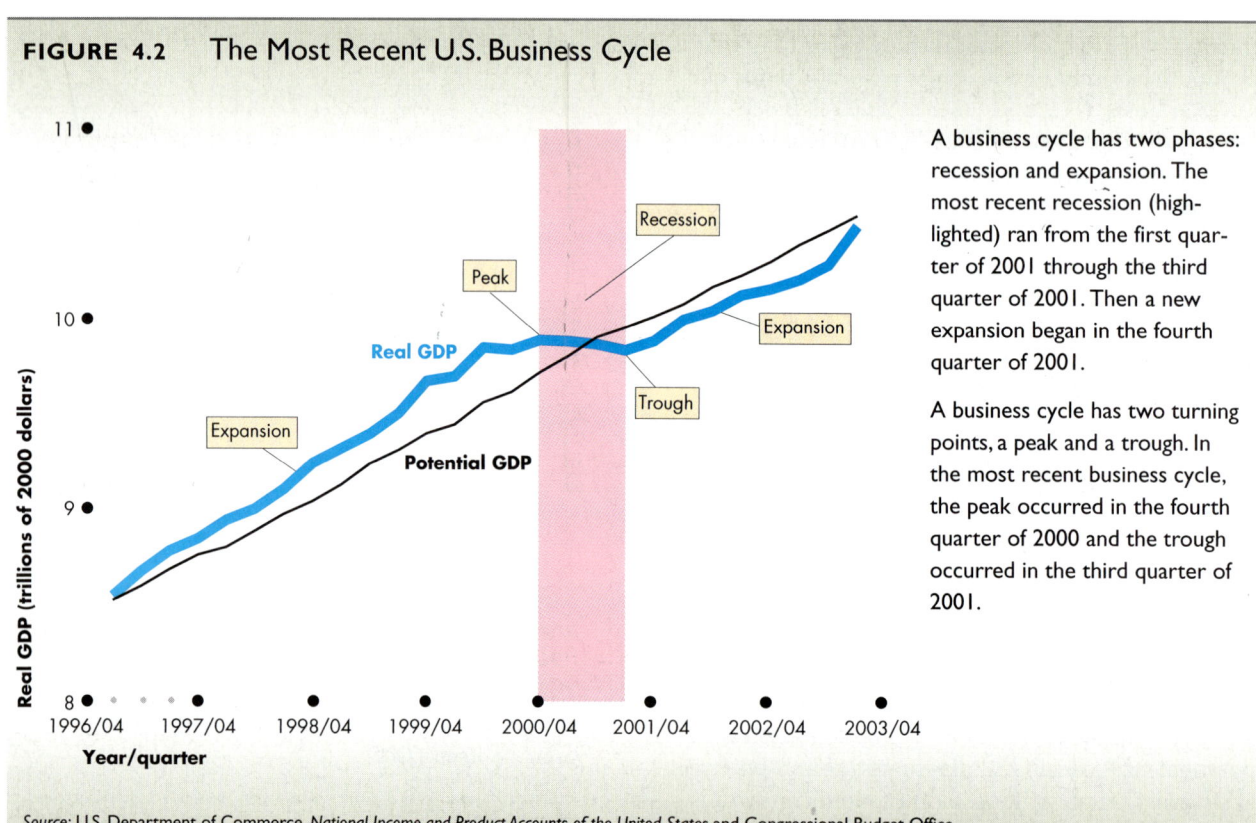

**FIGURE 4.2** The Most Recent U.S. Business Cycle

A business cycle has two phases: recession and expansion. The most recent recession (highlighted) ran from the first quarter of 2001 through the third quarter of 2001. Then a new expansion began in the fourth quarter of 2001.

A business cycle has two turning points, a peak and a trough. In the most recent business cycle, the peak occurred in the fourth quarter of 2000 and the trough occurred in the third quarter of 2001.

*Source:* U.S. Department of Commerce, *National Income and Product Accounts of the United States* and Congressional Budget Office.

**The Most Recent Recession in Historical Perspective** The recession of 2001 was milder than the recessions of 1990–1991 and 1982, but compared to earlier recessions these recessions were mild. You can see how mild they were by looking at Fig. 4.3, which shows a longer history of U.S. economic growth. The biggest decrease in real GDP occurred during the Great Depression of the 1930s. A large decrease also occurred in 1946 and 1947, after a huge World War II expansion. In more recent times, serious recessions occurred during the mid-1970s and during the early 1980s.

Each of these economic downturns was more severe than those in 1990–1991 and 2001. But you can see that the Great Depression was much more severe than anything that followed it. This episode was so extreme that we don't call it a recession. We call it a *depression*.

This last truly great depression occurred before the government started taking policy actions to stabilize the economy. It also occurred before the birth of modern macroeconomics. Is the absence of another great depression a sign that macroeconomics has contributed to economic stability? Some people believe it is. Others doubt it. We'll evaluate these opinions on a number of occasions in this book.

We've looked at real GDP growth and fluctuations in the United States. But is the U.S. experience typical? Do other countries share our experience? Let's see whether they do.

## Economic Growth Around the World

All countries experience economic growth, but the growth rate varies both over time and across countries. The fluctuations in economic growth rates over time tend to be correlated across countries, but some countries experience greater volatility in growth rates than others. And some growth rate differences across countries persist over a number of years.

We'll compare U.S. economic growth over time with that in other countries. And we'll look at longer term differences in growth rates among countries and groups of countries.

**Growth Rates over Time** First, we'll compare the growth rate of real GDP in the United States with that for the rest of the world as a whole. Figure 4.4(a)

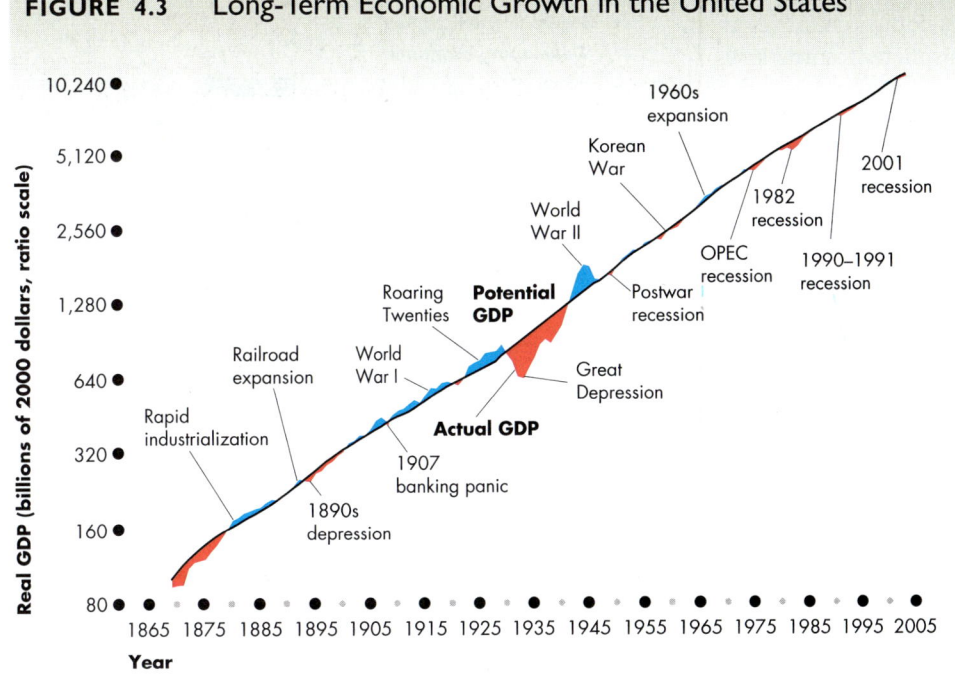

**FIGURE 4.3** Long-Term Economic Growth in the United States

The thin black line shows potential GDP. Along this line, real GDP grew at an average rate of 3.7 percent a year between 1870 and 2002. The blue areas show when real GDP was above potential GDP, and the red areas show when it was below potential GDP. During some periods, such as World War II, real GDP expanded quickly. During other periods, such as the Great Depression and more recently in 1975, 1982, 1990–1991, and 2001, real GDP declined.

Sources: 1869–1928, Christina Romer, "The Prewar Business Cycle Reconsidered: New Estimates of Gross National Product, 1869–1908," *Journal of Political Economy* 97, (1989) 1–37. 1929–2002, U.S. Department of Commerce, *National Income and Product Accounts of the United States*.

shows these two growth rates from 1972 to 2002. (Note that this figure graphs *growth rates* of real GDP and not *levels* of real GDP that the three previous figures showed. So the number on the *y*-axis of this graph is a rate of growth expressed as percent per year.)

You can see a striking fact in Fig. 4.4(a). The U.S. real GDP growth rate fluctuates much more than the real GDP growth rate in the rest of the world as a whole. In several years, U.S. real GDP actually falls—a negative growth rate—but the rest of the world never has negative growth during the 30 years shown in the figure.

**Persistent Differences in Growth Rates** Second, we'll look at longer term persistent differences across countries. Figure 4.4(b) compares the growth of the U.S. economy with that of several other countries and regions from 1992 through 2002. Among the advanced economies (the red bars), Japan has grown the slowest and the newly industrialized Asian economies have grown fastest. The United States is in the middle of these two growth rates.

Among the developing economies (the green bars) the most rapid growth has occurred in Asia, where the average growth rate was almost 8 percent a year. The slowest growing developing countries are in Africa and the Western Hemisphere (Central and South America).

The transition economies (purple bar) didn't grow at all during the ten years covered by Fig. 4.4(b). These are countries such as Russia and the other countries of Central Europe that are making a transition from a state-managed economy to a market economy. Production shrank in these countries.

World average growth (the blue bar) has been a bit more than 3 percent a year, and slightly greater than the U.S. growth rate.

**Consequences of Persistent Differences** The persistent differences in growth rates are bringing dramatic change to the share of some nations in world real GDP. Because the U.S. real GDP growth rate almost equals that of the rest of the world, the U.S. share of world real GDP is almost constant and is about 21 percent. But some fast-growing nations such as China are becoming a significantly bigger part of the global economy. China's share of world real GDP has increased from 4 percent in 1982 to 13 percent in 2002 and the share continues to grow.

**FIGURE 4.4  Economic Growth Around the World**

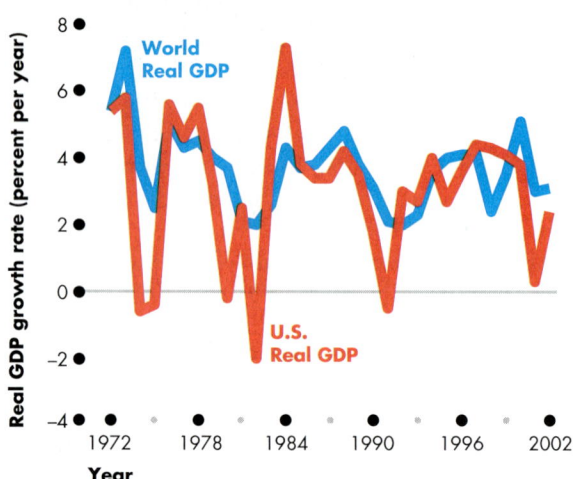

(a) The United States and the rest of the world: 1972–2002

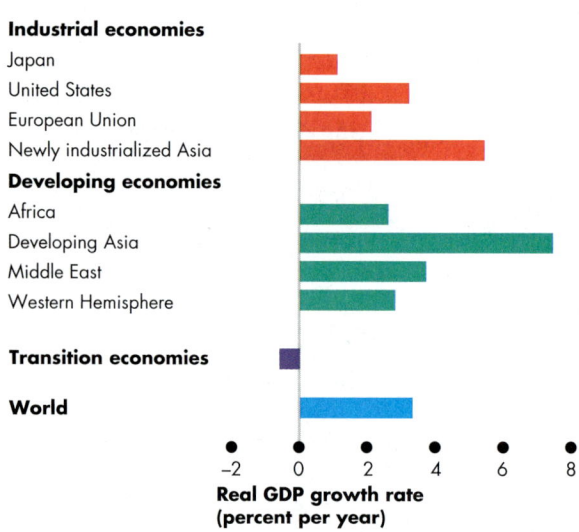

(b) Countries and regions compared: 1992–2002 average

In part (a), U.S. economic growth fluctuates much more than that in the rest of the world as a whole, but the fluctuations across countries are correlated.

In part (b), growth rate differences persist. Between 1992 and 2002, Asian economies grew fastest and transition economies shrank. The U.S. growth rate is in the middle of the pack and is similar to the world average growth rate.

*Source:* International Monetary Fund, *World Economic Outlook*, September 2003, Washington, D.C.

## The Lucas Wedge and the Okun Gap

You've seen that productivity growth slowed during the 1970s. And you've seen that real GDP growth fluctuates so that real GDP falls below potential GDP from time to time. How costly are the growth slowdown and lost output over the business cycle?

The answers are provided by two measures:

- The Lucas wedge
- The Okun gap

**The Lucas Wedge** The **Lucas wedge** is the accumulated loss of output that results from a slowdown in the growth rate of real GDP per person. It is given this name because Robert E. Lucas Jr., a leading macroeconomist, drew attention to it and remarked that once you begin to think about the benefits of faster economic growth, it is hard to think about anything else!

Figure 4.5(a) shows the Lucas wedge that arises from the productivity growth slowdown of the 1970s. The black line in the figure tracks the path that potential GDP would have followed if its 1960s growth rate had been maintained through the next 33 years to 2003.

The Lucas wedge is a staggering $50 trillion—almost five years' real GDP at the 2003 level. This number is a measure of the cost of slower productivity growth.

**The Okun Gap** The **Okun gap** is the gap between real GDP and potential GDP, and so is another name for the *output gap*. It is given this name because Arthur M. Okun, a policy economist who was chairman of President Lyndon Johnson's council of economic advisors during the 1960s, drew attention to it as a source of loss from economic fluctuations.

Figure 4.5(b) shows the Okun gap from the recessions that occurred over the same years as those for which we've just calculated the Lucas wedge.

The Okun gap is $2.7 trillion—about one quarter of real GDP in 2003. This number is a measure of the cost of business cycle fluctuations.

You can see that the Lucas wedge is a much bigger deal than the Okun gap—almost *twenty* times as big a deal! Smoothing the business cycle saves spells of high unemployment and lost output. But maintaining a high rate of productivity growth makes a dramatic difference to the standard of living over a number of years.

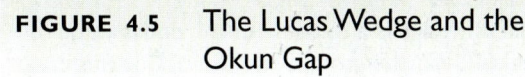

**FIGURE 4.5** The Lucas Wedge and the Okun Gap

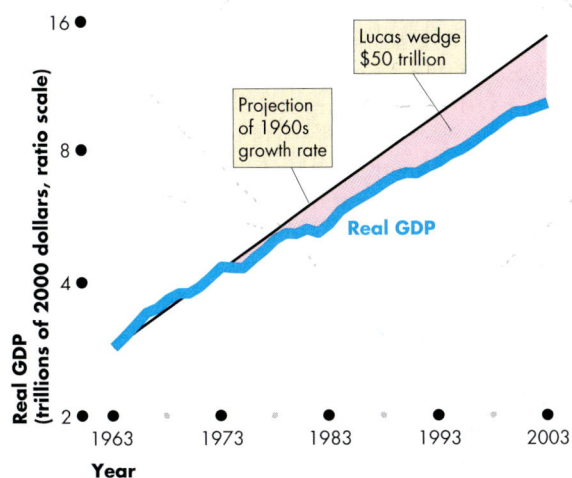

(a) The Lucas wedge

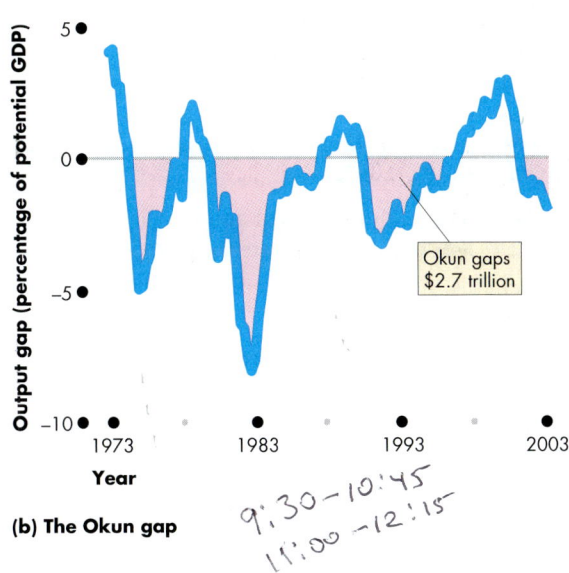

(b) The Okun gap

In part (a), the Lucas wedge that arises from the productivity growth slowdown of the 1970s is a staggering $50 trillion or almost 5 times the real GDP of 2003.

In part (b), the Okun gap that arises from the lost production in recessions since the early 1970s amount to $2.7 trillion or about one quarter of real GDP in 2003.

Over this 33-year period, the Lucas wedge is almost 20 times as large as the Okun gap.

*Source:* Bureau of Economic Analysis and author's assumptions.

### Benefits and Costs of Economic Growth

The Lucas wedge is a measure of the dollar value of lost real GDP if the growth rate slows. But this cost translates into real goods and services. It is a cost in terms of less health care for the poor and elderly, less cancer and AIDS research, less space research and exploration, worse roads, and less housing. We even have less to spend on cleaner lakes, more trees, and cleaner air.

But fast growth is also costly. Its main cost is forgone *current* consumption. To sustain a high growth rate, resources must be devoted to advancing technology and accumulating capital rather than to *current* consumption. This cost cannot be avoided. But it brings the benefit of greater consumption in the future. (See Chapter 2, p. 38.)

Two other possible costs of faster growth are a more rapid depletion of exhaustible natural resources such as oil and natural gas and increased pollution of the air, rivers, and oceans. But neither of these two costs is inevitable. The technological advances that bring economic growth help us to economize on natural resources and to clean up the environment. For example, more efficient auto engines cut gasoline use and tailpipe emissions.

#### REVIEW QUIZ

1. What is economic growth and how is the long-term economic growth rate measured?
2. What is the distinction between real GDP and potential GDP?
3. What is a business cycle and what are its phases?
4. What is a recession?
5. In what phase of the business cycle was the U.S. economy during 2003?
6. What happened to economic growth in the United States during the 1970s?
7. What are the benefits and the costs of long-term economic growth?

We've seen that real GDP grows and that it fluctuates over the business cycle. The business cycle brings fluctuations in jobs and unemployment. Let's now examine these core macroeconomic problems.

## Jobs and Unemployment

WHAT KIND OF LABOR MARKET WILL YOU ENTER when you graduate? Will there be plenty of good jobs to choose from, or will there be so much unemployment that you will be forced to take a low-paying job that doesn't use your education? The answer depends, to a large degree, on the total number of jobs available and on the unemployment rate.

### Jobs

The U.S. economy is an incredible job-creating machine. In 2003, 137 million people had jobs—17 million more than in 1993 and 37 million more than in 1983. But the pace of job creation fluctuates and during a recession, the number of jobs shrinks. For example, during the recession of 1990–1991, more than 1 million jobs were lost, and during the 2001 recession, 2 million jobs disappeared.

Through the expansions that follow a recession, more jobs are created than the number previously lost. For example, during the expansion of the 1990s, 2 million jobs were created each year. During the expansion of 2002 and 2003, job creation was slow and the number of jobs returned to its 2001 peak only toward the end of 2003.

The jobs created are not the same as those lost. Most new jobs are in the service industries. Jobs in manufacturing shrink each year because we buy more of our consumer goods from cheaper foreign sources. Some people worry that we are exporting our best jobs, but the truth is that, on the average, the new jobs are better than the ones lost and pay higher wages.

### Unemployment

Not everyone who wants a job can find one. On any one day in a normal or average year, 7 million people are unemployed, and during a recession or depression, unemployment rises above this level. For example, in the recession of 1991 and again in 2003, almost 9 million people were looking for jobs. In the booming economic conditions of 1999, the number of job seekers fell to 6 million.

These unemployment numbers are large. The number of people unemployed during a recession is equivalent to the population of Los Angeles. And even in a boom, the number is equivalent to the population of Chicago!

To place the number of unemployed people in perspective, we use a measure called the unemployment rate. The **unemployment rate** is the number of unemployed people expressed as a percentage of all the people who have jobs or are looking for one. (The concept of the unemployment rate, along with some other measures of the labor market, is explained more fully in Chapter 6.)

The unemployment rate is not a perfect measure of the underutilization of labor for two main reasons. First, it excludes people who are so discouraged that they've given up the effort to find work. Second, the unemployment rate measures unemployed people rather than unemployed labor hours. So the unemployment rate doesn't tell us about the numbers of part-time workers who want full-time jobs.

Despite these two limitations, the unemployment rate is the best available measure of underused labor resources. Let's look at some facts about unemployment.

## Unemployment in the United States

Figure 4.6 shows the unemployment rate in the United States from 1928 through 2003. Three features stand out. First, during the Great Depression of the 1930s, the unemployment rate climbed to an all-time high of 25 percent in 1933 and remained high throughout the 1930s. After 1934, the official rate probably overstates unemployment because it counts as unemployed the people who had make-work jobs created by the government.

Second, although in recent years we have not experienced anything as devastating as the Great Depression, we have seen some high unemployment rates during recessions. The figure highlights three of them—the OPEC recession of the mid-1970s, the 1982 recession, and the 1990–1991 recession.

Third, unemployment never falls to zero. In the period since World War II, the average unemployment rate has been close to 6 percent.

How does U.S. unemployment compare with unemployment in other countries?

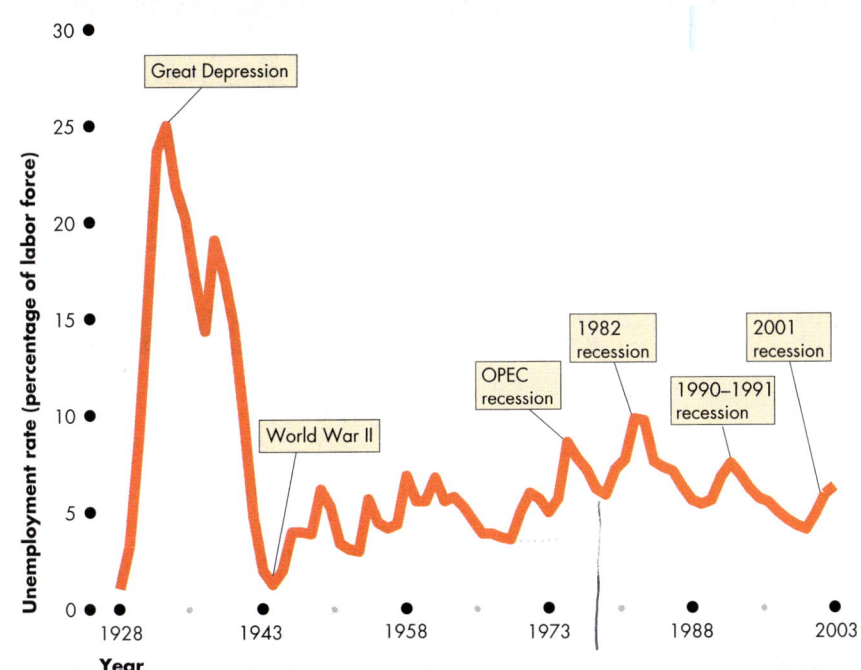

**FIGURE 4.6** Unemployment in the United States

Unemployment is a persistent feature of economic life, but its rate varies. At its worst—during the Great Depression—25 percent of the labor force was unemployed. In the 1982 recession, the unemployment rate climbed toward 10 percent. In the 1990–1991 and 2001 recessions, the unemployment rate climbed above 5 percent. Between the late 1960s and 1982, there was a general tendency for the unemployment rate to increase. Since then the unemployment rate has remained below its 1982 peak. The unemployment rate fell during the 1990s expansion.

*Source:* Bureau of Labor Statistics.

## Unemployment Around the World

Figure 4.7 shows the unemployment rate in Canada, Western Europe, and Japan, and compares them with the unemployment rate in the United States. Over the period shown in this figure, U.S. unemployment averaged 6.3 percent, much higher than Japanese unemployment, which averaged 3.1 percent, but lower than Canadian unemployment, which averaged 9.1 percent and European unemployment, which averaged 9 percent.

U.S. unemployment fluctuates over the business cycle. It increases during a recession and decreases during an expansion. Like U.S. unemployment, Canadian and European unemployment increase during recessions and decrease during expansions. The cycle in Canadian unemployment is similar to that in U.S. unemployment, but the European cycle is out of phase with the U.S. cycle. Also, European unemployment was on a rising trend through the 1980s. In contrast with other countries, Japanese unemployment has remained relatively stable, but has drifted upward in recent years.

We've looked at some facts about unemployment in the United States and in other countries. Let's now look at some of the consequences of unemployment that make it a serious problem.

## Why Unemployment Is a Problem

Unemployment is a serious economic, social, and personal problem for two main reasons:

- Lost production and incomes
- Lost human capital

**Lost Production and Incomes** The loss of a job brings an immediate loss of income and production. These losses are devastating for the people who bear them and make unemployment a frightening prospect for everyone. Employment insurance creates a safety net, but it does not provide the same living standard that having a job provides.

**Lost Human Capital** Prolonged unemployment can permanently damage a person's job prospects. For example, a manager loses his job when his employer downsizes. Short of income, he becomes a taxi driver. After a year in this work, he discovers that he can't compete with new MBA graduates. He eventually gets hired as a manager but in a small firm and at a low wage. He has lost some of his human capital.

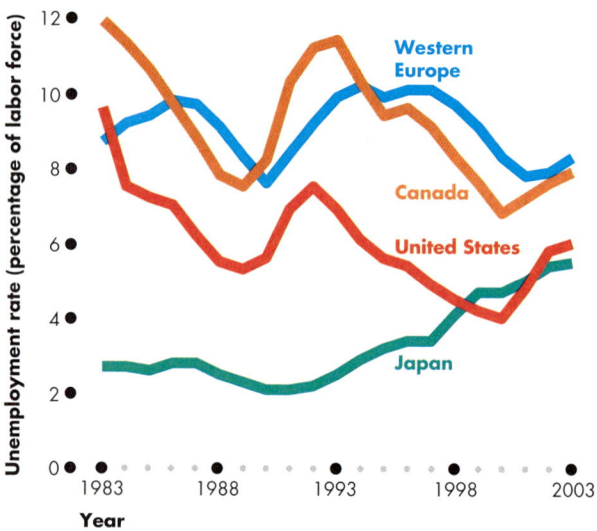

**FIGURE 4.7** Unemployment in Industrial Economies

The unemployment rate in the United States has been lower than that in Canada and Western Europe but higher than that in Japan. The cycle in Canadian unemployment is similar to that in the United States. Western European unemployment has a cycle that is out of phase with the U.S. unemployment cycle. Unemployment in Japan has drifted upward in recent years.

*Source:* International Monetary Fund, *World Economic Outlook*, September 2003, Washington, D.C.

The costs of unemployment are spread unequally, which makes unemployment a highly charged political problem as well as a serious economic problem.

### REVIEW QUIZ

1. What is unemployment?
2. What have been the main trends and cycles in the U.S. unemployment rate since 1926?
3. How does unemployment in the United States compare with unemployment in Canada, Western Europe, and Japan?
4. What are the main costs of unemployment that make it a serious problem?

Let's now turn to the third major macroeconomic issue: inflation.

# Inflation

PRICES ON THE AVERAGE CAN BE RISING, FALLING, or stable. **Inflation** is a process of rising prices. We measure the *inflation rate* as the percentage change in the *average* level of prices or the **price level**. A common measure of the price level is the *Consumer Price Index* (CPI). The CPI tells us how the average price of all the goods and services bought by a typical urban household changes from month to month. (The CPI is explained in Chapter 6.)

So that you can see how the inflation rate is measured, let's do a calculation. In August 2003, the CPI was 184.5, and in August 2002, it was 180.7, so the inflation rate during the year to August 2003 was 2.1 percent.

## Inflation in the United States

Figure 4.8 shows the U.S. inflation rate from 1963 through 2003. During the early 1960s, the inflation rate was between 1 and 2 percent a year. It began to increase during the late 1960s at the time of the Vietnam War. But the largest increases occurred in 1974 and 1980, years in which the actions of the Organization of Petroleum Exporting Countries (OPEC) resulted in exceptionally large increases in the price of oil. Inflation was brought under control in the early 1980s when Federal Reserve Chairman Paul Volcker pushed interest rates up and people cut back on their spending. Since 1983, inflation has been relatively mild, and during the 1990s its rate continued to fall until 1999, when it increased but fell again after 2000.

The inflation rate rises and falls over the years, but it rarely becomes negative. If the inflation rate is negative, the price *level* is falling and we have **deflation**. Since the 1930s, the price level has generally increased—the inflation rate has been positive. Thus even when the inflation rate is low, as it was in 2003, the price level is rising. But in 2003, some people feared that the United States might be on the edge of a new period of deflation.

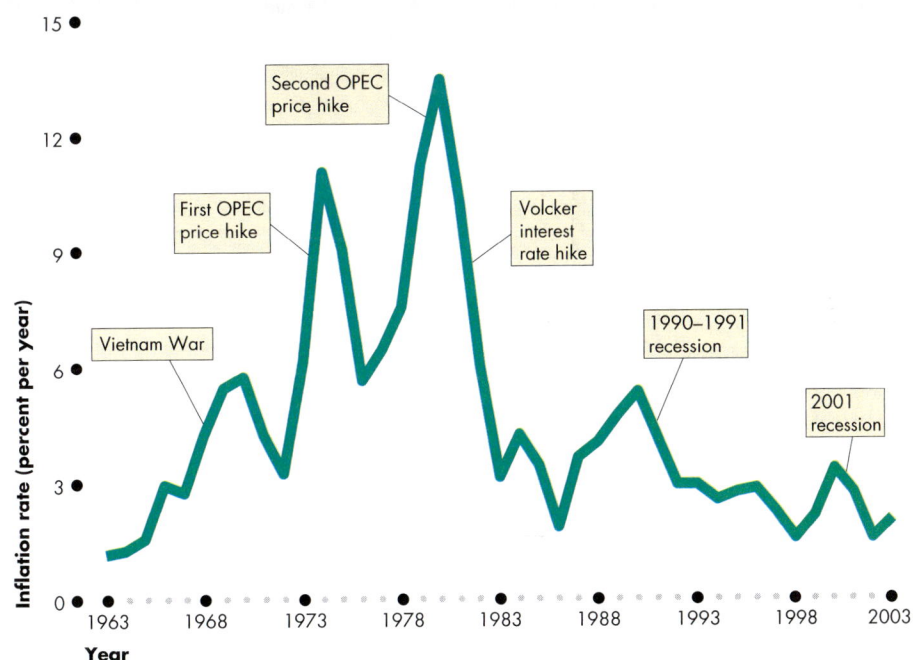

**FIGURE 4.8** Inflation in the United States

Inflation is a persistent feature of economic life in the United States. The inflation rate was low in the first half of the 1960s, but it increased during the late 1960s at the time of the Vietnam War. It increased further with the OPEC oil price hikes, but it eventually declined in the early 1980s because of policy actions taken by the Federal Reserve. Since 1983, inflation has been mild, and during the 1990s, it fell further. In the late 1990s, the inflation rate increased slightly before falling again in the early 2000s.

*Source*: Bureau of Labor Statistics.

### Inflation Around the World

Figure 4.9 shows inflation around the world since 1983. It also shows the U.S. inflation rate in a broader perspective. Part (a) shows that U.S. inflation has been similar to that of other industrial countries. All industrial countries, including the United States, had falling inflation during the early 1980s, rising inflation during the late 1980s, and falling and low inflation during the 1990s.

Part (b) shows that the average inflation rate of industrial countries has been very low compared with that of the developing counties. Among the developing countries, the most extreme inflation in recent times has occurred in the former Yugoslavia, where its rate has exceeded 6,000 percent per year.

### Is Inflation a Problem?

If inflation were predictable, it would not be much of a problem. But inflation is not predictable. Unpredictable inflation makes the economy behave a bit like a casino in which some people gain and some lose and no one can predict where the gains and losses will fall. Gains and losses occur because of unpredictable changes in the value of money. Money is used as a measuring rod of value in the transactions that we undertake. Borrowers and lenders, workers and employers, all make contracts in terms of money. If the value of money varies unpredictably over time, then the amounts *really* paid and received—the quantity of goods that the money will buy—also fluctuate unpredictably. Measuring value with a measuring rod whose units vary is a bit like trying to measure a piece of cloth with an elastic ruler. The size of the cloth depends on how tightly the ruler is stretched.

In a period of rapid, unpredictable inflation, resources get diverted from productive activities to forecasting inflation. It becomes more profitable to forecast the inflation rate correctly than to invent a new product. Doctors, lawyers, accountants, farmers—just about everyone—can make themselves better off, not by specializing in the profession for which they have been trained but by spending more of their time dabbling as amateur economists and inflation forecasters and managing their investment portfolios.

From a social perspective, this diversion of talent resulting from inflation is like throwing scarce resources onto the garbage heap. This waste of resources is a cost of inflation.

The most serious type of inflation is called *hyperinflation*—an inflation rate that exceeds 50 percent a

**FIGURE 4.9** Inflation Around the World

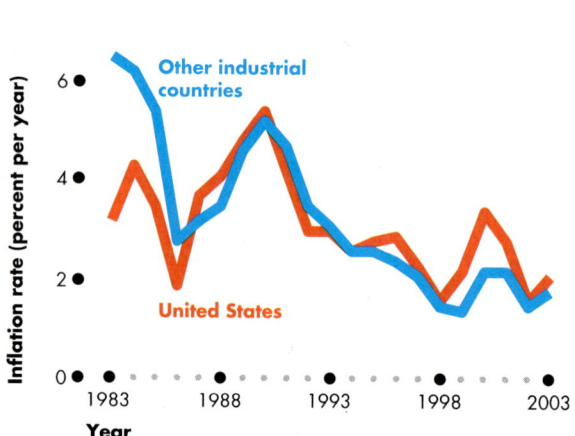

(a) The United States and other industrial countries

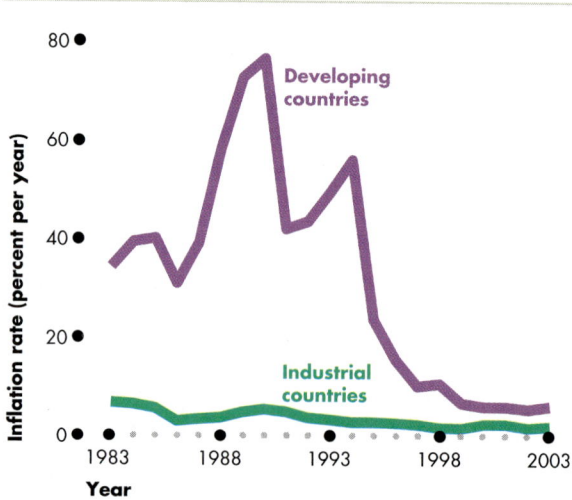

Inflation in the United States is similar to that in the other industrial countries. Compared with the developing countries, inflation in the industrial countries is low.

*Source*: International Monetary Fund, *World Economic Outlook*, September 2003.

month. At the height of a hyperinflation, workers are often paid twice a day because money loses its value so quickly. As soon as workers are paid, they rush out to spend their wages before they lose too much value.

Hyperinflation is rare, but there have been some spectacular examples of it. Several European countries experienced hyperinflation during the 1920s after World War I and again during the 1940s after World War II. But hyperinflation is more than just a historical curiosity. It occurs in today's world. In 1994, the African nation of Zaire had a hyperinflation that peaked at a *monthly* inflation rate of 76 percent, which is 88,000 percent a year! Brazil has also been close to the hyperinflation stratosphere with a monthly inflation rate of 40 percent. A cup of coffee that cost 15 cruzeiros in 1980 cost 22 *billion* cruzeiros in 1994.

Inflation imposes costs, but getting rid of inflation is also costly. Policies that lower the inflation rate increase the unemployment rate. Most economists think the increase in the unemployment rate that accompanies a fall in the inflation rate is temporary. But some economists say that higher unemployment is a permanent cost of low inflation. The cost of lowering inflation must be evaluated when an anti-inflation policy is pursued. You will learn more about inflation and the costs of curing it in Chapter 12.

### REVIEW QUIZ

1. What is inflation and how does it influence the value of money?
2. How is inflation measured?
3. What has been the U.S. inflation record since 1963?
4. How does inflation in the United States compare with inflation in other industrial countries and in developing countries?
5. What are some of the costs of inflation that make it a serious economic problem?

Now that you've studied economic growth and fluctuations, unemployment, and inflation, let's turn to the fourth macroeconomic issue: surpluses and deficits. What happens when a government spends more than it collects in taxes? And what happens when a nation buys more from other countries than it sells to them? Do governments and nations face the problem that you and I would face if we spent more than we earned? Do they run out of funds? Let's look at these questions.

## Surpluses and Deficits

IN 1998, FOR THE FIRST TIME IN ALMOST 30 YEARS, the U.S. federal government had a budget surplus. At the same time, the United States had a large international deficit. What are the government budget surplus and the nation's international deficit?

### Government Budget Surplus and Deficit

If a government collects more in taxes than it spends, it has a surplus—a **government budget surplus**. If a government spends more than it collects in taxes, it has a deficit—a **government budget deficit**. The U.S. federal government had a surplus from 1998 to 2000 and a deficit each year after 2001.

Figure 4.10(a) shows the federal government surplus and deficit measured as a percentage of GDP since 1962. (The concept of GDP, which is explained more fully in Chapter 5, equals total income in the economy.)

We measure the budget surplus or deficit as a percentage of GDP so that we can compare the surplus or deficit in one year with that in another year. You can think of this measure as the number of cents of surplus or deficit per dollar of income earned by an average person.

The government had a budget surplus in 1969 and from 1998 to 2001. In every year from 1970 through 1997, the government had a deficit that fluctuated and swelled during recessions. From 1980 through 1995, the deficit was never less than 2 percent of GDP.

Since 1992, the federal government deficit has shrunk and in 1998 a surplus emerged. In 2000, the government budget surplus was a bit more than 2 percent of GDP. In 2001, the federal government surplus turned into a deficit again.

### International Deficit

When we import goods and services from the rest of the world, we make payments to foreigners. When we export goods and services to the rest of the world, we receive payments from foreigners. If our imports exceed our exports, we have an international deficit.

Figure 4.10(b) shows the history of the U.S. international balance from 1962 to 2002. The figure shows the balance on the **current account**, which includes U.S. exports minus U.S. imports but also takes into account interest payments paid to and

## FIGURE 4.10 Government Budget and International Surpluses and Deficits

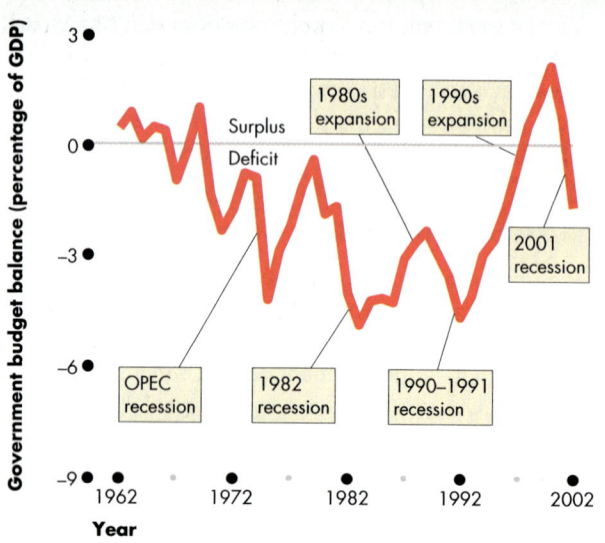

(a) U.S. government budget deficit

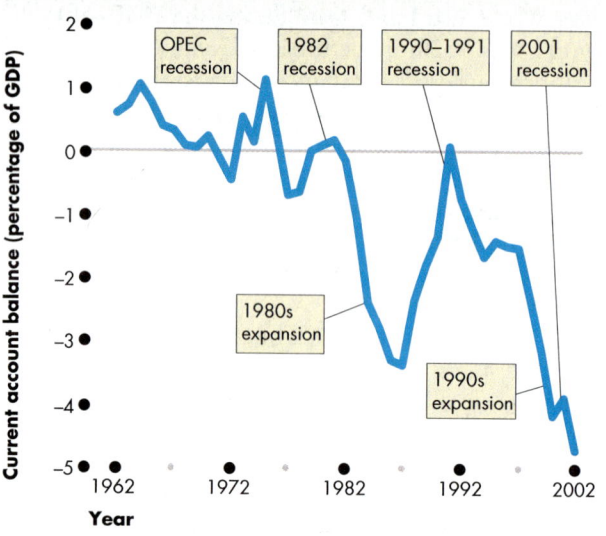

(b) U.S. international deficit

In part (a), the federal government deficit as a percentage of GDP increased during recessions and shrunk during the recoveries. A surplus emerged in 1998, but in 2001 the deficit reappeared. In part (b), the U.S. current account shows the balance of U.S exports minus U.S imports. Until the early 1980s, the U.S. current account was generally in surplus. During the 1980s expansion, a large current account deficit emerged. It almost disappeared during the 1990-1991 recession, but it reappeared during the 1990s expansion.

*Sources*: The U.S. federal government's budget and *Economic Report of the President, 2003.*

---

received from the rest of the world. To compare one year with another, the figure shows the current account as a percentage of GDP. The U.S. current account has fluctuated, and since 1980, it has ranged from close to zero to almost 5 percent of GDP. U.S. imports have exceeded U.S. exports.

### Do Deficits Matter?

Why do deficits cause anxiety? What happens when a government cannot cover its spending with taxes, or when a country buys more from other countries than it sells to them?

If you spend more than you earn, you have a deficit. And to cover your deficit, you go into debt. But when you borrow, you must pay interest on your debt. Just like you, if a government or a nation has a deficit, it must borrow. And like you, the government and the nation must pay interest on their debts.

Whether borrowing and paying out huge amounts of interest is a good idea depends on what the borrowed funds are used for. If you borrow to finance a vacation, you must eventually tighten your belt, cut spending, and repay your debt as well as pay interest on the debt. But if you borrow to invest in a business that earns a large profit, you might be able to repay your debt and pay the interest on it while continuing to increase your spending. It is the same with a government and a nation. A government or a nation that borrows to increase its consumption might be heading for trouble later. But a government or a nation that borrows to buy assets that earn a profit might be making a sound investment.

You will learn more about the government budget in Chapter 15 and about the international current account deficit in Chapter 18.

> **REVIEW QUIZ**
>
> 1. What determines a government's budget deficit?
> 2. How has the U.S. federal government budget evolved since 1962?
> 3. What is a country's international deficit?
> 4. How has the U.S. international deficit changed since the 1960s?

## Macroeconomic Policy Challenges and Tools

FROM THE TIME OF ADAM SMITH'S *Wealth of Nations* in 1776 until the publication of Keynes' *General Theory of Employment, Interest, and Money* in 1936, it was widely believed that the only economic role for government was to enforce property rights. The economy behaved best, it was believed, if the government left people free to pursue their own best interests. The macroeconomics of Keynes challenged this view. Keynes' central point was that the economy will not fix itself and that government actions are needed to achieve and maintain full employment. The U.S. government declared full employment as a policy goal soon after World War II ended.

### Policy Challenges and Tools

Today, the five widely agreed challenges for macroeconomic policy are to

1. Boost economic growth
2. Keep inflation low
3. Stabilize the business cycle
4. Reduce unemployment
5. Reduce government and international deficits

But how can we do all these things? What are the tools available to pursue the macroeconomic policy challenges? Macroeconomic policy tools are divided into two broad categories:

- Fiscal policy
- Monetary policy

**Fiscal Policy** Making changes in tax rates and in government spending programs is called **fiscal policy**. This range of actions is under the control of the federal government. Fiscal policy can be used to try to boost long-term growth by creating incentives that encourage saving, investment, and technological change. Fiscal policy can also be used to try to smooth out the business cycle. When the economy is in a recession, the government might cut taxes or increase its spending. Conversely, when the economy is in a rapid expansion, the government might increase taxes or cut its spending in an attempt to slow real GDP growth and prevent inflation from increasing. Fiscal policy is discussed in Chapter 15.

**Monetary Policy** Changing interest rates and changing the amount of money in the economy is called **monetary policy**. These actions are under the control of the Federal reserve (the Fed). The principal aim of monetary policy is to keep inflation in check. To achieve this objective, the Fed prevents the quantity of money from expanding too rapidly. Monetary policy can also be used to smooth the business cycle. When the economy is in recession, the Fed might lower interest rates and inject money into the economy. And when the economy is in a rapid expansion, the Fed might increase interest rates in an attempt to slow real GDP growth and prevent inflation from increasing. We study monetary policy in Chapter 16.

> **REVIEW QUIZ**
>
> 1. What are the main challenges of macroeconomic policy?
> 2. What are the main tools of macroeconomic policy?
> 3. Can you distinguish between fiscal policy and monetary policy?

◆ In the following chapters, you will learn about the causes of economic growth, business cycles, unemployment, inflation, and deficits as well as the policy choices and challenges that the government and the Fed face. But first, *Reading Between the Lines* on pp. 102–103 gives you a close-up view of the 2003 expansion in the U.S. economy.

# READING BETWEEN THE LINES

## *The 2003 Expansion*

**THE ATLANTA JOURNAL-CONSTITUTION, NOVEMBER 26, 2003**

### Economy perks up with rising profits

The economy's third quarter surge was even more stunning than first reported, as growth soared to an 8.2 percent pace and offered new evidence that businesses are spending again.

The Commerce Department's preliminary estimate for the three months ending in September, at 7.2 percent, already was the fastest expansion in two decades.

Behind Tuesday's revision upward was data showing that companies had not slashed inventories as deeply as first reported, while exports picked up and, most encouragingly, both business spending and profits were higher.

"To me, the new news is the profit data," said Paul Kasriel, chief of economic research at Northern Trust in Chicago. "Without profits, businesses don't tend to hire people."

Corporate profits soared 11.8 percent after surging 9.9 percent in the prior quarter. A year ago, profits were negative for three consecutive quarters.

So the increasingly rosy view in the rear-view mirror is coloring the vista.

"We will have a more balanced expansion going forward," Kasriel said. "More subdued, but more balanced."

Consumer confidence has also leaped to its highest level in more than a year, the Conference Board said Tuesday. And it was the biggest one-month improvement since December 2001.

Economists have repeatedly warned that consumer spending depends on the jobs picture. So perhaps the most promising piece of the survey was the growing conclusion that the job market is improving. ....

© The Atlanta Journal-Constitution
All rights reserved.

### Essence of the Story

- Real GDP grew at an 8.2 percent annual rate during the third quarter of 2003, up from a preliminary estimate of 7.2 percent.

- Companies had not lowered inventories as much as first reported, and exports increased.

- Business spending and profits were also higher.

- Economist Paul Kasriel said that the expansion would continue and would be "more subdued, but more balanced."

- Consumer confidence increased, and the job market improved.

## Economic Analysis

- The growth rate of real GDP during the third quarter of 2003 was a rapid 8.2 percent.

- This growth rate refers to the third quarter of the year but is expressed as a percentage *annual* growth rate.

- Real GDP actually grew by $192 billion, which is 2 percent of its level during the second quarter of 2003.

- How does the third-quarter growth rate compare with those for earlier quarters?

- The figure provides the answer.

- During 2001, the U.S. economy was in recession and real GDP shrank—the real GDP growth rate was negative.

- From the fourth quarter of 2001 when the expansion began through the second quarter of 2003, real GDP grew at an average annual rate of 2.7 percent.

- So the growth rate in the third quarter of 2003 was extraordinarily rapid—three times the average of the previous seven quarters.

- The black line in the figure is potential GDP.

- Potential GDP grows at an annual average rate of about 3 percent.

- Until the third quarter of 2003, real GDP was growing a bit below its potential growth rate and the Okun gap—the gap between actual and potential GDP—remained roughly constant.

- An expansion that leaves the Okun gap constant creates enough new jobs to match the growing population but not enough to lower the unemployment rate. Such an episode is called a jobless recovery.

- The accumulated value of lost output—the accumulated Okun gap—during 2002 and 2003 was about $1 trillion, or 10 percent of annual real GDP.

- Can a growth rate of around 8 percent a year be maintained over a number of years? Or will growth become more subdued as predicted by economist Paul Kasriel?

- The figure shows a reason why Paul Kasriel is almost certainly correct.

- In the long run, real GDP growth cannot exceed the growth rate of potential GDP.

- A growth rate of 8.2 percent even for one more quarter would take real GDP above potential GDP and bring inflation. Eventually, real GDP growth must slow.

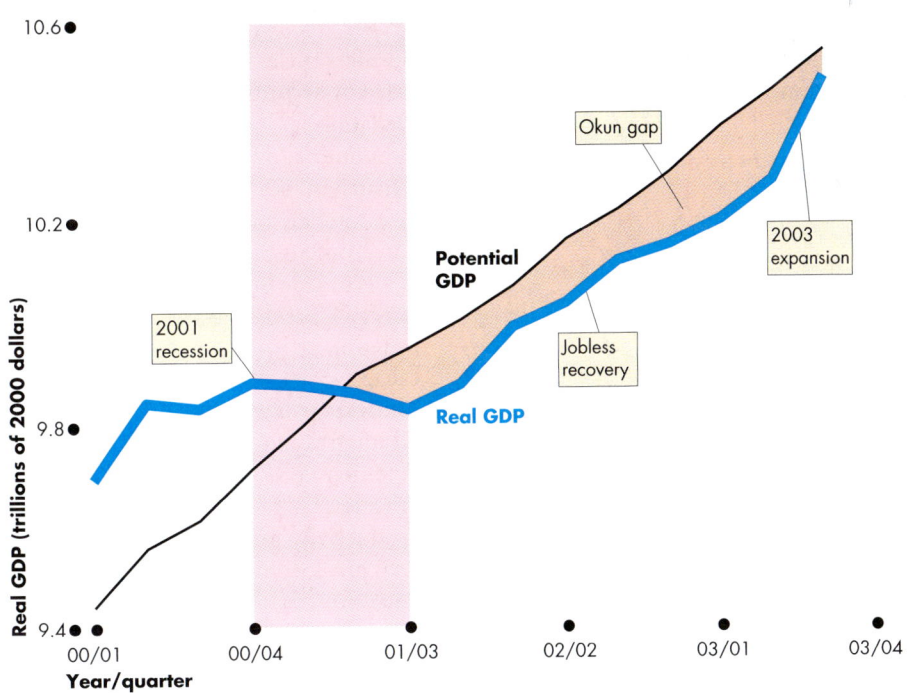

Figure 1 The 2001 recession and jobless recovery

# SUMMARY

## KEY POINTS

### Origins and Issues of Macroeconomics (p. 88)
- Macroeconomics studies economic growth and fluctuations, unemployment, inflation, and surpluses and deficits.

### Economic Growth and Fluctuations (pp. 89–94)
- Economic growth is the expansion of potential GDP. Real GDP fluctuates around potential GDP in a business cycle.
- The main benefit of long-term economic growth is higher future consumption, and the main cost is lower current consumption.
- Slow productivity growth (the Lucas wedge) is more costly than the business cycle (the Okun gap).

### Jobs and Unemployment (pp. 94–96)
- The U.S. economy creates 1.8 million jobs a year, but unemployment persists.
- Unemployment increases during a recession and decreases during an expansion.
- The U.S. unemployment rate is lower than that in Canada and Western Europe but higher than that in Japan.
- Unemployment can permanently damage a person's job prospects.

### Inflation (pp. 97–99)
- Inflation, a process of rising prices, is measured by the percentage change in the CPI.
- Inflation is a problem because it lowers the value of money and makes money less useful as a measuring rod of value.

### Surpluses and Deficits (pp. 99–101)
- When the government collects more in taxes than it spends, the government has a budget surplus. When the government spends more than it collects in taxes, the government has a budget deficit.
- When imports exceed exports, a nation has an international deficit.
- Deficits are financed by borrowing.

### Macroeconomic Policy Challenges and Tools (p. 101)
- The macroeconomic policy challenge is to use fiscal policy and monetary policy to boost long-term growth, stabilize the business cycle, lower unemployment, tame inflation, and prevent large deficits.

## KEY FIGURES

Figure 4.1   Economic Growth in the United States, 89
Figure 4.2   The Most Recent U.S. Business Cycle, 90
Figure 4.3   Long-Term Economic Growth in the United States, 91
Figure 4.5   The Lucas Wedge and the Okun Gap, 93
Figure 4.6   Unemployment in the United States, 95
Figure 4.8   Inflation in the United States, 97
Figure 4.10  Government Budget and International Surpluses and Deficits, 100

## KEY TERMS

Business cycle, 90
Current account, 99
Deflation, 97
Economic growth, 89
Expansion, 90
Fiscal policy, 101
Government budget deficit, 99
Government budget surplus, 99
Great Depression, 88
Inflation, 97
Lucas wedge, 93
Monetary policy, 101
Okun gap, 93
Potential GDP, 89
Price level, 97
Productivity growth slowdown, 89
Real gross domestic product (real GDP), 89
Recession, 90
Unemployment rate, 95

# PROBLEMS

*1. Use Data Graphing on **MyEconLab** to answer the following questions. In which country in 2002 was
   a. The growth rate of real GDP highest: Canada, Japan, or the United States?
   b. The unemployment rate highest: Canada, Japan, the United Kingdom, or the United States?
   c. The inflation rate lowest: Canada, Germany, the United Kingdom, or the United States?
   d. The government budget deficit (as a percentage of GDP) largest: Canada, Japan, the United Kingdom, or the United States?

2. Use Data Graphing on **MyEconLab** to answer the following questions. In which country in 1996 was
   a. The growth rate of real GDP highest: Canada, Japan, or the United States?
   b. The unemployment rate lowest: Canada, Japan, the United Kingdom, or the United States?
   c. The inflation rate lowest: Canada, the United Kingdom, Japan, or the United States?
   d. The government budget surplus (as a percentage of GDP) smallest: Canada, the United Kingdom, or the United States?
   e. Is it possible to say in which country consumption possibilities are growing fastest? Why or why not?

*3. The figure shows the real GDP growth rates in India and Pakistan from 1989 to 1996.

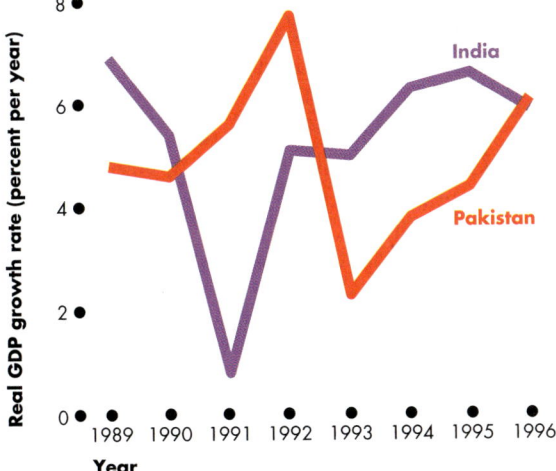

In which years did economic growth in
   a. India increase? And in which year was growth the fastest?
   b. Pakistan decrease? And in which year was growth the slowest?
   c. Compare the paths of economic growth in India and Pakistan during this period.

4. The figure shows real GDP per person in Australia and Japan from 1989 to 1996.

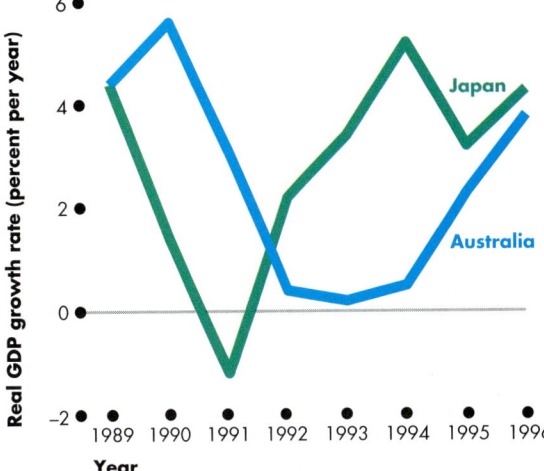

In which years did economic growth in
   a. Australia increase? And in which year was growth the fastest?
   b. Japan decrease? And in which year was growth the slowest?
   c. Compare the paths of economic growth in Australia and Japan during this period.

*5. The figure shows real GDP in Germany from the first quarter of 1991 to the fourth quarter of 1994.

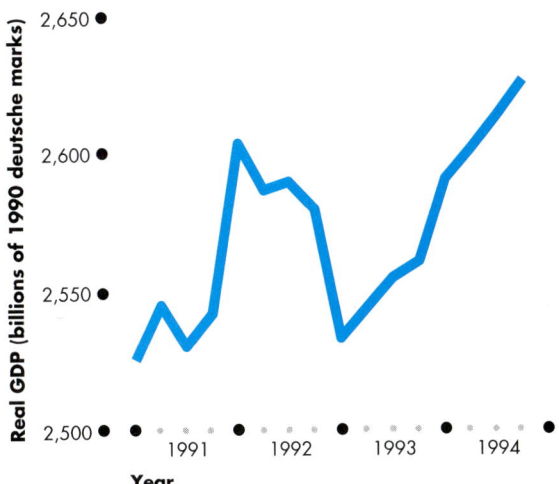

\* Solutions to odd-numbered problems are available on **MyEconLab**.

a. How many recessions did Germany experience during this period?
b. In which quarters, if any, did Germany experience a business cycle peak?
c. In which quarters, if any, did Germany experience a business cycle trough?
d. In which quarters, if any, did Germany experience an expansion?

6. Use the links on **MyEconLab** to obtain data on quarterly real GDP for the United States since the fourth quarter of 2002 and update Fig. 2. Use what you have discovered to answer the following questions:
   a. Is the U.S. economy now in a recession or an expansion?
   b. If the economy is now in an expansion, how long has the expansion lasted? If the economy is now in recession, how long has the economy been in recession?
   c. During the last year, has the growth rate sped up or slowed down?

*7. Use Data Graphing on **MyEconLab** to answer the following questions. Which country, in 2002, had
   a. The largest budget deficit: Canada, Japan, the United Kingdom, or the United States?
   b. A current account surplus: Canada, Japan, Germany, or the United States?

8. Use Data Graphing on **MyEconLab** to answer the following questions. Which country, in 2002, had
   a. The largest budget surplus: Canada, Japan, the United Kingdom, or the United States?
   b. The largest current account deficit: Canada, Japan, Germany, or the United States?

*9. Use Data Graphing on **MyEconLab** to make a scatter diagram of the inflation rate and the unemployment rate in the United States.
   a. Describe the relationship.
   b. Do you think that low unemployment brings an increase in the inflation rate?

10. Use Data Graphing on **MyEconLab** to make a scatter diagram of the government budget deficit as a percentage of GDP and the unemployment rate in the United States.
    a. Describe the relationship.
    b. Do you think that low unemployment brings a decrease in the budget deficit?

# CRITICAL THINKING

1. Study *Reading Between the Lines* on pp. 102–103 and then answer the following questions:
   a. When did the most recent recession end and expansion begin?
   b. Why was the 2002 and 2003 expansion called a jobless recovery?
   c. Why do you expect the growth rate of the third quarter of 2003 to be temporary?
   d. Can you think of reasons why the growth rate of potential GDP might have increased?
   e. Can you think of any actions of the federal government that might have contributed to the strong expansion of the third quarter of 2003?

# WEB EXERCISES

**Use the links on MyEconLab to work the following exercises.**

1. Obtain the latest data on real GDP, unemployment, and inflation in the United States.
   a. Update Fig. 4.2, 4.6, and 4.8.
   b. What dangers does the U.S. economy face today?
   c. What actions, if any, do you think might be needed to keep the economy strong?
2. Obtain data on unemployment in your home state.
   a. Compare unemployment in your home state with that in the United States as a whole.
   b. Why do you think your state might have a higher or a lower unemployment rate than the U.S. average?
3. Obtain data on the Consumer Price Index for the capital city in your home state.
   a. Compare the inflation rate in your home state with that in the United States as a whole.
   b. Compare the inflation rate in your home state with that of the capital cities in neighboring states.
4. Obtain data on the following variables for the United States for the most recent period. Describe how the variables have changed over the last year.
   a. The unemployment rate
   b. The inflation rate
   c. The government budget surplus or deficit
   d. The international deficit

# Measuring GDP and Economic Growth

CHAPTER 5

## An Economic Barometer

Will our economy keep expanding through 2004 and 2005? And will the expansion be rapid or slow? Or are we going to slip into recession again? Many U.S. corporations wanted to know the answers to these questions at the beginning of 2004. AOL wanted to know whether to expand its server network or delay for a while. Amazon.com wanted to know whether to increase its warehousing facilities. To assess the severity of a recession and to make big decisions about business expansion, firms such as AOL and Amazon use forecasts of GDP. What exactly is GDP and how can we use it to tell us whether we are in a recession or how rapidly our economy is expanding?

To reveal the rate of growth or shrinkage of GDP, we must remove the effects of inflation and assess how *real* GDP is changing. How do we remove the inflation component of GDP to reveal *real* GDP?

Some countries are rich while others are poor. How do we compare economic well-being in one country with that in another? How can we make international comparisons of GDP?

◆ In this chapter, you will find out how economic statisticians measure GDP, real GDP, and the economic growth rate. You will also learn about the limitations of these measures. In *Reading Between the Lines* at the end of the chapter, we'll look at real GDP during the 2003 expansion.

### After studying this chapter, you will be able to

- **Define GDP and use the circular flow model to explain why GDP equals aggregate expenditure and aggregate income**
- **Explain the two ways of measuring GDP**
- **Explain how we measure *real* GDP and the GDP deflator**
- **Explain how we use real GDP to measure economic growth and describe the limitations of our measure**

## Gross Domestic Product

WHAT EXACTLY IS GDP, HOW IS IT CALCULATED, what does it mean, and why do we care about it? You are going to discover the answers to these questions in this chapter. First, what *is* GDP?

### GDP Defined

**GDP**, or **gross domestic product**, is the market value of all the final goods and services produced within a country in a given time period. This definition has four parts:

- Market value
- Final goods and services
- Produced within a country
- In a given time period

We'll examine each in turn.

**Market Value** To measure total production, we must add together the production of apples and oranges, computers and popcorn. Just counting the items doesn't get us very far. For example, which is the greater total production: 100 apples and 50 oranges, or 50 apples and 100 oranges?

GDP answers this question by valuing items at their *market values*—the prices at which each item is traded in markets. If the price of an apple is 10 cents, the market value of 50 apples is $5. If the price of an orange is 20 cents, the market value of 100 oranges is $20. By using market prices to value production, we can add the apples and oranges together. The market value of 50 apples and 100 oranges is $5 plus $20, or $25.

**Final Goods and Services** To calculate GDP, we value the *final goods and services* produced. A **final good** (or service) is an item that is bought by its final user during a specified time period. It contrasts with an **intermediate good** (or service), which is an item that is produced by one firm, bought by another firm, and used as a component of a final good or service.

For example, a Ford SUV is a final good, but a Firestone tire on the SUV is an intermediate good. A Dell computer is a final good, but an Intel Pentium chip inside it is an intermediate good.

If we were to add the value of intermediate goods and services produced to the value of final goods and services, we would count the same thing many times—a problem called *double counting*. The value of an SUV already includes the value of the tires, and the value of a Dell PC already includes the value of the Pentium chip inside it.

Some goods can be an intermediate good in some situations and a final good in other situations. For example, the ice cream that you buy on a hot summer day is a final good, but the ice cream that a diner buys and uses to make sundaes is an intermediate good. The sundae is the final good. So whether a good is an intermediate good or a final good depends on what it is used for, not what it is.

Some items that people buy are neither final goods nor intermediate goods. Examples of such items include financial assets—stocks and bonds—and second-hand goods—used cars or existing homes.

These items are not part of GDP. But a used car and an existing home were part of GDP in the year in which they were produced.

**Produced Within a Country** Only goods and services that are produced *within a country* count as part of that country's GDP. Nike Corporation, a U.S. firm, produces sneakers in Vietnam, and the market value of those shoes is part of Vietnam's GDP, not part of U.S. GDP. Toyota, a Japanese firm, produces automobiles in Georgetown, Kentucky, and the value of this production is part of U.S. GDP, not part of Japan's GDP.

**In a Given Time Period** GDP measures the value of production *in a given time period*—normally either a quarter of a year—called the quarterly GDP data—or a year—called the annual GDP data.

GDP measures not only the value of total production but also total income and total expenditure. The equality between the value of total production and total income is important because it shows the direct link between productivity and living standards. Our standard of living rises when our incomes rise and we can afford to buy more goods and services. But we must produce more goods and services if we are to be able to buy more goods and services.

Rising incomes and a rising value of production go together. They are two aspects of the same phenomenon—increasing productivity. To see why, we study the circular flow of expenditure and income.

## GDP and the Circular Flow of Expenditure and Income

Figure 5.1 illustrates the circular flow of expenditure and income. The economy consists of households, firms, governments, and the rest of the world (the purple diamonds), which trade in factor markets, goods (and services) markets, and financial markets. We focus first on households and firms.

**Households and Firms** Households sell and firms buy the services of labor, capital, and land in factor markets. For these factor services, firms pay income to households: wages for labor services, interest for the use of capital, and rent for the use of land. A fourth factor of production, entrepreneurship, receives profit.

Firms' retained earnings—profits that are not distributed to households—are part of the household sector's income. You can think of retained earnings as being income that households save and lend back to firms. Figure 5.1 shows the total income—*aggregate income*—received by households, including retained earnings, by the blue dots labeled $Y$.

Firms sell and households buy consumer goods and services—such as inline skates and haircuts—in the markets for goods and services. The total payment for these goods and services is **consumption expenditure**, shown by the red dots labeled $C$.

Firms buy and sell new capital equipment—such as computer systems, airplanes, trucks, and assembly line equipment—in the goods market. Some of what firms produce is not sold but is added to inventory. For example, if GM produces 1,000 cars and sells 950 of them, the other 50 cars remain in GM's inventory of unsold cars, which increases by 50 cars. When a firm adds unsold output to inventory, we can think of the firm as buying goods from itself. The

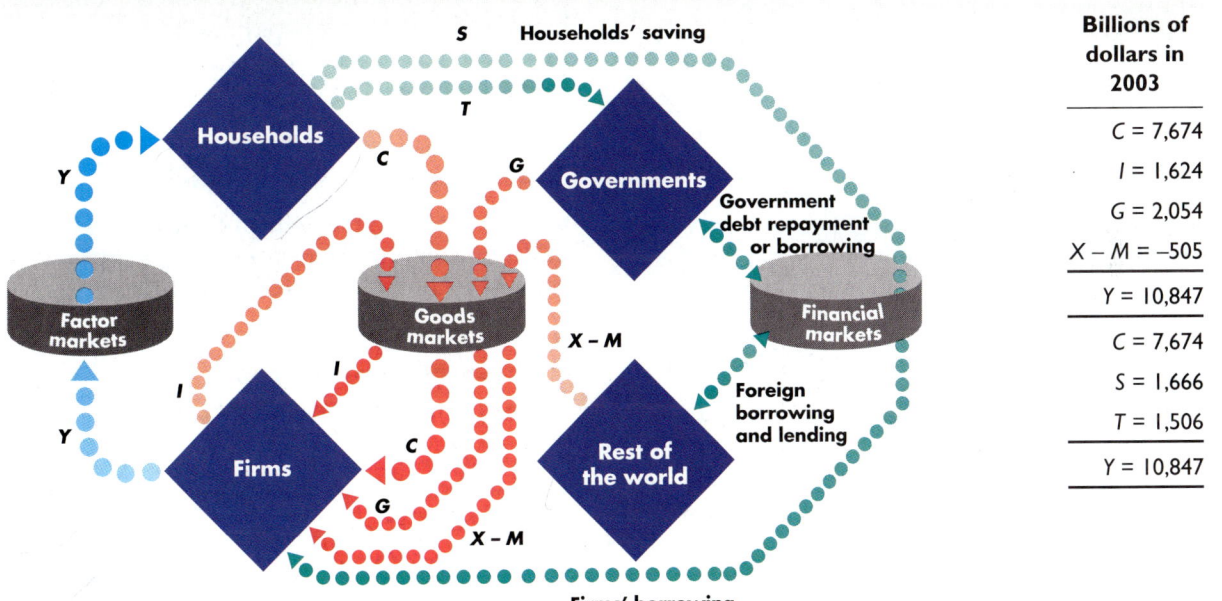

**FIGURE 5.1  The Circular Flow of Expenditure and Income**

| Billions of dollars in 2003 |
| --- |
| $C = 7{,}674$ |
| $I = 1{,}624$ |
| $G = 2{,}054$ |
| $X - M = -505$ |
| $Y = 10{,}847$ |
| $C = 7{,}674$ |
| $S = 1{,}666$ |
| $T = 1{,}506$ |
| $Y = 10{,}847$ |

In the circular flow of expenditure and income, households make consumption expenditures ($C$); firms make investment expenditures ($I$); governments purchase goods and services ($G$); and the rest of the world purchases net exports ($X - M$) —(red flows). Households receive income ($Y$) from firms (blue flow).

Aggregate income (blue flow) equals aggregate expenditure (red flows). Households use their income to consume, ($C$), save ($S$), and pay net taxes ($T$). Firms borrow to finance their investment expenditures, and governments and the rest of the world borrow to finance their deficits or lend their surpluses (green flows).

*Source*: U.S. Department of Commerce, Bureau of Economic Analysis. (The data are for the second quarter of 2003 annual rate.)

purchase of new plant, equipment, and buildings and the additions to inventories are **investment**, shown by the red dots labeled *I*.

**Governments** Governments buy goods and services, called **government purchases**, from firms. In Fig. 5.1, government purchases of goods and services are shown as the red flow *G*. Governments use taxes to pay for their purchases. Figure 5.1 shows taxes as net taxes by the green dots labeled *T*. **Net taxes** are equal to taxes paid to governments minus transfer payments received from governments and minus interest payments on the governments' debt. *Transfer payments* are cash transfers from governments to households and firms such as social security benefits, unemployment compensation, and subsidies.

**Rest of the World** Firms sell goods and services to the rest of the world—**exports**—and buy goods and services from the rest of the world—**imports**. Exports (*X*) minus imports (*M*) are called **net exports**, which Fig. 5.1 shows by the red flow *X* − *M*.

If net exports are positive (if exports exceed imports), there is a net flow of goods and services from U.S. firms to the rest of the world. If net exports are negative (if imports exceed exports), there is net flow of goods and services from the rest of the world to U.S. firms.

**GDP Equals Expenditure Equals Income** Gross domestic product can be determined in two ways: By the total expenditure on goods and services or by the total income earned producing goods and services.

The total expenditure—*aggregate expenditure*—is the sum of the red flows in Fig. 5.1. Aggregate expenditure equals consumption expenditure plus investment plus government purchases plus net exports.

Aggregate income earned producing goods and services is equal to the total amount paid for the factors of production used—wages, interest, rent, and profit. This amount is shown by the blue flow in Fig. 5.1. Because firms pay out as incomes (including retained profits) everything they receive from the sale of their output, income (the blue flow) equals expenditure (the sum of the red flows). That is,

$$Y = C + I + G + X - M.$$

The table in Fig. 5.1 shows the numbers for 2003. You can see that the sum of the expenditures is $10,847 billion, which also equals aggregate income.

Because aggregate expenditure equals aggregate income, these two methods of valuing GDP give the same answer. So

GDP equals aggregate expenditure and equals aggregate income.

The circular flow model is the foundation on which the national economic accounts are built.

### Financial Flows

The circular flow model also enables us to see the connection between the expenditure and income flows and flows through the financial markets that finance deficits and pay for investment. These flows are shown in green in Fig. 5.1. Household **saving** (*S*) is the amount that households have left after they have paid their taxes and bought their consumption goods and services. Government borrowing finances a government budget deficit. (Government lending arises when the government has a budget surplus.) And foreign borrowing pays for a deficit with the rest of the world. These financial flows are the sources of the funds that firms use to pay for their investment in new capital. Let's look a bit more closely at how investment is financed.

### How Investment Is Financed

Investment adds to the stock of capital and is one of the determinants of the rate at which production grows. Investment is financed from three sources:

1. Private saving
2. Government budget surplus
3. Borrowing from the rest of the world

Private saving is the green flow labeled *S* in Fig. 5.1. Notice that households' income is consumed, saved, or paid in taxes. That is,

$$Y = C + S + T.$$

But you've seen that *Y* also equals the sum of the components of aggregate expenditure. That is,

$$Y = C + I + G + X - M.$$

By using these two equations, you can see that

$$I + G + X - M = S + T.$$

Now subtract *G* and *X* from both sides of the last equation and add *M* to both sides to obtain

$$I = S + (T - G) + (M - X).$$

In this equation, $(T - G)$ is the government budget surplus and $(M - X)$ is borrowing from the rest of the world.

If taxes $(T)$ exceed government purchases $(G)$, the government has a budget surplus equal to $(T - G)$, and this surplus contributes toward paying for investment. If taxes are less than government purchases, the government has a budget deficit equal to $(T - G)$, which is now negative. This deficit subtracts from the sources that finance investment.

If we import $(M)$ more than we export $(X)$, we borrow an amount equal to $(M - X)$ from the rest of the world. So part of the rest of the world's saving finances investment in the United States. If we export more than we import, we lend an amount equal to $(X - M)$ to the rest of the world. So part of U.S. saving is used to finance investment in other countries.

The sum of private saving, $S$, and government saving, $(T - G)$ is called **national saving**. So investment is financed by national saving and foreign borrowing.

Every year since the early 1980s, the United States has borrowed from the rest of the world—total foreign borrowing of more that $1.5 trillion over that period. In 2003, the United States increased its international debt by $505 billion.

## Gross and Net Domestic Product

What does the "gross" in GDP mean? Gross means before accounting for the depreciation of capital. The opposite of gross is net, which means after accounting for the depreciation of capital. To understand what the depreciation of capital is and how it affects aggregate expenditure and income, we need to expand the accounting framework that we use and distinguish between flows and stocks.

**Flows and Stocks in Macroeconomics** A **flow** is a quantity per unit of time. The water that is running from an open faucet into a bathtub is a flow. So are the number of CDs that you buy during a month, and the amount of income that you earn during a month. GDP is a flow—the value of the goods and services produced in a country *during a given time period*. Saving and investment are also flows.

A **stock** is a quantity that exists at a point in time. The water in a bathtub is a stock. So are the number of CDs that you own, and the amount of money in your savings account. The two key stocks in macroeconomics are wealth and capital. And the flows of saving and investment change these stocks. Let's see how.

**Wealth and Saving** **Wealth** is the value of all the things that people own. What people own, a stock, is related to what they earn, a flow. People earn an income, which is the amount they receive during a given time period from supplying the services of resources. Income that is left after paying taxes is either consumed or saved. *Consumption expenditure* is the amount spent on consumption goods and services. *Saving* is the amount of income remaining after consumption expenditures are met. So saving adds to wealth.

For example, suppose that at the end of the school year, you have $250 in a savings account and some textbooks that are worth $300. That's all you own. Your wealth is $550. Suppose that you take a summer job and earn an income of $5,000. You are extremely careful and spend only $1,000 through the summer on consumption goods and services. At the end of the summer, when school starts again, you have $4,250 in your savings account. Your wealth is now $4,550. Your wealth has increased by $4,000, which equals your saving of $4,000. Your saving of $4,000 equals your income of $5,000 minus your consumption expenditure of $1,000.

National wealth and national saving work just like this personal example. The wealth of a nation at the start of a year equals its wealth at the start of the previous year plus its saving during the year. Its saving equals its income minus its consumption expenditure.

**Capital and Investment** *Capital* is the plant, equipment, buildings, and inventories of raw materials and semifinished goods that are used to produce other goods and services. The amount of capital in the economy exerts a big influence on GDP.

Two flows change the stock of capital: investment and depreciation. *Investment*, the purchase of new capital, increases the stock of capital. (Investment includes additions to inventories.) **Depreciation** is the decrease in the stock of capital that results from wear and tear and obsolescence. Another name for depreciation is **capital consumption**. The total amount spent on purchases of new capital and on replacing depreciated capital is called **gross investment**. The amount by which the stock of capital increases is called **net investment**. Net investment equals gross investment minus depreciation.

Figure 5.2 illustrates these concepts. On January 1, 2003, Tom's CDs, Inc., had 3 machines. This quantity was its initial capital. During 2003, Tom's scrapped an older machine. This quantity is its depreciation. After depreciation, Tom's stock of capital was down to 2 machines. But also during 2003, Tom's bought 2 new machines. This amount is its gross investment. By December 31, 2003, Tom's CDs had 4 machines, so its capital had increased by 1 machine. This amount is Tom's net investment. Tom's net investment equals its gross investment (the purchase of 2 new machines) minus its depreciation (1 machine scrapped).

The example of Tom's CDs can be applied to the economy as a whole. The nation's capital stock decreases because capital depreciates and increases because of gross investment. The change in the nation's capital stock from one year to the next equals its net investment.

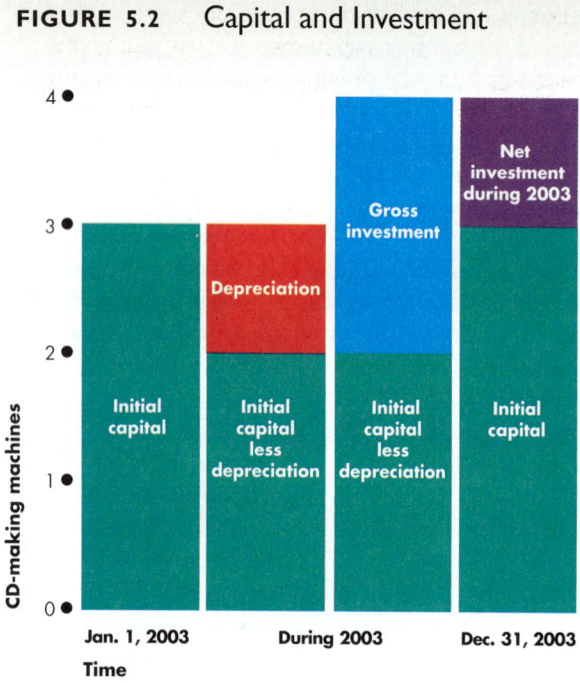

**FIGURE 5.2  Capital and Investment**

Tom's CDs has a capital stock at the end of 2003 that equals its capital stock at the beginning of the year plus its net investment. Net investment is equal to gross investment less depreciation. Tom's gross investment is the 2 new machines bought during the year, and its depreciation is the 1 machine that Tom's scrapped during the year. Tom's net investment is 1 machine.

**Back to the Gross in GDP**  We can now see the distinction between gross domestic product and net domestic product. On the income side of the flows that measure GDP, a firm's *gross* profit is its profit *before* subtracting *depreciation*. A firm's gross profit is part of aggregate income, so depreciation is counted as part of gross income and GDP. Similarly, on the expenditure side of the flows that measure GDP, *gross investment* includes depreciation, so depreciation is counted as part of aggregate expenditure, and total expenditure is a gross measure.

Net domestic product excludes depreciation. Like GDP, it can be viewed as the sum of incomes or expenditures. Net income includes firms' *net* profits—profits *after* subtracting depreciation. And net expenditure includes *net* investment, which also excludes depreciation.

**The Short Term Meets the Long Term**  The flows and stocks that you've just studied influence GDP growth and fluctuations. One of the reasons why GDP grows is that the capital stock grows. Investment adds to capital, so GDP grows because of investment. But investment fluctuates, which brings fluctuations to GDP. So capital and investment along with wealth and saving are part of the key to understanding both the growth and the fluctuations of GDP.

Investment and saving interact with income and consumption expenditure in a circular flow of expenditure and income. In this circular flow, income equals expenditure, which also equals the value of production. This equality is the foundation on which a nation's economic accounts are built and from which its GDP is measured.

> ### REVIEW QUIZ
> 1  Define GDP and distinguish between a final good and an intermediate good. Provide examples.
> 2  Why does GDP equal aggregate income and also equal aggregate expenditure?
> 3  How is U.S. investment financed? What determines national saving? national savings / Foreign borrow
> 4  What is the distinction between gross and net? before taxes, after taxes

Let's now see how the ideas that you've just studied are used in practice. We'll see how GDP and its components are measured in the United States today.

# Measuring U.S. GDP

The BUREAU OF ECONOMIC ANALYSIS (BEA) uses the concepts that you met in the circular flow model to measure GDP and its components in the *National Income and Product Accounts*. Because the value of aggregate output equals aggregate expenditure and aggregate income, there are two approaches available for measuring GDP, and both are used. They are

- The expenditure approach
- The income approach

## The Expenditure Approach

The *expenditure approach* measures GDP as the sum of consumption expenditure ($C$), investment ($I$), government purchases of goods and services ($G$), and net exports of goods and services ($X - M$), corresponding to the red flows in the circular flow model in Fig. 5.1. Table 5.1 shows the result of this approach for 2003. The table uses the terms in the *National Income and Product Accounts*.

*Personal consumption expenditures* are the expenditures by households on goods and services produced in the United States and in the rest of the world. They include goods such as CDs and books and services such as banking and legal advice. They do *not* include the purchase of new homes, which is counted as part of investment. But they do include the purchase of consumer durable goods, which technically are capital like homes.

*Gross private domestic investment* is expenditure on capital equipment and buildings by firms and expenditure on new homes by households. It also includes the change in business inventories.

*Government purchases of goods and services* are the purchases of goods and services by all levels of government. This item includes expenditures on national defense and garbage collection. But it does *not* include transfer payments because they are not purchases of goods and services.

*Net exports of goods and services* are the value of exports minus the value of imports. This item includes computers that IBM sells to Volkswagen, the German auto producer (a U.S. export), and Japanese DVD players that Circuit City buys from Sony (a U.S. import).

Table 5.1 shows the relative magnitudes of the four items of aggregate expenditure.

### TABLE 5.1 GDP: The Expenditure Approach

| Item | Symbol | Amount in 2003 (billions of dollars) | Percentage of GDP |
|---|---|---|---|
| Personal consumption expenditures | C | 7,674 | 70.7 |
| Gross private domestic investment | I | 1,624 | 15.0 |
| Government purchases of goods and services | G | 2,054 | 18.9 |
| Net exports of goods and services | X – M | –505 | –4.7 |
| **Gross domestic product** | Y | 10,847 | 100.0 |

The expenditure approach measures GDP as the sum of personal consumption expenditures ($C$), gross private domestic investment ($I$), government purchases of goods and services ($G$), and net exports ($X - M$). In 2003, GDP measured by the expenditure approach was $10,847 billion. Two thirds of aggregate expenditure is on personal consumption goods and services.

*Source:* U.S. Department of Commerce, Bureau of Economic Analysis.

## The Income Approach

The *income approach* measures GDP by summing the incomes that firms pay households for the factors of production they hire—wages for labor, interest for capital, rent for land, and profits for entrepreneurship. Let's see how the income approach works.

The *National Income and Product Accounts* divide incomes into five categories:

1. Compensation of employees
2. Net interest
3. Rental income
4. Corporate profits
5. Proprietors' income

*Compensation of employees* is the payment for labor services. It includes net wages and salaries (called "take-home pay") that workers receive plus taxes withheld on earnings plus fringe benefits such as social security and pension fund contributions.

*Net interest* is the interest households receive on loans they make minus the interest households pay on their own borrowing.

*Rental income* is the payment for the use of land and other rented resources.

*Corporate profits* are the profits of corporations, some of which are paid to households in the form of dividends and some of which are retained by corporations as undistributed profits. They are all income.

*Proprietors' income* is a mixture of the previous four items. The BEA cannot split the income earned by the owner-operator of a business into compensation for labor, payment for the use of capital, and profit, so the BEA lumps them into this single category.

Table 5.2 shows these five incomes and their relative magnitudes.

The sum of the incomes is called *net domestic income at factor cost*. The term *factor cost* is used because it is the cost of the factors of production used to produce final goods. When we sum all the expenditures on final goods, we arrive at a total called *domestic product at market prices*. Market prices and factor cost would be the same except for indirect taxes and subsidies.

An *indirect tax* is a tax paid by consumers when they buy goods and services. (In contrast, a *direct tax* is a tax on income.) State sales taxes and taxes on alcohol, gasoline, and tobacco products are indirect taxes. Because of indirect taxes, consumers pay more for some goods and services than producers receive. Market price exceeds factor cost. For example, if the sales tax is 7 percent, when you buy a $1 chocolate bar you pay $1.07. The factor cost of the chocolate bar including profit is $1. The market price is $1.07.

A *subsidy* is a payment by the government to a producer. Payments made to grain growers and dairy farmers are subsidies. Because of subsidies, consumers pay less for some goods and services than producers receive. Factor cost exceeds market price.

To get from factor cost to market price, we add indirect taxes and subtract subsidies. Making this adjustment brings us one step closer to GDP, but it does not quite get us there.

The final step is to add depreciation (or capital consumption). You can see the reason for this adjustment by recalling the distinction between gross and net profit and between gross and net investment. Total income is a net number because it includes firms' net profits, which exclude depreciation. Total expenditure is a gross number because it includes gross investment. So to get from total income to GDP, we must add depreciation to total income.

**TABLE 5.2** GDP: The Income Approach

| Item | Amount in 2003 (billions of dollars) | Percentage of GDP |
|---|---|---|
| Compensation of employees | 6,165 | 56.8 |
| Net interest | 582 | 5.4 |
| Rental income | 153 | 1.4 |
| Corporate profits | 1,023 | 9.4 |
| Proprietors' income | 839 | 7.7 |
| Indirect taxes less subsidies | 782 | 7.2 |
| Capital consumption (depreciation) | 1,303 | 12.0 |
| **Gross domestic product** | **10,847** | **100.0** |

The sum of all incomes equals net domestic income at factor cost. GDP equals net domestic income at factor cost plus indirect taxes less subsidies plus capital consumption (depreciation). In 2003, GDP measured by the income approach was $10,847 billion. The compensation of employees—labor income—was by far the largest part of aggregate income.

*Source:* U.S. Department of Commerce, Bureau of Economic Analysis.

### REVIEW QUIZ

1 What is the expenditure approach to measuring GDP?
2 What is the income approach to measuring GDP?
3 What adjustments must be made to total income to make it equal GDP?

You now know how GDP is defined and measured. The dollar value of GDP can change because either prices change or the volume of goods and services produced changes. You are next going to learn how we unscramble these two sources of change in GDP to reveal changes in the volume of goods and services produced—changes in what we call *real* GDP.

# Real GDP and the Price Level

YOU'VE SEEN THAT GDP MEASURES TOTAL expenditure on final goods and services in a given period. In 2003, GDP was $10,847 billion. A year before, in 2002, GDP was $10,428 billion. Because GDP in 2003 was greater than in 2002, we know that one or two things must have happened during 2003:

- We produced more goods and services in 2003 than in 2002.
- We paid higher prices for our goods and services in 2003 than we paid in 2001.

Producing more goods and services contributes to an improvement in our standard of living. Paying higher prices means that our cost of living has increased but our standard of living has not. So it matters a great deal why GDP has increased.

You're now going to learn how economists at the Bureau of Economic Analysis split GDP into two parts. One part tells us the change in production, and the other part tells us the change in prices. The method that is used has changed in recent years, and you are going to learn about the new method.

We measure the change in production by using a number that we call real GDP. **Real GDP** is the value of final goods and services produced in a given year when valued at constant prices. By comparing the value of the goods and services produced at constant prices, we can measure the change in the volume of production.

## Calculating Real GDP

Table 5.3 shows the quantities produced and the prices in 2002 for an economy that produces only two goods: balls and bats. The first step toward calculating real GDP is to calculate **nominal GDP**, which is the value of the final goods and services produced in a given year valued at the prices that prevailed in that same year. Nominal GDP is just a more precise name for GDP that we use when we want to be emphatic that we are not talking about real GDP.

**Nominal GDP Calculation** To calculate nominal GDP in 2002, sum the expenditures on balls and bats in 2002 as follows:

Expenditure on balls = 100 balls × $1 = $100.
Expenditure on bats = 20 bats × $5 = $100.
Nominal GDP in 2002 = $100 + $100 = $200.

Table 5.4 shows the quantities produced and the prices in 2003. The quantity of balls produced increased to 160, and the quantity of bats produced increased to 22. The price of a ball fell to 50¢, and the price of a bat increased to $22.50. To calculate nominal GDP in 2003, we sum the expenditures on balls and bats in 2003 as follows:

Expenditure on balls = 160 balls × $0.50 = $80.
Expenditure on bats = 22 bats × $22.50 = $495.
Nominal GDP in 2003 = $80 + $495 = $575.

To calculate real GDP, we choose one year, called the *base year*, against which to compare the other years. In the United States today, the base year is 2000. The choice of the base year is not important. It is just a common reference point. We'll use 2002 as the base year. By definition, real GDP equals nominal GDP in the base year. So real GDP in 2002 is $200.

**Base-Year Prices Value of Real GDP** The base-year prices method of calculating real GDP, which is the traditional method, values the quantities produced in a year at the prices of the base year. Table 5.5 shows the prices for 2002 and the quantities in 2003 (based on the information in Tables 5.3 and 5.4). The value

### TABLE 5.3  GDP Data for 2002

| Item | Quantity | Price |
|---|---|---|
| Balls | 100 | $1.00 |
| Bats | 20 | $5.00 |

### TABLE 5.4  GDP Data for 2003

| Item | Quantity | Price |
|---|---|---|
| Balls | 160 | $0.50 |
| Bats | 22 | $22.50 |

### TABLE 5.5  2003 Quantities and 2002 Prices

| Item  | Quantity | Price  |
|-------|----------|--------|
| Balls | 160      | $1.00  |
| Bats  | 22       | $5.00  |

of the 2003 quantities at the 2002 prices is calculated as follows:

Expenditure on balls = 160 balls × $1.00 = $160.
Expenditure on bats = 22 bats × $5.00 = $110.
Value of the 2003 quantities at 2002 prices = $270.

Using the traditional base-year prices method, $270 would be recorded as real GDP in 2003.

**Chain-Weighted Output Index Calculation** The **chain-weighted output index** method, which is the new method of calculating real GDP, uses the prices of two adjacent years to calculate the real GDP growth rate. So to find the real GDP growth rate in 2003, we compare the quantities produced in 2002 and 2003 by using both the 2002 prices and the 2003 prices. We then average the two sets of numbers in a special way that we'll now describe.

To compare the quantities produced in 2002 and 2003 at 2003 prices, we need to calculate the value of 2002 quantities at 2003 prices. Table 5.6 summarizes these quantities and prices. The value of the 2002 quantities at the 2003 prices is calculated as follows:

Expenditure on balls = 100 balls × $0.50 = $50.
Expenditure on bats = 20 bats × $22.50 = $450.
Value of the 2002 quantities at 2003 prices = $500.

We now have two comparisons between 2002 and 2003. At the 2002 prices, the value of production

### TABLE 5.6  2002 Quantities and 2003 Prices

| Item  | Quantity | Price   |
|-------|----------|---------|
| Balls | 100      | $0.50   |
| Bats  | 20       | $22.50  |

increased from $200 in 2002 to $270 in 2003. The increase in value is $70, and the percentage increase is ($70 ÷ $200) × 100, which is 35 percent.

At the 2003 prices, the value of production increased from $500 in 2002 to $575 in 2003. The increase in value is $75, and the percentage increase is ($75 ÷ $500) × 100, which is 15 percent.

The new method of calculating real GDP uses the average of these two percentage increases. The average of 35 percent and 15 percent is (35 + 15) ÷ 2, which equals 25 percent. Real GDP is 25 percent greater in 2003 than in 2002. Real GDP in 2002 is $200, so real GDP in 2003 is $250.

**Chain Linking** The calculation that we've just described is repeated each year. Each year is compared with its preceding year. So in 2004, the calculations are repeated but using the prices and quantities of 2003 and 2004. Real GDP in 2004 equals real GDP in 2003 increased by the calculated percentage change in real GDP for 2004. For example, suppose that real GDP for 2004 is calculated to be 20 percent greater than that in 2003. You know that real GDP in 2003 is $250. So real GDP in 2004 is 20 percent greater than this value and is $300. In every year, real GDP is valued in base-year (2002) dollars.

By applying the calculated percentage change to the real GDP of the preceding year, real GDP in each year is linked back to the dollars of the base year like the links in a chain.

### Calculating the Price Level

You've seen how real GDP is used to reveal the change in the quantity of goods and services produced. We're now going to see how we can find the change in prices that increases our cost of living.

The average level of prices is called the **price level**. One measure of the price level is the **GDP deflator**, which is an average of current-year prices expressed as a percentage of base-year prices. We calculate the GDP deflator by using the formula:

GDP deflator = (Nominal GDP ÷ Real GDP) × 100.

You can see why the GDP deflator is a measure of the price level. If nominal GDP rises but real GDP remains unchanged, it must be that the price level has risen. The formula gives a higher value for the GDP deflator. The larger the nominal GDP for a given real GDP, the higher is the price level and the larger is the GDP deflator.

TABLE 5.7  Calculating the GDP Deflator

| Year | Nominal GDP | Real GDP | GDP Deflator |
|---|---|---|---|
| 2002 | $200 | $200 | 100 |
| 2003 | $575 | $250 | 230 |

Table 5.7 shows how the GDP deflator is calculated. In 2002, the deflator is 100. In 2003, it is 230, which equals nominal GDP of $575 divided by real GDP of $250 and then multiplied by 100.

### Deflating the GDP Balloon

You can think of GDP as a balloon that is blown up by growing production and rising prices. In Fig. 5.3, the GDP deflator lets the inflation air out of the nominal GDP balloon—the contribution of rising prices—so that we can see what has happened to *real* GDP. The red balloon for 1991 shows real GDP in that year. The green balloon shows *nominal* GDP in 2001. The red balloon for 2001 shows real GDP for that year. To see real GDP in 2001, we *deflate* nominal GDP using the GDP deflator.

### REVIEW QUIZ

1  What is the distinction between nominal GDP and real GDP?
2  What is the traditional method of calculating real GDP?
3  What is the new method of calculating real GDP?
4  How is the GDP deflator calculated?

You now know how to calculate real GDP and the GDP deflator. Your next task is to learn how to use real GDP to calculate economic growth and to make economic welfare comparisons. We also look at some limitations of real GDP as a measure of economic welfare and as a tool for comparing living standards across countries.

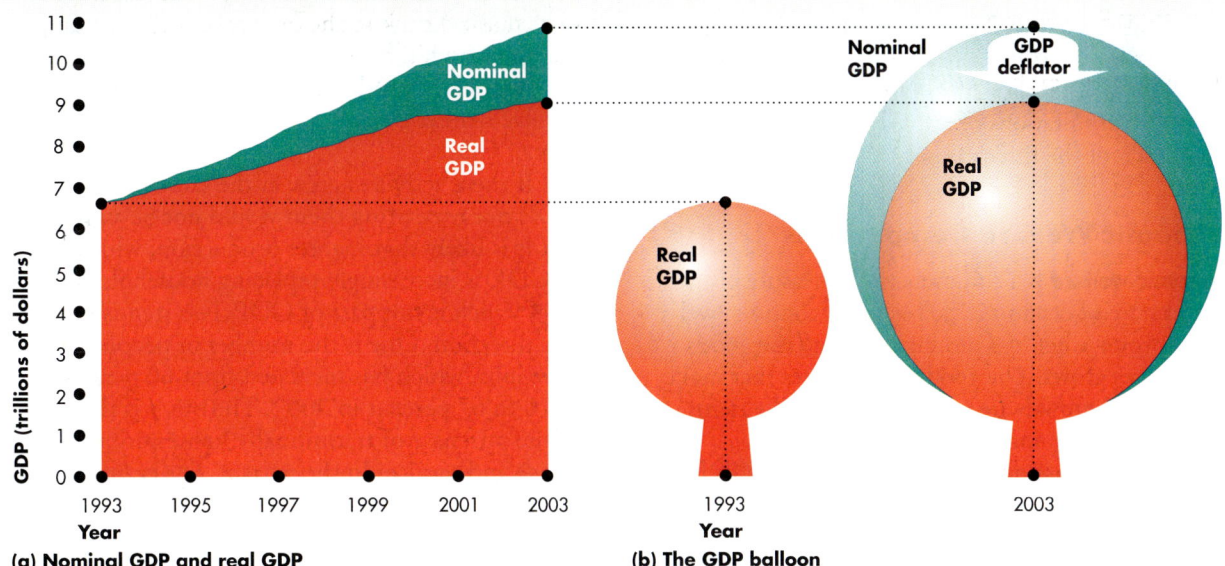

**FIGURE 5.3  The U.S. GDP Balloon**

(a) Nominal GDP and real GDP

(b) The GDP balloon

Part of the rise in GDP comes from inflation and part from increased production—an increase in real GDP. The GDP deflator lets some air out of the GDP balloon so that we can see the extent to which production has increased.

Source: U.S. Department of Commerce, Bureau of Economic Analysis.

# Measuring Economic Growth

WE USE ESTIMATES OF REAL GDP TO CALCULATE the economic growth rate. The **economic growth rate** is the percentage change in the quantity of goods and services produced from one year to the next. To calculate the economic growth rate, we use the formula:

$$\text{Economic growth rate} = \frac{\text{Real GDP this year} - \text{Real GDP last year}}{\text{Real GDP last year}} \times 100.$$

For example, real GDP was $10,288 billion in 2003 and $10,045 billion in 2002. So the economic growth rate (percent per year) during 2003 was:

$$\text{Economic growth rate} = \frac{(\$10{,}288 - \$10{,}045)}{\$10{,}045} \times 100$$

$$= 2.42 \text{ percent per year.}$$

We want to measure the economic growth rate so that we can make

- Economic welfare comparisons
- International comparisons
- Business cycle forecasts

Although the real GDP growth rate is used for these three purposes, it is not a perfect measure for any of them. Nor is it a totally misleading measure. We'll evaluate the limitations of real GDP and its growth rate in each of the three cases.

## Economic Welfare Comparisons

**Economic welfare** is a comprehensive measure of the general state of economic well-being. Economic welfare improves when the production of *all* the goods and services grows. The goods and services that make up real GDP growth are only a part of all the items that influence economic welfare.

Today, because of real GDP growth, real GDP per person in the United States of $39,000 is twice what it was in 1966. But are we twice as well off? Does this growth of real GDP provide a full and accurate measure of the change in economic welfare?

It does not. The reason is that economic welfare depends on many other factors that are either not measured accurately by real GDP or not measured at all by real GDP. Some of these factors are

- Overadjustment for inflation
- Household production
- Underground economic activity
- Health and life expectancy
- Leisure time
- Environment quality
- Political freedom and social justice

**Overadjustment for Inflation** The price indexes that are used to measure inflation give an upward-biased estimate of true inflation. (You will learn about the sources of this bias on p. 143.) If we overestimate the rise in prices, we underestimate the growth of real GDP. When car prices rise because cars have improved (safer, more fuel efficient, more comfortable), the GDP deflator counts the price increase as inflation. So what is really an increase in production is counted as an increase in price rather than an increase in real GDP. It is deflated away by the wrongly measured higher price level. The magnitude of this bias is probably less than 1 percentage point a year, but its exact magnitude is not known.

**Household Production** An enormous amount of production takes place every day in our homes. Preparing meals, cleaning the kitchen, changing a light bulb, cutting the grass, washing the car, and helping a high school student with homework are all examples of productive activities that do not involve market transactions and are not counted as part of GDP.

If these activities grew at the same rate as real GDP, not measuring them would not be a problem. But it is likely that market production, which is part of GDP, is increasingly replacing household production, which is not part of GDP. Two trends point in this direction. One is the number of people who have jobs, which has increased from 60 percent in 1970 to 67 percent in 2002. The other is the trend in the purchase of traditionally home-produced goods and services in the market. For example, more and more families now eat in fast-food restaurants—one of the fastest-growing industries in the United States—and use day-care services. This trend means that an increasing proportion of food preparation and child care that were part of household production are now measured as part of GDP. So real GDP grows more rapidly than does real GDP plus home production.

**Underground Economic Activity** The *underground economy* is the part of the economy that is purposely hidden from the view of the government to avoid taxes and regulations or because the goods and services being produced are illegal. Because underground economic activity is unreported, it is omitted from GDP.

The underground economy is easy to describe, even if it is hard to measure. It includes the production and distribution of illegal drugs, production that uses illegal labor that is paid less than the minimum wage, and jobs done for cash to avoid paying income taxes. This last category might be quite large and includes tips earned by cab drivers, hairdressers, and hotel and restaurant workers.

Estimates of the scale of the underground economy range between 9 and 30 percent of GDP ($800 billion to $2,800 billion) in the United States and much more in some countries. It is particularly large in some Eastern European countries that are making a transition from communist economic planning to a market economy.

Provided that the underground economy is a reasonably stable proportion of the total economy, the growth rate of real GDP still gives a useful estimate of changes in economic welfare. But sometimes production shifts from the underground economy to the rest of the economy, and sometimes it shifts the other way. The underground economy expands relative to the rest of the economy if taxes become especially high or if regulations become especially restrictive. And the underground economy shrinks relative to the rest of the economy if the burdens of taxes and regulations are eased. During the 1980s, when tax rates were cut, there was an increase in the reporting of previously hidden income and tax revenues increased. So some part (but probably a very small part) of the expansion of real GDP during the 1980s represented a shift from the underground economy rather than an increase in production.

**Health and Life Expectancy** Good health and a long life—the hopes of everyone—do not show up in real GDP, at least not directly. A higher real GDP does enable us to spend more on medical research, health care, a good diet, and exercise equipment. And as real GDP has increased, our life expectancy has lengthened—from 70 years at the end of World War II to approaching 80 years today. Infant deaths and death in childbirth, two fearful scourges of the nineteenth century, have almost been eliminated.

But we face new health and life expectancy problems every year. AIDS and drug abuse are taking young lives at a rate that causes serious concern. When we take these negative influences into account, we see that real GDP growth overstates the improvements in economic welfare.

**Leisure Time** Leisure time is an economic good that adds to our economic welfare. Other things being equal, the more leisure we have, the better off we are. Our working time is valued as part of GDP, but our leisure time is not. Yet from the point of view of economic welfare, that leisure time must be at least as valuable to us as the wage that we earn on the last hour worked. If it were not, we would work instead of taking the leisure. Over the years, leisure time has steadily increased. The workweek has become shorter, more people take early retirement, and the number of vacation days has increased. These improvements in economic well-being are not reflected in real GDP.

**Environment Quality** Economic activity directly influences the quality of the environment. The burning of hydrocarbon fuels is the most visible activity that damages our environment. But it is not the only example. The depletion of exhaustible resources, the mass clearing of forests, and the pollution of lakes and rivers are other major environmental consequences of industrial production.

Resources that are used to protect the environment are valued as part of GDP. For example, the value of catalytic converters that help to protect the atmosphere from automobile emissions is part of GDP. But if we did not use such pieces of equipment and instead polluted the atmosphere, we would not count the deteriorating air that we were breathing as a negative part of GDP.

An industrial society possibly produces more atmospheric pollution than an agricultural society does. But pollution does not always increase as we become wealthier. Wealthy people value a clean environment and are willing to pay for one. Compare the pollution that was discovered in East Germany in the late 1980s with pollution in the United States. East Germany, a poor country, polluted its rivers, lakes, and atmosphere in a way that is unimaginable in the United States or in wealthy West Germany.

**Political Freedom and Social Justice** Most people in the Western world value political freedoms such as those provided by the U.S. Constitution. And they value social justice or fairness—equality of opportunity and of access to social security safety nets that protect people from the extremes of misfortune.

A country might have a very large real GDP per person but have limited political freedom and equity. For example, a small elite might enjoy political liberty and extreme wealth while the vast majority are effectively enslaved and live in abject poverty. Such an economy would generally be regarded as having less economic welfare than one that had the same amount of real GDP but in which political freedoms were enjoyed by everyone. Today, China has rapid real GDP growth but limited political freedoms, while Russia has slow real GDP growth and an emerging democratic political system. Economists have no easy way to determine which of these countries is better off.

**The Bottom Line** Do we get the wrong message about the growth in economic welfare by looking at the growth of real GDP? The influences that are omitted from real GDP are probably important and could be large. Developing countries have a larger underground economy and a larger amount of household production than do developed countries. So as an economy develops and grows, part of the apparent growth might reflect a switch from underground to regular production and from home production to market production. This measurement error overstates the rate of economic growth and the improvement in economic welfare.

Other influences on living standards include the amount of leisure time available, the quality of the environment, the security of jobs and homes, and the safety of city streets. It is possible to construct broader measures that combine the many influences that contribute to human happiness. Real GDP will be one element in those broader measures, but it will by no means be the whole of them.

### International Comparisons

All the problems we've just reviewed affect the economic welfare of every country, so to make international comparisons of economic welfare, factors in addition to real GDP must be used. But real GDP comparisons are major components of international welfare comparisons, and two special problems arise in making these comparisons. First, the real GDP of one country must be converted into the *same currency units* as the real GDP of the other country. Second, the *same prices* must be used to value the goods and services in the countries being compared. Let's look at these two problems by using a striking example, a comparison of the United States and China.

In 2003, real GDP per person in the United States was $39,000. The official Chinese statistics published in the International Monetary Fund's (IMF) World Economic Outlook (WEO) says that real GDP per person in China in 2003 was 9,500 yuan. (The yuan is the currency of China.) On the average, during 2003, $1 U.S. was worth 8.276 yuan. If we use this exchange rate to convert Chinese yuan into U.S. dollars, we get a value of $1,150. This comparison of China and the United States makes China look extremely poor. In 2003, GDP per person in the United States was 34 times that in China.

Figure 5.4 shows the story of real GDP in China from 1983 to 2003 based on converting the yuan to the U.S. dollar at the market exchange rate. Figure 5.4 also shows another story based on an estimate of real GDP per person that is much larger than the official measure. Let's see how this alternative measurement is made. GDP in the United States is measured by using prices that prevail in the United States. China's GDP is measured by using prices that prevail in China. But the relative prices in the two countries are very different. Some goods that are expensive in the United States cost very little in China. These items have a small weight in China's real GDP. If, instead of using China's prices, all the goods and services produced in China are valued at the prices prevailing in the United States, then a more valid comparison can be made of GDP in the two countries. Such a comparison uses prices called *purchasing power parity prices* or *PPP*.

Robert Summers and Alan Heston, economists in the Center for International Comparisons at the University of Pennsylvania, have used PPP prices to construct real GDP data for more than 100 countries. And the IMF now uses methods similar to those of Summers and Heston to calculate PPP estimates of GDP in all countries. The PPP comparisons tell a remarkable story about China.

According to the PPP comparisons, GDP per person in the United States in 2003 was 6 times that of China, not the 34 times shown at the market exchange rate. Figure 5.4 shows the PPP view of China's real GDP and compares it with the market exchange rate view.

A prominent China scholar, Thomas Rawski of the University of Pittsburgh, doubts both sets of data shown in Fig. 5.4. He believes that the growth rate of

# Measuring Economic Growth

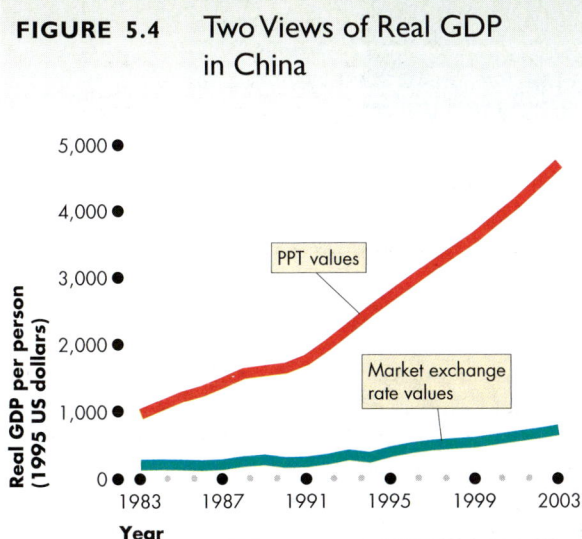

**FIGURE 5.4** Two Views of Real GDP in China

Valuing GDP at the market exchange rate, China is a poor developing country in which income per person is less than 3 percent of the U.S. level. But valuing GDP at purchasing power parity prices, China's real GDP is 16 percent of the U.S. level. Some China scholars think that even the market exchange rate numbers are too big. So there is much uncertainty about China's real GDP.

*Sources:* International Monetary Fund, *World Economic Outlook*, September 2003, Washington, D.C.

China's real GDP has been exaggerated for some years and that even the market exchange rate data overstate real GDP in China.

U.S. real GDP is measured pretty reliably. But China's is not. The alternative measures of China's real GDP are unreliable, and the truth about GDP in China is not known. But China is expanding, and many businesses are paying close attention to the prospects of expanding their activities in China and other fast-growing Asian economies.

## Business Cycle Forecasts

If policymakers plan to raise interest rates to slow an expansion that they believe is too strong, they look at the latest estimates of real GDP. But suppose that for the reasons that we've just discussed, real GDP is mismeasured. Does this mismeasurement hamper our ability to identify the phases of the business cycle? It does not. The reason is that although the omissions from real GDP do change over time, they probably do not change in a systematic way with the business cycle. So inaccurate measurement of real GDP does not necessarily cause a wrong assessment of the phase of the business cycle.

The fluctuations in economic activity measured by real GDP tell a reasonably accurate story about the phase of the business cycle that the economy is in. When real GDP grows, the economy is in a business cycle expansion; when real GDP shrinks (for two quarters), the economy is in a recession. Also, as real GDP fluctuates, so do production and jobs.

But real GDP fluctuations probably exaggerate or overstate the fluctuations in total production and economic welfare. The reason is that when business activity slows in a recession, household production increases and so does leisure time. When business activity speeds up in an expansion, household production and leisure time decrease. Because household production and leisure time increase in a recession and decrease in an expansion, real GDP fluctuations tend to overstate the fluctuations in both total production and economic welfare. But the directions of change of real GDP, total production, and economic welfare are probably the same.

### REVIEW QUIZ

1. Does real GDP measure economic welfare? If not, why not?
2. Does real GDP measure total production of goods and services? If not, what are the main omissions?
3. How can we make valid international comparisons of real GDP?
4. Does the growth of real GDP measure the economic growth rate accurately?
5. Do the fluctuations in real GDP measure the business cycle accurately?

◆ You've now studied the methods used to measure GDP, economic growth, and the price level. And you've learned about some of the limitations of these measures. *Reading Between the Lines* on pp. 122–123 looks at real GDP in the 2003 U.S. expansion.

Your next task is to learn how we measure employment and unemployment and inflation.

# READING BETWEEN THE LINES

## *Real GDP in the 2003 Expansion*

**LOS ANGELES TIMES, NOVEMBER 26, 2003**

### Economy Expands at Fastest Clip Since 1984

The American economy grew even faster in the third quarter than the government first thought, thanks to fresh evidence that business was finally opening its pocketbook.

The Commerce Department said Tuesday that growth of the gross domestic product was a robust 8.2% from July through September—a percentage point, or about $24 billion, greater than it had estimated last month. It was the most robust quarterly expansion since 1984.

The department attributed most of the increase in the nation's total output of goods and services to a substantial jump in business spending. ...

The biggest news in the GDP numbers seemed to be that corporate America, which has been portrayed as hunkered down and cautious about expanding, is actually flush with cash and ready to invest—at least in computers and software.

Business investment grew at an annualized rate of 14% during the July-through-September quarter, the department said, better than the 11.1% rate the government initially estimated. Equipment and software investment climbed at an 18.4% pace, its best showing in five years.

The buying binge was fueled by corporate profits, which the government said grew at an annual pace of more than 30%. ...

Commerce officials said consumer spending grew at a 6.4% rate in the quarter, less than the 6.6% they originally estimated. ....

©2003 Los Angeles Times, November 26, 2003. Reprinted with permission. Further reproduction prohibited.

### Essence of the Story

■ Real GDP grew at an annual rate of 8.2 percent from July through September 2003 (revised up from 7.2 percent).

■ It was the fastest quarterly growth since 1984.

■ Business investment grew at an annual rate of 14 percent (revised up from 11.1 percent).

■ Consumer spending grew at an annual rate of 6.4 percent (revised *down* from 6.6 percent).

■ Corporate profits grew at an annual rate of more than 30 percent.

## Economic Analysis

- This news article reports revised real GDP numbers for the third quarter of 2003.

- The preliminary estimates of a month earlier were revised upward as more complete data became available.

- The data for this quarter were the first to show a large increase following the recession of 2001.

- Figure 1 shows the real GDP growth rate (annualized) quarter by quarter from the first quarter of 1997 to the third quarter of 2003.

- You can see the high growth rates of the 1990s, a slowing of the growth rate during 2000, a recession in 2001, and growth through 2002 and 2003.

- Figure 2 shows the components of real GDP. You can see that most of the growth of real GDP comes from consumption growth and that, during 2000 and 2001, investment, shown by the red bars, decreased.

- The news article reports increases in business investment and business profit. Investment is part of aggregate expenditure and profit is part of aggregate income. So these items are on opposite sides of the circular flow of income and expenditure.

- The 2002–2003 expansion was a weak one.

- Figure 3 emphasizes the weakness of the 2002–2003 expansion.

- After eight quarters, real GDP was 7 percent above its trough level.

- At a similar point in the average of the previous six expansions, real GDP was 11 percent above its trough level.

- Despite the rapid growth in the third quarter of 2003, the current expansion is close to the weakest of the past six expansions.

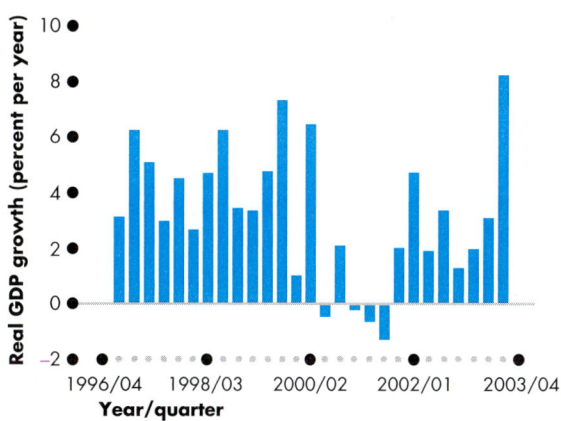

Figure 1 Real GDP growth rates: 1997–2003

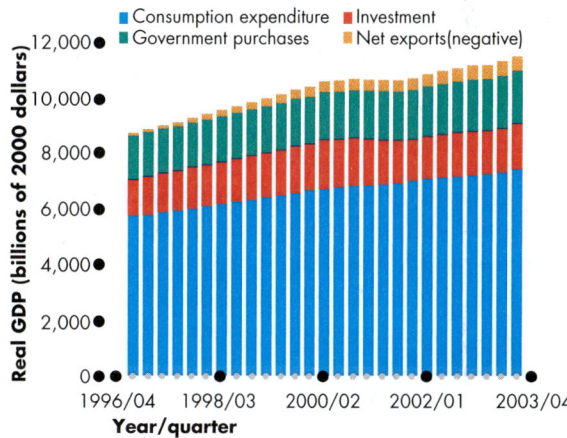

Figure 2 Real GDP and components: 1997–2003

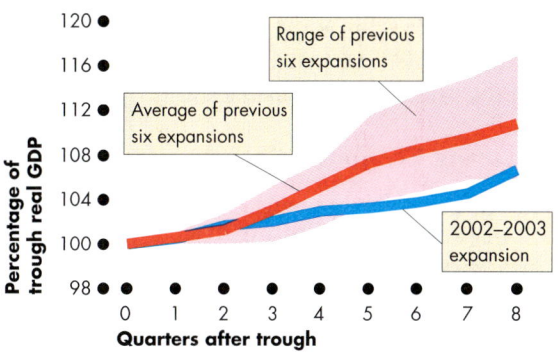

Figure 3 The jobless recovery

# SUMMARY

## KEY POINTS

### Gross Domestic Product (pp. 108–112)

- GDP, or gross domestic product, is the market value of all the final goods and services produced in a country during a given period.
- A final good is an item that is bought by its final user during a specified time period, and contrasts with an intermediate good, which is a component of a final good.
- GDP is calculated by using the expenditure and income totals in the circular flow of expenditure and income.
- Aggregate expenditure on goods and services equals aggregate income and GDP.

### Measuring U.S. GDP (pp. 113–114)

- Because aggregate expenditure, aggregate income, and the value of aggregate production are equal, we can measure GDP by using the expenditure approach or the income approach.
- The expenditure approach sums consumption expenditure, investment, government purchases of goods and services, and net exports.
- The income approach sums wages, interest, rent, and profit (and indirect taxes and depreciation).

### Real GDP and the Price Level (pp. 115–117)

- Real GDP is measured by a chain-weighted output index that compares the value of production each year with its value at the previous year's prices.
- The GDP deflator measures the price level based on the prices of the items that make up GDP.

### Measuring Economic Growth (pp. 118–121)

- We measure the economic growth rate as the percentage change in real GDP.
- Real GDP growth is not a perfect measure of economic growth because it excludes quality improvements, household production, the underground economy, health and life expectancy, leisure time, environmental damage, political freedom, and social justice.
- The growth rate of real GDP gives a good indication of the phases of the business cycle.

## KEY FIGURES AND TABLES

Figure 5.1   The Circular Flow of Expenditure and Income, 109
Figure 5.2   Capital and Investment, 112
Table 5.1    GDP: The Expenditure Approach, 113
Table 5.2    GDP: The Income Approach, 114

## KEY TERMS

Capital consumption, 111
Chain-weighted output index, 116
Consumption expenditure, 109
Depreciation, 111
Economic growth rate, 118
Economic welfare, 118
Exports, 110
Final good, 108
Flow, 111
GDP deflator, 116
Government purchases, 110
Gross domestic product (GDP), 108
Gross investment, 111
Imports, 110
Intermediate good, 108
Investment, 110
National saving, 111
Net exports, 110
Net investment, 111
Net taxes, 110
Nominal GDP, 115
Price level, 116
Real GDP, 115
Saving, 110
Stock, 111
Wealth, 111

# PROBLEMS

*1. The figure at the bottom of the page shows the flows of expenditure and income on Lotus Island. During 2002, $A$ was $20 million, $B$ was $60 million, $C$ was $24 million, $D$ was $30 million, and $E$ was $6 million. Calculate
   a. Aggregate expenditure.
   b. Aggregate income.
   c. GDP.
   d. Government budget deficit.
   e. Household saving.
   f. Government saving.
   g. National saving.
   h. Borrowing from the rest of the world.

2. In problem 1, during 2003, $A$ was $25 million, $B$ was $100 million, $C$ was $30 million, $D$ was $30 million, and $E$ was –$10 million. Calculate the quantities in problem 1 during 2003.

*3. Martha owns a copy shop that has 10 copiers. One copier wears out each year and is replaced. In addition, this year Martha will expand her business to 14 copiers. Calculate Martha's initial capital stock, depreciation, gross investment, net investment, and final capital stock.

4. Wendy operates a weaving shop with 20 looms. One loom wears out each year and is replaced. But this year, Wendy will expand her business to 24 looms. Calculate Wendy's initial capital stock, depreciation, gross investment, net investment, and final capital stock.

*5. The transactions in Ecoland last year were

| Item | Dollars |
|---|---|
| Wages paid to labor | 800,000 |
| Consumption expenditure | 600,000 |
| Taxes | 250,000 |
| Transfer payments | 50,000 |
| Profits | 200,000 |
| Investment | 250,000 |
| Government purchases | 200,000 |
| Exports | 300,000 |
| Saving | 300,000 |
| Imports | 250,000 |

   a. Calculate Ecoland's GDP.
   b. Did you use the expenditure approach or the income approach to make this calculation?
   c. How is investment financed?

6. The transactions in Highland last year were

| Item | Dollars |
|---|---|
| Wages paid to labor | 400,000 |
| Consumption expenditure | 350,000 |
| Net taxes | 125,000 |
| Profits | 140,000 |
| Investment | 150,000 |
| Government purchases | 130,000 |
| Exports | 120,000 |
| Saving | 135,000 |
| Imports | 140,000 |

   a. Calculate Highland's GDP.
   b. What extra information do you need to calculate net domestic product at factor cost?
   c. Where does Highland get the funds to finance its investment?

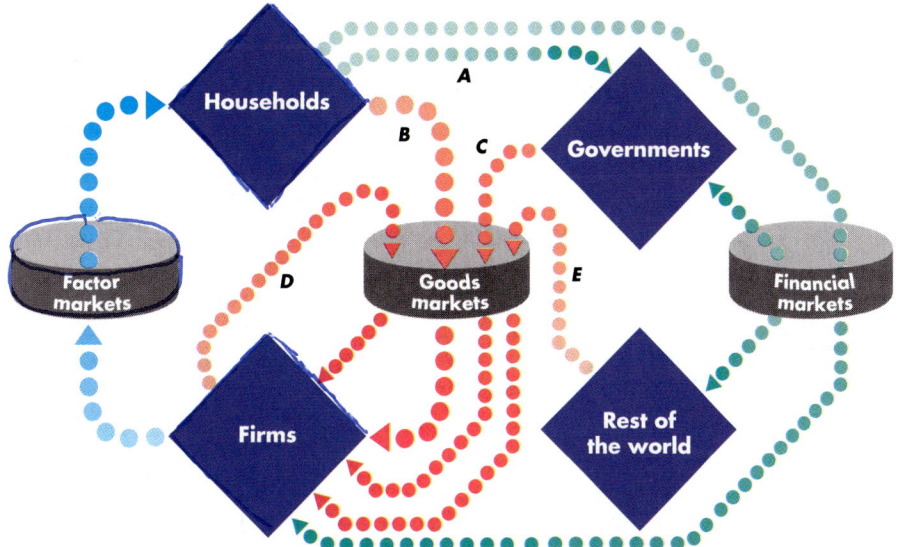

* Solutions to odd-numbered problems are available on MyEconLab.

*7. Bananaland produces only bananas and sunscreen. The base year is 2002, and the tables give the quantities produced and prices.

| | Quantity | |
|---|---|---|
| Good | 2002 | 2003 |
| Bananas | 1,000 bunches | 1,100 bunches |
| Sunscreen | 500 bottles | 525 bottles |

| | Price | |
|---|---|---|
| Good | 2002 | 2003 |
| Bananas | $2 a bunch | $3 a bunch |
| Sunscreen | $10 a bottle | $8 a bottle |

Calculate Bananaland's
  a. Nominal GDP in 2002 and 2003.
  b. Real GDP in 2003 using the base-year prices method.

8. Sea Island produces only lobsters and crabs. The base year is 2003, and the tables give the quantities produced and the prices.

| | Quantity | |
|---|---|---|
| Good | 2003 | 2004 |
| Lobsters | 1,000 | 1,100 |
| Crabs | 500 | 525 |

| | Price | |
|---|---|---|
| Good | 2003 | 2004 |
| Lobsters | $20 each | $25 each |
| Crabs | $10 each | $12 each |

Calculate Sea Island's
  a. Nominal GDP in 2003 and 2004.
  b. Real GDP in 2004 using the base-year prices method.

*9. Bananaland (described in problem 7) decides to use the chain-weighted output index method to calculate real GDP. Using this method:
  a. Calculate the growth rate of real GDP in 2003.
  b. Calculate the GDP deflator in 2003.
  c. Compare and comment on the differences in real GDP using the base-year prices and chain-weighted output index methods.

10. Sea Island (described in problem 8) decides to use the chain-weighted output index method to calculate real GDP. Using this method:
  a. Calculate the growth rate of real GDP in 2004.
  b. Calculate the GDP deflator in 2004.
  c. Compare and comment on the differences in real GDP using the base-year prices and chain-weighted output index methods.

## CRITICAL THINKING

1. Study *Reading Between the Lines* on pp. 122–123 and then answer the following questions:
  a. Which components of aggregate expenditure increased at the fastest rate in the third quarter of 2003?
  b. Which components of aggregate expenditure increased at the slowest rate in the third quarter of 2003?
  c. Explain why we do *not* add the change in profits to the change in investment and the other components of aggregate expenditure to find the total change in real GDP.
  d. For how long has the U.S. economy been expanding since the last business cycle trough?
  e. How does the current expansion compare with previous expansions? Did it start out weak and then strengthen, or start out strong and then weaken? Or has it been weak from the outset?
  f. Can you think of any reasons why the current expansion might be weak?

## WEB EXERCISES

**Use the links on MyEconLab to work the following exercise.**

1. Visit the Bureau of Economic Analysis. There you can obtain all the available data on GDP and the components of aggregate expenditure and aggregate income. You will find data in current price (nominal GDP) and constant prices (real GDP).
  a. What is the value of nominal GDP in the current quarter?
  b. What is the value of real GDP in the current quarter using the chain-weighted index method?
  c. What is the GDP deflator in the current quarter?
  d. What was the value of real GDP in the same quarter of the previous year?
  e. By how much has real GDP changed over the past year? (Express your answer as a percentage.)
  f. Did real GDP increase or decrease and what does the change tell you about the state of the economy over the past year?

# Monitoring Cycles, Jobs, and the Price Level

## Vital Signs

**The last U.S. recession began in March 2001 and** ended in November 2001. What exactly is a recession, who decides when it begins and ends, and what criteria are used to make these decisions?

Each month, we chart the course of the unemployment rate as a measure of U.S. economic health. How do we measure the unemployment rate? What does it tell us? Is it a reliable vital sign for the economy?

Every month, we also chart the number of people working, the number of hours they work, and the wages they receive. Are most new jobs full time or part time? And are they high-wage jobs or low-wage jobs?

As the U.S. economy expanded during 2002 and 2003, job growth was weak and these questions about the health of the labor market became of vital importance to millions of American families. We put the spotlight on the labor market during the so-called "jobless recovery" of 2002 and 2003 in *Reading Between the Lines* at the end of this chapter.

Having a good job that pays a decent wage is only half of the equation that translates into a good standard of living. The other half is the cost of living. We track the cost of the items that we buy with another number that is published every month, the Consumer Price Index, or CPI. What is the CPI? How is it calculated? And does it provide a reliable guide to the changes in our cost of living?

◆ These are the questions we study in this chapter. We begin by looking at the way in which a recession is identified and dated.

## After studying this chapter, you will be able to

- **Explain how we date business cycles**
- **Define the unemployment rate, the labor force participation rate, the employment-to-population ratio, and aggregate hours**
- **Describe the sources of unemployment, its duration, the groups most affected by it, and how it fluctuates over a business cycle**
- **Explain how we measure the price level and the inflation rate using the CPI**

# The Business Cycle

We defined the business cycle in Chapter 4 as the periodic but irregular up-and-down movement in production and jobs. A business cycle has two phases—expansion and recession—and two turning points—peak and trough. One definition of **recession** is a two-quarter decrease in real GDP. The National Bureau of Economic Research (NBER), which dates the phases of the U.S. cycle, defines a recession a bit differently from this common definition as follows.

> A **recession** is a significant decline in activity spread across the economy, lasting more than a few months, visible in industrial production, employment, real income, and wholesale-retail trade. A recession begins just after the economy reaches a **peak** of activity and ends as the economy reaches its **trough**. Between trough and peak, the economy is in an **expansion**.[1]

Real GDP is the broadest measure of economic activity, and another popular working definition of a recession is a decrease in real GDP that lasts for at least two quarters. But we don't measure real GDP each month, so the NBER does not use the real GDP numbers. Instead, it looks at employment, which is the broadest *monthly* indicator of economic activity, along with other monthly measures that include personal income, sales of manufactures, and industrial production.

The NBER Dating Committee waits until it sees a large enough decline before declaring that a recession has begun. It also waits until it sees a large enough expansion before declaring that a recession has ended.

## Business Cycle Dates

Each recession, expansion, and turning point has been dated by the NBER, which has identified 16 recessions and 17 expansions since 1919. Table 6.1 lists the dates of their peaks and troughs. On the average, recessions have lasted for just over a year and real GDP has fallen from peak to trough by more than 6 percent. Expansions have lasted for almost 4 years on the average, and real GDP has increased from trough to peak by an average of 22 percent.

But the averages hide huge variations from one cycle to another. The Great Depression, which began with a recession that ran from August 1929 to March 1933, was the most severe contraction of economic activity ever experienced. Over a 43-month period, real GDP shrank by 33 percent. The second most severe recession was also in the 1930s. Another relatively severe fall in real GDP occurred at the end of World War II in 1945. The only other recession that comes close to these is that of 1974–1975, which resulted from a fourfold rise in the price of oil, lasted for 16 months, and saw real GDP fall by 5 percent. The biggest expansion occurred during World War II, but the longest was in the 1990s. Other big expansions were in the 1960s and 1980s. There is no correlation between the length of an expansion and the length of the preceding recession.

Figure 6.1 shows the range of variation across the different recessions and expansions. Figure 6.1 shows

| TABLE 6.1 | Business Cycle Reference Dates |
|---|---|
| **Trough** | **Peak** |
| March 1919 | January 1920 |
| July 1921 | May 1923 |
| July 1924 | October 1926 |
| November 1927 | August 1929 |
| March 1933 | May 1937 |
| June 1938 | February 1945 |
| October 1945 | November 1948 |
| October 1949 | July 1953 |
| May 1954 | August 1957 |
| April 1958 | April 1960 |
| February 1961 | December 1969 |
| November 1970 | November 1973 |
| March 1975 | January 1980 |
| July 1980 | July 1981 |
| November 1982 | July 1990 |
| March 1991 | March 2001 |
| November 2001 | — |

Seventeen cycles between 1919 and 2001 had average recessions that lasted for a bit more than a year and expansions that had average lengths of almost 4 years. Recessions have been getting shorter and expansions longer.

*Source:* National Bureau of Economic Research.

---

[1] "The NBER's Business-Cycle Dating Procedure," January 10, 2002, NBER Web site (www.nber.org). (Boldfacing of key terms added.)

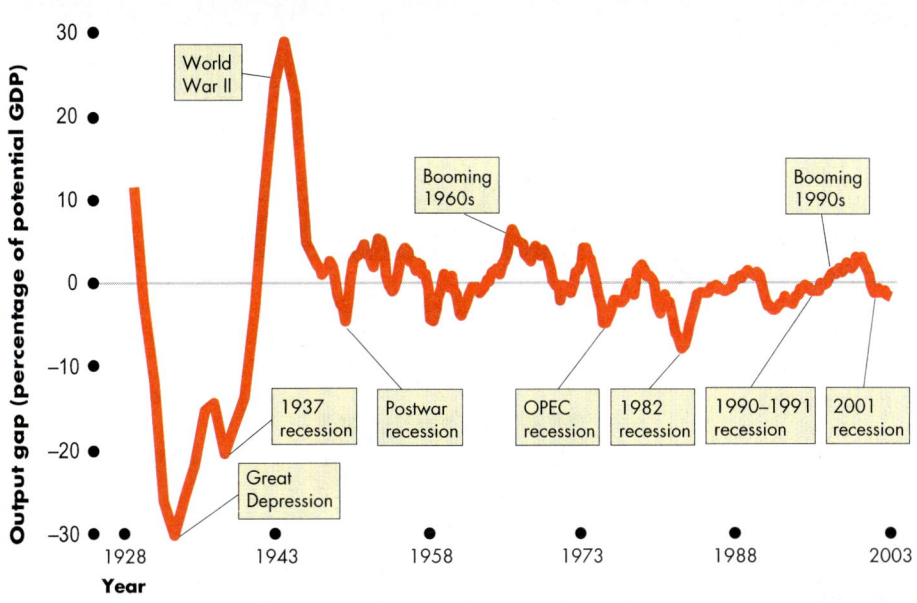

FIGURE 6.1  Business Cycle Patterns

Recessions have lasted from 43 months during the Great Depression, when real GDP fell by 33 percent, to 6 months in 1980, when real GDP fell by 2.5 percent. The mildest recession lasted through most of 1970, when real GDP fell by less than 1 percent. The 2001 recession was the second mildest. Recessions have been less severe in the post–World War II period. Expansions have lasted from 6 months in 1980 to 120 months from 1991 to 2001. Expansions are becoming longer and stronger.

*Sources:* National Bureau of Economic Research, Bureau of Economic Analysis, and author's calculations.

the total percentage change in real GDP during successive recessions and expansions. The figure also shows that expansions last much longer than recessions. Expansions are the normal state of the economy. Recessions are relatively short-lived interruptions of that normal process.

### The 2001 Recession

The NBER identified March 2001 as the month in which the most recent recession began and November 2001 as the month in which it ended. This recession was the second mildest ever experienced (the recession of 1970 was the mildest on record). Real GDP fell by only 0.6 percent from the peak in the fourth quarter of 2000 to the trough in the third quarter of 2001.

The level of employment, which peaked in March 2001, was the major indicator of recession used by the NBER. Industrial production was another indicator used by the NBER, but it had already peaked in the summer of 2000. A third indicator, manufacturing trade sales, fluctuated so erratically during 2001 that it provided no clear information about the timing of the onset of recession. A fourth indicator, personal incomes, continued to rise but eventually peaked in the fall of 2001.

Although the recession was declared over by November 2001, the economy remained weak throughout 2002 and 2003. It is normal for real GDP to remain below its pre-recession peak for some time after an expansion begins. And in the recovery from the 2001 recession, this tendency was pronounced. Real GDP grew at an annual rate of less than 3 percent, and the number of people employed continued to fall in what came to be called a jobless recovery.

The Federal Reserve kept interest rates low to aid recovery and to avoid the risk (small though it was) that the economy would slip into a further recession.

### REVIEW QUIZ

1. What are the phases of the business cycle?
2. How do we know when a recession has begun?
3. How do we know when a recession has ended?
4. Have recessions been getting worse?
5. What was unusual about the 2001 recession?

## Jobs and Wages

YOU HAVE SEEN THAT EMPLOYMENT IS ONE OF the key features of the economy that helps the NBER determine the onset of recession. The state of the labor market has a large impact on our incomes and our lives. We become concerned when jobs are hard to find and more relaxed when they are plentiful. But we want a good job, which means that we want a well-paid and interesting job. You are now going to learn how economists track the health of the labor market.

### Population Survey

Every month, the U.S. Census Bureau surveys 60,000 households and asks a series of questions about the age and job market status of the members of each household. This survey is called the **Current Population Survey**. The Census Bureau uses the answers to describe the anatomy of the labor force.

Figure 6.2 shows the population categories used by the Census Bureau and the relationships among the categories. It divides the population into two groups: the working-age population and others who are too young to work or who live in institutions and are unable to work. The **working-age population** is the total number of people aged 16 years and over who are not in jail, a hospital, or some other form of institutional care. The Census Bureau divides the working-age population into two groups: those in the labor force and those not in the labor force. It also divides the labor force into two groups: the employed and the unemployed. So the **labor force** is the sum of the employed and the unemployed.

To be counted as employed in the Current Population Survey, a person must have either a full-time job or a part-time job. To be counted as *un*employed, a person must be available for work and must be in one of three categories:

1. Without work but has made specific efforts to find a job within the previous four weeks
2. Waiting to be called back to a job from which he or she has been laid off
3. Waiting to start a new job within 30 days

Anyone surveyed who satisfies one of these three criteria is counted as unemployed. People in the working-age population who are neither employed nor unemployed are classified as not in the labor force.

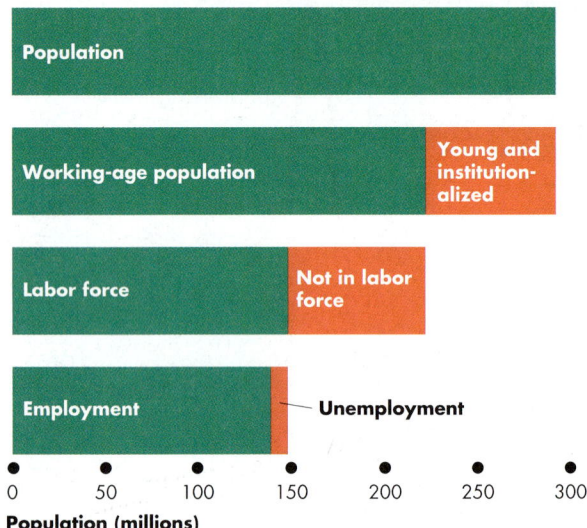

**FIGURE 6.2  Population Labor Force Categories**

The total population is divided into the working-age population and the young and institutionalized. The working-age population is divided into those in the labor force and those not in the labor force. The labor force is divided into the employed and the unemployed.

*Source:* Bureau of Labor Statistics.

In 2003, the population of the United States was 292 million. There were 70.8 million people under 16 years of age or living in institutions. The working age population was 221.2 million. Of this number, 73.4 million were not in the labor force. Most of these people were in school full time or had retired from work. The remaining 147.8 million people made up the U.S. labor force. Of these, 138.5 million were employed and 9.3 million were unemployed.

### Three Labor Market Indicators

The Census Bureau calculates three indicators of the state of the labor market, which are shown in Fig. 6.3. They are

- The unemployment rate
- The labor force participation rate
- The employment-to-population ratio

**The Unemployment Rate** The amount of unemployment is an indicator of the extent to which people who want jobs can't find them. The **unemployment rate** is the percentage of the people in the labor force who are unemployed. That is,

$$\text{Unemployment rate} = \frac{\text{Number of people unemployed}}{\text{Labor force}} \times 100$$

and

$$\text{Labor force} = \frac{\text{Number of people employed} +}{\text{Number of people unemployed}}.$$

In 2003, the number of people employed was 138.5 million and the number unemployed was 9.3 million. By using the above equations, you can verify that the labor force was 147.8 million (138.5 million plus 9.3 million) and the unemployment rate was 6.3 percent (9.3 million divided by 147.8 million, multiplied by 100).

Figure 6.3 shows the unemployment rate (the orange line) and two other labor market indicators between 1963 and 2003. The average unemployment rate has been 6 percent, and it reached peak values at the end of the recessions of 1974, 1982, and 1990–1991.

**The Labor Force Participation Rate** The number of people who join the labor force is an indicator of the willingness of people of working age to take jobs. The **labor force participation rate** is the percentage of the working-age population who are members of the labor force. That is,

$$\text{Labor force participation rate} = \frac{\text{Labor force}}{\text{Working-age population}} \times 100.$$

In 2002, the labor force was 147.8 million and the working-age population was 221.2 million. By using the above equation, you can calculate the labor force participation rate. It was 66.8 percent (147.8 million divided by 221.1 million, multiplied by 100).

Figure 6.3 shows the labor force participation rate (graphed in red and plotted on the left-hand scale). It had an upward trend from 59 percent during the early 1960s to 67 percent in 2000. But it has fallen since 2000. It has also had some mild fluctuations, which result from unsuccessful job seekers becoming discouraged workers. **Discouraged workers** are people who are available and willing to work but have not made specific efforts to find a job within the previous four weeks. These workers often temporarily leave the labor force during a recession and reenter during an expansion and become active job seekers.

**FIGURE 6.3** Employment, Unemployment, and the Labor Force: 1963–2003

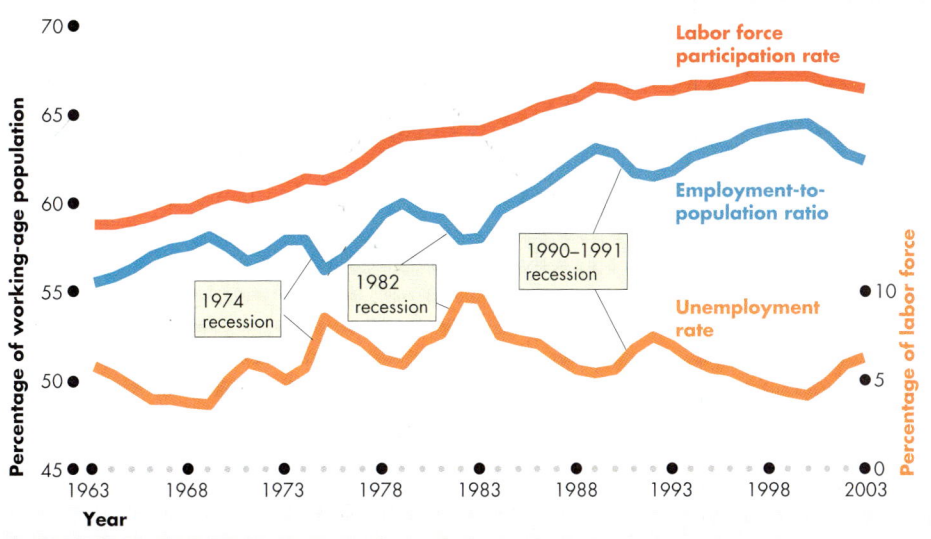

The unemployment rate increases in recessions and decreases in expansions. The labor force participation rate and the employment-to-population ratio have upward trends and fluctuate with the business cycle. The employment-to-population ratio fluctuates more than the labor force participation rate and reflects cyclical fluctuations in the unemployment rate. Fluctuations in the labor force participation rate arise mainly because of discouraged workers.

Source: Bureau of Labor Statistics.

**The Employment-to-Population Ratio** The number of people of working age who have jobs is an indicator of both the availability of jobs and the degree of match between people's skills and jobs. The **employment-to-population ratio** is the percentage of people of working age who have jobs. That is,

$$\text{Employment-to-population ratio} = \frac{\text{Number of people employed}}{\text{Working-age population}} \times 100.$$

In 2003, employment was 138.5 million and the working-age population was 221.2 million. By using the above equation, you can calculate the employment-to-population ratio. It was 62.6 percent (138.5 million divided by 221.2 million, multiplied by 100).

Figure 6.3 shows the employment-to-population ratio (graphed in blue and plotted against the left-hand scale). It increased from 55 percent during the early 1960s to 64 percent in 2000. The increase in the employment-to-population ratio means that the U.S. economy has created jobs at a faster rate than the working-age population has grown. This labor market indicator also fluctuates, and its fluctuations coincide with but are opposite to those in the unemployment rate. It falls during a recession and increases during an expansion.

Why have the labor force participation rate and the employment-to-population ratio increased? The main reason is an increase in the number of women in the labor force. Figure 6.4 shows this increase. Between 1963 and 2003, the female labor force participation rate increased from 38 percent to 60 percent. Shorter work hours, higher productivity, and an increased emphasis on white-collar jobs have expanded the job opportunities and wages available to women. At the same time, technological advances have increased productivity in the home and freed up women's time to take jobs outside the home.

Figure 6.4 also shows another remarkable trend in the U.S. labor force: The labor force participation rate and the employment-to-population ratio for men have *decreased*. Between 1963 and 2003, the male labor force participation rate decreased from 81 percent to 74 percent. It decreased because increasing numbers of men were remaining in school longer and because some were retiring earlier.

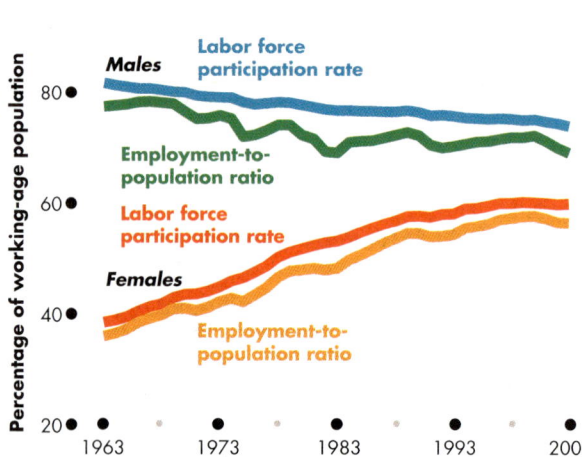

**FIGURE 6.4** The Changing Face of the Labor Market

The upward trends in the labor force participation rate and the employment-to-population ratio are accounted for mainly by the increasing participation of women in the labor market. The male labor force participation rate and employment-to-population ratio have decreased.

*Source:* Bureau of Labor Statistics.

## Aggregate Hours

The three labor market indicators that we've just examined are useful signs of the health of the economy and directly measure what matters to most people: jobs. But these three indicators don't tell us the quantity of labor used to produce real GDP, and we cannot use them to calculate the productivity of labor. The productivity of labor is significant because it influences the wages people earn.

The reason why the number of people employed does not measure the quantity of labor employed is that all jobs are not the same. People in part-time jobs might work just a few hours a week. People in full-time jobs work around 35 to 40 hours a week. And some people regularly work overtime. For example, a 7-11 store might hire six students who work for three hours a day each. Another 7-11 store might hire two full-time workers who work nine hours a day each. The number of people employed in these two stores is eight, but the total hours worked by six of the eight is the same as the total hours worked by the other two. To determine the total amount of labor used to produce real GDP, we measure labor in hours rather than in jobs. **Aggregate hours** are the total number of hours worked by all the people employed, both full time and part time, during a year.

Figure 6.5(a) shows aggregate hours in the U.S. economy from 1963 to 2003. Like the employment-to-population ratio, aggregate hours have an upward trend. But aggregate hours have not grown as quickly as has the number of people employed. Between 1963 and 2003, the number of people employed in the U.S. economy increased by 160 percent. During that same period, aggregate hours increased by a bit more than 100 percent. Why the difference? Because average hours per worker decreased.

Figure 6.5(b) shows average hours per worker. After hovering at almost 39 hours a week during the early 1960s, average hours per worker decreased to about 34 hours a week during the 1990s. This shortening of the average workweek arose partly because of a decrease in the average hours worked by full-time workers but mainly because the number of part-time jobs increased faster than the number of full-time jobs.

Fluctuations in aggregate hours and average hours per worker line up with the business cycle. Figure 6.5 highlights the past three recessions, during which aggregate hours decreased and average hours per worker decreased more quickly than trend.

### Real Wage Rate

The **real wage rate** is the quantity of goods and services that an hour's work can buy. It is equal to the money wage rate (dollars per hour) divided by the price level. If we use the GDP deflator to measure the price level, the real wage rate is expressed in 2000 dollars because the GDP deflator is 100 in 2000. The real wage rate is a significant economic variable because it measures the reward for labor.

What has happened to the real wage rate in the United States? Figure 6.6 answers this question. It shows three measures of the average hourly real wage rate in the U.S. economy between 1963 and 2003.

The first measure of the real wage rate is the Department of Labor's calculation of the average hourly earnings of private manufacturing nonsupervisory workers. This measure increased to $12.44 in 1978 (in 2000 dollars) and then remained almost

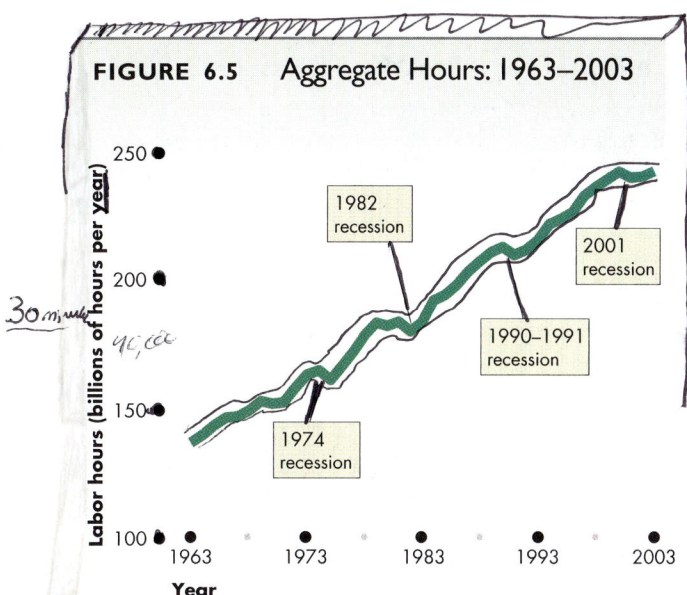

(a) Aggregate hours

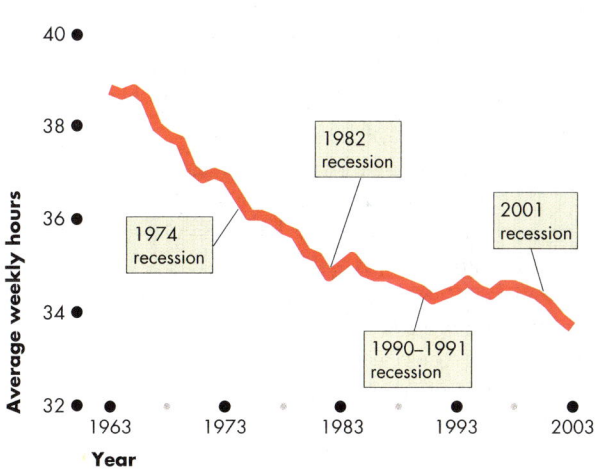

(b) Average weekly hours per person

Aggregate hours (part a) measure the total labor used to produce real GDP more accurately than does the number of people employed because an increasing proportion of jobs are part time. Between 1963 and 2003, aggregate hours increased by an average of 1.9 percent a year. Fluctuations in aggregate hours coincide with the business cycle. Aggregate hours have increased at a slower rate than the number of jobs because the average workweek has shortened (part b).

*Source*: Bureau of Labor Statistics, and the author's calculations.

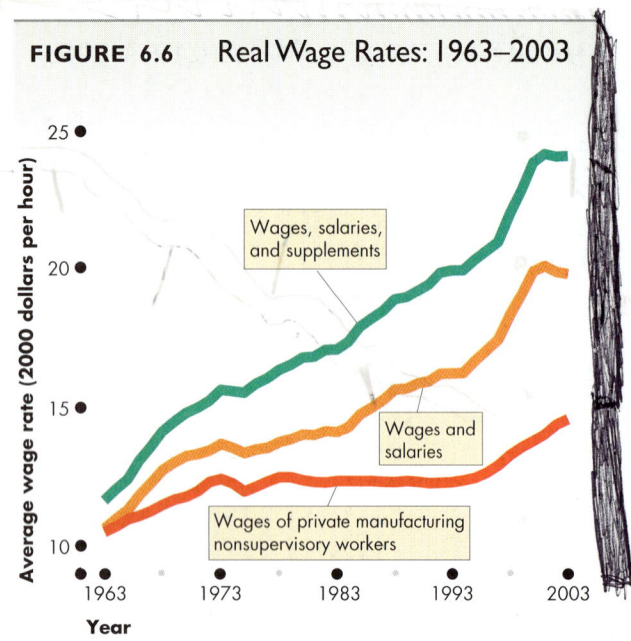

**FIGURE 6.6** Real Wage Rates: 1963–2003

The average hourly real wage rate of private manufacturing nonsupervisory workers peaked in 1978, was constant through 1993, then increased again through 2003. Broader measures of hourly real wage rates increased, but all show a growth slowdown during the 1970s.

*Sources:* Bureau of Economic Analysis, Bureau of Labor Statistics, and the author's calculations.

constant at around $12.30 for 15 years. From the mid-1990s, the real wage rate increased again and reached $14.55 in 2003.

The second measure of the real wage rate is calculated by dividing total wages and salaries in the *National Income and Product Accounts* by aggregate hours. This measure is broader than the first and includes the incomes of all types of labor, whether their rate of pay is calculated by the hour or not. This broader measure did not stop growing after 1978, but its growth rate slowed during the mid-1970s and remained low through the early 1980s. It then speeded up during the late 1980s, sagged during the early 1990s, and then grew very rapidly from 1996 through 2000. After 2000, this measure of labor income per hour fell slightly.

Fringe benefits such as pension contributions and the payment by employers of health insurance premiums have become an increasing part of labor compensation. Figure 6.6 shows a third measure of the hourly real wage rate that reflects this trend. It is *total labor compensation*—wages, salaries, *and supplements*—divided by aggregate hours. This measure is the most comprehensive one available, and it shows that the real wage rate increased almost every year until 2000 but then became flat.

The data in Fig. 6.6 show us that no matter how we measure the wage rate, its growth rate slowed during the 1970s. This slowdown in wage growth coincided with a slowdown in productivity growth—in the growth rate of real GDP per hour of work. The average wage rate of workers in manufacturing was the most severely affected by the productivity growth slowdown but the broader measures also slowed.

The fall in hourly compensation on the broader measures during the 2000s is most unusual. The 2001 recession probably played a role in this decrease. But it was a mild recession and the long period of a flat wage rate is not found in previous, even more severe, recessions.

### REVIEW QUIZ

1 What are the trends in the unemployment rate, the labor force participation rate, and the employment-to-population ratio?
2 How do the unemployment rate, the labor force participation rate, and the employment-to-population ratio fluctuate over the business cycle?
3 Has the female labor force participation rate been similar to or different from the male labor force participation rate?
4 How have aggregate hours changed since 1961?
5 How did average hourly real wage rates change during the 1990s and 2000s?

You've now seen how we measure employment, unemployment, and real wage rate. Your next task is to study the anatomy of unemployment and see why it never disappears, even at full employment.

# Unemployment and Full Employment

How do people become unemployed, and how does a period of unemployment end? How long do people remain unemployed on the average? Who is at greatest risk of becoming unemployed? Let's answer these questions by looking at the anatomy of unemployment.

## The Anatomy of Unemployment

People become unemployed if they

1. Lose their jobs and search for another job.
2. Leave their jobs and search for another job.
3. Enter or reenter the labor force to search for a job.

People end a spell of unemployment if they

1. Are hired or recalled.
2. Withdraw from the labor force.

People who are laid off, either permanently or temporarily, from their jobs are called *job losers*. Some job losers become unemployed, but some immediately withdraw from the labor force. People who voluntarily quit their jobs are called *job leavers*. Like job losers, some job leavers become unemployed and search for a better job while others either withdraw from the labor force temporarily or permanently retire from work. People who enter or reenter the labor force are called *entrants* and *reentrants*. Entrants are mainly people who have just left school. Some entrants get a job right away and are never unemployed, but many spend time searching for their first job, and during this period, they are unemployed. Reentrants are people who have previously withdrawn from the labor force. Most of these people are formerly discouraged workers. Figure 6.7 shows these labor market flows.

Let's see how much unemployment arises from the three different ways in which people can become unemployed.

**The Sources of Unemployment** Figure 6.8 shows unemployment by reason for becoming unemployed. Job losers are the biggest source of unemployment. On the average, they account for around half of total

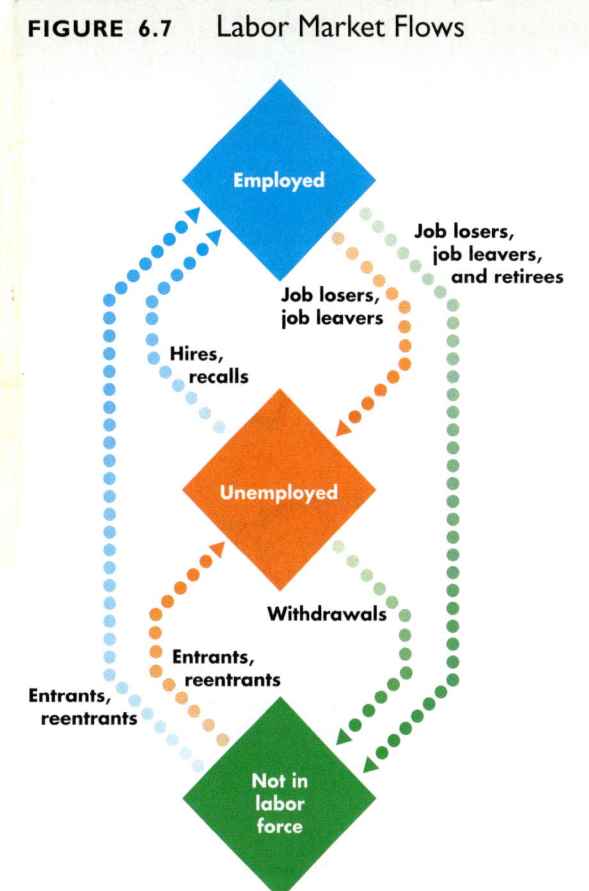

FIGURE 6.7 Labor Market Flows

Unemployment results from employed people losing or leaving their jobs (job losers and job leavers) and from people entering the labor force (entrants and reentrants). Unemployment ends because people get hired or recalled or because they withdraw from the labor force.

unemployment. Also, their number fluctuates a great deal. At the trough of the recession of 1990–1991, on any given day, more than 5 million of the 9.4 million unemployed were job losers. In contrast, at the business cycle peak in March 2001, only 3.3 million of the 6 million unemployed were job losers.

Entrants and reentrants also make up a large component of the unemployed. Their number fluctuates but more mildly than the fluctuations in the number of job losers.

Job leavers are the smallest and most stable source of unemployment. On any given day, fewer than 1 million people are unemployed because they

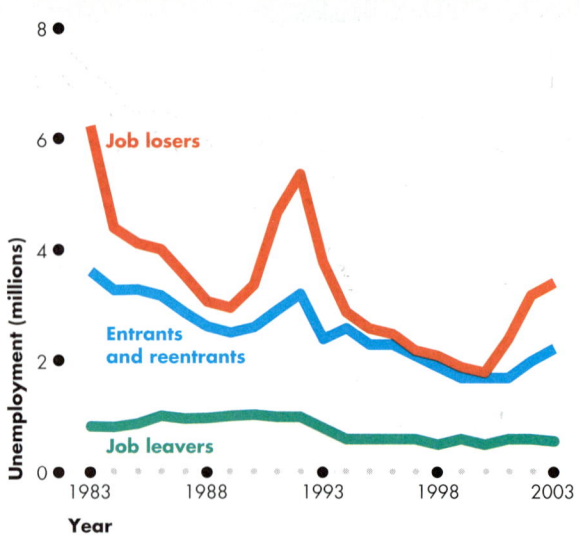

**FIGURE 6.8** Unemployment by Reason

Everyone who is unemployed is a job loser, a job leaver, or an entrant or reentrant into the labor force. Most unemployment results from job loss. The number of job losers fluctuates more closely with the business cycle than do the numbers of job leavers and entrants and reentrants. Entrants and reentrants are the second most common type of unemployed people. Their number fluctuates with the business cycle because of discouraged workers. Job leavers are the least common type of unemployed people.

*Source:* Bureau of Labor Statistics.

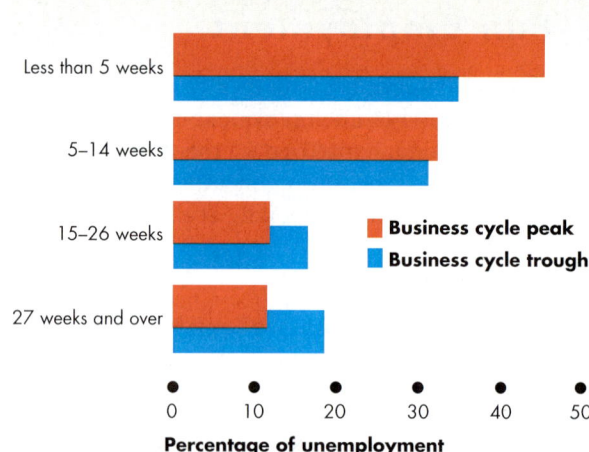

**FIGURE 6.9** Unemployment by Duration

Close to a business cycle peak in 2000, when the unemployment rate was 4 percent, 45 percent of unemployment lasted for less than 5 weeks and 30 percent lasted for 5 to 14 weeks. So 75 percent of unemployment lasted for less than 15 weeks and 25 percent lasted for 15 weeks or more.

Close to a business cycle trough in 2002, when the unemployment rate was 5.8 percent, 35 percent of unemployment lasted for less than 5 weeks and 31 percent lasted for 5 to 14 weeks. So 65 percent of unemployment lasted for less than 15 weeks, and 35 percent lasted for 15 weeks or more.

*Source:* Bureau of Labor Statistics.

are job leavers. The number of job leavers is remarkably constant. To the extent that this number fluctuates, it does so in line with the business cycle: A slightly larger number of people leave their jobs in good times than in bad times.

**The Duration of Unemployment** Some people are unemployed for a week or two, and others are unemployed for periods of a year or more. The longer the spell of unemployment, the greater the personal cost to the unemployed. The average duration of unemployment varies over the business cycle. Figure 6.9 compares the duration of unemployment close to a business cycle peak in 2000, when the unemployment rate was low, with that close to a business cycle trough in 2002, when the unemployment rate was high. In 2000, when the unemployment rate hit a low of 4 percent, 45 percent of the unemployed were in that situation for less than 5 weeks and only 11 percent of the unemployed were jobless for more than 27 weeks. In 2002, when unemployment approached 5.8 percent, only 35 percent of the unemployed found a new job in less than 5 weeks and 18 percent were unemployed for more than 27 weeks. At both low and high unemployment rates, about 30 percent of the unemployed take between 5 weeks and 14 weeks to find a job.

**The Demographics of Unemployment** Figure 6.10 shows unemployment rates for different demographic groups. The figure shows that high unemployment rates occur among young workers and also among blacks. In the business cycle trough in 1992, the unemployment rate of black teenage males was 42 percent.

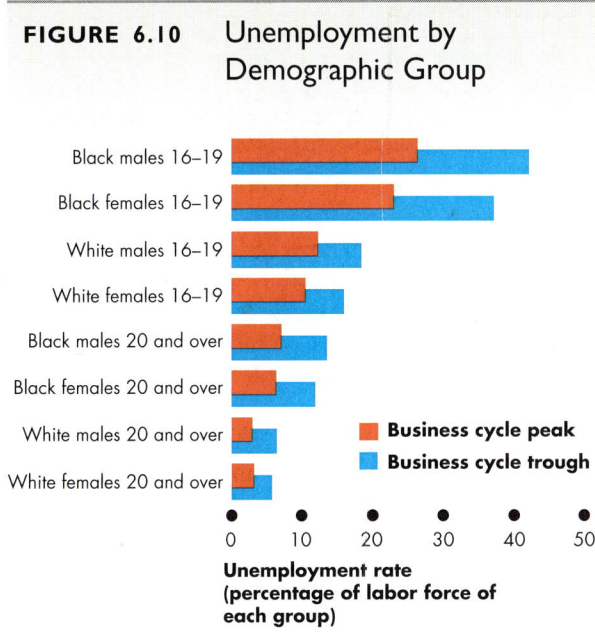

**FIGURE 6.10 Unemployment by Demographic Group**

Black teenagers experience unemployment rates that average twice those of white teenagers, and teenage unemployment rates are much higher than those for people aged 20 years and over. Even in a business cycle trough, when unemployment is at its highest rate, only 6 percent of whites aged 20 years and over are unemployed.

*Source:* Bureau of Labor Statistics.

Even in 2000, when the unemployment rate was 4 percent, the black teenage unemployment rates were more than 20 percent. The unemployment rates for white teenagers are less than half those of black teenagers. The racial differences also exist for workers aged 20 years and over. The highest unemployment rates that whites 20 years and over experience are lower than the lowest rates experienced by the other groups.

Why are teenage unemployment rates so high? There are three reasons. First, young people are still in the process of discovering what they are good at and trying different lines of work. So they leave their jobs more frequently than do older workers. Second, firms sometimes hire teenagers on a short-term trial basis. So the rate of job loss is higher for teenagers than for other people. Third, most teenagers are in school and not in the labor force. This fact means that the percentage of the teenage population that is unemployed is much lower than the percentage of the teenage labor force that is unemployed. In 2003, for example, 1 million teenagers were unemployed and 6 million were employed. So the teenage unemployment rate (all races) was 17 percent. But 9 million teenagers were in school. If we considered being in school to be the equivalent of having a job and measured teenage unemployment as a percentage of the teenage labor force plus the school population, we would record that 6 percent of teenagers are unemployed.

## Types of Unemployment

Unemployment is classified into three types that are based on its origins. They are

- Frictional — *normal labor turnover*
- Structural — *changes in technology "and can't adapt"*
- Cyclical — *normal within business cycle*

**Frictional Unemployment** The unemployment that arises from normal labor turnover—from people entering and leaving the labor force and from the ongoing creation and destruction of jobs—is **frictional unemployment**. Frictional unemployment is a permanent and healthy phenomenon in a dynamic, growing economy.

The unending flow of people into and out of the labor force and the processes of job creation and job destruction create the need for people to search for jobs and for businesses to search for workers. There are always businesses with unfilled jobs and people seeking jobs. Look in your local newspaper, and you will see that there are always some jobs being advertised. Businesses don't usually hire the first person who applies for a job, and unemployed people don't usually take the first job that comes their way. Instead, both firms and workers spend time searching out what they believe will be the best match available. By this process of search, people can match their own skills and interests with the available jobs and find a satisfying job and a good income. While these unemployed people are searching, they are frictionally unemployed.

The amount of frictional unemployment depends on the rate at which people enter and reenter the labor force and on the rate at which jobs are created and destroyed. During the 1970s, the amount of frictional unemployment increased as a consequence of the postwar baby boom that began during the 1940s. By the late 1970s, the baby boom had created a bulge in the number of people leaving school. As these people entered the labor force, the amount of frictional unemployment increased.

The amount of frictional unemployment is influenced by unemployment compensation. The greater the number of unemployed people covered by unemployment insurance and the more generous the unemployment benefit they receive, the longer is the average time taken in job search and the greater is the amount of frictional unemployment. In the United States in 2001, 45 percent of the unemployed received unemployment benefit. And the average benefit check was $205 a week. Canada and Western Europe have more generous benefits than those in the United States and have higher unemployment rates.

**Structural Unemployment** The unemployment that arises when changes in technology or international competition change the skills needed to perform jobs or change the locations of jobs is **structural unemployment**. Structural unemployment usually lasts longer than frictional unemployment because workers must usually retrain and possibly relocate to find a job. For example, when a steel plant in Gary, Indiana, is automated, some jobs in that city are eliminated. Meanwhile, new jobs for security guards, retail clerks, and life-insurance salespeople are created in Chicago, Indianapolis, and other cities. The unemployed former steelworkers remain unemployed for several months until they move, retrain, and get one of these jobs. Structural unemployment is painful, especially for older workers for whom the best available option might be to retire early or take a lower-skilled, lower-paying job.

At some times the amount of structural unemployment is modest. At other times it is large, and at such times, structural unemployment can become a serious long-term problem. It was especially large during the late 1970s and early 1980s. During those years, oil price hikes and an increasingly competitive international environment destroyed jobs in traditional U.S. industries, such as auto and steel, and created jobs in new industries, such as electronics and bioengineering, as well as in banking and insurance. Structural unemployment was also present during the early 1990s as many businesses and governments "downsized."

**Cyclical Unemployment** The fluctuating unemployment over the business cycle is **cyclical unemployment**. Cyclical unemployment increases during a recession and decreases during an expansion. An autoworker who is laid off because the economy is in a recession and who gets rehired some months later when the expansion begins has experienced cyclical unemployment.

## Full Employment

There is always *some* unemployment—someone looking for a job or laid off and waiting to be recalled. So what do we mean by *full employment*? **Full employment** occurs when there is no cyclical unemployment or, equivalently, when all the unemployment is frictional and structural. The divergence of the unemployment rate from full employment is cyclical unemployment. The unemployment rate at full employment is called the **natural rate of unemployment**.

There can be a lot of unemployment at full employment, and the term "full employment" is an example of a technical economic term that does not correspond with everyday language. The term "natural rate of unemployment" is another technical economic term whose meaning does not correspond with everyday language. For most people—especially for unemployed workers—there is nothing *natural* about unemployment.

So why do economists call a situation with a lot of unemployment one of "full employment"? And why is the unemployment at full employment called "natural"?

The reason is that the economy is a complex mechanism that is always changing. In 2003, the U.S. economy employed 138.5 million people. More than 2.5 million workers retired during that year, and more than 3 million new workers entered the labor force. All these people worked in some 20 million businesses that produced goods and services valued at more than $10 trillion. Some of these businesses downsized and failed, and others expanded. This process of change creates frictions and dislocations that are unavoidable. And they create unemployment.

There is not much controversy about the existence of a natural rate of unemployment. Nor is there much disagreement that it changes. The natural rate of unemployment arises from the existence of frictional and structural unemployment, and it fluctuates because the frictions and the amount of structural change fluctuate. But economists don't agree about the size of the natural rate of unemployment and the extent to which it fluctuates. Some economists believe that the natural rate of unemployment fluctuates frequently and that at times of rapid demographic and technological change, the natural rate of unemployment can be high. Others think that the natural rate of unemployment changes slowly.

### Real GDP and Unemployment Over the Cycle

The quantity of real GDP at full employment is called **potential GDP**. You will study the forces that determine potential GDP in Chapter 8 (pp. 196–199). Over the business cycle, real GDP fluctuates around potential GDP and the unemployment rate fluctuates around the natural rate of unemployment. Figure 6.11 illustrates these fluctuations in the United States between 1983 and 2003—real GDP in part (a) and the unemployment rate in part (b).

When the economy is at full employment, the unemployment rate equals the natural rate of unemployment and real GDP equals potential GDP. When the unemployment rate is less than the natural rate of unemployment, real GDP is greater than potential GDP. And when the unemployment rate is greater than the natural rate of unemployment, real GDP is less than potential GDP.

Figure 6.11(b) shows one view of the natural rate of unemployment. Keep in mind that economists do not know the magnitude of the natural rate of unemployment and the natural rate shown in the figure is only one estimate. In Fig. 6.11(b), the natural rate of unemployment is 6.1 percent in 1983 and it falls steadily through the 1980s and 1990s to 5.2 percent by 2003. This estimate of the natural rate of unemployment in the United States is one that many, but not all, economists would accept.

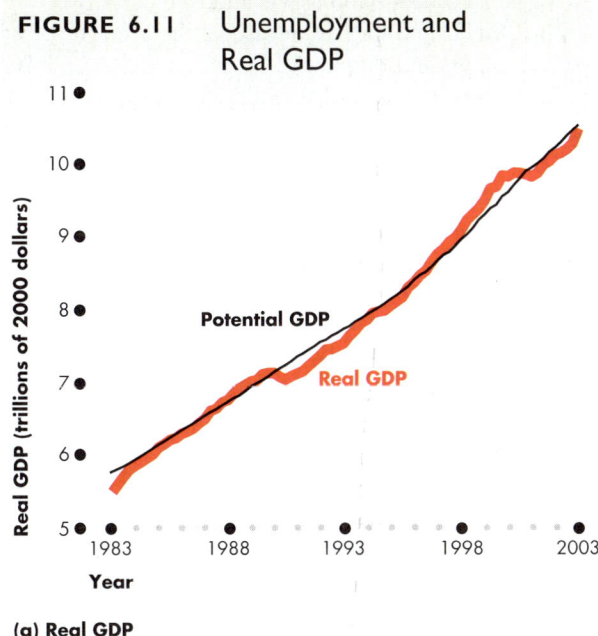

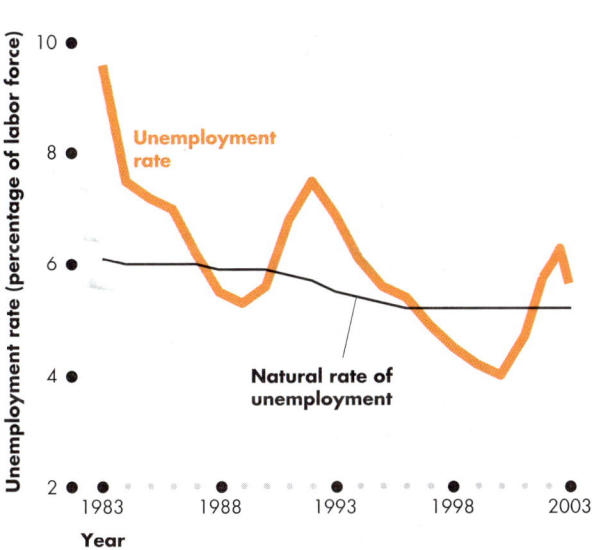

**FIGURE 6.11  Unemployment and Real GDP**

(a) Real GDP

(b) Unemployment rate

As real GDP fluctuates around potential GDP (part a), the unemployment rate fluctuates around the natural rate of unemployment (part b). Following a deep recession in the early 1980s, the unemployment rate reached almost 10 percent. In the milder recessions of 1990–1991 and 2001, unemployment peaked at lower rates. The natural rate of unemployment decreased somewhat during the 1980s and 1990s.

*Sources:* Bureau of Economic Analysis, Bureau of Labor Statistics, and Congressional Budget Office.

### REVIEW QUIZ

1. What are the categories of people who become unemployed?
2. Define frictional unemployment, structural unemployment, and cyclical unemployment. Give examples of each type of unemployment.
3. What is the natural rate of unemployment?
4. How might the natural rate of unemployment change and what factors might make it change?
5. How does the unemployment rate fluctuate over the business cycle?

Your final task in this chapter is to learn about another vital sign that gets monitored every month, the Consumer Price Index (CPI). What is the CPI, how do we measure it, and what does it mean?

# The Consumer Price Index

The **Bureau of Labor Statistics (BLS)** calculates the Consumer Price Index every month. The **Consumer Price Index (CPI)** is a measure of the average of the prices paid by urban consumers for a fixed "basket" of consumer goods and services. What you learn in this section will help you to make sense of the CPI and relate it to your own economic life. The CPI tells you what has happened to the value of the money in your pocket.

## Reading the CPI Numbers

The CPI is defined to equal 100 for a period called the **reference base period**. Currently, the reference base period is 1982–1984. That is, for the average of the 36 months from January 1982 through December 1984, the CPI equals 100.

In 2003, the CPI was 183.9. This number tells us that the average of the prices paid by urban consumers for a fixed market basket of consumer goods and services was 83.9 percent higher in 2003 than it was on the average during 1982–1984.

In 2003, the CPI was 183.9 and in 2002, the CPI was 179.9. Comparing the 2003 CPI with the 2002 CPI tells us that the index of the prices paid by urban consumers for a fixed basket of consumer goods and services increased between 2002 and 2003 by 4 points—from 179.9 to 183.9—or by 2.2 percent.

## Constructing the CPI

Constructing the CPI is a huge operation that costs millions of dollars and involves three stages:

- Selecting the CPI basket
- Conducting the monthly price survey
- Calculating the CPI

**The CPI Basket** The first stage in constructing the CPI is to select what is called the *CPI basket*. This "basket" contains the goods and services represented in the index and the relative importance attached to each of them. The idea is to make the relative importance of the items in the CPI basket the same as that in the budget of an average urban household. For example, because people spend more on housing than on bus rides, the CPI places more weight on the price of housing than on the price of bus rides.

The BLS uses two baskets and calculates two CPIs. One, called CPI-U, measures the average price paid by *all* urban households. The other, called CPI-W, measures the average price paid by urban wage earners and clerical workers. Here, we will focus on CPI-U, the broader measure.

To determine the spending patterns of households and to select the CPI basket, the BLS conducts a Consumer Expenditure Survey. This survey is costly and so is undertaken infrequently. Today's CPI basket is based on data gathered in a Consumer Expenditure Survey of 1993–1995. Before 1998, the CPI basket was based on a 1982–1984 Consumer Expenditure Survey. The BLS plans more frequent updates of the CPI basket in the future.

Until recently, the time period covered by the Consumer Expenditure Survey was also the reference base period. But when the BLS switched to the 1993–1995 basket, it decided to retain 1982–1984 as the reference base period.

Figure 6.12 shows the CPI basket at the end of 2001. The basket contains around 80,000 goods and

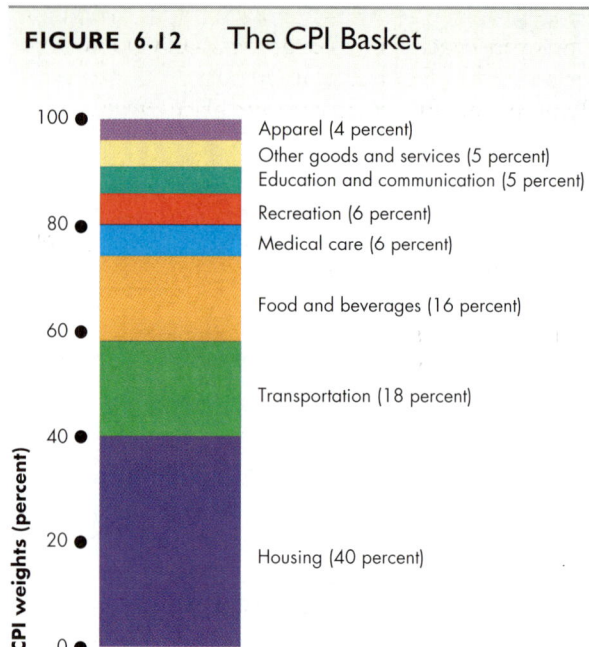

**FIGURE 6.12   The CPI Basket**

The CPI basket consists of the items that an average urban household buys. It consists mainly of housing (40 percent), transportation (18 percent), and food and beverages (16 percent). All other items add up to 26 percent of the total.

*Sources:* United States Census Bureau and Bureau of Labor.

services arranged in the eight large groups shown in the figure. The most important item in a household's budget is housing, which accounts for 40 percent of total expenditure. Transportation comes next at 18 percent. Third in relative importance are food and beverages at 16 percent. These three groups account for almost three quarters of the average household budget. Medical care and recreation each take 6 percent, and education and communication take 5 percent. Another 5 percent is spent on other goods and services, and apparel (clothing and footwear) takes 4 percent.

The BLS breaks down each of these categories into smaller ones. For example, the education and communication category breaks down into textbooks and supplies, tuition, telephone services, and personal computer services.

As you look at the relative importance of the items in the CPI basket, remember that they apply to the *average* household. *Individual* households are spread around the average. Think about your own expenditure and compare the basket of goods and services you buy with the CPI basket.

**The Monthly Price Survey** Each month, BLS employees check the prices of the 80,000 goods and services in the CPI basket in 30 metropolitan areas. Because the CPI aims to measure price *changes*, it is important that the prices recorded each month refer to exactly the same item. For example, suppose the price of a box of jelly beans has increased but a box now contains more beans. Has the price of jelly beans increased? The BLS employee must record the details of changes in quality or packaging so that price changes can be isolated from other changes.

Once the raw price data are in hand, the next task is to calculate the CPI.

**Calculating the CPI** The CPI calculation has three steps:

1. Find the cost of the CPI basket at base period prices.
2. Find the cost of the CPI basket at current period prices.
3. Calculate the CPI for the base period and the current period.

We'll work through these three steps for a simple example. Suppose the CPI basket contains only two goods and services: oranges and haircuts. We'll construct an annual CPI rather than a monthly CPI with the reference base period 2003 and the current period 2004.

Table 6.2 shows the quantities in the CPI basket and the prices in the base period and current period.

Part (a) contains the data for the base period. In that period, consumers bought 10 oranges at $1 each and 5 haircuts at $8 each. To find the cost of the CPI basket in the base period prices, multiply the quantities in the CPI basket by the base period prices. The cost of oranges is $10 (10 at $1 each), and the cost of haircuts is $40 (5 at $8 each). So total expenditure in the base period on the CPI basket is $50 ($10 + $40).

Part (b) contains the price data for the current period. The price of an orange increased from $1 to $2, which is a 100 percent increase ($1 ÷ $1 × 100 = 100). The price of a haircut increased from $8 to $10, which is a 25 percent increase ($2 ÷ $8 × 100 = 25).

The CPI provides a way of averaging these price increases by comparing the cost of the basket rather than the price of each item. To find the cost of the CPI basket in the current period, 2004, multiply the quantities in the basket by their 2004 prices. The cost of oranges is $20 (10 at $2 each), and the cost of haircuts is $50 (5 at $10 each) So total expenditure on the fixed CPI basket at current period prices is $70 ($20 + $50).

**TABLE 6.2** The CPI: A Simplified Calculation

**(a) The cost of the CPI basket at base period prices: 2003**

| Item | CPI basket Quantity | Price | Cost of CPI Basket |
|---|---|---|---|
| Oranges | 10 | $1.00 | $10 |
| Haircuts | 5 | $8.00 | $40 |
| Cost of CPI basket at base period prices | | | $50 |

**(b) The cost of the CPI basket at current period prices: 2004**

| Item | CPI basket Quantity | Price | Cost of CPI Basket |
|---|---|---|---|
| Oranges | 10 | $2.00 | $20 |
| Haircuts | 5 | $10.00 | $50 |
| Cost of CPI basket at current period prices | | | $70 |

You've now taken the first two steps toward calculating the CPI: calculating the cost of the CPI basket in the base period and the current period. The third step uses the numbers you've just calculated to find the CPI for 2003 and 2004.

The formula for the CPI is

$$\text{CPI} = \frac{\text{Cost of CPI basket at current period prices}}{\text{Cost of CPI basket at base period prices}} \times 100.$$

In Table 6.2, you have established that in 2003, the cost of the CPI basket was $50 and in 2001, it was $70. You also know that the base period is 2003. So the cost of the CPI basket at base year prices is $50. If we use these numbers in the CPI formula, we can find the CPI for 2000 and 2001. For 2003, the CPI is

$$\text{CPI in 2003} = \frac{\$50}{\$50} \times 100 = 100.$$

For 2004, the CPI is

$$\text{CPI in 2004} = \frac{\$70}{\$50} \times 100 = 140.$$

The principles that you've applied in this simplified CPI calculation apply to the more complex calculations performed every month by the BLS.

## Measuring Inflation

A major purpose of the CPI is to measure *changes* in the cost of living and in the value of money. To measure these changes, we calculate the **inflation rate**, which is the percentage change in the price level from one year to the next. To calculate the inflation rate, we use the formula:

$$\text{Inflation rate} = \frac{(\text{CPI this year} - \text{CPI last year})}{\text{CPI last year}} \times 100.$$

We can use this formula to calculate the inflation rate in 2002. The CPI in December 2002 was 180.9, and the CPI in December 2001 was 176.7. So the inflation rate during 2001 was

$$\text{Inflation rate} = \frac{(180.9 - 176.7)}{176.7} \times 100 = 2.4\%.$$

Figure 6.13 shows the CPI and the inflation rate in the United States during the 30 years between 1973 and 2003. The two parts of the figure are related.

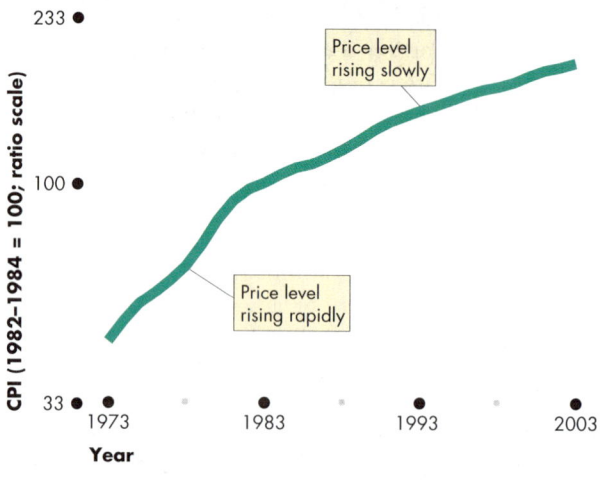

**FIGURE 6.13   The CPI and the Inflation Rate**

(a) CPI: 1973–2003

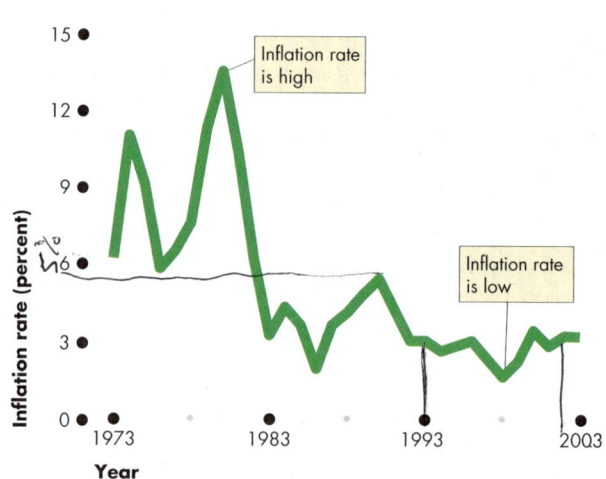

(b) Inflation rate: 1973–2003

In part (a), the CPI (the price level) has increased every year. In part (b), the inflation rate has averaged 5 percent a year. During the 1970s and early 1980s, the inflation rate was high and sometimes exceeded 10 percent a year. But after 1983, the inflation rate fell to an average of 3 percent a year.

*Source:* Bureau of Labor Statistics.

Figure 6.13 shows that when the price *level* in part (a) rises rapidly, the inflation rate in part (b) is high, and when the price level in part (a) rises slowly, the inflation rate in part (b) is low. Notice in part (a) that the CPI increased every year during this period. During the late 1970s and 1980, the CPI was increasing rapidly, but its rate of increase slowed during the 1980s and 1990s.

The CPI is not a perfect measure of the price level, and changes in the CPI probably overstate the inflation rate. Let's look at the sources of bias.

### The Biased CPI

The main sources of bias in the CPI are

- New goods bias
- Quality change bias
- Commodity substitution bias
- Outlet substitution bias

**New Goods Bias**  If you want to compare the price level in 2003 with that in 1973, you must somehow compare the price of a computer today with that of a typewriter in 1973. Because a PC is more expensive than a typewriter was, the arrival of the PC puts an upward bias into the CPI and its inflation rate.

**Quality Change Bias**  Cars, CD players, and many other items get better every year. Part of the rise in the prices of these items is a payment for improved quality and is not inflation. But the CPI counts the entire price rise as inflation and so overstates inflation.

**Commodity Substitution Bias**  Changes in relative prices lead consumers to change the items they buy. For example, if the price of beef rises and the price of chicken remains unchanged, people buy more chicken and less beef. Suppose they switch from beef to chicken on a scale that provides the same amount of protein and the same enjoyment as before and their expenditure is the same as before. The price of protein has not changed. But because it ignores the substitution of chicken for beef, the CPI says the price of protein has increased.

**Outlet Substitution Bias**  When confronted with higher prices, people use discount stores more frequently and convenience stores less frequently. This phenomenon is called *outlet substitution*. The CPI surveys do not monitor outlet substitutions.

### The Magnitude of the Bias

You've reviewed the sources of bias in the CPI. But how big is the bias? This question was tackled in 1996 by a Congressional Advisory Commission on the Consumer Price Index chaired by Michael Boskin, an economics professor at Stanford University. This commission said that the CPI overstates inflation by 1.1 percentage points a year. That is, if the CPI reports that inflation is 3.1 percent a year, most likely inflation is actually 2 percent a year.

### Some Consequences of the Bias

The bias in the CPI distorts private contracts and increases government outlays. Many private agreements, such as wage contracts, are linked to the CPI. For example, a firm and its workers might agree to a three-year wage deal that increases the wage rate by 2 percent a year *plus* the percentage increase in the CPI. Such a deal ends up giving the workers more real income than the firm intended.

Close to a third of federal government outlays, including Social Security checks, are linked directly to the CPI. And while a bias of 1 percent a year seems small, accumulated over a decade it adds up to almost a trillion dollars of additional expenditures.

**Reducing the Bias**  To reduce the bias in the CPI, the BLS has decided to undertake consumer spending surveys at more frequent intervals and to revise the basket that is used for calculating the CPI every two years.

---

#### REVIEW QUIZ

1 What is the CPI and how is it calculated?
2 How do we calculate the inflation rate and what is the relationship between the CPI and the inflation rate?
3 What are the four main ways in which the CPI is an upward-biased measure of the price level?
4 What problems arise from the CPI bias?

---

◆ You've now completed your study of the measurement of macroeconomic performance. Your task in the following chapters is to learn what determines that performance and how policy actions might improve it. But first, take a close-up look at the jobless recovery of 2002 and 2003 in *Reading Between the Lines* on pp. 144–145.

# READING BETWEEN THE LINES

## *The Jobless Recovery of 2002–2003*

**THE BOSTON GLOBE, NOVEMBER 6, 2003**

### Flickers of Job Growth Seen

Falling numbers of Americans filing for unemployment benefits and strong gains in productivity growth may be setting the stage for the recovering economy to begin putting laid-off employees back to work.

"The odds do increasingly favor a revival of job creation," the Federal Reserve chairman, Alan Greenspan, said yesterday in a televised speech to the Securities Industries Association.

Many economists have talked about a "jobless recovery"—one even quipped the country is experiencing a "job-loss" recovery—as companies have shied away from hiring even as the economy gained momentum, shoring up their bottom lines through layoffs and squeezing more out of remaining workers. But two reports released yesterday yielded tentative evidence that existing work forces are close to being maxed out and that companies may finally start hiring again. More details could emerge today when the Labor Department is set to release its October employment report…

"We're seeing the light at the end of the tunnel," said Nariman Behravesh, chief economist for the forecasting firm Global Insight. "You get this picture that businesses are coming out of their shell and starting to spend more and hire more." ….

Copyright 2003 by GLOBE NEWSPAPER CO (MA). Reproduced with permission. Further reproduction prohibited.

### Essence of the Story

■ Economists have talked about a "jobless recovery" as companies have increased production without hiring more workers.

■ But two reports issued in November 2003 suggest that companies may finally start hiring again.

■ The October employment report might provide more information.

# Economic Analysis

■ This news article reports that during the expansion of 2002 and 2003, production increased, but the number of jobs did not increase in line with increased production.

■ The figures show the jobless recovery and place it in a longer term historical perspective.

■ In Fig. 1, the y-axis shows the level of employment as a percentage of its level at the business cycle trough and the x-axis shows the number of months since the business cycle trough.

■ By October 2003, the expansion had been running for 23 months.

■ The blue line in the figure shows the growth of employment during the 2002–2003 expansion.

■ In October 2003, employment was only 1.3 percent higher than it had been at the cycle trough in November 2001.

■ The red line in the figure shows the growth of employment on the average during the previous five expansions.

■ On the average, after 23 months of expansion, employment has expanded by 4.3 percent—more than three times that of the current expansion.

■ The shaded area shows the range of experience over the previous five expansions.

■ You can see that the current expansion follows the weakest of the previous ones and after 23 months is the weakest.

■ Figure 2 shows the same comparison for the unemployment rate.

■ In an average expansion, the unemployment rate falls after 23 months to 89 percent of its trough level.

■ But in the current expansions, the unemployment rate actually increased and after 23 months stood at 7 percent *above* its trough level.

■ Again, the current expansion is the weakest of the past six expansions.

■ The jobless recovery arises partly from a weaker than average recovery of production (see p. 123) and partly from an increase in output per worker.

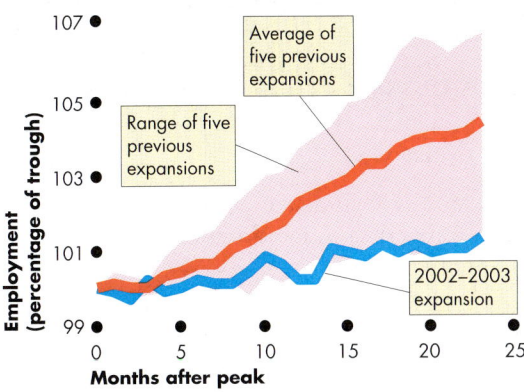

Figure 1 Employment during the 2002–2003 expansion

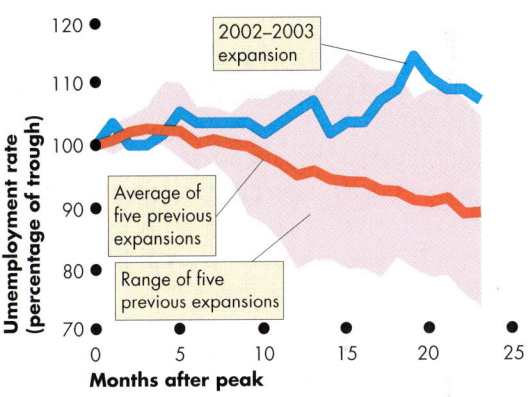

Figure 2 The unemployment rate during the 2002–2003 expansion

# SUMMARY

## KEY POINTS

### The Business Cycle (pp. 128–129)

- A recession is a significant decline in activity spread across the economy and lasting more than a few months.
- Another definition of recession is a decrease in real GDP that lasts for at least two quarters.
- The NBER has identified 16 recessions and 17 expansions since 1919.

### Jobs and Wages (pp. 130–134)

- The unemployment rate has averaged 6 percent. It increases in recessions and decreases in expansions.
- The labor force participation rate and the employment-to-population ratio have an upward trend and fluctuate with the business cycle.
- The labor force participation rate has increased for females and decreased for males.
- Aggregate hours have an upward trend, and they fluctuate with the business cycle.
- Real hourly wage rates grow but their growth rates slowed during the 1970s.

### Unemployment and Full Employment (pp. 135–139)

- People are constantly entering and leaving the state of unemployment.
- The duration of unemployment fluctuates over the business cycle. But the demographic patterns of unemployment are constant.
- Unemployment can be frictional, structural, and cyclical.
- When all the unemployment is frictional and structural, the unemployment rate equals the natural rate of unemployment, the economy is at full employment, and real GDP equals potential GDP.
- Over the business cycle, real GDP fluctuates around potential GDP and the unemployment rate fluctuates around the natural rate of unemployment.

### The Consumer Price Index (pp. 140–143)

- The Consumer Price Index (CPI) is a measure of the average of the prices paid by urban consumers for a fixed basket of consumer goods and services.
- The CPI is defined to equal 100 for a reference base period—currently 1982–1984.
- The inflation rate is the percentage change in the CPI from one year to the next.
- Changes in the CPI probably overstate the inflation rate because of the bias that arises from new goods, quality changes, commodity substitution, and outlet substitution.
- The bias in the CPI distorts private contracts and increases government outlays.

## KEY FIGURES

Figure 6.1    Business Cycle Patterns, 129
Figure 6.2    Population Labor Force Categories, 130
Figure 6.7    Labor Market Flows, 135
Figure 6.11   Unemployment and Real GDP, 139
Figure 6.12   The CPI Basket, 140

## KEY TERMS

Aggregate hours, 133
Consumer Price Index (CPI), 140
Cyclical unemployment, 138
Discouraged workers, 131
Employment-to-population ratio, 132
Expansion, 128
Frictional unemployment, 137
Full employment, 138
Inflation rate, 142
Labor force, 130
Labor force participation rate, 131
Natural rate of unemployment, 138
Peak, 128
Potential GDP, 139
Real wage rate, 133
Recession, 128
Reference base period, 140
Structural unemployment, 138
Trough, 128
Unemployment rate, 131
Working-age population, 130

# PROBLEMS

*1. The Bureau of Labor Statistics reported the following data for December 2000:
   Labor force: 141,544,000
   Employment: 135,888,000
   Working-age population: 210,743,000
   Calculate for that month the
   a. Unemployment rate.
   b. Labor force participation rate.
   c. Employment-to-population ratio.

2. The Bureau of Labor Statistics reported the following data for December 2001:
   Labor force: 142,314,000
   Employment: 134,055,000
   Working-age population: 212,927,000
   Calculate for that month the
   a. Unemployment rate.
   b. Labor force participation rate.
   c. Employment-to-population ratio.

*3. During 2000, the working-age population increased by 1,911,000, employment increased by 1,375,000, and the labor force increased by 1,311,000. Use these numbers and the data in problem 1 to calculate the change in unemployment and the change in the number of people not in the labor force during 2000.

4. During 2001, the working-age population increased by 2,184,000, employment decreased by 1,833,000, and the labor force increased by 770,000. Use these numbers and the data in problem 2 to calculate the change in unemployment and the change in the number of people not in the labor force during 2001.

*5. In August 2000, the unemployment rate was 4.1 percent. In August 2001, the unemployment rate was 4.9 percent. Use this information to predict what happened between August 2000 and August 2001 to the numbers of
   a. Job losers and job leavers.
   b. Labor force entrants and reentrants.

6. In January 2001, the unemployment rate was 4.2 percent. In January 2002, the unemployment rate was 5.6 percent. Use these data to predict what happened in 2002 to the numbers of
   a. Job losers and job leavers.
   b. Labor force entrants and reentrants.

*7. In July 2002, in the economy of Sandy Island, 10,000 people were employed, 1,000 were unemployed, and 5,000 were not in the labor force. During August 2002, 80 people lost their jobs, 20 people quit their jobs, 150 people were hired or recalled, 50 people withdrew from the labor force, and 40 people entered or reentered the labor force. Calculate for July 2002
   a. The labor force.
   b. The unemployment rate.
   c. The working-age population.
   d. The employment-to-population ratio.
   And calculate for the end of August 2002
   e. The number of people unemployed.
   f. The number of people employed.
   g. The labor force.
   h. The unemployment rate.

8. In July 2003, in the economy of Sandy Island, 11,000 people were employed, 900 were unemployed, and 5,000 were not in the labor force. During August 2002, 40 people lost their jobs, 10 people quit their jobs, 180 people were hired or recalled, 20 people withdrew from the labor force, and 60 people entered or reentered the labor force. Calculate for July 2003
   a. The labor force.
   b. The unemployment rate.
   c. The working-age population.
   d. The employment-to-population ratio.
   And calculate for the end of August 2003
   e. The number of people unemployed.
   f. The number of people employed.
   g. The labor force.
   h. The unemployment rate.

*9. A typical family on Sandy Island consumes only juice and cloth. Last year, which was the base year, the family spent $40 on juice and $25 on cloth. In the base year, juice was $4 a bottle and cloth was $5 a length. This year, juice is $4 a bottle and cloth is $6 a length. Calculate
   a. The basket used in the CPI.
   b. The CPI in the current year.
   c. The inflation rate in the current year.

10. A typical family on Lizard Island consumes only mangoes and nuts. In the base year, the family spent $60 on nuts and $10 on mangoes. In the base year, mangoes were $1 each and nuts were $3 a bag. This year, mangoes are $1.50 each and nuts are $4 a bag. Calculate
    a. The basket used in the CPI.
    b. The CPI in the current year.
    c. The inflation rate in the current year.

* Solutions to odd-numbered problems are available on MyEconLab.

## CRITICAL THINKING

1. Study *Reading Between the Lines* on pp. 144–145 and then answer the following questions:
   a. Why was the expansion of 2002 and 2003 called a jobless expansion?
   b. Compare the performance of employment and unemployment in 2002 and 2003 with that in previous expansions.
   c. Can you think of reasons why the 2002 and 2003 expansion didn't create many jobs?
   d. Do you think the U.S. government should help to create more jobs? Why? How?
2. Thinking about the economy of Sandy Island in problems 7 and 8:
   a. In what phase of its business cycle was Sandy Island during 2003?
   b. What do you predict would be happening to real GDP on Sandy Island? Why?
   c. What do you predict would be happening to standard of living on Sandy Island? Why?
3. Describe the main features of the labor market at the peak of the business cycle.
4. Describe the main features of the labor market at the trough of the business cycle.
5. You've seen in this chapter that the average workweek has shortened over the years. Do you think that shorter work hours are a problem or a benefit? Do you expect the average workweek to keep getting shorter? Why or why not?
6. An increasing number of jobs are part-time jobs. Can you think of some reasons for this trend? Who benefits from part-time jobs, the employer or the worker or both? Explain with examples.
7. You've seen that the CPI is biased and overstates the true inflation rate. It would be a simple matter to adjust the CPI for the known average bias. Yet we continue to keep a flawed measure of inflation in place. Why do you think we don't adjust the CPI for the known average bias so that its measure of the inflation rate is more accurate? Explain who gains from the biased measure and who loses from it. Try to think of reasons why those who lose have not persuaded those who win to adopt a more accurate measure.

## WEB EXERCISES

**Use the links on MyEconLab to work the following exercises.**

1. Review the Federal Reserve's *Beige Book*. In which phase of the business cycle is the economy in your region? How does your region compare to the nation as a whole?
2. Visit the Bureau of Labor Statistics and find labor market data for your own state.
   a. What have been the trends in employment, unemployment, and labor force participation in your own state during the past two years?
   b. On the basis of what you know about your own region, how would you set about explaining these trends?
   c. Try to identify those industries that have expanded most and those that have shrunk.
   d. What are the problems with your own regional labor market that you think need state government action to resolve?
   e. What actions do you think your state government must take to resolve these problems? Answer this question by using the demand and supply model of the labor market and predict the effects of the actions you prescribe.
   f. Compare the labor market performance of your own state with that of the nation as a whole.
   g. If your state is performing better than the national average, to what do you attribute the success? If your region is performing worse than the national average, to what do you attribute its problems? What federal actions are needed in your state labor market?
3. Visit the Bureau of Labor Statistics and find CPI data for your own region.
   a. What have been the trends in the CPI in your region during the past two years?
   b. Compare the CPI performance of your own region with that of the nation as a whole.
   c. On the basis of what you know about your own region, how would you set about explaining its deviation from the national average?

# Aggregate Supply and Aggregate Demand

CHAPTER 7

## Production and Prices

**During the 10 years from 1993 to 2003, U.S.** real GDP increased by 37 percent. Expanding at this pace, real GDP almost doubles every 20 years. What forces bring persistent and rapid expansion of real GDP?

Expanding real GDP brings a rising standard of living. Inflation—rising prices—brings a rising *cost of living*. Because of inflation, you need $2 today to buy what $1 bought in 1983. What causes inflation?

Our economy expands and prices rise at an uneven pace. They ebb and flow over the business cycle. After 10 years of rapid expansion, our economy came to a grinding halt in 2001. Why do we have a business cycle?

Economists know the answers to some of the questions we've just posed, but not to all of them. Active research on these issues divides economists into schools of thought about the most likely answers and the best way to find them.

◆ This chapter explains a *model* of real GDP and the price level—the *aggregate supply–aggregate demand model* or *AS-AD model*. This model represents the consensus view of macroeconomists on how real GDP and the price level are determined. The model provides a framework for understanding the forces that make our economy expand, that bring inflation, and that cause business cycle fluctuations. The model also provides a framework within which we can see the range of views of macroeconomists in different schools of thought.

### After studying this chapter, you will be able to

- ■ **Explain what determines aggregate supply**
- ■ **Explain what determines aggregate demand**
- ■ **Explain macroeconomic equilibrium**
- ■ **Explain the effects of changes in aggregate supply and aggregate demand on economic growth, inflation, and the business cycle**
- ■ **Explain the main schools of thought in macroeconomics today**

## Aggregate Supply

The AGGREGATE SUPPLY–AGGREGATE DEMAND model enables us to understand three features of macroeconomic performance:

- Growth of potential GDP
- Inflation
- Business cycle fluctuations

The model uses the concepts of *aggregate* supply and *aggregate* demand to determine *real GDP* and the *price level* (the GDP deflator). We begin by looking at the limits to production that influence aggregate supply.

### Aggregate Supply Fundamentals

The *quantity of real GDP supplied* ($Y$) depends on

1. The quantity of labor ($L$)
2. The quantity of capital ($K$)
3. The state of technology ($T$)

The influence of these three factors on the quantity of real GDP supplied is described by the **aggregate production function**, which is written as the equation:

$$Y = F(L, K, T).$$

In words, the quantity of real GDP supplied is determined by (is a function $F$ of) the quantities of labor and capital and the state of technology. The larger is $L$, $K$, or $T$, the greater is $Y$.

At any given time, the quantity of capital and the state of technology are fixed. They depend on decisions that were made in the past. The population is also fixed. But the quantity of labor is not fixed. It depends on decisions made by people and firms about the supply of and demand for labor.

The labor market can be in any one of three states: at full employment, above full employment, or below full employment.

Even at full employment, there are always some people looking for jobs and some firms looking for people to hire. The reason is that there is a constant churning of the labor market. Every day, some jobs are destroyed as businesses reorganize or fail. Some jobs are created as new businesses start up or existing ones expand. Some workers decide, for any of a thousand personal reasons, to quit their jobs. And other people decide to start looking for a job. This constant churning in the labor market prevents unemployment from ever disappearing. The unemployment rate at full employment is called the **natural rate of unemployment**.

Another way to think about **full employment** is as a state of the labor market in which the quantity of labor demanded equals the quantity supplied. Firms demand labor only if it is profitable to do so. And the lower the wage rate, which is the cost of labor, the greater is the quantity of labor demanded. People supply labor only if doing so is the most valuable use of their time. And the higher the wage rate, which is the return to labor, the greater is the quantity of labor supplied. The wage rate that makes the quantity of labor demanded equal to the quantity of labor supplied is the equilibrium wage rate. At this wage rate, there is full employment. (You can study the labor market at full employment further in Chapter 8 on pp. 182–186.)

The quantity of real GDP at full employment is *potential GDP*, which depends on the full-employment quantity of labor, the quantity of capital, and the state of technology. Over the business cycle, employment fluctuates around full employment and real GDP fluctuates around potential GDP.

To study aggregate supply in different states of the labor market, we distinguish two time frames:

- Long-run aggregate supply
- Short-run aggregate supply

### Long-Run Aggregate Supply

The economy is constantly bombarded by events that move real GDP away from potential GDP and, equivalently, move employment away from full employment. Following such an event, forces operate to take real GDP back toward potential GDP and restore full employment. The **macroeconomic long run** is a time frame that is sufficiently long for these forces to have done their work so that real GDP equals potential GDP and full employment prevails.

The **long-run aggregate supply curve** is the relationship between the quantity of real GDP supplied and the price level in the long run when real GDP equals potential GDP. Figure 7.1 shows this relationship as the vertical line labeled *LAS*. Along the long-run aggregate supply curve, as the price level changes, real GDP remains at potential GDP, which in Fig. 7.1 is $10 trillion. The long-run aggregate supply curve is always vertical and is located at potential GDP.

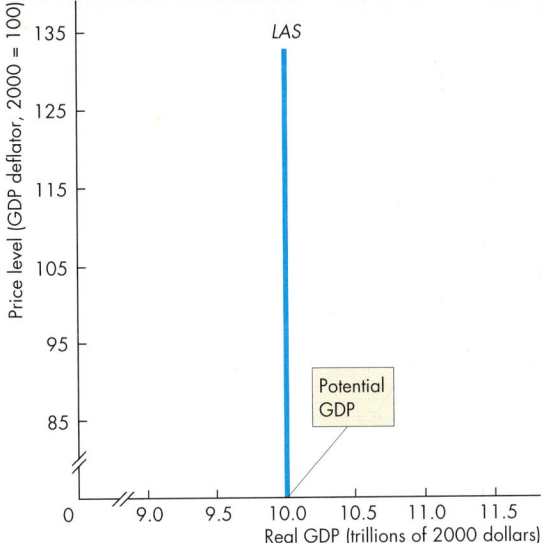

**FIGURE 7.1  Long-Run Aggregate Supply**

The long-run aggregate supply curve (LAS) shows the relationship between potential GDP and the price level. Potential GDP is independent of the price level, so the LAS curve is vertical at potential GDP.

The long-run aggregate supply curve is vertical because potential GDP is independent of the price level. The reason for this independence is that a movement along the LAS curve is accompanied by a change in *two* sets of prices: the prices of goods and services—the price level—and the prices of productive resources. A 10 percent increase in the prices of goods and services is matched by a 10 percent increase in the money wage rate and other resource prices. That is, the price level, wage rate, and other resource prices all change by the same percentage, and *relative prices* and the *real wage rate* remain constant. When the price level changes but relative prices and the real wage rate remain constant, real GDP remains constant.

**Production at a Pepsi Plant** You can see why real GDP remains constant when all prices change by the same percentage by thinking about production decisions at a Pepsi bottling plant. The plant is producing the quantity of Pepsi that maximizes profit. The plant can increase production but only by incurring a higher *marginal cost* (see Chapter 2, p. 35). So the firm has no incentive to change production.

## Short-Run Aggregate Supply

The **macroeconomic short run** is a period during which some money prices are sticky and real GDP might be below, above, or at potential GDP and the unemployment rate might be above, below, or at the natural rate of unemployment.

The **short-run aggregate supply curve** is the relationship between the quantity of real GDP supplied and the price level in the short run when the money wage rate, the prices of other resources, and potential GDP remain constant. Figure 7.2 shows a short-run aggregate supply curve as the upward-sloping curve labeled *SAS*. This curve is based on the short-run aggregate supply schedule, and each point on the aggregate supply curve corresponds to a row of the aggregate supply schedule. For example, point *A* on the short-run aggregate supply curve and row *A* of the schedule tell us that if the price level is 100, the quantity of real GDP supplied is $9 trillion.

At point *C*, the price level is 105 and the quantity of real GDP supplied is $10 trillion, which equals potential GDP. If the price level is higher than 105, real GDP exceeds potential GDP; if the price level is below 105, real GDP is less than potential GDP.

**Back at the Pepsi Plant** You can see why the short-run aggregate supply curve slopes upward by returning to the Pepsi bottling plant. The plant produces the quantity that maximizes profit. If the price of Pepsi rises and the money wage rate and other costs don't change, Pepsi can earn a profit on a greater quantity and has an incentive to increase production. The higher relative price of Pepsi covers the higher marginal cost of producing more Pepsi, so the firm increases production.

Similarly, if the price of Pepsi falls and the money wage rate and other costs don't change, the lower relative price is not sufficient to cover the marginal cost of Pepsi, so the firm decreases production.

Again, what's true for Pepsi bottlers is true for the producers of all goods and services. So when the price level rises and the money wage rate and other resource prices remain constant, the quantity of real GDP supplied increases.

## FIGURE 7.2 Short-Run Aggregate Supply

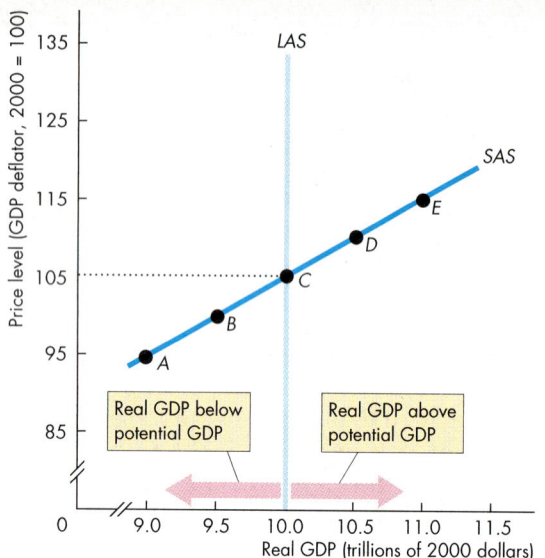

| | Price Level (GDP deflator) | Real GDP (trillions of 2000 dollars) |
|---|---|---|
| A | 95 | 9.0 |
| B | 100 | 9.5 |
| C | 105 | 10.0 |
| D | 110 | 10.5 |
| E | 115 | 11.0 |

The short-run aggregate supply curve shows the relationship between the quantity of real GDP supplied and the price level when the money wage rate, other resource prices, and potential GDP remain the same. The short-run aggregate supply curve, SAS, is based on the schedule in the table. This curve is upward-sloping because firms' costs increase as the rate of output increases, so a higher price is needed, relative to the prices of productive resources, to bring forth an increase in the quantity produced.

On the SAS curve, when the price level is 105, real GDP equals potential GDP. If the price level is greater than 105, real GDP exceeds potential GDP; if the price level is below 105, real GDP is less than potential GDP.

## Movements Along the LAS and SAS Curves

Figure 7.3 summarizes what you've just learned about the LAS and SAS curves. When the price level, the money wage rate, and other resource prices rise by the same percentage, relative prices remain constant and real GDP remains at potential GDP. There is a *movement along* the LAS curve.

When the price level rises but the money wage rate and other resource prices remain the same, the quantity of real GDP supplied increases and there is a *movement along* the SAS curve.

Let's next study the influences that bring changes in aggregate supply.

## FIGURE 7.3 Movements Along the Aggregate Supply Curves

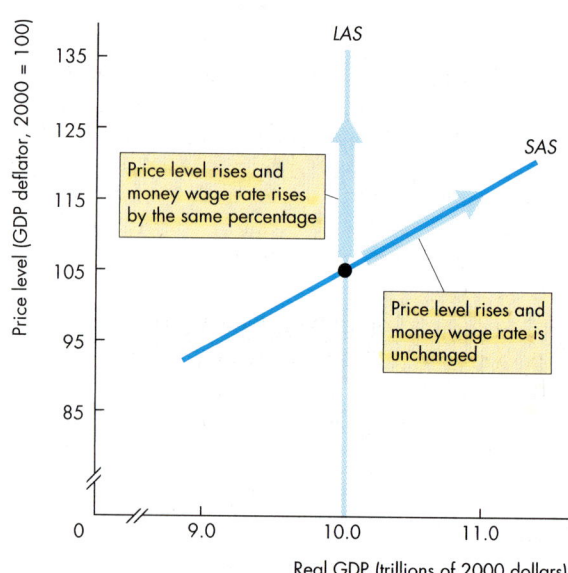

A rise in the price level with no change in the money wage rate and other resource prices brings an increase in the quantity of real GDP supplied and a movement along the short-run aggregate supply curve, SAS.

A rise in the price level with equal percentage increases in the money wage rate and other resource prices keeps the quantity of real GDP supplied constant at potential GDP and brings a movement along the long-run aggregate supply curve, LAS.

## Changes in Aggregate Supply

You've just seen that a change in the price level brings a movement along the aggregate supply curves but does not change aggregate supply. Aggregate supply changes when influences on production plans other than the price level change. Let's begin by looking at factors that change potential GDP.

### Changes in Potential GDP

When potential GDP changes, both long-run aggregate supply and short-run aggregate supply change. Potential GDP changes for three reasons:

1. Change in the full-employment quantity of labor
2. Change in the quantity of capital
3. Advance in technology

An increase in the full-employment quantity of labor, an increase in the quantity of capital, or an advance in technology increases potential GDP. And an increase in potential GDP changes both long-run aggregate supply and short-run aggregate supply.

Figure 7.4 shows these effects of a change in potential GDP. Initially, the long-run aggregate supply curve is $LAS_0$ and the short-run aggregate supply curve is $SAS_0$. If an increase in the quantity of capital or a technological advance increases potential GDP to $11 trillion, long-run aggregate supply increases and the long-run aggregate supply curve shifts rightward to $LAS_1$. Short-run aggregate supply also increases, and the short-run aggregate supply curve shifts rightward to $SAS_1$.

Let's look more closely at the influences on potential GDP and the aggregate supply curves.

### A Change in the Full-Employment Quantity of Labor

A Pepsi bottling plant that employs 100 workers bottles more Pepsi than an otherwise identical plant that employs 10 workers. The same is true for the economy as a whole. The larger the quantity of labor employed, the greater is GDP.

Over time, potential GDP increases because the labor force increases. But (with constant capital and technology) *potential* GDP increases only if the full-employment quantity of labor increases. Fluctuations in employment over the business cycle bring fluctuations in real GDP. But these changes in real GDP are fluctuations around potential GDP. They are not changes in potential GDP and long-run aggregate supply.

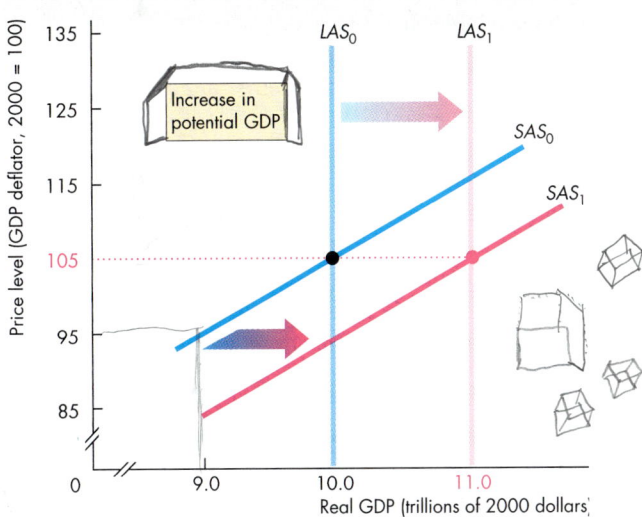

**FIGURE 7.4  A Change in Potential GDP**

An increase in potential GDP increases both long-run aggregate supply and short-run aggregate supply and shifts both aggregate supply curves rightward from $LAS_0$ to $LAS_1$ and from $SAS_0$ to $SAS_1$.

### A Change in the Quantity of Capital

A Pepsi bottling plant with two production lines bottles more Pepsi than an otherwise identical plant that has only one production line. For the economy, the larger the quantity of capital, the more productive is the labor force and the greater is its potential GDP. Potential GDP per person in the capital-rich United States is vastly greater than that in capital-poor China and Russia.

Capital includes *human capital*. One Pepsi plant is managed by an economics major with an MBA and has a labor force with an average of 10 years of experience. This plant produces a much larger output than an otherwise identical plant that is managed by someone with no business training or experience and that has a young labor force that is new to bottling. The first plant has a greater amount of human capital than the second. For the economy as a whole, the larger the quantity of *human capital*—the skills that people have acquired in school and through on-the-job training—the greater is potential GDP.

***An Advance in Technology*** A Pepsi plant that has pre–computer age machines produces less than one that uses the latest robot technology. Technological change enables firms to produce more from any given amount of inputs. So even with fixed quantities of labor and capital, improvements in technology increase potential GDP.

Technological advances are by far the most important source of increased production over the past two centuries. Because of technological advances, one farmer in the United States today can feed 100 people and one autoworker can produce almost 14 cars and trucks in a year.

Let's now look at the effects of changes of money wages.

### Changes in the Money Wage Rate and Other Resource Prices
When the money wage rate (or the money price of any resource such as oil) changes, short-run aggregate supply changes but long-run aggregate supply does not change.

Figure 7.5 shows the effect of an increase in the money wage rate. Initially, the short-run aggregate supply curve is $SAS_0$. A rise in the money wage rate *decreases* short-run aggregate supply and shifts the short-run aggregate supply curve leftward to $SAS_2$.

A rise in the money wage rate decreases short-run aggregate supply because it increases firms' costs. With increased costs, the quantity that firms are willing to supply at each price level decreases, which is shown by a leftward shift of the *SAS* curve.

A change in the money wage rate does not change long-run aggregate supply because on the *LAS* curve, the change in the money wage rate is accompanied by an equal percentage change in the price level. With no change in *relative* prices, firms have no incentive to change production and real GDP remains constant at potential GDP. With no change in potential GDP, the long-run aggregate supply curve remains at *LAS*.

### What Makes the Money Wage Rate Change?
The money wage rate can change for two reasons: departures from full employment and expectations about inflation. Unemployment above the natural rate puts downward pressure on the money wage rate, and unemployment below the natural rate puts upward pressure on the money wage rate. An expected increase in the inflation rate makes the money wage rate rise faster, and an expected decrease in the inflation rate slows the rate at which the money wage rate rises.

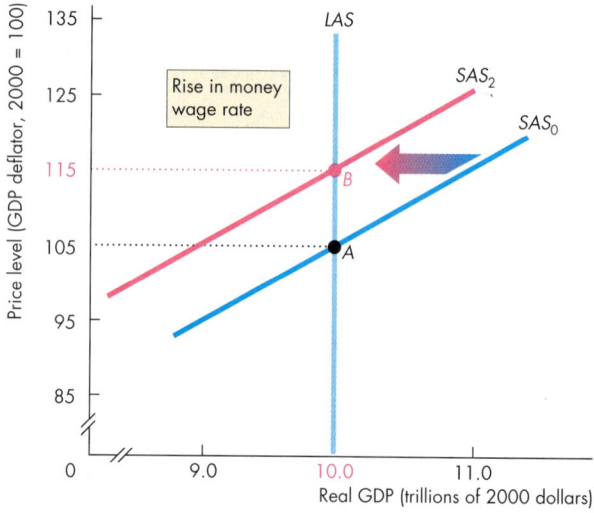

**FIGURE 7.5** A Change in the Money Wage Rate

A rise in the money wage rate decreases short-run aggregate supply and shifts the short-run aggregate supply curve leftward from $SAS_0$ to $SAS_2$. A rise in the money wage rate does not change potential GDP, so the long-run aggregate supply curve does not shift.

### REVIEW QUIZ

1. If the price level rises and if the money wage rate also rises by the same percentage, what happens to the quantity of real GDP supplied? Along which aggregate supply curve does the economy move?
2. If the price level rises and the money wage rate remains constant, what happens to the quantity of real GDP supplied? Along which aggregate supply curve does the economy move?
3. If potential GDP increases, what happens to aggregate supply? Is there a shift of or a movement along the *LAS* curve and the *SAS* curve?
4. If the money wage rate rises and potential GDP remains the same, what happens to aggregate supply? Is there a shift of the *LAS* curve and the *SAS* curve or a movement along them?

# Aggregate Demand

THE QUANTITY OF REAL GDP DEMANDED IS the sum of the real consumption expenditure (*C*), investment (*I*), government expenditures (*G*), and exports (*X*) minus imports (*M*). That is,

$$Y = C + I + G + X - M.$$

The *quantity of real GDP demanded* is the total amount of final goods and services produced in the United States that people, businesses, governments, and foreigners plan to buy.

These buying plans depend on many factors. Some of the main ones are

- The price level
- Expectations
- Fiscal policy and monetary policy
- The world economy

We first focus on the relationship between the quantity of real GDP demanded and the price level. To study this relationship, we keep all other influences on buying plans the same and ask: How does the quantity of real GDP demanded vary as the price level varies?

## The Aggregate Demand Curve

Other things remaining the same, the higher the price level, the smaller is the quantity of real GDP demanded. This relationship between the quantity of real GDP demanded and the price level is called **aggregate demand**. Aggregate demand is described by an *aggregate demand schedule* and an *aggregate demand curve*.

Figure 7.6 shows an aggregate demand curve (*AD*) and an aggregate demand schedule. Each point on the *AD* curve corresponds to a row of the schedule. For example, point *C'* on the *AD* curve and row *C'* of the schedule tell us that if the price level is 105, the quantity of real GDP demanded is $10 trillion.

The aggregate demand curve slopes downward for two reasons:

- Wealth effect
- Substitution effects

**Wealth Effect** When the price level rises but other things remain the same, *real* wealth decreases. Real

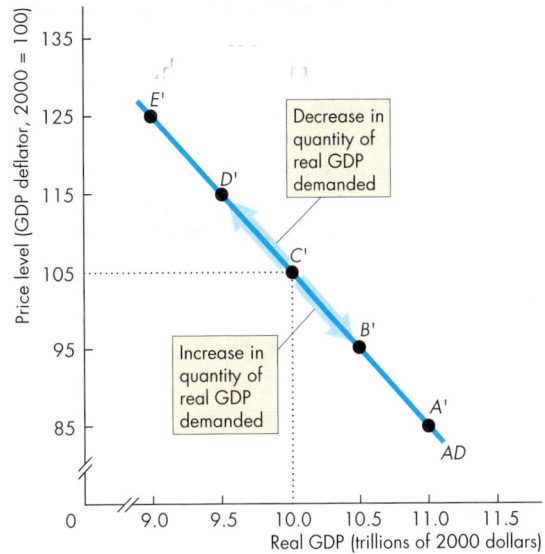

FIGURE 7.6  Aggregate Demand

|    | Price Level (GDP deflator) | Real GDP (trillions of 2000 dollars) |
|----|---|---|
| A' | 85  | 11.0 |
| B' | 95  | 10.5 |
| C' | 105 | 10.0 |
| D' | 115 | 9.5  |
| E' | 125 | 9.0  |

The aggregate demand curve (*AD*) shows the relationship between the quantity of real GDP demanded and the price level. The aggregate demand curve is based on the aggregate demand schedule in the table. Each point *A'* through *E'* on the curve corresponds to the row in the table identified by the same letter. Thus when the price level is 105, the quantity of real GDP demanded is $10 trillion, shown by point *C'* in the figure. A change in the price level, when all other influences on aggregate buying plans remain the same, brings a change in the quantity of real GDP demanded and a movement along the *AD* curve.

wealth is the amount of money in the bank, bonds, stocks, and other assets that people own, measured not in dollars but in terms of the goods and services that this money, bonds, and stock will buy.

People save and hold money, bonds, and stocks for many reasons. One reason is to build up funds for education expenses. Another reason is to build up enough funds to meet possible medical expenses or other big bills. But the biggest reason is to build up enough funds to provide a retirement income.

If the price level rises, real wealth decreases. People then try to restore their wealth. To do so, they must increase saving and, equivalently, decrease current consumption. Such a decrease in consumption is a decrease in aggregate demand.

***Maria's Wealth Effect*** You can see how the wealth effect works by thinking about Maria's buying plans. Maria lives in Moscow, Russia. She has worked hard all summer and saved 20,000 rubles (the ruble is the currency of Russia), which she plans to spend attending graduate school when she has finished her economics degree. So Maria's wealth is 20,000 rubles. Maria has a part-time job, and her income from this job pays her current expenses. The price level in Russia rises by 100 percent, and now Maria needs 40,000 rubles to buy what 20,000 once bought. To try to make up some of the fall in value of her savings, Maria saves even more and cuts her current spending to the bare minimum.

**Substitution Effects** When the price level rises and other things remain the same, interest rates rise. The reason is related to the wealth effect that you've just studied. A rise in the price level decreases the real value of the money in people's pockets and bank accounts. With a smaller amount of real money around, banks and other lenders can get a higher interest rate on loans. But faced with higher interest rates, people and businesses delay plans to buy new capital and consumer durable goods and cut back on spending.

This substitution effect involves substituting *goods in the future for goods in the present* and is called an *intertemporal* substitution effect—a substitution across time. Saving increases to increase future consumption.

To see this intertemporal substitution effect more clearly, think about your own plan to buy a new computer. At an interest rate of 5 percent a year, you might borrow $2,000 and buy the new computer. But at an interest rate of 10 percent a year, you might decide that the payments would be too high. You don't abandon your plan to buy the computer, but you decide to delay your purchase.

A second substitution effect works through international prices. When the U.S. price level rises and other things remain the same, U.S.-made goods and services become more expensive relative to foreign-made goods and services. This change in *relative prices* encourages people to spend less on U.S.-made items and more on foreign-made items. For example, if the U.S. price level rises relative to the Canadian price level, Canadians buy fewer U.S.-made cars (U.S. exports decrease) and Americans buy more Canadian-made cars (U.S. imports increase). U.S. GDP decreases.

***Maria's Substitution Effects*** In Moscow, Russia, Maria makes some substitutions. She was planning to trade in her old motor scooter and get a new one. But with a higher price level and higher interest rates, she decides to make her old scooter last one more year. Also, with the prices of Russian goods sharply increasing, Maria substitutes a low-cost dress made in Malaysia for the Russian-made dress she had originally planned to buy.

**Changes in the Quantity of Real GDP Demanded**
When the price level rises and other things remain the same, the quantity of real GDP demanded decreases—a movement up the aggregate demand curve as shown by the arrow in Fig. 7.6. When the price level falls and other things remain the same, the quantity of real GDP demanded increases—a movement down the aggregate demand curve.

We've now seen how the quantity of real GDP demanded changes when the price level changes. How do other influences on buying plans affect aggregate demand?

## Changes in Aggregate Demand

A change in any factor that influences buying plans other than the price level brings a change in aggregate demand. The main factors are

- Expectations
- Fiscal policy and monetary policy
- The world economy

**Expectations** An increase in expected future income increases the amount of consumption goods (especially big-ticket items such as cars) that people plan to buy today and increases aggregate demand.

An increase in the expected **future inflation** rate increases aggregate demand because people decide to buy more goods and services at today's relatively lower prices.

An increase in expected **future profit** increases the investment that firms plan to undertake today and increases aggregate demand.

**Fiscal Policy and Monetary Policy** The government's attempt to influence the economy by setting and changing taxes, making transfer payments, and purchasing goods and services is called **fiscal policy**. A tax cut or an increase in transfer payments—for example, unemployment benefits or welfare payments—increases aggregate demand. Both of these influences operate by increasing households' *disposable* income. **Disposable income is aggregate income minus taxes plus transfer payments**. The greater the disposable income, the greater is the quantity of consumption goods and services that households plan to buy and the greater is aggregate demand.

Government purchases of goods and services are one component of aggregate demand. So if the government spends more on spy satellites, schools, and highways, aggregate demand increases.

**Monetary policy** consists of changes in interest rates and in the quantity of money in the economy. The quantity of money is determined by the Federal Reserve (the Fed) and the banks (in a process described in Chapters 10 and 11). An increase in the quantity of money in the economy increases aggregate demand. To see why money affects aggregate demand, imagine that the Fed borrows the army's helicopters, loads them with millions of new $10 bills, and sprinkles them like confetti across the nation. People gather the newly available money and plan to spend some of it. So the quantity of goods and services demanded increases. But people don't plan to spend all the new money. They plan to save some of it and lend it to others through the banks. Interest rates fall, and with lower interest rates, people plan to buy more consumer durables and firms plan to increase their investment.

**The World Economy** Two main influences that the world economy has on aggregate demand are the foreign exchange rate and foreign income. The *foreign exchange rate* is the amount of a foreign currency that you can buy with a U.S. dollar. Other things remaining the same, a rise in the foreign exchange

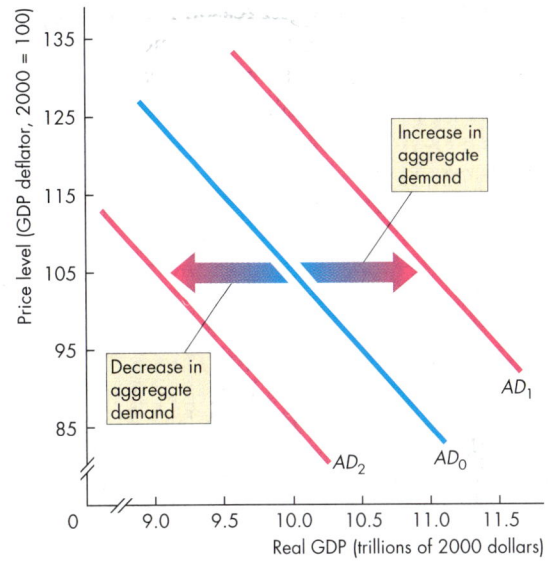

**FIGURE 7.7** Changes in Aggregate Demand

**Aggregate demand**

| Decreases if: | Increases if: |
|---|---|
| ■ Expected future income, inflation, or profits decrease | ■ Expected future income, inflation, or profits increase |
| ■ Fiscal policy decreases government purchases, increases taxes, or decreases transfer payments | ■ Fiscal policy increases government purchases, decreases taxes, or increases transfer payments |
| ■ Monetary policy decreases the quantity of money and increases interest rates | ■ Monetary policy increases the quantity of money and decreases interest rates |
| ■ The exchange rate increases or foreign income decreases | ■ The exchange rate decreases or foreign income increases |

rate decreases aggregate demand. To see how the foreign exchange rate influences aggregate demand, suppose that the exchange rate is 1.20 euros per U.S. dollar. A Nokia cell phone made in Finland costs 120 euros, and an equivalent Motorola phone made in the United States costs $110. In U.S. dollars, the

Nokia phone costs $100, so people around the world buy the cheaper phone from Finland. Now suppose the exchange rate falls to 1 euro per U.S. dollar. The Nokia phone now costs $120 and is more expensive than the Motorola phone. People will switch from the Nokia phone to the Motorola phone. U.S. exports will increase and U.S. imports will decrease, so U.S. aggregate demand will increase.

An increase in foreign income increases U.S. exports and increases U.S. aggregate demand. For example, an increase in income in Japan and Germany increases Japanese and German consumers' and producers' planned expenditures on U.S.-made goods and services.

**Shifts of the Aggregate Demand Curve** When aggregate demand changes, the aggregate demand curve shifts. Figure 7.7 shows two changes in aggregate demand and summarizes the factors that bring about such changes.

Aggregate demand increases and the aggregate demand curve shifts rightward from $AD_0$ to $AD_1$ when expected future income, inflation, or profit increases; government purchases of goods and services increase; taxes are cut; transfer payments increase; the quantity of money increases and interest rates fall; the foreign exchange rate falls; or foreign income increases.

Aggregate demand decreases and the aggregate demand curve shifts leftward from $AD_0$ to $AD_2$ when expected future income, inflation, or profit decreases; government purchases of goods and services decrease; taxes increase; transfer payments decrease; the quantity of money decreases and interest rates rise; the foreign exchange rate rises; or foreign income decreases.

### REVIEW QUIZ

1 What does the aggregate demand curve show, what factors change, and what factors remain the same when there is a movement along the aggregate demand curve?
2 Why does the aggregate demand curve slope downward?
3 How do changes in expectations, fiscal policy and monetary policy, and the world economy change aggregate demand and the aggregate demand curve?

## Macroeconomic Equilibrium

THE PURPOSE OF THE AGGREGATE SUPPLY–aggregate demand model is to explain changes in real GDP and the price level. To achieve this purpose, we combine aggregate supply and aggregate demand and determine macroeconomic equilibrium. There is a macroeconomic equilibrium for each of the time frames for aggregate supply: a long-run equilibrium and a short-run equilibrium. Long-run equilibrium is the state toward which the economy is heading. Short-run equilibrium is the normal state of the economy as it fluctuates around potential GDP.

We'll begin our study of macroeconomic equilibrium by looking first at the short run.

### Short-Run Macroeconomic Equilibrium

The aggregate demand curve tells us the quantity of real GDP demanded at each price level, and the short-run aggregate supply curve tells us the quantity of real GDP supplied at each price level. **Short-run macroeconomic equilibrium** occurs when the quantity of real GDP demanded equals the quantity of real GDP supplied. That is, short-run macroeconomic equilibrium occurs at the point of intersection of the *AD* curve and the *SAS* curve. Figure 7.8 shows such an equilibrium at a price level of 105 and real GDP of $10 trillion (points *C* and *C'*).

To see why this position is the equilibrium, think about what happens if the price level is something other than 105. Suppose, for example, that the price level is 115 and that real GDP is $11 trillion (at point *E* on the *SAS* curve). The quantity of real GDP demanded is less than $11 trillion, so firms are unable to sell all their output. Unwanted inventories pile up, and firms cut both production and prices. Production and prices are cut until firms can sell all their output. This situation occurs only when real GDP is $10 trillion and the price level is 105.

Now suppose the price level is 95 and real GDP is $9 trillion (at point *A* on the *SAS* curve). The quantity of real GDP demanded exceeds $9 trillion, so firms are unable to meet the demand for their output. Inventories decrease, and customers clamor for goods and services. So firms increase production and raise prices. Production and prices increase until

# MACROECONOMIC EQUILIBRIUM

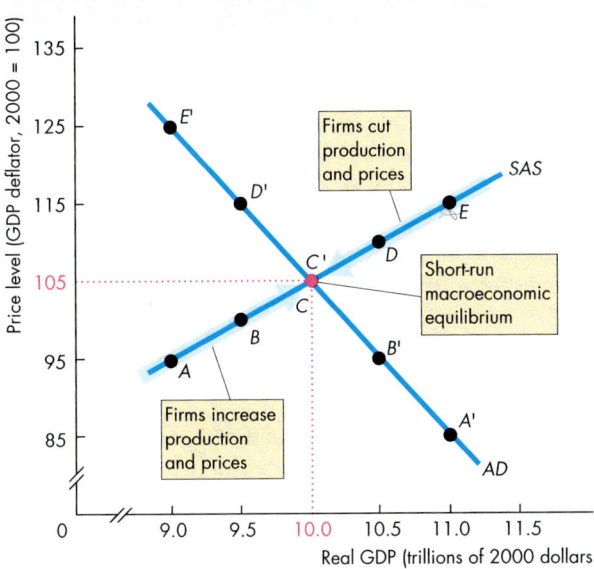

**FIGURE 7.8** Short-Run Equilibrium

Short-run macroeconomic equilibrium occurs when real GDP demanded equals real GDP supplied—at the intersection of the aggregate demand curve (*AD*) and the short-run aggregate supply curve (*SAS*). Here, such an equilibrium occurs at points *C* and *C'*, where the price level is 105 and real GDP is $10 trillion. If the price level is 115 and real GDP is $11 trillion (point *E*), firms will not be able to sell all their output. They will decrease production and cut prices. If the price level is 95 and real GDP is $9 trillion (point *A*), people will not be able to buy all the goods and services they demand. Firms will increase production and raise their prices. Only when the price level is 105 and real GDP is $10 trillion can firms sell all that they produce and can people buy all the goods and services they demand. This is the short-run macroeconomic equilibrium.

firms can meet demand. This situation occurs only when real GDP is $10 trillion and the price level is 105.

In short-run equilibrium, the money wage rate is fixed. It does not adjust to bring full employment. So in the short run, real GDP can be greater than or less than potential GDP. But in the long run, the money wage rate does adjust and real GDP moves toward potential GDP. We are going to study this adjustment process. But first, let's look at the economy in long-run equilibrium.

## Long-Run Macroeconomic Equilibrium

**Long-run macroeconomic equilibrium** occurs when real GDP equals potential GDP—equivalently, when the economy is on its *long-run* aggregate supply curve. Figure 7.9 shows the long-run macroeconomic equilibrium, which occurs at the intersection of the *AD* curve and the *LAS* curve (the blue curves). Long-run macroeconomic equilibrium comes about because the money wage rate adjusts. Potential GDP and aggregate demand determine the price level, and the price level influences the money wage rate. In long-run equilibrium, the money wage rate has adjusted to put the (green) *SAS* curve through the long-run equilibrium point.

We'll look at this money wage adjustment process later in this chapter. But first, let's see how the *AS-AD* model helps us to understand economic growth and inflation.

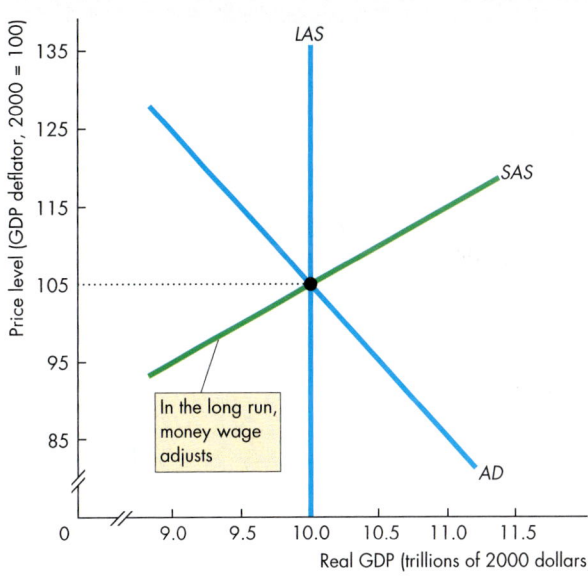

**FIGURE 7.9** Long-Run Equilibrium

In long-run macroeconomic equilibrium, real GDP equals potential GDP. So long-run equilibrium occurs where the aggregate demand curve *AD* intersects the long-run aggregate supply curve *LAS*. In the long run, aggregate demand determines the price level and has no effect on real GDP. The money wage rate adjusts in the long run, so the *SAS* curve intersects the *LAS* curve at the long-run equilibrium price level.

## Economic Growth and Inflation

Economic growth occurs because over time, the quantity of labor grows, capital is accumulated, and technology advances. These changes increase potential GDP and shift the *LAS* curve rightward. Figure 7.10 shows such a shift. The growth rate of potential GDP is determined by the pace at which labor grows, capital is accumulated, and technology advances.

Inflation occurs when over time, the increase in aggregate demand is greater than the increase in long-run aggregate supply. That is, inflation occurs if the *AD* curve shifts rightward by more than the rightward shift in the *LAS* curve. Figure 7.10 shows such shifts.

If aggregate demand increased at the same pace as long-run aggregate supply, we would experience real GDP growth with no inflation.

In the long run, the main influence on aggregate demand is the growth rate of the quantity of money.

At times when the quantity of money increases rapidly, aggregate demand increases quickly and the inflation rate is high. When the growth rate of the quantity of money slows, other things remaining the same, the inflation rate eventually decreases.

Our economy experiences periods of growth and inflation, like those shown in Fig. 7.10. But it does not experience *steady* growth and *steady* inflation. Real GDP fluctuates around potential GDP in a business cycle, and inflation fluctuates. When we study the business cycle, we ignore economic growth. By doing so, we can see the business cycle more clearly.

## The Business Cycle

The business cycle occurs because aggregate demand and short-run aggregate supply fluctuate but the money wage rate does not adjust quickly enough to keep real GDP at potential GDP. Figure 7.11 shows three types of short-run macroeconomic equilibrium.

In part (a), there is a below full-employment equilibrium. A **below full-employment equilibrium** is a macroeconomic equilibrium in which potential GDP exceeds real GDP. The amount by which potential GDP exceeds real GDP is the *Okun gap* that you saw in Chapter 4, p. 93. This gap is also called a **recessionary gap**. This name reminds us that a gap has opened up between potential GDP and real GDP either because the economy has experienced a recession or because real GDP, while growing, has grown more slowly than potential GDP.

The below full-employment equilibrium shown in Fig. 7.11(a) occurs where the aggregate demand curve $AD_0$ intersects short-run aggregate supply curve $SAS_0$ at a real GDP of $9.8 trillion and a price level of 105. Potential GDP is $10 trillion, so the recessionary gap is $0.2 trillion. The U.S. economy was in a situation similar to that shown in Fig. 7.11(a) in the early 2000s.

Figure 7.11(b) is an example of *long-run equilibrium*, in which real GDP equals potential GDP. In this example, the equilibrium occurs where the aggregate demand curve $AD_1$ intersects the short-run aggregate supply curve $SAS_1$ at an actual and potential GDP of $10 trillion. The U.S. economy was in a situation such as that shown in Fig. 7.11(b) in 1998.

Figure 7.11(c) shows an above full-employment equilibrium. An **above full-employment equilibrium**

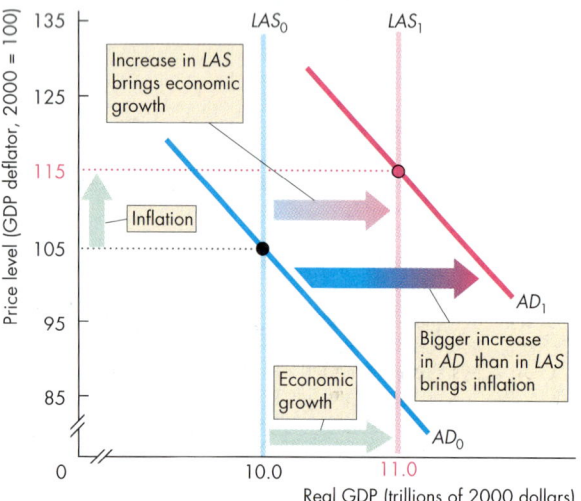

**FIGURE 7.10** Economic Growth and Inflation

Economic growth is the persistent increase in potential GDP. Economic growth is shown as an ongoing rightward shift of the *LAS* curve. Inflation is the persistent rise in the price level. Inflation occurs when the increase in aggregate demand is greater than the increase in long-run aggregate supply.

is a macroeconomic equilibrium in which real GDP exceeds potential GDP. The amount by which real GDP exceeds potential GDP is called an **inflationary gap**. This name reminds us that a gap has opened up between real GDP and potential GDP and that this gap creates inflationary pressure.

The above full-employment equilibrium shown in Fig. 7.11(c) occurs where the aggregate demand curve $AD_2$ intersects the short-run aggregate supply curve $SAS_2$ at a real GDP of $10.2 trillion and a price level of 105. There is an inflationary gap of $0.2 trillion. The U.S. economy was in a situation similar to that depicted in Fig. 7.11(c) in 1999 and 2000.

The economy moves from one type of equilibrium to another as a result of fluctuations in aggregate demand and in short-run aggregate supply. These fluctuations produce fluctuations in real GDP and the price level. Figure 7.11(d) shows how real GDP fluctuates around potential GDP.

Let's now look at some of the sources of these fluctuations around potential GDP.

## FIGURE 7.11  The Business Cycle

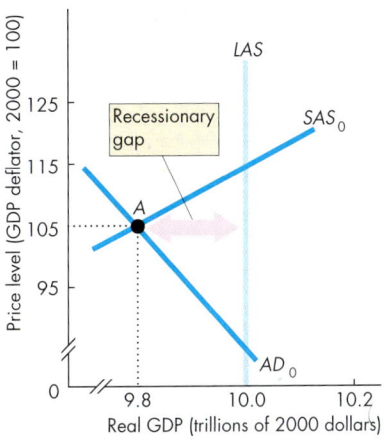

(a) Below full-employment equilibrium

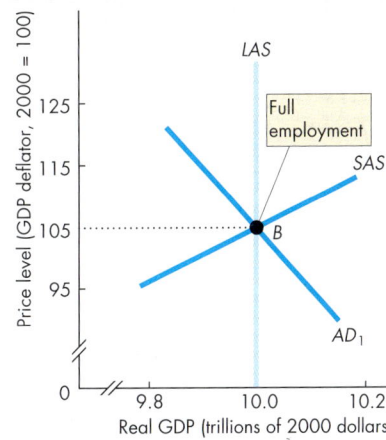

(b) Long-run equilibrium

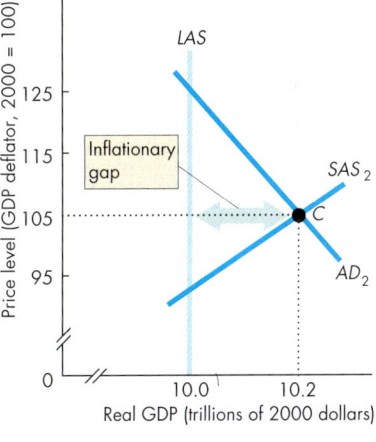

(c) Above full-employment equilibrium

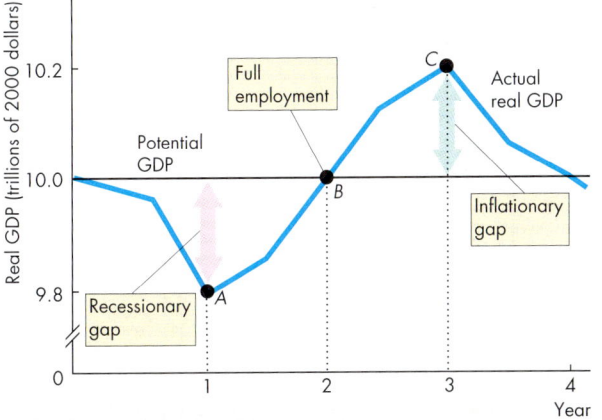

(d) Fluctuations in real GDP

Part (a) shows a below full-employment equilibrium in year 1; part (b) shows a long-run equilibrium in year 2; and part (c) shows an above full-employment equilibrium in year 3. Part (d) shows how real GDP fluctuates around potential GDP in a business cycle.

In year 1, a recessionary gap exists and the economy is at point A (in parts a and d). In year 2, the economy is in long-run equilibrium and the economy is at point B (in parts b and d). In year 3, an inflationary gap exists and the economy is at point C (in parts c and d).

## Fluctuations in Aggregate Demand

One reason real GDP fluctuates around potential GDP is that aggregate demand fluctuates. Let's see what happens when aggregate demand increases.

Figure 7.12(a) shows an economy in long-run equilibrium. The aggregate demand curve is $AD_0$, the short-run aggregate supply curve is $SAS_0$, and the long-run aggregate supply curve is $LAS$. Real GDP equals potential GDP at $10 trillion, and the price level is 105.

Now suppose that the world economy expands and that the demand for U.S.-made goods increases in Japan and Europe. The increase in U.S. exports increases aggregate demand in the United States and the aggregate demand curve shifts rightward from $AD_0$ to $AD_1$ in Fig. 7.12(a).

Faced with an increase in demand, firms increase production and raise prices. Real GDP increases to $10.5 trillion, and the price level rises to 110. The economy is now in an above full-employment equilibrium. Real GDP exceeds potential GDP, and there is an inflationary gap.

The increase in aggregate demand has increased the prices of all goods and services. Faced with higher prices, firms have increased their output rates. At this stage, prices of goods and services have increased but wage rates have not changed. (Recall that as we move along a short-run aggregate supply curve, the money wage rate is constant.)

The economy cannot produce in excess of potential GDP forever. Why not? What are the forces at work that bring real GDP back to potential GDP?

Because the price level has increased and the money wage rate is unchanged, workers have experienced a fall in the buying power of their wages and firms' profits have increased. In these circumstances, workers demand higher wages and firms, anxious to maintain their employment and output levels, meet those demands. If firms do not raise the money wage rate, they will either lose workers or have to hire less productive ones.

As the money wage rate rises, the short-run aggregate supply curve begins to shift leftward. In Fig. 7.12(b), the short-run aggregate supply curve moves

**FIGURE 7.12  An Increase in Aggregate Demand**

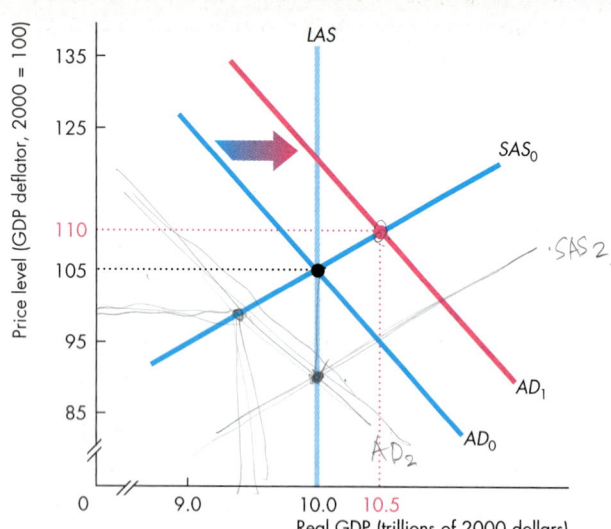

(a) Short-run effect

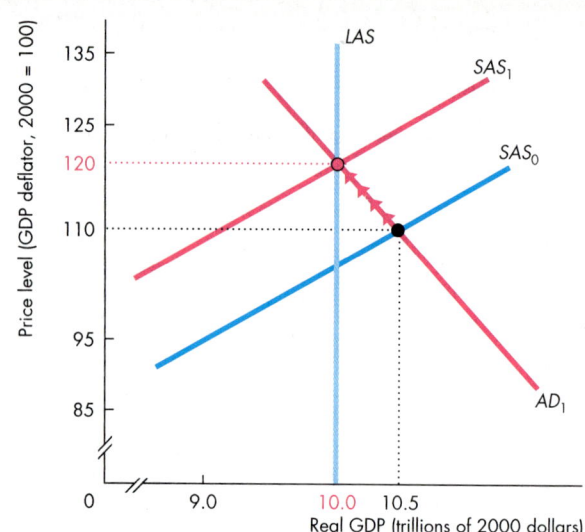

(b) Long-run effect

An increase in aggregate demand shifts the aggregate demand curve from $AD_0$ to $AD_1$. In short-run equilibrium, real GDP increases to $10.5 trillion and the price level rises to 110. In this situation, an inflationary gap exists. In the long run, the money wage rate rises and the short-run aggregate supply curve shifts leftward from $SAS_0$ to $SAS_1$ in part (b). As short-run aggregate supply decreases, the SAS curve shifts and intersects the aggregate demand curve $AD_1$ at higher price levels and real GDP decreases. Eventually, the price level rises to 120 and real GDP decreases to $10 trillion—potential GDP.

from $SAS_0$ toward $SAS_1$. The rise in the wage rate and the shift in the SAS curve produce a sequence of new equilibrium positions. Along the adjustment path, real GDP decreases and the price level rises. The economy moves up along its aggregate demand curve as shown by the arrowheads in the figure.

Eventually, the money wage rate rises by the same percentage as the price level. At this time, the aggregate demand curve $AD_1$ intersects $SAS_1$ at a new long-run equilibrium. The price level has risen to 120, and real GDP is back where it started, at potential GDP.

A decrease in aggregate demand has similar but opposite effects to those of an increase in aggregate demand. That is, a decrease in aggregate demand shifts the aggregate demand curve leftward. Real GDP decreases to less than potential GDP, and a recessionary gap emerges. Firms cut prices. The lower price level increases the purchasing power of wages and increases firms' costs relative to their output prices because the wage rate remains unchanged. Eventually, the money wage rate falls and the short-run aggregate supply curve shifts rightward. But the wage rate changes slowly, so real GDP slowly returns to potential GDP and the price level falls slowly.

Let's now work out how real GDP and the price level change when aggregate supply changes.

## Fluctuations in Aggregate Supply

Fluctuations in short-run aggregate supply can bring fluctuations in real GDP around potential GDP. Suppose that initially real GDP equals potential GDP. Then there is a large but temporary rise in the price of oil. What happens to real GDP and the price level?

Figure 7.13 answers this question. The aggregate demand curve is $AD_0$, the short-run aggregate supply curve is $SAS_0$, and the long-run aggregate supply curve is LAS. Real GDP is $10 trillion, which equals potential GDP, and the price level is 105. Then the price of oil rises. Faced with higher energy and transportation costs, firms decrease production. Short-run aggregate supply decreases, and the short-run aggregate supply curve shifts leftward to $SAS_1$. The price level rises to 115, and real GDP decreases to $9.5 trillion. Because real GDP decreases, the economy experiences recession. Because the price level increases, the economy experiences inflation. A combination of recession and inflation, called **stagflation**, actually occurred in the United States in the mid-1970s and early 1980s. But events like this are not common.

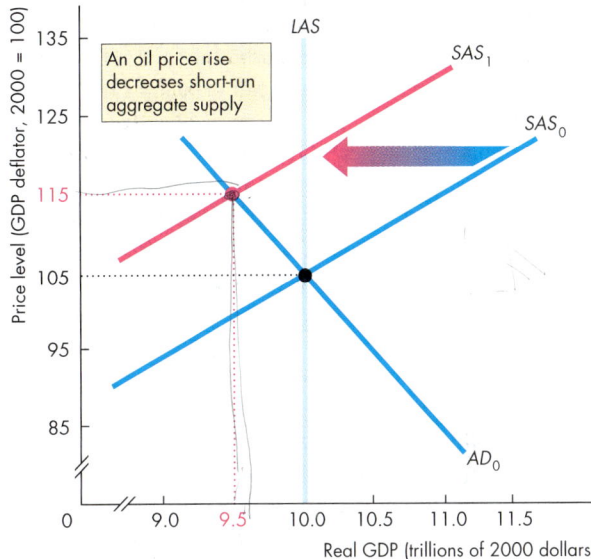

**FIGURE 7.13** A Decrease in Aggregate Supply

An increase in the price of oil decreases short-run aggregate supply and shifts the short-run aggregate supply curve from $SAS_0$ to $SAS_1$. Real GDP falls from $10 trillion to $9.5 trillion, and the price level increases from 105 to 115. The economy experiences stagflation.

### REVIEW QUIZ

1. Does economic growth result from increases in aggregate demand, short-run aggregate supply, or long-run aggregate supply?
2. Does inflation result from increases in aggregate demand, short-run aggregate supply, or long-run aggregate supply?
3. Describe three types of short-run macroeconomic equilibrium.
4. How do fluctuations in aggregate demand and short-run aggregate supply bring fluctuations in real GDP around potential GDP?

Let's put our new knowledge of aggregate supply and aggregate demand to work and see how we can explain recent U.S. macroeconomic performance.

## U.S. Economic Growth, Inflation, and Cycles

THE ECONOMY IS CONTINUALLY CHANGING. If you imagine the economy as a video, then an aggregate supply–aggregate demand figure such as Fig. 7.13 is a freeze-frame. We're going to run the video—an instant replay—but keep our finger on the freeze-frame button and look at some important parts of the previous action. Let's run the video from 1963.

Figure 7.14 shows the economy in 1963 at the point of intersection of its aggregate demand curve, $AD_{63}$, and short-run aggregate supply curve, $SAS_{63}$. Real GDP was $2.8 trillion, and the GDP deflator was 22 (about a fifth of its 2003 level). In 1963, real GDP equaled potential GDP—the economy was on its long-run aggregate supply curve, $LAS_{63}$.

By 2003, the economy had reached the point marked by the intersection of aggregate demand curve $AD_{03}$ and short-run aggregate supply curve $SAS_{03}$. Real GDP was $10.3 trillion, and the GDP deflator was 105.

Potential GDP in 2003 was $10.5 trillion so equilibrium real GDP was less that potential GDP on $LAS_{03}$.

The path traced by the blue and red dots in Fig. 7.14 shows three key features:

- Economic growth
- Inflation
- Business cycles

### Economic Growth

Over the years, real GDP grows—shown in Fig. 7.14 by the rightward movement of the dots. The faster real GDP grows, the larger is the horizontal distance between successive dots. The forces that generate economic growth are those that increase potential GDP. Potential GDP grows because the quantity of labor grows, we accumulate physical capital and human capital, and our technologies advance.

These forces that bring economic growth were strongest during the 1960s and 1990s. During the late 1970s, economic growth was slow.

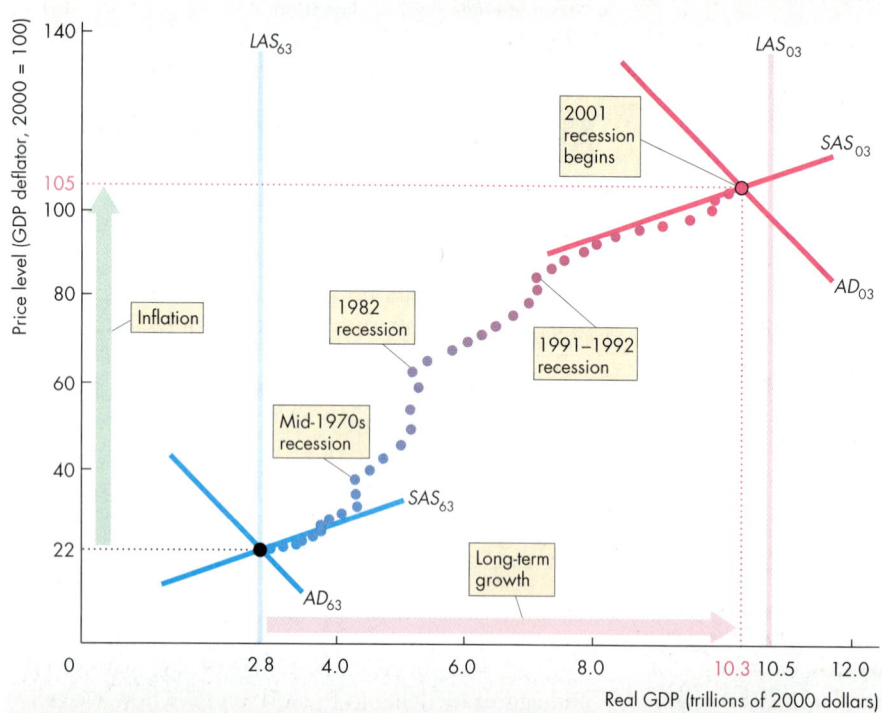

**FIGURE 7.14 Aggregate Supply and Aggregate Demand: 1963–2003**

Each point shows the GDP deflator and real GDP in a given year. In 1963 the aggregate demand curve, $AD_{63}$, and the short-run aggregate supply curve, $SAS_{63}$, determined these variables. Each point is generated by the gradual shifting of the AD and SAS curves. By 2003, the curves were $AD_{03}$ and $SAS_{03}$. Real GDP grew, and the price level increased. Real GDP grew quickly and inflation was moderate during the 1960s; real GDP growth sagged in 1974–1975 and again in 1982. Inflation was rapid during the 1970s but slowed after the 1982 recession. The period from 1982 to 1989 was one of strong, persistent expansion. A recession began in 1991, and a further strong and sustained expansion then followed until the 2001 recession. The recovery after 2001 was weak.

*Source:* Bureau of Economic Analysis and author's assumptions.

## Inflation

The price level rises over the years—shown in Fig. 7.14 by the upward movement of the points. The larger the rise in the price level, the larger is the vertical distance between successive dots in the figure. The main force generating the persistent increase in the price level is a tendency for aggregate demand to increase at a faster pace than the increase in long-run aggregate supply. All of the factors that increase aggregate demand and shift the aggregate demand curve influence the pace of inflation. But one factor—the growth of the quantity of money—is the main source of *persistent* increases in aggregate demand and persistent inflation.

## Business Cycles

Over the years, the economy grows and shrinks in cycles—shown in Fig. 7.14 by the wavelike pattern made by the dots, with the recessions highlighted. The cycles arise because both the expansion of short-run aggregate supply and the growth of aggregate demand do not proceed at a fixed, steady pace. Although the economy has cycles, recessions do not usually follow quickly on the heels of their predecessors; "double-dip" recessions like the one in the cartoon are rare.

## The Evolving Economy: 1963–2003

During the 1960s, real GDP growth was rapid and inflation was low. This was a period of rapid increases in aggregate supply and of moderate increases in aggregate demand.

The mid-1970s were years of rapid inflation and recession—of stagflation. The major sources of these developments were a series of massive oil price increases that decreased short-run aggregate supply and rapid increases in the quantity of money that increased aggregate demand. Recession occurred because short-run aggregate supply decreased at a faster pace than aggregate demand increased.

The rest of the 1970s saw high inflation—the price level increased quickly—but slow growth in real GDP. By 1980, inflation was a major problem and the Fed decided to take strong action against it. It drove interest rates to previously unknown levels and decreased aggregate demand. By 1982, the decrease in aggregate demand put the economy in a deep recession.

During the years 1983–1990, capital accumulation and steady technological advance resulted in a

"Please stand by for a series of tones. The first indicates the official end of the recession, the second indicates prosperity, and the third the return of the recession."

© The New Yorker Collection 1991
Robert Mankoff from cartoonbank.com. All Rights Reserved.

sustained increase in potential GDP. Wage growth was moderate, the price of oil fell, and short-run aggregate supply increased. Aggregate demand growth kept pace with the growth of aggregate supply. Sustained but steady growth in aggregate supply and aggregate demand kept real GDP growing and inflation steady. The economy moved from a recession with real GDP less than potential GDP in 1982 to above full employment in 1990.

The economy was in this condition when a decrease in aggregate demand led to the 1991 recession. The economy again embarked on a path of expansion through 2001. During the late 1990s and 2000, the expansion increased real GDP to a level that exceeded potential GDP and took employment to above full employment. Then in late 2000 and early 2001, aggregate demand decreased and another recession occurred. This recession was mild and was followed by a slow recovery. In 2003, although real GDP had grown above its 2001 recession level, it remained below potential GDP.

You've now reviewed the *AS-AD* model and seen how that model can provide an account of the forces that move real GDP and the price level to bring economic growth, inflation, and the business cycle. The account that we've just given is the consensus account. But it isn't the only one. We're going to end this chapter by using the *AS-AD* model as a framework for a quick look at the alternative schools of thought in macroeconomics.

## Macroeconomic Schools of Thought

MACROECONOMICS IS AN ACTIVE FIELD OF research and much remains to be learned about the forces that make our economy grow and fluctuate. There is a greater degree of consensus and certainty about economic growth and inflation—the longer term trends in real GDP and the price level—than there is about the business cycle—the short-term fluctuations in these variables. Here, we'll look only at differences of view about short-term fluctuations.

The aggregate supply–aggregate demand model that you've studied in this chapter provides a good foundation for understanding the range of views that macroeconomists hold about this topic. But what you will learn here is just a first glimpse at the scientific controversy and debate. We'll return to these issues at various later points in the text and deepen your appreciation of the alternative views.

Classification usually requires simplification. And classifying macroeconomists is no exception to this general rule. The classification that we'll use here is simple, but it is not misleading. We're going to divide macroeconomists into three broad schools of thought and examine the views of each group in turn. The groups are

- Keynesian
- Classical
- Monetarist

### The Keynesian View

A **Keynesian** macroeconomist believes that left alone, the economy would rarely operate at full employment and that to achieve and maintain full employment, active help from fiscal policy and monetary policy is required.

The term "Keynesian" derives from the name of one of the twentieth century's most famous economists, John Maynard Keynes (see p. 174).

The Keynesian view is based on beliefs about the forces that determine aggregate demand and short-run aggregate supply.

**Aggregate Demand Fluctuations** In the Keynesian view, *expectations* are the most significant influence on aggregate demand. And expectations are based on herd instinct or, what Keynes himself called "animal spirits." A wave of pessimism about future profit prospects can lead to a fall in aggregate demand and plunge the economy into recession.

**Aggregate Supply Response** In the Keynesian view, the money wage rate that lies behind the short-run aggregate supply curve is extremely sticky in the downward direction. Basically, the money wage rate doesn't fall. So if there is a recessionary gap, there is no automatic mechanism for getting rid of it. If it were to happen, a fall in the money wage rate would increase short-run aggregate supply and restore full employment. But the money wage rate doesn't fall, so the economy remains stuck in recession.

A modern version of the Keynesian view known as the **new Keynesian** view holds that not only is the money wage rate sticky but that prices of goods and services are also sticky. With a sticky price level, the short-run aggregate supply curve is horizontal at a fixed price level.

**Policy Response Needed** The Keynesian view calls for fiscal policy and monetary policy to actively offset changes in aggregate demand that bring recession.

By stimulating aggregate demand in a recession, full employment can be restored.

### The Classical View

A **classical** macroeconomist believes that the economy is self-regulating and that it is always at full employment. The fluctuations that occur are efficient responses of a well-functioning market economy that is bombarded by shocks, mainly coming from the uneven pace of technological change.

The term "classical" derives from the name of the founding school of economics that includes Adam Smith, David Ricardo, and John Stuart Mill (see p. 52).

Like the Keynesian view, the classical view can be understood in terms of beliefs, different from those of a Keynesian, about aggregate demand and aggregate supply.

**Aggregate Demand Fluctuations** In the classical view, technological change is the most significant influence on both aggregate demand and aggregate supply. For this reason, classical macroeconomists don't use the *AS-AD* framework. But their views can be interpreted in this framework. A technological change that increases the productivity of capital brings an increase in aggregate demand because firms increase their expenditure on new plant and equipment. A technological change that lengthens the useful life of existing capital decreases the demand for new capital, which decreases aggregate demand.

**Aggregate Supply Response** In the classical view, the money wage rate that lies behind the short-run aggregate supply curve is instantly and completely flexible. The money wage rate adjusts so quickly to maintain equilibrium in the labor market that real GDP always adjusts to equal potential GDP.

Potential GDP itself fluctuates for the same reasons that aggregate demand fluctuates—technological change. When the pace of technological change is rapid, potential GDP increases quickly and so does real GDP. And when the pace of technological change slows, so does the growth rate of potential GDP.

**Classical Policy** The classical view of policy emphasizes the potential for taxes to stunt incentives and create inefficiency. By minimizing the disincentive effects of taxes, employment, investment, and technological advance are at their efficient levels and the economy expands at an appropriate and rapid pace.

## The Monetarist View

A **monetarist** is a macroeconomist believes that the economy is self-regulating and that it will normally operate at full employment, provided that monetary policy is not erratic and that the pace of money growth is kept steady.

The term "monetarist" was coined by an outstanding twentieth century economist, Karl Brunner, to describe his own views and those of Milton Friedman (see p. 300).

The monetarist view can be interpreted in terms of beliefs about the forces that determine aggregate demand and short-run aggregate supply.

**Aggregate Demand Fluctuations** In the monetarist view, *the quantity of money* is the most significant influence on aggregate demand. And the quantity of money is determined by the Federal Reserve (the Fed). If the Fed keeps money growing at a steady pace, aggregate demand fluctuations will be minimized and the economy will operate close to full employment. But if the Fed decreases the quantity of money or even just slows its growth rate too abruptly, the economy will go into recession. In the monetarist view, all recessions result from inappropriate monetary policy.

**Aggregate Supply Response** The monetarist view of short-run aggregate supply is the same as the Keynesian view—the money wage rate is sticky. If the economy is in recession, it will take an unnecessarily long time for it to return unaided to full employment.

**Monetarist Policy** The monetarist view of policy is the same as the classical view on fiscal policy. Taxes should be kept low to avoid disincentive effects that decrease potential GDP. Provided that the quantity of money is kept on a steady growth path, no active stabilization is needed to offset changes in aggregate demand.

## The Way Ahead

In the chapters that follow, you're going to encounter Keynesian, classical, and monetarist views again. The popular way to study macroeconomics today is to begin with the classical model and that's what we do in the next chapter. We then build on that model and study the growing economy. From there, we study money and inflation and lay the foundation for a deeper look at the sources of macroeconomic fluctuations. And we finish with a closer look at fiscal policies and monetary policies that try to achieve faster growth, stable prices, and a smoother cycle.

This order for learning macroeconomics was not always followed. And some teachers today prefer to move next to a study of economic fluctuations. That sequence can be followed in this text. To do so, the reader will jump to Chapter 13 to study the Keynesian model and then backtrack through money and end with the classical model and economic growth.

◆ The *AS-AD* model explains economic growth, inflation, and the business cycle. The *AS-AD* model enables us to keep our eye on the big picture, but it lacks detail. It does not tell us as much as we need to know about the deeper forces that lie behind aggregate supply and aggregate demand. The chapters that follow begin to fill in the details. We begin with the supply side and study the forces that make our economy grow. But before you embark on this next stage, take a look at *Reading Between the Lines* on pp. 168–169, which gives you a look at the expanding U.S. economy in 2003.

# READING BETWEEN THE LINES

## *Aggregate Supply and Aggregate Demand in Action*

**THE WALL STREET JOURNAL, NOVEMBER 25, 2003**

## U.S. 3rd Qtr GDP Revised To Up 8.2% Rate From Up 7.2%

The U.S. economy, spurred by powerful business and consumer spending, galloped ahead during the summer at a pace faster than earlier estimated.

Gross domestic product increased in July through September at an 8.2% annual rate, the Commerce Department said Tuesday.

The economy's blistering run in the third quarter marked its best quarterly performance since a 9.0% surge in the first three months of 1984....

The economy has been accelerating all year. It advanced 1.4% in the first three months of 2003 and 3.3% in the second quarter.

Analysts think the economy will cool after the torrid third quarter. Nonetheless, solid growth is expected to continue. A prominent panel of forecasters is predicting GDP to climb 4.5% in 2004, higher than they earlier estimated. The National Association for Business Economics said Monday the expected growth will prod the Federal Reserve to begin raising interest rates....

The government report showed inflation edged up in July through September a bit less than first thought. The price index for gross domestic purchases rose at a 1.8% rate; it was first estimated as climbing 1.9%. The index advanced 0.4% in the second quarter. ....

©2003 The Wall Street Journal. Reprinted with permission. Further reproduction prohibited.

### Essence of the Story

■ Real GDP grew during the third quarter of 2003 at an 8.2 percent annual rate—the highest since 1984.

■ Inflation also edged upward. The GDP deflator rose at a 1.8 percent annual rate.

■ The economy has accelerated all year. It advanced 1.4 percent in the first quarter 2003 and 3.3 percent in the second quarter.

■ A panel of forecasters predicts GDP to grow by 4.5 percent in 2004.

■ The National Association for Business Economics says it expects the Federal Reserve to begin raising interest rates.

## Economic Analysis

- U.S. real GDP grew spectacularly during the third quarter of 2003, at an 8.2 percent annual rate, and the price level rose at only a 1.8 percent annual rate.

- Real GDP increased steadily throughout 2003 and the inflation rate was modest.

- Most forecasters were optimistic that the economy would continue to grow through 2004 but at a much lower rate than that of the third quarter.

- The strong growth of 2003 occurred as real GDP expanded to close a large recessionary gap.

- Figure 1 illustrates this gap a year earlier, in the third quarter of 2002.

- In the third quarter of 2002, real GDP was $10.04 trillion and the price level was 104 at the intersection of the aggregate demand curve, $AD_{02}$ and the short-run aggregate supply curve, $SAS_{02}$.

- But potential GDP in the third quarter of 2002 was $10.17 trillion, so long-run aggregate supply was at $LAS_{02}$ and there was a recessionary gap of $0.13 trillion or close to one percent of potential GDP.

- With this amount of slack in the economy, real GDP had plenty of room to expand without stimulating inflation.

- Also, potential GDP was growing, so real GDP needed to grow more rapidly than potential GDP to close the recessionary gap.

- That is what happened during the year to the third quarter of 2003.

- Potential GDP increased by just under 4 percent to $10.56 trillion; real GDP increased by almost 4.5 percent to $10.49 trillion; the recessionary gap shrank to $0.07 trillion; and the price level increased to 106—an inflation rate of only 1.9 percent over the year.

- Figure 2 illustrates these changes. Because potential GDP increased, the LAS curve shifted rightward to $LAS_{03}$ and the SAS curve shifted rightward to $SAS_{03}$.

- "Spurred by powerful business and consumer spending," as the news article says, aggregate demand increased by more than aggregate supply and the AD curve shifted rightward to $AD_{03}$.

- The economy will continue to grow in 2004 but at a slower pace because by late 2003, real GDP was approaching full employment and if an inflationary gap emerged, the Fed would act to lower aggregate demand.

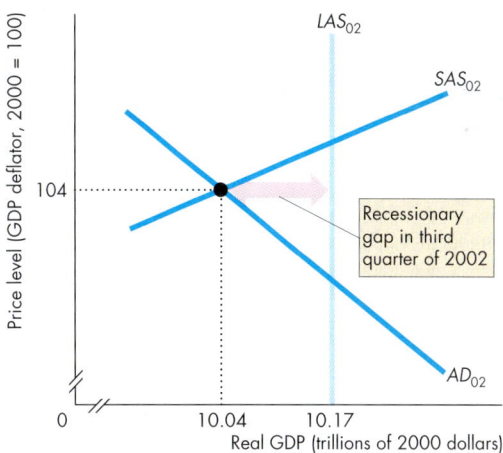

Figure 1 The economy in the third quarter of 2002

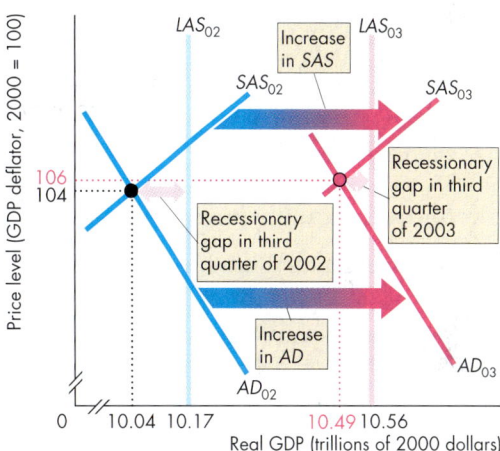

Figure 2 The action in 2002–2003

# SUMMARY

## KEY POINTS

### Aggregate Supply (pp. 150–154)

- In the long run, the quantity of real GDP supplied is potential GDP.
- In the short run, a rise in the price level increases the quantity of real GDP supplied.
- A change in potential GDP changes long-run and short-run aggregate supply. A change in the money wage rate changes only short-run aggregate supply.

### Aggregate Demand (pp. 155–158)

- A rise in the price level decreases the quantity of real GDP demanded because of a wealth effect and substitution effects.
- Changes in expected future income, inflation, and profits; in fiscal policy and monetary policy; and in world real GDP and the foreign exchange rate change aggregate demand.

### Macroeconomic Equilibrium (pp. 158–163)

- Aggregate demand and short-run aggregate supply determine real GDP and the price level.
- In the long run, real GDP equals potential GDP and aggregate demand determines the price level.
- Economic growth occurs because potential GDP increases and inflation occurs because aggregate demand grows more quickly than potential GDP.
- The business cycle occurs because aggregate demand and aggregate supply fluctuate.

### U.S. Economic Growth, Inflation, and Cycles (pp. 164–165)

- Potential GDP grew fastest during the 1960s and 1990s and slowest during the 1970s.
- Inflation persists because aggregate demand grows faster than potential GDP.
- Business cycles occur because aggregate supply and aggregate demand change at an uneven pace.

### Macroeconomic Schools of Thought (pp. 166–167)

- Keynesian economists believe that full employment can be achieved only with active policy.
- Classical economists believe that the economy is self-regulating and always at full employment.
- Monetarist economists believe that recessions result from inappropriate monetary policy.

## KEY FIGURES

Figure 7.2   Short-Run Aggregate Supply, 152
Figure 7.3   Movements Along the Aggregate Supply Curves, 152
Figure 7.6   Aggregate Demand, 155
Figure 7.7   Changes in Aggregate Demand, 157
Figure 7.8   Short-Run Equilibrium, 159
Figure 7.9   Long-Run Equilibrium, 159
Figure 7.10  Economic Growth and Inflation, 160
Figure 7.11  The Business Cycle, 161
Figure 7.12  An Increase in Aggregate Demand, 162
Figure 7.14  Aggregate Supply and Aggregate Demand: 1963–2003, 164

## KEY TERMS

Above full-employment equilibrium, 160
Aggregate demand, 155
Aggregate production function, 150
Below full-employment equilibrium, 160
Classical, 166
Disposable income, 157
Fiscal policy, 157
Inflationary gap, 161
Keynesian, 166
Long-run aggregate supply curve, 150
Long-run macroeconomic equilibrium, 159
Macroeconomic long run, 150
Macroeconomic short run, 151
Monetarist, 167
Monetary policy, 157
Natural rate of unemployment, 150
New Keynesian, 166
Recessionary gap, 160
Short-run aggregate supply curve, 151
Short-run macroeconomic equilibrium, 158
Stagflation, 163

# PROBLEMS

*1. The following events occur that influence the economy of Toughtimes:
   - A deep recession hits the world economy.
   - Oil prices rise sharply.
   - Businesses expect huge losses in the near future.
   a. Explain the separate effects of each of these events on real GDP and the price level in Toughtimes, starting from a position of long-run equilibrium.
   b. Explain the combined effects of these events on real GDP and the price level in Toughtimes, starting from a position of long-run equilibrium.
   c. Explain what the Toughtimes government and the Fed can do to overcome the problems faced by the economy.

2. The following events occur that influence the economy of Coolland:
   - There is a strong expansion in the world economy.
   - Businesses expect huge profits in the near future.
   - The government cuts its purchases.
   a. Explain the separate effects of each of these events on real GDP and the price level in Coolland, starting from a position of long-run equilibrium.
   b. Explain the combined effects of these events on real GDP and the price level in Coolland, starting from a position of long-run equilibrium.
   c. Explain why the Coolland government or central bank might want to take action to influence the Coolland economy.

*3. The economy of Mainland has the following aggregate demand and supply schedules:

| Price level | Real GDP demanded | Real GDP supplied in the short run |
|---|---|---|
| | (billions of 2000 dollars) | |
| 90 | 450 | 350 |
| 100 | 400 | 400 |
| 110 | 350 | 450 |
| 120 | 300 | 500 |
| 130 | 250 | 550 |
| 140 | 200 | 600 |

   a. In a figure, plot the aggregate demand curve and the short-run aggregate supply curve.
   b. What are the values of real GDP and the price level in Mainland in a short-run macroeconomic equilibrium?
   c. Mainland's potential GDP is $500 billion. Plot the long-run aggregate supply curve in the figure in part (a).

4. The economy of Miniland has the following aggregate demand and supply schedules:

| Price level | Real GDP demanded | Real GDP supplied in the short run |
|---|---|---|
| | (billions of 2000 dollars) | |
| 90 | 600 | 150 |
| 100 | 500 | 200 |
| 110 | 400 | 250 |
| 120 | 300 | 300 |
| 130 | 200 | 350 |
| 140 | 100 | 400 |

   a. In a figure, plot the aggregate demand curve and the short-run aggregate supply curve.
   b. What are the values of real GDP and the price level in Miniland in a short-run macroeconomic equilibrium?
   c. Miniland's potential GDP is $250 billion. Plot the long-run aggregate supply curve in the figure in part (a).

*5. In problem 3, aggregate demand increases by $100 billion. How do real GDP and the price level change in the short run?

6. In problem 4, aggregate demand decreases by $150 billion. How do real GDP and the price level change in the short run?

*7. In problem 3, aggregate supply decreases by $100 billion. What now is the short-run macroeconomic equilibrium?

8. In problem 4, aggregate supply increases by $150 billion. What now is the short-run macroeconomic equilibrium?

*9. In the economy shown in the figure on the next page, initially the short-run aggregate supply is $SAS_0$ and aggregate demand is $AD_0$. Then some events change aggregate demand, and the aggregate demand curve shifts rightward to $AD_1$. Later, some other events change aggregate supply, and the short-run aggregate supply curve shifts leftward to $SAS_1$.

* Solutions to odd-numbered problems are available on MyEconLab.

172   CHAPTER 7   AGGREGATE SUPPLY AND AGGREGATE DEMAND

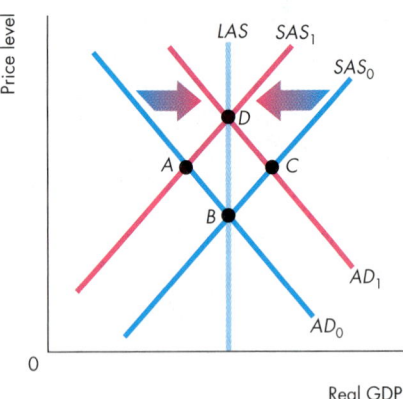

a. What is the equilibrium point after the change in aggregate demand?
b. What is the equilibrium point after the change in aggregate supply?
c. What events could have changed aggregate demand from $AD_0$ to $AD_1$?
d. What events could have changed aggregate supply from $SAS_0$ to $SAS_1$?

10. In the economy shown in the figure, initially long-run aggregate supply is $LAS_0$, short-run aggregate supply is $SAS_0$, and aggregate demand is $AD$. Then some events change aggregate supply, and the aggregate supply curves shift rightward to $LAS_1$ and $SAS_1$.

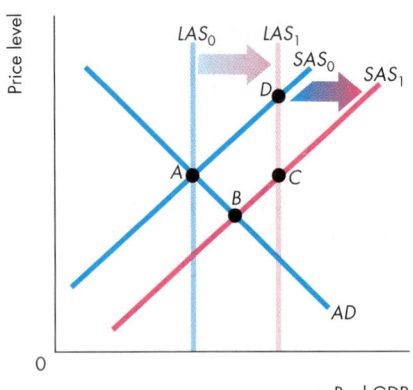

a. What is the equilibrium point after the change in aggregate supply?
b. What events could have changed long-run aggregate supply from $LAS_0$ to $LAS_1$?
c. What events could have changed short-run aggregate supply from $SAS_0$ to $SAS_1$?
d. After the increase in aggregate supply, is real GDP greater than or less than potential GDP?
e. What change in aggregate demand will make real GDP equal to potential GDP?

## CRITICAL THINKING

1. After you have studied the account of the U.S. economy in 2003 in *Reading Between the Lines* on pp. 168–169,
   a. Describe the main features of the U.S. economy in the third quarter of 2002.
   b. Did the United States have a recessionary gap or an inflationary gap in 2002? How do you know?
   c. Use the *AS-AD* model to show the changes in aggregate demand and aggregate supply that brought the increase in real GDP and modest rise in the price level between the third quarter of 2002 and the same quarter of 2003.
   d. Use the *AS-AD* model to show the changes in aggregate demand and aggregate supply that would occur if the Federal Reserve raised the interest rate.
   e. Use the *AS-AD* model to show the changes in aggregate demand and aggregate supply that would occur if the federal government increased its purchases of goods and services or cut taxes further.

## WEB EXERCISES

**Use the links on MyEconLab to work the following exercises.**

1. Find data on recent changes in and forecasts of real GDP and the price level in the United States.
   a. What is your forecast of next year's real GDP?
   b. What is your forecast of next year's price level?
   c. What is your forecast of the inflation rate?
   d. What is your forecast of the growth rate of real GDP?
   e. Do you think there will be a recessionary gap or an inflationary gap next year?
2. Find data on recent changes in and forecasts of real GDP and the price level in Japan.
   a. What is your forecast of next year's real GDP?
   b. What is your forecast of next year's price level?
   c. What is your forecast of the inflation rate?
   d. What is your forecast of the growth rate of real GDP?
   e. Compare and contrast the forecasts for the U.S. and Japanese economies.

# UNDERSTANDING THE THEMES OF MACROECONOMICS

PART 3

## *The Big Picture*

Macroeconomics is a large and controversial subject that is interlaced with political ideological disputes. And it is a field in which charlatans as well as serious thinkers have much to say. This page is a map that looks back at the road you've just traveled and forward at the path you will take from here.

You began your study of macroeconomics in Chapter 4 with the core questions of the subject. What are the causes of

- Economic growth?
- Business cycles?
- Unemployment?
- Inflation?
- Deficits?

In Chapter 5, you learned how we measure the economy's output and the price level. These measures are used to calculate the rate of economic growth, business cycle fluctuations, and inflation. You discovered that making these measurements is not straightforward and that small measurement errors can have a big effect on our perceptions about how we are doing. In Chapter 6, you learned how we measure the state of the labor market—the levels of employment and unemployment and wages. And in Chapter 7, you studied the macroeconomic version of supply and demand—*aggregate supply* and *aggregate demand*. You saw that the aggregate supply–aggregate demand model is the big picture model. It explains both the long-term trends in economic growth and inflation and the short-term business cycle fluctuations in production, jobs, and inflation.

The chapters that lie ahead of you look behind aggregate supply and aggregate demand. In Chapters 8 and 9, you study aggregate supply and economic growth. This material is central to the oldest question in macroeconomics that Adam Smith tried to answer. You'll begin in Chapter 8 by looking at the economy at full employment and study the forces that determine potential GDP and make it change as well as the role played by saving and investment in increasing the amount of capital and creating economic growth. Then, in Chapter 9, you will study the growth process and the roles of capital accumulation and technological change in bringing about economic growth.

In Chapters 10 through 12, you will study aggregate demand, money, and inflation. And in Chapters 13 through 16, you will study fluctuations and stabilization policy. This material is central to the macroeconomics that Keynes developed as a response to the Great Depression. Here you will learn about economic fluctuations and the policies that might limit their severity.

Before continuing your study of macroeconomics, spend a few minutes with John Maynard Keynes and Jean Baptiste Say, the leading scholars who developed this subject, and with one of today's leading macroeconomists, Robert Barro of Harvard University.

# PROBING THE IDEAS

## Macroeconomic Revolutions

### THE ECONOMIST

**John Maynard Keynes**, *born in England in 1883, was one of the outstanding minds of the twentieth century. He wrote on probability as well as economics, represented Britain at the Versailles peace conference at the end of World War I, was a master speculator on international financial markets (an activity he conducted from bed every morning and which made and lost him several fortunes), and played a prominent role in creating the International Monetary Fund.*

*He was a member of the Bloomsbury Group, a circle of outstanding artists and writers that included E. M. Forster, Bertrand Russell, and Virginia Woolf.*

*Keynes was a controversial and quick-witted figure. A critic once complained that Keynes had changed his opinion on some matter, to which Keynes retorted: "When I discover I am wrong, I change my mind. What do you do?"*

*"The ideas of economists and political philosophers, both when they are right and when they are wrong, are more powerful than is commonly understood. Indeed the world is ruled by little else."*

JOHN MAYNARD KEYNES
*The General Theory of Employment, Interest, and Money*

### THE ISSUES

During the Industrial Revolution, as technological change created new jobs and destroyed old ones, people began to wonder whether the economy could create enough jobs and sufficient demand to buy all the things that the new industrial economy could produce.

Jean-Baptiste Say argued that production creates incomes that are sufficient to buy everything that is produced—supply creates its own demand—an idea that came to be called *Say's Law*.

Say and Keynes would have had a lot to disagree about. Jean-Baptiste Say, born in Lyon, France, in 1767 (he was 9 years old when Adam Smith's *Wealth of Nations* was published), suffered the wrath of Napoleon for his views on government and the economy. In today's world, Say would be leading a radical conservative charge for a smaller and leaner government. Say was the most famous economist of his era on both sides of the Atlantic. His book, *Traité d'économie politique (A Treatise in Political Economy)*, published in 1803, became a best-selling university economics textbook in both Europe and North America.

As the Great Depression of the 1930s became more severe and more prolonged, Say's Law looked less and less relevant. John Maynard Keynes revolutionized macroeconomic thinking by turning Say's Law on its head, arguing that production does not depend on supply. Instead, it depends on what people are willing to buy—on demand. Or as Keynes put it, production depends on *effective demand*. It is possible, argued Keynes, for people to refuse to spend all of their incomes. If businesses fail to spend on new capital the amount that people plan to save, demand might be less than supply. In this situation, resources might go unemployed and remain unemployed indefinitely.

The influence of Keynes persists even today, more than 60 years after the publication of his main work. But during the past 20 years, Nobel Laureate Robert E. Lucas, Jr., with significant contributions from a list of outstanding macroeconomists too long to name, has further revolutionized macroeconomics. Today, we know a lot about economic growth, unemployment, inflation, and business cycles. And we know how to use fiscal policy and monetary policy to improve macroeconomic performance. But we don't yet have all the answers. Macroeconomics remains a field of lively controversy and exciting research.

## NOW

Advances in computer technology have made it possible for us to dial our own telephone calls to any part of the world and get connected in a flash. A task that was once performed by telephone operators, who made connections along copper wires, is now performed faster and more reliably by computers along fiber-optic cables. Just as the Industrial Revolution transformed the textile industry, so today's Information Revolution is transforming the telecommunications industry. In the process, the mix of jobs is changing. There are fewer jobs for telephone operators but more jobs for telephone systems designers, builders, managers, and marketers. In the long run, as people spend the income they earn in their changing jobs, supply creates its own demand, just as Say predicted. But does supply create its own demand in the short run, when displaced workers are unemployed?

## THEN

In 1776, James Hargreaves, an English weaver and carpenter, developed a simple hand-operated machine called a spinning jenny (pictured here). Using this machine, a person could spin 80 threads at once. Thousands of hand-wheel spinners, operators of machines that could spin only one thread, lost their jobs. They protested by wrecking spinning jennies. In the long run, the displaced hand-wheel spinners found work, often in factories that manufactured the machines that had destroyed their previous jobs. From the earliest days of the Industrial Revolution to the present day, people have lost their jobs as new technologies have automated what human effort had previously been needed to accomplish.

*Robert Barro, whom you can meet on the following pages, is one of the most distinguished macroeconomists. He has contributed to our understanding of economic growth, inflation, and the business cycle and played a significant role in the contemporary macroeconomic revolution.*

175

# TALKING WITH

**Robert J. Barro** *is Robert C. Waggoner Professor of Economics at Harvard University and a senior fellow at the Hoover Institution of Stanford University. Born in 1944 in New York City, he was a physics undergraduate at the California Institute of Technology and an economics graduate student at Harvard. Professor Barro is one of the world's leading economists and has done research on every aspect of macroeconomics, with a focus in recent years on economic growth. In addition to his many scholarly books and articles, he writes extensively for a wider audience. His book,* Getting it Right: Markets and Choices in a Free Society *(MIT Press, 1996) explains, in non-technical language, the importance of property rights and free markets for achieving economic growth and a high standard of living. A new book,* Nothing Is Sacred: Economic Ideas for the New Millennium *(MIT Press, 2002), expands on these ideas. And his regular articles in* Business Week *and the* Wall Street Journal *provide an accessible analysis of an incredible range of current economic issues.*

*Michael Parkin talked with Robert Barro about his work and the progress that economists have made in understanding macroeconomic performance since the pioneering work of Keynes.*

*Professor Barro, your first degree was in physics. Why did you switch to economics when you went to graduate school?*

For me, economics provided an ideal combination of technical analysis with applications to social problems and policies. Physics—or really mathematics—provided a strong background for economic theory and econometrics, but it was not until later in graduate school that I thought I acquired good economic insights. Overall, the transition from physics to economics was a relatively easy one for me, and I have never regretted the choice to switch fields. (Perhaps it also helped that, after taking courses from the great Richard Feynman at Caltech, I recognized that I would never be an outstanding theoretical physicist.)

*Your recent research has focused on the determinants of economic growth. What do we know about determinants of growth? And what do we still need to discover?*

A lot of progress has been made over the last decade in attaining an empirical understanding of the determinants of economic growth. There are no "silver bullets" for growth, but there are a number of favorable policies, institutions, and national characteristics that have been identified.

For example, growth is stimulated by a strong rule of law, high levels of human capital in the forms of education and health, low levels of non-productive government spending (and associated taxes), international openness, low fertility rates, and macroeconomic stability (including low and stable inflation). Given these and other factors, growth tends to be higher if a country starts off poorer. That is, convergence—in the sense of the poor tending to grow faster than the rich—holds in a conditional sense, when

*There are no "silver bullets" for growth, but there are a number of favorable policies, institutions, and national characteristics that have been identified.*

one holds constant an array of policies and national characteristics. However, convergence does not apply in an absolute sense because the poorest countries tend to have the worst policies and characteristics (which explains why they are observed to be poor).

**Is there anything that rich countries can do to help poor countries grow faster? Or does successful economic growth come only from self-help?**

Mostly economic growth has to come from internal improvements in institutions and policies and from domestic accumulations of human and physical capital. There is no evidence that the rich countries can help through welfare programs, such as foreign aid and debt relief. On the contrary, there is some evidence that, because of the low quality of governance in most developing countries, foreign aid goes mainly to increased government spending and corruption. In the bad old days, the rich countries also provided governance (though not aimed especially at the interests of the governed). However, no one wants to return to the era of colonialism.

**You've identified international openness as a characteristic that encourages growth. Is this an area in which the rich countries might do more by opening themselves to free trade with poor countries? Or is it enough for poor countries to just get on with opening their doors?**

The rich countries could help to spur economic development by opening themselves more to trade in goods and services, technology, and financial transactions. Protectionist policies, notably in agriculture and textiles, are harmful to developing countries as well as to consumers in rich countries. President Bush's policies have been disgraceful in this area, notably in his protectionism during 2002 for steel and agriculture.

**Inflation has been subdued in the United States for most of the 1990s and 2000s. Is this now a problem of the past that we can stop worrying about?**

I am optimistic that the monetary authorities of the United States and many other countries have become committed to price stability and have learned that high inflation does not stimulate growth. Central banks seem also to have learned a lot about the mechanics of achieving price stability. One worry,

*I am optimistic that the monetary authorities of the United States and many other countries have become committed to price stability and have learned that high inflation does not stimulate growth.*

however, is that monetary authorities—including the Federal Reserve—will become overconfident and will come to believe that they can fine-tune the real economy without losing price stability. For example, the Fed's sharp reductions in interest rates during the 2001 recession may have stimulated too much and could lead eventually to higher inflation.

**How do economic growth and inflation interact? Why can't a country grow faster by keeping demand growth strong and inflating?**

Inflation is inversely related to economic growth over the medium term—for example, periods of five years or more. This relationship is particularly evident at high inflation rates—say, above 10-15% per year— ut probably also applies for more moderate inflation. The likely reason for the inverse relation is that high and volatile inflation makes it difficult for the price system to operate efficiently. It is possible that unanticipated monetary stimulus expands the real economy in the short run. However, this short-term benefit is not worth the cost over the medium and long term. Moreover, the stimulus works mainly when it comes as a surprise, and it is hard to be surprising in a systematic way.

*Some years ago, you worked on the business cycle. What is your current view on the nature and causes of aggregate fluctuations? Are they primarily an efficient response to the uneven pace of technical change, or are they primarily the consequence of market failure and demand fluctuations?*

Many factors are sources of business cycles, and economists have not been very successful at isolating the precise causes. Influences that seem to matter include variations in the rate of technological progress, shifts in the terms of trade, fiscal effects (particularly important during wartime), and monetary fluctuations. In some countries, shifts in labor relations and in regulatory policies are important. Other countries are influenced by major changes in the quality of governance, such as the recent deterioration of public institutions in Argentina.

I do not think that we know what portion of fluctuations represents efficient responses to shocks as opposed to excess volatility associated with market failure. We do know that many observed fluctuations stem from failures of government policy and institutions, so it is inappropriate to think of governments as typically smoothing out the excesses of the private sector.

*What remains in today's macroeconomics of the contribution of Keynes?*

Probably Keynesian economics is most influential today in analyses that stress the real effects of monetary policy—either as sources of business fluctuations or as ways to smooth out the cycle. This situation is ironic because Keynes himself deemphasized monetary shocks as a source of fluctuations. He stressed the excesses of the private economy—including the amplifying effects of multipliers and the sensitivity of investment to shifting expectations—and the potentially beneficial role of offsetting fiscal policies. Empirically, the multiplier seems to have existed only in the mind of Keynes.

*What advice do you have for a student who is just starting to study economics? Is it a good subject in which to major? If so, what other subjects would you urge students to study alongside economics? Or is the path that you followed, starting with physics (or perhaps math) and then moving to economics for graduate school more effective?*

Economics is an excellent field for an undergraduate to study whether one chooses to become an economist or—more likely—if one goes into other fields, such as business or law. Economists have found the framework or methodology that makes economics the core social science, and its impact has been felt greatly by other fields, such as political science, law, and history. These days, economic reasoning is being applied to the study of an array of social topics, including marriage and fertility, crime, democracy, and legal structure. As another example, I am currently participating in a project that involves the interactions between economics and religion (see www.wcfia.harvard.edu/religion for a description). Partly this work is about how economic development and government policies affect religiosity and partly about how religious beliefs and participation influence economic and political outcomes. So, perhaps in the future economics will also be important for studies in theology. No doubt, many economists (including me) have imperialistic tendencies, but this is because they have a great product to sell. As to other complementary subjects to study, the most

> *Economists have found the framework or methodology that makes economics the core social science …*

valuable one is probably mathematics, which provides many of the useful tools to carry out theoretical and empirical inquiries.

# PART 4     Aggregate Supply and Economic Growth

# The Economy at Full Employment: The Classical Model

CHAPTER 8

## Our Economy's Compass

**The path followed by the economy is a bit like** that of an explorer searching for a new route through unknown terrain. The explorer's progress is like the economy's growth that brings an ever rising standard of living. Sometimes the explorer strays off course to either the left or the right. These departures from the main course are like the alternation between recessionary gap and inflationary gap as the economy fluctuates through the business cycle.

But the explorer has a compass that helps to keep finding the main path and avoid departing from it too far. The explorer's compass is like the forces that prevent the economy from fluctuating too wildly and keep returning it to its forward path. These are the forces that determine full employment equilibrium.

◆ We're going to study the economy's compass in this chapter. We'll investigate the forces that determine the level of employment and the real wage rate at full employment. And we'll see how potential GDP is determined. We'll also see how the real interest rate adjusts to allocate potential GDP between consumption and investment.

### After studying this chapter, you will be able to

- Describe the relationship between the quantity of labor employed and real GDP
- Explain what determines the demand for labor and the supply of labor and how labor market equilibrium determines employment, the real wage rate, and potential GDP
- Explain how business investment decisions and household saving decisions are made
- Explain how investment and saving interact to determine the real interest rate
- Use the classical model to explain the forces that change potential GDP

## The Classical Model: A Preview

Economists have made progress in understanding how the economy works by dividing the variables that describe macroeconomic performance into two lists:

- Real variables
- Nominal variables

Real variables—real GDP, employment and unemployment, the real wage rate, consumption, saving, investment, and the real interest rate—describe the real economy and tell us what is *really* happening to economic well-being.

Nominal variables—the price level (CPI or GDP deflator), the inflation rate, nominal GDP, the nominal wage rate, and the nominal interest rate—tell us how *dollar values* and the cost of living are changing.

This separation of macroeconomic performance into a real part and a nominal part is the basis of a huge discovery called the **classical dichotomy**, which states:

At full employment, the forces that determine real variables are independent of those that determine nominal variables.

In practical terms, the classical dichotomy means that we can explain why real GDP per person in the United States is 20 times that in Nigeria by looking only at the real parts of the two economies and ignoring differences in their price levels and inflation rates. Similarly, we can explain why real GDP per person in 2003 was around twice that in 1963 without considering what has happened to the value of the dollar between those two years.

The **classical model** is a model of an economy that determines the real variables—real GDP, employment and unemployment, the real wage rate, consumption, saving, investment, and the real interest rate—at full employment.

Most economists believe that the economy is rarely at full employment and that the business cycle is a fluctuation around full employment. Classical economists think that the economy is always at full employment and that the business cycle is a fluctuation of the full-employment economy.

Regardless of which view of the cycle an economist takes, all agree that the classical model that you're now going to study provides powerful insights into macroeconomic performance.

## Real GDP and Employment

To produce more output, we must use more inputs. We can increase real GDP by employing more labor, increasing the quantity of capital, or developing technologies that are more productive. In the short term, the quantity of capital and the state of technology are fixed. So to increase real GDP in the short term, we must increase the quantity of labor employed. Let's look at the relationship between real GDP and the quantity of labor employed.

### Production Possibilities

When you studied the limits to production in Chapter 2 (see p. 32), you learned about the *production possibilities frontier*, which is the boundary between those combinations of goods and services that can be produced and those that cannot. We can think about the production possibilities frontier for any pair of goods or services when we hold the quantities of all other goods and services constant. Let's think about the production possibilities frontier for two special items: real GDP and the quantity of leisure time.

Real GDP is a measure of the final goods and services produced in the economy in a given time period (see Chapter 5, p. 108). We measure real GDP as a number of 1996 dollars, but the measure is a *real* one. Real GDP is not a pile of dollars. It is a pile of goods and services. Think of it as a number of big shopping carts filled with goods and services. Each cart contains some of each kind of different goods and services produced, and one cartload of items costs $1 trillion. To say that real GDP is $10 trillion means that real GDP is 10 very big shopping carts of goods and services.

The quantity of leisure time is the number of hours we spend not working. It is the time we spend playing or watching sports, seeing movies, and hanging out with friends. Leisure time is a special type of good or service.

Each hour that we spent pursuing fun could have been spent working. So when the quantity of leisure time increases by one hour, the quantity of labor employed decreases by one hour. If we spent all our time having fun rather than working, we would not produce anything. Real GDP would be zero. The more leisure time we forgo to work, the greater is the quantity of labor employed and the greater is real GDP.

The relationship between leisure time and real GDP is a *production possibilities frontier* (*PPF*). Figure 8.1(a) shows an example of this frontier. The economy has 450 billion hours of leisure time available. If people use all these hours to pursue leisure, no labor is employed and real GDP is zero. As people forgo leisure and work more, real GDP increases. If people spent 200 billion hours working and took 250 billion hours in leisure, real GDP would be $10 trillion at point *A*. If people spent all the available hours working, real GDP would be $15 trillion.

The bowed-out *PPF* displays increasing opportunity cost. In this case, the opportunity cost of a given amount of real GDP is the amount of leisure time forgone to produce it. As real GDP increases, each additional unit of real GDP costs an increasing amount of forgone leisure. The reason is that we use the most productive labor first, and as we use more labor, we use increasingly less productive labor.

## The Production Function

The **production function** is the relationship between real GDP and the quantity of labor employed when all other influences on production remain the same. The production function shows how real GDP varies as the quantity of labor employed varies, other things remaining the same.

Because one more hour of labor employed means one less hour of leisure, the production function is like a mirror image of the leisure time–real GDP *PPF*. Figure 8.1(b) shows the production function for the economy whose *PPF* is shown in Fig. 8.1(a). You can see that when the quantity of labor employed is zero, real GDP is also zero. And as the quantity of labor employed increases, so does real GDP. When 200 billion labor hours are employed, real GDP is $10 trillion (at point *A*).

A decrease in leisure hours and the corresponding increases in the quantity of labor employed and real GDP bring a movement along the production possibilities frontier and along the production function. The arrows along the *PPF* and the production function in Fig. 8.1 show these movements. Such movements occurred when employment and real GDP surged during World War II.

The *PPF* tells us how real GDP and employment are linked. But what determines the levels of employment and real GDP at which the economy operates? We're now going to answer this question.

**FIGURE 8.1** Production Possibilities and the Production Function

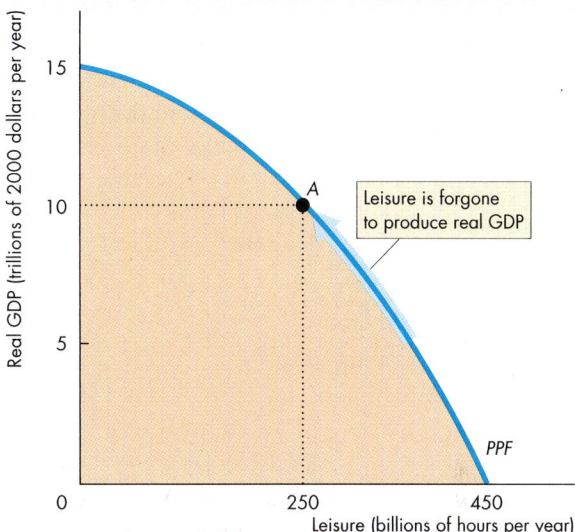

(a) Production possibility frontier

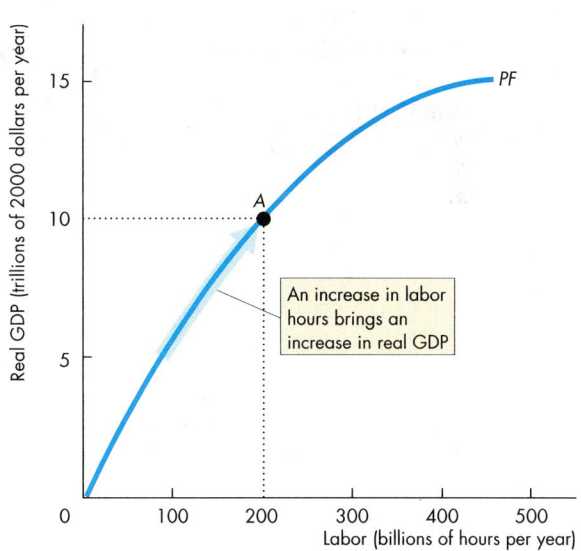

(b) Production function

On the production possibilities frontier in part (a), if we enjoy 450 billion hours of leisure, we produce no real GDP. If we forgo 200 billion hours of leisure time to work and spend 250 billion hours of leisure time, we produce a real GDP of $10 trillion, at point *A*.

At point *A* on the production function in part (b), we use 200 billion hours of labor to produce $10 trillion of real GDP.

## The Labor Market and Potential GDP

YOU'VE SEEN THAT IN A GIVEN YEAR, WITH A given amount of physical and human capital and given technology, real GDP depends on the quantity of labor hours employed. To produce more real GDP, we must employ more labor hours. The labor market determines the quantity of labor hours employed and the quantity of real GDP supplied. We'll learn how by studying

- The demand for labor
- The supply of labor
- Labor market equilibrium
- Potential GDP

### The Demand for Labor

The **quantity of labor demanded** is the number of labor hours hired by all the firms in the economy. The **demand for labor** is the relationship between the quantity of labor demanded and the real wage rate when all other influences on firms' hiring plans remain the same. The **real wage rate** is the quantity of goods and services that an hour of labor earns. In contrast, the **money wage rate** is the number of dollars that an hour of labor earns. A real wage rate is equal to a money wage rate divided by the price of a good. For the economy as a whole, the average real wage rate equals the average money wage rate divided by the price level multiplied by 100. So we express the real wage rate in constant dollars. (Today, we express this real wage rate in 1996 dollars.)

The *real* wage rate influences the quantity of labor demanded because what matters to firms is not the number of dollars they pay (money wage rate) but how much output they must sell to earn those dollars.

We can represent the demand for labor as either a demand schedule or a demand curve. The table in Fig. 8.2 shows part of a demand for labor schedule. It tells us the quantity of labor demanded at three different real wage rates. For example, if the real wage rate falls from $40 an hour to $35 an hour, the quantity of labor demanded increases from 150 billion hours a year to 200 billion hours a year. (You can find these numbers in rows *A* and *B* of the table.)

The demand for labor curve is *LD*. Points *A*, *B*, and *C* on the curve correspond to rows *A*, *B*, and *C* of the demand schedule.

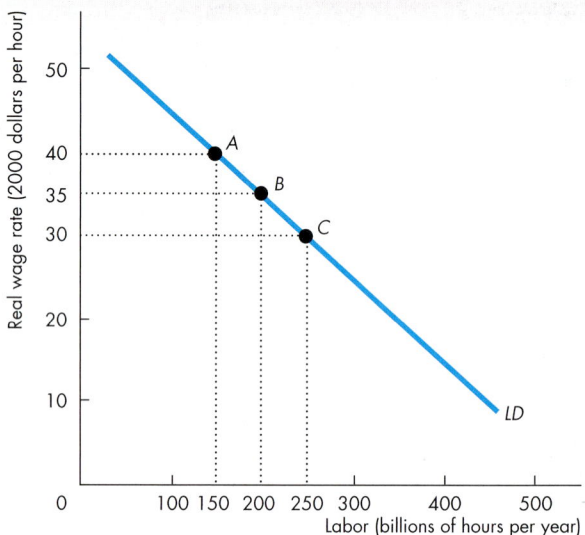

**FIGURE 8.2**  The Demand for Labor

|   | Real wage rate (1996 dollars per hour) | Quantity of labor demanded (billions of hours per year) |
|---|---|---|
| A | 40 | 150 |
| B | 35 | 200 |
| C | 30 | 250 |

The table shows part of a demand for labor schedule. Points A, B, and C on the demand for labor curve correspond to the rows of the table. The lower the real wage rate, the greater is the quantity of labor demanded.

Why does the quantity of labor demanded *increase* as the real wage rate *decreases*? That is, why does the demand for labor curve slope downward? To answer these questions, we must learn about the marginal product of labor.

**The Marginal Product of Labor**  The **marginal product of labor** is the additional real GDP produced by an additional hour of labor when all other influences on production remain the same. The marginal product of labor is governed by the **law of diminishing returns**, which states that as the quantity of labor increases, other things remaining the same, the marginal product of labor decreases.

**The Law of Diminishing Returns** Diminishing returns arise because the amount of capital is fixed. Two people operating one machine are not twice as productive as one person operating one machine. Eventually, as more labor hours are hired, workers get in each other's way and output increases barely at all.

**Marginal Product Calculation** We calculate the marginal product of labor as the change in real GDP divided by the change in the quantity of labor employed. Figure 8.3(a) shows some calculations, and Fig. 8.3(b) shows the marginal product curve.

In Fig. 8.3(a), when the quantity of labor employed increases from 100 billion hours to 200 billion hours, an increase of 100 billion hours, real GDP increases from $6 trillion to $10 trillion, an increase of $4 trillion, or $4,000 billion. The marginal product of labor equals the increase in real GDP ($4,000 billion) divided by the increase in the quantity of labor employed (100 billion hours), which is $40 an hour.

When the quantity of labor employed increases from 200 billion hours to 300 billion hours, an increase of 100 billion hours, real GDP increases from $10 trillion to $13 trillion, an increase of $3 trillion, or $3,000 billion. The marginal product of labor equals $3,000 billion divided by 100 billion hours, which is $30 an hour.

In Fig. 8.3(b), as the quantity of labor employed increases, the marginal product of labor diminishes. Between 100 billion and 200 billion hours (at 150 billion hours), marginal product is $40 an hour. And between 200 billion and 300 billion hours (at 250 billion hours), marginal product is $30 an hour.

The diminishing marginal product of labor limits the demand for labor.

**Diminishing Marginal Product and the Demand for Labor** Firms are in business to maximize profits. Each hour of labor that a firm hires increases output and adds to costs. Initially, an extra hour of labor produces more output than the real wage that the labor costs. Marginal product exceeds the real wage rate. But each additional hour of labor produces less additional output than the previous hour—the marginal product of labor diminishes.

As a firm hires more labor, eventually the extra output from an extra hour of labor is exactly what that hour of labor costs. At this point, marginal product equals the real wage rate. Hire one less hour and marginal product exceeds the real wage rate. Hire one

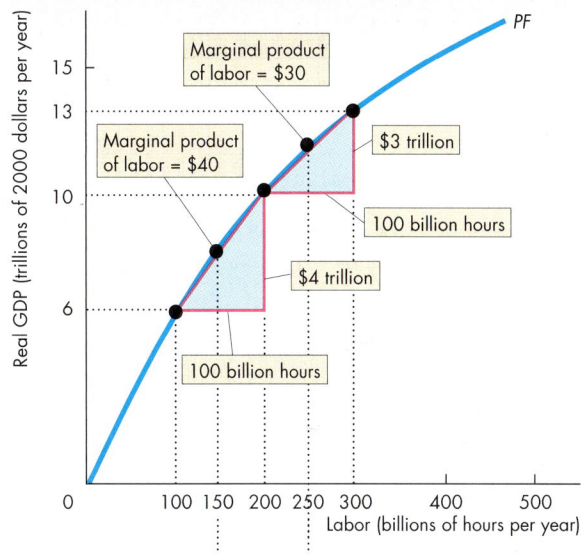

**FIGURE 8.3** Marginal Product and the Demand for Labor

(a) Calculating marginal product

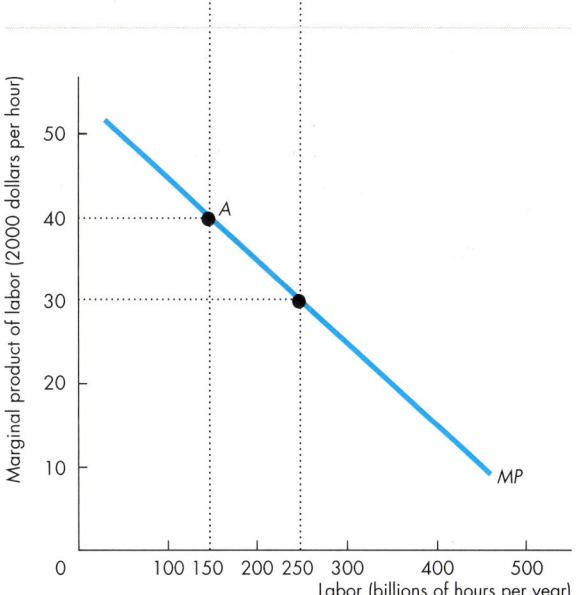

(b) The marginal product curve

Between 100 billion and 200 billion hours, the marginal product of labor is $40 an hour. Between 200 billion and 300 billion hours, the marginal product of labor is $30 an hour. At point A on the MP curve, the marginal product of labor is $40 an hour at 150 billion hours (the midpoint between 100 billion and 200 billion). The MP curve is the demand for labor curve.

more hour and the real wage rate exceeds the marginal product. In either case, profit is less.

Because marginal product diminishes as the quantity of labor employed increases, the lower the real wage rate, the greater is the quantity of labor that a firm can profitably hire. The marginal product curve is the same as the demand for labor curve.

You might gain a clearer understanding of the demand for labor by looking at an example.

### The Demand for Labor in a Soda Factory

Suppose that when a soda factory employs one additional hour of labor, output increases by 11 bottles. Marginal product is 11 bottles an hour. If the money wage rate is $5.50 an hour and soda sells for 50¢ a bottle, the real wage rate is 11 bottles an hour. (We calculate the real wage rate for the soda factory as the money wage rate of $5.50 an hour divided by a price of 50¢ a bottle, which equals a real wage rate of 11 bottles an hour.) Because marginal product diminishes, we know that if the firm did not hire this hour of labor, marginal product would exceed 11 bottles. Because the firm can hire the hour of labor for a real wage rate of 11 bottles, it just pays it to do so.

If the price of soda remains at 50¢ a bottle and the money wage rate falls to $5.00 an hour, the real wage rate falls to 10 bottles an hour and the firm increases the quantity of labor demanded.

Similarly, if the money wage rate remains at $5.50 an hour and the price of soda rises to 55¢ a bottle, the real wage rate falls to 10 bottles an hour and the firm increases the quantity of labor demanded.

When the firm pays a real wage rate equal to the marginal product of labor, it is maximizing profit.

**Changes in the Demand for Labor** A change in the real wage rate brings a change in the quantity of labor demanded, which is shown by a movement along the demand curve. A change in any other influence on a firm's decision to hire labor brings a change in the demand for labor, which is shown by a shift of the demand curve. These other influences are the quantities of physical and human capital and technology. An increase in capital or an advance in technology shifts the production function upward. These same forces increase the marginal product of labor and shift the demand for labor curve rightward. Labor-saving technological change decreases the demand for some types of labor, but overall advances in technology increase the demand for labor.

### The Supply of Labor

The **quantity of labor supplied** is the number of labor hours that all the households in the economy plan to work. The **supply of labor** is the relationship between the quantity of labor supplied and the real wage rate when all other influences on work plans remain the same.

We can represent the supply of labor as a supply schedule or a supply curve. The table in Fig. 8.4 shows a supply of labor schedule. It tells us the quantity of labor supplied at different real wage rates. For example, if the real wage rate rises from $15 an hour (row A) to $35 an hour (row B), the quantity of labor supplied increases from 150 billion

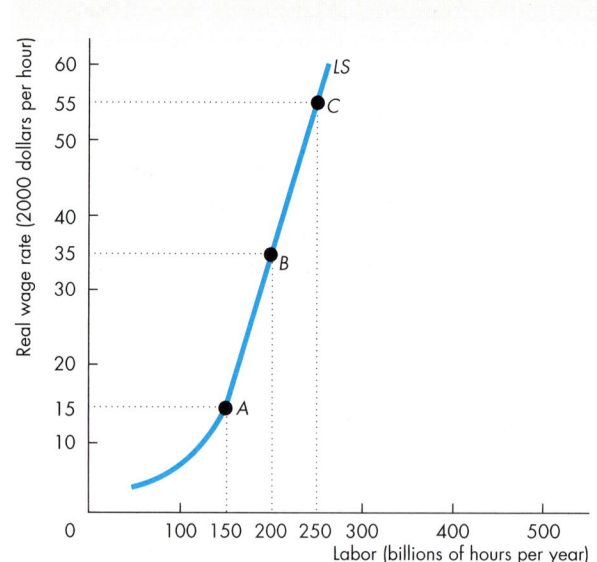

**FIGURE 8.4** The Supply of Labor

| | Real wage rate (1996 dollars per hour) | Quantity of labor supplied (billions of hours per year) |
|---|---|---|
| A | 15 | 150 |
| B | 35 | 200 |
| C | 55 | 250 |

The table shows part of a supply of labor schedule. Points A, B, and C on the supply of labor curve correspond to the rows of the table. The higher the real wage rate, the greater is the quantity of labor supplied.

hours a year to 200 billion hours a year. The curve LS is a supply of labor curve. Points A, B, and C on the curve correspond to rows A, B, and C of the supply schedule.

The *real* wage rate influences the quantity of labor supplied because what matters to people is not the number of dollars they earn (the money wage rate) but what those dollars will buy.

The quantity of labor supplied increases as the real wage rate increases for two reasons:

- Hours per person increase
- Labor force participation increases

**Hours per Person** In choosing how many hours to work, a household considers the opportunity cost of not working. This opportunity cost is the real wage rate. The higher the real wage rate, the greater is the opportunity cost of taking leisure and not working. And as the opportunity cost of taking leisure rises and other things remain the same, the more the household chooses to work.

But other things don't remain the same. The higher the real wage rate, the greater is the household's income. And the higher the household's income, the more it wants to consume. One item that it wants to consume more of is leisure.

So a rise in the real wage rate has two opposing effects. By increasing the opportunity cost of leisure, it makes the household want to consume less leisure and to work more. And by increasing the household's income, it makes the household want to consume more leisure and to work fewer hours. For most households, the opportunity cost effect is stronger than the income effect. So the higher the real wage rate, the greater is the amount of work that the household chooses to do.

**Labor Force Participation** Some people have productive opportunities outside the labor force. These people choose to work only if the real wage rate exceeds the value of these other productive activities. For example, a parent might spend time caring for her or his child. The alternative is day care. The parent will choose to work only if he or she can earn enough per hour to pay the cost of child care and have enough left to make the work effort worthwhile. The higher the real wage rate, the more likely it is that a parent will choose to work and so the greater is the labor force participation rate.

**Labor Supply Response** The quantity of labor supplied increases as the real wage rate rises. But the quantity of labor supplied is not highly responsive to the real wage rate. A large percentage change in the real wage rate brings a small percentage change in the quantity of labor supplied.

**Changes in the Supply of Labor** A change in the real wage rate brings a change in the quantity of labor supplied, which is shown by a movement along the supply curve. A change in any other influence on a household's decision to work brings a change in the supply of labor, which is shown by a shift of the supply curve.

The other major influence on the supply of labor is the working-age population. Over time, as the working-age population increases—either because the number of births exceeds the number of deaths, or from immigration—the supply of labor increases.

Other factors that include technology in the home and social attitudes also influence the supply of labor and especially the supply of female labor. Advances in technology in the home along with greater opportunities for women have shifted the supply of labor curve rightward.

Let's now see how the labor market determines employment, the real wage rate, and potential GDP.

## Labor Market Equilibrium and Potential GDP

The forces of supply and demand operate in labor markets just as they do in the markets for goods and services. The price of labor is the real wage rate. A rise in the real wage rate eliminates a shortage of labor by decreasing the quantity demanded and increasing the quantity supplied. A fall in the real wage rate eliminates a surplus of labor by increasing the quantity demanded and decreasing the quantity supplied. If there is neither a shortage nor a surplus, the labor market is in equilibrium.

In macroeconomics, we study the economy-wide labor market to determine the total quantity of labor employed and the average real wage rate.

**Labor Market Equilibrium** Figure 8.5(a) shows a labor market in equilibrium. The demand curve LD and the supply curve LS are the same as those in Fig. 8.2 and Fig. 8.4, respectively.

If the real wage rate exceeds $35 an hour, the quantity of labor supplied exceeds the quantity

**FIGURE 8.5** The Labor Market and Potential GDP

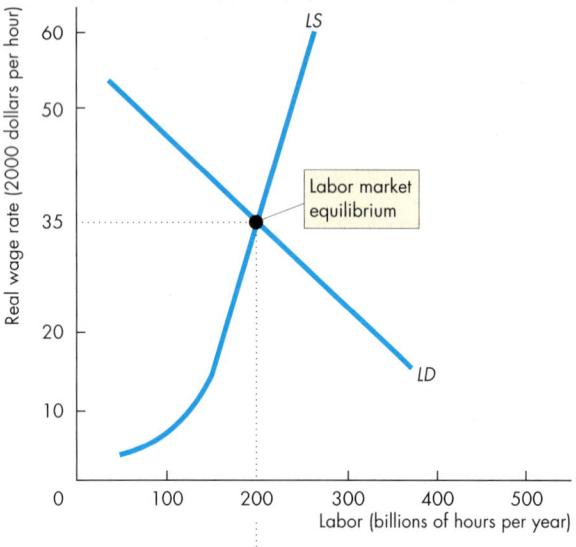

(a) The labor market

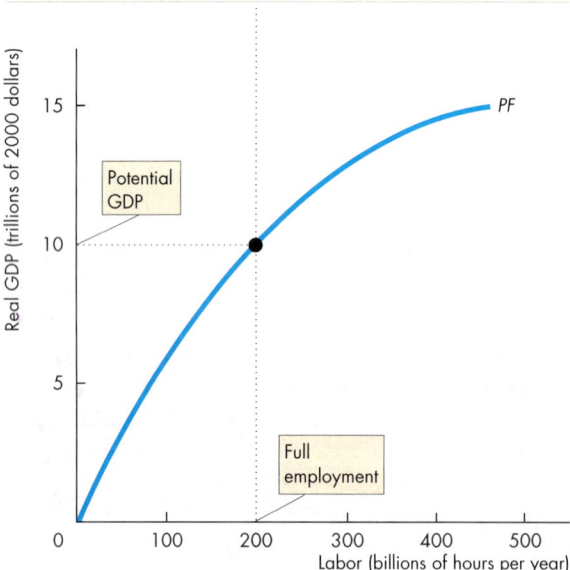

(b) Potential GDP

Full employment occurs (part a) when the quantity of labor demanded equals the quantity of labor supplied. The real wage rate is $35 an hour, and employment is 200 billion hours a year. Part (b) shows potential GDP. It is the quantity of real GDP determined by the production function at the full-employment quantity of labor.

demanded and there is a surplus of labor. In this situation, the real wage rate falls.

If the real wage rate is less than $35 an hour, the quantity of labor demanded exceeds the quantity supplied and there is a shortage of labor. In this situation, the real wage rate rises.

If the real wage rate is $35 an hour, the quantity of labor demanded equals the quantity supplied and there is neither a shortage nor a surplus of labor. In this situation, the labor market is in equilibrium and the real wage rate remains constant. The equilibrium level of employment is 200 billion hours a year. This equilibrium level of employment is *full employment*.

**Potential GDP** You've seen that the quantity of real GDP depends on the quantity of labor employed. The production function tells us how much real GDP a given amount of employment can produce. At the equilibrium level of employment, the economy is at full employment. And the level of real GDP at full employment is *potential GDP*. So the equilibrium level of employment produces potential GDP.

Figure 8.5(b) shows potential GDP. The equilibrium level of employment in Fig. 8.5(a) is 200 billion hours. The production function in Fig. 8.5(b) tells us that 200 billion hours of labor can produce a real GDP of $10 trillion. This amount is potential GDP.

### REVIEW QUIZ

1 What is the relationship between the leisure time–real GDP *PPF* and the production function?
2 What does the outward-bowed shape of the leisure time–real GDP *PPF* imply about the opportunity cost of real GDP and why is the *PPF* bowed outward?
3 Why does a rise in the real wage rate bring a decrease in the quantity of labor demanded, other things remaining the same?
4 Why does a rise in the real wage rate bring an increase in the quantity of labor supplied, other things remaining the same?
5 What happens in the labor market if the real wage rate is above or below the full-employment level?
6 How is potential GDP determined?

# Unemployment at Full Employment

SO FAR, WE'VE FOCUSED ON THE FORCES THAT determine the real wage rate, the quantity of labor employed, and potential GDP. We're now going to bring unemployment into the picture and study the real factors that influence the natural unemployment rate.

In Chapter 6 (p. 130), we learned how unemployment is measured. We described how people become unemployed—they lose jobs, leave jobs, and enter or reenter the labor force—and we classified unemployment—it can be frictional, structural, and cyclical. We also learned that we call the unemployment rate at full employment the *natural rate of unemployment*.

But measuring, describing, and classifying unemployment do not *explain* it. Why is there always some unemployment? Why does its rate fluctuate? Why was the unemployment rate lower during the 1960s and the late 1990s than during the 1980s and early 1990s?

Part of the answer is that fluctuations in aggregate demand bring fluctuations in the unemployment rate around the natural rate. But the churning economy also brings fluctuations in the natural unemployment rate. Here we look at the forces that determine the natural unemployment rate.

Unemployment is always present for two broad reasons:

- Job search
- Job rationing

## Job Search

**Job search** is the activity of looking for an acceptable vacant job. There are always some people who have not yet found a suitable job and who are actively searching for one. The reason is that the labor market is in a constant state of change. The failure of existing businesses destroys jobs. The expansion of existing businesses and the startup of new businesses that use new technologies and develop new markets create jobs. As people pass through different stages of life, some enter or reenter the labor market. Others leave their jobs to look for better ones, and still others retire. This constant churning in the labor market means that there are always some people looking for jobs, and these people are the unemployed.

The amount of job search depends on a number of factors, one of which is the real wage rate. In Fig. 8.6, when the real wage rate is $35 an hour, the economy is at full-employment equilibrium. The amount of job search that takes place at this wage rate generates unemployment at the natural rate. If the real wage rate is above the full-employment equilibrium—for example, at $45 an hour—there is a surplus of labor. At this higher real wage rate, more job search takes place and unemployment exceeds the natural rate. If the real wage rate is below the full-employment equilibrium—for example, at $25 an hour—there is a shortage of labor. At this real wage rate, less job search takes place and unemployment falls below the natural rate.

The market forces of demand and supply move the real wage rate toward the full-employment equilibrium. And these same forces move the amount of

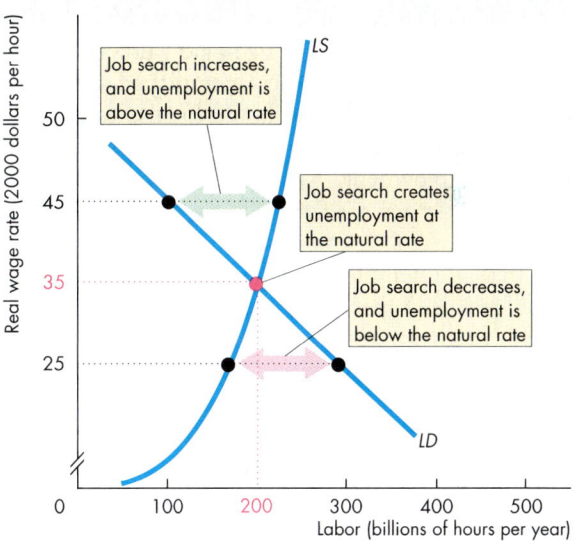

**FIGURE 8.6** Job Search Unemployment

When the real wage rate is at its full-employment level—$35 an hour in this example—job search puts unemployment at the natural rate. If the real wage rate is above the full-employment level, there is a surplus of labor. Job search increases, and unemployment rises above the natural rate. If the real wage rate is below the full-employment level, there is a shortage of labor. Job search decreases, and unemployment falls below the natural rate.

job search toward the level that creates unemployment at the natural rate.

But other influences on the amount of job search bring changes in the natural rate of unemployment. The main sources of these changes are

- Demographic change
- Unemployment compensation
- Structural change

**Demographic Change** An increase in the proportion of the population that is of working age brings an increase in the entry rate into the labor force and an increase in the unemployment rate. This factor has been important in the U.S. labor market in recent years. The bulge in the birth rate that occurred from the late 1940s through the late 1950s increased the proportion of new entrants into the labor force during the 1970s and brought an increase in the unemployment rate.

As the birth rate declined, the bulge moved into higher age groups, and the proportion of new entrants declined during the 1980s. During this period, the natural rate of unemployment decreased.

Another demographic trend is an increase in the number of households with two paid workers. When one of these workers becomes unemployed, it is possible, with income still flowing in, to take longer to find a new job. This factor might have increased frictional unemployment.

**Unemployment Compensation** The length of time that an unemployed person spends searching for a job depends, in part, on the opportunity cost of job search. An unemployed person who receives no unemployment compensation faces a high opportunity cost of job search. In this situation, search is likely to be short and the person is likely to accept a less attractive job rather than continue a costly search process. An unemployed person who receives generous unemployment compensation faces a low opportunity cost of job search. In this situation, search is likely to be prolonged. The unemployed worker will continue to search for an ideal job.

The extension of unemployment compensation to larger groups of workers during the late 1960s and 1970s lowered the opportunity cost of job search. Consequently, the amount of job search and the natural rate of unemployment increased during those years.

**Structural Change** Labor market flows and unemployment are influenced by the pace and direction of technological change. Sometimes, technological change brings a *structural slump*, a condition in which some industries die and some regions suffer while other industries are born and other regions flourish. When these events occur, labor turnover is high—the flows between employment and unemployment increase and the number of unemployed people increases. The decline of industries in the "Rust Belt" and the rapid expansion of industries in the "Sun Belt" illustrate the effects of technological change and were a source of the increase in unemployment during the 1970s and early 1980s. While these changes were taking place, the natural rate of unemployment increased.

## Job Rationing

You've learned that markets *allocate* scarce resources by adjusting the market price to make buying plans and selling plans agree. Another word that has a meaning similar to "allocate" is "ration." Markets *ration* scarce resources by adjusting prices. In the labor market, the real wage rate rations employment and therefore rations jobs. Changes in the real wage rate keep the number of people seeking work and the number of jobs available in balance.

But the real wage rate is not the only possible instrument for rationing jobs. And in some industries, the real wage rate is set above the market equilibrium level. **Job rationing** is the practice of paying a real wage rate above the equilibrium level and then rationing jobs by some method.

Two reasons why the real wage rate might be set above the equilibrium level are

- Efficiency wage
- Minimum wage

**Efficiency Wage** It is costly for a firm to pay its workers more than the market wage rate. But doing so also brings benefits. An **efficiency wage** is a real wage rate set above the full-employment equilibrium wage rate that balances the costs and benefits of this higher wage rate to maximize the firm's profit.

The cost of paying a higher wage is direct. It is the addition to the firm's wage bill. The benefits of paying a higher wage rate are indirect.

First, a firm that pays a high wage rate can attract the most productive workers. Second, the firm can get greater productivity from its work force if it threatens to fire those who do not perform at the desired standard. The threat of losing a well-paid job stimulates greater work effort. Third, workers are less likely to quit their jobs, so the firm faces a lower rate of labor turnover and lower training costs. Fourth, the firm's recruiting costs are lower. The firm always faces a steady stream of available new workers.

Faced with benefits and costs, a firm offers a wage rate that balances productivity gains from the higher wage rate against its additional cost. This wage rate maximizes the firm's profit and is the efficiency wage.

**Minimum Wage** A **minimum wage** is the lowest wage rate at which a firm may legally hire labor. If the minimum wage is set *below* the equilibrium wage, the minimum wage has no effect. The minimum wage and market forces are not in conflict. But if a minimum wage is set *above* the equilibrium wage, the minimum wage is in conflict with the market forces and does have some effects on the labor market.

The minimum wage in the United States is set by the federal government's Fair Labor Standards Act. The federal minimum wage increases from time to time and has fluctuated between 35 percent and more than 50 percent of the average wage of production workers. It was last set in 1997 at $5.15 an hour. Some state governments have passed state minimum wage laws that exceed the federal minimum.

### Job Rationing and Unemployment

Regardless of the reason, if the real wage rate is set above the equilibrium level, the natural rate of unemployment increases. The above-equilibrium real wage rate decreases the quantity of labor demanded and increases the quantity of labor supplied. So even at full employment, the quantity of labor supplied exceeds the quantity of labor demanded.

The surplus of labor is an addition to the amount of unemployment. The unemployment that results from a nonmarket wage rate and job rationing increases the natural rate of unemployment because it is added to the job search that takes place at full-employment equilibrium.

Economists broadly agree that efficiency wages can create persistent unemployment. And most economists believe that the minimum wage contributes to unemployment, especially among low-skilled young workers. But David Card of the University of California at Berkeley and Alan Krueger of Princeton University have challenged this view. And the challenge has been rebutted.

Card and Krueger say that an increase in the minimum wage works like an efficiency wage. It makes workers more productive and less likely to quit. Most economists remain skeptical about this suggestion. If higher wages make workers more productive and reduce labor turnover, why don't firms freely pay the wage rates that encourage the correct work habits? Daniel Hamermesh of the University of Texas at Austin says that firms anticipate increases in the minimum wage and cut employment *before* they occur. Looking for the effects of an increase in the minimum wage *after* it has occurred misses its effects. Finis Welch of Texas A&M University and Kevin Murphy of the University of Chicago say that regional differences in economic growth and not changes in the minimum wage explain the facts that Card and Krueger found.

### REVIEW QUIZ

1. Why does the economy experience unemployment at full employment?
2. Why does the natural rate of unemployment fluctuate?
3. What is job rationing and why does it occur?
4. How does an efficiency wage influence the real wage rate, employment, and unemployment?
5. How does the minimum wage create unemployment?

You've now studied the forces that determine the real wage rate, the quantity of labor employed, and potential GDP as well as the natural rate of unemployment during a given period.

You've also seen that the classical model makes predictions about what happens when the quantities of factors of production change. Capital accumulation and technological advances are the major ongoing changes that bring economic growth. To lay a foundation for your study of economic growth in Chapter 9, we're going to see what the classical model tells us about capital and the interest rate.

## Investment, Saving, and the Interest Rate

Potential GDP depends on the quantities of our productive resources, one of which is the economy's **capital stock**—the total quantity of plant, equipment, buildings, and inventories. The capital stock includes business capital such as communication satellites and computers as well as the inventories that businesses carry. It includes houses and apartments. And it includes government-owned *social infrastructure capital* such as highways, dams and canals, schools, state universities, national defense systems, and the justice system that establishes and enforces property rights.

Investment and saving decisions determine the size of the capital stock. The purchase of new capital, called *gross investment*, increases the capital stock. The wearing out and scrapping of capital, called *depreciation*, decreases the capital stock. The capital stock changes by the amount of *net investment*, which equals gross investment minus depreciation (see Chapter 5, p. 111). Investment is financed by *saving*, which equals income minus consumption.

The return on capital is the **real interest rate**, which is equal to the *nominal* interest rate adjusted for inflation. The nominal interest rate is the interest rate expressed in terms of money. The real interest rate is approximately equal to the nominal interest rate minus the inflation rate.[1] For example, if the nominal interest rate is 10 percent a year and the inflation rate is 4 percent a year, the real interest rate (approximately) is 6 percent a year. Think about the following example. You borrow $1,000 for one year. If the real interest rate is 6 percent a year, the people who loaned you the money must be able to buy goods and services valued in today's prices at $1,060 when you repay them. But after a year in which prices rise by 4 percent, they will need $1,100 to buy goods and services that today cost $1,060. So if you pay them $1,100, you are paying them only $1,060 in today's prices and the *real* interest paid is $60—6 percent a year.

We're going to see how investment and saving decisions are made and how they determine the equilibrium real interest rate.

### Investment Decisions

Investment consists of private investment and government investment. We'll look at the role of government in Chapter 15. In this chapter, we focus on private investment decisions.

How does Amazon.com decide how much to spend on servers, software, and warehouses? How does AT&T decide how much to spend on fiber-optic cables? Business investment decisions are influenced by

- The expected profit rate
- The real interest rate

To decide whether to invest in a new Internet book-distribution system, Amazon.com compares the expected profit rate with the real interest rate. The real interest rate is the opportunity cost of an investment. Let's look more closely at the expected profit rate and the real interest rate.

**The Expected Profit Rate** Other things remaining the same, the greater the expected profit rate from new capital, the greater is the amount of investment.

Imagine that Amazon.com is trying to decide whether to build a new Internet book-distribution system that will operate for one year and then be scrapped and replaced by an even better system. Amazon.com expects net revenue of $120 million from operating the system. Net revenue is equal to total revenue from sales minus the cost of labor and materials. The firm's expected profit from this investment is $20 million, which equals $120 million (net revenue) minus $100 million (cost of the system). The expected *profit rate* is 20 percent a year—($20 million ÷ $100 million) × 100.

Of the many influences on the expected profit rate, the three that stand out are

1. The phase of the business cycle
2. Advances in technology
3. Taxes

The phase of the business cycle influences the expected profit rate because sales fluctuate over the business cycle. In an expansion, an increase in sales brings a higher profit rate. In a recession, a decrease in sales brings a lower profit rate.

---

[1] The *exact* real interest rate formula allows for the change in the purchasing power of the interest as well as the amount of the loan. The exact formula is: Real interest rate = (Nominal interest rate − Inflation rate) ÷ (1 + Inflation rate/100). If the nominal interest rate is 10 percent and the inflation rate is 4 percent, the real interest rate is (10 − 4) ÷ (1 + 0.04) = 5.77 percent. The lower the inflation rate, the better is the approximation.

As technologies advance, profit expectations change. When a new technology first becomes available, firms expect to be on a learning curve and so expect a modest profit rate from the new technology. But as firms gain experience with a new technology, they expect costs to fall and the profit rate to increase.

It is the *after-tax* profit rate that a firm receives, so changes in tax rates influence the firm's after-tax profit rate. Firms go to extreme lengths to avoid taxes, and for multinational firms, the decision about *where* to invest often depends on the effect of taxes on profit.

**The Real Interest Rate** Other things remaining the same, the lower the real interest rate, the greater is the amount of investment.

The funds used to finance investment might be borrowed, or they might be the financial resources of the firm's owners (the firm's retained earnings). But regardless of the source of the funds, the opportunity cost of the funds is the real interest rate. The real interest paid on borrowed funds is an obvious cost. The real interest rate is also the cost of using retained earnings because these funds could be loaned to another firm. The real interest income forgone is the opportunity cost of using retained earnings to finance an investment project.

In the Amazon.com example, the expected profit rate is 20 percent a year. So it is profitable for Amazon to invest as long as the real interest rate is less than 20 percent a year. That is, at real interest rates below 20 percent a year, Amazon.com will invest in the new system, and at real interest rates in excess of 20 percent a year, it will not. Some projects are profitable at high real interest rates, but other projects are profitable only at low real interest rates. Consequently, the higher the real interest rate, the smaller is the number of projects that are worth undertaking and the smaller is the amount of investment.

We summarize the influences on investment decisions in an investment demand curve.

## Investment Demand

Other things remaining the same, investment decreases if the real interest rate rises and increases if the real interest rate falls. Figure 8.7 illustrates this relationship. The table highlights the amounts of investment that occur at three real interest rates. The relationship between investment and the real interest rate, other things remaining the same, is called **investment demand**.

Figure 8.7 shows an investment demand curve. Each point (*A* through *C*) on the investment demand curve corresponds to a row in the table. If the real interest rate is 6 percent a year, investment is $1 trillion. A change in the real interest rate brings a movement along the investment demand curve. If the real interest rate rises to 8 percent a year, investment decreases to $0.8 trillion; there is a movement up the investment demand curve. If the real interest rate falls to 4 percent a year, investment increases to $1.2 trillion; there is a movement down the investment demand curve.

A change in any other influence on investment plans changes investment demand and shifts the investment demand curve. Fluctuations in the

**FIGURE 8.7   Investment Demand**

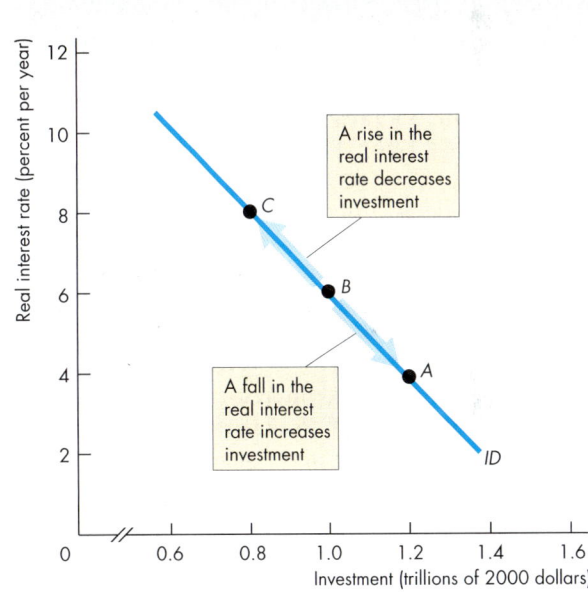

| | Real interest rate (percent per year) | Investment (trillions of 2000 dollars) |
|---|---|---|
| A | 4 | 1.2 |
| B | 6 | 1.0 |
| C | 8 | 0.8 |

The investment demand curve shows the effects of a change in the real interest rate on investment, other things remaining the same. A change in the real interest rate brings a movement along the investment demand curve.

expected profit rate are the main source of fluctuations in investment demand.

## Saving Decisions

Investment is financed by saving—by not consuming. The supply of financial resources from saving can come from three sources: households, governments, and the rest of the world.

Government saving arises if there is a budget surplus. We study the effects of this source of saving in Chapter 15. Saving in the rest of the world comes into our economy through international trade deficits and international borrowing. We study these aspects of the economy in Chapter 18. Here, we focus on household saving.

Households must decide how to allocate their *disposable income* between saving and consumption. Of the many factors that influence a household's saving decision, the more important ones are

- The real interest rate
- Disposable income
- Wealth
- Expected future income

**The Real Interest Rate**  Other things remaining the same, the lower the real interest rate, the smaller is the amount of saving and the greater is the amount of consumption. The real interest rate is the opportunity cost of consumption. A dollar consumed is a dollar not saved, so the interest that could have been earned on that saving is forgone. This opportunity cost arises regardless of whether a person is a lender or a borrower. For a lender, saving less this year means receiving less interest next year. For a borrower, saving less this year means paying less off a loan this year and paying more interest next year.

You can see why the real interest rate influences saving by thinking about student loans. If the real interest rate on student loans jumped to 20 percent a year, students would save more (buying cheaper food and finding lower-rent accommodations) to pay off their loans as quickly as possible. If the real interest rate on student loans fell to 1 percent a year, students would save less and take out larger loans.

**Disposable Income**  The greater a household's disposable income, other things remaining the same, the greater is its saving. For example, suppose a student works during the summer and earns a disposable income of $10,000. She spends the entire $10,000 on consumption during the year and saves nothing. When she graduates as an economics major, her disposable income jumps to $20,000 a year. She now saves $4,000 and spends $16,000 on consumption. The increase in disposable income of $10,000 has increased saving by $4,000.

**Wealth**  A household's *wealth* equals its assets (what it *owns*) minus its debts (what it *owes*). The purchasing power of a household's wealth is the *real* value of its wealth. It is the quantity of goods and services that the household's wealth can buy. The greater a household's real wealth, other things remaining the same, the less is its saving.

Patty is a department store executive who earns a disposable income of $30,000 a year. She has been saving and now has $15,000 in the bank and no debts. That is, Patty's wealth is $15,000. Patty's colleague, Tony, also earns a disposable income of $30,000, but he has no money in the bank. Tony's wealth is zero. Patty decides that this year, she will take a vacation and save only $1,000. But Tony decides to skip a vacation and save $5,000. With greater wealth and other things the same, Patty saves less than Tony.

**Expected Future Income**  The lower a household's expected future income, other things remaining the same, the greater is its saving. That is, if two households have the same disposable income in the current year, the household with the larger expected future income will spend a larger portion of current disposable income on consumption goods and services and will save less.

Look at Patty and Tony again. Patty has just been promoted and will receive a $10,000 pay raise next year. Tony has just been told that he will be fired at the end of the year. On receiving this news, Patty buys a new car—increases her consumption and decreases her saving. Tony sells his car and takes the bus—decreases his consumption and increases his saving.

A young household expects to have a higher future income for some years and then to have a lower income during retirement. Because of this life-cycle income pattern, young people and retired people save least, and middle-aged people save most.

Saving plans interact with investment plans to determine the real interest rate and the amount of investment and saving. Before we can understand these interactions, we need to learn about the saving supply curve.

## Saving Supply

If the real interest rate rises, other things remaining the same, saving increases. The relationship between saving and the real interest rate, other things remaining the same, is called **saving supply**.

Figure 8.8 illustrates saving supply. The table shows a saving supply schedule, and the graph shows the saving supply curve. The points *A* through *C* on the saving supply curve *SS* in Fig. 8.8 correspond to the rows of the table. For example, point *B* indicates that when the real interest rate is 6 percent a year, saving is $1.0 trillion. If the real interest rate rises from 6 percent a year to 8 percent a year, saving increases from $1 trillion to $1.1 trillion and there is a movement along the saving supply curve from *B* to *C*.

Along the saving supply curve, all influences on saving except the interest rate remain the same. A change in any other influence on saving changes saving supply and shifts the saving supply curve. An increase in disposable income, a decrease in wealth, or a decrease in expected future income increases saving supply, and the saving supply curve shifts rightward. Changes in these factors in the opposite direction decrease saving and shift the saving supply curve leftward.

In the short run, saving supply is probably not very responsive to changes in the interest rate and is most responsive to changes in income. But in the long run, the response of saving to the interest rate is probably large.

## Equilibrium in the Capital Market

We're now going to see how investment decisions and saving decisions determine the real interest rate. To do so, we study the capital market.

In the U.S. economy, there are many interrelated capital markets. There are markets in which the stocks of corporations are traded. Stocks are securities issued by corporations that pay a dividend based on each firm's profits. These markets determine the prices and rates of return earned by the stocks of each corporation. The New York Stock Exchange is an example of this type of capital market.

There are markets in which bonds are traded. Bonds are securities issued by governments and corporations that pay a fixed number of dollars each year but that have a price that fluctuates. These markets determine the interest rate on bonds.

There are markets in all types of loans. One of these markets is in credit card loans and another is in housing loans—called the mortgage market.

All these different capital markets determine interest rates that differ mainly because of differences in the amount of risk that attaches to a specific loan—the riskier the loan, the higher the interest rate, other things remaining the same.

**FIGURE 8.8** Saving Supply

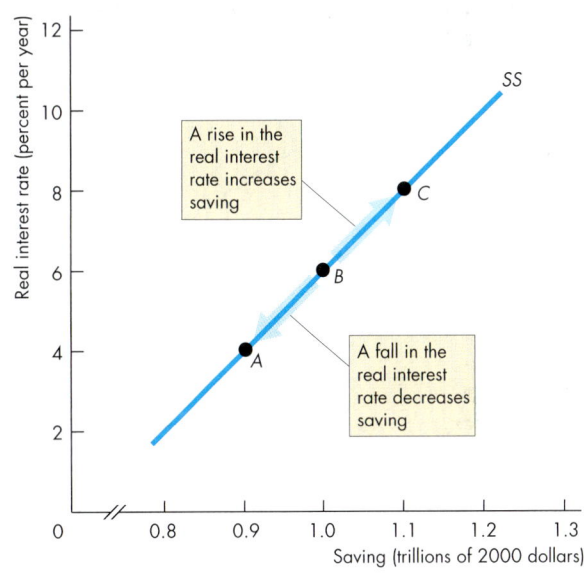

| | Real interest rate (percent per year) | Saving (trillions of 2000 dollars) |
|---|---|---|
| A | 4 | 0.9 |
| B | 6 | 1.0 |
| C | 8 | 1.1 |

The saving supply curve shows the effects of a change in the real interest rate on saving, other things remaining the same. A change in the real interest rate brings a movement along the saving supply curve.

We're going to think about the capital market as the total of all these individual markets. It makes good sense to do so because the individual markets are so tightly interrelated. If the interest rate got too high in one part of the capital market, funds would flow into that part of the market and depress the interest rate. And if the interest rate got too low in one part of the market, funds would leave that part of the market and its interest rate would rise.

So it is in the capital market as whole—the aggregate of all the individual bits of the market—in which the average interest rate is determined.

Figure 8.9 shows how investment and saving determine the real interest rate. The *ID* curve is the investment demand curve. The *SS* curve is the saving supply curve. The higher the real interest rate, the greater is the amount of saving and the smaller is the amount of investment.

In Fig. 8.9, when the real interest rate exceeds 6 percent a year, saving exceeds investment. Borrowers have an easy time finding the loans they want, but lenders are unable to lend all the funds they have available. The real interest rate falls. The interest rate continues to fall until saving equals investment. Alternatively, when the interest rate is less than 6 percent a year, saving is less than investment. Borrowers can't find the loans they want, but lenders are able to lend all the funds they have available. So the real interest rate rises and continues to rise until saving equals investment. Regardless of whether there is a surplus or a shortage of saving, the real interest rate changes and is pulled toward an equilibrium level.

In Fig. 8.9, this equilibrium is 6 percent a year. At this interest rate, there is neither a surplus nor a shortage of saving. Investors can get the funds they demand, and savers can lend all the funds they have available. The plans of savers and investors are consistent with each other.

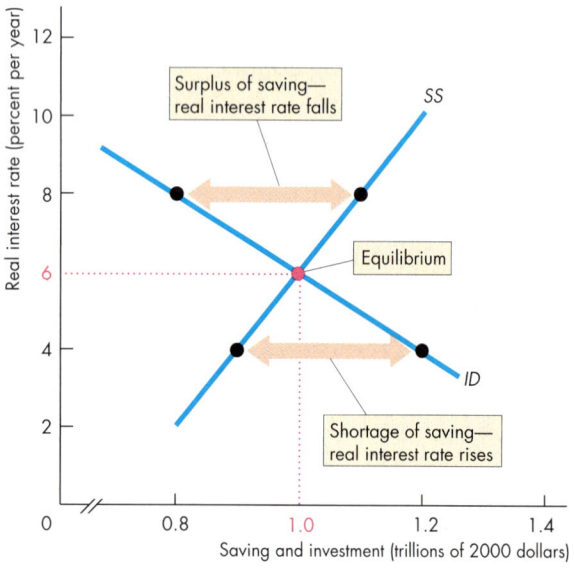

**FIGURE 8.9  Equilibrium in the Capital Market**

|   | Real interest rate (percent per year) | Investment | Saving |
|---|---|---|---|
|   |   | (trillions of 2000 dollars) | |
| A | 4 | 1.2 | 0.9 |
| B | 6 | 1.0 | 1.0 |
| C | 8 | 0.8 | 1.1 |

The table shows investment and saving at three interest rates, and the figure shows the investment demand curve, *ID*, and saving supply curve, *SS*. If the real interest rate were 4 percent a year, investment would exceed saving and the real interest rate would rise. If the real interest rate were 8 percent a year, saving would exceed investment and the real interest rate would fall. When the real interest rate is 6 percent a year, investment equals saving and the real interest rate is at its equilibrium.

### REVIEW QUIZ

1 Use the investment demand curve to illustrate what happens to investment if the real interest rate falls and other things remain the same; and if the real interest rate rises and other things remain the same.
2 Use the investment demand curve to illustrate what happens to investment if the expected profit rate increases and other things remain the same; and if the expected profit rate decreases and other things remain the same.
3 How do the real interest rate, disposable income, wealth, and expected future income influence saving?
4 How is the real interest rate determined?

# The Dynamic Classical Model

THE CLASSICAL MODEL HAS RICH IMPLICATIONS for how the economy changes over time in response to population growth and technological change and an increasing quantity of capital. We're now going to look at some of these dynamic aspects of the full-employment economy. We'll begin by looking at the sources and effects of changes in productivity.

## Changes in Productivity

When we talk about *productivity*, we usually mean labor productivity. **Labor productivity** is real GDP per hour of labor. Three factors influence labor productivity:

- Physical capital
- Human capital
- Technology

**Physical Capital** A farm worker equipped with only a stick and primitive tools can cultivate almost no land and grow barely enough food to feed a single family. A farmer equipped with a steel plow pulled by an animal can cultivate more land and produce enough food to feed a small village. A farmer equipped with a modern tractor, plow, and harvester can cultivate thousands of acres and produce enough food to feed hundreds of people.

By using physical capital on our farms and in our factories, shops, and offices, we enormously increase labor productivity.

**Human Capital** An economy's **human capital** is the knowledge and skill that people have obtained from education and on-the-job training. The average college graduate has a greater amount of human capital than the average high school graduate possesses. Consequently, the college graduate is able to perform some tasks that are beyond the ability of the high school graduate. The college graduate is more productive. For the nation as a whole, the greater the amount of schooling its citizens complete, the greater is its real GDP, other things remaining the same.

Regardless of how much schooling a person has completed, not much production is accomplished on the first day at work. Learning about the new work environment consumes the newly hired worker. But as time passes and experience accumulates, the worker becomes more productive. We call this on-the-job education activity **learning-by-doing**.

Learning-by-doing can bring incredible increases in labor productivity. The more experienced the labor force, the greater is its labor productivity, and other things remaining the same, the greater is real GDP.

**Technology** A student equipped with a pen can complete a readable page of writing in perhaps 10 minutes. This same task takes 5 minutes with a typewriter and 2 minutes with a computer. This is an example of the enormous impact of technology on productivity.

Any influence on production that increases labor productivity shifts the production function upward. Real GDP increases at each level of labor hours. In Fig. 8.10, the production function is initially $PF_0$. Then an increase in physical capital or human capital or an advance in technology occurs. The production function shifts upward to $PF_1$.

Labor productivity in the United States increases on the average by almost 2 percent a year.

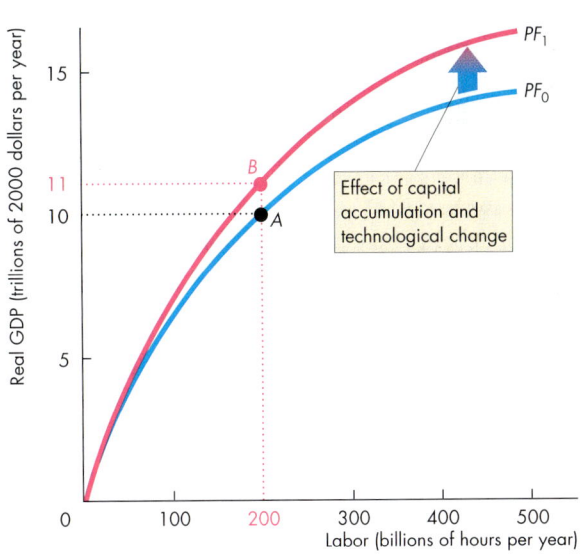

**FIGURE 8.10** An Increase in Labor Productivity

On $PF_0$, 200 billion labor hours produce a real GDP of $10 trillion (point A). An increase in capital or an advance in technology increases labor productivity and shifts the production function upward to $PF_1$. Now, 200 billion labor hours produce a real GDP of $11 trillion (point B).

The classical model also helps us to understand how changes in labor productivity and other factors change real GDP. Real GDP will increase if

1. The economy recovers from recession.
2. Potential GDP increases.

Recovery from recession means that the economy moves along the leisure time–real GDP *PPF* from a point at which real GDP and employment are too low to the full-employment equilibrium point. Equivalently, the economy moves along the short-run aggregate supply curve. Economists have a lot to say about such a move. And you learned about this type of short-term change in real GDP in Chapter 7.

Increasing potential GDP means expanding production possibilities. We're going to study such an expansion in the rest of this chapter and in Chapter 9. We begin this process here by examining two influences on potential GDP:

- An increase in population
- An increase in labor productivity

## An Increase in Population

As the population increases and the additional people reach working age, the supply of labor increases. With more labor available, the economy's production possibilities expand. But does the expansion of production possibilities mean that potential GDP increases? And does it mean that potential GDP *per person* increases?

The answers to these questions have intrigued economists for many years. And they cause heated political debate today. In China, for example, families are under enormous pressure to limit the number of children they have. In other countries, such as France, the government encourages large families. We can study the effects of an increase in population by using the model of the full-employment economy in Fig. 8.11.

In Fig. 8.11(a), the demand for labor is $LD$ and initially the supply of labor is $LS_0$. At full employment, the real wage rate is $35 an hour and the level of employment is 200 billion hours a year. In Fig. 8.11(b), the production function (*PF*) shows that with 200 billion hours of labor employed, potential GDP is $10 trillion. We're now going to work out what happens when the population increases.

An increase in the population increases the number of people of working age, and the supply of labor

**FIGURE 8.11** The Effects of an Increase in Population

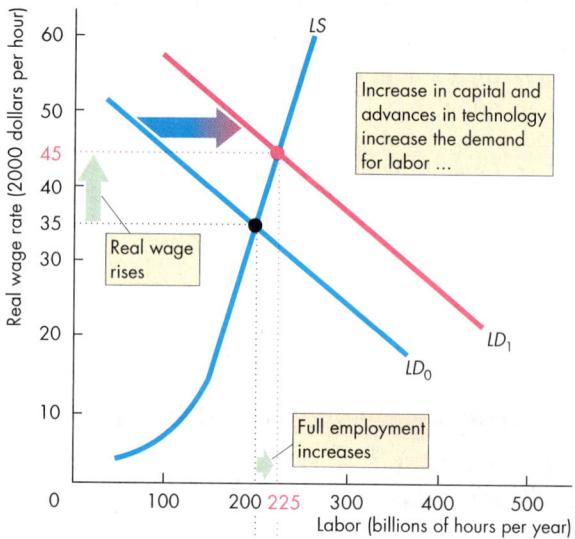

(a) The labor market

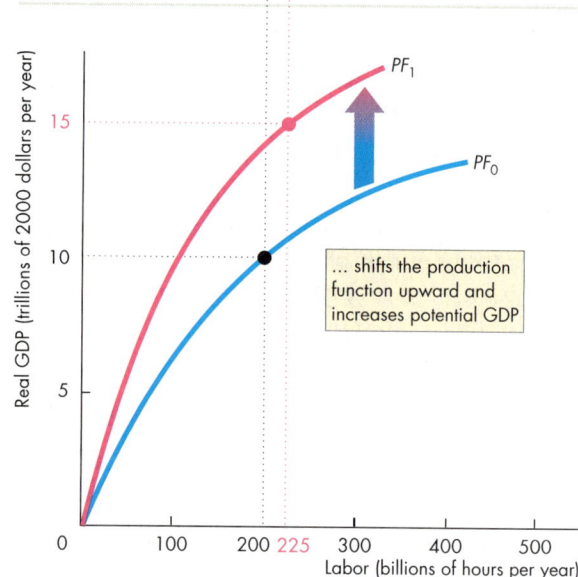

(b) Potential GDP

An increase in population increases the supply of labor. In part (a), the real wage rate falls, and the full-employment quantity of labor increases. In part (b), the increase in full employment increases potential GDP. Because the marginal product of labor diminishes, the increased population increases potential GDP but potential GDP per hour of work decreases.

increases. The labor supply curve shifts rightward to $LS_1$. At a real wage rate of $35 an hour, there is now a surplus of labor. So the real wage rate falls. In this example, it falls until it reaches $25 an hour. At $25 an hour, the quantity of labor demanded equals the quantity of labor supplied. Equilibrium employment increases to 300 billion hours a year.

Figure 8.11(b) shows the effect of the increase in equilibrium employment on real GDP. As the full-employment quantity of labor increases from 200 billion hours to 300 billion hours, potential GDP increases from $10 trillion to $13 trillion.

So at full employment, an increase in population increases employment, increases potential GDP, and lowers the real wage rate.

An increase in population also decreases potential GDP per hour of work. You can see this decrease by dividing potential GDP by total labor hours. Initially, with potential GDP at $10 trillion and labor hours at 200 billion, potential GDP per hour of work was $50. With the increase in population, potential GDP is $13 trillion and labor hours are 300 billion. Potential GDP per hour of work is $43.33. Diminishing returns are the source of the decrease in potential GDP per hour of work.

You've seen that an increase in population increases potential GDP and decreases potential GDP per hour of work. Some people challenge this conclusion and argue that people are the ultimate economic resource. They claim that a larger population brings forth a greater amount of scientific discovery and technological advance. Consequently, according to this argument, an increase in population never takes place in isolation. It is always accompanied by an increase in labor productivity. Let's now look at the effects of this influence on potential GDP.

## An Increase in Labor Productivity

We've seen that three factors increase labor productivity:

- An increase in physical capital
- An increase in human capital
- An advance in technology

Saving and investment increase the quantity of physical capital over time. We studied the factors that influence the decisions that determine how quickly capital grows earlier in this chapter. Education and on-the-job training and experience increase human capital. Research and development efforts bring advances in technology. In Chapter 9, we study how all these forces interact to determine the growth rate of potential GDP.

Here, we study the *effects* of an increase in physical capital, an increase in human capital, or an advance in technology on the labor market and potential GDP. We'll see how potential GDP, employment, and the real wage rate change when any of these three influences on labor productivity changes.

**An Increase in Physical Capital** If the quantity of physical capital increases, labor productivity increases. With labor being more productive, the economy's production possibilities expand. How does such an expansion of production possibilities change the real wage rate, employment, and potential GDP?

The additional capital increases the real GDP that each quantity of labor can produce. It also increases the marginal product of labor and so increases the demand for labor. Some physical capital replaces some types of labor. So the demand for those types of labor decreases when capital increases. But an increase in physical capital creates a demand for the types of labor that build, sell, and maintain the additional capital. The increases in demand for labor are always larger than the decreases in demand, and the economy-wide demand for labor increases.

With an increase in the economy-wide demand for labor, the real wage rate rises and the quantity of labor supplied increases. Equilibrium employment increases.

Potential GDP now increases for two reasons. First, a given level of employment produces more real GDP. Second, equilibrium employment increases.

**An Increase in Human Capital** If the quantity of human capital increases, labor productivity increases. Again, with labor being more productive, the economy's production possibilities expand. And this expansion of production possibilities changes the equilibrium real wage rate, employment, and potential GDP in a similar manner to the effects of a change in physical capital.

**An Advance in Technology** As technology advances, labor productivity increases. And exactly as in the case of an increase in capital, the economy's production possibilities expand. Again, just as in the case of an increase in capital, the new technology increases the real GDP that each quantity of labor can produce and increases the marginal product of labor and the demand for labor.

With an increase in the demand for labor, the real wage rate rises, the quantity of labor supplied increases, and equilibrium employment increases. And again, potential GDP increases because a given level of employment produces more real GDP and because equilibrium employment increases.

**Illustrating the Effects of an Increase in Labor Productivity** Figure 8.12 shows the effects of an increase in labor productivity that results from an increase in capital or an advance in technology. In part (a), the demand for labor initially is $LD_0$ and the supply of labor is $LS$. The real wage rate is $35 an hour, and full employment is 200 billion hours a year.

In part (b), the production function initially is $PF_0$. With 200 billion hours of labor employed, potential GDP is $10 trillion.

Now an increase in capital or an advance in technology increases the productivity of labor. In Fig. 8.12(a), the demand for labor increases and the demand curve shifts rightward to $LD_1$. In Fig. 8.12(b), the productivity of labor increase shifts the production function upward to $PF_1$.

In Fig. 8.12(a), at the original real wage rate of $35 an hour, there is now a shortage of labor. So the real wage rate rises. In this example, it keeps rising until it reaches $45 an hour. At $45 an hour, the quantity of labor demanded equals the quantity of labor supplied and full employment increases to 225 billion hours a year.

Figure 8.12(b) shows the effects on potential GDP of the increase in full employment combined with the new production function. As full employment increases from 200 billion hours to 225 billion hours, potential GDP increases from $10 trillion to $15 trillion.

Potential GDP per hour of work also increases. You can see this increase by dividing potential GDP by total labor hours. Initially, with potential GDP at $10 trillion and labor hours at 200 billion, potential GDP per hour of work was $50. With the increase in labor productivity, potential GDP is $15 trillion and labor hours are 225 billion, so potential GDP per hour of work is $66.67.

We've just studied the effects of a change in population and an increase in labor productivity separately. In reality, these changes occur together. We can see the combined effects by examining an episode in the life of the U.S. economy.

**FIGURE 8.12  The Effects of an Increase in Labor Productivity**

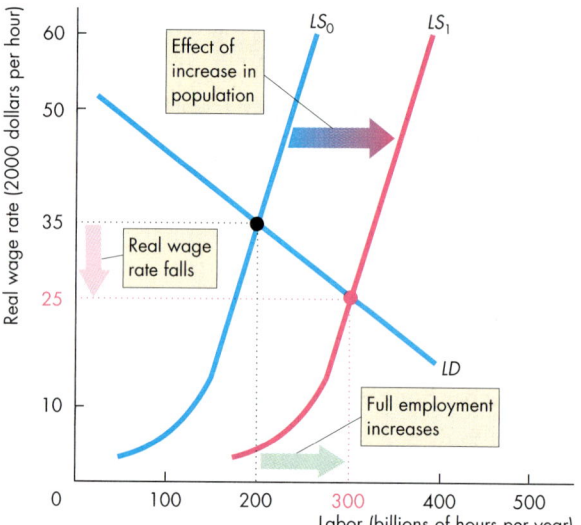

(a) The labor market

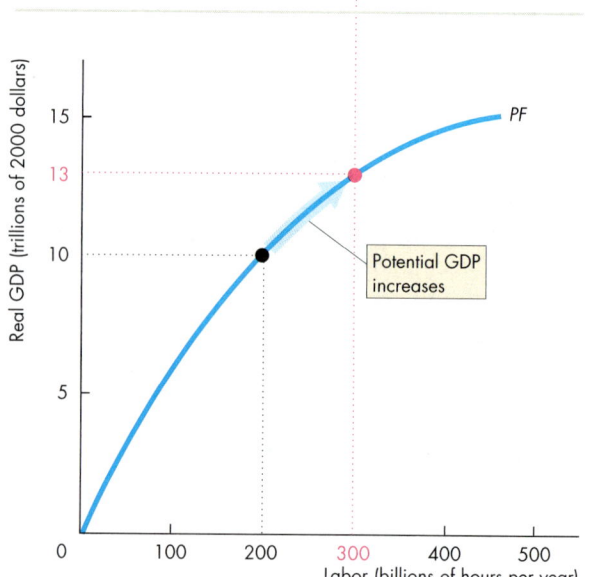

(b) Potential GDP

An increase in labor productivity shifts the demand for labor curve rightward from $LD_0$ to $LD_1$ (part a) and the production function upward from $PF_0$ to $PF_1$ (part b). The real wage rate rises to $45 an hour, and full employment increases from 200 billion to 225 billion hours. Potential GDP increases from $10 trillion to $15 trillion.

# The Dynamic Classical Model   199

## Population and Productivity in the United States

The U.S. economy was close to full employment in 2001. It was also close to full employment 20 years earlier, in 1981. We're going to compare these two years and look at the forces that moved the economy from one full-employment equilibrium to another.

In 1981, real GDP in the United States was $5.4 trillion, employment was 159 billion hours, and the real wage rate was $17 an hour. (We are using 2000 dollars.)

By 2001, real GDP had increased to $9.9 trillion, labor hours had increased to 231 billion, and the real wage rate had risen to $24 an hour. (Again, we are using 2000 dollars.)

The factors that you've just studied—an increase in population, increases in physical and human capital, and advances in technology—brought these changes.

Figure 8.13 shows these effects. In 1981, the demand for labor was $LD_{81}$, the supply of labor was $LS_{81}$, the real wage rate was $17, and 159 billion hours of labor were employed. The production function was $PF_{81}$ and potential GDP was $5.4 trillion. By 2001, the increase in population had increased the supply of labor to $LS_{01}$. And the accumulation of capital and advances in technology had increased the demand for labor to $LD_{01}$ and shifted the production function upward to $PF_{01}$. The real wage rate increased to $24, employment increased to 231 billion hours, and potential GDP increased to $9.9 trillion.

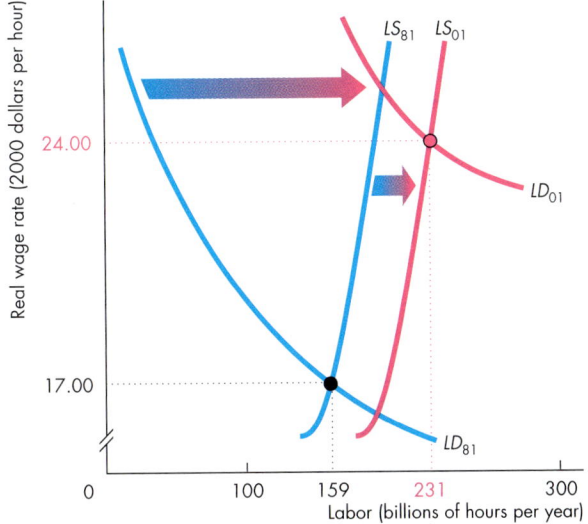

**FIGURE 8.13** Full Employment in the United States: 1981 and 2001

(a) The labor market

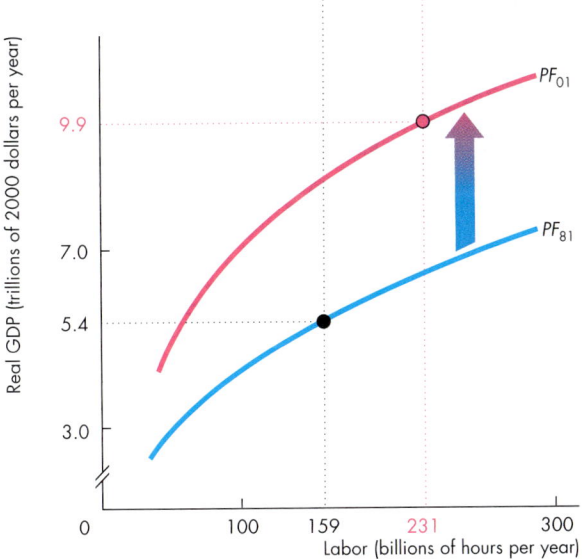

(b) The U.S. production function in 1981 and 2001

In 1981, the real wage rate was $17 an hour and the quantity of labor employed was 159 billion hours (part a). Potential GDP was $5.4 trillion on $PF_{81}$ (part b). By 2001, the real wage rate was $24 an hour and 231 billion hours of labor were employed. Potential GDP had increased to $9.9 trillion on $PF_{01}$.

### REVIEW QUIZ

1. When the population increases but nothing else changes, why does real GDP per hour of work decrease?
2. How does an increase in capital change the real wage rate, full employment, and potential GDP?
3. How do advances in technology change the real wage rate, full employment, and potential GDP?

You've seen how potential GDP is determined and what makes it change. *Reading Between the Lines* on pp. 200–201 looks at the productivity change in 2003.

# READING BETWEEN THE LINES

## Productivity Growth in 2003

**THE WALL STREET JOURNAL, DECEMBER 4, 2003**

### Productivity Jumped in Quarter

In a performance with bullish implications for Americans' standard of living, the productivity of U.S. workers rose at the fastest rate in 20 years in the third quarter, revised data show.

Output per worker at nonagricultural businesses in the third quarter rose at an annual rate of 9.4%, the Labor Department said, even better than its earlier estimate of 8.1%. That is the best quarterly performance since 1983, and brought the 12-month rate of increase to 5%. For the two years ended Sept. 30, productivity growth averaged 5.5%, the best two-year performance since 1953, according to Banc of America Securities.

Increased productivity means companies can produce more per worker, earn more profits and pay higher wages without raising prices. It is the key to rising standards of living over the long run....

In the short run, the strong productivity performance bolsters corporate profits and encourages the Federal Reserve to take its time about raising interest rates. "This is going to be extremely important for the sustainability of the recovery," said Scott Anderson, a senior economist with Wells Fargo & Co. in Minneapolis. "It means corporate profitability will remain strong, and that will allow businesses to ramp up hiring and investment spending while keeping costs contained."

In the long run, the recent performance likely means the economy's long-term growth rate could have risen to as much as 4%, from about 2.5% between the early 1970s and mid-1990s. ....

©2003 The Wall Street Journal. Reprinted with permission.
Further reproduction prohibited.

### Essence of the Story

■ Labor productivity in the United States grew at annual rate of 9.4 percent, the fastest rate in 20 years, during the third quarter of 2003.

■ In the short run, strong productivity growth increases profits and encourages the Federal Reserve to delay raising the interest rate.

■ In the long run, the economy's long-term growth rate might have increased to as much as 4 percent, from about 2.5 percent between the early 1970s and mid-1990s.

## Economic Analysis

- Productivity growth during the two years since the 2001 recession has been rapid.

- The production function has shifted upward.

- Figure 1 shows the production function in 2001, $PF_{01}$. In 2001, the economy was at point A, where 231 billion hours of labor produced $9.87 trillion dollars worth of goods and services.

- By 2003, the production function had shifted to $PF_{03}$ in Fig. 1. In 2003, the economy was at point B, where 233 billion hours of labor produced $10.29 trillion dollars worth of goods and services.

- The economy was not at full employment in 2003. According to the Congressional Budget Office, potential GDP was $10.53 trillion. To produce this amount of real GDP on the 2003 production function would have needed 236 billion hours of labor, at point C in Fig. 1.

- The increase in productivity and shift of the production function also increased the demand for labor.

- Figure 2 shows the effects of the productivity increase on the demand for labor.

- The demand for labor curve shifted from $LD_{01}$ in 2001 to $LD_{03}$ in 2003.

- This shift is not as large as might have been expected because much of the productivity gain resulted from more productive capital rather than more productive labor.

- In Fig. 2, the economy moved from point A in 2001 to point B in 2003. There was a small increase in employment and virtually no change in the real wage rate.

- If real GDP had increased to equal potential GDP, the real wage rate would need to fall to bring a movement along the demand for labor curve $LD_{03}$ to point C in Fig. 2.

- It was not possible to say on the basis of the data available at the end of 2003 whether the increase in productivity would boost the economy's long-term growth rate or whether it would be a short-lived boost to the growth rate.

- The news article says that faster productivity growth will delay a rise in the interest rate. The reason would be that faster productivity growth would leave real GDP below potential GDP and with plenty of space to expand.

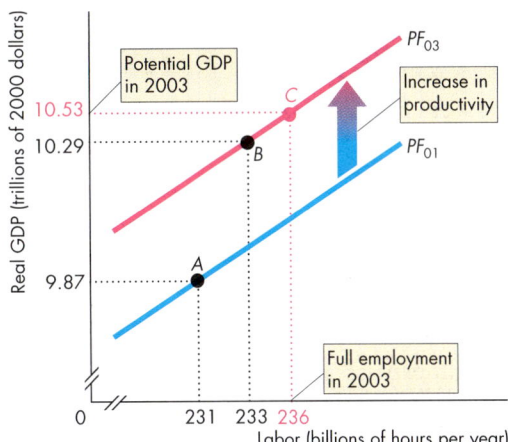

Figure 1 The shift of the production function

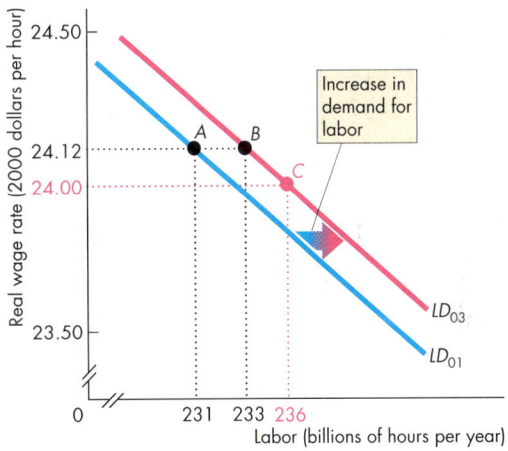

Figure 2 The shift of the demand for labor curve

# SUMMARY

## KEY POINTS

### The Classical Model: A Preview (p. 180)

- The classical model explains how real GDP, employment, the real wage rate, investment, saving, and the real interest rate are determined at full employment.

### Real GDP and Employment (pp. 180–181)

- To produce real GDP, we must forgo leisure time.
- As the quantity of labor increases, real GDP increases.

### The Labor Market and Potential GDP (pp. 182–186)

- Other things remaining the same, as the real wage rate falls, the quantity of labor demanded increases and the quantity of labor supplied decreases.
- At full-employment equilibrium, the quantity of labor demanded equals the quantity of labor supplied and real GDP equals potential GDP.

### Unemployment at Full Employment (pp. 187–189)

- The unemployment rate at full employment is the natural rate of unemployment.
- Persistent unemployment arises from search and job rationing.

### Investment, Saving, and the Interest Rate (pp. 190–194)

- Other things remaining the same, as the real interest rate falls, investment increases and saving decreases.
- The equilibrium real interest rate makes saving equal to investment.

### The Dynamic Classical Model (pp. 195–199)

- An increase in capital or a technological advance increases both employment and the real wage and increases potential GDP.
- An increase in population increases the supply of labor, lowers the real wage rate, increases the quantity of labor employed, and increases potential GDP. It decreases potential GDP per hour of work.
- An increase in capital or an advance in technology increases labor productivity. It shifts the production function upward and the demand for labor curve rightward. The real wage rate rises, the quantity of labor employed increases, and potential GDP increases.

## KEY FIGURES

Figure 8.1   Production Possibilities and the Production Function, 181
Figure 8.2   The Demand for Labor, 182
Figure 8.3   Marginal Product and the Demand for Labor, 183
Figure 8.4   The Supply of Labor, 184
Figure 8.5   The Labor Market and Potential GDP, 186
Figure 8.7   Investment Demand, 191
Figure 8.8   Saving Supply, 193
Figure 8.9   Equilibrium in the Capital Market, 194

## KEY TERMS

Capital stock, 190
Classical dichotomy, 180
Classical model, 180
Demand for labor, 182
Efficiency wage, 188
Human capital, 195
Investment demand, 191
Job rationing, 188
Job search, 187
Labor productivity, 195
Law of diminishing returns, 182
Learning-by-doing, 195
Marginal product of labor, 182
Minimum wage, 189
Money wage rate, 182
Production function, 181
Quantity of labor demanded, 182
Quantity of labor supplied, 184
Real interest rate, 190
Real wage rate, 182
Saving supply, 193
Supply of labor, 184

# PROBLEMS

*1. Robinson Crusoe lives on a desert island on the equator. He has 12 hours of daylight every day to allocate between leisure and work. The table shows seven alternative combinations of leisure and real GDP in Crusoe's economy:

| Possibility | Leisure (hours per day) | Real GDP (dollars per day) |
|---|---|---|
| A | 12 | 0 |
| B | 10 | 10 |
| C | 8 | 18 |
| D | 6 | 24 |
| E | 4 | 28 |
| F | 2 | 30 |
| G | 0 | 30 |

  a. Make a table and a graph of Crusoe's production function.
  b. Find the marginal product of labor for Crusoe at different quantities of labor.

2. The people of Nautica have 100 hours every day to allocate between leisure and work. The table shows the combinations of real GDP and leisure in the economy of Nautica:

| Possibility | Leisure (hours per day) | Real GDP (dollars per day) |
|---|---|---|
| A | 0 | 75 |
| B | 20 | 70 |
| C | 40 | 60 |
| D | 60 | 45 |
| E | 80 | 25 |
| F | 100 | 0 |

  a. Make a table and a graph of Nautica's production function.
  b. Find the marginal product of labor for Nautica at different quantities of labor.

*3. Use the information provided in problem 1 about Robinson Crusoe's economy. Also, use the information that at a real wage rate of $4.50 an hour, Crusoe is willing to work any number of hours between zero and the total available to him.
  a. Make a table that shows Crusoe's demand for labor schedule and draw Crusoe's demand for labor curve.
  b. Make a table that shows Crusoe's supply of labor schedule and draw Crusoe's supply of labor curve.

  c. What are the full-employment equilibrium real wage rate and quantity of labor in Crusoe's economy?
  d. Find Crusoe's potential GDP.

4. Use the information provided in problem 2 about the economy of Nautica. Also, use the information that the people of Nautica are willing to work 10 hours a day for a real wage rate of $10 an hour. And for each 50¢ an hour *increase* in the real wage, they are willing to work an *additional* hour a day.
  a. Make a table that shows Nautica's demand for labor schedule and draw Nautica's demand for labor curve.
  b. Make a table that shows Nautica's supply of labor schedule and draw Nautica's supply of labor curve.
  c. Find the full-employment equilibrium real wage rate and quantity of labor in Nautica's economy.
  d. Find Nautica's potential GDP.

*5. A cellular phone assembly plant costs $10 million and has a life of one year. The firm will have to hire labor at a cost of $3 million and buy parts and fuel at a cost of a further $3 million. If the firm builds the plant, it will be able to produce cellular telephones that will sell for a total revenue of $17 million. Does it pay the firm to invest in this new production line at the following real interest rates:
  a. 5 percent a year?
  b. 10 percent a year?
  c. 15 percent a year?

6. A natural gas deposit contains gas that can be pumped out in one year and sold for a total revenue of $40 million. It will take a $36 million investment in equipment and pipelines to access the gas and deliver it to the buyers. Does it pay to undertake this investment at the following real interest rates:
  a. 5 percent a year?
  b. 10 percent a year?
  c. 15 percent a year?

*7. In 1999, the Batman family (Batman and Robin) had a disposable income of $50,000, wealth of $100,000, and an expected future income of $50,000 a year. At an interest rate of 4 percent a year, the Batmans would save $10,000. At an interest rate of 6 percent a year, they would save $12,500. And at an

* Solutions to odd-numbered problems are available on **MyEconLab**.

interest rate of 8 percent a year, they would save $15,000.
   a. Draw a graph of the Batman family's saving supply curve for 1999.
   b. In 2000, everything remained the same as the year before except that the Batmans expected their future income to rise to $60,000 a year. Show the influence of this change on the Batman family's saving supply curve.
8. It is now 2002, and the Batman family has wealth of $120,000. Its disposable income is $60,000, and its expected future income is also $60,000 a year. The Batmans will save $15,000 at an interest rate of 6 percent a year. If the interest rate falls to 4 percent a year, they will cut their saving to $10,000. And if the interest rate rises to 8 percent a year, they will increase their saving to $20,000.
   a. Draw a graph of the Batman family's saving supply curve for 2002.
   b. In 2002, the stock market boomed and the Batmans' wealth increased by 50 percent. Indicate the direction of influence of this change on the Batman family's saving supply curve.
*9. If the United States cracked down on illegal immigrants and returned millions of workers to their countries of origin, what would happen in the United States to
   a. Potential GDP
   b. Employment
   c. The real wage rate
10. If the United States freed up its immigrants laws and admitted millions of new workers, what would happen in the United States to
    a. Potential GDP
    b. Employment
    c. The real wage rate
*11. If a large increase in investment increased productivity, what would happen to
    a. Potential GDP
    b. Employment
    c. The real wage rate
12. If a severe drought brought a fall in productivity, what would happen to
    a. Potential GDP
    b. Employment
    c. The real wage rate

# CRITICAL THINKING

1. Study the news article about labor productivity in 2001 to 2003 in the United States in *Reading Between the Lines* on pp. 200–201 and then
   a. Describe what happened to productivity during 2002 and 2003 and illustrate the changes using the tools of the production function and the demand for labor curve.
   b. Explain why we can't be sure that the increase in productivity is the beginning of a new era of more rapid economic expansion.
   c. List and consider the possible contribution of each of the factors that might have led to the increase in productivity.
2. You are working for the President's Council of Economic Advisors and must write a memo for the President that provides a checklist of policy initiatives that will increase potential GDP. Be as imaginative as possible, but justify each of your suggestions with reference to the concepts and tools that you have learned about in this chapter.

# WEB EXERCISES

**Use the links on MyEconLab to work the following exercises.**

1. Obtain information about the economy of Russia during the 1990s. Try to figure out what happened to the production possibilities frontier and production function and to the demand for labor and supply of labor in Russia during the 1990s. Tell a story about the Russian economy during those years using only the concepts and tools that you have learned about in this chapter.
2. Obtain information about the economy of China during the 1990s. Try to figure out what happened to the production possibilities frontier and production function and to the demand for labor and supply of labor in China during the 1990s. Tell a story about the Chinese economy during those years using only the concepts and tools that you have learned about in this chapter.

# Economic Growth

**CHAPTER 9**

## Transforming People's Lives

Real GDP *per person* in the United States more than doubled between 1963 and 2003. If you live in a dorm, chances are it was built during the 1960s and equipped with two electrical outlets, one for a desk lamp and one for a bedside lamp. Today, with the help of a power bar (or two), your room bulges with a personal computer, television and VCR or DVD player, stereo system, microwave, refrigerator, coffeemaker, and toaster—the list goes on. What has brought about this growth in production, incomes, and living standards?

We see even greater economic growth if we look at modern Asia. On the banks of the Li River in Southern China, Songman Yang breeds cormorants, amazing birds that he trains to fish and to deliver their catch to a basket on his simple bamboo raft. Songman's work, the capital equipment and technology he uses, and the income he earns are similar to those of his ancestors going back some 2,000 years. Yet all around Songman, in China's bustling cities, people are participating in an economic miracle. They are creating businesses, investing in new technologies, developing local and global markets, and transforming their lives. Why are incomes in China growing so rapidly?

◆ In this chapter, we study the forces that make real GDP grow, that make some countries grow faster than others, and that make our own growth rate sometimes slow down and sometimes speed up.

In *Reading Between the Lines* at the end of the chapter, we return to the economic growth of China and see how it compares with the economic growth of the United States.

### After studying this chapter, you will be able to

- Describe the long-term growth trends in the United States and other countries and regions
- Identify the main sources of long-term real GDP growth
- Explain the productivity growth slowdown in the United States during the 1970s and the speedup during the 1990s
- Explain the rapid economic growth rates being achieved in Asia
- Explain the theories of economic growth

## Long-Term Growth Trends

THE LONG-TERM GROWTH TRENDS THAT WE study in this chapter are the trends in *potential GDP*. We are interested in long-term growth primarily because it brings rising incomes *per person*. So we begin by looking at some facts about the level and the growth rate of real GDP per person in the United States and around the world. Let's look first at real GDP per person in the United States over the past hundred years.

### Growth in the U.S. Economy

Figure 9.1 shows real GDP per person in the United States for the hundred years from 1903 to 2003. In the middle of the graph are two extraordinary events: the Great Depression of the 1930s and World War II of the 1940s. The fall in real GDP during the depression and the bulge during the war obscure any changes in the long-term growth trend that might have occurred within these years.

For the century as a whole, the average growth rate was 2 percent a year. But from 1903 to the onset of the Great Depression in 1929, the average growth rate was only 1.4 percent a year. Between 1930 and 1950, averaging out the depression and the war, the long-term growth rate was 2.2 percent a year. Then, after World War II, the average growth rate was 2 percent a year. Growth was especially rapid during the 1960s and late 1990s and slower during the period from 1973 to 1983.

Figure 9.1 shows the productivity growth slowdown of 1973–1983 in a longer perspective. It also shows that productivity growth slowdowns have occurred before. The early years of the 1900s and the mid-1950s had even slower growth than we had during the 1970s and 1980s. The rapid growth of the 1960s and 1990s is not unusual either. The 1920s were years of similarly rapid growth.

A major goal of this chapter is to explain why our economy grows and why the long-term growth rate varies. Another goal is to explain variations in the economic growth rate across countries. Let's look at some facts about growth rates.

**FIGURE 9.1** A Hundred Years of Economic Growth in the United States

During the 100 years from 1903 to 2003, real GDP per person in the United States grew by 2 percent a year, on the average. The growth rate was greater after World War II than before the Great Depression.

Sources: Christina D. Romer, "The Prewar Business Cycle Reconsidered: New Estimates of Gross National Product, 1869–1908," *Journal of Political Economy*, Vol. 97 1989; Bureau of Economic Analysis; and author's calculations to link these two sources.

## Real GDP Growth in the World Economy

Figure 9.2 shows real GDP per person in the United States and in other countries between 1963 and 2003. Part (a) looks at the seven richest countries—known as the G7 nations. Among these nations, the United States has the highest real GDP per person. In 2003, Canada had the second-highest real GDP per person, ahead of Japan and France, Germany, Italy, and the United Kingdom (collectively the Europe Big 4).

During the forty years shown here, the gaps between the United States, Canada, and Europe's Big 4 have widened slightly. But starting from a long way back, Japan grew fastest. It caught up to Europe in 1973 and Canada in 1990. But during the 1990s, Japan's economy stagnated.

Most other countries are growing slower than, and falling further behind, the United States. Figure 9.2(b) looks at some of these countries. Western Europe (other than the Big 4) grew faster than the United States before 1975, but then slowed during the 1980s, and fell behind the U.S. growth rate during the 1990s. After a brief period of catch-up, the former Communist countries of Central Europe have fallen increasingly behind the United States, and by 2001, they were as far behind as they had been 30 years earlier.

Africa and Central and South America have grown more slowly than the United States. Real GDP per person in Central and South America slipped from a comparative high of 29 percent of the U.S. level of real GDP per person in 1963 to 20 percent in 2003. Africa slipped from 12 percent of the U.S. level of real GDP per person in 1963 to 6 percent in 2003.

**FIGURE 9.2  Economic Growth Around the World: Catch-Up or Not?**

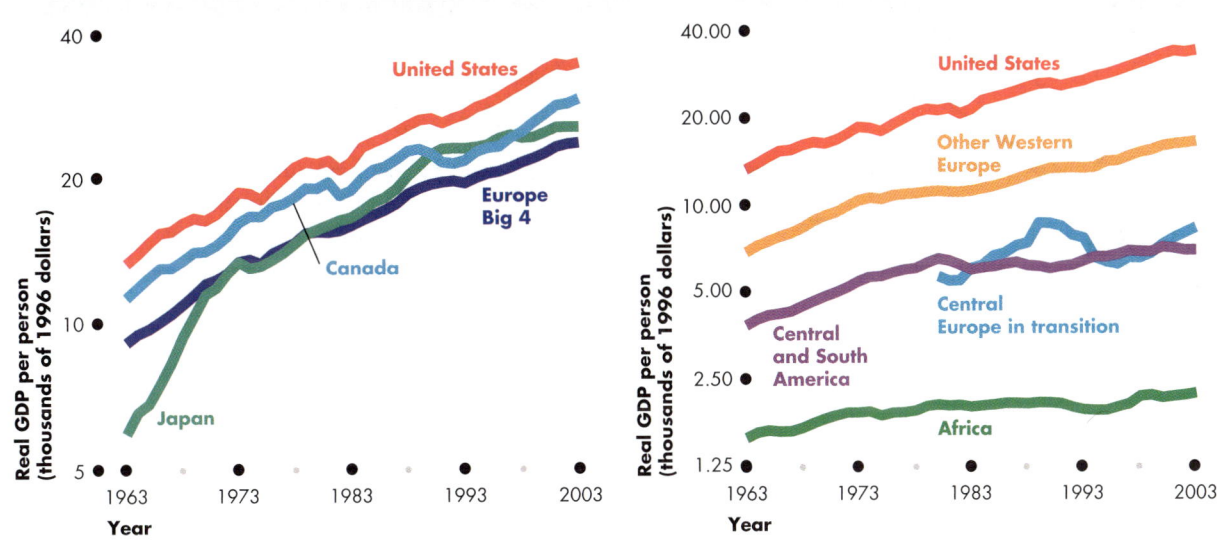

(a) Catch-up?

(b) No catch-up?

Real GDP per person has grown throughout the world economy. Among the rich industrial countries (part a), real GDP has grown slightly faster in the United States than in Canada and the four big countries of Europe (France, Germany, Italy, and the United Kingdom). Japan had the fastest growth rate before 1973 but then slowed and stagnated during the 1990s.

Among a wider range of countries (part b), growth rates have been lower than that of the United States and the gaps between the levels of real GDP per person in the United States have widened. The gaps between the United States and Central Europe and Africa have widened by a large amount.

Sources: (1963–2000) Alan Heston, Robert Summers and Bettina Aten, Penn World Table Version 6.1, Center for International Comparisons at the University of Pennsylvania (CICUP), October 2002 and (2001–2003) and International Monetary Fund, *World Economic Outlook*, October 2003.

A group of Asian economies provides a strong contrast to the persistent gaps between the United States and other economies shown in Fig. 9.2(b). Hong Kong, Korea, Singapore, and Taiwan have experienced spectacular growth, which you can see in Fig. 9.3. During the 1960s, real GDP per person in these economies ranged from 13 to 30 percent of that in the United States. But by 2003, real GDP per person in Hong Kong and Singapore had reached 80 percent of that in the United States.

Figure 9.3 shows that China is also catching up, but from a long way behind. China's real GDP per person increased from 5 percent of the U.S. level in 1963 to 13 percent in 2003.

The Asian economies shown in Fig. 9.3 are like fast trains running on the same track at similar speeds and with a roughly constant gap between them. Hong Kong is the lead train and runs about 15 years in front of Korea and 40 years in front of the rest of China, which is the last train. Real GDP per person in Korea in 2003 was similar to that in Hong Kong in 1986, and real GDP in China in 2003 was similar to that of Hong Kong in 1963. Between 1963 and 2003, Hong Kong transformed itself from a poor developing economy into one of the richest in the world.

The rest of China is now doing what Hong Kong has done. If China continues its rapid growth, the world economy will become a dramatically different place. China has a population 200 times that of Hong Kong and almost 5 times that of the United States.

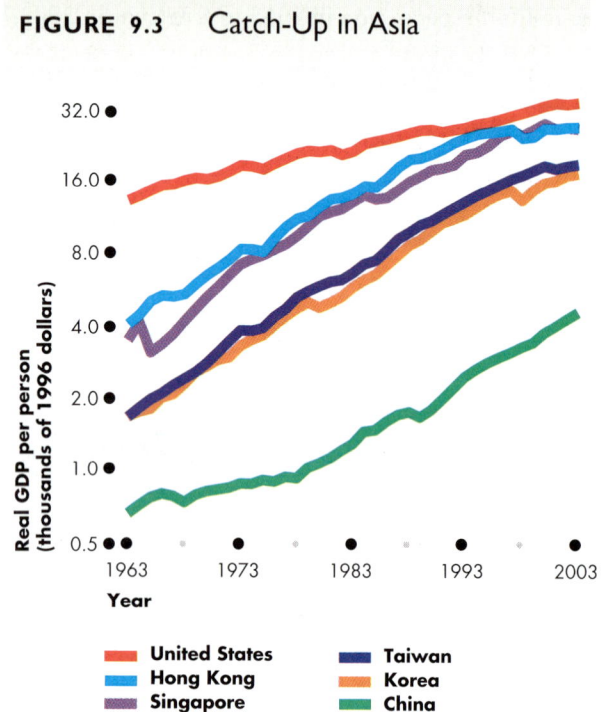

**FIGURE 9.3    Catch-Up in Asia**

United States | Taiwan
Hong Kong | Korea
Singapore | China

Catch-up has occurred in five economies in Asia. After starting out in 1963 with real GDP per person as low as 13 percent of that in the United States, Hong Kong, Korea, Singapore, and Taiwan have substantially narrowed the gap between them and the United States. And from being a very poor developing country in 1963, China now has a real GDP per person that equals that of Hong Kong in 1963. China is growing at a rate that is enabling it to continue to catch up with the United States.

*Sources:* See Fig. 9.2.

### REVIEW QUIZ

1. What has been the average economic growth rate in the United States over the past 100 years? In which periods was growth the most rapid and in which periods was it the slowest?
2. Describe the gaps between the levels of real GDP per person in the United States and other countries. For which countries are the gaps narrowing? For which countries are the gaps widening? And for which countries are the gaps remaining unchanged?
3. Compare the growth rates and levels of real GDP per person in Hong Kong, Korea, Singapore, Taiwan, China, and the United States. How far is China behind the other Asian economies?

The facts about economic growth in the United States and around the world raise some big questions that we're now going to answer. We'll study the causes of economic growth in three stages. First, we'll look at the preconditions for growth and the activities that sustain it. Second, we'll learn how economists measure the relative contributions of the sources of growth—an activity called *growth accounting*. And third, we'll study three theories of economic growth that seek to explain how the influences on growth interact to determine the growth rate. Let's take our first look at the causes of economic growth.

# The Causes of Economic Growth: A First Look

Most human societies have lived for centuries and even thousands of years, like Songman Yang, with no economic growth. The key reason is that they have lacked some fundamental social institutions and arrangements that are essential preconditions for economic growth. Let's see what these preconditions are.

## Preconditions for Economic Growth

The most basic precondition for economic growth is an appropriate *incentive* system. Three institutions are crucial to the creation of incentives:

1. Markets
2. Property rights
3. Monetary exchange

Markets enable buyers and sellers to get information and to do business with each other, and market prices send signals to buyers and sellers that create incentives to increase or decrease the quantities demanded and supplied. Markets enable people to specialize and trade and to save and invest. But markets need property rights and monetary exchange.

Property rights are the social arrangements that govern the ownership, use, and disposal of factors of production and goods and services. They include the rights to physical property (land, buildings, and capital equipment), to financial property (claims by one person against another), and to intellectual property (such as inventions). Clearly established and enforced property rights give people an assurance that a capricious government will not confiscate their income or savings.

Monetary exchange facilitates transactions of all kinds, including the orderly transfer of private property from one person to another. Property rights and monetary exchange create incentives for people to specialize and trade, to save and invest, and to discover new technologies.

No unique political system is necessary to deliver the preconditions for economic growth. Liberal democracy, founded on the fundamental principle of the rule of law, is the system that does the best job. It provides a solid base on which property rights can be established and enforced. But authoritarian political systems have sometimes provided an environment in which economic growth has occurred.

Early human societies, based on hunting and gathering, did not experience economic growth because they lacked these preconditions. Economic growth began when societies evolved the three key institutions that create incentives. But the presence of an incentive system and the institutions that create it does not guarantee that economic growth will occur. It permits economic growth but does not make that growth inevitable.

The simplest way in which growth happens when the appropriate incentive system exists is that people begin to specialize in the activities at which they have a comparative advantage and trade with each other. You saw in Chapter 2 how everyone can gain from such activity. By specializing and trading, everyone can acquire goods and services at the lowest possible cost. Equivalently, people can obtain a greater volume of goods and services from their labor.

As an economy moves from one with little specialization to one that reaps the gains from specialization and exchange, its production and consumption grow. Real GDP per person increases, and the standard of living rises.

But for growth to be persistent, people must face incentives that encourage them to pursue three activities that generate ongoing economic growth:

- Saving and investment in new capital
- Investment in human capital
- Discovery of new technologies

These three sources of growth, which interact with each other, are the primary sources of the extraordinary growth in productivity during the past 200 years. Let's look at each in turn.

## Saving and Investment in New Capital

Saving and investment in new capital increase the amount of capital per worker and increase real GDP per hour of labor—labor productivity. Labor productivity took the most dramatic upturn when the amount of capital per worker increased during the Industrial Revolution. Production processes that use hand tools can create beautiful objects, but production methods that use large amounts of capital per worker, such as auto plant assembly lines, are much more productive. The accumulation of capital on farms, in textile factories, in iron foundries and steel mills, in coal mines, on building sites, in chemical plants, in auto plants, in banks and insurance companies, and in shopping malls has added incredibly to the productivity of our economy. The next time you see a movie set in the Old West or colonial times, look carefully at the small amount of capital around. Try to imagine how productive you would be in such circumstances compared with your productivity today.

### Investment in Human Capital

Human capital—the accumulated skill and knowledge of human beings—is the most fundamental source of economic growth. It is a source of both increased productivity and technological advance.

The development of one of the most basic human skills—writing—was the source of some of the earliest major gains in productivity. The ability to keep written records made it possible to reap ever-larger gains from specialization and exchange. Imagine how hard it would be to do any kind of business if all the accounts, invoices, and agreements existed only in people's memories.

Later, the development of mathematics laid the foundation for the eventual extension of knowledge about physical forces and chemical and biological processes. This base of scientific knowledge was the foundation for the technological advances of the Industrial Revolution 200 years ago and of today's information revolution.

But a lot of human capital that is extremely productive is much more humble. It takes the form of millions of individuals learning and repetitively doing simple production tasks and becoming remarkably more productive in those tasks.

One carefully studied example illustrates the importance of this kind of human capital. Between 1941 and 1944 (during World War II), U.S. shipyards produced some 2,500 units of a cargo ship, called the Liberty Ship, to a standardized design. In 1941, it took 1.2 million person-hours to build one ship. By 1942, it took 600,000 person-hours, and by 1943, it took only 500,000. Not much change occurred in the capital employed during these years. But an enormous amount of human capital was accumulated. Thousands of workers and managers learned from experience and accumulated human capital that more than doubled their productivity in two years.

### Discovery of New Technologies

Saving and investment in new capital and the accumulation of human capital have made a large contribution to economic growth. But technological change—the discovery and the application of new technologies and new goods—has made an even greater contribution.

People are many times more productive today than they were a hundred years ago. We are not more productive because we have more steam engines and more horse-drawn carriages per person. Rather, it is because we have engines and transportation equipment that use technologies that were unknown a hundred years ago and that are more productive than the old technologies were. Technological change makes an enormous contribution to our increased productivity. It arises from formal research and development programs and from informal trial and error, and it involves discovering new ways of getting more out of our resources.

To reap the benefits of technological change, capital must increase. Some of the most powerful and far-reaching fundamental technologies are embodied in human capital—for example, language, writing, and mathematics. But most technologies are embodied in physical capital. For example, to reap the benefits of the internal combustion engine, millions of horse-drawn carriages and horses had to be replaced by automobiles; more recently, to reap the benefits of computerized word processing, millions of typewriters had to be replaced by PCs and printers.

> **REVIEW QUIZ**
>
> 1 What economic activities that lead to economic growth do markets, property rights, and monetary exchange facilitate?
> 2 How do saving and investment in new capital, the growth of human capital, and the discovery of new technologies generate economic growth?
> 3 Provide some examples of how human capital has created new technologies that are embodied in both human and physical capital.

What is the quantitative contribution of the sources of economic growth? To answer this question, economists use growth accounting.

# Growth Accounting

You've seen that saving and investment in new capital, investment in human capital, and the discovery of new technologies bring economic growth. But how much does each of these sources of growth contribute? Knowing the answer to this question is crucial if we're going to understand the growth process and be able to achieve faster growth.

Edward F. Denison, an economist at the Brookings Institution, answered this question by developing **growth accounting**, a tool that calculates the quantitative contribution to real GDP growth of each of its sources.

The key tool of growth accounting is the aggregate production function, which is written as the equation:

$$Y = F(L, K, T)$$

In words, the real GDP, $Y$, is determined by (is a function $F$ of) the quantities of labor, $L$, and capital, $K$, and of the state of technology, $T$. The larger is $L$, $K$, or $T$, the greater is $Y$. And the faster $L$ and $K$ grow and the faster $T$ advances, the faster $Y$ grows.

Labor growth depends primarily on population growth. And the growth rate of capital and the pace of technological advance determine the growth rate of labor productivity.

## Labor Productivity

**Labor productivity** is real GDP per hour of labor. It is calculated by dividing real GDP by aggregate labor hours. That is, labor productivity equals $Y$ divided by $L$.

Labor productivity determines how much income an hour of labor generates. Figure 9.4 shows labor productivity for the period 1963–2003. Productivity growth was most rapid during the 1960s. It slowed down in 1973 and remained low for about 10 years. Productivity growth then speeded up again in what has been called the new economy of the 1990s.

Why did productivity grow fastest during the 1960s and late 1990s? Why did it slow down in 1973 and then speed up again after 1983?

Growth accounting answers these questions by dividing the growth in labor productivity into two components and then measuring the contribution of each. The components are

- Growth in capital per hour of labor
- Technological change

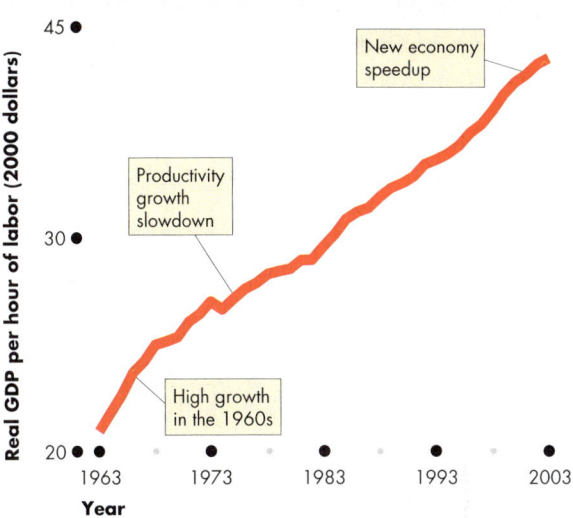

**FIGURE 9.4** Real GDP per Hour of Labor

Real GDP divided by aggregate hours equals real GDP per hour of labor, which is a broad measure of productivity. During the 1960s and late 1990s, the productivity growth rate was high. It slowed between 1973 and 1983.

*Sources*: Bureau of Economic Analysis, Bureau of Labor Statistics, and author's calculations.

Capital is physical capital. Technological change includes everything that contributes to labor productivity growth that is not included in growth in capital per hour. In particular, technological change includes human capital growth. Human capital growth and technological change are intimately related. Technology advances because knowledge advances. And knowledge is part of human capital. So "technological change" is a broad, catchall concept.

The analytical engine of growth accounting is a relationship called the productivity curve. Let's learn about this relationship and see how it is used.

## The Productivity Curve

The **productivity curve** is a relationship that shows how real GDP per hour of labor changes as the amount of capital per hour of labor changes with a given state of technology. Figure 9.5 illustrates the productivity curve. Capital per hour of labor is measured on the $x$-axis, and real GDP per hour of labor is measured on the *y*-axis. The figure shows *two* productivity curves. One is the curve labeled $PC_0$, and the other is the curve labeled $PC_1$.

An increase in the quantity of capital per hour of labor increases real GDP per hour of labor, which is shown by a movement along a productivity curve. For example, on $PC_0$, when capital per hour of labor is $30, real GDP per hour of labor is $20. If capital per hour of labor increases to $60, real GDP per hour of labor increases to $25.

Technological change increases the amount of GDP per hour of labor that can be produced by a given amount of capital per hour of labor. Technological change shifts the productivity curve upward. For example, if capital per hour of labor is $30 and a technological change increases real GDP per hour of labor from $20 to $25, the productivity curve shifts upward from $PC_0$ to $PC_1$ in Fig. 9.5. Similarly, if capital per hour of labor is $60, the same technological change increases real GDP per hour of labor from $25 to $32 and shifts the productivity curve upward from $PC_0$ to $PC_1$.

To calculate the contributions of capital growth and technological change to productivity growth, we need to know the shape of the productivity curve. The shape of the productivity curve reflects a fundamental economic law—the law of diminishing returns. The **law of diminishing returns** states that as the quantity of one input increases with the quantities of all other inputs remaining the same, output increases but by ever smaller increments. For example, in a factory that has a given amount of capital, as more labor is hired, production increases. But each *additional* hour of labor produces less *additional* output than the previous hour produced. Two typists working with one computer type fewer than twice as many pages per day as one typist working with one computer.

Applied to capital, the law of diminishing returns states that if a given number of hours of labor use more capital (with the same technology), the *additional* output that results from the *additional* capital gets smaller as the amount of capital increases. One typist working with two computers types fewer than twice as many pages per day as one typist working with one computer. More generally, one hour of labor working with $40 of capital produces less than twice the output of one hour of labor working with $20 of capital. But how much less? The answer is given by the *one third rule*.

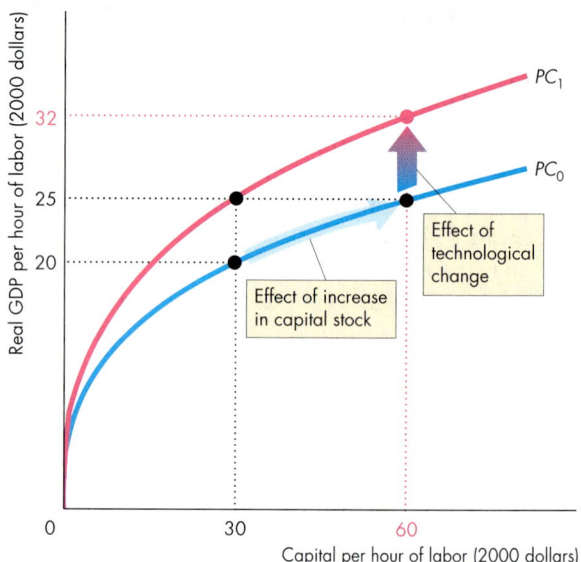

**FIGURE 9.5** How Productivity Grows

Productivity is measured by real GDP per hour of labor, and it can grow for two reasons: (1) Capital per hour of labor increases, and (2) technological advances occur. The productivity curve, $PC_0$, shows the effects of an increase in capital per hour of labor on productivity. Here, when capital per hour of labor increases from $30 to $60, real GDP per hour of labor increases from $20 to $25 along the productivity curve $PC_0$. Technological advance shifts the productivity curve upward. Here, an advance in technology shifts the productivity curve from $PC_0$ to $PC_1$. When capital per hour of labor is $60, real GDP per hour of labor increases from $25 to $32.

**The One Third Rule** Robert Solow of MIT estimated a U.S. productivity curve and discovered the **one third rule**, that on the average, with no change in technology, a 1 percent increase in capital per hour of labor brings a *one third of 1 percent* increase in real GDP per hour of labor. This one third rule is used to calculate the contributions of an increase in capital per hour of labor and technological change to the growth of real GDP. Let's do such a calculation.

Suppose that capital per hour of labor grows by 3 percent a year and real GDP per hour of labor grows by 2.5 percent a year. The one third rule tells us that capital growth has contributed one third of

3 percent, which is 1 percent. The rest of the 2.5 percent growth of real GDP per hour of labor comes from technological change. That is, technological change has contributed 1.5 percent, which is the 2.5 percent growth of real GDP per hour of labor minus the estimated 1 percent contribution of capital growth.

## Accounting for the Productivity Growth Slowdown and Speedup

We can use the one third rule to study U.S. productivity growth and the productivity growth slowdown. Figure 9.6 tells the story, starting in 1963.

**Booming Sixties** In 1963, the economy was at the point marked 63 on $PC_0$. During the next 10 years, the growth of capital per hour of labor moved the economy to point $A$ on $PC_0$ and rapid technological change shifted the productivity curve upward to $PC_1$, so the economy moved to the point marked 73.

**Slowdown** From 1973 to 1983, growth of capital per hour of labor moved the economy to point $B$ on $PC_1$ and a tiny contribution from technological change shifted the productivity curve upward to $PC_2$. The economy moved to the point marked 83.

The contribution of capital growth was almost the same after 1973 as it had been during the 1960s, and the productivity growth slowdown occurred because the contribution of technological change to real GDP growth slowed.

**Speedup** From 1983 to 1993, growth of capital per hour of labor moved the economy to point $C$ on $PC_2$, and a return of rapid technological change shifted the productivity curve upward to $PC_3$. The economy moved to the point marked 93.

**New Economy** From 1993 to 2003, growth of capital per hour of labor moved the economy to point $D$ on $PC_3$ and continued rapid technological change shifted the productivity curve upward to $PC_4$. The economy moved to the point marked 03.

The speedup in the growth rate and the new economy of the 1990s, like the slowdown of the 1970s, came from the contribution of technological change, not from the growth of capital. But the "new economy" of the 1990s was not so new after all. The growth rate of the 1990s, while more rapid than the 1970s and 1980s, still lagged that of the 1960s.

**FIGURE 9.6** Growth Accounting and the Productivity Changes

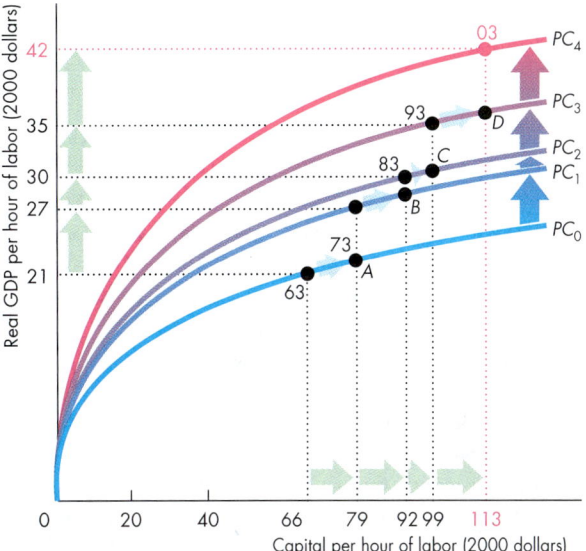

(a) The shifting productivity curve

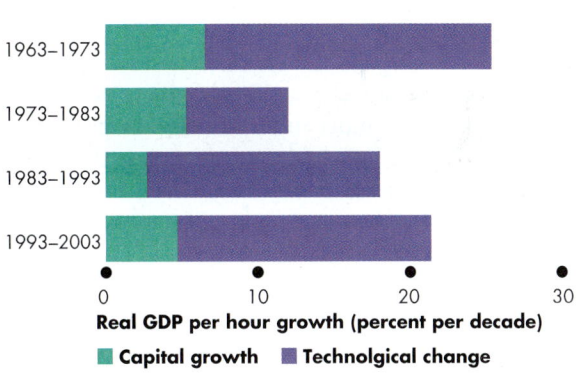

(b) The sources of growth

Part (a) shows the productivity curve each decade between 1963 and 2003. The points labeled 63, 73, 83, 93, and 03 show the actual levels of capital per hour of labor and real GDP per hour of labor. The points labeled $A$, $B$, $C$, and $D$ show where the economy would have moved to if there had been no technological change.

Part (b) shows the contributions of capital growth and technological change. Growth from technological change slowed between 1973 and 1983 and then speeded up. But the growth of the 1990s did not return to the rate of the 1960s.

*Sources:* Bureau of Economic Analysis, Bureau of Labor Statistics, and the author's calculations.

## Technological Change During the Productivity Growth Slowdown

Technological change did not stop during the productivity growth slowdown. But its focus changed from increasing productivity to coping with

- Energy price shocks
- The environment

**Energy Price Shocks** Energy price increases that occurred in 1973–1974 and in 1979–1980 diverted research efforts toward saving energy rather than increasing productivity. Airplanes became more fuel efficient, but they didn't operate with smaller crews. Real GDP per gallon of fuel increased faster, but real GDP per hour of labor increased more slowly.

**The Environment** The 1970s saw an expansion of laws and resources devoted to protecting the environment and improving the quality of the workplace. The benefits of these actions—cleaner air and water and safer factories—are not counted as real GDP. So the growth of these benefits is not measured as part of productivity growth.

## Achieving Faster Growth

Growth accounting tells us that to achieve faster economic growth, we must either increase the growth rate of capital per hour of labor or increase the pace of technological advance (which includes improving human capital). The main suggestions for achieving these objectives are

- Stimulate saving
- Stimulate research and development
- Target high-technology industries
- Encourage international trade
- Improve the quality of education

**Stimulate Saving** Saving finances investment, which brings capital accumulation. So stimulating saving can stimulate economic growth. The East Asian economies have the highest growth rates and the highest saving rates. Some African economies have the lowest growth rates and the lowest saving rates.

Tax incentives can increase saving. Individual Retirement Accounts (IRAs) are a tax incentive to save. Economists claim that a tax on consumption rather than income provides the best saving incentive.

**Stimulate Research and Development** Everyone can use the fruits of *basic* research and development efforts. For example, all biotechnology firms can use advances in gene-splicing technology. Because basic inventions can be copied, the inventor's profit is limited, and the market allocates too few resources to this activity.

Governments can direct public funds toward financing basic research, but this solution is not foolproof. It requires a mechanism for allocating the public funds to their highest-valued use. The National Science Foundation is one possibly efficient channel for allocating public funds to universities to finance and stimulate basic research.

**Target High-Technology Industries** Some people say that by providing public funds to high-technology firms and industries, a country can become the first to exploit a new technology and can earn above-average profits for a period while others are busy catching up. This strategy is risky and just as likely to use resources inefficiently as to speed growth.

**Encourage International Trade** Free international trade stimulates growth by extracting all the available gains from specialization and exchange. The fastest-growing nations today are those with the fastest-growing exports and imports.

**Improve the Quality of Education** The free market produces too little education because it brings benefits beyond those valued by the people who receive the education. By funding basic education and by ensuring high standards in basic skills such as language, mathematics, and science, governments can contribute to a nation's growth potential. Education can also be stimulated and improved by using tax incentives to encourage improved private provision.

### REVIEW QUIZ

1 List some examples of scarcity in the United States today.
2 Use the headlines in today's news to provide some examples of scarcity around the world.
3 Use today's news to illustrate the distinction between microeconomics and macroeconomics.

# Growth Theories

We've seen that real GDP grows when the quantities of labor and capital (which includes human capital) grow and when technology advances. Does this mean that the growth of labor and capital and technological advances *cause* economic growth? It might. But there are other possibilities. *One* of these factors might be the cause of real GDP growth, and the others might be the *effect*. We must try to discover how the influences on economic growth interact with each other to make some economies grow quickly and others grow slowly. And we must probe the reasons why a country's long-term growth rate sometimes speeds up and sometimes slows down.

Growth theories are designed to study the interactions among the several factors that contribute to growth and to disentangle cause and effect. They are also designed to enable us to study the way the different factors influence each other.

Growth theories are also designed to be universal. They are not theories about the growth of only poor countries or rich countries. They are theories about why and how poor countries become rich and rich countries continue to get richer.

We're going to study three theories of economic growth, each of which gives some insights into the process of economic growth. But none provides a definite answer to the basic questions: What causes economic growth and why do growth rates vary? Economics has some way to go before it can provide a definite answer to these questions. The three growth theories we study are

- Classical growth theory
- Neoclassical growth theory
- New growth theory

## Classical Growth Theory

**Classical growth theory** is the view that real GDP growth is temporary and that when real GDP per person rises above the subsistence level, a population explosion eventually brings real GDP per person back to the subsistence level. Adam Smith, Thomas Robert Malthus, and David Ricardo, the leading economists of the late eighteenth century and early nineteenth century, proposed this theory, but the view is most closely associated with the name of Malthus and is sometimes called the *Malthusian theory*.

Many people today are Malthusians! They say that if today's global population of 6.2 billion explodes to 11 billion by 2200, we will run out of resources and return to a primitive standard of living. We must act, say the Malthusians, to contain the population growth.

**The Basic Classical Idea** To understand classical growth theory, let's transport ourselves back to the world of 1776, when Adam Smith is first explaining the idea. Most of the 2.5 million people who live in the newly independent United States of America work on farms or on their own land and perform their tasks using simple tools and animal power. They earn an average of 2 shillings (a bit less than 12 dollars in today's money) for working a 10-hour day.

Then advances in farming technology bring new types of plows and seeds that increase farm productivity. As farm productivity increases, farm production increases and some farm workers move from the land to the cities, where they get work producing and selling the expanding range of farm equipment. Incomes rise, and the people seem to be prospering. But will the prosperity last? Classical growth theory says it will not.

Advances in technology—in both agriculture and industry—lead to an investment in new capital, which makes labor more productive. More and more businesses start up and hire the now more productive labor. The greater demand for labor raises the real wage rate and increases employment.

At this stage, economic growth has occurred and everyone has benefited from it. Real GDP has increased, and the real wage rate has increased. But the classical economists believe that this new situation can't last because it will induce a population explosion.

**Classical Theory of Population Growth** When the classical economists were developing their ideas about population growth, an unprecedented population explosion was under way. In Britain and other Western European countries, improvements in diet and hygiene had lowered the death rate while the birth rate remained high. For several decades, population growth was extremely rapid. For example, after being relatively stable for several centuries, the population of Britain increased by 40 percent between 1750 and 1800 and by a further 50 percent between 1800 and 1830. Meanwhile, an estimated 1 million people (about 20 percent of the 1750 population) left Britain for America and Australia before 1800, and outward migration continued on a similar scale through the nineteenth century. These facts are the empirical basis for the classical theory of population growth.

To explain the high rate of population growth, the classical economists used the idea of a **subsistence real wage rate**, which is the minimum real wage rate needed to maintain life. If the actual real wage rate is less than the subsistence real wage rate, some people cannot survive and the population decreases. In classical theory, when the real wage rate exceeds the subsistence real wage rate, the population grows. But a rising population brings diminishing returns to labor. So labor productivity eventually decreases. This dismal implication led to economics being called the *dismal science*. The dismal implication is that no matter how much technological change occurs, real wage rates are always pushed back toward the subsistence level.

### Classical Theory and the Productivity Curve

Figure 9.7 illustrates the classical growth theory using the productivity curve. Initially, the productivity curve is $PC_0$. Subsistence real GDP is $20 an hour, shown by the horizontal line in the graph. The economy starts out at point A, with $60 of capital per hour of labor and $20 of real GDP per hour of labor, the subsistence level. Because real GDP is at the subsistence level, the population is constant.

Then a technological advance occurs, which shifts the productivity curve upward to $PC_1$. The economy now moves to point B on $PC_1$, and real GDP per hour of labor rises to $30. Now earning more than the subsistence wage, people have more children and live longer. The population grows.

A growing population means that labor hours grow, so capital per hour of labor falls. As capital per hour of labor falls, there is a movement down along the productivity curve $PC_1$. Real GDP per hour of labor falls and keeps falling as long as the population grows and capital per hour of labor falls.

This process ends when real GDP per hour of labor is back at the subsistence level at point C on productivity curve $PC_1$. The population stops growing and capital per hour of labor stops falling.

Repeated advances in technology play out in the same way as the advance that we've just studied. No matter how productive our economy becomes, population growth lowers capital per hour of labor and drives real GDP per hour of labor toward the subsistence level. Living standards temporarily improve while the population is expanding, but when the

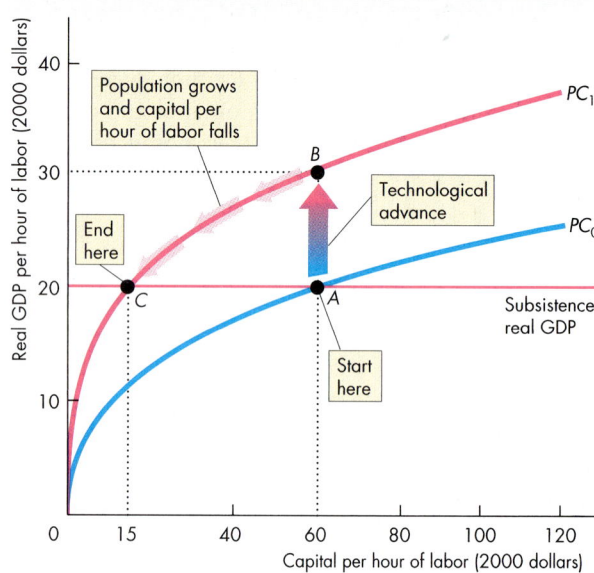

**FIGURE 9.7** Classical Growth Theory

The economy starts out at point A with capital per hour of labor of $60 and real GDP per hour of labor of $20—the subsistence level—on productivity curve $PC_0$. A technological advance increases productivity and shifts the productivity curve upward to $PC_1$. The economy moves to point B. The population now grows, and both capital and real GDP per hour of labor fall. The process ends at point C when real GDP per hour of labor is back at its subsistence level.

population expansion ends, the standard of living is back at the subsistence level.

### Classical Theory and Capital Accumulation
In the story you've just worked through, the total quantity of capital didn't change. Suppose that people save and invest, so capital grows. Doesn't a growing quantity of capital prevent the dismal conclusion of classical theory? It does not. *Anything* that raises real GDP per hour of labor above the subsistence level triggers a population explosion that eventually wipes out the gains from greater productivity.

The dismal conclusion of classical growth theory is a direct consequence of the assumption that the population explodes if real GDP per hour of labor exceeds the subsistence level. To avoid this conclusion, we need a different view of population growth.

The neoclassical growth theory that we'll now study provides a different view.

## Neoclassical Growth Theory

**Neoclassical growth theory** is the proposition that that real GDP per person grows because technological change induces a level of saving and investment that makes capital per hour of labor grow. Growth ends only if technological change stops.

Robert Solow of MIT suggested the most popular version of neoclassical growth theory in the 1950s. But Frank Ramsey of Cambridge University in England first developed this theory in the 1920s.

Neoclassical theory's big break with its classical predecessor is its view about population growth. So we'll begin our account of neoclassical theory by examining its views about population growth.

### The Neoclassical Economics of Population Growth
The population explosion of eighteenth century Europe that created the classical theory of population eventually ended. The birth rate fell, and while the population continued to increase, its rate of increase became moderate. This slowdown in population growth seemed to make the classical theory less relevant. It also eventually led to the development of a modern economic theory of population growth.

The modern view is that although the population growth rate is influenced by economic factors, the influence is not a simple and mechanical one like that proposed by the classical economists. Key among the economic influences on population growth is the opportunity cost of a woman's time. As women's wage rates increase and their job opportunities expand, the opportunity cost of having children increases. Faced with a higher opportunity cost, families choose to have fewer children and the birth rate falls.

A second economic influence works on the death rate. The technological advance that brings increased productivity and increased incomes brings advances in health care that extends lives.

These two opposing economic forces influence the population growth rate. As incomes increase, both the birth rate and the death rate decrease. It turns out that these opposing forces almost offset each other, so the rate of population growth is independent of the rate of economic growth.

This modern view of population growth and the historical trends that support it contradict the views of the classical economists. They also call into question the modern doomsday conclusion that the planet will one day be swamped with too many people to feed.

Neoclassical growth theory adopts this modern view of population growth. Forces other than real GDP and its growth rate determine population growth.

### Technological Change
In the neoclassical theory, the rate of technological change influences the rate of economic growth but economic growth does not influence the pace of technological change. It is assumed that technological change results from chance. When we get lucky, we have rapid technological change, and when bad luck strikes, the pace of technological advance slows.

### Target Rate of Return and Saving
The key assumption in the neoclassical growth theory concerns saving. Other things remaining the same, the higher the real interest rate, the greater is the amount that people save. To decide how much to save, people compare the real interest rate with a *target rate of return*. If the real interest rate exceeds the target rate of return, saving is sufficient to make capital per hour of labor grow. If the target rate of return exceeds the real interest rate, saving is not sufficient to maintain the current level of capital per hour of labor, so capital per hour of labor shrinks. And if the real interest rate equals a target rate of return, saving is just sufficient to maintain the quantity of capital per hour of labor at its current level.

### The Basic Neoclassical Idea
To understand neoclassical growth theory, imagine the world of the mid-1950s, when Robert Solow is explaining his idea. Americans are enjoying post–World War II prosperity. Income per person is around $12,000 a year in today's money. The population is growing at about 1 percent a year. People are saving and investing about 20 percent of their incomes, enough to keep the quantity of capital per hour of labor constant. Income per person is growing, but not by much.

Then technology begins to advance at a more rapid pace across a range of activities. The transistor revolutionizes an emerging electronics industry. New plastics revolutionize the manufacture of household appliances. The interstate highway system revolutionizes road transportation. Jet airliners start to replace piston-engine airplanes and speed air transportation.

These technological advances bring new profit opportunities. Businesses expand, and new businesses are created to exploit the newly available profitable technologies. Investment and saving increase. The economy enjoys new levels of prosperity and growth. But will the prosperity last? And will the growth last? Neoclassical growth theory says that the *prosperity* will last but the *growth* will not last unless technology keeps advancing.

According to the neoclassical growth theory, the prosperity will persist because there is no classical population growth to induce lower wages.

But growth will stop if technology stops advancing, for two related reasons. First, high profit rates that result from technological change bring increased saving and capital accumulation. But second, capital accumulation eventually results in diminishing returns that lower the real interest rate, and that eventually decrease saving and slow the rate of capital accumulation.

**Neoclassical Theory and the Productivity Curve**
Figure 9.8 illustrates the neoclassical growth theory. Initially, the productivity curve is $PC_0$ and the economy is at point $A$, with $60 of capital per hour of labor and real GDP of $20 an hour.

The slope of the productivity curve measures the real interest rate. If the quantity of capital is small, the productivity curve is steep and the real interest rate is high. If the quantity of capital is large, the productivity curve is less steep and the real interest rate is low. A straight line with a slope equal to the target rate of return illustrates the target rate of return.

At point $A$ on productivity curve $PC_0$, the slope of the productivity curve equals the slope of the target rate of return line. If the quantity of capital per hour of labor were less than $60, the real interest rate would exceed the target rate of return and capital per hour of labor would grow. If the quantity of capital per hour of labor were greater than $60, the real interest rate would be less than the target rate of return and capital per hour of labor would shrink. But when the quantity of capital per hour of labor is $60, the real interest rate equals the target rate of return and capital per hour of labor is constant.

Now a technological advance occurs that shifts the productivity curve upward to $PC_1$. The economy now moves to point $B$ on $PC_1$, and real GDP per hour of labor rises to $30. It is at this point in the classical theory that forces kick in to drive real GDP back to the subsistence level. But in the neoclassical theory, no such forces operate. Instead, at point $B$, the real interest rate exceeds the target rate of return. (You can see why by comparing the slopes of $PC_1$ at

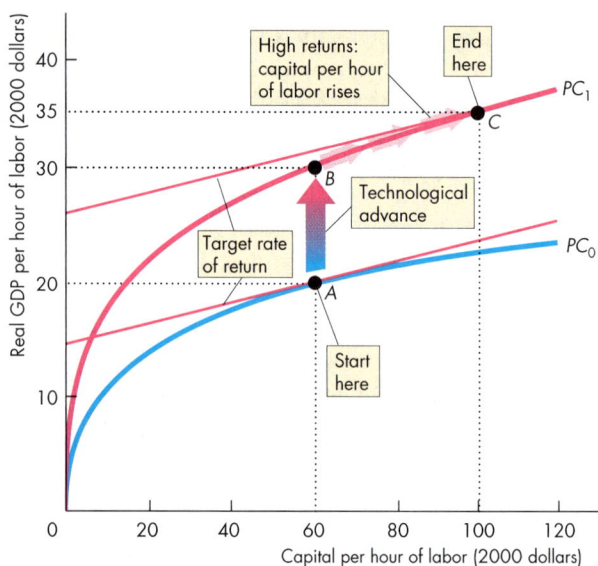

**FIGURE 9.8    Neoclassical Growth Theory**

The economy starts on productivity curve $PC_0$ at point $A$. The slope of the productivity curve measures the real interest rate, so at point $A$ the real interest rate equals the target rate of return.

A technological advance shifts the productivity curve upward to $PC_1$ and the economy moves to point $B$. The real interest rate exceeds the target rate of return, and the quantity of capital per hour of labor rises—a movement up along the productivity curve $PC_1$. Growth ends when the real interest rate again equals the target rate of return at point $C$.

point $B$ and the target rate of return line.)

With a high real interest rate available, saving and investment increase and the quantity of capital per hour of labor rises. There is a movement up along the productivity curve $PC_1$, and real GDP per hour of labor increases.

This growth process eventually ends because, as the quantity of capital per hour of labor increases, the real interest rate falls. At point $C$, where the process ends, the real interest rate again equals the target rate of return.

Throughout the process you've just studied, real GDP per hour of labor grows but the growth rate gradually decreases and growth eventually ends.

But if another advance in technology occurs, the

process you've just seen repeats. Ongoing advances in technology constantly increase the real interest rate, inducing the saving that increases capital per hour of labor. The growth process persists as long as technology advances. And the growth rate fluctuates because technological progress occurs at a variable rate.

### A Problem with Neoclassical Growth Theory

All economies have access to the same technologies, and capital is free to roam the globe seeking the highest available real interest rate. Given these facts, neoclassical growth theory implies that growth rates and income levels per person around the globe will converge. While there is some sign of convergence among the rich countries, as Fig. 9.2(a) shows, convergence is slow, and it does not appear to be imminent for all countries, as Fig. 9.2(b) shows.

New growth theory attempts to overcome this shortcoming of neoclassical growth theory. It also attempts to explain how the rate of technological change is determined.

### New Growth Theory

**New growth theory** holds that real GDP per person grows because of the choices people make in the pursuit of profit and that growth can persist indefinitely. Paul Romer of Stanford University developed this theory during the 1980s, but the ideas go back to work by Joseph Schumpeter during the 1930s and 1940s.

The theory begins with two facts about market economies:

- Discoveries result from choices.
- Discoveries bring profit and competition destroys profit.

**Discoveries and Choices** When people discover a new product or technique, they think of themselves as being lucky. They are right. But the pace at which new discoveries are made—and at which technology advances—is not determined by chance. It depends on how many people are looking for a new technology and how intensively they are looking.

**Discoveries and Profits** Profit is the spur to technological change. The forces of competition squeeze profits, so to increase profit, people constantly seek either lower-cost methods of production or new and better products for which people are willing to pay a higher price. Inventors can maintain a profit for several years by taking out a patent or copyright. But eventually, a new discovery is copied, and profits disappear.

Two further facts play a key role in the new growth theory:

- Discoveries are a public capital good.
- Knowledge is capital that is not subject to the law of diminishing returns.

**Discoveries Are a Public Capital Good** Economists call a good a *public good* when no one can be excluded from using it and when one person's use does not prevent others from using it. National defense is one example of a public good. Knowledge is another.

When in 1992, Marc Andreesen and his friend Eric Bina developed a browser they called Mosaic, they laid the foundation for Netscape Navigator and Internet Explorer, two pieces of capital that have increased productivity unimaginably.

While patents and copyrights protect the inventors or creators of new products and production processes and enable them to reap the returns from their innovative ideas, once a new discovery has been made, everyone can benefit from its use. And one person's use of a new discovery does not prevent others from using it. Your use of a Web browser doesn't prevent someone else from using that same code simultaneously.

Because knowledge is a public good, as the benefits of a new discovery spread, free resources become available. These resources are free because nothing is given up when they are used. They have a zero opportunity cost. Knowledge is even more special because it is not subject to diminishing returns.

**Knowledge Capital Is Not Subject to Diminishing Returns** Production is subject to diminishing returns when one resource is fixed and the quantity of another resource changes. Adding labor to a fixed amount of equipment, or adding equipment to a fixed amount of labor both bring diminishing marginal product—diminishing returns.

But increasing the stock of knowledge makes labor and machines more productive. Knowledge capital does not bring diminishing returns.

The fact that knowledge capital does *not* experience diminishing returns is the central novel proposition of the new growth theory. And the implication of this simple and appealing idea is astonishing. Unlike the other two theories, the new growth theory has no growth-stopping mechanism. As physical capital accumulates, the real interest rate falls. But the incentive to innovate and earn a higher profit becomes stronger. So innovation occurs, which increases the real interest rate. Real GDP per hour of labor grows indefinitely as people find new technologies that yield a higher real interest rate.

The growth rate depends on people's ability to innovate and the real interest rate. Over the years, the ability to innovate has changed. The invention of language and writing (the two most basic human capital tools) and later the development of the scientific method and the establishment of universities and research institutions brought huge increases in the real interest rate. Today, a deeper understanding of genes is bringing profit in a growing biotechnology industry. And advances in computer technology are creating an explosion of profit opportunities in a wide range of information age industries.

### New Growth Theory and the Productivity Curve

Figure 9.9 illustrates new growth theory. Like Fig. 9.8, which illustrates neoclassical growth theory, Fig. 9.9 contains a productivity curve and a target rate of return curve.

But unlike in neoclassical theory, in the new growth theory, the productivity curve never stands still. The pursuit of profit means that technology is always advancing and human capital is always growing. The result is an ever upward-shifting productivity curve. As physical capital is accumulated, diminishing returns lower its rate of return. But ever-advancing productivity counteracts this tendency and keeps the rate of return above the target rate of return.

Advancing technology and human capital growth keep the productivity curve shifting upward from $PC_0$ to $PC_1$ to $PC_2$ and beyond. As the productivity curve shifts upward, capital and real GDP per hour of labor rise together along the line labeled as the $Ak$ line in the figure.

The new growth theory implies that although the productivity curve shows diminishing returns, if capital is interpreted more broadly as physical capital, human capital, and the technologies they embody, then real GDP per hour of labor grows at the same rate as the growth in capital per hour of labor. Real GDP per hour of labor is proportional to capital per hour of labor.

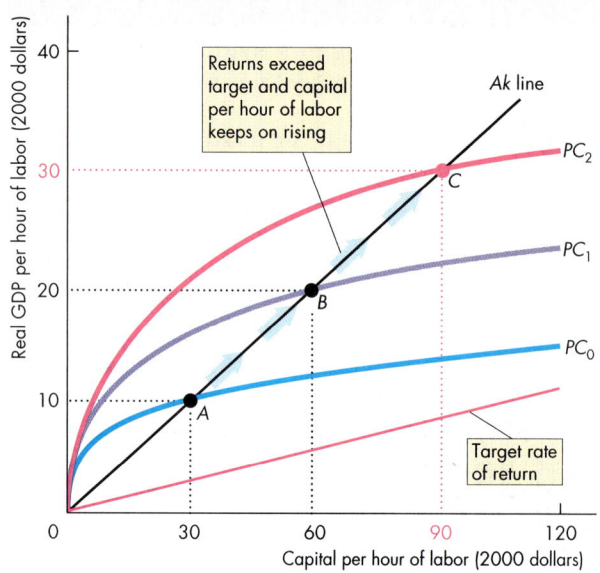

**FIGURE 9.9** New Growth Theory

In new growth theory, economic growth results from incentives to innovate and from capital that does not experience diminishing returns. The productivity curve, PC, keeps shifting upward, and real GDP per hour of labor and capital per hour of labor grow along the $Ak$ line.

Capital is $k$, real GDP is $y$, and real GDP is related to capital by the equation:

$$y = Ak.$$

In Fig. 9.9, $A = (1/3)$. When capital per hour of labor is $30, real GDP per hour of labor is $10 at point A. People look for yet more profit and accumulate yet more capital. The economy expands to point B, with capital per hour of labor of $60 and real GDP per hour of labor of $20. In pursuit of further profit, technology keeps advancing and capital per hour of labor rises to $90 with real GDP per hour of labor of $30, at point C. Real GDP per hour of labor and capital per hour of labor increase without limit.

**A Perpetual Motion Economy** The new growth theory sees the economy as a perpetual motion machine, which Fig. 9.10 illustrates. Insatiable wants lead us to pursue profit, innovate, and create new and better products. New firms start up and old firms go out of business. As firms start up and die, jobs are

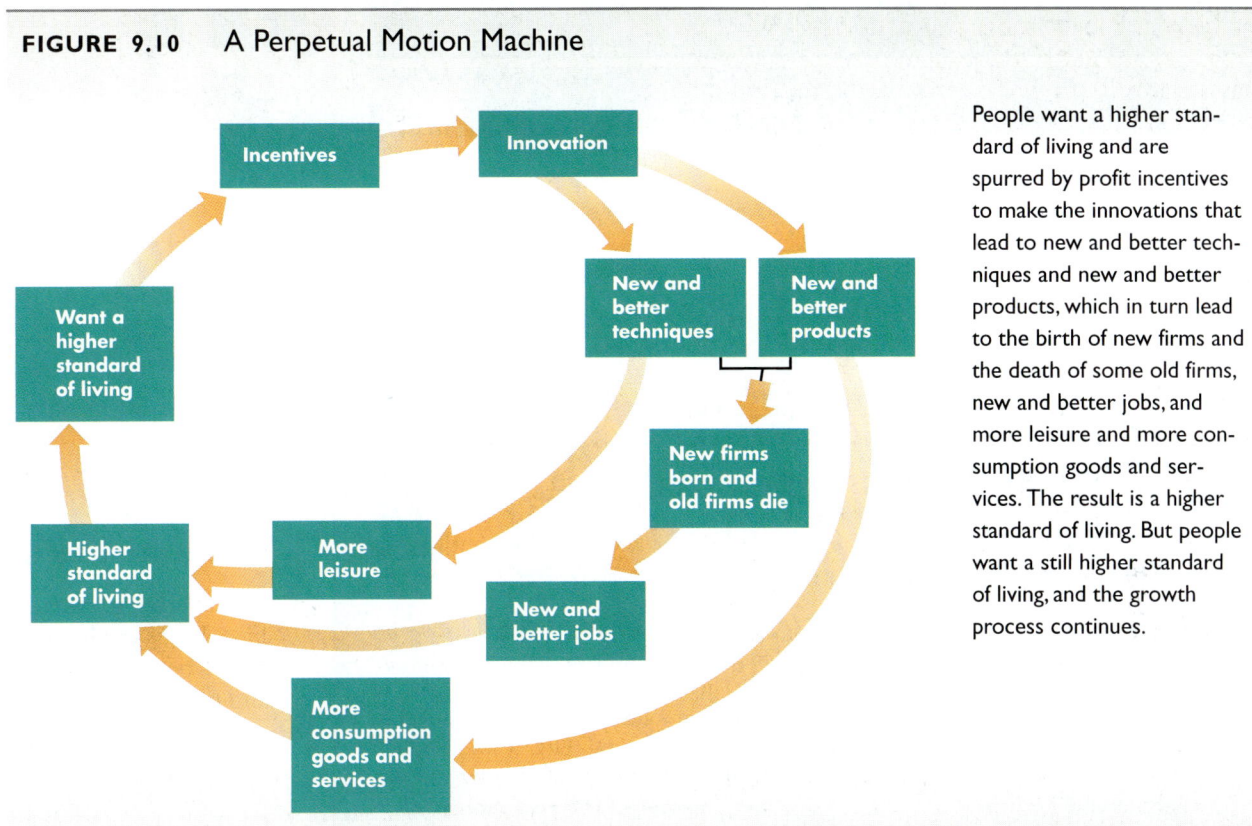

FIGURE 9.10  A Perpetual Motion Machine

People want a higher standard of living and are spurred by profit incentives to make the innovations that lead to new and better techniques and new and better products, which in turn lead to the birth of new firms and the death of some old firms, new and better jobs, and more leisure and more consumption goods and services. The result is a higher standard of living. But people want a still higher standard of living, and the growth process continues.

Source: Based on a similar figure in *These Are the Good Old Days: A Report on U.S. Living Standards*, Federal Reserve Bank of Dallas 1993 Annual Report.

created and destroyed. New and better jobs lead to more leisure and more consumption. But our insatiable wants are still there, so the process continues, going round and round a circle of wants, profits, innovation, and new products.

### Sorting Out the Theories

Which theory is correct? Probably none, but they all teach us something of value. The classical theory reminds us that our physical resources are limited and that with no advances in technology, we must eventually hit diminishing returns. Neoclassical theory reaches the same conclusion, but not because of a population explosion. Instead, it emphasizes diminishing returns to capital and reminds us that we cannot keep growth going just by accumulating physical capital. We must also advance technology and accumulate human capital. We must become more creative in our use of scarce resources. New growth theory emphasizes the possible capacity of human resources to innovate at a pace that offsets diminishing returns.

### REVIEW QUIZ

1  What is the key idea of classical growth theory that leads to the dismal outcome?
2  What, according to the neoclassical growth theory, is the fundamental cause of economic growth?
3  What is the key proposition of the new growth theory that makes growth persist?

◆ Economic growth is the single most decisive factor influencing a country's living standard. But another is the extent to which the country fully employs its scarce resources. In the next part, we study economic fluctuations and recessions. But before embarking on this new topic, take a look at *Reading Between the Lines* on pp. 222–223 and see how economic growth is transforming the economy of China.

# READING BETWEEN THE LINES

**POLICY WATCH**

## *Economic Growth in Asia*

### ADB sees higher East Asia economic growth in 2003

East Asian economies will grow 6.1 percent this year and 6.6 percent in 2004 on the back of an improving external environment and strong domestic demand, according to the Asian Development Bank (ADB)'s Asia Economic Monitor (AEM) released Thursday.

The new forecast for 2003 represents a 0.5 percentage point upgrade from the AEM's July forecast of 5.6 percent growth. The new forecast for 2004 is up 0.3 percentage point from the July estimate, the report said.

...

China's economy is an increasingly important engine of East Asian growth. Economies in the region are benefiting from the sharp third-quarter rebound of China's economy after the outbreak of severe acute respiratory syndrome, or SARS, and the consequent increase in imports, according to the report.

"The last two years have seen a surge in production and trade integration between the PRC (the People's Republic of China) and the rest of East Asia," it notes. "The PRC has emerged as a center for global production networks and a market for exports of specialized components and other intermediate inputs. The PRC's importance as the driver of intra-regional trade is increasing."

Powered by strong fixed investment, steady private consumption, and a vibrant export sector, China's GDP is forecast to grow 8.5 percent this year, up a full percentage point from the July estimate, and 7.9 percent in 2004, according to the AEM. ...

www.chinaview.cn
December 11, 2003

### Essence of the Story

■ Real GDP growth in East Asia is predicted to be 6.1 percent in 2003 and 6.6 percent in 2004.

■ The Asian economies are benefiting from China's rebound from the effects of SARS.

■ China has strong fixed investment, steady private consumption, and a vibrant export sector, and it is forecast to grow by 8.5 percent in 2003 and 7.9 percent in 2004.

■ China's economy is an engine of East Asian growth because it has extensive trade links with the other Asian economies.

## Economic Analysis

■ Starting around 1983, China began to open up its economy to international investment and trade and permitted its citizens to seek graduate education abroad.

■ At the same time, private enterprise increasingly replaced state-owned enterprise as the method of production.

■ Although it is a stretch, let's assume that the productivity curve in China after 1983 became the same as that in the United States.

■ Using this assumption, Fig. 1 shows the positions of China and the United States on the productivity curves for 1983 and 2003.

■ In 1983, the United States had $92 of capital per hour of labor and produced $30 of real GDP per hour of labor.

■ By 2003, the United States had $113 of capital per hour of labor and produced $42 of real GDP per hour of labor. Capital per hour of labor had increased by 23 percent, and real GDP per hour of labor had increased by 40 percent.

■ China is too far behind the United States to see the changes in China in Fig. 1.

■ But Fig. 2 zooms in on China and shows the incredibly large changes that have occurred in that economy.

■ In 1983, China had 3 cents of capital per hour of labor and produced $2 of real GDP per hour of labor. (The values are in 2000 U.S. dollars.)

■ By 2003, China had 40 cents of capital per hour of labor and produced $6.25 of real GDP per hour of labor. Capital per hour of labor had increased by 1,500 percent, and real GDP per hour of labor had increased by 152 percent.

■ These data for China in 2003 are based on official Chinese statistics. Some scholars think that the official data exaggerate China's real GDP and growth rate.

■ Based on the official data, China is converging on the United States but has a long way to go. At the current rate of convergence, real GDP per person will be equal in the two countries in the mid-2040s.

■ But the population of China is 4.5 times that of the United States, so at current growth rates, the two countries will have the same real GDP in 2010.

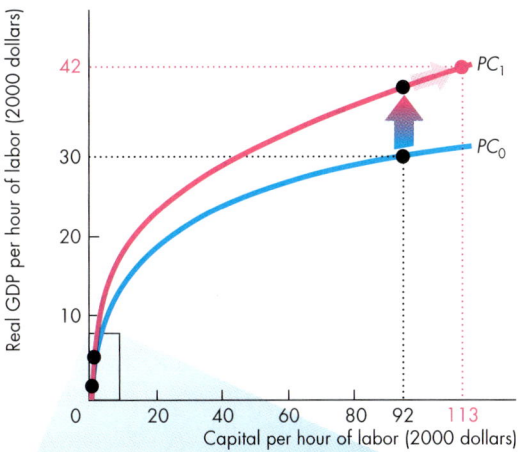

**Figure 1 Productivity curves in China and the United States**

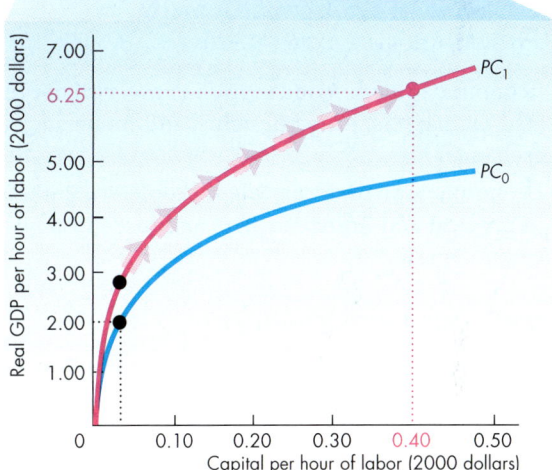

**Figure 2 Zoom in on the productivity curves in China**

■ After 2010, China will have the world's largest economy, and it will become larger every year.

## You're The Voter

■ Do you think the United States can learn any lessons from China to make the U.S. economy grow faster?

■ What effects do you think the Chinese policies described in the news article will have on China's growth rate?

■ Can you think of any tax reforms that might increase the U.S. growth rate? Would you vote for these reforms? Why or why not?

# SUMMARY

## KEY POINTS

### Long-Term Growth Trends (pp. 206–208)

- Between 1903 and 2003, real GDP per person in the United States grew at an average rate of 2 percent a year. Growth was rapid during the 1960s and late 1990s.
- The real GDP gap between the United States and Central and South America has persisted. The gaps between the United States and Hong Kong, Korea, Taiwan, and China have narrowed. The gaps between the United States and Africa and Central Europe have widened.

### The Causes of Economic Growth: A First Look (pp. 209–210)

- Economic growth requires an *incentive* system created by markets, property rights, and monetary exchange.
- Economic growth occurs when people save, invest in physical and human capital, and discover new technologies.

### Growth Accounting (pp. 211–214)

- Growth accounting measures the contributions of capital accumulation and technological change to productivity growth.
- Growth accounting uses the productivity curve and the one third rule: A 1 percent increase in capital per hour of labor brings a one third of 1 percent increase in real GDP per hour of labor.
- During the productivity growth slowdown of the 1970s, technological change made no contribution to real GDP growth.
- It might be possible to achieve faster growth by stimulating saving, stimulating research and development, targeting high-technology industries, encouraging more international trade, and improving the quality of education.

### Growth Theories (pp. 215–221)

- In classical theory, when a technological advance increases real GDP per person above the *subsistence* level, a population explosion brings diminishing returns to labor and real GDP per person returns to the subsistence level.
- In neoclassical growth theory, when a technological advance increases saving and investment, an increase in the capital stock brings diminishing returns to capital and eventually, without further technological change, the capital stock and real GDP per person stop growing.
- In new growth theory, when technological advances increase saving and investment, an increase in the capital stock *does not* bring diminishing returns to capital and growth persists indefinitely.

## KEY FIGURES

Figure 9.1   A Hundred Years of Economic Growth in the United States, 206
Figure 9.5   How Productivity Grows, 212
Figure 9.6   Growth Accounting and the Productivity Changes, 213
Figure 9.7   Classical Growth Theory, 216
Figure 9.8   Neoclassical Growth Theory, 218
Figure 9.9   New Growth Theory, 220

## KEY TERMS

Classical growth theory, 215
Growth accounting, 211
Labor productivity, 211
Law of diminishing returns, 212
Neoclassical growth theory, 217
New growth theory, 219
One third rule, 212
Productivity curve, 211
Subsistence real wage rate, 216

# PROBLEMS

*1. The following information has been discovered about the economy of Longland. The economy's productivity curve is

| Capital per hour of labor (2000 dollars per hour) | Real GDP per hour of labor (2000 dollars per hour) |
|---|---|
| 10 | 3.80 |
| 20 | 5.70 |
| 30 | 7.13 |
| 40 | 8.31 |
| 50 | 9.35 |
| 60 | 10.29 |
| 70 | 11.14 |
| 80 | 11.94 |

Does this economy conform to the one third rule? If so, explain why. If not, explain why not and explain what rule, if any, it does conform to. Explain how you would do the growth accounting for this economy.

2. The following information has been discovered about the economy of Flatland. The economy's productivity curve is

| Capital per hour of labor (2000 dollars per hour) | Real GDP per hour of labor (2000 dollars per hour) |
|---|---|
| 20 | 6.00 |
| 40 | 7.50 |
| 60 | 8.44 |
| 80 | 9.14 |
| 100 | 9.72 |
| 120 | 10.20 |
| 140 | 10.62 |
| 160 | 11.00 |

Does this economy conform to the one third rule? If so, explain why. If not, explain why not and explain what rule, if any, it does conform to. Explain how you would do the growth accounting for this economy.

*3. In Longland, described in problem 1, capital per hour of labor in 1999 was $40 and real GDP per hour of labor was $8.31. In 2001, capital per hour of labor was $50 and real GDP per hour of labor was $10.29 an hour.
   a. Does Longland experience diminishing returns? Explain why or why not.
   b. Use growth accounting to find the contribution of the change in capital between 1999 and 2001 to the growth of productivity in Longland.
   c. Use growth accounting to find the contribution of technological change between 1999 and 2001 to the growth of productivity in Longland.

4. In Flatland, described in problem 2, capital per hour of labor in 1999 was $60 and real GDP per hour of labor was $8.44. In 2001, capital per hour of labor was $120 and real GDP per hour of labor was $12.74 an hour.
   a. Does Flatland experience diminishing returns? Explain why or why not.
   b. Use growth accounting to find the contribution of the change in capital between 1999 and 2001 to the growth of productivity in Flatland.
   c. Use growth accounting to find the contribution of technological change between 1999 and 2001 to the growth of productivity in Flatland.

*5. The following information has been discovered about the economy of Cape Despair. Subsistence real GDP is $15 an hour. Whenever real GDP per hour rises above this level, the population grows, and when real GDP per hour of labor falls below this level, the population falls. The productivity curve in Cape Despair is as follows:

| Capital per hour of labor (2000 dollars per hour) | Real GDP per hour of labor (2000 dollars per hour) |
|---|---|
| 20 | 8 |
| 40 | 15 |
| 60 | 21 |
| 80 | 26 |
| 100 | 30 |
| 120 | 33 |
| 140 | 35 |
| 160 | 36 |

Initially, the population of Cape Despair is constant, and real GDP is at its subsistence level. Then a technological advance shifts the productivity curve upward by $7 at each level of capital per hour of labor.
   a. What are the initial capital per hour of labor and real GDP per hour of labor?

* Solutions to odd-numbered problems are available on MyEconLab.

b. What happens to real GDP per hour of labor immediately following the technological advance?
c. What happens to the population growth rate following the technological advance?
d. What is the eventual quantity of capital per hour of labor in Cape Despair?

6. Martha's Island is an economy that behaves according to the neoclassical growth model. The economy has no growth, a target rate of return of 10 percent a year, and the following productivity curve:

| Capital per hour of labor (2000 dollars per hour) | Real GDP per hour of labor (2000 dollars per hour) |
|---|---|
| 40 | 16 |
| 80 | 30 |
| 120 | 42 |
| 160 | 52 |
| 200 | 60 |
| 240 | 66 |
| 280 | 70 |
| 320 | 72 |

A technological advance shifts the productivity curve upward.
a. What is the initial capital per hour of labor on Martha's Island?
b. What is the initial real GDP per hour of labor?
c. What happens to the return from capital immediately following the technological advance?
d. What happens to the return on capital and the quantity of capital per hour of labor?

*7. Romeria is a country that behaves according to the predictions of new growth theory. The target rate is 3 percent a year. A technological advance increases the demand for capital and raises the real interest rate to 5 percent a year. Describe the events that happen in Romeria and contrast them with the events in Martha's Island in problem 6.

8. Suppose that in Romeria, described in problem 7, technological advance slows and the real interest rate falls to 3 percent a year. Describe what happens in Romeria.

# CRITICAL THINKING

1. After studying *Reading Between the Lines* on pp. 222–223, answer the following questions:
   a. What is the growth rate of the Asian economies predicted to be in 2003 and 2004?
   b. Is real GDP per hour of labor in China growing because capital per hour of labor is increasing, because of other factors, or both? How would you determine the contribution of each factor?
   c. Is China narrowing the gap between real GDP per person in China and real GDP per person in the United States?
   d. At the current rate of convergence, how long will it take for real GDP per person in China to equal that in the United States?

2. Is faster economic growth always a good thing? Argue the case for faster growth and the case for slower growth and then reach a conclusion on whether growth should be increased or decreased.

# WEB EXERCISES

**Use the links on MyEconLab to work the following exercises.**

1. Obtain data on real GDP per person for the United States, China, South Africa, and Mexico since 1960.
   a. Draw a graph of the data.
   b. Which country has the lowest real GDP per person and which has the highest?
   c. Which country has experienced the fastest growth rate since 1960 and which the slowest?
   d. Explain why the growth rates in these four countries are ranked in the order you have discovered.
   e. Return to the Penn World Table Web site and obtain data for any four other countries that interest you. Describe and explain the patterns that you find for these countries.

2. Write a memo to your member of Congress in which you set out the policies you believe the U.S. government must follow to speed up the growth rate of real GDP in the United States.

# UNDERSTANDING AGGREGATE SUPPLY AND ECONOMIC GROWTH

PART 4

## Expanding the Frontier

Economics is about how we cope with scarcity. We cope by making choices that balance marginal benefits and marginal costs so that we use our scarce resources efficiently.

These choices determine how much work we do; how hard we work at school to learn the mental skills that form our human capital and that determine the kinds of jobs we get and the incomes we earn; and how much we save for future big-ticket expenditures. These choices also determine how much businesses and governments spend on new capital—on auto assembly lines, computers and fiber cables for improved Internet services, shopping malls, highways, bridges, and tunnels; and how intensively existing capital and natural resources are used and therefore how quickly they wear out or are used up. Most significant of all, these choices determine the problems that scientists, engineers, and other inventors work on to develop new technologies.

All the choices we've just described determine two vital measures of economic performance:

- Real GDP
- Economic growth

Real GDP is determined by the quantity of labor, the quantity of capital, and the state of technological knowledge. And economic growth—the growth rate of real GDP—is determined by growth in the quantity of labor, capital accumulation, and technological advances.

Economic growth, maintained at a steady rate over a number of decades, is the single most powerful influence on any society. It brings a transformation that continues to amaze thoughtful people. Economic growth that is maintained at a rapid rate can transform a society in years, not decades. Such transformations are taking place right now in many Asian countries. These transformations are economic miracles.

The two chapters in this part studied the miracle of rapid economic growth and the forces that shape our capacity to produce goods and services.

Chapter 8 explained how potential GDP and the full-employment quantity of labor, employment, and unemployment are determined by equilibrium in the labor market.

Chapter 8 also explained how capital accumulation results from saving and investment decisions that are coordinated in the capital market.

Chapter 9 studied the process of economic growth in the fast-growing economies of Asia and the United States. It explained how growth is influenced by technological change and the incentives that stimulate it.

Modern ideas about economic growth owe much to two economists, Joseph Schumpeter and Paul Romer, whom you can meet on the following pages.

# PROBING THE IDEAS

## Incentives to Innovate

"*Economic progress, in capitalist society, means turmoil.*"

JOSEPH
SCHUMPETER
*Capitalism, Socialism, and Democracy*

### THE ECONOMIST

**Joseph Schumpeter,** *the son of a textile factory owner, was born in Austria in 1883. He moved from Austria to Germany during the tumultuous 1920s when those two countries experienced hyperinflation. In 1932, in the depths of the Great Depression, he came to the United States and became a professor of economics at Harvard University.*

*This creative economic thinker wrote about economic growth and development, business cycles, political systems, and economic biography. He was a person of strong opinions who expressed them strongly and delighted in verbal battles.*

*Schumpeter has become the unwitting founder of modern growth theory. He saw the development and diffusion of new technologies by profit-seeking entrepreneurs as the source of economic progress. But he saw economic progress as a process of creative destruction—the creation of new profit opportunities and the destruction of currently profitable businesses. For Schumpeter, economic growth and the business cycle were a single phenomenon.*

*When Schumpeter died, in 1950, he had achieved his self-expressed life ambition: He was regarded as the world's greatest economist.*

### THE ISSUES

Technological change, capital accumulation, and population growth all interact to produce economic growth. But what is cause and what is effect? And can we expect productivity and income per person to keep growing?

The classical economists of the eighteenth and nineteenth centuries believed that technological advances and capital accumulation were the engines of growth. But they also believed that no matter how successful people were at inventing more productive technologies and investing in new capital, they were destined to live at the subsistence level. These economists based their conclusion on the belief that productivity growth causes population growth, which in turn causes productivity to decline. These classical economists believed that whenever economic growth raises incomes above the subsistence level, the population will increase. They went on to reason that the increase in population brings diminishing returns that lower productivity. As a result, incomes must always return to the subsistence level. Only when incomes are at the subsistence level is population growth held in check.

A new approach, called neoclassical growth theory, was developed by Robert Solow of MIT, during the 1950s. Solow, who was one of Schumpeter's students, received the Nobel Prize for Economic Science for this work.

Solow challenged the conclusions of the classical economists. But the new theories of economic growth developed during the 1980s and 1990s went further. They stand the classical belief on its head. Today's theory of population growth is that rising income slows the population growth rate because it increases the opportunity cost of having children and lowers the opportunity cost of investing in children and equipping them with

228

more human capital, which makes them more productive. Productivity and income grow because technology advances, and the scope for further productivity growth, which is stimulated by the search for profit, is practically unlimited.

## THEN

In 1830, a strong and experienced farm worker could harvest three acres of wheat in a day. The only capital employed was a scythe to cut the wheat, which had been used since Roman times, and a cradle on which the stalks were laid, which had been invented by Flemish farmers in the fifteenth century. With newly developed horse-drawn plows, harrows, and planters, farmers could plant more wheat than they could harvest. But despite big efforts, no one had been able to make a machine that could replicate the swing of a scythe. Then in 1831, 22-year-old Cyrus McCormick built a machine that worked. It scared the horse that pulled it, but it did in a matter of hours what three men could accomplish in a day. Technological change has increased productivity on farms and brought economic growth. Do the facts about productivity growth mean that the classical economists, who believed that diminishing returns would push us relentlessly back to a subsistence living standard, were wrong?

## NOW

Today's technologies are expanding our horizons beyond the confines of our planet and are expanding our minds. Geosynchronous satellites bring us global television, voice and data communication, and more accurate weather forecasts, which, incidentally, increase agricultural productivity. In the foreseeable future, we might have superconductors that revolutionize the use of electric power, virtual reality theme parks and training facilities, pollution-free hydrogen cars, wristwatch telephones, and optical computers that we can talk to. Equipped with these new technologies, our ability to create yet more dazzling technologies increases. Technological change begets technological change in an (apparently) unending process and makes us ever more productive and brings ever higher incomes.

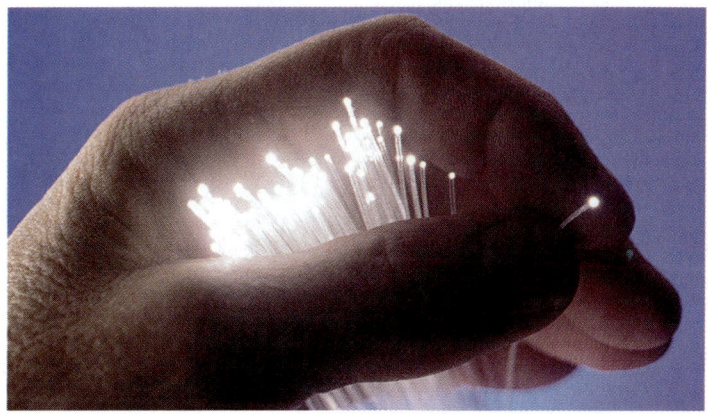

*Today's revolution in the way economists think about economic growth has been led by Paul Romer, a professor of economics at Stanford University, whom you can meet on the following pages.*

# TALKING WITH

Paul Romer

*Paul Romer* is Professor of Economics at the Graduate School of Business at Stanford University and the Royal Bank Fellow of the Canadian Institute for Advanced Research. Born in 1955 in Denver, Colorado, he earned his B.S. in Mathematics (1977) and his Ph.D. in Economics (1983) from the University of Chicago.

Professor Romer has transformed the way economists think about economic growth. He believes that sustained economic growth arises from competition among firms. Firms try to increase their profits by devoting resources to creating new products and developing new ways of making existing products.

Michael Parkin talked with Professor Romer about his work, how he was influenced by Joseph Schumpeter and Robert Solow, and the insights economic growth offers us.

**Professor Romer, why did you decide to become an economist?**

As an undergraduate, I studied math and physics and was interested in becoming a cosmologist. During my senior year, I concluded that job prospects in physics were not very promising, so I decided to go to law school. I was an undergraduate at the University of Chicago, where the law and economics movement first emerged. In the fall of my senior year, I took my first economics course to prepare for law school. My economics professor, Sam Peltzman, presented a simple piece of economic analysis that changed my life. He argued that the demand for economists was likely to grow for decades. The government, which employs economists, would grow in size. Businesses that deal with the government would want their own economists. The legal profession that serves businesses would also need more economists. Because of all these demands, many students would want to take economics courses. This meant that there would be many job openings for economists at universities. Moreover, he claimed, being a professor of economics was a lot like being a cosmologist and far more fun than being a lawyer. I could take fragmentary bits of evidence and try to make sense of them using mathematical equations. So I tore up my law school applications, applied to graduate school in economics, and never looked back.

**What are the truly important lessons about the causes of economic growth?**

As a physics major, I felt that the description economists used for growth violated a basic law of physics: the conservation of mass. Economists seemed to be saying that GDP, the output of a nation, was a bunch of stuff that was "produced" and that the quantity of stuff produced has grown steadily over time and will continue to do so. But this can't be right. We have the same amount of stuff, or elements from the periodic table, that we had 100,000 years ago because there are many more people now. In terms of kilograms of matter per person, we know that we are vastly poorer than our ancestors were 100,000 years ago. Yet we clearly have a higher standard of living. How could this be? This basic question indicates that thinking about growth as a production process that generates stuff is a dead-end. Instead, economic growth has to be about rearranging the fixed amount of matter that we have to work with and making new combinations that seem a lot more valuable. The key insight is that economic growth comes from increases in value, not increases in the amount of matter.

*Can you give us an example of an increase in value?*
For tens of thousands of years, we treated iron oxide, ordinary rust, like dirt. When we lived in caves, we learned how to use it as a pigment for decorating cave walls. We took the low-value dirt and put it to the higher-valued use of making cave paintings. Later, we learned how to extract the iron from iron ore to make bridges and rails. Later still, we learned how to arrange the iron atoms together with carbon atoms and make steel. Recently, we learned how to take iron oxide and put it on magnetic tape and use it to store sound and pictures. The iron, oxygen, and carbon atoms have always been here. We have a higher standard of living because we have learned how to arrange these atoms in ways that we find more valuable.

*What kind of policy implications does this kind of thinking lead to?*
Policy makers must encourage institutions to become more efficient at discovering new recipes to rearrange matter. Consider the transistor as an example. We take silicon and mix it with a few impurities and some metal in just the right way, and we get a computer chip worth thousands of times what the raw ingredients were worth. Research grants, subsidies for education, and institutions like the nonprofit private university encourage the production of new recipes

> *We take silicon and mix it with a few impurities and some metal in just the right way, and we get a computer chip worth thousands of times what the raw ingredients were worth.*

or ideas. But so do venture capitalists who help new-technology startups, competitive markets that allow the firms with better instructions or ideas to quickly displace existing firms, and labor laws that let inefficient firms lay off workers when more efficient new firms come on the scene. We must let firms like Digital Electronics or Wang Computers shrink, maybe even fail, if we want to make room for new firms like Intel to enter the scene and thrive.

*Were the classical economists wrong in their view that population growth and diminishing returns are the dominant long-term influences on production and incomes? Or is the current global population explosion part of a process that will ultimately prove them correct?*
Classical economists like Malthus and Ricardo were right when they argued that we have a fixed amount of natural resources to work with. Malthus pointed out that resource scarcity will lead to falling standards of living if we continue to work with the same set of recipes or instructions for using our resources. Where he went wrong was in assuming that there was little scope for us to find new recipes for taking resources such as land, water, carbon dioxide, nitrogen, and sunshine and converting them into carbohydrates and proteins that we can eat.

The classical economists got half of the story right. We do live in a world with scarce resources. They missed the other half. There is an incomprehensibly large number of different formulas we can use to recombine these scarce resources into things we value, such as protein or entertainment.

Scarcity is a very important part of economics and our lives. For example, we know that there is an absolute limit on the number of people who can live on the earth. One way or another, we know that the rate of population growth will slow down. It's only a question of how and when. But will this ultimately lead to a period when standards of living fall as Malthus predicted? I doubt it. As countries get rich, population growth slows. As a larger fraction of the worldwide population becomes educated, these people will help us to discover new things, like plants that are more efficient at taking carbon dioxide out of the atmosphere, and more efficient distribution systems. Thus standards of living for all humans will continue to improve.

*During the past decade, China and several other economies in East Asia have experienced rapid, unheralded growth rates. Why?*

These countries took some of the recipes, formulas, and instructions for generating value that already existed in the advanced countries of the world and put them to use within their borders. It's the same process that the Japanese followed after the Meiji restoration at the end of the last century. These countries noticed that other people in the world knew a lot about how to create value and realized that by trading with these people, they could share in the gains.

*What lessons from East Asia can, in principle, be applied in Africa and Central Europe?*

The basic insight is that there are huge potential gains from trade. Poor countries can supply their natural and human resources. Rich countries can supply their know-how. When these are combined, everyone can be better off. The challenge is for a country to arrange its laws and institutions so that both sides can profitably engage in trade. If there are barriers to trade or if the government cannot protect basic property rights and prevent crime, trade can't take place. For example, the Japanese have been able to borrow many ideas about manufacturing and design and even to improve on some of these ideas. But because they have barriers that limit entry of foreign firms into the retail sector, they still waste vast quantities of resources on a very inefficient distribution system.

*What does today's thinking about economic growth owe to Joseph Schumpeter and Robert Solow?*

Schumpeter worked at a time before most economists had learned to work with equations. He coined the phrase "creative destruction," which describes the process by which companies like Wang shrink or go out of business when new firms come in. He also described in words how important monopoly profits are in the process of innovation. There were many other economists, including Alfred Marshall, who described these same issues in verbal terms and also struggled to express these ideas in terms of equations.

Robert Solow was part of the post–World War II generation of economists who truly mastered the use of equations and wrote eloquently using both words and equations. As a result, his ideas have been far more influential than Schumpeter's. Many economists in the 1950s were trying to get a grasp on the economic effects of knowledge, formulas, recipes, and instructions. Solow called these things "technology" and gave us a wonderfully concise and workable way to think about how technology interacts with other economic inputs such as capital and labor. He also linked the methods that he and several economists were using to measure technology with this framework for thinking about the behavior of the economy as a whole. His work on growth was a masterful piece of invention, synthesis, and exposition.

Recent economists have taken Solow's mathematical framework and extended it to bring in some of the elements that Schumpeter described in words, like creative destruction and monopoly power. One of the great things about ideas is that they build on each other. In Isaac Newton's famous phrase, those of us working on growth today are "able to see farther because we stand on the shoulders of giants." Newton was another person who was pretty good with equations and could turn a good phrase.

*Is economics a worthwhile subject to major in? What can one do with an economics degree?*

Economics is an excellent training ground for developing mathematical and verbal skills. But students should supplement the courses in economics with courses in mathematics and science that force them to practice working with equations, graphs, and numbers. There is no substitute for such practice. Innate ability is far less important than most students think.

They should also take courses that force them to

*If you can learn how to write readable prose and use the basic tools of mathematics, you can do almost anything.*

write, revise, and edit. I took an English course in college that taught me the basics of how to edit, and it is one of the best investments I made. You can't tell what you will end up doing or what skills you will need later in life. But if you can learn how to write readable prose and use the basic tools of mathematics, you can do almost anything.

# PART 5  Aggregate Demand, Money, and Inflation

# Money, Banks, and the Federal Reserve

CHAPTER 10

## Money Makes the World Go Around

Money, like fire and the wheel, has been around for a long time. And it has taken many forms. Money was wampum (beads made from shells) for North American Indians, whale's teeth for Fijians, and tobacco for early American colonists. Cakes of salt served as money in Ethiopia and Tibet. Today, when we want to buy something, we use coins or bills, write a check, or present a debit card or a credit card. Tomorrow, we'll use a "smart card" that keeps track of spending and that our pocket computer can read. Are all these things money?

When we deposit some coins or notes into a bank, is that still money? And what happens when the bank lends the money we've deposited to someone else? How can we get our money back if it has been lent out?

The quantity of money in our economy is regulated by the Federal Reserve—the Fed. How does the Fed influence the quantity of money?

◆ In this chapter, we study the functions of money, the banks that create it, and the control of its quantity by the Federal Reserve. In *Reading Between the Lines* at the end of the chapter, we look at recent changes in the types of money that we use when we go shopping.

### After studying this chapter, you will be able to

- Define money and describe its functions
- Explain the economic functions of banks and other depository institutions and describe how they are regulated
- Explain how banks create money
- Describe the structure of the Federal Reserve System (the Fed), and the tools used by the Fed to conduct monetary policy
- Explain what an open market operation is, how it works, and how it changes the quantity of money

# What Is Money?

What do wampum, tobacco, and nickels and dimes have in common? Why are they all examples of money? To answer these questions, we need a definition of money. **Money** is any commodity or token that is generally acceptable as a means of payment. A **means of payment** is a method of settling a debt. When a payment has been made, there is no remaining obligation between the parties to a transaction. So what wampum, tobacco, and nickels and dimes have in common is that they have served (or still do serve) as the means of payment. But money has three other functions:

- Medium of exchange
- Unit of account
- Store of value

## Medium of Exchange

A *medium of exchange* is any object that is generally accepted in exchange for goods and services. Without a medium of exchange, goods and services must be exchanged directly for other goods and services—an exchange called **barter**. Barter requires a *double coincidence of wants*, a situation that rarely occurs. For example, if you want a hamburger, you might offer a CD in exchange for it. But you must find someone who is selling hamburgers and who wants your CD.

A medium of exchange overcomes the need for a double coincidence of wants. And money acts as a medium of exchange because people with something to sell will always accept money in exchange for it. But money isn't the only medium of exchange. You can buy with a credit card. But a credit card isn't money. It doesn't make a final payment, and the debt it creates must eventually be settled by using money.

## Unit of Account

A *unit of account* is an agreed measure for stating the prices of goods and services. To get the most out of your budget, you have to figure out whether seeing one more movie is worth its opportunity cost. But that cost is not dollars and cents. It is the number of ice-cream cones, sodas, or cups of coffee that you must give up. It's easy to do such calculations when all these goods have prices in terms of dollars and cents (see Table 10.1). If a movie costs $6 and a six-pack of soda costs $3, you know right away that

**TABLE 10.1** The Unit of Account Function of Money Simplifies Price Comparisons

| Good | Price in money units | Price in units of another good |
|---|---|---|
| Movie | $6.00 each | 2 six-packs of soda |
| Soda | $3.00 per six-pack | 2 ice-cream cones |
| Ice cream | $1.50 per cone | 3 packs of jelly beans |
| Jelly beans | $0.50 per pack | 2 cups of coffee |
| Gum | $0.25 per stick | 1 local phone call |

*Money as a unit of account*: The price of a movie is $6 and the price of a stick of gum is 25¢, so the opportunity cost of a movie is 24 sticks of gum ($6.00 ÷ 25¢ = 24).

*No unit of account*: You go to a movie theater and learn that the price of a movie is 2 six-packs of soda. You go to a candy store and learn that a pack of jelly beans costs 2 sticks of gum. But how many sticks of gum does seeing a movie cost you? To answer that question, you go to the convenience store and find that a six-pack of soda costs 2 ice-cream cones. Now you head for the ice-cream shop, where an ice-cream cone costs 3 packs of jelly beans. Now you get out your pocket calculator: 1 movie costs 2 six-packs of soda, or 4 ice-cream cones, or 12 packs of jelly beans, or 24 sticks of gum!

seeing one more movie costs you 2 six-packs of soda. If jelly beans are 50¢ a pack, one more movie costs 12 packs of jelly beans. You need only one calculation to figure out the opportunity cost of any pair of goods and services.

But imagine how troublesome it would be if your local movie theater posted its price as 2 six-packs of soda, and if the convenience store posted the price of a six-pack of soda as 2 ice-cream cones, and if the ice-cream shop posted the price of an ice-cream cone as 3 packs of jelly beans, and if the candy store priced a pack of jelly beans as 2 sticks of gum! Now how much running around and calculating would you have to do to figure out how much that movie is going to cost you in terms of the soda, ice cream, jelly beans, or gum that you must give up to see it? You get the answer for soda right away from the sign posted on the movie theater. But for all the other goods, you're going to have to visit many different stores to establish the price of each commodity in terms of another and then calculate prices in units that are relevant for your own decision. Cover up the column labeled "Price in money units" in Table 26.1 and see how hard it is to figure out the number of local phone calls it costs to see one movie. It's enough to make a person swear off movies! You can see how much simpler it is if all the prices are expressed in dollars and cents.

## Store of Value

Money is a *store of value* in the sense that it can be held and exchanged later for goods and services. If money were not a store of value, it could not serve as a means of payment.

Money is not alone in acting as a store of value. A physical object such as a house, a car, a work of art, or a computer can act as a store of value.

The most reliable and useful stores of value are items that have a stable value. The more stable the value of a commodity or token, the better it can act as a store of value and the more useful it is as money. No store of value has a completely stable value. The value of a house, a car, or a work of art fluctuates over time. The value of the commodities and tokens that are used as money also fluctuate over time. And when there is inflation, their values persistently fall.

Because inflation brings a falling value of money, a low inflation rate is needed to make money as useful as possible as a store of value.

## Money in the United States Today

In the United States today, money consists of

- Currency
- Deposits at banks and other depository institutions

**Currency** The bills and coins that we use in the United States today are known as **currency**. Bills are money because the government declares them so with the words "This note is legal tender for all debts, public and private." You can see these words on every dollar bill.

**Deposits** Deposits at banks and other depository institutions such as savings and loan associations are also money. Deposits are money because they can be converted into currency and because they are used to settle debts.

**Official Measures of Money** The two main official measures of money in the United States today are known as M1 and M2. Figure 10.1 shows the items that make up these two measures. **M1** consists of currency and traveler's checks plus checking deposits owned by individuals and businesses. M1 does *not* include currency held by banks, and it does not include currency and checking deposits owned by the U.S. government. **M2** consists of M1 plus time deposits, savings deposits, and money market mutual funds and other deposits. You can see that M2 is almost five times as large as M1. You can also see that currency is a small part of our money.

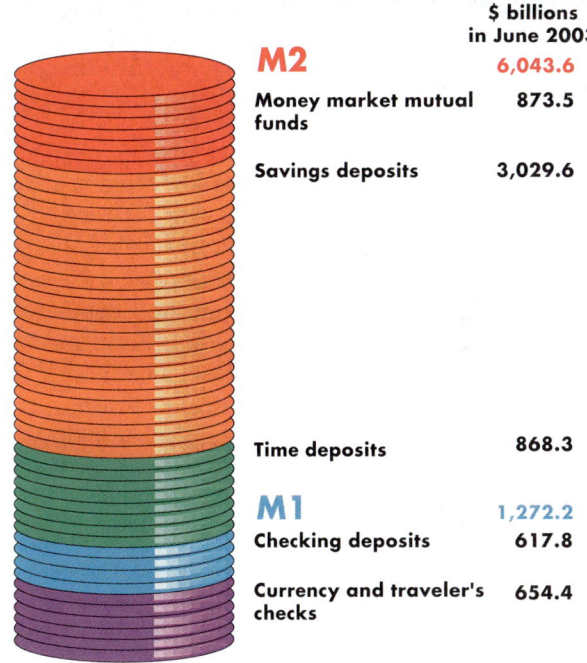

**FIGURE 10.1**  Two Measures of Money

M1
- Currency held outside banks and traveler's checks
- Checking deposits at commercial banks, savings and loan associations, savings banks, and credit unions

M2
- M1
- Time deposits
- Savings deposits
- Money market mutual funds and other deposits

*Source:* The Federal Reserve Board.

**Are M1 and M2 Really Money?** Money is the means of payment. So the test of whether an asset is money is whether it serves as a means of payment. Currency passes the test. But what about deposits? Checking deposits are money because they can be transferred from one person to another by writing a check or using a debit card. Such a transfer of ownership is equivalent to handing over currency. Because M1 consists of currency plus checking deposits and each of these is a means of payment, *M1 is money*.

But what about M2? Some of the savings deposits in M2 are just as much a means of payment as the checking deposits in M1. You can use the ATM at the grocery store checkout or gas station and transfer funds directly from your savings account to pay for your purchase. But other savings deposits are not means of payment. These deposits are known as *liquid assets*. **Liquidity** is the property of being instantly convertible into a means of payment with little loss in value. Because most of the deposits in M2 are quickly and easily converted into currency or checking deposits, they are similar to M1, but they are not means of payment.

**Deposits Are Money but Checks Are Not** In defining money, we include, along with currency, deposits at banks and other depository institutions. But we do not count the checks that people write as money. Why are deposits money and checks not?

To see why deposits are money but checks are not, think about what happens when Colleen buys some roller-blades for $200 from Rocky's Rollers. When Colleen goes to Rocky's shop, she has $500 in her deposit account at the Laser Bank. Rocky has $1,000 in his deposit account—at the same bank, as it happens. The total deposits of these two people are $1,500. Colleen writes a check for $200. Rocky takes the check to the bank right away and deposits it. Rocky's bank balance rises from $1,000 to $1,200, and Colleen's balance falls from $500 to $300. The total deposits of Colleen and Rocky are still the same as before: $1,500. Rocky now has $200 more than before, and Colleen has $200 less.

This transaction has transferred money from Colleen to Rocky. The check itself was never money. There wasn't an extra $200 worth of money while the check was in circulation. The check instructs the bank to transfer money from Colleen to Rocky.

If Colleen and Rocky use different banks, there is an extra step. Rocky's bank credits the check to Rocky's account and then takes the check to a check-clearing center. The check is then sent to Colleen's bank, which pays Rocky's bank $200 and then debits Colleen's account $200. This process can take a few days, but the principles are the same as when two people use the same bank.

**Credit Cards Are Not Money** So checks are not money. But what about credit cards? Isn't having a credit card in your wallet and presenting the card to pay for your roller-blades the same thing as using money? Why aren't credit cards somehow valued and counted as part of the quantity of money?

When you pay by check, you are frequently asked to prove your identity by showing your driver's license. It would never occur to you to think of your driver's license as money. It's just an ID card. A credit card is also an ID card but one that lets you take out a loan at the instant you buy something. When you sign a credit card sales slip, you are saying, "I agree to pay for these goods when the credit card company bills me." Once you get your statement from the credit card company, you must make at least the minimum payment due. To make that payment, you need money—you need to have currency or a checking deposit to pay the credit card company. So although you use a credit card when you buy something, the credit card is not the *means of payment* and it is not money.

> ### REVIEW QUIZ
> 1 What makes something money? What functions does money perform? Why do you think packs of chewing gum don't serve as money?
> 2 What are the problems that arise when a commodity is used as money?
> 3 What are the main components of money in the United States today?
> 4 What are the official measures of money? Are all the measures really money?
> 5 Why are checks and credit cards not money?

We've seen that the main component of money in the United States is deposits at banks and other depository institutions. Let's take a closer look at these institutions.

# Depository Institutions

A FIRM THAT TAKES DEPOSITS FROM HOUSEHOLDS and firms and makes loans to other households and firms is called a **depository institution**. The deposits of three types of depository institution make up the nation's money:

- Commercial banks
- Thrift institutions
- Money market mutual funds

## Commercial Banks

A **commercial bank** is a firm that is licensed by the Comptroller of the Currency (at the U.S. Treasury) or by a state agency to receive deposits and make loans. About 8,000 commercial banks operate in the United States today. A commercial bank's balance sheet summarizes its business and Table 10.2 shows the aggregate balance sheet of the commercial banks in the United States at the end of June 2003.

A bank's *balance sheet* lists its assets, liabilities, and net worth. *Assets* are what the bank *owns*, *liabilities* are what the bank *owes*, and *net worth*, which is equal to assets minus liabilities, is the value of the bank to its stockholders—its owners. Among a bank's liabilities are the deposits that are part of the nation's money. Your deposit at the bank is a liability to your bank (and an asset to you) because the bank must repay your deposit whenever you decide to take your money out of the bank.

**Profit and Prudence: A Balancing Act** The aim of a bank is to maximize the net worth of its stockholders. To achieve this objective, the interest rate at which a bank lends exceeds the rate at which it borrows. But a bank must perform a delicate balancing act. Lending is risky, and the more a bank ties up its deposits in high-risk, high-interest rate loans, the bigger is its chance of not being able to repay its depositors. And if depositors perceive a high risk of not being repaid, they withdraw their funds and create a crisis for the bank. So a bank must be prudent in the way it uses its deposits, balancing security for the depositors against profit for its stockholders.

**Reserves and Loans** To achieve security for its depositors, a bank divides its funds into two parts: reserves and loans. **Reserves** are the cash in a bank's

**TABLE 10.2** Commercial Banks' Balance Sheet June 2003

| Assets (billions of dollars) | | Liabilities (billions of dollars) | |
|---|---|---|---|
| Reserves and liquid assets | 331 | Deposits | 4,702 |
| Investment securities | 1,863 | Borrowing | 1,478 |
| Loans | 4,653 | Other liabilities (net) and net worth | 667 |
| Total assets | 6,847 | Total liabilities | 6,847 |

*Source:* Federal Reserve Board.

vault plus its deposits at Federal Reserve banks. (We'll study the Federal Reserve banks later in this chapter.) The cash in a bank's vaults is a reserve to meet its depositors' demands for currency. This cash keeps the ATM replenished every time you and your friends raid it for money for a midnight pizza. The account of a bank at the Federal Reserve is similar to your own bank account. Commercial banks use these accounts to receive and make payments. A commercial bank deposits cash into or draws cash out of its account at the Federal Reserve and writes checks on that account to settle debts with other banks.

If a bank kept all its deposits as reserves, it wouldn't make any profit. In fact, it keeps only a small fraction of its funds in reserves and lends the rest. A bank has three types of assets:

1. *Liquid assets* are U.S. government Treasury bills and commercial bills. These assets are the banks' first line of defense if they need cash. Liquid assets can be sold and instantly converted into cash with virtually no risk of loss. Because they are virtually risk free, they have a low interest rate.

2. *Investment securities* are longer-term U.S. government bonds and other bonds. These assets can be sold quickly and converted into cash but at prices that fluctuate. Because their prices fluctuate, these assets are riskier than liquid assets, but they also have a higher interest rate.

3. *Loans* are commitments of fixed amounts of money for agreed-upon periods of time. Most banks' loans are made to corporations to finance the purchase of capital equipment and inventories and to households—personal loans—to

finance consumer durable goods, such as cars or boats. The outstanding balances on credit card accounts are also bank loans. Loans are the riskiest assets of a bank because they cannot be converted into cash until they are due to be repaid. And some borrowers default and never repay. Because they are the riskiest of a bank's assets, loans carry the highest interest rate.

Commercial bank deposits are one component of the nation's money. But thrift institutions and money market mutual funds also take deposits that form part—an increasing part—of the nation's money. We'll now describe the other institutions whose deposits form part of the nation's money.

### Thrift Institutions

The **thrift institutions** are

- Savings and loan associations
- Savings banks
- Credit unions

**Savings and Loan Association** A **savings and loan association** (S&L) is a depository institution that receives checking deposits and savings deposits and that makes personal, commercial, and home-purchase loans.

**Savings Bank** A **savings bank** is a depository institution that accepts savings deposits and makes mostly mortgage loans. Some savings banks (called *mutual* savings banks) are owned by their depositors.

**Credit Union** A **credit union** is a depository institution owned by a social or economic group such as a firm's employees that accepts savings deposits and makes mostly consumer loans.

### Money Market Mutual Funds

A **money market mutual fund** is a fund operated by a financial institution that sells shares in the fund and holds liquid assets such as U.S. Treasury bills or short-term commercial bills.

Money market mutual fund shares act like bank deposits. Shareholders can write checks on their money market mutual fund accounts. But there are restrictions on most of these accounts. For example, the minimum deposit accepted might be $2,500, and the smallest check a depositor is permitted to write might be $500.

### The Economic Functions of Depository institutions

All depository institutions make a profit from the spread between the interest rate they pay on deposits and the interest rate at which they lend. Why can depository institutions get deposits at a low interest rate and lend at a higher one? What services do they perform that make their depositors willing to put up with a low interest rate and their borrowers willing to pay a higher one?

Depository institutions provide four main services that people are willing to pay for:

- Creating liquidity
- Minimizing the cost of obtaining funds
- Minimizing the cost of monitoring borrowers
- Pooling risk

**Creating Liquidity** Depository institutions create liquidity. *Liquid assets* are those that are easily convertible into money with little loss of value. Some of the liabilities of depository institutions are themselves money; others are highly liquid assets that are easily converted into money.

Depository institutions create liquidity by borrowing short and lending long. *Borrowing short* means taking deposits but standing ready to repay them on short notice (and even on no notice in the case of checking deposits). *Lending long* means making loan commitments for a prearranged, and often quite long, period of time. For example, when a person makes a deposit with a savings and loan association, that deposit can be withdrawn at any time. But the S&L makes a lending commitment for perhaps more than 20 years to a homebuyer.

**Minimizing the Cost of Obtaining Funds** Finding someone from whom to borrow can be a costly business. Imagine how troublesome it would be if there were no depository institutions. A firm that was looking for $1 million to buy a new factory would probably have to hunt around for several dozen people from whom to borrow to acquire enough funds for its capital project. Depository institutions lower the costs of this search. The firm that needs $1 million can go to a single depository institution to obtain those funds. The depository institution has to borrow from a large number of people, but it's not doing that just for this one firm and the million dollars it wants to borrow. The depository institution can establish an organization that is capable of raising funds from a large number of depositors and can spread the cost of this activity over a large number of borrowers.

### Minimizing the Cost of Monitoring Borrowers

Lending money is a risky business. There's always a danger that the borrower will not repay. Most of the money that is lent gets used by firms to invest in projects that they hope will return a profit. But sometimes those hopes are not fulfilled. Checking up on the activities of a borrower and ensuring that the best possible decisions are being made for making a profit and avoiding a loss are costly and specialized activities. Imagine how costly it would be if each household that lent money to a firm had to incur the costs of monitoring that firm directly. By depositing funds with a depository institution, households avoid those costs. The depository institution performs the monitoring activity by using specialized resources that have a much lower cost than what the households would incur if they had to undertake the activity individually.

### Pooling Risk

As we noted above, lending money is risky. There is always a chance of not being repaid—of default. Lending to a large number of different individuals can reduce the risk of default. In such a situation, if one person defaults on a loan, it is a nuisance but not a disaster. In contrast, if only one person borrows and that person defaults on the loan, the entire loan is a write-off. Depository institutions enable people to pool risk in an efficient way. Thousands of people lend money to any one institution, and, in turn, the institution relends the money to hundreds, perhaps thousands, of individual firms. If any one firm defaults on its loan, that default is spread across all the people who deposited money with the institution, and no individual depositor is left exposed to a high degree of risk.

We are interested in banks and other depository institutions because they *create* money. But these firms are highly regulated, and this regulation limits their ability to create money. So next, we'll examine these regulations. We'll also look at the deregulation and innovation that have occurred in the financial sector during the past 20 years.

## Financial Regulation, Deregulation, and Innovation

Depository institutions are highly regulated firms. But regulation is not static, and during the 1980s, some important changes in their regulation as well as deregulation took place. Also, the institutions are not static. In their pursuit of profit, they constantly seek lower-cost ways of obtaining funds, monitoring borrowers, pooling risk, and creating liquidity. They also are inventive in seeking ways to avoid the costs imposed on them by financial regulation. Depository institutions face two types of regulation:

- Deposit insurance
- Balance sheet rules

**Deposit Insurance** The deposits of most depository institutions are insured by the Federal Deposit Insurance Corporation (FDIC). The FDIC is a federal agency that receives its income from compulsory insurance premiums paid by commercial banks and other depository institutions. The FDIC operates two separate insurance funds: the Bank Insurance Fund (BIF), which insures deposits in commercial banks, and the Saving Association Insurance Fund (SAIF), which insures the deposits of S&Ls, savings banks, and credit unions. Each of these funds insures deposits of up to $100,000.

The existence of deposit insurance provides protection for depositors in the event that a depository institution fails. Both depositors and banks benefit from this protection. Depositors benefit because they face no greater risk from placing their wealth in a bank deposit than from holding it in currency. And banks benefit because the risk of a bank run is minimized. A *bank run* is a process in which depositors rush to withdraw their deposits and the banks run out of reserves with which to repay the depositors. Without deposit insurance, a bank run can seriously destabilize the entire financial system.

But deposit insurance does have an adverse side effect. It weakens the incentive for the owner of a depository institution to make safe investments and loans. Some economists believe that deposit insurance played a role in creating a crisis for S&Ls during the 1980s. During the 1970s, a surge in the inflation rate sent the interest rates that the S&Ls had to pay to attract deposits to levels that exceeded the interest rates on the long-term home purchase loans they had made. In an attempt to recoup some of these losses, S&L owners made high-risk loans. They did so because they knew they were making a one-way bet. If their loans paid off, they made a high rate of return. If they failed and could not meet their obligations to the depositors, the insurance fund would step in. Depositors didn't worry about risk because their deposits were insured. The bad loans were good business!

Because of this type of problem, all depository institutions face regulation of their balance sheets.

**Balance Sheet Rules** The most important balance sheet regulations are

- Equity capital requirements
- Reserve requirements
- Deposit rules
- Lending rules

*Equity capital requirements* are the minimum amount of an owner's own financial resources—called *equity capital*—that must be put into a depository institution. This amount must be sufficiently large to discourage owners from making loans that are too risky.

*Reserve requirements* are rules setting out the minimum percentages of deposits that must be held in currency or other safe, liquid assets. These minimum percentages vary across the different types of depository institutions and deposits; they are largest for checking deposits and smallest for long-term savings deposits.

*Deposit rules* are restrictions on the different types of deposits that an institution may accept. These are the rules that historically have created the sharpest distinctions between the various institutions. For example, in the past, commercial banks provided checking accounts while other institutions provided only savings accounts.

*Lending rules* are restrictions on the proportions of different types of loans that a depository institution may make. Like deposit rules, these rules also helped to create distinctions between the institutions. Before 1980, commercial banks were the only institutions that were permitted to make commercial loans, and S&Ls and savings banks were restricted to making mostly mortgage loans to homebuyers.

## Deregulation in the 1980s and 1990s

In 1980, Congress passed the Depository Institutions' Deregulation and Monetary Control Act (DIDMCA). The DIDMCA removed many of the distinctions between commercial banks and other depository institutions. It permitted nonbank depository institutions to compete with commercial banks in a wider range of lending business. At the same time, it permitted the payment of interest on checking deposits so that NOW accounts and ATS accounts could be offered by all deposit-taking institutions—banks and nonbanks.[1] It also extended the powers of the Federal Reserve to place reserve requirements on all depository institutions. Despite the general direction of deregulation, this move brought a greater measure of central control over the financial system than had previously existed and represented a strengthening of the Fed's control.

The ability of S&Ls and savings banks to compete for lending business with commercial banks was further strengthened in 1982 with the passage of the Garn–St. Germain Depository Institutions Act. This legislation further eased restrictions on the scale of commercial lending that S&Ls and savings banks could undertake.

The most significant deregulation during the 1990s was the Riegle–Neal Interstate Banking and Branching Efficiency Act of 1994. This law permits U.S. banks for the first time to establish branches in any state.

This new law brought large changes in the structure of the banking industry. The most visible was the wave of mergers of large banks and the appearance on the American banking scene of some major international banks. These changes will make the U.S. banking industry more efficient.

## Financial Innovation

The development of new financial products—of new ways of borrowing and lending—is called **financial innovation**. The aim of financial innovation is to lower the cost of deposits or to increase the return from lending or, more simply, to increase the profit from financial intermediation. There are three main influences on financial innovation:

- Economic environment
- Technology
- Regulation

The pace of financial innovation was remarkable during the 1980s and 1990s, and all three of these forces played a role.

---

[1] A NOW account is a Negotiable Order of Withdrawal account; "negotiable order of withdrawal" is another name for a check. An ATS account is an Automatic-Transfer Savings account—a savings account that is linked to a checking account. Funds are automatically transferred between the two accounts.

**Economic Environment** During the late 1970s and early 1980s, a high inflation rate brought high interest rates. For example, homebuyers were paying interest rates as high as 15 percent a year on mortgages.

High inflation and high interest rates created an incentive for financial innovation. Traditionally, house purchases were financed by mortgage loans at a guaranteed interest rate. The high interest rates of the early 1980s brought high borrowing costs for S&Ls. But because they were committed to fixed interest rates on their mortgages, the industry incurred severe losses.

To overcome this situation, the S&Ls developed variable interest rate mortgages—loans on which the interest rate would change in response to changing economic conditions. The creation of variable interest rate mortgages has taken some of the risk out of long-term lending for house purchases.

**Technology** The major technological change of the 1980s and 1990s was the development of low-cost computing and long distance communication. These new technologies had profound effects on financial products and led to much financial innovation.

Some examples of financial innovation that resulted from these new technologies are the widespread use of credit cards, the spread of daily interest deposit accounts, and the increased use of the U.S. dollar abroad, an extension of the use of Eurodollars.[2]

The cost of keying in transactions data and of calculating interest on deposits or on outstanding credit card balances was too great to make these financial products widely available before the 1980s. But with today's technologies, these products are highly profitable for banks and widely used.

**Regulation** A good deal of financial innovation takes place to avoid regulation. For example, a regulation known as Regulation Q prevented banks from paying interest on checking deposits. This restriction created an incentive for the banks to devise new types of deposits on which checks could be written and interest paid, thereby getting around the regulation.

**Deregulation, Innovation, and Money**

Deregulation and financial innovation that have led to the development of new types of deposit accounts have brought important changes in the composition of the nation's money. In 1960, M1 consisted of only currency and checking deposits at commercial banks. In the 1990s, new types of checking deposits expanded while traditional checking deposits declined. Similar changes have taken place in the composition of M2. Savings deposits have declined, while time deposits and money market mutual funds have expanded.

### REVIEW QUIZ

1. What are the functions of commercial banks, savings and loan associations, savings banks, credit unions, and money market mutual funds? What functions do they have in common and how do they differ from each other?
2. What is liquidity and how do depository institutions create it?
3. How do depository institutions lower the cost of borrowing and lending and of monitoring borrowers?
4. How do depository institutions pool risks?
5. Is everyone free to open a bank, take deposits, and make loans with no restrictions on these activities? What are the main restrictions that regulators impose on banks? Why?
6. Did the financial deregulation of the 1980s make commercial banks more like or less like other depository institutions?
7. What are the main factors that stimulate depository institutions constantly to develop new financial products and services?
8. What have deregulation and financial innovation done to the composition of the nation's money?

We're now ready to learn how banks create money. In the following section, we'll use the term "banks" to refer to all the institutions whose deposits are part of the nation's money. Let's see how money is created.

---

[2] Eurodollars are U.S. dollar bank accounts held in other countries, mainly in Europe. They were "invented" during the 1960s when the Soviet Union wanted the security and convenience of holding funds in U.S. dollars but was unwilling to place deposits in U.S. banks.

## How Banks Create Money

BANKS CREATE MONEY. BUT THIS DOESN'T MEAN that they have smoke-filled back rooms in which counterfeiters are busily working. Remember, most money is deposits, not currency. What banks create is deposits, and they do so by making loans. But the amount of deposits they can create is limited by their reserves.

### Reserves: Actual and Required

The fraction of a bank's total deposits that are held in reserves is called the **reserve ratio**. The reserve ratio changes when a bank's customers make a deposit or withdrawal. Making a deposit increases the reserve ratio, and making a withdrawal decreases the reserve ratio.

The **required reserve ratio** is the ratio of reserves to deposits that banks are required, by regulation, to hold. A bank's *required reserves* are equal to its deposits multiplied by the required reserve ratio. Actual reserves minus required reserves are **excess reserves**. Whenever banks have excess reserves, they are able to create money. To see how, we'll look at a model banking system.

### Creating Deposits by Making Loans

In the model banking system that we'll study, the required reserve ratio is 25 percent. That is, for each dollar deposited, the bank keeps 25¢ in reserves and lends the rest.

Figure 10.2 is going to keep track of what is happening in the money creation process, which begins when Art decides to decrease his currency holding and put $100,000 on deposit. Art's bank now has $100,000 of new deposits and $100,000 of additional reserves. With a required reserve ratio of 25 percent, the bank keeps $25,000 on reserve and lends $75,000 to Amy. Amy writes a check for $75,000 to buy a copy-shop franchise from Barb. At this point, Art's bank has a new deposit of $100,000, new loans of $75,000, and new reserves of $25,000. You can see this situation in Fig. 10.2 as the first row of the running tally.

For Art's bank, that is the end of the story. But it's not the end of the story for the entire banking system. Barb deposits her check for $75,000 in another bank. Its deposits and reserves increase by $75,000. This bank puts 25 percent of its increase in deposits ($18,750) into reserve and lends $56,250 to Bob. Bob then writes a check to Carl to pay off a business loan. The current state of play is seen in Fig. 26.2. Now total reserves of the banking system have increased by $43,750 ($25,000 plus $18,750), total loans have increased by $131,250 ($75,000 plus $56,250), and total deposits have increased by $175,000 ($100,000 plus $75,000).

When Carl takes his check to his bank, its deposits and reserves increase by $56,250, $14,063 of which it keeps in reserve and $42,187 of which it lends. This process continues until there are no excess reserves in the banking system. But the process takes a lot of further steps. Figure 10.2 shows one additional step. It also shows the final tallies: Reserves increase by $100,000, loans increase by $300,000, and deposits increase by $400,000.

The sequence in Fig. 10.2 shows the first four stages of the process. To work out the entire process, look closely at the numbers in the figure. The initial deposit is $100,000. Call this amount $A$ ($A = \$100,000$). At each stage, the loan is 75 percent (0.75) of the previous loan and the deposit is 0.75 of the previous deposit. Call that proportion $L$ ($L = 0.75$). The complete sequence is

$$A + AL + AL^2 + AL^3 + \ldots$$

Remember, $L$ is a fraction, so at each stage in this sequence, the amount of new loans gets smaller. The total number of loans made at the end of the process is the above sum, which is[3]

$$\frac{A}{(1 - L)}.$$

---

[3] The sequence of values is called a convergent geometric series. To find the sum of a series such as this, begin by calling the sum $S$. Then write out the sum as

$$S = A + AL + AL^2 + AL^3 + \ldots$$

Multiply by $L$ to get

$$SL = AL + AL^2 + AL^3 + \ldots$$

Subtract the second equation from the first to get

$$S(1 - L) = A$$

or

$$S = \frac{A}{(1 - L)}.$$

## FIGURE 10.2   The Multiple Creation of Bank Deposits

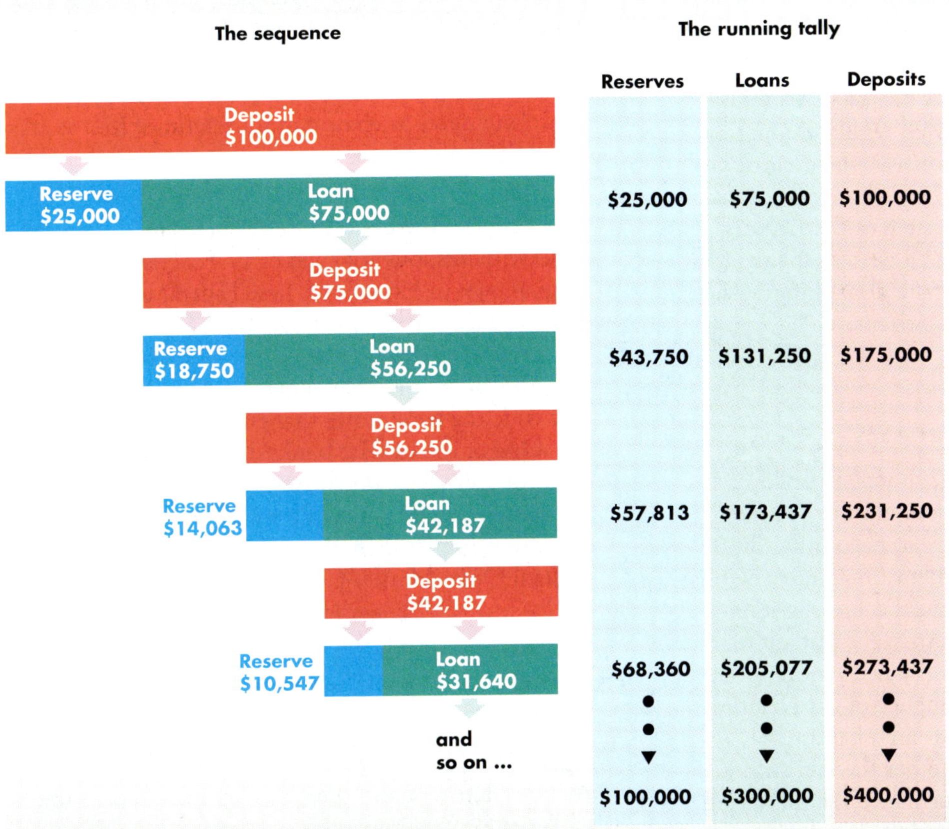

**The sequence**

Deposit $100,000
→ Reserve $25,000 | Loan $75,000
→ Deposit $75,000
→ Reserve $18,750 | Loan $56,250
→ Deposit $56,250
→ Reserve $14,063 | Loan $42,187
→ Deposit $42,187
→ Reserve $10,547 | Loan $31,640
and so on ...

**The running tally**

| Reserves | Loans | Deposits |
|---|---|---|
| $25,000 | $75,000 | $100,000 |
| $43,750 | $131,250 | $175,000 |
| $57,813 | $173,437 | $231,250 |
| $68,360 | $205,077 | $273,437 |
| ⋮ | ⋮ | ⋮ |
| $100,000 | $300,000 | $400,000 |

When a bank receives deposits, it keeps 25 percent in reserves and lends 75 percent. The amount lent becomes a new deposit at another bank. The next bank in the sequence keeps 25 percent and lends 75 percent, and the process continues until the banking system has created enough deposits to eliminate its excess reserves. The running tally tells us the amounts of deposits and loans created at each stage. At the end of the process, an additional $100,000 of reserves creates an additional $400,000 of deposits.

---

If we use the numbers from the example, the total increase in deposits is

$$\$100,000 + 75,000 + 56,250 + 42,187 + \ldots$$
$$= \$100,000(1 + 0.75 + 0.5625 + 0.42187 + \ldots)$$
$$= \$100,000(1 + 0.75 + 0.75^2 + 0.75^3 + \ldots)$$
$$= \$100,000 \times \frac{1}{(1 - 0.75)}$$
$$= \$100,000 \times \frac{1}{(0.25)}$$
$$= \$100,000 \times 4$$
$$= \$400,000.$$

By using the same method, you can check that the totals for reserves and loans are the ones shown in Fig. 10.2.

### REVIEW QUIZ

1. How do banks create deposits by making loans, and what are the factors that limit the amount of deposits and loans they can create?
2. A bank manager tells you that he doesn't create money. He just lends the money that people deposit in the bank. How do you explain to him that he's wrong and that he does create money?
3. If the banks receive new deposits of $100 million, what determines the total change in deposits that the banking system can create?

You now know what money is and how banks create it. Your next task is to learn about the Federal Reserve System and see how the Fed influences the quantity of money circulating in the economy.

## The Federal Reserve System

THE CENTRAL BANK OF THE UNITED STATES IS the **Federal Reserve System**. A **central bank** is a bank's bank and a public authority that regulates a nation's depository institutions and controls the quantity of money. As the banks' bank, the Fed provides banking services to commercial banks such as the Bank of America. A central bank is not a citizens' bank. That is, the Fed does not provide general banking services for businesses and individual citizens.

### The Fed's Goals and Targets

The Fed conducts the nation's **monetary policy**, which means that it adjusts the quantity of money in circulation. The Fed's goals are to keep inflation in check, maintain full employment, moderate the business cycle, and contribute toward achieving long-term growth. Complete success in the pursuit of these goals is impossible, and the Fed's more modest goal is to improve the performance of the economy and to get closer to the goals than a hands-off approach would achieve. Whether the Fed succeeds in improving economic performance is a matter on which there is a range of opinion.

In pursuit of its ultimate goals, the Fed pays close attention to interest rates and pays special attention to one interest rate, the **federal funds rate**, which is the interest rate that the banks charge each other on overnight loans of reserves. The Fed sets a target for the federal funds rate that is consistent with its ultimate goals and then takes actions to achieve its target.

This chapter examines the tools available to the Fed in its conduct of monetary policy. (The next chapter looks at the effects of the Fed's actions on the economy.) We begin by describing the structure of the Fed.

### The Structure of the Fed

The key elements in the structure of the Federal Reserve System are

- The Board of Governors
- The Regional Federal Reserve Banks
- The Federal Open Market Committee

**The Board of Governors** The Board of Governors has seven members, who are appointed by the President of the United States and confirmed by the Senate, each for a 14-year term. The terms are staggered so that one seat on the board becomes vacant every two years. The President appoints one of the board members as chairman for a term of four years, which is renewable.

**The Federal Reserve Banks** There are 12 Federal Reserve banks, one for each of 12 Federal Reserve districts shown in Fig. 10.3. These Federal Reserve banks provide check clearing services to commercial banks and other depository institutions, hold the reserve accounts of commercial banks, lend reserves to banks, and issue the bank notes that circulate as currency.

One of the district banks, the Federal Reserve Bank of New York (known as the New York Fed), occupies a special place in the Federal Reserve System because it implements the policy decisions of the Federal Open Market Committee.

**The Federal Open Market Committee** The **Federal Open Market Committee** (FOMC) is the main policy-making organ of the Federal Reserve System. The FOMC consists of the following voting members:

- The chairman and the other six members of the Board of Governors
- The president of the Federal Reserve Bank of New York
- The presidents of the other regional Federal Reserve banks (of whom, on a yearly rotating basis, only four vote)

The FOMC meets approximately every six weeks to review the state of the economy and to decide the actions to be carried out by the New York Fed.

### The Fed's Power Center

A description of the formal structure of the Fed gives the impression that power in the Fed resides with the Board of Governors. In practice, it is the chairman of the Board of Governors who has the largest influence on the Fed's monetary policy actions, and some remarkable individuals have held this position. One of these is Alan Greenspan, the current chairman, who was appointed by President Reagan in 1987, reappointed by President Bush in 1992, and again

# THE FEDERAL RESERVE SYSTEM 245

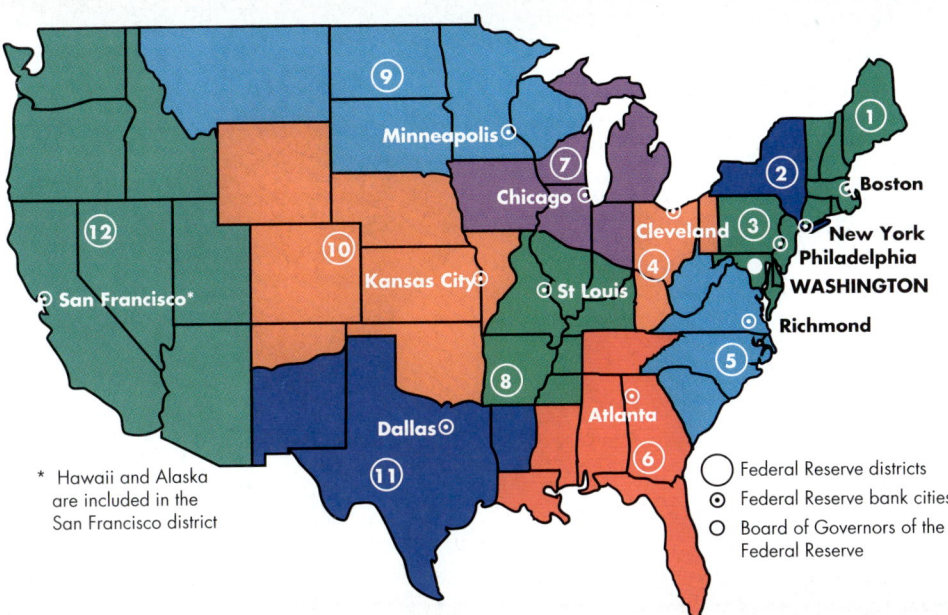

**FIGURE 10.3** The Federal Reserve System

The nation is divided into 12 Federal Reserve districts, each having a Federal Reserve bank. (Some of the larger districts also have branch banks.) The Board of Governors of the Federal Reserve System is located in Washington, D.C.

* Hawaii and Alaska are included in the San Francisco district

○ Federal Reserve districts
◉ Federal Reserve bank cities
○ Board of Governors of the Federal Reserve

*Source: Federal Reserve Bulletin.*

by President Clinton in 1996 and 2000. Another is Paul Volcker, who was appointed in 1979 by President Carter and reappointed in 1983 by President Reagan. Volcker eradicated inflation but at the cost of one of the most severe postwar recessions.

The chairman's power and influence stem from three sources. First, it is the chairman who controls the agenda and who dominates the meetings of the FOMC. Second, day-to-day contact with a large staff of economists and other technical experts provides the chairman with detailed background briefings on monetary policy issues. Third, the chairman is the spokesperson for the Fed and the main point of contact of the Fed with the President and government and with foreign central banks and governments.

## The Fed's Policy Tools

The Federal Reserve System has many responsibilities, but we'll examine its single most important one: regulating the amount of money floating around in the United States. How does the Fed control the quantity of money? It does so by adjusting the reserves of the banking system. Also, it is by adjusting the reserves of the banking system and by standing ready to make loans to banks that the Fed is able to prevent bank failures. The Fed uses three main policy tools to achieve its objectives:

- Required reserve ratios
- Discount rate
- Open market operations

**Required Reserve Ratios** All depository institutions in the United States are required to hold a minimum percentage of deposits as reserves. This minimum percentage is known as a *required reserve ratio*. The Fed determines a required reserve ratio for each type of deposit. In 2002, banks were required to hold minimum reserves equal to 3 percent of checking deposits up to $42.8 million and 10 percent of these deposits in excess of $42.8 million. The required reserves on other types of deposits were zero.

**Discount Rate** The **discount rate** is the interest rate at which the Fed stands ready to lend reserves to depository institutions. A change in the discount rate is proposed to the FOMC by the Board of Directors of at least one of the 12 Federal Reserve banks and is approved by the Board of Governors.

**Open Market Operations** An **open market operation** is the purchase or sale of government securities—U.S. Treasury bills and bonds—by the Federal Reserve System in the open market. When the Fed conducts an open market operation, it makes a transaction with a bank or some other business but it does not transact with the federal government.

Figure 10.4 summarizes the structure and policy tools of the Fed. To understand how the tools work, we need to know about the Fed's balance sheet.

## The Fed's Balance Sheet

Table 10.3 shows the balance sheet of the Federal Reserve System for February 2002. The assets on the left side are what the Fed owns, and the liabilities on the right side are what it owes. The Fed's assets are

1. Gold and foreign exchange
2. U.S. government securities
3. Loans to banks

Gold and foreign exchange are the Fed's holdings of international reserves, which consist of deposits at other central banks and an account called Special Drawing Rights, which the Fed holds at the International Monetary Fund.

The Fed's major assets are its holdings of U.S. government securities. These securities are mainly short-term Treasury bills and bonds.

When the banks are short of reserves, they can borrow reserves from the Fed. These borrowed reserves are an asset, "loans to banks," in the Fed's balance sheet.

The Fed's assets are the backing for its liabilities:

1. Federal Reserve notes in circulation
2. Banks' deposits

The Federal Reserve notes in circulation are the dollar bills that we use in our daily transactions. Some of these bills are held by the public; others are in the tills and vaults of banks and other financial institutions. Banks' deposits are the deposits of depository institutions and part of their reserves.

You might be wondering why Federal Reserve notes are considered a liability of the Fed. When bank notes were invented, they gave their owner a claim on the gold reserves of the issuing bank. Such notes were *convertible paper money*. The holder of such a note could convert the note on demand into gold (or some other commodity such as silver) at a guaranteed price. So when a bank issued a note, it was holding itself

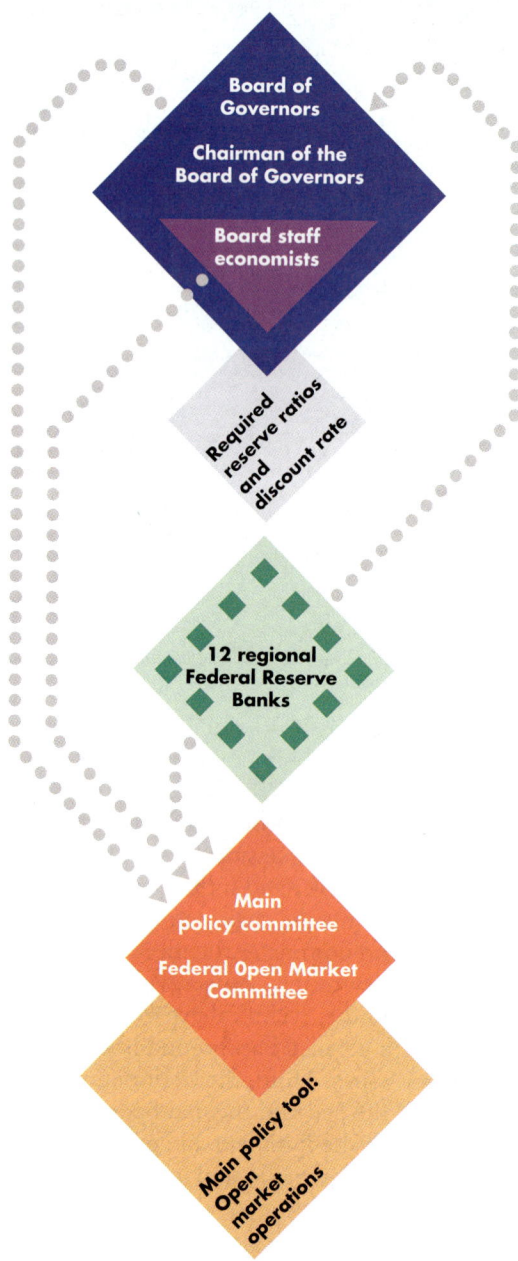

**FIGURE 10.4 The Structure of the Fed**

The Board of Governors sets required reserve ratios and, on the proposal of the 12 Federal Reserve banks, sets the discount rate. The Board of Governors and presidents of the regional Federal Reserve banks sit on the FOMC to determine open market operations.

## TABLE 10.3 The Fed's Balance Sheet, February 2002

| Assets (billions of dollars) | | Liabilities (billions of dollars) | |
|---|---|---|---|
| Gold and foreign exchange | 47 | Federal Reserve notes | 609 |
| U.S. government securities | 569 | Banks' deposits | 15 |
| Loans to banks | 30 | Other assets (net) | 22 |
| Total assets | 646 | Total liabilities | 646 |

Source: Federal Reserve Board.

liable to convert that note into gold or silver. Modern bank notes are nonconvertible. A *nonconvertible note* is a bank note that is not convertible into any commodity and that obtains its value by government fiat—hence the term "fiat money." Such notes are the legal liability of the bank that issues them, and they are backed by holdings of securities and loans. Federal Reserve notes are backed by the Fed's holdings of U.S. government securities.

The Fed's liabilities together with coins in circulation (coins are issued by the Treasury and are not liabilities of the Fed) make up the monetary base. That is, the **monetary base** is the sum of Federal Reserve notes, coins, and banks' deposits at the Fed. The monetary base is so named because it acts like a base that supports the nation's money supply. The larger the monetary base, the greater is the quantity of money.

### REVIEW QUIZ

1. What is the central bank of the United States and what functions does it perform?
2. Who appoints the Fed board members and chairman and for how long do they serve?
3. Can you name the Fed's three policy tools?
4. What is the Federal Open Market Committee and what are its main functions?
5. How often does the FOMC meet?

Next, we're going to see how the Fed controls the quantity of money. We'll see how the Fed's monetary policy instruments change the monetary base and how changes in the monetary base change the quantity of money.

## Controlling the Quantity of Money

THE FED CONSTANTLY MONITORS AND ADJUSTS the quantity of money in the economy. To change the quantity of money, the Fed can use any of its three tools: required reserve ratios, discount rate, and open market operations. Required reserve ratios are changed infrequently. The discount rate and open market operations are used more frequently. Let's see how these tools work.

### How Required Reserve Ratios Work

When the Fed *increases* the required reserve ratio, the banks must hold more reserves. To increase their reserves, the banks must *decrease* their lending, which *decreases* the quantity of money. When the Fed *decreases* the required reserve ratio, the banks may hold less reserves. To decrease their reserves, the banks *increase* their lending, which *increases* the quantity of money.

### How the Discount Rate Works

When the Fed *increases* the discount rate, banks must pay a higher price for any reserves that they borrow from the Fed. Faced with the higher cost of reserves, the banks try to get by with smaller reserves. But with a given required reserve ratio, banks must also *decrease* their lending to decrease their borrowed reserves. So the quantity of money *decreases*. When the Fed *decreases* the discount rate, banks pay a lower price for any reserves that they borrow from the Fed. Faced with lower cost of reserves, banks are willing to borrow more reserves and *increase* their lending. So the quantity of money *increases*.

### How an Open Market Operation Works

When the Fed *buys* securities in an open market operation, bank reserves *increase*, banks *increase* their lending, and the quantity of money *increases*. When the Fed *sells* securities in an open market operation, bank reserves *decrease*, banks *decrease* their lending, and the quantity of money *decreases*. Open market operations are used more frequently than the other two tools and are the most complex in their operation. So we'll study this tool in greater detail than the other two.

The key to understanding how an open market operation works is to see how it changes the reserves of the banking system. We'll trace the effects of an open market operation when the Fed *buys* securities.

**The Fed Buys Securities**  Suppose the Fed buys $100 million of U.S. government securities in the open market. There are two cases to consider: when the Fed buys from a commercial bank and when it buys from the public (a person or business that is not a commercial bank). The outcome is essentially the same in both cases, but you might need to be convinced of this fact, so we'll study the two cases. We'll start with the simpler case, in which the Fed buys from a commercial bank.

*Buys from Commercial Bank*  When the Fed buys $100 million of securities from the Manhattan Commercial Bank, two things happen:

1. The Manhattan Commercial Bank has $100 million less in securities, and the Fed has $100 million more in securities.
2. The Fed pays for the securities by crediting the Manhattan Commercial Bank's deposit account at the Fed with $100 million.

Figure 10.5(a) shows the effects of these actions on the balance sheets of the Fed and the Manhattan Commercial Bank. Ownership of the securities passes from the commercial bank to the Fed, so the bank's assets decrease by $100 million and the Fed's assets increase by $100 million, as shown by the blue arrow running from the Manhattan Commercial Bank to the Fed. The Fed pays for the securities by crediting the Manhattan Commercial Bank's deposit account—its reserves—at the Fed with $100 million, as shown by the green arrow running from the Fed to the Manhattan Commercial Bank. This action increases the monetary base and increases the reserves of the banking system.

The Fed's assets increase by $100 million, and its liabilities also increase by $100 million. The commercial bank's total assets remain constant, but their composition changes. Its holdings of government securities decrease by $100 million, and its deposits at the Fed increase by $100 million. So the bank has additional reserves, which it can use to make loans.

We've just seen that when the Fed buys government securities from a bank, the bank's reserves increase. But what happens if the Fed buys government securities from the public—say, from Goldman Sachs, a financial services company?

**FIGURE 10.5**  The Fed Buys Securities in the Open Market

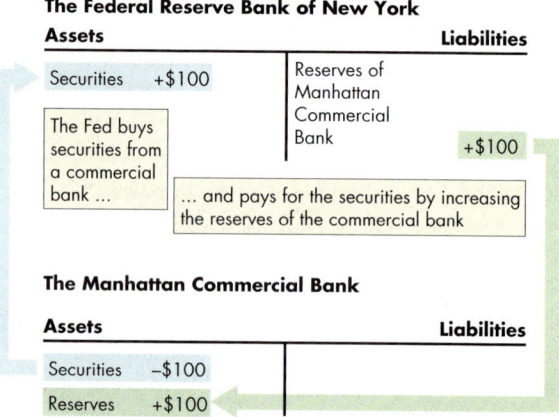

(a) The Fed buys securities from a commercial bank

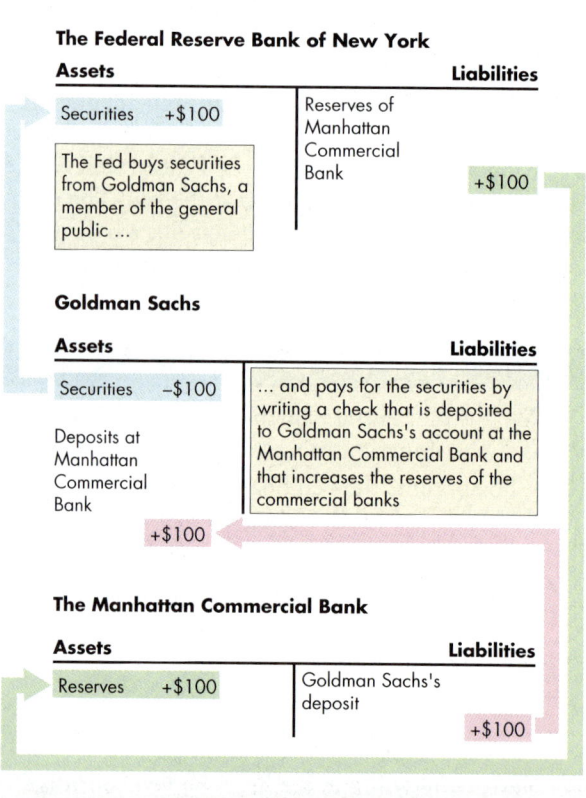

(b) The Fed buys securities from the public

***Buys from Public*** When the Fed buys $100 million of securities from Goldman Sachs, three things happen:

1. Goldman Sachs has $100 million less in securities, and the Fed has $100 million more in securities.
2. The Fed pays for the securities with a check for $100 million drawn on itself, which Goldman Sachs deposits in its account at the Manhattan Commercial Bank.
3. The Manhattan Commercial Bank collects payment of this check from the Fed, and $100 million is deposited in Manhattan's deposit account at the Fed.

Figure 10.5(b) shows the effects of these actions on the balance sheets of the Fed, Goldman Sachs, and the Manhattan Commercial Bank. Ownership of the securities passes from Goldman Sachs to the Fed, so Goldman Sachs's assets decrease by $100 million and the Fed's assets increase by $100 million, as shown by the blue arrow running from Goldman Sachs to the Fed. The Fed pays for the securities with a check payable to Goldman Sachs, which Goldman Sachs deposits in the Manhattan Commercial Bank. This payment increases Manhattan's reserves by $100 million, as shown by the green arrow running from the Fed to the Manhattan Commercial Bank. It also increases Goldman Sachs's deposit at the Manhattan Commercial Bank by $100 million, as shown by the red arrow running from the Manhattan Commercial Bank to Goldman Sachs. Just as when the Fed buys from a bank, this action increases the monetary base and increases the reserves of the banking system.

Again, the Fed's assets increase by $100 million, and its liabilities also increase by $100 million. Goldman Sachs has the same total assets as before, but their composition has changed. It now has more money and fewer securities. The Manhattan Commercial Bank's total assets increase, and so do its liabilities. Its deposits at the Fed—its reserves—increase by $100 million, and its deposit liability to Goldman Sachs increases by $100 million. Because its reserves have increased by the same amount as its deposits, the bank has excess reserves, which it can use to make loans.

When the Fed *sells* securities, all the transactions and events you've just studied work in reverse. (Trace the process again but with the Fed selling and the banks or public buying securities.)

## The Monetary Base, the Quantity of Money, and the Money Multiplier

The *monetary base* is the sum of Federal Reserve notes, coins, and banks' deposits at the Fed. An open market purchase increases the banks' deposits at the Fed and increases the monetary base. And a change in the monetary base brings a change in the quantity of money. The **money multiplier** determines the change in the quantity of money that results from a given change in the monetary base. For example, if a $1 million increase in the monetary base brings a $3 million increase in the quantity of money, the money multiplier is 3.

A change in the monetary base has a multiplier effect on the quantity of money because banks create deposits when they have excess reserves. So the process of money creation that follows an open market operation is similar to the one that you have just studied. But there is another factor that comes into play. When the banks use new reserves to make loans, bank deposits and currency held outside the banks increase. An increase in currency held outside the banks, called a **currency drain**, decreases the amount of money that banks can create from a given increase in the monetary base.

Figure 10.6 shows the multiplier effect of an open market purchase. Initially, banks' reserves increase, but the quantity of money does not change. But the banks have excess reserves, and the following sequence of events takes place:

- Banks lend excess reserves.
- The quantity of money increases.
- New deposits are used to make payments.
- Some of the new money is held as currency—a *currency drain*.
- Some of the new money remains on deposit in banks.
- Banks' required reserves increase.
- Excess reserves decrease but remain positive.

The sequence repeats in a series of rounds, but each round begins with a smaller quantity of excess reserves than did the previous one. The process continues until excess reserves have finally been eliminated.

Figure 10.5 keeps track of the magnitudes of the increases in reserves, loans, deposits, currency, and money that result from an open market purchase of $100,000. In this figure, the *required reserve ratio* is 10 percent of deposits and the *currency drain* is 50 percent of deposits (assumed numbers).

The Fed buys $100,000 of securities from the banks. The banks' reserves increase by this amount, but deposits do not change. The banks have excess reserves of $100,000, and they lend those reserves. When the banks lend $100,000 of excess reserves, $66,667 remains in the banks as deposits and $33,333 drains off and is held outside the banks as currency. The quantity of money has now increased by $100,000—the increase in deposits plus the increase in currency holdings.

The increased bank deposits of $66,667 generate an increase in required reserves of 10 percent of that amount, which is $6,667. Actual reserves have increased by the same amount as the increase in deposits: $66,667. So the banks now have excess reserves of $60,000. At this stage, we have gone around the circle shown in Fig. 10.6 once. The process we've just described repeats but begins with excess reserves of $60,000. Figure 10.7 shows the next two rounds. At the end of the process, the quantity of money has increased by a multiple of the increase in the monetary base. In this case, the increase is $250,000, which is 2.5 times the increase in the monetary base.

An open market *sale* works similarly to an open market purchase, but it *decreases* the quantity of money. (Trace the process again but with the Fed selling and the banks or public buying securities.)

## The Size of the Money Multiplier

In the example we've just worked through, the money multiplier is 2.5. Why? The size of the money multiplier depends on the magnitudes of the required reserve ratio and the ratio of currency to deposits. To see how these two ratios influence the size of the money multiplier, call required reserves $R$, the required reserve ratio $r$, currency $C$, the ratio of currency to deposits $c$, deposits $D$, the quantity of money $M$, and the monetary base $B$.

Required reserves $R = rD$ and currency $C = cD$. The quantity of money is $M = C + D$, or,

$$M = (1 + c)D. \tag{1}$$

The monetary base $B = R + C$, or

$$B = (r + c)D. \tag{2}$$

**FIGURE 10.6** A Round in the Multiplier Process Following an Open Market Purchase

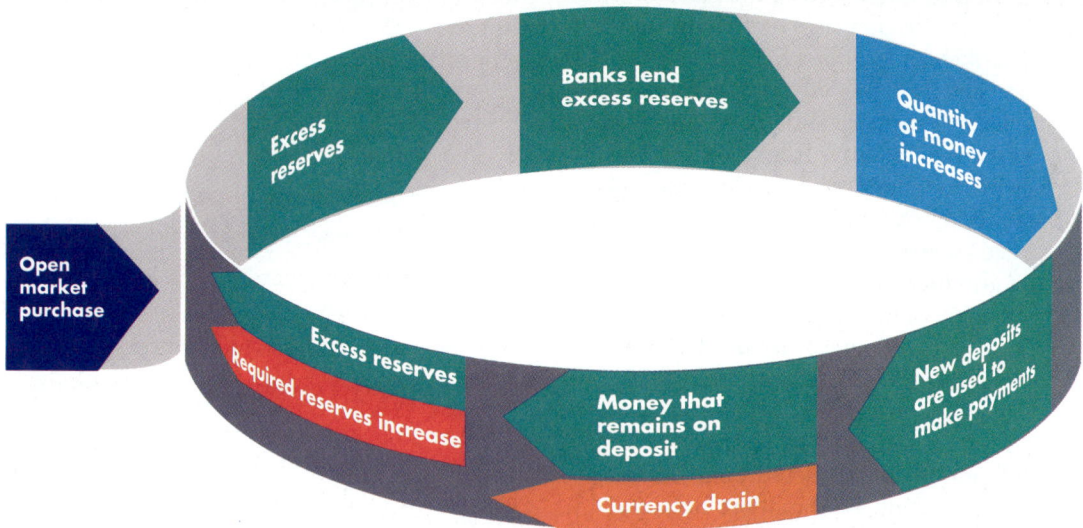

An open market purchase increases bank reserves and creates excess reserves. Banks lend the excess reserves, and new loans are used to make payments. Households and firms receiving payments keep some of the receipts in the form of currency—a currency drain—and place the rest on deposit in banks.

The increase in bank deposits increases banks' reserves but also increases banks' required reserves. Required reserves increase by less than actual reserves, so the banks still have some excess reserves, though less than before. The process repeats until excess reserves have been eliminated.

# FIGURE 10.7 The Multiplier Effect of an Open Market Purchase

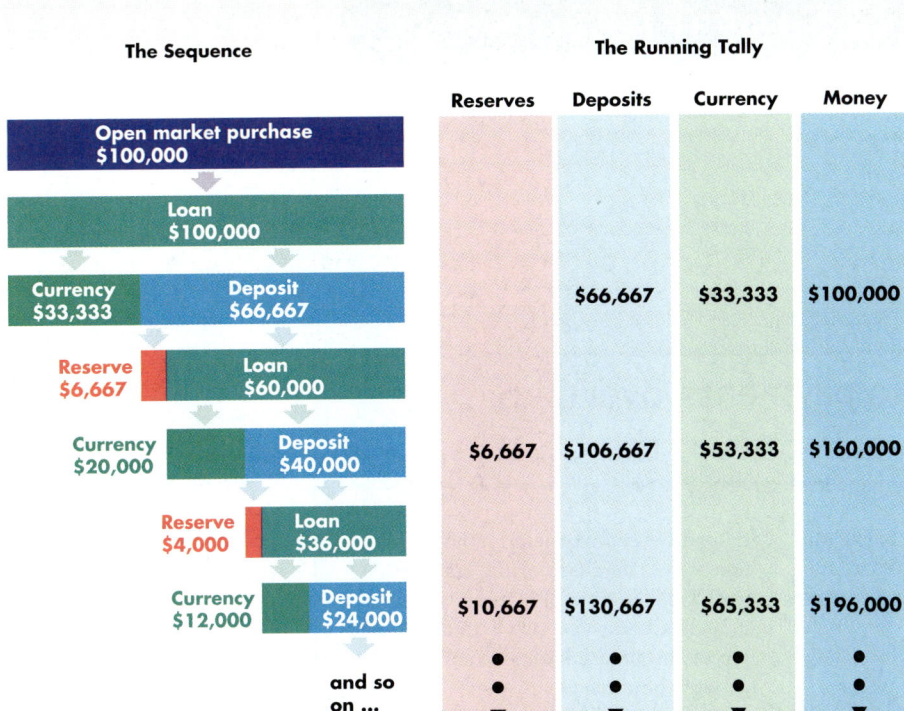

When the Fed provides the banks with $100,000 of additional reserves in an open market operation, the banks lend those reserves. Of the amount lent, $33,333 (50 percent of deposits) leaves the banks in a currency drain and $66,667 remains on deposit. With additional deposits, required reserves increase by $6,667 (10 percent required reserve ratio) and the banks lend $60,000. Of this amount, $20,000 leaves the banks in a currency drain and $40,000 remains on deposit. The process repeats until the banks have created enough deposits to eliminate their excess reserves. An additional $100,000 of reserves creates $250,000 of money.

Divide equation (1) by equation (2) to get

$$\frac{M}{B} = \frac{(1+c)}{(r+c)}$$

or

$$M = \left[\frac{(1+c)}{(r+c)}\right] \times B.$$

With $r = 0.1$ (10 percent) and $c = 0.5$ (50 percent), $(1+c)/(r+c) = (1.5/0.6) = 2.5$, which is the magnitude of the money multiplier that we found in the above exercise.

The magnitude of the U.S. money multiplier depends on the definition of money that we use. For M1, $r = 0.08$ (8 percent) and $c = 1.06$ (106 percent), so the money multiplier is 1.8. For M2, $r = 0.01$ (1 percent) and $c = 0.12$ (12 percent) so the money multiplier is 8.6. That is, in the United States, a $1 million increase in the monetary base brings a $1.8 million increase in M1 and an $8.6 million increase in M2. Currency increases by $930,000 and bank reserves increase by $70,000.

### REVIEW QUIZ

1. What happens when the Fed buys or sells securities in the open market?
2. What do the banks do when they have excess reserves and how do their actions influence the quantity of money?
3. What do the banks do when they are short of reserves and how do their actions influence the quantity of money?

♦ You've now seen how the Fed influences the quantity of money. Your task in the next chapter is to see how changes in the quantity of money influence the interest rate, expenditure plans, real GDP, and the price level. But first, take a look at *Reading Between the Lines* on pp. 252–253 and see how the way we use money is changing.

# READING BETWEEN THE LINES

## *Electronic Money*

### Electronic payments overtake checks and cash in the US

For the first time, electronic payments have surpassed cash and checks as the preferred payment method for US consumers when shopping on the high street, according to a nationwide study conducted by the American Bankers Association and Boston-based strategy consulting firm Dove Consulting.

The 2003/2004 study, conducted among 2008 US consumers, found that cash and checks now account for 47% of in-store purchases, as compared to 57% in 1999 and 51% in 2001.

Much of the slack appears to be taken up by growth in debit cards, which now account for nearly one-in-three in-store purchases, up from 21% four years ago.

While cash remains the single most frequently used payment method on the high street, its share of the transaction mix has fallen from 39% in 1999 to 32% in 2003. Checks also play a diminishing role at the point-of-sale, accounting for just 15% of purchases.

Comparatively, consumer use of credit cards for in-store purchases has remained relatively constant at 21%. At 2%, the "other" payments category is made up of prepaid cards.

The study finds check usage is also on the wane for bill payments, falling from 72% in 2001 to 60% today, with online bill payment gaining in popularity. The survey finds 41% of consumers currently use online bill payment to settle recurring bills.

Copyright finextra.com
16 December 2003
http://www.finextra.com/topstory.asp?id=10825

### Essence of the Story

■ In 2003, cash accounted for 32 percent of in-store purchases, down from 39 percent in 1999 and checks accounted for 15 percent of purchases, down from 18 percent in 1999.

■ Debit cards accounted for 32 percent of in-store purchases, up from 21 percent in 1999.

■ Credit cards accounted for a constant 21 percent of in-store purchases.

■ Check usage for bill payments fell from 72 percent in 2001 to 60 percent in 2003, and online bill payment increased.

## Economic Analysis

- The news article reports the changes that occurred between 1999 and 2003 in the way transactions are done in retail stores.

- Figure 1 provides a graphic description of the changes: cash down from 39 percent to 32 percent; checks down from 18 percent to 15 percent; and debit cards up from 21 percent to 32 percent.

- Checks and debit cards are alternative ways of paying with a bank deposit. It is the bank deposit that is money.

- Credit cards, constant at 21 percent, are not a method of *payment*. Payment occurs when the credit card balance is paid off. Most of these payments are made by writing a check.

- If all credit card balances are paid by using a check, electronic forms of payment are not yet more common than paper forms of payment.

- The cost of conducting a transaction determines the method of payment that a person uses.

- All forms of payment incur a transaction cost.

- The main cost using cash arises from theft. Carrying cash is more risky than carrying a plastic card that needs a PIN to be used.

- Electronic forms of payment are used only if they provide a lower transaction cost than cash or a check.

- Transaction costs make a huge difference to the way a market works.

- Figure 2 shows the effects of transaction costs in the market for music downloads.

- The demand curve for downloads is $D$, and the supply curve, which includes a transaction cost of 33¢ per transaction, is $S_0$. The equilibrium number of downloads is 2 million tracks per week.

- If the transaction cost were zero, the supply curve would be $S_1$. The equilibrium number of downloads would increase to 3 million tracks per week. (The numbers are hypothetical.)

- PayPal currently charges 33¢ per transaction and is planning to cut this price.

- As the cost of electronic transactions falls, we can expect the use of these methods of transaction to increase and the use of cash and checks to decrease further.

- Improved transactions technologies increase the quantities of goods and services that we are able to consume.

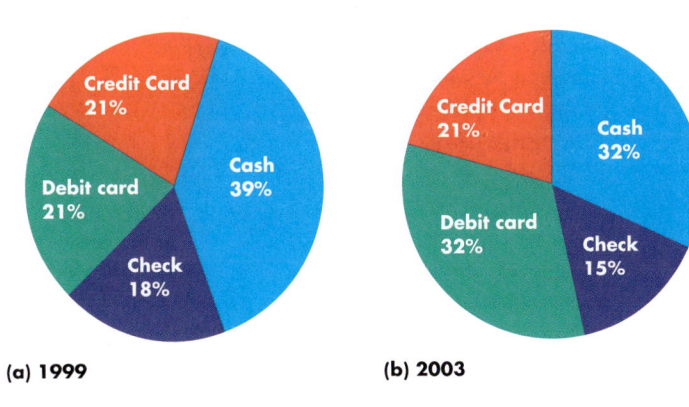

**Figure 1 The changing methods of payment**

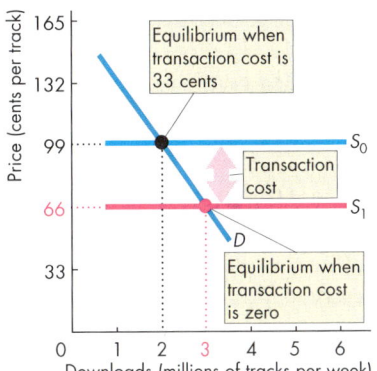

**Figure 2 How transactions costs change market outcome**

# SUMMARY

## KEY POINTS

### What Is Money? (pp. 234–236)

- Money is the means of payment, a medium of exchange, a unit of account, and a store of value.
- M1 consists of currency, traveler's checks, and checking deposits owned by individuals and businesses. M2 consists of M1 plus savings deposits, time deposits, and money market mutual funds.

### Depository Institutions (pp. 237–241)

- Commercial banks, S&Ls, savings banks, credit unions, and money market mutual funds are depository institutions whose liabilities are money.
- Depository institutions provide four main economic services: They create liquidity, minimize the cost of obtaining funds, minimize the cost of monitoring borrowers, and pool risks.
- Financial regulation to protect depositors includes deposit insurance and balance sheet rules such as minimum equity capital rules, required reserves, and deposit and lending rules.

### How Banks Create Money (pp. 242–243)

- Banks create money by making loans.
- The total quantity of deposits that can be supported by a given amount of reserves (the deposit multiplier) is determined by the required reserve ratio.

### The Federal Reserve System (pp. 244–247)

- The Federal Reserve System is the central bank of the United States.
- The Fed influences the economy by setting the required reserve ratio for banks, by setting the discount rate—the interest rate at which it is willing to lend reserves to the banking system, and by open market operations.

### Controlling the Quantity of Money (pp. 247–251)

- By buying government securities in the market (an open market purchase), the Fed increases the monetary base and bank reserves; and by selling government securities in the market (an open market sale), the Fed decreases the monetary base and bank reserves.
- A change in the monetary base and bank reserves has a multiplier effect on the quantity of money. The multiplier is larger, the smaller the required reserve ratio and the smaller the currency drain.

## KEY FIGURES

Figure 10.1   Two Measures of Money, 235
Figure 10.2   The Multiple Creation of Bank Deposits, 243
Figure 10.4   The Structure of the Fed, 246
Figure 10.7   The Multiplier Effect of an Open Market Purchase, 251

## KEY TERMS

Barter, 234
Central bank, 244
Commercial bank, 237
Credit union, 238
Currency, 235
Currency drain, 249
Depository institution, 237
Discount rate, 245
Excess reserves, 242
Federal funds rate, 244
Federal Open Market Committee, 244
Federal Reserve System, 244
Financial innovation, 240
Liquidity, 236
M1, 235
M2, 235
Means of payment, 234
Monetary base, 247
Monetary policy, 244
Money, 234
Money market mutual fund, 238
Money multiplier, 249
Open market operation, 246
Required reserve ratio, 242
Reserve ratio, 242
Reserves, 237
Savings and loan association, 238
Savings bank, 238
Thrift institutions, 238

# PROBLEMS

*1. In the United States today, money includes which of the following items?
   a. Federal Reserve banknotes in the Bank of America's cash machines
   b. Your Visa card
   c. The quarters inside public phones
   d. U.S. dollar bills in your wallet
   e. The check you have just written to pay for your rent
   f. The loan you took out last August to pay for your school fees

2. Which of the following items are money? Which are deposit money?
   a. Checking deposits at Citicorp
   b. Yahoo! stock held by individuals
   c. An American Express traveler's check
   d. State of Florida securities
   e. NOW accounts

   Explain your answer by referring to the three basic functions of money.

*3. Sara withdraws $1,000 from her savings account at the Lucky S&L, keeps $50 in cash, and deposits the balance in her checking account at the Bank of Illinois. What is the immediate change in M1 and M2?

4. Monica takes $10,000 from her money market mutual fund and puts the funds into her savings account at the Bank of Alaska. What is the immediate change in M1 and M2?

*5. The commercial banks in Zap have

   | | |
   |---|---|
   | Reserves | $250 million |
   | Loans | $1,000 million |
   | Deposits | $2,000 million |
   | Total assets | $2,500 million |

   a. Construct the commercial banks' balance sheet. If you are missing any assets, call them "other assets"; if you are missing any liabilities, call them "other liabilities."
   b. Calculate the banks' reserve ratio.
   c. If banks hold no excess reserves, calculate the deposit multiplier.

6. The commercial banks in Zip have

   | | |
   |---|---|
   | Reserves | $250 million |
   | Loans | $3,750 million |
   | Deposits | $4,000 million |
   | Total assets | $4,200 million |

   a. Construct the commercial banks' balance sheet. If you are missing any assets, call them "other assets"; if you are missing any liabilities, call them "other liabilities."
   b. Calculate the banks' reserve ratio.
   c. If banks hold no excess reserves, calculate the deposit multiplier.

*7. An immigrant arrives in New Transylvania with $1,200. The $1,200 is deposited in a bank. All the banks in New Transylvania have a required reserve ratio of 10 percent, and they have no excess reserves when the immigrant arrives.
   a. What is the initial increase in the quantity of money in New Transylvania?
   b. What is the initial increase in the quantity of bank deposits when the immigrant arrives?
   c. How much does the immigrant's bank lend initially?
   d. Set out the transactions that take place and calculate the amount lent and the amount of deposits created if all the funds lent are returned to the banking system in the form of deposits.
   e. By how much has the quantity of money increased after the banks have made 2 loans?
   f. What is the total increase in the quantity of money, in bank loans, and in bank deposits?

8. An Internet thief in Chicago steals $1 million from a bank in Buenos Aires, Argentina. He transfers the funds to a bank account in Chicago. The Chicago bank has a required reserve ratio of 5 percent, and it has no excess reserves when the transfer occurs.
   a. What is the initial increase in the quantity of money in the United States?
   b. What is the initial increase in the quantity of bank deposits when the theft occurs?
   c. How much does the thief's bank lend out?
   d. Set out the transactions that take place and calculate the amount lent and the amount of deposits created if all the funds lent are returned to the banking system in the form of deposits.
   e. By how much has the quantity of money increased after the banks have made 2 loans?
   f. What is the total increase in the quantity of money, in bank loans, and in bank deposits?

* Solutions to odd-numbered problems are available on **MyEconLab**.

*9. You are given the following information about the economy of Nocoin: The banks have deposits of $300 billion. Their reserves are $15 billion, two thirds of which is in deposits with the central bank. There are $30 billion notes outside the banks. There are no coins! Calculate
   a. The monetary base.
   b. The quantity of money.
   c. The banks' reserve ratio.
   d. The currency drain as a percentage of the quantity of money.

10. You are given the following information about the economy of Fredzone: The people and businesses in Fredzone have bank deposits of $500 billion and hold $100 billion in notes and coins. The banks hold deposits at the Fredzone Fed of $5 billion, and they keep $5 billion in notes and coins in their vaults and ATM machines. Calculate
    a. The monetary base.
    b. The quantity of money.
    c. The banks' reserve ratio.
    d. The currency drain as a percentage of the quantity of money.

*11. Suppose that in problem 1, the Bank of Nocoin, the central bank, undertakes an open market purchase of securities of $0.5 billion.
    a. What happens to the quantity of money?
    b. Explain why the change in the quantity of money is not equal to the change in the monetary base.
    c. Calculate the money multiplier.

12. Suppose that in problem 2, the Fredzone Fed undertakes an open market sale of securities of $1 billion.
    a. What happens to the quantity of money?
    b. Explain why the change in the quantity of money is not equal to the change in the monetary base.
    c. Calculate the money multiplier.

# CRITICAL THINKING

1. Study *Reading Between the Lines* on pp. 252–253 and then
   a. Describe what has happened to the use of cash, checks, debit cards, and credit cards between 1999 and 2003.
   b. Explain why the use of cash and checks has decreased and the use of debit cards has increased.
2. Rapid inflation in Brazil caused the cruzeiro to lose its ability to function as money. Which of these commodities do you think would be most likely to take the place of the cruzeiro in the Brazilian economy? Explain why.
   a. Tractor parts
   b. Packs of cigarettes
   c. Loaves of bread
   d. Impressionist paintings
   e. Baseball trading cards

# WEB EXERCISES

**Use the links on MyEconLab to work the following exercise.**

1. Visit Roy Davies's Web site, "Money—Past, Present, and Future," and study the section on e-money. Then answer the following questions:
   a. What is e-money and what are the alternative forms that it takes?
   b. Do you think that the widespread use of e-money will limit the ability of the Federal Reserve to control the quantity of money? Why or why not?
   c. When you buy an item on the Internet and pay for it using PayPal, are you using money? Explain why or why not.
   d. Why might e-money be superior to cash as a means of payment?

# Money, Interest, Real GDP, and the Price Level

CHAPTER 11

## Ripple Effects of Money

**There is enough money in the United States** today for everyone to have a wallet stuffed with $2,300 in notes and coins and another $19,000 in the bank. Why do we hold all this money? What influences the quantity of money that we decide to hold?

Through 2001, as the U.S. economy slowed to a near standstill, the Fed, anxious to keep the economy expanding, cut interest rates 11 times from more than 6 percent at the start of the year to less than 2 percent at the year's end. In 2002 and 2003, the Fed cut interest rates even further to historically low levels. A few years earlier, in 1999 and 2000, the Fed was more concerned about inflation than recession and it raised interest rates.

How does the Fed change interest rates? And how do interest rates influence the economy? How do lower interest rates fight recession? How do higher interest rates keep inflation in check?

◆ In this chapter, you'll discover the answers to these questions. In *Reading Between the Lines* at the end of the chapter, you'll see what happens when money gets out of control, as it did in Argentina during the late 1980s. The demand for money and the supply of money determine the interest rate. So we begin by studying the influences on the quantity of money that people decide to hold.

### After studying this chapter, you will be able to

- Explain what determines the demand for money
- Explain how the Fed influences interest rates
- Explain how the Fed's actions influence spending plans, real GDP, and the price level in the short run
- Explain how the Fed's actions influence real GDP and the price level in the long run and explain the quantity theory of money

## The Demand for Money

THERE IS NO LIMIT TO THE AMOUNT OF MONEY we would like to *receive* in payment for our labor or as interest on our savings. But there *is* a limit to how big an inventory of money—the money that we hold in our wallet or in a deposit account at the bank—we would like to hold onto and not either spend or use to buy assets that generate an income. The demand for money is the demand for the inventory of money that people plan to hold.

### The Influences on Money Holding

The quantity of money that people plan to hold depends on four main factors:

- The price level
- The interest rate
- Real GDP
- Financial innovation

**The Price Level** The quantity of money measured in dollars is *nominal money*. The quantity of nominal money demanded is proportional to the price level, other things remaining the same. If the price level rises by 10 percent, people hold 10 percent more nominal money than before, other things remaining the same. If you hold $20 to buy your weekly movies and soda, you will increase your money holding to $22 if the prices of movies and soda—and your wage rate—increase by 10 percent.

The quantity of money measured in constant dollars (for example, in 2000 dollars) is *real money*. Real money is equal to nominal money divided by the price level and is the quantity of money measured in terms of what it will buy. In the above example, when the price level rises by 10 percent and you increase your money holding by 10 percent, your *real* money holding is constant. Your $22 at the new price level buys the same quantity of goods and is the same quantity of *real money* as your $20 at the original price level. The quantity of real money demanded is independent of the price level.

**The Interest Rate** A fundamental principle of economics is that as the opportunity cost of something increases, people try to find substitutes for it. Money is no exception. The higher the opportunity cost of holding money, other things remaining the same, the lower is the quantity of real money demanded. But what is the opportunity cost of holding money? It is the interest rate that you can earn by holding money minus the interest rate that you must forgo on other assets that you could hold instead of money.

The interest rate that you earn on currency and checking deposits is zero. So the opportunity cost of holding these items is the interest rate on other assets such as a savings bond or Treasury bill. By holding money instead, you forgo the interest that you otherwise would have received. This forgone interest is the opportunity cost of holding money.

Money loses value because of inflation. So why isn't the inflation rate part of the cost of holding money? It is: Other things remaining the same, the higher the expected inflation rate, the higher is the interest rate and the higher, therefore, is the opportunity cost of holding money. (The forces that make the interest rate change to reflect changes in the expected inflation rate are described in Chapter 12, p. 293.)

**Real GDP** The quantity of money that households and firms plan to hold depends on the amount they are spending, and the quantity of money demanded in the economy as a whole depends on aggregate expenditure—real GDP.

Again, suppose that you hold an average of $20 to finance your weekly purchases of movies and soda. Now imagine that the prices of these goods and of all other goods remain constant but that your income increases. As a consequence, you now spend more and you also keep a larger amount of money on hand to finance your higher volume of expenditure.

**Financial Innovation** Technological change and the arrival of new financial products change the quantity of money held. Financial innovations include

1. Daily interest checking deposits
2. Automatic transfers between checking and saving deposits
3. Automatic teller machines
4. Credit cards and debit cards
5. Internet banking and bill paying

These innovations have occurred because of the development of computing power that has lowered the cost of calculations and record keeping.

We summarize the effects of the influences on money holding by using a demand for money curve.

## The Demand for Money Curve

The demand for money curve is the relationship between the quantity of real money demanded and the interest rate when all other influences on the amount of money that people wish to hold remain the same.

Figure 11.1 shows a demand for money curve, $MD$. When the interest rate rises, everything else remaining the same, the opportunity cost of holding money rises and the quantity of real money demanded decreases—there is a movement up along the demand for money curve. Similarly, when the interest rate falls, the opportunity cost of holding money falls, and the quantity of real money demanded increases—there is a movement down along the demand for money curve.

When any influence on money holding other than the interest rate changes, there is a change in the demand for money and the demand for money curve shifts. Let's study these shifts.

## Shifts in the Demand for Money Curve

A change in real GDP or financial innovation changes the demand for money and shifts the demand curve for real money.

Figure 11.2 illustrates the change in the demand for money. A decrease in real GDP decreases the demand for money and shifts the demand curve leftward from $MD_0$ to $MD_1$. An increase in real GDP has the opposite effect: It increases the demand for money and shifts the demand curve rightward from $MD_0$ to $MD_2$.

The influence of financial innovation on the demand for money curve is more complicated. It might increase the demand for some types of deposits, decrease the demand for others, and decrease the demand for currency.

We'll look at the effects of changes in real GDP and financial innovation by studying the demand for money in the United States.

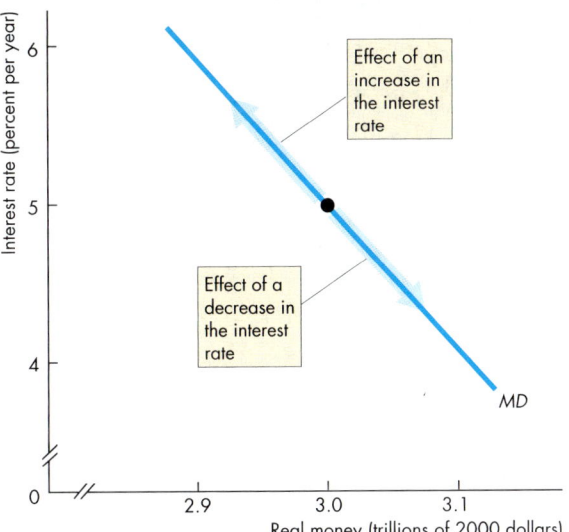

**FIGURE 11.1  The Demand for Money**

The demand for money curve, $MD$, shows the relationship between the quantity of money that people plan to hold and the interest rate, other things remaining the same. The interest rate is the opportunity cost of holding money. A change in the interest rate brings a movement along the demand curve.

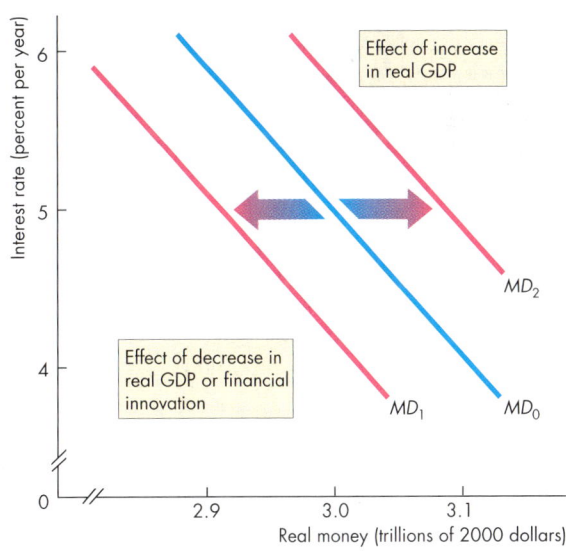

**FIGURE 11.2  Changes in the Demand for Money**

A decrease in real GDP decreases the demand for money. The demand curve shifts leftward from $MD_0$ to $MD_1$. An increase in real GDP increases the demand for money. The demand curve shifts rightward from $MD_0$ to $MD_2$. Financial innovation generally decreases the demand for money.

## The Demand for Money in the United States

Figure 11.3 shows the relationship between the interest rate and the quantity of real money demanded in the United States between 1970 and 2003. Each dot shows the interest rate and the amount of real money held in a given year. In 1970, the demand for M1 (shown in part a) was $MD_0$. During the early 1970s, the spread of credit cards decreased the demand for M1 (currency and checking deposits) and this financial innovation shifted the demand for M1 curve leftward to $MD_1$. But over the years, real GDP growth increased the demand for M1, and by 1994, the demand for M1 curve had shifted rightward to $MD_2$.

Further financial innovation arising from a continued increase in the use of credit cards and the spread of ATMs decreased the demand for M1 and shifted the demand curve leftward again.

In 1970, the demand for M2 (shown in part b) was $MD_0$. The spread of credit cards that decreased the demand for M1 during the period did not decrease demand for M2. The reason is that many new financial products were M2 deposits. So from 1970 through 1989, the demand for M2 increased and the demand for M2 curve shifted rightward to $MD_1$. But between 1989 and 1994, innovations in financial products that compete with deposits of all kinds occurred and the demand for M2 decreased. The demand for M2 curve shifted leftward to $MD_2$. Finally, after 1994, the expanding economy brought rising real GDP. The demand for M2 increased again, and the demand curve shifted rightward to $MD_3$.

### FIGURE 11.3 The Demand for Money in the United States

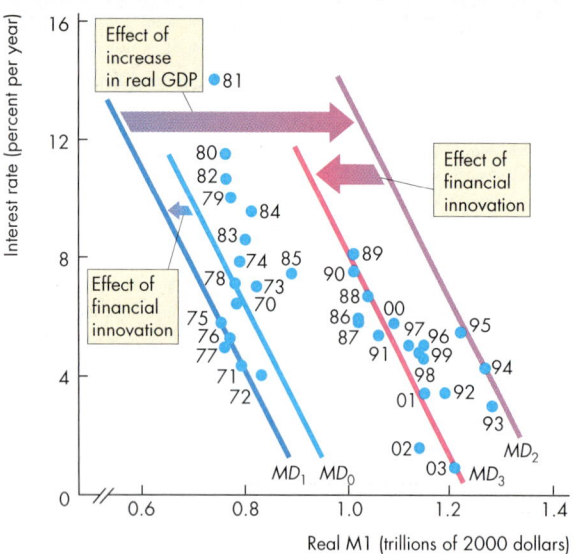

(a) M1 demand

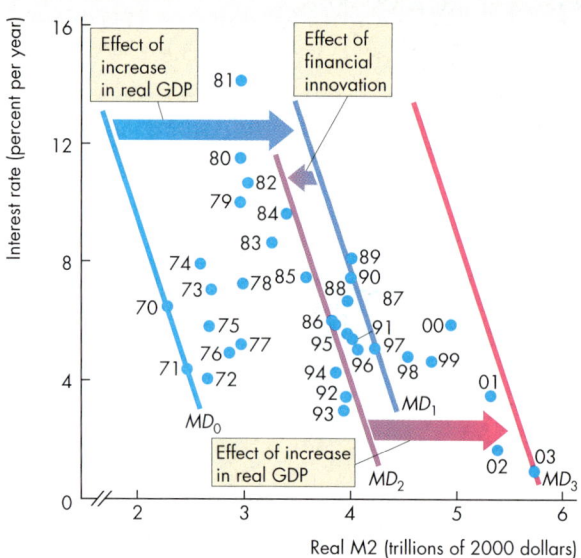

(b) M2 demand

The dots show the quantity of real money and the interest rate in each year between 1970 and 2003. In 1970, the demand for M1 was $MD_0$ in part (a). The demand for M1 decreased during the early 1970s because of financial innovation, and the demand curve shifted leftward to $MD_1$. But real GDP growth increases the demand for M1 and by 1994, the demand curve had shifted rightward to $MD_2$. Further financial innovation decreased the demand for M1 during the 1990s and 2000s and shifted the demand curve leftward again to $MD_3$. In 1970, the demand for M2 curve was $MD_0$ in part (b). The growth of real GDP increased the demand for M2, and by 1989, the demand curve had shifted rightward to $MD_1$. During the early 1990s, new substitutes for M2 decreased the demand for M2 and the demand curve shifted leftward to $MD_2$. But during the late 1990s, rapid growth of real GDP increased the demand for M2. By 2003, the demand curve had shifted rightward to $MD_3$.

*Sources:* Bureau of Economic Analysis and Federal Reserve Board.

### REVIEW QUIZ

1. What are the main influences on the quantity of real money that people and businesses plan to hold?
2. What does the demand for money curve show?
3. How does an increase in the interest rate change the quantity of money demanded and how would you show the effect by using the demand for money curve?
4. How does an increase in real GDP change the demand for money and how would you show the effect by using the demand for money curve?
5. How have financial innovations changed the demand for M1 and the demand for M2?

We now know what determines the demand for money. And we've seen that a key factor is the interest rate—the opportunity cost of holding money. But what determines the interest rate? Let's find out.

## Interest Rate Determination

AN INTEREST RATE IS THE PERCENTAGE YIELD ON a financial security such as a *bond* or a *stock*. The higher the price of a financial security, other things remaining the same, the lower is the interest rate. An example will make this relationship clear. Suppose the federal government sells a bond that promises to pay $10 a year. If the price of the bond is $100, the interest rate is 10 percent per year—$10 is 10 percent of $100. If the price is $50, the interest rate is 20 percent—$10 is 20 percent of $50. And if the price is $200, the interest rate is 5 percent—$10 is 5 percent of $200.

You've just seen the link between the price of a bond and the interest rate. People divide their wealth between bonds (along with other interest-bearing financial assets) and money, and the amount they hold as money depends on the interest rate. We can study these forces that determine the interest rate in either the market for bonds or the market for money.

Because the Fed can influence the *quantity of money*, we focus on the market for money.

### Money Market Equilibrium

The interest rate is determined by the supply of money and the demand for money. The quantity of money supplied is determined by the actions of the banking system and the Fed. On any given day, the quantity of money is fixed. The *real* quantity of money supplied is equal to the nominal quantity supplied divided by the price level. At a given moment in time, there is a particular price level, and so the quantity of real money supplied is a fixed amount. In Fig. 11.4, the quantity of real money supplied is $3.0 trillion and the supply of money curve is *MS*.

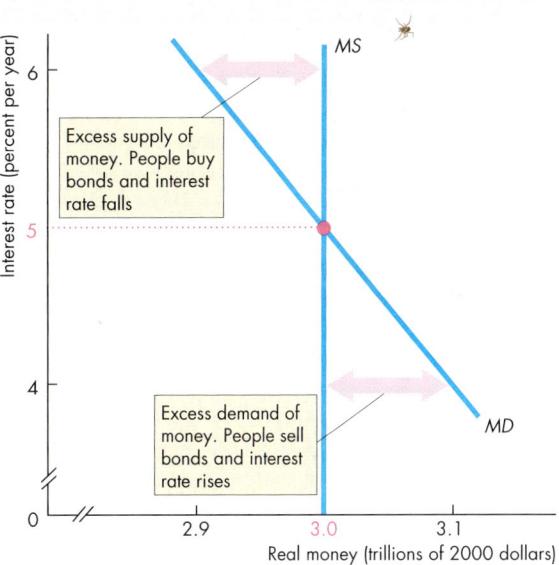

**FIGURE 11.4** Money Market Equilibrium

Money market equilibrium occurs when the interest rate has adjusted to make the quantity of money demanded equal to the quantity supplied. Here, equilibrium occurs at an interest rate of 5 percent. At interest rates above 5 percent, the quantity of money demanded is less than the quantity supplied, so people buy bonds and the interest rate falls. At interest rates below 5 percent, the quantity of money demanded exceeds the quantity supplied, so people sell bonds and the interest rate rises. Only at 5 percent is the quantity of money in existence willingly held.

On any given day, all the influences on the demand for money except the interest rate are constant. That is, real GDP and the price level are given. But the interest rate fluctuates daily. And the lower the interest rate, the greater is the quantity of money demanded. In Fig. 11.4, the demand for money curve is $MD$.

When the quantity of money supplied equals the quantity of money demanded, the money market is in equilibrium. Figure 11.4 illustrates money market equilibrium. Equilibrium is achieved by changes in the interest rate. If the interest rate is too high, people demand a smaller quantity of money than the quantity supplied. They are holding too much money. In this situation, they try to get rid of money by buying bonds. As they do so, the price of a bond rises and the interest rate falls toward the equilibrium rate. Conversely, if the interest rate is too low, people demand a larger quantity of money than the quantity supplied. They are holding too little money. In this situation, they try to get more money by selling bonds. The supply of bonds increases, the price of a bond falls, and the interest rate rises toward the equilibrium rate. Only when the interest rate is at the level at which the quantity of money demanded equals the quantity supplied do people willingly hold the money and take no actions that change the interest rate.

## Changing the Interest Rate

Suppose that the economy is overheating and the Fed fears inflation. It decides to take action to decrease aggregate demand and spending. To do so, it wants to raise interest rates and discourage borrowing and expenditure on goods and services. What does the Fed do?

The Fed sells securities in the open market. As it does so, it mops up bank reserves and induces the banks to cut their lending. The banks make a smaller quantity of new loans each day until the stock of loans outstanding has fallen to a level that is consistent with the new lower level of reserves. The quantity of money decreases.

Suppose that the Fed undertakes open market operations on a sufficiently large scale to decrease the quantity of money from $3.0 trillion to $2.9 trillion in Fig. 11.5. As a consequence, the supply of money curve shifts leftward, from $MS_0$ to $MS_1$. The demand for money curve is $MD$. With an interest rate of 5 percent, and with $2.9 trillion of money in the economy, firms and households are now holding less money than they wish to hold. They attempt to increase their money holding by selling financial assets. As they do

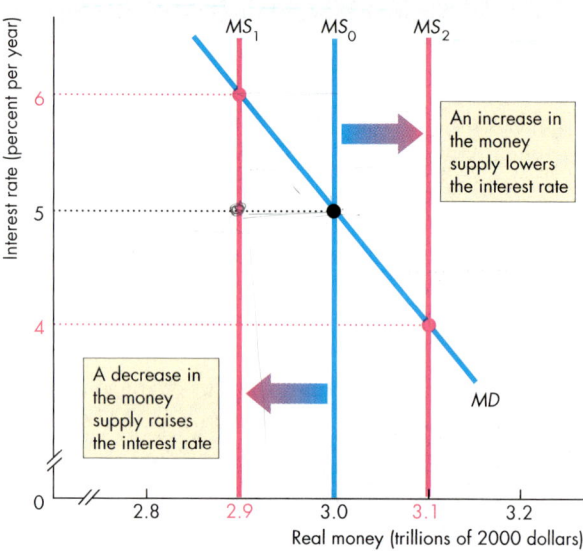

**FIGURE 11.5** Interest Rate Changes

An open market sale of securities shifts the money supply curve leftward to $MS_1$, and the interest rate rises to 6 percent. An open market purchase of securities shifts the money supply curve rightward to $MS_2$, and the interest rate falls to 4 percent.

so, the price of a bond falls and the interest rate rises. When the interest rate has increased to 6 percent, people are willing to hold the smaller $2.9 trillion of money that the Fed and the banks have created.

Conversely, suppose that the Fed fears recession and decides to stimulate spending by increasing the quantity of money. If the Fed increases the quantity of real money to $3.1 trillion, the supply of money curve shifts rightward from $MS_0$ to $MS_2$. Equilibrium occurs when the interest rate has fallen to 4 percent.

### REVIEW QUIZ

1. How is the short-term interest rate determined?
2. What do people do if they are holding more money than they plan to hold and what happens to the interest rate?
3. What actions does the Fed take if it wants to increase the interest rate? What actions does it take if it wants to decrease the interest rate?

# Short-Run Effects of Money on Real GDP and the Price Level

YOU'VE NOW SEEN HOW THE FED INFLUENCES the quantity of money and how a change in the quantity of money changes the interest rate. We're now going to look at the wider effects of the Fed's actions on the economy. We'll begin with an overview of their ripple effects.

## Ripple Effects of Interest Rate

If the Fed raises the interest rate, three events follow:

- Investment and consumption expenditure decrease.
- The dollar rises, and net exports decrease.
- A multiplier process unfolds.

**Investment and Consumption** The real interest rate is the *opportunity cost* of the funds used to finance investment and the purchase of big-ticket consumer items. So when the real interest rate rises, expenditure on these items falls. In the long run, the real interest rate is determined by demand and supply in the capital market (Chapter 8, pp. 193–194). But in the short run, the Fed changes the real interest rate by changing the nominal interest rate.

**The Dollar and Net Exports** A rise in the interest rate, other things remaining the same, means that the U.S. interest rate rises relative to the interest rates in other countries. Some people will want to move funds from other countries into the United States to take advantage of the higher interest rate they can now earn on their U.S. bank deposits and bonds. When money is moved into the United States, people buy dollars and sell other currencies, such as Japanese yen or British pounds. With more dollars demanded, the price of the dollar rises on the foreign exchange market.

The higher price of the dollar means that foreigners must now pay more for U.S.-made goods and services. So the quantity demanded and the expenditure on U.S.-made items decrease. U.S. exports decrease. Similarly, the higher dollar means that Americans now pay less for foreign-made goods and services. So the quantity demanded and the expenditure on foreign-made items increase. U.S. imports increase.

**Multiplier Process** A multiplier process occurs because the decrease in expenditure that we've just described brings a decrease in income, which induces a further decrease in consumption expenditure. (This multiplier effect is described in detail in Chapter 13, but you don't need to know the details to understand the basic idea.) The decreased consumption expenditure lowers aggregate expenditure still further. Real GDP growth slows, and the inflation rate slows.

If the Fed lowers the interest rate, the events that we've just described occur in the opposite directions, so real GDP growth and the inflation rate speed up.

Figure 11.6 summarizes the process that we've just described. It begins with the Fed's open market

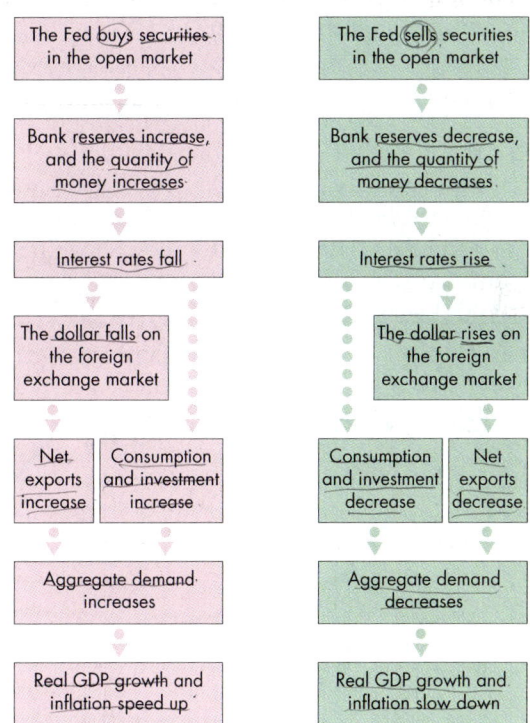

**FIGURE 11.6  Ripple Effects of the Fed's Actions**

The Fed's open market operations change the quantity of money and the interest rate. Expenditure plans change, and so does aggregate demand. Eventually, the Fed's open market operation has ripple effects that change real GDP and the price level.

operations that change the quantity of money and the interest rate and ends with the effects on real GDP and the price level.

We've described the broad outline of how the Fed's actions influence real GDP and the price level. We're now going to take a closer look at how those actions work in the *macroeconomic short run*, a period during which some money prices are sticky and real GDP might be below, above, or at potential GDP. (In the next section, we'll look at the long-run effects of money.)

To see the short-run effects of money on real GDP and the price level, we're going to bring together the *AS-AD* model that you met in Chapter 7 and the model of the money market that you've just studied in the current chapter. We'll look at two cases. In the first case, the Fed seeks to avoid inflation and in the second, to avoid recession. To keep the story as clear as possible, we'll suppose (unrealistically) that the Fed can control the economy with enormous precision, so it takes exactly the correct actions to restore full employment.

### The Fed Tightens to Avoid Inflation

Suppose that real GDP exceeds potential GDP—there is an inflationary gap—and the Fed decides to try to eliminate the inflationary gap and return real GDP to potential GDP. Figure 11.7 shows how the Fed would achieve this outcome if it were able to control the economy with precision.

Figure 11.7(a) shows the money market. Initially, the supply of money curve is $MS_0$ and with demand for money curve $MD$, the equilibrium interest rate is 5 percent a year.

In Fig. 11.7(b), the curve *ISE* shows the relationship between the interest rate and aggregate expenditure plans—interest-sensitive expenditure. With an interest rate of 5 percent a year, interest-sensitive expenditure is $2 trillion.

Figure 11.7(c) shows the aggregate supply and aggregate demand curves. With interest-sensitive expenditure at $2 trillion, aggregate demand is $AD_0$. The aggregate supply curve is *SAS*, so equilibrium real GDP is $10.2 trillion, which exceeds potential GDP.

The Fed now conducts an open market sale that decreases the quantity of money. The money supply curve shifts leftward to $MS_1$ in part (a), and the interest rate rises to 6 percent a year. Interest-sensitive expenditure decreases to $1.9 trillion in part (b). In part (c), aggregate demand decreases to $AD_0 - \Delta I$. With the decrease in aggregate demand, real GDP, aggregate expenditure, and aggregate income decrease. The decrease in income induces a further decrease in consumption expenditure, and aggregate demand decreases further. The aggregate demand curve shifts farther leftward to $AD_1$.

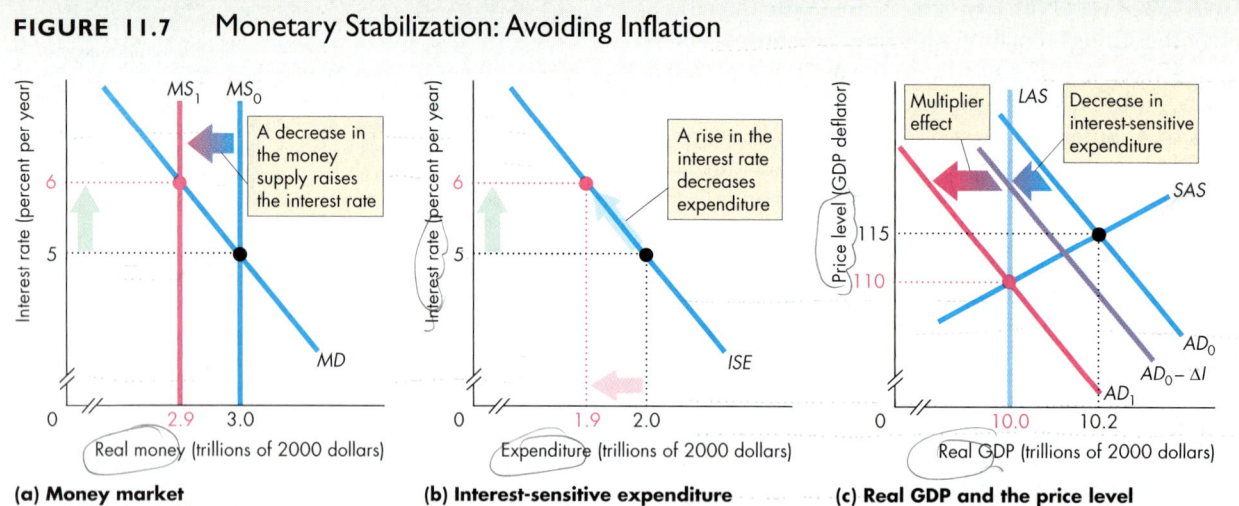

**FIGURE 11.7** Monetary Stabilization: Avoiding Inflation

Real GDP is $10.2 trillion, which exceeds potential GDP of $10 trillion in part (c). The Fed raises the interest rate (part a), investment decreases (part b), and aggregate demand decreases with a multiplier effect (part c).

# SHORT-RUN EFFECTS OF MONEY ON REAL GDP AND THE PRICE LEVEL 265

## FIGURE 11.8 Monetary Stabilization: Avoiding Recession

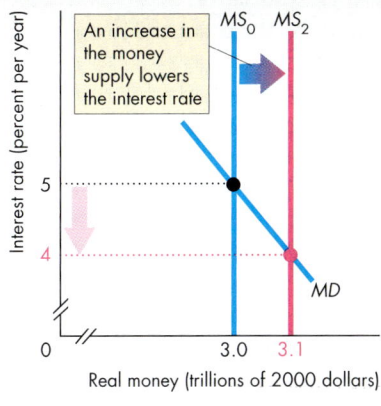
(a) Money market

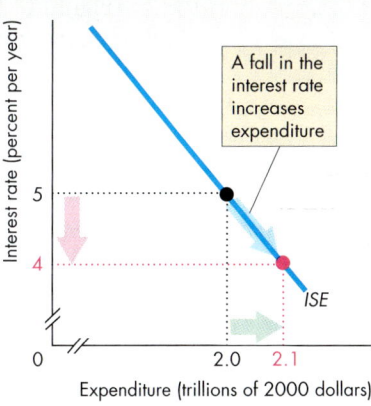
(b) Interest-sensitive expenditure

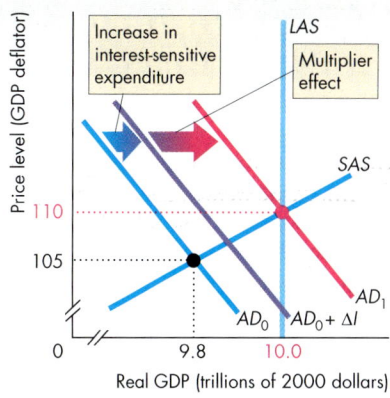
(c) Real GDP and the price level

Real GDP is $9.8 trillion, which is below potential GDP of $10 trillion in part (c). The Fed lowers the interest rate (part a), investment increases (part b), and aggregate demand increases with a multiplier effect (part c).

The Fed's actions have eliminated an inflation threat and brought real GDP to equal potential GDP at $10 trillion and the price level to 110.

In reality, because real GDP is growing and the price level is rising, the Fed's actions would slow real GDP growth and slow inflation rather than decrease real GDP and lower the price level as they do in this example.

### The Fed Eases to Avoid Recession

Now suppose that real GDP is less than potential GDP—there is a recessionary gap—and the Fed decides to try to eliminate the recessionary gap and return real GDP to potential GDP.

Figure 11.8 shows how the Fed would achieve this outcome (again if it were able to control the economy with precision). In parts (a) and (b) of Fig. 11.8, the starting point is the same as in Fig. 11.7. The interest rate is 5 percent a year, and interest-sensitive expenditure is $2 trillion.

In part (c), the aggregate demand curve is $AD_0$, the aggregate supply curve is $SAS$, and equilibrium real GDP is $9.8 trillion, which is less than potential GDP.

The Fed now conducts an open market purchase that increases the quantity of money. The $MS$ curve shifts rightward to $MS_2$. The interest rate falls to 4 percent a year. In part (b), interest-sensitive expenditure increases to $2.1 trillion. And in part (c), aggregate demand increases to $AD_0 + \Delta I$.

With the increase in aggregate demand, real GDP, aggregate expenditure, and aggregate income increase. The increase in income induces a further increase in consumption expenditure, and aggregate demand increases further. The aggregate demand curve shifts farther rightward to $AD_1$.

The Fed's actions have eliminated a recession and brought real GDP to equal potential GDP at $10 trillion and the price level to 110.

> ### REVIEW QUIZ
> 1. Sketch the ripple effects of an open market operation that decreases the quantity of money.
> 2. Which components of aggregate expenditure change when the interest rate changes?
> 3. Why are net exports sensitive to the interest rate?
> 4. Use the *AS-AD* model to show the effects of the Fed's attempts in 2001–2003 to avoid and then speed the recovery from a recession.
> 5. Use the *AS-AD* model to show the effects of the Fed's attempts in 2000 to eliminate an inflationary gap.

You now know the short-run effects of the Fed's actions on real GDP and the price level. We're now going to look at the long-run effects.

## Long-Run Effects of Money on Real GDP and the Price Level

THE MACROECONOMIC LONG RUN IS A PERIOD that is sufficiently long for the forces that move real GDP toward potential GDP to have had their full effects. In the macroeconomic long run, real GDP equals potential GDP. To study the long run effects of money on real GDP and the price level, we begin and end at a full-employment equilibrium. We'll study the effects of an increase in the quantity of money at full employment.

### An Increase in the Quantity of Money at Full Employment

Suppose that real GDP is equal to potential GDP and the Fed increases the quantity of money. The reason for increasing the quantity of money is less obvious than in the case that we examined earlier in which there was a recessionary gap. One possibility is that the Fed isn't sure about the state of the economy and it believes, incorrectly, that there actually is a recessionary gap.

Figure 11.9 shows the situation before and after the Fed's action. In part (a) the quantity of real money is $3 trillion and the interest rate is 6 percent a year at the intersection of $MS_0$ and $MD$. And in part (b), real GDP is $10 trillion, which equals potential GDP, and the price level is 100.

The Fed now conducts an open market purchase that increases the quantity of money by 10 percent to $3.3 trillion. The $MS$ curve shifts rightward to $MS_1$. The interest rate falls to 4 percent a year. In part (b), aggregate demand increases to $AD_1$. The price level rises to 105 and real GDP increases to $10.2 trillion. There is now an inflationary gap. Real GDP is greater than potential GDP, and in the labor market the unemployment rate is below the natural rate.

A shortage of labor brings a rise in the money wage rate and a decrease in short-run aggregate supply. The $SAS$ curve now starts to shift toward $SAS_1$. As short-run aggregate supply decreases, the price level rises and real GDP decreases. The money wage rate stops rising and the $SAS$ curve stops shifting when full

**FIGURE 11.9** Long-Run Effects of a Change in the Quantity of Money

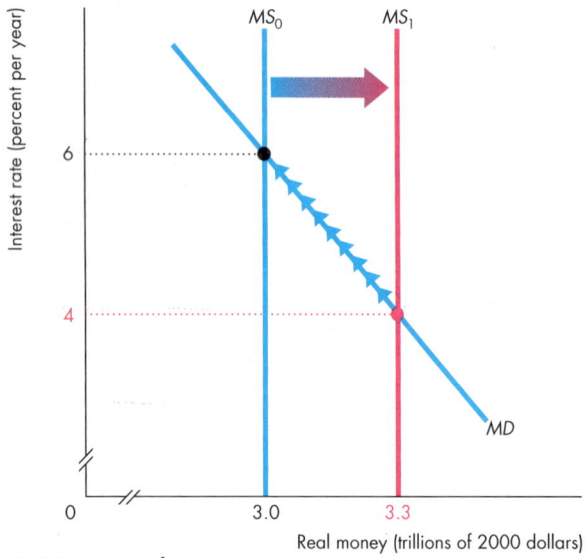

(a) Money market

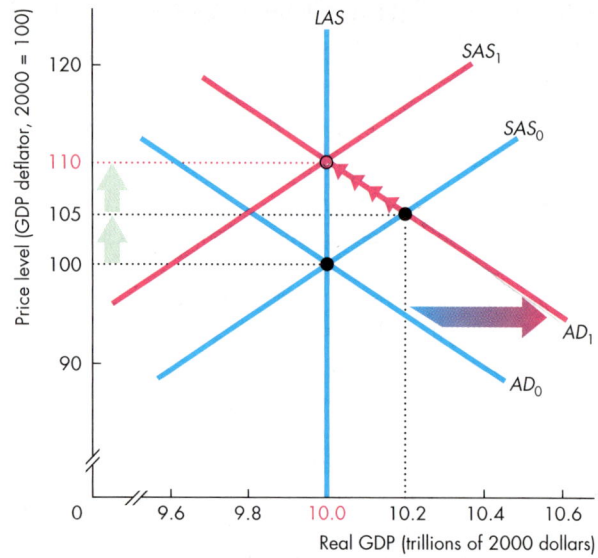

(b) AS–AD

In part (a), a 10 percent increase in the quantity of money shifts the $MS$ curve from $MS_0$ to $MS_1$ and lowers the interest rate. In part (b), aggregate demand increases from $AD_0$ to $AD_1$. The price level rises to 105 and real GDP increases to $10.2 trillion. Real GDP exceeds potential GDP, so the money wage rate rises and the $SAS$ curve shifts leftward from $SAS_0$ to $SAS_1$. Real GDP returns to potential GDP, and the price level rises to 110. In part (a), the real quantity of money returns to its initial level. In the long run, the increase in the quantity of money increases the price level and has no effect on real GDP.

employment is restored with real GDP back at $10 trillion and a price level of 110. Notice that the price level has increased from 100 to 110, a 10 percent increase in the price level. Back in part (a), with a price level of 110, the real quantity of money has decreased to $3 trillion, its initial level ($3.3 × 100/110 = $3).

So when the quantity of money increases at full employment, after a period of adjustment in which real GDP exceeds potential GDP, the price level eventually rises by the same percentage as the increase in the quantity of money and real GDP remains at potential GDP. In the long run, money has no real effects and the price level is proportional to the quantity of money.

## The Quantity Theory of Money

The **quantity theory of money** is the proposition that in the long run, an increase in the quantity of money brings an equal percentage increase in the price level. The original basis of the quantity theory of money is a concept known as *the velocity of circulation* and an equation called *the equation of exchange*.

The **velocity of circulation** is the average number of times a dollar of money is used annually to buy the goods and services that make up GDP. GDP is equal to the price level ($P$) multiplied by real GDP ($Y$). That is,

$$GDP = PY.$$

Call the quantity of money $M$. The velocity of circulation, $V$, is determined by the equation:

$$V = PY/M.$$

For example, if GDP is $6 trillion and the quantity of money is $3 trillion, the velocity of circulation is 2. On the average, each dollar of money circulates twice in its use to purchase the final goods and services that make up GDP; that is, each dollar of money is used twice in a year to buy GDP.

Figure 11.10 shows the velocity of circulation of both M1 and M2, the two main official measures of money, since 1963. You can see that the velocity of circulation of M1 increased through 1980 and fluctuated during the 1980s and 1990s. In contrast, the velocity of circulation of M2 has been remarkably stable. The reason why the velocity of M1 has increased is that deregulation and financial innovation have created new types of deposits and payments technologies that are substitutes for M1. As a result, the quantity of M1 per dollar of GDP has decreased, and equivalently, the velocity of circulation of M1

**FIGURE 11.10**   The Velocity of Circulation in the United States: 1963–2003

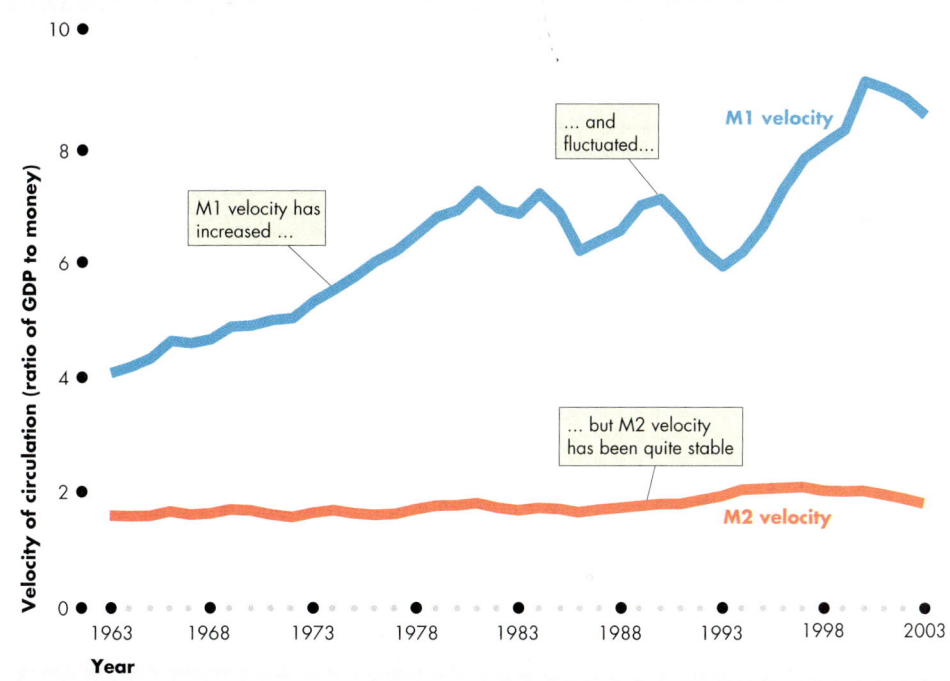

The velocity of circulation of M1 has increased over the years because deregulation and financial innovation have created M1 substitutes. The velocity of circulation of M2 has been relatively stable because the M1 substitutes that have resulted from deregulation and financial innovation are new types of deposits that are part of M2.

*Sources:* The Federal Reserve Board and Bureau of Economic Analysis.

has increased. The reason why the velocity of M2 has been almost constant is that the new types of deposits that have replaced M1 are part of M2. So the ratio of M2 to GDP and the velocity of circulation of M2 have been much more stable.

The **equation of exchange** states that the quantity of money ($M$) multiplied by the velocity of circulation ($V$) equals GDP, or

$$MV = PY.$$

Given the definition of the velocity of circulation, this equation is always true—it is true by definition. With $M$ equal to $3 trillion and $V$ equal to 2, $MV$ is equal to $6 trillion, the value of GDP.

The equation of exchange becomes the quantity theory of money by making two assumptions:

1. The velocity of circulation is not influenced by the quantity of money.
2. Potential GDP is not influenced by the quantity of money.

If these two assumptions are true, the equation of exchange tells us that a change in the quantity of money brings about an equal proportional change in the price level. You can see why by solving the equation of exchange for the price level. Dividing both sides of the equation by real GDP ($Y$) gives

$$P = (V/Y)M.$$

In the long run, real GDP, $Y$, equals potential GDP, so if potential GDP and velocity are not influenced by the quantity of money, the relationship between the change in the price level ($\Delta P$) and the change in the quantity of money ($\Delta M$) is

$$\Delta P = (V/Y)\Delta M.$$

Divide this equation by the previous one, $P = (V/Y)M$, to get

$$\Delta P/P = \Delta M/M.$$

($\Delta P/P$) is the proportional increase in the price level, and ($\Delta M/M$) is the proportional increase in the quantity of money. So this equation is the quantity theory of money: In the long run, the percentage increase in the price level equals the percentage increase in the quantity of money.

## The Quantity Theory and the AS-AD Model

The quantity theory of money can be interpreted in terms of the AS-AD model. The aggregate demand curve is a relationship between the quantity of real GDP demanded ($Y$) and the price level ($P$), other things remaining constant. We can obtain such a relationship from the equation of exchange:

$$MV = PY.$$

Dividing both sides of this equation by real GDP ($Y$) gives

$$P = MV/Y.$$

This equation may be interpreted as describing an aggregate demand curve. In Chapter 7 (p. 155), you saw that the aggregate demand curve slopes downward. As the price level increases, the quantity of real GDP demanded decreases. The above equation also shows such a relationship between the price level and the quantity of real GDP demanded. For a given quantity of money ($M$) and a given velocity of circulation ($V$), the higher the price level ($P$), the smaller is the quantity of real GDP demanded ($Y$).

In general, when the quantity of money changes, the velocity of circulation might also change. But the quantity theory asserts that velocity is not influenced by the quantity of money. If this assumption is correct, an increase in the quantity of money increases aggregate demand and shifts the aggregate demand curve upward by the same amount as the percentage change in the quantity of money.

The quantity theory of money also asserts that real GDP, which in the long run equals potential GDP, is not influenced by the quantity of money. This assertion is true in the AS-AD model in the long run when the economy is on its long-run aggregate supply curve. Figure 11.9 shows the quantity theory result in the AS-AD model. Initially, the economy is on the long-run aggregate supply curve $LAS$ and at the intersection of the aggregate demand curve $AD_0$ and the short-run aggregate supply curve $SAS_0$. A 10 percent increase in the quantity of money shifts the aggregate demand curve from $AD_0$ to $AD_1$. This shift, measured by the vertical distance between the two demand curves, is 10 percent. In the long run, the money wage rate rises (also by 10 percent) and shifts the SAS curve leftward to $SAS_1$. A new long-run equilibrium occurs at the intersection of $AD_1$ and $SAS_1$. Real GDP remains at potential GDP of $10 trillion, and the price level rises to 110. The new price level is 10 percent higher than the initial one of 100.

So the AS-AD model predicts the same outcome as the quantity theory of money. The AS-AD model also predicts a less precise relationship between the quantity of money and the price level in the short run than in the long run. For example, Fig. 11.8 shows that if we start out at a below-full employment equilibrium, an increase in the quantity of money increases real GDP. In this case, a 10 percent increase in the quantity of money increases the price level from 105 to 110—a 2.8 percent increase. That is, the price level increases by a smaller percentage than the percentage increase in the quantity of money.

How good a theory is the quantity theory of money? Let's answer this question by looking at some historical and international data.

## Historical Evidence on the Quantity Theory of Money

The percentage increase in the price level is the inflation rate, and the percentage increase in the quantity of money is the money growth rate. So the quantity theory predictions can be cast in terms of money growth and inflation. The quantity theory predicts that at a given potential GDP and in the long run, the inflation rate will equal the money growth rate. But over time, potential GDP expands. Taking this expansion into account, the quantity theory predicts that in the long run, the inflation rate will equal the money growth rate minus the growth rate of potential GDP.

We can test the quantity theory of money by looking at the historical relationship between money growth and inflation in the United States. Figure 11.11 shows two views of this relationship for the years between 1963 and 2003. In both parts of the figure, the inflation rate is the percentage change in the GDP deflator and the money growth rate is the growth rate of M2. Part (a) shows year-to-year changes in the quantity of money and the price level. These changes show the short-run relationship between money growth and inflation. Part (b) shows decade average changes. These changes average out the year-to-year fluctuations and enable us to see the long-run relationship between the variables. If the quantity theory is a reasonable guide to reality, there should be a strong correlation between inflation and money growth in the decade average data and a weak correlation in the year-to-year data.

That is what the data show. The year-to-year fluctuations in part (a) show a weak correlation, and the decade average fluctuations in part (b) show a stronger correlation. The rising inflation rate during the 1970s came from a speedup in money growth.

And the falling inflation rate of the 1980s came from a slowing of money growth.

But during the late 1990s when money growth increased, the inflation rate remained low and even fell somewhat. Part of the reason is that the demand for M2 increased and the velocity of circulation of M2 decreased during this period. But if M2 growth remains at its early 2000s rate, the inflation rate will turn up again.

## International Evidence on the Quantity Theory of Money

Another way to test the quantity theory of money is to look at the cross-country data. Figure 11.12(a) shows the relationship between money growth and inflation in 60 countries during the 1980s. Figure 11.12(b) shows the relationship for 13 regions and countries that cover the entire world during the 1990s. By looking at a decade average, we again smooth out the short-run effects of money growth and focus on the long-run effects. These data show that rapid money growth is associated with high inflation.

## Correlation, Causation, and Other Influences

Both the historical evidence for the United States and the international data tell us that in the long run, money growth and inflation are correlated. But the correlation between money growth and inflation does not tell us that money growth causes inflation. Money growth might cause inflation; inflation might cause money growth; or some third variable might simultaneously cause inflation and money growth.

According to the quantity theory and according to the *AS-AD* model, causation runs from money growth to inflation. But neither theory denies the possibility that at different times and places, causation might run in the other direction or that some third factor might be the root cause of both rapid money growth and inflation. One possible third factor is a large and persistent government budget deficit that gets financed by creating money.

Some occasions provide an opportunity to test our assumptions about causation. One of these is World War II and the years immediately following it. Rapid money growth during the war years was accompanied by controls that held prices down during the war but allowed them to rise immediately after the war. The inflationary consequence of

## FIGURE 11.11 Money Growth and Inflation in the United States: 1963–2003

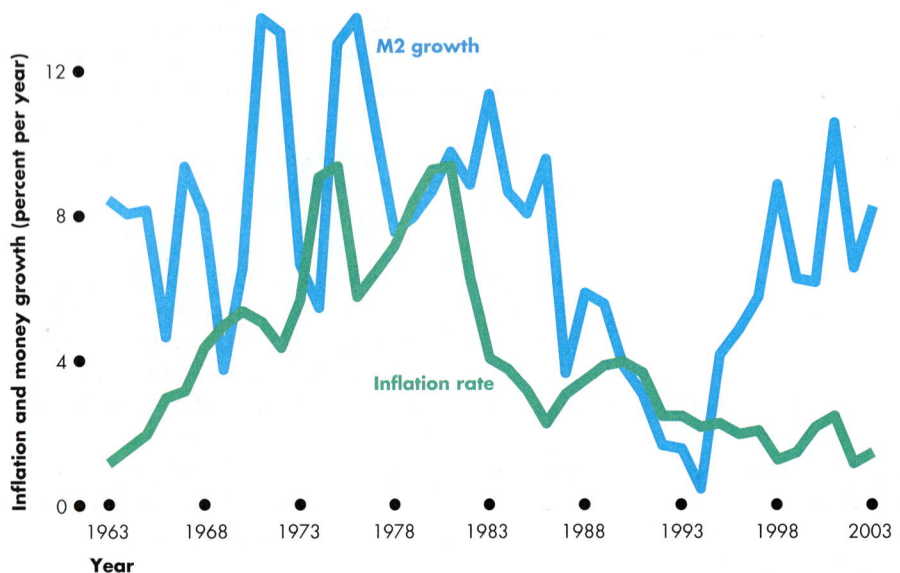

(a) Year-to-year change in M2 and the price level

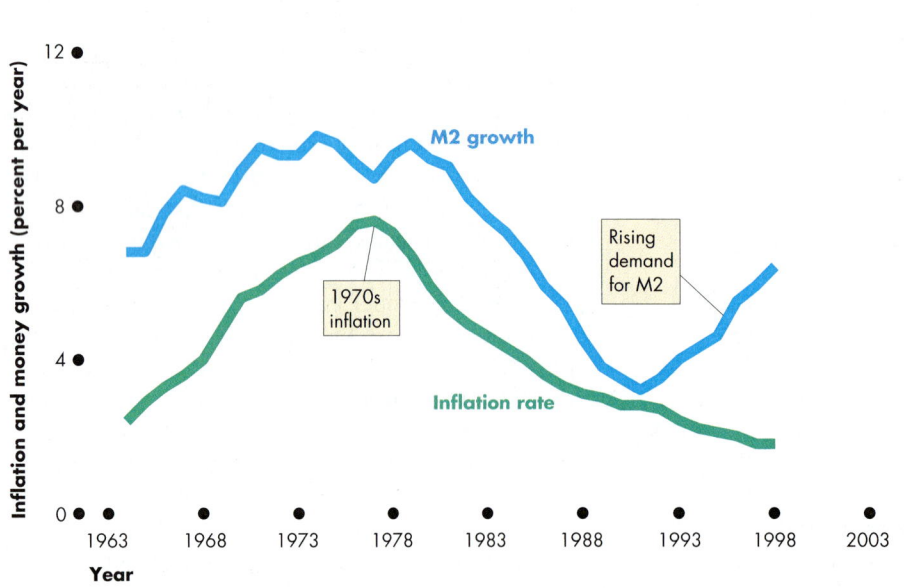

(b) Decade average change in M2 and the price level

*Sources:* The Federal Reserve Board and the Bureau of Economic Analysis.

Year-to-year fluctuations in money growth and inflation (part a) are loosely correlated, but decade average fluctuations in money growth and inflation (part b) are more closely correlated. The burst of inflation during the 1970s was caused by a speedup in money growth. The slowing of inflation during the 1980s came from slower money growth. The increase in money growth during the late 1990s came from an increase in the demand for money, but if the high money growth rate is maintained, the inflation rate will rise.

# LONG-RUN EFFECTS OF MONEY ON REAL GDP AND THE PRICE LEVEL 271

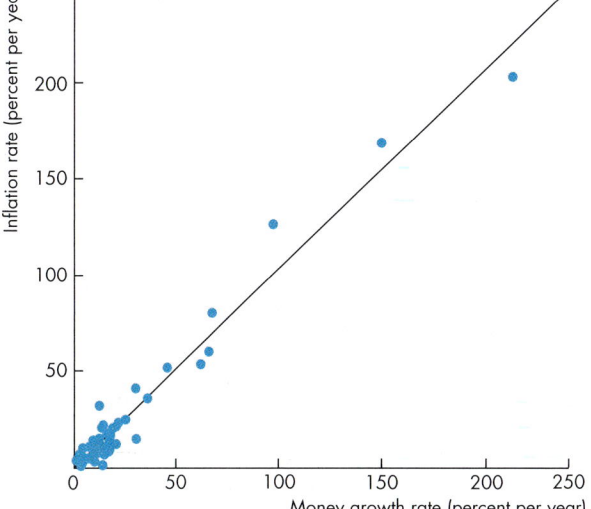

**FIGURE 11.12  Money Growth and Inflation in the World Economy**

**(a) 60 countries during the 1980s**

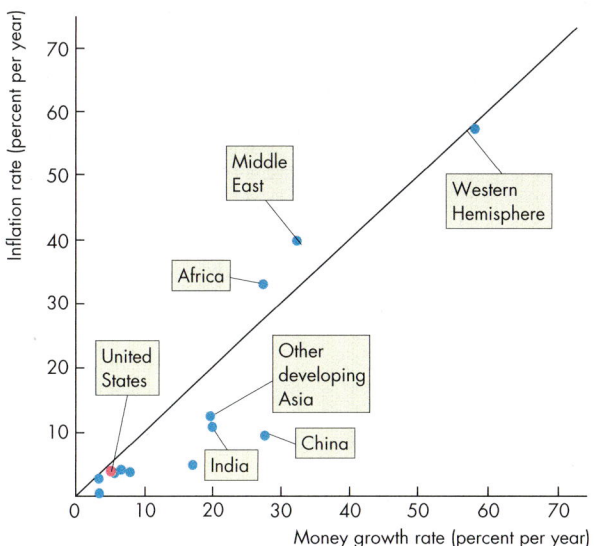

**(b) 13 regions and countries during the 1990s**

Inflation and money growth in 60 countries in part (a) and in the low-inflation countries in part (b) show a clear positive relationship.

*Sources:* The Federal Reserve Bank of St. Louis, *Review*, May/June 1988, p. 15 and International Monetary Fund.

wartime money growth was delayed by price controls but not avoided. And the wartime money growth caused the postwar inflation. The late 1960s and 1970s provide another test. Rapid money growth that began during the 1960s caused higher inflation during the 1970s. The combination of historical and international correlations between money growth and inflation and independent evidence about the direction of causation leads to the conclusion that the quantity theory is correct in the long run. It explains the long-term fundamental source of inflation. It also implies that the only way to slow inflation, in the long run, is to slow money growth.

But the quantity theory is not correct in the short run. To understand the short-term fluctuations in inflation, the joint effects of a change in the quantity of money on real GDP, the velocity of circulation, and the price level must be explained. The *AS-AD* model provides this explanation, and points to other factors that influence the inflation rate independently of the money growth rate in the short run.

### REVIEW QUIZ

1. Do the short-run effects of an increase in the quantity of money on the price level and real GDP differ from the long-run effects? What are the differences? Why are there different effects?
2. What is the quantity theory of money? Are the predictions of the quantity theory in conflict with the predictions of the *AS-AD* model?
3. Do the long-run historical evidence and the international evidence on the relationship between money growth and inflation support the quantity theory?

◆ Before you leave the subject of this chapter, look at *Reading Between the Lines* on pp. 272–273 and see how rapid money growth brought inflation in Argentina during the late 1980s. In the next chapter, we'll return to the problem of inflation and explore more deeply its causes and its consequences.

# READING BETWEEN THE LINES

## *The Quantity Theory of Money in Argentina*

**THE WASHINGTON POST, JANUARY 6, 2002**

### Argentines Prepare To Face Fallout of Economic 'D-Day'

BUENOS AIRES, Jan. 5—Enter a bustling, warehouse-style superstore and the first impression is of a coming storm. A 31-year-old music teacher wearing a black Paris Opera T-shirt is stocking up on light bulbs and Diet Coke. A woman, jittery and arguing with her accountant husband, wheels around a cart brimming with enough coffee and beef to last a month. But the line of people at the register—desperate to buy computers, stereos and televisions—is the tip-off that the disaster here is man-made.

With the announcement Friday that Argentina's bankrupt government will devalue the peso and end its decade-old parity with the U.S. dollar, a latent panic began to resurface today, the fear of hyperinflation.

Ten years ago, when annual inflation reached 5,000 percent, people would rush down the aisles of supermarkets, desperate to grab goods before clerks could stamp on higher prices. Imported goods such as computers and VCRs were often scarce or expensive or both. Now, with financial collapse about to break the peso-dollar peg that tamed inflation, Argentina's unprecedented era of monetary stability is coming to an end. And many fear inflation will return.

"I'm broke, but I'm still buying before D-Day—Devaluation Day," said Paula Cardoso, 57, a chain-smoking librarian who picked out a Sony television for $275. She, like so many, feared the prices of imported electronics would be the first to rise. "We had 10 years of stability, but the party is over, my friend. We're going back to the old Argentina. Just you wait."...

Inflation has become part of national mythology, a boogeyman story passed down from generation to generation.

"My father told me all about those years—about getting to the grocery store in the morning because he didn't know what prices would be like after he got out of work," said Jorge Villegas, 22, a college student who spent most of his savings today on a $950 Compaq computer at Carrefour, a French chain similar to Wal-Mart, in the upper-middle class Palermo neighborhood.

"I was going to wait a few months before I bought the computer, but now, I didn't think I could afford to wait," he said.

...

© 2002 The Washington Post. Reprinted with permission. Further reproduction prohibited.

### Essence of the Story

■ In January 2002, Argentines were stocking up on all types of goods: light bulbs, Diet Coke, coffee, beef, computers, stereos, and televisions.

■ The reason was that they feared hyperinflation.

The government had announced that it would devalue the peso and end its 10-year-long fixed link with the U.S. dollar.

■ Ten years earlier, the inflation rate had been 5,000 percent a year.

## Economic Analysis

- Argentina has long suffered from a high inflation rate.

- During the 1970s, its average inflation rate was 130 percent a year. During the 1980s, the inflation rate climbed to an average of 570 percent a year. And in 1989, the inflation rate exceeded 3,000 percent a year.

- To appreciate an inflation rate of 3,000 percent a year, translate it to a monthly inflation rate. Every month, on the average, prices rise by 33 percent. Table 1 shows what happens to the price of a coffee that in January was $3.00 a cup. After six months, the price is $12.50!

- When people expect prices to rise rapidly, they expect the money they hold to fall in value rapidly. So they spend and hold goods rather than money.

- Figure 1 shows the inflation record in Argentina from 1971 through 2001.

- During the 1970s and 1980s, when the inflation rate was high, the money growth rate in Argentina was also high—as predicted by the quantity theory of money.

- The very high inflation rate of 1989–1990 created a crisis of confidence in the ability of Argentina to achieve a stable value of money.

- To instill confidence, the government adopted a U.S. dollar standard. One unit of the national currency was defined to be worth one U.S. dollar.

- For a decade, this arrangement kept money growth and inflation in check and Argentina had a stable price level.

- But other problems—slow economic growth, a high unemployment rate, and government budget deficits—led the Argentine government to abandon the fixed link with the U.S. dollar in 2001.

- With a return to the monetary system of the 1980s, people feared a return to the inflation of the 1980s, so they spent their money on a wide range of goods.

- The increased spending increased the velocity of circulation of money and increased the inflation rate by more than the increase in the money growth rate.

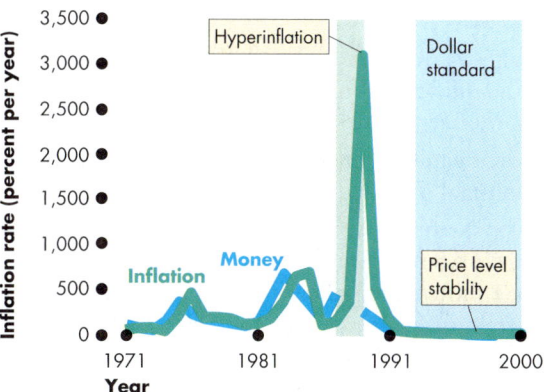

Figure 1 Inflation in Argentina

| Month | Price of coffee (dollars per cup) |
|---|---|
| January | 3.00 |
| February | 4.00 |
| March | 5.30 |
| April | 7.00 |
| May | 9.49 |
| June | 12.50 |

Table 1 A 33-percent-a-year inflation

# SUMMARY

## KEY POINTS

**The Demand for Money** (pp. 258–261)

- The quantity of money demanded is the amount of money that people plan to hold.
- The quantity of real money equals the quantity of nominal money divided by the price level.
- The quantity of real money demanded depends on the interest rate and real GDP. A higher interest rate induces a smaller quantity of real money demanded.

**Interest Rate Determination** (pp. 261–262)

- Changes in interest rates achieve equilibrium in the markets for money and financial assets.
- Money market equilibrium achieves an interest rate (and an asset price) that makes the quantity of real money available willingly held.
- If the quantity of real money is increased by the actions of the Fed, the interest rate falls and the prices of financial assets rise.

**Short-Run Effects of Money on Real GDP and the Price Level** (pp. 263–265)

- When the Fed raises interest rates, investment, consumption expenditure, and net exports decrease and a multiplier effect brings a greater decrease in aggregate demand.
- When the Fed lowers interest rates, investment, consumption expenditure, and net exports increase and a multiplier effect brings a greater increase in aggregate demand.
- An increase in the quantity of money lowers the interest rate, increases interest-sensitive expenditure, and increases aggregate demand.
- In the short run, the increase in aggregate demand brings an increase in real GDP and a rise in the price level.

**Long-Run Effects of Money on Real GDP and the Price Level** (pp. 266–271)

- In the long run, an increase in the quantity of money that increases aggregate demand brings a rise in the money wage rate, a decrease in short-run aggregate supply, a rise in the price level, and no change in real GDP.
- The quantity theory of money is an alternative way of looking at the long-run relationship between the growth rate of money and the inflation rate.

## KEY FIGURES

Figure 11.1  The Demand for Money, 259
Figure 11.2  Changes in the Demand for Money, 259
Figure 11.4  Money Market Equilibrium, 261
Figure 11.5  Interest Rate Changes, 262
Figure 11.7  Monetary Stabilization: Avoiding Inflation, 264
Figure 11.8  Monetary Stabilization: Avoiding Recession, 265
Figure 11.9  Long-Run Effects of a Change in the Quantity of Money, 266

## KEY TERMS

Equation of exchange, 268
Quantity theory of money, 267
Velocity of circulation, 267

# PROBLEMS

*1. The spreadsheet provides information about the demand for money in Minland. Column A is the interest rate, $R$. Columns B, C, and D show the quantity of money demanded at three different levels of real GDP. $Y_0$ is $10 billion, $Y_1$ is $20 billion, and $Y_2$ is $30 billion. The quantity of money is $3 billion. Initially, real GDP is $20 billion.

|   | A | B | C | D |
|---|---|---|---|---|
| 1 | $R$ | $Y_0$ | $Y_1$ | $Y_2$ |
| 2 | 7 | 1.0 | 1.5 | 2.0 |
| 3 | 6 | 1.5 | 2.0 | 2.5 |
| 4 | 5 | 2.0 | 2.5 | 3.0 |
| 5 | 4 | 2.5 | 3.0 | 3.5 |
| 6 | 3 | 3.0 | 3.5 | 4.0 |
| 7 | 2 | 3.5 | 4.0 | 4.5 |
| 8 | 1 | 4.0 | 4.5 | 5.0 |

What happens in Minland
 a. If the interest rate exceeds 4 percent a year?
 b. If the interest rate is less than 4 percent a year?
 c. If the interest rate equals 4 percent a year?

2. The Minland economy in problem 1 experiences a severe recession. Real GDP decreases to $10 billion. The Minland Fed takes no actions to change the quantity of money.
 a. What happens in Minland if the interest rate is 4 percent a year?
 b. What is the equilibrium interest rate in Minland?
 c. Compared with the situation in problem 1, does the interest rate in Minland rise or fall? Why?

*3. The Minland economy in problem 1 experiences a severe business cycle. Real GDP increses to $30 billion and then decreases to $10 billion. The Minland Fed takes no actions to change the quantity of money. What happens to the interest rate in Minland
 a. During the expansion phase of the cycle?
 b. During the recession phase of the cycle?

4. Financial innovation in Minland changes the demand for money. People now plan to hold $0.5 billion less than the numbers provided in the spreadsheet in problem 1.
 a. What happens to the interest rate if the Minland Fed takes no actions?
 b. What happens to the interest rate if the Minland Fed decreases the quantity of money by $0.5 billion? Explain.

*5. The figure shows the demand for money in Upland.
 a. In the figure, draw the supply of money curve if the interest rate is 3 percent a year.
 b. Suppose that the Upland Fed wants to lower the interest rate by 1 percentage point. By how much must it change the quantity of real money? Draw the new supply of money curve.

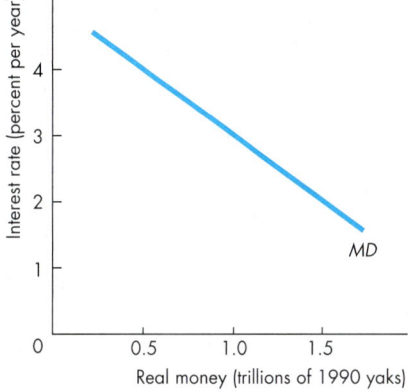

Suppose that to change the quantity of money in part (b) of the problem, the Upland Fed uses open market operations. Does it make an open market purchase or an open market sale of securities?

6. In Upland, in problem 5, a new smart card replaces currency and the demand for money changes. Also, the new smart card causes business to boom. Real GDP increases.
 a. Draw a new demand for money curve that is consistent with the events just described.
 b. Suppose that the Upland Fed wants to prevent the interest rate from changing. What must it do to the quantity of money? Draw the new supply of money curve.
 c. Does the Upland Fed make an open market purchase or an open market sale of securities?

*7. Starting from above full-employment equilibrium, briefly explain with the aid of the *AS-AD* model the short-run effect on the price level and real GDP of an open market sale. Does such an action help to avoid inflation? Does it lower real GDP in the long run?

\* Solutions to odd-numbered problems are available on **MyEconLab**.

8. Starting from unemployment equilibrium, briefly explain with the aid of the *AS-AD* model the short-run effect on the price level and real GDP of an open market purchase. Does such an action help to avoid inflation? Does it increase real GDP in the long run?

*9. Slowcon is a country in which the quantity theory of money operates in the long run but not in the short run. Slowcon has some unemployment when banks begin to make new loans and increase the quantity of money.
   a. What is the effect of the banks' actions on aggregate demand?
   b. What are the effects of the banks' actions on real GDP and the price level in the short run?
   c. What are the effects of the banks' actions on real GDP and the price level in the long run?

10. Banks in Japan make bad loans that don't get repaid, and several banks fail. The banks' customers lose their deposits.
    a. What is the effect of the bank failures on the quantity of money?
    b. What is the effect of the bank failures on aggregate demand?
    c. What are the effects of the bank failures on real GDP and the price level in the short run?
    d. What are the effects of the bank failures on real GDP and the price level in the long run?

*11. Quantecon is a country in which the quantity theory of money operates. The country has a constant population, capital stock, and technology. In year 1, real GDP was $400 million, the price level was 200, and the velocity of circulation of money was 20. In year 2, the quantity of money was 20 percent higher than in year 1.
    a. What was the quantity of money in year 1?
    b. What was the quantity of money in year 2?
    c. What was the price level in year 2?
    d. What was the level of real GDP in year 2?
    e. What was the velocity of circulation in year 2?

12. In Quantecon described in problem 11, in year 3, the quantity of money falls to one fifth of its year 2 level.
    a. What is the quantity of money in year 3?
    b. What is the price level in year 3?
    c. What is the level of real GDP in year 3?
    d. What is the velocity of circulation in year 3?
    e. If it takes more than one year for the full quantity theory effect to occur, what do you predict happens to real GDP in Quantecon in year 3? Why?

# CRITICAL THINKING

1. Study the news article about inflation in Argentina in *Reading Between the Lines* on pp. 272–273 and then answer the following questions:
   a. How has Argentina coped with the problem of finding a stable unit of account?
   b. What happened to the velocity of circulation of money in Argentina in 2001?
   c. How do people protect themselves from a falling value of money in Argentina?
2. What did the Fed do during 2001, 2002, and 2003 to try to avoid recession? What were the risks in the Fed's actions? Do you think the Fed acted appropriately? Explain why or why not.
3. What was the Fed's main challenge in 2004? What did the Fed do to meet this challenge? Do you think the Fed acted appropriately? Explain why or why not.

# WEB EXERCISES

**Use the links on MyEconLab to work the following exercises.**

1. Visit the Federal Reserve Board and obtain the latest data on M1, M2, and some short-term interest rates. Then answer the following questions.
   a. Is the Fed trying to slow the economy or speed it up? How can you tell which?
   b. What open market operations do you think the Fed has undertaken during the past month?
   c. Skim the latest minutes of the FOMC, which you can find at the Fed's Web site, and see whether you can discover the open market operations that are planned.
   d. In light of the Fed's recent actions, what ripple effects do you expect over the coming months?
2. Visit the Federal Reserve Board and look at the current economic conditions described in the Beige Book. On the basis of current forecasts by the Fed, do you predict that the Fed will raise interest rates, lower interest rates, or hold interest rates steady? Write a brief summary of your predictions and reasons.

# Inflation

## From Rome to Rio de Janeiro

**At the end of the third century A.D., Roman** Emperor Diocletian struggled to contain an inflation that raised prices by more than 300 percent a year. At the end of the twentieth century, Brazil's president, Fernando Henrique Cardoso, struggled to contain an inflation that hit a rate of 40 percent *per month*—or 5,600 percent a year.

Today, the United States has remarkable price stability, but during the 1970s, the U.S. price level more than doubled—an inflation of more than 100 percent over the decade. Why do inflation rates vary? And why do serious inflations break out from time to time?

Will inflation increase so our savings buy less? Or will inflation decrease so our debts are harder to repay? To make good decisions, we need good forecasts of inflation, and not for just next year but for many years into the future. How do people try to forecast inflation? And how do expectations of inflation influence the economy?

Does the Fed face a tradeoff between inflation and unemployment? And does a low unemployment rate signal a rising inflation rate? How does inflation affect the interest rate?

◆ We'll answer these questions in this chapter. We'll begin by reviewing what inflation is and how it is measured. And we'll end, in *Reading Between the Lines*, by returning to links between inflation and unemployment in the United States today.

## After studying this chapter, you will be able to

- **Distinguish between inflation and a one-time rise in the price level**
- **Explain how demand-pull inflation is generated**
- **Explain how cost-push inflation is generated**
- **Describe the effects of inflation**
- **Explain the short-run and long-run relationships between inflation and unemployment**
- **Explain the short-run and long-run relationships between inflation and interest rates**

## Inflation and the Price Level

WE DON'T HAVE MUCH INFLATION TODAY, BUT during the 1970s, inflation was a major problem. *Inflation* is a process in which the *price level is rising* and *money is losing value*.

If the price level rises persistently, then people need more and more money to make transactions. Incomes rise, so firms must pay out more in wages and other payments to owners of factors of production. And prices rise, so consumers must take more money with them when they go shopping. But the value of money gets smaller and smaller.

A change in one price is not inflation. For example, if the price of a hot dog jumps to $25 and all other money prices fall slightly so that the price level remains constant, there is no inflation. Instead, the relative price of a hot dog has increased. If the price of a hot dog and all other prices rise by a similar percentage, there is inflation.

But a one-time jump in the price level is not inflation. Instead, inflation is an ongoing *process*. Figure 12.1 illustrates this distinction. The red line shows the price level rising continuously. That is inflation. The blue line shows a one-time jump in the price level. This economy is not experiencing inflation. Its price level is constant most of the time.

Inflation is a serious problem, and preventing inflation is the main task of monetary policy and the actions of the Fed. We are going to learn how inflation arises and see how we can avoid the situation shown in the cartoon. But first, let's see how we calculate the inflation rate.

"I told you the Fed should have tightened."

© The New Yorker Collection 1997
Robert Mankoff from cartoonbank.com. All rights reserved.

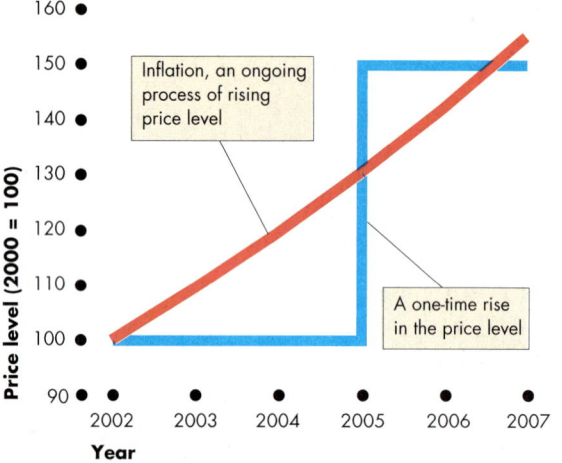

**FIGURE 12.1** Inflation Versus a One-Time Rise in the Price Level

Along the red line, an economy experiences inflation because the price level is rising persistently. Along the blue line, an economy experiences a one-time rise in the price level.

To measure the inflation *rate*, we calculate the annual percentage change in the price level. For example, if this year's price level is 126 and last year's price level was 120, the inflation rate is

$$\text{Inflation rate} = \frac{126 - 120}{120} \times 100$$

$$= 5 \text{ percent per year.}$$

This equation shows the connection between the *inflation rate* and the *price level*. For a given price level last year, the higher the price level in the current year, the higher is the inflation rate. If the price level is *rising*, the inflation rate is *positive*. If the price level rises at a *faster* rate, the inflation rate *increases*. Also, the higher the new price level, the lower is the value of money and the higher is the inflation rate.

Inflation can result from either an increase in aggregate demand or a decrease in aggregate supply. These two sources of impulses are called

- Demand-pull
- Cost-push

We'll first study a demand-pull inflation.

# Demand-Pull Inflation

AN INFLATION THAT RESULTS FROM AN INITIAL increase in aggregate demand is called **demand-pull inflation**. Demand-pull inflation can arise from *any* factor that increases aggregate demand, such as an

1. Increase in the quantity of money
2. Increase in government purchases
3. Increase in exports

## Initial Effect of an Increase in Aggregate Demand

Suppose that last year the price level was 105 and real GDP was $10 trillion. Potential GDP was also $10 trillion. Figure 12.2(a) illustrates this situation. The aggregate demand curve is $AD_0$, the short-run aggregate supply curve is $SAS_0$, and the long-run aggregate supply curve is $LAS$.

In the current year, aggregate demand increases to $AD_1$. Such a situation arises if, for example, the Fed loosens its grip on the quantity of money, or the government increases its purchases of goods and services, or exports increase.

With no change in potential GDP, and with no change in the money wage rate, the long-run aggregate supply curve and the short-run aggregate supply curve remain at $LAS$ and $SAS_0$, respectively.

The price level and real GDP are determined at the point where the aggregate demand curve $AD_1$ intersects the short-run aggregate supply curve. The price level rises to 108, and real GDP increases above potential GDP to $10.5 trillion. The economy experiences a 2.9 percent rise in the price level (a price level of 108 compared with 105 in the previous year) and a rapid expansion of real GDP. Unemployment falls below its natural rate. The next step in the unfolding story is a rise in the money wage rate.

## Money Wage Rate Response

Real GDP cannot remain above potential GDP forever. With unemployment below its natural rate, there is a shortage of labor. In this situation, the

## FIGURE 12.2    A Demand-Pull Rise in the Price Level

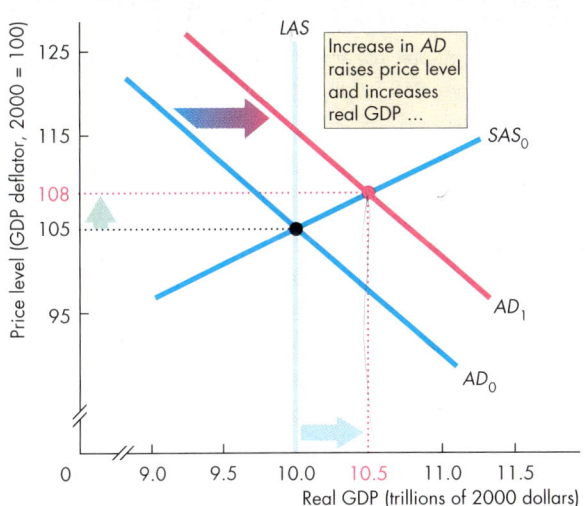

(a) Initial effect

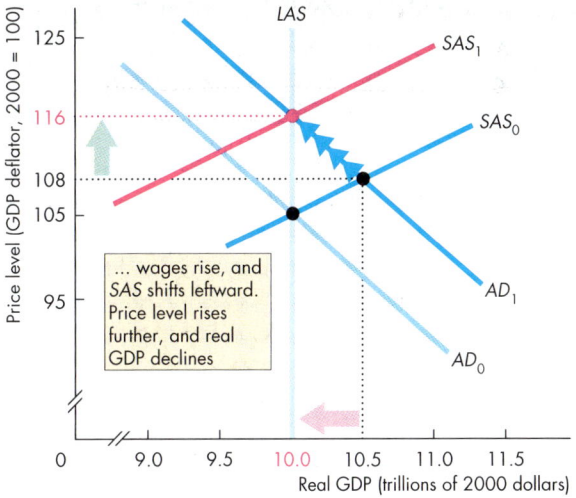

(b) Wages adjust

In part (a), the aggregate demand curve is $AD_0$, the short-run aggregate supply curve is $SAS_0$, and the long-run aggregate supply curve is $LAS$. The price level is 105, and real GDP is $10 trillion, which equals potential GDP. Aggregate demand increases to $AD_1$. The price level rises to 108, and real GDP increases to $10.5 trillion. In part (b), starting from above full employment, the money wage rate begins to rise and the short-run aggregate supply curve shifts leftward toward $SAS_1$. The price level rises further, and real GDP returns to potential GDP.

money wage rate begins to rise. As it does so, short-run aggregate supply decreases and the SAS curve starts to shift leftward. The price level rises further, and real GDP begins to decrease.

With no further change in aggregate demand—that is, the aggregate demand curve remains at $AD_1$—this process ends when the short-run aggregate supply curve has shifted to $SAS_1$ in Fig. 12.2(b). At this time, the price level has increased to 116 and real GDP has returned to potential GDP of $10 trillion, the level from which it started.

## A Demand-Pull Inflation Process

The process we've just studied eventually ends when, for a given increase in aggregate demand, the money wage rate has adjusted enough to restore the real wage rate to its full-employment level. We've studied a one-time rise in the price level like that described in Fig. 12.1. For inflation to proceed, aggregate demand must persistently increase.

The only way in which aggregate demand can persistently increase is <u>if the quantity of money persistently increases</u>. Suppose the government has a budget deficit that it finances by selling bonds. Also suppose that the Fed buys some of these bonds. When the Fed buys bonds, it creates more money. In this situation, aggregate demand increases year after year. The aggregate demand curve keeps shifting rightward. This <u>persistent increase in aggregate demand puts continual upward pressure on the price level</u>. The economy now experiences demand-pull inflation.

Figure 12.3 illustrates the process of demand-pull inflation. The starting point is the same as that shown in Fig. 12.2. The aggregate demand curve is $AD_0$, the short-run aggregate supply curve is $SAS_0$, and the long-run aggregate supply curve is LAS. Real GDP is $10 trillion, and the price level is 105. Aggregate demand increases, shifting the aggregate demand curve to $AD_1$. Real GDP increases to $10.5 trillion, and the price level rises to 108. The economy is at an above full-employment equilibrium. There is a shortage of labor, and the money wage rate rises. The short-run aggregate supply curve shifts to $SAS_1$. The price level rises to 116, and real GDP returns to potential GDP.

But the Fed increases the quantity of money again, and aggregate demand continues to increase. The aggregate demand curve shifts rightward to $AD_2$. The price level rises further to 120, and real GDP

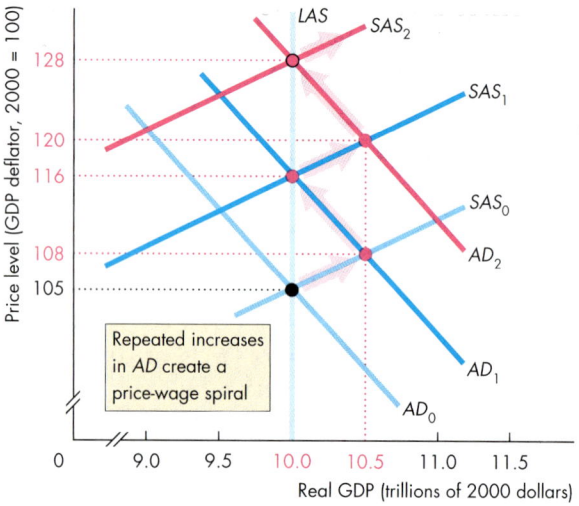

**FIGURE 12.3    A Demand-Pull Inflation Spiral**

Each time the quantity of money increases, aggregate demand increases, and the aggregate demand curve shifts rightward from $AD_0$ to $AD_1$ to $AD_2$, and so on. Each time real GDP goes above potential GDP, the money wage rate rises and the short-run aggregate supply curve shifts leftward from $SAS_0$ to $SAS_1$ to $SAS_2$, and so on. The price level rises from 105 to 108, 116, 120, 128, and so on. There is a perpetual demand-pull inflation. Real GDP fluctuates between $10 trillion and $10.5 trillion.

again exceeds potential GDP at $10.5 trillion. Yet again, the money wage rate rises and decreases short-run aggregate supply. The SAS curve shifts to $SAS_2$, and the price level rises further, to 128. As the quantity of money continues to grow, aggregate demand increases and the price level rises in an ongoing demand-pull inflation process.

The process you have just studied generates inflation—an ongoing process of a rising price level.

**Demand-Pull Inflation in Kalamazoo** You may better understand the inflation process that we've just described by considering what is going on in an individual part of the economy, such as a Kalamazoo soda-bottling plant. Initially, when aggregate demand increases, the demand for soda increases and the price of soda rises. Faced with a higher price, the soda plant works overtime and increases production. Conditions are good for workers in Kalamazoo, and the soda factory finds it hard to hang onto its best people. To do so, it offers a higher money wage rate. As the wage rate rises, so do the soda factory's costs.

What happens next depends on what happens to aggregate demand. If aggregate demand remains constant (as in Fig. 12.2b), the firm's costs are increasing, but the price of soda is not increasing as quickly as its costs. Production is scaled back. Eventually, the money wage rate and costs increase by the same percentage as the rise in the price of soda. In real terms, the soda factory is in the same situation as it was initially—before the increase in aggregate demand. The plant produces the same amount of soda and employs the same amount of labor as before the increase in demand.

But if aggregate demand continues to increase, so does the demand for soda and the price of soda rises at the same rate as wages. The soda factory continues to operate above full employment, and there is a persistent shortage of labor. Prices and wages chase each other upward in an unending spiral.

**Demand-Pull Inflation in the United States** A demand-pull inflation like the one you've just studied occurred in the United States during the 1960s. In 1960, inflation was a moderate 2 percent a year, but its rate increased slowly to 3 percent by 1966. Then, in 1967, a large increase in government purchases on the Vietnam War and an increase in spending on social programs, together with an increase in the growth rate of the quantity of money, increased aggregate demand more quickly. Consequently, the rightward shift of the aggregate demand curve speeded up and the price level increased more quickly. Real GDP moved above potential GDP, and the unemployment rate fell below its natural rate.

With unemployment below its natural rate, the money wage rate started to rise more quickly and the short-run aggregate supply curve shifted leftward. The Fed responded with a further increase in the money growth rate, and a demand-pull inflation spiral unfolded. By 1970, the inflation rate had reached 5 percent a year.

For the next few years, aggregate demand grew even more quickly and the inflation rate kept rising. By 1975, the inflation rate had almost reached 10 percent a year.

### REVIEW QUIZ

1. How does demand-pull inflation begin? What are the initial effects of demand-pull inflation on real GDP?
2. When real GDP moves above potential GDP, what happens to the money wage rate and short-run aggregate supply? How do real GDP and the price level respond?
3. What must happen to create a demand-pull inflation spiral?

Next, let's see how shocks to aggregate supply can create cost-push inflation.

## Cost-Push Inflation

An inflation that results from an initial increase in costs is called **cost-push inflation**. The two main sources of increases in costs are

1. An increase in money wage rates
2. An increase in the money prices of raw materials

At a given price level, the higher the cost of production, the smaller is the amount that firms are willing to produce. So if money wage rates rise or if the prices of raw materials (for example, oil) rise, firms decrease their supply of goods and services. Aggregate supply decreases, and the short-run aggregate supply curve shifts leftward.[1] Let's trace the effects of such a decrease in short-run aggregate supply on the price level and real GDP.

### Initial Effect of a Decrease in Aggregate Supply

Suppose that last year the price level was 105 and real GDP was $10 trillion. Potential real GDP was also $10 trillion. Figure 12.4 illustrates this situation. The aggregate demand curve was $AD_0$, the short-run

---

[1] Some cost-push forces, such as an increase in the price of oil accompanied by a decrease in the availability of oil, can also decrease long-run aggregate supply. We'll ignore such effects here and examine cost-push factors that change only short-run aggregate supply.

## FIGURE 12.4 A Cost-Push Rise in the Price Level

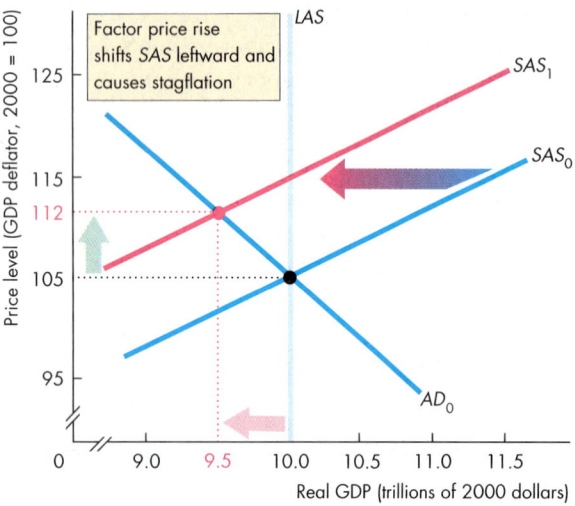

Initially, the aggregate demand curve is $AD_0$, the short-run aggregate supply curve is $SAS_0$, and the long-run aggregate supply curve is $LAS$. A decrease in aggregate supply (for example, resulting from a rise in the world price of oil) shifts the short-run aggregate supply curve to $SAS_1$. The economy moves to the point where the short-run aggregate supply curve $SAS_1$ intersects the aggregate demand curve $AD_0$. The price level rises to 112, and real GDP decreases to $9.5 trillion. The economy experiences stagflation.

aggregate supply curve was $SAS_0$, and the long-run aggregate supply curve was $LAS$. In the current year, the world's oil producers form a price-fixing organization that strengthens their market power and increases the relative price of oil. They raise the price of oil, and this action decreases short-run aggregate supply. The short-run aggregate supply curve shifts leftward to $SAS_1$. The price level rises to 112, and real GDP decreases to $9.5 trillion. The combination of a rise in the price level and a fall in real GDP is called stagflation.

This event is a one-time rise in the price level, like that in Fig. 12.1. It is not inflation. In fact, a supply shock on its own cannot cause inflation. Something more must happen to enable a one-time supply shock, which causes a one-time rise in the price level, to be converted into a process of money growth and ongoing inflation. The quantity of money must persistently increase. And it often does increase, as you will now see.

### Aggregate Demand Response

When real GDP falls, unemployment rises above its natural rate. In such a situation, there is usually an outcry of concern and a call for action to restore full employment. Suppose that the Fed increases the quantity of money. Aggregate demand increases. In Fig. 12.5, the aggregate demand curve shifts rightward to $AD_1$. The increase in aggregate demand has restored full employment. But the price level rises further to 116.

### A Cost-Push Inflation Process

The oil producers now see the prices of everything that they buy is increasing. So they increase the price of oil again to restore its new high relative price. Figure 12.6 continues the story.

## FIGURE 12.5 Aggregate Demand Response to Cost-Push

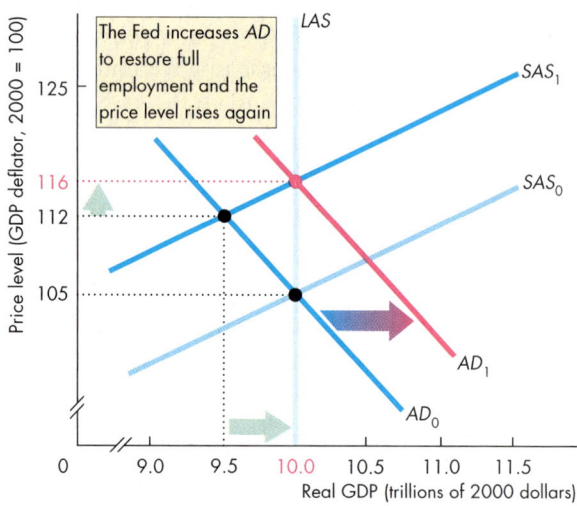

Following a cost-push increase in the price level, real GDP is below potential GDP and unemployment is above its natural rate. If the Fed responds by increasing aggregate demand to restore full employment, the aggregate demand curve shifts rightward to $AD_1$. The economy returns to full employment but the price level rises to 116.

The short-run aggregate supply curve now shifts to $SAS_2$, and another bout of stagflation ensues. The price level rises further, to 124, and real GDP decreases to $9.5 trillion. Unemployment increases above its natural rate. If the Fed responds yet again with an increase in the quantity of money, aggregate demand increases and the aggregate demand curve shifts to $AD_2$. The price level rises even higher—to 128—and full employment is again restored. A cost-push inflation spiral results. But if the Fed does not respond, the economy remains below full employment.

You can see that the Fed has a dilemma. If it increases the quantity of money to restore full employment, it invites another oil price hike that will call forth yet a further increase in the quantity of money.

Inflation will rage along at a rate decided by the oil-exporting nations. If the Fed keeps the lid on money growth, the economy operates with a high level of unemployment.

**Cost-Push Inflation in Kalamazoo** What is going on in the Kalamazoo soda-bottling plant when the economy is experiencing cost-push inflation? When the oil price increases, so do the costs of bottling soda. These higher costs decrease the supply of soda, increasing its price and decreasing the quantity produced. The soda plant lays off some workers. This situation will persist until either the Fed increases aggregate demand or the price of oil falls. If the Fed increases aggregate demand, the demand for soda increases and so does its price. The higher price of soda brings higher profits, and the bottling plant increases its production. The soda factory rehires the laid-off workers.

**Cost-Push Inflation in the United States** A cost-push inflation like the one you've just studied occurred in the United States during the 1970s. It began in 1974 when the Organization of Petroleum Exporting Countries (OPEC) raised the price of oil fourfold. The higher oil price decreased aggregate supply, which caused the price level to rise more quickly and real GDP to shrink. The Fed then faced a dilemma: Would it increase the quantity of money and accommodate the cost-push forces, or would it keep aggregate demand growth in check by limiting money growth? In 1975, 1976, and 1977, the Fed repeatedly allowed the quantity of money to grow quickly and inflation proceeded at a rapid rate. In 1979 and 1980, OPEC was again able to push oil prices higher. On that occasion, the Fed decided not to respond to the oil price hike with an increase in the quantity of money. The result was a recession but also, eventually, a fall in inflation.

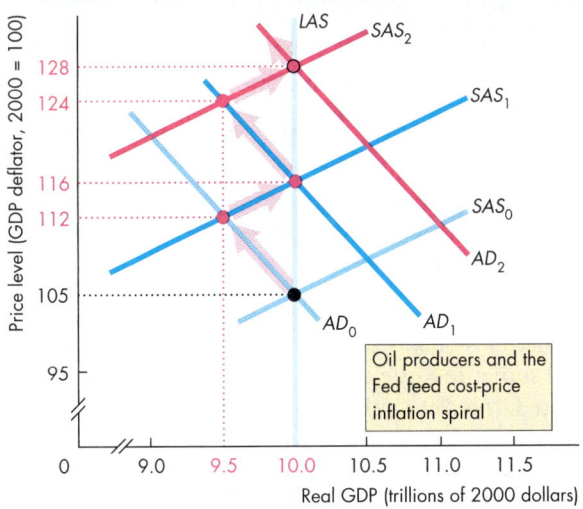

FIGURE 12.6  A Cost-Push Inflation Spiral

When a cost increase decreases short-run aggregate supply from $SAS_0$ to $SAS_1$, the price level rises to 112 and real GDP decreases to $9.5 trillion. The Fed responds with an increase in the quantity of money. The aggregate demand curve shifts from $AD_0$ to $AD_1$, the price level rises to 116, and real GDP returns to $10 trillion. A further cost increase occurs, which shifts the short-run aggregate supply curve again, this time to $SAS_2$. Stagflation is repeated, and the price level rises to 124. The Fed responds again, and the cost-price inflation spiral continues.

### REVIEW QUIZ

1 How does cost-push inflation begin? What are the initial effects of a cost-push rise in the price level?
2 What is stagflation and why does cost-push inflation cause stagflation?
3 What must the Fed do to convert a one-time rise in the price level into a freewheeling cost-push inflation?

## Effects of Inflation

REGARDLESS OF WHETHER INFLATION IS DEMAND-pull or cost-push, the failure to correctly *anticipate* it results in unintended consequences. These unintended consequences impose costs in both labor markets and capital markets. Let's examine these costs.

### Unanticipated Inflation in the Labor Market

Unanticipated inflation has two main consequences for the operation of the labor market:

- Redistribution of income
- Departure from full employment

**Redistribution of Income** Unanticipated inflation redistributes income between employers and workers. Sometimes employers gain at the expense of workers, and sometimes they lose. If an unexpected increase in aggregate demand increases the inflation rate, then the money wage rate will not have been set high enough. Profits will be higher than expected, and real wages will buy fewer goods than expected. In this case, employers gain at the expense of workers. But if aggregate demand is expected to increase at a rapid rate and it fails to do so, workers gain at the expense of employers. With a high inflation rate anticipated, the money wage rate is set too high and profits are squeezed. Redistribution between employers and workers creates an incentive for both firms and workers to try to forecast inflation correctly.

**Departures from Full Employment** Redistribution brings gains to some and losses to others. But departures from full employment impose costs on everyone. To see why, let's return to the soda-bottling plant.

If the bottling plant and its workers do not anticipate inflation but inflation occurs, the money wage rate does not rise to keep up with inflation. The real wage rate falls, and the firm tries to hire more labor and increase production. But because the real wage rate has fallen, the firm has a hard time attracting the labor it wants to employ. It pays overtime rates to its existing work force, and because it runs its plant at a faster pace, it incurs higher plant maintenance and parts replacement costs. But also, because the real wage rate has fallen, workers begin to quit the bottling plant to find jobs that pay a real wage rate that is closer to one that prevailed before the outbreak of inflation. This labor turnover imposes additional costs on the firm. So even though its production increases, the firm incurs additional costs and its profits do not increase as much as they otherwise would. The workers incur additional costs of job search, and those who remain at the bottling plant wind up feeling cheated. They've worked overtime to produce the extra output, and when they come to spend their wages, they discover that prices have increased so their wages buy a smaller quantity of goods and services than expected.

If the bottling plant and its workers anticipate a high inflation rate that does not occur, they increase the money wage rate by too much and the real wage rate rises. At the higher real wage rate, the firm lays off some workers and the unemployment rate increases. The workers who keep their jobs gain, but those who become unemployed lose. Also, the bottling plant loses because its output and profits fall.

### Unanticipated Inflation in the Market for Financial Capital

Unanticipated inflation has two consequences for the operation of the market for financial capital:

- Redistribution of income
- Too much or too little lending and borrowing

**Redistribution of Income** Unanticipated inflation redistributes income between borrowers and lenders. Sometimes borrowers gain at the expense of lenders, and sometimes they lose. When inflation is unexpected, interest rates are not set high enough to compensate lenders for the falling value of money. In this case, borrowers gain at the expense of lenders. But if inflation is expected and then fails to occur, interest rates are set too high. In this case, lenders gain at the expense of borrowers. Redistributions of income between borrowers and lenders create an incentive for both groups to try to forecast inflation correctly.

**Too Much or Too Little Lending and Borrowing** If the inflation rate turns out to be either higher or lower than expected, the interest rate does not incorporate a correct allowance for the falling value of money and the real interest rate is either lower or higher than it otherwise would be. When the real interest rate turns out to be too low, which occurs when inflation is *higher* than expected, borrowers wish they had borrowed more and lenders wish they had lent less. Both groups would have made different lending and borrowing decisions with greater foresight about the inflation rate. When the real interest rate turns out to be too high, which occurs when inflation is *lower* than expected, borrowers wish they had borrowed less and lenders wish they had lent more. Again, both groups would have made different lending and borrowing decisions with greater foresight about the inflation rate.

So unanticipated inflation imposes costs regardless of whether the inflation turns out to be higher or lower than anticipated. The presence of these costs gives everyone an incentive to forecast inflation correctly. Let's see how people go about this task.

## Forecasting Inflation

Inflation is difficult to forecast for two reasons. First, there are several sources of inflation—the demand-pull and cost-push sources you've just studied. Second, the speed with which a change in either aggregate demand or aggregate supply translates into a change in the price level varies. This speed of response also depends on the extent to which the inflation is anticipated, as you will see below.

Because inflation is costly and difficult to forecast, people devote considerable resources to improving inflation forecasts. Some people specialize in forecasting, and others buy forecasts from specialists. The specialist forecasters are economists who work for public and private macroeconomic forecasting agencies and for banks, insurance companies, labor unions, and large corporations. The returns these specialists make depend on the quality of their forecasts, so they have a strong incentive to forecast as accurately as possible. The most accurate forecast possible is the one that is based on all the relevant information and is called a **rational expectation**.

A rational expectation is not necessarily a correct forecast. It is simply the best forecast available. It will often turn out to be wrong, but no other forecast that could have been made with the information available could be predicted to be better.

You've seen the effects of inflation when people fail to anticipate it. And you've seen why it pays to try to anticipate inflation. Let's now see what happens if inflation is correctly anticipated.

## Anticipated Inflation

In the demand-pull and cost-push inflations that we studied earlier, the money wage rate is sticky. When aggregate demand increases, either to set off a demand-pull inflation or to accommodate cost-push inflation, the money wage rate does not change immediately. But if people correctly anticipate increases in aggregate demand, they will adjust the money wage rate so as to keep up with anticipated inflation.

In this case, inflation proceeds with real GDP equal to potential GDP and unemployment at its natural rate. Figure 12.7 explains why. Suppose that last year the price level was 105 and real GDP was $10 trillion, which is also potential GDP. The aggregate demand curve was $AD_0$, the aggregate supply curve was $SAS_0$, and the long-run aggregate supply curve was $LAS$.

Suppose that potential GDP does not change, so the $LAS$ curve does not shift. Also suppose that aggregate demand is expected to increase and that the expected aggregate demand curve for this year is $AD_1$. In anticipation of this increase in aggregate demand, the money wage rate rises and the short-run aggregate supply curve shifts leftward. If the money wage rate rises by the same percentage as the price level rises, the short-run aggregate supply curve for next year is $SAS_1$.

If aggregate demand turns out to be the same as expected, the aggregate demand curve is $AD_1$. The short-run aggregate supply curve, $SAS_1$, and $AD_1$ determine the actual price level at 116. Between last year and this year, the price level increased from 105 to 116 and the economy experienced an inflation rate of 10 percent, the same as the inflation rate that was anticipated. If this anticipated inflation is ongoing, in the following year aggregate demand increases (as anticipated) and the aggregate demand curve shifts to $AD_2$. The money wage rate rises to reflect the anticipated inflation, and the short-run aggregate supply curve shifts to $SAS_2$. The price level rises by a further 10 percent to 128.

What has caused this inflation? The immediate answer is that because people expected inflation, the wage rate was increased and prices increased. But the expectation was correct. Aggregate demand was expected to increase, and it did increase. Because aggregate demand was *expected* to increase from $AD_0$ to $AD_1$, the short-run aggregate supply curve shifted from $SAS_0$ to $SAS_1$. Because aggregate demand actually did increase by the amount that was expected, the actual aggregate demand curve shifted from $AD_0$

to $AD_1$. The combination of the anticipated and actual shifts of the aggregate demand curve rightward produced an increase in the price level that was anticipated.

Only if aggregate demand growth is correctly forecasted does the economy follow the course described in Fig. 12.7. If the expected growth rate of aggregate demand is different from its actual growth rate, the expected aggregate demand curve shifts by an amount that is different from the actual aggregate demand curve. The inflation rate departs from its expected level, and to some extent, there is unanticipated inflation.

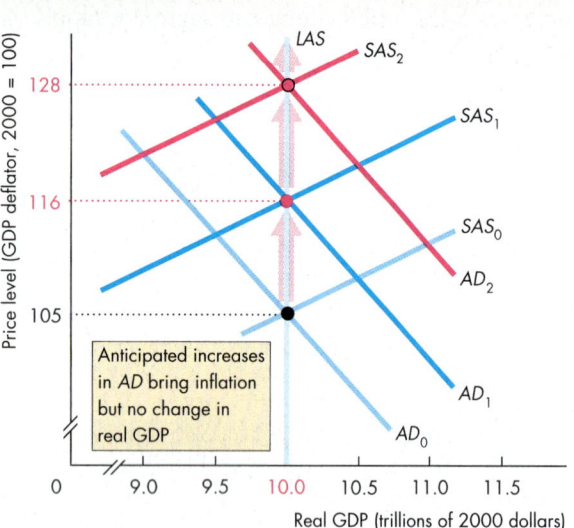

FIGURE 12.7  Anticipated Inflation

Potential real GDP is $10 trillion. Last year, aggregate demand was $AD_0$, and the short-run aggregate supply curve was $SAS_0$. The actual price level was the same as the expected price level—105. This year, aggregate demand is expected to increase to $AD_1$. The rational expectation of the price level changes from 105 to 116. As a result, the money wage rate rises and the short-run aggregate supply curve shifts to $SAS_1$. If aggregate demand actually increases as expected, the actual aggregate demand curve $AD_1$ is the same as the expected aggregate demand curve. Real GDP is $10 trillion and the actual price level is 116. The inflation is correctly anticipated. Next year, the process continues with aggregate demand increasing as expected to $AD_2$ and the money wage rate rising to shift the short-run aggregate supply curve to $SAS_2$. Again, real GDP remains at $10 trillion, and the price level rises, as anticipated, to 128.

## Unanticipated Inflation

When aggregate demand increases by *more* than expected, there is some unanticipated inflation that looks just like the demand-pull inflation that you studied earlier. Some inflation is expected, and the money wage rate is set to reflect that expectation. The *SAS* curve intersects the *LAS* curve at the expected price level. Aggregate demand then increases, but by more than expected. So the *AD* curve intersects the *SAS* curve at a level of real GDP that exceeds potential GDP. With real GDP above potential GDP and unemployment below its natural rate, the money wage rate rises. So the price level rises further. If aggregate demand increases again, a demand-pull inflation spiral unwinds.

When aggregate demand increases by *less* than expected, there is some unanticipated inflation that looks like the cost-push inflation that you studied earlier. Again, some inflation is expected, and the money wage rate is set to reflect that expectation. The *SAS* curve intersects the *LAS* curve at the expected price level. Aggregate demand then increases, but by less than expected. So the *AD* curve intersects the *SAS* curve at a level of real GDP below potential GDP. Aggregate demand increases to restore full employment. But if aggregate demand is expected to increase by more than it actually does, the money wage rate again rises, short-run aggregate supply again decreases, and a cost-push spiral unwinds.

We've seen that only when inflation is unanticipated does real GDP depart from potential GDP. When inflation is anticipated, real GDP remains at potential GDP. Does this mean that an anticipated inflation has no costs?

## The Costs of Anticipated Inflation

The costs of an anticipated inflation depend on its rate. At a moderate rate of 2 or 3 percent a year, the cost is probably small. But as the anticipated inflation rate rises, so does its cost, and an anticipated inflation at a rapid rate can be extremely costly.

Anticipated inflation decreases potential GDP and slows economic growth. These adverse consequences arise for three major reasons:

- Transactions costs
- Tax effects
- Increased uncertainty

**Transactions Costs** The first transactions costs are known as the "shoe leather costs." These are costs that arise from an increase in the velocity of circulation of money and an increase in the amount of running around that people do to try to avoid incurring losses from the falling value of money.

When money loses value at a rapid anticipated rate, it does not function well as a store of value and people try to avoid holding money. They spend their incomes as soon as they receive them, and firms pay out incomes—wages and dividends—as soon as they receive revenue from their sales. The velocity of circulation increases. During the 1920s in Germany, when inflation reached *hyperinflation* levels (rates more than 50 percent a month), wages were paid and spent twice in a single day!

The range of estimates of the shoe leather costs is large. Some economists put them at close to zero. Others estimate them to be as much as 2 percent of GDP for a 10 percent inflation. For a rapid inflation, these costs are much more.

The shoe leather costs of inflation are just one of several transactions costs that are influenced by the inflation rate. At high anticipated inflation rates, people seek alternatives to money as means of payment and use tokens and commodities or even barter, all of which are less efficient than money as a means of payment. For example, when inflation reached 1,000 percent a year in Israel during the 1980s, the U.S. dollar started to replace the increasingly worthless shekel. Consequently, people had to keep track of the exchange rate between the shekel and the dollar hour by hour and had to engage in many additional and costly transactions in the foreign exchange market.

Because anticipated inflation increases transactions costs, it diverts resources from producing goods and services and it decreases potential GDP. The faster the anticipated inflation rate, the greater is the decrease in potential GDP and the farther leftward the *LAS* curve shifts.

**Tax Consequences** Anticipated inflation interacts with the tax system and creates serious distortions in incentives. Its major effect is on real interest rates.

Anticipated inflation swells the dollar returns on investments. But dollar returns are taxed, so the effective tax rate rises. This effect becomes serious at even modest inflation rates. Let's consider an example.

Suppose the real interest rate is 4 percent a year and the tax rate is 50 percent. With no inflation, the nominal interest rate is also 4 percent a year and 50 percent of this rate is taxable. The real *after-tax* interest rate is 2 percent a year (50 percent of 4 percent). Now suppose the inflation rate is 4 percent a year and the nominal interest rate is 8 percent a year. (See p. 293.) The *after-tax* nominal rate is 4 percent a year (50 percent of 8 percent). Now subtract the 4 percent inflation rate from this amount, and you see that the *after-tax real interest rate* is zero! The true tax rate on interest income is 100 percent.

The higher the inflation rate, the higher is the effective tax rate on income from capital. And the higher the tax rate, the higher is the interest rate paid by borrowers and the lower is the after-tax interest rate received by lenders.

With a low after-tax real interest rate, the incentive to save is weakened and the saving rate falls. With a high cost of borrowing, the amount of investment decreases. And with a fall in saving and investment, the pace of capital accumulation slows and so does the long-term growth rate of real GDP.

**Increased Uncertainty** When the inflation rate is high, there is increased uncertainty about the long-term inflation rate. Will inflation remain high for a long time, or will price stability be restored? This increased uncertainty makes long-term planning difficult and gives people a shorter-term focus. Investment falls, and so the growth rate slows.

But this increased uncertainty also misallocates resources. Instead of concentrating on the activities at which they have a comparative advantage, people find it more profitable to search for ways of avoiding the losses that inflation inflicts. As a result, creative people who might otherwise work on productive innovations work on finding ways of profiting from the inflation instead.

The implications of inflation for economic growth have been estimated to be enormous. Peter Howitt of Brown University, building on work by Robert Barro of Harvard University, has estimated that if inflation is lowered from 3 percent a year to zero, the growth rate of real GDP will rise by between 0.06 and 0.09 percentage point a year. These numbers might seem small, but they are growth rates. After 30 years, real GDP would be 2.3 percent higher and the present value of all the future output would by 85 percent of current GDP—$8.5 trillion! In the rapid anticipated inflations of Brazil and Russia, the costs are much greater than the numbers given here.

> **REVIEW QUIZ**
>
> 1. What is a rational expectation? Are people who form rational expectations ever wrong?
> 2. Why do people forecast inflation and what information do they use to do so?
> 3. How does anticipated inflation occur?
> 4. What are the effects of a rapid anticipated inflation? Does anticipated inflation bring an increase in real GDP?

You've seen that an increase in aggregate demand that is not fully anticipated increases both the price level and real GDP. It also decreases unemployment. Similarly, a decrease in aggregate demand that is not fully anticipated decreases the price level and real GDP. It also increases unemployment. Do these relationships mean that there is a tradeoff between inflation and unemployment? Does low unemployment always bring inflation and does low inflation bring high unemployment? We explore these questions.

## Inflation and Unemployment: The Phillips Curve

THE AGGREGATE SUPPLY–AGGREGATE DEMAND model focuses on the price level and real GDP. Knowing how these two variables change, we can work out what happens to the inflation rate and the unemployment rate. But the model does not place inflation and unemployment at center stage.

A more direct way of studying inflation and unemployment uses a relationship called the Phillips curve. The Phillips curve approach uses the same basic ideas as the *AS-AD* model, but it focuses directly on inflation and unemployment. The Phillips curve is so named because New Zealand economist A.W. Phillips popularized it. A **Phillips curve** shows the relationship between inflation and unemployment. There are two time frames for Phillips curves:

- The short-run Phillips curve
- The long-run Phillips curve

### The Short-Run Phillips Curve

The **short-run Phillips curve** shows the relationship between inflation and unemployment, holding constant:

1. The expected inflation rate
2. The natural unemployment rate

You've just seen what determines the expected inflation rate. The natural rate of unemployment and the factors that influence it are explained in Chapter 8, pp. 187–189.

Figure 12.8 shows a short-run Phillips curve, *SRPC*. Suppose that the expected inflation rate is 10 percent a year and the natural rate of unemployment is 6 percent, point *A* in the figure. A short-run Phillips curve passes through this point. If inflation rises above its expected rate, unemployment falls

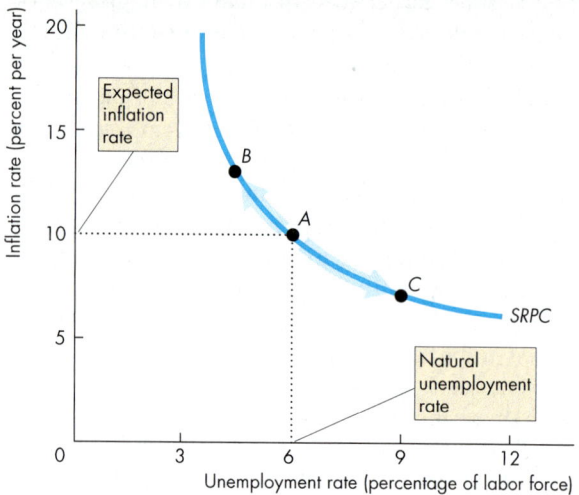

**FIGURE 12.8** A Short-Run Phillips Curve

The short-run Phillips curve (*SRPC*) shows the relationship between inflation and unemployment at a given expected inflation rate and a given natural unemployment rate. With an expected inflation rate of 10 percent a year and a natural unemployment rate of 6 percent, the short-run Phillips curve passes through point A. An unanticipated increase in aggregate demand lowers unemployment and increases inflation—a movement up the short-run Phillips curve. An unanticipated decrease in aggregate demand increases unemployment and lowers inflation—a movement down the short-run Phillips curve.

below its natural rate. This joint movement in the inflation rate and the unemployment rate is illustrated as a movement up along the short-run Phillips curve from point A to point B in the figure. Similarly, if inflation falls below its expected rate, unemployment rises above its natural rate. In this case, there is movement down along the short-run Phillips curve from point A to point C.

This negative relationship between inflation and unemployment along the short-run Phillips curve is explained by the aggregate supply–aggregate demand model. Figure 12.9 shows the connection between the two approaches. Initially, the aggregate demand curve is $AD_0$, the short-run aggregate supply curve is $SAS_0$, and the long-run aggregate supply curve is $LAS$. Real GDP is $10 trillion, and the price level is 100. Aggregate demand is expected to increase, and the aggregate demand curve is expected to shift rightward to $AD_1$. Anticipating this increase in aggregate demand, the money wage rate rises, which shifts the short-run aggregate supply curve to $SAS_1$. What happens to actual inflation and real GDP depends on the *actual* change in aggregate demand.

First, suppose that aggregate demand actually increases by the amount expected, so the aggregate demand curve shifts to $AD_1$. The price level rises from 100 to 110, and the inflation rate is an anticipated 10 percent a year. Real GDP remains at potential GDP, and unemployment remains at its natural rate—6 percent. The economy moves to point A in Fig. 12.9, and it can equivalently be described as being at point A on the short-run Phillips curve in Fig. 12.8.

Alternatively, suppose that aggregate demand is expected to increase to $AD_1$ but actually increases by more than expected, to $AD_2$. The price level now rises to 113, a 13 percent inflation rate. Real GDP increases above potential GDP, and unemployment falls below its natural rate. We can now describe the economy as moving to point B in Fig. 12.9 or as being at point B on the short-run Phillips curve in Fig. 12.8.

Finally, suppose that aggregate demand is expected to increase to $AD_1$ but actually remains at $AD_0$. The price level now rises to 107, a 7 percent inflation rate. Real GDP falls below potential GDP, and unemployment rises above its natural rate. We can now describe the economy as moving to point C in Fig. 12.9 or as being at point C on the short-run Phillips curve in Fig. 12.8.

**FIGURE 12.9    AS-AD and the Short-Run Phillips Curve**

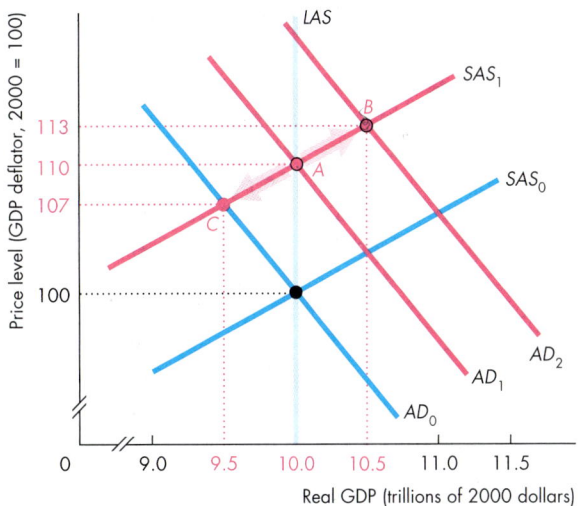

If aggregate demand is expected to increase and shift the aggregate demand curve from $AD_0$ to $AD_1$, then the money wage rate rises by an amount that shifts the short-run aggregate supply curve from $SAS_0$ to $SAS_1$. The price level rises to 110, a 10 percent rise, and the economy is at point A in this figure and at point A on the short-run Phillips curve in Fig. 12.8. If, with the same expectations, aggregate demand increases and shifts the aggregate demand curve from $AD_0$ to $AD_2$, the price level rises to 113, a 13 percent rise, and the economy is at point B in this figure and at point B on the short-run Phillips curve in Fig. 12.8. If, with the same expectations, aggregate demand does not change, the price level rises to 107, a 7 percent rise, and the economy is at point C in this figure and at point C on the short-run Phillips curve in Fig. 12.8.

The short-run Phillips curve is like the short-run aggregate supply curve. A movement along the *SAS* curve that brings a higher price level and an increase in real GDP is equivalent to a movement along the short-run Phillips curve that brings an increase in the inflation rate and a decrease in the unemployment rate. (Similarly, a movement along the *SAS* curve that brings a lower price level and a decrease in real GDP is equivalent to a movement along the short-run Phillips curve that brings a decrease in the inflation rate and an increase in the unemployment rate.)

### The Long-Run Phillips Curve

The **long-run Phillips curve** shows the relationship between inflation and unemployment when the actual inflation rate equals the expected inflation rate. The long-run Phillips curve is vertical at the natural unemployment rate. In Fig. 12.10, it is the vertical line $LRPC$. The long-run Phillips curve tells us that any anticipated inflation rate is possible at the natural unemployment rate. This proposition is consistent with the $AS$-$AD$ model, which predicts that when inflation is anticipated, real GDP equals potential GDP and unemployment is at its natural rate.

When the expected inflation rate changes, the short-run Phillips curve shifts but the long-run Phillips curve does not shift. If the expected inflation rate is 10 percent a year, the short-run Phillips curve is $SRPC_0$. If the expected inflation rate falls to 7 percent a year, the short-run Phillips curve shifts downward to $SRPC_1$. The distance by which the short-run Phillips curve shifts downward when the expected inflation rate falls is equal to the change in the expected inflation rate.

To see why the short-run Phillips curve shifts when the expected inflation rate changes, let's do a thought experiment. There is full employment, and a 10 percent a year anticipated inflation is raging. The Fed now begins an attack on inflation by slowing money growth. Aggregate demand growth slows, and the inflation rate falls to 7 percent a year. At first, this decrease in inflation is *un*anticipated, so the money wage rate continues to rise at its original rate. The short-run aggregate supply curve shifts leftward at the same pace as before. Real GDP decreases, and unemployment increases. In Fig. 12.10, the economy moves from point $A$ to point $C$ on $SRPC_0$.

If the actual inflation rate remains steady at 7 percent a year, this rate eventually comes to be expected. As this happens, wage growth slows and the short-run aggregate supply curve shifts leftward less quickly. Eventually, it shifts leftward at the same pace at which the aggregate demand curve is shifting rightward. The actual inflation rate equals the expected inflation rate, and full employment is restored. Unemployment is back at its natural rate. In Fig. 12.10, the short-run Phillips curve has shifted from $SRPC_0$ to $SRPC_1$ and the economy is at point $D$.

An increase in the expected inflation rate has the opposite effect to that shown in Fig. 12.10. Another important source of shifts in the Phillips curve is a change in the natural rate of unemployment.

### Changes in the Natural Rate of Unemployment

The natural rate of unemployment changes for many reasons (see Chapter 8, pp. 187–189). A change in the natural rate of unemployment shifts both the short-run and long-run Phillips curves. Figure 12.11 illustrates such shifts. If the natural rate of unemployment increases from 6 percent to 9 percent, the long-run Phillips curve shifts from $LRPC_0$ to $LRPC_1$, and if expected inflation is constant at 10 percent a year, the short-run Phillips curve shifts from $SRPC_0$ to $SRPC_1$. Because the expected inflation rate is constant, the short-run Phillips curve $SRPC_1$ intersects the long-run curve $LRPC_1$ (point $E$) at the same inflation rate at which the short-run Phillips curve $SRPC_0$ intersects the long-run curve $LRPC_0$ (point $A$).

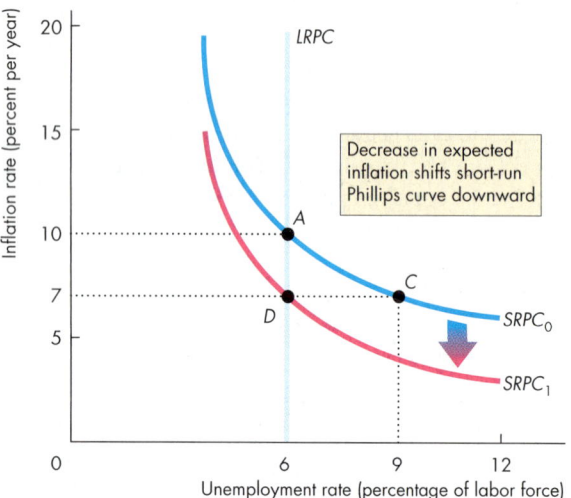

**FIGURE 12.10** Short-Run and Long-Run Phillips Curves

The long-run Phillips curve is $LRPC$. A fall in expected inflation from 10 percent a year to 7 percent a year shifts the short-run Phillips curve downward from $SRPC_0$ and $SRPC_1$. The new short-run Phillips curve intersects the long-run Phillips curve at the new expected inflation rate—point $D$. With the original expected inflation rate (of 10 percent a year), a fall in the actual inflation rate to 7 percent a year increases the unemployment rate to 9 percent, at point $C$.

# INFLATION AND UNEMPLOYMENT: THE PHILLIPS CURVE

## The U.S. Phillips Curve

Figure 12.12(a) is a scatter diagram of inflation and unemployment since 1960. We can interpret the data in terms of the shifting short-run Phillips curve in Fig. 12.12(b). During the 1960s, the short-run Phillips curve was $SRPC_0$, with a natural rate of unemployment of 4.5 percent and an expected inflation rate of 2 percent a year (point A). During the early 1970s, the short-run Phillips curve was $SRPC_1$ with a natural rate of unemployment of 5 percent and an expected inflation rate of 6 percent a year (point B). During the late 1970s, the natural unemployment rate increased to 8 percent (point C) and the short-run Phillips curve was $SRPC_2$. And briefly in 1975 and again in 1981, the expected inflation rate surged to 8 percent a year (point D) and the short-run Phillips curve was $SRPC_3$. During the 1980s and 1990s, the expected inflation rate and the natural rate of unemployment decreased and the short-run Phillips curve shifted leftward. By the early 1990s, it was back at $SRPC_1$. And by the mid-1990s, it was again $SRPC_0$.

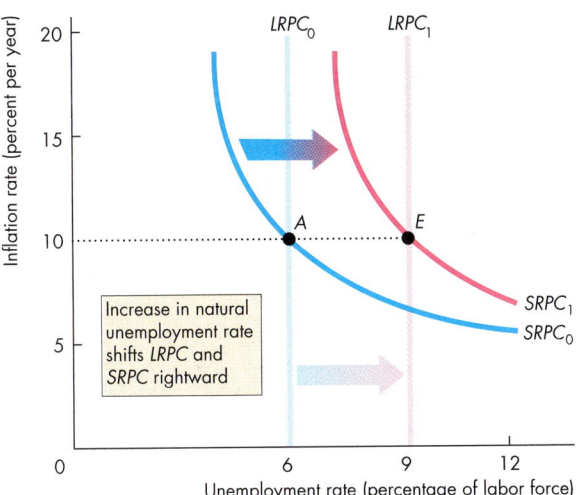

**FIGURE 12.11** A Change in the Natural Unemployment Rate

A change in the natural unemployment rate shifts both the short-run and long-run Phillips curves. Here, the natural unemployment rate increases from 6 percent to 9 percent, and the two Phillips curves shift right to $SRPC_1$ and $LRPC_1$. The new long-run Phillips curve intersects the new short-run Phillips curve at the expected inflation rate—point E.

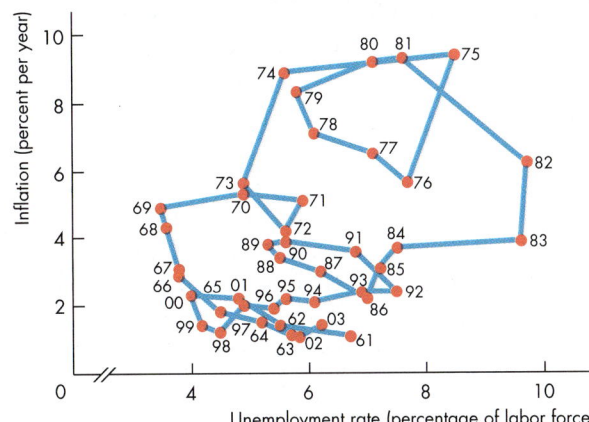

**FIGURE 12.12** Phillips Curves in the United States

**(a) Time sequence**

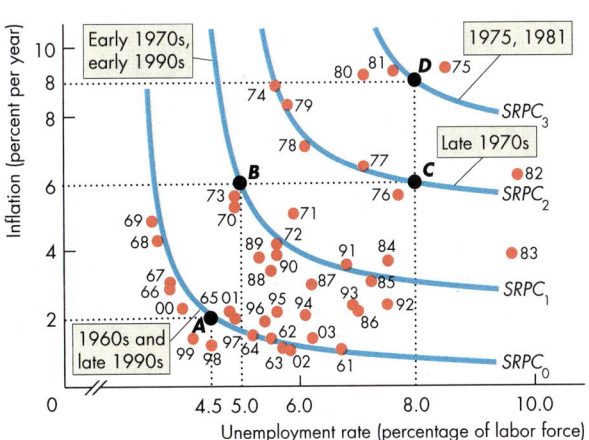

**(b) Four Phillips curves**

In part (a), each dot represents the combination of inflation and unemployment for a particular year in the United States. Part (b) interprets the data with a shifting short-run Phillips curve. The black dots A, B, C, and D show the combination of the natural rate of unemployment and the expected inflation rate in different periods. The short-run Phillips curve was $SRPC_0$ during the 1960s and the late 1990s and early 2000s. It was $SRPC_1$ during the early 1970s and early 1990s, $SRPC_2$ during the late 1970s, and $SRPC_3$ (briefly) in 1975 and 1981.

*Source:* Bureau of Labor Statistics and the author's calculations and assumptions.

## REVIEW QUIZ

1. How would you use the Phillips curve to illustrate an unanticipated change in the inflation rate?
2. What are the effects of an unanticipated increase in the inflation rate on the unemployment rate?
3. If the expected inflation rate increases by 10 percentage points, how does the short-run Phillips curve and the long-run Phillips curve change?
4. If the natural unemployment rate increases, what happens to the short-run Phillips curve, the long-run Phillips curve, and the expected inflation rate?
5. Does the United States have a stable short-run Phillips curve? Explain why or why not.
6. Does the United States have a stable long-run Phillips curve?

So far, we've studied the effects of inflation on real GDP, real wages, employment, and unemployment. But inflation lowers the value of money and changes the real value of the amounts borrowed and repaid. As a result, interest rates are influenced by inflation. Let's see how.

## Interest Rates and Inflation

TODAY, BUSINESSES IN THE UNITED STATES CAN borrow at interest rates of around 6 percent a year. Businesses in Russia pay interest rates of 20 percent a year, and those in Turkey pay 30 percent a year. Although U.S. interest rates have never been as high as these two cases, U.S. businesses faced interest rates of 16 percent or higher during the 1980s. Why do interest rates vary so much both across countries and over time? Part of the answer is because risk differences make *real interest rates* vary across countries. High-risk countries pay higher interest rates than do low-risk countries. But another part of the answer is that the inflation rate varies.

Figure 12.13 shows that the higher the inflation rate, the higher is the nominal interest rate. This proposition is true for the United States over time in part (a) and the world in 2000 in part (b).

**FIGURE 12.13** Inflation and the Interest Rate

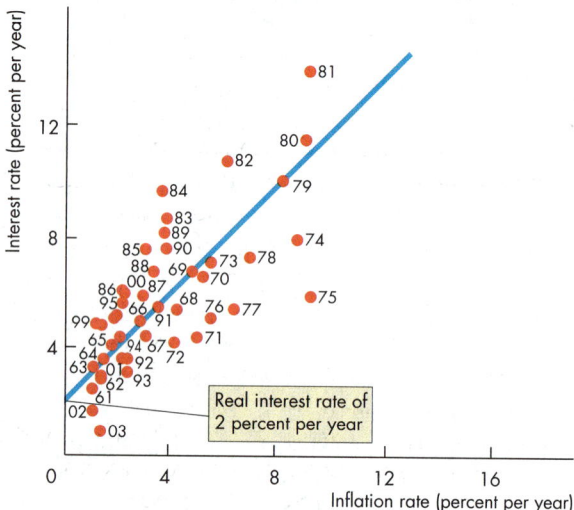

(a) United States

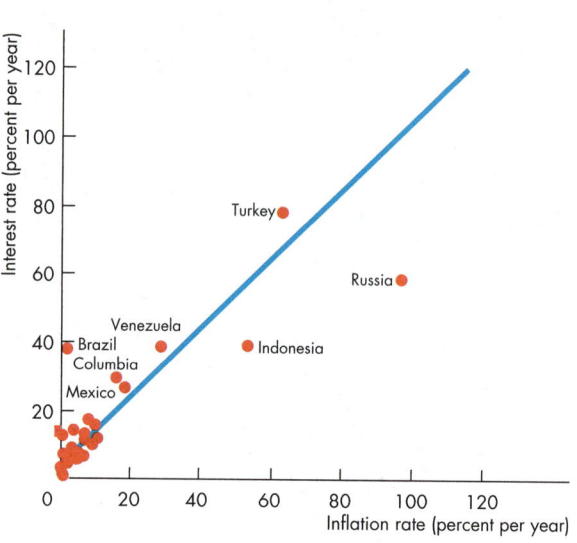

(b) Around the world

Other things remaining the same, the higher the inflation rate, the higher is the nominal interest rate. Part (a) shows this relationship between nominal interest rates and the inflation rate in the United States, and part (b) shows the relationship across a number of countries in 2000.

Sources: Federal Reserve Board, Bureau of Labor Statistics, and International Monetary Fund.

## How Interest Rates Are Determined

Investment demand and saving supply determine the *real* interest rate in the market for financial capital. Investment demand and saving supply depend on the real interest rate, and the real interest rate adjusts to make investment plans and saving plans equal. (Chapter 8, pp. 193–194, explains the forces that determine the equilibrium real interest rate.)

The demand for money and the supply of money determine the *nominal* interest rate in the money market. The demand for money depends on the nominal interest rate, the supply of money is determined by the Fed's monetary policy, and the nominal interest rate adjusts to make the quantity of money demanded equal to the quantity supplied. (Chapter 11, pp. 261–262, explains the forces that determine the equilibrium nominal interest rate.)

Because the real interest rate is determined in the capital market and the nominal interest rate is determined in the money market, it might seem that there is no connection between the two interest rates. But there is a very tight connection. On the average, the nominal interest rate equals the real interest rate plus the expected inflation rate. Other things remaining the same, a 1 percentage point rise in the expected inflation rate leads to a 1 percentage point rise in the nominal interest rate. Why? The answer is that investment and saving decisions in the capital market and demand for money decisions in the money market are interrelated.

Let's see why expected inflation influences the nominal interest rate.

## Why Expected Inflation Influences the Nominal Interest Rate

To see why the nominal interest rate equals the real interest rate plus the expected inflation rate, think about the investment, saving, and demand for money decisions that people make. Imagine first that there is no inflation and none is expected. Investment equals saving at a real interest rate of 6 percent a year. The demand for money equals the supply of money at a nominal interest rate of 6 percent a year.

Walt Disney Corporation is willing to pay an interest rate of 6 percent a year to get the funds it needs to pay for its global investment in new theme parks. Sue and thousands of people like her are willing to save and lend Disney the amount it needs for its theme parks if they can get a *real* return of 6 percent a year. (Sue is saving to buy a new car.) And Disney, Sue, and everyone else are willing to hold the quantity of money supplied by the Fed.

If the nominal interest rate was 7 percent a year, Disney Corporation would put its investment plans on hold and buy bonds. It would make an extra one percent interest by doing so. As Disney and others bought bonds, the demand for bonds would increase, the price of bonds would rise, and the nominal interest rate would fall. Only when the nominal interest rate on a bond equaled the real interest rate on a theme park would Disney be in equilibrium.

Now imagine that the inflation rate is a steady and expected 4 percent a year. All dollar amounts, including theme park profits and car prices, are rising by 4 percent a year. If Disney was willing to pay a 6 percent interest rate when there was no inflation, it is now willing to pay a 10 percent interest rate. Its profits are rising by 4 percent a year, so it is *really* paying only a 6 percent interest rate. Similarly, if Sue was willing to lend at a 6 percent interest rate when there was no inflation, she is now willing to lend only if she gets a 10 percent interest rate. The price of the car Sue is planning on buying is rising by 4 percent a year, so she is *really* getting only a 6 percent interest rate.

Because borrowers are willing to pay the higher rate and lenders are willing to lend only if they receive the higher rate when inflation is expected, the *nominal interest rate* increases by an amount equal to the expected inflation rate. The *real interest rate* remains constant at 6 percent a year.

> **REVIEW QUIZ**
>
> 1 What is the relationship between the real interest rate, the nominal interest rate, and the expected inflation rate?
> 2 Why does a change in inflation change the nominal interest rate?

◆ Before leaving this chapter, look at *Reading Between the Lines* on pp. 294–295, which examines the relationship between inflation and unemployment in the United States during the past few years and gives you a look at today's short-run Phillips curve.

Your task in the next chapter is to focus on the business cycle. What causes cycles in economic activity? What brought the recession of 2001? And why was the expansion of 2002 and 2003 so weak?

# READING BETWEEN THE LINES

## The U.S. Phillips Curve: 2000–2003

**PITTSBURGH POST-GAZETTE, July 27, 2000**

### Links More Tenuous Between Inflation, Jobless Rates

Federal Reserve Chairman Alan Greenspan last week took aim at the favorite theory of anyone who thinks U.S. interest rates have to rise just because the jobless rate is close to a 30-year low.

That theory holds that at a certain point unemployment goes too low for the economy's good, driving up wage demands and, ultimately, inflation. Some economists say the figure is as high as 6 percent, some say 5 percent. The Fed chairman said the relationship between unemployment and inflation is tenuous at best.

Such a theory may have been "very useful" at one time, but "is probably going to fail in the years ahead as a useful indicator," Greenspan told the Senate Banking Committee in his twice-yearly economic report card.

His comments may give a clue to how the Fed will deal with future developments in the U.S. labor market. If unemployment sticks near 4 percent, Greenspan probably will continue to resist the once automatic reaction of Fed Governor Lawrence Meyer and other members of the policy-setting Open Market Committee to raise rates in an effort to curtail consumer and business borrowing and slow growth. ...

That evidence doesn't support Meyer and other so-called hawks on the Fed. Unemployment dropped below 5 percent in 1996, a level many of them thought would lead directly to higher prices.

Still, consumer price inflation, not including food and energy items, has held below 3 percent the entire time. ...

In a speech last month, Meyer dismissed "the broader interpretation of the New Economy concept"—meaning the notion that there's no link between low unemployment and accelerating inflation.

A jobless rate of 4 percent or so is probably too low, he said. And if the level of unemployment that leads to accelerating inflation "turns out to be closer to 5 percent, then the task is more demanding," and more workers might have to lose their jobs to bring the economy back into balance, he suggested. ...

But Greenspan can marshal some reasons Meyer's theory hasn't held true: Higher worker productivity has allowed companies to make do with fewer workers.

Also, inflation expectations remain low, so workers are less likely to demand outsized wage increases. ...

© 2000 Pittsburgh Post-Gazette
Reprinted with permission. Further reproduction prohibited.

### Essence of the Story

■ Federal Reserve Chairman Alan Greenspan challenged the view that U.S. interest rates must rise if the unemployment rate gets too low.

■ He said the relationship between unemployment and inflation is weak and not very useful.

■ Federal Reserve Governor Lawrence Meyer and other members of Federal Open Market Committee say that if the unemployment rate goes too low, inflation will increase.

■ Economists differ on what that unemployment rate is. Some say it is as high as 6 percent, and some say 5 percent. But most say that 4 percent is too low.

■ The unemployment rate fell below 5 percent in 1996, but the inflation rate remained below 3 percent a year.

■ Inflation expectations remain low, so workers are less likely to demand outsized wage increases.

## Economic Analysis

■ This news article is about the U.S. Phillips curve.

■ During 2000, when the news article was written, the unemployment rate fluctuated between 3.9 percent and 4.1 percent and was 4.0 percent on the average.

■ Inflation did not take off at this low average unemployment rate. But the inflation rate did edge upward slightly from 2.5 percent a year in January 2000 to 3.8 percent a year in July 2000.

■ We can interpret the data in 2000 as being on the long-run Phillips curve for that year.

■ Figure 1 shows the long-run Phillips curve for 2000. The natural unemployment rate was 4 percent, and the expected inflation rate was about 3.8 percent a year.

■ Starting in December 2000, the unemployment rate increased almost every month. By December 2001, it had reached 5.8 percent.

■ Through this same period, the inflation rate decreased almost every month. In January 2001, the inflation rate was 3.8 percent a year, and by December 2001, it had fallen to 1.6 percent a year.

■ The figure shows how we can interpret the data for 2001. The natural unemployment rate remained at 4 percent, so the long-run Phillips curve did not shift.

■ The expected inflation rate remained constant at (an approximate guess) 4 percent a year, so the short-run Phillips curve did not shift.

■ As 2001 unfolded, the economy moved downward along its short-run Phillips curve.

■ During 2002 and 2003, the unemployment rate remained close to 6 percent and the inflation rate fluctuated but around an average of about 1.5 percent a year.

■ The data for these years are consistent with a new long-run Phillips curve at a natural rate of unemployment of 5.8 percent.

■ The figure shows the short-run Phillips curve for 2002 and 2003 as being the same as that for 2000 and 2001. But in 2003 the natural rate of unemployment was higher and the expected inflation rate was lower than in 2000.

■ It is a coincidence that we can't rely on that the changes in the natural rate of unemployment and ex-

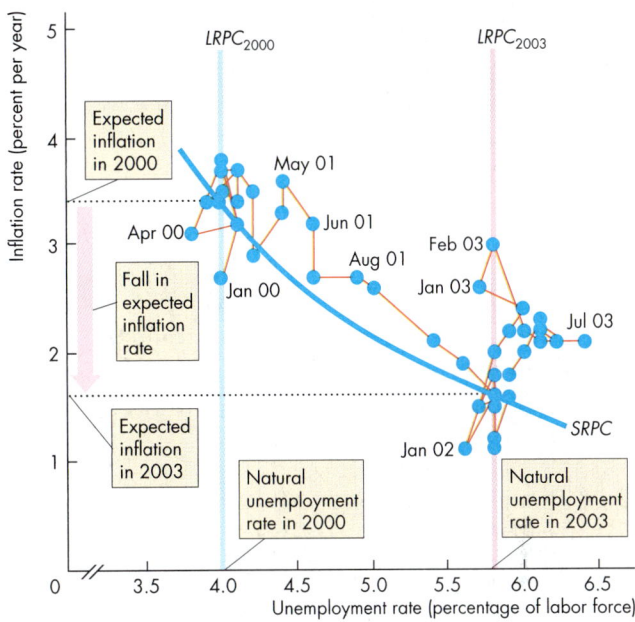

**Figure 1 U.S. Phillips Curves: 2000–2003**

pected inflation rate during the early 2000s left the short-run Phillips curve unchanged.

■ We cannot predict future changes in the natural unemployment rate and expected inflation rate, so the short-run tradeoff will shift in ways that we can't predict.

■ So Alan Greenspan is correct when he says the tradeoff has limited usefulness for policy.

# SUMMARY

## KEY POINTS

### Inflation and the Price Level (p. 278)

- Inflation is a process of persistently rising prices and falling value of money.

### Demand-Pull Inflation (pp. 279–281)

- Demand-pull inflation arises from increasing aggregate demand.
- Its main sources are increases in the quantity of money or in government purchases.

### Cost-Push Inflation (pp. 281–283)

- Cost-push inflation can result from any factor that decreases aggregate supply.
- Its main sources are increasing wage rates and increasing prices of key raw materials.

### Effects of Inflation (pp. 284–288)

- Inflation is costly when it is unanticipated because it creates inefficiencies and redistributes income and wealth.
- People try to anticipate inflation to avoid its costs.
- Forecasts of inflation based on all the available relevant information are called rational expectations.
- A moderate anticipated inflation has a small cost. But a rapid anticipated inflation is costly because it decreases potential GDP and slows growth.

### Inflation and Unemployment: The Phillips Curve (pp. 288–292)

- The short-run Phillips curve shows the tradeoff between inflation and unemployment when the expected inflation rate and the natural rate of unemployment are constant.
- The long-run Phillips curve, which is vertical, shows that when the actual inflation rate equals the expected inflation rate, the unemployment rate equals the natural rate of unemployment.
- Unexpected changes in the inflation rate bring movements along the short-run Phillips curve.
- Changes in expected inflation shift the short-run Phillips curve.
- Changes in the natural rate of unemployment shift both the short-run and long-run Phillips curves.

### Interest Rates and Inflation (pp. 292–293)

- The higher the expected inflation rate, the higher is the nominal interest rate.
- As the anticipated inflation rate rises, borrowers willingly pay a higher interest rate and lenders successfully demand a higher interest rate.
- The nominal interest rate adjusts to equal the real interest rate plus the expected inflation rate.

## KEY FIGURES

Figure 12.2   A Demand-Pull Rise in the Price Level, 279
Figure 12.3   A Demand-Pull Inflation Spiral, 280
Figure 12.4   A Cost-Push Rise in the Price Level, 282
Figure 12.6   A Cost-Push Inflation Spiral, 283
Figure 12.7   Anticipated Inflation, 286
Figure 12.8   A Short-Run Phillips Curve, 288
Figure 12.10  Short-Run and Long-Run Phillips Curves, 290

## KEY TERMS

Cost-push inflation, 281
Demand-pull inflation, 279
Inflation, 278
Long-run Phillips curve, 290
Phillips curve, 288
Rational expectation, 285
Short-run Phillips curve, 288

# PROBLEMS

*1. The figure shows an economy's long-run aggregate supply curve LAS; three aggregate demand curves $AD_0$, $AD_1$, and $AD_2$; and three short-run aggregate supply curves $SAS_0$, $SAS_1$, and $SAS_2$. The economy starts out on the curves $AD_0$ and $SAS_0$. Some events then occur that generate a demand-pull inflation.
   a. List the events that might cause a demand-pull inflation.
   b. Using the figure, describe the initial effects of a demand-pull inflation.
   c. Using the figure, describe what happens as a demand-pull inflation spiral unwinds.

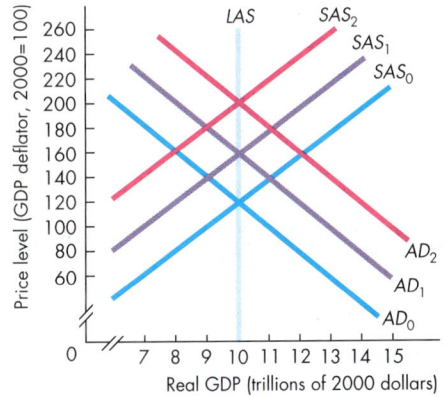

2. The economy described in problem 1 starts out on the curves $AD_0$ and $SAS_0$. Some events then occur that generate a cost-push inflation.
   a. List the events that might cause a cost-push inflation.
   b. Using the figure, describe the initial effects of a cost-push inflation.
   c. Using the figure, describe what happens as a cost-push inflation spiral unwinds.

*3. The economy described in problem 1 starts out on the curves $AD_0$ and $SAS_0$. Some events then occur that generate a perfectly anticipated inflation.
   a. List the events that might cause a perfectly anticipated inflation.
   b. Using the figure, describe the initial effects of an anticipated inflation.
   c. Using the figure, describe what happens as an anticipated inflation proceeds.

4. In the economy described in problem 1, suppose that people anticipate deflation (a falling price level), but aggregate demand turns out to not change.
   a. What happens to the short-run and long-run aggregate supply curves? (Draw some new curves if you need to.)
   b. Using the figure, describe the initial effects of an anticipated deflation.
   c. Using the figure, describe what happens as it becomes obvious to everyone that the anticipated deflation is not going to occur.

*5. An economy has an unemployment rate of 4 percent and an inflation rate of 5 percent at point A in the figure. Some events then occur that move the economy to point D.

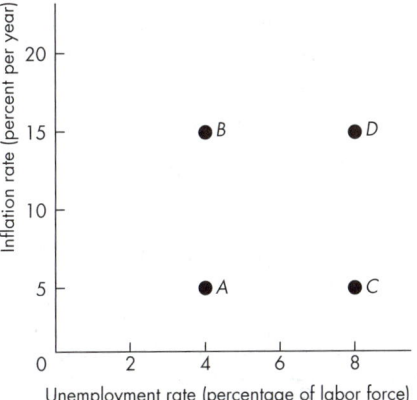

   a. Describe the events that could move the economy from point A to point D.
   b. Draw in the diagram the economy's short-run and long-run Phillips curves when the economy is at point A.
   c. Draw in the diagram the economy's short-run and long-run Phillips curves when the economy is at point D.

6. The economy described in problem 5 is initially at point B. Some events occur that move the economy from point B to point C.
   a. Describe the events that could move the economy from point B to point C.
   b. Draw in the diagram the economy's short-run and long-run Phillips curves when the economy is at point B.
   c. Draw in the diagram the economy's short-run and long-run Phillips curves when the economy is at point C.

* Solutions to odd-numbered problems are available on **MyEconLab**.

*7. In the economy described in problem 5, some events occur that move the economy in a clockwise loop from A to B to D to C and back to A.
   a. Describe the events that could create this sequence.
   b. Draw in the figure the sequence of the economy's short-run and long-run Phillips curves.
   c. Has the economy experienced demand-pull inflation, cost-push inflation, anticipated inflation, or none of these?

8. In the economy described in problem 5, some events occur that move the economy in a counterclockwise loop from A to C to D to B and back to A.
   a. Describe the events that could create this sequence.
   b. Draw in the figure the sequence of the economy's short-run and long-run Phillips curves.
   c. Has the economy experienced demand-pull inflation, cost-push inflation, anticipated inflation, or none of these?

*9. An economy with a natural rate of unemployment of 4 percent and an expected inflation rate of 6 percent a year has the following inflation and unemployment history:

| Year | Inflation rate (percent per year) | Unemployment rate (percent) |
|---|---|---|
| 1999 | 10 | 2 |
| 2000 | 8 | 3 |
| 2001 | 6 | 4 |
| 2002 | 4 | 5 |
| 2003 | 2 | 6 |

   a. Draw a figure that shows the economy's short-run and long-run Phillips curves.
   b. If the actual inflation rate rises from 6 percent a year to 8 percent a year, what is the change in the unemployment rate? Explain why it occurs.

10. For the economy described in problem 9, the natural rate of unemployment rises to 5 percent and the expected inflation rate falls to 5 percent. Draw the new short-run and long-run Phillips curves in a figure.

# CRITICAL THINKING

1. Study *Reading Between the Lines* on pp. 294–295 and then answer the following questions:
   a. What does Alan Greenspan say about the tradeoff between inflation and unemployment?
   b. What does Federal Reserve Governor Lawrence Meyer say about the tradeoff between inflation and unemployment?
   c. Whom do you think is correct, Greenspan or Meyer, and why?
   d. Do you think the evidence of 2000–2003 is consistent with the view that the natural rate of unemployment is 6 percent? Explain why or why not.

2. In light of what you have learned in this chapter, what do you think the Fed should do during the next few months to keep the economy expanding and to keep inflation in check?

# WEB EXERCISES

**Use the links on MyEconLab to work the following exercises.**

1. Obtain data on the growth rate of the quantity of money and the inflation rate in the United States since 2000.
   a. Calculate the average growth rate of the quantity of money since 2000.
   b. Calculate the average inflation rate since 2000.
   c. Make a graph of the growth rate of the quantity of money and the inflation rate since 2000.
   d. Interpret your graph and explain what it tells you about the forces that generate inflation and the relationship between money growth and inflation.

2. Obtain data on the inflation rate and the unemployment rate in Canada during the 1990s and 2000s.
   a. Make a graph using the data you've obtained that is similar to Fig. 12.12.
   b. Describe the similarities and the differences in relationship between inflation and unemployment found in the United States and in Canada.

# UNDERSTANDING AGGREGATE DEMAND, MONEY, AND INFLATION

## PART 5

## *Money Chasing Goods*

Aggregate demand fluctuations bring recessions and expansions. If aggregate demand expands more rapidly than long-run aggregate supply, we get inflation. So understanding the forces that determine aggregate demand helps us to understand both the business cycle and inflation.

It took economists a long time to achieve this knowledge, and we still don't know enough about aggregate demand to be able to forecast it more than a few months ahead. But we do know the basic factors that influence aggregate demand. And we know a lot about how those factors interact to send shock waves rippling through the economy.

Fundamentally, aggregate demand is a monetary phenomenon. The quantity of money is the single most significant influence on aggregate demand. This insight was first outlined more than 200 years ago by David Hume, a Scottish philosopher and close friend of Adam Smith. Milton Friedman and other economists known as *monetarists* also emphasize the central role of money. Money lies at the center of Keynes' theory of aggregate demand as well. But Keynes also called attention to the power of independent changes in government purchases, taxes, and business investment to influence aggregate demand. In the modern world, we also recognize the effect of changes in exports on aggregate demand.

The chapters in this part explain the role of money and its influence on aggregate demand. Chapter 10 explained exactly what money is, how banks create it, and how the Federal Reserve influences its quantity by using open market operations. Chapter 11 showed how the quantity of money influences the interest rate, the exchange rate, expenditure plans, and aggregate demand. Chapter 12 returned to the aggregate supply–aggregate demand framework and explained inflation. It showed how the trends in inflation are determined by the trend in the money supply and how fluctuations in aggregate demand bring fluctuations in inflation, employment, and unemployment.

Today, the short-run relationship between inflation and unemployment is called the Phillips curve, honoring the work of Bill Phillips in the 1960s. But Irving Fisher and even David Hume understood this relationship. Hume wrote "In every Kingdom into which money begins to flow in greater abundance than formerly, every thing takes a new face: labor and industry gain life; the merchant becomes more enterprising, the manufacturer more diligent and skilful, and even the farmer follows his plow with greater alacrity and attention."

Many economists have developed the insights you've learned in these chapters. One of the truly outstanding ones is Milton Friedman, whom you can meet on the next page. Another, and one of today's leading macroeconomists, is Michael Woodford of Princeton University, whom you can also meet on the following pages.

299

# PROBING THE IDEAS

## Understanding Inflation

### THE ECONOMIST

"Inflation is always and everywhere a monetary phenomenon."

MILTON FRIEDMAN
*The Counter-Revolution in Monetary Theory*

**Milton Friedman** *was born into a poor immigrant family in New York City in 1912. He was an undergraduate at Rutgers and graduate student at Columbia University during the Great Depression. Today, Professor Friedman is a Senior Fellow at the Hoover Institution at Stanford University. But his reputation was built between 1946 and 1983, when he was a leading member of the "Chicago School," an approach to economics developed at the University of Chicago and based on the views that free markets allocate resources efficiently and that stable and low money supply growth delivers macroeconomic stability.*

*Friedman has advanced our understanding of the forces that determine aggregate demand and clarified the effects of the quantity of money and for this work, he was awarded the (much overdue, in the opinion of his many admirers) 1977 Nobel Prize for Economic Science.*

*By reasoning from basic economic principles, Friedman predicted that persistent demand stimulation would not increase output but would cause inflation. When output growth slowed and inflation broke out in the 1970s, Friedman seemed like a prophet, and for a time, his policy prescription, known as monetarism, was embraced around the world.*

### THE ISSUES

The combination of history and economics has taught us a lot about the causes of inflation. Severe inflation—hyperinflation—arises from a breakdown of the normal fiscal policy processes at times of war or political upheaval. Tax revenues fall short of government spending, and newly printed money fills the gap between them. As inflation increases, the quantity of money that is needed to make payments increases, and a shortage of money can even result. So the rate of money growth increases yet further, and prices rise yet faster. Eventually, the monetary system collapses. Such was the experience of Germany during the 1920s and Brazil during the 1990s.

In earlier times, when commodities were used as money, inflation resulted from the discovery of new sources of money. The most recent occurrence of this type of inflation was at the end of the nineteenth century when gold, then used as money, was discovered in Australia, the Klondike, and South Africa.

In modern times, inflation has resulted from increases in the money supply that has accommodated increases in costs. The most dramatic such inflations occurred during the 1970s when the Fed and other central banks around the world accommodated oil price increases.

To avoid inflation, money supply growth must be held in check. But at times of severe cost pressure, central banks feel a strong tug in the direction of avoiding recession and accommodating the cost pressure.

Yet some countries have avoided inflation more effectively than others have. One source of success is central bank independence. In low-inflation countries, such as Germany and Japan, the central bank decides how much money to create and at what level to set interest rates, and does not take instructions from the government. In high-inflation countries, such as the United Kingdom and Italy, the central bank takes direct orders from the government about interest rates and money supply growth. The architects of the new monetary system for the European Community based on the euro noticed this connection between central bank independence and inflation and modeled the constitution for the European Central Bank on the independent German central bank.

## THEN

When inflation is especially rapid, as it was in Germany in 1923, money becomes almost worthless. In Germany at that time, bank notes were more valuable as fire kindling than as money, and the sight of people burning Reichmarks was a common one. To avoid having to hold money for too long, wages were paid and spent twice a day. Banks took deposits and made loans, but at interest rates that compensated both depositors and the bank for the falling value of money—interest rates that could exceed 100 percent a month. The price of a dinner would increase during the course of an evening, making lingering over coffee a very expensive pastime.

## NOW

In 1994, Brazil had a computer-age hyperinflation, an inflation rate that was close to 50 percent a month. Banks installed ATMs on almost every street corner and refilled them several times an hour. Brazilians tried to avoid holding currency. As soon as they were paid, they went shopping and bought enough food to get them through to the next payday. Some shoppers filled as many as six carts on a single monthly trip to the supermarket. Also, instead of using currency, Brazilians used credit cards whenever possible. But they paid their card balances off quickly because the interest rate on unpaid balances was 50 percent a month. Only at such a high interest rate did it pay banks to lend to cardholders, because banks themselves were paying interest rates of 40 percent a month to induce depositors to keep their money in the bank.

*Many economists today are working on aggregate demand and inflation. One distinguished contributor, whom you can meet on the following pages, is Michael Woodford of Princeton University.*

# TALKING WITH

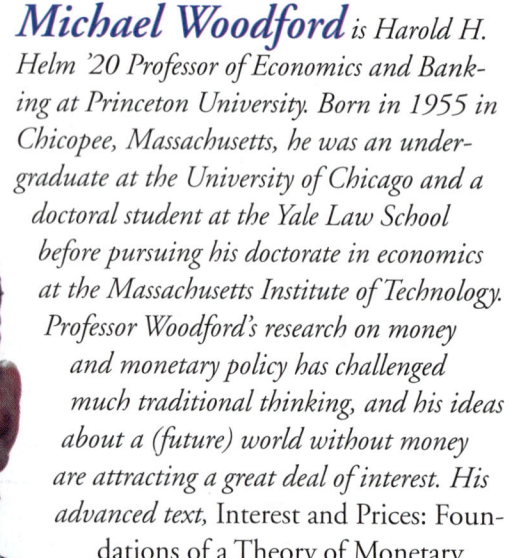

Michael Woodford

**Michael Woodford** *is Harold H. Helm '20 Professor of Economics and Banking at Princeton University. Born in 1955 in Chicopee, Massachusetts, he was an undergraduate at the University of Chicago and a doctoral student at the Yale Law School before pursuing his doctorate in economics at the Massachusetts Institute of Technology. Professor Woodford's research on money and monetary policy has challenged much traditional thinking, and his ideas about a (future) world without money are attracting a great deal of interest. His advanced text,* Interest and Prices: Foundations of a Theory of Monetary Policy *is being published by Princeton University Press.*
*Michael Parkin talked with Michael Woodford about his work and the progress that economists have made in designing effective monetary policy rules.*

### Why, after completing law school, did you decide to become an economist?

Almost every class in law school was full of economic reasoning. I became fascinated by economic analysis, and thought that I would have to get a better foundation in economics in order to think clearly about legal issues. In the end I found that I liked economics enough to become an economist.

I am able to address questions of public policy, which is what had originally drawn me to law, but in a way that also allows me to indulge a taste for thinking about what the world might be like or should be like, and not simply the way that it already is.

In a world as rapidly changing as ours is, I think that the perspective provided by economics is essential for understanding which kinds of laws and rules make sense.

### You are a supporter of rules for monetary policy. Why are rules so important?

In my view, rules are important not because central bankers can't be relied upon to take the public interest to heart, or because they don't know what they're doing, but because the effects of monetary policy depend critically upon what the private sector expects about future policy, and hence about the future course of the economy. Thus effective monetary policy depends more on the successful *management of expectations* than on any direct consequences of the current level of interest rates.

In order to steer people's expectations about future monetary policy in the way that it would like, a central bank needs to communicate details about how policy will be conducted in the future. The best way to do this is by being explicit about the *rule* that guides its decision making. The central bank also needs to establish a reputation for actually following the rule.

Following the rule means *not* always doing what might seem best in given current conditions. What is best for the economy now will be independent of what people may have expected in the past. But if the central bank doesn't feel bound to follow through on its prior commitments, people will learn that they don't mean anything. Then those commitments will not shape people's expectations in the desired way.

There is actually a strong parallel between monetary policy rules and the law, and the desirability of rules is an example of the perspective that I gained from the study of law. A judge doesn't simply seek to determine, in each individual case, what outcome would do the most good, given the individual circumstances. Instead, the judge makes a decision based on rules established either by precedent or by statute. Because the law is rule-based, people are able to forecast more accurately the consequences of their contemplated actions.

> *"Following the rule means **not** always doing what might seem best in given current conditions."*

A central banker is often portrayed as the captain of the economic ship, steering it skillfully between the rocks of inflation and unemployment in a choppy sea. But a ship's captain doesn't need to care about how the ocean will interpret his actions. So the parallel isn't a good one. In my view, the role of a central banker is more similar to that of a judge than to that of a ship's captain. Both central bankers and judges care enormously about the effects of their decisions on the expectations of people whose behavior depends on expected future decisions.

### The rule that you favor is different from that suggested by Milton Friedman. What is wrong with the Friedman rule?

Friedman's rule involves a target for the growth rate of some definition of the quantity of money. I don't think that the best monetary rule involves a target of any kind for the growth rate of a monetary aggregate. Friedman's rule is not the worst sort of rule, as simple rules go, but we can do better.

Just a century ago, no one had any idea how to establish a reasonably predictable monetary standard except by guaranteeing the convertibility of money into a precious metal such as gold. We didn't have the surprisingly modern concept of index numbers and today's routinely calculated price indexes like the CPI that enable us to measure, to a decent approximation, the purchasing power of the dollar.

We now understand that pegging the value of money to something like gold is a cruder solution to the problem than is necessary. We don't need to leave the value of money hostage to the vagaries of the gold market simply in order to maintain confidence that a dollar means *something*.

Friedman recognizes the value of a well-managed fiat currency, but supposes that there is unlikely to be much predictability to the value of money unless the central bank is committed to a fixed target growth path for the quantity of money. But that again is a more indirect solution to the problem of maintaining a stable and predictable value for money than is necessary.

And there is a potentially large cost of such a crude approach when the relation between one's favorite monetary aggregate and the value of money shifts over time. A focus on stabilizing a monetary aggregate means less stability than would otherwise have been possible in the purchasing power of money.

### So what would be a good monetary rule?

First, there should be a clearly defined target in terms of variables that policymakers actually care about, such as the inflation rate, rather than an "intermediate target" such as a monetary aggregate. Second, the central bank should be as clear as possible about the decision making process through which it determines the level of interest rates that is believed to be consistent with achieving the target.

"Inflation targeting," as currently practiced in the United Kingdom, Canada, and New Zealand, is an example of the general approach that I would advocate. But I think that central banks of an inflation-targeting country could do a better job of explaining the procedures used to determine the interest rate that is judged to be consistent with the inflation target—they could be more transparent.

And all of these countries could better explain to the public the ways in which variables other than inflation are also taken into consideration. I'm not sure that inflation targeting needs to be *stricter*, in the sense that considerations other than inflation should be more scrupulously ruled out. But I think that it is desirable to make it more of a *rule*.

### One of the most intriguing issues that you've worked on is the question of what determines the price level in a "cashless economy." How would we control inflation in such a world?

One advantage of the approach to monetary policy that I've just mentioned is that the form of policy rule that is appropriate need not change much at all if we were to progress to a "cashless economy." As long as the central bank can still control the overnight interest rates—the federal funds rate in the United States—the *rule* for adjusting the interest rate need not change. Yet there might no longer be any meaning to a target path for a monetary aggregate in such a world.

The critical question is whether a central bank would still be able to control overnight interest rates in such a world. Some argue that central banks only control interest rates in the interbank market for reserves because the private sector cannot supply a good substitute for reserves and the central bank is therefore a monopoly supplier. They then worry that if private substitutes for reserves were available, central banks would lose control of the interest rate.

But this line of reasoning assumes, as do most textbooks (even the good ones!), that central banks can change the interest rate *only* by changing the *opportunity cost* of holding reserves, which should only be possible in the presence of market power. But central banks can change the overnight interest rate *without* changing the opportunity cost of holding reserves. Indeed, the Bank of Canada already does so. It pays interest on reserves and maintains a fixed difference between the interest rate on reserves and the discount rate—the rate at which it stands willing to lend reserves to the banks. The overnight rate fluctuates inside the range of these two rates, so by changing the interest rate on reserves, the Bank of Canada controls the overnight rate but doesn't change the opportunity cost of holding reserves.

Every central bank, including the Fed, would have to adjust the interest rate in a way similar to this in a "cashless economy."

*Where do you stand on the sources of aggregate fluctuations? Are they primarily an efficient response to the uneven pace of technical change, or are they primarily the consequence of market failure and demand fluctuations?*

I don't think that they are primarily an *efficient* response to variations in technical progress or to other real disturbances of that kind. I think that there are important distortions that often result in *inefficient* responses of the economy to real disturbances, and this is why monetary policy matters. But I do think that real disturbances are important—for example, I don't think that exogenous variations in monetary policy have been responsible for too much of the economic instability in the U.S. economy in recent decades—and I think that their supply-side effects are important, too.

The important issue, to my mind, is not whether the disturbances are thought to have more to do with supply or demand factors; it is whether the economy can be relied upon to respond efficiently to them, regardless of the nature of monetary policy. I don't think that that occurs automatically. The goal of good monetary policy is to bring about such a world: one in which monetary policy is not itself a source of disturbances, and in which the responses to real disturbances are efficient ones. The first part simply requires that monetary policy be systematic, but the second part depends upon the choice of a monetary policy rule of the right sort.

*What advice do you have for a student who is just starting to study economics? Is it a good subject in which to major? What other subjects would you urge students to study alongside economics?*

I think economics is an excellent major for students with many different interests. Most people who study economics are probably looking for an edge in the business world, and economics is valuable for that. But it's also an extremely valuable background for people interested in careers in law, government, or public policy. And of course, for some of us, the subject is interesting in its own right. I find that the challenges just get deeper the farther I get into the subject.

Probably the most important other subject for someone thinking of actually becoming an economist is mathematics. This is often the determining factor as to how well a student will do in graduate study, because the research literature is a good deal more mathematical than many people suspect from their undergraduate economics courses. But economics is not a branch of mathematics. It's a subject that seeks to understand people and social institutions, and so all sorts of other subjects—history, politics, sociology, psychology, moral and political philosophy—are useful background for an economist, too. I don't at all regret the amount of time I spent in liberal arts courses as an undergraduate.

# PART 6    Economic Fluctuations and Stabilization Policy

# Expenditure Multipliers: The Keynesian Model

CHAPTER 13

## Economic Amplifier or Shock Absorber?

**Erykah Badu sings into a microphone in a barely** audible whisper. Increasing in volume, through the magic of electronic amplification, her voice fills Central Park.

    Michael Bloomberg, the mayor of New York, and a secretary are being driven to a business meeting along one of the city's less well-repaired streets. The car's wheels bounce and vibrate over some of the worst potholes in the nation, but its passengers are completely undisturbed and the secretary's notes are written without a ripple, thanks to the car's efficient shock absorbers.

    Investment and exports fluctuate like the volume of Erykah Badu's voice and the uneven surface of a New York City street. How does the economy react to those fluctuations? Does it behave like an amplifier, blowing up the fluctuations and spreading them out to affect the many millions of participants in an economic rock concert? Or does it react like a limousine, absorbing the shocks and providing a smooth ride for the economy's passengers?

◆   You will explore these questions in this chapter. You will learn how a recession or an expansion begins when a change in investment or exports induces an amplified change in aggregate expenditure and real GDP. And you'll learn the crucial role played by business inventories in the transition from expansion to recession and back to expansion. *Reading Between the Lines* at the end of the chapter looks at the role played by business inventories during the 2001 recession.

### After studying this chapter, you will be able to

- Explain how expenditure plans and real GDP are determined when the price level is fixed
- Explain the expenditure multiplier
- Explain how recessions and expansions begin
- Explain the relationship between aggregate expenditure and aggregate demand
- Explain how the multiplier gets smaller as the price level changes

305

## Fixed Prices and Expenditure Plans

The Keynesian model that we study in this chapter describes the economy in the very short run. It isolates and places in focus the forces that operate at a business cycle peak when an expansion ends and a recession begins and at a trough, when recession turns into expansion.

In this model, all the firms are like your local supermarket. They set their prices, advertise their products and services, and sell the quantities their customers are willing to buy. If they persistently sell a greater quantity than they plan to and are constantly running out of inventory, they eventually raise their prices. And if they persistently sell a smaller quantity than they plan to and have inventories piling up, they eventually cut their prices. But in the very short term, their prices are fixed. They hold the prices they have set, and the quantities they sell depend on demand, not supply.

Fixed prices have two immediate implications for the economy as a whole:

1. Because each firm's price is fixed, the *price level* is fixed.
2. Because demand determines the quantities that each firm sells, *aggregate demand* determines the aggregate quantity of goods and services sold, which equals real GDP.

So to understand the fluctuations in real GDP when the price level is fixed, we must understand aggregate demand fluctuations. The Keynesian aggregate expenditure model explains fluctuations in aggregate demand by identifying the forces that determine expenditure plans.

### Expenditure Plans

Aggregate expenditure has four components:

1. Consumption expenditure
2. Investment
3. Government purchases of goods and services
4. Net exports (exports *minus* imports)

These four components of aggregate expenditure sum to real GDP (see Chapter 5, pp. 109–110). **Aggregate planned expenditure** is equal to *planned* consumption expenditure plus *planned* investment plus *planned* government purchases of goods and services plus *planned* exports minus *planned* imports.

In the very short term, *planned* investment, *planned* government purchases, and *planned* exports are fixed. But *planned* consumption expenditure and *planned* imports are not fixed. They depend on the level of real GDP itself.

**A Two-Way Link Between Aggregate Expenditure and GDP** Because real GDP influences consumption expenditure and imports, and because consumption expenditure and imports are components of aggregate expenditure, there is a two-way link between aggregate expenditure and GDP. Other things remaining the same,

- An increase in real GDP increases aggregate expenditure, and
- An increase in aggregate expenditure increases real GDP.

You are going to learn how this two-way link between aggregate expenditure and real GDP determines real GDP when the price level is fixed. The starting point is to consider the first piece of the two-way link: the influence of real GDP on planned consumption expenditure and saving.

### Consumption Function and Saving Function

Several factors influence consumption expenditure and saving. The more important ones are

- Real interest rate
- Disposable income
- Wealth
- Expected future income

Chapter 8 (see p. 192) explains how these factors influence consumption expenditure and saving. The second factor, **disposable income**, is aggregate income minus taxes plus transfer payments. And aggregate income equals real GDP. So to explore the two-way link between real GDP and planned consumption expenditure, we focus on the relationship between consumption expenditure and disposable income when the other factors are constant.

**Consumption and Saving Plans** The table in Fig. 13.1 shows an example of the relationship among planned consumption expenditure, planned saving, and disposable income. It lists the consumption expenditure and the saving that people plan to undertake at each level of disposable income. Notice that at each level of disposable income, consumption expenditure plus saving always equals disposable income. Households can only consume or save their disposable income, so planned consumption plus planned saving always equals disposable income.

The relationship between consumption expenditure and disposable income, other things remaining the same, is called the **consumption function**. The relationship between saving and disposable income, other things remaining the same, is called the **saving function**. Let's begin by studying the consumption function.

## FIGURE 13.1  Consumption Function and Saving Function

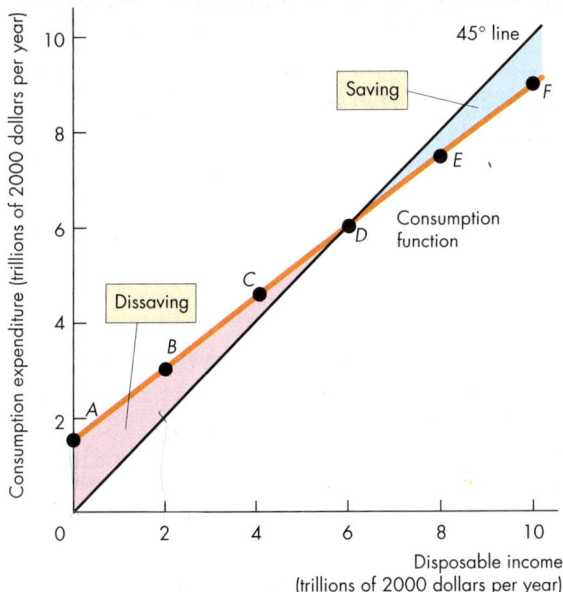

(a) Consumption function

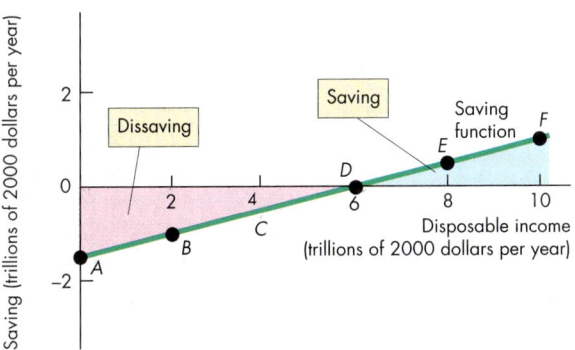

(b) Saving function

| | Disposable income | Planned consumption expenditure | Planned saving |
|---|---|---|---|
| | (trillions of 2000 dollars per year) | | |
| A | 0 | 1.5 | −1.5 |
| B | 2 | 3.0 | −1.0 |
| C | 4 | 4.5 | −0.5 |
| D | 6 | 6.0 | 0 |
| E | 8 | 7.5 | 0.5 |
| F | 10 | 9.0 | 1.0 |

The table shows consumption expenditure and saving plans at various levels of disposable income. Part (a) of the figure shows the relationship between consumption expenditure and disposable income (the consumption function). The height of the consumption function measures consumption expenditure at each level of disposable income. Part (b) shows the relationship between saving and disposable income (the saving function). The height of the saving function measures saving at each level of disposable income. Points A through F on the consumption and saving functions correspond to the rows in the table. The height of the 45° line in part (a) measures disposable income. So along the 45° line, consumption expenditure equals disposable income. Consumption expenditure plus saving equals disposable income. When the consumption function is above the 45° line, saving is negative (dissaving occurs). When the consumption function is below the 45° line, saving is positive. At the point where the consumption function intersects the 45° line, all disposable income is consumed and saving is zero.

**Consumption Function** Figure 13.1(a) shows a consumption function. The *y*-axis measures consumption expenditure and the *x*-axis measures disposable income. Along the consumption function, the points labeled *A* through *F* correspond to the rows of the table. For example, point *E* shows that when disposable income is $8 trillion, consumption expenditure is $7.5 trillion. Along the consumption function, as disposable income increases, consumption expenditure also increases.

At point *A* on the consumption function, consumption expenditure is $1.5 trillion even though disposable income is zero. This consumption expenditure is called *autonomous consumption*, and it is the amount of consumption expenditure that would take place in the short run even if people had no current income. Consumption expenditure in excess of this amount is called *induced consumption*, which is expenditure that is induced by an increase in disposable income.

**45° Line** Figure 13.1(a) also contains a 45° line, the height of which measures disposable income. At each point on this line, consumption expenditure equals disposable income. In the range over which the consumption function lies above the 45° line—between *A* and *D*—consumption expenditure exceeds disposable income. In the range over which the consumption function lies below the 45° line—between *D* and *F*—consumption expenditure is less than disposable income. And at a point at which the consumption function intersects the 45° line—at point *D*—consumption expenditure equals disposable income.

**Saving Function** Figure 13.1(b) shows a saving function. The *x*-axis is exactly the same as that in part (a). The *y*-axis measures saving. Again, the points marked *A* through *F* correspond to the rows of the table. For example, point *E* shows that when disposable income is $8 trillion, saving is $0.5 trillion. Along the saving function, as disposable income increases, saving also increases. At disposable income less than $6 trillion (point *D*), saving is negative. Negative saving is called *dissaving*. At disposable income greater than $6 trillion, saving is positive, and at $6 trillion, saving is zero.

Notice the connection between the two parts of Fig. 13.1. When consumption expenditure exceeds disposable income in part (a), saving is negative in part (b). When disposable income exceeds consumption expenditure in part (a), saving is positive in part (b). And when consumption expenditure equals disposable income in part (a), saving is zero in part (b).

When saving is negative (when consumption expenditure exceeds disposable income), past savings are used to pay for current consumption. Such a situation cannot last forever, but it can occur if disposable income falls temporarily.

### Marginal Propensities to Consume and Save

The extent to which consumption expenditure changes when disposable income changes depends on the marginal propensity to consume. The **marginal propensity to consume** (*MPC*) is the fraction of a change in disposable income that is consumed. It is calculated as the *change* in consumption expenditure ($\Delta C$) divided by the *change* in disposable income ($\Delta YD$) that brought it about. That is,

$$MPC = \frac{\Delta C}{\Delta YD}.$$

In the table in Fig. 13.1, when disposable income increases from $6 trillion to $8 trillion, consumption expenditure increases from $6 trillion to $7.5 trillion. The $2 trillion increase in disposable income increases consumption expenditure by $1.5 trillion. The *MPC* is $1.5 trillion divided by $2 trillion, which equals 0.75.

The **marginal propensity to save** (*MPS*) is the fraction of a *change* in disposable income that is saved. It is calculated as the *change* in saving ($\Delta S$) divided by the *change* in disposable income ($\Delta YD$) that brought it about. That is,

$$MPS = \frac{\Delta S}{\Delta YD}.$$

In the table in Fig. 13.1, an increase in disposable income from $6 trillion to $8 trillion increases saving from zero to $0.5 trillion. The $2 trillion increase in disposable income increases saving by $0.5 trillion. The *MPS* is $0.5 trillion divided by $2 trillion, which equals 0.25.

The marginal propensity to consume plus the marginal propensity to save always equals 1. They sum to 1 because consumption expenditure and saving exhaust disposable income. Part of each dollar increase in disposable income is consumed, and the remaining part is saved. You can see that these two marginal propensities sum to 1 by using the equation:

$$\Delta C + \Delta S = \Delta YD.$$

Divide both sides of the equation by the change in disposable income to obtain

$$\frac{\Delta C}{\Delta YD} + \frac{\Delta S}{\Delta YD} = 1.$$

$\Delta C/\Delta YD$ is the marginal propensity to consume (*MPC*), and $\Delta S/\Delta YD$ is the marginal propensity to save (*MPS*), so

$$MPC + MPS = 1.$$

### Slopes and Marginal Propensities

The slopes of the consumption function and the saving function are the marginal propensities to consume and save. Figure 13.2(a) shows the *MPC* as the slope of the consumption function. A $2 trillion increase in disposable income from $6 trillion to $8 trillion is the base of the red triangle. The increase in consumption expenditure that results from this increase in disposable income is $1.5 trillion and is the height of the triangle. The slope of the consumption function is given by the formula "slope equals rise over run" and is $1.5 trillion divided by $2 trillion, which equals 0.75—the *MPC*.

Figure 13.2(b) shows the *MPS* as the slope of the saving function. A $2 trillion increase in disposable income from $6 trillion to $8 trillion (the base of the red triangle) increases saving by $0.5 trillion (the height of the triangle). The slope of the saving function is $0.5 trillion divided by $2 trillion, which equals 0.25—the *MPS*.

### Other Influences on Consumption Expenditure and Saving

You've seen that a change in disposable income leads to changes in consumption expenditure and saving. A change in disposable income brings movements along the consumption function and saving function.

Along the consumption function and saving function, all other influences on consumption expenditure and saving (such as the real interest rate, wealth, and expected future income) are fixed. A change in any of these other influences shifts both the consumption function and the saving function.

**FIGURE 13.2  Marginal Propensities to Consume and Save**

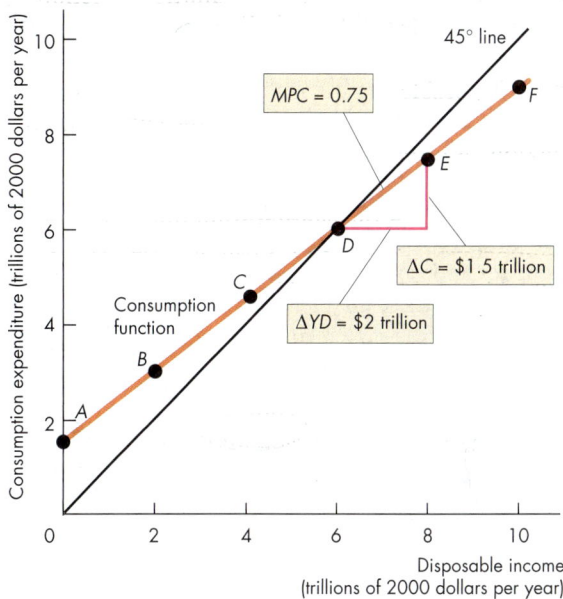

**(a) Consumption function**

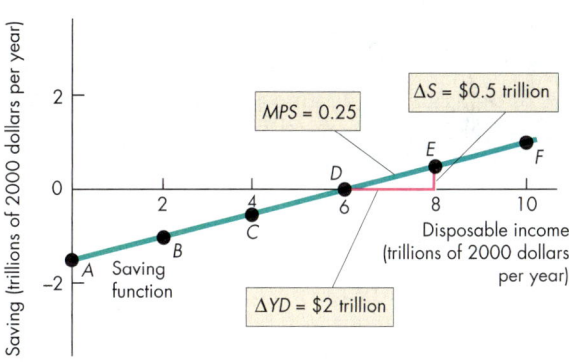

**(b) Saving function**

The marginal propensity to consume, *MPC*, is equal to the change in consumption expenditure divided by the change in disposable income, other things remaining the same. It is measured by the slope of the consumption function. In part (a), the *MPC* is 0.75. The marginal propensity to save, *MPS*, is equal to the change in saving divided by the change in disposable income, other things remaining the same. It is measured by the slope of the saving function. In part (b), the *MPS* is 0.25.

When the real interest rate falls or when wealth or expected future income increases, consumption expenditure increases and saving decreases. Figure 13.3 shows the effects of these changes on the consumption function and the saving function. The consumption function shifts upward from $CF_0$ to $CF_1$, and the saving function shifts downward from $SF_0$ to $SF_1$. Such shifts commonly occur during the expansion phase of the business cycle because, at such a time, expected future income increases.

When the real interest rate rises or when wealth or expected future income decreases, consumption decreases and saving increases. Figure 13.3 also shows the effects of these changes on the consumption function and the saving function. The consumption function shifts downward from $CF_0$ to $CF_2$, and the saving function shifts upward from $SF_0$ to $SF_2$. Such shifts often occur when a recession begins because, at such a time, expected future income decreases.

We've studied the theory of the consumption function. Let's now see how that theory applies to the U.S. economy.

## The U.S. Consumption Function

Figure 13.4 shows the U.S. consumption function. Each point identified by a blue dot represents consumption expenditure and disposable income for a particular year. (The dots are for the years 1961–2003. Five of the years are identified in the figure.) The line labeled $CF_0$ is an estimate of the U.S. consumption function in 1961 and the line labeled $CF_1$ is an estimate of the U.S. consumption function in 2003.

The slope of the consumption function in Fig. 13.4 is 0.9, which means that a $1 trillion increase in disposable income brings a $0.9 trillion increase in consumption expenditure. This slope, which is an estimate of the marginal propensity to consume, is an assumption that is at the upper end of the range of values that economists have estimated for the marginal propensity to consume.

The consumption function shifts upward over time as other influences on consumption expenditure change. Of these other influences, the real interest rate and wealth fluctuate and so bring upward and downward shifts in the consumption function. But rising expected future income brings a steady upward shift in the consumption function. As the consumption function shifts upward, autonomous consumption expenditure increases.

**FIGURE 13.3** Shifts in the Consumption and Saving Functions

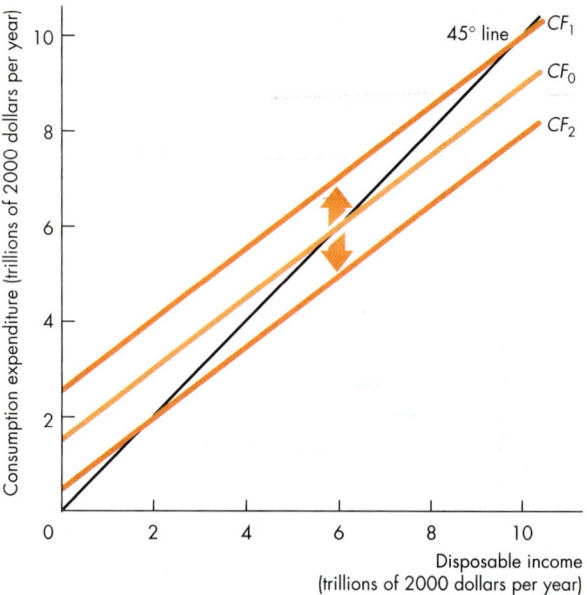

(a) Consumption function

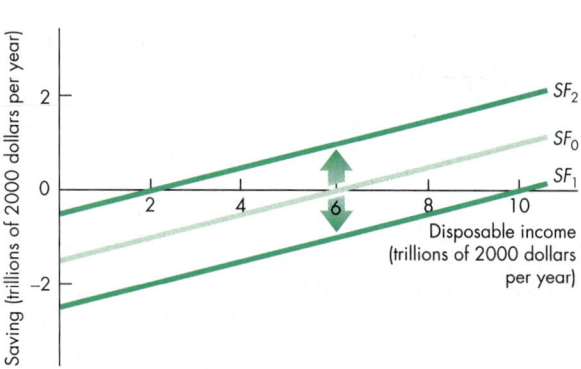

(b) Saving function

A fall in the real interest rate, an increase in wealth, or an increase in expected future income increases consumption expenditure and decreases saving. It shifts the consumption function upward from $CF_0$ to $CF_1$ and shifts the saving function downward from $SF_0$ to $SF_1$. A rise in the real interest rate or a decrease in either wealth or expected future income shifts the consumption function downward from $CF_0$ to $CF_2$ and shifts the saving function upward from $SF_0$ to $SF_2$.

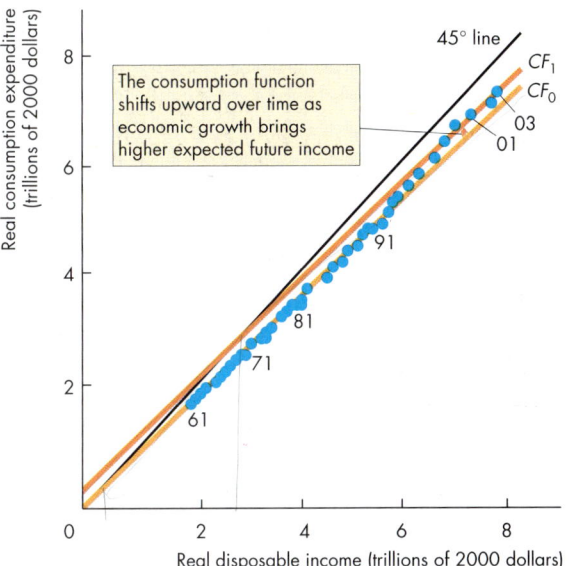

**FIGURE 13.4** The U.S. Consumption Function

Each blue dot shows consumption expenditure and disposable income for a particular year. The lines $CF_0$ and $CF_1$ are estimates of the U.S. consumption function in 1961 and 2003, respectively. Here, the (assumed) marginal propensity to consume is 0.9.

## Consumption as a Function of Real GDP

You've seen that consumption expenditure changes when disposable income changes. Disposable income changes when either real GDP changes or net taxes change. If tax rates don't change, real GDP is the only influence on disposable income. So consumption depends not only on disposable income but also on real GDP. We use this link between consumption and real GDP to determine equilibrium expenditure. But before we do so, we need to look at one further component of aggregate expenditure: imports. Like consumption expenditure, imports also are influenced by real GDP.

## Import Function

U.S. imports are determined by many factors, but in the short run, one factor dominates: U.S. real GDP.

Other things remaining the same, the greater the U.S. real GDP, the larger is the quantity of U.S. imports.

The relationship between imports and real GDP is determined by the marginal propensity to import. The **marginal propensity to import** is the fraction of an increase in real GDP that is spent on imports. It is calculated as the change in imports divided by the change in real GDP that brought it about, other things remaining the same. For example, if a $1 trillion increase in real GDP increases imports by $0.25 trillion, the marginal propensity to import is 0.25.

In recent years, since the North American Free Trade Agreement (NAFTA) was implemented, U.S. imports have surged. For example, between 1991 and 2001, real GDP increased by $2,657 billion and imports increased by $861 billion. If no factors other than real GDP influenced imports during the 1990s, these numbers would imply a marginal propensity to import of 0.32. But other factors, such as NAFTA, increased imports, so the marginal propensity to import is smaller than 0.32. The marginal propensity to import is probably as large as 0.2, and it has been increasing as the global economy has become more integrated.

> **REVIEW QUIZ**
>
> 1 Which components of aggregate expenditure are influenced by real GDP?
> 2 Define the marginal propensity to consume. What is your estimate of your own marginal propensity to consume? After you graduate, will it change? Why or why not?
> 3 How do we calculate the effects of real GDP on consumption expenditure and imports by using the marginal propensity to consume and the marginal propensity to import?

Real GDP influences consumption expenditure and imports. But consumption expenditure and imports along with investment, government purchases, and exports influence real GDP. Your next task is to study this second piece of the two-way link between aggregate expenditure and real GDP and see how all the components of aggregate planned expenditure interact to determine real GDP.

# Real GDP with a Fixed Price Level

You are now going to discover how aggregate expenditure plans interact to determine real GDP when the price level is fixed. First, we will study the relationship between aggregate planned expenditure and real GDP. Second, we'll learn about the key distinction between *planned* expenditure and *actual* expenditure. And third, we'll study equilibrium expenditure, a situation in which aggregate planned expenditure and actual expenditure are equal.

The relationship between aggregate planned expenditure and real GDP can be described by either an aggregate expenditure schedule or an aggregate expenditure curve. The *aggregate expenditure schedule* lists aggregate planned expenditure generated at each level of real GDP. The *aggregate expenditure curve* is a graph of the aggregate expenditure schedule.

## FIGURE 13.5 Aggregate Expenditure

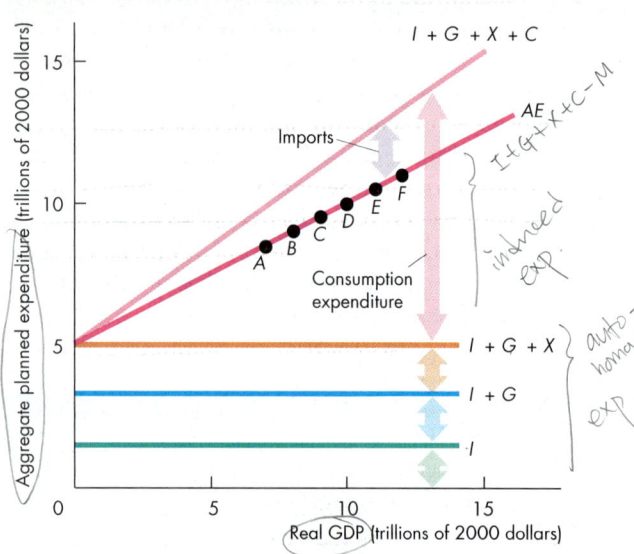

Aggregate planned expenditure is the sum of planned consumption expenditure, investment, government purchases of goods and services, and exports minus imports. For example, in row B of the table, when real GDP is $8 trillion, planned consumption expenditure is $5.6 trillion, planned investment is $1.5 trillion, planned government purchases of goods and services are $1.8 trillion, planned exports are $1.7 trillion, and planned imports are $1.6 trillion. So when real GDP is $8 trillion, aggregate planned expenditure is $9 trillion ($5.6 + $1.5 + $1.8 + $1.7 − $1.6). The schedule shows that aggregate planned expenditure increases as real GDP increases. This relationship is graphed as the aggregate expenditure curve *AE*. The components of aggregate expenditure that increase with real GDP are consumption expenditure and imports. The other components—investment, government purchases, and exports—do not vary with real GDP.

|   | Real GDP (Y) | Consumption expenditure (C) | Investment (I) | Government purchases (G) | Exports (X) | Imports (M) | Aggregate planned expenditure (AE = C + I + G + X − M) |
|---|---|---|---|---|---|---|---|
|   | (trillions of 2000 dollars) | | | | | | |
|   | 0 | 0 | 1.5 | 1.8 | 1.7 | 0.0 | 5.0 |
| A | 7 | 4.9 | 1.5 | 1.8 | 1.7 | 1.4 | 8.5 |
| B | 8 | 5.6 | 1.5 | 1.8 | 1.7 | 1.6 | 9.0 |
| C | 9 | 6.3 | 1.5 | 1.8 | 1.7 | 1.8 | 9.5 |
| D | 10 | 7.0 | 1.5 | 1.8 | 1.7 | 2.0 | 10.0 |
| E | 11 | 7.7 | 1.5 | 1.8 | 1.7 | 2.2 | 10.5 |
| F | 12 | 8.4 | 1.5 | 1.8 | 1.7 | 2.4 | 11.0 |

## Aggregate Planned Expenditure and Real GDP

The table in Fig. 13.5 sets out an aggregate expenditure schedule together with the components of aggregate planned expenditure. To calculate aggregate planned expenditure at a given real GDP, we add the various components together. The first column of the table shows real GDP, and the second column shows the consumption expenditure generated by each level of real GDP. A $1 trillion increase in real GDP generates a $0.7 trillion increase in consumption expenditure—the *MPC* is 0.7.

The next two columns show investment and government purchases of goods and services. Investment depends on the real interest rate and the expected rate of profit (see Chapter 8, pp. 190–191). At a given point in time, these factors generate a particular level of investment. Suppose this level of investment is $1.5 trillion. Also, suppose that government purchases of goods and services are $1.8 trillion.

The next two columns show exports and imports. Exports are influenced by events in the rest of the world, prices of foreign-made goods and services relative to the prices of similar U.S.-made goods and services, and foreign exchange rates. But they are not directly affected by U.S. real GDP. Exports are a constant $1.7 trillion. Imports increase as U.S. real GDP increases. A $1 trillion increase in U.S. real GDP generates a $0.2 trillion increase in imports—the marginal propensity to import is 0.2.

The final column shows aggregate planned expenditure—the sum of planned consumption expenditure, investment, government purchases of goods and services, and exports minus imports.

Figure 13.5 plots an aggregate expenditure curve. Real GDP is shown on the *x*-axis, and aggregate planned expenditure is shown on the *y*-axis. The aggregate expenditure curve is the red line *AE*. Points *A* through *F* on that curve correspond to the rows of the table. The *AE* curve is a graph of aggregate planned expenditure (the last column) plotted against real GDP (the first column).

Figure 13.5 also shows the components of aggregate expenditure. The constant components—investment (*I*), government purchases of goods and services (*G*), and exports (*X*)—are shown by the horizontal lines in the figure. Consumption expenditure (*C*) is the vertical gap between the lines labeled *I* + *G* + *X* and *I* + *G* + *X* + *C*.

To construct the *AE* curve, subtract imports (*M*) from the *I* + *G* + *X* + *C* line. Aggregate expenditure is expenditure on U.S.-made goods and services. But the components of aggregate expenditure—*C*, *I*, and *G*—include expenditure on imported goods and services. For example, if you buy a new cell phone, your expenditure is part of consumption expenditure. But if the cell phone is a Nokia made in Finland, your expenditure on it must be subtracted from consumption expenditure to find out how much is spent on goods and services produced in the United States—on U.S. real GDP. Money paid to Nokia for cell phone imports from Finland does not add to aggregate expenditure in the United States.

Because imports are only a part of aggregate expenditure, when we subtract imports from the other components of aggregate expenditure, aggregate planned expenditure still increases as real GDP increases, as you can see in Fig. 13.5.

Consumption expenditure minus imports, which varies with real GDP, is called **induced expenditure**. The sum of investment, government purchases, and exports, which does not vary with real GDP, is called **autonomous expenditure**. Consumption expenditure and imports can also have an autonomous component—a component that does not vary with real GDP. Another way of thinking about autonomous expenditure is that it would be the level of aggregate planned expenditure if real GDP were zero.

In Fig. 13.5, autonomous expenditure is $5 trillion—aggregate planned expenditure when real GDP is zero. For each $1 trillion increase in real GDP, induced expenditure increases by $0.5 trillion.

The aggregate expenditure curve summarizes the relationship between aggregate *planned* expenditure and real GDP. But what determines the point on the aggregate expenditure curve at which the economy operates? What determines *actual* aggregate expenditure?

## Actual Expenditure, Planned Expenditure, and Real GDP

*Actual* aggregate expenditure is always equal to real GDP, as we saw in Chapter 5 (p. 110). But aggregate *planned* expenditure is not necessarily equal to actual aggregate expenditure and therefore is not necessarily equal to real GDP. How can actual expenditure and planned expenditure differ from each other? Why don't expenditure plans get implemented? The main reason is that firms might end up with inventories that are greater or smaller than planned. People carry out their consumption expenditure plans, the government implements its planned purchases of goods and services, and net exports are as planned. Firms carry out their plans to purchase new buildings, plant, and equipment. But one component of investment is the change in firms' inventories of goods. If aggregate planned expenditure is less than real GDP, firms don't sell all the goods they produce and they end up with inventories they hadn't planned. If aggregate planned expenditure exceeds real GDP, firms sell more than they produce and inventories decrease below the level that firms had planned.

## Equilibrium Expenditure

**Equilibrium expenditure** is the level of aggregate expenditure that occurs when aggregate *planned* expendi-

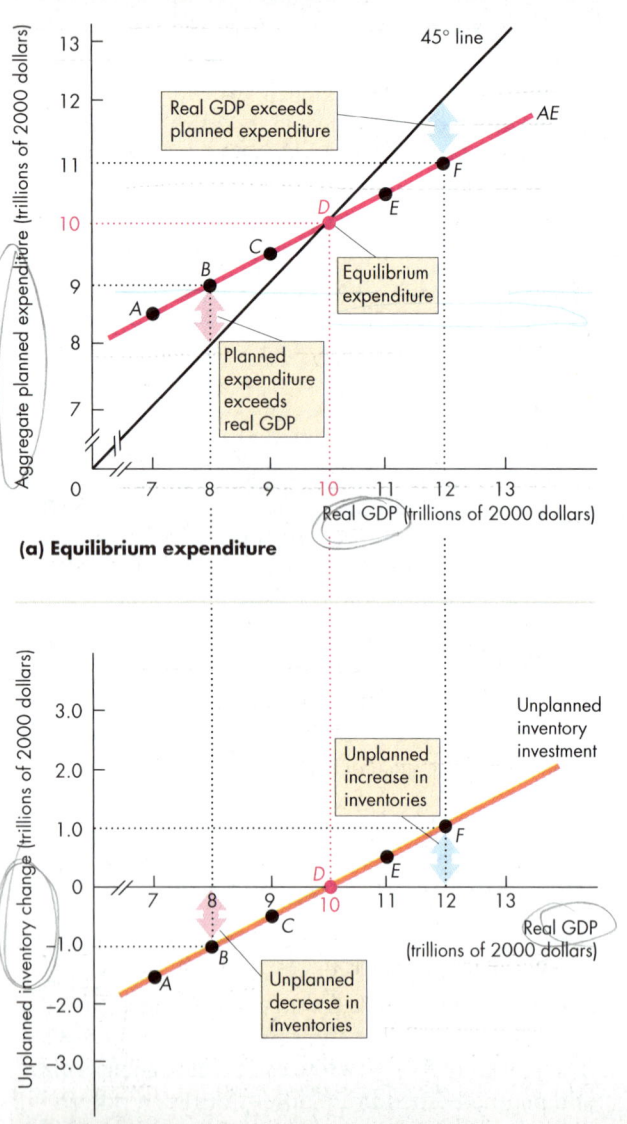

**FIGURE 13.6  Equilibrium Expenditure**

(a) Equilibrium expenditure

(b) Unplanned inventory changes

|   | Real GDP (Y) | Aggregate planned expenditure (AE) | Unplanned inventory change (Y − AE) |
|---|---|---|---|
|   | (trillions of 2000 dollars) | | |
| A | 7 | 8.5 | −1.5 |
| B | 8 | 9.0 | −1.0 |
| C | 9 | 9.5 | −0.5 |
| D | 10 | 10.0 | 0 |
| E | 11 | 10.5 | 0.5 |
| F | 12 | 11.0 | 1.0 |

The table shows expenditure plans at different levels of real GDP. When real GDP is $10 trillion, aggregate planned expenditure equals real GDP.

Part (a) of the figure illustrates equilibrium expenditure, which occurs when aggregate planned expenditure equals real GDP at the intersection of the 45° line and the AE curve. Part (b) of the figure shows the forces that bring about equilibrium expenditure. When aggregate planned expenditure exceeds real GDP, inventories decrease—for example, at point B in both parts of the figure. Firms increase production, and real GDP increases.

When aggregate planned expenditure is less than real GDP, inventories increase—for example, at point F in both parts of the figure. Firms decrease production, and real GDP decreases. When aggregate planned expenditure equals real GDP, there are no unplanned inventory changes and real GDP remains constant at equilibrium expenditure.

ture equals real GDP. Equilibrium expenditure is a level of aggregate expenditure and real GDP at which everyone's spending plans are fulfilled. When the price level is fixed, equilibrium expenditure determines real GDP. When aggregate planned expenditure and actual aggregate expenditure are unequal, a process of convergence toward equilibrium expenditure occurs. And throughout this convergence process, real GDP adjusts. Let's examine equilibrium expenditure and the process that brings it about.

Figure 13.6(a) illustrates equilibrium expenditure. The table sets out aggregate planned expenditure at various levels of real GDP. These values are plotted as points A through F along the AE curve. The 45° line shows all the points at which aggregate planned expenditure equals real GDP. Thus where the AE curve lies above the 45° line, aggregate planned expenditure exceeds real GDP; where the AE curve lies below the 45° line, aggregate planned expenditure is less than real GDP; and where the AE curve intersects the 45° line, aggregate planned expenditure equals real GDP. Point D illustrates equilibrium expenditure. At this point, real GDP is $10 trillion.

## Convergence to Equilibrium

What are the forces that move aggregate expenditure toward its equilibrium level? To answer this question, we must look at a situation in which aggregate expenditure is away from its equilibrium level. Suppose that in Fig. 13.6, real GDP is $8 trillion. With real GDP at $8 trillion, actual aggregate expenditure is also $8 trillion. But aggregate *planned* expenditure is $9 trillion, point B in Fig. 13.6(a). Aggregate planned expenditure exceeds *actual* expenditure. When people spend $9 trillion and firms produce goods and services worth $8 trillion, firms' inventories fall by $1 trillion, point B in Fig. 13.6(b). Because the change in inventories is part of investment, actual investment is $1 trillion less than planned investment.

Real GDP doesn't remain at $8 trillion for very long. Firms have inventory targets based on their sales. When inventories fall below target, firms increase production to restore inventories to the target level. To increase inventories, firms hire additional labor and increase production. Suppose that they increase production in the next period by $1 trillion. Real GDP increases by $1.0 trillion to $9.0 trillion. But again, aggregate planned expenditure exceeds real GDP. When real GDP is $9.0 trillion, aggregate planned expenditure is $9.5 trillion, point C in Fig. 13.6(a). Again, inventories decrease, but this time by less than before. With real GDP of $9.0 trillion and aggregate planned expenditure of $9.5 trillion, inventories decrease by $0.5 trillion, point C in Fig. 13.6(b). Again, firms hire additional labor, and production increases; real GDP increases yet further.

The process that we've just described—planned expenditure exceeds real GDP, inventories decrease, and production increases to restore inventories—ends when real GDP has reached $10 trillion. At this real GDP, there is equilibrium. Unplanned inventory changes are zero. Firms do not change their production.

You can do an experiment similar to the one we've just done but starting with a level of real GDP greater than equilibrium expenditure. In this case, planned expenditure is less than actual expenditure, inventories pile up, and firms cut production. As before, real GDP keeps on changing (decreasing this time) until it reaches its equilibrium level of $10.0 trillion.

### REVIEW QUIZ

1. What is the relationship between aggregate planned expenditure and real GDP at expenditure equilibrium?
2. How does equilibrium expenditure come about? What adjusts to achieve equilibrium?
3. If real GDP and aggregate expenditure are less than their equilibrium levels, what happens to firms' inventories? How do firms change their production? And what happens to real GDP?
4. If real GDP and aggregate expenditure are greater than equilibrium expenditure, what happens to firms' inventories? How do firms change their production? And what happens to real GDP?

We've learned that when the price level is fixed, real GDP is determined by equilibrium expenditure. And we have seen how unplanned changes in inventories and the production response they generate bring a convergence toward equilibrium. We're now going to study *changes* in equilibrium and discover an economic amplifier called the *multiplier*.

# The Multiplier

INVESTMENT AND EXPORTS CAN CHANGE FOR many reasons. A fall in the real interest rate might induce firms to increase their planned investment. A wave of innovation, such as occurred with the spread of multimedia computers in the 1990s, might increase expected future profits and lead firms to increase their planned investment. An economic boom in Western Europe and Japan might lead to a large increase in their expenditure on U.S.-produced goods and services—on U.S. exports. These are all examples of increases in autonomous expenditure.

When autonomous expenditure increases, aggregate expenditure increases, and so does equilibrium expenditure and real GDP. But the increase in real GDP is *larger* than the change in autonomous expenditure. The multiplier is the amount by which a change in autonomous expenditure is magnified or multiplied to determine the change in equilibrium expenditure and real GDP.

It is easiest to get the basic idea of the multiplier if we work with an example economy in which there are no income taxes and no imports. So we'll first assume that these factors are absent. Then, when you understand the basic idea, we'll bring these factors back into play and see what difference they make to the multiplier.

## The Basic Idea of the Multiplier

Suppose that investment increases. The additional expenditure by businesses means that aggregate expenditure and real GDP increase. The increase in real GDP increases disposable income, and with no income taxes, real GDP and disposable income increase by the same amount. The increase in disposable income brings an increase in consumption expenditure. And the increased consumption expenditure adds even more to aggregate expenditure. Real GDP and disposable income increase further, and so does consumption expenditure. The initial increase in investment brings an even bigger increase in aggregate expenditure because it induces an increase in consumption expenditure. The magnitude of the increase in aggregate expenditure that results from an increase in autonomous expenditure is determined by the *multiplier*.

The table in Fig. 13.7 sets out an aggregate planned expenditure schedule. Initially, when real GDP is $9 trillion, aggregate planned expenditure is $9.25 trillion. For each $1 trillion increase in real GDP, aggregate planned expenditure increases by $0.75 trillion. This aggregate expenditure schedule is shown in the figure as the aggregate expenditure curve $AE_0$. Initially, equilibrium expenditure is $10 trillion. You can see this equilibrium in row *B* of the table and in the figure where the curve $AE_0$ intersects the 45° line at the point marked *B*.

Now suppose that autonomous expenditure increases by $0.5 trillion. What happens to equilibrium expenditure? You can see the answer in Fig. 13.7. When this increase in autonomous expenditure is added to the original aggregate planned expenditure, aggregate planned expenditure increases by $0.5 trillion at each level of real GDP. The new aggregate expenditure curve is $AE_1$. The new equilibrium expenditure, highlighted in the table (row *D'*), occurs where $AE_1$ intersects the 45° line and is $12 trillion (point *D'*). At this real GDP, aggregate planned expenditure equals real GDP.

## The Multiplier Effect

In Fig. 13.7, the increase in autonomous expenditure of $0.5 trillion increases equilibrium expenditure by $2 trillion. That is, the change in autonomous expenditure leads, like Erykah Badu's electronic equipment, to an amplified change in equilibrium expenditure. This amplified change is the *multiplier effect*—equilibrium expenditure increases by *more than* the increase in autonomous expenditure. The multiplier is greater than 1.

Initially, when autonomous expenditure increases, aggregate planned expenditure exceeds real GDP. As a result, inventories decrease. Firms respond by increasing production so as to restore their inventories to the target level. As production increases, so does real GDP. With a higher level of real GDP, *induced expenditure* increases. Thus equilibrium expenditure increases by the sum of the initial increase in autonomous expenditure and the increase in induced expenditure. In this example, induced expenditure increases by $1.5 trillion, so equilibrium expenditure increases by $2 trillion.

Although we have just analyzed the effects of an *increase* in autonomous expenditure, the same analysis applies to a decrease in autonomous expenditure. If initially the aggregate expenditure curve is $AE_1$, equilibrium expenditure and real GDP are $12 trillion. A decrease in autonomous expenditure of $0.5 trillion

# The Multiplier

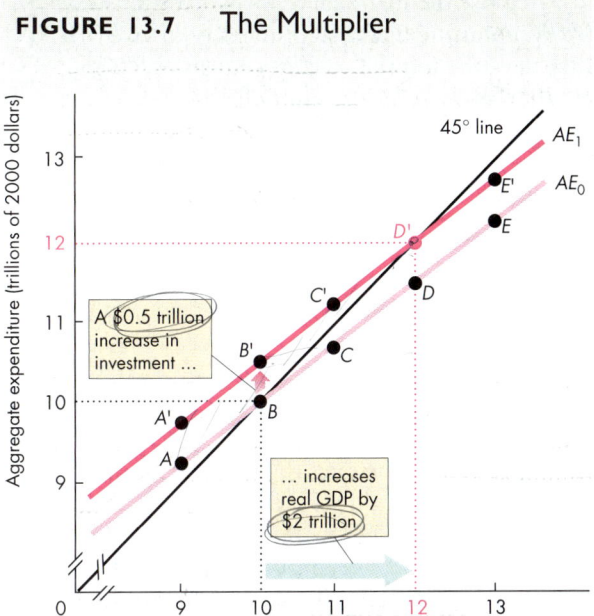

FIGURE 13.7 The Multiplier

| Real GDP (Y) | Aggregate planned expenditure | | | |
|---|---|---|---|---|
| | Original (AE₀) | | New (AE₁) | |
| | (trillions of 2000 dollars) | | | |
| 9 | A | 9.25 | A' | 9.75 |
| 10 | B | 10.00 | B' | 10.50 |
| 11 | C | 10.75 | C' | 11.25 |
| 12 | D | 11.50 | D' | 12.00 |
| 13 | E | 12.25 | E' | 12.75 |

A $0.5 trillion increase in autonomous expenditure shifts the AE curve upward by $0.5 trillion from AE₀ to AE₁. Equilibrium expenditure increases by $2 trillion from $10 trillion to $12 trillion. The increase in equilibrium expenditure is 4 times the increase in autonomous expenditure, so the multiplier is 4.

shifts the aggregate expenditure curve downward by $0.5 trillion to AE₀. Equilibrium expenditure decreases from $12 trillion to $10 trillion. The decrease in equilibrium expenditure ($2 trillion) is larger than the decrease in autonomous expenditure that brought it about ($0.5 trillion). The multiplier is 4.

## Why Is the Multiplier Greater Than 1?

We've seen that equilibrium expenditure increases by more than the increase in autonomous expenditure. This makes the multiplier greater than 1. How come? Why does equilibrium expenditure increase by more than the increase in autonomous expenditure?

The multiplier is greater than 1 because induced expenditure increases—an increase in autonomous expenditure induces further increases in expenditure. Each time NASA launches a space shuttle, it spends $450 million. If NASA increases its program by one flight, aggregate expenditure and real GDP immediately increase by $450 million. But that is not the end of the story. Astronauts and engineers now have more income, and they spend part of the extra income on cars, flat-screen TVs, vacations, and a host of other goods and services. Real GDP now rises by the initial $450 million plus the extra consumption expenditure induced by the $450 million increase in income. The producers of cars, flat-screen TVs, vacations, and other goods and services now have increased incomes, and they, in turn, spend part of the increase in their incomes on consumption goods and services. Additional income induces additional expenditure, which creates additional income.

We have seen that a change in autonomous expenditure has a multiplier effect on real GDP. But how big is the multiplier effect?

## The Size of the Multiplier

Suppose that the economy is in a recession. Profit prospects start to look better, and firms are making plans for large increases in investment. The world economy is also heading toward expansion, and exports are increasing. The question on everyone's lips is: How strong will the expansion be? This is a hard question to answer. But an important ingredient in the answer is working out the size of the multiplier.

The *multiplier* is the amount by which a change in autonomous expenditure is multiplied to determine the change in equilibrium expenditure that it generates. To calculate the multiplier, we divide the change in equilibrium expenditure by the change in autonomous expenditure. Let's calculate the multiplier for the example in Fig. 13.7. Initially, equilibrium expenditure is $10 trillion. Then autonomous expenditure increases by $0.5 trillion, and equilibrium expenditure increases by $2 trillion, to $12 trillion. Then

$$\text{Multiplier} = \frac{\text{Change in equilibrium expenditure}}{\text{Change in autonomous expenditure}}$$

$$= \frac{\$2 \text{ trillion}}{\$0.05 \text{ trillion}} = 4.$$

### The Multiplier and the Marginal Propensities to Consume and Save

The magnitude of the multiplier depends on the marginal propensity to consume. The larger the marginal propensity to consume, the larger is the multiplier. To see why, let's do a calculation.

Aggregate expenditure and real GDP change because consumption expenditure changes and investment changes. The change in real GDP ($\Delta Y$) equals the change in consumption expenditure ($\Delta C$) plus the change in investment ($\Delta I$). That is,

$$\Delta Y = \Delta C + \Delta I.$$

But the change in consumption expenditure is determined by the change in real GDP and the marginal propensity to consume. It is

$$\Delta C = MPC \times \Delta Y.$$

Now substitute $MPC \times \Delta Y$ for $\Delta C$ in the previous equation to give

$$\Delta Y = MPC \times \Delta Y + \Delta I.$$

Now, solve for $\Delta Y$ as

$$(1 - MPC) \times \Delta Y = \Delta I$$

and rearrange

$$\Delta Y = \frac{\Delta I}{(1 - MPC)}.$$

Finally, divide both sides of this equation by $\Delta I$ to give

$$\text{Multiplier} = \frac{\Delta Y}{\Delta I} = \frac{1}{(1 - MPC)}.$$

Using the numbers for Fig. 13.7, $MPC$ is 0.75, so the multiplier is

$$\text{Multiplier} = \frac{1}{(1 - 0.75)} = \frac{1}{0.25} = 4.$$

Because the marginal propensity to consume ($MPC$) plus the marginal propensity to save ($MPS$) sum to 1, the term ($1 - MPC$) equals $MPS$. So another formula for the multiplier is

$$\text{Multiplier} = \frac{1}{MPS}.$$

Again using the numbers in Fig. 13.7, we have

$$\text{Multiplier} = \frac{1}{0.25} = 4.$$

Because the marginal propensity to save ($MPS$) is a fraction—a number between 0 and 1—the multiplier is greater than 1.

Figure 13.8 illustrates the multiplier process. Autonomous expenditure increases by $0.5 trillion. At this time, real GDP increases by $0.5 trillion (the green bar in round 1). This increase in real GDP induces more consumption expenditure in round 2. Induced expenditure increases by 0.75 times the increase in real GDP, so the increase in real GDP of $0.5 trillion induces a further increase in expenditure of $0.375 trillion. This change in induced expenditure (the green bar in round 2) when added to the previous increase in expenditure (the blue bar in round 2) increases real GDP by $0.875 trillion. The round 2 increase in real GDP induces a round 3 increase in consumption expenditure. The process repeats through successive rounds. Each increase in real GDP is 0.75 times the previous increase and eventually real GDP increases by $2 trillion.

So far, we've ignored imports and income taxes. Let's now see how these two factors influence the multiplier.

### Imports and Income Taxes

The multiplier is determined, in general, not only by the marginal propensity to consume but also by the marginal propensity to import and by the marginal tax rate. Imports make the multiplier smaller than it otherwise would be. To see why, think about what happens following an increase in investment. An increase in investment increases real GDP, which in turn increases consumption expenditure. But part of the increase in investment and consumption expenditure is expenditure on imported goods and services, not U.S.-produced goods and services. Only expenditure on U.S.-produced goods and services increases U.S. real GDP. The larger the marginal propensity to import, the smaller is the change in U.S. real GDP.

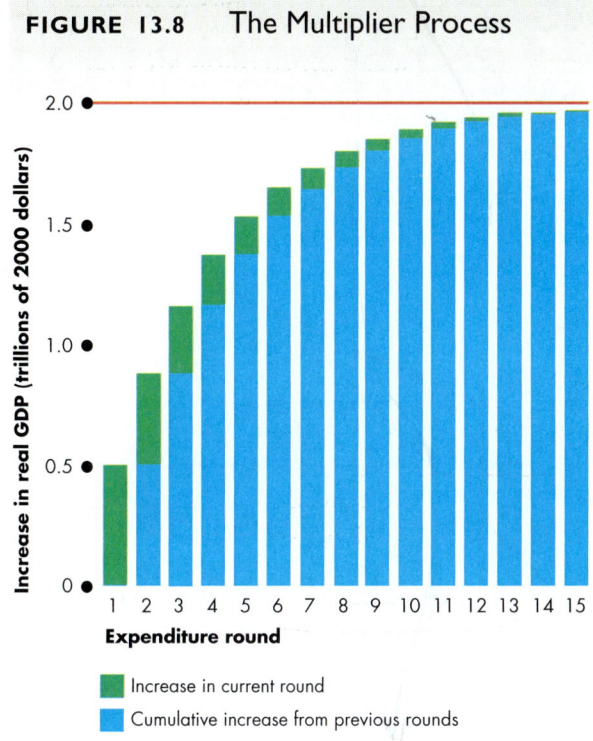

**FIGURE 13.8** The Multiplier Process

- Increase in current round
- Cumulative increase from previous rounds

Autonomous expenditure increases by $0.5 trillion. In round 1, real GDP increases by the same amount. With a marginal propensity to consume of 0.75, each additional dollar of real GDP induces an additional 0.75 of a dollar of consumption expenditure. The round 1 increase in real GDP induces an increase in consumption expenditure of $0.375 trillion in round 2. At the end of round 2, real GDP has increased by $0.875 trillion. The extra $0.375 trillion of real GDP in round 2 induces a further increase in consumption expenditure of $0.281 trillion in round 3. Real GDP increases yet further to $1.156 trillion. This process continues with real GDP increasing by ever-smaller amounts. When the process comes to an end, real GDP has increased by a total of $2 trillion.

Income taxes also make the multiplier smaller than it otherwise would be. Again, think about what happens following an increase in investment. An increase in investment increases real GDP. But because income taxes increase, disposable income increases by less than the increase in real GDP. Consequently, consumption expenditure increases by less than it would if taxes had not changed. The larger is the marginal tax rate, the smaller is the change in disposable income and real GDP.

The marginal propensity to import and the marginal tax rate together with the marginal propensity to consume determine the multiplier. And their combined influence depends on the slope of the *AE* curve.

$$\text{Multiplier} = \frac{1}{(1 - \text{Slope of the } AE \text{ curve})}$$

Figure 13.9 compares two situations. In Fig. 13.9(a), there are no imports and no taxes. The slope of the *AE* curve equals the marginal propensity to consume, which is 0.75, and the multiplier is 4. In Fig. 13.9(b), imports and income taxes decrease the slope of the *AE* curve to 0.5. The multiplier is 2.

Over time, the value of the multiplier changes as tax rates change and as the marginal propensity to consume and the marginal propensity to import change. These ongoing changes make the multiplier hard to predict. But they do not change the fundamental fact that an initial change in autonomous expenditure leads to a magnified change in aggregate expenditure and real GDP.

Pages 328–329 of the math note show the effects of taxes, imports, and the *MPC* on the multiplier.

Now that we've studied the multiplier and the factors that influence its magnitude, let's use what we've learned to gain some insights into business cycle turning points.

## Business Cycle Turning Points

At business cycle turning points, the economy moves from expansion to recession or from recession to expansion. Economists understand these turning points as seismologists understand earthquakes. They know quite a lot about the forces and mechanisms that produce them, but they can't predict them. The forces that bring business cycle turning points are the swings in autonomous expenditure such as investment and exports. The mechanism that gives momentum to the economy's new direction is the multiplier. Let's use what we've now learned to examine these turning points.

**A Recession Begins** A recession is triggered by a decrease in autonomous expenditure that decreases aggregate planned expenditure. At the moment the economy turns the corner into recession, real GDP exceeds aggregate planned expenditure. In this situation, firms see unplanned inventories piling up. The recession now begins. To reduce their inventories, firms cut production, and real GDP begins to

## FIGURE 13.9  The Multiplier and the Slope of the AE Curve

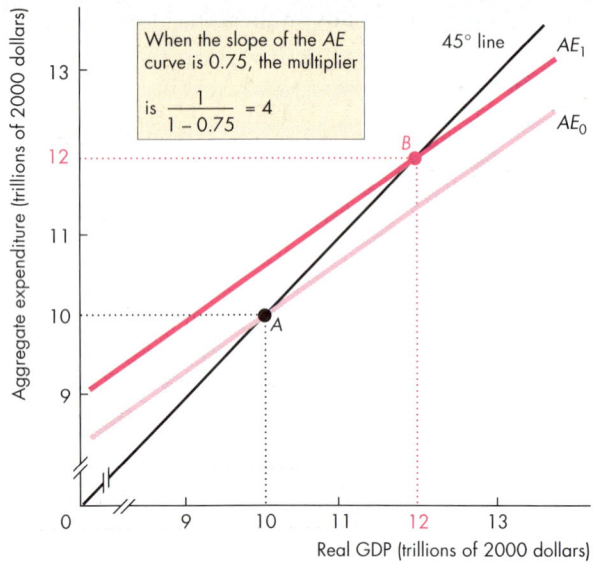

(a) Multiplier is 4

Imports and income taxes make the AE curve less steep and reduce the value of the multiplier. In part (a), with no imports and income taxes, the slope of the AE curve is 0.75 (the marginal propensity to consume) and the multiplier is 4.

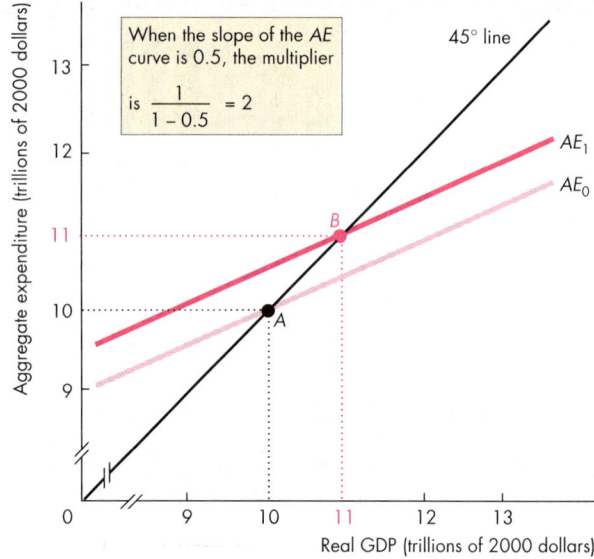

(b) Multiplier is 2

But with imports and income taxes, the slope of the AE curve is less than the marginal propensity to consume. In part (b), the slope of the AE curve is 0.5. In this case, the multiplier is 2.

decrease. This initial decrease in real GDP brings lower incomes that cut consumption expenditure. The multiplier process kicks in, and the recession takes hold.

**An Expansion Begins** The process we've just described works in reverse at a business cycle trough. An expansion is triggered by an increase in autonomous expenditure that increases aggregate planned expenditure. At the moment the economy turns the corner into an expansion, aggregate planned expenditure exceeds real GDP. In this situation, firms see their inventories taking an unplanned dive. The expansion now begins. To meet their inventory targets, firms increase production, and real GDP begins to increase. This initial increase in real GDP brings higher incomes that stimulate consumption expenditure. The multiplier process kicks in, and the expansion picks up speed.

**The 2002–2003 Expansion** The NBER declared November 2001 as the start of the most recent expansion. During 2001, the year before the expansion, business inventories fell relative to their desired levels. Through 2002 and 2003, inventories increased, but not by as much as planned. So even in late 2003, firms were stepping up production to restore their planned inventory levels. *Reading Between the Lines* on pp. 326–327 looks at this episode.

### REVIEW QUIZ

1. What is the multiplier? What does it determine? Why does it matter?
2. How do the marginal propensity to consume, the marginal propensity to import, and the marginal tax rate influence the multiplier?
3. How do fluctuations in autonomous expenditure influence real GDP? If autonomous expenditure decreases, which phase of the business cycle does the economy enter?

The economy's potholes are changes in investment and exports. And the economy does not operate like the shock absorbers on Michael Bloomberg's car. While the price level is fixed, the effects of the economic potholes are not smoothed out. Instead, they are amplified like Erykah Badu's voice. But we've considered only the adjustments in spending that occur in the very short term when the price level is fixed. What happens after a long enough time lapse for the price level to change? Let's answer this question.

## The Multiplier and the Price Level

WHEN FIRMS CAN'T KEEP UP WITH SALES AND their inventories fall below target, they increase production, but at some point, they raise their prices. Similarly, when firms find unwanted inventories piling up, they decrease production, but eventually they cut their prices. So far, we've studied the macroeconomic consequences of firms changing their production levels when their sales change, but we haven't looked at the effects of price changes. When individual firms change their prices, the economy's price level changes.

To study the simultaneous determination of real GDP and the price level, we use the *aggregate supply–aggregate demand model*, which is explained in Chapter 7. But to understand how aggregate demand adjusts, we need to work out the connection between the aggregate supply–aggregate demand model and the equilibrium expenditure model that we've used in this chapter. The key to understanding the relationship between these two models is the distinction between the aggregate *expenditure* and aggregate *demand* and the related distinction between the aggregate *expenditure curve* and the aggregate *demand curve*.

### Aggregate Expenditure and Aggregate Demand

The aggregate expenditure curve is the relationship between the aggregate planned expenditure and real GDP, all other influences on aggregate planned expenditure remaining the same. The aggregate demand curve is the relationship between the aggregate quantity of goods and services demanded and the price level, all other influences on aggregate demand remaining the same. Let's explore the links between these two relationships.

### Aggregate Expenditure and the Price Level

When the price level changes, aggregate planned expenditure changes and the quantity of real GDP demanded changes. The aggregate demand curve slopes downward. Why? There are two main reasons:

- Wealth effect
- Substitution effects

**Wealth Effect** Other things remaining the same, the higher the price level, the smaller is the purchasing power of people's real wealth. For example, suppose you have $100 in the bank and the price level is 105. If the price level rises to 125, your $100 buys fewer goods and services. You are less wealthy. With less wealth, you will probably want to try to spend a bit less and save a bit more. The higher the price level, other things remaining the same, the lower is aggregate planned expenditure.

**Substitution Effects** A rise in the price level today, other things remaining the same, makes current goods and services more expensive relative to future goods and services and results in a delay in purchases—an *intertemporal substitution*. A rise in the price level, other things remaining the same, makes U.S.-produced goods more expensive relative to foreign-produced goods and services. As a result, U.S. imports increase and U.S. exports decrease—an *international substitution*.

When the price level rises, each of these effects reduces aggregate planned expenditure at each level of real GDP. As a result, when the price level *rises*, the aggregate expenditure curve shifts *downward*. A fall in the price level has the opposite effect. When the price level *falls*, the aggregate expenditure curve shifts *upward*.

Figure 13.10(a) shows the shifts of the *AE* curve. When the price level is 105, the aggregate expenditure curve is $AE_0$, which intersects the 45° line at point *B*. Equilibrium expenditure is $10 trillion. If the price level increases to 125, the aggregate expenditure curve shifts downward to $AE_1$, which intersects the 45° line at point *A*. Equilibrium expenditure is

$9 trillion. If the price level decreases to 85, the aggregate expenditure curve shifts upward to $AE_2$, which intersects the 45° line at point C. Equilibrium expenditure is $11 trillion.

We've just seen that when the price level changes, other things remaining the same, the aggregate expenditure curve shifts and the equilibrium expenditure changes. And when the price level changes, other things remaining the same, there is a movement along the aggregate demand curve.

Figure 13.10(b) shows the movements along the aggregate demand curve. At a price level of 105, the aggregate quantity of goods and services demanded is $10 trillion—point B on the AD curve. If the price level rises to 125, the aggregate quantity of goods and services demanded decreases to $9 trillion. There is a movement up along the aggregate demand curve to point A. If the price level falls to 85, the aggregate quantity of goods and services demanded increases to $11 trillion. There is a movement down along the aggregate demand curve to point C.

Each point on the aggregate demand curve corresponds to a point of equilibrium expenditure. The equilibrium expenditure points A, B, and C in Fig. 13.10(a) correspond to the points A, B, and C on the aggregate demand curve in Fig. 13.10(b).

A change in the price level, other things remaining the same, shifts the aggregate expenditure curve and brings a movement along the aggregate demand curve. A change in any other influence on aggregate planned expenditure shifts *both* the aggregate expenditure curve and the aggregate demand curve. For example, an increase in investment or in exports increases both aggregate planned expenditure and aggregate demand and shifts both the AE curve and the AD curve. Figure 13.11 illustrates the effect of such an increase.

Initially, the aggregate expenditure curve is $AE_0$ in part (a) and the aggregate demand curve is $AD_0$ in part (b). The price level is 105, real GDP is $10 trillion, and the economy is at point A in both parts of Fig. 13.11. Now suppose that investment increases by $1 trillion. At a constant price level of 105, the aggregate expenditure curve shifts upward to $AE_1$. This curve intersects the 45° line at an equilibrium expenditure of $12 trillion (point B). This equilibrium expenditure of $12 trillion is the aggregate quantity of goods and services demanded at a price level of 105, as shown by point B in part (b). Point B lies on a new aggregate demand curve. The aggregate demand curve has shifted rightward to $AD_1$.

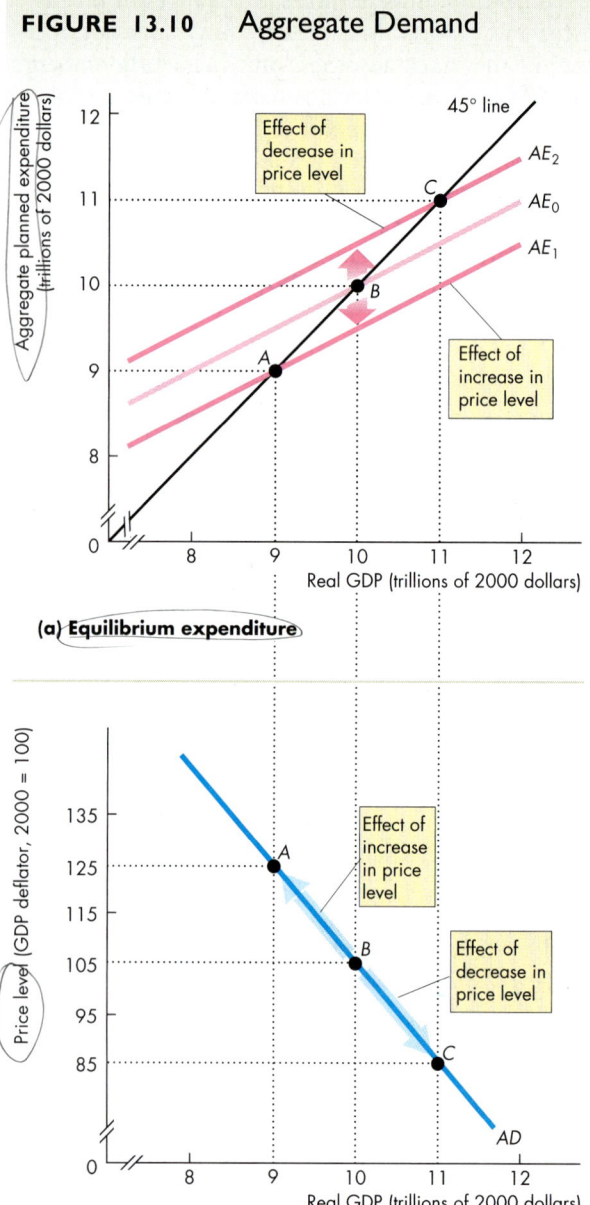

FIGURE 13.10 Aggregate Demand

(a) Equilibrium expenditure

(b) Aggregate demand

A change in the price level *shifts* the AE curve and results in a *movement along* the AD curve. When the price level is 105, the AE curve is $AE_0$ and equilibrium expenditure is $10 trillion at point B. When the price level rises to 125, the AE curve is $AE_1$ and equilibrium expenditure is $9 trillion at point A. When the price level falls to 85, the AE curve is $AE_2$ and equilibrium expenditure is $11 trillion at point C. Points A, B, and C on the AD curve in part (b) correspond to the equilibrium expenditure points A, B, and C in part (a).

## The Multiplier and the Price Level

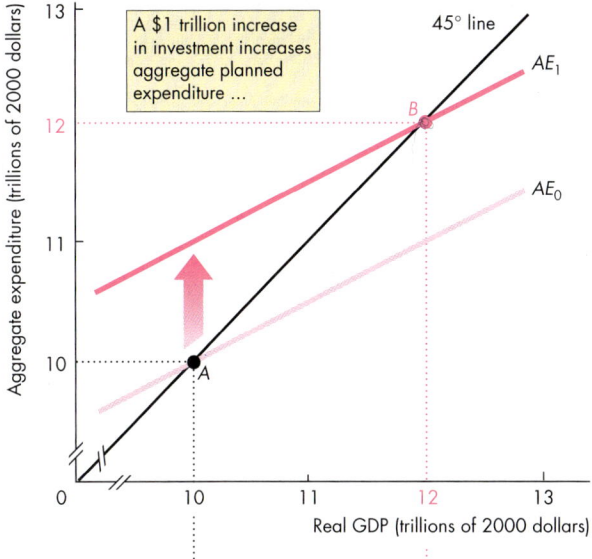

**FIGURE 13.11  A Change in Aggregate Demand**

(a) Aggregate expenditure

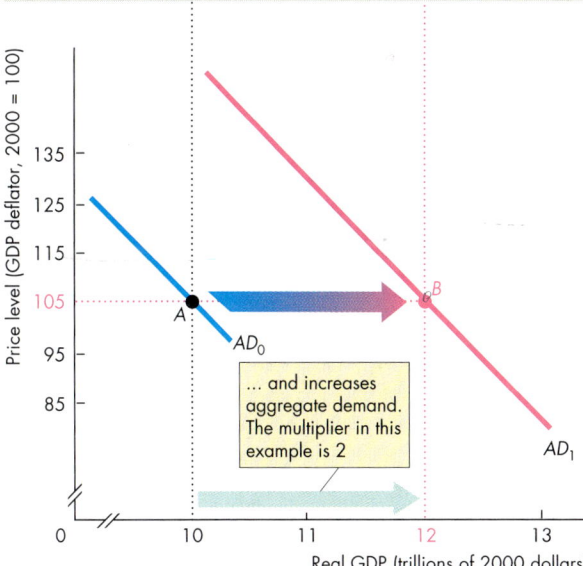

(b) Aggregate demand

The price level is 105. When the aggregate expenditure curve is $AE_0$ (part a), the aggregate demand curve is $AD_0$ (part b). An increase in autonomous expenditure shifts the AE curve upward to $AE_1$. In the new equilibrium, real GDP is $12 trillion (at point B). Because the quantity of real GDP demanded at a price level of 105 increases to $12 trillion, the AD curve shifts rightward to $AD_1$.

But how do we know by how much the AD curve shifts? The multiplier determines the answer. The larger the multiplier, the larger is the shift in the aggregate demand curve that results from a given change in autonomous expenditure. In this example, the multiplier is 2. A $1 trillion increase in investment produces a $2 trillion increase in the aggregate quantity of goods and services demanded at each price level. That is, a $1 trillion increase in autonomous expenditure shifts the aggregate demand curve rightward by $2 trillion.

A decrease in autonomous expenditure shifts the aggregate expenditure curve downward and shifts the aggregate demand curve leftward. You can see these effects by reversing the change that we've just described. If the economy is initially at point B on the aggregate expenditure curve $AE_1$, the aggregate demand curve is $AD_1$. A decrease in autonomous expenditure shifts the aggregate planned expenditure curve downward to $AE_0$. The aggregate quantity of goods and services demanded falls from $12 trillion to $10 trillion, and the aggregate demand curve shifts leftward to $AD_0$.

Let's summarize what we have just discovered:

If some factor other than a change in the price level increases autonomous expenditure, the AE curve shifts upward and the AD curve shifts rightward.

The size of the AD curve shift depends on the change in autonomous expenditure and the multiplier.

### Equilibrium Real GDP and the Price Level

In Chapter 7, we learned that aggregate demand and short-run aggregate supply determine equilibrium real GDP and the price level. We've now put aggregate demand under a more powerful microscope and have discovered that a change in investment (or in any component of autonomous expenditure) changes aggregate demand and shifts the aggregate demand curve. The magnitude of the shift depends on the multiplier. But whether a change in autonomous expenditure results ultimately in a change in real GDP, a change in the price level, or a combination of the two depends on aggregate supply. There are two time frames to consider: the short run and the long run. First we'll see what happens in the short run.

### ggregate Demand in the

13.12 describes the economy. the aggregate expenditure curve um expenditure is $10 trillion— aggregate demand is $AD_0$ and the supply curve is *SAS*. (Chapter 7, pp. 151–152 explains the *SAS* curve.) Equilibrium is at point *A*, where the aggregate demand and short-run aggregate supply curves intersect. The price level is 105, and real GDP is $10 trillion.

Now suppose that investment increases by $1 trillion. With the price level fixed at 105, the aggregate expenditure curve shifts upward to $AE_1$. Equilibrium expenditure increases to $12 trillion—point *B* in part (a). In part (b), the aggregate demand curve shifts rightward by $2 trillion, from $AD_0$ to $AD_1$. How far the aggregate demand curve shifts is determined by the multiplier when the price level is fixed. But with this new aggregate demand curve, the price level does not remain fixed. The price level rises, and as it does, the aggregate expenditure curve shifts downward. The short-run equilibrium occurs when the aggregate expenditure curve has shifted downward to $AE_2$ and the new aggregate demand curve, $AD_1$, intersects the short-run aggregate supply curve. Real GDP is $11.3 trillion, and the price level is 118 (at point *C*).

When price level effects are taken into account, the increase in investment still has a multiplier effect on real GDP, but the multiplier is smaller than it would be if the price level were fixed. The steeper the slope of the short-run aggregate supply curve, the larger is the increase in the price level and the smaller is the multiplier effect on real GDP.

**An Increase in Aggregate Demand in the Long Run** Figure 13.13 illustrates the long-run effect of an increase in aggregate demand. In the long run, real GDP equals potential GDP and there is full employment. Potential GDP is $10 trillion, and the long-run aggregate supply curve is *LAS*. Initially, the economy is at point *A* in parts (a) and (b).

Investment increases by $1 trillion. In Fig. 13.13, the aggregate expenditure curve shifts to $AE_1$ and the aggregate demand curve shifts to $AD_1$. With no change in the price level, the economy would move to point *B* and real GDP would increase to $12 trillion. But in the short run, the price level rises to 118 and real GDP increases to only $11.3 trillion. With the higher price level, the *AE* curve shifts from $AE_1$ to

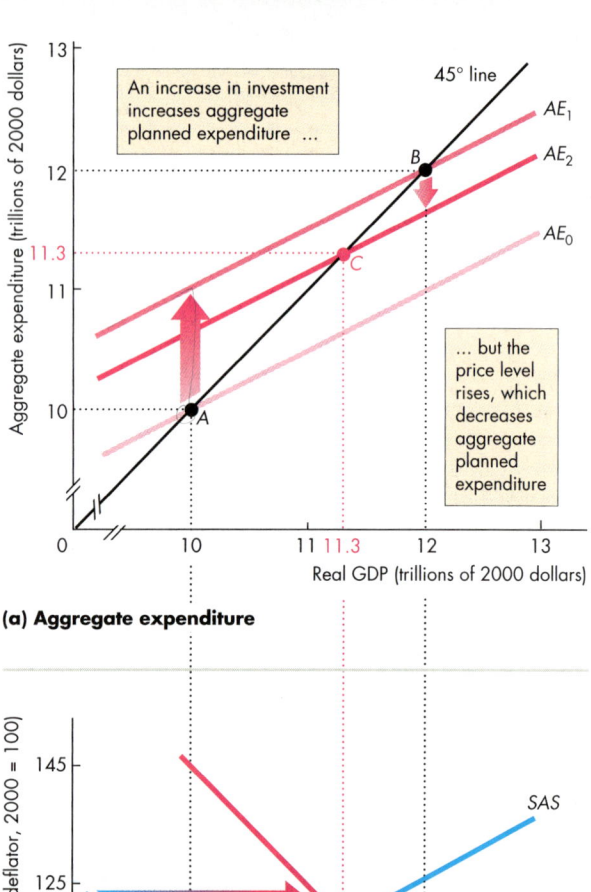

**FIGURE 13.12  The Multiplier in the Short Run**

(a) Aggregate expenditure

(b) Aggregate demand

An increase in investment shifts the *AE* curve from $AE_0$ to $AE_1$ and the *AD* curve from $AD_0$ to $AD_1$. The price level rises, and the higher price level shifts the *AE* curve downward from $AE_1$ to $AE_2$. The economy moves to point *C* in both parts. In the short run, when prices are flexible, the multiplier effect is smaller than when the price level is fixed.

THE MULTIPLIER AND THE PRICE LEVEL    325

## FIGURE 13.13  The Multiplier in the Long Run

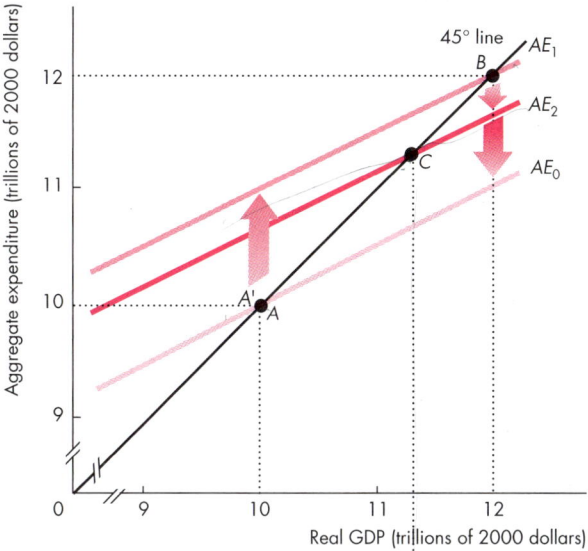

**(a) Aggregate expenditure**

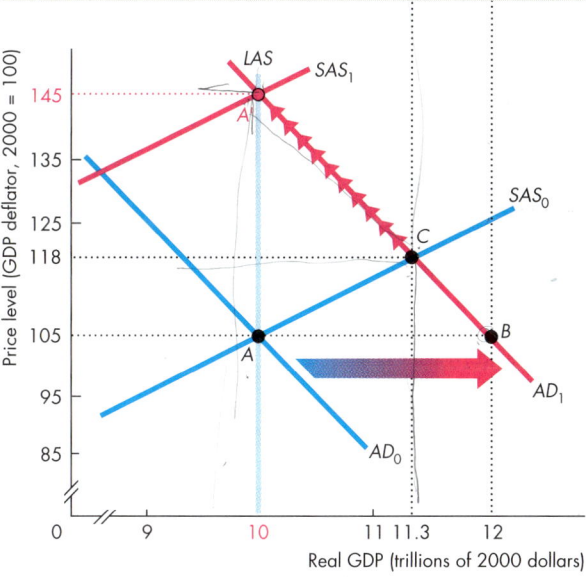

**(b) Aggregate demand**

Starting from point A, an increase in investment shifts the AE curve to $AE_1$ and the AD curve to $AD_1$. In the short run, the economy moves to point C. In the long run, the money wage rate rises, and the SAS curve shifts to $SAS_1$. As the price level rises, the AE curve shifts back to $AE_0$, and the economy moves to point A'. In the long run, the multiplier is zero.

$AE_2$. The economy is now in a short-run equilibrium at point C in both part (a) and part (b). Real GDP now exceeds potential GDP. The labor force is more than fully employed, and shortages of labor increase the money wage rate. The higher money wage rate increases firms' costs, which decreases short-run aggregate supply and shifts the SAS curve leftward to $SAS_1$. The price level rises further, and real GDP decreases. There is a movement along $AD_1$, and the AE curve shifts downward from $AE_2$ toward $AE_0$. When the money wage rate and the price level have increased by the same percentage, real GDP is again equal to potential GDP and the economy is at point A'. In the long run, the multiplier is zero.

### REVIEW QUIZ

1 How does a change in the price level influence the AE curve and the AD curve?
2 If autonomous expenditure increases with no change in the price level, what happens to the AE curve and the AD curve? Which curve shifts by an amount that is determined by the multiplier and why?
3 How does an increase in autonomous expenditure change real GDP in the short-run? Does real GDP change by the same amount as the change in aggregate demand? Why or why not?
4 How does real GDP change in the long run when autonomous expenditure increases? Does real GDP change by the same amount as the change in aggregate demand? Why or why not?

◆ You are now ready to build on what you've learned about aggregate expenditure fluctuations and study the business cycle and the roles of fiscal policy and monetary policy in smoothing the cycle, while achieving price stability and sustained economic growth. In Chapter 14, we study the business cycle and in Chapters 15 and 16, we study fiscal policy and monetary policy. But before you leave the current topic, look at *Reading Between the Lines* on pp. 326–327 and see the model you've studied in this chapter in action in the U.S. economy during the 2003 expansion.

# READING BETWEEN THE LINES

## *Inventories in Expansion*

**THE WALL STREET JOURNAL, DECEMBER 11, 2003**

## US Business Inventories +0.4% in October

U.S. business inventories climbed higher than expected during October, indicating companies might be growing more comfortable with the economic recovery.

Inventories increased 0.4% to a seasonally adjusted level of $1.18 trillion, following a revised 0.4% advance in September, the Commerce Department said Thursday.

The October increase was bigger than expected on Wall Street. Forecasters projected an advance of 0.2%.

With the economy heating up, demand for goods has drained inventories. Analysts see firms rebuilding depleted stocks in a process that will, in turn, elevate demand, boost production and push the economy.

Gross domestic product has advanced all year. Analysts expect solid economic growth through 2004. ...

The inventory-to-sales ratio was 1.35; it was 1.36 in September. The inventory-to-sales ratio, an indicator of how well firms are matching supply with demand, measures how long it would take in months for a firm to sell all of its current inventory.

Retail inventories increased by 0.6% in October, after rising by 1.1% in the prior month. ...

General merchandise stores climbed by 0.4%. Food store inventories went down 1.0%. Stockpiles at furniture stores rose by 1.9%, while inventories at building materials, garden equipment and supplies stores were flat. There was a 0.7% decline in clothing inventories.

October wholesale inventories increased by 0.5% and factory inventories remained unchanged....

Year over year, business inventories climbed by 1.9% from October 2002 to October 2003. Sales increased by 5.1% during the same period.

© 2003 The Wall Street Journal
Reprinted with permission
Further reproduction prohibited.

### Essence of the Story

- U.S. business inventories increased by 0.4 percent to $1.18 trillion during October 2003.

- This increase was larger than expected.

- Year over year, business inventories increased by 1.9 percent from October 2002 to October 2003, but the value of goods sold increased by 5.1 percent during the same period.

- So the ratio of inventories to the value of goods sold fell, and the rebuilding of depleted inventories was predicted to boost production and further expand the economy during 2004.

## Economic Analysis

- This news article is about inventories and their effect on real GDP.

- The effect of an increase in inventories on real GDP depends on whether the increase is planned or unplanned.

- A planned increase in inventories increases aggregate planned expenditure, shifts the AE curve upward, and increases equilibrium expenditure.

- An unplanned increase in inventories has no direct effect on the AE curve but means that actual expenditure exceeds planned expenditure.

- When actual expenditure exceeds planned expenditure, real GDP grows more slowly and sometimes decreases.

- The news article implies that the increase in inventories in October 2003 was planned, so the increase is predicted to bring faster expansion of real GDP during 2004.

- The article also says that the planned increase in inventories is a response to a previous unplanned decrease during the earlier part of 2003.

- This interpretation is correct, and the figures illustrate why.

- In the third quarter of 2003 (the quarter that ended September 30, 2003), real GDP was $10,493 billion, up $205 billion on the second quarter. (All the values are 2000 dollars.)

- Business inventories decreased during the third quarter by $9 billion.

- But with real GDP increasing, firms planned larger inventories.

- Based on trends in the ratio of inventories to sales, we can estimate that planned inventory investment during the third quarter of 2003 was $21 billion.

- Assuming this estimate to be correct, there was an unplanned decrease in inventories of $30 billion—see part (b) of the figure.

- Aggregate *planned* expenditure was $30 billion greater than actual expenditure and was $10,523 billion—in part (a) of the figure.

- With an assumption about the slope of the AE curve, we can calculate equilibrium expenditure.

- In the figure, the slope of the AE curve is 0.457 (a value that is based on the assumption that the MPC = 0.9, the marginal tax rate is 0.27, and the marginal propensity to import is 0.2).

- Equilibrium expenditure, based on these assumptions, is $10,548 billion.

- Regardless of the exact values, equilibrium expenditure exceeds actual expenditure and the pace of real GDP growth will increase as stated in the news article.

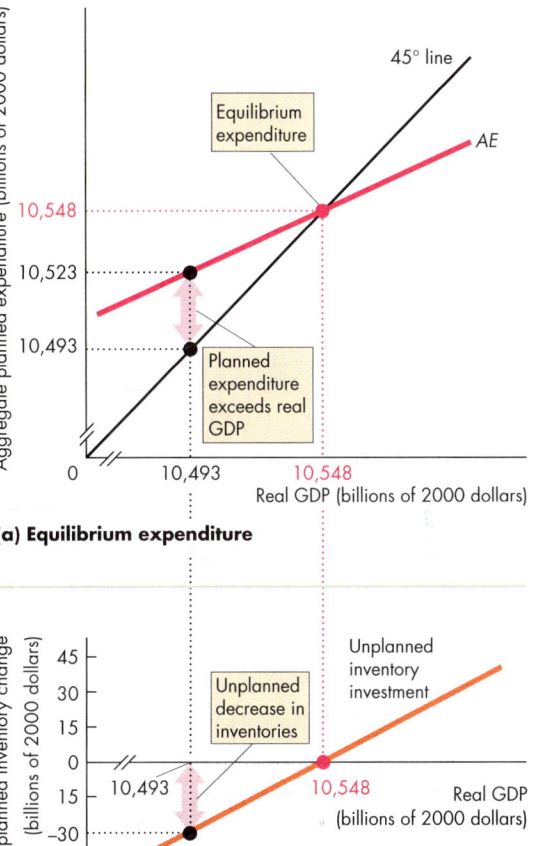

**(a) Equilibrium expenditure**

**(b) Unplanned inventory changes**

## Mathematical Note
### The Algebra of the Keynesian Model

THIS MATHEMATICAL NOTE DERIVES FORMULAS FOR the expenditure equilibrium and the multipliers. We begin by defining the symbols we need

- Aggregate planned expenditure, $AE$
- Real GDP, $Y$
- Consumption expenditure, $C$
- Investment, $I$
- Government purchases, $G$
- Exports, $X$
- Imports, $M$
- Net taxes, $T$
- Autonomous consumption expenditure, $a$
- Lump-sum taxes, $T_a$
- Marginal propensity to consume, $b$
- Marginal propensity to import, $m$
- Marginal tax rate, $t$
- Autonomous expenditure, $A$

### Aggregate Expenditure

Aggregate planned expenditure ($AE$) is the sum of the planned amounts of consumption expenditure ($C$), investment ($I$), government purchases ($G$), and exports ($X$) minus the planned amount of imports ($M$).

$$AE = C + I + G + X - M.$$

**Consumption Function** Consumption expenditure ($C$) depends on disposable income ($YD$), and we write the consumption function as

$$C = a + bYD.$$

Disposable income ($YD$) equals real GDP minus net taxes ($Y - T$). So if we replace $YD$ with ($Y - T$), the consumption function becomes

$$C = a + b(Y - T).$$

Net taxes equals lump-sum taxes plus induced taxes. Induced taxes equal real GDP ($Y$) multiplied by the marginal tax rate. So

$$T = T_a + tY.$$

Use this last equation to replace $T$ in the consumption function. The consumption function becomes

$$C = a - bT_a + b(1 - t)Y.$$

This equation describes consumption expenditure as a function of real GDP.

**Import Function** Imports depend on real GDP, and the import function is

$$M = mY.$$

**Aggregate Expenditure Curve** Use the consumption function and the import function to replace $C$ and $M$ in the $AE$ equation. That is,

$$AE = a - bT_a + b(1 - t)Y + I + G + X - mY.$$

Collect the terms on the right side of the equation that involve $Y$ to obtain

$$AE = (a - bT_a + I + G + X) + [b(1 - t) - m]Y.$$

Autonomous expenditure ($A$) is $(a - bT_a + I + G + X)$, and the slope of the $AE$ curve is $[b(1 - t) - m]$. So the equation for the $AE$ curve, which is shown in Fig. 1, is

$$AE = A + [b(1 - t) - m]Y.$$

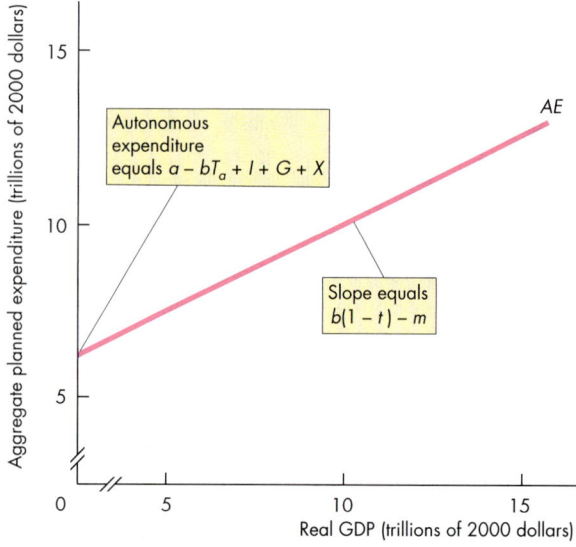

**Figure 1 The $AE$ curve**

## Equilibrium Expenditure

Equilibrium expenditure occurs when aggregate planned expenditure (AE) equals real GDP (Y). That is,

$$AE = Y.$$

In Fig. 2, the scales of the x-axis (real GDP) and the y-axis (aggregate planned expenditure) are identical, so the 45° line shows the points at which aggregate planned expenditure equals real GDP.

Figure 2 shows the point of equilibrium expenditure at the intersection of the AE curve and the 45° line.

To calculate equilibrium expenditure, solve the equations for the AE curve and the 45° line for the two unknown quantities AE and Y. So starting with

$$AE = A + [b(1 - t) - m]Y$$
$$AE = Y,$$

replace AE with Y in the AE equation to obtain

$$Y = A + [b(1 - t) - m]Y.$$

The solution for Y is

$$Y = \frac{1}{1 - [b(1 - t) - m]} A.$$

## The Multiplier

The multiplier equals the change in equilibrium expenditure and real GDP (Y) that results from a change in autonomous expenditure (A) divided by the change in autonomous expenditure.

A change in autonomous expenditure ($\Delta A$) changes equilibrium expenditure and real GDP by

$$\Delta Y = \frac{1}{1 - [b(1 - t) - m]} \Delta A,$$

$$\text{Multiplier} = \frac{1}{1 - [b(1 - t) - m]}.$$

The size of the multiplier depends on the slope of the AE curve, $b(1 - t) - m$. The larger the slope, the larger is the multiplier. So the multiplier is larger,

- The greater the marginal propensity to consume ($b$)
- The smaller the marginal tax rate ($t$)
- The smaller the marginal propensity to import ($m$)

An economy with no imports and no marginal taxes has $m = 0$ and $t = 0$. In this special case, the multiplier equals $1/(1 - b)$. If $b$ is 0.75, then the multiplier is 4, as shown in the figure below. In an economy with $b = 0.75$, $t = 0.2$, and $m = 0.1$, the multiplier is 1 divided by 1 minus $0.75(1 - 0.02) - 0.1$, which equals 2. Make up some more examples to show the effects of $b$, $t$, and $m$ on the multiplier.

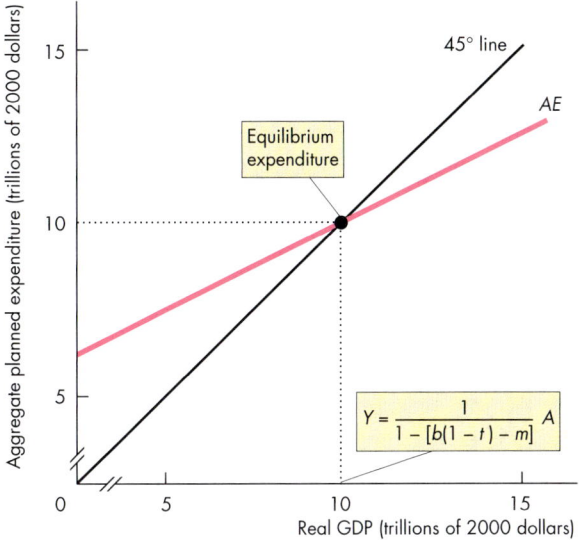

Figure 2 Equilibrium expenditure

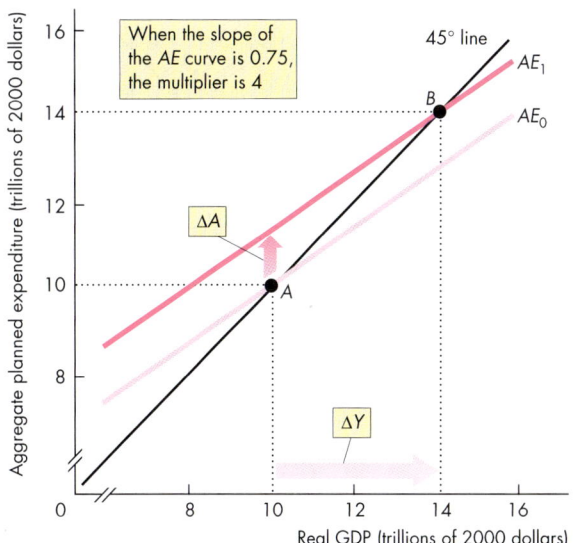

Figure 3 The multiplier

## Government Purchases Multiplier

The government purchases multiplier equals the change in equilibrium expenditure ($Y$) that results from a change in government purchases ($G$) divided by the change in government purchases. Because autonomous expenditure is equal to

$$A = a - bT_a + I + G + X,$$

the change in autonomous expenditure equals the change in government purchases. That is,

$$\Delta A = \Delta G.$$

You can see from the solution for equilibrium expenditure $Y$ that

$$\Delta Y = \frac{1}{1 - [b(1 - t) - m]} \Delta G.$$

The government purchases multiplier equals

$$\frac{1}{1 - [b(1 - t) - m]}.$$

In an economy in which $t = 0$ and $m = 0$, the government purchases multiplier is $1/(1 - b)$. With $b = 0.75$, the government purchases multiplier is 4, as Fig. 4 shows. Make up some examples and use the above formula to show how $b$, $m$, and $t$ influence the government purchases multiplier.

## Lump-Sum Taxes Multiplier

The lump-sum taxes multiplier equals the change in equilibrium expenditure ($Y$) that results from a change in lump-sum taxes ($T_a$) divided by the change in lump-sum taxes. Because autonomous expenditure is equal to

$$A = a - bT_a + I + G + X,$$

the change in autonomous expenditure equals *minus* $b$ multiplied by the change in lump-sum taxes. That is,

$$\Delta A = -b \Delta T_a.$$

You can see from the solution for equilibrium expenditure $Y$ that

$$\Delta Y = \frac{-b}{1 - [b(1 - t) - m]} \Delta T_a.$$

The lump-sum taxes multiplier equals

$$\frac{-b}{1 - [b(1 - t) - m]}.$$

In an economy in which $t = 0$ and $m = 0$, the lump-sum taxes multiplier is $-b/(1 - b)$. In this special case, with $b = 0.75$, the lump-sum taxes multiplier equals $-3$, as Fig. 5 shows. Make up some examples and use the above formula to show how $b$, $m$, and $t$ influence the lump-sum taxes multiplier.

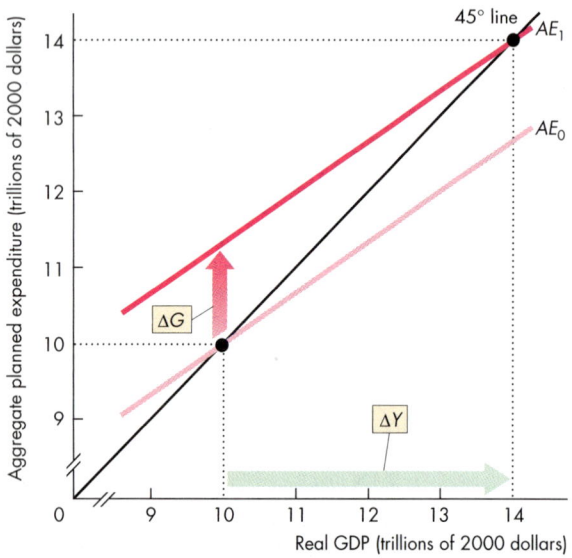

**Figure 4 Government purchases multiplier**

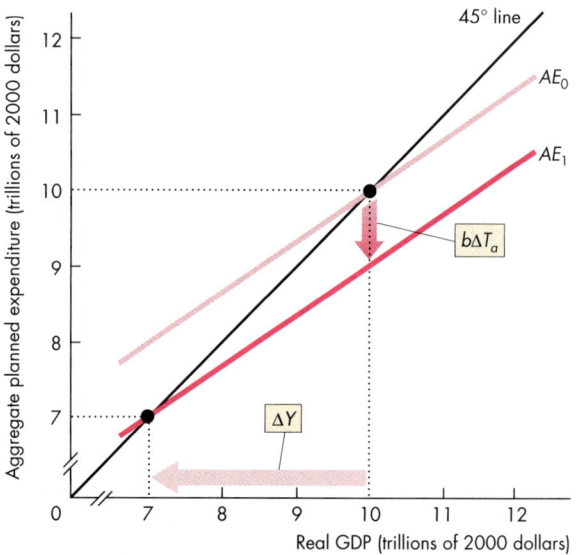

**Figure 5 Lump-sum tax multiplier**

## Balanced Budget Multiplier

The balanced budget multiplier equals the change in equilibrium expenditure ($Y$) that results from equal changes in government purchases and lump-sum taxes divided by the change in government purchases. Because government purchases and lump-sum taxes change by the same amount, the budget balance does not change.

The change in equilibrium expenditure that results from the change in government purchases is

$$\Delta Y = \frac{1}{1 - [b(1 - t) - m]}\Delta G.$$

And the change in equilibrium expenditure that results from the change in lump-sum taxes is

$$\Delta Y = \frac{-b}{1 - [b(1 - t) - m]}\Delta T_a.$$

So the change in equilibrium expenditure resulting from the changes in government purchases and lump-sum taxes is

$$\Delta Y = \frac{1}{1 - [b(1 - t) - m]}\Delta G + \frac{-b}{1 - [b(1 - t) - m]}\Delta T_a.$$

Notice that

$$\frac{1}{1 - [b(1 - t) - m]}$$

is common to both terms on the right side. So we can rewrite the equation as

$$\Delta Y = \frac{1}{1 - [b(1 - t) - m]}[\Delta G - b\Delta Ta]$$

The $AE$ curve shifts upward by $\Delta G - b\Delta T_a$ as shown in Fig. 6.

But the change in government purchases equals the change in lump-sum taxes. That is,

$$\Delta G = \Delta T_a.$$

And

$$\Delta Y = \frac{1 - b}{1 - [b(1 - t) - m]}\Delta G.$$

The balance budget multiplier equals

$$\frac{1 - b}{1 - [b(1 - t) - m]}.$$

In an economy in which $t = 0$ and $m = 0$, the balance budget multiplier is $(1 - b)/(1 - b)$, which equals 1, as Fig. 6 shows. Make up some examples and use the above formula to show how $b$, $m$, and $t$ influence the balance budget multiplier.

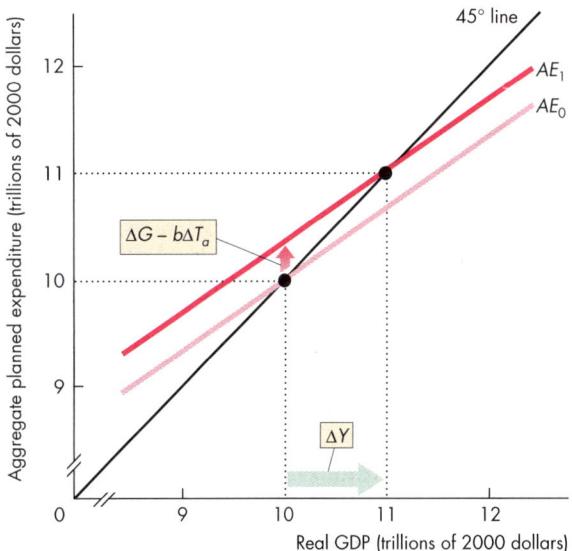

**Figure 6 Balanced budget multiplier**

# SUMMARY

## KEY POINTS

### Fixed Prices and Expenditure Plans (pp. 306–311)

- When the price level is fixed, expenditure plans determine real GDP.
- Consumption expenditure is determined by disposable income, and the marginal propensity to consume (*MPC*) determines the change in consumption expenditure brought about by a change in disposable income. Real GDP determines disposable income.
- Imports are determined by real GDP, and the marginal propensity to import determines the change in imports brought about by a change in real GDP.

### Real GDP with a Fixed Price Level (pp. 312–315)

- Aggregate *planned* expenditure depends on real GDP.
- Equilibrium expenditure occurs when aggregate planned expenditure equals actual expenditure and real GDP.

### The Multiplier (pp. 316–321)

- The multiplier is the magnified effect of a change in autonomous expenditure on real GDP.
- The multiplier is influenced by the marginal propensity to consume, the marginal propensity to import, and the marginal income tax rate.

### The Multiplier and the Price Level (pp. 321–325)

- The aggregate demand curve is the relationship between the quantity of real GDP demanded and the price level, other things remaining the same.
- The aggregate expenditure curve is the relationship between aggregate planned expenditure and real GDP, other things remaining the same.
- At a given price level, there is a given aggregate expenditure curve. A change in the price level changes aggregate planned expenditure and shifts the aggregate expenditure curve. A change in the price level also creates a movement along the aggregate demand curve.
- A change in autonomous expenditure that is not caused by a change in the price level shifts the aggregate expenditure curve and shifts the aggregate demand curve. The magnitude of the shift of the aggregate demand curve depends on the multiplier and on the change in autonomous expenditure.
- The multiplier decreases as the price level changes, and the long-run multiplier is zero.

## KEY FIGURES

Figure 13.1   Consumption Function and Saving Function, 307
Figure 13.2   Marginal Propensities to Consume and Save, 309
Figure 13.5   Aggregate Expenditure, 312
Figure 13.6   Equilibrium Expenditure, 314
Figure 13.7   The Multiplier, 317
Figure 13.8   The Multiplier Process, 319
Figure 13.9   The Multiplier and the Slope of the *AE* Curve, 320
Figure 13.10  Aggregate Demand, 322
Figure 13.11  A Change in Aggregate Demand, 323
Figure 13.12  The Multiplier in the Short Run, 324
Figure 13.13  The Multiplier in the Long Run, 325

## KEY TERMS

Aggregate planned expenditure, 306
Autonomous expenditure, 313
Consumption function, 307
Disposable income, 306
Equilibrium expenditure, 314
Induced expenditure, 313
Marginal propensity to consume, 308
Marginal propensity to import, 311
Marginal propensity to save, 308
Multiplier, 316
Saving function, 307

# PROBLEMS

*1. You are given the following information about the economy of Heron Island:

| Disposable income (millions of dollars per year) | Consumption expenditure (millions of dollars per year) |
|---|---|
| 0 | 5 |
| 10 | 10 |
| 20 | 15 |
| 30 | 20 |
| 40 | 25 |

Calculate Heron Island's:
a. Marginal propensity to consume.
b. Saving at each level of disposable income.
c. Marginal propensity to save.

2. You are given the following information about the economy of Spendthrift Island:

| Disposable income (millions of dollars per year) | Saving (millions of dollars per year) |
|---|---|
| 0 | −10 |
| 50 | −5 |
| 100 | 0 |
| 150 | 5 |
| 200 | 10 |
| 250 | 15 |
| 300 | 20 |

a. Calculate the marginal propensity to save.
b. Calculate consumption at each level of disposable income.
c. Calculate the marginal propensity to consume.
d. Why is the island called "spendthrift"?

*3. Turtle Island has no imports or exports, the people of Turtle Island pay no incomes taxes, and the price level is fixed. The figure illustrates the components of aggregate planned expenditure on Turtle Island. On Turtle Island,
a. What is autonomous expenditure?
b. What is the marginal propensity to consume?
c. What is aggregate planned expenditure when real GDP is $6 billion?
d. If real GDP is $4 billion, what is happening to inventories?
e. If real GDP is $6 billion, what is happening to inventories?
f. What is the multiplier?

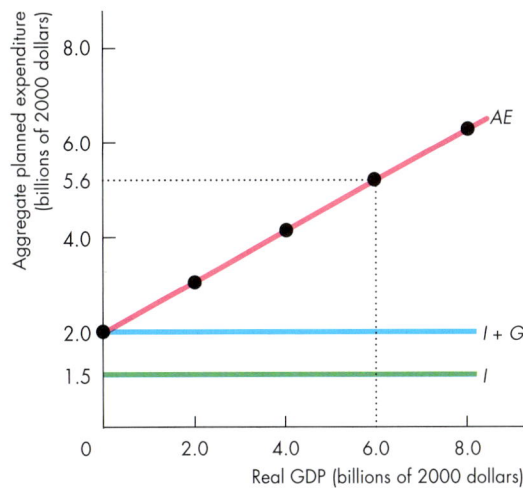

4. The spreadsheet lists the components of aggregate planned expenditure in Spice Bay. The numbers are in billions of cloves, the currency of Spice Bay.

|   | A | B | C | D | E | F | G |
|---|---|---|---|---|---|---|---|
| 1 |   | Y | C | I | G | X | M |
| 2 | a | 100 | 110 | 50 | 60 | 60 | 15 |
| 3 | b | 200 | 170 | 50 | 60 | 60 | 30 |
| 4 | c | 300 | 230 | 50 | 60 | 60 | 45 |
| 5 | d | 400 | 290 | 50 | 60 | 60 | 60 |
| 6 | e | 500 | 350 | 50 | 60 | 60 | 75 |
| 7 | f | 600 | 410 | 50 | 60 | 60 | 90 |

In Spice Bay,
a. What is autonomous expenditure?
b. What is the marginal propensity to consume?
c. What is aggregate planned expenditure when real GDP is 200 billion cloves?
d. If real GDP is 200 billion cloves, what is happening to inventories?
e. If real GDP is 500 billion cloves, what is happening to inventories?
f. What is the multiplier in Spice Bay?

*5. You are given the following information about the economy of Zeeland: Autonomous consumption expenditure is $100 billion, and the marginal propensity to consume is 0.9. Investment is $460 billion, government purchases of goods and services are $400 billion, and net taxes are a constant $400 billion—they do not vary with income.
a. What is the consumption function?

* Solutions to odd-numbered problems are available on **MyEconLab**.

b. What is the equation that describes the aggregate expenditure curve?
c. Calculate equilibrium expenditure.
d. If investment falls to $360 billion, what is the change in equilibrium expenditure and what is the size of the multiplier?

6. You are given the following information about the economy of Antarctica: Autonomous consumption expenditure is $1 billion, and the marginal propensity to consume is 0.9. Investment is $5 billion, government purchases of goods and services are $4 billion, and net taxes are a constant $4 billion—they do not vary with income.
   a. What is the consumption function?
   b. What is the equation that describes the aggregate expenditure curve?
   c. Calculate equilibrium expenditure.
   d. If investment falls to $3 billion, what is the change in equilibrium expenditure and what is the size of the multiplier?

*7. Suppose that in problem 5, the price level is 100 and real GDP equals potential GDP.
   a. If investment increases by $100 billion, what happens to the quantity of real GDP demanded?
   b. In the short run, does real GDP increase by more than, less than, or the same amount as the increase in the quantity of real GDP demanded?
   c. In the long run, does real GDP increase by more than, less than, or the same amount as the increase in the quantity of real GDP demanded?
   d. In the short run, does the price level in Zeeland rise, fall, or remain unchanged?
   e. In the long run, does the price level in Zeeland rise, fall, or remain unchanged?

8. Suppose that in problem 6, the price level is 100 and real GDP equals potential GDP.
   a. If investment increases by $1 billion, what happens to the quantity of real GDP demanded?
   b. In the long run, does real GDP increase by more than, less than, or the same amount as the increase in the quantity of real GDP demanded?
   c. In the short run, does the price level in Antarctica rise, fall, or remain unchanged?

## CRITICAL THINKING

1. Study *Reading Between the Lines* on pp. 326–327 and then answer the following questions:
   a. If the 2003 changes in inventories were part of *planned* investment, what role did they play in shifting the *AE* curve and changing equilibrium expenditure? Use a figure similar to that on p. 327 to answer this question.
   b. If the 2003 changes in inventories were part of *unplanned* investment, what role did they play in shifting the *AE* curve and changing equilibrium expenditure? Use a figure similar to that on p. 327 to answer this question.
   c. What do you think will happen to real GDP, aggregate expenditure, and inventory investment in 2004? What clues do you get from the news article?
   d. Is a build-up of business inventories a cause or a consequence of expansion?

## WEB EXERCISES

**Use the links on MyEconLab to work the following exercises.**

1. Obtain data on real GDP per person and consumption as a percentage of real GDP for the United States, China, South Africa, and Mexico since 1960.
   a. In a spreadsheet, multiply your real GDP data by the consumption percentage and divide by 100 to obtain data on real consumption expenditure per person.
   b. Make graphs like Fig. 13.4 to show the relationship between consumption and real GDP for these four countries.
   c. On the basis of the numbers you've obtained, in which country do you expect the multiplier to be largest (other things remaining the same)?
   d. What other data would you need to be able to calculate the multipliers for these countries?

2. You are a research assistant in the office of the President's Council of Economic Advisors. Draft a note for the President that explains the power and limitations of the multiplier. The President wants only 250 words of crisp, clear, jargon-free explanation together with a lively example.

# The Business Cycle

**CHAPTER 14**

## Must What Goes Up Always Come Down?

**The 1990s were years of rapid expansion for the** U.S. economy—so much so that people began to talk of a "new economy," one fueled by information technologies in which recession was a disease that had been cured. Then came the 2001 recession, which was mild in comparison with its predecessors but a recession nonetheless.

Like the 1990s, the 1920s were years of expansion and unprecedented prosperity. After the horrors of World War I (1914–1918), Americans were back at work, producing such technological marvels as cars and airplanes, telephones and vacuum cleaners. Houses and apartments were being built at a frantic pace. Then, almost without warning, in October 1929, came a devastating stock market crash. Overnight, the values of stocks and shares trading on Wall Street fell by 30 percent. During the next four years, there followed the most severe economic contraction in recorded history. By 1933, real GDP had fallen by 26 percent, unemployment had increased to 25 percent of the labor force, and employment was down 20 percent.

Our economy has experienced 16 recessions since 1920 and 10 since the end of World War II in 1945. Most of these recessions were short-lived and were followed by another, much longer spell of expansion.

◆ What causes a repeating sequence of recessions and expansions in our economy? Must what goes up always come down? This chapter explores these questions. And *Reading Between the Lines* at the end of the chapter looks at the expansion of 2002–2003.

### After studying this chapter, you will be able to

- **Distinguish among the different theories of the business cycle**
- **Explain the Keynesian and monetarist theories of the business cycle**
- **Explain the new classical and new Keynesian theories of the business cycle**
- **Explain real business cycle theory**
- **Describe the origins of, and the mechanisms at work during, the expansion of the 1990s, the recession of 2001, and the Great Depression**

# Cycle Patterns, Impulses, and Mechanisms

You've looked at the business cycle at several points in your study of macroeconomics. You met it first in Chapter 4, which defines the phases of the cycle and describes its history. You saw in Chapter 6 how unemployment fluctuates over the business cycle. In Chapter 7, you learned about a framework for studying the business cycle: the *AS-AD* model. In Chapters 11 through 13, you saw how money influences economic fluctuations and how inflation and the business cycle intertwine. Finally, in Chapter 13, you focused on business cycle turning points and the inventory changes and multiplier effects that operate as the economy swings from expansion to recession and back to expansion.

You've also looked at another type of economic fluctuation: the productivity growth slowdown of the 1970s. This slowdown is not classified as a business cycle event, but it has some similarities. It is part of an overall process of economic growth, the pace of which fluctuates. The processes of growth and the business cycle are intimately connected. In fact, according to one view, they are all manifestations of the same phenomenon.

This chapter brings all these strands in your previous study of macroeconomics together and gives you an opportunity to review what you have learned and to put it to work in a focused way in interpreting and making sense of particular episodes in our economic history. We'll get moving by first returning to the facts about the business cycle and looking at the complex patterns it makes.

## Business Cycle Patterns

The *business cycle* is an irregular and nonrepeating up-and-down movement of business activity that takes place around a generally rising trend and that shows great diversity. Each recession, expansion, and turning point has been dated by the National Bureau of Economic Research (NBER). The NBER has identified 16 recessions and expansions since 1920. On the average, recessions have lasted for just over a year, and real GDP has fallen from peak to trough by more than 6 percent. On the average, expansions have lasted for almost 4 years, and real GDP has increased from trough to peak by 22 percent. But these averages hide huge variations from one cycle to another.

Table 14.1 shows the range of variation. You can see that the Great Depression was much more severe than anything that followed it. Over a 43-month period (August 1929 to March 1933), real GDP shrank by 32.6 percent. The second most severe recession was also in the 1930s. Another relatively severe recession occurred at the end of World War II, in 1945. The only other recession that comes close to these is that of 1974–1975, which resulted from a fourfold rise in the price of oil, lasted for 16 months, and saw real GDP fall by 4.9 percent. The other recessions since 1950, including the most recent 2001 recession, have been much milder than those of the 1930s. The biggest expansion occurred during World War II. The other two big expansions were in the 1960s and 1990s. There is no correlation between the length of an expansion and the length of the preceding recession.

With this enormous diversity of experience, there is no simple explanation for the business cycle. Also, there is no currently available way of forecasting when the next turning point will come. But there is a body of theory about the business cycle that helps us to understand its causes. A good place to begin studying this theory is to distinguish the possible ways in which cycles can be created.

## Cycle Impulses and Mechanisms

Cycles are a widespread physical phenomenon. In a tennis match, the ball cycles from one side of the court to the other and back again. Every day, the earth cycles from day to night and back to day. A child on a rocking horse creates a cycle as the horse swings back and forth.

The tennis ball cycle is the simplest. It is caused by the actions of the players. Each time the ball changes direction (at each turning point), the racket (an outside force) is applied. The day-night-day cycle is the most subtle. This cycle is caused by the rotation of the earth. No new force is applied each day to make the sun rise and set. It happens because of the design of the objects that interact to create the cycle. Nothing happens at a turning point (sunrise and sunset) that is any different from what is happening at other points except that the sun comes into or goes out of view. The child's rocking horse cycle is a combination of these two cases. To start the horse rocking, some outside force must be exerted (as in the tennis ball cycle). But once the horse is rocking, the to-and-fro cycle continues for some time with no further force being applied (as in the day-night-day cycle). The rocking horse cycle eventually dies out unless the horse is pushed again, and each time the horse is pushed, the cycle temporarily becomes more severe.

The economy is a bit like all three of these examples. It can be hit by shocks (like a tennis ball) that send it in one direction or another, it can cycle indefinitely (like the turning of day into night), and it can cycle in swings that get milder until another shock sets off a new burst of bigger swings (like a rocking horse). While none of these analogies is perfect, they all contain some insights into the business cycle. Different theories of the cycle emphasize different outside forces (different tennis rackets) and different cycle mechanisms (different solar system and rocking horse designs).

Although there are several different theories of the business cycle, they all agree about one aspect of the cycle: the central role played by investment and the accumulation of capital.

## The Central Role of Investment and Capital

Whatever the shocks are that hit the economy, they hit one crucial variable: investment. Recessions begin when investment in new capital slows down, and they turn into expansions when investment speeds up. Investment and capital interact like the spinning earth and the sun to create an ongoing cycle.

### TABLE 14.1 Business Cycle Dates Since 1920

| Business cycle dates | | Duration in months | | | | |
|---|---|---|---|---|---|---|
| Peak | Trough | Contraction (previous peak to trough) | Expansion (trough to this peak) | Cycle (trough from previous trough) | Cycle (peak from previous peak) | Fall in real GDP (peak to trough, percent) |
| Jan-20 | Jul-21 | 18 | 10 | 28 | 17 | 8.7 |
| May-23 | Jul-24 | 14 | 22 | 36 | 40 | 4.1 |
| Oct-26 | Nov-27 | 13 | 27 | 40 | 41 | 2.0 |
| Aug-29 | Mar-33 | 43 | 21 | 64 | 34 | 32.6 |
| May-37 | Jun-38 | 13 | 50 | 63 | 93 | 18.2 |
| Feb-45 | Oct-45 | 8 | 80 | 88 | 93 | 11.0 |
| Nov-48 | Oct-49 | 11 | 37 | 48 | 45 | 1.5 |
| Jul-53 | May-54 | 10 | 45 | 55 | 56 | 3.2 |
| Aug-57 | Apr-58 | 8 | 39 | 47 | 49 | 3.3 |
| Apr-60 | Feb-61 | 10 | 24 | 34 | 32 | 1.2 |
| Dec-69 | Nov-70 | 11 | 106 | 117 | 116 | 1.0 |
| Nov-73 | Mar-75 | 16 | 36 | 52 | 47 | 4.9 |
| Jan-80 | Jul-80 | 6 | 58 | 64 | 74 | 2.5 |
| Jul-81 | Nov-82 | 16 | 12 | 28 | 18 | 3.0 |
| Jul-90 | Mar-91 | 8 | 92 | 100 | 108 | 1.4 |
| Mar-01 | Nov-01 | 8 | 120 | 128 | 128 | 0.5 |

*Sources:* National Bureau of Economic Research and Bureau of Economic Analysis.

In an expansion, investment proceeds at a rapid rate and the capital stock grows quickly. But rapid capital growth means that the amount of capital per hour of labor is growing. Equipped with more capital, labor becomes more productive. But the *law of diminishing returns* begins to operate. The law of diminishing returns states that as the quantity of capital increases, with the quantity of labor remaining the same, the gain in productivity from the additional units of capital eventually diminishes. Diminishing returns to capital bring a fall in the profit rate, and with a lower profit rate, the incentive to invest weakens. As a result, investment eventually falls. When it falls by a large amount, recession begins.

In a recession, investment is low and the capital stock grows slowly. In a deep recession, the capital stock might actually fall. Slow capital growth (or even a falling capital stock) means that the amount of capital per hour of labor is falling. With a low amount of capital per hour of labor, businesses begin to see opportunities for profitable investment and the pace of investment eventually picks up. As it does so, recession turns into expansion.

## The AS-AD Model

Investment and capital are a crucial part of the business cycle mechanism, but they are just one part. To study the broader business cycle mechanism, we need a broader framework. That framework is the *AS-AD* model of Chapter 7. All the theories of the business cycle can be described in terms of the *AS-AD* model. Theories differ both in what they identify as the impulse and in the cycle mechanism. But all theories can be thought of as making assumptions about the factors that make either aggregate supply or aggregate demand fluctuate and assumptions about how they interact with each other to create a business cycle. Business cycle impulses can affect either the supply side or the demand side of the economy or both. But there are no pure supply-side theories. We will classify all theories of the business cycle as either

- Aggregate demand theories or
- Real business cycle theory

We'll study the aggregate demand theories first. Then we'll study real business cycle theory, which is a more recent approach that isolates a shock that has both aggregate supply and aggregate demand effects.

## Aggregate Demand Theories of the Business Cycle

THREE TYPES OF AGGREGATE DEMAND THEORY OF the business cycle have been proposed:

- Keynesian theory
- Monetarist theory
- Rational expectations theories

### Keynesian Theory

The **Keynesian theory of the business cycle** regards volatile expectations as the main source of economic fluctuations. This theory is distilled from Keynes's *General Theory of Employment, Interest, and Money*. We'll explore the Keynesian theory by looking at its main impulse and the mechanism that converts that impulse into a real GDP cycle.

**Keynesian Impulse** The *impulse* in the Keynesian theory of the business cycle is *expected future sales and profits*. A change in expected future sales and profits changes the demand for new capital and changes the level of investment.

Keynes had a sophisticated theory about *how* expected sales and profits are determined. He reasoned that these expectations would be volatile because most of the events that shape the future are unknown and impossible to forecast. So, he reasoned, news or even rumors about any of the thousands of relevant factors that influence sales and profits—such as future tax rate changes, interest rate changes, advances in technology, global economic and political events—change expectations in ways that can't be quantified but that have large effects.

To emphasize the volatility and diversity of sources of changes in expected sales and profits, Keynes described these expectations as *animal spirits*. In using this term, Keynes was not saying that expectations are irrational. Rather, he meant that because future sales and profits are impossible to forecast, it might be rational to take a view about them based on rumors, guesses, intuition, and instinct. Further, it might be rational to *change* one's view of the future, perhaps radically, in light of scraps of new information.

**Keynesian Cycle Mechanism** In the Keynesian theory, once a change in animal spirits has changed investment, a cycle mechanism begins to operate that has two key elements. First, the initial change in investment has a multiplier effect. The change in investment changes *aggregate* expenditure, real GDP, and disposable income. The change in disposable income changes consumption expenditure, and aggregate demand changes by a multiple of the initial change in investment. (This mechanism is described in detail in Chapter 13, pp. 316–319.) The aggregate demand curve shifts rightward in an expansion and leftward in a recession.

The second element of the Keynesian cycle mechanism is the response of real GDP to a change in aggregate demand. The short-run aggregate supply curve is horizontal (or nearly so). With a horizontal *SAS* curve, swings in aggregate demand translate into swings in real GDP with no changes in the price level. But the short-run aggregate supply curve depends on the money wage rate. If the money wage rate is fixed (sticky), the *SAS* curve does not move. And if the money wage rate changes, the *SAS* curve shifts. In the Keynesian theory, the response of the money wage rate to changes in aggregate demand are *asymmetric*.

On the downside, when aggregate demand decreases and unemployment rises, the money wage rate does not change. It is completely rigid in the downward direction. With a decrease in aggregate demand and no change in the money wage rate, the economy gets stuck in a below full-employment equilibrium. There are no natural forces operating to restore full employment. The economy remains in that situation until animal spirits are lifted and investment increases again.

On the upside, when aggregate demand increases and unemployment falls below its natural rate, the money wage rate rises quickly. It is flexible in the upward direction. At above full employment, the horizontal *SAS* curve plays no role and only the vertical *LAS* curve is relevant. With an increase in aggregate demand and an accompanying rise in the money wage rate, the price level rises quickly to eliminate the shortages and bring the economy back to full employment. The economy remains in that situation until animal spirits fall and investment and aggregate demand decrease.

Figures 14.1 and 14.2 illustrate the Keynesian theory of the business cycle by using the aggregate

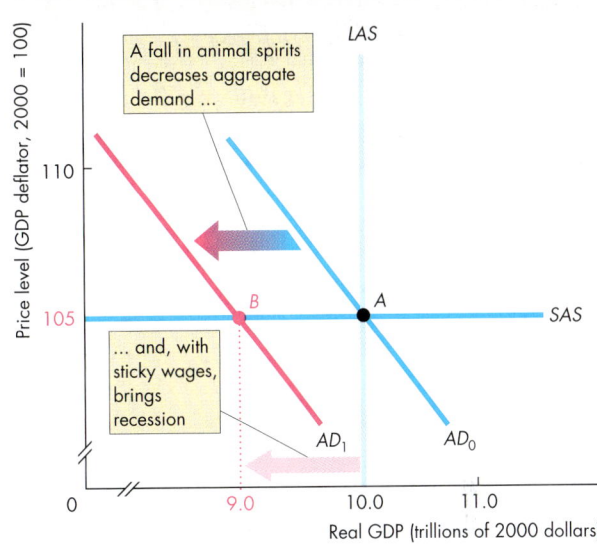

**FIGURE 14.1    A Keynesian Recession**

The economy is operating at point A at the intersection of the long-run aggregate supply curve, *LAS*; the short-run aggregate supply curve, *SAS*; and the aggregate demand curve, $AD_0$. A Keynesian recession begins when a fall in animal spirits causes investment demand to decrease. Aggregate demand decreases, and the *AD* curve shifts leftward to $AD_1$. With a sticky money wage rate, real GDP decreases to $9 trillion and the price level does not change. The economy moves to point B.

supply–aggregate demand model. In Fig. 14.1, the economy is initially at full employment (point *A*) on the long-run aggregate supply curve, *LAS*; the aggregate demand curve, $AD_0$; and the short-run aggregate supply curve, *SAS*. A fall in animal spirits decreases investment, and a multiplier process decreases aggregate demand. The aggregate demand curve shifts leftward to $AD_1$. With a fixed money wage rate, real GDP falls to $9 trillion and the economy moves to point *B*. Unemployment has increased and there is a surplus of labor, but the money wage rate does not fall and the economy remains at point *B* until some force moves it away.

That force is shown in Fig. 14.2. Here, starting out at point *B*, a rise in animal spirits increases investment. The multiplier process kicks in, and aggregate demand increases. The *AD* curve shifts to $AD_2$, and real GDP begins to increase. An expansion

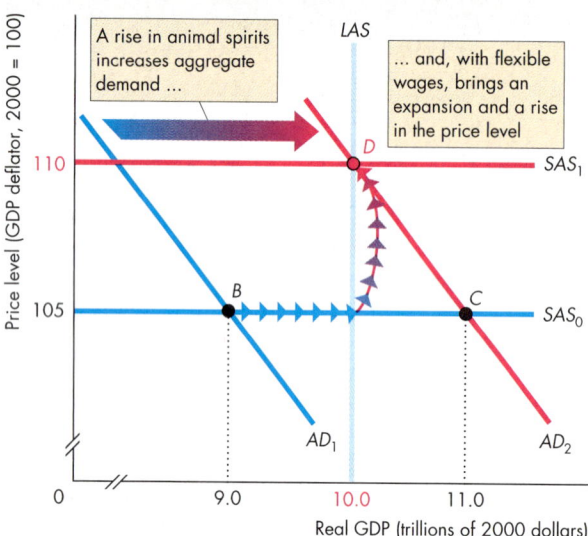

**FIGURE 14.2  A Keynesian Expansion**

Starting at point $B$, a Keynesian expansion begins when a rise in animal spirits causes investment demand to increase. Aggregate demand increases, and the $AD$ curve shifts rightward to $AD_2$. If the money wage rate is sticky, real GDP increases to $10 trillion. But the economy does not go all the way to point $C$. When full employment is reached, the money wage rate rises and the $SAS$ curve shifts upward toward $SAS_1$. The price level rises as the economy heads toward point $D$.

is underway. As long as real GDP remains below potential GDP ($10 trillion in this example), the money wage rate and the price level remain constant. But real GDP never increases to point $C$, the point of intersection of $SAS_0$ and $AD_2$. The reason is that once real GDP exceeds potential GDP and unemployment falls below its natural rate, the money wage rate begins to rise and the $SAS$ curve starts to shift upward toward $SAS_1$. As the money wage rate rises, the price level also rises and real GDP growth slows. The economy follows a path like the one shown by the arrows connecting point $B$, the initial equilibrium, with point $D$, the final equilibrium.

The Keynesian business cycle is like a tennis match. It is caused by outside forces—animal spirits—that change direction and set off a process that ends at an equilibrium that must be hit again by the outside forces to disturb it.

## Monetarist Theory

The **monetarist theory of the business cycle** regards fluctuations in the quantity of money as the main source of economic fluctuations. This theory is distilled from the writings of Milton Friedman and several other economists. We'll explore the monetarist theory, as we did the Keynesian theory, by looking first at its main impulse and second at the mechanism that creates a cycle in real GDP.

**Monetarist Impulse** The *impulse* in the monetarist theory of the business cycle is the *growth rate of the quantity of money*. A speedup in money growth brings expansion, and a slowdown in money growth brings recession. The source of the change in the growth rate of the quantity of money is the monetary policy actions of the Fed.

**Monetarist Cycle Mechanism** In the monetarist theory, once the Fed has changed the money growth rate, a cycle mechanism begins to operate that, like the Keynesian mechanism, first affects aggregate demand. When the money growth rate increases, the quantity of real money in the economy increases and interest rates fall. The foreign exchange rate also falls—the dollar loses value on the foreign exchange market. These initial financial market effects begin to spill over into other markets. Investment and exports increase, and consumers spend more on durable goods. These initial changes in expenditure have a multiplier effect, just as investment has in the Keynesian theory. Through these mechanisms, a speedup in money growth shifts the aggregate demand curve rightward and brings an expansion. Similarly, a slowdown in money growth shifts the aggregate demand curve leftward and brings a recession.

The second element of the monetarist cycle mechanism is the response of aggregate supply to a change in aggregate demand. The short-run aggregate supply curve is upward-sloping. With an upward-sloping $SAS$ curve, swings in aggregate demand translate into swings in both real GDP and the price level. But monetarists believe that real GDP deviations from full employment are temporary in both directions.

In monetarist theory, the money wage rate is only *temporarily sticky*. When aggregate demand decreases and unemployment rises, the money wage rate eventually begins to fall. As the money wage rate falls, so does the price level, and after a period of adjustment, full employment is restored. When aggregate demand increases and unemployment falls below its natural rate, the money wage rate begins to rise. As the money wage rate rises, so does the price level, and through a period of adjustment, real GDP returns to potential GDP and the unemployment rate returns to the natural rate.

Figure 14.3 illustrates the monetarist theory. In part (a), the economy is initially at full employment (point $A$) on the long-run aggregate supply curve, $LAS$; the aggregate demand curve, $AD_0$; and the short-run aggregate supply curve, $SAS_0$. A slowdown in the money growth rate decreases aggregate demand, and the aggregate demand curve shifts leftward to $AD_1$.

Real GDP decreases to $9.5 trillion, and the economy goes into recession (point $B$). Unemployment increases, and there is a surplus of labor. The money wage rate begins to fall. As the money wage falls, the short-run aggregate supply curve starts to shift rightward toward $SAS_1$. The price level falls, and real GDP begins to expand as the economy moves to point $C$, its new full-employment equilibrium.

Figure 14.3(b) shows the effects of the opposite initial money shock—a speedup in money growth. Here, starting out at point $C$, a rise in the money growth rate increases aggregate demand and shifts the $AD$ curve to $AD_2$. Both real GDP and the price level increase as the economy moves to point $D$, the point of intersection of $SAS_1$ and $AD_2$. With real GDP above

## FIGURE 14.3 A Monetarist Business Cycle

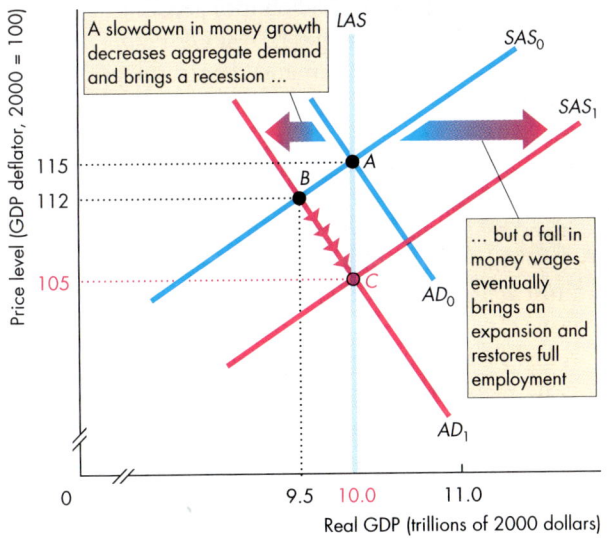

(a) Recession

A monetarist recession begins when a slowdown in money growth decreases aggregate demand. The $AD$ curve shifts leftward from $AD_0$ to $AD_1$ (in part a). With a sticky money wage rate, real GDP decreases to $9.5 trillion and the price level falls to 112 as the economy moves from point $A$ to point $B$. With a surplus of labor, the money wage rate falls and the $SAS$ curve shifts rightward to $SAS_1$. The price level falls further, and real GDP returns to potential GDP at point $C$.

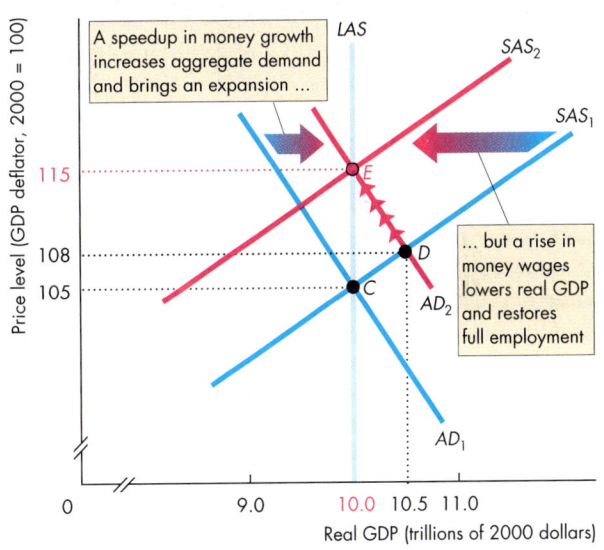

(b) Expansion

Starting at point $C$ (part b), a monetarist expansion begins when an increase in money growth increases aggregate demand and shifts the $AD$ curve rightward to $AD_2$. With a sticky money wage rate, real GDP rises to $10.5 trillion, the price level rises to 108, and the economy moves to point $D$. With a shortage of labor, the money wage rate rises and the $SAS$ curve shifts toward $SAS_2$. The price level rises, and real GDP decreases to potential GDP as the economy heads toward point $E$.

potential GDP and unemployment below its natural rate, the money wage rate begins to rise and the *SAS* curve starts to shift leftward toward $SAS_2$. As the money wage rate rises, the price level also rises and real GDP decreases. The economy moves from point *D* to point *E*, its new full-employment equilibrium.

The monetarist business cycle is like a rocking horse. It needs an outside force to get it going, but once going, it rocks back and forth (but just once). It doesn't matter in which direction the force initially hits. If it is a money growth slowdown, the economy cycles with a recession followed by expansion. If it is a money growth speedup, the economy cycles with an expansion followed by recession.

## Rational Expectations Theories

A *rational expectation* is a forecast that is based on all the available relevant information (see Chapter 12, p. 285). Rational expectations theories of the business cycle are based on the view that the money wage rate is determined by a rational expectation of the price level. Two distinctly different rational expectations theories of the cycle have been proposed. A **new classical theory of the business cycle** regards *unanticipated* fluctuations in aggregate demand as the main source of economic fluctuations. This theory is based on the work of Robert E. Lucas, Jr. and several other economists, including Thomas J. Sargent and Robert J. Barro (see pp. 176–178). A different **new Keynesian theory of the business cycle** also regards *unanticipated* fluctuations in aggregate demand as the main source of economic fluctuations but also leaves room for *anticipated* aggregate demand fluctuations to play a role.

We'll explore these theories, as we did the Keynesian and monetarist theories, by looking first at the main impulse and second at the cycle mechanism.

**Rational Expectations Impulse** The *impulse* that distinguishes the rational expectations theories from the other aggregate demand theories of the business cycle is the *unanticipated change in aggregate demand*. A larger than anticipated increase in aggregate demand brings an expansion, and a smaller than anticipated increase in aggregate demand brings a recession. Any factor that influences aggregate demand—for example, fiscal policy, monetary policy, or developments in the world economy that influence exports—whose change is not anticipated can bring a change in real GDP.

**Rational Expectations Cycle Mechanisms** To describe the rational expectations cycle mechanisms, we'll deal first with the new classical version. When aggregate demand decreases, if the money wage rate doesn't change, real GDP and the price level both decrease. The fall in the price level increases the *real* wage rate, and employment decreases and unemployment rises. In the new classical theory, these events occur only if the decrease in aggregate demand is not anticipated. If the decrease in aggregate demand *is* anticipated, the price level is expected to fall and both firms and workers will agree to a lower money wage rate. By doing so, they can prevent the real wage rate from rising and avoid a rise in the unemployment rate.

Similarly, if firms and workers anticipate an increase in aggregate demand, they expect the price level to rise and will agree to a higher money wage rate. By doing so, they can prevent the real wage rate from falling and avoid a fall in the unemployment rate below the natural rate.

Only fluctuations in aggregate demand that are unanticipated and not taken into account in wage agreements bring changes in real GDP. *Anticipated* changes in aggregate demand change the price level, but they leave real GDP and unemployment unchanged and do not create a business cycle.

New Keynesian economists, like new classical economists, believe that the money wage rate is influenced by rational expectations of the price level. But new Keynesians emphasize the long-term nature of most wage contracts. They say that *today's* money wage rate is influenced by *yesterday's* rational expectations. These expectations, which were formed in the past, are based on old information that might now be known to be incorrect. After they have made a long-term wage agreement, both firms and workers might anticipate a change in aggregate demand, which they expect will change the price level. But because they are locked into their agreement, they are unable to change the money wage rate. So the money wage rate is sticky in the new Keynesian theory, and with sticky money wages, even an *anticipated* change in aggregate demand changes real GDP.

New classical economists believe that long-term contracts are renegotiated when conditions change to make them outdated. So they do not regard long-term contracts as an obstacle to money wage flexibility, provided that both parties to an agreement recognize the changed conditions. If both firms and workers expect the price level to change, they will change the agreed money wage rate to reflect that shared expectation. In this situation, anticipated changes in aggregate demand change the money wage rate and the price level and leave real GDP unchanged.

The distinctive feature of both versions of the rational expectations theory of the business cycle is the role of unanticipated changes in aggregate demand. Figure 14.4 illustrates its effect on real GDP and the price level.

Potential GDP is $10 trillion, and the long-run aggregate supply curve is LAS. Aggregate demand is expected to be EAD. Given potential GDP and EAD, the money wage rate is set at the level that is expected to bring full employment. At this money wage rate, the short-run aggregate supply curve is SAS. Imagine that initially aggregate demand equals expected aggregate demand, so there is full employment, and the economy is at point A. Real GDP is $10 trillion, and the price level is 105. Then, unexpectedly, aggregate demand turns out to be less than expected, and the aggregate demand curve shifts leftward to $AD_0$ (in Fig. 14.4a). Many different aggregate demand shocks, such as a slowdown in the money growth rate or a collapse of exports, could have caused this shift. A recession begins. Real GDP decreases to $9.5 trillion, and the price level falls to 102. The economy moves to point B. Unemployment increases, and there is a surplus of labor. But aggregate demand is expected to be at EAD, so the money wage rate doesn't change and the short-run aggregate supply curve remains at SAS.

## FIGURE 14.4  A Rational Expectations Business Cycle

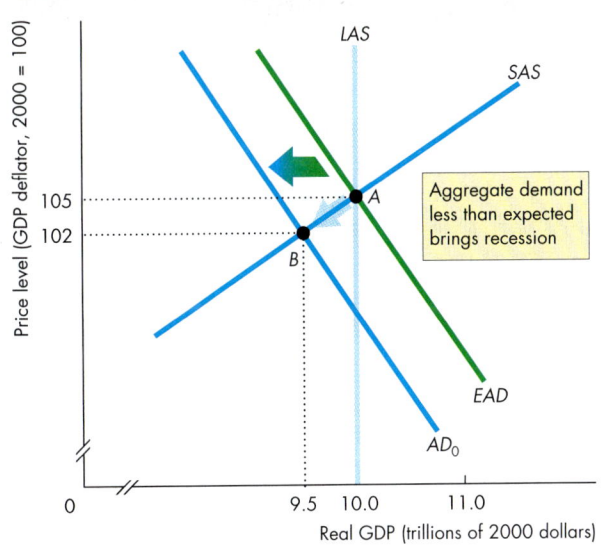

(a) Recession

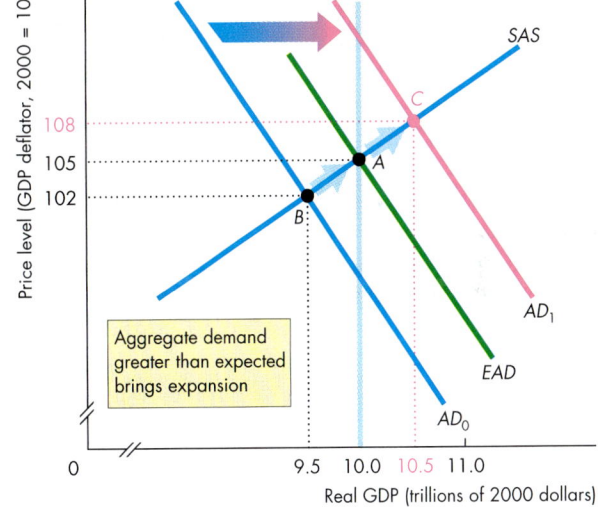

(b) Expansion

The economy is expected to be at point A at the intersection of the long-run aggregate supply curve, LAS; the short-run aggregate supply curve, SAS; and the *expected* aggregate demand curve, EAD. A rational expectations recession begins when an unanticipated fall in aggregate demand shifts the AD curve leftward to $AD_0$. With money wage rates based on the expectation that aggregate demand will be EAD, real GDP falls to $9.5 trillion and the price level falls to 102 as the economy moves to point B. As long as aggregate demand is *expected* to be EAD, there is no change in the money wage rate.

A rational expectations expansion begins when an unanticipated rise in aggregate demand shifts the AD curve rightward from $AD_0$ to $AD_1$. With money wage rates based on the expectation that aggregate demand will be EAD, real GDP increases to $10.5 trillion and the price level rises to 108 as the economy moves to point C. Again, as long as aggregate demand is *expected* to be EAD, there is no change in the money wage rate.

The recession ends when aggregate demand increases again to its expected level. And a larger shock that takes aggregate demand to a level that exceeds $EAD$ brings an expansion. In Fig. 14.4(b), the aggregate demand curve shifts rightward to $AD_1$. Such an increase in aggregate demand might be caused by a speedup in the money growth rate or an export boom. Real GDP now increases to $10.5 trillion, and the price level rises to 108. The economy moves to point $C$. Unemployment is now below the natural rate. But aggregate demand is expected to be at $EAD$, so the money wage rate doesn't change and the short-run aggregate supply curve remains at $SAS$.

Fluctuations in aggregate demand between $AD_0$ and $AD_1$ around expected aggregate demand $EAD$ bring fluctuations in real GDP and the price level between points $B$ and $C$.

The two versions of the rational expectations theory differ in their predictions about the effects of a change in expected aggregate demand. The new classical theory predicts that as soon as expected aggregate demand changes, the money wage rate also changes, so the $SAS$ curve shifts. The new Keynesian theory predicts that the money wage rate changes only gradually when new contracts are made, so the $SAS$ curve moves only slowly. This difference between the two theories is crucial for policy. According to the new classical theory, anticipated policy actions change the price level only and have no effect on real GDP and unemployment. The reason is that when policy is expected to change, the money wage rate changes, so the $SAS$ curve shifts and offsets the effects of the policy action on real GDP. In contrast, in the new Keynesian theory, because the money wage rate changes only when new contracts are made, even anticipated policy actions change real GDP and can be used in an attempt to stabilize the cycle.

Like the monetarist business cycle, these rational expectations cycles are similar to rocking horses. They need an outside force to get them going, but once they are going, the economy rocks around its full employment point. The new classical horse rocks faster and comes to rest more quickly than the new Keynesian horse.

### AS-AD General Theory

All the theories of the business cycle that we've considered can be viewed as particular cases of the more general $AS$-$AD$ theory. In this more general theory, the impulses of both the Keynesian and monetarist theories can change aggregate demand. A multiplier effect makes aggregate demand change by more than any initial change in one of its components. The money wage rate can be viewed as responding to changes in the expected price level. Even if the money wage is flexible, it will change only to the extent to which price level expectations change. As a result, the money wage rate will adjust gradually.

Although in all three types of business cycle theory that we've considered, the cycle is caused by fluctuations in aggregate demand, we cannot rule out the possibility that an occasional aggregate supply shock might occur. A recession could occur because aggregate supply falls. For example, a widespread drought that cuts agricultural production could cause a recession in an economy that has a large agricultural sector. But the aggregate demand theories of the cycle regard aggregate supply shocks as rare rather than normal events. Aggregate demand fluctuations are the normal ongoing sources of fluctuations.

### REVIEW QUIZ

1. What, according to Keynesian theory, causes the business cycle? What are the roles of *animal spirits*, the multiplier, and the sticky money wage rate in this theory?
2. What, according to monetarist theory, causes the business cycle? What are the roles of the Fed and money growth in this theory?
3. What, according to new classical theory and new Keynesian theory, causes the business cycle? What are the roles of rational expectations and unanticipated fluctuations in aggregate demand in these theories?
4. What are the differences between the new classical theory and the new Keynesian theory concerning the money wage rate over the business cycle?

A new theory of the business cycle challenges the mainstream and traditional aggregate demand theories that you've just studied. It is called the real business cycle theory. Let's look at this new theory of the business cycle.

## Real Business Cycle Theory

THE NEWEST THEORY OF THE BUSINESS CYCLE, known as **real business cycle theory** (or RBC theory), regards random fluctuations in productivity as the main source of economic fluctuations. These productivity fluctuations are assumed to result mainly from fluctuations in the pace of technological change, but they might also have other sources, such as international disturbances, climate fluctuations, or natural disasters. The origins of real business cycle theory can be traced to the rational expectations revolution set off by Robert E. Lucas, Jr., but the first demonstrations of the power of this theory were given by Edward Prescott and Finn Kydland and by John Long and Charles Plosser. Today, real business cycle theory is part of a broad research agenda called *dynamic general equilibrium analysis*, and hundreds of young macroeconomists do research on this topic.

Like our study of the aggregate demand theories, we'll explore RBC theory by looking first at its impulse and then at the mechanism that converts that impulse into a cycle in real GDP.

### The RBC Impulse

The *impulse* in RBC theory is the *growth rate of productivity that results from technological change*. RBC theorists believe this impulse to be generated mainly by the process of research and development that leads to the creation and use of new technologies.

Most of the time, technological change is steady and productivity grows at a moderate pace. But sometimes productivity growth speeds up, and occasionally productivity *decreases*—labor becomes less productive, on the average.

A period of rapid productivity growth brings a strong business cycle expansion, and a *decrease* in productivity triggers a recession.

It is easy to understand why technological change brings productivity growth. But how does it *decrease* productivity? All technological change eventually increases productivity. But if initially, technological change makes a sufficient amount of existing capital, especially human capital, obsolete, productivity

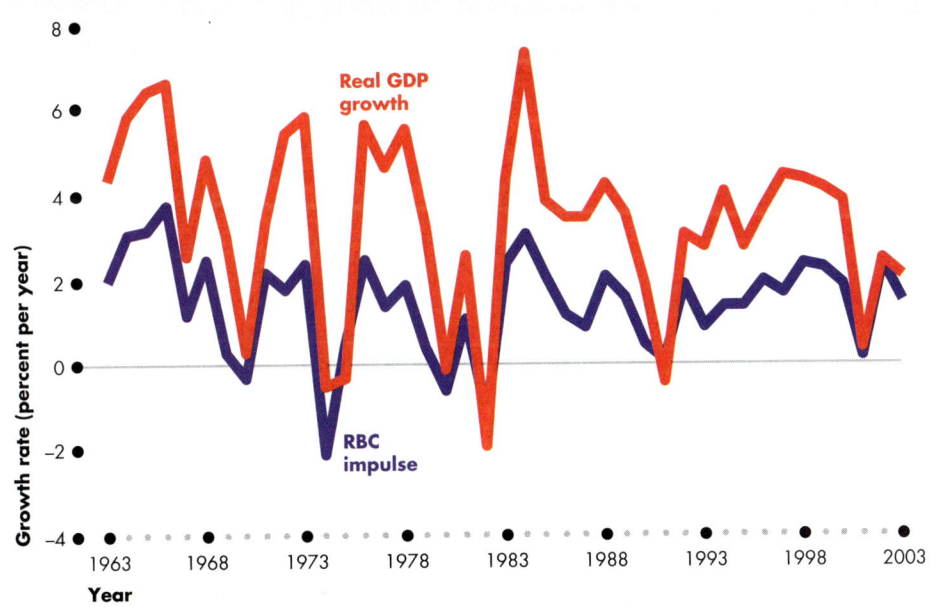

**FIGURE 14.5** The Real Business Cycle Impulse

The real business cycle is caused by changes in technology that bring fluctuations in the growth rate of productivity. The fluctuations in productivity growth shown here are calculated by using growth accounting (the one third rule) to remove the contribution of capital accumulation to productivity growth. Productivity fluctuations are correlated with real GDP fluctuations. Economists are not sure what the productivity variable actually measures or what causes it to fluctuate.

*Source:* Bureau of Economic Analysis and the author's calculations.

temporarily decreases. At such a time, more jobs are destroyed than created and more businesses fail than start up.

To isolate the RBC theory impulse, economists use growth accounting, which is explained in Chapter 9, pp. 211–214. Figure 14.5 shows the RBC impulse for the United States from 1963 through 2003. You can see that fluctuations in productivity growth are correlated with real GDP fluctuations. But this RBC impulse variable is a catch-all, and no one knows what it actually measures or what causes it to fluctuate.

## The RBC Mechanism

According to RBC theory, two immediate effects follow from a change in productivity that gets an expansion or a contraction going:

1. Investment demand changes.
2. The demand for labor changes.

We'll study these effects and their consequences during a recession. In an expansion, they work in the direction opposite to what is described here.

Technological change makes some existing capital obsolete and temporarily decreases productivity. Firms expect the future profits to fall and see their labor productivity falling. With lower profit expectations, they cut back their purchases of new capital, and with lower labor productivity, they plan to lay off some workers. So the initial effect of a temporary fall in productivity is a decrease in investment demand and a decrease in the demand for labor.

Figure 14.6 illustrates these two initial effects of a decrease in productivity. Part (a) shows investment demand, $ID$, and saving supply, $SS$ (both of which are explained in Chapter 8, pp. 191, 193). Initially, investment demand is $ID_0$, and the equilibrium investment and saving are $2 trillion at a real interest rate of 6 percent a year. A decrease in productivity decreases investment demand, and the $ID$ curve shifts leftward to $ID_1$. The real interest rate falls to 4 percent, and investment and saving decrease to $1.7 trillion.

Part (b) shows the demand for labor, $LD$, and the supply of labor, $LS$ (which are explained in Chapter 8, pp. 182–185). Initially, the demand for labor is $LD_0$, and equilibrium employment is 200 billion hours a year at a real wage rate of $35 an hour. The decrease in productivity decreases the demand for labor, and the $LD$ curve shifts leftward to $LD_1$.

Before we can determine the new level of employment and real wage rate, we need to take a ripple effect into account—the key ripple effect in RBC theory.

### The Key Decision: When to Work?

According to RBC theory, people decide *when* to work by doing a cost-benefit calculation. They compare the return from working in the current period with the *expected* return from working in a later period. You make such a comparison every day in school. Suppose your goal in this course is to get an A. To achieve this goal, you work pretty hard most of the time. But during the few days before the midterm and final exams, you work especially hard. Why? Because you believe that the return from studying close to the exam is greater than the return from studying when the exam is a long time away. So during the term, you take time off for the movies and other leisure pursuits, but at exam time, you work every evening and weekend.

Real business cycle theory says that workers behave like you. They work fewer hours, sometimes zero hours, when the real wage rate is temporarily low, and they work more hours when the real wage rate is temporarily high. But to properly compare the current wage rate with the expected future wage rate, workers must use the real interest rate. If the real interest rate is 6 percent a year, a real wage of $1 an hour earned this week will become $1.06 a year from now. If the real wage rate is expected to be $1.05 an hour next year, today's real wage of $1 looks good. By working longer hours now and shorter hours a year from now, a person can get a 1 percent higher real wage. But suppose the real interest rate is 4 percent a year. In this case, $1 earned now is worth $1.04 next year. Working fewer hours now and more next year is the way to get a 1 percent higher real wage.

So the when-to-work decision depends on the real interest rate. The lower the real interest rate, other things remaining the same, the smaller is the supply of labor. Many economists believe this *intertemporal substitution* effect to be of negligible size. RBC theorists believe that the effect is large, and it is the key element in the RBC mechanism.

You saw in Fig. 14.6(a) that the decrease in investment demand lowers the real interest rate. This fall in the real interest rate lowers the return to current work and decreases the supply of labor. In Fig. 14.6(b), the labor supply curve shifts leftward to $LS_1$. The effect of a productivity shock on the demand for

## FIGURE 14.6   Capital and Labor Markets in a Real Business Cycle

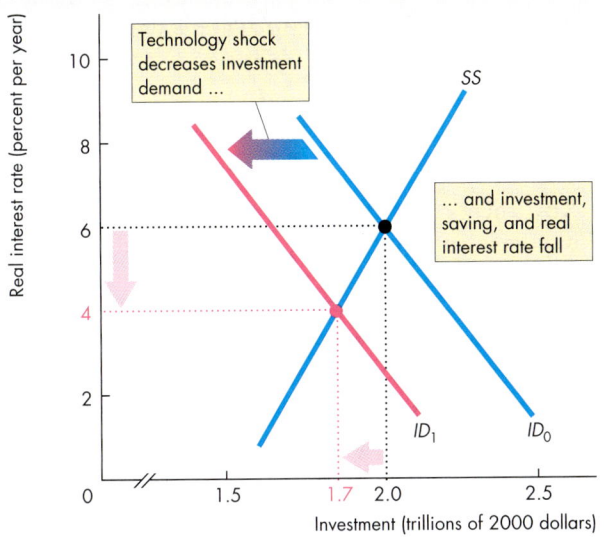

(a) Investment, saving, and interest rate

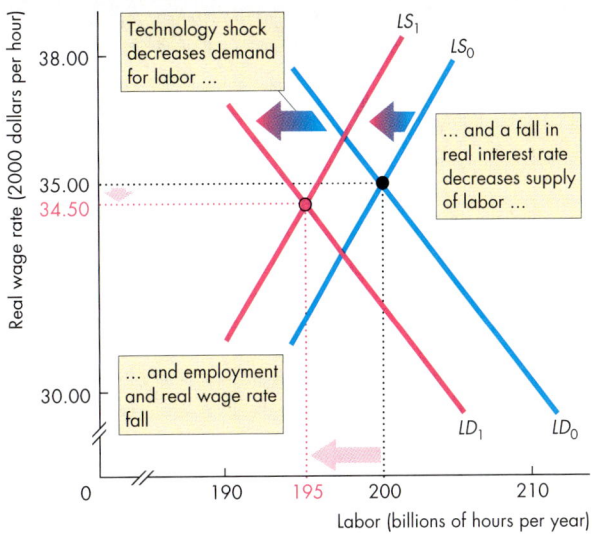

(b) Labor and wage rate

Saving supply is SS (part a), and initially, investment demand is $ID_0$. The real interest rate is 6 percent a year, and saving and investment are $2 trillion. In the labor market (part b), the demand for labor is $LD_0$ and the supply of labor is $LS_0$. The real wage rate is $35 an hour, and employment is 200 billion hours. A technological change temporarily decreases productivity, and both investment demand and the demand for labor decrease. The two demand curves shift leftward to $ID_1$ and $LD_1$. In part (a), the real interest rate falls to 4 percent a year and investment and saving decrease. In part (b), the fall in the real interest rate decreases the supply of labor (the when-to-work decision) and the supply curve shifts leftward to $LS_1$. Employment decreases to 195 billion hours, and the real wage rate falls to $34.50 an hour. A recession is underway.

---

labor is larger than the effect of the fall in the real interest rate on the supply of labor. That is, the LD curve shifts farther leftward than does the LS curve. As a result, the real wage rate falls to $34.50 an hour and the level of employment decreases to 195 billion hours. A recession has begun and is intensifying.

**Real GDP and the Price Level**   The next part of the RBC story traces the consequences of the changes you've just seen for real GDP and the price level. With a decrease in employment, aggregate supply decreases, and with a decrease in investment, aggregate demand decreases. Figure 14.7 illustrates these effects, using the AS-AD model. Initially, the long-run aggregate supply curve is $LAS_0$, and the aggregate demand curve is $AD_0$. The price level is 105, and real GDP is $10 trillion. There is no short-run aggregate supply curve in this figure because in RBC theory, the SAS curve has no meaning. The labor market moves relentlessly toward its equilibrium, and the money wage rate adjusts freely (either upward or downward) to ensure that the real wage rate keeps the quantity of labor demanded equal to the quantity supplied. In RBC theory, unemployment is always at the natural rate, and the natural rate fluctuates over the business cycle because the amount of job search fluctuates.

The decrease in employment decreases total production, and aggregate supply decreases. The LAS curve shifts leftward to $LAS_1$. The decrease in investment decreases aggregate demand, and the AD curve shifts leftward to $AD_1$. The price level falls to 102, and real GDP decreases to $9.8 trillion. The economy has gone through a recession.

**What Happened to Money?**   The name *real* business cycle theory is no accident. It reflects the central prediction of the theory. Real things, not nominal or monetary things, cause the business cycle. If the

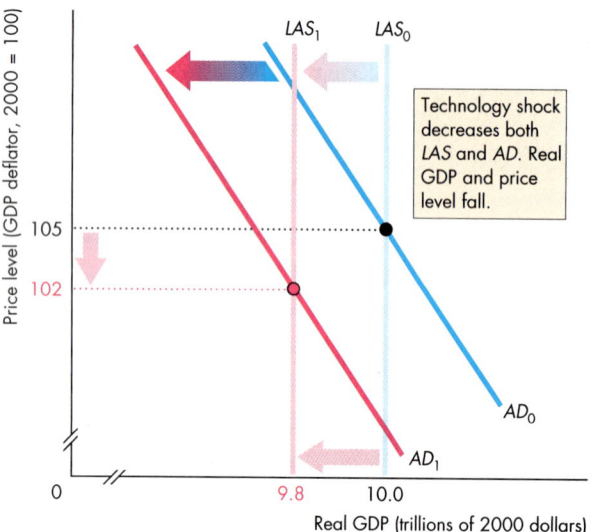

**FIGURE 14.7** AS-AD in a Real Business Cycle

Initially, the long-run aggregate supply curve is $LAS_0$, and the aggregate demand curve is $AD_0$. Real GDP is $10 trillion (which equals potential GDP), and the price level is 105. There is no SAS curve in RBC theory because the money wage rate is flexible. The technological change described in Fig. 30.6 temporarily decreases potential GDP, and the LAS curve shifts leftward to $LAS_1$. The fall in investment demand decreases aggregate demand, and the AD curve shifts leftward to $AD_1$. Real GDP falls to $9.8 trillion, and the price level falls to 102. The economy has gone into recession.

pp. 211–214. There, we focused on slow-changing trends in productivity growth. Real business cycle theory uses the same idea but says that there are frequent shocks to productivity that are mostly positive but that are occasionally negative.

## Criticisms of Real Business Cycle Theory

RBC theory is controversial, and when economists discuss it, they often generate more heat than light. Its detractors claim that its basic assumptions are just too incredible. Money wages *are* sticky, they claim, so to assume otherwise is at odds with a clear fact. Intertemporal substitution is too weak, they say, to account for large fluctuations in labor supply and employment with small real wage rate changes.

But what really kills the RBC story, say most economists, is an implausible impulse. Technology shocks are not capable of creating the swings in productivity that growth accounting reveals. These swings in productivity are caused by something, they concede, but they are as likely to be caused by *changes in aggregate demand* as by technology. If the fluctuations in productivity are caused by aggregate demand fluctuations, then the traditional aggregate demand theories are needed to explain them. Fluctuations in productivity do not cause the cycle but are caused by it!

Building on this theme, the critics point out that the so-called productivity fluctuations that growth accounting measures are correlated with changes in the growth rate of money and other indicators of changes in aggregate demand.

## Defense of Real Business Cycle Theory

The defenders of RBC theory claim that the theory works. It explains the macroeconomic facts about the business cycle and is consistent with the facts about economic growth. In effect, a single theory explains *both growth and cycles*. The growth accounting exercise that explains slowly changing trends also explains the more frequent business cycle swings. Its defenders also claim that RBC theory is consistent with a wide range of *micro*economic evidence about labor supply decisions, labor demand and investment demand decisions, and information on the distribution of income between labor and capital.

RBC theorists acknowledge that money and the business cycle are correlated. That is, rapid money

quantity of money changes, aggregate demand changes. But if there is no real change—with no change in the use of resources and no change in potential GDP—the change in the quantity of money changes only the price level. In real business cycle theory, this outcome occurs because the aggregate supply curve is the LAS curve, which pins real GDP down at potential GDP, so when AD changes, only the price level changes.

**Cycles and Growth** The shock that drives the business cycle of RBC theory is the same as the force that generates economic growth: technological change. On the average, as technology advances, productivity grows. But it grows at an uneven pace. You saw this fact when you studied growth accounting in Chapter 9,

growth and expansion go together, and slow money growth and recession go together. But, they argue, causation does not run from money to real GDP as the traditional aggregate demand theories state. Instead, they view causation as running from real GDP to money—so-called reverse causation. In a recession, the initial fall in investment demand that lowers the interest rate decreases the demand for bank loans and lowers the profitability of banking. So banks increase their reserves and decrease their loans. The quantity of bank deposits and hence the quantity of money decrease. This reverse causation is responsible for the correlation between money growth and real GDP, according to real business cycle theory.

Its defenders also argue that the RBC view is significant because it at least raises the possibility that the business cycle is efficient. The business cycle does not signal an economy that is misbehaving; it is business as usual. If this view is correct, it means that policy designed to smooth the cycle is misguided. Only by taking out the peaks can the troughs be smoothed out. But peaks are bursts of investment to take advantage of new technologies in a timely way. So smoothing the cycle means delaying the benefits of new technologies.

### REVIEW QUIZ

1 According to real business cycle theory, what causes the business cycle? What is the role of fluctuations in the rate of technological change?
2 According to real business cycle theory, how does a fall in productivity growth influence investment demand, the real interest rate, the demand for labor, the supply of labor, employment, and the real wage rate?
3 According to real business cycle theory, how does a fall in productivity growth influence long-run aggregate supply, aggregate demand, real GDP, and the price level?

You've now reviewed the main theories of the business cycle. Your next task is to examine some actual business cycles. We'll focus on three episodes: the expansion of the 1990s, the recession of 2001, and the Great Depression of the 1930s.

# Expansion and Recession During the 1990s and 2000s

IN THE THEORIES OF THE BUSINESS CYCLE THAT you've studied, recessions and expansions can be triggered by a variety of forces, some on the aggregate demand side and some on the aggregate supply side. We'll study the events and the processes at work during two recent episodes:

- The U.S. expansion of the 1990s
- The U.S. recession of 2001

## The U.S. Expansion of the 1990s

From March 1991 through March 2001, the U.S. economy enjoyed 120 months of uninterrupted expansion, the longest period of sustained expansion in the nation's history and more than a year longer than the previous all-time record of the 1960s. Real GDP grew by 40 percent during this period. What caused this long and strong expansion?

### Productivity Growth in the Information Age

The most significant feature of the 1990s was an explosion in the use of computers. The growth of the Internet is the single most visible consequence of this explosion. But it is just one of many transformations of economic life that occurred during the 1990s.

The personal computer changed the way we write, keep financial and other records, and communicate with each other. The microprocessor that is at the heart of the PC has also, in other specialized forms, revolutionized the way we listen to music, drive a car, use a camera, get cash from the bank, make a microwave dinner, and check out at the supermarket. It has revolutionized even more the way firms produce goods and services.

All this technological change created profit opportunities but required a large amount of investment to realize those profits. Also, most of the world shared in this technological revolution. And its global nature brought a large increase in U.S. exports.

The increase in investment and exports, with their multiplier effects on consumption expenditure, brought a large and persistent increase in aggregate demand.

The hot pace of technological change brought a correspondingly large increase in aggregate supply by increasing capital and increasing productivity.

**Fiscal Policy and Monetary Policy** The expansion of the 1990s was to some degree made possible by the fiscal policy and monetary policy that accompanied it. The expansion was not caused by these policies, but they encouraged sustained real GDP growth.

**Aggregate Demand and Aggregate Supply During the Expansion** Figure 14.8 shows the 1990s expansion using the *AS-AD* model. In 1991, the economy was on aggregate demand curve $AD_{91}$ and short-run aggregate supply curve $SAS_{91}$ with real GDP at $7.1 trillion and the price level at 84. The long-run aggregate supply curve was $LAS_{91}$, and potential GDP exceeded real GDP. There was a recessionary gap. By 2001, capital accumulation, increased labor hours, and technological change had increased potential GDP to $9.9 trillion and the long-run aggregate supply curve had shifted to $LAS_{01}$. The large increase in investment demand and exports with their multiplier effects increased aggregate demand, and the aggregate demand curve shifted to $AD_{01}$.

The increase in potential GDP increased short-run aggregate supply, but a higher money wage rate decreased short-run aggregate supply. The net effect of these effects was a small decrease in short-run aggregate supply to $SAS_{01}$. Real GDP increased to $9.9 trillion—equal to potential GDP—and the price level increased to 102.

**A Real Business Cycle Expansion Phase** The description of the expansion of the 1990s that we've just reviewed looks exactly like the events that real business cycle theory predicts. A strong and sustained burst of technological change brought rising productivity. The result was an increase in investment demand, an increase in the demand for labor, and an increase in the supply of labor. The real interest rate increased, and the real wage rate increased but only slightly.

The increases in the demand for labor and supply of labor brought a falling unemployment rate. The lower unemployment rate is a lower *natural* rate and not a sign that the economy is overheating.

### The U.S. Recession of 2001

The 2001 recession was the mildest recession on record. It turned out to be so mild through 2001 that it barely qualified as a recession. If the NBER dating

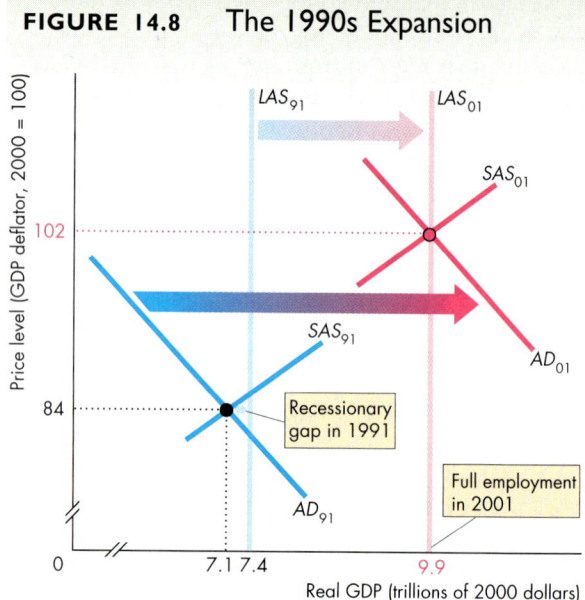

**FIGURE 14.8  The 1990s Expansion**

In 1991, the economy was on its aggregate demand curve, $AD_{91}$, and its short-run aggregate supply curve, $SAS_{91}$, with real GDP at $7.1 trillion and a price level of 84. Potential GDP exceeded real GDP and there was a recessionary gap. Technological advances increased both aggregate demand and aggregate supply. The aggregate demand curve shifted to $AD_{01}$, and the long-run aggregate supply curve shifted to $LAS_{01}$. But a higher money wage rate shifted the short-run aggregate supply curve to $SAS_{01}$. The result of these shifts was an increase in real GDP to $9.9 trillion (equal to potential GDP) and an increase in the price level to 102.

committee ever felt tempted to cancel a recession, this one was a prime candidate!

**Absence of External Shocks** The recession did not originate from any clearly visible external shocks. The huge shock of the September 11 attacks, while they strongly influenced the economy in the final part of 2001, could not have been at work at the onset of the recession.

**Fiscal Policy** There were no major fiscal policy shocks to trigger the recession. On the contrary, six months after the recession began, government purchases increased to strengthen defense and security in the wake of September 11. Tax revenues decreased and the deficit increased as the normal automatic stabilizers began to operate (see Chapter 15, p. 379).

**Monetary Policy** There were no major monetary policy shocks to trigger the recession, although the Fed had raised interest rates very slightly and held the M2 money growth rate steady during 2000.

**Real Business Cycle Effects** The real business cycle impulse (see Fig. 14.5, p. 345) pointed downward strongly during 2001. The growth rate of productivity arising from technological change and other factors slowed from 1.7 percent in 2000 to 0.5 percent in 2001. This slowdown would have been enough to slow real GDP growth rate but not to bring the economy to a full-blown recession.

The exact technological events that brought a slowing of the pace of productivity growth are hard to identify with certainty. But it seems likely that much of the slowdown came in the overgrown "dot-com" sector. Judging by the movements in stock prices, it was the high-tech sector generally that was hit hardest during the slowdown.

Whatever the exact source of the productivity growth slowdown, it hit investment hard. Business investment fell, and this was the major source of the decrease in aggregate demand. No other component of aggregate demand fell.

**Labor Market and Productivity** Although real GDP barely fell, employment and aggregate hours did fall and the unemployment rate increased. Labor productivity increased, and so did the real wage rate.

The tendency for labor productivity and the real wage rate to rise during a recession is not unusual. But the strength of these effects during the 2001 recession was unusual.

The money wage rate rose by 4 percent during 2001, and the real wage rate rose by 3.4 percent. The slowdown in productivity growth and the strong rise in the money wage rate decreased short-run aggregate supply during 2001.

**Aggregate Demand and Aggregate Supply**
Figure 14.9 illustrates the 2001 recession in terms of the shifting aggregate demand and aggregate supply curves. In the first quarter of 2001, the economy was on aggregate demand curve $AD_{Q1}$ and short-run aggregate supply curve $SAS_{Q1}$ with real GDP at $9.88 trillion and the price level at 101.4. In the second quarter of 2001, the short-run aggregate supply curve had shifted to $SAS_{Q2}$ and the aggregate demand curve had shifted to $AD_{Q2}$. Real GDP had decreased to $9.87 trillion. The price level had increased to 102.2.

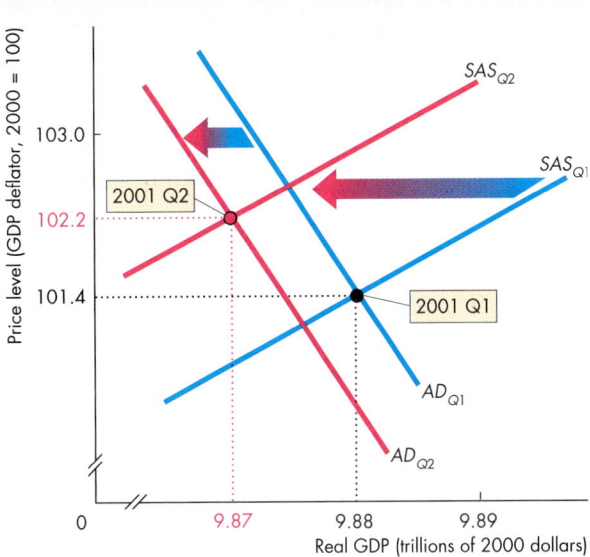

**FIGURE 14.9 The 2001 Recession**

In the first quarter of 2001, the economy was on its aggregate demand curve, $AD_{Q1}$, and its short-run aggregate supply curve, $SAS_{Q1}$, with real GDP at $9.88 trillion and a price level of 101.4. A rise in the money wage rate decreased aggregate supply and shifted the SAS curve to $SAS_{Q2}$. A fall in investment decreased aggregate demand and shifted the AD curve to $AD_{Q2}$. The combination of a decrease in both aggregate supply and aggregate demand put the economy into a mild recession.

### REVIEW QUIZ

1. What factors brought the long and strong expansion in the United States during the 1990s?
2. What factors contributed to the recession of 2001?

You've now seen how business cycle theory can be used to interpret the expansion of the 1990s and the recession of 2001. But can we use business cycle theory to explain the greatest of recessions—the Great Depression? Let's find out.

## The Great Depression

THE LATE 1920S WERE YEARS OF ECONOMIC boom. New houses and apartments were built on an unprecedented scale, new firms were created, and the nation's capital expanded. At the beginning of 1929, U.S. real GDP exceeded potential GDP and the unemployment rate was a low 3.2 percent. But as that eventful year unfolded, increasing signs of economic weakness began to appear. The most dramatic events occurred in October when the stock market collapsed, losing more than one third of its value in two weeks. The four years that followed were ones of monstrous economic depression.

Figure 14.10 shows the dimensions of the Great Depression. On the eve of the Great Depression in 1929, the economy was on aggregate demand curve $AD_{29}$ and short-run aggregate supply curve $SAS_{29}$. Real GDP was $865 billion (2000 dollars), and the price level was 12.0.

In 1930, there was a widespread expectation that the price level would fall, and the money wage rate fell. With a lower money wage rate, the short-run aggregate supply curve shifted from $SAS_{29}$ to $SAS_{30}$. But increased pessimism and uncertainty decreased both investment and the demand for consumer durables, and aggregate demand decreased to $AD_{30}$. In 1930, real GDP decreased to $791 billion (a 9 percent decrease) and the price level fell to 11.5 (a 4 percent fall).

In a normal recession, the economy might have remained below full employment for a year or so and then started to expand. But the recession of 1930 was not a normal one. In 1930 and the next two years, the economy was further bombarded with huge negative demand shocks (the sources of which we'll look at in a moment). The aggregate demand curve shifted leftward all the way to $AD_{33}$. With a depressed economy, the price level was expected to fall, and wages fell in line with those expectations. The money wage fell from 55¢ an hour in 1930 to 44¢ an hour by 1933. As a result of lower wages, the aggregate supply curve shifted from $SAS_{30}$ to $SAS_{33}$. But the size of the shift of the short-run aggregate supply curve was much less than the decrease in aggregate demand. As a result, the aggregate demand curve and the short-run aggregate supply curve intersected in 1933 at a real GDP of $636 billion (a decrease of 26 percent from 1929) and a price level of 8.9 (a decrease of 26 percent from 1929).

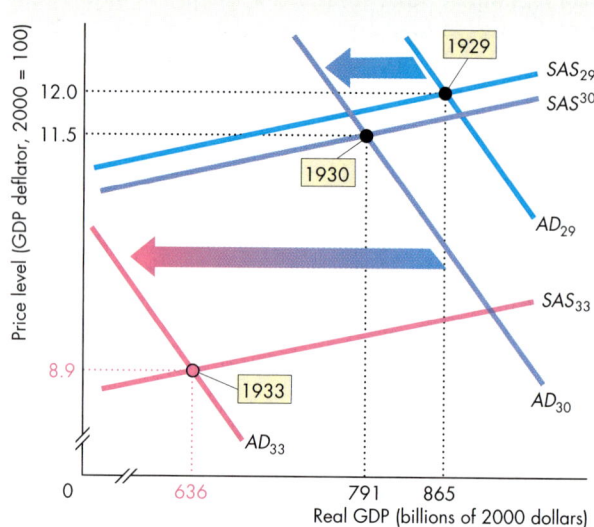

FIGURE 14.10 The Great Depression

In 1929, real GDP was $865 billion and the price level was 12.0—at the intersection of $AD_{29}$ and $SAS_{29}$. Increased pessimism and uncertainty resulted in a decrease in investment, and aggregate demand decreased to $AD_{30}$. Capital increased and wages decreased, so the short-run aggregate supply curve shifted to $SAS_{30}$. Real GDP and the price level fell. In the next three years, decreases in the quantity of money and investment decreased aggregate demand, shifting the aggregate demand curve to $AD_{33}$. Again, to some degree, the decrease in aggregate demand was anticipated, so the money wage rate fell and the short-run aggregate supply curve shifted to $SAS_{33}$. By 1933, real GDP had fallen to $636 billion (74 percent of its 1929 level) and the price level had fallen to 8.9 (74 percent of its 1929 level).

Although the Great Depression brought enormous hardship, the distribution of that hardship was uneven. Twenty-five percent of the work force had no jobs at all. Also at that time, there were virtually no organized social security and unemployment programs in place. So for many families, there was virtually no income. But the pocketbooks of those who kept their jobs barely noticed the Great Depression. It is true that wages fell from 57¢ an hour in 1929 to 44¢ an hour in 1933. But at the same time, the price level fell by a larger percentage, so real wages actually increased. Thus people who had jobs became better off during the Great Depression.

You can begin to appreciate the magnitude of the Great Depression if you compare it with the two most recent recessions. Between mid-1990 and mid-1991, real GDP fell by 0.6 percent. And during the 2001 recession, real GDP also fell by about 0.6 percent. A hypothetical 2003 Great Depression would lower real GDP by 26 percent to its mid-1990s level.

## Why the Great Depression Happened

The late 1920s were years of economic boom, but they were also years of increasing uncertainty. The main source of increased uncertainty was international. The world economy was going through tumultuous times. The patterns of world trade were changing as Britain, the traditional economic powerhouse of the world, began its period of relative economic decline and new economic powers such as Japan began to emerge. International currency fluctuations and the introduction of restrictive trade policies (see Chapter 17) by many countries further increased the uncertainty faced by firms. There was also domestic uncertainty arising from the fact that there had been such a strong boom in recent years, especially in the capital goods sector and housing. No one believed that this boom would last forever, but many people thought it had a lot farther to run, and there was great uncertainty about how demand would change.

This environment of uncertainty led to a slowdown in consumer spending, especially on new homes and household appliances. By the fall of 1929, the uncertainty had reached a critical level and contributed to the stock market crash. The stock market crash, in turn, heightened people's fears about economic prospects in the foreseeable future. Fear fed fear. Investment collapsed. The building industry almost disappeared. An industry that had been operating flat out just two years earlier was now building virtually no new houses and apartments. It was this drop in investment and a drop in consumer spending on durables that led to the initial leftward shift of the aggregate demand curve from $AD_{29}$ to $AD_{30}$ in Fig. 14.10.

At this stage, what became the Great Depression was no worse than many previous recessions had been. What distinguishes the Great Depression from previous recessions are the events that followed between 1930 and 1933. But economists, even to this day, have not come to agreement on how to interpret those events. One view, argued by Peter Temin,[1] is that spending continued to fall for a wide variety of reasons—including a continuation of increasing pessimism and uncertainty. According to Temin's view, the continued contraction resulted from a collapse of expenditure that was independent of the decrease in the quantity of money. The investment demand curve shifted leftward. Milton Friedman and Anna J. Schwartz have argued that the continuation of the contraction was almost exclusively the result of the subsequent worsening of financial and monetary conditions.[2] According to Friedman and Schwartz, it was a severe cut in the quantity of money that lowered aggregate demand, prolonging the contraction and deepening the depression.

Although there is disagreement about the causes of the contraction phase of the Great Depression, the disagreement is not about the elements at work but about the degree of importance attached to each. Everyone agrees that increased pessimism and uncertainty lowered investment demand, and everyone agrees that there was a massive contraction of the quantity of real money. Temin and his supporters assign primary importance to the fall in autonomous expenditure and secondary importance to the fall in the quantity of money. Friedman and Schwartz and their supporters assign primary responsibility to the quantity of money and regard the other factors as being of limited importance.

Let's look at the contraction of aggregate demand a bit more closely. Between 1930 and 1933, nominal money decreased by 20 percent. This decrease in the quantity of money was not directly induced by the Fed's actions. The *monetary base* (currency in circulation and bank reserves) hardly fell at all. But the bank deposits component of money suffered an enormous collapse. It did so primarily because a large number of banks failed. Before the Great Depression, increasing stock prices and booming business conditions fueled an expansion of bank loans. But after the stock market crash and the downturn, many borrowers found themselves in hard economic times. They

---

[1] Peter Temin, *Did Monetary Forces Cause the Great Depression?* (New York: W.W. Norton, 1976).
[2] Milton Friedman and Anna J. Schwartz developed this explanation in *A Monetary History of the United States: 1867–1960* (Princeton, N.J.: Princeton University Press, 1963), Chapter 22.

could not pay the interest on their loans, and they could not meet the agreed repayment schedules. Banks had deposits that exceeded the realistic value of the loans that they had made. When depositors withdrew funds from the banks, the banks lost reserves. Many of them simply couldn't meet their depositors' demands to be repaid.

Bank failures feed on themselves and create additional failures. Seeing banks fail, people become anxious to protect themselves and so take their money out of the banks. Such were the events of 1930. The quantity of notes and coins in circulation increased, and the volume of bank deposits declined. But the very action of taking money out of the bank to protect one's wealth accentuated the process of banking failure. Banks were increasingly short of cash and unable to meet their obligations.

What role did the stock market crash of 1929 play in producing the Great Depression? It certainly created an atmosphere of fear and panic and probably also contributed to the overall air of uncertainty that dampened investment spending. It also reduced the wealth of stockholders, encouraging them to cut back on their consumption spending. But the direct effect of the stock market crash on consumption, although a contributing factor to the Great Depression, was not the major source of the drop in aggregate demand. It was the collapse in investment arising from increased uncertainty that brought the 1930 decline in aggregate demand.

The stock market crash was a predictor of severe recession. It reflected the expectations of stockholders concerning future profit prospects. As those expectations became pessimistic, people sold their stocks. There were more sellers than buyers, and the prices of stocks were bid lower and lower. That is, the behavior the stock market was a consequence of expectations about future profitability, and those expectations were lowered as a result of increased uncertainty.

## Can It Happen Again?

Because we have an incomplete understanding of the causes of the Great Depression, we cannot be sure whether such an event will happen again. The economic turmoil of the 1920s that preceded the Depression certainly can happen again. But there are some significant differences between the current economy and that of the 1930s that make a severe depression much less likely today than it was 60 years ago. The most significant features of the economy that make severe depression less likely today are

- Bank deposit insurance
- The Fed's role as lender of last resort
- Taxes and government spending
- Multi-income families

Let's examine each of these in turn.

**Bank Deposit Insurance**   As a result of the Great Depression, the federal government established, in the 1930s, the Federal Deposit Insurance Corporation (FDIC). The FDIC insures bank deposits for up to $100,000 per deposit, so most depositors need no longer fear bank failure. If a bank fails, the FDIC pays the deposit holders. With federally insured bank deposits, the key event that turned a fairly ordinary recession into the Great Depression is most unlikely to occur. It was the fear of bank failure that caused people to withdraw their deposits from banks. The aggregate consequence of these individually rational acts was to cause the very bank failures that were feared. With deposit insurance, most depositors have nothing to lose if a bank fails and so have no incentive to take actions that are likely to give rise to that failure.

Some recent events reinforce this conclusion. With massive failures of S&Ls in the 1980s and with bank failures in New England in 1990 and 1991, there was no tendency for depositors to panic and withdraw their funds in a self-reinforcing run on similar institutions.

**Lender of Last Resort**   The Fed is the lender of last resort in the U.S. economy. If a single bank is short of reserves, it can borrow reserves from other banks. If the entire banking system is short of reserves, banks can borrow from the Fed. By making reserves available (at a suitable interest rate), the Fed is able to make the quantity of reserves in the banking system respond flexibly to the demand for those reserves. Bank failure can be prevented or at least contained to cases in which bad management practices are the source of the problem. Widespread failures of the type that occurred in the Great Depression can be prevented.

It is now generally agreed that the Fed made a serious mistake in its handling of monetary policy during the Great Depression. With one eye on the international situation, the Fed *increased* the discount rate sharply from 1.5 percent to 3.5 percent just when the banks needed to borrow more. It was only long after the event, when Friedman and Schwartz examined the contraction years of the Great Depression, that economists came to realize that the Fed would have had to *decrease* the discount rate and *increase* the monetary base to have prevented the intensification of the contraction. Now that this lesson has been learned and there is such widespread agreement about the matter, there is at least some chance that the mistake will not be repeated.

The last time the Fed was confronted by a similar problem, although on a much smaller scale, was in October 1987. At that time, a severe stock market crash triggered fears of a new Great Depression. The Fed Chairman, Alan Greenspan, told the U.S. banking and financial community that the Fed had both the ability and the intent to maintain calm financial conditions and to supply sufficient reserves to ensure that the banking system did not begin to contract.

**Taxes and Government Spending** The government sector was a much smaller part of the economy in 1929 than it is today. On the eve of that earlier recession, government purchases of goods and services were less than 9 percent of GDP. Today, government purchases exceed 18 percent of GDP. Government transfer payments were less than 6 percent of GDP in 1929. Today, they exceed 15 percent of GDP.

A larger level of government purchases of goods and services means that when recession hits, a large component of aggregate demand does not decline. But government transfer payments are the most sensitive economic stabilizer. When the economy goes into recession and depression, more people qualify for unemployment compensation and social security. As a consequence, although disposable income decreases, the extent of the decrease is moderated by the existence of such programs. Consumption expenditure, in turn, does not decline by as much as it would in the absence of such government programs. The limited decline in consumption spending further limits the overall decrease in aggregate expenditure, thereby limiting the magnitude of an economic downturn.

**Multi-Income Families** At the time of the Great Depression, families with more than one wage earner were much less common than they are today. The labor force participation rate in 1929 was around 55 percent. Today, it is 67 percent. So even if the unemployment rate increased to around 25 percent today, close to 50 percent of the adult population would actually have jobs. During the Great Depression, less than 40 percent of the adult population had work. Multi-income families have greater security than single-income families. The chance of both (or all) income earners in a family losing their jobs simultaneously is much lower than the chance of a single earner losing work. With greater family income security, family consumption is likely to be less sensitive to fluctuations in family income that are seen as temporary. So when aggregate income falls, it might not induce a cut in consumption. For example, during the OPEC recession, as real GDP fell, personal consumption expenditure actually increased. And during the 2001 recession when real GDP fell by $53 billion, consumption expenditure increased by $79 billion.

For the four reasons we have just reviewed, it appears that the economy has better shock-absorbing characteristics today than it had in the 1920s and 1930s. Even if there is a collapse of confidence, leading to a fall in investment, today's shock absorbers will not translate that initial shock into the large and prolonged fall in real GDP and rise in unemployment that occurred more than 60 years ago.

Because the economy is now more immune to severe recession than it was in the 1930s, even a stock market crash of the magnitude that occurred in 1987 had barely noticeable effects on spending. A crash of a similar magnitude in 1929 resulted in the near collapse of housing investment and consumer durable purchases. In the period following the 1987 stock market crash, investment and spending on durable goods hardly changed. None of this is to say that there might not be a deep recession or even a Great Depression in the twenty-first century. But it would take a very severe shock to trigger one.

◆ We have now completed our study of the business cycle. Before you leave this topic, take a look at *Reading Between the Lines* on pp. 356–357, which provides a further examination of the U.S. economy during the expansion of 2002–2003.

We have also completed our study of the science of macroeconomics and learned about the influences on long-term economic growth and inflation as well as the business cycle. We have discovered that these issues pose huge policy challenges. How can we speed up the rate of economic growth while at the same time keep inflation low and avoid big swings of the business cycle? Our task in the next chapter is to study these macroeconomic policy challenges and the debate that surrounds them.

# READING BETWEEN THE LINES

## *Explaining the 2002–2003 Expansion*

**THE WALL STREET JOURNAL, OCTOBER 31, 2003**

### Economy Turned In Its Best Growth Rate In Nearly Two Decades

The U.S. economy shot out of the doldrums to its best quarterly growth rate in nearly two decades, giving a potentially powerful political lift to President Bush despite chronic weakness in the job market. ...

Spending by consumers, exports and residential construction all registered sharp gains. But the news economists found most significant was that investment by businesses grew at an 11% annual clip, the fastest rate since early 2000.

The burst of growth was in different measures both an economic and a political achievement for President Bush. ...

Mr. Bush isn't out of the economic woods yet. For voters, jobs and income matter far more than GDP statistics—and by those measures, the president's record is still weak. The unemployment rate remains near a nine-year high, and even during the third-quarter boom, the economy shed 41,000 jobs.

Since Mr. Bush took office, businesses have slashed a whopping 2.7 million jobs, a record that—Democrats never tire of pointing out—is the worst for any president since Herbert Hoover presided over the Great Depression. Even under the most optimistic forecasts for the next year, the economy will likely end up having lost jobs during all of Mr. Bush's first term. "A jobless economic recovery is a little bit like going on a diet and gaining weight—what's the point?" says Clark aide Chris Lehane.

Because businesses are operating more efficiently and getting more output out of each worker, rapid economic growth may not guarantee a better job market soon. "Any good news on the economy is welcome, but it would be premature for President Bush to declare 'mission accomplished' on the economic front while we still have a jobless recovery and a huge jobs deficit to erase," said Rep. Pete Stark of California, ranking Democrat on the Joint Economic Committee. ...

"It's the old Ronald Reagan question—are you better or worse off than when George Bush took office," says Mark Penn, Mr. Lieberman's pollster. "That is still going to work against him."

....

©2003 The Wall Street Journal. Reprinted with permission. Further reproduction prohibited.

### Essence of the Story

■ The U.S. economy had its best quarterly growth rate in nearly twenty years in the third quarter of 2003.

■ Consumer spending, exports, residential construction, and business investment all grew rapidly.

■ Businesses are getting more output out of each worker, so rapid economic growth might not create more jobs.

■ Since President Bush took office, businesses have cut 2.7 million jobs–the worst since the Great Depression.

■ Even under optimistic forecasts, the economy might end up having lost jobs during all of Mr. Bush's first term.

## Economic Analysis

- The expansion of real GDP during the third quarter of 2003 was part of an expansion that began at a trough in the third quarter of 2001.

- Figure 1 traces this expansion using the AS-AD model.

- In the third quarter of 2001, aggregate demand was $AD_0$, long-run aggregate supply was $LAS_0$, and short-run aggregate supply was $SAS_0$.

- Real GDP was $9,834 billion, and the price level was 102. Potential GDP was $10,070 billion, so there was a recessionary gap of $236 billion. (All values are in 2000 dollars.)

- By the third quarter of 2003, aggregate demand had increased to $AD_1$, long-run aggregate supply to $LAS_1$, and short-run aggregate supply to $SAS_1$.

- Real GDP was $10,493 billion, and the price level was 106. Potential GDP was $10,693 billion, so there was still a recessionary gap but a bit smaller than in 2001 at $200 billion.

- Figure 2 shows the components of aggregate demand that increased most over these two years of the expansion. They were personal consumption and government purchases.

- Business investment increased only modestly. And although exports increased, so did imports, and net exports actually fell.

- The news article says that real GDP increased because labor productivity increased but the number of jobs fell. This description is not correct.

- GDP is produced by employed and self-employed persons.

- Figure 3 shows the facts about employment. The number of people with jobs decreased (blue line), but total employment increased (red line) during 2002 and 2003. By October 2003, employment exceeded its level at the beginning of 2001.

- Labor productivity did grow during the expansion, but not at an unusually rapid rate.

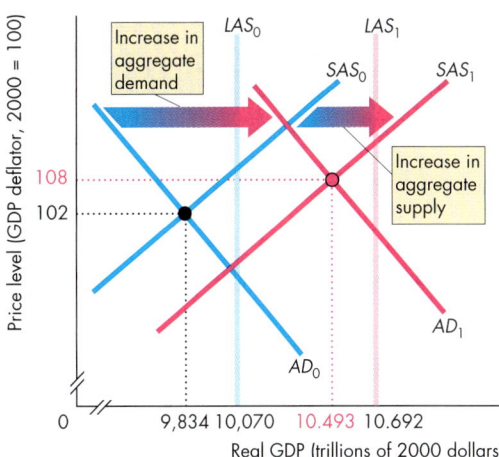

Figure 1 *AS* and *AD* during 2002–2003 expansion

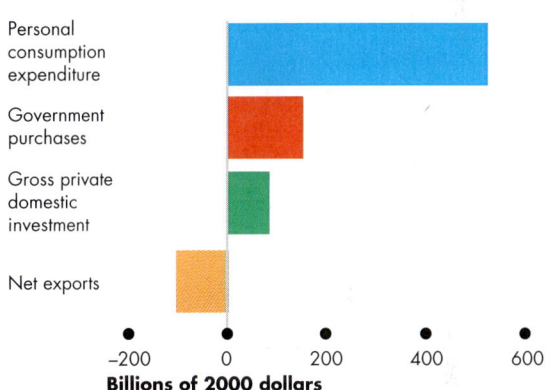

Figure 2 The components of aggregate demand

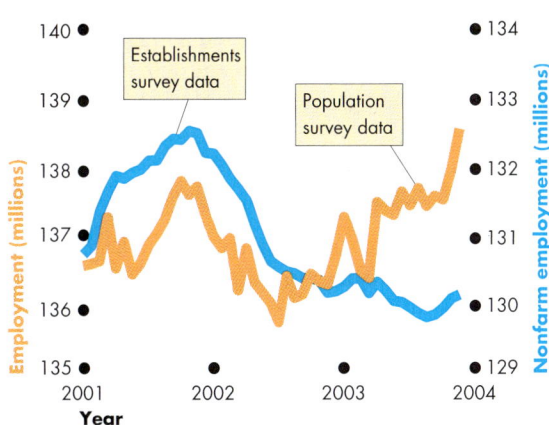

Figure 3 Two views of the jobless recovery

# SUMMARY

## KEY POINTS

### Cycle Patterns, Impulses, and Mechanisms (pp. 336–338)

- Since 1920, there have been 16 recessions and expansions.
- The Great Depression was the most severe contraction of real GDP, and the post–World War II recessions have been milder than the prewar recessions.

### Aggregate Demand Theories of the Business Cycle (pp. 338–344)

- Keynesian business cycle theory identifies volatile expectations about future sales and profits as the main source of economic fluctuations.
- Monetarist business cycle theory identifies fluctuations in the quantity of money as the main source of economic fluctuations.
- Rational expectations theory identifies unanticipated fluctuations in aggregate demand as the main source of economic fluctuations.

### Real Business Cycle Theory (pp. 345–349)

- In real business cycle (RBC) theory, economic fluctuations are caused by fluctuations in the influence of technological change on productivity growth.
- A temporary slowdown in the pace of technological change decreases investment demand and both the demand for labor and supply of labor.

### Expansion and Recession During the 1990s and 2000s (pp. 349–351)

- The 1990s expansion resulted from a large increase in the rate of productivity growth that increased investment demand and the demand for and supply of labor and that increased both aggregate demand and aggregate supply.
- The 2001 recession was accompanied by a slowdown in the growth rate of productivity from technological change, which was probably concentrated in the high-tech sectors.

### The Great Depression (pp. 352–355)

- The Great Depression started with increased uncertainty, which brought a fall in investment (especially in housing) and spending on consumer durables.
- There followed a near total collapse of the financial system. Banks failed, and the quantity of money decreased, resulting in a continued fall in aggregate demand.
- The Great Depression itself produced a series of reforms that make a repeat of such a depression much less likely.

## KEY FIGURES

Figure 14.1   A Keynesian Recession, 339
Figure 14.2   A Keynesian Expansion, 340
Figure 14.3   A Monetarist Business Cycle, 341
Figure 14.4   A Rational Expectations Business Cycle, 343
Figure 14.6   Capital and Labor Markets in a Real Business Cycle, 347
Figure 14.7   *AS-AD* in a Real Business Cycle, 348
Figure 14.8   The 1990s Expansion, 350
Figure 14.9   The 2001 Recession, 351

## KEY TERMS

Keynesian theory of the business cycle, 338
Monetarist theory of the business cycle, 340
New classical theory of the business cycle, 342
New Keynesian theory of the business cycle, 342
Real business cycle theory, 345

# PROBLEMS

*1. The figure shows the economy of Virtual Reality. When the economy is in a long-run equilibrium, it is at points *B*, *F*, and *J*. When a recession occurs in Virtual Reality, the economy moves away from these points to one of the other points identified in each of the three parts of the figure.
   a. If the Keynesian theory is the correct explanation for the recession, to which points does the economy move?
   b. If the monetarist theory is the correct explanation for the recession, to which points does the economy move?
   c. If the new classical rational expectations theory is the correct explanation for the recession, to which points does the economy move?
   d. If the new Keynesian rational expectations theory is the correct explanation for the recession, to which points does the economy move?
   e. If real business cycle theory is the correct explanation for the recession, to which points does the economy move?

2. The figure also shows the economy of Vital Signs. When the economy is in a long-run equilibrium, it is at points *A*, *E*, and *I*. When an expansion occurs in Vital Signs, the economy moves away from these points to one of the other points identified in each of the three parts of the figure.
   a. If the Keynesian theory is the correct explanation for the recession, to which points does the economy move?
   b. If the monetarist theory is the correct explanation for the recession, to which points does the economy move?
   c. If the new classical rational expectations theory is the correct explanation for the recession, to which points does the economy move?
   d. If the new Keynesian rational expectations theory is the correct explanation for the recession, to which points does the economy move?
   e. If real business cycle theory is the correct explanation for the recession, to which points does the economy move?

\* Solutions to odd-numbered problems are available on **MyEconLab**.

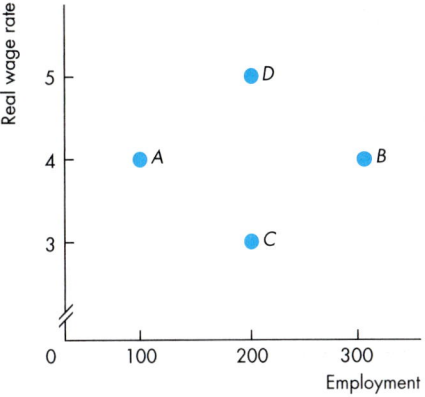

**(a) Labor market**

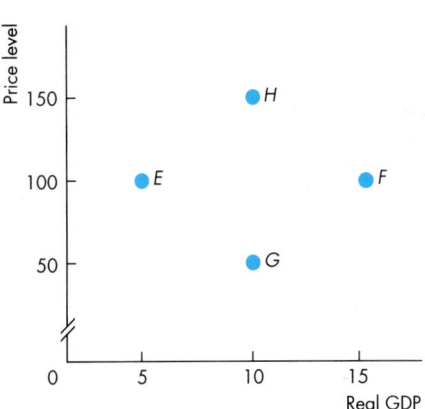

**(b) AS-AD**

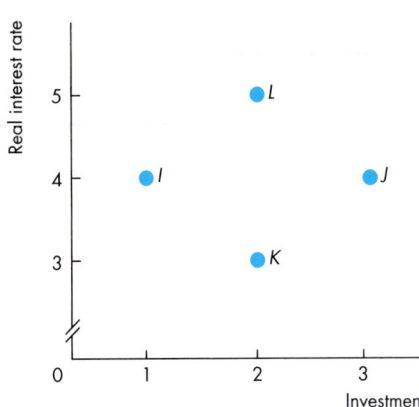

**(c) Investment**

*3. Suppose that when the recession occurs in Virtual Reality, the economy moves to *D*, *G*, and *K*. Which theory of the business cycle, if any, explains this outcome?

4. Suppose that when the expansion occurs in Vital Signs, the economy moves to D, H, and L. Which theory of the business cycle, if any, explains this outcome?

*5. Suppose that when the recession occurs in Virtual Reality, the economy moves to C, G, and K. Which theory of the business cycle, if any, explains this outcome?

6. Suppose that when the expansion occurs in Vital Signs, the economy moves to C, H, and L. Which theory of the business cycle, if any, explains this outcome?

*7. Suppose that when the recession occurs in Virtual Reality, the economy moves to D, H, and K. Which theory of the business cycle, if any, explains this outcome?

8. Suppose that when the expansion occurs in Vital Signs, the economy moves to D, G, and L. Which theory of the business cycle, if any, explains this outcome?

*9. Suppose that when the recession occurs in Virtual Reality, the economy moves to C, H, and K. Which theory of the business cycle, if any, explains this outcome?

10. Suppose that when the expansion occurs in Vital Signs, the economy moves to C, G, and L. Which theory of the business cycle, if any, explains this outcome?

*11. Suppose that when the recession occurs in Virtual Reality, the economy moves to D, G, and L. Which theory of the business cycle, if any, explains this outcome?

12. Suppose that when the expansion occurs in Vital Signs, the economy moves to C, H, and K. Which theory of the business cycle, if any, explains this outcome?

*13. Suppose that when the recession occurs in Virtual Reality, the economy moves to C, G, and L. Which theory of the business cycle, if any, explains this outcome?

14. Suppose that when the expansion occurs in Vital Signs, the economy moves to D, H, and K. Which theory of the business cycle, if any, explains this outcome?

# CRITICAL THINKING

1. *Study Reading Between the Lines* on pp. 356–357 and then answer the following questions:
   a. What brought the 2002–2003 expansion: an increase in aggregate demand, and increase in aggregate supply, or an increase in both?
   b. Does the expansion appear to be consistent with the Keynesian theory of the business cycle? Explain why or why not.
   c. Does the expansion appear to be consistent with the monetarist theory of the business cycle? Explain why or why not.
   d. Does the expansion appear to be consistent with the real business cycle theory? Explain why or why not.
2. Describe the changes in real GDP, employment and unemployment, and the price level that occurred during the Great Depression years of 1929–1933.

# WEB EXERCISES

**Use the links on MyEconLab to work the following exercises.**

1. Obtain data on the current state of the U.S. economy.
   a. List all of the features of the U.S. economy during the current year that you can think of that are consistent with a pessimistic outlook for the next two years.
   b. List all of the features of the U.S. economy during the current year that you can think of that are consistent with an optimistic outlook for the next two years.
   c. How do you think the U.S. economy is going to evolve over the next year or two? Explain your predictions, drawing on the pessimistic and optimistic factors that you have listed in the previous two questions and on your knowledge of macroeconomic theory.
2. Obtain data on the current state of the global economy. How do you think the global economy is going to evolve over the next year or two? Explain your predictions, drawing on the pessimistic and optimistic factors that you have listed in the previous two questions and on your knowledge of macroeconomic theory.

# Fiscal Policy

**CHAPTER 15**

## Balancing Acts on Capitol Hill

**In 2004, the federal government planned to** collect in taxes 17.3 cents of every dollar Americans earned and it planned to spend 20 cents of every dollar that Americans earned. So the government planned a deficit of almost 3 cents in every dollar earned—a total deficit of more than $300 billion. Federal government deficits are not new. Aside from the four years 1998–2001, the government's budget has been in deficit every year since 1970. Deficits bring debts, and your share of the federal government's debt is around $13,000.

What are the effects of taxes on the economy? Do they harm employment and production?

Does it matter if the government doesn't balance its books? What are the effects of an ongoing government deficit and accumulating debt? Do they slow economic growth? Do they impose a burden on future generations—on you and your children?

What are the effects of government spending on the economy? Does a dollar spent by the government on goods and services have the same effect as a dollar spent by someone else? Does it create jobs, or does it destroy them?

◆ These are the fiscal policy issues that you will study in this chapter. In *Reading Between the Lines* at the end of the chapter, we look at the federal budget in 2004 and compare it with that of 2000, the last year of the Clinton administration.

## After studying this chapter, you will be able to

- Describe the federal budget process and the recent history of expenditures, taxes, deficits, and debt
- Explain the supply-side effects of fiscal policy on employment and potential GDP
- Explain the effects of deficits on saving, investment, and economic growth
- Explain how fiscal policy choices redistribute benefits and costs across generations
- Explain how fiscal policy can be used to stabilize the business cycle

361

## The Federal Budget

THE ANNUAL STATEMENT OF THE EXPENDITURES and tax revenues of the government of the United States together with the laws and regulations that approve and support those expenditures and taxes make up the **federal budget**. The federal budget has two purposes:

1. To finance the activities of the federal government
2. To achieve macroeconomic objectives

The first purpose of the federal budget was its only purpose before the Great Depression years of the 1930s. The second purpose arose as a reaction to the Great Depression. The use of the federal budget to achieve macroeconomic objectives such as full employment, sustained economic growth, and price level stability is called **fiscal policy**. It is on this second purpose that we focus in this chapter.

### The Institutions and Laws

Fiscal policy is made by the President and Congress on an annual timeline that is shown in Fig. 15.1 for the 2004 budget.

### The Roles of the President and Congress

The President *proposes* a budget to Congress each February and, after Congress has passed the budget acts in September, either signs those acts into law or vetoes the *entire* budget bill. He does not have the veto power to eliminate specific items in a budget bill and approve others—known as a *line-item veto*. Many state governors have long had line-item veto authority, and Congress attempted to grant these powers to the President of the United States in 1996. But in a 1998 Supreme Court ruling, the line-item veto for the President was declared unconstitutional. Although the President proposes and ultimately approves the budget, the task of making the tough decisions on spending and taxes rests with Congress.

Congress begins its work on the budget with the President's proposal. The House of Representatives and the Senate develop their own budget ideas in their respective House and Senate Budget Committees. Formal conferences between the two houses eventually resolve differences of view, and a series of spending acts and an overall budget act are usually passed by both houses before the start of the fiscal year. A

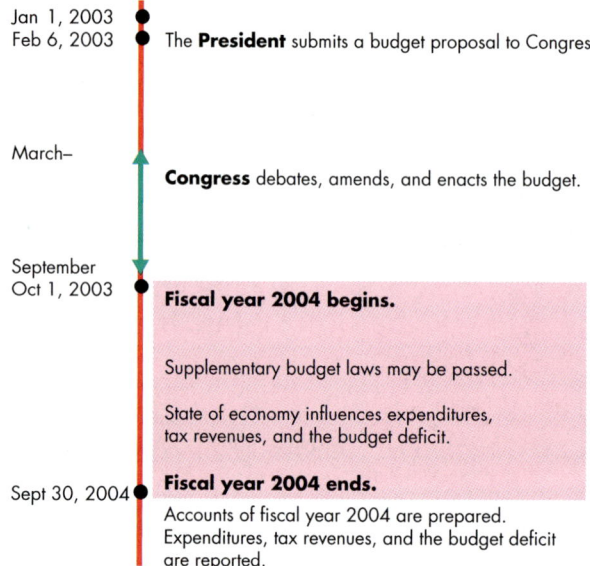

**FIGURE 15.1** The Federal Budget Timeline in Fiscal 2004

The federal budget process begins with the President's proposals in February. Congress debates and amends these proposals and enacts a budget before the start of the fiscal year on October 1. The President signs the budget acts into law or vetoes the entire budget bill. Throughout the fiscal year, Congress might pass supplementary budget laws. The budget outcome is calculated after the end of the fiscal year.

*fiscal year* is a year that runs from October 1 to September 30 in the next calendar year. *Fiscal* 2004 is the fiscal year that *begins* on October 1, 2003.

During a fiscal year, Congress often passes supplementary budget laws, and the budget outcome is influenced by the evolving state of the economy. For example, if a recession begins, tax revenues fall and welfare payments increase.

**The Employment Act of 1946** Fiscal policy operates within the framework of the landmark **Employment Act of 1946** in which Congress declared that

> … it is the continuing policy and responsibility of the Federal Government to use all practicable means … to coordinate and utilize all its plans, functions, and resources … to promote maximum employment, production, and purchasing power.

This act recognized a role for government actions to keep unemployment low, keep the economy expanding, and keep inflation in check. The *Full Employment and Balanced Growth Act of 1978,* more commonly known as the *Humphrey-Hawkins Act,* went farther than the 1946 employment act and set a specific target of 4 percent for the unemployment rate. But this target has never been treated as an unwavering policy goal. Under the 1946 act, the President must describe the current economic situation and the policies he believes are needed in an annual *Economic Report of the President,* which the Council of Economic Advisers writes.

**The Council of Economic Advisers** The President's Council of Economic Advisers was established in 1946 by the Employment Act. The Council consists of a chairperson and two other members, all of whom are economists on a one- or two-year leave from their regular university or public service jobs. In 2003, the chair of President Bush's Council of Economic Advisers was Gregory Mankiw of Harvard University. The **Council of Economic Advisers** monitors the economy and keeps the President and the public well informed about the current state of the economy and the best available forecasts of where it is heading. This economic intelligence activity is one source of data that informs the budget-making process.

Let's look at the most recent federal budget.

### Highlights of the 2004 Budget

Table 15.1 shows the main items in the federal budget proposed by President Bush for 2004. The numbers are projected amounts for the fiscal year beginning on October 1, 2003—fiscal 2004. Notice the three main parts of the table: *Tax revenues* are the government's receipts, *expenditures* are the government's outlays, and the *deficit* is the amount by which the government's expenditures exceed its tax revenues.

**Tax Revenues** Tax revenues were projected to be $1,955 billion in fiscal 2004. These revenues come from four sources:

1. Personal income taxes
2. Social security taxes
3. Corporate income taxes
4. Indirect taxes

The largest source of revenue is *personal income taxes,* which in 2004 are expected to be $841 billion. These taxes are paid by individuals on their incomes. The second largest source is *social security taxes*. These taxes are paid by workers and their employers to finance the government's social security programs. Third in size are *corporate income taxes*. These taxes are paid by companies on their profits. Finally, the smallest source of federal revenue is what are called *indirect taxes*. These taxes are on the sale of gasoline, alcoholic beverages, and a few other items.

**Expenditures** Expenditures are classified in three categories:

1. Transfer payments
2. Purchases of goods and services
3. Debt interest

The largest item of expenditure, *transfer payments*, are payments to individuals, businesses, other levels of government, and the rest of the world. In 2004, this item is expected to be $1,387 billion. It includes Social Security benefits, Medicare and Medicaid, unemployment checks, welfare payments, farm subsidies, grants to state and local governments, aid to developing countries, and dues to international

**TABLE 15.1** Federal Budget in Fiscal 2004

| Item | Projections (billions of dollars) |
|---|---|
| **Tax Revenues** | **1,955** |
| Personal income taxes | 841 |
| Social security taxes | 807 |
| Corporate income taxes | 191 |
| Indirect taxes | 116 |
| **Expenditures** | **2,256** |
| Transfer payments | 1,387 |
| Purchases of goods and services | 647 |
| Debt interest | 222 |
| **Deficit** | **301** |

*Source:* Budget of the United States Government, Fiscal Year 2004, Table 14.1, Federal Transactions in the National Income and Product Accounts.

organizations such as the United Nations. Transfer payments, especially those for Medicare and Medicaid, are sources of persistent growth in government expenditures and are a major source of concern and political debate.

*Purchases of goods and services* are expenditures on final goods and services, and in 2004, they are expected to total $647 billion. These expenditures, which include those on national defense, homeland security, research on cures for AIDS, computers for the Internal Revenue Service, government cars and trucks, federal highways, and dams, have decreased in recent years. This component of the federal budget is *government purchases of goods and services* that appears in the circular flow of expenditure and income and in the National Income and Product Accounts (see Chapter 5, pp. 109–110 and 113).

*Debt interest* is the interest on the government debt. In 2004, this item is expected to be $222 billion—about 10 percent of total expenditure. This interest payment is large because the government has a debt approaching $4 trillion, which has arisen from many years of budget deficits during the 1970s, 1980s, 1990s, and 2000s.

**Surplus or Deficit** The government's budget balance is equal to tax revenues minus expenditures.

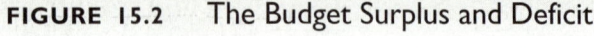

Budget balance = Tax revenues – Expenditures.

If tax revenues exceed expenditures, the government has a **budget surplus**. If expenditures exceed tax revenues, the government has a **budget deficit**. If tax revenues equal expenditures, the government has a **balanced budget**. In fiscal 2004, with projected expenditures of $2,256 billion and tax revenues of $1,955 billion, the government projected a budget deficit of $301 billion.

Big numbers like these are hard to visualize and hard to compare over time. To get a better sense of the magnitude of taxes, spending, and the deficit, we often express them as percentages of GDP. Expressing them in this way lets us see how large government is relative to the size of the economy and also helps us to study *changes* in the scale of government over time.

How typical is the federal budget of 2004? Let's look at the recent history of the budget.

### The Budget in Historical Perspective

Figure 15.2 shows the government's tax revenues, expenditures, and budget surplus or deficit since 1980. Through 1997, there was a budget deficit. The federal government began running a deficit in 1970, and the 1983 deficit shown in the figure was the highest on record at 5.2 percent of GDP. The deficit declined through 1989 but climbed again during the 1990–1991 recession. During the 1990s

**FIGURE 15.2  The Budget Surplus and Deficit**

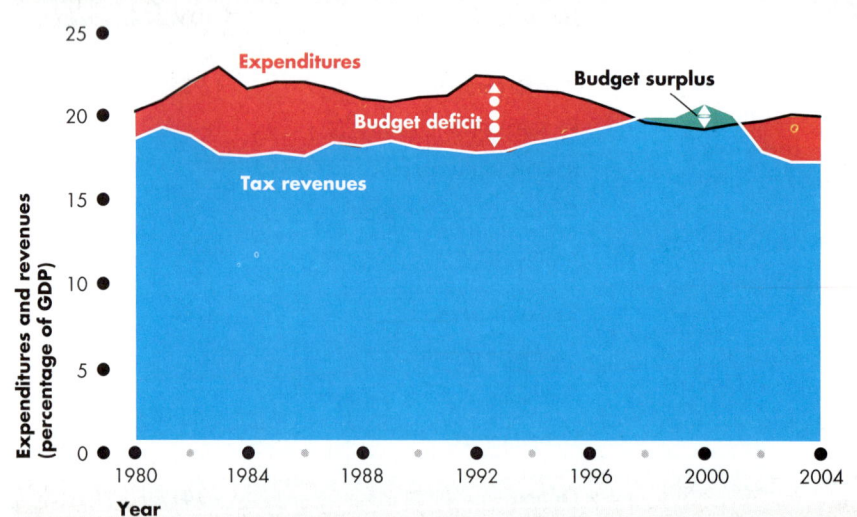

The figure records the federal government's expenditures, tax revenues, and budget surplus/deficit from 1980 to 2004. During the 1980s, a large and persistent budget deficit arose from the combination of a decrease in tax revenues and an increase in expenditures. In 1998, rising revenues and falling expenditures (as percentages of GDP) created a budget surplus, but a deficit emerged again in 2002 as expenditure on security increased and taxes were cut.

*Source: Budget of the United States Government, Fiscal Year 2004, Table 14.2, Federal Transactions in the National Income and Product Accounts.*

expansion, the deficit gradually shrank, and in 1998, the first surplus since 1969 emerged. But by 2002, the budget was again in deficit.

Why did the budget deficit grow during the 1980s and vanish in the late 1990s? The answer lies in the changes in expenditures and tax revenues. But which components of expenditures and tax revenues changed to swell and then shrink the deficit? Let's look at tax revenues and expenditures in a bit more detail.

**Tax Revenues** Figure 15.3(a) shows the components of tax revenues as percentages of GDP from 1980 to 2004. Cuts in corporate and personal income taxes lowered total tax revenues between 1983 and 1986. The decline resulted from tax cuts that had been passed during 1981. From 1986 through 1991, tax revenues did not change much as a percentage of GDP. Personal income tax payments increased through the 1990s but fell sharply after 2000.

**FIGURE 15.3** Federal Government Tax Revenues and Expenditures

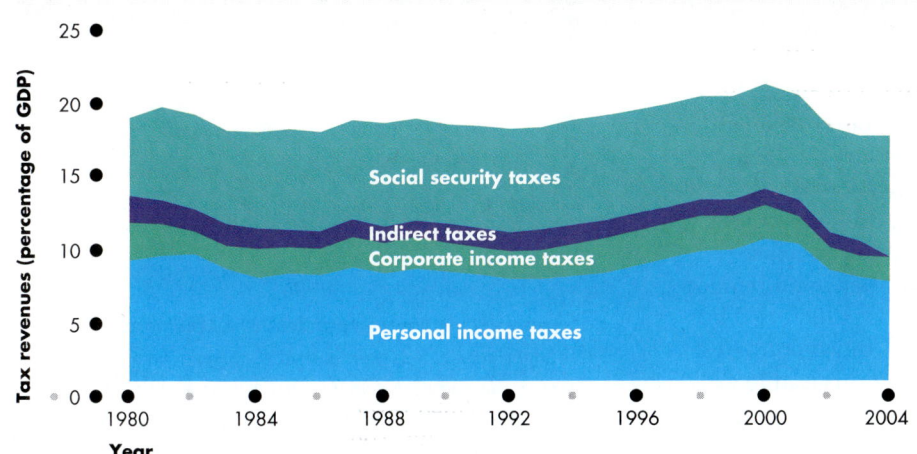

(a) Tax revenues

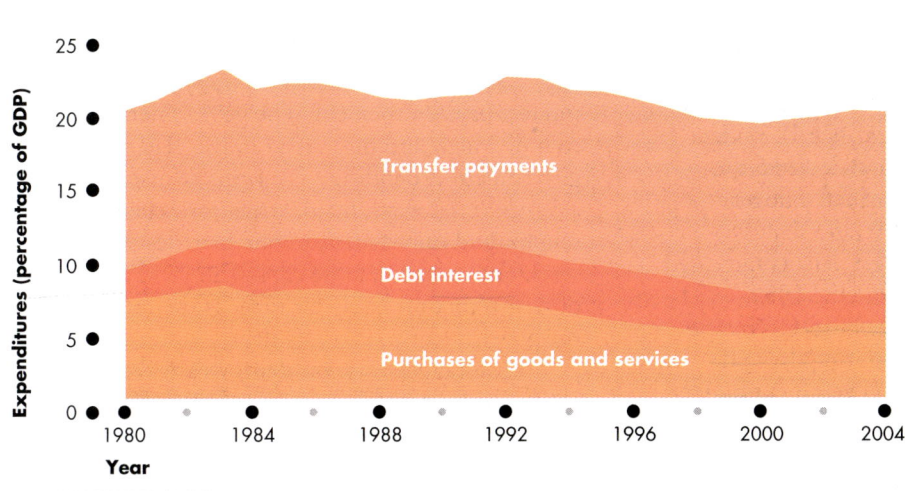

(b) Expenditures

In part (a), revenues from personal and corporate income taxes as a percentage of GDP were approximately constant during the 1980s, increased during the 1990s, and decreased sharply during the 2000s. The other components of tax revenues remained steady.

In part (b), purchases of goods and services decreased as a percentage of GDP through 2001, but then increased because purchases of security-related goods and services increased sharply in 2002. Transfer payments increased over the entire period. Debt interest held steady during the 1980s and decreased during the 1990s and 2000s, helped by a shrinking deficit during the 1990s and low interest rates during 2002 and 2003.

*Source: Budget of the United States Government, Fiscal Year 2004*, Table 14.2, Federal Transactions in the National Income and Product Accounts.

**Expenditures** Figure 15.3(b) shows the components of government expenditures as percentages of GDP from 1980 to 2004. Total expenditures decreased slightly through 1989, increased during the early 1990s, decreased steadily until 2001, and then increased again. Purchases of goods and services decreased through 2001. They increased when expenditures on security-related goods and services increased sharply in 2002 in the wake of the attacks that occurred on September 11, 2001. Debt interest was a constant percentage of GDP during the 1980s and fell slightly during the late 1990s and 2000s. To understand the role of debt interest, we need to see the connection between the government budget surplus or deficit and government debt.

**Surplus, Deficit, and Debt** The government borrows when it has a deficit and makes repayments when it has a surplus. **Government debt** is the total amount that the government has borrowed. It is the sum of past budget deficits minus the sum of past budget surpluses. A government budget deficit increases government debt. And a persistent budget deficit feeds itself. The deficit leads to increased borrowing; increased borrowing leads to larger interest payments; and larger interest payments lead to a larger deficit. That is the story of the increasing budget deficit during the 1970s and 1980s.

Figure 15.4 shows the story of two definitions of government debt since 1940. Gross debt includes the amounts that the government owes to future generations in social security payments. Net debt is the debt held by the public, and it excludes social security obligations.

As a percentage of GDP, government debt was at an all-time high at the end of World War II. Budget surpluses and rapid economic growth lowered the debt-to-GDP ratio through 1974. Small budget deficits increased the debt-to-GDP ratio slightly through the 1970s, and large budget deficits increased it dramatically during the 1980s and the 1990–1991 recession. The growth rate of the debt-to-GDP ratio slowed as the economy expanded during the mid-1990s and began to fall when the government budget went into surplus in the late 1990s.

**Debt and Capital** Businesses and individuals incur debts to buy capital—assets that yield a return. In fact, the main point of debt is to enable people to buy assets that will earn a return that exceeds the

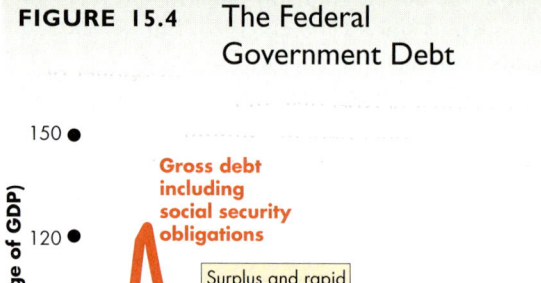

**FIGURE 15.4** The Federal Government Debt

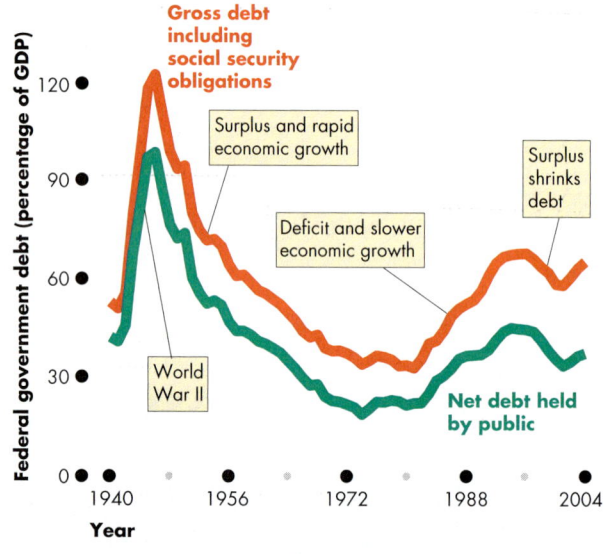

Gross and net government debt (the accumulation of past budget deficits less past budget surpluses) was at its highest at the end of World War II. Debt as a percentage of GDP fell through 1974 but then started to increase. After a further brief decline during the late 1970s, it exploded during the 1980s and continued to increase through 1995, after which it began to fall.

Source: Budget of the United States Government, Fiscal Year 2003, Table 7.1, Federal Debt.

interest paid on the debt. The government is similar to individuals and businesses in this regard. Much government expenditure is on public assets that yield a return. Highways, major irrigation schemes, public schools and universities, public libraries, and the stock of national defense capital all yield a social rate of return that probably far exceeds the interest rate the government pays on its debt.

But total government debt, which is almost $6 trillion, is four times the value of the government's capital stock. So some government debt has been incurred to finance public consumption expenditure and transfer payments, which do not have a social return. Future generations bear the cost of this debt.

How does the U.S. government budget balance compare with those in other countries?

## The U.S. Government Budget in Global Perspective

Figure 15.5 places the U.S. government budget of 2003 in a global perspective. In that year, almost all countries had budget deficits. Summing the deficits of all the governments, the world as a whole had a deficit of 3.1 percent of world GDP—a total government deficit of about $1.6 trillion.

The government of Japan had the largest deficit, as a percentage of GDP. The United States and France came next, followed by the developing countries. Of the other advanced economies, Italy, the United Kingdom, and the entire European Union had large deficits.

Even the newly industrialized economies of Asia (Hong Kong, Korea, Singapore, and Taiwan) had deficits along with the other advanced countries as a group. Of the world's major economies, only Canada had a surplus in 2003.

## State and Local Budgets

The *total government* sector of the United States includes state and local governments as well as the federal government. In 2002, when federal government expenditures were $2,000 billion, state and local expenditures were almost $1,900 billion. Most of these expenditures were on public schools, colleges, and universities ($564 billion), local police and fire services, and roads.

It is the combination of federal, state, and local government taxes, expenditures, and budget deficits that influences the economy. But state and local budgets are not designed to stabilize the aggregate economy or to make it more efficient. So sometimes, when the federal government cuts taxes or expenditures, state and local governments do the reverse and to a degree cancel out the effects of the federal actions. For example, during 2001, when federal taxes began to decrease as a percentage of GDP, state and local taxes increased.

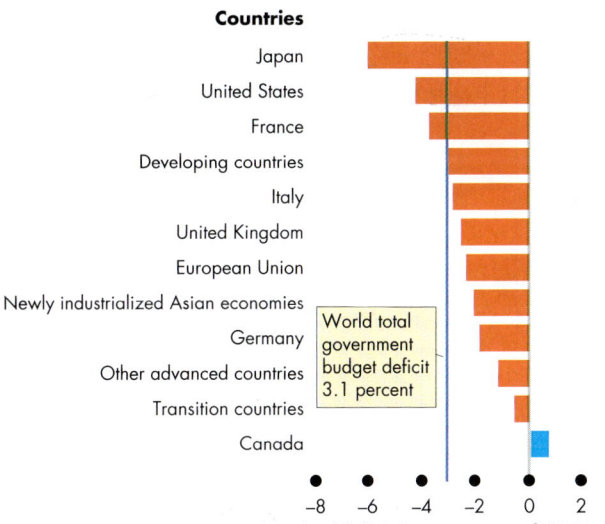

**FIGURE 15.5** Government Budgets Around the World in 2003

Governments in most countries had budget deficits in 2003. The largest ones were in Japan, followed by the United States and France. The developing countries, Italy, and the United Kingdom also had large deficits. Of the major countries, only Canada had a surplus.

*Source:* International Monetary Fund, *World Economic Outlook,* September 2003.

### REVIEW QUIZ

1. What is fiscal policy, who makes it, and what is it designed to influence?
2. What special role does the President play in creating fiscal policy?
3. What special roles do the Budget Committees of the House of Representatives and the Senate play in creating fiscal policy?
4. What is the timeline for the U.S. federal budget each year? When does a fiscal year begin and end?
5. Is the federal government budget today in surplus or deficit?

Now that you know what the federal budget is and what the main items of revenue and expenditure are, it is time to study the *effects* of fiscal policy. We'll begin by learning about the effects of taxes on employment, aggregate supply, and potential GDP. Then we'll study the effects of deficits and see how fiscal policy brings redistribution across generations. Finally, we'll look at the demand-side effects of fiscal policy and see how it provides a tool for stabilizing the business cycle.

## The Supply Side: Employment and Potential GDP

FISCAL POLICY HAS IMPORTANT EFFECTS ON employment, potential GDP, and aggregate supply that we'll now examine. These effects are known as **supply-side effects**, and economists who believe these effects to be large ones are generally referred to as *supply-siders*. To study these effects, we'll begin with a refresher on how full employment and potential GDP are determined in the absence of taxes. Then we'll introduce an income tax and see how it changes the economic outcome.

### Full Employment and Potential GDP

You learned in Chapter 8 (pp. 185–186) how the full-employment quantity of labor and potential GDP are determined. At full employment, the real wage rate adjusts to make the quantity of labor demanded equal the quantity of labor supplied. Potential GDP is the real GDP that the full-employment quantity of labor can produce using the existing quantity of physical capital and human capital and the current state of technology.

Figure 15.6 illustrates a full-employment situation. In part (a), the demand for labor is *LD*, the supply of labor is *LS*, and full employment equilibrium occurs at a wage rate of $30 an hour with 250 billion hours a year of labor employed.

In Fig. 15.6(b), the production function is *PF*. When 250 billion hours of labor are employed, real GDP—which is also potential GDP—is $11 trillion.

Let's now see how an income tax changes this full-employment equilibrium.

### The Effects of the Income Tax

The tax on labor income influences potential GDP and aggregate supply by changing the full-employment quantity of labor. The income tax weakens the incentive to work and drives a wedge between the take-home wage of workers and the cost of labor to firms. The result is a smaller quantity of labor and a lower potential GDP.

Figure 15.6 shows this outcome. In the labor market, the income tax has no effect on the demand for labor, which remains at *LD*. The reason is that the quantity of labor that firms plan to hire depends only on how productive labor is and what it costs—its real wage. The slope of the demand for labor

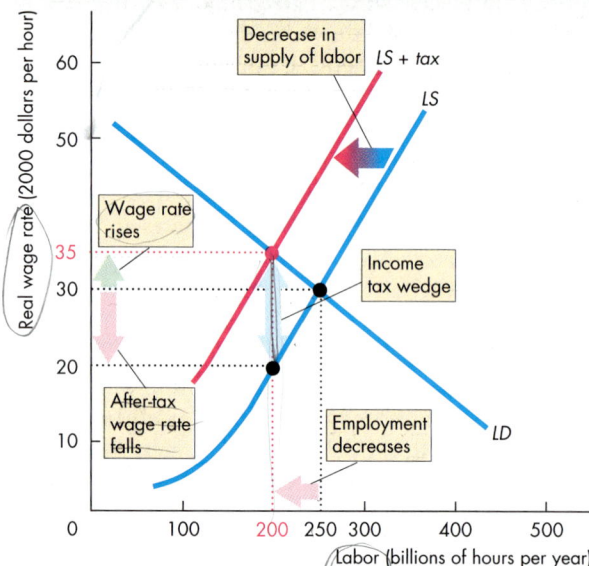

**FIGURE 15.6** The Effects of the Income Tax on Aggregate Supply

(a) Income tax and the labor market

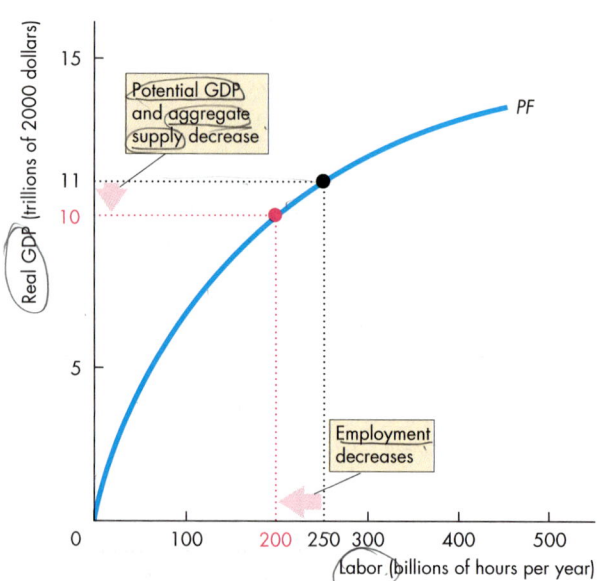

(b) Income tax and potential GDP

In part (a), the demand for labor curve is *LD*, and the supply of labor curve is *LS*. With no income tax, the real wage rate is $30 an hour and employment is 250 billion hours. In part (b), the production function is *PF*, and potential GDP is $11 trillion. An income tax shifts the supply of labor curve leftward to *LS + tax*. The before-tax wage rate rises to $35 an hour, the after-tax wage rate falls to $20 an hour, and the quantity of labor employed decreases. With less labor, potential GDP decreases.

curve tells us how the quantity of labor demanded responds to a change in the cost of labor—a change in the real wage rate. The position of the demand curve tells us how productive labor is.

But the supply of labor *does* change. With no income tax, the real wage rate is $30 an hour and 250 billion hours of labor a year are employed. An income tax weakens the incentive to work and decreases the supply of labor. The reason is that for each dollar of before-tax earnings, workers must pay the government an amount determined by the income tax code. So workers look at the after-tax wage rate when they decide how much labor to supply. When an income tax is imposed, the supply curve shifts leftward to *LS + tax*. The amount of income tax payable is measured by the vertical distance between the *LS* curve and the *LS + tax* curve. With this smaller supply of labor, the *before-tax* wage rate rises to $35 an hour, but the *after-tax* wage rate falls to $20 an hour. The gap between the before-tax and after-tax wage rates is like a wedge and is called the **tax wedge**.

The new equilibrium quantity of labor employed is 200 billion hours a year—a smaller quantity than in the no tax case.

Because the full-employment quantity of labor decreases, so does potential GDP. In this example, the tax rate is high—$15 tax on a $35 wage rate, about 43 percent. A lower tax rate would have a smaller effect on employment and potential GDP.

A tax increase would decrease the supply of labor by more than that shown in Fig. 15.6. Equilibrium employment and potential GDP would also decrease still further. A tax cut would increase the supply of labor, increase equilibrium employment, and increase potential GDP.

### Taxes on Expenditure and the Tax Wedge

The tax wedge that we've just considered is only a part of the wedge that affects labor-supply decisions. Taxes on consumption expenditure add to the wedge. The reason is that a tax on consumption raises the prices paid for consumption goods and services and is equivalent to a cut in the real wage rate.

The incentive to supply labor depends on the goods and services that an hour of labor can buy. The higher the prices of goods and services and the lower the wage rate, the less is the incentive to supply labor.

Suppose the income tax rate is 25 percent and the tax rate on consumption expenditure is 10 percent. The worker now faces a combined tax of 35 percent.

### Some Real World Tax Wedges

Edward Prescott, an economist at the University of Minnesota, has estimated the tax wedges for a number of countries. The U.S. tax wedge is a combination of 13 percent tax on consumption and 32 percent tax on incomes. The income tax rate includes Social Security taxes and is a *marginal* tax rate.

Among the industrial countries, the U.S. tax wedge is relatively small. Prescott estimates that in France, taxes on consumption are 33 percent and on incomes 49 percent. The estimates for the United Kingdom fall between these numbers. Figure 15.7 shows these components of the tax wedges in the three countries.

### Does the Tax Wedge Matter?

According to Prescott's estimates, the tax wedge has a powerful effect on employment and potential GDP. Potential GDP in France is 31 percent below that of the United States (per person), and the entire difference can be attributed to the difference in the tax wedge in the two countries.

Potential GDP in the United Kingdom is 41 percent below that of the United States (per person), and about a third of the difference arises from the different tax wedges. (The rest is due to different productivities.) If these estimates are correct, the income tax cuts implemented by the Bush administration (see *Reading Between the Lines* on pp. 382–383) will have large effects on potential GDP.

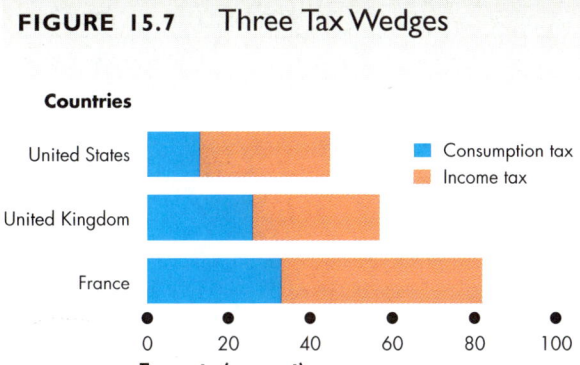

**FIGURE 15.7** Three Tax Wedges

Tax rates are much higher in France and the United Kingdom than in the United States and can account for much of the difference in potential GDP per person.

*Source:* Edward C. Prescott, *American Economic Review*, 2003.

## Tax Revenues and the Laffer Curve

You've just seen that an increase in the tax rate decreases the quantity of employment and decreases potential GDP.

An interesting consequence of this fact is that a higher tax rate does not always bring greater tax revenue. A higher tax rate brings in more revenue per dollar earned. But because a higher tax rate decreases the number of dollars earned, two forces operate in opposite directions on total taxes collected.

The relationship between the tax rate and the amount of tax revenue collected is called the **Laffer curve**. The curve is so named because Arthur B. Laffer, a member of President Reagan's Economic Policy Advisory Board, drew such a curve on a table napkin and launched the idea that tax *cuts* could *increase* tax revenue.

Figure 15.8 shows a Laffer curve. The tax *rate* is measured on the *x*-axis, and total tax *revenue* on the *y*-axis. For tax rates below $t^*$, an increase in the tax rate increases tax revenue. When the tax rate reaches $t^*$, tax revenue is maximized. But a tax rate increase beyond $t^*$ decreases tax revenue.

Most people think that the United States is on the upward-sloping part of the Laffer curve. So is the United Kingdom. But France might be close to the maximum point, or perhaps even beyond it.

## The Supply-Side Debate

Before 1980, few economists paid attention to the supply-side effects of taxes on employment and potential GDP. Then, when Ronald Reagan took office as President, a group of supply-siders began to argue the virtues of cutting taxes. Arthur Laffer was one of them. Laffer and his supporters were not held in high esteem among mainstream economists, but they did become influential for a period. They correctly argued that tax cuts would increase employment and increase output. But they incorrectly argued that tax cuts would increase tax revenues and decrease the budget deficit. For this prediction to be correct, the United States would have had to be on the "wrong" side of the Laffer curve. Given that U.S. tax rates are among the lowest in the industrial world, it is unlikely that this condition was met. And the fact that when the Reagan administration did cut taxes, the budget deficit increased reinforces this view.

Supply-side economics became tarnished because of its association with Laffer and came to be called "voodoo economics." But mainstream economists, including Martin Feldstein, a Harvard professor who was Reagan's chief economic advisor, recognized the power of tax cuts as incentives but took the standard view that tax cuts without spending cuts would swell the budget deficit and bring serious further problems. This view is now widely accepted by economists of all political persuasions.

### FIGURE 15.8 A Laffer Curve

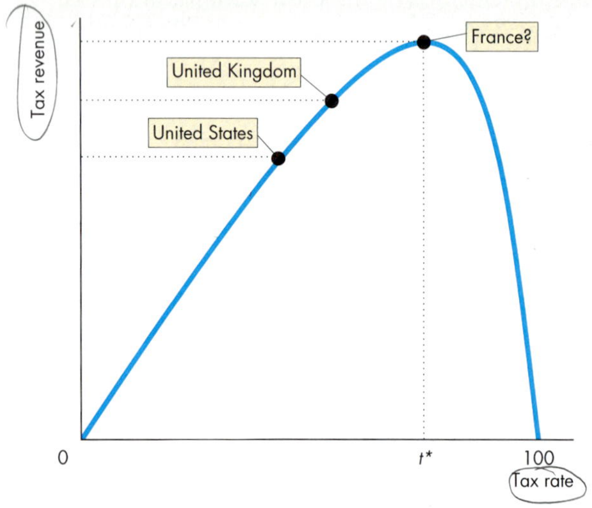

A Laffer curve shows the relationship between the tax rate and tax revenues. For tax rates below $t^*$, an increase in the tax rate increases tax revenue. At the tax rate $t^*$, tax revenue is maximized. For tax rates above $t^*$, an increase in the tax rate decreases tax revenue.

> **REVIEW QUIZ**
>
> 1. How does a tax on labor income influence the quantity of employment at full employment?
> 2. How does the tax wedge influence potential GDP?
> 3. Why are consumption taxes relevant for measuring the tax wedge?
> 4. What is the Laffer curve and why is it unlikely that the United States is on the "wrong" side of it?

You now know the effects of taxes on potential GDP. The effects that we've studied influence the *level* of real GDP but not its *growth rate*. We're now going to look at the effects of taxes and the budget deficit on saving and investment, which in turn influence the pace of economic growth.

# The Supply Side: Investment, Saving, and Economic Growth

You learned in Chapter 5 how investment is financed by national saving and foreign borrowing. Later in Chapter 8, you studied the factors that influence investment and saving decisions and how the real interest rate adjusts in the capital market to coordinate saving and investment plans. Then in Chapter 9, you saw how investment and saving bring an increasing quantity of capital and contribute to the growth of real GDP.

When we studied the capital market in Chapter 8, we ignored the influence of government. We're now going to bring government saving into the picture and see how fiscal policy interacts with private saving and investment decisions to influence the rate of economic growth.

We begin with a quick refresher of what you learned in Chapter 5 about the sources of finance for investment.

## The Sources of Investment Finance

GDP equals the sum of consumption expenditure, $C$, investment, $I$, government purchases, $G$, and net exports, $(X - M)$ (Chapter 5, pp. 110–111). That is,

$$GDP = C + I + G + (X - M).$$

GDP also equals the sum of consumption expenditure, saving, $S$, and net taxes, $T$. That is,

$$GDP = C + S + T.$$

By combining these two ways of looking at GDP, you can see that

$$I + G + (X - M) = S + T$$

or

$$I = S + T - G + (M - X).$$

This equation tells us that investment, $I$, is financed by saving, $S$, government saving, $T - G$, and foreign borrowing, $(M - X)$.

Saving and foreign borrowing are the private sources of saving, $PS$, and

$$PS = S + (M - X).$$

Investment is equal to the sum of private saving and government saving. That is,

$$I = PS + (T - G).$$

- If net taxes, $T$, exceed government purchases, $G$, the government sector has a budget surplus and government saving is positive.
- If government purchases exceed net taxes, the government sector has a budget deficit and government saving is negative.

When the government sector has a budget surplus, it contributes toward financing investment. Its saving must be added to private saving. But when the government sector has a budget deficit, it competes with businesses for private saving. In this situation, government saving must be subtracted from private saving.

Figure 15.9 shows the sources of investment finance in the United States from 1973 through 2003. You can see that during the 1990s, investment increased sharply but domestic saving was flat. The increase in investment was financed partly by an increase in government saving—a falling government deficit—and by a surge in foreign borrowing.

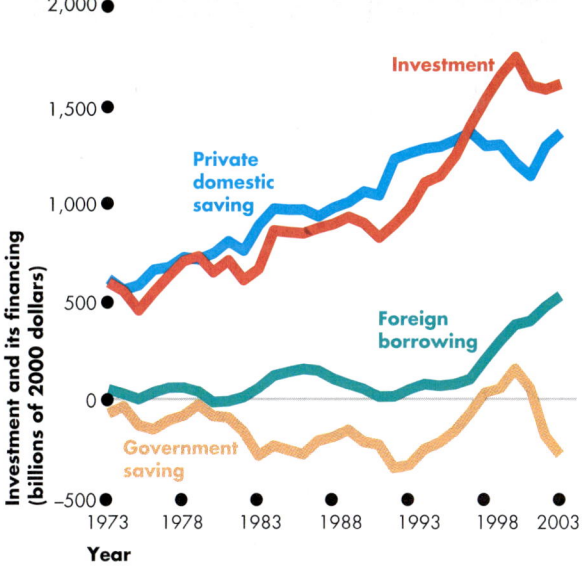

**FIGURE 15.9** Financing U.S. Investment

During the 1990s, rising U.S. investment was financed by surging foreign borrowing and a falling government budget deficit. For most of the period shown here, the government budget has been in deficit.

*Sources:* Bureau of Economic Analysis and Office of Management and Budget.

Fiscal policy can influence the capital market in two ways:

- Taxes affect the incentive to save.
- Government saving—the budget surplus or deficit—is a component to total saving.

## Taxes and the Incentive to Save

A tax on interest income weakens the incentive to save and drives a wedge between the after-tax interest rate earned by savers and the interest rate paid by firms. These effects are analogous to those of a tax on labor income. But they are more serious for two reasons.

First, a tax on labor income lowers the quantity of labor employed and lowers potential GDP, while a tax on capital income lowers the quantity of saving and investment and *slows the growth rate of real GDP*. A tax on capital income creates a Lucas wedge (Chapter 4, p. 93)—an ever widening gap between potential GDP and the potential GDP that might have been.

Second, the true tax rate on interest income is much higher than that on labor income because of the way that inflation and taxes on interest interact. We'll examine this interaction before we study the effects of taxes on saving and investment.

**Real Tax Rate on Real Interest Rate** The interest rate that influences investment and saving plans is the *real after-tax interest rate*. You learned in Chapter 12 (p. 293) that the *real* interest rate is equal to the *nominal* interest rate adjusted for inflation and (approximately) equals the nominal interest rate minus the inflation rate. The real *after-tax* interest rate subtracts the income tax paid on interest income from the real interest rate.

But the tax law imposes the income tax on the nominal interest rate, not the real interest rate. So the higher the inflation rate, the higher is the true tax rate on interest income. You can see why by considering two cases. In both cases, we'll keep the real interest rate the same at 4 percent a year and the tax rate on nominal interest income the same at 40 percent.

First, suppose there is no inflation so the nominal interest rate equals the real interest rate of 4 percent a year. The tax on 4 percent interest is 1.6 percent (40 percent of 4 percent), so the real after-tax interest rate is 4 percent minus 1.6 percent, which equals 2.4 percent.

Second, suppose the inflation rate is 6 percent. The nominal interest rate is now 10 percent. The tax on 10 percent interest is 4 percent (40 percent of 10 percent), so the real after-tax interest rate is 4 percent minus 4 percent, which equals zero. The true tax rate in this case is not 40 percent but 100 percent!

**Effect of Income Tax on Saving and Investment**
In Fig. 15.10, initially there are no taxes. The investment demand curve, *ID*, shows the quantity of investment at each real interest rate, and the saving supply curve, *SS*, shows the quantity of saving at each real interest rate. The interest rate is 3 percent a year, and investment and saving are $2 trillion a year.

A tax on interest income has no effect on investment demand, which remains at *ID*. The reason is that the quantity of investment that firms plan to undertake depends only on how productive capital is and what it costs—its real interest rate. But a tax on interest income weakens the incentive to save and decreases saving supply. For each dollar of before-tax earnings, savers must

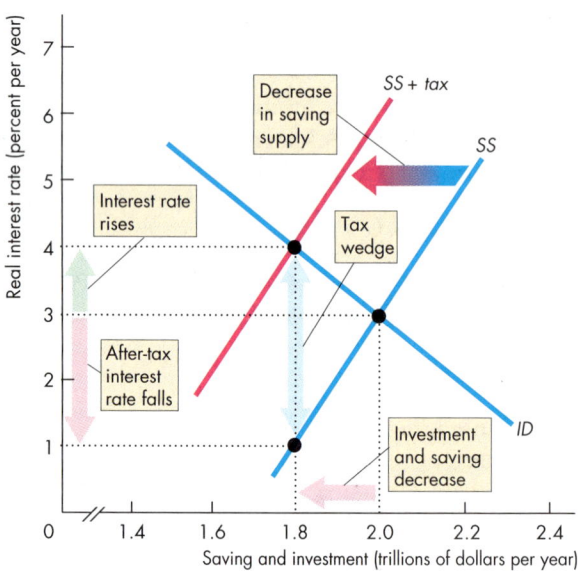

**FIGURE 15.10** The Effects of a Tax on Capital Income

The investment demand curve is *ID*, and the saving supply curve is *SS*. With no income tax, the real interest rate is 3 percent a year and saving and investment are $2 trillion. An income tax shifts the saving supply curve leftward to *SS + tax*. The interest rate rises to 4 percent a year, the after-tax interest rate falls to 1 percent a year, and saving and investment decrease. With less investment, the real GDP growth rate falls.

pay the government an amount determined by the tax code. So savers look at the after-tax real interest rate when they decide how much saving to supply.

When a tax is imposed, the saving supply curve shifts leftward to SS + *tax*. The amount of tax payable is measured by the vertical distance between the SS curve and the SS + *tax* curve. With this smaller saving supply, the interest rate rises to 4 percent a year, but the *after-tax* interest rate falls to 1 percent a year. The gap between the interest rate and the after-tax interest rate is a tax wedge.

The new equilibrium level of saving and investment is $1.8 trillion a year—a smaller quantity than in the no tax case.

The effects of the income tax on saving and investment are likely to be large. And at a high inflation rate, they are likely to be especially large.

You've seen how taxes affect private saving. Let's now see how government saving affects the capital market.

## Government Saving

Government saving is positive when the budget is in surplus, negative when the budget is in deficit, and zero when the budget is balanced.

In Fig. 15.11, the investment demand curve, *ID*, shows the quantity of investment at each real interest rate. The curve labeled *PS* shows the relationship between *private* saving and the real interest rate. If government saving were zero, the *PS* curve would be the saving supply curve. The real interest rate would be 4 percent, and saving and investment would be equal at $1.8 trillion a year.

We will now see what happens when the government budget is in deficit—when government saving is *negative*. We must subtract the budget deficit from private saving to find the saving supply curve. This curve, labeled *SS*, lies to the left of the private saving supply curve. And the horizontal distance between the *PS* curve and the *SS* curve is government saving, which in this example is a negative $0.3 trillion. (This number, like all the other numbers in Fig. 15.9, is similar to the actual value in the United States in 2003.)

The effect of negative government saving, which is also called *dissaving*, is to decrease saving supply and increase the real interest rate. Investment decreases. In Fig. 15.11, with a government deficit of $0.3 trillion, the saving supply curve shifts leftward and the real interest rate rises from 4 percent to 5 percent a year. Investment decreases from $1.8 trillion to $1.6 trillion. Investment does not decrease by the full amount of the government deficit because the higher real interest rate induces an increase in private saving. In Fig. 15.11, private saving increases by $0.1 trillion to $1.9 trillion.

The tendency for a government budget deficit to decrease investment is called a **crowding-out effect**. By raising the real interest rate, the government deficit crowds out private investment. A government surplus has the opposite effect to what we've just seen. It increases saving supply, lowers the real interest rate, and stimulates investment.

In the crowding-out case that you've just seen, the *quantity of private saving* changes because the real interest rate changes. There is a movement along the *PS* curve. But private saving supply does not change. That is, the *PS* curve does not shift. But suppose that a change in government saving changes private saving supply and shifts the *PS* curve. This possibility is called the Ricardo-Barro effect, so named because it was first suggested by the English economist David

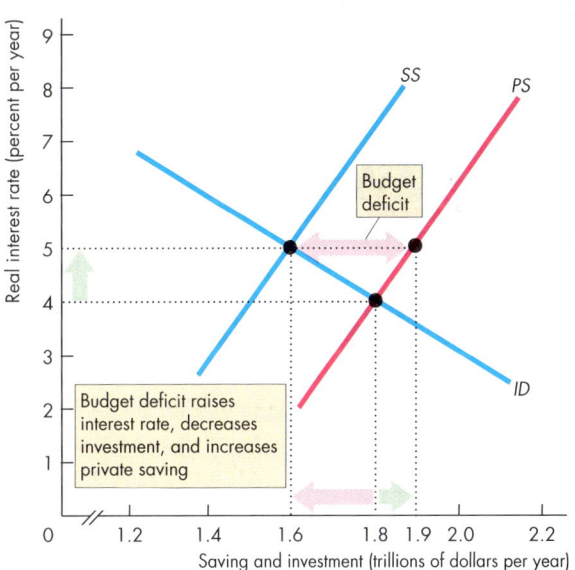

**FIGURE 15.11    A Crowding-Out Effect**

The investment demand curve is *ID*, and the private saving supply curve is *PS*. With a balanced government budget, the real interest rate is 4 percent a year and investment equals saving at $1.8 trillion a year. A government budget deficit is negative government saving (dissaving). We subtract the government deficit from private saving to determine the saving supply curve *SS*. The real interest rate rises, investment decreases (is crowded out), and private saving increases.

Ricardo in the eighteenth century and refined by Robert J. Barro of Harvard University during the 1980s. The **Ricardo-Barro effect** holds that a government budget deficit has no effect on the real interest rate or investment and that financing government purchases by taxes or by borrowing are equivalent.

The reasoning behind the Ricardo-Barro effect is the following. A government that runs a deficit must sell bonds to pay for the goods and services that are not paid for by taxes. And the government must pay interest on those bonds. It must also collect more taxes *in the future* to pay the interest on the larger quantity of bonds that are outstanding. Taxpayers are rational and have good foresight. They can see that their taxes will be higher in the future and so their disposable income will be lower. Lower expected future disposable income increases saving. And if taxpayers want to neutralize the effects of the government deficit on their own consumption plans, they increase their own saving by the same amount that the government is dissaving through its deficit.

This outcome is extreme and probably does not actually occur. Taxpayers probably respond in the *direction* suggested by Ricardo and Barro but not in the *amount* they suggest. So the effect of a government deficit probably lies between the case shown in Fig. 15.11 and the Ricardo-Barro case in which there is no effect. That is, a government deficit increases the real interest rate and partly crowds out private investment, but it also induces an increase in private saving in anticipation of lean times later when taxes will rise to pay the interest on the increasing debt.

### REVIEW QUIZ

1 Why does the tax on interest income have more serious effects than the tax on labor income?
2 How does a tax on interest income affect saving, investment, and the real interest rate?
3 Does a government budget deficit crowd out investment? How?
4 What is the Ricardo-Barro effect and why is it unlikely to operate fully?

You now know the effects of a deficit on saving and investment. Because a deficit crowds out investment, it slows the growth rate of real GDP. Next we'll look at the effects of fiscal policy on intergenerational redistribution.

# Generational Effects of Fiscal Policy

Is A BUDGET DEFICIT A BURDEN ON FUTURE generations? If it is, how will the burden be borne? And is the budget deficit the only burden on future generations? What about off-budget deficits such as that of the Social Security fund? Does it matter who owns the bonds that the government sells to finance its deficit? What about the bonds owned by foreigners? Won't repaying those bonds impose a bigger burden than repaying bonds owned by Americans?

To answer questions like these, we use a tool called **generational accounting**—an accounting system that measures the lifetime tax burden and benefits of each generation. This accounting system was developed by Alan Auerbach of the University of Pennsylvania and Laurence Kotlikoff of Boston University. The most recent generational accounts for the United States were prepared by Jagadeesh Gokhale of the Federal Reserve Bank of Cleveland and Kent Smetters of the University of Pennsylvania.

## Generational Accounting and Present Value

Income taxes and social security taxes are paid by people who have jobs. Social Security benefits are paid to people after they retire. So to compare taxes and benefits, we must compare the value of taxes paid by people during their working years with the benefits received in their retirement years. To compare the value of an amount of money at one date with that at a later date, we use the concept of present value. A **present value** is an amount of money that, if invested today, will grow to equal a given future amount when the interest that it earns is taken into account. We can compare dollars today with dollars in 2030 or any other future year by using present values.

For example, if the interest rate is 5 percent a year, $1,000 invested today will grow, with interest, to $11,467 after 50 years. So the present value (in 2004) of $11,467 in 2054 is $1,000.

By using present values, we can assess the magnitude of the government's debts to older Americans in the form of pensions and medical benefits.

But the assumed interest rate and growth rate of taxes and benefits critically influence the answers we get. For example, at an interest rate of 3 percent a year, the present value (in 2004) of $11,467 in 2054 is $2,616. The lower the interest rate, the greater is the present value of a given future amount.

Because there is uncertainty about the proper interest rate to use to calculate present values, plausible alternative numbers are used to estimate a range of present values.

Using generational accounting and present values, economists have studied the situation facing the federal government arising from its social security obligations. And they have found a time bomb!

## The Social Security Time Bomb

When social security was introduced in the New Deal of the 1930s, today's demographic situation was not envisaged. The age distribution of the U.S. population is dominated by a surge in the birth rate that occurred after World War II that created what is called the "baby boom generation."

It is estimated that in 2008, 77 million "baby boomers" will start collecting Social Security pensions and in 2011, they will become eligible for Medicare benefits. By 2030, all the baby boomers will have retired and, compared to 2003, the population supported by social security will have doubled.

Under the existing Social Security laws, the federal government has an obligation to these citizens to pay pensions and Medicare benefits on an already declared scale. These obligations are a debt owed by the government and are just as real as the bonds that the government issues to finance its current deficit.

To assess the full extent of the government's obligations, economists use the concept of fiscal imbalance. **Fiscal imbalance** is the present value of the government's commitments to pay benefits minus the present value of its tax revenues. Fiscal imbalance is an attempt to measure the scale of the government's true liabilities.

In 2003, the fiscal imbalance was estimated to be $45 trillion. (Using alternative assumptions about interest rates and growth rates, the number might be as low as $29 trillion or as high as $65 trillion.)

To put $45 trillion in perspective, note that U.S. GDP in 2003 was a bit more than $10 trillion. So this debt is 4.5 times a year's production. Another perspective is to compare the fiscal imbalance with the government's official explicit debt—the value of its outstanding bonds. That number was $3.7 trillion in 2003, so the government's fiscal imbalance is about 12 times its market debt.

How could the federal government meet its social security obligations? Gokhale and Smetters consider four alternatives:

- Raise income taxes
- Raise social security taxes
- Cut social security benefits
- Cut federal government discretionary spending

If one of these actions had been taken in 2003, the magnitude of the change required to keep the government solvent is staggering. Income taxes would need to be raised by 69 percent; or social security taxes raised by 95 percent; or benefits cut by 56 percent. Even if the government shut down all its so-called discretionary activities—that includes national defense—it still would not be able to pay its bills.

Of course, by combining the four measures, the pain from each could be lessened. But the pain would still be severe. And worse, delay makes all these numbers rise. If nothing is done until 2008, for example, the fiscal imbalance climbs to $54 trillion.

## Generational Imbalance

A fiscal imbalance must eventually be corrected and when it is, people pay either with higher taxes or lower benefits. The concept of generational imbalance tells us who will pay. **Generational imbalance** is the division of the fiscal imbalance between the current and future generations, assuming that the current generation will enjoy the existing levels of taxes and benefits.

Figure 15.12 shows an estimate of how today's fiscal imbalance is distributed across the current (born before 1988) and future (born in or after 1988) generations. It also shows that the major source of the imbalances is Medicare. Social Security pension benefits create a fiscal imbalance, but these benefits are more than fully paid for by the current generation. But the current generation will pay less than 50 percent of its Medicare costs, and the balance will fall on future generations.

Summing all the items, the current generation will pay 43 percent and future generations pay 57 percent of the fiscal imbalance.

Because the estimated fiscal imbalance is so large, it is not possible to predict how the imbalance will be resolved. But we can predict that the outcome involves a combination of lower benefits and higher taxes. One of these taxes could be the inflation tax—paying bills with new money and creating inflation.

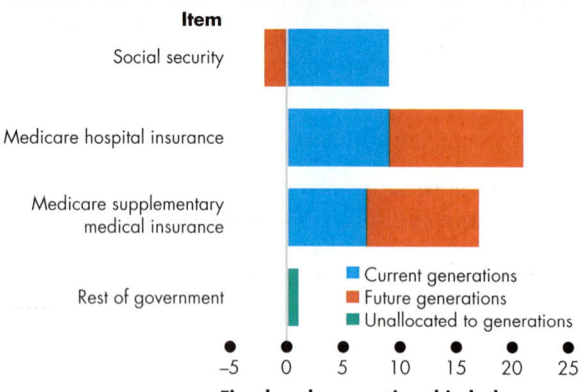

**FIGURE 15.12  Fiscal and Generational Imbalances**

The largest components of the fiscal imbalance are Medicare benefits. These benefits are also the main component of the generational imbalance. Social security pension benefits are entirely paid for by the current generation.

*Source:* Jagadeesh Gokhale and Kent Smetters, "Fiscal and Generational Imbalances: New Budget Measures For New Budget Priorities," April 2003.

## International Debt

So far in our discussion of government deficits and debts, we've ignored the role played by the rest of the world. We'll conclude this discussion by considering the role and magnitude of international debt.

You've seen that foreign borrowing is one source of investment finance. And you've also seen that this source of investment finance became large during the late 1990s and 2000s.

How large is the contribution of the rest of the world? How much investment have we paid for by borrowing from abroad? And how much government debt is held abroad?

Table 15.2 answers these questions. Part (a) shows that at the end of June 2003, the United States had a net debt to the rest of the world of $4 trillion. Of that debt, a bit more than half ($2.1 trillion) was U.S. government debt. U.S. corporations had used $2.5 trillion of foreign funds ($1.1 trillion in bonds and $1.4 trillion in equities), not much more than the borrowing of the U.S. government.

Part (b) shows how total government debt divides between domestic and foreign holdings. More than a half of the outstanding $3.9 trillion of debt is held by foreigners.

The international debt of the United States is important because, when that debt is repaid, the United States will transfer real resources to the rest of the world. Instead of running a large net exports deficit, the United States will need a surplus of exports over imports. To make a surplus possible, U.S. saving must increase and consumption must decrease. Some tough choices lie ahead.

**TABLE 15.2  What the United States Owed the Rest of the World in June 2003**

|  | $ trillions |
|---|---|
| **(a) U.S. Liabilities** | |
| Deposits in U.S. banks | 0.7 |
| U.S. government securities | 2.1 |
| U.S. corporate bonds | 1.1 |
| U.S. corporate equities | 1.4 |
| Other (net) | −1.3 |
| **Total** | **4.0** |
| **(b) U.S. government securities** | |
| Held by rest of world | 2.1 |
| Held in the United States | 1.8 |
| **Total** | **3.9** |

*Source:* Federal Reserve Board.

### REVIEW QUIZ

1. What is a present value?
2. Can you distinguish between fiscal imbalance and generational imbalance?
3. How large was the estimated U.S. fiscal imbalance in 2003 and how did it divide between current and future generations?
4. What is the source of the fiscal imbalance and what are the painful choices that face current and future generations?
5. How much of the fiscal imbalance is accounted for by debt to the rest of the world?

You now know how economists assess a government's fiscal imbalance and how they divide the cost of covering an imbalance across generations. And you've seen the extent and implication of U.S. debt (government and private) held in the rest of the world. We conclude this chapter by looking at the role of fiscal policy as a tool for stabilizing the business cycle.

# Stabilizing the Business Cycle

FISCAL POLICY ACTIONS THAT SEEK TO STABILIZE the business cycle work by changing aggregate demand. These policy actions can be either

- Discretionary or
- Automatic

A fiscal action initiated by an act of Congress is called **discretionary fiscal policy**. It requires a change in a spending program or in a tax law. For example, an increase in defense spending or a cut in the income tax rate is a discretionary fiscal policy.

A fiscal action that is triggered by the state of the economy is called **automatic fiscal policy**. For example, an increase in unemployment induces an increase in payments to the unemployed. A fall in incomes induces a decrease in tax revenues.

Changes in government purchases and changes in taxes have multiplier effects on aggregate demand. Chapter 13 explains the basic idea of the multiplier and pages 329–331 of its math note show the algebra of the fiscal policy multipliers that we'll now study.

## The Government Purchases Multiplier

The **government purchases multiplier** is the magnification effect of a change in government purchases of goods and services on aggregate demand. Government purchases are a component of aggregate expenditure, so when government purchases change, aggregate demand changes. Real GDP changes and induces a change in consumption expenditure, which brings a further change in aggregate expenditure. A multiplier process ensues.

**A Homeland Security Multiplier** The terrorist attacks of September 11, 2001, brought a reappraisal of the nation's homeland security requirements and an increase in government purchases. This increase in purchases initially increased the incomes of producers of airport and border security equipment and security workers. Better-off security workers increased their consumption expenditures. With rising revenues, other businesses in all parts of the nation boomed and expanded their payrolls. A second round of increased consumption expenditures increased incomes yet further. The increase in security expenditures and its multiplier effect helped to end the 2001 recession.

## The Tax Multiplier

The **tax multiplier** is the magnification effect of a change in taxes on aggregate demand. A *decrease* in taxes *increases* disposable income, which increases consumption expenditure. A decrease in taxes works like an increase in government purchases. But the magnitude of the tax multiplier is smaller than the government purchases multiplier. The reason is that a $1 tax cut generates *less than* $1 of additional expenditure. The marginal propensity to consume determines the increase in expenditure induced by a tax cut. For example, if the marginal propensity to consume is 0.75, then a $1 tax cut increases consumption expenditure by only 75 cents. In this case, the tax multiplier is 0.75 times the magnitude of the government purchases multiplier.

**A Bush Tax Cut Multiplier** Congress enacted the Bush tax cut package that lowered taxes starting in 2002. These tax cuts had a multiplier effect. With more disposable income, people increased consumption expenditure. This spending increased other people's incomes, which spurred yet more consumption expenditure. Like the increase in security expenditures, the tax cut and its multiplier effect helped to end the 2001 recession.

## The Balanced Budget Multiplier

The **balanced budget multiplier** is the magnification effect on aggregate demand of a *simultaneous* change in government purchases and taxes that leaves the budget balance unchanged. The balanced budget multiplier is positive because a $1 increase in government purchases increases aggregate demand by more than a $1 increase in taxes decreases aggregate demand. So when both government purchases and taxes increase by $1, aggregate demand increases.

## Discretionary Fiscal Stabilization

If real GDP is below potential GDP, discretionary fiscal policy might be used in an attempt to restore full employment. The government might increase its purchases of goods and services, cut taxes, or do some of both. These actions would increase aggregate demand. If they were timed correctly and were of the correct magnitude, they could restore full employment. Figure 15.13 shows how. Potential GDP is $10 trillion, but real GDP is below potential at $9 trillion and there is a $1 trillion *recessionary gap* (see Chapter 7, p. 160). To eliminate the recessionary gap and restore full employment, the government takes a discretionary fiscal policy action. An increase in government purchases or a tax cut increases aggregate expenditure by $\Delta E$. If this were the only change in spending plans, the $AD$ curve would become $AD_0 + \Delta E$ in Fig. 15.13. But the increase in government purchases or the tax cut sets off a multiplier process, which increases consumption expenditure. As the multiplier process plays out, aggregate demand increases and the $AD$ curve shifts rightward to $AD_1$.

With no change in the price level, the economy would move from the initial equilibrium point $A$ to point $B$ on $AD_1$. But the increase in aggregate demand combined with the upward-sloping aggregate supply curve brings a rise in the price level. So the economy moves to a new equilibrium at point $C$. The price level rises to 105, and real GDP increases to $10 trillion. Full employment is restored.

Figure 15.14 illustrates the opposite case in which discretionary fiscal policy is used to eliminate inflationary pressure. The government decreases its purchases of goods and services or raises taxes to decrease aggregate demand. In the figure, the decrease in government purchases or rise in taxes decreases aggregate expenditure by $\Delta E$ and the $AD$ curve shifts to $AD_0 - \Delta E$. The initial decrease in aggregate expenditure sets off a multiplier process, which decreases consumption expenditure. As the multiplier process plays out, aggregate demand decreases and the $AD$ curve shifts leftward to $AD_1$.

With no change in the price level, the economy would move from the initial equilibrium point $A$ to point $B$ on $AD_1$ in Fig. 15.14. But the decrease in aggregate demand combined with the upward-sloping $AS$ curve brings a fall in the price level. So the economy moves to a new equilibrium at point $C$. The price level falls to 105, and real GDP decreases to $10 trillion. The inflationary gap has been eliminated, inflation has been avoided, and the economy is back at full employment.

Figures 15.13 and 15.14 make fiscal policy look easy. Calculate the recessionary gap or the inflationary gap and the multiplier, change government purchases or taxes, and eliminate the gap. In reality, things are not that easy.

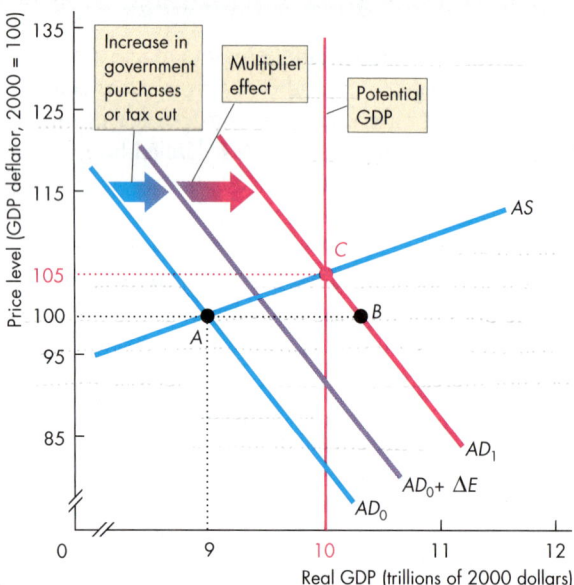

**FIGURE 15.13  Expansionary Fiscal Policy**

Potential GDP is $10 trillion, real GDP is $9 trillion, and there is a $1 trillion recessionary gap. An increase in government purchases or a tax cut increases expenditure by $\Delta E$. The multiplier increases induced expenditure. The $AD$ curve shifts rightward to $AD_1$, the price level rises to 105, real GDP increases to $10 trillion, and the recessionary gap is eliminated.

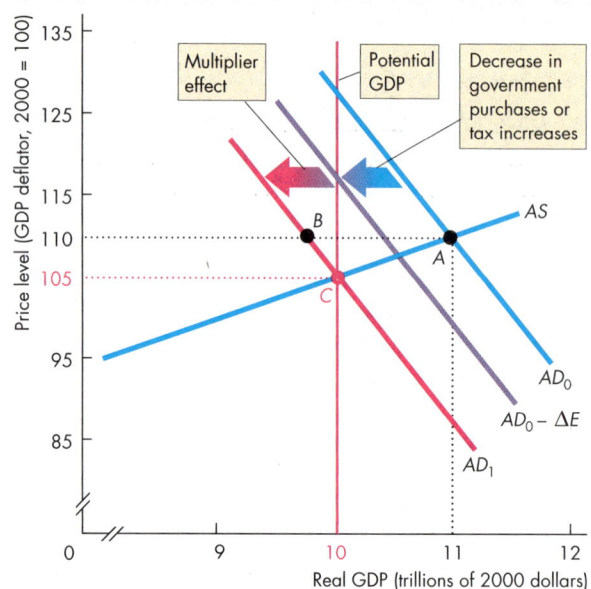

**FIGURE 15.14  Contractionary Fiscal Policy**

Potential GDP is $10 trillion, real GDP is $11 trillion, and there is a $1 trillion inflationary gap. A decrease in government purchases or a rise in taxes decreases expenditure by $\Delta E$. The multiplier increases induced expenditure. The $AD$ curve shifts leftward to $AD_1$, the price level falls to 105, real GDP decreases to $10 trillion, and the inflationary gap is eliminated.

## Limitations of Discretionary Fiscal Policy

The use of discretionary fiscal policy is seriously hampered by three time lags:

- Recognition lag
- Law-making lag
- Impact lag

**Recognition Lag** The recognition lag is the time it takes to figure out that fiscal policy actions are needed. This process has two aspects: figuring out the current state of the economy and forecasting its future state.

**Law-Making Lag** The law-making time lag is the amount of time it takes Congress to pass the laws needed to change taxes or spending. This process takes time because each member of Congress has a different idea about what is the best tax or spending program to change, so long debates and committee meetings are needed to reconcile conflicting views. The economy might benefit from fiscal stimulation today, but by the time Congress acts, a different fiscal medicine might be needed.

**Impact Lag** The impact lag is the time it takes from passing a tax or spending change to implementing the new arrangements and their effects on real GDP being felt. This lag depends partly on the speed with which government agencies can act and partly on the timing of changes in spending plans by households and businesses.

Economic forecasting has improved enormously in recent years, but it remains inexact and subject to error. So, because of these three time lags, discretionary fiscal action might end up moving real GDP *away* from potential GDP and creating the very problems it seeks to correct.

Let's now look at automatic fiscal policy.

## Automatic Stabilizers

Automatic fiscal policy is a consequence of tax revenues and expenditures that fluctuate with real GDP. These features of fiscal policy are called **automatic stabilizers** because they work to stabilize real GDP without explicit action by the government. Their name is borrowed from engineering and conjures up images of shock absorbers, thermostats, and sophisticated devices that keep airplanes and ships steady in turbulent air and seas.

**Induced Taxes** On the revenues side of the budget, tax laws define tax *rates*, not tax *dollars*. Tax dollars paid depend on tax rates and incomes. But incomes vary with real GDP, so tax revenues depend on real GDP. Taxes that vary with real GDP are called **induced taxes**. When real GDP increases in an expansion, wages and profits rise, so the taxes on these incomes—induced taxes—rise. When real GDP decreases in a recession, wages and profits fall, so the induced taxes on these incomes fall.

**Needs-Tested Spending** On the expenditure side of the budget, the government creates programs that pay benefits to suitably qualified people and businesses. The spending on such programs is called **needs-tested spending**, and it results in transfer payments that depend on the economic state of individual citizens and businesses. When the economy is in a recession, unemployment is high and the number of people experiencing economic hardship increases, but needs-tested spending on unemployment benefits and food stamps also increases. When the economy expands, unemployment falls, the number of people experiencing economic hardship decreases, and needs-tested spending decreases.

Induced taxes and needs-tested spending decrease the multiplier effects of changes in autonomous expenditure (such as investment and exports). So they moderate both expansions and recessions and make real GDP more stable. They achieve this outcome by weakening the link between real GDP and disposable income and so reduce the effect of a change in real GDP on consumption expenditure. When real GDP increases, induced taxes increase and needs-tested spending decreases, so disposable income does not increase by as much as the increase in real GDP. As a result, consumption expenditure does not increase by as much as it otherwise would and the multiplier effect is reduced.

We can see the effects of automatic stabilizers by looking at the way that the government budget deficit fluctuates over the business cycle.

**Budget Deficit Over the Business Cycle** Figure 15.15 shows the business cycle and fluctuations in the budget deficit between 1983 and 2003. Part (a) shows the fluctuations of real GDP around potential GDP. Part (b) shows the federal budget deficit. Both parts highlight recessions by shading those periods. By comparing the two parts of the figure, you can see the relationship between the business cycle and the budget deficit. As a rule, when the economy is in an expansion the budget deficit declines. (In the figure, a declining deficit means a deficit that is getting closer to zero.) As the expansion slows before the recession begins, the budget deficit increases. It continues to increase during the recession and for a period after the recession is over. Then, when the expansion is well under way, the budget deficit declines again.

The budget deficit fluctuates with the business cycle because both tax revenues and expenditures fluctuate with real GDP. As real GDP increases during an expansion, tax revenues increase and transfer payments decrease, so the budget deficit automatically decreases. As real GDP decreases during a recession, tax revenues decrease and transfer payments increase, so the budget deficit automatically increases. Fluctuations in investment and exports have a multiplier effect on real GDP. But fluctuations in tax revenues (and the budget deficit) act as an automatic stabilizer. They decrease the swings in disposable income and make the multiplier effect smaller. They dampen both expansions and recessions.

**Cyclical and Structural Balances** Because the government budget balance fluctuates with the business cycle, we need a method of measuring the balance that tells us whether it is a temporary cyclical phenomenon or a persistent phenomenon. A temporary cyclical surplus or deficit vanishes when full employment returns. A persistent surplus or deficit requires government action to remove it.

To determine whether the budget balance is persistent or temporary and cyclical, economists have developed the concepts of the structural budget balance and the cyclical budget balance. The **structural surplus or deficit** is the budget balance that would occur if the economy were at full employment and real GDP were equal to potential GDP. The **cyclical surplus or deficit** is the actual surplus or deficit minus the structural surplus or deficit. That is, the cyclical surplus or deficit is the part of the budget balance that arises purely because real GDP does not equal potential GDP. For example, suppose that the budget deficit is $100 billion. And suppose that economists have determined that there is a structural deficit of $25 billion. Then there is a cyclical deficit of $75 billion.

Figure 15.16 illustrates the concepts of the cyclical surplus or deficit and the structural surplus or deficit. The blue curve shows government expenditures. The expenditures curve slopes downward because transfer payments, a component of government expenditures, decreases as real GDP increases.

**FIGURE 15.15** The Business Cycle and the Budget Deficit

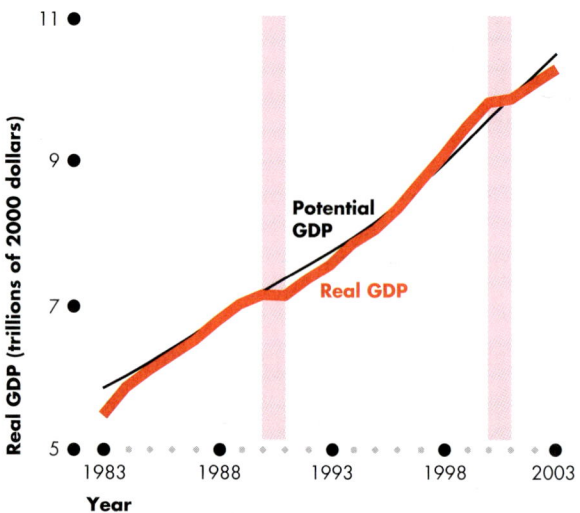

(a) Growth and recessions

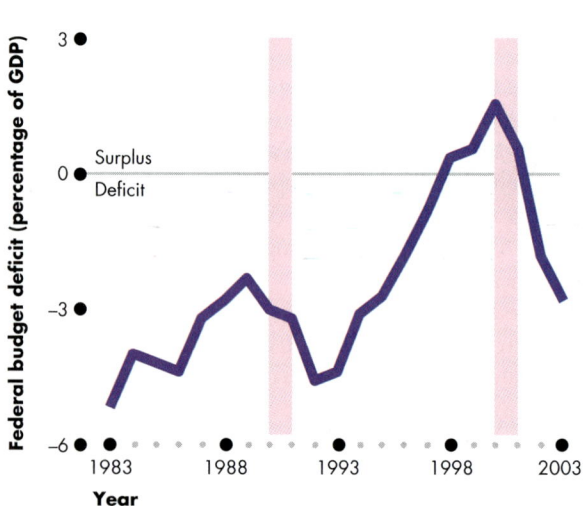

(b) Federal budget deficit

As real GDP fluctuates around potential GDP (part a), the budget deficit fluctuates (part b). During a recession (shaded years), tax revenues decrease, transfer payments increase, and the budget deficit increases. The deficit also increases *before* a recession as real GDP growth slows and *after* a recession before real GDP growth speeds up.

Sources: Bureau of Economic Analysis, Congressional Budget Office, and Office of Management and the Budget.

## FIGURE 15.16  Cyclical and Structural Surpluses and Deficits

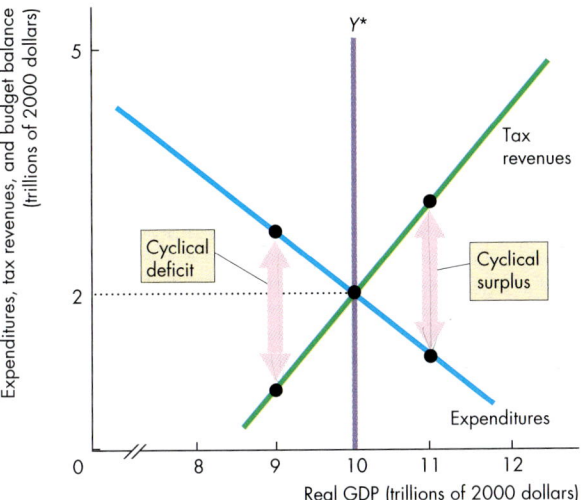

**(a) Cyclical deficit and cyclical surplus**

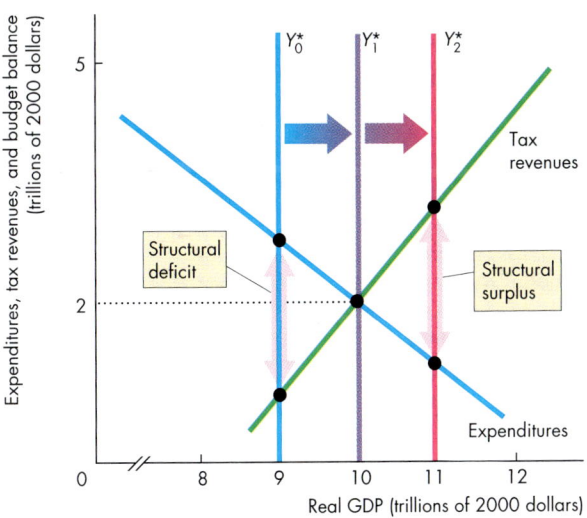

**(b) Structural deficit and structural surplus**

In part (a), potential GDP is $10 trillion. When real GDP is less than potential GDP, the budget is in a *cyclical deficit*. When real GDP exceeds potential GDP, the budget is in a *cyclical surplus*. The government has a *balanced budget* when real GDP equals potential GDP. In part (b), when potential GDP is $9 trillion, there is a *structural deficit*. But when potential GDP is $11 trillion, there is a *structural surplus*.

The green curve shows tax revenues. The tax revenues curve slopes upward because most components of tax revenues increase as incomes and real GDP increase.

In Fig. 15.16(a), potential GDP is $10 trillion. If real GDP equals potential GDP, the government has a *balanced budget*. Expenditures and tax revenues each equal $2 trillion. If real GDP is less than potential GDP, expenditures exceed tax revenues and there is a *cyclical deficit*. If real GDP is greater than potential GDP, expenditures are less than tax revenues and there is a *cyclical surplus*.

In Fig. 15.16(b), potential GDP grows but the tax revenues curve and the expenditure curve do not change. When potential GDP is $9 trillion ($Y^*_0$), there is a *structural deficit*. When potential GDP grows to $10 trillion ($Y^*_1$), there is a *structural balance* of zero (neither a deficit nor a surplus). And when potential GDP grows to $11 trillion ($Y^*_2$), there is a *structural surplus*.

The U.S. federal budget was in a structural deficit starting in the mid-1970s and continuing through the mid-1990s. That is, even if the economy had been at full employment, the budget would have been in deficit. Worse, the structural deficit was so large that even at the peak of a business cycle, the budget was in deficit. The budget surplus that emerged at the end of the 1990s was at least partly a cyclical surplus and as the economy slowed during 2001, a deficit emerged.

### REVIEW QUIZ

1. How can the federal government use fiscal policy to stabilize the business cycle?
2. Why is the government purchases multiplier larger than the taxes multiplier?
3. Why does a balanced budget increase in spending and taxes increase aggregate demand?
4. How do income taxes and needs-tested programs work as automatic stabilizers to dampen the business cycle?
5. How do we tell whether a budget deficit needs government action to remove it?

◆ You've seen how fiscal policy influences potential GDP, the growth rate of real GDP, and real GDP fluctuations. *Reading Between the Lines* on pp. 382–383 looks further at the 2004 budget and President Bush's fiscal policy.

# READING BETWEEN THE LINES

## POLICY WATCH

## Fiscal Policy Today

**THE BOSTON GLOBE, DECEMBER 4, 2003**

### Federal Spending Per Household Is Most Since WWII

...Such programs as the No Child Left Behind education law have combined with wartime costs and a generous farm bill to increase government spending by 16 percent in the last two years, compared with an average of 3.5 percent a year during the 1990s. The recent passage of a $396 billion Medicare expansion and overhaul bill is expected to drive spending even higher in future years.

The Heritage Foundation and other conservative groups expressed concerns yesterday about the spending habits of a Republican Congress that had promised fiscal restraint. The foundation said this Congress's spending increases went well beyond outlays for defense and homeland security: Subtracting those, spending still went up 11 percent over the past two years.

...Brian M. Riedl, a Heritage Foundation economist...found that per-household spending this year reached $20,000 in inflation-adjusted dollars for the first time since World War II—a trend he said makes a tax increase nearly inevitable. "People haven't felt the pain yet because ... spending has been financed by budget deficits," he said.

The Center for Budget and Policy Priorities (CBPP), a group that has defended spending on social programs in the past, arrived at similar conclusions. Looking at "discretionary spending "—appropriations that exclude entitlement programs such as Social Security and Medicare, whose payments are largely out of the control of the president—spending in inflation-adjusted dollars has increased 8.7 percent a year under the current administration. That's up from an average of 4.2 percent a year in the last three years of the Clinton administration, CBPP economist Richard Kogan said....

©2003 by Globe Newspaper Co (MA). Reprinted with permission. Further reproduction prohibited.

### Essence of the Story

- Federal spending increased by 8.7 percent a year under the Bush administration, up from an average of 4.2 percent a year in the last three years of the Clinton administration.

- The passage of a $396 billion bill to expand Medicare will send spending even higher in future years.

- Conservative groups as well as defenders of spending on social programs agree that federal spending is out of control.

- A Heritage Foundation report says that spending per-household is at its highest level since World War II.

## Economic Analysis

- The news article compares some features of the federal budget today with those during the years of the Clinton administration.

- Figure 1 shows the broad facts about the federal budget in 2000 and 2004. The 2000 numbers are those for the last Clinton year, and the 2004 numbers are for the current year.

- You can see that expenditures have increased substantially. Transfer payments increased by $274 billion; defense spending increased by $95 billion; and other expenditures increased by $62 billion. Total outlays were up by $431 billion.

- You can also see that tax revenues *decreased*. Personal income taxes fell by $157 billion, and corporate income taxes fell by $36 billion. Social security taxes and indirect taxes increased, but by less than the decrease in other taxes. So total taxes decreased by $65 billion.

- The balance of the federal budget turned from a surplus of $152 billion in 2000 to a deficit of $301 billion in 2004.

- Figure 2 expresses the budget data as percentages of GDP. This way of looking at the budget highlights the allocation of resources between the federal government and the rest of the economy.

- Relative to GDP, the increase in expenditures is small. You can see that transfer payments and nondefense expenditures increased by more than the increase in defense expenditures.

- Figure 2 also highlights the dramatic decrease in personal and corporate income taxes. These tax cuts and the consequent swing from surplus to deficit are the major fiscal policy events of the Bush administration.

- These fiscal policy actions have supply-side effects on the labor market and capital market, generational effects, and stabilization effects.

- The swing from surplus to deficit, a swing of $453 billion, has been financed by a $170 billion *increase* in borrowing from the rest of the world and a $283 billion crowding out of private expenditures.

- The tax cuts have positive supply-side effects, but the spending increase has a negative crowding-out effect.

- The increased deficit increases the burden that is transferred to future generations.

- The combined spending increase and tax cut increased aggregate demand and helped bring the economy back from recession. But it didn't move real GDP back to potential GDP.

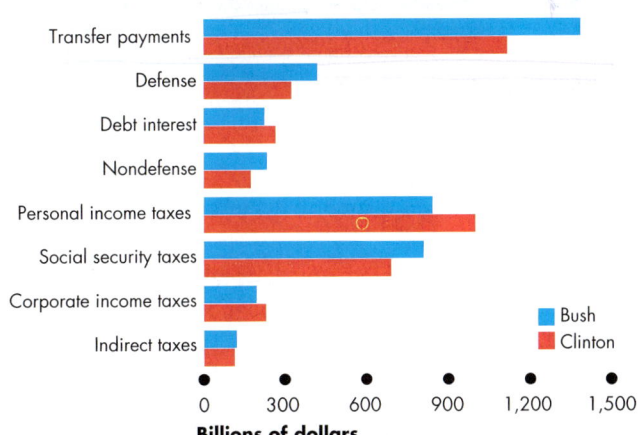

**Figure 1** Bush and Clinton budgets compared, billions of dollars

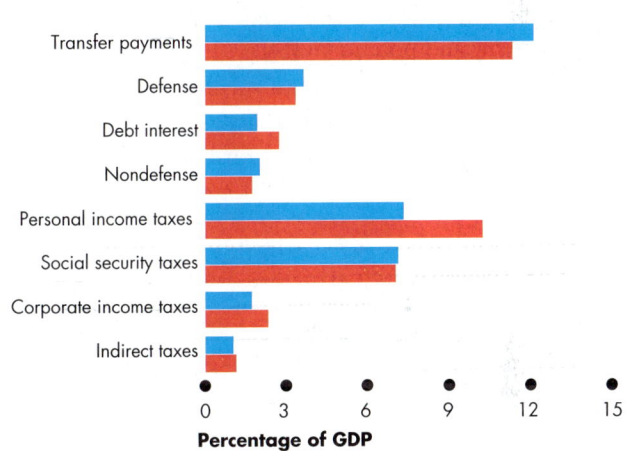

**Figure 2** Bush and Clinton budgets compared, percentage of GDP

### You're The Voter

- Do you think the current federal fiscal policy is appropriate?

- Would you vote for further tax cuts and spending cuts or for tax and spending increases? Explain.

# SUMMARY

## KEY POINTS

### The Federal Budget (pp. 362–367)

- The federal budget is used to achieve macroeconomic objectives.
- Tax revenues can exceed, equal, or fall short of expenditures—the budget can be in surplus, balanced, or deficit.
- Budget deficits create government debt.

### The Supply Side: Employment and Potential GDP (pp. 368–370)

- Fiscal policy has supply-side effects because taxes weaken the incentive to work and decrease employment and potential GDP.
- The U.S. tax wedge is large but smaller than those of the United Kingdom and France.
- The Laffer curve shows the relationship between the tax rate and the amount of tax collected.

### The Supply Side: Investment, Saving, and Economic Growth (pp. 371–374)

- Fiscal policy has supply-side effects because taxes weaken the incentive to save and invest, which lowers the growth rate of real GDP.
- A government budget deficit decreases saving, raises the real interest rate, and crowds out some investment.
- The Ricardo-Barro effect lessens crowding-out.

### Generational Effects of Fiscal Policy (pp. 374–376)

- Generational accounting measures the lifetime tax burden and benefits of each generation.
- In 2003, the U.S. fiscal imbalance was estimated to be $45 trillion—4.5 times annual GDP.
- Future generations will pay for 57 percent of the benefits of the current generation.
- Foreigners hold a half of U.S. government debt.

### Stabilizing the Business Cycle (pp. 377–381)

- Fiscal stabilization can be discretionary or automatic.
- Discretionary changes in government purchases or taxes can change aggregate demand but are hampered by law-making lags and the difficulty of correctly diagnosing and forecasting the state of the economy.
- Automatic changes in fiscal policy moderate the business cycle.

## KEY FIGURES

Figure 15.6   The Effects of the Income Tax on Aggregate Supply, 368
Figure 15.10   The Effects of a Tax on Capital Income, 372
Figure 15.13   Expansionary Fiscal Policy, 378
Figure 15.14   Contractionary Fiscal Policy, 378

## KEY TERMS

Automatic fiscal policy, 377
Automatic stabilizer, 379
Balanced budget, 364
Balanced budget multiplier, 377
Budget deficit, 364
Budget surplus, 364
Council of Economic Advisers, 363
Crowding-out effect, 373
Cyclical surplus or deficit, 380
Discretionary fiscal policy, 377
Employment Act of 1946, 362
Federal budget, 362
Fiscal imbalance, 375
Fiscal policy, 362
Generational accounting, 374
Generational imbalance, 375
Government debt, 366
Government purchases multiplier, 377
Induced taxes, 379
Laffer curve, 370
Needs-tested spending, 379
Present value, 374
Ricardo-Barro effect, 374
Structural surplus or deficit, 380
Supply-side effects, 368
Tax multiplier, 377
Tax wedge, 369

# PROBLEMS

*1. The government is proposing to increase the tax rate on labor income and asks you to report on the supply-side effects of such an action. Answer the following questions using appropriate diagrams. You are being asked about directions of change, not exact magnitudes.
   a. What will happen to the supply of labor and why?
   b. What will happen to the demand for labor and why?
   c. What will happen to the equilibrium level of employment and why?
   d. What will happen to the equilibrium pre-tax wage rate?
   e. What will happen to the equilibrium after-tax wage rate?
   f. What will happen to potential GDP?
   g. What evidence would you present to the government to support the view that a lower tax on labor income will have a significant effect on the labor market?

2. The government is proposing to lower the tax rate on labor income and asks you to report on the supply-side effects of such an action. Answer the following questions using appropriate diagrams. You are being asked about directions of change, not exact magnitudes.
   a. What will happen to the supply of labor and why?
   b. What will happen to the demand for labor and why?
   c. What will happen to the equilibrium level of employment and why?
   d. What will happen to the equilibrium pre-tax wage rate?
   e. What will happen to the equilibrium after-tax wage rate?
   f. What will happen to potential GDP?
   g. How would your answers to the above questions change if at the same time as cutting the labor income tax rate, the government increased the rate of sales tax to keep the amount of tax collected constant?
   h. What evidence would you present to the government to support the view that a higher tax on labor income will have a significant effect on the labor market?

*3. Suppose that in the United States in 2004, investment is $1,600 billion, saving is $1,400 billion, government purchases are $1,500 billion, exports are $2,000 billion, and imports are $2,500 billion.
   a. What is the amount of tax revenue?
   b. What is the government budget balance?
   c. Is the government exerting a positive or negative impact on investment?
   d. What fiscal policy action might increase investment and speed economic growth? Explain how the policy action would work.

4. Suppose that in China in 2004, investment is $400 billion, saving is $400 billion, tax revenues are $500 billion, exports are $300 billion, and imports are $200 billion.
   a. What is the amount of government purchases?
   b. What is the government budget balance?
   c. Is the government exerting a positive or negative impact on investment?
   d. What fiscal policy action might increase investment and speed economic growth? Explain how the policy action would work.

*5. Government expenditures are increased by $100 billion.
   a. Explain how saving, investment, and the real interest rate respond to this fiscal policy.
   b. How does your answer to the previous question depend on the strength of the Ricardo-Barro effect?

6. Government expenditures are decreased by $100 billion.
   a. Explain how saving, investment, and the real interest rate respond to this fiscal policy.
   b. How does your answer to the previous question depend on the strength of the Ricardo-Barro effect?

*7. Suppose that instead of taxing nominal capital income, the tax code is changed and the inflation rate is subtracted from the interest rate before calculating taxable income from capital. Explain and illustrate using the appropriate diagrams, the effect that this change would have on
   a. The true tax rate on capital income.
   b. Saving supply.
   c. Investment demand.
   d. The equilibrium amount of investment and the equilibrium real interest rate.

* Solutions to odd-numbered problems are available on **MyEconLab**.

8. Suppose that capital income taxes are based (as they are in the United States and most countries) on nominal interest rates. And suppose that the inflation rate increases by 5 percent. Explain and illustrate using the appropriate diagrams, the effect that this change would have on
   a. The true tax rate on capital income.
   b. Saving supply.
   c. Investment demand.
   d. The equilibrium amount of investment and the equilibrium real interest rate.

*9. The economy is in a recession and there is a large recessionary gap.
   a. Describe the discretionary and automatic fiscal policy actions that might occur.
   b. Describe a discretionary fiscal stimulation package that could be used that would *not* bring a budget deficit.
   c. Explain the risks of discretionary fiscal policy in this situation.

10. The economy is in a boom and there is a large inflationary gap.
    a. Describe the discretionary and automatic fiscal policy actions that might occur.
    b. Describe a discretionary fiscal restraint package that could be used that would *not* produce serious negative supply-side effects.
    c. Explain the risks of discretionary fiscal policy in this situation.

*11. The economy is in a recession. There is a large recessionary gap and there is a budget deficit.
    a. Do we know whether the budget deficit is structural or cyclical? Explain your answer.
    b. Do we know whether automatic stabilizers are increasing or decreasing aggregate demand? Explain your answer.
    c. If a discretionary increase in government purchases occurs, what happens to the structural deficit or surplus? Explain.

12. The economy is in a boom. There is a large inflationary gap and there is a budget deficit.
    a. Do we know whether the budget deficit is structural or cyclical? Explain your answer.
    b. Do we know whether automatic stabilizers are increasing or decreasing aggregate demand? Explain your answer.
    c. If a discretionary decrease in government purchases occurs, what happens to the structural deficit or surplus? Explain your answer.

# CRITICAL THINKING

1. Study *Reading Between the Lines* on pp. 382–383.
   a. Describe the main differences between the budgets of President Clinton in 2000 and President Bush in 2004.
   b. Does the Bush budget show that government spending is out of control as claimed by some in the news article? Explain why or why not.
   c. Do you think the 2004 budget should be balanced? If so, do you think the government should cut spending or raise taxes? If you think the budget should not be balanced, explain why.
2. Think about the supply-side effects of 2004 budget.
   a. What would be the main effects of lower income tax rates on the level of potential GDP?
   b. How would lower income taxes influence the real wage rate and the real interest rate?
   c. What are the main costs of lower income taxes?

# WEB EXERCISES

**Use the links on MyEconLab to work the following exercises.**

1. Visit the National Center for Policy Analysis Idea House. Click on "Dick Armey Flat Tax" and "The Liberal Case for a Flat Tax." When you have studied these two pages, answer the following questions:
   a. What are the main features of Dick Armey's plan?
   b. What is the liberal case for a flat tax?
   c. Why do you think a flat tax is usually associated with conservatives rather than liberals?
2. Visit the U.S. government budget Web site. Use the information that you can find on this site to describe the main features of the budget for the current fiscal year. Analyze the demand side and supply-side effects of the current year's budget.

# Monetary Policy

**CHAPTER 16**

## What Can Monetary Policy Do?

**During the 1990s, the U.S. economy performed** well. Real GDP expanded by between 3 percent and 4 percent each year in one of the most stable and sustained episodes of growth the economy has seen. The unemployment rate fell steadily from around 7 percent in 1991 to 4 percent in 2000. While the economy was expanding and unemployment falling, the inflation rate remained below 3 percent a year and showed no sign of turning upward.

But by 2000, growth was slowing, and in 2001, real GDP shrank and unemployment increased.

The United States was not alone in facing a growth slowdown. Every other major country saw its economy slow. Alan Greenspan and his fellow central bankers began to cut interest rates to stimulate production and jobs.

Were these actions the right ones? Can and should monetary policy try to counter recessions? Or should monetary policy focus more narrowly on price stability?

◆ In this chapter, we're going to study the Federal Reserve's challenges of avoiding inflation and achieving sustainable long-term growth and low unemployment. We're also going to review the alternative views on these issues. In *Reading Between the Lines* at the end of the chapter, we'll look at the Fed's decisions at the end of 2003 to keep the interest rate low and aid the recovery from recession.

### After studying this chapter, you will be able to

- Distinguish among the instruments, ultimate goals, and intermediate targets of monetary policy and review the Fed's performance
- Describe and compare the performance of a *monetarist fixed rule* and *Keynesian feedback rules* for monetary policy
- Explain why the outcome of monetary policy crucially depends on the Fed's credibility
- Describe and compare the *new monetarist* and *new Keynesian* feedback rules for monetary policy

# Instruments, Goals, Targets, and the Fed's Performance

It helps to keep a clear head when thinking about monetary policy if we distinguish among:

- Instruments
- Goals
- Intermediate targets

The *instruments* of monetary policy are the tools that you learned about in Chapter 10. They are open market operations, the discount rate, and required reserve ratios. The Fed conducts open market operations and sets the discount rate and the required reserve ratios to achieve the goals of its monetary policy.

The *goals* of monetary policy are the ultimate objectives that the Fed seeks. The Fed's primary goal is to maintain *price level stability*. But there is a short-run tradeoff between price level stability and real GDP. So a secondary goal of monetary policy is to keep real GDP as close as possible to potential GDP and help maintain *sustainable real GDP growth*.

The effects of changes in the Fed's instruments on the goals of monetary policy cannot be predicted with certainty, and they occur with a long and variable time lag. For these reasons, the Fed needs some way of assessing whether its actions are on the right track. It makes these assessments by watching the evolution of intermediate targets.

The possible *intermediate targets* of monetary policy include monetary aggregates such as M1 and M2, the *monetary base*—the sum of notes, coins, and banks' deposits at the Fed—and the *federal funds rate*—the interest rate on overnight loans among banks.

The Fed's open market operations and discount rate changes influence the M1 and M2 measures of money indirectly along with other influences that stem from the lending decisions of the banks and the borrowing decisions of households and firms. Because the Fed does not have immediate and tight control of these aggregates, it does not use them as intermediate targets.

In contrast, open market operations and the discount rate *directly* affect the monetary base and the federal funds rate. These effects are fast and easy for the Fed to monitor. The Fed might target either the monetary base or the federal funds rate, but it cannot independently target both at the same time and must decide which one to target. In recent years, the Fed's choice has been the federal funds rate.

## Price Level Stability

Why does the Fed want to achieve price level stability? And what exactly is price level stability?

**Why Price Level Stability?** The economy works best when the price level is stable and predictable. If the inflation rate fluctuates unpredictably, money becomes less useful as a measuring rod for conducting transactions. Borrowers and lenders and employers and workers must take on extra risks.

If the inflation rate is higher than expected, the real interest rate turns out to be lower than expected, which favors borrowers and hurts lenders. Conversely, if the inflation rate is lower than expected, the real interest rate turns out to be higher than expected, which favors lenders and hurts borrowers.

Similarly, if the inflation rate is higher than expected, the real wage rate turns out to be lower than expected, which favors employers and hurts workers. And if the inflation rate is lower than expected, the real wage rate turns out to be higher than expected, which favors workers and hurts employers.

Keeping the inflation rate steady and predictable avoids these problems. Some economists say that the inflation *rate* doesn't matter so long as the rate is *predictable*. It is *predictability* that avoids the problems and risks that we've just described. A high inflation rate that is correctly anticipated means that the nominal interest rate is high but the real interest rate is unaffected by the inflation. Similarly the money wage rate is set in anticipation of the inflation that is present and the real wage rate is immune from inflation.

While accepting the logic of the argument that a high anticipated inflation has few adverse effects, most economists believe that when the inflation rate is high, its rate becomes harder to predict. So the inflation rate *does* matter and price level stability is the only sustainable goal.

**What Is Price Level Stability?** Alan Greenspan once defined price level stability as a condition in which the inflation rate does not feature in people's economic calculations. An inflation rate close enough to zero but not exactly zero would qualify as price stability on this definition. Most economists agree with Alan Greenspan and view an inflation rate of between 0 and 3 percent a year as being consistent with price level stability.

Price level measurement bias is the main reason why a low inflation rate is considered to be price level stability. Quality improvements that create the measurement bias imply that a *measured* inflation rate of between 0 and 3 percent a year is close to a zero true inflation rate and so is equivalent to price level stability.

## Sustainable Real GDP Growth

Price level stability is the primary goal of monetary policy. But it is only a means to a deeper end—a high and rising standard of living. And the standard of living depends crucially on the growth rate of *real* GDP. With a real GDP growth rate of 3 percent a year, it takes 24 years for production to double. But with a growth rate of 8 percent a year, as China and some other Asian countries are achieving, production doubles in just 9 years.

The limits to *sustainable* growth are determined not by the actions of the Fed, but by the availability of natural resources, by environmental considerations, and by the willingness of people to save and invest in new capital and new technologies rather than consume everything they produce.

But the Fed's actions have indirect effects on real GDP growth: they affect the trend growth rate and the cyclical fluctuations around the trend.

### Monetary Policy and Potential GDP Growth

Price level stability contributes to potential GDP growth by creating a climate that favors a high rate of saving and investment. So by pursuing its primary policy goal, the Fed indirectly furthers its second goal.

### Monetary Policy and the Business Cycle

Fluctuations in the pace of technological advance and in the pace of investment in new capital bring fluctuations in potential GDP. So some fluctuations in real GDP are fluctuations in potential GDP. But when real GDP grows less quickly than potential GDP, output is lost, and when real GDP grows more quickly than potential GDP, bottlenecks arise. Keeping real GDP growth steady and equal to potential GDP growth avoids these problems.

It is not known how smooth real GDP growth can be made. Real business cycle theory regards all the fluctuations in real GDP as fluctuations in potential GDP. Keynesian and monetarist aggregate demand theories of the cycle regard most of the fluctuations in real GDP as being avoidable deviations from potential GDP.

Monetary policy can both create and help to avoid fluctuations around potential GDP. It creates fluctuations if the Fed incorrectly anticipates swings in aggregate demand and reinforces them with inappropriately timed swings in the interest rate and the money growth rate. And monetary policy helps to smooth out fluctuations if the Fed correctly anticipates swings in aggregate demand and offsets them with appropriately timed swings in the interest rate and the money growth rate.

Smoothing real GDP fluctuations also helps to keep the unemployment rate close to the natural rate of unemployment. And keeping unemployment at its natural rate prevents the waste and social problems of high unemployment and the inflation that come when the unemployment rate sinks too low.

## The Fed's Performance: 1973–2003

The Fed's performance depends on two broad factors:

- Shocks to the price level
- Monetary policy actions

**Shocks to the Price Level** Shocks to the price level during the 1970s and 1980s made the Fed's job harder and shocks in the 1990s made its job easier.

During the 1970s, world oil price hikes, large and increasing budget deficits, and a productivity slowdown intensified inflationary pressures. These shocks imparted upward pressure on the price level and decreased real GDP.

During the 1990s, falling world oil prices, decreasing budget deficits (and eventually a budget surplus) eased the pressure on inflation, and the new information economy brought more rapid productivity growth. These shocks imparted downward pressure on the price level and increased real GDP.

**Monetary Policy Actions** Figure 16.1 provides a snapshot of monetary policy during the 30 years from 1973 to 2003.

The figure identifies the terms of office of the Presidents and the Fed chairmen. The Fed has had four chairmen during this period. Notice that the term of a Fed chairman does not coincide with the term of a President. Arthur Burns (whose term began in 1969) served until 1978. William Miller had a short term and was replaced by Paul Volcker in 1979. The current chairman, Alan Greenspan, was appointed by President Reagan in 1987 and has served through the terms of four Presidents.

The figure shows three broad measures of monetary policy. They are the federal funds rate, the real federal funds rate, and the growth rate of M2.

The federal funds rate tells us how the Fed was changing its key intermediate target. And the real federal funds rate tells us how the Fed's actions were changing the opportunity cost of short-term funds that influences spending plans. The M2 growth rate provides a broader indication of how monetary policy was influencing aggregate demand.

First, let's look at some of the monetary policy trends. The federal funds rate trended upward from 1973 through 1981, downward through 1993, was flat through 2001, and then trended downward again in 2002 and 2003.

The real federal funds rate fell through 1975 and then increased to a peak in 1981. It then followed the trends of the federal funds rate.

During the early 1970s, M2 grew at a rapid rate that hit a peak of 14 percent in 1976. The M2 growth rate remained high until 1983 and then fell steadily from 12 percent in 1983 to less than 1 percent in 1994. After 1994, the M2 growth rate trended upward.

The high M2 growth brought the 1970s inflation, which brought rising *nominal* interest rates but, at first, falling real interest rates. The subsequent sharp downward trend in M2 growth brought falling inflation and falling nominal interest rates, but it was accompanied by high real interest rates. M2 growth increased during the late 1990s and remained high through 2003.

Notice a remarkable fact about the monetary policy cycles: There is a tendency for the federal funds rate to rise and the M2 growth rate to decrease immediately following an election and for the federal funds rate to fall and the M2 growth rate to increase as the next election approaches.

Usually, the incumbent President or his party's successor has won the election. There are two exceptions. In 1980, M2 growth increased but not as quickly as the demand for money. Interest rates increased, the economy slowed, and Jimmy Carter lost his reelection bid. In 1992, M2 growth slowed, interest rates rose, and George Bush lost his reelection bid. A coincidence? Perhaps, but Presidents take a keen interest in what the Fed is up to. And as the 2004 election approached, the White House was watching anxiously, hoping that the Fed would continue to favor a low federal funds rate and keep the economy expanding.

**Inflation and Real GDP: Hits and Misses**  We've described the shocks to the price level that monetary policy had to cope with. And we've reviewed the main trends in the intermediate policy targets. How well has the Fed done? How close has it come to

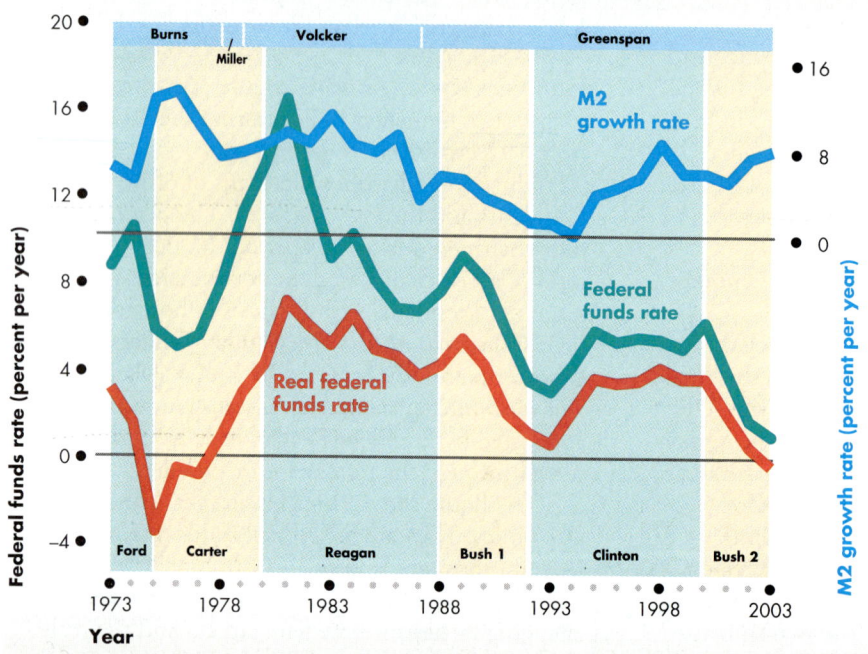

**FIGURE 16.1**  The Monetary Policy Record: A Summary

The monetary policy record is summarized here by the federal funds rate and the growth rate of M2. Fluctuations in the interest rate and M2 growth have coincided with elections, with monetary growth usually increasing just before an election.

Exceptions are 1979–1980 and 1991–1992, when monetary growth did not increase and the incumbent President lost the election.

*Source*: Federal Reserve Board.

## FIGURE 16.2 Macroeconomic Performance: Inflation and Real GDP

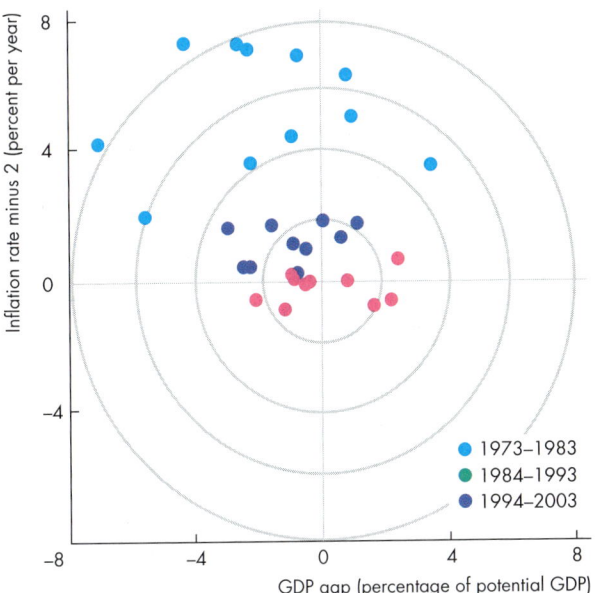

The inflation rate was high and the real GDP fluctuated a long way below potential GDP during the 1970s and early 1980s. This macroeconomic performance falls short of the goals of price level stability and sustainable real GDP growth. During the 1990s and 2000s, both inflation and fluctuations of real GDP around potential GDP have been less severe. This recent macroeconomic performance comes close to achieving the goals of price level stability and sustainable real GDP growth.

*Source:* Bureau of Economic Analysis.

achieving the ultimate monetary policy goals of price level stability and sustained real GDP growth?

Figure 16.2 provides a neat way of answering these questions. An inflation rate of about 2 percent a year is consistent with price stability. So the *y*-axis shows how close to this goal the Fed has come by measuring deviations of the inflation rate from 2 percent.

Achieving sustained real GDP growth means keeping real GDP close to potential GDP. So the *x*-axis shows how close the Fed has come to this goal by measuring deviations of real GDP from potential GDP. The origin, at which real GDP equals potential GDP (full employment) and the inflation rate is 2 percent a year, is like the bull's eye of a target.

The dots show how well the Fed has done in aiming for this ideal outcome. The blue dots show the Fed's performance between 1973 and 1983. You can see that during this period, the inflation rate was high and real GDP was substantially below potential GDP. The purple dots show how the Fed performed between 1984 and 1993. During this period, the inflation rate fell and real GDP remained closer to potential GDP. The red dots show the Fed's performance between 1994 and 2003. Over this decade, the United States enjoyed an unusual period of price level stability and sustained growth of real GDP, which remained close to potential GDP.

What you've just learned helps to explain why the Fed did so badly during the 1970s and early 1980s, missing its goals by a large margin, and why the Fed did so well during the 1990s and 2000s, coming very close to achieving its goals.

The shocks to the price level during the 1970s and 1980s pushed the inflation rate up and sent real GDP well below potential—the blue dots. The Fed allowed the quantity of money to grow rapidly during the 1970s, which reinforced these shocks.

The shocks to the price level of the 1990s lowered the inflation rate and kept real GDP close to potential GDP—the red dots.

By the 1990s, the Fed had learned from its past challenges and its policy strategy had evolved so that even if we had been confronted with the shocks of the 1970s, performance would most likely be better than it then was during those inflationary years.

### REVIEW QUIZ

1 What are the instruments, goals, and intermediate targets of monetary policy?
2 Why is price level stability the main goal of monetary policy?
3 What were the main features of monetary policy between 1973 and 2003? In which periods was monetary policy inflationary? In which periods was it most successful in achieving its goals?

You now know what monetary policy seeks to achieve. We're now going to look at the effects of using alternative monetary policy strategies to keep the price level stable and sustain economic growth.

## Achieving Price Level Stability

THERE ARE TWO PRICE LEVEL STABILITY problems. When the price level *is* stable, the problem is to prevent inflation from breaking out. When inflation is already present, the problem is to reduce its rate and restore price level stability while doing the least possible damage to real GDP growth.

Preventing inflation from breaking out means avoiding excessive increases in aggregate demand, which bring demand-pull inflation, and avoiding decreases in aggregate supply, which bring cost-push inflation.

Avoiding demand-pull inflation is the flip side of avoiding demand-driven recession and is achieved by stabilizing aggregate demand. Many different monetary policy regimes can be used to stabilize aggregate demand. But they all fall into three broad categories:

- Fixed-rule policies
- Feedback-rule policies
- Discretionary policies

### Fixed-Rule Policies

A **fixed-rule policy** specifies an action to be pursued independently of the state of the economy. An everyday example of a fixed rule is a stop sign. It says, "Stop regardless of the state of the road ahead—even if no other vehicle is trying to use the road." One fixed-rule policy, proposed by Milton Friedman, is to keep the quantity of money growing at a constant rate year in and year out, regardless of the state of the economy, to make the *average* inflation rate zero. Fixed rules are rarely followed in practice, but they have some merits in principle. Later in this chapter, we will study how fixed rules would work if they were pursued.

### Feedback-Rule Policies

A **feedback-rule policy** specifies how policy actions respond to changes in the state of the economy. A yield sign is an everyday feedback rule. It says, "Stop if another vehicle is attempting to use the road ahead, but otherwise, proceed." A monetary policy feedback-rule is one that changes the money supply or the interest rate in response to the state of the economy. For example, the Fed's Federal Open Market Committee uses a feedback rule when it pushes the interest rate ever higher in response to rising inflation and strong real GDP growth.

### Discretionary Policies

A **discretionary policy** responds to the state of the economy in a possibly unique way that uses all the information available, including perceived lessons from past "mistakes." An everyday discretionary policy occurs at an unmarked intersection. Each driver uses discretion in deciding whether to stop and how slowly to approach the intersection. Most macroeconomic policy actions have an element of discretion because every situation is to some degree unique. For example, through 1998, the Fed cut interest rates several times to maintain economic growth in the face of a sagging Asian economy. The Fed might have delayed cutting interest rates until it was sure that lower interest rates were needed and then cut them in larger increments. The Fed used discretion based on lessons it had learned from earlier expansions. But despite the fact that all policy actions have an element of discretion, they can be regarded as modifications of a feedback-rule policy.

We'll study the effects of monetary policy by comparing the performance of the price level and real GDP under alternative fixed rules and feedback rules. Because price level instability and real GDP fluctuations can result from demand shocks or supply shocks, we need to consider these two cases. The easy case is that of demand shocks, which we'll study first.

### A Monetarist Fixed Rule with Aggregate Demand Shocks

Aggregate demand fluctuates for the many reasons that you reviewed in Chapter 7 and elaborated in Chapters 13 and 14. These reasons include fluctuations in profit expectations that change investment and fluctuations in the world economy that bring fluctuations in the demand for exports. When aggregate demand fluctuates for one of these reasons, the behavior of the price level and real GDP depend on how policy responds. You saw in Chapter 15 that automatic fiscal policy dampens the effects of expenditure fluctuations because tax revenues and transfer payments are linked to the state of the economy. But automatic fiscal policy doesn't eliminate fluctuations in aggregate demand. The remaining fluctuations leave a role for monetary policy.

If monetary policy follows the fixed rule that a monetarist (see Chapter 7, p. 167) advocates, the quantity of money does not respond to the state of aggregate demand. It remains the same regardless of what happens to the price level and real GDP.

Consequently, the price level and real GDP fluctuate in the same direction as the fluctuations in aggregate demand.

Figure 16.3 illustrates these fluctuations. *On the average*, the economy is on aggregate demand curve $AD_0$ and short-run aggregate supply curve $SAS$. These curves intersect at point $A$ on the long-run aggregate supply curve, $LAS$. The price level is 105, and real GDP is $10 trillion. That is, on the average, the economy is at full employment with a stable price level.

But because investment and exports fluctuate, aggregate demand fluctuates between a low level of $AD_{LOW}$ and a high level of $AD_{HIGH}$. These fluctuations in aggregate demand bring related fluctuations in the price level and real GDP.

When the aggregate demand curve shifts leftward to $AD_{LOW}$, equilibrium occurs at point $B$. The price level has fallen to 100 and real GDP has decreased to $9.5 trillion. The economy is in a recession. Real GDP is less than potential GDP (a recessionary gap), and unemployment is above its natural rate.

Because aggregate demand fluctuates between $AD_{LOW}$ and $AD_{HIGH}$, the price level and real GDP don't remain at their recession levels. When profit expectations improve, investment increases, or as economic expansion proceeds in the rest of the world, exports increase. As a result, the aggregate demand curve shifts rightward toward $AD_0$. The price level rises and real GDP increases toward potential GDP.

Conversely, when the aggregate demand curve shifts rightward to $AD_{HIGH}$, equilibrium occurs at point $C$. The price level has risen to 110, and real GDP has increased to $10.5 trillion. The economy is in a boom. Real GDP exceeds potential GDP (an inflationary gap), and unemployment is below its natural rate.

Again, because aggregate demand fluctuates, the price level and real GDP don't remain at their boom levels. When profit expectations worsen, investment expenditure decreases, or as economic expansion ends in the rest of the world, exports decrease. As a result, the aggregate demand curve shifts leftward toward $AD_0$. The price level falls and real GDP decreases toward potential GDP.

(In the above analysis, you should think of the price level as rising and falling relative to a trend rate of increase so that the price level never actually falls.)

Let's contrast the adjustment under this fixed-policy rule with that under a feedback-rule policy.

## A Keynesian Feedback Rule with Aggregate Demand Shocks

If monetary policy follows the feedback rule that a Keynesian (see Chapter 7, p. 166) advocates, the interest rate and the quantity of money respond to the state of the economy. A decrease in aggregate demand sends the price level below target and real GDP below potential GDP, and an increase in aggregate demand sends the price level above target and real GDP above potential GDP. So the feedback rule raises the interest rate and decreases the quantity of money when aggregate demand increases and cuts the interest rate and increases the quantity of money when aggregate demand decreases.

The response of the price level and real GDP to this feedback rule depends on how well it is implemented. Figure 16.4 illustrates the behavior of the price level and real GDP under this feedback-rule policy if the policy is well implemented.

As before, in the absence of a feedback rule, aggregate demand fluctuates between $AD_{LOW}$ and

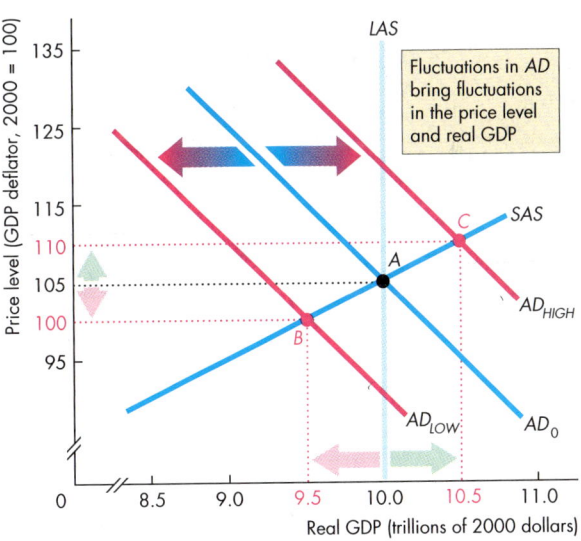

**FIGURE 16.3  A Fixed Rule with AD Shocks**

Aggregate demand fluctuates between $AD_{LOW}$ and $AD_{HIGH}$ and on the average is $AD_0$. Potential GDP is $10 trillion and the short-run aggregate supply curve is $SAS$. The price level and real GDP fluctuate as aggregate demand fluctuates and swing between recession at point $B$, full employment at point $A$, and boom at point $C$. A fixed-rule monetary policy does not respond to the changing state of the economy.

$AD_{HIGH}$, and the price level and real GDP fluctuate in the same direction as aggregate demand.

But with a feedback rule, when a decrease in investment or exports decreases aggregate demand and shifts the aggregate demand curve to $AD_{LOW}$, the Fed cuts the interest rate and increases the quantity of money. The aggregate demand curve then begins to shift rightward toward $AD_0$.

Similarly, when an increase in investment or exports increases aggregate demand and shifts the aggregate demand curve to $AD_{HIGH}$, the Fed raised the interest rate and decreases the quantity of money. The aggregate demand curve then begins to shift leftward toward $AD_0$.

Ideally the feedback rule will keep aggregate demand close to $AD_0$ so that the price level remains almost constant and real GDP remains close to potential GDP.

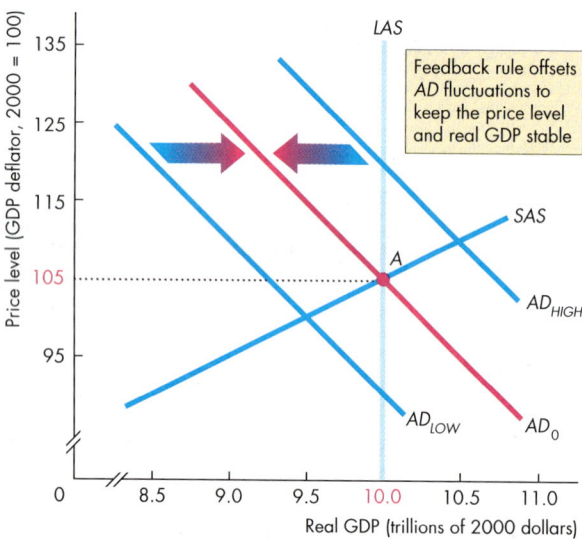

**FIGURE 16.4  A Feedback Rule with AD Shocks**

With no feedback policy, aggregate demand fluctuates between $AD_{LOW}$ and $AD_{HIGH}$ and the price level and real GDP fluctuate between recession and boom. A feedback-rule monetary policy responds to the changing state of the economy. When aggregate demand shifts to $AD_{LOW}$, a cut in the interest rate and an increase in the quantity of money shift it back toward $AD_0$. And when aggregate demand shifts to $AD_{HIGH}$, a rise in the interest rate and a decrease in the quantity of money shift it back toward $AD_0$.

A feedback policy might not be implemented as well as the one described in Fig. 16.4. And it might be implemented so badly that it results in fluctuations in the price level and real GDP of even greater amplitude than those that occur when a fixed rule is followed. The main reason why a feedback rule might not work well is that the effects of policy actions are spread out over a future period that is longer than the Fed's forecast horizon.

## Policy Lags and the Forecast Horizon

The effects of policy actions taken today are spread out over the next two years or even more. But the Fed cannot forecast that far ahead. Its forecast horizon is less than one year. Further, the Fed can't predict the precise timing and magnitude of the effects of its policy actions. So a feedback policy that reacts to *today's* economy might be wrong for the economy at that uncertain future date when the policy's effects are felt.

For example, suppose that today the economy is in recession. The Fed reacts with an interest rate cut and an increase in the quantity of money. Some time later, investment and purchases of consumer durable goods increase. Some time still later, this increase in expenditure increases income; higher income in turn induces higher consumption expenditure. Later yet, the higher expenditure increases the demand for labor, and eventually, the money wage rate and prices rise.

Nine months to two years later, aggregate demand is responding to the Fed's actions. But by the time the Fed's actions are having their maximum effect, the economy has moved on to a new situation. Perhaps a world economic slowdown has added a new negative effect on aggregate demand that is offsetting the Fed's expansionary actions. Or perhaps a boost in expected profit has stimulated investment and increased aggregate demand yet further, adding to the Fed's own expansionary policy action.

Whatever the situation, the Fed can take the appropriate actions today only if it can forecast future shocks to aggregate demand. To smooth the fluctuations in aggregate demand, the Fed needs to take actions that are based on a reliable forecast of what will be happening over a period stretching two or more years into the future. If the Fed is good at economic forecasting and bases its policy actions on its forecasts, then it can deliver the type of aggregate-demand-smoothing performance illustrated in Fig. 16.4. But if the Fed takes policy actions that are based on today's economy or on unreliable forecasts of the economy a year into the future, then those actions will often be inappropriate ones.

Some economists who advocate fixed rules believe that the Fed's own reactions to the current state of the economy are a main source of fluctuations in aggregate demand and a major factor that people must forecast to make their own economic choices.

During recent years, the Fed has tried to avoid the problems just described. In 1994, it increased interest rates early in the expansion and by small increments. In 1995, after real GDP growth slowed but before any signs of recession were on the horizon, the Fed began to cut interest rates. In 1997, before inflation turned seriously upward, the Fed hit the monetary brake. And in 1998, while the economy expanded strongly, the Fed cut interest rates to avoid the effects of the Asian recession.

But the Fed was far too late in its 2001 interest rate cuts to deal with the recession that began in March of that year. The Fed would have needed to start the cutting a year earlier to have been effective.

So whether a feedback rule or a fixed rule deals more effectively with aggregate demand fluctuations is not easily determined and depends on the quality of the forecasts that are used to inform the policy actions.

We're now going to turn from aggregate demand fluctuations to aggregate supply fluctuations. You will see that these fluctuations bring greater challenges for monetary policy.

## Stabilizing Aggregate Supply Shocks

Two types of shock occur to bring fluctuations in aggregate supply:

- Productivity growth fluctuations
- Fluctuations in cost-push pressure

**Productivity Growth Fluctuations** Real business cycle theorists believe that all fluctuations in real GDP are caused not by fluctuations in aggregate demand but by fluctuations in productivity growth. According to real business cycle theory, there is no distinction between long-run aggregate supply and short-run aggregate supply. Because the money wage rate is flexible, the labor market is always in equilibrium and unemployment is always at its natural rate. So the vertical long-run aggregate supply curve is also the short-run aggregate supply curve. The price level and real GDP fluctuate because of shifts in the long-run aggregate supply curve.

Regardless of whether real business cycle theory is correct, there is little doubt that the trend growth rate of productivity changes. For example, the productivity growth trend slowed during the 1970s and speeded up again during the 1990s. A productivity growth slowdown lowers potential GDP (and the $LAS$ curve) relative to what it otherwise would have been and a productivity growth speedup increases potential GDP (and the $LAS$ curve) relative to what it otherwise would have been.

**Fluctuations in Cost-Push Pressure** Cost-push inflation has its origins in cost increases (see Chapter 12, p. 281). Cost-push inflation pressures fluctuate and bring changes in short-run aggregate supply. In 1973–1974 and again in 1979, the world oil price exploded and produced an increase in cost-push pressure. The $SAS$ curve shifted leftward. During the 1990s, the world oil price fell and weakened cost-push inflation. The $SAS$ curve shifted rightward.

The response of the price level and real GDP to the aggregate supply shocks that we've just reviewed depend on monetary policy. First, we'll see what happens if the monetarist fixed rule is used. And we'll consider the two types of shock—a productivity shock that affects long-run aggregate supply and a cost-push shock that affects short-run aggregate supply.

## Monetarist Fixed Rule with a Productivity Shock

As in the case of aggregate demand shocks, a fixed-rule policy keeps the quantity of money constant regardless of what happens to the price level and real GDP. Figure 16.5 shows how the price level and real GDP respond to a negative productivity shock like the productivity growth slowdown of the 1970s.

In the absence of a productivity shock, the economy would have been at point $A$ on aggregate demand curve $AD_0$ and long-run aggregate supply curve $LAS_0$ at a price level of 105 and with real GDP equal to \$10 trillion.

Suppose that instead of being at $LAS_0$, slower productivity growth means that the long-run aggregate supply curve is $LAS_1$. With a fixed rule, the lower level of long-run aggregate supply has no effect on the quantity of money and no effect on aggregate demand. The aggregate demand curve remains at $AD_0$ regardless of the level of long-run aggregate supply.

With the lower long-run aggregate supply, real GDP falls to \$9.5 trillion, and the price level rises to 120 at point $B$.

## FIGURE 16.5 A Fixed Rule with an LAS Shock

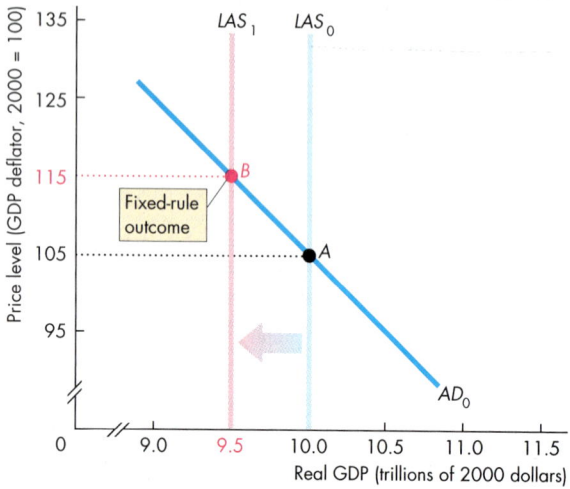

With normal productivity growth, the economy would have been at point A on $LAS_0$. A productivity growth slowdown puts the long-run aggregate supply curve at $LAS_1$. With a monetarist rule, there is no change in the quantity of money and aggregate demand remains at $AD_0$. Real GDP decreases to $9.5 trillion, and the price level rises to 120 at point B.

The decrease in real GDP is an inevitable consequence of a real productivity shock and no monetary policy can change that outcome. But the rise in the price level is a consequence of the fixed-rule monetarist policy. The price level rises because the $AD$ curve is downward sloping. A decrease in potential GDP with constant aggregate demand must bring a rise in the price level.

Can a feedback rule improve on the outcome of a fixed rule?

### Feedback Rules with Productivity Shock

An aggregate demand shock sends the price level and real GDP in the same direction. So a feedback rule that seeks to stabilize both variables is easy to define. It increases aggregate demand when the price level and real GDP fall and it decreases aggregate demand when the price level and real GDP rise.

But an aggregate supply shock sends the price level and real GDP in opposite directions. So a feedback policy might seek to stabilize either the price level or real GDP. But it can't stabilize both. And the desire to stabilize real GDP conflicts with the goal of price stability.

Figure 16.6 shows the effects of two alternative feedback rules. The first rule seeks to stabilize real GDP and the second rule seeks to stabilize the price level.

**Feedback Rule to Stabilize Real GDP** Suppose that the Fed's feedback rule is: When real GDP decreases, increase the quantity of money to increase aggregate demand. In this example, seeking to keep real GDP close to $10 trillion, the Fed increases the quantity of money to shift the aggregate demand curve to $AD_1$. Because the long-run aggregate supply curve is $LAS_1$, potential GDP and actual real GDP are $9.5 trillion.

The increase in aggregate demand cannot bring forth an increase in output if the economy does not have the capacity to produce that output. So real GDP remains at $9.5 trillion, and the price level rises by even more than it does with a fixed rule. In this example, the price level rises to 125 at point C.

## FIGURE 16.6 Feedback Rules with an LAS Shock

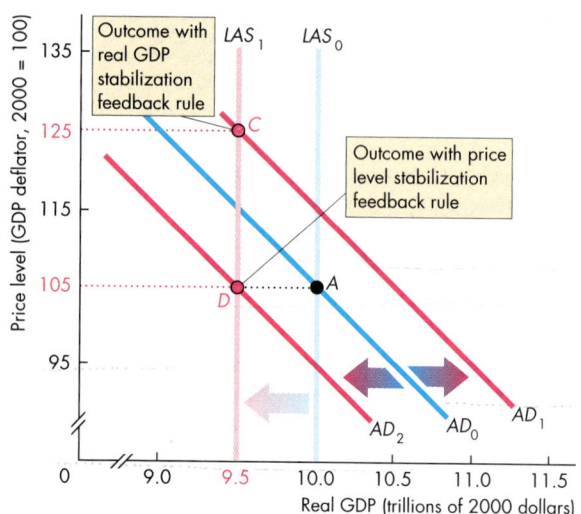

With a feedback rule to stabilize real GDP, the Fed increases the quantity of money, intending to increase real GDP. Aggregate demand shifts to $AD_1$. The price level rises to 125 and real GDP remains at $9.5 trillion at point C. With a feedback rule to stabilize the price level, the Fed decreases the quantity of money. Aggregate demand shifts to $AD_2$. The price level remains constant at 105 at point D.

You can see that in this case the attempt to stabilize real GDP using a feedback rule policy has no effect on real GDP but destabilizes the price level.

**Feedback Rule to Stabilize the Price Level** Now suppose that the Fed's feedback rule is: When the price level rises, *decrease* the quantity of money to decrease aggregate demand. In this example, seeking to keep price level close to 105, the Fed decreases the quantity of money to shift the aggregate demand curve to $AD_2$.

The decrease in aggregate demand keeps the price level at 105 at point $D$. Real GDP remains at $9.5 trillion, the same as it does with a fixed rule and a feedback rule to stabilize real GDP.

We've seen that when a productivity shock occurs, a feedback rule that responds to deviations of the price level from some target can deliver a more stable price level and has no adverse effects on real GDP.

What about a cost-push inflation shock? Do the same conclusions apply to it? Let's find out.

## Monetarist Fixed Rule with a Cost-Push Inflation Shock

Figure 16.7 shows the economy at full employment. Aggregate demand is $AD_0$, short-run aggregate supply is $SAS_0$, and long-run aggregate supply is $LAS$. Real GDP is $10 trillion, and the price level is 105 at point $A$. Now suppose that OPEC tries to gain a temporary advantage by increasing the price of oil. The short-run aggregate supply curve shifts leftward from $SAS_0$ to $SAS_1$.

Figure 16.7(a) shows what happens if the Fed follows a monetarist fixed rule. The Fed ignores the fact that there has been a surge in the price of oil. No policy action is taken. The short-run aggregate supply curve has shifted to $SAS_1$, but the aggregate demand curve remains at $AD_0$. The price level rises to 115, and real GDP decreases to $9.5 trillion at point $B$. The economy has experienced *stagflation*.

In the new short-run equilibrium, there is a recessionary gap. With real GDP below potential GDP, OPEC isn't selling as much oil as before and the price of oil might begin to fall. Also, with unemployment above its natural rate, the money wage rate will begin to fall. These events shift the short-run aggregate supply curve back toward $SAS_0$. As short-run aggregate supply increases, the price level begins to fall and real GDP begins to increase.

Eventually, the price level returns to 105, and real GDP returns to $10 trillion. But this adjustment takes a long time.

## Feedback Rules with Cost-Push Inflation Shock

Again, there are two feedback rules:

- Feedback rule to stabilize real GDP
- Feedback rule to stabilize the price level

**Feedback Rule to Stabilize Real GDP** Figure 16.7(b) shows what happens if the Fed operates a feedback rule to stabilize real GDP. The starting point $A$ is the same as before—the economy is on $SAS_0$ and $AD_0$ with a price level of 105 and real GDP of $10 trillion. OPEC raises the price of oil, and the short-run aggregate supply curve shifts to $SAS_1$. Real GDP decreases to $9.5 trillion, and the price level rises to 115 at point $B$.

With real GDP below potential GDP, the Fed increases the quantity of money. Aggregate demand increases, and the aggregate demand curve shifts rightward to $AD_1$. The price level rises to 120, and real GDP returns to $10 trillion at point $C$. The economy moves back to full employment but at a higher price level. The economy has experienced *cost-push inflation*.

The Fed responded in this way to the first wave of OPEC price increases in the mid-1970s. OPEC saw the same advantage in forcing up the price of oil again. A new rise in the price of oil decreased aggregate supply, and the short-run aggregate supply curve shifted leftward once more. If the Fed had chased it with an increase in aggregate demand, the economy would have been in a freewheeling inflation.

**Feedback Rule to Stabilize the Price Level** Figure 16.7(c) shows what happens if the Fed operates a feedback rule to stabilize the price level. The economy starts at point $A$ and moves to point $B$, as before.

But now, with the price level above target, the Fed *decreases* the quantity of money. Aggregate demand decreases, and the aggregate demand curve shifts leftward to $AD_2$. The price level falls to 105, and real GDP decreases to $8.5 trillion at point $D$. The Fed has averted *cost-push inflation*.

Realizing the danger of cost-push inflation and having experienced it during the 1970s, the Fed responded in this way to the second wave of OPEC price increases in the early 1980s. The Fed held firm and slowed the growth of aggregate demand to dampen the inflation consequences of OPEC's actions. But we paid a big price in the form of the deep recession of 1981–1982.

## FIGURE 16.7 Three Stabilization Polices: Cost-Push Inflation Shock

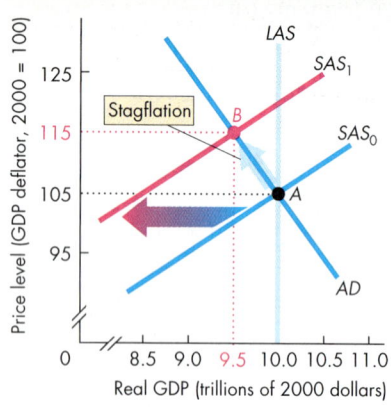
(a) Fixed rule: temporary supply shock

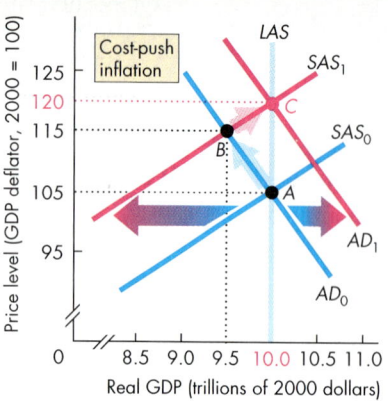
(b) Feedback rule: stabilize real GDP

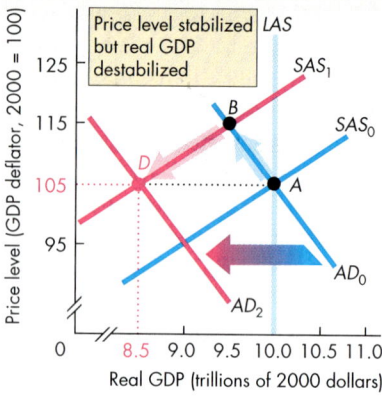
(c) Feedback rule: stabilize the price level

The economy starts out at point A on $AD_0$ and $SAS_0$, with a price level of 105 and real GDP of $10 trillion. OPEC forces up the price of oil, and the short-run aggregate supply curve shifts to $SAS_1$. Real GDP decreases to $9.5 trillion, and the price level increases to 115 at point B.

With a fixed-rule policy (part a), the Fed makes no change to aggregate demand. The economy stays in a recession at point B until the price of oil falls again and the economy returns to point A.

With a feedback rule to stabilize real GDP (part b), the Fed increases aggregate demand to $AD_1$. Real GDP returns to $10 trillion, but the price level rises to 120 at point C. The economy is set for another round of cost-push inflation.

With a feedback rule to stabilize the price level (part c), the Fed decreases aggregate demand to $AD_2$. Real GDP falls to $8.5 trillion, but the price level is stabilized at 105—point D. The Fed has avoided cost-push inflation at the cost of recession.

**Incentives to Push Up Costs** You can see that there are no checks on the incentives to push up *nominal* costs if the Fed accommodates price hikes. If some group sees a temporary gain from pushing up the price at which they are selling their resources and if the Fed always accommodates the increase to prevent unemployment and slack business conditions from emerging, then cost-push elements will have a free rein.

But when the Fed pursues a fixed-rule policy or a feedback policy that responds to the price level rather than to real GDP, the incentive to attempt to steal a temporary advantage from a price increase is severely weakened. The cost of higher unemployment and lower output is a consequence that each group must face and recognize. So a fixed rule or a feedback rule that reacts to the price level can deliver steady inflation, while a feedback rule that responds to real GDP leaves cost-push pressures free to generate inflation.

The key feature of monetary policy that can avoid cost-push inflation is credibility. If it is known and expected that the Fed will fight cost-push pressures, the incentive to create them is weakened.

> ### REVIEW QUIZ
> 1 What is a fixed-rule monetary policy? Provide two (new) examples of fixed rules in everyday life.
> 2 What is a feedback monetary policy? Provide two (new) examples of feedback rules in everyday life.
> 3 Why might feedback rules not necessarily deliver a better macroeconomic performance than a fixed rule?
> 4 What rules prevent inflation in the face of a productivity growth slowdown?
> 5 What rules protect the price level from cost-push pressures?

You've reviewed the effects of alternative monetary policy strategies in the face of shocks to aggregate demand and aggregate supply. In the next section we're going to learn more about the role of the credibility of monetary policy.

## Policy Credibility

WE'RE NOW GOING TO FOCUS ON THE ROLE OF policy credibility. To illustrate its role, we're going to switch a focus from *avoiding* inflation to *eradicating* a high inflation rate. We'll contrast two cases that illustrate the extremes of the absence and presence of credibility:

- A surprise inflation reduction
- A credible announced inflation reduction

### A Surprise Inflation Reduction

We can study the role of credibility by using either the AS-AD model or the Phillips curve. The AS-AD model tells us about real GDP and the price level, while the Phillips curve, which is explained in Chapter 12 (pp. 288–291), lets us keep track of inflation and unemployment.

Figure 16.8 illustrates the economy at full employment with inflation raging at 10 percent a year. In part (a), the economy is on aggregate demand curve $AD_0$ and short-run aggregate supply curve $SAS_0$. Real GDP is $10 trillion, and the price level is 105. With real GDP equal to potential GDP on the $LAS$ curve, the economy is at full employment. Equivalently, in part (b), the economy is on its long run Phillips curve, $LRPC$, and short-run Phillips curve, $SRPC_0$. The inflation rate of 10 percent a year is anticipated, so unemployment is at its natural rate, 6 percent of the labor force.

Next year, aggregate demand is *expected* to increase and the aggregate demand curve in Fig. 16.8(a) is expected to shift rightward from $AD_0$ to $AD_1$. In expectation of this increase in aggregate demand, the

**FIGURE 16.8** The Role of Credibility

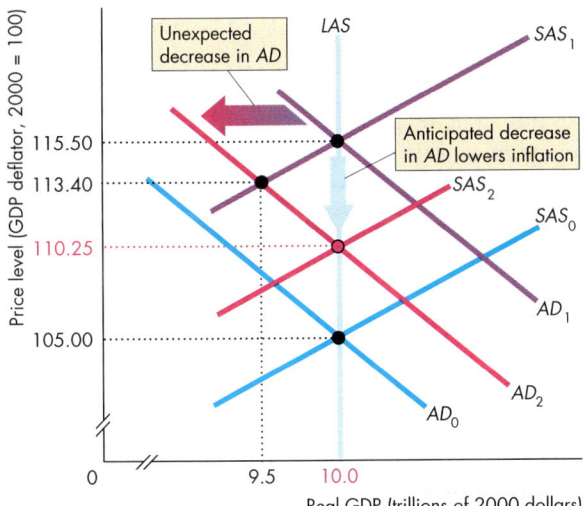

(a) Aggregate demand and aggregate supply

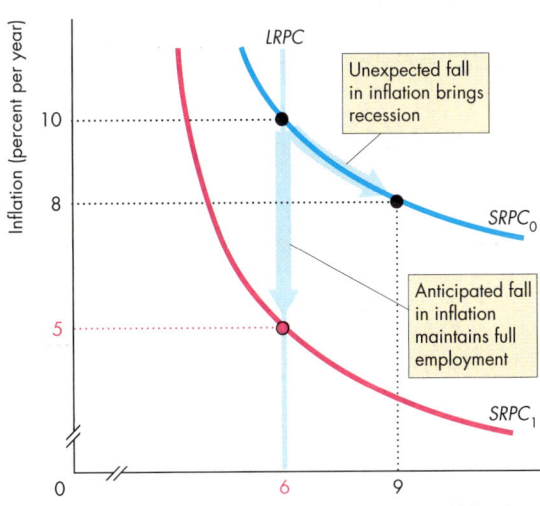

(b) Phillips curves

In part (a), the aggregate demand curve is expected to shift and actually shifts from $AD_0$ to $AD_1$. The short-run aggregate supply curve shifts from $SAS_0$ to $SAS_1$. The price level rises to 115.5, but real GDP remains at $10 trillion. Inflation is 10 percent a year, and this inflation rate is anticipated. Part (b) shows this same situation: Unemployment is at the natural rate of 6 percent, and inflation is 10 percent a year.

An unexpected slowdown in aggregate demand growth shifts the aggregate demand curve from $AD_0$ to $AD_2$. Real GDP decreases to $9.5 trillion, and inflation slows to 8 percent (price level is 113.4). Unemployment rises to 9 percent as the economy slides down $SRPC_0$.

An anticipated, credible, announced slowdown in aggregate demand growth shifts the aggregate demand curve from $AD_0$ to $AD_2$. The short-run aggregate supply curve shifts from $SAS_0$ to $SAS_2$. The short-run Phillips curve shifts to $SRPC_1$. Inflation slows to 5 percent a year, real GDP remains at $10 trillion, and unemployment remains at its natural rate of 6 percent.

money wage rate increases and shifts the short-run aggregate supply curve from $SAS_0$ to $SAS_1$. If expectations are fulfilled, the price level rises to 115.5—a 10 percent inflation—and real GDP remains at potential GDP. In part (b), the economy remains at its original position—unemployment is at its natural rate, and the inflation rate is 10 percent a year.

Now suppose that no one is expecting the Fed to change its policy, but the Fed actually tries to slow inflation. It raises interest rates and slows money growth. Aggregate demand growth slows, and the aggregate demand curve (in part a) shifts rightward from $AD_0$, not to $AD_1$ as people expect, but to $AD_2$.

With no change in the expected inflation rate, the money wage rate rises by the same amount as before and the short-run aggregate supply curve shifts leftward from $SAS_0$ to $SAS_1$. Real GDP decreases to $9.5 trillion, and the price level rises to 113.4—an inflation rate of 8 percent a year. In Fig. 16.8(b), the economy moves along the short-run Phillips curve $SRPC_0$ as unemployment rises to 9 percent and inflation falls to 8 percent a year. The Fed's policy has succeeded in slowing inflation, but at the cost of recession. Real GDP is below potential GDP, and unemployment is above its natural rate.

## A Credible Announced Inflation Reduction

Suppose that instead of simply slowing down the growth of aggregate demand, the Fed announces its intention ahead of its action and in a credible and convincing way so that its announcement is believed. That is, the Fed's policy is anticipated. Because the lower level of aggregate demand is expected, the money wage rate increases at a pace that is consistent with the lower level of aggregate demand. The short run aggregate supply curve (in Fig. 16.8a) shifts leftward from $SAS_0$ but only to $SAS_2$. Aggregate demand increases by the amount expected, and the aggregate demand curve shifts from $AD_0$ to $AD_2$. The price level rises to 110.25—an inflation rate of 5 percent a year—and real GDP remains at potential GDP. In Fig. 16.8(b), the lower expected inflation rate shifts the short-run Phillips curve downward to $SRPC_1$, and inflation falls to 5 percent a year, while unemployment remains at its natural rate of 6 percent. A credible announced inflation reduction lowers inflation but with no accompanying recession or increase in unemployment.

## Inflation Reduction in Practice

When the Fed in fact slowed inflation in 1981, we paid a high price. The Fed's policy action to end inflation was not credible. It occurred in the face of a money wage rate that had been set at too high a level to be consistent with the growth of aggregate demand that the Fed subsequently allowed. The consequence was recession—a decrease in real GDP and a rise in unemployment. Could the Fed have lowered inflation without causing recession by telling people far enough ahead of time that it did indeed plan to lower inflation?

The answer appears to be no. The main reason is that people expect the Fed to behave in line with its record, not with its stated intentions. How many times have you told yourself that it is your firm intention to take off 10 unwanted pounds or to keep within your budget and put a few dollars away for a rainy day, only to discover that, despite your very best intentions, your old habits win out in the end?

To form expectations of the Fed's *actions*, people look at the Fed's past actions, not its stated intentions. On the basis of such observations—called Fed watching—people try to work out what the Fed's policy is, to forecast its future actions, and to forecast the effects of those actions on aggregate demand and inflation. The Greenspan Fed, like the Volcker Fed that preceded it, has built a reputation for being anti-inflationary. That reputation is valuable because it helps the Fed to contain inflation and lowers the cost of eliminating inflation if it temporarily returns. The reason is that with a low expected inflation rate, the short-run Phillips curve is in a favorable position (like $SRPC_1$ in Fig. 16.8b). The Fed's actions during the 1990s were designed to keep inflation expectations low and prevent the gains made during the 1980s recession from being eroded.

### REVIEW QUIZ

1 Why does a recession usually result as inflation is being tamed?
2 How does establishing a credible reputation of being an inflation fighter improve the Fed's ability to maintain low inflation?

We're going to end this chapter by looking at two new rules that pay attention to the need for credibility in the conduct of monetary policy.

# New Monetarist and New Keynesian Feedback Rules

YOU'VE SEEN THAT THE MONETARIST FIXED RULE prevents cost-push pressure from becoming ongoing cost-push inflation. But it achieves this goal at the cost of lost real GDP. Also, the monetarist fixed rule does not avoid price level fluctuations in the face of productivity shocks. And it does not prevent price level and real GDP fluctuations in the face of known or forecasted fluctuations in aggregate demand.

You've also seen that a Keynesian feedback rule that targets real GDP unleashes the forces of cost-push inflation. This rule might or might not moderate fluctuations in the price level and real GDP that stem from aggregate demand shocks. And you've seen that a feedback rule that targets the price level avoids cost-push inflation but at an even greater cost in terms of lost real GDP than the loss inflicted by a monetarist fixed rule. None of these rules work well, and none is a sufficiently credible rule for the Fed to commit to.

In an attempt to develop a rule that is credible and that works well, economists have explored policies that respond to both the price level and real GDP.

Two such policy rules are the

- McCallum Rule
- Taylor Rule

## The McCallum Rule

Suggested by Bennett T. McCallum, an economics professor at Carnegie-Mellon University, the **McCallum rule** adjusts the growth rate of the monetary base to target the inflation rate but also to take into account changes in the trend productivity growth rate and fluctuations in aggregate demand.

The McCallum rule is in the spirit of the monetarist fixed rule, but it is a feedback rule and might be called the *new monetarist rule*. The rule is derived from the equation of exchange that you met in Chapter 11, p. 268. The equation of exchange states that

$$MV = PY,$$

where $M$ is the quantity of money, $V$ is the velocity of circulation, $P$ is the price level, and $Y$ is real GDP.

The equation of exchange implies that the price level is

$$P = MV/Y.$$

This equation implies that the inflation rate (the rate at which $P$ increases) equals the growth rate of the quantity of money (the rate at which $M$ increases) plus the growth rate of the velocity of circulation (the rate at which $V$ increases), minus the growth rate of real GDP (the rate at which $Y$ increases).

To make the equation of exchange operational, we need a working definition of money. Monetary aggregates such as M1 and M2 can be influenced by the Fed but not precisely controlled by it. In contrast, the Fed directly controls the *monetary base*. For this reason, Bennett McCallum uses the monetary base as his definition of the quantity of money. And $V$ is the velocity of circulation of the monetary base.

To take account of changes in trend productivity growth, the McCallum rule makes the growth rate of the monetary base respond to the average growth rate of real GDP over the past 10 years. The 10-year period moves forward one year each year—an average called a *moving average*.

To take account of changes in the velocity of circulation, which change aggregate demand, the McCallum rule makes the growth rate of the monetary base respond to the average growth rate of the velocity of circulation over the past 4 years—a 4-year moving average.

Summarizing, the McCallum rule says:

Make the monetary base grow at a rate equal to the target inflation rate plus the 10-year moving average growth rate of real GDP minus the 4-year moving average of the growth rate of the velocity of circulation of the monetary base.

If the Fed had a specific target for the inflation rate, the McCallum rule would tell the Fed the growth rate of monetary base that would achieve that target, on the average.

Figure 16.9 shows how the monetary base has grown and how it would have grown if it had followed the McCallum rule. The blue line is the actual growth rate of the monetary base. (The large swing in the growth in 1999 and 2000 is not important for monetary policy and occurred because the Fed wanted to be sure there was enough currency in the economy in case the banking system's computers caught the so-called "millennium bug.")

The grey lines show the McCallum rule growth rate of the monetary base for two target inflation rates—zero and 4 percent a year. This range spans the range that the Fed would regard as being consistent with price level stability.

You can see that during the 1970s, the Fed permitted the monetary base to grow too rapidly. This rapid money growth brought the high inflation rate of the 1970s. You can also see that for most of the 1990s and 2000s, the monetary base has grown at a rate that falls inside the range of growth rates that the McCallum rule says will deliver price level stability.

## The Taylor Rule

Suggested by John Taylor, formerly an economics professor at Stanford University and now Undersecretary of the Treasury for International Affairs in the Bush administration, the **Taylor rule** adjusts the federal funds rate to target the inflation rate and to take into account deviations of the inflation rate from its target and deviations of real GDP from potential GDP.

The Taylor rule is in the spirit of the Keynesian feedback rule, but it is designed first and foremost to achieve price level stability. It also places a great weight to deviations of real GDP from potential GDP, so it might be called the *new Keynesian rule*.

If the Fed followed the Taylor rule, it would make the federal funds rate adjust in the following way:

Set the federal funds rate equal to the target inflation rate plus 2.5 percent plus one half of the gap between the actual inflation rate and the target inflation rate plus one half of the percentage deviation of real GDP from potential GDP.

Figure 16.10 shows the federal funds rate and the rate if the Taylor rule were followed. The blue line is the actual federal funds rate, and the grey lines show what the rate would have been if the Fed had followed the Taylor rule with inflation rate targets of zero and 4 percent a year. Again, this range spans the inflation rates that the Fed might regard as being consistent with price level stability.

You can see that during the 1970s, the federal funds rate was much lower than that required for

**FIGURE 16.9** The McCallum Rule

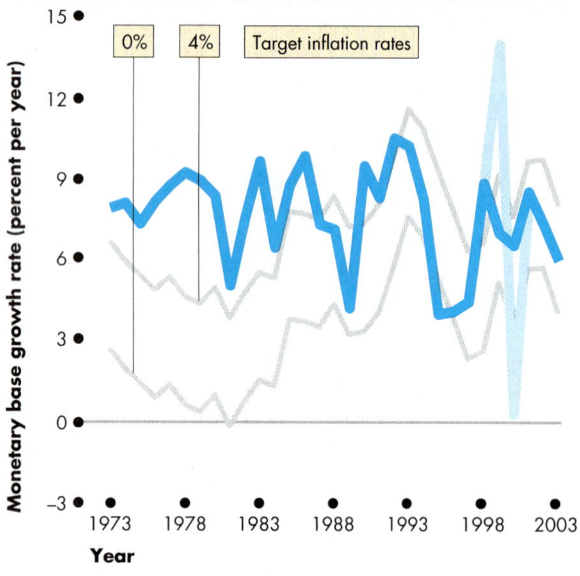

During the 1970s, monetary base growth was more rapid than the McCallum rule would have delivered and the inflation rate was high. During the 1990s and 2000s, monetary base growth was similar to what the McCallum rule would have delivered and the inflation rate was moderate.

*Sources:* Federal Reserve Bank of St Louis and author's calculations.

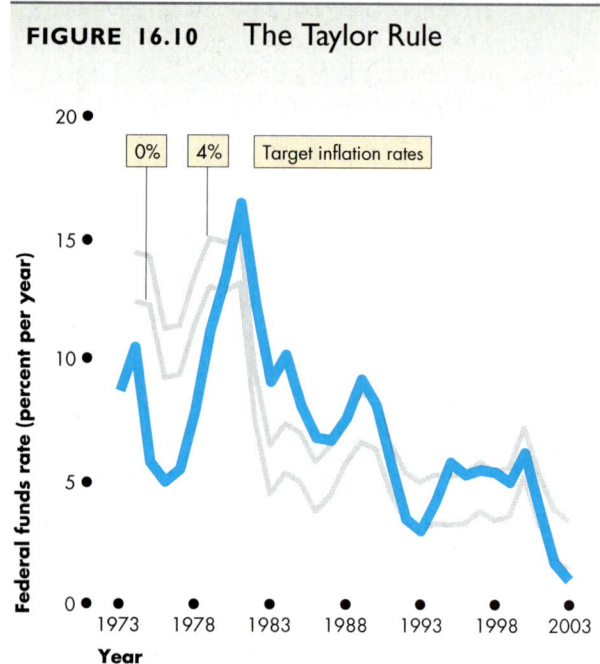

**FIGURE 16.10** The Taylor Rule

During the 1970s, the Federal funds rate was lower than the Taylor rule would have delivered and the inflation rate was high. During the 1990s and 2000s, the federal funds rate was in line with the Taylor rule and the inflation rate was moderate.

*Sources:* Federal Reserve Bank of St Louis and author's calculations.

price level stability. If the Fed had followed the Taylor rule during those years, the inflation rate would not have exploded as it did.

During the 1980s, the federal funds rate was slightly higher than the level suggested by the Taylor rule, but not by much. And during the 1990s and 2000s, the Fed's actual policy was similar to the Taylor rule.

## Differences Between the Rules

The McCallum rule and the Taylor rule tell a similar story about the inflation of the 1970s and the price level stability of the 1990s and 2000s. During the 1970s, the quantity of money grew too rapidly (McCallum rule) and the federal funds rate was too low (Taylor rule). During the 1990s and 2000s, both the growth rate of the quantity of money (McCallum rule) and the federal funds rate (Taylor rule) were consistent with low inflation and price level stability.

Although the two rules deliver a similar conclusion about the inflationary 1970s and the more stable 1990s and 2000s, they differ in two important ways:

- Strength of response to output fluctuations
- Targeting money versus the interest rate

### Strength of Response to Output Fluctuations

The McCallum rule pays little attention to current real GDP. The current growth rate of real GDP changes the 10-year moving average and gets a weight of one-tenth in the updated average growth rate.

In contrast, the Taylor rule responds powerfully to the current level of real GDP. If real GDP is below potential GDP, the Fed cuts the federal funds rate by an amount equal to half the GDP gap. Similarly, if real GDP exceeds potential GDP, the Fed raises the federal funds rate by half the output gap.

This difference in the two rules means that the McCallum rule focuses almost exclusively on the goal of price stability and downplays the role of monetary policy in stabilizing the business cycle while the Taylor rule pursues its basic goal of price stability but pays a lot of attention to the current state of the business cycle.

### Targeting Money Versus the Interest Rate

The McCallum rule targets the monetary base, which means that it permits the federal funds rate to fluctuate to achieve equilibrium in the market for overnight loans among banks.

In contrast, the Taylor rule targets the federal funds rate, which means that it permits the monetary base to fluctuate in response to changes in the demand for monetary base.

The Taylor rule is much closer to a description of what the Fed actually does day by day. The Fed does target the federal funds rate and does permit the monetary base to fluctuate in response to changes in the demand for it.

Why does McCallum favor targeting the monetary base? And which rule is better?

## Choosing Between the Rules

Monetarists favor targeting the monetary base because they believe that it provides a more solid anchor for the price level than does the interest rate. The equation of exchange ties the price level to the monetary base, its velocity of circulation, and real GDP. By responding to changes in real GDP and velocity, a monetary base growth rule can deliver a guaranteed inflation rate on the average over the longer term.

Targeting the interest rate leaves the monetary base growth rate to be determined by the growth in the demand for money. And the price level is a major influence on the quantity of money demanded. So there is a potential indeterminacy. Set the interest rate too low, money grows too rapidly, inflation is too rapid, and money grows ever more rapidly.

This potential problem actually disappears if the interest rate rule follows the Taylor principle, which raises the interest rate when the inflation rate rises and by *more* than the rise in the inflation rate.

So the Taylor rule is immune to the monetarist objection to interest rate targeting.

Keynesians say that targeting the quantity of money would bring excessive swings in the interest rate, which in turn would bring excessive swings in aggregate expenditure. For this reason, Keynesians favor interest rate targeting.

### REVIEW QUIZ

1 Describe the McCallum rule.
2 Describe the Taylor rule.

◆ Before you leave this chapter, take a look at *Reading Between the Lines* on pp. 404–405 and see the challenge the Fed faced at the end of 2003 as it contemplated whether to hold interest rates at their historically low level or begin to move them upward.

# READING BETWEEN THE LINES

## POLICY WATCH

## Monetary Policy Today

THE WASHINGTON POST, DECEMBER 10, 2003

### Fed Indicates Boost in Rates is Unlikely

Federal Reserve officials made no change in interest rates at a policy-making meeting yesterday and signaled that any rate hike remains well into the future.

However, in a subtly worded statement issued after the meeting, the Federal Open Market Committee, the central bank's top policymaking group, acknowledged that the economic recovery has gathered speed and that the likelihood of a further drop in inflation has largely disappeared.

But the key sentence in the statement said that the committee had concluded that "with inflation quite low and resource use slack," very low interest rates "can be maintained for a considerable period." The Fed's current target for overnight rates is 1 percent, the lowest level in more than 40 years.

The words "resource use slack" refer to the fact that the nation's unemployment rate is still close to 6 percent, well above the level usually associated with rising inflation, while only about 75 percent of available U.S. factory production capacity is in use.

Many analysts and investors had expected the officials to drop the "considerable period" phrasing as the first step toward raising rates. That expectation was based primarily on the strength in recent indicators, such as the third quarter's extremely strong 8.2 percent annual rate of economic growth, increases in payroll jobs for four months in a row and a half-percentage point drop in the nation's unemployment rate, to 5.9 percent last month from 6.4 percent in June. Increases in many commodity prices had also caused some analysts to warn that inflation, which has been running at only about a 1 percent annual rate by some measures, was about to increase.

What the committee did instead was refine the language of the statement issued after its October meeting to take account of the economic developments since then. Some analysts praised the new wording as a real advance in the Fed's ability to let the public know what its policymakers are thinking.

....

©2003 The Washington Post. Reprinted with permission. Further reproduction prohibited.

### Essence of the Story

■ The Federal Open Market Committee (FOMC) left its target for the federal funds rate unchanged at 1 percent at its December 2003 meeting.

■ The FOMC noted that economic recovery has gathered speed and that a further fall in the inflation rate is unlikely.

■ But with an unemployment rate of 6 percent and 75 percent of production capacity in use, the FOMC declared that "a very low interest rate can be maintained for a considerable period."

■ Many analysts and investors had expected the FOMC to indicate an earlier start to a period of rising interest rates.

## Economic Analysis

- At the beginning of 2001, the federal funds rate was 6.5 percent a year.

- Through 2001, the growth rate of real GDP slowed and the unemployment rate increased. To counter this development, the Fed gradually lowered the federal funds rate.

- The economy remained weak in 2002, and the Fed cut the interest rate even further to a historically low level.

- Figure 1 shows the course of the federal funds rate each month from 1999 through 2003.

- Figure 1 shows the Taylor rule for the federal funds rate if the long-run inflation rate target is 2 percent a year (see pp. 774–775).

- When the federal funds rate exceeds the Taylor rule level, as it did in 2000 and the first half of 2001, the Fed is showing more concern about restraining inflation than about sagging real GDP growth.

- When the federal funds rate is below the Taylor rule level, as it has been since mid-2001, the Fed is showing more concern about boosting real GDP growth than about rising inflation.

- At the end of 2003, was the FOMC correct to be more concerned about real GDP growth than about inflation?

- Figure 2 shows a reason to be concerned. The recessionary gap of 2002 and 2003 was becoming very small by the end of 2003.

- When real GDP moves above potential GDP and an inflationary gap opens up, as it seems will happen early in 2004, the inflation rate will turn upward.

- Given that monetary policy operates with a considerable time lag, a more cautious Fed would already have begun to raise the interest rate.

- It is a fairly safe prediction that the Fed will begin to raise the federal funds rate some time during 2004. And as so often in the past, the move will be too little too late.

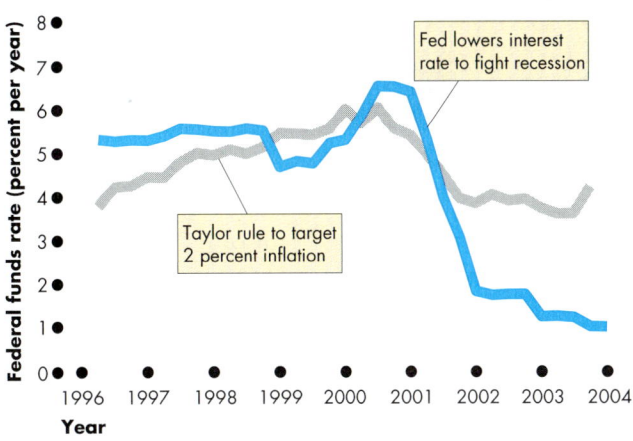

Figure 1 The federal funds rate and the Taylor rule

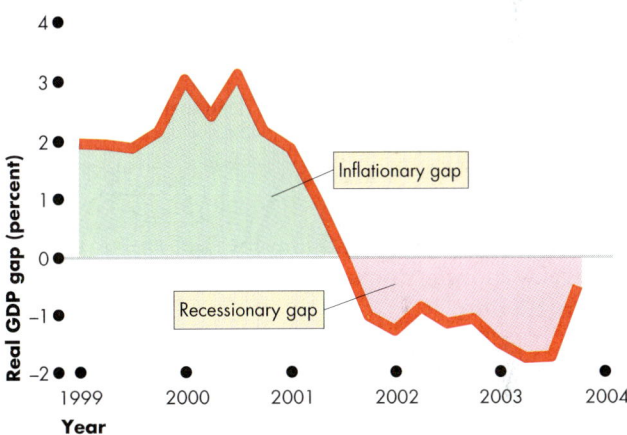

Figure 2 The GDP gap

## You're The Voter

- Do you think the current FOMC monetary policy is appropriate?

- If you were a member of the FOMC, would you vote for an immediate rise in the federal funds rate or would you vote to maintain the rate at a low level? Explain.

# SUMMARY

## KEY POINTS

### Instruments, Goals, Targets, and the Fed's Performance (pp. 388–391)

- Open market operations, the discount rate, and required reserve ratios are the instruments of monetary policy.
- Price stability and sustained real GDP growth are the goals of monetary policy.
- The federal funds rate is the main intermediate target of monetary policy.

### Achieving Price Level Stability (pp. 392–398)

- Monetary policy can follow a fixed rule, a feedback rule, or be discretionary.
- Fixed-rule policies leave the price level and real GDP to fluctuate in the face of demand shocks and supply shocks.
- Feedback rules seek to respond to the state of the economy and dampen the effects of shocks.
- A feedback rule might not improve on a fixed rule because monetary policy operates with a long and variable time lag.
- A feedback rule that responds to real GDP fluctuations makes the economy vulnerable to cost-push inflation.

### Policy Credibility (pp. 399–400)

- Monetary policy actions that are unexpected affect real GDP.
- Monetary policy actions that are expected and credible impact the price level and leave real variables unaffected.

### New Monetarist and New Keynesian Feedback Rules (pp. 401–403)

- The McCallum new monetarist feedback rule adjusts the growth rate of the monetary base to target the inflation rate while responding to changes in the long term growth rate of real GDP and changes in the velocity of circulation.
- The Taylor new Keynesian feedback rule adjusts the federal funds rate to target the inflation rate but responds equally strongly to deviations of real GDP from potential GDP.

## KEY FIGURES

Figure 16.3  A Fixed Rule with *AD* Shocks, 393
Figure 16.4  A Feedback Rule with *AD* Shocks, 394
Figure 16.5  A Fixed Rule with an *LAS* Shock, 396
Figure 16.6  Feedback Rules with an *LAS* Shock, 396
Figure 16.7  Three Stabilization Polices: Cost-Push Shock, 398
Figure 16.8  The Role of Credibility, 399

## KEY TERMS

Discretionary policy, 392
Feedback-rule policy, 392
Fixed-rule policy, 392
McCallum rule, 401
Taylor rule, 402

# PROBLEMS

*1. The economy shown in the figure is initially on aggregate demand curve $AD_0$ and short-run aggregate supply curve $SAS$. Then aggregate demand decreases, and the aggregate demand curve shifts leftward to $AD_1$.

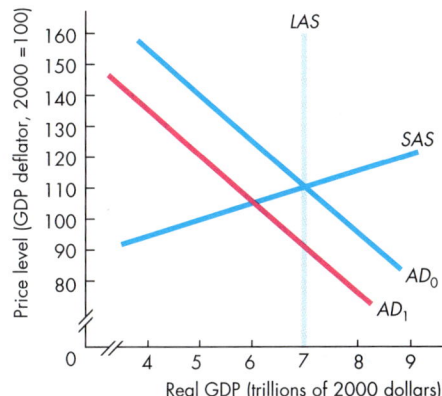

a. What is the initial equilibrium real GDP and price level?
b. If the decrease in aggregate demand is temporary and the Fed follows a fixed-rule monetary policy, what happens to the price level and real GDP? Trace the immediate effects and the adjustment as aggregate demand returns to its original level.
c. If the decrease in aggregate demand is temporary and the Fed follows a feedback-rule monetary policy, what happens to the price level and real GDP? Trace the immediate effects and the adjustment as aggregate demand returns to its original level.
d. If the decrease in aggregate demand is permanent and the Fed follows a fixed-rule monetary policy, what happens to the price level and real GDP?
e. If the decrease in aggregate demand is permanent and the Fed follows a feedback-rule monetary policy, what happens to the price level and real GDP?

2. The economy shown in the figure is initially on aggregate demand curve $AD$ and short-run aggregate supply curve $SAS_0$. Then short-run aggregate supply decreases, and the short-run aggregate supply curve shifts leftward to $SAS_1$.

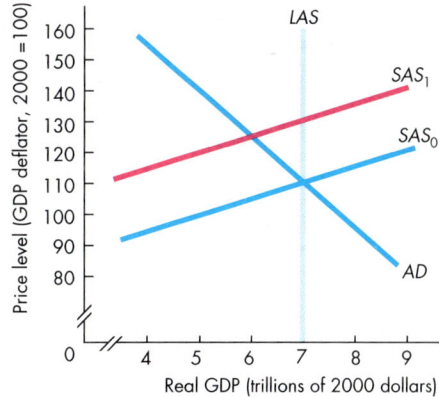

a. What is the initial equilibrium real GDP and price level?
b. What type of event could have caused the decrease in short-run aggregate supply?
c. If the Fed follows a fixed-rule monetary policy, what happens to the price level and real GDP? Trace the immediate effects and the adjustment as aggregate demand and short-run aggregate supply return to their original level.
d. If the Fed follows a feedback-rule monetary policy, what happens to the price level and real GDP? Trace the immediate effects and the adjustment as aggregate demand and short-run aggregate supply respond to the policy action.

*3. The economy is experiencing 10 percent a year inflation and 7 percent unemployment. Real GDP growth has sagged to 1 percent a year. The stock market has crashed.
a. Explain how the economy might have gotten into its current state.
b. Set out policies for the Fed to pursue that will lower inflation, lower unemployment, and speed real GDP growth.
c. Explain how and why your proposed policies will work.

4. The inflation rate has fallen to less than 1 percent a year, and the unemployment rate has fallen to less then 4 percent. Real GDP is growing at almost 5 percent a year. The stock market is at a record high.
a. Explain how the economy might have gotten into its current state.
b. Set out policies for the Fed to pursue that will lower inflation, lower unemployment, and speed real GDP growth.

* Solutions to odd-numbered problems are available on **MyEconLab**.

c. Explain how and why your proposed policies will work.
*5. When the economies of Indonesia, South Korea, Thailand, Malaysia, and the Philippines entered into recession in 1997, the International Monetary Fund (IMF) made loans, but only on the condition that the recipients of the loans increase interest rates, raise taxes, and cut government purchases.
  a. Would you describe the IMF prescription as a feedback-rule policy or a fixed-rule policy?
  b. What do you predict the effects of the IMF policies would be?
  c. Do you have any criticisms of the IMF policies? What would you have required these countries to do? Why?
6. As the U.S. economy continued to expand and its stock market soared to new record levels during 1998, the Fed cut interest rates.
  a. Would you describe the Fed's actions as a feedback-rule policy or a fixed-rule policy?
  b. What do you predict the effects of the Fed's policies would be?
  c. Do you have any criticisms of the Fed's policies? What monetary policy would you have pursued? Why?
*7. A productivity growth slowdown has occurred.
  a. Explain its possible origins.
  b. Explain the limits of monetary policy in helping to speed up growth again.
8. A nation is experiencing a falling saving rate.
  a. Explain its possible origins.
  b. Explain the limits of monetary policy in helping to lift the saving rate back to its previous level.

# CRITICAL THINKING

1. Study *Reading Between the Lines* on pp. 404–405 and then answer the following questions.
   a. What did the FOMC decide at its December 2003 meeting? Explain the committee's reasoning.
   b. Is the federal funds rate at 1 percent a year an unusually low rate? Why do you think the Fed lowered the rate so much more in the recession of the early 2000s than it did in the recession of the early 1990s?
   c. What do you think is the greater threat today: inflation or recession and unemployment? Explain.
   d. Do you think the Fed was playing a political game in 2003 and 2004? Explain.
2. Suppose the economy is booming and inflation is beginning to rise, but it is widely agreed that a massive recession is just around the corner. Weigh the advantages and disadvantages of the Fed pursuing a fixed-rule policy and a feedback-rule policy.
3. Suppose the economy is in a recession and inflation is falling. It is widely agreed that a strong recovery is just around the corner. Weigh the advantages and disadvantages of the Fed pursuing a fixed-rule policy and a feedback-rule policy.

# WEB EXERCISES

**Use the links on MyEconLab to work the following exercises.**

1. Review the most recent *Beige Book*.
   a. Review the current state of the economy.
   b. Write a brief note to the FOMC suggesting the appropriate change in the federal funds rate and providing reasons.
2. Review the latest *World Economic Outlook*.
   a. What are the major monetary policy problems in the world economy today?
   b. What is the general direction in which monetary policy actions are pushing the global economy?

# UNDERSTANDING ECONOMIC FLUCTUATIONS AND STABILIZATION POLICY

PART 6

## *Boom and Bust*

To cure a disease, doctors must first understand how the disease responds to different treatments. It helps to understand the mechanisms that operate to cause the disease, but sometimes, a workable cure can be found even before the full story of the causes has been told.

Curing economic ills is similar to curing our medical ills. We need to understand how the economy responds to the treatments we might prescribe for it. And sometimes, we want to try a cure even though we don't fully understand the reasons for the problem we're trying to control.

You've seen how the pace of capital accumulation and technological change determine the long-term growth trend. You've learned how fluctuations around the long-term trend can be generated by changes in aggregate demand and aggregate supply. And you've learned about the key sources of fluctuations in aggregate demand and aggregate supply.

The four chapters in this part have built on everything you've studied in macroeconomics. The central tools they use are the demand and supply model of Chapter 3 and the *AS-AD* model of Chapter 7. But they use these models to explain the big picture or grand vision that different schools of thought hold concerning the way the economy operates and what is important.

Chapter 13 explained the effects of changes in business investment and the multiplier effect they have on consumption expenditure and aggregate demand. This chapter also explained how changes in business inventories trigger changes in production and incomes.

In Chapter 14, you learned about alternative visions of the business cycle. All of these visions can be translated into the *AS-AD* model. And doing so helps us to compare and contrast the competing visions. But the new real business cycle (RBC) theory is more at home with the demand and supply model of microeconomics than the *AS-AD* model. Most economists have not embraced the real business cycle approach. It is an extreme view. But the method that real business cycle theory uses is here to stay. This method is to build a (mathematical) model of the entire economy and then see, in a computer simulation, what kind of cycle the model creates. The economy on the computer is then calibrated to the real economy, and the cycles are compared. The computer model can be treated with a variety of "medications" and their effects observed. This new style of business cycle research cannot be explained in detail without using advanced mathematical ideas. But Chapter 30 explained the economics that underlies it and showed you the type of model that real business cycle theorists use.

Chapter 15 reviewed a wide range of fiscal policy issues and problems, and Chapter 16 described the monetary policy debate and explained the alternative approaches that have been proposed to contain inflation while sustaining economic growth and smoothing the business cycle.

The economist you're going to meet on the following page, Irving Fisher, developed ideas about business cycles and policy that have never been in the mainstream but that are becoming fashionable today.

# PROBING THE IDEAS

## Business Cycles

### THE ECONOMIST

**Irving Fisher** *(1867–1947) ranks among the greatest American-born economists. The son of a Congregational minister who died as Irving was finishing high school, he paid his way through Yale and earned enough to keep his mother and younger brother by tutoring his fellow students.*

*Irving Fisher came to economics by way of mathematics. He was Yale's first Ph.D. student in pure economics, but in the math department!*

*The contributions that Fisher made to economics cover the entire subject. He is best known for his work on the quantity theory of money (Chapter 11, pp. 267–269) and the relation between interest rates and inflation (Chapter 13, pp. 292–293). But he also wrote on the business cycle. He believed that the Great Depression was caused because the fall in the price level increased the real burden of debts. He wrote from experience. He had borrowed heavily to buy stocks in the rising market of the late 1920s and lost a fortune of perhaps 10 million dollars in the crash of 1929.*

### THE ISSUES

Economic activity has fluctuated between boom and bust for as long as we've had records. And understanding the sources of economic fluctuations has turned out to be difficult. One reason is that there are no simple patterns. Every new episode of the business cycle is different from its predecessor in some way. Some cycles are long and some short, some are mild and some severe, some begin in the United States and some abroad. We never know with any certainty when the next turning point (down or up) is coming or what will cause it. A second reason is that the apparent waste of resources during a recession or a depression seems to contradict the very foundation of economics: Resources are limited and people have unlimited wants—there is scarcity. A satisfactory theory of the business cycle must explain why scarce resources don't *always* get fully employed.

One theory is that recessions result from insufficient aggregate demand. The solution is to increase government spending, cut taxes, and cut interest rates. But demand stimulation must not be overdone. Countries that stimulate aggregate demand too much, such as Brazil, find their economic growth rates sagging, unemployment rising, and inflation accelerating.

Today's new theory, real business cycle theory, predicts that fluctuations in aggregate demand have *no* effect on output and employment and change only the price level and inflation rate. But this theory ignores the *real* effects of financial collapse of the type that occurred in the 1930s. If banks fail on a large scale and people lose their wealth, other firms also begin to fail and jobs are destroyed. Unemployed people cut their spending, and output falls yet further. Demand stimulation might not be called for, but

*"…in the great booms and depressions, … the two big bad actors are debt disturbances and price level disturbances."*

IRVING FISHER
"The Debt Deflation Theory of Depressions"
ECONOMETRICA, 1933

action to ensure that sound banks survive certainly is.

While economists are trying to understand the sources of the business cycle, the government and the Fed are doing the best they can to moderate the cycle. In the years since World War II, there appears to have been some success. Although the business cycle has not disappeared, it has become much less severe.

## THEN

What happens to the economy when people lose confidence in banks? They withdraw their funds. These withdrawals feed on themselves, creating a snowball of withdrawals and, eventually, panic. Short of funds with which to repay depositors, banks call in loans and previously sound businesses are faced with financial distress. They close down and lay off workers. And recession deepens and turns into depression. Bank failures and the resulting decline in the nation's supply of money and credit were a significant factor in deepening and prolonging the Great Depression. But they taught us the importance of stable financial institutions and gave rise to the establishment of federal deposit insurance to prevent future financial collapse.

## NOW

How can a building designed as a shop have no better use than to be boarded up and left empty? Not enough aggregate demand, say the Keynesians. Not so, say the real business cycle theorists. Technological change has reduced the building's current productivity as a shop to zero. But its expected future productivity is sufficiently high that it is not efficient to refit the building for some other purpose.

All unemployment, whether of buildings or people, can be explained in a similar way. For example, how can it be that during a recession, a person trained as a shop clerk is without work? Not enough aggregate demand is one answer. Another is that the current productivity of shop clerks is low but their expected future productivity is sufficiently high that it does not pay an unemployed clerk to retrain for a job that is currently available.

*It is now over 70 years since the Great Depression began. Although we've had many recessions since then, none of them compare with the severity of that event. Some credit for avoiding another major depression must go to the Federal Reserve Board and the monetary policy it has pursued. Next you can meet Peter Ireland, an economics professor at Boston College and former research economist at the Federal Reserve Bank of Richmond.*

# TALKING WITH

**Peter N. Ireland** is Professor of Economics at Boston College. Born in Cambridge, Massachusetts, he was an undergraduate and graduate student at the University of Chicago. Professor Ireland began his career as a research economist at the Federal Reserve Bank of Richmond and also taught at Rutgers University before returning home to the Boston area. His research has spanned a large range of theoretical, empirical, and policy issues in macroeconomics and monetary economics.

Michael Parkin talked with Peter Ireland about his work and the challenges of conducting economic policy.

### What attracted you to economics?

When I first started college, I wasn't quite sure which field I wanted to choose for my major. But after taking a number of courses in different fields, I decided that economics was what I liked best.

Most of all, I enjoyed how economics takes advantage of the quantitative precision of math and statistics—two other fields that I've always found interesting—while at the same time addressing many of the political and social issues that always seemed important to me.

Also, as an undergraduate at Chicago, I was lucky enough to work as a research assistant for Professor Robert Fogel who, as you know, went on to win the Nobel Prize in economics. That was a great experience; more than anything else, it taught me the value of patience and perseverance in conducting economic research. Often, the answer to a tough economics question is just waiting there for anyone to find—it's just a matter of who is willing to put the time and effort into finding and sifting though the relevant data.

### What does a research economist at a regional Federal Reserve Bank do?

Reserve Bank economists perform many tasks. Through their writings and public speeches, they serve as liaisons between the Fed and the local communities. Also, through their basic research, they help find ways to improve monetary policymaking in the United States.

But perhaps the most important job that research economists at the Fed perform involves briefing their Reserve Bank president prior to each meeting of the Federal Open Market Committee. Eight times per year, members of each Bank's research staff sit down with their president to review the most recent economic data and to interpret those data using their theoretical and statistical models. All of the work that's done feeds into answering one important question: at the FOMC meeting, should the president recommend that interest rates be raised, lowered, or held steady?

I really enjoyed that part of my job at the Richmond Fed. It was exciting to be able to apply the economics that I learned in graduate school to address a specific policy issue. And it was nice to think that my work might be making a difference, however small, in helping senior Fed officials make the right policy decisions.

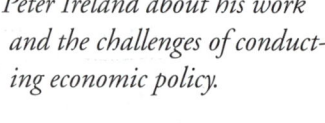
Peter N. Ireland

*Can you summarize what you think we currently know about aggregate fluctuations? Do sticky wages have a role to play? What is the role of the technology shocks that real business cycle theory emphasizes?*

Identifying the source of business cycle fluctuations remains an important and lively topic of research in macroeconomics. Different economists have different opinions on this issue, but I myself like to take a fairly eclectic view.

> *…perhaps the most important insight provided by real business cycle theory is the idea that there are some types of shocks that hit the economy to which monetary and fiscal policymakers cannot or should not respond.*

I agree with monetarist and Keynesian economists who argue that monetary policy can have important real effects in the short run, due to rigidity in nominal prices and wages. At the same time, however, I think that there is a strong element of truth in real business cycle theory, with its emphasis on technology shocks. In my view, perhaps the most important insight provided by real business cycle theory is the idea that there are some types of shocks that hit the economy to which monetary and fiscal policymakers cannot or should not respond.

Suppose, for example, that the price of imported oil rises sharply and suddenly, as it has done on a number of occasions in postwar U.S. history. When that type of shock—which resembles a negative technology shock—hits the economy, inflation and unemployment are both going to rise—one won't see the usual Phillips-curve trade-off between those two variables. And anything that the Fed tries to do to offset the joint rise in inflation and unemployment is probably just going to make matters worse.

But there's a happy side to this same story. Suppose that the economy experiences a period of unusually rapid growth in productivity—like the one we enjoyed in the United States during the 1990s and may still be enjoying today. That's like a positive technology shock in the real business cycle model, and it will be accompanied by low inflation and falling unemployment. Once again, there is no Phillips-curve trade-off: in this case, the Fed can just sit back and enjoy the best of both worlds.

*Some economists advocate a monetary policy rule that adjusts the federal funds rate in response to the latest inflation and output data—a Taylor Rule. What is your view of such a rule?*

I consider the Taylor rule to be very useful, because it gives monetary policymakers a simple but systematic way of comparing the present to the past. Suppose, for example, that today's federal funds rate turns out to be lower than the level that is recommended by the Taylor rule. Then FOMC members know that monetary policy today is more expansionary, relative to the state of the economy, than it has been in the past. So if FOMC members want policy to be more expansionary, then they can have confidence that they're on the right track. But if, on the other hand, FOMC members would prefer that policy be closer to neutral, or even somewhat restrictive, then the Taylor rule warns them that the federal funds rate soon might need to move higher.

*Other economists advocate a monetary policy rule that gradually adjusts the growth rate of the monetary base to long-term trends in real GDP and velocity—a McCallum Rule. What is your view of this rule?*

Again on this topic, my views are a bit eclectic: I also think that McCallum's rule is a valuable guide for monetary policymaking—and for the very same reasons that I find the Taylor rule useful!

Too often, I think, economists fall into the trap of concluding that if there are two models—call them models A and B—and if model A has been helpful in understanding the data, then it necessarily follows that model B must be false. Of course, if model B has been shown to make predictions that are systematically inaccurate, then it should be abandoned in favor of its more successful competitor. But in many cases, different models can serve as complements rather than competitors.

Consider the situation that prevails in the U.S. economy today, in the Fall of 2003. The federal funds rate is unusually low, so the Taylor rule tells us that monetary policy is accommodative—as, presumably, it should be to help pull the economy out of recession. At the same time, the monetary base and the broader monetary aggregates are growing at a robust pace as well, so the McCallum rule leads us to the same conclusion that monetary policy is appropriately expansionary. So in this case, by seeing that two very different models lead to exactly the same conclusion, we can be all the more confident that the Fed is on track.

***Thinking about what we know and don't know about aggregate fluctuations, how would you describe the task of macroeconomic stabilization policy?***

Somewhat paradoxically, perhaps, the two most important lessons about stabilization policy that macroeconomists have learned in recent decades both apply to the long run. The first lesson is that in the long run, the inflation rate is constrained by the central bank's choice of money growth rate; put another way, the central bank is responsible for controlling inflation. And the second lesson is that in the long run, there is little or no trade-off between inflation and unemployment.

> *…the Federal Reserve's job first and foremost is to provide for a low and stable rate of inflation.*

Taken together, these two lessons imply that the Federal Reserve's job first and foremost is to provide for a low and stable rate of inflation. That is something that the Fed can achieve without sacrificing anything in terms of its goals for employment.

Constrained by that long-run objective, the Fed can then do what it can to help stabilize the real economy. But a difficult issue goes back to something that we talked about earlier: the fact that different shocks can call for different policy responses from the Fed. So Federal Reserve officials and their research advisors must work hard to continue building models that help us identify exactly what types of shocks might be hitting the economy at any given point in time. And above all, in pursuing its stabilization objectives, the Fed should act cautiously, so as to avoid repeating the large policy mistakes of the past—even if that means it can't always respond to developments in the economy as vigorously or as quickly as some observers might like.

***What advice do you have for a student who is just starting to study economics? Is economics a good subject in which to major? What other subjects would you urge students to study along side economics?***

I definitely think that economics is a great choice for an undergraduate major. In addition to what I said before—about how economics combines some of the most interesting aspects of many other fields—an economics major can also serve as a stepping-stone toward a wide variety of careers. Of course, many economics majors go on to work in business or finance, but others find that they are equally well-prepared for a career in law or in public policy. Or, if you major in economics today, who knows: you might even go on to graduate school and become the professor who writes the next best-selling Principles textbook! More seriously, the point is, you can do a lot of different things with an economics degree.

To someone who is just starting to study economics, I'd recommend taking at least a few additional courses in statistics, econometrics (which is just statistics applied specifically to economics), and mathematics—because the field continues to become more and more quantitative. But I'd also say that taking courses in political science, sociology, and psychology can also be really useful, especially if they suggest new problems that haven't yet been addressed from an economic point of view.

# PART 7 The Global Economy

# Trading with the World

## Silk Routes and Sucking Sounds

**Since ancient times, people have expanded** their trading as far as technology allowed. Marco Polo opened up the silk route between Europe and China in the thirteenth century. Today, container ships laden with cars and electronics and Boeing 747s stuffed with farm-fresh foods ply sea and air routes, carrying billions of dollars worth of goods. Why do people go to such great lengths to trade with those in other nations?

In 1994, the United States entered into a free trade agreement with Canada and Mexico—the North American Free Trade Agreement, or NAFTA. Some people predicted a "giant sucking sound" as jobs were transferred from high-wage Michigan to low-wage Mexico. Can we compete with a country that pays its workers a fraction of U.S. wages?

Workers in China earn even less than those in Mexico, and today, just about every manufactured object that we buy seems to be made in China. How can we compete with low-wage China and the other low-wage Asian nations? Are there any industries, besides perhaps making Hollywood movies and building large passenger jets, in which we have an advantage?

Would it be a good idea to limit imports from China and other countries by putting a tariff or a quota on those imports?

◆ In this chapter, we're going to learn about international trade and discover how all nations can gain from trading with other nations. You will discover that all nations can compete, no matter how high their wages. But you will also learn why, despite the fact that international trade brings benefits to all, governments restrict trade. In *Reading Between the Lines* at the end of the chapter, we'll look at the growing trade with China and see why we all benefit from it.

## CHAPTER 17

### After studying this chapter, you will be able to

■ Describe the trends and patterns in international trade

■ Explain comparative advantage and explain why all countries can gain from international trade

■ Explain why international trade restrictions reduce the volume of imports and exports and reduce our consumption possibilities

■ Explain the arguments that are used to justify international trade restrictions and show how they are flawed

■ Explain why we have international trade restrictions

## Patterns and Trends in International Trade

The goods and services that we buy from people in other countries are called **imports**. The goods and services that we sell to people in other countries are called **exports**. What are the most important things that we import and export? Most people would probably guess that a rich nation such as the United States imports raw materials and exports manufactured goods. Although that is one feature of U.S. international trade, it is not its most important feature. The bulk of our exports *and* imports is manufactured goods. We sell foreigners earth-moving equipment, airplanes, supercomputers, and scientific equipment, and we buy televisions, DVD players, blue jeans, and T-shirts from them. Also, we are a major exporter of agricultural products and raw materials. And we import and export a huge volume of services.

### Trade in Goods

Manufactured goods account for 55 percent of our exports and 68 percent of our imports. Industrial materials (raw materials and semi-manufactured items) account for 14 percent of our exports and 15 percent of our imports, and agricultural products account for only 8 percent of our exports and 4 percent of our imports. Our largest individual export and import items are capital goods and automobiles. But goods account for only 70 percent of our exports and 84 percent of our imports. The rest of our international trade is in services.

### Trade in Services

You may be wondering how a country can "export" and "import" services. Here are some examples.

If you take a vacation in France and travel there on an Air France flight from New York, you import transportation services from France. The money you spend in France on hotel bills and restaurant meals is also classified as the import of services. Similarly, the money spent by a French student on vacation in the United States is a U.S. export of services to France.

When we import TV sets from South Korea, the owner of the ship that transports them might be Greek and the company that insures them might be British. The payments that we make for transportation and insurance are imports of services. Similarly, when an American shipping company transports California wine to Tokyo, the transportation cost is an export of a service to Japan. Our international trade in these types of services is large and growing.

### Geographical Patterns of International Trade

The United States has trading links with every part of the world, but Canada is our biggest trading partner. In 2003, 20 percent of our exports went to Canada and 17 percent of our imports came from Canada. Japan is our second biggest trading partner, accounting for 8 percent of exports and 9 percent of imports in 2003. The regions in which our trade is largest are the European Union—with 24 percent of our exports and 23 percent of our imports in 2003—and Latin America—with 20 percent of our exports and 18 percent of our imports in 2003.

### Trends in the Volume of Trade

In 1960, we exported 3.5 percent of total output and imported 4 percent of the goods and services that we bought. In 2003, we exported 10 percent of total output and imported 15 percent of the goods and services that we bought.

On the export side, capital goods, automobiles, food, and raw materials have remained large items and held a roughly constant share of total exports. But the composition of imports has changed. Food and raw material imports have fallen steadily. Imports of fuel increased dramatically during the 1970s but fell during the 1980s. Imports of machinery have grown and today approach 50 percent of total imports.

### Net Exports and International Borrowing

The value of exports minus the value of imports is called **net exports**. In 2003, U.S. net exports were a negative $500 billion. Our imports were $500 billion more than our exports. When we import more than we export, as we did in 2003, we borrow from foreigners or sell some of our assets to them. When we export more than we import, we make loans to foreigners or buy some of their assets.

# The Gains from International Trade

THE FUNDAMENTAL FORCE THAT GENERATES international trade is *comparative advantage*. And the basis of comparative advantage is divergent *opportunity costs*. You met these ideas in Chapter 2 (pp. 40–43), when we learned about the gains from specialization and exchange between Tom and Nancy.

Tom and Nancy each specialize in producing just one good and then trade with each other. Most nations do not go to the extreme of specializing in a single good and importing everything else. But nations can increase the consumption of all goods if they redirect their scarce resources toward the production of those goods and services in which they have a comparative advantage.

To see how this outcome occurs, we'll apply the same basic ideas that we learned in the case of Tom and Nancy to trade among nations. We'll begin by recalling how we can use the production possibilities frontier to measure opportunity cost. Then we'll see how divergent opportunity costs bring comparative advantage and gains from trade for countries as well as for individuals even though no country completely specializes in the production of just one good.

## Opportunity Cost in Farmland

Farmland (a fictitious country) can produce grain and cars at any point inside or along its production possibilities frontier, *PPF*, shown in Fig. 17.1. (We're holding constant the output of all the other goods that Farmland produces.) The Farmers (the people of Farmland) are consuming all the grain and cars that they produce, and they are operating at point *A* in the figure. That is, Farmland is producing and consuming 15 billion bushels of grain and 8 million cars each year. What is the opportunity cost of a car in Farmland?

We can answer that question by calculating the slope of the production possibilities frontier at point *A*. The magnitude of the slope of the frontier measures the opportunity cost of one good in terms of the other. To measure the slope of the frontier at point *A*, place a straight line tangential to the frontier at point *A* and calculate the slope of that straight line. Recall that the formula for the slope of a line is the change in the value of the variable measured on the *y*-axis divided by the change in the value of the variable

measured on the *x*-axis as we move along the line. Here, the variable measured on the *y*-axis is billions of bushels of grain, and the variable measured on the *x*-axis is millions of cars. So the slope is the change in the number of bushels of grain divided by the change in the number of cars.

As you can see from the red triangle at point *A* in Fig. 17.1, if the number of cars produced increases by 2 million, grain production decreases by 18 billion bushels. Therefore the magnitude of the slope is 18 billion divided by 2 million, which equals 9,000. To get one more car, the people of Farmland must give up 9,000 bushels of grain. So the opportunity cost of 1 car is 9,000 bushels of grain. Equivalently, 9,000 bushels of grain cost 1 car. For the people of Farmland, these opportunity costs are the prices they face. The price of a car is 9,000 bushels of grain, and the price of 9,000 bushels of grain is 1 car.

**FIGURE 17.1  Opportunity Cost in Farmland**

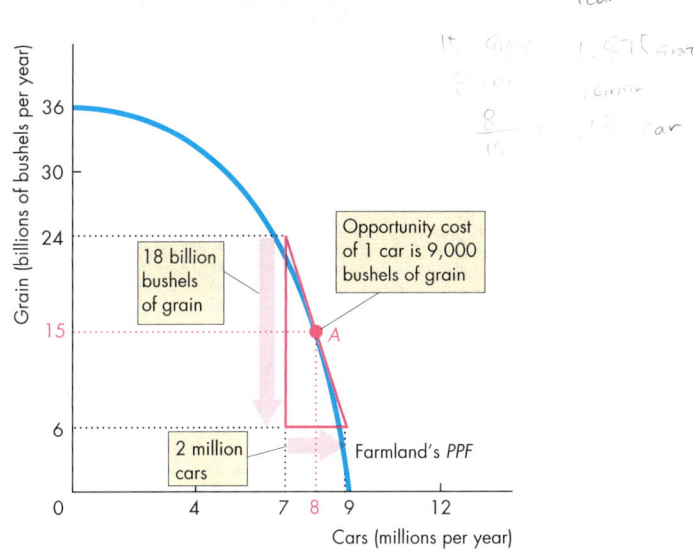

Farmland produces and consumes 15 billion bushels of grain and 8 million cars a year. That is, it produces and consumes at point *A* on its production possibilities frontier. Opportunity cost is equal to the magnitude of the slope of the production possibilities frontier. The red triangle tells us that at point *A*, 18 billion bushels of grain must be forgone to get 2 million cars. That is, at point *A*, 2 million cars cost 18 billion bushels of grain. Equivalently, 1 car costs 9,000 bushels of grain or 9,000 bushels cost 1 car.

## Opportunity Cost in Mobilia

Figure 17.2 shows the production possibilities frontier of Mobilia (another fictitious country). Like the Farmers, the Mobilians consume all the grain and cars that they produce. Mobilia consumes 18 billion bushels of grain a year and 4 million cars, at point $A'$.

Let's calculate the opportunity costs in Mobilia. At point $A'$, the opportunity cost of a car is equal to the magnitude of the slope of the red line tangential to Mobilia's *PPF*. You can see from the red triangle that the magnitude of the slope of Mobilia's *PPF* is 6 billion bushels of grain divided by 6 million cars, which equals 1,000 bushels of grain per car. To get one more car, the Mobilians must give up 1,000 bushels of grain. So the opportunity cost of 1 car is 1,000 bushels of grain, or equivalently, the opportunity cost of 1,000 bushels of grain is 1 car. These are the prices faced in Mobilia.

## Comparative Advantage

Cars are cheaper in Mobilia than in Farmland. One car costs 9,000 bushels of grain in Farmland but only 1,000 bushels of grain in Mobilia. But grain is cheaper in Farmland than in Mobilia—9,000 bushels of grain cost only 1 car in Farmland, while that same amount of grain costs 9 cars in Mobilia.

Mobilia has a comparative advantage in car production. Farmland has a comparative advantage in grain production. A country has a **comparative advantage** in producing a good if it can produce that good at a lower opportunity cost than any other country. Let's see how opportunity cost differences and comparative advantage generate gains from international trade.

## The Gains from Trade: Cheaper to Buy Than to Produce

If Mobilia bought grain for what it costs Farmland to produce it, then Mobilia could buy 9,000 bushels of grain for 1 car. That is much lower than the cost of growing grain in Mobilia, for there it costs 9 cars to produce 9,000 bushels of grain. If the Mobilians can buy grain at the low Farmland price, they will reap some gains.

If the Farmers can buy cars for what it costs Mobilia to produce them, they will be able to obtain a car for 1,000 bushels of grain. Because it costs 9,000 bushels of grain to produce a car in Farmland, the Farmers would gain from such an opportunity.

In this situation, it makes sense for Mobilians to buy their grain from Farmers and for Farmers to buy their cars from Mobilians. But at what price will Farmland and Mobilia engage in mutually beneficial international trade?

## The Terms of Trade

The quantity of grain that Farmland must pay Mobilia for a car is Farmland's **terms of trade** with Mobilia. Because the United States exports and imports many different goods and services, we measure the terms of trade in the real world as an index number that averages the terms of trade over all the items we trade.

The forces of international supply and demand determine the terms of trade. Figure 17.3 illustrates these forces in the Farmland–Mobilia international car market. The quantity of cars *traded internationally* is measured on the *x*-axis. On the *y*-axis, we measure the price of a car. This price is expressed as the *terms of trade*: bushels of grain per car. If no international trade takes place, the price of a car in

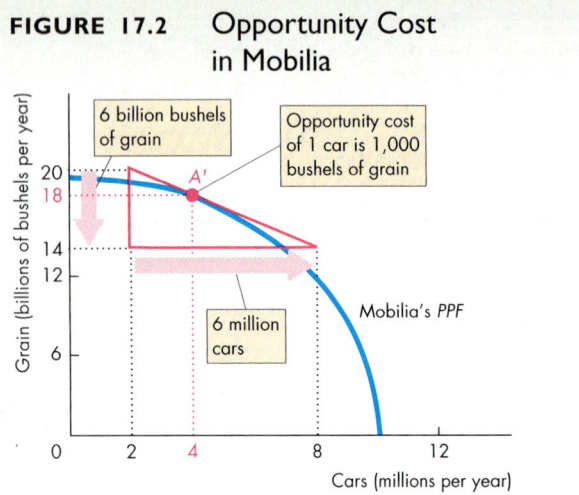

**FIGURE 17.2 Opportunity Cost in Mobilia**

Mobilia produces and consumes 18 billion bushels of grain and 4 million cars a year at point A' on its production possibilities frontier. Opportunity cost is equal to the magnitude of the slope of the production possibilities frontier. The red triangle tells us that at point A', 6 billion bushels of grain must be forgone to get 6 million cars. That is, at point A', 6 million cars cost 6 billion bushels of grain. Equivalently, 1 car costs 1,000 bushels of grain or 1,000 bushels cost 1 car.

# THE GAINS FROM INTERNATIONAL TRADE

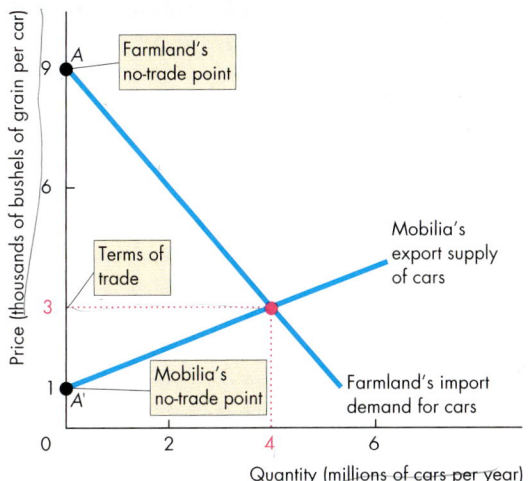

**FIGURE 17.3** International Trade in Cars

Farmland's import demand curve for cars is downward sloping, and Mobilia's export supply curve of cars is upward sloping. With no international trade, the price of a car is 9,000 bushels of grain in Farmland (point A) and 1,000 bushels of grain in Mobilia (point A').

With free international trade, the price (terms of trade) is determined where the export supply curve intersects the import demand curve: 3,000 bushels of grain per car. At that price, 4 million cars a year are imported by Farmland and exported by Mobilia. The value of grain exported by Farmland and imported by Mobilia is 12 billion bushels a year, the quantity required to pay for the cars imported.

Farmland is 9,000 bushels of grain, its opportunity cost, indicated by point A in the figure. Again, if no trade takes place, the price of a car in Mobilia is 1,000 bushels of grain, its opportunity cost, indicated by point A' in the figure. The no-trade points A and A' in Fig. 17.3 correspond to point A in Fig. 17.1 and point A' in Fig. 17.2. The lower the price of a car (terms of trade), the greater is the quantity of cars that the Farmers are willing to import from the Mobilians. This fact is illustrated by the downward-sloping curve, which shows Farmland's import demand for cars.

The Mobilians respond in the opposite direction. The higher the price of a car, the greater is the quantity of cars that Mobilians are willing to export to Farmers. This fact is reflected in Mobilia's export supply of cars—the upward-sloping line in Fig. 17.3.

The international market in cars determines the equilibrium terms of trade (price) and quantity traded. This equilibrium occurs where the import demand curve intersects the export supply curve. In this case, the equilibrium terms of trade are 3,000 bushels of grain per car. Mobilia exports and Farmland imports 4 million cars a year. Notice that the terms of trade are lower than the initial price in Farmland but higher than the initial price in Mobilia.

## Balanced Trade

The number of cars exported by Mobilia—4 million a year—is exactly equal to the number of cars imported by Farmland. How does Farmland pay for its cars? The answer is by exporting grain. How much grain does Farmland export? You can find the answer by noticing that for 1 car, Farmland must pay 3,000 bushels of grain. So for 4 million cars, Farmland pays 12 billion bushels of grain. Farmland's exports of grain are 12 billion bushels a year, and Mobilia imports this same quantity of grain.

Mobilia exchanges 4 million cars for 12 billion bushels of grain each year, and Farmland exchanges 12 billion bushels of grain for 4 million cars. Trade is balanced. For each country, the value received from exports equals the value paid out for imports.

## Changes in Production and Consumption

We've seen that international trade makes it possible for Farmers to buy cars at a lower price than they can produce them and sell their grain for a higher price. International trade also enables Mobilians to sell their cars for a higher price and buy grain for a lower price. Everyone gains. How is it possible for *everyone* to gain? What are the changes in production and consumption that accompany these gains?

An economy that does not trade with other economies has identical production and consumption possibilities. Without trade, the economy can consume only what it produces. But with international trade, an economy can consume different quantities of goods from those that it produces. The production possibilities frontier describes the limit of what a country can produce, but it does not describe the limits to what it can consume. Figure 17.4 will help you to see the distinction between production possibilities and consumption possibilities when a country trades with other countries.

## FIGURE 17.4  Expanding Consumption Possibilities

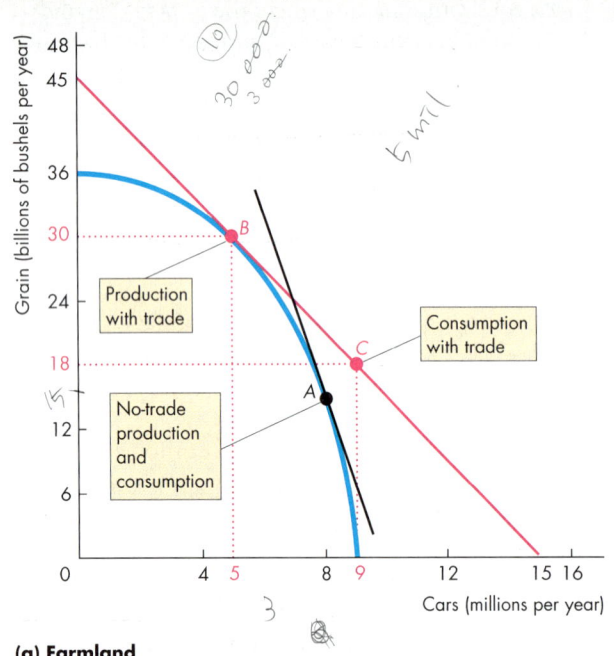

**(a) Farmland**

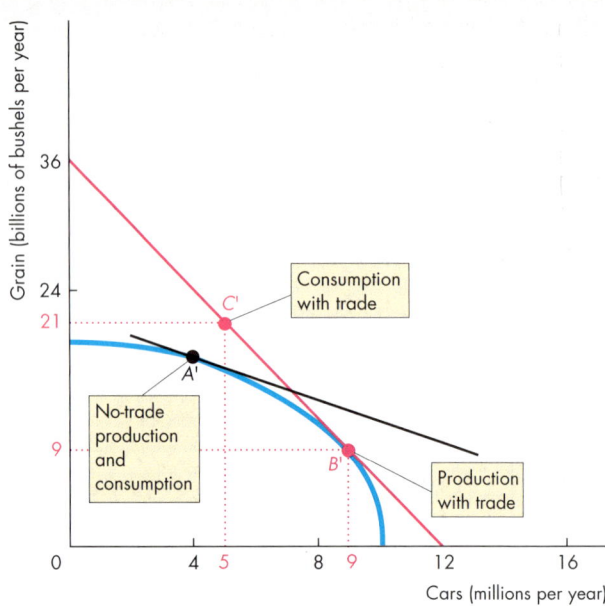

**(b) Mobilia**

With no international trade, the Farmers produce and consume at point A and the opportunity cost of a car is 9,000 bushels of grain (the slope of the black line in part a). Also, with no international trade, the Mobilians produce and consume at point A' and the opportunity cost of 1,000 bushels of grain is 1 car (the slope of the black line in part b). Goods can be exchanged internationally at a price of 3,000 bushels of grain for 1 car along the red line in each part of the figure.

In part (a), Farmland decreases its production of cars and increases its production of grain, moving from A to B. It exports grain and imports cars, and it consumes at point C. The Farmers have more of both cars and grain than they would if they produced all their own consumption goods—at point A.

In part (b), Mobilia increases car production and decreases grain production, moving from A' to B'. Mobilia exports cars and imports grain, and it consumes at point C'. The Mobilians have more of both cars and grain than they would if they produced all their own consumption goods—at point A'.

First of all, notice that the figure has two parts: part (a) for Farmland and part (b) for Mobilia. The production possibilities frontiers that you saw in Figs. 17.1 and 17.2 are reproduced here. The slopes of the two black lines in the figure represent the opportunity costs in the two countries when there is no international trade. Farmland produces and consumes at point A, and Mobilia produces and consumes at A'. Cars cost 9,000 bushels of grain in Farmland and 1,000 bushels of grain in Mobilia.

**Consumption Possibilities**  The red line in each part of Fig. 17.4 shows the country's consumption possibilities with international trade. These two red lines have the same slope, and the magnitude of that slope is the opportunity cost of a car in terms of grain on the world market: 3,000 bushels per car. The *slope* of the consumption possibilities line is common to both countries because its magnitude equals the *world* price. But the position of a country's consumption possibilities line depends on the country's production possibilities. A country cannot produce outside its production possibilities curve, so its consumption possibilities curve touches its production possibilities curve. So Farmland could choose to consume at point B with no international trade or, with international trade, at any point on its red consumption possibilities line.

**Free Trade Equilibrium** With international trade, the producers of cars in Mobilia can get a higher price for their output. As a result, they increase the quantity of car production. At the same time, grain producers in Mobilia get a lower price for their grain, and so they reduce production. Producers in Mobilia adjust their output by moving along their production possibilities frontier until the opportunity cost in Mobilia equals the world price (the opportunity cost in the world market). This situation arises when Mobilia is producing at point $B'$ in Fig. 17.4(b).

But the Mobilians do not consume at point $B'$. That is, they do not increase their consumption of cars and decrease their consumption of grain. Instead, they sell some of their car production to Farmland in exchange for some of Farmland's grain. They trade internationally. But to see how that works out, we first need to check in with Farmland to see what's happening there.

In Farmland, producers of cars now get a lower price and producers of grain get a higher price. As a consequence, producers in Farmland decrease car production and increase grain production. They adjust their outputs by moving along the production possibilities frontier until the opportunity cost of a car in terms of grain equals the world price (the opportunity cost on the world market). They move to point $B$ in part (a). But the Farmers do not consume at point $B$. Instead, they trade some of their additional grain production for the now cheaper cars from Mobilia.

The figure shows us the quantities consumed in the two countries. We saw in Fig. 17.3 that Mobilia exports 4 million cars a year and Farmland imports those cars. We also saw that Farmland exports 12 billion bushels of grain a year and Mobilia imports that grain. So Farmland's consumption of grain is 12 billion bushels a year less than it produces, and its consumption of cars is 4 million a year more than it produces. Farmland consumes at point $C$ in Fig. 17.4(a).

Similarly, we know that Mobilia consumes 12 billion bushels of grain more than it produces and 4 million cars fewer than it produces. Mobilia consumes at point $C'$ in Fig. 17.4(b).

## Calculating the Gains from Trade

You can now literally see the gains from trade in Fig. 17.4. Without trade, Farmers produce and consume at $A$ (part a)—a point on Farmland's production possibilities frontier. With international trade, Farmers consume at point $C$ in part (a)—a point *outside* the production possibilities frontier. At point $C$, Farmers are consuming 3 billion bushels of grain a year and 1 million cars a year more than before. These increases in consumption of both cars and grain, beyond the limits of the production possibilities frontier, are the Farmers' gains from international trade.

Mobilians also gain. Without trade, they consume at point $A'$ in part (b)—a point on Mobilia's production possibilities frontier. With international trade, they consume at point $C'$—a point outside their production possibilities frontier. With international trade, Mobilia consumes 3 billion bushels of grain a year and 1 million cars a year more than they would without trade. These are the gains from international trade for Mobilia.

### Gains for All

Trade between the Farmers and the Mobilians does not create winners and losers. It creates only winners. Farmers selling grain and Mobilians selling cars face an increased demand for their products because the net demand by foreigners is added to domestic demand. With an increase in demand, the price rises.

Farmers buying cars and Mobilians buying grain face an increased supply of these products because the net foreign supply is added to domestic supply. With an increase in supply, the price falls.

### Gains from Trade in Reality

The gains from trade between Farmland and Mobilia that we have just studied occur in a model economy—in a world economy that we have imagined. But these same phenomena occur every day in the real global economy.

**Comparative Advantage in the Global Economy** We buy TVs and DVD players from Korea, machinery from Europe, and fashion goods from Hong Kong. In exchange, we sell machinery, grain and lumber, airplanes, computers and financial services. All this international trade is generated by comparative advantage, just like the international trade between Farmland and Mobilia in our model economy. All international trade arises from comparative advantage, even when trade is in similar goods such as tools and machines. At first thought, it seems puzzling that countries exchange manufactured goods. Why doesn't each developed country produce all the manufactured goods its citizens want to buy?

**Trade in Similar Goods** Why does the United States produce automobiles for export and at the same time import large quantities of automobiles from Canada, Japan, Korea, and Western Europe? Wouldn't it make more sense to produce all the cars that we buy here in the United States? After all, we have access to the best technology available for producing cars. Autoworkers in the United States are surely as productive as their fellow workers in Canada, Western Europe, and Asian countries. So why does the United States have a comparative advantage in some types of cars and Japan and Europe in others?

**Diversity of Taste and Economies of Scale** The first part of the answer is that people have a tremendous diversity of taste. Let's stick with the example of cars. Some people prefer a sports car, some prefer a limousine, some prefer a regular, full-size car, some prefer a sport utility vehicle, and some prefer a minivan. In addition to size and type of car, there are many other dimensions in which cars vary. Some have low fuel consumption, some have high performance, some are spacious and comfortable, some have a large trunk, some have four-wheel drive, some have front-wheel drive, some have a radiator grill that looks like a Greek temple, others resemble a wedge. People's preferences across these many dimensions vary. The tremendous diversity in tastes for cars means that people value variety and are willing to pay for it in the marketplace.

The second part of the answer to the puzzle is economies of scale—the tendency for the average cost to be lower, the larger the scale of production. In such situations, larger and larger production runs lead to ever lower average costs. Production of many goods, including cars, involves economies of scale. For example, if a car producer makes only a few hundred (or perhaps a few thousand) cars of a particular type and design, the producer must use production techniques that are much more labor-intensive and much less automated than those employed to make hundreds of thousands of cars in a particular model. With short production runs and labor-intensive production techniques, costs are high. With very large production runs and automated assembly lines, production costs are much lower. But to obtain lower costs, the automated assembly lines have to produce a large number of cars.

It is the combination of diversity of taste and economies of scale that determines opportunity cost, produces comparative advantages, and generates such a large amount of international trade in similar commodities. With international trade, each car manufacturer has the whole world market to serve. Each producer can specialize in a limited range of products and then sell its output to the entire world market. This arrangement enables large production runs on the most popular cars and feasible production runs even on the most customized cars demanded by only a handful of people in each country.

The situation in the market for cars is also present in many other industries, especially those producing specialized equipment and parts. For example, the United States exports computer central processor chips but imports memory chips, exports mainframe computers but imports PCs, exports specialized video equipment but imports DVD players. International trade in similar but slightly different manufactured products is profitable.

---

### REVIEW QUIZ

1  What is the fundamental source of the gains from international trade?
2  In what circumstances can countries gain from international trade?
3  What determines the goods and services that a country will export?
4  What determines the goods and services that a country will import?
5  What is a comparative advantage and what role does it play in determining the amount and type of international trade that occurs?
6  How can it be that all countries gain from international trade and that there are no losers?
7  Provide some examples of comparative advantage in today's world.
8  Why does the United States both export and import automobiles?

---

You've now seen how free international trade brings gains for all. But international trade is not free in our world. We'll now take a brief look at the history and the effects of international trade restrictions. We'll see that free trade brings the greatest possible benefits and that international trade restrictions are costly.

# International Trade Restrictions

GOVERNMENTS RESTRICT INTERNATIONAL TRADE to protect domestic industries from foreign competition by using two main tools:

1. Tariffs
2. Nontariff barriers

A **tariff** is a tax that is imposed by the importing country when an imported good crosses its international boundary. A **nontariff barrier** is any action other than a tariff that restricts international trade. Examples of nontariff barriers are quantitative restrictions and licensing regulations limiting imports. First, let's look at tariffs.

## The History of Tariffs

U.S. tariffs today are modest in comparison with their historical levels. Figure 17.5 shows the average tariff rate—total tariffs as a percentage of total imports. You can see in this figure that this average reached a peak of 20 percent in 1933. In that year, three years after the passage of the Smoot-Hawley Act, one third of our imports was subject to a tariff and on those imports the tariff rate was 60 percent. The average tariff in Fig. 17.5 for 1933 is 60 percent multiplied by 0.33, which equals 20 percent. Today, the average tariff rate is less than 2 percent.

The reduction in tariffs after World War II followed the signing in 1947 of the **General Agreement on Tariffs and Trade** (GATT). From its formation, GATT organized a series of "rounds" of negotiations that resulted in a steady process of tariff reduction. One of these, the Kennedy Round that began in the early 1960s, resulted in large tariff cuts starting in 1967. Another, the Tokyo Round, resulted in further tariff cuts in 1979. The final round, the Uruguay Round, started in 1986 and was completed in 1994.

The Uruguay Round was the most ambitious and comprehensive of the rounds and led to the creation of the **World Trade Organization** (WTO). Membership of the WTO brings greater obligations for countries to observe the GATT rules. The United States signed the Uruguay Round agreements, and Congress ratified them in 1994.

**FIGURE 17.5** U.S. Tariffs: 1930–2003

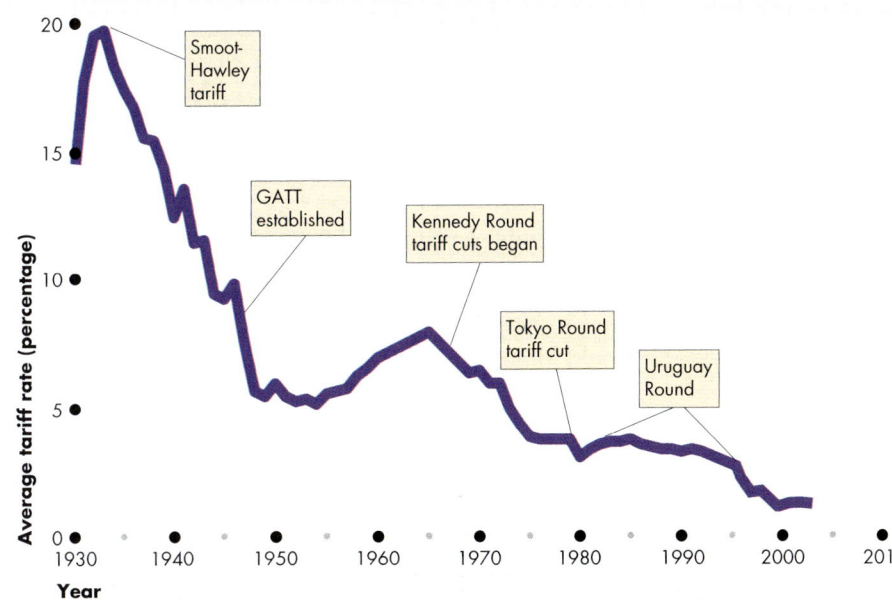

The Smoot-Hawley Act, which was passed in 1930, took U.S. tariffs to a peak average rate of 20 percent in 1933. (One third of imports was subject to a tariff rate of 60 percent.) Since the establishment of GATT in 1947, tariffs have steadily declined in a series of negotiating rounds, the most significant of which are identified in the figure. Tariffs are now as low as they have ever been.

Sources: U.S. Bureau of the Census, *Historical Statistics of the United States, Colonial Times to 1970*, Bicentennial Edition, Part 1 (Washington, D.C., 1975); Series U-212: updated from *Statistical Abstract of the United States*: various editions.

In addition to the agreements under the GATT and the WTO, the United States is a party to the **North American Free Trade Agreement** (NAFTA), which became effective on January 1, 1994, and under which barriers to international trade between the United States, Canada, and Mexico will be virtually eliminated after a 15-year phasing-in period.

In other parts of the world, trade barriers have virtually been eliminated among the member countries of the European Union, which has created the largest unified tariff-free market in the world. In 1994, discussions among the Asia-Pacific Economic group (APEC) led to an agreement in principle to work toward a free-trade area that embraces China, all the economies of East Asia and the South Pacific, Chile, Peru, Mexico, and the United States and Canada. These countries include the fastest-growing economies and hold the promise of heralding a global free-trade area.

The effort to achieve freer trade underlines the fact that trade in some goods is still subject to a high tariff. Textiles and footwear are among the goods that face the highest tariffs, and rates on these items average more than 10 percent. Some individual items face a tariff much higher than the average. For example, when you buy a pair of blue jeans for $30, you pay about $7 more than you would if there were no tariffs on textiles. Other goods that are protected by tariffs are agricultural products, energy and chemicals, minerals, and metals. The meat, cheese, and sugar that you consume cost significantly more because of protection than they would with free international trade.

The temptation for governments to impose tariffs is a strong one. First, tariffs provide revenue to the government. Second, they enable the government to satisfy special interest groups in import-competing industries. But, as we'll see, free international trade brings enormous benefits that are reduced when tariffs are imposed. Let's see how.

## How Tariffs Work

To see how tariffs work, let's return to the example of trade between Farmland and Mobilia. Figure 17.6 shows the international market for cars in which these two countries are the only traders. The volume of trade and the price of a car are determined at the point of intersection of Mobilia's export supply curve of cars and Farmland's import demand curve for cars.

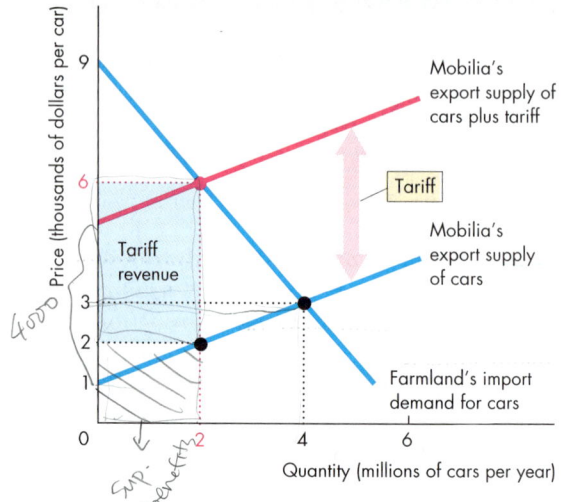

**FIGURE 17.6  The Effects of a Tariff**

Farmland imposes a tariff on car imports from Mobilia. The tariff increases the price that Farmers have to pay for a car and shifts the supply curve of cars in Farmland leftward. The vertical distance between the original supply curve and the new one is the amount of the tariff, $4,000 per car. The price of a car in Farmland increases, and the quantity of cars imported decreases. The government of Farmland collects a tariff revenue of $4,000 per car—a total of $8 billion on the 2 million cars imported. Farmland's exports of grain decrease because Mobilia now has a lower income from its exports of cars.

In Fig. 17.6, these two countries trade cars and grain in exactly the same way that we saw in Fig. 17.3. Mobilia exports cars, and Farmland exports grain. The volume of car imports into Farmland is 4 million a year, and the world market price of a car is 3,000 bushels of grain. Figure 17.6 expresses prices in dollars rather than in units of grain and is based on a money price of grain of $1 a bushel. With grain costing $1 a bushel, the money price of a car is $3,000.

Now suppose that the government of Farmland, perhaps under pressure from car producers, decides to impose a tariff on imported cars. In particular, suppose that a tariff of $4,000 per car is imposed. (This is a huge tariff, but the car producers of Farmland are pretty fed up with competition from Mobilia.) What happens?

- The supply of cars in Farmland decreases.
- The price of cars in Farmland rises.
- The quantity of cars imported by Farmland decreases.
- The government of Farmland collects the tariff revenue.
- Resource use is inefficient.
- The *value* of exports changes by the same amount as the *value* of imports, and trade remains balanced.

**Change in the Supply of Cars** Farmland cannot buy cars at Mobilia's export supply price. It must pay that price plus the $4,000 tariff. So the supply curve in Farmland shifts leftward. The new supply curve is that labeled "Mobilia's export supply of cars plus tariff." The vertical distance between Mobilia's original export supply curve and the new supply curve is the tariff of $4,000 a car.

**Rise in Price of Cars** A new equilibrium occurs where the new supply curve intersects Farmland's import demand curve for cars. That equilibrium is at a price of $6,000 a car, up from $3,000 with free trade.

**Fall in Imports** Car imports fall from 4 million to 2 million cars a year. At the higher price of $6,000 a car, domestic car producers increase their production. Domestic grain production decreases as resources are moved into the expanding car industry.

**Tariff Revenue** Total expenditure on imported cars by the Farmers is $6,000 a car multiplied by the 2 million cars imported ($12 billion). But not all of that money goes to the Mobilians. They receive $2,000 a car, or $4 billion for the 2 million cars. The difference—$4,000 a car, or a total of $8 billion for the 2 million cars—is collected by the government of Farmland as tariff revenue.

**Inefficiency** The people of Farmland are willing to pay $6,000 for the marginal car imported. But the opportunity cost of that car is $2,000. So there is a gain from trading an extra car. In fact, there are gains—willingness to pay exceeds opportunity cost—all the way up to 4 million cars a year. Only when 4 million cars are being traded is the maximum price that a Farmer is willing to pay equal to the minimum price that is acceptable to a Mobilian. Restricting trade reduces the gains from trade.

**Trade Remains Balanced** With free trade, Farmland was paying $3,000 a car and buying 4 million cars a year from Mobilia. The total amount paid to Mobilia for imports was $12 billion a year. With a tariff, Farmland's imports have been cut to 2 million cars a year and the price paid to Mobilia has also been cut to only $2,000 a car. The total amount paid to Mobilia for imports has been cut to $4 billion a year. Doesn't this fact mean that Farmland now has a balance of trade surplus? It does not.

The price of cars in Mobilia has fallen. But the price of grain remains at $1 a bushel. So the relative price of cars has fallen, and the relative price of grain has increased. With free trade, the Mobilians could buy 3,000 bushels of grain for one car. Now they can buy only 2,000 bushels for a car. With a higher relative price of grain, the quantity demanded by the Mobilians decreases and Mobilia imports less grain. But because Mobilia imports less grain, Farmland exports less grain. In fact, Farmland's grain industry suffers from two sources. First, there is a decrease in the quantity of grain sold to Mobilia. Second, there is increased competition for inputs from the now-expanded car industry. The tariff leads to a contraction in the scale of the grain industry in Farmland.

It seems paradoxical at first that a country imposing a tariff on cars hurts its own export industry, lowering its exports of grain. It may help to think of it this way: Mobilians buy grain with the money they make from exporting cars to Farmland. If they export fewer cars, they cannot afford to buy as much grain. In fact, in the absence of any international borrowing and lending, Mobilia must cut its imports of grain by exactly the same amount as the loss in revenue from its export of cars. Grain imports into Mobilia are cut back to a value of $4 billion, the amount that can be paid for by the new lower revenue from Mobilia's car exports. Trade is still balanced. The tariff cuts imports and exports by the same amount. The tariff has no effect on the *balance* of trade, but it reduces the *volume* of trade.

The result that we have just derived is perhaps one of the most misunderstood aspects of international economics. On countless occasions, politicians and others call for tariffs to remove a balance of trade deficit or argue that lowering tariffs would produce a balance of trade deficit. They reach this conclusion by failing to work out all the implications of a tariff.

Let's now look at nontariff barriers.

## Nontariff Barriers

The two main forms of nontariff barrier are

1. Quotas
2. Voluntary export restraints

A **quota** is a quantitative restriction on the import of a particular good, which specifies the maximum amount of the good that may be imported in a given period of time. A **voluntary export restraint** (VER) is an agreement between two governments in which the government of the exporting country agrees to restrain the volume of its own exports.

Quotas are especially prominent in textiles and agriculture. Voluntary export restraints are used to regulate trade between Japan and the United States.

## How Quotas and VERs Work

To see how a quota works, suppose that Farmland imposes a quota that restricts its car imports to 2 million cars a year. Figure 17.7 shows the effects of this action. The quota is shown by the vertical red line at 2 million cars a year. Because it is illegal to exceed the quota, car importers buy only that quantity from Mobilia, for which they pay $2,000 a car. But because the import supply of cars is restricted to 2 million cars a year, people in Farmland are willing to pay $6,000 per car. This is the price of a car in Farmland.

The value of imports falls to $4 billion, exactly the same as in the case of the tariff. So with lower incomes from car exports and with a higher relative price of grain, Mobilians cut back on their imports of grain in exactly the same way that they did under a tariff.

The key difference between a quota and a tariff lies in who collects the gap between the import supply price and the domestic price. In the case of a tariff, it is the government of the importing country. In the case of a quota, it goes to the person who has the right to import under the import quota regulations.

A voluntary export restraint is like a quota arrangement in which quotas are allocated to each exporting country. The effects of a VER are similar to those of a quota but differ from them in that the gap between the domestic price and the export price is captured not by domestic importers but by the foreign exporter. The government of the exporting country has to establish procedures for allocating the restricted volume of exports among its producers.

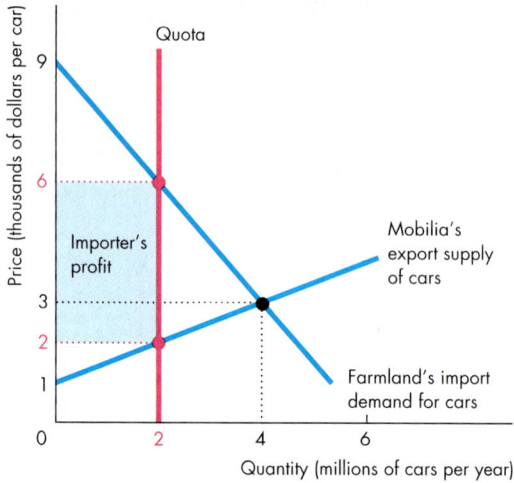

**FIGURE 17.7** The Effects of a Quota

Farmland imposes a quota of 2 million cars a year on car imports from Mobilia. That quantity appears as the vertical line labeled "Quota." Because the quantity of cars supplied by Mobilia is restricted to 2 million, the price at which those cars will be traded increases to $6,000. Importing cars is profitable because Mobilia is willing to supply cars at $2,000 each. There is competition for import quotas.

### REVIEW QUIZ

1. What happens to a country's consumption possibilities when it opens itself up to international trade and trades freely at world market prices?
2. What do international trade restrictions do to the gains from international trade?
3. Which is best for a country: restricted trade, no trade, or free trade? Why?
4. What does a tariff on imports do to the volume of imports and the volume of exports?
5. In the absence of international borrowing and lending, how do tariffs and other international trade restrictions influence the total value of imports and exports and the balance of trade?

We're now going to look at some commonly heard arguments for restricting international trade and see why they are almost never correct.

# The Case Against Protection

For as long as nations and international trade have existed, people have debated whether a country is better off with free international trade or with protection from foreign competition. The debate continues, but for most economists, a verdict has been delivered and is the one you have just seen. Free trade promotes prosperity for all; protection is inefficient. We've seen the most powerful case for free trade in the example of how Farmland and Mobilia both benefit from their comparative advantage. But there is a broader range of issues in the free trade versus protection debate. Let's review these issues.

Three arguments for restricting international trade are

- The national security argument
- The infant-industry argument
- The dumping argument

Let's look at each in turn.

## The National Security Argument

The national security argument for protection is that a country must protect the industries that produce defense equipment and armaments and those on which the defense industries rely for their raw materials and other intermediate inputs. This argument for protection does not withstand close scrutiny.

First, it is an argument for international isolation, for in a time of war, there is no industry that does not contribute to national defense. Second, if the case is made for boosting the output of a strategic industry, it is more efficient to achieve this outcome with a subsidy to the firms in the industry financed out of taxes. Such a subsidy would keep the industry operating at the scale judged appropriate, and free international trade would keep the prices faced by consumers at their world market levels.

## The Infant-Industry Argument

The so-called **infant-industry argument** for protection is that it is necessary to protect a new industry to enable it to grow into a mature industry that can compete in world markets. The argument is based on the idea of *dynamic comparative advantage*, which can arise from *learning-by-doing* (see Chapter 2).

Learning-by-doing is a powerful engine of productivity growth, and comparative advantage does evolve and change because of on-the-job experience. But these facts do not justify protection.

First, the infant-industry argument is valid only if the benefits of learning-by-doing *not only* accrue to the owners and workers of the firms in the infant industry but also *spill over* to other industries and parts of the economy. For example, there are huge productivity gains from learning-by-doing in the manufacture of aircraft. But almost all of these gains benefit the stockholders and workers of Boeing and other aircraft producers. Because the people making the decisions, bearing the risk, and doing the work are the ones who benefit, they take the dynamic gains into account when they decide on the scale of their activities. In this case, almost no benefits spill over to other parts of the economy, so there is no need for government assistance to achieve an efficient outcome.

Second, even if the case is made for protecting an infant industry, it is more efficient to do so by a subsidy to the firms in the industry, with the subsidy financed out of taxes.

## The Dumping Argument

**Dumping** occurs when a foreign firm sells its exports at a lower price than its cost of production. Dumping might be used by a firm that wants to gain a global monopoly. In this case, the foreign firm sells its output at a price below its cost to drive domestic firms out of business. When the domestic firms have gone, the foreign firm takes advantage of its monopoly position and charges a higher price for its product. Dumping is usually regarded as a justification for temporary countervailing tariffs.

But there are powerful reasons to resist the dumping argument for protection. First, it is virtually impossible to detect dumping because it is hard to determine a firm's costs. As a result, the test for dumping is whether a firm's export price is below its domestic price. But this test is a weak one because it can be rational for a firm to charge a low price in markets in which the quantity demanded is highly sensitive to price and a higher price in a market in which demand is less price-sensitive.

Second, it is hard to think of a good that is produced by a natural *global* monopoly. So even if all the domestic firms in some industry were driven out of business, it would always be possible to find many alternative foreign sources of supply and to buy the good at prices determined in competitive markets.

Third, if a good or service were a truly global natural monopoly, the best way of dealing with it would be by regulation—just as in the case of domestic monopolies. Such regulation would require international cooperation.

The three arguments for protection that we've just examined have an element of credibility. The counterarguments are in general stronger, however, so these arguments do not make the case for protection. But they are not the only arguments that you might encounter. The many other arguments that are commonly heard are quite simply wrong. They are fatally flawed. The most common of them are that protection

- Saves jobs
- Allows us to compete with cheap foreign labor
- Brings diversity and stability
- Penalizes lax environmental standards
- Protects national culture
- Prevents rich countries from exploiting developing countries

### Saves Jobs

The argument that protection saves jobs goes as follows: When we buy shoes from Brazil or shirts from Taiwan, U.S. workers in these industries lose their jobs. With no earnings and poor prospects, these workers become a drain on welfare and spend less, causing a ripple effect of further job losses. The proposed solution to this problem is to ban imports of cheap foreign goods and protect U.S. jobs. The proposal is flawed for the following reasons.

First, free trade does cost some jobs, but it also creates other jobs. It brings about a global rationalization of labor and allocates labor resources to their highest-valued activities. Because of international trade in textiles, tens of thousands of workers in the United States have lost jobs as textile mills and other factories have closed. But tens of thousands of workers in other countries have gotten jobs because textile mills have opened there. And tens of thousands of U.S. workers have gotten better-paying jobs than textile workers because other export industries have expanded and created more jobs than have been destroyed.

Second, imports create jobs. They create jobs for retailers that sell imported goods and firms that service those goods. They also create jobs by creating incomes in the rest of the world, some of which are spent on imports of U.S.-made goods and services.

Although protection does save particular jobs, it does so at inordinate cost. For example, textile jobs are protected in the United States by quotas imposed under an international agreement called the Multifiber Arrangement. The U.S. International Trade Commission (ITC) has estimated that because of quotas, 72,000 jobs exist in textiles that would otherwise disappear and annual clothing expenditure in the United States is $15.9 billion or $160 per family higher than it would be with free trade. Equivalently, the ITC estimates that each textile job saved costs $221,000 a year.

### Allows Us to Compete with Cheap Foreign Labor

With the removal of tariffs in U.S. trade with Mexico, people said we would hear a "giant sucking sound" as jobs rushed to Mexico (shown in the cartoon). Let's see what's wrong with this view.

The labor cost of a unit of output equals the wage rate divided by labor productivity. For example, if a U.S. autoworker earns $30 an hour and produces 15 units of output an hour, the average labor cost of a

"I don't know what the hell happened—one minute I'm at work in Flint, Michigan, then there's a giant sucking sound and suddenly here I am in Mexico."

© The New Yorker Collection 1993
Mick Stevens from Cartoonbank.com. All Rights Reserved.

unit of output is $2. If a Mexican auto assembly worker earns $3 an hour and produces 1 unit of output an hour, the average labor cost of a unit of output is $3. Other things remaining the same, the higher a worker's productivity, the higher is the worker's wage rate. High-wage workers have high productivity. Low-wage workers have low productivity.

Although high-wage U.S. workers are more productive, on the average, than low-wage Mexican workers, there are differences across industries. U.S. labor is relatively more productive in some activities than in others. For example, the productivity of U.S. workers in producing movies, financial services, and customized computer chips is relatively higher than their productivity in the production of metals and some standardized machine parts. The activities in which U.S. workers are relatively more productive than their Mexican counterparts are those in which the United States has a *comparative advantage*. By engaging in free trade, increasing our production and exports of the goods and services in which we have a comparative advantage and decreasing our production and increasing our imports of the goods and services in which our trading partners have a comparative advantage, we can make ourselves and the citizens of other countries better off.

## Brings Diversity and Stability

A diversified investment portfolio is less risky than one that has all the eggs in one basket. The same is true for an economy's production. A diversified economy fluctuates less than an economy that produces only one or two goods.

But big, rich, diversified economies such as those of the United States, Japan, and Europe do not have this type of stability problem. Even a country such as Saudi Arabia that produces only one good (in this case, oil) can benefit from specializing in the activity at which it has a comparative advantage and then investing in a wide range of other countries to bring greater stability to its income and consumption.

## Penalizes Lax Environmental Standards

Another argument for protection is that many poorer countries, such as Mexico, do not have the same environmental policies that we have and, because they are willing to pollute and we are not, we cannot compete with them without tariffs. So if they want free trade with the richer and "greener" countries, they must clean up their environments to our standards.

This argument for international trade restrictions is weak. First, not all poorer countries have significantly lower environmental standards than the United States has. Many poor countries and the former communist countries of Eastern Europe do have bad environmental records. But some countries enforce strict laws. Second, a poor country cannot afford to be as concerned about its environment as a rich country can. The best hope for a better environment in Mexico and in other developing countries is rapid income growth through free trade. As their incomes grow, developing countries will have the *means* to match their desires to improve their environment. Third, poor countries have a comparative advantage at doing "dirty" work, which helps rich countries achieve higher environmental standards than they otherwise could.

## Protects National Culture

The national culture argument for protection is not heard much in the United States, but it is a commonly heard argument in Canada and Europe.

The expressed fear is that free trade in books, magazines, movies, and television programs means U.S. domination and the end of local culture. So, the reasoning continues, it is necessary to protect domestic "culture" industries from free international trade to ensure the survival of a national cultural identity.

Protection of these industries is common and takes the form of nontariff barriers. For example, local content regulations on radio and television broadcasting and in magazines is often required.

The cultural identity argument for protection has no merit, and it is one more example of rent seeking. Writers, publishers, and broadcasters want to limit foreign competition so that they can earn larger economic profits. There is no actual danger to national culture. In fact, many of the creators of so-called American cultural products are not Americans but the talented citizens of other countries, ensuring the survival of their national cultural identities in Hollywood! Also, if national culture is in danger, there is no surer way of helping it on its way out than by impoverishing the nation whose culture it is. And protection is an effective way of doing just that.

### Prevents Rich Countries from Exploiting Developing Countries

Another argument for protection is that international trade must be restricted to prevent the people of the rich industrial world from exploiting the poorer people of the developing countries, forcing them to work for slave wages.

Wage rates in some developing countries are indeed very low. But by trading with developing countries, we increase the demand for the goods that these countries produce and, more significantly, we increase the demand for their labor. When the demand for labor in developing countries increases, the wage rate also increases. So, far from exploiting people in developing countries, trade improves their opportunities and increases their incomes.

We have reviewed the arguments that are commonly heard in favor of protection and the counterarguments against them. There is one counterargument to protection that is general and quite overwhelming. Protection invites retaliation and can trigger a trade war. The best example of a trade war occurred during the Great Depression of the 1930s when the Smoot-Hawley tariff was introduced in the United States. Country after country retaliated with its own tariff, and in a short period, world trade had almost disappeared. The costs to all countries were large and led to a renewed international resolve to avoid such self-defeating moves in the future. They also led to the creation of GATT and are the impetus behind NAFTA, APEC, and the European Union.

### REVIEW QUIZ

1. Can we achieve national security goals, stimulate the growth of new industries, or restrain foreign monopoly by restricting international trade?
2. Can we save jobs, compensate for low foreign wages, make the economy more diversified, compensate for costly environmental policies, protect national culture, or protect developing countries from being exploited by restricting international trade?
3. Is there any merit to the view that we should restrict international trade for any reason? What is the main argument against international trade restrictions?

## Why Is International Trade Restricted?

WHY, DESPITE ALL THE ARGUMENTS AGAINST protection, is trade restricted? There are two key reasons:

- Tariff revenue
- Rent seeking

### Tariff Revenue

Government revenue is costly to collect. In the developed countries such as the United States, a well-organized tax collection system is in place that can generate billions of dollars of income tax and sales tax revenues. This tax collection system is made possible by the fact that most economic transactions are done by firms that must keep properly audited financial records. Without such records, the revenue collection agencies (the Internal Revenue Service in the United States) would be severely hampered in the work. Even with audited financial accounts, some proportion of potential tax revenue is lost. Nonetheless, for the industrialized countries, the income tax and sales taxes are the major sources of revenue and the tariff plays a very small role.

But governments in developing countries have a difficult time collecting taxes from their citizens. Much economic activity takes place in an informal economy with few financial records, so only a small amount of revenue is collected from income taxes and sales taxes. The one area in which economic transactions are well recorded and audited is in international trade. So this activity is an attractive base for tax collection in these countries and is used much more extensively than in the developed countries.

### Rent Seeking

Rent seeking is the major reason why international trade is restricted. **Rent seeking** is lobbying and other political activity that seek to capture the gains from trade. Free trade increases consumption possibilities *on the average*, but not everyone shares in the gain and some people even lose. Free trade brings benefits to some and imposes costs on others, with total benefits exceeding total costs. It is the uneven distribution of costs and benefits that is the principal source of impediment to achieving more liberal international trade.

Returning to our example of trade in cars and grain between Farmland and Mobilia, the benefits from free trade accrue to all the producers of grain and to those producers of cars who would not have to bear the costs of adjusting to a smaller car industry. Those costs are transition costs, not permanent costs. The costs of moving to free trade are borne by those car producers and their employees who have to become grain producers. The number of people who gain will, in general, be enormous in comparison with the number who lose. The gain per person will therefore be rather small. The loss per person to those who bear the loss will be large. Because the loss that falls on those who bear it is large, it will pay those people to incur considerable expense to lobby against free trade. On the other hand, it will not pay those who gain to organize to achieve free trade. The gain from trade for any one individual is too small for that individual to spend much time or money on a political organization to achieve free trade. The loss from free trade will be seen as being so great by those bearing that loss that they *will* find it profitable to join a political organization to prevent free trade. Each group is optimizing—weighing benefits against costs and choosing the best action for themselves. The anti-free-trade group will, however, undertake a larger quantity of political lobbying than the pro-free-trade group.

### Compensating Losers

If, in total, the gains from free international trade exceed the losses, why don't those who gain compensate those who lose so that everyone is in favor of free trade? To some degree, such compensation does take place. When Congress approved the NAFTA deal with Canada and Mexico, it set up a $56 million fund to support and retrain workers who lost their jobs because of the new trade agreement. During the first six months of the operation of NAFTA, only 5,000 workers applied for benefits under this scheme.

The losers from freer international trade are also compensated indirectly through the normal unemployment compensation arrangements. But only limited attempts are made to compensate those who lose from free international trade. The main reason why full compensation is not attempted is that the costs of identifying all the losers and estimating the value of their losses would be enormous. Also, it would never be clear whether a person who has fallen on hard times is suffering because of free trade or for other reasons that might be largely under his or her control. Furthermore, some people who look like losers at one point in time may, in fact, wind up gaining. The young autoworker who loses his job in Michigan and becomes a computer assembly worker in Minneapolis resents the loss of work and the need to move. But a year or two later, looking back on events, he counts himself fortunate. He has made a move that has increased his income and given him greater job security.

It is because we do not, in general, compensate the losers from free international trade that protectionism is such a popular and permanent feature of our national economic and political life.

### REVIEW QUIZ

1 What are the two main reasons for imposing tariffs on imports?
2 What type of country most benefits from the revenue from tariffs? Provide some examples of such countries.
3 Does the United States need to use tariffs to raise revenue for the government? Explain why or why not.
4 If international trade restrictions are costly, why do we use them? Why don't the people who gain from trade organize a political force that is strong enough to ensure that their interests are protected?

♦ You've now seen how free international trade enables all nations to gain from specialization and trade. By producing goods in which we have a comparative advantage and trading some of our production for that of others, we expand our consumption possibilities. Placing impediments on that trade restricts the extent to which we can gain from specialization and trade. By opening our country up to free international trade, the market for the things that we sell expands and the relative price rises. The market for the things that we buy also expands, and the relative price falls.

*Reading Between the Lines* on pp. 432–433 looks at the globalization of production and the gains that are being reaped by Americans and Asians as production in China and trade between China and the United States expand.

# READING BETWEEN THE LINES

## POLICY WATCH

## *The Gains from Globalization*

**THE WALL STREET JOURNAL, OCTOBER 6, 2003**

### Textile-Sector Changes Stir Up Southeast Asia

A dozen women wearing Muslim headscarves bend over whirring sewing machines in Prolexus Bhd.'s training room, practicing the most complicated techniques used to stitch the Nike and Gap outfits that are made on the factory floor downstairs.

Workers at this factory, tucked amid the leafy hills that surround this southern Malaysian town, have sewn all kinds of garments for big U.S. brands for 27 years.

But ... China's entry in late 2001 into the World Trade Organization, and the looming end of the textile-quota system among WTO members, are reshaping Southeast Asia's textile industry. These developments are forcing companies across the region to relocate basic jobs to countries with lower-paid labor, including China, while pushing the companies themselves to boost productivity and know-how among workers at home.

In 1994 WTO members agreed to phase out by the end of 2004 textile quotas that have restricted global trade in garments since they were imposed in 1974 by European and North American countries. This is expected to increase the dominance in this sector by China, which enjoys economies of scale, low-cost labor and an integrated domestic industry that spans cotton farming to clothing design. The World Bank estimates China's share of global clothing exports will more than double to 47% by 2010 from 20% today.

China has already seen big gains in the few categories that have gained quota-free status in recent years, such as brassieres and dressing gowns. China's textile and garment exports to the U.S. market more than doubled to $4.96 billion in 2002, and the American Manufacturing Trade Action Coalition predicts a doubling this year. ....

©2003 The Wall Street Journal. Reprinted with permission. Further reproduction prohibited.

### Essence of the Story

■ In 1994, WTO members agreed to end textile quotas by 2004.

■ China entered the WTO in 2001, and the end of quotas is expected to increase China's dominance in textiles.

■ The World Bank estimates China's share of global clothing exports will more than double to 47 percent by 2010, up from 20 percent in 2003.

## Economic Analysis

■ With free trade, goods are produced where they cost the least.

■ Clothing can be produced at lower cost in Asia than in the United States.

■ By specializing in items at which we have a comparative advantage and buying our clothes from China, we gain and the Chinese gain.

■ We gain because our clothes cost less; the Chinese gain because they can sell clothing to us for a higher price than their cost of production.

■ We also gain because we sell items to China such as large passenger jets for more than our cost of production, and the Chinese gain because they can buy items like passenger jets for a lower price that their cost of producing them.

■ The table contains some illustrative numbers, and Fig. 1 shows these numbers graphically.

■ The United States can produce Nike outfits or other goods and services. The opportunity cost in the United States of 1 unit of Nike outfits is 1 unit of other goods and services.

■ China can also produce Nike outfits or other goods and services. The opportunity cost in China of 1 unit of Nike outfits is 0.5 units of other goods and services.

■ If the countries do not trade, their consumption possibilities are limited to their production possibilities.

■ But if China produces Nike outfits and the United States produces other goods and services, the two countries can expand their consumption possibilities.

■ In Fig. 2, China produces 40 units of Nike outfits and the United States produces 100 units of other goods and services.

■ If the two countries trade 1 unit of Nike outfits for 0.75 units of other goods and services, the United States gets Nike outfits for less than its opportunity cost of producing them and China sells the outfits for more than its opportunity cost of producing them.

■ Table 1 shows the trading possibilities, and each country can trade along its trade line in Fig. 2.

■ The United States buys goods from China, but China also buys goods from the United States.

### You're The Voter

■ Do you think that U.S. trade with China and other low-income Asian countries should be free?

■ Would you vote for measures to keep the jobs that produce clothing in the United States? Explain why or why not.

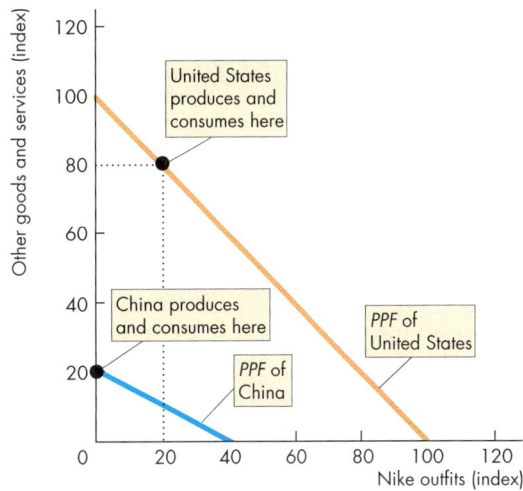

**Figure 1** No trade

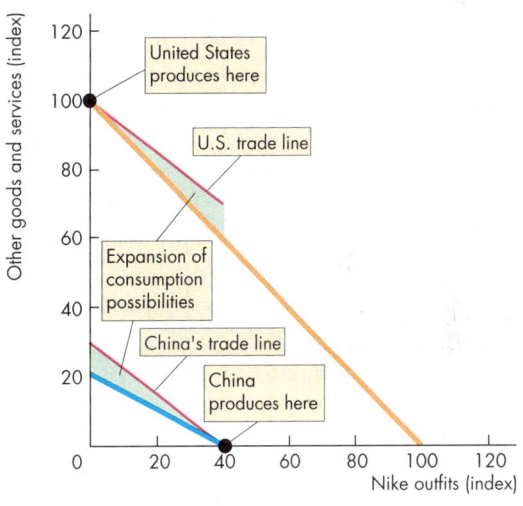

**Figure 2** Free trade

|  | Other goods and services | | | |
|---|---|---|---|---|
|  | Production possibilities | | Trading possibilities | |
| Nike outfits | United States | China | United States | China |
| 0 | 100 | 20 | 100 | 30 |
| 20 | 80 | 10 | 85 | 15 |
| 40 | 60 | 0 | 70 | 0 |
| 100 | 0 |  |  |  |

**Table 1** Production possibilities and trading possibilities for China and the United States

# SUMMARY

## KEY POINTS

### Patterns and Trends in International Trade (p. 416)

- Large flows of trade take place between countries, most of which is in manufactured goods exchanged among rich industrialized countries.
- Since 1960, the volume of U.S. trade has more than doubled.

### The Gains from International Trade (pp. 417–422)

- Comparative advantage is the fundamental source of the gains from trade.
- Comparative advantage exists when opportunity costs between countries diverge.
- By increasing its production of goods in which it has a comparative advantage and then trading some of the increased output, a country can consume at points outside its production possibilities frontier.
- In the absence of international borrowing and lending, trade is balanced as prices adjust to reflect the international supply of and demand for goods.
- The world price balances the production and consumption plans of the trading parties. At the equilibrium price, trade is balanced.
- Comparative advantage explains the international trade that takes place in the world.
- But trade in similar goods arises from economies of scale in the face of diversified tastes.

### International Trade Restrictions (pp. 423–426)

- Countries restrict international trade by imposing tariffs and quotas.
- International trade restrictions raise the domestic price of imported goods, lower the volume of imports, and reduce the total value of imports.
- They also reduce the total value of exports by the same amount as the reduction in the value of imports.

### The Case Against Protection (pp. 427–430)

- Arguments that protection is necessary for national security, to protect infant industries, and to prevent dumping are weak.
- Arguments that protection saves jobs, allows us to compete with cheap foreign labor, makes the economy diversified and stable, penalizes lax environmental standards, protects national culture, and prevents rich countries from exploiting developing countries are fatally flawed.

### Why Is International Trade Restricted? (pp. 430–431)

- Trade is restricted because tariffs raise government revenue and because protection brings a small loss to a large number of people and a large gain per person to a small number of people.

## KEY FIGURES

Figure 17.1    Opportunity Cost in Farmland, 417
Figure 17.2    Opportunity Cost in Mobilia, 418
Figure 17.3    International Trade in Cars, 419
Figure 17.4    Expanding Consumption Possibilities, 420
Figure 17.6    The Effects of a Tariff, 424
Figure 17.7    The Effects of a Quota, 426

## KEY TERMS

Comparative advantage, 418
Dumping, 427
Exports, 416
General Agreement on Tariffs and Trade, 423
Imports, 416
Infant-industry argument, 427
Net exports, 416
Nontariff barrier, 423
North American Free Trade Agreement, 424
Quota, 426
Rent Seeking, 430
Tariff, 423
Terms of trade, 418
Voluntary export restraint, 426
World Trade Organization, 423

# PROBLEMS

*1. The table provides information about Virtual Reality's production possibilities.

| TV sets (per day) | | Computers (per day) |
|---|---|---|
| 0 | and | 36 |
| 10 | and | 35 |
| 20 | and | 33 |
| 30 | and | 30 |
| 40 | and | 26 |
| 50 | and | 21 |
| 60 | and | 15 |
| 70 | and | 8 |
| 80 | and | 0 |

  a. Calculate Virtual Reality's opportunity cost of a TV set when it produces 10 sets a day.
  b. Calculate Virtual Reality's opportunity cost of a TV set when it produces 40 sets a day.
  c. Calculate Virtual Reality's opportunity cost of a TV set when it produces 70 sets a day.
  d. Using the answers to parts (a), (b), and (c), sketch the relationship between the opportunity cost of a TV set and the quantity of TV sets produced in Virtual Reality.

2. The table provides information about Vital Sign's production possibilities.

| TV sets (per day) | | Computers (per day) |
|---|---|---|
| 0 | and | 18.0 |
| 10 | and | 17.5 |
| 20 | and | 16.5 |
| 30 | and | 15.0 |
| 40 | and | 13.0 |
| 50 | and | 10.5 |
| 60 | and | 7.5 |
| 70 | and | 4.0 |
| 80 | and | 0 |

  a. Calculate Vital Sign's opportunity cost of a TV set when it produces 10 sets a day.
  b. Calculate Vital Sign's opportunity cost of a TV set when it produces 40 sets a day.
  c. Calculate Vital Sign's opportunity cost of a TV set when it produces 70 sets a day.
  d. Using the answers to parts (a), (b), and (c), sketch the relationship between the opportunity cost of a TV set and the quantity of TV sets produced in Virtual Reality.

*3. Suppose that with no international trade, Virtual Reality in problem 1 produces and consumes 10 TV sets a day and Vital Signs produces and consumes 60 TV sets a day. Now suppose that the two countries begin to trade with each other.
  a. Which country exports TV sets?
  b. What adjustments are made to the amount of each good produced by each country?
  c. What adjustments are made to the amount of each good consumed by each country?
  d. What can you say about the terms of trade (the price of a TV set expressed as computers per TV set) under free trade?

4. Suppose that with no international trade, Virtual Reality in problem 1 produces and consumes 50 TV sets a day and Vital Signs produces and consumes 20 TV sets a day. Now suppose that the two countries begin to trade with each other.
  a. Which country exports TV sets?
  b. What adjustments are made to the amount of each good produced by each country?
  c. What adjustments are made to the amount of each good consumed by each country?
  d. What can you say about the terms of trade (the price of a TV set expressed as computers per TV set) under free trade?

*5. Compare the total quantities of each good produced in problems 1 and 2 with the total quantities of each good produced in problems 3 and 4.
  a. Does free trade increase or decrease the total quantities of TV sets and computers produced in both cases? Why?
  b. What happens to the price of a TV set in Virtual Reality in the two cases? Why does it rise in one case and fall in the other?
  c. What happens to the price of a computer in Vital Signs in the two cases? Why does it rise in one case and fall in the other?

6. Compare the international trade in problem 3 with that in problem 4.
  a. Why does Virtual Reality export TV sets in one of the cases and import them in the other case?
  b. Do the TV producers or the computer producers gain in each case?
  c. Do consumers gain in each case?

* Solutions to odd-numbered problems are available on **MyEconLab**.

*7. The figure depicts the international market for soybeans.

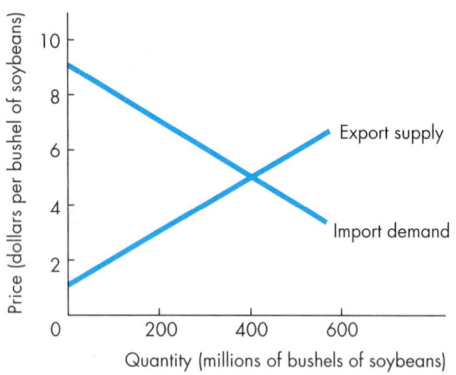

a. If the two countries did not engage in international trade, what would be the prices of soybeans in the two countries?
b. What is the world price of soybeans if there is free trade between these countries?
c. What quantities of soybeans are exported and imported?
d. What is the balance of trade?

8. If the country in problem 7 that imports soybeans imposes a tariff of $2 per bushel, what is the world price of soybeans and what quantity of soybeans gets traded internationally? What is the price of soybeans in the importing country? Calculate the tariff revenue.

*9. The importing country in problem 7 imposes a quota of 300 million bushels on imports of soybeans.
a. What is the price of soybeans in the importing country?
b. What is the revenue from the quota?
c. Who gets this revenue?

10. The exporting country in problem 7 imposes a VER of 300 million bushels on its exports of soybeans.
a. What is the world price of soybeans now?
b. What is the revenue of soybean growers in the exporting country?
c. Which country gains from the VER?

# CRITICAL THINKING

1. Study *Reading Between the Lines* on pp. 432–433 and then answer the following questions.
   a. What changes are occurring in the global market for clothing?
   b. Why is China going to become the biggest producer of clothing?
   c. Do you think that Americans should be concerned about who makes their clothes?
   d. Will the United States run out of activities at which it has a comparative advantage? Explain your answer.

# WEB EXERCISES

**Use the links on MyEconLab to work the following exercises.**

1. Study the Web *Reading Between the Lines* on steel dumping, and then answer the following questions:
   a. What is the argument in the news article for limiting steel imports?
   b. Evaluate the argument. Is it correct or incorrect in your opinion? Why?
   c. Would you vote to eliminate steel imports? Why or why not?
   d. Would you vote differently if you lived in another steel-producing country? Why or why not?

2. Visit the Public Citizen Global Trade Watch and the State of Arizona Department of Commerce Web sites. Review the general message provided by the two sites about NAFTA and then answer the following questions:
   a. What is the message that the Public Citizen Global Trade Watch wants to give?
   b. What is the message that the State of Arizona Department of Commerce wants to give?
   c. Which message do you think is correct and why?
   d. Would you vote to maintain NAFTA? Why or why not?

# International Finance

**CHAPTER 18**

## ¥€$!

**The yen (¥), the euro (€), and the dollar ($) are** the world's three big currencies. The yen (the currency of Japan) and the dollar (the currency of the United States) have been around for a long time. The euro is the currency of 12 members of the European Union. It was created in the early 1990s but didn't come into everyday use as notes and coins until January 1, 2002. Most of the world's international trade and finance are conducted using these three currencies.

In February 2002, one U.S. dollar bought 134 Japanese yen. Through 2002 and 2003, the dollar sank and by December 2003, one dollar bought only 108 yen. The dollar also sank against the euro, falling from 1.14 euros at the start of 2002 to 0.81 euros at the end of 2003.

Why has the dollar fallen in value against the other major currencies? Is there anything we can do or should do to stabilize the value of the dollar?

In 1988, Americans owned foreign assets equal in value to the assets that foreigners owned in the United States. Before 1988, American ownership of foreign assets exceeded foreign ownership of U.S. assets. But every year since 1988, the balance has tipped increasingly the other way. Foreign entrepreneurs such as Australian-born Rupert Murdoch and Sony's Akio Mori have roamed the United States with giant virtual shopping carts and loaded them up with such items as Twentieth Century Fox, the Rockefeller Center, and MGM. Why have foreigners been buying more U.S. real estate and businesses than Americans have been buying abroad?

◆ In this chapter, you're going to discover why the U.S. economy has become attractive for foreign investors, what determines the amount of international borrowing and lending, and why the dollar fluctuates against other currencies. At the end of the chapter, in *Reading Between the Lines*, we'll return to the falling dollar in 2003.

## After studying this chapter, you will be able to

- **Explain how international trade is financed**
- **Describe a country's balance of payments accounts**
- **Explain what determines the amount of international borrowing and lending**
- **Explain why the United States changed from being a lender to being a borrower in the mid-1980s**
- **Explain how the foreign exchange value of the dollar is determined**
- **Explain why the foreign exchange value of the dollar fluctuates**

## Financing International Trade

WHEN SONY STORES IN THE UNITED STATES imports CD players from Japan, it does not pay for them with U.S. dollars—it uses Japanese yen. And when a French construction company buys an earth mover from Caterpillar, Inc., it uses U.S. dollars. Whenever we buy things from another country, we use the currency of that country to make the transaction. It doesn't make any difference what the item being traded is; it might be a consumption good or a capital good, a building, or even a firm.

We're going to study the markets in which money—different types of currency—is bought and sold. But first we're going to look at the scale of international trading, borrowing, and lending and at the way in which we keep our records of these transactions. Such records are called the balance of payments accounts.

### Balance of Payments Accounts

A country's **balance of payments accounts** records its international trading, borrowing, and lending. There are in fact three balance of payments accounts:

1. Current account
2. Capital account
3. Official settlements account

The **current account** records payments for imports of goods and services from abroad, receipts from exports of goods and services sold abroad, net interest income paid abroad, and net transfers (such as foreign aid payments). The *current account balance* equals the sum of exports minus imports, net interest income, and net transfers.

The **capital account** records foreign investment in the United States minus U.S. investment abroad. (This account also has a statistical discrepancy that arises from errors and omissions in measuring capital transactions.)

The **official settlements account** records the change in **U.S. official reserves**, which are the government's holdings of foreign currency. If U.S. official reserves *increase*, the official settlements account balance is *negative*. The reason is that holding foreign money is like investing abroad. U.S. investment abroad is a minus item in the capital account and in the official settlements account.

The sum of the balances on the three accounts always equals zero. That is, to pay for our current account deficit, either we must borrow more from abroad than we lend abroad or our official reserves must decrease to cover the shortfall.

Table 18.1 shows the U.S. balance of payments accounts in 2003. Items in the current account and capital account that provide foreign currency to the United States have a plus sign; items that cost the United States foreign currency have a minus sign. The table shows that in 2003, U.S. imports exceeded U.S. exports and the current account had a deficit of $558 billion. How do we pay for imports that exceed the value of our exports? That is, how do we pay for our current account deficit? We pay by borrowing from the rest of the world. The capital account tells us by how much. We borrowed $1,051 billion (foreign investment in the United States) but made loans of

**TABLE 18.1** U.S. Balance of Payments Accounts in 2003

| Current account | Billions of dollars |
|---|---|
| Imports of goods and services | –1,487 |
| Exports of goods and services | +990 |
| Net interest income | +7 |
| Net transfers | –68 |
| Current account balance | –558 |

| Capital account | |
|---|---|
| Foreign investment in the United States | +1,051 |
| U.S. investment abroad | –456 |
| Statistical discrepancy | –36 |
| Capital account balance | +559 |

| Official settlements account | |
|---|---|
| Official settlements account balance | –1 |

*Source:* Bureau of Economic Analysis. The data are for 2003, second quarter, seasonally adjusted at annual rate.

$456 billion (U.S. investment abroad). Our *net* foreign borrowing was $1,051 billion minus $456 billion, which equals $595 billion. There is almost always a statistical discrepancy between our capital account and current account transactions and in 2003, the discrepancy was –$36 billion. Combining the discrepancy with the measured net foreign borrowing gives a capital account balance of $559 billion.

Our capital account balance plus our current account balance equals the change in official U.S. reserves. In 2003, our capital account balance of $559 billion plus our current balance of –$558 billion equals $1 billion. Our reserves *increased* in 2003 by $1 billion. This amount appears in Table 34.1 as –$1 billion. Recall that when our reserves *increase* we record this as a negative number in our international accounts because an increase in our reserves is like making a loan to the rest of the world—the government increases its deposits in foreign central banks.

The numbers in Table 18.1 give a snapshot of the balance of payments accounts in 2003. Figure 18.1 puts that snapshot into perspective by showing the balance of payments between 1983 and 2003. Because the economy grows and the price level rises, changes in the dollar value of the balance of payments do not convey much information. To remove the influences of growth and inflation, Fig. 18.1 shows the balance of payments as a percentage of nominal GDP.

As you can see, the capital account balance is almost a mirror image of the current account balance. The official settlements balance is very small in comparison with the balances on these other two accounts. A large current account deficit (and capital account surplus) emerged during the 1980s but declined from 1987 to 1991. The deficit then increased every year through 2000, decreased slightly in 2001, and then increased again.

You might find it easier to understand the balance of payments accounts if you think about the income and expenditure, borrowing and lending, and bank account of an individual.

**Individual Analogy** An individual's current account records the income from supplying the services of factors of production and the expenditure on goods and services. Consider, for example, Joanne. She worked in 2003 and earned an income of $25,000. Joanne has $10,000 worth of investments that earned her an interest income of $1,000. Joanne's current account shows an income of $26,000. Joanne spent

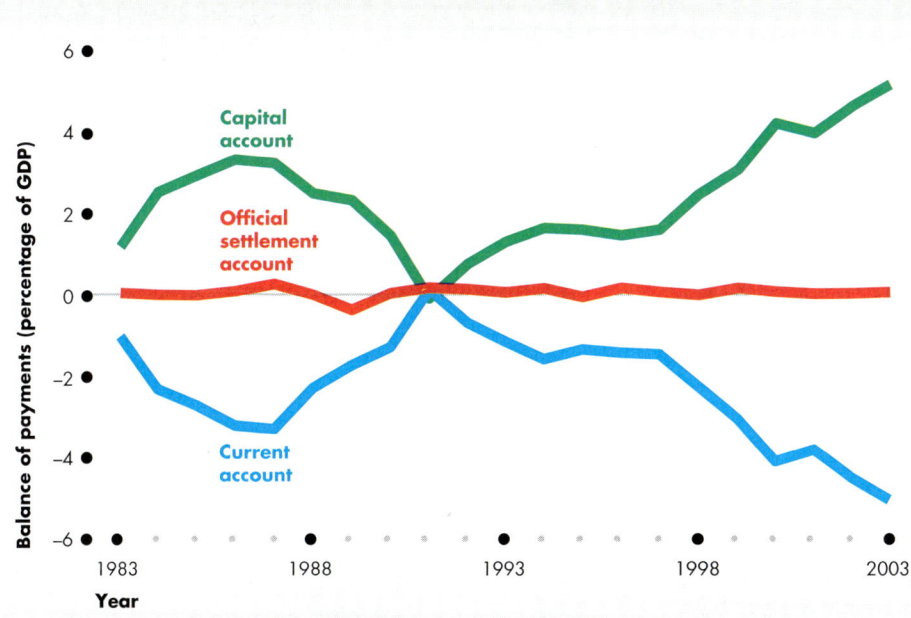

FIGURE 18.1  The Balance of Payments: 1983–2003

During the 1980s, a large current account deficit arose. That deficit decreased in the late 1980s but increased again through 2000, decreased slightly in the 2001 recession, and then increased again. The capital account balance mirrors the current account balance. When the current account balance is negative, the capital account balance is positive—we borrow from the rest of the world. Fluctuations in the official settlements balance are small.

*Source*: Bureau of Economic Analysis.

$18,000 buying goods and services for consumption. She also bought a new house, which cost her $60,000. So Joanne's total expenditure was $78,000. The difference between her expenditure and her income is $52,000 ($78,000 minus $26,000). This amount is Joanne's current account deficit.

To pay for expenditure of $52,000 in excess of her income, Joanne has to use the money that she has in the bank or she has to take out a loan. In fact, Joanne took out a mortgage of $50,000 to help buy her house. This mortgage was the only borrowing that Joanne did, so her capital account surplus was $50,000. With a current account deficit of $52,000 and a capital account surplus of $50,000, Joanne is still $2,000 short. She got that $2,000 from her own bank account. Her cash holdings decreased by $2,000.

Joanne's income from her work is analogous to a country's income from its exports. Her income from her investments is analogous to a country's interest income from foreigners. Her purchases of goods and services, including her purchase of a house, are analogous to a country's imports. Joanne's mortgage—borrowing from someone else—is analogous to a country's borrowing from the rest of the world. The change in Joanne's bank account is analogous to the change in the country's official reserves.

## Borrowers and Lenders, Debtors and Creditors

A country that is borrowing more from the rest of the world than it is lending to it is called a **net borrower**. Similarly, a **net lender** is a country that is lending more to the rest of the world than it is borrowing from it.

The United States is a net borrower, but it has not always been in this situation. Throughout the 1960s and most of the 1970s, the United States was a net lender to the rest of the world. It had a surplus on its current account and a deficit on its capital account. It was not until 1983 that the United States became a significant net borrower from the rest of the world. Between 1983 and 1987, its borrowing increased each year. It then decreased and was briefly zero in 1991, after which it started to increase again. The total net foreign borrowing by the United States between 1983 and 2003 was $3.8 trillion—35 percent of the value of the nation's production of goods and services.

Most countries are net borrowers like the United States. But a small number of countries, including Japan and oil-rich Saudi Arabia, are net lenders.

A net borrower might be reducing its net assets held in the rest of the world, or it might be going deeper into debt. A nation's total stock of foreign investment determines whether it is a debtor or creditor. A **debtor nation** is a country that during its entire history has borrowed more from the rest of the world than it has lent to it. It has a stock of outstanding debt to the rest of the world that exceeds the stock of its own claims on the rest of the world. A **creditor nation** is a country that during its entire history has invested more in the rest of the world than other countries have invested in it.

At the heart of the distinction between a net borrower/net lender and a debtor/creditor nation is the distinction between flows and stocks, which you have encountered many times in your study of macroeconomics. Borrowing and lending are flows—amounts borrowed or lent per unit of time. Debts are stocks—amounts owed at a point in time. The flow of borrowing and lending changes the stock of debt.

The United States was a debtor nation through the nineteenth century as we borrowed from Europe to finance our westward expansion, railroads, and industrialization. We paid off our debt and became a creditor nation for most of the twentieth century. But following a string of current account deficits, we became a debtor nation again in 1989.

Since 1989, total stock of U.S. borrowing from the rest of the world has exceeded U.S. lending to the rest of the world. The largest debtor nations are the capital-hungry developing countries (such as the United States was during the nineteenth century). The international debt of these countries grew from less than a third to more than a half of their gross domestic product during the 1980s and created what was called the "Third World debt crisis."

Should we be concerned that the United States is a net borrower? The answer to this question depends mainly on what the net borrower is doing with the borrowed money. If borrowing is financing investment that in turn is generating economic growth and higher income, borrowing is not a problem. If the borrowed money is being used to finance consumption, then higher interest payments are being incurred, and consequently, consumption will eventually have to be reduced. In this case, the more the borrowing and the longer it goes on, the greater is the reduction in consumption that will eventually be necessary. We'll see below whether the United States is borrowing for investment or for consumption.

## Current Account Balance

What determines a country's current account balance and net foreign borrowing? You've seen that net exports (*NX*) is the main item in the current account. We can define the current account balance (*CAB*) as:

*CAB* = *NX* + Net interest income + Net transfers.

We can study the current account balance by looking at what determines net exports because the other two items are small and do not fluctuate much.

## Net Exports

Net exports are determined by the government budget and private saving and investment. To see how net exports are determined, we need to recall some of the things that we learned about the *National Income and Product Accounts* in Chapter 5. Table 18.2 will refresh your memory and summarize some calculations.

Part (a) lists the national income variables that are needed, with their symbols. Part (b) defines three balances. **Net exports** is exports of goods and services minus imports of goods and services.

The **government sector surplus or deficit** is equal to net taxes minus government purchases of goods and services. If that number is positive, a government sector surplus is lent to other sectors; if that number is negative, a government deficit must be financed by borrowing from other sectors. The government sector deficit is the sum of the deficits of the federal, state, and local governments.

The **private sector surplus or deficit** is saving minus investment. If saving exceeds investment, a private sector surplus is lent to other sectors. If investment exceeds saving, a private sector deficit is financed by borrowing from other sectors.

Part (b) also shows the values of these balances for the United States in 2003. As you can see, net exports were –$506 billion, a deficit of $506 billion. The government sector's revenue from net taxes was $1,506 billion, and it purchased $2,054 billion worth of goods and services. The government sector deficit was $548 billion. The private sector saved $1,666 billion and invested $1,624 billion, so it had a surplus of $42 billion.

Part (c) shows the relationship among the three balances. From the *National Income and Product Accounts*, we know that real GDP, *Y*, is the sum of consumption expenditure (*C*), investment, government purchases, and net exports. It also equals the sum of consumption expenditure, saving, and taxes. Rearranging these equations tells us that net exports is the sum of the government sector deficit and the private sector deficit. In the United States in 2001,

**TABLE 18.2  Net Exports, the Government Budget, Saving, and Investment**

| | Symbols and equations | United States in 2003 (billions of dollars) |
|---|---|---|
| **(a) Variables** | | |
| Exports* | X | 1,020 |
| Imports* | M | 1,526 |
| Government purchases | G | 2,054 |
| Net taxes | T | 1,506 |
| Investment | I | 1,624 |
| Saving | S | 1,666 |
| **(b) Balances** | | |
| Rest of world | X – M | 1,020 – 1,526 = –506 |
| Government sector | T – G | 1,506 – 2,054 = –548 |
| Private sector | S – I | 1,666 – 1,624 = 42 |
| **(c) Relationship among balances** | | |
| National accounts | Y = C + I + G + X – M | |
| | = C + S + T | |
| Rearranging: | X – M = S – I + T – G | |
| Net exports | X – M | –506 |
| equals: | | |
| Government sector | T – G | –548 |
| plus | | |
| Private sector | S – I | 42 |

*Source:* Bureau of Economic Analysis. The data are 2003, second quarter, seasonally adjusted at annual rate.

* The *National Income and Product Accounts* measures of exports and imports are slightly different from the balance of payments accounts measures in Table 34.1 on p. 810.

the government sector had a surplus of $360 billion and the private sector had a deficit of $690 billion. The government sector deficit plus the private sector deficit equals net exports of –$330 billion.

## The Three Sector Balances

You've seen that net exports equal the sum of the government balance and the private balance. How do these three sector balances fluctuate over time? Figure 18.2 answers this question. It shows the government sector balance (the red line), net exports (the blue line), and the private sector balance (the green line).

You can see that there is a strong tendency for the private sector balance and the government sector balance to move in opposite directions. During the 1980s, when the government went into deeper deficit, the private sector went into a larger surplus.

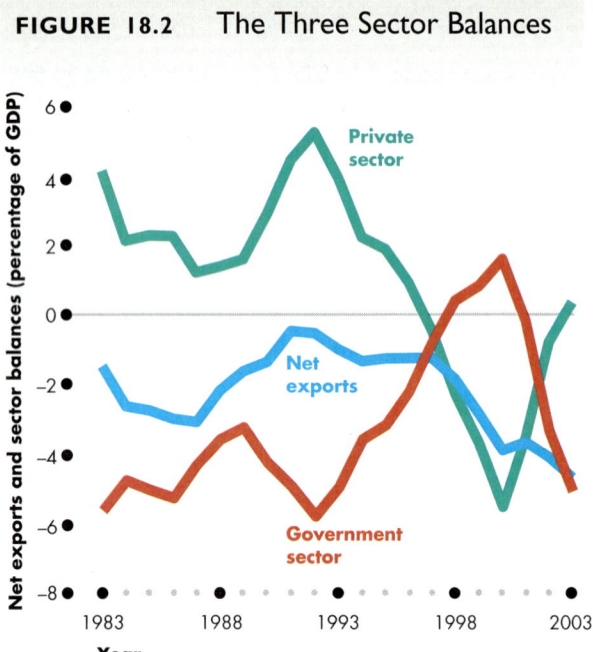

**FIGURE 18.2    The Three Sector Balances**

The private sector balance and the government sector balance tend to move in opposite directions. Net exports respond to the *sum* of the government sector and private sector balances. When the private sector and the government sector together are in deficit, that deficit is financed by net foreign borrowing.

*Source:* Bureau of Economic Analysis.

Between 1998 and 2001, the government had a surplus and the private sector a deficit. And in 2002 and 2003, the government again had deficit and the private sector a small surplus.

The relationship between net exports and the other two sector balances is not a strong one. Sometimes, when the government sector balance becomes increasingly negative (a larger deficit), as it did during the first half of the 1980s, net exports become negative. But through the 1990s and into the 2000s, net exports did not follow the government sector balance closely. Net exports respond to the *sum* of the government sector and private sector balances. When the private sector and the government sector together are in deficit, that deficit is financed by net foreign borrowing.

## Is U.S. Borrowing for Consumption or Investment?

In 2003, net exports were a negative $506 billion and we borrowed this amount from abroad. Did we borrow for consumption or investment? In 2003, private investment in buildings, plant, and equipment was $1,624 billion. Government investment in defense equipment and public structures such as highways and dams was $336 billion. All this investment added to the nation's capital, and much of it increased productivity. Government also spends on education and health care services, which increase *human capital*. Our international borrowing is financing private and public investment, not consumption.

### REVIEW QUIZ

1. When an American art dealer buys a painting from a French gallery, which currency gets used to make the transaction?
2. When a German car maker buys parts from a Detroit car maker, which currency gets used to make the transaction?
3. What transactions does the current account record? What transactions does the capital account record? What transactions does the official settlements account record?
4. How are net exports, the government sector balance, and the private sector balance related?

# The Exchange Rate

WHEN WE BUY FOREIGN GOODS OR INVEST IN another country, we have to obtain some of that country's currency to make the transaction. When foreigners buy U.S.-produced goods or invest in the United States, they have to obtain some U.S. dollars. We get foreign currency, and foreigners get U.S. dollars in the foreign exchange market. The **foreign exchange market** is the market in which the currency of one country is exchanged for the currency of another. The foreign exchange market is not a place like a downtown flea market or a produce market. The market is made up of thousands of people—importers and exporters, banks, and specialists in the buying and selling of foreign exchange, called foreign exchange brokers. The foreign exchange market opens on Monday morning in Hong Kong, which is still Sunday evening in New York. As the day advances, markets open in Singapore, Tokyo, Frankfurt, London, New York, Chicago, and San Francisco. As the West Coast markets close, Hong Kong is only an hour away from opening for the next day of business. The sun barely sets on the foreign exchange market. Dealers around the world are in continual contact by telephone, and on a typical day, $1.5 trillion changes hands.

The price at which one currency exchanges for another is called a **foreign exchange rate**. For example, in December 2003, one U.S. dollar bought 108 Japanese yen. The exchange rate was 108 yen per dollar.

Figure 18.3 shows the exchange rate of the U.S. dollar in terms of the Japanese yen and the European euro between 1993 and 2003. Over this period, the dollar has both depreciated and appreciated.

**Currency depreciation** is the fall in the value of one currency in terms of another currency. For example, if the dollar falls from 100 yen to 80 yen, the dollar depreciates by 20 percent. The U.S. dollar depreciated against the Japanese yen during 2003.

**Currency appreciation** is the rise in the value of one currency in terms of another currency. For example, if the dollar rises from 100 yen to 120 yen, the dollar appreciates by 20 percent. The U.S. dollar appreciated against the yen in 2001 and 2002.

We've just expressed the value of the U.S. dollar in terms of the yen. But we can express the value of the dollar in terms of any currency. We can also

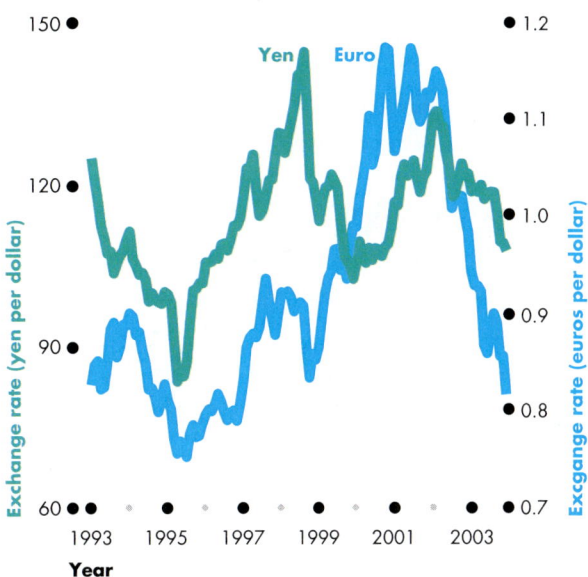

**FIGURE 18.3** The Yen-Dollar and the Euro-Dollar Exchange Rates

The exchange rate is the price at which a currency can be traded for another currency. The yen–dollar exchange rate (yen per dollar) and the euro–dollar exchange rate (euros per dollar) show that the dollar fluctuates a great deal against these other two major currencies.

*Source:* The Pacific Exchange Rate Service.

express the exchange rate of the yen in terms of the dollar as a number of dollars per yen. When the U.S. dollar appreciates against the yen, the yen depreciates against the dollar.

Why does the U.S. dollar fluctuate in value? Why does it sometimes depreciate and sometimes appreciate? What happened during 2001 to make the dollar appreciate against the yen and in 2000 to make it depreciate? To answer these questions, we need to understand what determines the exchange rate.

The exchange rate is a price—the price of one country's money in terms of another country's money. And like all prices, demand and supply determine the exchange rate. So to understand what determines the exchange rate, we need to study demand and supply in the foreign exchange market. We'll begin by looking at the demand side of the market.

## Demand in the Foreign Exchange Market

The quantity of dollars demanded in the foreign exchange market is the amount that traders plan to buy during a given time period at a given exchange rate. This quantity depends on three main factors:

1. The exchange rate
2. Interest rates in the United States and other countries
3. The expected future exchange rate

We first look at the relationship between the quantity of dollars demanded and the exchange rate.

## The Law of Demand for Foreign Exchange

People do not buy dollars because they enjoy them. The demand for dollars is a *derived demand*. People demand dollars so that they can buy U.S.-made goods and services (U.S. exports). They also demand dollars so that they can buy U.S. assets such as bonds, stocks, businesses, and real estate. Nevertheless, the law of demand applies to dollars just as it does to anything else that people value.

Other things remaining the same, the higher the exchange rate, the smaller is the quantity of dollars demanded in the foreign exchange market. For example, if the price of the U.S. dollar rises from 100 yen to 120 yen but nothing else changes, the quantity of U.S. dollars that people plan to buy in the foreign exchange market decreases. Why does the exchange rate influence the quantity of dollars demanded?

There are two separate reasons, and they are related to the two sources of the derived demand for dollars:

- Exports effect
- Expected profit effect

**Exports Effect** The larger the value of U.S. exports, the larger is the quantity of dollars demanded on the foreign exchange market. But the value of U.S. exports depends on the exchange rate. The lower the exchange rate, with everything else the same, the cheaper are U.S.-produced goods and services, so the more the United States exports and the greater is the quantity of U.S. dollars demanded on the foreign exchange market to pay for these exports.

**Expected Profit Effect** The larger the expected profit from holding dollars, the greater is the quantity of dollars demanded in the foreign exchange market. But expected profit depends on the exchange rate. The lower the exchange rate, other things remaining the same, the larger is the expected profit from buying dollars and the greater is the quantity of dollars demanded on the foreign exchange market.

To understand this effect, suppose you think the dollar will be worth 120 yen by the end of the month. If today, a dollar costs 115 yen, you buy dollars today. But a person who thinks that the dollar will be worth 115 yen at the end of the month does not buy dollars today. Now suppose the exchange rate falls to 110 yen per dollar. More people think they can profit from buying dollars, so the quantity of dollars demanded today increases.

For the two reasons we've just reviewed, other things remaining the same, when the foreign exchange rate rises, the quantity of dollars demanded decreases, and when the foreign exchange rate falls, the quantity of dollars demanded increases. Figure 34.4 shows the demand curve for U.S. dollars in the foreign exchange market. In this figure, when the foreign exchange rate rises, other things remaining the same, there is a decrease in the quantity of dollars demanded and a movement up along the demand curve as shown by the arrow. When the exchange rate falls, other things remaining the same, there is an increase in the quantity of dollars demanded and a movement down along the demand curve as shown by the arrow.

## Changes in the Demand for Dollars

A change in any influence on the dollars that people plan to buy in the foreign exchange market other than the exchange rate brings a change in the demand for dollars and a shift in the demand curve for dollars. Demand either increases or decreases. These other influences are

- Interest rates in the United States and other countries
- The expected future exchange rate

**Interest Rates in the United States and Other Countries** People and businesses buy financial assets to make a return. The higher the interest rate that people can make on U.S. assets compared with foreign assets, the more U.S. assets they buy. What

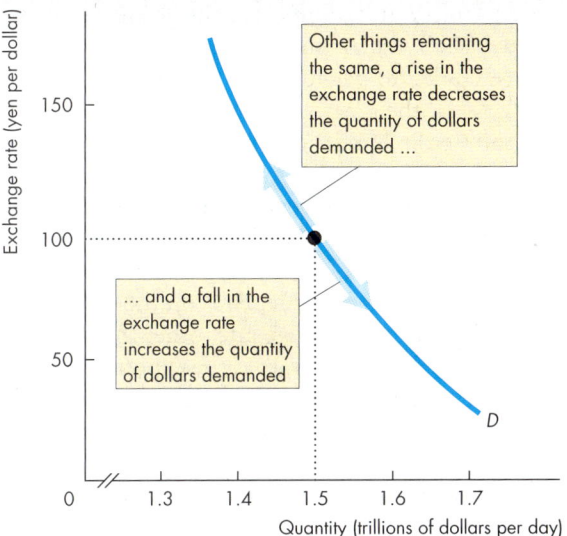

**FIGURE 18.4** The Demand for Dollars

The quantity of dollars that people plan to buy depends on the exchange rate. Other things remaining the same, if the exchange rate rises, the quantity of dollars demanded decreases and there is a movement up along the demand curve for dollars. If the exchange rate falls, the quantity of dollars demanded increases and there is a movement down along the demand curve for dollars.

matters is not the level of U.S. interest rates, but the U.S. interest rate minus the foreign interest rate, a gap that is called the **U.S. interest rate differential**. If the U.S. interest rate rises and the foreign interest rate remains constant, the U.S. interest rate differential increases. The larger the U.S. interest rate differential, the greater is the demand for U.S. assets and the greater is the demand for dollars on the foreign exchange market.

**The Expected Future Exchange Rate** Other things remaining the same, the higher the expected future exchange rate, the greater is the demand for dollars. To see why, suppose you are Toyota's finance manager. The exchange rate is 100 yen per dollar, and you think that by the end of the month, it will be 120 yen per dollar. You spend 100,000 yen today and buy $1,000. At the end of the month, the dollar is 120 yen, as you predicted it would be, and you sell the $1,000. You get 120,000 yen. You've made a profit of 20,000 yen, or almost $167. The higher the expected future exchange rate, other things remaining the same, the greater is the expected profit and the greater is the demand for dollars.

Figure 18.5 summarizes the above discussion of the influences on the demand for dollars. A rise in the U.S. interest rate differential or a rise in the expected future exchange rate increases the demand for dollars and shifts the demand curve rightward from $D_0$ to $D_1$. A fall in the U.S. interest rate differential or a fall in the expected future exchange rate decreases the demand for dollars and shifts the demand curve leftward from $D_0$ to $D_2$.

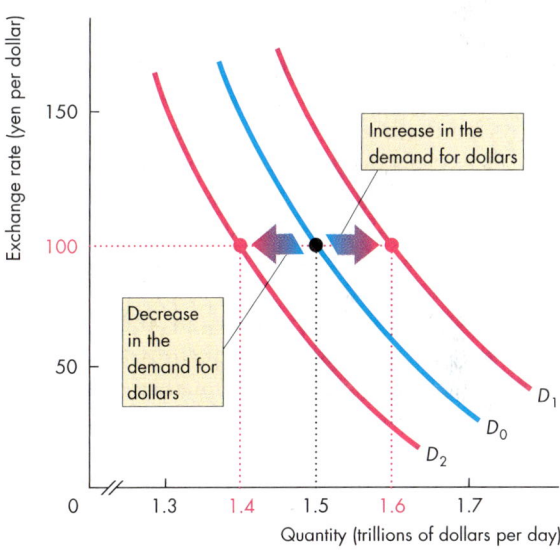

**FIGURE 18.5** Changes in the Demand for Dollars

A change in any influence on the quantity of dollars that people plan to buy, other than the exchange rate, brings a change in the demand for dollars.

*The demand for dollars*

Increases if:
- The U.S. interest rate differential increases
- The expected future exchange rate rises

Decreases if:
- The U.S. interest rate differential decreases
- The expected future exchange rate falls

## Supply in the Foreign Exchange Market

The quantity of U.S. dollars supplied in the foreign exchange market is the amount that traders plan to sell during a given time period at a given exchange rate. This quantity depends on three main factors:

1. The exchange rate
2. Interest rates in the United States and other countries
3. The expected future exchange rate

Let's look first at the relationship between the quantity of dollars supplied in the foreign exchange market and the exchange rate.

## The Law of Supply of Foreign Exchange

People in the United States supply dollars in the foreign exchange market when they buy other currencies. And they buy other currencies so that they can buy foreign-made goods and services (U.S. imports). They also supply dollars and buy foreign currencies so that they can buy foreign assets such as bonds, stocks, businesses, and real estate. The law of supply applies to dollars just as it does to anything else that people plan to sell.

Other things remaining the same, the higher the exchange rate, the greater is the quantity of dollars supplied in the foreign exchange market. For example, if the price of the U.S. dollar rises from 100 yen to 120 yen but nothing else changes, the quantity of U.S. dollars that people plan to buy in the foreign exchange market increases. Why does the exchange rate influence the quantity of dollars supplied?

There are two reasons, and they parallel the two reasons on the demand side of the market:

- Imports effect
- Expected profit effect

**Imports Effect** The larger the value of U.S. imports, the larger is the quantity of foreign currency demanded to pay for these imports. And when people buy foreign currency, they supply dollars. So the larger the value of U.S. imports, the greater is the quantity of dollars supplied in the foreign exchange market. But the value of U.S. imports depends on the exchange rate. The higher the exchange rate, with everything else the same, the cheaper are foreign-produced goods and services to Americans, so the more the United States imports and the greater is the quantity of U.S. dollars supplied in the foreign exchange market to pay for these imports.

**Expected Profit Effect** The larger the expected profit from holding a foreign currency, the greater is the quantity of that currency demanded and the greater is the quantity of dollars supplied in the foreign exchange market. But the expected profit from holding a foreign currency depends on the exchange rate. The higher the exchange rate, other things remaining the same, the larger is the expected profit from selling dollars and the greater is the quantity of dollars supplied in the foreign exchange market.

For the two reasons we've just reviewed, other things remaining the same, when the foreign

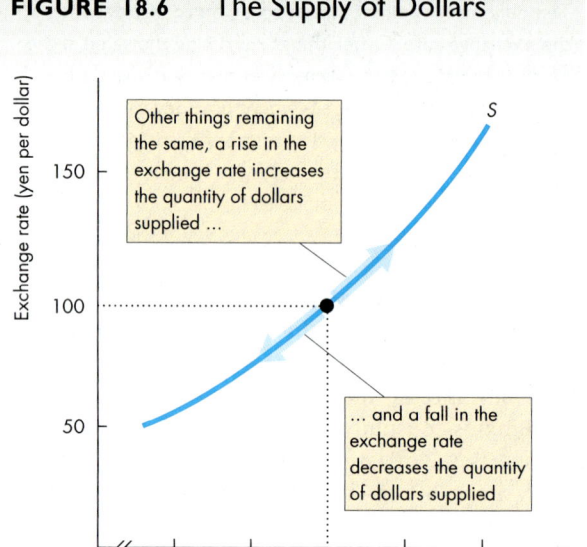

**FIGURE 18.6** The Supply of Dollars

Other things remaining the same, a rise in the exchange rate increases the quantity of dollars supplied ...

... and a fall in the exchange rate decreases the quantity of dollars supplied

The quantity of dollars that people plan to sell depends on the exchange rate. Other things remaining the same, if the exchange rate rises, the quantity of dollars supplied increases and there is a movement up along the supply curve for dollars. If the exchange rate falls, the quantity of dollars supplied decreases and there is a movement down along the supply curve for dollars.

exchange rate rises, the quantity of dollars supplied increases and when the foreign exchange rate falls, the quantity of dollars supplied decreases. Figure 18.6 shows the supply curve for U.S. dollars in the foreign exchange market. In this figure, when the foreign exchange rate rises, other things remaining the same, there is an increase in the quantity of dollars supplied and a movement up along the supply curve as shown by the arrow. When the foreign exchange rate falls, other things remaining the same, there is a decrease in the quantity of dollars supplied and a movement down along the supply curve as shown by the arrow.

## Changes in the Supply of Dollars

A change in any influence on the amount of dollars that people plan to sell in the foreign exchange market other than the exchange rate brings a change in the supply of dollars and a shift in the supply curve for dollars. Supply either increases or decreases. These other influences parallel the other influences on demand but have exactly the opposite effects. These influences are

- Interest rates in the United States and other countries
- The expected future exchange rate

**Interest Rates in the United States and Other Countries** The larger the U.S. interest rate differential, the smaller is the demand for foreign assets and the smaller is the supply of dollars on the foreign exchange market.

**The Expected Future Exchange Rate** Other things remaining the same, the higher the expected future exchange rate, the smaller is the supply of dollars. To see why, suppose the dollar is trading at 100 yen per dollar today and you think that by the end of the month, the dollar will be 120 yen per dollar. You were planning on selling dollars today, but you decide to hold off and wait until the end of the month. If you supply dollars today, you get only 100 yen per dollar. But at the end of the month, if the rate is 120 yen per dollar as you predict, you'll get 120 yen for each dollar you supply. You'll make a profit of 20 percent. So the higher the expected future exchange rate, other things remaining the same, the smaller is the

expected profit from selling U.S. dollars today and the smaller is the supply of dollars today.

Figure 18.7 summarizes the above discussion of the influences on the supply of dollars. A rise in the U.S. interest rate differential or a rise in the expected future exchange rate decreases the supply of dollars and shifts the demand curve leftward from $S_0$ to $S_1$. A fall in the U.S. interest rate differential or a fall in the expected future exchange rate increases the supply of dollars and shifts the supply curve rightward from $S_0$ to $S_2$.

**FIGURE 18.7** Changes in the Supply of Dollars

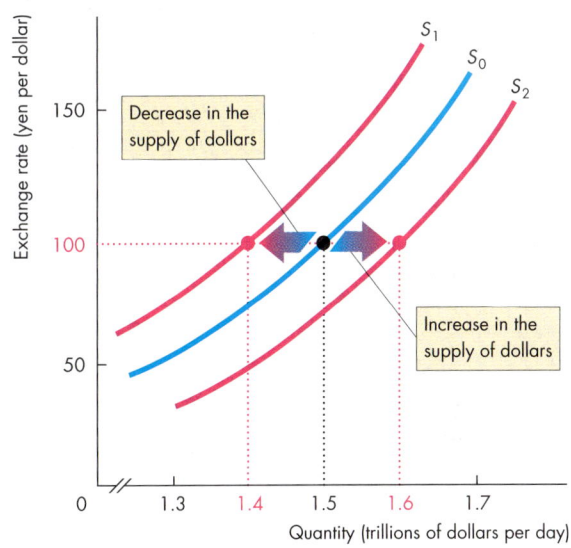

A change in any influence on the quantity of dollars that people plan to sell, other than the exchange rate, brings a change in the supply for dollars.

*The supply of dollars*

Increases if:

- The U.S. interest rate differential decreases
- The expected future exchange rate falls

Decreases if:

- The U.S. interest rate differential increases
- The expected future exchange rate rises

## Market Equilibrium

Figure 18.8 shows how demand and supply in the foreign exchange market determine the exchange rate. The demand curve is $D$, and the supply curve is $S$. As in all the other markets you've studied, the price (the exchange rate) acts as a regulator.

If the exchange rate is too high, there is a surplus—the quantity supplied exceeds the quantity demanded. In Fig. 18.8, if the exchange rate is 150 yen, there is a surplus of dollars. If the exchange rate is too low, there is a shortage—the quantity supplied is less than the quantity demanded. In Fig. 18.8, if the exchange rate is 50 yen, there is a shortage of dollars.

At the equilibrium exchange rate, there is neither a shortage nor a surplus. The quantity supplied equals the quantity demanded. In Fig. 18.8, the equilibrium exchange rate is 100 yen. At this exchange rate, the quantity demanded and the quantity supplied are both $1.5 trillion a day.

The foreign exchange market is constantly pulled to its equilibrium by the forces of supply and demand. Foreign exchange dealers are constantly looking for the best price they can get. If they are selling, they want the highest price available. If they are buying, they want the lowest price available. Information flows from dealer to dealer through the worldwide computer network, and the price adjusts second by second to keep buying plans and selling plans in balance. That is, price adjusts minute by minute to keep the market at its equilibrium.

## Changes in the Exchange Rate

If the demand for dollars increases and the supply of dollars does not change, the exchange rate rises. If the demand for dollars decreases and the supply of dollars does not change, the exchange rate falls. Similarly, if the supply of dollars decreases and the demand for dollars does not change, the exchange rate rises. If the supply of dollars increases and the demand for dollars does not change, the exchange rate falls.

These predictions about the effects of changes in demand and supply are exactly the same as those for any other market.

**Why the Exchange Rate Is Volatile** Sometimes the dollar depreciates, and at other times, it appreciates but the quantity of dollars traded each day barely changes. Why? The main reason is that supply and demand are not independent of each other in the foreign exchange market.

When we studied the demand for dollars and the supply of dollars, we saw that unlike the situation in other markets, the demand side and the supply side of the market have some common influences. A change in the expected future exchange rate or a change in the U.S. interest rate differential changes both demand and supply and in opposite directions. These common influences on both demand and supply explain why the exchange rate can be volatile at times even though the quantity of dollars traded does not change.

Everyone in the market is potentially either a demander or a supplier. Each has a price above which he or she will sell and below which he or she will buy. Let's see how these common supply and demand effects work by looking at two episodes: one in which the dollar appreciated and one in which it depreciated.

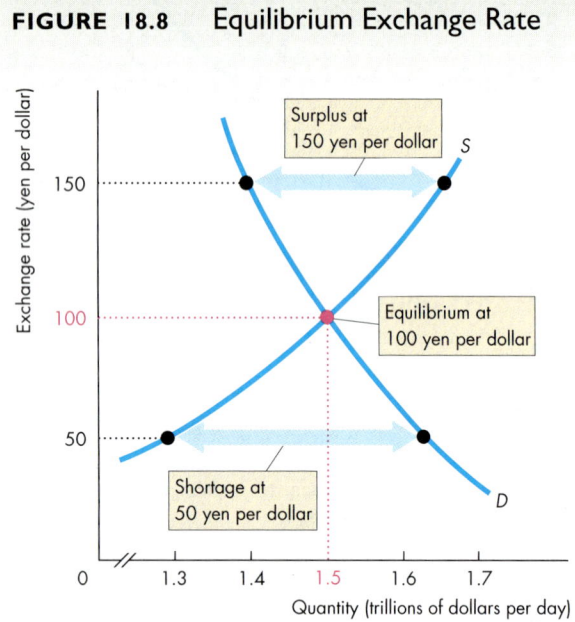

**FIGURE 18.8** Equilibrium Exchange Rate

The demand curve for dollars is $D$, and the supply curve is $S$. If the exchange rate is 150 yen per dollar, there is a surplus of dollars and the exchange rate falls. If the exchange rate is 50 yen per dollar, there is a shortage of dollars and the exchange rate rises. If the exchange rate is 100 yen per dollar, there is neither a shortage nor a surplus of dollars and the exchange rate remains constant. The market is in equilibrium.

**An Appreciating Dollar: 1999–2001** Between 1999 and 2001, the dollar appreciated against the yen. It rose from 103 yen to 127 yen per dollar. Figure 18.9(a) explains why this happened. In 1999, the demand and supply curves were those labeled $D_{99}$ and $S_{99}$. The exchange rate was 103 yen—where the supply and demand curves intersect. During the next two years, currency traders expected the yen to depreciate against the dollar. The demand for yen decreased. As a result, the demand for dollars increased, and the supply of dollars decreased. The demand curve shifted from $D_{99}$ to $D_{01}$, and the supply curve shifted from $S_{99}$ to $S_{01}$. These two shifts reinforced each other, and the exchange rate rose to 127 yen per dollar.

**A Depreciating Dollar: 2001–2003** Between 2001 and 2003, the dollar fell from 127 yen to 108 yen per dollar. Figure 18.9(b) explains this fall. In 2001, the demand and supply curves were those labeled $D_{01}$ and $S_{01}$. The exchange rate was 127 yen per dollar.

During 2003, traders expected the U.S. dollar to depreciate against the yen. They expected a lower exchange rate. As a result, the demand for dollars decreased and the supply of dollars increased. The demand curve shifted leftward to $D_{03}$, and the supply curve shifted rightward to $S_{03}$. The exchange rate fell to 108 yen per dollar.

### Exchange Rate Expectations

The changes in the exchange rate that we've just examined occurred in part because the exchange rate was *expected to change*. This explanation sounds a bit like a self-fulfilling prophecy. But what makes expectations change? The answer is new information about the deeper forces that influence the value of money. There are two such forces:

- Purchasing power parity
- Interest rate parity

### FIGURE 18.9 Exchange Rate Fluctuations

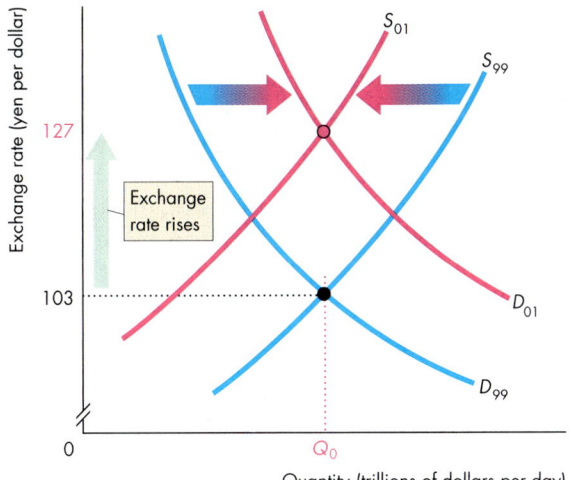
(a) 1999 to 2001

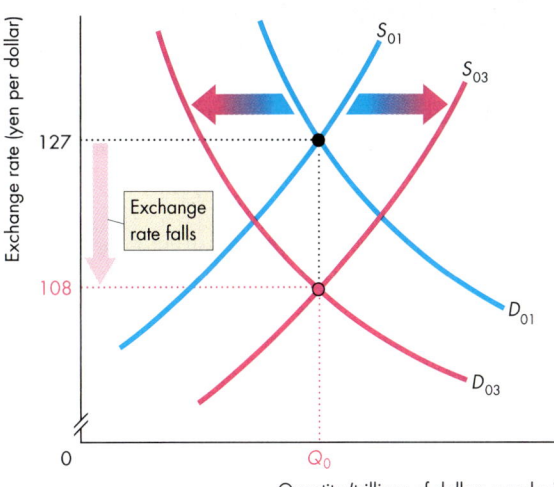
(b) 2001 to 2003

The exchange rate fluctuates because in the foreign exchange market changes in demand and supply are not independent of each other. Everyone is a potential buyer and seller in the foreign exchange market. Between 1999 and 2001 (in part a), currency traders expected the dollar to appreciate. The demand for dollars increased, the supply of dollars decreased, and the dollar appreciated. Between 2001 and 2003 (in part b), currency traders expected the dollar to depreciate. The demand for dollars decreased, the supply of dollars increased, and the dollar depreciated.

**Purchasing Power Parity** Money is worth what it will buy. But two kinds of money—U.S. dollars and Canadian dollars, for example—might buy different amounts of goods and services. Suppose a Big Mac costs $4 (Canadian) in Toronto and $3 (U.S.) in New York. If the Canadian dollar exchange rate is $1.33 Canadian per U.S. dollar, the two monies have the same value. You can buy a Big Mac in either Toronto or New York for either $4 Canadian or $3 U.S.

The situation we've just described is called **purchasing power parity**, which means *equal value of money*. If purchasing power parity does not prevail, some powerful forces go to work. To understand these forces, let's suppose that the price of a Big Mac in New York rises to $4 U.S., but in Toronto it remains at $4 Canadian. Suppose the exchange rate remains at $1.33 Canadian per U.S. dollar. In this case, a Big Mac in Toronto still costs $4 Canadian or $3 U.S. But in New York, it costs $4 U.S. or $5.33 Canadian. Money buys more in Canada than in the United States. Money is not of equal value in both countries.

If all (or most) prices have increased in the United States and not increased in Canada, then people will generally expect that the value of the U.S. dollar on the foreign exchange market must fall. In this situation, the exchange rate is expected to fall. The demand for U.S. dollars decreases, and the supply of U.S. dollars increases. The exchange rate falls, as expected. If the exchange rate falls to $1.00 Canadian and there are no further price changes, purchasing power parity is restored. A Big Mac now costs $4 in either U.S. or Canadian dollars in both New York and Toronto.

If prices increase in Canada and other countries but remain constant in the United States, then people will generally expect that the value of the U.S. dollar on the foreign exchange market is too low and that it is going to rise. In this situation, the exchange rate is expected to rise. The demand for U.S. dollars increases and the supply of U.S. dollars decreases. The exchange rate rises, as expected.

Ultimately, the value of money is determined by the price level, which in turn is determined by aggregate supply and aggregate demand (see Chapter 7, pp. 158–159). So the deeper forces that influence the exchange rate have tentacles that spread throughout the economy. If prices in the United States rise faster than those in other countries, the exchange rate falls. And if prices rise more slowly in the United States than in other countries, the exchange rate rises.

**Interest Rate Parity** Money is worth what it can earn. Again, two kinds of money—Canadian dollars and U.S. dollars, for example—might earn different amounts. For example, suppose a Canadian dollar bank deposit in Toronto earns 5 percent a year and a U.S. dollar bank deposit in New York earns 3 percent a year. In this situation, why does anyone deposit money in New York? Why doesn't all the money flow to Toronto? The answer is because of exchange rate expectations. Suppose people expect the Canadian dollar to depreciate by 2 percent a year. This 2 percent depreciation must be subtracted from the 5 percent interest to obtain the net return of 3 percent a year that an American can earn by depositing funds in a Toronto bank. The two returns are equal. This situation is one of **interest rate parity**, which means *equal rates of return*.

Adjusted for risk, interest rate parity always prevails. Funds move to get the highest return available. If for a few seconds a higher return is available in New York than in Toronto, the demand for U.S. dollars rises and the exchange rate rises until expected rates of return are equal.

### The Fed in the Foreign Exchange Market

Interest rates in the United States are determined by the demand for and supply of money (see Chapter 11, pp. 261–262). But the supply of money is influenced by the Fed, so ultimately, the exchange rate is influenced by monetary policy. When interest rates in the United States rise relative to those in other countries, the demand for U.S. dollars increases, the supply of U.S. dollars decreases, and the exchange rate rises. (Similarly, when interest rates in the United States fall relative to those in other countries, the demand for U.S. dollars decreases, the supply of U.S. dollars increases, and the exchange rate falls.)

But the Fed can intervene directly in the foreign exchange market. It can buy or sell dollars and try to smooth out fluctuations in the exchange rate. Let's look at the foreign exchange interventions the Fed can make.

Suppose the Fed wants the exchange rate to be steady at 100 yen per dollar. If the exchange rate rises above 100 yen, the Fed sells dollars. If the exchange rate falls below 100 yen, the Fed buys dollars. By these actions, the Fed changes the supply of dollars and keeps the exchange rate close to its target rate of 100 yen.

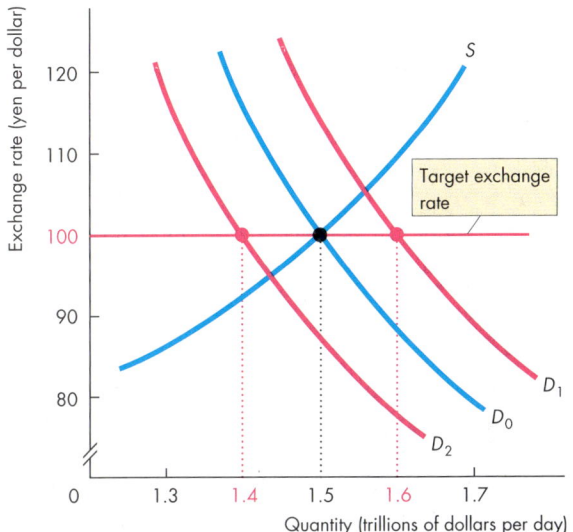

**FIGURE 18.10** Foreign Exchange Market Intervention

Initially, the demand for dollars is $D_0$, the supply of dollars is S, and the exchange rate is 100 yen per dollar. The Fed can intervene in the foreign exchange market to keep the exchange rate close to its target rate (100 yen in this example). If demand increases from $D_0$ to $D_1$, the Fed sells dollars to increase supply. If demand decreases from $D_0$ to $D_2$, the Fed buys dollars to decrease supply. Persistent intervention on one side of the market cannot be sustained.

Figure 18.10 shows this Fed intervention in the foreign exchange market. The supply of dollars is S, and initially, the demand for dollars is $D_0$. The equilibrium exchange rate is 100 yen per dollar. This exchange rate is the Fed's target rate, shown by the horizontal red line in the figure.

When the demand for dollars increases and the demand curve shifts rightward to $D_1$, the Fed sells $0.1 trillion. This action increases the supply of dollars by $0.1 trillion and prevents the exchange rate from rising. When the demand for dollars decreases and the demand curve shifts leftward to $D_2$, the Fed buys $0.1 trillion. This action decreases the supply of dollars by $0.1 trillion and prevents the exchange rate from falling.

If the demand for dollars fluctuates between $D_1$ and $D_2$ and on the average is $D_0$, the Fed can repeatedly intervene in the way we've just seen. Sometimes the Fed buys and sometimes it sells, but on the average, it neither buys nor sells.

But suppose the demand for dollars increases permanently from $D_0$ to $D_1$. The Fed cannot now maintain the exchange rate at 100 yen per dollar indefinitely. To do so, the Fed would have to sell dollars every day. When the Fed sells dollars in the foreign exchange market, it buys foreign currency. So the Fed would be piling up foreign currency.

Now suppose the demand for dollars decreases permanently from $D_0$ to $D_2$. Again the Fed cannot maintain the exchange rate at 100 yen per dollar indefinitely. To do so, the Fed would have to buy dollars every day. When the Fed buys dollars in the foreign exchange market, it uses its holdings of foreign currency. So the Fed would be losing foreign currency. Eventually, it would run out of foreign currency and would then have to abandon its attempt to fix the exchange rate.

### REVIEW QUIZ

1. What is the exchange rate and how is it determined?
2. What are the influences of interest rates and the expected future exchange rate on the demand for and supply of dollars in the foreign exchange market?
3. How do changes in the expected future exchange rate influence the actual exchange rate?
4. How do purchasing power parity and interest rate parity affect exchange rate expectations?
5. How can the Fed influence the foreign exchange market?

◆ *Reading Between the Lines* on pp. 452–453 looks at the sinking U.S. dollar in 2003.

You have now reached the end of your economics course. Go back to the big questions and ideas that define economics and the economic way of thinking (on pp. 2–11) and see how much more they mean to you now than they did when you first encountered them. I hope that your instructor and I have opened your eyes and shown you a new way of viewing the world. Keep your economics text handy and use it to refresh your memory of the economic principles that help you to make sense of your world. And keep reading between the lines!

# READING BETWEEN THE LINES

## The Sinking Dollar

**THE WALL STREET JOURNAL, DECEMBER 30, 2003**

### U.S. Dollar Loses Ground as Euro Notches New High

The euro notched yet another all-time record high against the dollar Tuesday, as the broad downward pressure on the greenback in global currency markets refused to lift. The U.S. currency also reached fresh 11-year lows against sterling and six-year lows against the Australian dollar.

At late morning, the euro was trading at $1.2531, up from $1.2485 late Monday in New York. The dollar was at ¥106.88, down from ¥107, and also weaker against the Swiss franc at 1.2432 francs versus 1.25 francs Monday. Sterling was at $1.7810, a new high, up from $1.7735 late Monday in New York. ...

"Higher interest rates may be the dollar's salvation, but for the moment, this scenario appears to be at the outer edges of the radar screen," wrote Michael Woolfolk, senior currency strategist at Bank of New York in New York. "Hence, it is [unnervingly] difficult to escape the conclusion that there is still plenty of downside to the dollar ahead of us."...

Some European Central Bank officials say the euro's exchange rate is merely in line with long-term averages, but others are starting to express concern that its strength is starting to hurt exports and the region's overall economic growth.

"They were ineffective in curbing the euro's decline [in 1999 and 2000], so I can't see them being any more effective in curbing its strength three years later," said Robert Lynch, senior currency strategist at BNP Paribas in New York, referring to ECB officials' jawboning.

Until specific action is taken, any rhetoric will remain just that, and the lack of action to back up the words may end up "inviting speculators, potentially, to just push the euro even higher," Mr. Lynch said. ....

©2003 The Wall Street Journal. Printed with permission. Further reproduction prohibited.

### Essence of the Story

- The U.S. dollar reached an all time low against the euro, an 11-year low against the U.K. pound, and 6-year low against the Australian dollar.

- The dollar also fell against the Japanese yen and the Swiss franc.

- A currency expert said that a higher U.S. interest rate might stop the dollar from falling but a higher interest rate seems unlikely.

- Some Europeans say the euro exchange rate is appropriate, but others say that it is too high and is lowering European exports and economic growth.

- The ECB is not expected to stop the euro's current rise.

## Economic Analysis

- Exchange rates changed a lot during 2002 and 2003. The dollar fell, the euro rose, and the yen rose against the dollar but fell against the euro.

- Figure 1 shows the path of the sinking dollar. The value of the dollar fell from a high of 134 yen in February 2002 to a low of 108 yen in December 2003.

- And the value of the dollar fell from a high of 1.15 euros in February 2002 to a low of 81 euro cents in December 2003.

- Figure 2 shows the path of the rising euro. The value of the euro rose from a low of 87 U.S cents in February 2002 to a high of $.23 in December 2003.

- And the value of the euro rose from a low of 116 yen in February 2002 to a high of 138 yen in June 2003. The euro then fell to 132 yen in December 2003.

- Figure 3 shows the paths of the yen. These paths are implied by the paths of the dollar and the euro that we've just described.

- Describing exchange rate movements is easy. Explaining them is hard. If we could predict exchange rate movements, we could make a lot of money!

- The news article suggests that interest rates can explain exchange rate changes.

- In 2003, the interest rates on similar assets were 1.2 percent in the United States, 2.3 percent in Europe, and 0.1 percent in Japan.

- If interest rate differences explained the exchange rates, the yen would be falling, the euro rising, and the dollar rising against the yen and falling against the euro—not what we see in the data.

- Purchasing power parity estimates say that the yen was overvalued by 38 percent at the end of 2003 and that the euro was overvalued by 18 percent. If these estimates are correct, the dollar should be rising—at least in the long run!

- But the United States has a very large balance of payments deficit and large scale of foreign borrowing. Concerns about this fact might be the source of the falling dollar.

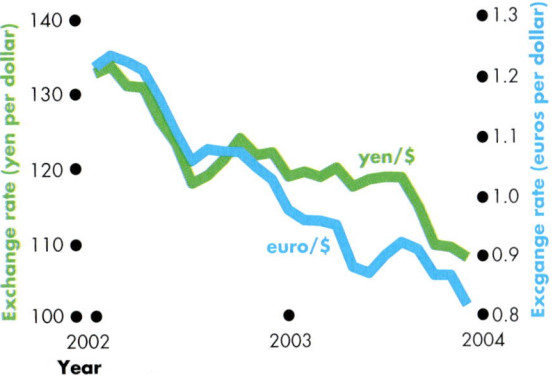

**Figure 1** The sinking dollar

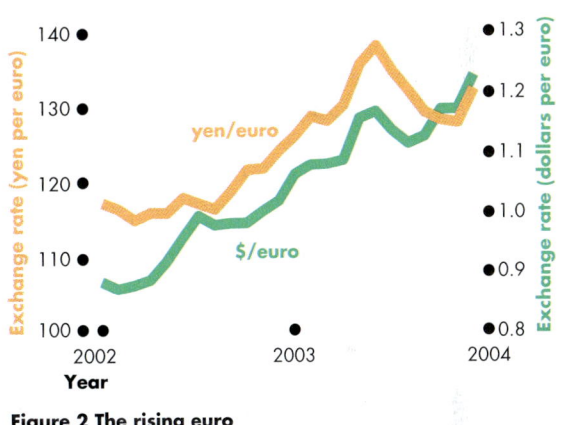

**Figure 2** The rising euro

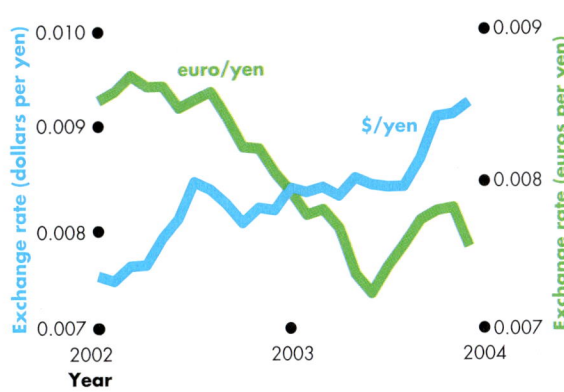

**Figure 3** The ambiguous yen

# SUMMARY

## KEY POINTS

### Financing International Trade (pp. 438–442)

- International trade, borrowing, and lending are financed by using foreign currency.
- A country's international transactions are recorded in its balance of payments accounts.
- The balance of payments has three accounts: current account, capital account, and official settlement account.
- Historically, the United States has been a net lender to the rest of the world, but in 1989, that situation changed and the United States became a net borrower and a net debtor.
- Net exports equal the government sector balance plus the private sector balance.

### The Exchange Rate (pp. 443–451)

- Foreign currency is obtained in exchange for domestic currency in the foreign exchange market.
- The exchange rate is determined by demand and supply in the foreign exchange market.
- The lower the exchange rate, the greater is the quantity of dollars demanded. A change in the exchange rate brings a movement along the demand curve for dollars.
- Changes in the expected future exchange rate and the U.S. interest rate differential change the demand for dollars and shift the demand curve.
- The lower the exchange rate, the smaller is the quantity of dollars supplied. A change in the exchange rate brings a movement along the supply curve for dollars.
- Changes in the expected future exchange rate and the U.S. interest rate differential change the supply of dollars and shift the supply curve.
- Fluctuations in the exchange rate occur because the fluctuations in the demand for and supply of dollars are not independent.
- The Fed can intervene in the foreign exchange market to smooth fluctuations in the dollar.

## KEY FIGURES AND TABLE

Figure 18.1  The Balance of Payments, 1983–2003, 439
Figure 18.3  The Yen-Dollar and the Euro-Dollar Exchange Rates, 443
Figure 18.8  Equilibrium Exchange Rate, 448
Figure 18.9  Exchange Rate Fluctuations, 449
Figure 18.10 Foreign Exchange Market Intervention, 451
Table 18.2   Net Exports, the Government Budget, Saving, and Investment, 441

## KEY TERMS

Balance of payments accounts, 438
Capital account, 438
Creditor nation, 440
Currency appreciation, 443
Currency depreciation, 443
Current account, 438
Debtor nation, 440
Foreign exchange market, 443
Foreign exchange rate, 443
Government sector surplus or deficit, 441
Interest rate parity, 450
Net borrower, 440
Net exports, 441
Net lender, 440
Official settlements account, 438
Private sector surplus or deficit, 441
Purchasing power parity, 450
U.S. interest rate differential, 445
U.S. official reserves, 438

# PROBLEMS

*1. The citizens of Silecon, whose currency is the grain, conduct the following transactions in 2003:

| Item | Billions of grains |
| --- | --- |
| Imports of goods and services | 350 |
| Exports of goods and services | 500 |
| Borrowing from the rest of the world | 60 |
| Lending to the rest of the world | 200 |
| Increase in official holdings of foreign currency | 10 |

a. Set out the three balance of payments accounts for Silecon.
b. Does the central bank intervene in the foreign exchange market?

2. The citizens of Spin, whose currency is the wheel, conduct the following transactions in 2003:

| Item | Wheels |
| --- | --- |
| Imports of goods and services | 100 |
| Exports of goods and services | 120 |
| Borrowing from the rest of the world | 4 |
| Lending to the rest of the world | 24 |
| Increase in official holdings of foreign currency | 0 |

a. Set out the three balance of payments accounts for Spin.
b. Does the central bank intervene in the foreign exchange market?

*3. The figure at the bottom of the page shows the flows of income and expenditure in Dream Land in 2002. The amounts are in millions of dollars. GDP in Dream Land is $120 million.
a. Calculate Dream Land's net exports.
b. Calculate saving in Dream Land.
c. How is Dream Land's investment financed?

4. The figure shows the flows of income and expenditure in Dream Land in 2003. The amounts are in millions of dollars. Dream Land's GDP has increased to $130 million, but all the other items whose values are provided in the figure remain the same as they were in 2002.
a. Calculate Dream Land's net exports in 2003.
b. Calculate saving in Dream Land in 2003.
c. How is Dream Land's investment financed?

*5. The table on the next page tells you about Ecflex, a country whose currency is the band. The official settlements balance is zero. Net interest income and net transfers from abroad are zero.
Calculate the following for Ecflex:
a. Imports of goods and services
b. Current account balance
c. Capital account balance
d. Net taxes
e. Private sector balance

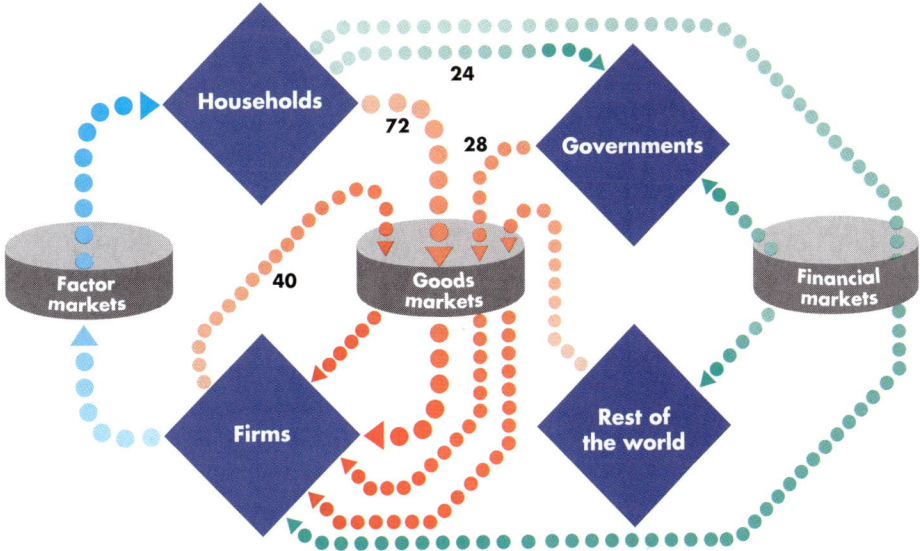

* Solutions to odd-numbered problems are available on MyEconLab.

| Item | Billion bands |
|---|---|
| GDP | 100 |
| Consumption expenditure | 60 |
| Government purchases of goods and services | 24 |
| Investment | 22 |
| Exports of goods and services | 20 |
| Government budget deficit | 4 |

6. You are told the following about Ecfix, a country whose currency is the rock. The central bank intervenes to keep the exchange rate fixed.

| Item | Billion rocks |
|---|---|
| GDP | 400 |
| Consumption expenditure | 240 |
| Government purchases of goods and services | 100 |
| Investment | 100 |
| Exports of goods and services | 80 |
| Saving | 90 |

Calculate the following for Ecfix:
 a. Imports of goods and services
 b. Current account balance
 c. Government sector balance
 d. Net taxes
 e. Private sector balance

*7. A country's currency appreciates, and its official holdings of foreign currency increase. What can you say about:
 a. The central bank's intervention in the foreign exchange market?
 b. The country's current account balance?
 c. The country's official settlements account?

8. A country has a lower inflation rate than all other countries. It has more rapid economic growth. The central bank does not intervene in the foreign exchange market. What can you say about each of the following (and why):
 a. The exchange rate?
 b. The current account balance?
 c. The expected exchange rate?
 d. The interest rate differential?
 e. Interest rate parity?
 f. Purchasing power parity?

# CRITICAL THINKING

1. Study *Reading Between the Lines* on pp. 452–453 and then answer the following questions.
 a. Do you think the falling dollar is a problem for Americans or the source of potential benefit?
 b. Do you think the rising euro is a problem for Europeans or the source of potential benefit?
 c. What, if anything, could the Fed do to stop the sinking dollar? Should the Fed act in this way?
 d. What, if anything, could the European Central Bank (ECB) do to stop the rising euro? Should the ECB act in this way?

# WEB EXERCISES

**Use the links on MyEconLab to work the following exercises.**

1. Visit the Bureau of Economic Analysis and find data on the United States balance of payments accounts.
 a. When did the United States last have a current account surplus?
 b. Does the United States have a surplus or a deficit in trade in goods?
 c. Does the United States have a surplus or a deficit in trade in services?
 d. What has happened to foreign investment in the United States during the past 10 years?
 e. Do you think the U.S. balance of payments record is a matter for concern? Why or why not?

2. Visit PACIFIC (an exchange rate service) and read the page on purchasing power parity.
 a. What is purchasing power parity?
 b. Which currencies are the most overvalued relative to the U.S. dollar today?
 c. Which currencies are the most undervalued relative to the U.S. dollar today?
 d. Can you offer some suggestions as to why some currencies are overvalued and some are undervalued?
 e. Do you think that the information on overvaluation and undervaluation is useful to currency speculators? Why or why not?

# UNDERSTANDING THE GLOBAL ECONOMY

PART 7

## *It's a Small World*

The scale of international trade, borrowing, and lending, both in absolute dollar terms and as a percentage of total world production expands every year. One country, Singapore, imports and exports goods and services in a volume that exceeds its Gross Domestic Product. The world's largest nation, China, returned to the international economic stage during the 1980s and is now a major producer of manufactured goods.

International economic activity is large because today's economic world is small and because communication is so incredibly fast. But today's world is not a new world. From the beginning of recorded history, people have traded over large and steadily increasing distances. The great Western civilizations of Greece and Rome traded not only around the Mediterranean but also into the Gulf of Arabia. The great Eastern civilizations traded around the Indian Ocean. By the Middle Ages, the East and the West were trading routinely overland on routes pioneered by Venetian traders and explorers such as Marco Polo. When, in 1497, Vasco da Gama opened a sea route between the Atlantic and Indian Oceans around Africa, a new trade between East and West began, which brought tumbling prices of Eastern goods in Western markets.

The European discovery of America and the subsequent opening up of Atlantic trade continued the process of steady globalization. So, the developments of the 1990s, amazing though many of them are, represent a continuation of an ongoing expansion of human horizons.

These two chapters studied the interaction of nations in today's global economy.

Chapter 17 described and explained international trade in goods and services. In this chapter, you came face to face with one of the biggest policy issues of all ages, free trade versus protection and the globalization debate. The chapter explained how all nations can benefit from free international trade.

Chapter 18 explained some of the fundamentals of international borrowing and lending and the exchange rate. It explained the poorly understood fact that the size of a nation's international deficit depends not on how efficient it is, but on how much its citizens save relative to how much they invest. Nations with low saving rates, everything else being the same, have international deficits.

This chapter also explained why foreign exchange rates fluctuate so much.

The global economy is big news these days. And it has always attracted attention. On the next page, you can meet the economist who first understood comparative advantage, David Ricardo. And you can meet one of today's leading international economists, Jagdish Bhagwati of Columbia University.

# PROBING THE IDEAS

## Gains from International Trade

*Gains from International Trade "Under a system of perfectly free commerce, each country naturally devotes its capital and labor to such employments as are most beneficial to each."*

DAVID RICARDO
*The Principles of Political Economy and Taxation,*
1817

### THE ECONOMIST

**David Ricardo** (1772–1832) was a highly successful 27-year-old stockbroker when he stumbled on a copy of Adam Smith's Wealth of Nations *(see p. 52)* on a weekend visit to the country. He was immediately hooked and went on to become the most celebrated economist of his age and one of the all-time great economists. One of his many contributions was to develop the principle of comparative advantage, the foundation on which the modern theory of international trade is built. The example he used to illustrate this principle was the trade between England and Portugal in cloth and wine.

The General Agreement on Tariffs and Trade was established as a reaction against the devastation wrought by beggar-my-neighbor tariffs imposed during the 1930s. But it is also a triumph for the logic first worked out by Smith and Ricardo.

### THE ISSUES

Until the mid-eighteenth century, it was generally believed that the purpose of international trade was to keep exports greater than imports and pile up gold. If gold was accumulated, it was believed, the nation would prosper; if gold was lost through an international deficit, the nation would be drained of money and impoverished. These beliefs are called *mercantilism*, and the *mercantilists* were pamphleteers who advocated with missionary fervor the pursuit of an international surplus. If exports did not exceed imports, the mercantilists wanted imports restricted.

In the 1740s, David Hume explained that as the quantity of money (gold) changes, so also does the price level, and the nation's *real* wealth is unaffected. In the 1770s, Adam Smith argued that import restrictions would lower the gains from specialization and make a nation poorer. Thirty years later, David Ricardo proved the law of comparative advantage and demonstrated the superiority of free trade. Mercantilism was intellectually bankrupt but remained politically powerful.

Gradually, through the nineteenth century, the mercantilist influence waned and North America and Western Europe prospered in an environment of increasingly free international trade. But despite remarkable advances in economic understanding, mercantilism never quite died. It had a brief and devastating revival in the 1920s and 1930s when tariff hikes brought about the collapse of international trade and accentuated the Great Depression. It subsided again after World War II with the establishment of the General Agreement on Tariffs and Trade (GATT).

But mercantilism lingers on. The often expressed view that the United States should restrict Japanese imports and reduce its deficit with Japan and fears that NAFTA will bring economic ruin to the United States are modern manifestations of mercantilism. It would be interesting to have David Hume, Adam Smith, and David Ricardo commenting on these views. But we know what they would say—the same things that they said to the eighteenth-century mercantilists. And they would still be right today.

## THEN

In the eighteenth century, when mercantilists and economists were debating the pros and cons of free international exchange, the transportation technology that was available limited the gains from international trade. Sailing ships with tiny cargo holds took close to a month to cross the Atlantic Ocean. But the potential gains were large, and so was the incentive to cut shipping costs. By the 1850s, the clipper ship had been developed, cutting the journey from Boston to Liverpool to only 12 1/4 days. Half a century later, 10,000-ton steamships were sailing between America and England in just 4 days. As sailing times and costs declined, the gains from international trade increased and the volume of trade expanded.

## NOW

The container ship has revolutionized international trade and contributed to its continued expansion. Today, most goods cross the oceans in containers—metal boxes—packed into and piled on top of ships like this one. Container technology has cut the cost of ocean shipping by economizing on handling and by making cargoes harder to steal, lowering insurance costs. It is unlikely that there would be much international trade in goods such as television sets and VCRs without this technology. High-value and perishable cargoes such as flowers and fresh foods, as well as urgent courier packages, travel by air. Every day, dozens of cargo-laden 747s fly between every major U.S. city and to destinations across the Atlantic and Pacific oceans.

*Jagdish Bhagwati, whom you can meet on the following pages, is one of the most distinguished international economists. He has contributed to our understanding of the effects of international trade and trade policy on economic growth and development and has played a significant role in helping to shape today's global trading arrangements.*

# TALKING WITH

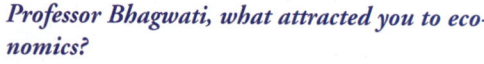
Jagdish Bhagwati

**Jagdish Bhagwati** is University Professor at Columbia University. Born in India in 1934, he studied at Cambridge University in England, MIT, and Oxford University before returning to India. He returned to teach at MIT in 1968 and moved to Columbia in 1980. A prolific scholar, Professor Bhagwati also writes in leading newspapers and magazines throughout the world. He has been much honored for both his scientific work and his impact on public policy. His greatest contributions are in international trade but extend also to developmental problems and the study of political economy. Michael Parkin talked with Jagdish Bhagwati about his work and the progress that economists have made in understanding the benefits of international economic integration since the pioneering work of Ricardo.

### Professor Bhagwati, what attracted you to economics?

When you come from India where poverty hits the eye, it is easy to be attracted to economics which can be used to bring prosperity and create jobs to pull up the poor into gainful employment.

I learned later that there are two broad types of economist: those who treat the subject as an arid mathematical toy, and those who see it as a serious social science.

If Cambridge, where I went as an undergraduate, had been interested in esoteric mathematical economics, I would have opted for something else. But the Cambridge economists from whom I learned — many among the greatest figures in the discipline — saw economics as a social science. I therefore saw the power of economics as a tool to address India's poverty and was immediately hooked.

### Who had the greatest impact on you at Cambridge?

Most of all, it was Harry Johnson, a young Canadian of immense energy and profound analytical gifts. Quite unlike the shy and reserved British dons, Johnson was friendly, effusive, and supportive of students who flocked around him. He would later move to Chicago where he became one of the most influential members of the market-oriented Chicago school. Another was Joan Robinson, arguably the world's most impressive female economist.

When I left Cambridge for MIT, going from one Cambridge to the other, I was lucky to transition from one phenomenal set of economists to another. At MIT, I learned much from future Nobel laureates Paul Samuelson and Robert Solow: Both would later become great friends and colleagues when I joined the MIT faculty in 1968.

### After Cambridge and MIT, you went to Oxford and then back to India. What did you do in India?

I joined the Planning Commission in New Delhi, where my first big job was to find ways of raising the bottom thirty percent of India's population out of poverty to a "minimum income" level.

### And what did you prescribe?

My main prescription was to "grow the pie". My research suggested that the share of the bottom 30 percent of the pie did not seem to

460

vary dramatically with differences in economic and political systems. So, growth in the pie seemed to be the principal (but not the only) component of an anti-poverty strategy. To supplement growth's good effects on the poor, the Indian planners were also dedicated to education, health, social reforms, and land reforms. Also, the access of the lowest-income

> *My main prescription was to "grow the pie"… Today, this strategy has no rivals. Much empirical work shows that where growth has occurred, poverty has lessened.*

and socially disadvantaged groups to the growth process and its benefits was to be improved in many ways, such as extension of credit without collateral.

Today, this strategy has no rivals. Much empirical work shows that where growth has occurred, poverty has lessened. It is nice to know that one's basic take on an issue of such central importance to humanity's well-being has been borne out by experience!

**You left India in 1968 to come to America and an academic job at MIT. Why?**

While the decision to emigrate often reflects personal factors — and they were present in my case — the offer of a Professorship from MIT certainly helped me make up my mind. At the time, it was easily the world's most celebrated Department: Serendipitously, the highest-ranked Departments at MIT were not in engineering and the sciences but in linguistics (which had Noam Chomsky) and economics (which had Paul Samuelson). Joining the MIT faculty was a dramatic breakthrough: I felt stimulated each year by several fantastic students and by several of the world's most creative economists.

**We hear a lot in the popular press about fair trade and level playing fields. What's the distinction between free trade and fair trade? How can the playing field be unlevel?**

Free trade simply means allowing no trade barriers such as tariffs, subsidies, and quotas. Trade barriers make domestic prices different from world prices for traded goods. When this happens, resources are not being used efficiently. Basic economics from the time of Ricardo tells us why free trade is good for us and why barriers to trade harm us, though our understanding of this doctrine today is far more nuanced and profound than it was at its creation.

Fair trade, on the other hand, is almost always a sneaky way of objecting to free trade. If your rivals are hard to compete with, you are not likely to get protection simply by saying that you cannot hack it. But if you say that your rival is an "unfair" trader, that is an easier sell! As international competition has

> *Fair trade … is almost always a sneaky way of objecting to free trade.*

grown fiercer, cries of "unfair trade" have therefore multiplied. The lesser rogues among the protectionists ask for "free and fair trade," whereas the worst ones ask for "fair, not free, trade."

**At the end of World War II, the General Agreement of Tariffs and Trade (GATT) was established and there followed several rounds of multilateral trade negotiations and reductions in barriers to trade. How do you assess the contribution of GATT and its successor, the World Trade Organization (WTO)?**

The GATT has made a huge contribution by overseeing massive trade liberalization in industrial goods among the developed countries. GATT rules, which "bind" tariffs to negotiated ceilings, prevent the raising of tariffs and have prevented tariff wars like those of the 1930s in which mutual and retaliatory tariff barriers were raised to the detriment of everyone.

The GATT was folded into the WTO at the end of the Uruguay Round of trade negotiations and is institutionally stronger. For instance, it has a binding Dispute Settlement Mechanism, whereas the GATT had no such teeth. It is also more ambitious in its scope, extending to new areas such as environment, intellectual property protection, and investment rules.

*Running alongside the pursuit of multilateral free trade has been the emergence of bilateral trade agreements such as NAFTA and the EU. How do you view the bilateral free trade areas in today's world?*

Unfortunately, there has been an explosion of bilateral free trade areas today. By some estimates, the ones in place and others being plotted approach 400! Each bilateral agreement gives preferential treatment to its trading partner over others. Because there are now so many bilateral agreements, such as between United States and Israel and between United States and Jordan, the result is a chaotic pattern of different tariffs depending on where a product comes from. Also, "rules of origin" must be agreed upon to determine whether a product is, say, Jordanian or Taiwanese if Jordan qualifies for a preferential tariff but Taiwan does not, and Taiwanese inputs enter the Jordanian manufacture of the product.

I have called the resulting criss-crossing of preferences and rules of origin the "spaghetti bowl" problem. The world trading system is choking under these proliferating bilateral deals. Contrast this complexity against the simplicity of a multilateral system with common tariffs for all WTO members.

> *We now have a world of uncoordinated and inefficient trade policies.*

We now have a world of uncoordinated and inefficient trade policies. The EU makes bilateral free trade agreements with different non-EU countries, so the United States follows with its own bilateral agreements; and with Europe and the United States doing it, the Asian countries, long wedded to multilateralism, have now succumbed to the mania.

Instead, if the United States had provided leadership by rewriting rules to make the signing of such bilateral agreements extremely difficult, this plague on the trading system today might well have been averted.

*Despite the benefits that economics points to from multilateral free trade, the main organization that pursues this goal, the WTO, is having a very hard time with the anti-globalization movement. What can we say about globalization that puts the WTO and its work in proper perspective?*

The anti-globalization movement contains a diverse set of activists. Essentially, they all claim to be stakeholders in the globalization phenomenon. But there are those who want to drive a stake through the system, as in Dracula films, and there are those who want to exercise their stake in the system. The former want to be heard; the latter, to be listened to. For a while, the two disparate sets of critics were milling around together, seeking targets of opportunity at international conferences such as WTO's November 2000 meeting in Seattle where the riots broke out. Now things have settled down; and the groups that want to work systematically and seriously at improving the global economy's functioning are much more in play.

But the WTO is also seen, inaccurately for the most part, as imposing trade sanctions that override concerns such as environmental protection. For example, U.S. legislation bans the importing of shrimp that is harvested without the use of turtle-excluding devices. India and others complained, but the WTO upheld the U.S. legislation. Ignorant of the facts, demonstrators took to the streets dressed as turtles protesting the WTO decision!

*What advice do you have for a student who is just starting to study economics? Is economics a good subject in which to major?*

I would say: enormously so. In particular, we economists bring three unique insights to good policymaking.

First, economists look for second and subsequent-round effects of actions.

Second, we correctly emphasize that a policy cannot be judged without using a counterfactual. It is a witticism that an economist, when asked how her husband was, said: compared to what?

Third, we uniquely and systematically bring the principle of social cost and benefit to our policy analysis.

# GLOSSARY

**Above full-employment equilibrium** A macroeconomic equilibrium in which real GDP exceeds potential GDP. (p. 160)

**Absolute advantage** A person has an absolute advantage if that person can produce more of goods with a given amount of resources than another person can; a country has an absolute advantage if its output per unit of inputs of all goods is larger than that of another country. (p. 43)

**Aggregate demand** The relationship between the quantity of real GDP demanded and the price level. (p. 155)

**Aggregate hours** The total number of hours worked by all the people employed, both full time and part time, during a year. (p. 133)

**Aggregate planned expenditure** The expenditure that households, firms, governments, and foreigners plan to undertake in given circumstances. It is the sum of planned consumption expenditure, planned investment, planned government purchases of goods and services, and planned exports minus planned imports. (p. 306)

**Aggregate production function** The relationship between the quantity of real GDP supplied and the quantities of labor and capital and the state of technology. (p. 150)

**Allocative efficiency** A situation in which we cannot produce more of any good without giving up some of another good that we value more highly. (p. 37)

**Automatic fiscal policy** A change in fiscal policy that is triggered by the state of the economy. (p. 377)

**Automatic stabilizers** Mechanisms that stabilize real GDP without explicit action by the government. (p. 379)

**Autonomous expenditure** The sum of those components of aggregate planned expenditure that are not influenced by real GDP. Autonomous expenditure equals investment, government purchases, exports, and the autonomous parts of consumption expenditure and imports. (p. 313)

**Balanced budget** A government budget in which tax revenues and expenditures are equal. (p. 364)

**Balanced budget multiplier** The magnification on aggregate demand of a *simultaneous* change in government purchases and taxes that leaves the budget balance unchanged. (p. 377)

**Balance of payments accounts** A country's record of international trading, borrowing, and lending. (p. 438)

**Barter** The direct exchange of one good or service for other goods and services. (p. 234)

**Below full-employment equilibrium** A macroeconomic equilibrium in which potential GDP exceeds real GDP. (p. 160)

**Big tradeoff** A tradeoff between equity and efficiency. (p. 10)

**Budget deficit** A government's budget balance that is negative—expenditures exceed tax revenues. (p. 364)

**Budget surplus** A government's budget balance that is positive—tax revenues exceed expenditures. (p. 364)

**Business cycle** The periodic but irregular up-and-down movement in production. (p. 90)

**Capital** The tools, equipment, buildings, and other constructions that businesses now use to produce goods and services. (p. 4)

**Capital account** A record of foreign investment in a country minus its investment abroad. (p. 438)

**Capital accumulation** The growth of capital resources. (p. 38)

**Capital consumption** The decrease in the capital stock that results from wear and tear and obsolescence. (p. 111)

**Capital stock** The total quantity of plant, equipment, buildings, and inventories. (p. 190)

**Central bank** A bank's bank and a public authority that regulates a nation's depository institutions and controls the quantity of money. (p. 244)

*Ceteris paribus* Other things being equal—all other relevant things remaining the same. (p. 13)

**Chain-weighted output index** An index that uses the prices of two adjacent years to calculate the real GDP growth rate. (p. 116)

**Change in demand** A change in buyers' plans that occurs when some influence on those plans other than the price of the good changes. It is illustrated by a shift of the demand curve. (p. 60)

**Change in supply** A change in sellers' plans that occurs when some influence on those plans other than the price of the good changes. It is illustrated by a shift of the supply curve. (p. 65)

**Change in the quantity demanded** A change in buyers' plans that occurs when the price of a good changes but all other influences on buyers' plans remain unchanged. It is illustrated by a movement along the demand curve. (p. 63)

**Change in the quantity supplied** A change in sellers' plans that occurs when the price of a good changes but all other influences on sellers' plans remain unchanged. It is illustrated by a movement along the supply curve. (p. 66)

**Classical** A macroeconomist who believes that the economy is self-regulating and that it is always at full employment. (p. 166)

G–1

**Classical dichotomy** At full employment, the forces that determine real variables are independent of those that determine nominal variables. (p. 180)

**Classical growth theory** A theory of economic growth based on the view that real GDP growth is temporary and that when real GDP per person increases above subsistence level, a population explosion brings real GDP back to subsistence level. (p. 215)

**Classical model** A model of an economy that determines the real variables—real GDP, employment and unemployment, the real wage rate, consumption, saving, investment, and the real interest rate—at full employment. (p. 180)

**Commercial bank** A firm that is licensed by the Comptroller of the Currency in the U.S. Treasury) or by a state agency to receive deposits and make loans. (p. 237)

**Comparative advantage** A person or country has a comparative advantage in an activity if that person or country can perform the activity at a lower opportunity cost than anyone else or any other country. (pp. 40, 418)

**Competitive market** A market that has many buyers and many sellers, so no single buyer or seller can influence the price. (p. 58)

**Complement** A good that is used in conjunction with another good. (p. 61)

**Consumer Price Index (CPI)** An index that measures the average of the prices paid by urban consumers for a fixed "basket" of the consumer goods and services. (p. 140)

**Consumption expenditure** The total payment for consumer goods and services. (p. 109)

**Consumption function** The relationship between consumption expenditure and disposable income, other things remaining the same. (p. 307)

**Cost-push inflation** An inflation that results from an initial increase in costs. (p. 281)

**Council of Economic Advisers** The President's council whose main work is to monitor the economy and keep the President and the public well informed about the current state of the economy and the best available forecasts of where it is heading. (p. 363)

**Creditor nation** A country that during its entire history has invested more in the rest of the world than other countries have invested in it. (p. 440)

**Credit union** A depository institution owned by a social or economic group such as firm's employees that accepts savings deposits and makes mostly consumer loans. (p. 238)

**Cross-section graph** A graph that shows the values of an economic variable for different groups in a population at a point in time. (p. 18)

**Crowding-out effect** The tendency for a government budget deficit to decrease in investment. (p. 373)

**Currency** The bills and coins that we use today. (p. 235)

**Currency appreciation** The rise in the value of one currency in terms of another currency. (p. 443)

**Currency depreciation** The fall in the value of one currency in terms of another currency. (p. 443)

**Currency drain** An increase in currency held outside the banks. (p. 249)

**Current account** A record of the payments for imports of goods and services, receipts from exports of goods and services, the interest income, and net transfers. (pp. 99, 438)

**Cyclical surplus or deficit** The actual surplus or deficit minus the structural surplus or deficit. (p. 380)

**Cyclical unemployment** The fluctuations in unemployment over the business cycle. (p. 138)

**Debtor nation** A country that during its entire history has borrowed more from the rest of the world than it has lent to it. (p. 440)

**Deflation** A process in which the price level falls—a negative inflation. (p. 97)

**Demand** The relationship between the quantity of a good that consumers plan to buy and the price of the good when all other influences on buyers' plans remain the same. It is described by a demand schedule and illustrated by a demand curve. (p. 59)

**Demand curve** A curve that shows the relationship between the quantity demanded of a good and its price when all other influences on consumers' planned purchases remain the same. (p. 60)

**Demand for labor** The relationship between the quantity of labor demanded and the real wage rate when all other influences on firm's hiring plans remain the same. (p. 182)

**Demand-pull inflation** An inflation that results from an initial increase in aggregate demand. (p. 279)

**Depository institution** A firm that takes deposits from households and firms and makes loans to other households and firms. (p. 237)

**Depreciation** The decrease in the capital stock that results from wear and tear and obsolescence. (p. 111)

**Direct relationship** A relationship between two variables that move in the same direction. (p. 20)

**Discount rate** The interest rate at which the Fed stands ready to lend reserves to depository institutions. (p. 245)

**Discouraged workers** People who are available and willing to work but have not made specific efforts to find a job within the previous four weeks. (p. 131)

**Discretionary fiscal policy** A policy action that is initiated by an act of Congress. (p. 377)

**Discretionary policy** A policy that responds to the state of the economy in a possibly unique way that uses all the information available, including perceived lessons from past "mistakes." (p. 392)

**Disposable income** Aggregate income minus taxes plus transfer payments. (pp. 157, 306)

**Dumping** The sale by a foreign firm of exports at a lower price that the cost of production. (p. 427)

**Dynamic comparative advantage** A comparative advantage that a person or country possesses as a result of having specialized in a particular activity and then, as a result of learning-by-doing, having become the producer with the lowest opportunity cost. (p. 43)

**Economic growth** The expansion of production possibilities that results from capital accumulation and technological change. (pp. 38, 89)

**Economic growth rate** The percentage change in the quantity of goods and services produced from one year to the next. (p. 118)

**Economic model** A description of some aspect of the economic world that includes only those features of the world that are needed for the purpose at hand. (p. 12)

**Economics** The social science that studies the *choices* that individuals, businesses, governments, and entire societies make and how they cope with *scarcity* and the *incentives* that influence and reconcile those choices. (p. 2)

**Economic theory** A generalization that summarizes what we think we understand about the economic choices that people make and the performance of industries and entire economies. (p. 12)

**Economic welfare** A comprehensive measure of the general state of economic well-being. (p. 118)

**Efficiency wage** A real wage rate that is set above the full-employment equilibrium wage rate and that balances the costs and benefits of this higher wage rate to maximize the firm's profit. (p. 188)

**Employment Act of 1946** A landmark Congressional act that recognized a role for government actions to keep unemployment, keep the economy expanding, and keep inflation in check. (p. 362)

**Employment-to-population ratio** The percentage of people of working age who have jobs. (p. 132)

**Entrepreneurship** The human resource that organizes labor, land, and capital. Entrepreneurs come up with new ideas about what and how to produce, make business decisions, and bear the risk that arise from their decisions. (p. 4)

**Equation of exchange** An equation that states that the quantity of money multiplied by the velocity of circulation equals GDP. (p. 268)

**Equilibrium expenditure** The level of aggregate expenditure that occurs when aggregate planned expenditure equals real GDP. (p. 314)

**Equilibrium price** The price at which the quantity demanded equals the quantity supplied. (p. 68)

**Equilibrium quantity** The quantity bought and sold at the equilibrium price. (p. 68)

**Excess reserves** A bank's actual reserves minus its required reserves. (p. 242)

**Expansion** A business cycle phase between a trough and a peak—phase in which real GDP increases. (pp. 90, 128)

**Exports** The goods and services that we sell to people in other countries. (pp. 110, 416)

**Factors of production** The productive resources that businesses use to produce goods and services. (p. 3)

**Federal budget** The annual statement of the expenditures and tax revenues of the government of the United States together with the laws and regulations that approve and support those expenditures and taxes. (p. 362)

**Federal funds rate** The interest rate that banks charge each other on overnight loans of reserves. (p. 244)

**Federal Open Market Committee** The main policy-making organ of the Federal Reserve System. (p. 244)

**Federal Reserve System** The central bank of the United States. (p. 244)

**Feedback-rule policy** A rule that specifies how policy actions respond to changes in the state of the economy. (p. 392)

**Final good** An item that is bought by its final user during the specified time period. (p. 108)

**Financial innovation** The development of new financial products—new ways of borrowing and lending. (p. 240)

**Firm** An economic unit that hires factors of production and organizes those factors to produce and sell goods and services. (p. 44)

**Fiscal imbalance** The present value of the government's commitments to pay benefits minus the present value of its tax revenues. (p. 375)

**Fiscal policy** The government's attempt to achieve macroeconomic objectives such as full employment, sustained economic growth, and price level stability by setting and changing taxes, making transfer payments, and purchasing goods and services. (pp. 101, 157, 362)

**Fixed-rule policy** A rule that specifies an action to be pursued independently of the state of the economy. (p. 392)

**Flow** A quantity per unit of time. (p. 111)

**Foreign exchange market** The market in which the currency of one country is exchanged for the currency of another. (p. 443)

**Foreign exchange rate** The price at which one currency exchanges for another. (p. 443)

**Frictional unemployment** The unemployment that arises from normal labor turnover—from people entering and leaving the labor force and from the ongoing creation and destruction of jobs. (p. 137)

**Full employment** A situation in which the quantity of labor demanded equal the quantity supplied. At full employment, there is no cyclical unemployment—all unemployment is frictional and structural. (p. 138)

**GDP deflator** One measure of the price level, which is the average of current-year prices as a percentage of base-year prices. (p. 116)

**General Agreement on Tariffs and Trade** An international agreement signed in 1947 to reduce tariffs on international trade. (p. 423)

**Generational accounting** An accounting system that measures the lifetime tax burden and benefits of each generation. (p. 374)

**Generational imbalance** The division of the fiscal imbalance between the current and future generations, assuming that the current generation will enjoy the existing levels of taxes and benefits (p. 375)

**Goods and services** The objects that people value and produce to satisfy their wants. (p. 3)

**Government budget deficit** The deficit that arises when federal government spends more than it collects in taxes. (p. 99)

**Government budget surplus** The surplus that arises when the federal government collects more in taxes than it spends. (p. 99)

**Government debt** The total amount of borrowing that the government has borrowed. It equals the sum of past budget deficits minus budget surpluses. (p. 366)

**Government purchases** Goods and services bought by the government. (p. 110)

**Government purchases multiplier** The magnification effect of a change in government purchases of goods and services on aggregate demand. (p. 377)

**Government sector surplus or deficit** An amount equal to net taxes minus government purchases of goods and services. (p. 441)

**Great Depression** A decade (1929–1939) of high unemployment and stagnant production throughout the world economy. (p. 88)

**Gross domestic product (GDP)** The market value of all the final goods and services produced within a country during a given time period—usually a year. (p. 108)

**Gross investment** The total amount spent on purchases of new capital and on replacing depreciated capital. (p. 111)

**Growth accounting** A method of calculating how much real GDP growth results from growth of labor and capital and how much is attributable to technological change. (p. 211)

**Human capital** The knowledge and skill that people obtain from education, on-the-job training, and experience. (pp. 3, 195)

**Imports** The goods and services that we buy from people in other countries. (pp. 110, 416)

**Incentive** A reward that encourages or a penalty that discourages an action. (p. 2)

**Induced expenditure** The sum of the components of aggregate planned expenditure that vary with real GDP. Induced expenditure equals consumption expenditure minus imports. (p. 313)

**Induced taxes** Taxes that vary with real GDP. (p. 379)

**Infant-industry argument** The argument that it is necessary to protect a new industry to enable it to grow into a mature industry that can compete in world markets. (p. 427)

**Inferior good** A good for which demand decreases as income increases. (p. 62)

**Inflation** A process in which the price level is rising and money is losing value. (pp. 97, 278)

**Inflationary gap** The amount by which real GDP exceeds potential GDP. (p. 161)

**Inflation rate** The percentage change in the price level from one year to the next. (p. 142)

**Interest** The income that capital earns. (p. 4)

**Interest rate parity** A situation in which the rates of return on assets in different currencies are equal. (p. 450)

**Intermediate good** An item that is produced by one firm, bought by another firm, and used as a component of a final good or service. (p. 108)

**Inverse relationship** A relationship between variables that move in opposite directions. (p. 21)

**Investment** The purchase of new plant, equipment, and buildings and additions to inventories. (p. 110)

**Investment demand** The relationship between investment and real interest rate, other things remaining the same. (p. 191)

**Job rationing** The practice of paying a real wage rate above the equilibrium level and then rationing jobs by some method. (p. 188)

**Job search** The activity of looking for acceptable vacant jobs. (p. 187)

**Keynesian** An economist who believes that left alone, the economy would rarely operate at full employment and that to achieve full employment, active help from fiscal policy and monetary policy is required. (p. 166)

**Keynesian theory of the business cycle** A theory that regards volatile expectations as the main source of economic fluctuations. (p. 338)

**Labor** The work time and work effort that people devote to producing goods and services. (p. 3)

**Labor force** The sum of the people who are employed and who are unemployed. (p. 130)

**Labor force participation rate** The percentage of the working-age population who are members of the labor force. (p. 131)

**Labor productivity** Real GDP per hour of work. (pp. 195, 211)

**Laffer curve** The relationship between the tax rate and the amount of tax revenue collected. (p. 370)

**Land** The gifts of nature that we use to produce goods and services. (p. 3)

**Law of demand** Other things remaining the same, the higher the price of a good, the smaller is the quantity demanded of it. (p. 59)

**Law of diminishing returns** As a firm uses more of a variable input, with a given quantity of other inputs (fixed inputs), the marginal product of the variable input eventually diminishes. (pp. 182, 212)

**Law of supply** Other things remaining the same, the higher the price of a good, the greater is the quantity supplied of it. (p. 64)

**Learning-by-doing** People become more productive in an activity (learn) just by repeatedly producing a particular good or service (doing). (pp. 43, 195)

**Linear relationship** A relationship between two variables that is illustrated by a straight line. (p. 20)

**Liquidity** The property of being instantly convertible into a means of payment with little loss in value. (p. 236)

**Long-run aggregate supply curve** The relationship between the real GDP supplied and the price level in the long run when real GDP equals potential GDP. (p. 150)

**Long-run macroeconomic equilibrium** A situation that occurs when real GDP equals potential GDP—the economy is on its long-run aggregate supply curve. (p. 159)

**Long-run Phillips curve** A curve that shows the relationship between inflation and unemployment when the actual inflation rate equals the expected inflation rate. (p. 290)

**Lucas wedge** The accumulated loss of output that results from a slowdown in the growth rate of real GDP per person. (p. 93)

**M1** A measure of money that consists of currency and traveler's checks plus checking deposits owned by individuals and businesses. (p. 235)

**M2** A measure of money that consists of M1 plus time deposits, savings deposits, and money market mutual funds and other deposits. (p. 235)

**Macroeconomic long run** A time frame that is sufficiently long for real GDP to return to potential GDP so that full employment prevails. (p. 150)

**Macroeconomics** The study of the performance of the national economy and the global economy. (p. 2)

**Macroeconomic short run** A period during which some money prices are sticky and real GDP might be below, above, or at potential GDP and unemployment might be above, below, or at the natural rate of unemployment. (p. 151)

**Margin** When a choice is changed by a small amount or by a little at a time, the choice is made at the margin. (p. 11)

**Marginal benefit** The benefit that a person receives from consuming one more unit of a good or service. It is measured as the maximum amount that a person is willing to pay for one more unit of the good or service. (pp. 11, 36)

**Marginal benefit curve** A curve that shows the relationship between the marginal benefit of a good and the quantity of that good consumed. (p. 36)

**Marginal cost** The opportunity cost of producing one more unit of a good or service. It is the best alternative forgone. It is calculated as the increase in total cost divided by the increase in output. (pp. 11, 35)

**Marginal product of labor** The additional real GDP produced by an additional hour of labor when all other influences on production remain the same. (p. 182)

**Marginal propensity to consume** The fraction of a change in disposable income that is consumed. It is calculated as the change in consumption expenditure divided by the change in disposable income. (p. 308)

**Marginal propensity to import** The fraction of an increase in real GDP that is spent on imports. (p. 311)

**Marginal propensity to save** The fraction of an increase in disposable income that is saved. It is calculated as the change in saving divided by the change in disposable income. (p. 308)

**Market** Any arrangement that enables buyers and sellers to get information and to do business with each other. (p. 44)

**McCallum rule** A rule that adjusts the growth rate of the monetary base to target the inflation rate but also to take into account changes in the trend productivity growth rate and fluctuations in aggregate demand. (p. 401)

**Means of payment** A method of settling a debt. (p. 234)

**Microeconomics** The study of the choices that individuals and businesses make, the way those choices interact, and the influence governments exert on them. (p. 2)

**Minimum wage** A regulation that makes the hiring of labor below a specified wage rate illegal. (p. 189)

**Monetarist** An economist who believes that the economy is self-regulating and that it will normally operate at full employment, provided that monetary policy is not erratic and that the pace of money growth is kept steady. (p. 167)

**Monetarist theory of the business cycle** A theory that regards fluctuations in the quantity of money as the main source of economic fluctuations. (p. 340)

**Monetary base** The sum of the Federal Reserve notes, coins, and banks' deposits at the Fed. (p. 247)

**Monetary policy** The Fed conducts the nation's monetary policy by changing in interest rates and adjusting the quantity of money. (pp. 101, 157, 244)

**Money** Any commodity or token that is generally acceptable as a means of payment. (p. 234)

**Money market mutual fund** A fund operated by a financial institution that sells shares in the fund and holds liquid assets such as U.S. Treasury bills and short-term commercial bills. (p. 238)

**Money multiplier** The amount by which a change in the monetary base is multiplied to determine the resulting change in the quantity of money. (p. 249)

**Money price** The number of dollars that must be given up in exchange for a good or service. (p. 58)

**Money wage rate** The number of dollars that an hour of labor earns. (p. 182)

**Multiplier** The amount by which a change in autonomous expenditure is magnified or multiplied to determine the change in equilibrium expenditure and real GDP. (p. 316)

**National saving** The sum of private saving (saving by households and businesses) and government saving. (p. 111)

**Natural rate of unemployment** The unemployment rate when the economy is at full employment. There is no cyclical unemployment; all unemployment is frictional and structural. (pp. 138, 150)

**Needs-tested spending** Government spending on programs that pay benefits to suitably qualified people and businesses. (p. 379)

**Negative relationship** A relationship between variables that move in opposite directions. (p. 21)

**Neoclassical growth theory** A theory of economic growth that proposes that real GDP grows because technological change induces a level of saving and investment that makes capital per hour of labor grow. (p. 217)

**Net borrower** A country that is borrowing more from the rest of the world than it is lending to it. (p. 440)

**Net exports** The value of exports minus the value of imports. (pp. 110, 416, 441)

**Net investment** Net increase in the capital stock—gross investment minus depreciation. (p. 111)

**Net lender** A country that is lending more to the rest of the world than it is borrowing from it. (p. 440)

**Net taxes** Taxes paid to governments minus transfer payments received from governments. (p. 110)

**New classical theory of the business cycle** A rational expectations theory of the business cycle that regards unanticipated fluctuations in aggregate demand as the main source of economic fluctuations. (p. 342)

**New growth theory** A theory of economic growth based on the idea that real GDP per person grows because of the choices that people make in the pursuit of ever greater profit and that growth can persist indefinitely. (p. 219)

**New Keynesian** A Keynesian who holds the view that not only is the money wage rate sticky but that prices of goods and services are also sticky. (p. 166)

**New Keynesian theory of the business cycle** A rational expectations theory of the business cycle that regards unanticipated fluctuations in aggregate demand as the main source of economic fluctuations but leaves room for anticipated demand fluctuations to play a role. (p. 342)

**Nominal GDP** The value of the final goods and services produced in a given year valued at the prices that prevailed in that same year. It is a more precise name for GDP (p. 115)

**Nontariff barrier** Any action other than a tariff that restricts international trade. (p. 423)

**Normal good** A good for which demand increases as income increases. (p. 62)

**North American Free Trade Agreement** An agreement, which became effective on January 1, 1994, to eliminate all barriers to international trade between the United States, Canada, and Mexico after a 15-year phasing in period. (p. 424)

**Official settlements account** A record of the change in a country's official reserves. (p. 438)

**Okun gap** The gap between real GDP and potential GDP, and so is another name for the output gap. (p. 93)

**One third rule** The rule that, with no change in technology, a 1 percent increase in capital per hour of labor brings, on the average, a one third of 1 percent increase in real GDP per hour of labor. (p. 212)

**Open market operation** The purchase or sale of government securities—U.S. Treasury bills and bonds—by the Federal Reserve System in the open market. (p. 246)

**Opportunity cost** The highest-valued alternative that we give up to something. (p. 10)

**Peak** The point at which a business cycle turns from expansion into recession. (p. 128)

**Phillips curve** A curve that shows a relationship between inflation and unemployment. (p. 288)

**Positive relationship** A relationship between two variables that move in the same direction. (p. 20)

**Potential GDP** The quantity of real GDP at full employment. (pp. 89, 139)

**Preferences** A description of a person's likes and dislikes. (p. 36)

**Present value** The amount of money that, if invested today, will grow to be as large as a given future amount when the interest that it will earn is taken into account. (p. 374)

**Price level** The average level of prices as measured by a price index. (pp. 97, 116)

**Private sector surplus or deficit** An amount equal to saving minus investment. (p. 441)

**Production efficiency** A situation in which the economy cannot produce more of one good without producing less of some other good. (p. 33)

**Production function** The relationship between real GDP and the quantity of labor when all other influences on production remain the same. (p. 181)

**Production possibilities frontier** The boundary between the combinations of goods and services that can be produced and the combinations that cannot. (p. 32)

**Productivity curve** A relationship that shows how real GDP per hour of labor changes as the amount of capital per hour of labor changes with a given state of technology. (p. 211)

**Productivity growth slowdown** A slowdown in the growth rate of output per person. (p. 89)

**Profit** The income earned by entrepreneurship. (p. 4)

**Property rights** Social arrangements that govern the ownership, use, and disposal of resources or factors of production, goods, and services that are enforceable in the courts. (p. 44)

**Purchasing power parity** The equal value of different monies. (p. 450)

**Quantity demanded** The amount of a good or service that consumers plan to buy during a given time period at a particular price. (p. 59)

**Quantity of labor demanded** The labor hours hired by the firms in the economy. (p. 182)

**Quantity of labor supplied** The number of labor hours that all households in the economy plan to work. (p. 184)

**Quantity supplied** The amount of a good or service that producers plan to sell during a given time period at a particular price. (p. 64)

**Quantity theory of money** The proposition that in the long run, an increase in the quantity of money brings an equal percentage increase in the price level. (p. 267)

**Quota** A quantitative restriction on the import of a particular good, which specifies the maximum amount that can be imported in a given time period. (p. 426)

**Rational expectation** The most accurate forecast possible, a forecast that uses all the available information, including knowledge of the relevant economic forces that influence the variable being forecasted. (p. 285)

**Real business cycle theory** A theory that regards random fluctuations in productivity as the main source of economic fluctuations. (p. 345)

**Real Gross Domestic Product (real GDP)** The value of final goods and services produced in a given year when valued at constant prices. (pp. 89, 115)

**Real interest rate** The nominal interest rate adjusted for inflation; the nominal interest rate minus the inflation rate. (p. 190)

**Real wage rate** The quantity of goods ands services that an hour's work can buy. It is equal to the money wage rate divided by the price level. (pp. 133, 182)

**Recession** There are two common definitions of recession. They are (1) A business cycle phase in which real GDP decreases for at least two successive quarters. (p. 90) (2) A significant decline in activity spread across the economy, lasting for more than a few months, visible in industrial production, employment, real income, and wholesale-retail trade. (p. 128)

**Recessionary gap** The amount by which potential GDP exceeds real GDP. (p. 160)

**Reference base period** The period in which the CPI is defined to be 100. (p. 140)

**Relative price** The ratio of the price of one good or service to the price of another good or service. A relative price is an opportunity cost. (p. 58)

**Rent** The income that land earns. (p. 4)

**Rent seeking** Lobbying and other political activity that seek to capture the gains from trade. (p. 430)

**Required reserve ratio** The ratio of reserves to deposits that banks are required, by regulation, to hold. (p. 242)

**Reserve ratio** The fraction of a bank's total deposits that are held in reserves. (p. 242)

**Reserves** Cash in a bank's vault plus the bank's deposits at Federal Reserve banks. (p. 237)

**Ricardo-Barro effect** The equivalence of financing government purchases by taxes or by borrowing. (p. 374)

**Saving** The amount of income that households have left after they have paid their taxes and bought their consumption goods and services. (p. 110)

**Saving function** The relationship between saving and disposable income, other things remaining the same. (p. 307)

**Savings and loan association (S&L)** A depository institution that receives checking deposits and savings deposits and that makes personal, commercial, and home-purchase loans (p. 238)

**Savings bank** A depository institution, owned by its depositors, that accepts savings deposits and makes mortgage loans. (p. 238)

**Saving supply** The relationship between saving and the real interest rate, other things remaining the same. (p. 193)

**Scarcity** Our inability to satisfy all our wants. (p. 2)

**Scatter diagram** A diagram that plots the value of one economic variable against the value of another. (p. 19)

**Self-interest** The choices that you think are the best for you. (p. 5)

**Short-run aggregate supply curve** A curve that shows the relationship between the quantity of real GDP supplied and the price level in the short run when the money wage rate, other resource prices, and potential GDP remain constant. (p. 151)

**Short-run macroeconomic equilibrium** A situation that occurs when the quantity of real GDP demanded equals quantity of real GDP supplied—at the point of intersection of the $AD$ curve and the $SAS$ curve. (p. 158)

**Short-run Phillips curve** A curve that shows the tradeoff between inflation and unemployment, when the expected inflation rate and the natural rate of unemployment remain the same. (p. 288)

**Slope** The change in the value of the variable measured on the $y$-axis divided by the change in the value of the variable measured on the $x$-axis. (p. 24)

**Social interest** Choices that are the best for society as a whole. (p. 5)

**Stagflation** The combination of recession and inflation. (p. 163)

**Stock** A quantity that exists at a point in time. (p. 111)

**Structural surplus or deficit** The budget balance that would occur if the economy were at full employment and real GDP were equal to potential GDP. (p. 380)

**Structural unemployment** The unemployment that arises when changes in technology or international competition change the skills needed to perform jobs or change the locations of jobs. (p. 138)

**Subsistence real wage rate** The minimum real wage rate needed to maintain life. (p. 216)

**Substitute** A good that can be used in place of another good. (p. 61)

**Supply** The relationship between the quantity of a good that producers plan to sell and the price of the good when all other influences on sellers' plans remain the same. It is described by a supply schedule and illustrated by a supply curve. (p. 64)

**Supply curve** A curve that shows the relationship between the quantity supplied and the price of a good when all other influences on producers' planned sales remain the same. (p. 64)

**Supply of labor** The relationship between the quantity of labor supplied and the real wage rate when all other influences on work plans remain the same. (p. 184)

**Supply-side effects** The effects of fiscal policy on employment, potential GDP, and aggregate supply. (p. 368)

**Tariff** A tax that is imposed by the importing country when an imported good crosses its international boundary. (p. 423)

**Tax multiplier** The magnification effect of a change in taxes on aggregate demand. (p. 377)

**Tax wedge** The gap between the before-tax and after-tax wage rates. (p. 369)

**Taylor rule** A rule that adjusts the federal funds rate to target the inflation rate and to take into account deviations of the inflation rate from its target and deviations of real GDP from potential GDP. (p. 402)

**Technological change** The development of new goods and better ways of producing goods and services. (p. 38)

**Terms of trade** The quantity of goods and services that a country exports to pay for its imports of goods and services. (p. 418)

**Thrift institutions** Thrift institutions include savings and loan associations, savings banks, and credit unions. (p. 238)

**Time-series graph** A graph that measures time (for example, months or years) on the $x$-axis and the variable or variables in which we are interested on the $y$-axis. (p. 18)

**Tradeoff** An exchange—giving up one thing to get something else. (p. 9)

**Trend** The general tendency for a variable to move in one direction. (p. 18)

**Trough** The point at which a business cycle turns from recession into expansion. (p. 128)

**Unemployment rate** The percentage of the people in the labor force who are unemployed. (pp. 95, 131)

**U.S. interest rate differential** A gap equal to the U.S. interest rate minus the foreign interest rate. (p. 445)

**U.S. official reserves** The government's holdings of foreign currency. (p. 438)

**Velocity of circulation** The average number of times a dollar of money is used annually to buy the goods and services that make up GDP. (p. 267)

**Voluntary export restraint** An agreement between two governments in which the government of the exporting country agrees to restrain the volume of its own exports. (p. 426)

**Wages** The income that labor earns. (p. 4)

**Wealth** The market value of all the things that people own. (p. 111)

**Working-age population** The total number of people aged 16 years and over who are not in jail, hospital, or some other form of institutional care. (p. 130)

**World Trade Organization** An international organization that places greater obligations on its member countries to observe the GATT rules. (p. 423)

# INDEX

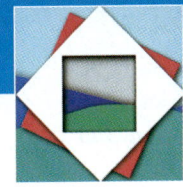

Key terms and pages on which they are defined appear in **boldface**.

**Above full-employment equilibrium, 160,** 160–161
**Absolute advantage, 43**
Account, money as unit of, 234–235
Africa. *See also specific countries*
 economic growth in, 207
 water in, 8
Age, unemployment and, 136, 137
**Aggregate demand, 155,** 155–158. *See also AS-AD* model
 changes in, 156–158
 classical view of fluctuations in, 166–167
 expansion of 1990s and, 350
 fluctuations in, macroeconomic equilibrium and, 162–163
 increase in, price level and, 324–325
 inflation and, 279, 282
 Keynesian view of fluctuations in, 166
 monetarist view of fluctuations in, 167
 real GDP and price level and, 321
 recession of 2001 and, 351
Aggregate demand curve, 155–156
 shifts of, 157, 158
 substitution effect and, 156
 wealth effect and, 155–156
Aggregate demand shocks
 Keynesian feedback rules with, 393–394
 monetarist fixed rules with, 392–393
Aggregate expenditure, 110
 algebra of, 328
 convergence toward equilibrium, 314, 315
 price level and, 321–323
 real GDP and, 321
Aggregate expenditure curve, 312

algebra of, 328
Aggregate expenditure schedule, 312
**Aggregate hours,** 132–133, **133**
Aggregate income, 109
**Aggregate planned expenditure, 306**
 real GDP and, 312, 313
**Aggregate production function, 150**
Aggregate supply. *See also AS-AD* model
 in action *(Reading Between the Lines),* 168–169
 changes in, 153–154
 classical view of fluctuations in, 167
 expansion of 1990s and, 350
 fluctuations in, macroeconomic equilibrium and, 163
 inflation and, 281–282
 Keynesian view of fluctuations in, 166
 long-run, 150–151
 monetarist view of fluctuations in, 167
 recession of 2001 and, 351
 short-run, 151, 152
Aggregate supply curve
 long-run, 150, 151
 movements along, 152
 movements along *LAS* and *SAS* curves and, 152
 short-run, 151
Aggregate supply shocks, stabilizing, 395
Agrarian Revolution, 6
Agricultural Revolution, 51
Airport security, cost and benefit of *(Reading Between the Lines),* 46–47
**Allocative efficiency, 37**
Amazon.com, 107
Amazon rainforest, disappearance of, 7–8
Andreesen, Marc, 219
Animal spirits, 338
AOL, 107
Appreciation of currencies, 443

Argentina, quantity theory of money in *(Reading Between the Lines),* 272–273
*AS-AD* model, 149–170, 409. *See also* Aggregate demand *entries;* Aggregate supply *entries*
 in action *(Reading Between the Lines),* 168–169
 aggregate demand and, 155–158
 aggregate supply and, 150–154
 business cycles and, 165, 338, 344
 classical view and, 166–167
 economic growth in U.S. and, 164
 evolving U.S. economy during 1963-2000 and, 165
 inflation in U.S. and, 165
 Keynesian view and, 166
 macroeconomic equilibrium and, 158–163
 monetarist view and, 167
 quantity theory of money and, 268–269
 real GDP and price level determination and, 321–325
Asia. *See also specific countries*
 economic growth in, 208
 economic growth in *(Reading Between the Lines),* 222–223
Asian-Pacific Economic Cooperation, 424
Assets
 on bank's balance sheet, 237
 liquid, 238
ATS accounts, 240
Auerbach, Alan, 374
Australia, water in, 8
**Automatic fiscal policy, 377**
**Automatic stabilizers, 379,** 379–381
Autonomous consumption, 308
**Autonomous expenditure, 313**
 multiplier and, 316–317
Axes of graphs, 17

Badu, Erykah, 305, 321
**Balanced budget, 364**

I-1

**Balanced budget multiplier, 377**
  algebra of, 331
Balanced trade, 419
  with tariffs, 425
**Balance of payments accounts, 438**
Balance sheets
  of banks, 237, 240
  of Fed, 246–247
Bank(s)
  central, 244
  commercial, 237–238
  Federal Reserve, 244, 245
  money creation by, 242–243
  savings, 238
Bank failures, 354
Bank Insurance Fund, 239
Bank runs, 239
Barro, Robert J., 176–178, 374
**Barter, 234**
Base year, 115–116
**Below full-employment equilibrium, 160**
Benefits
  of airport security *(Reading Between the Lines)*, 46–47
  marginal. *See* Marginal benefit
Berlin Wall, fall of, 5
Bhagwati, Jagdish, 460–462
Bias in CPI, 143
**Big tradeoff, 10**
Bina, Eric, 219
Bloomberg, Michael R., 305, 321
Board of Governors of Fed, 244
  chairman of, 244–245
Boeing, 427
Boorstin, Daniel J., 81
Borrowing short, 238
Brazil, hyperinflation in, 99, 277, 300, 301
Brunner, Karl, 167
Budget, federal. *See* Federal budget
**Budget deficits, 8, 364**
  cyclical, 380, 381
  of governments, 99
  over business cycle, 379–380
  planned, 361
  structural, 380, 381
**Budget surpluses, 364**
  cyclical, 380, 381
  of governments, 99
  structural, 380, 381
Bureau of Economic Analysis, 113
Bureau of Labor Statistics, CPI and, 140
Burns, Arthur, 389
Bush, George H. W., 244, 390
**Business cycle(s), 90,** 91, 128–129, 335–358, 410–411. *See also* Expansion(s); Great Depression; Recession(s)
  *AS-AD* model and, 338, 344
  budget deficits over, 379–380
  dates of, 128–129
  expansion of 2003, 102–103
  forecasts of, 121
  impulses and mechanisms of, 336–337
  investment and capital and, 337–338
  Keynesian theory of, 338–340
  macroeconomic equilibrium and, 160–161
  monetarist theory of, 340–342
  monetary policy and, 389
  during 1990s and 2000s, 349–351
  patterns of, 336, 337
  rational expectations theories of, 342–344
  real business cycle theory and, 345–349
  stabilization of, 377–381
  turning points of, 319–320
  in United States, 165
  in U.S. *(Reading Between the Lines),* 356–357

California, water in, 8
Canada
  economic growth in, 207
  NAFTA and. *See* North American Free Trade Agreement
  water in, 8
**Capital, 4,** 111
  business cycles and, 337–338
  change in quantity of, 153
  debt and, 366
  human. *See* Human capital
  new, investment in, economic growth and, 209–210
**Capital account, 438**

**Capital accumulation, 38**
  classical theory and, 216
**Capital consumption, 111**
Capital markets
  equilibrium in, 193–194
  unanticipated inflation in, 284–285
**Capital stock, 190**
Card, David, 189
Cardoso, Fernando Henrique, 277
Carter, Jimmy, 245, 390
Causation, correlation and, 20
Cause and effect, 13
Central America, economic growth in, 207
**Central banks, 244**
*Ceteris paribus* assumption, **13**
  graphing relationships involving more than two variables, 26–27
**Chain-weighted output index, 116**
**Change in demand, 60,** 60–63
  in aggregate demand, 156–158
  change in quantity demanded versus, 62–63
  for dollars, 444–445
  factors causing, 61–62
  price and quantity and, 70–71
**Change in supply, 65,** 65–67
  in aggregate supply, 153–154
  change in quantity supplied versus, 66–67
  of dollars, 447
  factors causing, 65–66
  of labor, 185
  price and quantity and, 71
**Change in the quantity demanded, 63**
  change in demand versus, 62–63
**Change in the quantity supplied, 66**
  change in supply versus, 66–67
Checks, 236
China
  competition with, 415
  economic growth in, 205, 208
  real GDP in, 120–121
Choice(s), 2. *See also* Preferences
  change associated with, 10
  at margin, 11
  new growth theory and, 219
  tradeoffs and, 9

Circular flow
  of expenditure and income, GDP and, 109–110
  household choices and, 44, 45
Circulation, velocity of, 267–268, 269
**Classical dichotomy, 180**
Classical economists, 228
**Classical growth theory, 215,** 215–216
**Classical model, 179–202, 180**
  changes in potential GDP and, 196–199
  dynamic aspects of, 195
  investment, saving, and interest rate in, 190–194
  labor market and potential GDP in, 182–186
  real GDP and employment in, 180–181
  unemployment at full employment in, 187–189
**Classical view, 166,** 166–167
Clinton, Bill, 245
**Commercial banks, 237,** 237–238
Communist states, 5
**Comparative advantage, 40,** 40–41, 417, **418,** 429
  dynamic, 43
  in global economy, 421
Compensation. *See also* Wage(s); Wage rate
  in GDP, 113
**Competitive market, 58**
**Complements, 61**
  in production, 66
Congress of United States, budgetary role of, 362
Consumer Expenditure Survey, 140
**Consumer price index (CPI), 97, 140,** 140–143
  biased, 143
  construction of, 140–142
  inflation measurement and, 142–143
Consumption
  autonomous, 308
  changes in, gains from trade and, 419–421
  as function of real GDP, 311
  induced, 308

  influences on, 308–310
  interest rate and, 263
  planned, 306–307
**Consumption expenditure, 109,** 111
  taxes on, 369
**Consumption function, 307,** 308
  algebra of, 328
  slope of, 309
  for United States, 310, 311
Convertible paper money, 246
Coordinates, 17
Corporate scandals, 7
Correlation, causation and, 20
Cost(s)
  of airport security (Reading Between the Lines), 46–47
  of anticipated inflation, 286–287
  of economic growth, 38
  incentives to push up, 398
  marginal. *See* Marginal cost
  opportunity. *See* Opportunity cost
**Cost-push inflation, 281,** 281–283
Cost-push inflation shocks, 395
  feedback rules with, 397–398
  monetarist fixed rules with, 397, 398
**Council of Economic Advisers, 363**
Cournot, Antoine-Augustin, 82
CPI basket, 140
Credibility, of monetary policy, 399–400
Credit cards, 236
**Creditor nations, 440**
**Credit unions, 238**
**Cross-section graphs, 18,** 19
**Crowding-out effect, 373**
**Currency, 235.** *See also* Dollar(s); Foreign exchange market
**Currency appreciation, 443**
**Currency depreciation, 443**
**Currency drain, 249**
**Current account, 99,** 99–100, **438**
  balance of, 438, 441
Curves, 20. *See also specific curves, e.g.* Demand curve
**Cyclical surpluses/deficits, 380**
**Cyclical unemployment, 138**

Debt
  capital and, 366

  federal, of United States, 8
  government, 366
  international, 376
Debt interest in federal budget, 364
**Debtor nations, 440**
Decisions, market coordination of, 45
Deficits
  budget. *See* Budget deficits
  government sector, 441
  international, 99–100
  private sector, 441
  significance of, 100
**Deflation, 97**
**Demand, 59,** 59–63
  aggregate. *See* Aggregate demand entries; AS-AD model
  change in. *See* Change in demand
  effective, 174
  in foreign exchange market, 444
  gasoline prices and (Reading Between the Lines), 74–77
  for investment, 191–192
  for labor. *See* Demand for labor
  law of, 59, 82–83, 444, 445
  for money, 258–261
**Demand curve, 60**
  aggregate, 155–156, 157, 158
  for money, 259
  movement along, 63
  shift of, 63
**Demand for labor, 182**
  changes in, 184
  diminishing marginal product and, 183–184
  potential GDP and, 182–184
Demand for money curve, 259
**Demand-pull inflation, 279,** 279–281
Demand schedule, 60
Demographics, of unemployment, 188
Denison, Edward F., 211
Deposit(s), 235, 236
Deposit insurance, 239–240
**Depository institutions, 237,** 237–241
  commercial banks as, 237–238
  economic functions of, 238–239
  financial innovation and, 240–241
  regulation and deregulation of,

239–240
thrift institutions as, 238
Depository Institutions Deregulation and Monetary Control Act of 1980, 240
Deposit rules, 240
**Depreciation, 111,** 190
of currencies, 443
Depressions, 91. *See also* Business cycle(s); Great Depression
Deregulation of depository institutions, 240, 241
Diminishing returns, law of, 182, 183, 212, 338
Diocletain, 277
**Direct relationships, 20,** 20–21
**Discount rate, 245,** 247
**Discouraged workers, 131**
Discoveries, new growth theory and, 219
**Discretionary fiscal policy, 377,** 377–379
**Discretionary policies, 392**
Dismal science, 216
**Disposable income, 157, 306**
consumption and saving plans and, 306–307
saving and, 192
Dissaving, 308, 373
Diversity as argument for protection, 429
Division of labor, 52–53
Dollar(s)
changes in demand for, 444–445
changes in supply of, 447
decline in value against euro *(Reading Between the Lines)*, 452–453
depreciation of, 449
Double coincidence of wants, 234
Double counting, 108
**Dumping, 427**
as argument for protection, 427–428
Dupuit, Jules, 83
**Dynamic comparative advantage, 43**
Dynamic general equilibrium analysis, 345

Economic coordination, 44–45

Economic environment, financial innovation and, 241
**Economic growth, 38,** 38–39, **89,** 89–94, 205–224
in Asia *(Reading Between the Lines)*, 222–223
benefits and costs of, 94
business cycles and, 348
causes of, 209–210
classical theory of, 215–216
cost of, 38
global, 91–92
growth accounting and, 211–214
long-term trends in, 206–208
Lucas wedge and, 93
macroeconomic equilibrium and, 160
measurement of, 118–121
neoclassical theory of, 217–219
new growth theory of, 219–221
Okun gap and, 93
rates of, 91–92
in United States, 164, 206
in U.S., 89–91
in United States and Hong Kong, 39
in world economy, 207–208
**Economic growth rate, 118**
**Economic models, 12**
building, 12
graphs used in, 20–23
testing, 12–13
unrelated variables in, 23
variables with maximums or minimums in, 22, 23
Economic Report of the President, 363
**Economics, 2**
defined, 2
as dismal science, 216
obstacles and pitfalls in, 13–14
scope of, 9, 51
as social science, 12–14
**Economic theories, 12**
Economic way of thinking, 9–11
**Economic welfare, 118**
bases for comparisons of, 118–120
business cycle forecasts and, 121
international comparisons of, 120–121
Economies of scale, gains from trade

and, 422
Economists, agreement/disagreement among, 14
Education, economic growth and, 214
Effective demand, 174
Efficiency. *See also* Inefficiency
allocative, 37
production, 37
**Efficiency wage, 188,** 188–189
Electronic money *(Reading Between the Lines)*, 252–253
Employment, 94. *See also* Job *entries*; Labor *entries*; Unemployment
aggregate hours and, 132–133
as argument for protection, 428
full, increase in quantity of money at, 266
full, potential GDP and, 368
real GDP and, 180–181
wages and. *See* Wage(s)
**Employment Act of 1946, 362,** 362–363
**Employment-to-population ratio, 132**
Energy price shocks, productivity growth slowdown and, 214
Enron, 7
Entrants, 135
**Entrepreneurship, 4**
Environment, economic, financial innovation and, 241
Environmental quality
as argument for protection, 429
economic welfare comparisons and, 119
productivity growth slowdown and, 214
**Equation of exchange, 268**
Equilibrium, 68–69
in capital market, 193–194
in foreign exchange market, 448
free trade, 421
labor market, 185–186
macroeconomic. *See* Macroeconomic equilibrium
in money market, 261–262
**Equilibrium expenditure, 314,** 314–315
algebra of, 329
**Equilibrium price, 68**

**Equilibrium quantity, 68**
Equity capital, requirements for, for banks, 240
Euro, dollar's decline against *(Reading Between the Lines),* 452–453
Eurodollars, 241
**Excess reserves, 242**
Exchange
 equation of, 268
 money as medium of, 234
Exchange rates. *See* Foreign exchange *entries*
**Expansion(s), 90, 128**
 inventories in *(Reading Between the Lines),* 326–328
 of 1990s, 349–350
 turning points of, 320
 of 2002–2003, 127
 of 2002–2003 *(Reading Between the Lines),* 102–103, 122–123, 356–357
 in United States, 336
Expectations
 aggregate demand and, 156–157
 for foreign exchange rate, 449–450
Expected future income
 changes in demand related to, 62
 saving and, 192–193
Expected future prices
 change in supply and, 66
 changes in demand related to, 61–62
Expected profit rate, investment and, 190–191
Expenditure(s)
 aggregate, 110, 314, 315, 321–323, 328
 autonomous, 313, 316–317
 circular flow of income and, 109–110
 consumption, 109, 111, 113
 equilibrium, 314–315, 329
 in federal budget, 363–364, 365, 366
 induced, 313, 316
 planned, 306–311
Expenditure approach to GDP, 113
Exploitation as argument for protection, 430
**Exports, 110, 416.** *See also* International trade; Trade restrictions
 net, 110, 113, 263, 416, 441–442

Factor markets, 44
**Factors of production, 3,** 3–4. *See also* Capital; Entrepreneurship; Labor; Land
Fair Labor Standards Act, 189
Fallacies
 of composition, 13
 *post hoc,* 13–14
**Federal budget, 362**
 deficits in. *See* Budget deficits
 historical perspective on, 364–366
 institutions and laws affecting, 362–363
 surpluses in, 364, 380, 381
 of 2004, 363–364
 U.S., in global perspective, 367
Federal Deposit Insurance Corporation, 239, 354
**Federal funds rate, 244**
**Federal Open Market Committee, 244**
**Federal Reserve System, 244,** 244–251. *See also* Monetary policy
 balance sheet of, 246–247
 chairman of Board of Governors of, 244–245
 control of quantity of money by, 247–251
 effect of actions on economy, 263–265
 in foreign exchange market, 450–451
 goals and targets of, 244
 Great Depression and, 354–355
 performance during 1973–2003, 389–391
 policy tools of, 245–246
 structure of, 244
**Feedback-rule policies, 392**
 with cost-push inflation shocks, 397–398
 Keynesian, with aggregate demand shocks, 393–394
 with monetarist fixed rules, 396–397

Feldstein, Martin, 370
**Final goods, 108**
**Financial innovation, 240,** 240–241
 quantity of money held and, 258
Financial property, 44
Finland, water in, 8
**Firms, 44**
**Fiscal imbalance, 375**
**Fiscal policy, 101, 157,** 361–384, **362**
 aggregate demand and, 157
 automatic, 377
 business cycle stabilization and, 377–381
 discretionary, 377–379
 employment and potential GDP and, 368–370
 expansion of 1990s and, 350
 federal budget and, 362–367
 generational effects of, 374–376
 investment, saving, and economic growth and, 371–374
 recession of 2001 and, 350
 of today *(Reading Between the Lines),* 382–383
Fiscal year, 362
Fisher, Irving, 299, 410
Fixed price(s), 306
Fixed price level, real GDP with, 312–315
**Fixed-rule policies, 392**
 monetarist, with aggregate demand shocks, 392–393
**Flows, 111**
Ford Motor Company, 10
**Foreign exchange market, 443**
 changes in demand for dollars in, 444–445
 changes in exchange rate and, 448–449
 changes in supply of dollars in, 447
 demand in, 444
 equilibrium in, 448
 exchange rate expectations and, 449–450
 Fed in, 450–451
 law of demand for foreign exchange and, 444, 445
 law of supply of foreign exchange

and, 446–447
supply in, 446
**Foreign exchange rates, 443**
aggregate demand and, 157
changes in, 448–449
expectations for, 449–450
Forster, E. M., 174
France, economic growth in, 207
Free trade equilibrium, 421
**Frictional unemployment, 137,** 137–138
Friedman, Milton, 167, 299, 300, 353, 392
**Full employment, 138**
increase in quantity of money at, 266
potential GDP and, 368
Full Employment and Balanced Growth Act of 1978, 363

Gains from trade, 40–43, 458–459
calculating, 421
gains from globalization *(Reading Between the Lines)*, 432–433
international trade and, 417–422
in reality, 421–422
Gama, Vasco da, 457
Garn-St. Germain Depository Institutions Act of 1982, 240
Gasoline price, supply and demand and *(Reading Between the Lines)*, 74–77
Gates, Bill, 4, 6, 7
GDP. *See* Gross domestic product (GDP)
**GDP deflator, 116,** 116–117
**General Agreement on Tariffs and Trade, 423,** 458
General Electric, 44
*General Theory of Employment, Interest, and Money* (Keynes), 88, 338
**Generational accounting, 374,** 374–375
**Generational imbalance, 375,** 376
Germany
economic growth in, 207
hyperinflation in, 287, 300, 301
reunification of, 5
Globalization, 6
Gokhale, Jagadeesh, 374, 375

Goods
complements, 61
final, 108
inferior, 62
intermediate, 108
normal, 62
substitutes, 61
trade in, 416
**Goods and services, 3.** *See also* Goods; Services
purchases of, in federal budget, 364
Goods markets, 44
Government
circular flow of expenditure and income and, 110
regulation by. *See* Regulation of United States. *See* Federal *entries*; United States
**Government budget deficits, 99.** *See also* Budget deficits
**Government budget surpluses, 99.** *See also* Budget surpluses
**Government debt, 366**
**Government purchases, 110,** 113
**Government purchases multiplier, 377**
algebra of, 329, 330
Government saving, 373–374
**Government sector surplus or deficit, 441**
Government spending
Great Depression and, 355
needs-tested, 379
Graphs, 17–28
cross-section, 18, 19
of data, 17–20
in economic models, 20–23
with maximum and minimum values, 22, 23
misleading, 20
of more than two variables, 26–27
of negative (inverse) relationships, 21–22
of positive (direct) relationships, 20–21
scatter diagrams, 19–20
slope and, 20, 24–26
time-series, 18
of unrelated variables, 23

**Great Depression,** 8, **88,** 91, 336, 352–355
causes of, 353–354
risk of recurrence, 354–355
trade war during, 430
unemployment during, 95
Greenspan, Alan, 14, 244–245, 355, 388
Grisham, John, 40
**Gross domestic product (GDP), 108,** 108–123
circular flow of expenditure and income and, 109–110
definition of, 108
economic growth measurement and, 118–121
equality with income, 110
expenditure approach to measurement of, 113
financial flows and, 110
government budget surpluses and deficits as percentage of, 99
income approach to measurement of, 113–114
investment and, 110–111
net domestic product and, 111–112
nominal, 115
potential. *See* Potential GDP
real. *See* Real GDP
**Gross investment, 111,** 190
Gross private domestic investment, 113
**Growth accounting, 208, 211,** 211–214

Hamermesh, Daniel, 189
Hargreaves, James, 175
Health, economic welfare comparisons and, 119
Heston, Alan, 120
High-technology industries, economic growth and, 214
HIV/AIDS, 7
Homeland security multiplier, 377
Hong Kong, economic growth in, 39, 208
Households
circular flow of expenditure and income and, 109–110
production of, economic welfare

comparisons and, 118
**Human capital, 3, 195**
   increase in, labor productivity and, 197
   investment in, economic growth and, 210
   labor productivity and, 195
   lost due to unemployment, 96
Human nature, 11
Hume, David, 299, 458
Humphrey-Hawkins Act, 363
Hyperinflation, 98–99, 300, 301

Impact lag, 379
**Import(s), 110, 416.** *See also* International trade; Trade restrictions
   multiplier and, 318
Import function, 311, 328
**Incentives, 2**
   economic growth and, 209
   to push up costs, 398
   responding to, 11
   to save, taxes and, 372–373
Income
   aggregate, 109
   changes in demand related to, 62
   circular flow of expenditure and, 109–110
   disposable, 157, 192, 306–307
   expected, saving and, 192–193
   lost due to unemployment, 96
Income approach to GDP, 113–114
Income effect, 59
Income taxes
   multiplier and, 318–319, 320
   potential GDP and, 368–369
   saving and investment effects of, 372–373
Indirect taxes, 114
Induced consumption, 308
**Induced expenditure, 313**
   multiplier and, 316
**Induced taxes, 379**
Industrial Revolution, 6, 51, 175
Inefficiency. *See also* Efficiency *entries*
   of tariffs, 425
**Infant-industry argument, 427**
**Inferior goods, 62**
**Inflation, 89, 97, 97–99, 278,** 277–296, 300–301. *See also* Price level(s)
   anticipated, 285–286
   cost-push, 281–283. *See also* Cost-push inflation shocks
   demand-pull, 279–281
   economic welfare comparisons and, 118
   Fed tightening to avoid, 264–265
   forecasting, 285
   global, 98
   interest rates and, 292–293
   macroeconomic equilibrium and, 160
   measurement of, 142–143
   monetary policy credibility and, 399–400
   price level and, 278
   problems due to, 98–99
   real GDP and, 390–391
   unanticipated, 284–285, 286–287
   unemployment and, 288–291
   in United States, 97, 165, 277, 281, 283
**Inflationary gap, 161**
**Inflation rate, 142,** 278
Information Revolution, 6, 51, 175
Innovation(s)
   financial, 240–241, 258
   incentives for, 228–229
Insurance
   deposit, 239–240
   Medicare, 375
   unemployment compensation, 188
Intel Corporation, 6, 7
Intellectual property, 44
**Interest, 4**
   net, in GDP, 114
*Interest and Prices: Foundations of a Theory of Monetary Policy* (Woodford), 302
Interest rate(s)
   changing, 262
   determination of, 261–262, 293
   discount rate, 245, 247
   federal funds rate, 244
   inflation and, 292–293
   nominal, expected inflation and, 293
   quantity of money held and, 258
   real, 190, 191, 192, 287, 292, 372
   ripple effects of, 263–264
**Interest rate parity, 450**
**Intermediate goods, 108**
International debt, 376
International deficits, 99–100
International finance, 437–454
   foreign exchange market and. *See* Foreign exchange market
   international trade and, 438–442
International substitution, 321
International trade, 415–434
   economic growth and, 214
   gains from, 417–422
   gains from globalization and *(Reading Between the Lines)*, 432–433
   geographical patterns of, 416
   in goods, 416
   net exports and international borrowing and, 416
   restrictions on. *See* Trade restrictions
   in services, 416
   volume of, trends in, 416
International Trade Commission, 428
Internet Explorer, 219
Intertemporal substitution, 321, 346
Intertemporal substitution effect, 156
Inventories in expansion *(Reading Between the Lines)*, 326–328
**Inverse relationships, 21,** 21–22
**Investment, 110**
   business cycles and, 337–338
   domestic, private, gross, 113
   financing of, 110–111
   gross, 111, 190
   in human capital, economic growth and, 210
   income tax effects on, 372–373
   interest rate and, 263
   net, 111, 190
   in new capital, economic growth and, 209–210
   private, decisions regarding, 190–191
   sources of investment finance and, 371–372
**Investment demand, 191,** 191–192
Ireland, Peter N., 412–414
Italy, economic growth in, 207

Japan, economic growth in, 207
Job(s). *See* Employment; Labor *entries;* Unemployment; Wage(s)
Job leavers, 135
Job losers, 135
**Job rationing, 188,** 188–189
 unemployment and, 189
**Job search, 187,** 187–188

Keynes, John Maynard, 88, 101, 166, 174
Keynesian feedback rules, with aggregate demand shocks, 393–394
**Keynesian theory of the business cycle, 338,** 338–340
**Keynesian view, 166,** 305–332
 algebra of, 328–331
 fixed prices and expenditure plans and, 306–311
 multiplier and. *See* Multiplier
 real GDP with fixed price level and, 312–315
Knowledge, new growth theory and, 219–220
Kopper, Michael, 7
Korea, economic growth in, 208
Kotlikoff, Laurence, 374
Krueger, Alan, 189
Kydland, Finn, 345

**Labor, 3,** 4
 change in full-employment quantity of, 153
 demand for. *See* Demand for labor
 division of, 52–53
 foreign, competition with, 428–429
 marginal product of, 182, 183–184
 quantity demanded, 182
 quantity supplied, 184
 supply of. *See* Supply of labor
**Labor force, 130**
**Labor force participation rate, 131,** 185
Labor markets
 competition with China and, 415
 equilibrium in, 185–186
 indicators for, 130–132
 potential GDP and, 182–186

recession of 2001 and, 351
unanticipated inflation in, 284
**Labor productivity, 195, 195,** 211, 211–213. *See also* Productivity *entries*
 economic growth and, 209–210
 growth in 2003 *(Reading Between the Lines),* 200–201
 increase in, potential GDP and, 197–198, 199
 increasing speed of growth and, 214
 recession of 2001 and, 351
 technological change during productivity growth slowdown and, 214
 in United States, 199
Laffer, Arthur B., 370
**Laffer curve, 370**
**Land, 3**
Lardner, Dionysus, 82–83
Law-making lag, 379
**Law of demand, 59,** 82–83
 for foreign exchange, 444, 445
**Law of diminishing returns, 182,** 183, **212,** 338
**Law of supply, 64,** 82–83
 of foreign exchange, 446–447
**Learning-by-doing, 43, 195,** 427
Leisure, production-possibilities frontier for real GDP and, 180–181
Leisure time, economic welfare comparisons and, 119
Lending long, 238
Lending rules, 240
Liabilities on bank's balance sheet, 237
Life expectancy, economic welfare comparisons and, 119
**Linear relationships, 20,** 20–21
Line-item veto, 362
Liquid assets, 238
**Liquidity, 236**
 creation by depository institutions, 238
Loans
 by banks, 237–238
 finding sources for, 238–239
Local budgets, 367
Long, John, 345
Long run
 macroeconomic, 150, 266–269
 macroeconomic issues and, 88

**Long-run aggregate supply curve, 150,** 151
**Long-run macroeconomic equilibrium, 159**
**Long-run Phillips curve, 290**
Lucas, Robert E., Jr., 93, 174–175, 345
**Lucas wedge, 93,** 94
Lump-sum taxes multiplier, algebra of, 330

**M1, 235,** 236, 241, 260
 velocity of circulation of, 267
**M2, 235,** 236, 241, 260
 velocity of circulation of, 267, 269
McCallum, Bennett T., 401
**McCallum rule, 401,** 401–402, 403
McCormick, Cyrus, 229
Macroeconomic equilibrium, 158–163
 business cycle and, 160–161
 economic growth and inflation and, 160
 fluctuations in aggregate demand and, 162–163
 fluctuations in aggregate supply and, 163
 long-run, 159
 short-run, 158–159
**Macroeconomic long run, 150**
 effects of money on real GDP and price level in, 266–269
Macroeconomic policy, 101
 classical view of, 167
 monetarist view of, 167
**Macroeconomics, 2**
 classical view of, 166–167
 Keynesian view of, 166
 monetarist view of, 167
 new Keynesian view of, 166
 origins and issues of, 88
**Macroeconomic short run, 151**
Malthus, Thomas Robert, 215
Malthusian theory, 215–216
**Margin, 11**
**Marginal benefit, 11, 36,** 60
 decreasing, principle of, 36
**Marginal benefit curve, 36**
**Marginal cost, 11, 35**
 production-possibilities frontier

and, 35
**Marginal product of labor, 182,** 183
diminishing, demand for labor and, 183–184
**Marginal propensity to consume, 308,** 308–309
multiplier and, 318, 319
**Marginal propensity to import, 311**
**Marginal propensity to save, 308,** 308–309
multiplier and, 318, 319
**Market(s), 44,** 58
circular flows through, 44, 45
competitive, 58
coordination of decisions by, 45
economic growth and, 209
factor, 44
goods, 44
Market equilibrium, 68–69
Market value, GDP and, 108
Marshall, Alfred, 82
Marshall, Mary Paley, 82
**Means of payment, 234**
Measurement, 12
Medicare, 375
Medium of exchange, money as, 234
Mercantilism, 458–459
Mexico, NAFTA and. *See* North American Free Trade Agreement
**Microeconomics, 2**
Microsoft Corporation, 6
Miller, William, 389
**Minimum wage, 189**
Models. *See* Economic models; *specific models*
Monetarist fixed rules
with aggregate demand shocks, 392–393
with cost-push inflation shocks, 397, 398
feedback rules with, 396–397
monetarist fixed rules with, 395–396
with productivity shocks, 395–396
**Monetarist theory of the business cycle, 340,** 340–342
**Monetarist view, 167**
**Monetary base, 247,** 249, 353
McCallum rule and, 401
Monetary exchange, economic growth and, 209
**Monetary policy, 101, 157, 244,** 387–406
aggregate demand and, 157
business cycle and, 389
credibility and, 399–400
expansion of 1990s and, 350
Fed's performance during 1973-2003 and, 389–391
goals of, 388
instruments of, 388
intermediate targets of, 388
McCallum rule and, 401–402, 403
during 1973–2003, 389–390
potential GDP growth and, 389
price level stability and, 388–389, 392–398
recession of 2001 and, 351
sustainable real GDP growth and, 389
Taylor rule and, 402–403
of today *(Reading Between the Lines)*, 404–405
**Money, 234,** 234–236
creation by banks, 242–243
demand for, 258–261
deregulation and financial innovation and, 241
electronic *(Reading Between the Lines)*, 252–253
Fed control of quantity of, 247–251
functions of, 234–235
increase in quantity at full employment, 266
influences on holding of, 258
nominal, 258
official measures of, 235–236
quantity theory of, 267–269, 271, 272–273
real, 258
ripple effects of, 257
in United States, 235–236
Money market, equilibrium in, 261–262
**Money market mutual funds, 238**
**Money multiplier, 249,** 249–251
size of, 250–251
**Money price, 58**
**Money wage rate, 182**
change in, change in aggregate supply and, 154
inflation and, 279–280
Moore, Gordon, 6
Moore's law, 6
Mori, Akio, 437
Mosaic, 219
Moving averages, 401
Multi-income families, 355
**Multiplier, 316,** 316–325
algebra of, 329
balanced budget, 331, 377
business cycle turning points and, 319–320
government purchases, 329, 330, 377
homeland security, 377
imports and income taxes and, 318–319, 320
interest rate and, 263–264
lump-sum taxes, 330
marginal propensities to consume and save and, 318, 319
multiplier effect and, 316–317
price level and, 321–325
size of, 317–318
tax, 377
Multiplier effect, 316
Murdoch, Rupert, 437
Murphy, Kevin, 189

National Bureau of Economic Research, 336
Business Cycle Dating Committee of, 128
National culture as argument for protection, 429
National Income and Product Accounts, 113, 134
**National saving, 111**
National security argument for protection, 427
**Natural rate of unemployment, 138, 150,** 187
changes in, inflation and, 290, 291
Natural resource(s), 3
*The Nature and the Causes of the Wealth of Nations* (Smith), 5
**Needs-tested spending, 379**
**Negative relationships, 21,** 21–22

**Neoclassical growth theory, 217,** 217–219, 228
**Net borrowers, 440**
Net domestic income at factor cost, 114
**Net exports, 110,** 113, **416, 441,** 441–442
  interest rate and, 263
  international borrowing and, 416
Net interest in GDP, 114
**Net investment, 111, 190**
**Net lenders, 440**
Netscape Navigator, 219
**Net taxes, 110**
Net worth on bank's balance sheet, 237
**New classical theory of the business cycle, 342**
New economy, 6–7
**New growth theory, 219,** 219–221
New Keynesian rule, 402–403
**New Keynesian theory of the business cycle, 342**
**New Keynesian view, 166**
New monetarist rule, 401–402, 403
**Nominal GDP, 115**
Nominal interest rate, expected inflation and, 293
Nominal money, 258
Nonconvertible notes, 247
**Nontariff barriers, 423,** 426
**Normal goods, 62**
Normative statements, 12
**North American Free Trade Agreement,** 311, 415, **424,** 431
NOW accounts, 240

Observation, 12
**Official settlements account, 438**
Okun, Arthur M., 93
**Okun gap, 93**
**One third rule, 212,** 212–213
OPEC, 97, 283
**Open market operations, 246,** 247–249
**Opportunity cost, 10,** 33–34
  comparative advantage and, 417–418
  increasing, 34
  as ratio, 33–34

Organization of Petroleum Exporting Countries, 97, 283
Origin of graph, 17

**Peaks,** 90, **128**
Personal consumption expenditures, 113
Phillips, A. W., 288, 299
**Phillips curve, 288,** 288–291, 299
  changes in natural rate of unemployment and, 290, 291
  long-run, 290
  short-run, 288–289
  in United States, 291
  in U.S. *(Reading Between the Lines),* 294–295
Physical capital
  increase in, labor productivity and, 197
  labor productivity and, 195
Plosser, Charles, 345
Plott, Charles R., 84–86
Policy lags, 394–395
Political freedom, economic welfare comparisons and, 119–120
Polo, Marco, 415, 457
Population
  changes in demand related to, 62
  of U.S., 130
Population growth
  classical theory of, 215–216
  neoclassical theory of, 217
  potential GDP and, 196–197, 199
  in United States, 199
**Positive relationships, 20,** 20–21
Positive statements, 12
*Post hoc* fallacy, 13–14
**Potential GDP, 89, 139**
  changes in, 153–154
  full employment and, 368
  income taxes and, 368–369
  labor market and, 182–186
  labor productivity increases and, 197–198, 199
  population increases and, 196–197, 199
  real GDP fluctuations about, 90
**Preferences, 36**
  changes in demand related to, 62
  diversity of, gains from trade

and, 422
Prescott, Edward, 345, 369
**Present value, 374**
  generational accounting and, 374–375
President of United States, budgetary role of, 362
Price(s), 58
  adjustments of, 69
  change in demand and, 70–71, 72–73
  change in supply and, 71, 72–73
  equilibrium, 68
  expected, change in demand related to, 61–62
  expected, change in supply and, 66
  fixed. See Fixed price(s)
  of gasoline, supply and demand and, 74–77
  money, 58
  of productive resources, change in supply and, 65
  as regulator, 68–69
  of related goods, changes in supply and demand and, 61, 65–66
  relative, 58
  of resources, 65
**Price level(s), 97, 116.** *See also* Inflation
  calculation of, 116–117
  equilibrium real GDP and, 323–325
  feedback rule to stabilize, 397
  fixed, real GDP with, 312–315
  inflation and, 278
  multiplier and, 321–325
  quantity of money held and, 258
  in RBC theory, 347, 348
  shocks to, during 1970s-1990s, 389
Price level stability, 388–389, 392–398
  aggregate demand shocks and, 392–394
  characteristics of, 388–389
  desirability of, 388
  discretionary policies and, 392
  feedback-rule policies and, 392, 393–394, 396–398
  fixed-rule policies and, 392–393, 395–396, 397, 398

policy lags and forecast horizon and, 394–395
productivity shocks and, 395–397
*The Principles of Economics* (Marshall), 82
Private saving, 373
**Private sector surplus or deficit, 441**
Privatization, 5–6
*Probing the Ideas*
 business cycles, 410–411
 gains from international trade, 458–459
 incentives to innovate, 228–229
 inflation, 300–301
 laws of supply and demand, 82–83
 macroeconomic revolutions, 174–175
 sources of economic wealth, 52–53
Production
 changes in, gains from trade and, 419–421
 factors of. *See* Capital; Entrepreneurship; Factors of production; Labor; Land
 household, economic welfare comparisons and, 118
 lost due to unemployment, 96
**Production efficiency, 33,** 37
**Production function, 181**
 aggregate, 150
**Production-possibilities frontier, 32,** 32–35
 gains from trade and, 40–42
 marginal cost and, 35
 opportunity cost and, 33–34
 for real GDP and leisure time, 180–181
 tradeoffs along, 33
**Productivity curve, 211,** 211–213
 classical theory and, 216
 new growth theory and, 220
Productivity growth, in information age, 349–350
**Productivity growth slowdown, 89**
Productivity of labor. *See* Labor productivity
Productivity theory, neoclassical growth theory and, 218–219
**Profit, 4**
 of banks, 237

expected, investment and, 190–191
 in GDP, 114
 new growth theory and, 219
**Property rights, 44**
 economic growth and, 209
Proprietor's income, in GDP, 114
**Purchasing power parity,** 120, **450**

Quantity
 change in demand and, 70–71, 72–73
 change in supply and, 71, 72–73
 equilibrium, 68
**Quantity demanded, 59**
**Quantity of labor demanded, 182**
**Quantity of labor supplied, 184**
**Quantity supplied, 64**
**Quantity theory of money, 267,** 267–269
 in Argentina *(Reading Between the Lines)*, 272–273
 AS-AD model and, 268–269
 historical evidence on, 269, 270
 international evidence on, 269, 271
**Quotas** (import), **426**

Race, unemployment and, 136–137
Rainforests, disappearance of, 7–8
Ramsey, Frank, 217
**Rational expectations, 285**
 business cycle and, 342–344
Rawski, Thomas, 120–121
RBC theory. *See* Real business cycle theory
*Reading Between the Lines*
 aggregate supply and demand in action, 168–169
 the cost and benefit of airport security, 46–47
 economic growth in Asia, 222–223
 electronic money, 252–253
 expansion of 2003, 102–103
 fiscal policy of today, 382–383
 gains from globalization, 432–433
 gasoline prices and, supply and demand and, 74–77
 inventories in expansion, 326–328
 jobless recovery of 2002–2003, 144–145

 monetary policy today, 404–405
 Phillips curve in United States, 294–295
 productivity growth in 2003, 200–201
 quantity theory of money in Argentina, 272–273
 real GDP in 2003 expansion, 122–123
 sinking dollar, 452–453
 U.S. expansion of 2002-2003, 356–357
Reagan, Ronald, 244, 245, 370
**Real business cycle theory, 345,** 345–349
 criticisms of, 348
 defense of, 348–349
 impulse and, 345–346
 mechanism and, 346–348
**Real GDP, 89, 115**
 aggregate expenditure and, 306
 aggregate planned expenditure and, 312, 313
 calculation of, 115–116
 changes in quantity demanded, 156
 consumption as function of, 311
 employment and, 180–181
 equilibrium, price level and, 323–325
 feedback rule to stabilize, 396–397
 with fixed price level, 312–315
 fluctuations around potential GDP, 90
 inflation and, 390–391
 price level and, 115–117
 production-possibilities frontier for leisure and, 180–181
 quantity of money held and, 258
 in RBC theory, 347, 348
 sustainable growth of, 389
 in 2003 expansion *(Reading Between the Lines)*, 122–123
 unemployment and, 139
**Real interest rate, 190,** 292
 after-tax, 287
 investment and, 191
 real tax rate on, 372
 saving and, 192
Real money, 258

Real property, 44
Real tax rate, on real interest rate, 372
**Real wage rate, 133,** 133–134, **182**
   subsistence, 216
**Recession(s), 90, 128,** 335
   Fed easing to avoid, 265
   turning points of, 319–320
   of 2001, 91, 127, 129, 350–351
   unemployment during, 95
   in United States, 336
**Recessionary gap, 160**
Recognition lag, 379
Reentrants, 135
**Reference base period, 140**
Regulation
   of banks' balance sheets, 240
   of depository institutions, 239
   financial innovation to avoid, 241
Related goods, prices of
   change in supply and, 65–66
   changes in demand related to, 61
**Relative price, 58**
Rent, 4
Rental income in GDP, 114
**Rent seeking, 430,** 430–431
**Required reserve ratios, 242,** 245, 247
Research and development, economic growth and, 214
**Reserve(s), 237,** 237–238
   excess, 242
   U.S. official, 438
**Reserve ratios, 242**
   required, 242, 245, 247
Reserve requirements, 240
Resource(s)
   misallocation of, 33
   natural, 3
Resource prices
   change in, change in aggregate supply and, 154
   change in supply and, 65
Revenue, from tariffs, 425, 430
Ricardo, David, 215, 373–374, 458
**Ricardo-Barro effect,** 373–374, **374**
Riegle-Neal Interstate Banking and Branching Efficiency Act of 1994, 240
Risk, pooling by depository institutions, 239

Rockefeller Center, 437
Romano, Ray, 4
Rome, hyperinflation in, 277
Romer, Paul, 219, 230–232
Russell, Bertrand, 174

Salaries in GDP, 113
**Saving, 110,** 111, 190
   decisions regarding, 192–193
   economic growth and, 209–210, 214
   government, 373–374
   income tax effects on, 372–373
   influences on, 308–310
   national, 111
   in neoclassical growth theory, 217
   planned, 306–307
   private, 373
   taxes and incentive to save and, 372–373
**Saving function, 307,** 308, 309
**Savings and loan associations, 238**
Savings Association Insurance Fund, 239
**Savings banks, 238**
**Saving supply, 193**
Say, Jean-Baptiste, 174
Say's Law, 174
Scale economies, 422
**Scarcity, 2**
**Scatter diagrams, 19,** 19–20
Schumpeter, Joseph, 219, 228
Schwartz, Anna J., 353
**Self-interest, 5**
Services. *See also* Goods and services
   trade in, 416
Shocks, 395
   aggregate demand, 392–394
   aggregate supply, 395
   cost-push inflation, 395, 397–398
   energy price, productivity growth slowdown and, 214
"Shoe leather costs," 287
Shortages, prices and, 69
Short run
   macroeconomic, 151
   macroeconomic issues and, 88
**Short-run aggregate supply curve, 151**
**Short-run macroeconomic equilib-**

   **rium, 158,** 158–159
**Short-run Phillips curve, 288,** 288–289
Singapore, economic growth in, 208
**Slope, 24,** 24–26
   across an arc, 25–26
   of consumption and saving functions, 309
   of curved lines, 25–26
   at point, 25
   of straight line, 24–25
Smetters, Kent, 374, 375
Smith, Adam, 5, 13, 52–53, 215, 299, 458
Smoot-Hawley tariff, 430
**Social interest, 5**
Social justice, economic welfare comparisons and, 120
Social security, viability of, 375
Solow, Robert, 212, 217–218, 228
Songman Yang, 205
Sony, 437, 438
South America. *See also specific countries*
   economic growth in, 207
Soviet Union, collapse of, 5
Special Drawing Rights, 246
Specialization, 40
Stability as argument for protection, 429
Stabilization of business cycles, 377–381
Stabilizers, automatic, 379–381
**Stagflation, 163,** 282, 397
State budgets, 367
**Stock(s), 111**
Stock market, crash of 1929, 335, 354
Store of value, money as, 235
**Structural surpluses/deficits, 380**
**Structural unemployment, 138**
Subsidies, 114
**Subsistence real wage rate, 216**
**Substitutes, 61**
   in production, 65–66
Substitution
   international, 321
   intertemporal, 321, 346
Substitution effect, 59
   aggregate demand and, 156
   aggregate expenditure and price

level and, 321–323
   intertemporal, 156
Sullivan, Scott, 7
Summers, Lawrence H., 54–56
Summers, Robert, 120
Suppliers, number of, change in supply and, 66
**Supply, 64,** 64–67
   aggregate. *See* Aggregate supply *entries;* AS-AD model
   change in, 65–67, 71
   in foreign exchange market, 446
   gasoline prices and *(Reading Between the Lines),* 74–77
   of labor. *See* Supply of labor
   law of, 64, 82–83
   minimum supply price and, 65
   saving, 193
**Supply curve, 64,** 64–65
   aggregate, 150, 151, 152
**Supply of labor, 184,** 184–185
   changes in, 185
Supply schedule, 64
**Supply-side effects, 368,** 368–374
   employment and potential GDP and, 368–370
   investment, saving, and economic growth and, 371–374
Surpluses
   budget, 99, 364, 380, 381
   government sector, 441
   prices and, 69
   private sector, 441

Taiwan, economic growth in, 208
*Talking with*
   Barro, Robert J., 176–178
   Bhagwati, Jagdish, 460–462
   Ireland, Peter N., 412–414
   Plott, Charles R., 84–86
   Romer, Paul, 230–232
   Summers, Lawrence H., 54–56
   Woodford, Michael, 302–304
Target rate of return in neoclassical growth theory, 217
**Tariffs, 423,** 423–425
   history of, 423–424
   operation of, 424–425
   revenue from, 430
   Smoot-Hawley, 430

Taxes
   on consumption expenditure, 369
   Great Depression and, 355
   incentive to save and, 372–373
   income. *See* Income taxes
   indirect, 114
   induced, 379
   inflation and, 287
   net, 110
**Tax multiplier, 377**
Tax revenues
   in federal budget, 363, 365
   Laffer curve and, 370
**Tax wedge, 369**
Taylor, John, 402
**Taylor rule, 402,** 402–403
**Technological change, 6–7, 38,** 175
   change in aggregate supply and, 154
   change in supply and, 66, 67
   computer chips and, 53
   financial innovation and, 241
   incentives to innovate and, 228–229
   increase in, labor productivity and, 197–198
   labor productivity and, 195
   in neoclassical growth theory, 217
   productivity growth and, 349–350
   during productivity growth slowdown, 214
   structural slumps and, 188
Temin, Peter, 353
**Terms of trade, 418,** 418–419
Terrorist attack of 9/11, economic response to, 7
**Thrift institutions, 238**
**Time-series graphs, 18**
Trade
   balanced, 419, 425
   gains from, 40–43
   international. *See* International trade; Trade restrictions
**Tradeoffs, 9**
   along production-possibilities frontier, 33
   big, 10
   classic, 9
   "what, how," and "for whom," 9–10
Trade restrictions, 423–431

   case for, 427–430
   nontariff, 423, 426
   reasons for, 430–431
   tariffs as, 423–425
Trade wars, 430
*Traité d'économie politique (A Treatise in Political Economy)* (Say), 174
Transfer payments, 110, 363–364
**Trends, 18**
Tropical rainforests, disappearance of, 7–8
**Troughs, 90, 128**
Twentieth Century Fox, 437

Uncertainty, inflation and, 287
Underground economy, economic welfare comparisons and, 119
Unemployment, 8, 94–96, 135–138
   cyclical, 138
   demographics of, 136–137
   duration of, 136
   frictional, 137–138
   at full employment, 187–189
   global, 96
   inflation and, 288–291
   jobless recovery of 2002–2003 *(Reading Between the Lines),* 144–145
   job rationing and, 189
   manner of becoming unemployed and, 135
   problems due to, 96
   real GDP and, 139
   sources of, 135–136
   structural, 138
   in United States, 95
Unemployment compensation, 188
**Unemployment rate, 95, 131**
   natural, 138, 150, 187, 290, 291
United Kingdom
   economic growth in, 207
   water in, 8
United States
   borrowing of, for consumption versus investment, 442
   budget deficits of, 8
   business cycles in, 128–129, 165, 336, 349–351
   business cycles in *(Reading Between the Lines),* 356–357

consumption function for, 310, 311
currency of, 444–445, 447, 449, 452–453
economic growth in, 39, 89–91, 164, 206
evolving economy during 1963–2003, 165
federal budget of. *See* Federal budget
GDP of, measurement of, 113–114
government debt of, 8
government of. *See* Federal *entries*
inflation in, 97, 165, 277, 281, 283
labor productivity in, 199
money in, 235–236
NAFTA and. *See* North American Free Trade Agreement
Phillips curve in, 291
Phillips curve in *(Reading Between the Lines)*, 294–295
population growth in, 199
population of, 130
quantity theory of money in, 269, 270
tariffs of, 423–424
unemployment in, 95
water in, 8
**U.S. interest rate differential, 445**
**U.S. official reserves, 438**
Unit of account, money as, 234–235

Value, money as store of, 235
**Velocity of circulation, 267,** 267–268, 269
Volcker, Paul, 97, 245, 389
**Voluntary export restraints, 426**

Wage(s), **4**
efficiency, 188–189
in GDP, 113
minimum, 189
money wage rate and, 182
real wage rate and, 133–134, 182

Wage rate, real, 133–134, 182, 216
Wal-Mart, 44
Walton, Sam, 44
Wants, 59
double coincidence of, 234
Water shortages, 8
**Wealth, 111**
saving and, 192
sources of, 52–53
Wealth effect
aggregate demand and, 155–156
aggregate expenditure and price level and, 321
*The Wealth of Nations* (Smith), 5, 13, 52, 458
Welch, Finis, 189
Woodford, Michael, 302–304
Woolf, Virginia, 174
**Working-age population, 130**
WorldCom, 7
**World Trade Organization, 423**

Zaire, hyperinflation in, 99

# The Addison-Wesley Series in Economics

**Abel/Bernanke**
*Macroeconomics*

**Bade/Parkin**
*Foundations of Microeconomics*

**Bade/Parkin**
*Foundations of Macroeconomics*

**Bierman/Fernandez**
*Game Theory with Economic Applications*

**Binger/Hoffman**
*Microeconomics with Calculus*

**Boyer**
*Principles of Transportation Economics*

**Branson**
*Macroeconomic Theory and Policy*

**Bruce**
*Public Finance and the American Economy*

**Byrns/Stone**
*Economics*

**Carlton/Perloff**
*Modern Industrial Organization*

**Caves/Frankel/Jones**
*World Trade and Payments: An Introduction*

**Chapman**
*Environmental Economics: Theory, Application, and Policy*

**Cooter/Ulen**
*Law and Economics*

**Downs**
*An Economic Theory of Democracy*

**Eaton/Mishkin**
*Online Readings to Accompany The Economics of Money, Banking, and Financial Markets*

**Ehrenberg/Smith**
*Modern Labor Economics*

**Ekelund/Tollison**
*Economics: Private Markets and Public Choice*

**Fusfeld**
*The Age of the Economist*

**Gerber**
*International Economics*

**Ghiara**
*Learning Economics: A Practical Workbook*

**Gordon**
*Macroeconomics*

**Gregory**
*Essentials of Economics*

**Gregory/Stuart**
*Russian and Soviet Economic Performance and Structure*

**Hartwick/Olewiler**
*The Economics of Natural Resource Use*

**Hubbard**
*Money, the Financial System, and the Economy*

**Hughes/Cain**
*American Economic History*

**Husted/Melvin**
*International Economics*

**Jehle/Reny**
*Advanced Microeconomic Theory*

**Klein**
*Mathematical Methods for Economics*

**Krugman/Obstfeld**
*International Economics: Theory and Policy*

**Laidler**
*The Demand for Money: Theories, Evidence, and Problems*

**Leeds/von Allmen**
*The Economics of Sports*

**Lipsey/Courant/Ragan**
*Economics*

**McCarty**
*Dollars and Sense: An Introduction to Economics*

**Melvin**
*International Money and Finance*

**Miller**
*Economics Today*

**Miller/Benjamin/North**
*The Economics of Public Issues*

**Mills/Hamilton**
*Urban Economics*

**Mishkin**
*The Economics of Money, Banking, and Financial Markets*

**Parkin**
*Economics*

**Parkin/Bade**
*Economics in Action Software*

**Perloff**
*Microeconomics*

**Phelps**
*Health Economics*

**Riddell/Shackelford/Stamos/ Schneider**
*Economics: A Tool for Critically Understanding Society*

**Ritter/Silber/Udell**
*Principles of Money, Banking, and Financial Markets*

**Rohlf**
*Introduction to Economic Reasoning*

**Ruffin/Gregory**
*Principles of Economics*

**Sargent**
*Rational Expectations and Inflation*

**Scherer**
*Industry Structure, Strategy, and Public Policy*

**Schotter**
*Microeconomics: A Modern Approach*

**Stock/Watson**
*Introduction to Econometrics*

**Studenmund**
*Using Econometrics: A Practical Guide*

**Tietenberg**
*Environmental and Natural Resource Economics*

**Tietenberg**
*Environmental Economics and Policy*

**Todaro/Smith**
*Economic Development*

**Waldman/Jensen**
*Industrial Organization: Theory and Practice*

**Williamson**
*Macroeconomics*

# Macroeconomic Data

These macroeconomic data series show some of the trends in GDP and its components, the price level, and other variables that provide information about changes in the standard of living and the cost of living—the central questions of macroeconomics. You will find these data in a spreadsheet that you can download from MyEconLab.

| | | NATIONAL INCOME AND PRODUCT ACCOUNTS | 1978 | 1979 | 1980 | 1981 | 1982 | 1983 | 1984 | 1985 | 1986 | 1987 |
|---|---|---|---|---|---|---|---|---|---|---|---|---|
| | | **EXPENDITURES APPROACH** | | | | | | | | | | |
| the sum of | 1 | Personal consumption expenditures | 1,428.5 | 1,592.2 | 1,757.1 | 1,941.1 | 2,077.3 | 2,290.6 | 2,503.3 | 2,720.3 | 2,899.7 | 3,100.2 |
| | 2 | Gross private domestic investment | 438.0 | 492.9 | 479.3 | 572.4 | 517.2 | 564.3 | 735.6 | 736.2 | 746.5 | 785.0 |
| | 3 | Government purchases | 453.6 | 500.8 | 566.2 | 627.5 | 680.5 | 733.5 | 797.0 | 879.0 | 949.3 | 999.5 |
| | 4 | Exports | 186.9 | 230.1 | 280.8 | 305.2 | 283.2 | 277.0 | 302.4 | 302.0 | 320.5 | 363.9 |
| less | 5 | Imports | 212.3 | 252.7 | 293.8 | 317.8 | 303.2 | 328.6 | 405.1 | 417.2 | 453.3 | 509.1 |
| equals | 6 | Gross domestic product | 2,294.7 | 2,563.3 | 2,789.5 | 3,128.4 | 3,255.0 | 3,536.7 | 3,933.2 | 4,220.3 | 4,462.8 | 4,739.5 |
| | | **INCOMES APPROACH** | | | | | | | | | | |
| the sum of | 7 | Compensation of employees | 1,336.1 | 1,500.8 | 1,651.8 | 1,825.8 | 1,925.8 | 2,042.6 | 2,255.6 | 2,424.7 | 2,570.1 | 2,750.2 |
| | 8 | Proprietors' income | 166.6 | 180.1 | 174.1 | 183.0 | 176.3 | 192.5 | 243.3 | 262.3 | 275.7 | 302.2 |
| | 9 | Rental income of persons | 22.1 | 23.8 | 30.0 | 38.0 | 38.8 | 37.8 | 40.2 | 41.9 | 33.5 | 33.5 |
| | 10 | Corporate profits | 216.6 | 223.2 | 201.1 | 226.1 | 209.7 | 264.2 | 318.6 | 330.3 | 319.5 | 368.8 |
| | 11 | Net interest | 115.0 | 138.9 | 181.8 | 232.3 | 271.1 | 285.3 | 327.1 | 341.3 | 366.8 | 366.4 |
| | 12 | Adjustments | 171.0 | 182.3 | 200.5 | 237.2 | 242.6 | 261.8 | 297.5 | 322.9 | 336.7 | 352.6 |
| equals | 13 | National Income | 2,027.4 | 2249.1 | 2,439.3 | 2,742.4 | 2,864.3 | 3,084.2 | 3,482.3 | 3,723.4 | 3,902.3 | 4,173.7 |
| plus | 14 | Indirect taxes minus subsidies | −16.6 | −17.8 | −27.0 | −35.0 | −72.7 | −28.4 | −58.0 | −36.3 | 11.4 | −14.0 |
| | 15 | Consumption of fixed capital | 262.3 | 300.1 | 343.0 | 388.1 | 426.9 | 443.8 | 472.6 | 506.7 | 531.3 | 561.9 |
| | 16 | Net factor incomes from rest of world | 21.6 | 31.9 | 34.2 | 32.9 | 36.5 | 37.1 | 36.3 | 26.5 | 17.8 | 17.9 |
| equals | 17 | Gross domestic product | 2,294.7 | 2,563.3 | 2,789.5 | 3,128.4 | 3,255.0 | 3,536.7 | 3,933.2 | 4,220.3 | 4,462.8 | 4,739.5 |
| | 18 | Real GDP (billions of 2000 dollars) | 5,015.0 | 5,173.4 | 5,161.7 | 5,291.7 | 5,189.3 | 5,423.8 | 5,813.6 | 6,053.7 | 6,263.6 | 6,475.1 |
| | 19 | Real GDP growth rate (percent per year) | 5.6 | 3.2 | −0.2 | 2.5 | −1.9 | 4.5 | 7.2 | 4.1 | 3.5 | 3.4 |
| | | **OTHER DATA** | | | | | | | | | | |
| | 20 | Population (millions) | 222.6 | 225.1 | 227.7 | 230.0 | 232.2 | 234.3 | 236.3 | 238.5 | 240.7 | 242.8 |
| | 21 | Labor force (millions) | 102.2 | 105.0 | 107.0 | 108.7 | 110.2 | 111.5 | 113.5 | 115.5 | 117.8 | 119.9 |
| | 22 | Employment (millions) | 96.0 | 98.8 | 99.3 | 100.4 | 99.5 | 100.8 | 105.0 | 107.2 | 109.6 | 112.4 |
| | 23 | Unemployment (millions) | 6.2 | 6.1 | 7.7 | 8.3 | 10.7 | 10.7 | 8.5 | 8.3 | 8.2 | 7.4 |
| | 24 | Labor force participation rate (percent) | 63.1 | 63.7 | 63.8 | 63.9 | 64.0 | 64.0 | 64.4 | 64.8 | 65.3 | 65.6 |
| | 25 | Unemployment rate (percent of labor force) | 6.1 | 5.8 | 7.2 | 7.6 | 9.7 | 9.6 | 7.5 | 7.2 | 7.0 | 6.2 |
| | 26 | Real GDP per person (2000 dollars per year) | 22,531 | 22,987 | 22,666 | 23,011 | 23,350 | 23,148 | 24,598 | 25,386 | 26,028 | 26,668 |
| | 27 | Growth rate of real GDP per person (percent per year) | 4.5 | 2.0 | −1.4 | 1.5 | −2.9 | 3.6 | 6.3 | 3.2 | 2.5 | 2.5 |
| | 28 | Quantity of money (M2, billions of dollars) | 1,365.6 | 1,473.3 | 1,599.4 | 1,754.9 | 1,909.8 | 2,125.9 | 2,309.6 | 2,494.9 | 2,731.6 | 2,830.6 |
| | 29 | GDP deflator (2000 = 100) | 45.8 | 49.5 | 54.0 | 59.1 | 62.7 | 65.2 | 67.7 | 69.7 | 71.3 | 73.2 |
| | 30 | GDP deflator inflation rate (percent per year) | 6.9 | 8.1 | 8.9 | 9.3 | 6.1 | 4.1 | 3.7 | 3.1 | 2.2 | 2.9 |
| | 31 | Consumer price index (1982–1984 = 100) | 65.2 | 72.6 | 82.4 | 90.9 | 96.5 | 99.6 | 103.9 | 107.5 | 109.6 | 113.6 |
| | 32 | CPI inflation rate (percent per year) | 7.6 | 11.3 | 13.5 | 10.3 | 6.2 | 3.2 | 4.3 | 3.5 | 2.0 | 3.6 |
| | 33 | Current account balance (billions of dollars) | −15.1 | −0.3 | 2.3 | 5.0 | −5.5 | −38.7 | −94.3 | −118.2 | −147.2 | −160.7 |